COMPUTING
TECHNOLOGY
INDUSTRY
ASSOCIATION™

A+

CERTIFICATION
PROGRAM

D1406126

A GUIDE TO
Managing and Maintaining Your PC

SECOND EDITION

COMPREHENSIVE

ENHANCED

Jean Andrews, Ph.D.

COURSE
TECHNOLOGY

ONE MAIN STREET, CAMBRIDGE, MA 02142

an International Thomson Publishing company I(T)P®

Cambridge • Albany • Bonn • Boston • Cincinnati • London • Madrid • Melbourne • Mexico City
New York • Paris • San Francisco • Singapore • Tokyo • Toronto • Washington

A Guide to Managing and Maintaining Your PC, Second Edition, Comprehensive Enhanced is published by Course Tech

Managing Editor:	Kristen Duerr
Senior Product Manager:	Jennifer Normandin
Production Editors:	Daphne E. Barbas, Barbara Worth
Development Editor:	Janet M. Weinrib
Composition House:	GEX, Inc.
Text Designer:	GEX, Inc.
Cover Designer:	Wendy J. Reifeiss
Marketing Manager:	Susan E. Ogar

© 1999 by Course Technology—I$\widehat{T}$P®

For more information contact:

Course Technology
One Main Street
Cambridge, MA 02142

ITP Europe
Berkshire House 168-173
High Holborn
London WCIV 7AA
England

Nelson ITP Australia
102 Dodds Street
South Melbourne, 3205
Victoria, Australia

ITP Nelson Canada
1120 Birchmount Road
Scarborough, Ontario
Canada M1K 5G4

International Thomson Editores
Seneca, 53
Colonia Polanco
11560 Mexico D.F. Mexico

ITP GmbH
Königswinterer Strasse 418
53227 Bonn
Germany

ITP Asia
60 Albert Street, #15-01
Albert Complex
Singapore 189969

ITP Japan
Hirakawacho Kyowa Building
2-2-1 Hirakawacho
Chiyoda-ku, Tokyo 102
Japan

All rights reserved. This publication is protected by federal copyright law. No part of this publication may be repro
stored in a retrieval system, or transmitted in any form or by any means, electronic, mechanical, photocopying, rec
or otherwise, or be used to make a derivative work (such as translation or adaptation), without prior permission i
ing from Course Technology.

Trademarks

Course Technology and the Open Book logo are registered trademarks and CourseKits is a trademark of
Technology. Custom Editions is a registered trademark of International Thomson Publishing.

I$\widehat{T}$P® The ITP logo is a registered trademark of International Thomson Publishing.

Some of the product names and company names used in this book have been used for identification pu
and may be trademarks or registered trademarks of their respective manufacturers and sellers.

Disclaimer

Course Technology reserves the right to revise this publication and make changes from time to time in its co
without notice.

ISBN 0-619-00064-3

Printed in Canada

1 2 3 4 5 6 WC 03 02 01 00 99

PHOTO CREDITS

FIGURE 1-1: Photographer Terry Vine/Tony Stone Images

FIGURE 1-8: Courtesy of Quantum

FIGURE 1-17: Courtesy of CompUSA, Inc.

FIGURE 3-2: Courtesy of Intel Corporation

FIGURE 3-3: Courtesy of AMD

FIGURE 3-4: Used with permission of Cyrix Corporation

FIGURE 3-6: Courtesy of Intel Corporation

FIGURE 4-20: Courtesy of Microsoft Corporation

FIGURE 4-21: © 1993 Steve Kahn

FIGURE 4-24 (top left and right): Used by Permission. Copyright Logitech 1997

FIGURE 4-24 (bottom): Courtesy of Sharp Electronics Corporation

FIGURE 5-44: Courtesy of DISCTEC

FIGURE 8-1: Courtesy of Microtek Lab, Inc.

FIGURE 8-2: © 1996 Adobe Systems Incorporated. All rights reserved.

FIGURE 13-9: Creative Labs, Inc.

FIGURE 13-10: Photo by Larry Marchant

FIGURE 13-28: Courtesy of Epson America, Inc.

FIGURE 13-30: Toshiba America Information Systems

FIGURE 13-32: Courtesy of Hewlett-Packard Company

FIGURE 13-37: Courtesy of Epson America, Inc.

FIGURES 14-1, 9, 10, 13, 14-16, 18-21, 24, 26-37, 39-43, 45-46, 48, 51-53, 57-61: Photos by Larry Marchant

FIGURE 15-4: Courtesy of Diamond Multimedia Systems, Inc.

FIGURE 15-7: Photo by Larry Marchant

FIGURE 16-7a: 3Com Corporation

FIGURE 16-7b: 3Com Corporation

FIGURE 16-7c: 3Com Corporation

FIGURE 17-6: Courtesy of Iomega Corporation

BRIEF CONTENTS

INTRODUCTION   XX

CHAPTER ONE   How Computers Work - An Overview   1

CHAPTER TWO   How Software and Hardware Work Together   45

CHAPTER THREE   The Systemboard   83

CHAPTER FOUR   Floppy Drives and Other Essential Devices   141

CHAPTER FIVE   Introduction to Hard Drives   191

CHAPTER SIX   Hard Drive Installation and Support   261

CHAPTER SEVEN   Troubleshooting Fundamentals   333

CHAPTER EIGHT   Customizing a Personal Computer System with Peripheral Equipment   381

CHAPTER NINE   Understanding and Managing Memory   429

CHAPTER TEN   Electricity and Power Supplies   485

CHAPTER ELEVEN   Supporting Windows 3.x and Windows 95   519

CHAPTER TWELVE   Understanding and Supporting Windows NT Workstations   587

CHAPTER THIRTEEN   Multimedia Technology   657

CHAPTER FOURTEEN   Purchasing a PC or Building Your Own   703

CHAPTER FIFTEEN   Communicating over Phone Lines   759

CHAPTER SIXTEEN   Networking Fundamentals and the Internet   809

CHAPTER SEVENTEEN   Viruses, Disaster Recovery, and a Maintenance Plan That Works   897

CHAPTER EIGHTEEN   The Professional PC Technician   941

Appendix A: Error Messages and Their Meanings   A-1
Appendix B: Hard Drive Types   B-1
Appendix C: ASCII Collating Sequence   C-1
Appendix D: The Hexidecimal Number System and Memory Addressing   D-1
Appendix E: Troubleshooting Guidelines   E-1

GLOSSARY
INDEX

TABLE OF CONTENTS

INTRODUCTION   XX

CHAPTER ONE
How Computers Work - An Overview   **1**
   Hardware   2
      Outside the Case   2
      Inside the Case   4
   Software   12
      Operating System   13
      Applications Software   25
   End-of-Chapter Material   36

CHAPTER TWO
How Software and Hardware Work Together   **45**
   How Software Manages Hardware Resources   46
      Configuration Data and How it is Stored   50
      Saving and Restoring Setup Information in CMOS   53
      ROM BIOS   56
      Device Drivers   58
      Interrupt Request Number (IRQ)   58
      Memory Used by BIOS and Device Drivers   60
      The I/O Address Table   60
      Summarizing How BIOS and Device Drivers Work   61
      DMA Controller Chip   63
      Summary of Computer Resources Required by Hardware 64

The Booting Process   64

    Power-On Self Test or POST, Step By Step   65

    Booting with MS-DOS   66

    Completion of the Boot Process   67

    Booting with Windows 95   69

Protecting Data, Software, and Hardware   71

    Keeping Rescue Disks   71

    Backups   72

    Documentation   72

    Written or Electronic Record of Setup   73

    Damage from Electricity   73

End-of-Chapter Material   74

CHAPTER THREE

The Systemboard   **83**

Types of Systemboards   84

The CPU and the Chip Set   87

    The Earlier Intel CPUs   88

    The Pentium and Its Competitors   90

    The Chip Set   96

ROM BIOS   99

    The Total BIOS in your System   100

    Plug-and-Play BIOS   101

    When BIOS is Incompatible with Hardware or Software   102

    Flash ROM   103

RAM (Random Access Memory)   105

    Dynamic Memory   105

    Static Cache Memory   107

Wait States   108

Buses and Expansion Slots   108

    What the System Bus Does   108

    The First ISA Bus   109

The Second ISA Bus   110

Microchannel Architecture (MCA) Bus   112

The EISA Bus   112

Local Buses   112

PCI Bus   114

Bus Comparisons and Bus Speeds   116

Universal Serial Bus   118

On-Board Ports   119

Hardware Configuration   119

Setup Stored on a CMOS Chip   120

Interrupt Request Number (IRQ)   121

DMA Controller   124

Power Supply Connections   124

End-of-Chapter Material   125

CHAPTER FOUR

Floppy Drives and Other Essential Devices   141

Floppy Drives   142

How Data is Physically Stored on a Disk   143

How Data is Logically Stored on a Disk   145

The Formatting Process   146

Using DOS to Manage a Floppy Disk   151

Using Windows 3.x to Manage a Floppy Drive   156

Using Windows 95 to Manage a Floppy Drive   158

Exchanging and Installing a Floppy Drive   160

Replacing a Floppy Drive   166

Keyboards   172

Computer Video   175

Monitors   175

Pointing Devices   179

Cleaning the Mouse   181

End-of-Chapter Material   181

CHAPTER FIVE

Introduction to Hard Drives   **191**

How a Hard Drive Is Physically Organized to Hold Data   192

How a Hard Drive Is Logically Organized to Hold Data   193

How the OS Views Data   194

Physical Drives and Logical Drives   195

Drive Capacity   196

The File Allocation Table (FAT)   201

The Root Directory   205

Using DOS to Manage a Hard Drive   208

MKDIR [drive:]path or MD [drive:]path Command   209

CHDIR [drive:]path or CD [drive]path or CD..   211

RMDIR [drive:]path or RD [drive:]path   211

DELTREE [drive:][path]   212

TREE [drive:][path] [/F] [/A]   212

ATTRIB   213

MIRROR   213

UNFORMAT   213

PATH   214

Using Batch Files   214

Using Windows 3.x to Manage a Hard Drive   214

Using Windows 95 to Manage a Hard Drive   217

Formatting and Optimizing the Hard Drive   220

Low-level Format and OS Format   220

Fragmentation   221

Cross-Linked and Lost Clusters   223

Disk Compression   225

Disk Caching   230

Using DOS under Windows 95 to Manage a Hard Drive   233

Hard Drive Technology   233

Hardware Components   233

Comparing SCSI Hard Drives and EIDE Hard Drives   244

Removable Drives   244

Why Use a Removable Drive?   245

Removable Drive Technologies 246
Available Products 246
Installing a Removable Drive 249
End-of-Chapter Material 249

CHAPTER SIX
Hard Drive Installation and Support **261**
Installing a Hard Drive 262
Physical Installation of a Hard Drive 262
Informing Setup of the New Drive 267
Making Partitions 268
OS or High-Level Format 271
Installing Software 271
When Things Go Wrong 272
Installing a SCSI Drive 275
Multiple Operating Systems 276
Utility Software 277
Norton Utilities 278
Nuts & Bolts 283
PC Tools 290
An Ounce of Prevention 290
Data Recovery 291
Returning to Floppy Disks 291
Summary of Disk Data Recovery 312
Hard Drive Troubleshooting and Data Recovery 313
Problems with Hard Drives 313
Setting Priorities Before You Start 313
Resolving Hard Drive Problems 314
Preparing for Disaster 317
Damaged Partition Table or Boot Record 318
Damaged FAT or Root Directory 321
Corrupted System Files 321
Corrupted Sector and Track Markings 322

Corrupted Data and Program Files 323
Virus Problems 323
Summary of Hard Drive Troubleshooting 324
Hard Drive Troubleshooting Guidelines 324
Hard Drive Does Not Boot 324
Drive Retrieves and Saves Data Slowly 325
Computer Will Not Recognize a Newly Installed
Hard Drive 325
End-of-Chapter Material 326

CHAPTER SEVEN
Troubleshooting Fundamentals 333

Troubleshooting Perspectives 334
Protect Yourself, the Hardware, and the Software 334
Tools to Help Support Personal Computers 337
Bootable Disk for DOS 338
Rescue Disk for Windows 95 338
POST Diagnostic Cards 339
Diagnostic Software 339
Utility Software for Updates and Fixes 340
General Purpose Utility Software 341
Handling Viruses 342
How to Isolate Computer Problems and Devise a Course of Action 343
Handling an Emergency 343
Fundamental Rules 345
Devising a Course of Action 347
Troubleshooting Guidelines: Peripheral Devices 351
Troubleshooting Keyboard Problems 351
Troubleshooting Monitor Problems 352
Troubleshooting Printer Problems 357
Problems with the Computer 361
When a PC Is Your Permanent Responsibility 364
Organize the Hard Drive Root Directory 365

Create a Boot or Rescue Disk 366

Documentation 366

Record of Setup Data 366

Practical Precautions to Protect Software and Data 367

Backup of Original Software 368

Backup of Data on the Hard Drive 368

End-of-Chapter Material 369

CHAPTER EIGHT
Customizing a Personal Computer System with Peripheral Equipment 381

The Right Tools for the Job 382

Desktop-Publishing Devices 383

Multimedia Devices 384

Bits Are Still Bits 386

Basic Principles 386

Hardware 387

Firmware 388

Device Drivers 389

Applications Software 391

Using Ports and Expansion Slots for Add-on Devices 393

Using Serial Ports 393

Using Parallel Ports 400

Examining a General-Purpose I/O Card 400

Resolving Resource Conflicts 403

Notebook Computers and the PC Card Slots 406

SCSI Devices 407

CD-ROM Drives 411

Caring for CD-ROM Drives 414

Installing a CD-ROM Drive 415

When Device Installations Create Problems 420

End-of-Chapter Material 420

CHAPTER NINE

Understanding and Managing Memory — **429**

Physical Memory — 430

SRAM, DRAM, and Memory Caching — 430

Memory on the Systemboard — 432

Memory on Expansion Boards — 436

How Memory Is Used by DOS and Windows 95 — 437

Physical Memory and Memory Addresses — 437

Areas of the Memory Map — 439

Shadow RAM or Shadowing ROM — 443

Virtual Memory — 444

RAM Drives — 444

Summary of How Memory is Managed — 445

Managing Memory with DOS or Windows 3.x — 445

Using HIMEM.SYS — 445

Using EMM386.EXE — 447

Managing Memory with Windows 3.x — 456

Swap Files and Virtual Memory — 456

Managing Memory with Windows 95 — 460

Windows 95 Swap File — 463

The Ultimate Solution: Windows NT — 464

Memory Troubleshooting Guidelines — 465

Upgrading Memory — 468

How Much Memory Can Fit on the Systemboard? — 468

Reading Ads about Memory Modules — 472

Installing Memory — 473

End-of-Chapter Material — 475

CHAPTER TEN

Electricity and Power Supplies — **485**

Introduction to Basic Electricity — 486

Voltage — 487

Amps — 488

The Relationship Between Voltage and Current 488
Ohms 489
Relationships Among Voltage, Current, and Resistance 489
Wattage 489
Measuring the Voltage of a Power Supply 490
Using a Multimeter 491
How to Measure the Voltage of a Power Supply 493
Exchanging the Power Supply 498
Power Supply Troubleshooting Guidelines 498
Upgrading the Power Supply 499
Installing a New Power Supply 500
Energy Star Computers (the Green Star) 501
Energy Star PCs 501
Energy Star Monitors 503
Surge Protection and Battery Backup 505
Surge Suppressors 505
Measuring Power Ranges of Devices 507
Power Conditioners 507
Uninterruptible Power Supply 508
The Line-Interactive UPS 510
End-of-Chapter Material 511

CHAPTER ELEVEN
Supporting Windows 3.x and Windows 95 **519**

Supporting Windows 3.1 and Windows 3.11 520
Windows 3.x Configuration and Application Information 520
Windows 3.x Installations 527
Conflicts and Problems with Applications Software in a
   Windows Environment 530
How Windows 3.x Manages Memory 540
Optimizing Windows 3.x 544
Supporting Windows 95 545
How Windows 95 Differs from Windows 3.x and DOS 545

Installing and Customizing Windows 95   551
Plug-and-Play and Hardware Installations   562
The Windows 95 Registry   570
Microsoft Support on the Internet   577
End-of-Chapter Material   578

CHAPTER TWELVE
Understanding and Supporting Windows NT Workstation   587
Windows NT vs. Windows 95   588
Features of Windows NT   589
Choosing Between Windows 95 and Windows NT   593
Upgrading from Windows 95 to Windows NT   594
Windows NT and a Dual Boot   597
The Windows NT Environment and Architecture   598
The Goals of Windows NT   598
The Modular Concept of Windows NT   599
Processes and Threads   607
Virtual DOS Machine Concept   608
Windows NT Networking   609
Installing and Customizing Windows NT   616
Preparing for the Installation   616
Step-by-Step Installation   618
Supporting Windows NT and Applications   624
The Windows NT Boot Process   624
Managing Legacy Software in the Windows NT
    Environment   634
The Windows NT Registry   637
How the Registry is Organized   637
Making Changes to the Registry   643
Backing Up the Registry   646
Windows NT Diagnostic Tools   646
The Task Manager   646

The Event Viewer 648
Windows NT Diagnostic 650
End-of-Chapter Material 650

CHAPTER THIRTEEN
Mutimedia Technology **657**
Multimedia on a PC 658
Why Multimedia? 658
Multimedia PC Requirements 661
The MPC Specifications 662
What CPU MMX Technology Does for Multimedia 667
Video Cards and Monitors 668
Video Cards 668
Choosing the Right Monitor 672
Devices Supporting Multimedia 674
Sound Cards 674
Troubleshooting Guidelines 686
Digital Cameras 687
Digital Video Disc (DVD) 688
Supporting Printers 690
Laser Printers 690
Ink-Jet Printers 695
Improving Printer Performance 695
End-of-Chapter Material 696

CHAPTER FOURTEEN
Purchasing a PC or Building Your Own **703**
Selecting a Personal Computer to Meet Your Needs 704
Brand-Name PC vs. Clone 706
Selecting Software 706
Selecting Hardware 707
Selecting a Total Package 707

Preparing to Build Your Own PC   708
  Getting Ready for Assembly: Selecting Parts   709
  Getting Ready for Assembly: Final Preparations   710
Building a Personal Computer, Step by Step   710
  Overview of the Assembly Process   711
  Step 1: Setting the Jumpers on the Systemboard   712
  Step 2: Installing the CPU and CPU Fan   719
  Step 3: Installing RAM on the Systemboard   722
  Step 4: Verifying That the Systemboard Is Working
          By Performing a Memory Test   723
  Step 5: Installing the Systemboard in the Computer Case   728
  Step 6: Connecting Serial and Parallel Ports
          to the Systemboard   732
  Step 7: Installing the Floppy Drive   733
  Step 8: Installing the Hard Drive   736
  Step 9: Installing the CD-ROM Drive   739
  Step 10: Installing the Sound Card   741
  Step 11: Installing the Modem   742
  Step 12: Installing the SCSI Host Adapter   745
  Step 13: Installing the Speaker   747
  Step 14: Installing the Video Card   748
  Step 15: Connecting Essential Peripherals   748
  Step 16: Setting CMOS and Installing the Operating System   748
  Step 17: Installing the Case Cover   751
  Step 18: Connecting the Scanner   753
  Finishing the Job   754
End-of-Chapter Material   754

CHAPTER FIFTEEN
Communicating over Phone Lines   759
  Communications Layers   760
  All About Modems   763
    How Modems Are Rated   764

Modem Features 774

Computer-Hardware-to-Modem Communication 775

Installing and Configuring a Modem 783

Communications Software 786

Software-to-Modem Communication 787

Software-to-Software Communication 792

File Transfer with pcANYWHERE 793

Remote Control with pcANYWHERE 794

Troubleshooting Guidelines 796

Faster Than Phone Lines 799

End-of-Chapter Material 802

CHAPTER SIXTEEN
Networking Fundamentals and the Internet **809**

An Overview of Networking 810

Types of Networks 810

Networking Hardware 819

The OSI Layer Network Model 823

Networking Software Overview 827

Networking with Windows 95 and Windows NT Workstation 831

Dial-Up Networking 832

Direct Cable Connect 838

Installing Network Adapters Using Windows 95
and Windows NT 840

Servicing PCs on a Network 843

PCs and the Internet 847

How the Internet Works 848

Connecting to the Internet 849

IP Addresses 849

Domain Name Resolution 852

The Internet, Networks, and Subnets 853

Connecting to the Internet 867

Some Examples of Network Services   870
   World Wide Web Browsers   872
   File Transfer   872
   Network Drive Map   875
   Print Services   880
Network Troubleshooting Guidelines   882
   Windows 95 Dial-Up Problems   882
   Problems with TCP/IP   883
   Problems with Network Printers   884
End-of-Chapter Material   885

CHAPTER SEVENTEEN
Viruses, Disaster Recovery, and a Maintenance Plan
That Works   897

Preventive Maintenance   898
   A Preventive Maintenance Plan   898
   When Moving Equipment   900
Viruses and Other Computer Infestations   901
   Understanding Computer Infestations   901
   Protecting Against Computer Infestations 907
All About Backups and Fault Tolerance   911
   Backup Hardware   912
   Backup Methods   917
   Backup Software   918
   RAID   929
   Planning for Disaster Recovery   931
End-of-Chapter Material   932

CHAPTER EIGHTEEN
The Professional PC Technician   941

What Customers Want   942
   Not Just Technical Proficiency   943

Providing Good Service on Support Calls 944
  Planning for Good Service 945
  Making a Service Call 947
  Phone Support 948
  Learning to Be a Better Communicator 949
  When You Can't Solve the Problem 954
Recordkeeping and Information Tools 954
  Tracking Service Calls and Help-Desk Calls 955
Professional Organizations and Certifications 959
  Why Certification? 961
Staying Abreast of New Technology 961
Protecting Software Copyrights 962
  What Does the Law Say? 963
  What Are Your Responsibilities to the Law? 964
End-of-Chapter Material 964

Appendix A: Error Messages and Their Meanings **A-1**
Appendix B: Hard Drive Types **B-1**
Appendix C: ASCII Collating Sequence **C-1**
**Appendix D: The Hexidecimal Number System
and Memory Addressing** **D-1**
Appendix E: Troubleshooting Guidelines **E-1**

GLOSSARY
INDEX

INTRODUCTION

A Guide to Managing and Maintaining Your PC, Comprehensive Enhanced was written to be the very best tool on the market today to prepare you to support personal computers. The book takes you from the just-a-user level to the I-can-fix-this level for the most common PC hardware and software concerns. The book achieves its goals with an unusually effective combination of tools that powerfully reinforce both concepts and hands-on real-world experience.

This book includes two pieces of software, Sylvan *RapidAssess* for A+–test preparation solution, and Nuts & Bolts–a powerful troubleshooting utility, on the enclosed single convenient CD. This software is integrated into the many Hands-On Projects in the book. The text was developed as a teaching tool, and contains many pedagogical features, including an itemized summary, review questions, comprehensive projects, and key-term definitions; there are also step-by-step guides on installation, maintenance, and optimizing system performance. A unique standalone troubleshooting guide (Appendix E), indexed for both hardware and software, distills all troubleshooting information from the book. Several in-depth, hands-on projects at the end of each chapter are designed to make certain that you not only understand the material, but can execute procedures and make decisions on your own. The carefully structured, clearly written text is accompanied by graphics that provide the visual input essential to learning. In addition, for instructors using the book in a classroom, a special CD-ROM is available that includes an instructor's manual, an online testing system, and a PowerPoint presentation.

Balanced coverage is given to new hardware as well as to the real work of PC repair, where some older technology is still in widespread use, and still needs support. For example, while the book covers the various Pentium processors, it also addresses the capabilities and maintenance of 486 processors because many are still in use. Also included is thorough coverage of operating system and applications support. While Windows 95 is the primary OS of choice for many PCs, DOS and Windows 3.x are still given comprehensive coverage because of their continuing widespread use. In addition, an entire chapter is dedicated to Windows NT, which has many powerful capabilities that make it an important option, especially in the business environment.

This book provides the most comprehensive preparation available for the newly revised A+ Certification examination. This certification credential's popularity among employers is growing exponentially, and obtaining certification increases your ability to gain employment and improve your salary. To get more information on A+ Certification and its sponsoring organization, the Computing Technology Industry Association, see their Web site at www.CompTIA.org.

FEATURES

In order to ensure a successful learning experience, this book includes the following pedagogical features:

- **Learning Objectives:** Every chapter opens with a list of learning objectives that sets the stage for you to absorb the lessons of the text.

- **Comprehensive Step-by-Step Troubleshooting Guidance:** Troubleshooting guidelines are included in almost every chapter. In addition, Appendix E is a unique compilation of troubleshooting information taken directly from the book, indexed for hardware and software problems. The guidelines are regularly updated and available on the Course Technology Web site, www.course.com (search on Andrews or the book title). You are invited to submit suggestions for these troubleshooting tips and guidelines on the Web site.

- **Step-by-Step Procedures:** The book is chock-full of step-by-step procedures covering subjects from hardware installation and maintenance to optimizing system performance.

 Notes: The Note icon is used whenever it is appropriate to present additional helpful material related to the subject being described.

- **Nuts & Bolts Utility Software:** The CD-ROM accompanying the book contains a copy of Nuts & Bolts, an award-winning diagnostic utility, receiving top ratings from *PC Advisor*, *Windows Sources*, *Home Office Computing*, *PC Computing*, and *Boot Magazine*. Many end-of-chapter projects direct you to use this software, which is designed to facilitate all aspects of installation, maintenance, diagnosis, repair, and optimization of system performance. The software comes with a 90-day license and with the ability to purchase online as well.

- **Sylvan *RapidAssess* for A+:** This test prep software is an exciting new way to prepare yourself for the A+ exams. Featuring test questions for both the Core and DOS exams, practice using the Study Mode, which provides answers and detailed explanations along the way. Next, test your acumen in the Certification Mode, which simulates the real exam. After your test, you are presented with a graphical representation of your score, as well as with a visual breakdown of how you performed on each test objective. Best of all, the questions are mapped to the pages in the book, so you have a road map from which to study. You can also buy a comprehensive set of 400 review questions to take the process one step further. Point your browser to www.course.com/Sylvan for more details.

- **End-of-Chapter Material:** Each chapter closes with the following features, which reinforce the material covered in the chapter and provide real-world, hands-on testing of the chapter's skill set:

  - **Summary:** This bulleted list of concise statements summarizes all major points of the chapter.

  - **Review Questions:** You can test your understanding of the chapter material with a comprehensive set of review questions.

  - **Key-Term List:** The content of each chapter is further reinforced by an end-of-chapter key-term list with definitions that are combined at the end of the book in a full-length glossary.

     Hands-On Projects: You get to test your real-world understanding with hands-on projects involving a full range of software and hardware problems. Chapters include exercises using Nuts & Bolts software as well. Each hands-on activity in this book is preceded by the Hands-On icon and a description of the exercise that follows.

- **In-Depth Behind-the-Scenes Technology:** Optional sections are included for an elective, more detailed study of the subject at hand, relying on technical tools such as DOS DEBUG. These sections are screened in light gray and may be skipped if desired.

SUPPLEMENTS

For instructors using this book in a classroom environment, the following teaching materials are available on a single CD-ROM:

Electronic Instructor's Manual: The Instructor's Manual that accompanies this textbook includes a list of objectives for each chapter, a detailed chapter outline, suggestions for classroom activities, and answers to end-of-chapter questions.

Course Test Manager 1.1: Accompanying this book is a powerful assessment tool known as the Course Test Manager. Designed by Course Technology, this cutting-edge Windows-based testing software helps instructors design and administer tests and pretests. In addition to being able to generate tests that can be printed and administered, this full-featured program also has an online testing component that allows students to take tests at the computer and have their exams automatically graded. The test bank that accompanies this book contains over 100 questions per chapter.

PowerPoint presentations: This book comes with Microsoft PowerPoint slides for each chapter. The presentation will walk you through all of the salient points of each chapter. These are included as a teaching aid for classroom presentation, to make available to students on the network for chapter review, or to be printed for classroom distribution. Instructors, please feel at liberty to add your own slides for additional topics you introduce to the class.

LAB MANUAL

The Lab Manual offers the most comprehensive method for learning PC Repair. When combined with *A Guide to Managing & Maintaining Your PC, Second Edition*, it gives users clear, concise instruction along with essential hands-on practice. Each of the 60 featured labs is mapped to the newly revised A+ certification objectives, and offers the hands-on experience essential for success in the quickly evolving PC industry. The Lab Manual was developed to assist users in merging tutorial and lab experiences for maximum understanding in a dynamic environment. To order a copy, consult your sales rep or point your browser to www.course.com.

ACKNOWLEDGMENTS

Working with the people at Course Technology has been nothing short of a delight. Kristen Duerr, Jennifer Normandin, and Daphne Barbas of CT, thanks for your support, encouragement, and diligence. Thank you, Janet Weinrib, the Developmental Editor, for keeping me on track. Thank you, Mike Walker, Beth Snider, and David Ridarick, for your tremendous research efforts.

Floyd Winters of Manatee Community College has made important contributions to the book. Thank you, Floyd, for help with the troubleshooting guidelines, review questions, key-term definitions, and hands-on projects. Without your contributions, the book would not be as powerful a learning tool as it is.

The reviewers all showed a genuine interest in the book's success; their help was invaluable. Thank you to: Cindy Childers, Roane State Community College; Melanie Guinn, Indian Hills Community College; Dan Heighton, Clark State Community College; David Koenig, Training Directions College; Shayan Mirabi, ITT Technical Institute; Richard Mossip, Rockland Community College; Don Myers, Vincennes University; Joe Sloop, Surry Community College; Raymond Ward, Garland County Community College; Lynn Wells, Muskingum Area Technical College; and Floyd Winters, Manatee Community College.

A very special thank you to my daughters, Jennifer and Joy. Thank you, girls, for your sincere support, for coffee at midnight, and for all the other many things you did to keep a home running while I wrote.

This book is dedicated to the covenant of God with man on earth.

Jean Andrews, Ph.D.

READ THIS BEFORE YOU BEGIN

The following hardware, software, and other equipment are needed to do the hands-on projects at the end of chapters:

- 8 MB RAM (16 MB recommended)
- You will need a working PC that can be taken apart and reassembled. Use a 486 or higher computer.
- Troubleshooting skills can better be practiced with an assortment of nonworking expansion cards that can be used to simulate problems.
- DOS, Microsoft Windows 3.x, and Microsoft Windows 95 are needed to complete projects in Chapters 1 through 11. Microsoft Windows NT Workstation is needed for Chapter 12. Chapters 13 through 18 use a combination of all these operating systems and environments.
- Equipment required to work on hardware includes a grounding mat and grounding strap and flat-head and Phillips-head screwdrivers. A multimeter is needed for Chapter 10 projects.
- Before undertaking any of the lab exercises, starting with Chapter 3, please review the safety guidelines below.

Installing Nuts & Bolts

Install Nuts & Bolts from the CD-ROM under either Windows 3.x or Windows 95.

PROTECT YOURSELF, THE HARDWARE, AND THE SOFTWARE

When you work on a computer it is possible to harm both the computer and yourself. The most common accident that happens when attempting to fix a computer problem is the erasing of software or data. Experimenting without knowing what you are doing can cause damage. To prevent these sorts of accidents, as well as the physically dangerous ones, take a few safety precautions. The text below describes the potential sources of damage to computers and how to protect against them.

Power to the Computer

To protect both yourself and the equipment, turn off the power before doing anything to the inside of a machine. Consider the monitor and the power supply to be "black boxes." Never remove the cover or put your hands inside this equipment unless you know about the hazards of charged capacitors. Both the power supply and the monitor can hold a dangerous level of electricity even after they are turned off and disconnected from a power source. When working inside a computer, turn off the power but leave the power cable plugged in to provide a good ground, unless the PC is on a grounded mat.

Static Electricity, or ESD

Electrostatic discharge (ESD), commonly known as static electricity, is an electrical charge at rest. A static charge can build up on the surface of a nongrounded conductor and on nonconductive surfaces such as clothing or plastic. When a nongrounded surface that has a static charge on it touches a grounded conductor, the charge is released. To see how this works, turn off the lights in a room, scuff your feet on the carpet, and touch another person. Occasionally you'll be able to see and feel the charge in your fingers. If you can feel the charge, then you discharged at least 3,000 volts of static electricity. If you hear the discharge, then you released at least 6,000 volts. If you see the discharge, then you released at least 8,000 volts of ESD. A charge of less than 3,000 volts can damage most electronic components. You can touch a chip on a card or systemboard and damage the chip with ESD and never feel, hear, or see the discharge.

There are two types of damage that ESD can cause in an electronic component: catastrophic failures and upset failures. A catastrophic failure destroys the component beyond use. An upset failure damages the component so that it does not perform well, even though it may still function to some degree. Upset failures are the most difficult to detect because they are not so easily observed.

Protect Against ESD

To protect the computer against ESD, always ground yourself before touching electronic components, including the hard drive, disk drive, systemboard, expansion cards, processors, and SIMMs. Ground yourself and the computer parts, using one or more of the following static control devices or methods:

- ***Ground bracelet or static strap:*** A ground bracelet is a strap you wear around your wrist. The other end is attached to a grounded conductor such as the computer case or a ground mat, or it can plug into a wall outlet (only the ground prong makes a connection!).

- ***Rubber mats or ground mats:*** Ground mats can come equipped with a cord to plug into a wall outlet to provide a grounded surface on which to work. Remember, if you lift the component off the mat, it is no longer grounded and is susceptible to ESD.

- ***Static shielding bags:*** New components come shipped in static shielding bags. Save the bags to store other devices that are not currently installed in a PC.

The best solution to protect against ESD is to use a ground bracelet together with a ground mat. If you do not have a ground mat or a ground bracelet, leave the power cord plugged into the electrical outlet so that the computer case is grounded, and touch the computer case before you touch a component. When passing a chip to another person, ground yourself. Leave components inside their protective bags until ready to use. Work on hard floors, not carpet, or use antistatic spray on the carpets. Generally, don't work on a computer if you or the computer have just come inside from the cold.

There is an exception to grounding yourself when working with computers. Inside a monitor case, there is substantial danger of stored voltage from capacitors. When working inside a monitor, you don't want to be grounded, as you would provide a conduit for the voltage to discharge through your body. In this situation, be careful *not* to ground yourself.

When handling systemboards and expansion cards, don't touch the chips on the boards. Don't stack boards on top of each other, which could accidentally dislodge a chip. Hold cards by the edges, but don't touch the edge connections on the card.

Don't touch a chip with a magnetized screwdriver. When using a multimeter to measure electricity, be careful not to touch a chip with the probes. When changing DIP switches, don't use a graphite pencil, because graphite is magnetized; a ballpoint pen works very well.

After you unpack a new device or software that has been wrapped in cellophane, remove the cellophane from the work area quickly. Don't allow anyone who is not properly grounded to touch components. Do not store cards within one foot of monitors, because they can discharge as much as 29,000 volts of ESD onto the screen.

Hold the component by the edges. Don't touch any of the soldered components on a card. If you need to put an electronic device down, place it on a grounded mat or on a static shielding bag. Keep components away from your hair and clothing.

Protect Hard Drives and Disks

Always turn off a computer before moving it, to protect the hard drive, which is always spinning when the computer is turned on (unless the drive has a sleep mode). Never jar a computer while the hard disk is running. Avoid placing a PC on the floor, where the user can accidentally kick it.

Never close the door of a double-sided 5¼-inch drive without either a disk or a cardboard shipping disk in the drive. If the two read/write heads touch each other, the heads may be scratched.

Follow the usual precautions to protect disks. Keep them away from magnetic fields, heat, and extreme cold. Don't open the floppy shuttle window or touch the surface of the disk inside the housing. Treat disks with care and they'll generally last for years.

How Computers Work - An Overview

Like millions of other computer users, you have probably used your microcomputer to play games, explore the Internet, write papers, build spreadsheets, or create a professional-looking proposal or flyer. You can perform all these applications without understanding exactly what goes on behind the computer case or monitor screen. But if you are curious to learn more about microcomputers, and if you want to graduate from simply being the end-user of your computer to becoming the master of your machine, then this book is for you. This book is written for anyone who wants to understand what is happening "behind the scenes" in order to install and set up new software for a user, install new hardware, diagnose both hardware and software problems, and make decisions about purchasing new hardware. This book provides the background you need to become a computer support person and helps prepare you for the A+ certification process, which is described in the Preface.

This chapter introduces you to the inside of your computer, a world of electronic and mechanical devices that has evolved over just a few short years to become one of the most powerful technical tools of our society. The only assumption made here are that you are a computer user, that is, you can turn on your machine, load a software package, and use that software to accomplish a task. Now this book will help you see what goes on behind the scenes when you do those things.

**IN THIS CHAPTER
YOU WILL LEARN:**

- How hardware components function together to make a microcomputer work
- How software interacts with hardware
- How an operating system and applications software interact

HARDWARE

The **hardware** of a computer is its physical equipment, such as the monitor, the keyboard, and memory chips. The **software** is the set of instructions that directs the computer to accomplish a task. Some software communicates with other software, which in turn instructs hardware. Ultimately, instructions must be translated into the electronic changes in hardware that actually execute processes. Most of the time, it's easy to distinguish hardware from software. For example, a floppy disk is hardware, but a file on the disk containing a set of instructions is software. This software file, sometimes called a **program**, might be written on the disk today, but you can erase that program file tomorrow and write a new one to the disk. In this case, it is clear that a floppy disk is a permanent physical entity whereas the program is not. Sometimes, however, hardware and software are not so easy to distinguish. For example, a **ROM** (read-only memory) microchip on a circuit board inside your computer has software instructions permanently etched into it during fabrication. This software is actually a part of the hardware and can never be erased. Here, you have an example of hardware and software married together, and it's difficult to separate the two, either physically or logically. Some even give a new name to such hybrid components, calling them **firmware**. This section will examine the hardware components of a microcomputer system.

OUTSIDE THE CASE

When you look at a computer, the first thing you notice is the hardware, the physical equipment (see Figure 1-1). Many hardware devices are designed to allow users to interact with the computer: some hardware displays the output of programs, and other hardware permits you to input data or instructions. These **input/output devices** outside the computer case are also called **peripheral devices**, and they communicate with what is inside the computer case through cables attached to the case at a connection called a **port**.

The **monitor** is the visual device that displays the primary output of the computer. Once, all monitors were monochrome (one color), but today they display text and graphics in color. Hardware manufacturers typically rate a monitor according to the size of its screen (in inches) and by the number of pixels displayed on the screen. A **pixel** is a dot or unit of color that is the smallest unit of display on a monitor. A **video card** (a board containing circuits and chips that controls video display) inside the computer controls the monitor.

The **keyboard** is the primary input device of a computer. Standard keyboards today are called enhanced keyboards and hold 102 keys. Some ergonomic keyboards are curved to be more comfortable to the hands and wrists. In addition, some keyboards come equipped with a mouse port—a plug into which a mouse, another input device, can be attached to the keyboard—although it is more common for the mouse port to be located directly on the computer case.

Figure 1-1 Typical components of a computer system

A **mouse** is a pointing device used to move a pointer on the screen and to make selections on the screen. The bottom of a mouse houses a rotating ball that is used to track movement and control the location of the pointer. The one, two, or three buttons on the top of the mouse serve different purposes for different software packages. For example, Windows 95 uses the left mouse button to execute a command and the right mouse button to display information about the command.

A very important output device is the **printer**, which produces output on paper, often called **hard copy**. The most popular printers available today are ink jet, laser, and dot matrix printers. Different printers understand data and commands according to different standards and protocols. As with any peripheral device, a printer needs a program to convert data and commands from applications software into the standards and protocols the printer can understand. This program is often called a **device driver**. Applications software often passes print requests to the printer driver, which communicates with the printer. With the device drivers doing the interpreting, applications software developers do not have to include the specific protocol and standards for every printer that might be used in the applications they write.

During installation of software written for DOS, a person installing software was asked to select a printer for the software to use. In Windows environments that selection during installation is no longer necessary. Instead, the application sends print jobs to Windows for printing. Windows uses the default Windows printer unless another printer from the Windows printer list is selected before printing.

All four input/output devices—the keyboard, the monitor, the mouse and the printer—communicate with the computer through cables attached to the computer at ports on the back of the computer case (see Figure 1-2). Most computers have the ports located on the back of the case, but some models put the ports on the front of the case for easy access.

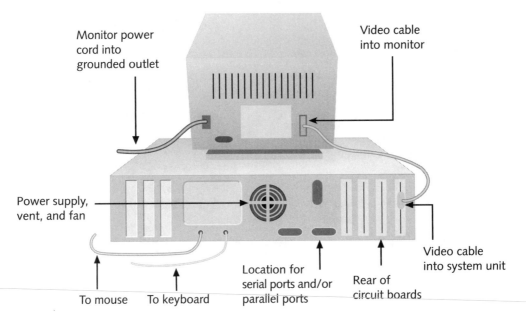

Monitor power cord into grounded outlet

Video cable into monitor

Power supply, vent, and fan

Video cable into system unit

To mouse   To keyboard

Location for serial ports and/or parallel ports

Rear of circuit boards

Figure 1-2   Cables connected to ports

The monitor and the printer each needs its own power supply. Electrical power cords for them connect to electrical outlets. Sometimes the computer case provides an electrical outlet for the monitor's power cord in order to eliminate the need of one more power outlet.

INSIDE THE CASE

Inside the case are the systemboard, at least one floppy disk drive, a power supply, hard drive, and circuit boards or cards, discussed below. Many components inside the case are designed for easy removal and installation so that users can change them to meet their individual needs (see Figure 1-3).

On the Systemboard

The **systemboard**, sometimes called the **motherboard**, is the most important circuit board inside the case (see Figure 1-4). A circuit board is a board that holds microchips and the circuitry that connects these chips. The systemboard contains the most crucial microchips and circuits in the computer. Smaller circuit boards are sometimes called circuit cards, adapter boards, expansion cards, interface cards, or simply **cards**. The video card discussed earlier is an example of an interface card.

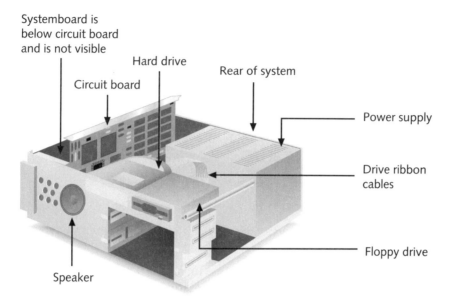

Figure 1-3 Inside the computer case

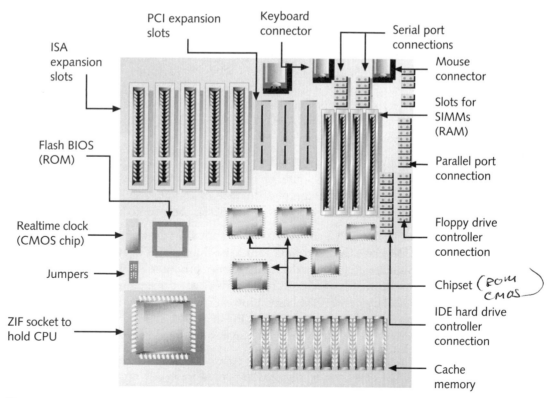

Figure 1-4 Components on a systemboard

The systemboard is the most complicated piece of equipment inside the case and is covered in detail in Chapter 3. The systemboard components introduced in this section and labeled in Figure 1-4 are:

- ZIF socket to hold the central processing unit (CPU), the computer's most important chip, in which all processes are ultimately executed on an electronic level

- 8-bit and 16-bit ISA expansion slots to connect circuit boards to the systemboard

- PCI expansion slots to connect new circuit boards on Pentium PCs

- Slots to hold SIMMs, which contain the system RAM, or random access memory

- Cache memory to speed up memory access

- Flash BIOS (basic input/output system) chip to control basic hardware functions

- Power supply connections to provide electricity to the system board and expansion cards

The systemboard holds the most important microchip in the computer system, called the **central processing unit (CPU)** or **microprocessor**, which does all the "thinking" of the computer. Well, almost all. Today most computers contain microchips that relieve the CPU of many tasks to increase the overall speed of the computer.

The CPU is the chip inside the computer on which most computer processes must ultimately be executed. CPUs are manufactured out of semiconductor material, which allows varying voltages to be carried along the same pathways, qualifying this material to transmit streams of bits and bytes that are the heart of basic computer processing (see Appendix D). While this book will touch on different types of machines, it will focus on the most common personal computers (PCs), referred to as IBM-compatible, which are built around a family of microprocessors manufactured by Intel Corporation. The Macintosh family of computers, manufactured by Apple Computer Corporation are built around a family of microprocessors manufactured by Motorola Corporation.

In addition to a CPU, some older systemboards also contain a chip that supports and enhances the function of some older CPUs. Many applications used this chip, called a **coprocessor**, to speed up the performance of certain CPU math functions. Most systemboards manufactured before 1995 have a special socket for the coprocessor.

In addition to the CPU, the systemboard contains two kinds of memory chips: ROM and RAM. ROM chips, as mentioned earlier, hold programs or software that tell the CPU how to perform many utility tasks that manage the computer. ROM chips are manufactured with programs permanently stored on them. If you want to upgrade these utility programs, usually you must buy new ROM chips. However, there are new ROM chips on the market that actually can be reprogrammed. Called **Flash ROM**, the software stored on these chips can be overwritten by new software that remains on the chip until it is overwritten.

The other type of memory chip on the systemboard is called a **RAM** (random access memory) chip. RAM chips can be installed individually directly on the systemboard or in banks of several chips on a small board that plugs into the systemboard. The most common type of board that holds memory chips is called a **SIMM** (single-in-line memory module). RAM chips hold both data and programming instructions while the CPU processes both. RAM chips are also called **primary storage**. Whatever information is stored in primary storage is lost when the computer is turned off, because RAM chips need a continuous supply of electrical power to hold the data or software stored in them. Memory that is dependent on a continuous power supply is lost every time power to the computer is interrupted. It is called **volatile** because it is by nature temporary. By contrast, memory that is in place permanently, such as that etched into ROM chips, is called **nonvolatile**.

The CPU uses memory addresses to access data or program instructions stored in memory. The CPU, as well as every other device in the computer, uses a binary (base 2) numbering scheme to identify memory addresses. These numbers are sometimes converted to hexadecimal (base 16) rather than to decimal (base 10) for display on screen. Base 16 is used instead of base 10 because it is easier for the computer to quickly convert binary to hexadecimal numbers rather than to decimal (base 10) numbers. See Appendix D for a discussion of the three number systems and how to convert from one system to another.

In DOS, memory is divided into different areas, as shown in Table 1-1. This division of memory began with DOS and later was used by Windows 3.1, 3.11, and Windows 95. We refine this simple view of memory in future chapters. Windows NT and OS/2 operating systems use a different method of organizing memory. Another entirely different method of managing memory is used by the Macintosh operating system for Apple computers.

Table 1-1   Divisions of Memory Under DOS

Range of Memory Addresses	Type of Memory
0 to 640K	Conventional or base memory
640K to 1024K	Upper memory
Above 1024K	Extended memory

Also on the systemboard is a **system clock** that times the activities of the chips on the systemboard. This clock ensures that all activities are performed in a synchronized fashion by providing a beat much like a metronome keeps the beat for a musician. In new computers, this chip contains memory or RAM, enough to hold configuration or setup information about the computer, and is called the **CMOS configuration chip**. The term CMOS stands for complementary metal oxide semiconductor and refers to the way the chip is manufactured. This chip is responsible for remembering how memory is allocated, which hard drives and floppy drives are present, and so forth. When the computer is first turned on, it looks to this CMOS chip to find out what hardware it should expect to find. A similar function is performed on Macintosh computers by a chip called the parameter Ram (PRAM) chip. The CMOS chip is powered by a very small trickle of electricity from a small battery that is located on the systemboard or computer case, usually close to the CMOS chip itself.

Chips are usually of two types: CMOS and TTL (transistor-transistor logic) chips. CMOS chips require less electricity, hold data longer after the electricity is turned off, are slower, and produce less heat than TTL chips do. There are many CMOS chips on the systemboard (most CPUs are CMOSs). In the computer industry, however, the term "CMOS chip" has come to mean the one chip on the systemboard that holds the configuration or setup information. If you hear the following: "What does CMOS say?" or "Let's change CMOS," the person is talking about the configuration or setup information stored on this one CMOS chip.

Besides the CPU and memory chips, the systemboard contains circuits or paths that enable data to move from chip to chip. You can see these data paths on the systemboard as lines, commonly called **traces**, on either the top or bottom of the board. The system of pathways along which data is passed from chip to chip on the board and the protocol and methods used for transmission together are referred to as the **bus**. One way a bus is rated is by the number of bits that can move down a data path simultaneously. Think of these bits as traveling side by side down the path just like cars travel on several lanes of a freeway. The data path is that part of the overall bus architecture that we are most familiar with. In Chapter 3 we discuss the other components that collectively make up the bus.

Data paths often terminate at expansion slots. An **expansion slot** is a slot or plug where you can add interface cards to enhance the hardware of your computer. The size and shape of the expansion slot is dependent on the kind of bus your computer uses. Therefore, one way to determine the kind of bus you have is to examine the expansion slots on the systemboard. For example, the video local bus (VL-bus) slot is one of the longest and is made for a video card and other expansion cards that require very fast data throughput. The newer slots on a Pentium systemboard, called PCI (peripheral component interconnect) slots, are some of the shortest, but fastest, slots of all.

The systemboard contains additional chips. These include the chip set, a group of chips designed to support various functions of the systemboard and a special kind of fast RAM called cache memory, switches that can hold setup information about the systemboard called jumpers, capacitors, and other components. You will read about these in more detail in Chapter 3, but you've got the basics now.

Interface Cards

As discussed above, most computers have one or more expansion slots, as shown in Figure 1-5. Some common circuit boards you might find plugged into the expansion slots on your computer are a video card, a hard drive adapter card, or a multi-input/output controller card. These cards control various peripheral devices. If your computer has an internal modem, that modem is installed as an expansion card. Another common kind of expansion card is a network card, which provides your computer with access to a network.

The easiest way to determine the function of a particular expansion card (short of seeing its name written on the card, which doesn't happen very often) is to look at the end of the card that fits against the back of the computer case. The card provides access to the outside of the case through a connector or port attached to the card (see Figure 1-6). A network card, for example, has a port designed to fit the network cable. An internal modem has one, usually two, telephone jacks as its ports. A standard I/O controller card usually has at least one parallel port designed to fit a printer cable connection and a serial port designed to fit a modem cable connection or some other serial device. Parallel and serial refer to the way in which data and instructions are transmitted along a cable. Parallel transmission refers to streams of bits flowing parallel to each other while serial transmission refers to one long stream of single-file bits. This is further explained in Chapter 4.

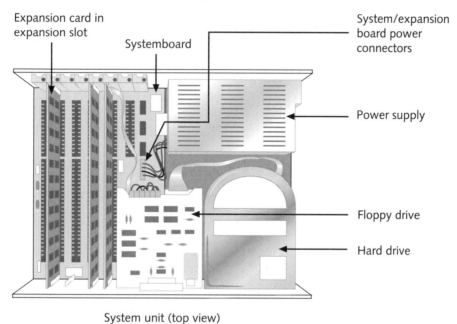

System unit (top view)

Figure 1-5   Circuit boards mounted in expansion slots

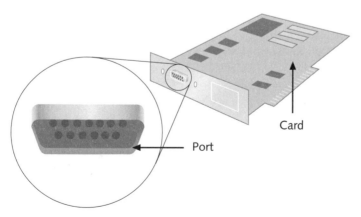

Figure 1-6   Expansion card and port

The Power Supply

Besides the systemboard and circuit boards, another essential hardware component inside the case is the power supply usually located near the rear of the case (see Figure 1-7). This power supply does not actually generate electricity but converts it and reduces it to a voltage that the computer can handle. Power cables from the power supply contain either 5 or 12 volts of DC current. In addition to supplying power for the computer, the power supply runs a conventional fan directly from the electrical output voltage to help keep the inside of the computer case cool. When a computer is running, this fan and the spinning of the hard drive are the two primary noise makers.

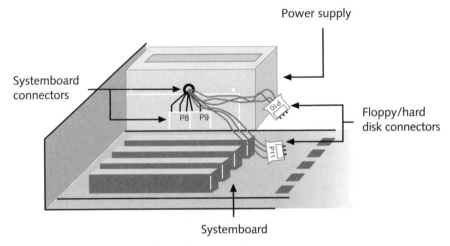

Figure 1-7   Power supply with connections

Secondary Storage

As you remember, the RAM on the systemboard is called primary storage. Primary storage holds both data and instructions as the CPU is processing both. These data and instructions are also stored on devices such as hard drives and floppy disks in locations that are remote from the CPU. This remote storage is called **secondary storage**. Data and instructions cannot be processed by the CPU from secondary storage, but must first be copied into primary storage (RAM) for processing. The most important difference between primary storage and secondary storage is that secondary storage is permanent storage. When you turn off your computer, the information in secondary storage remains intact. Conversely, the information in primary storage, or RAM, is lost when you turn off the machine. The four most popular secondary storage devices are hard disks, floppy disks, cassette tapes, and CD-ROMs.

The hard disk or hard drive usually is located near the front of the case and provides secondary storage for the computer. Data or programs written to the hard drive are stored permanently there until you erase them. Several years ago, hard drives were optional equipment but are now essential, primarily because of the larger storage capacity required by today's software.

1

The **hard drive** is a sealed case containing platters or discs that rotate at a high speed (see Figure 1-8). As the platters rotate, an arm with a sensitive read/write head reaches across the platters both writing new data to them and reading existing data from them. Managing a hard drive and understanding how one works are the subjects of Chapters 5 and 6. The hard drive requires a controller to manage it. The **hard drive controller** is a set of microchips both containing software to manage the hard drive and temporarily holding data that is passed back and forth to the hard drive. In the past, hard drives using older technology required a separate controller expansion card. Today, most hard drives have the controller on a circuit board attached directly to the hard drive. In this case, the data cable from the hard drive connects to a small adapter card in an expansion slot. The adapter card is the interface between the hard drive and the CPU; data passes from the hard drive to the adapter card to the systemboard to the CPU. Some computers have this adapter card built into the systemboard. In this case, the cable coming from the hard drive connects directly to the systemboard.

Figure 1-8   Hard drive with sealed cover removed

The older hard drives that had the controller on a large interface card in an expansion slot used two cables to connect the controller card to the hard drive: one cable was used to transmit instructions that controlled the hard drive from the controller card, and the other passed data back and forth. Regardless of the setup, the controller and the hard drive must use the same technology and be compatible for communication to be possible.

The read/write heads at the ends of the read/write arms on a hard drive get extremely close to the platters but do not actually touch them. The minute clearance between the heads and platters makes hard drives susceptible to destruction. Should a computer be bumped or moved while the hard drive is in operation, a head can easily bump against the platter and scratch the surface. Such an accident causes a "hard drive crash," often making the hard drive unusable. In addition, data sometimes "fades" off the hard drive over time.

Another secondary storage device inside the case is a floppy drive. Floppy drives come in two common sizes: 3½ inches and 5¼ inches. The newer 3½-inch disks use more advanced technology and actually hold more data than the older 5¼-inch disks did. Like hard drives, floppy drives must have controllers to manage them. Sometimes these controllers are on interface cards, and sometimes the floppy drive controller chips are located directly on the systemboard. You can tell which is the case for your computer by following the data cable from your floppy drive to the board. Floppy drives also require power, which they receive from the power supply through a power cord.

Figure 1-9 shows a complete floppy drive subsystem in a microcomputer. A disk is inserted into the front of the floppy drive. Electricity to the drive is provided by a power cord from the power supply that connects to a power port at the back of the drive. A data cable also is connected to the back of the drive and runs to either a controller card inserted into an expansion slot on the systemboard or directly to the systemboard that contains controller chips, which completes the subsystem.

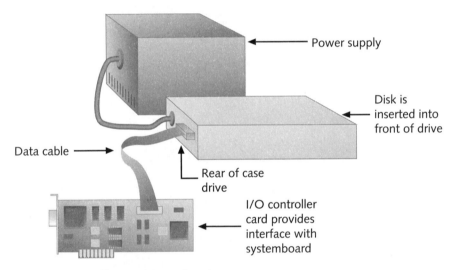

Figure 1-9   A floppy drive subsystem

SOFTWARE

Software consists of programs written by programmers that instruct computers to perform specific tasks. There are two kinds of programs written for microcomputers: operating systems and applications software. There are several operating systems and numerous applications software packages available. A microcomputer needs only one operating system (OS), but most users work with several applications software packages. Another important type of software made up of programs that instruct software how to communicate with hardware is referred to as the **basic input/output system** or **BIOS**. BIOS is the interface between software and hardware. BIOS programs can be stored on ROM chips either on the systemboard or on other circuit boards. This is called ROM BIOS or simply BIOS for short. The BIOS programs with instructions for peripheral devices are often together referred to as **System BIOS**. The BIOS Startup

Program, which is discussed below, runs many of the startup functions of the computer. (Note that there are other types of programs, called **device drivers**, that serve the same functions as BIOS programs but which are stored on secondary storage devices such as hard drives.)

OPERATING SYSTEM

The most common OS among IBM computers and IBM-compatible computers is DOS, the disk operating system. For years, DOS has been used with Windows, a program that is an intermediary between DOS and the user and is designed to provide a user-friendly interface. There have been a number of generations of Windows, including Windows 3.1 and Windows 3.11 (which is also called Windows for WorkGroups), which together are referred to as Windows 3.x. With Windows 3.x DOS continues to be the operating system. The more recent Windows 95 (and future Windows generations) provides both a user-friendly interface as well as actually conducting OS functions. Other operating systems include Macintosh for Apple computers, UNIX, OS/2, and Windows NT. This book looks at different operating systems, paying careful attention to their similarities and differences.

Today operating systems are stored on hard drives, but applications software can be stored on either hard drives, floppy disks, or CD-ROMs. Software is stored as files designated as **program files**. A **file** is a collection of data or programmed instructions that is stored on a secondary storage device and assigned a single name, which the OS uses to identify the file. Under DOS, a file's name has two parts. The first part, called the **filename**, contains up to eight characters. The second part, called the **file extension**, contains up to three characters. When you write the file extension in DOS commands, you separate the extension from the filename with a period. Acceptable file extensions for program files are .COM, .BAT, and .EXE. For example, the WordPerfect program file is named WP.EXE. Its filename is WP and file extension is .EXE.

With the introduction of Windows 95, long filenames traditionally used only by the Macintosh OS became available to IBM-compatible PCs. Under Windows 95 and Windows NT, filenames can be as long as 256 characters and may contain spaces. You must be careful when using long filenames with Windows 95 because Windows 95 still contains a portion of DOS, which can only understand an 8-character filename, 3-character extension format. When the DOS part of the system is operating, it will truncate long filenames and assign new 8-character ones. More information about naming files appears in Chapter 4.

Computers cannot function without an OS controlling them. Therefore, whenever a computer is turned on, one of the first things it does is look for an OS. This process of powering up and looking for an OS is called **booting** and is discussed next.

Although the OS is stored in files on the hard drive, these stored programs cannot be executed from their secondary storage locations. As explained above, these instructions first must be copied from secondary storage into RAM, or primary storage. The CPU can then read from one memory location in RAM to another to receive and follow instructions.

Figure 1-10 shows this two-step process. First, the computer startup program finds the OS program file stored on the hard drive and copies the file into RAM. The program file contains a list of instructions; each instruction is stored in a separate memory location with a memory address assigned to it. In the second step, control is given to these instructions in RAM. Beginning with the first memory address, the CPU executes the instruction stored at that address. Sometimes, an instruction causes control to be sent to a memory address other than the next one in sequential order. This action is called a program **jump**, as demonstrated in the move from Instruction 4 to Instruction 6 in Figure 1-10.

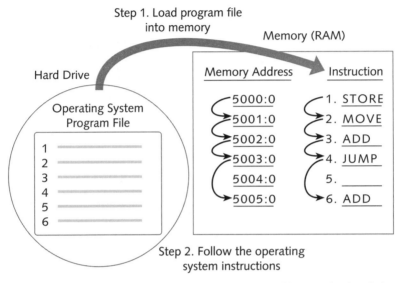

Figure 1-10   The operating system is stored in files on the hard drive but is executed from memory

Operating systems serve many functions. Among them are the following:

- Managing BIOS
- Managing files on secondary storage devices
- Managing primary memory (RAM)
- Diagnosing problems with software and hardware
- Interfacing hardware and software (that is, interpreting applications software needs to the hardware and interpreting hardware needs to applications software)
- Performing utility procedures requested by the user, often concerning secondary storage devices, such as formatting new disks, deleting files, copying files, and changing the system date

While DOS has served computing well over the years, it has some serious computing limitations primarily because it has been modified extensively as hardware capabilities increased. When computer users started using DOS in the early 1980s, computer systems were very small and the power and usefulness of the software and hardware were limited. The computer industry made assumptions and decisions based on limitations in power and memory that still limit us today

1

even though the power and memory have increased astronomically. Such outdated limitations particularly affect the way hardware and software interact through the OS. Some drawbacks of DOS were partly solved by Windows 3.1 and Windows 3.11. Windows 95, which contains parts of DOS and parts of a completely rewritten operating system, offers even greater improvements.

Interfacing with the Operating System

As explained above, an OS is loaded into memory and given control during the booting process. After booting is complete, the OS either automatically executes an applications software program or turns to you for its next instruction. You see an interface on the monitor screen. This interface can be one of three types:

A command-driven interface.   With a command-driven interface, you key in command lines to tell the OS to perform operations (see Figure 1-11). For instance, the command-driven interface of DOS is the C prompt, which looks like this:

    `C>` or `C:\>`

Computer users who are good typists and are very familiar with DOS commands often prefer this kind of OS interface.

A menu-driven interface.   Some operating systems allow you to choose from a list of options displayed on the screen. An example of such a menu-driven interface is File Manager in Windows 3.1. From the drop-down menus, you can format disks, rename files, copy and delete files, and perform many other operations to manage files and storage devices (see Figure 1-12).

```
C:\>copy autoexec.bat a:
        1 file(s) copied

C:\>date
Current date is Wed 10-15-1997
Enter new date (mm-dd-yy):

C:\>time
Current time is  6:12:09.41a
Enter new time:

C:\>ver


MS-DOS Version 6.22


C:\>copy config.sys config.bak
Overwrite CONFIG.BAK (Yes/No/All)?y

        1 file(s) copied

C:\>
```
⤒————————————————————————————————— C prompt

Figure 1-11   An operating system command-driven interface: the C prompt

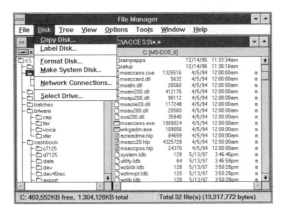

Figure 1-12   A menu-driven interface: File Manager in Windows 3.1

An icon-driven interface.   With an icon-driven interface, sometimes called **a graphical-user interface** or **GUI**, you perform operations by selecting icons (or pictures) on the screen. Examples of icon-driven interfaces are Macintosh, OS/2, and Windows. Figure 1-13 shows the Windows 3.1 Program Manager with an icon interface. You double-click an icon with the left button to execute an applications software program. In Figure 1-14, Windows 95 offers a slightly different icon-driven desktop with shortcuts to applications software. The **desktop** of the OS is the initial screen that appears together with its menus, commands, and icons. You double-click a shortcut icon on the desktop with the left mouse button to execute the applications software program. Today's operating systems are more likely to use a GUI than a command-driven desktop.

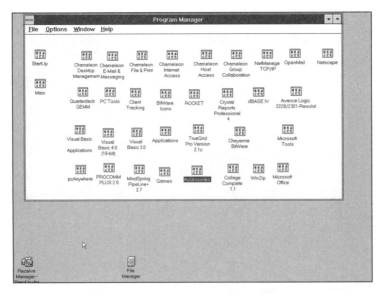

Figure 1-13   An icon-driven interface: Program Manager in Windows 3.1

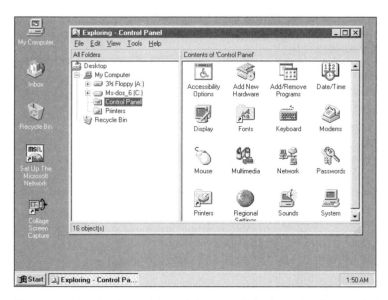

Figure 1-14   An icon-driven interface: Windows Explorer in Windows 95

Survey of Operating Systems

Operating systems continue to evolve as hardware and software technologies improve. As you look at several operating systems, you will see the evolution process from DOS to Windows 3.1, Windows 3.11, and Windows 95. To help you understand these gradual improvements in operating systems, you need to understand the following terms:

Multitasking.   Multitasking refers to the ability of a CPU to do more than one thing at a time. Only the newer Pentium CPU's discussed in Chapter 3 can do this. The older i386 and i486 CPUs could do only one thing at a time (80386 and 80486 CPUs are often abbreviated as i386 and i486 in documentation; the i stands for the chip manufacturer, Intel).

Environment.   Environment refers to the characteristics of software supporting and surrounding applications software. For example, for applications software to offer you a window with mouse movement, buttons to click, and icons to view, it must be supported by a GUI environment, such as Windows. Such an application is said to be in a "GUI environment" to work. Another example is the DOS environment that offers to its applications software only a "single-tasking environment." The software does not expect another applications software package to be running concurrently with it.

Multitasking environment.   Multitasking environment refers to an environment in which an OS allows you to run more than one application at a time. Actually, the computer only *appears* to be doing more than one thing at a time, while it is really switching back and forth between tasks, and programs. You observe a multitasking environment when you have two applications open, each in its own window. You don't need to close one application before opening another. DOS does not handle a multi-tasking environment, but Windows does.

Windows 3.x and Windows 95 accomplish multitasking by passing segments of the applications' processing needs one at a time to the CPU, thus sharing the CPU's resources. This allows you to move back and forth among applications, leaving more than one application open on the desktop at any given time (see Figure 1-15).

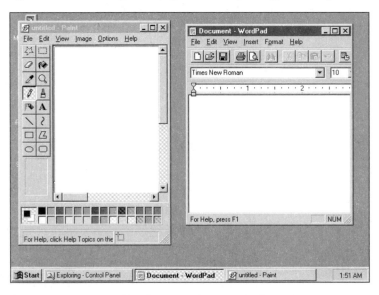

Figure 1-15   A multitasking environment allows two or more applications to run simultaneously

Operating Environment.   Operating environment refers to the overall support that software such as Windows 3.x provides to applications software, including multitasking or GUI (which DOS does not offer). Windows 95 moved forward in software development by providing an operating environment and an OS combined in a single package. Windows 3.x is the "middle man" that manages this pseudo-multitasking environment by passing tasks to DOS one at a time. DOS manages its single-tasking environment and relates to the hardware in single-task fashion. Windows provides the multitasking environment to the applications.

However, as Figure 1-16 shows, Windows 3.x both performs some of the functions of an OS and provides the environment within which the applications software works. Figure 1-16 shows that the applications software relates only to Windows. There is usually no attempt to make applications software interact directly with DOS, System BIOS, or the hardware in a Windows environment. Windows 3.x sometimes interfaces directly with hardware as when

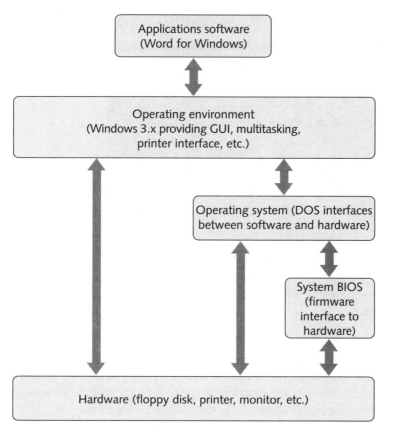

Figure 1-16 Windows 3.x and DOS supporting applications software

printing with one of its own printer drivers. In this case, Windows 3.x is serving as the OS. Sometimes, however, Windows passes such functions to DOS. DOS can choose to relate directly to the hardware or it can choose to pass the hardware request to System BIOS, firmware on the systemboard and interface cards, to process the request.

In this section we compare several operating systems based on these criteria:

- What kind of interface does the OS provide for the user?

- Can the OS do multitasking?

- Can the OS easily manage large quantities of primary memory (RAM) and secondary storage?

- How many and what kinds of applications are written to work with the OS (see Figure 1-17)?

- How powerful must the hardware be to make efficient use of the OS?

- How does the OS perform in a network?

Figure 1-17   A choice of operating systems is partially
determined by the variety of software that
uses it

Below is a list of the six main operating systems used on PCs, along with eight tables (see Tables 1-2 through 1-8) summarizing the advantages and disadvantages of each system. When choosing an operating system, consider all the criteria discussed below. Your choice will be determined by the size of your microcomputer system, your familiarity with the various operating systems, and the applications software you plan to use.

DOS (disk operating system).   The first operating system used by IBM microcomputers, for years DOS remained the unchallenged standard for operating systems used by IBM and IBM-compatible machines. Most seasoned microcomputer users are comfortable and familiar with DOS. Table 1-2 summarizes its advantages and disadvantages.

DOS with Windows 3.1 and 3.11 operating environments.   Written by the same software company that wrote DOS (Microsoft, Inc.), Windows 3.x gives DOS the icon-driven interface that is so popular with users. Windows 3.x is a middle layer or "go-between" program between the user and DOS that DOS runs to provide the operating environment for applications software packages. Windows 3.x, therefore, acts as a mediator linking DOS and the applications software. Table 1-3 summarizes the advantages and disadvantages of using Windows 3.x.

Table 1-2   Advantages and Disadvantages of DOS

Advantages	Disadvantages
Numerous applications software packages were written for DOS (although the number is now diminishing because of the newer, more powerful Windows environments).	Memory management is awkward and sometimes slow.
	DOS has no icon-driven interface.
DOS runs on small, inexpensive microcomputers with a minimum amount of memory and hard drive space.	DOS does only single-tasking; that is, it supports only a single application running at a time.
	DOS was not designed for use on networks. A separate applications software program is necessary for a DOS machine to access a network.
	The last version of DOS written to operate without an icon interface is DOS 6.22, which does not take advantage of the many new CPU features now available.

Table 1-3   Advantages and Disadvantages of DOS with Windows 3.x

Advantages	Disadvantages
DOS with Windows 3.x provides an icon-driven interface.	Memory management is awkward and sometimes slow.
A multitasking environment is provided by Windows managing more than one application by passing segments to DOS that then, in turn, interface with hardware.	DOS with Windows 3.x is sometimes slow due to the complexity of the middle layer or "go-between" concept.
DOS with Windows 3.x can run on relatively inexpensive microcomputer systems with a minimum amount of hard drive space.	The DOS/Windows 3.x combination does not take advantage of the full computing power of present-day CPUs.
Many applications software programs are available today to run with Windows 3.x.	
Windows 3.11, called Windows for Workgroups, was the first Windows environment designed to interface with a network without depending on separate applications software to do the job.	

Windows 95.   Windows 95 takes us one step closer to a new OS but does not completely eliminate DOS. Windows 95 is the marriage of Windows for Workgroups (Windows 3.11) with an updated version of DOS sometimes known as DOS 7.0, together with some completely new additions and improvements to the OS. Table 1-4 summarizes the advantages and disadvantages of Windows 95.

Table 1-4   Advantages and Disadvantages of Windows 95

Advantages	Disadvantages
Windows 95 offers almost complete compatibility for applications written for DOS and earlier versions of Windows.	Windows 95 requires at least a 386 CPU, 8 MB of RAM, and 30 MB of hard drive space.
Windows 95 is a mix of 16-bit and 32-bit processing. It is a mix because it attempts to move computer users forward into more advanced technology while maintaining backward compatibility with older software and hardware. Windows 95 is a bridge to a new OS.	Because of the attempt to bridge older 16-bit software applications with new technology, there are some problems with failures and errors created in this hybrid environment.
Windows 95 offers the ability for one PC to talk with another over phone lines without additional software. It works well for low-end network use, such as when two users want to exchange files.	
Windows 95 offers a very user-friendly and intuitive GUI interface.	
Disk access time is improved over DOS and Windows 3.x.	
Plug-and-play features make installing some new hardware devices easier than with earlier operating systems.	

Windows NT.   Windows NT breaks with previous versions of Windows. Although older applications written for DOS and DOS with Windows might work under Windows NT, Windows NT developers do not guarantee compatibility between the operating systems. The reason older software designed to be used by DOS might not be compatible with Windows NT is because NT is a true 32-bit OS. It takes an aggressive and altogether new approach toward managing hardware resources. Windows NT completely eliminates the underlying relationship with DOS. Table 1-5 summarizes the advantages and disadvantages of Windows NT.

OS/2.   OS/2, written by IBM in cooperation with Microsoft, Inc., provides an altogether new operating system to replace DOS. Errors in earlier versions and OS/2's large computer hardware requirements have made it slow to gain popularity. Table 1-6 summarizes the advantages and disadvantages of OS/2.

1

Table 1-5 Advantages and Disadvantages of Windows NT

Advantages	Disadvantages
Windows NT is designed to work within a powerful client-server architectural environment where networking is of major importance. With client-server arrangements, organizations are able to use their resources more efficiently. The **server** is a computer designated to store programs or data that can be used remotely by PCs and other computers networked with the server, which are referred to as **clients**.	Windows NT requires at least a 486 CPU, 16 MB of RAM, and 120 MB of hard drive space, thus eliminating it as a plausible option for low-end PCs.
	Windows NT is not compatible with some older hardware and software.
Windows NT offers a completely new file management system and file structure with a versatility and power similar to that of UNIX.	
Windows NT comes in two versions, Windows NT Workstation and Windows NT Server. As the names imply, Windows NT is targeting both ends of the client-server market.	
Windows NT Workstation offers both networking over a LAN as well as dial-up over phone lines.	
Windows NT Server offers powerful security as both a file server and in network administration.	

Table 1-6 Advantages and Disadvantages of OS/2

Advantages	Disadvantages
OS/2 can provide a multitasking environment.	Relatively few applications software packages are written for OS/2, although the number is increasing. Later versions of OS/2 run applications written for Windows. All versions of OS/2 run applications written for DOS, although these applications might not make use of the full computing power of OS/2.
OS/2 can handle large quantities of memory directly and quickly.	
OS/2 has an icon-driven interface.	
OS/2 works well in a networking environment.	
	Many microcomputer users are not familiar with OS/2 and avoid it for that reason.
	OS/2 requires a powerful computer system and large amounts of RAM and hard drive space to run efficiently.

Macintosh Operating System. Available only on Macintosh computers, several versions of the Macintosh OS have been written, the latest being System 7.5x. Rhapsody is the next up-and-coming OS for the Macintosh. Rhapsody features easy access to the Internet and has been designed to be Apple Computer's answer to Microsoft's Windows 95 and Windows NT Workstation. In addition, a new version of the Maintosh OS, code-named Tempo, will allow any Macintosh computer to become a web server for a small network. Table 1-7 summarizes the advantages and disadvantages of the Macintosh OS.

Table 1-7 Advantages and Disadvantages of the Macintosh Operating System

Advantages	Disadvantages
The Macintosh OS has an excellent icon-driven interface, and it is easy to learn and use.	Macintosh computers are relatively expensive.
The Macintosh OS provides a multitasking environment.	Historically, the Macintosh was not viewed as a professional's computer but rather was relegated to education and game-playing. Then the Mac gained a significant place in the professional desktop publishing market. Most recently, the availability of more powerful IBM-compatible PCs and operating systems has reduced the demand for the Mac.
The Macintosh OS manages large quantities of memory.	

UNIX Operating System. UNIX originally was written for mainframe computers in the early 1970s; only in the past few years has it become available for many different kinds of computers, including PCs, and it is now a popular OS for networking. UNIX computers are often used for Internet support. Problems with UNIX stem mostly from the lack of consistency from one vender's version to another. Table 1-8 summarizes the advantages and disadvantages of the Unix OS.

Table 1-8 Advantages and Disadvantages of the Unix Operating System

Advantages	Disadvantages
UNIX was written for powerful microcomputer systems and has a strong multitasking capability.	UNIX industry standards are not uniform, making it difficult for UNIX developers, administrators, and users to move from one UNIX vendor to another.
UNIX manages large quantities of memory.	
UNIX performance in a networking environment is excellent.	UNIX requires a powerful, large microcomputer system.
	Few business applications software packages have been written for UNIX for microcomputer systems (although there are several very powerful database packages available under UNIX, such as Informix and Oracle).

APPLICATIONS SOFTWARE

Applications software fits into six categories: word processing, spreadsheet, database management, graphics, communications, and games. There are many different products in each software category. For example, some popular database management packages include Access, Paradox, and Filemaker, and two popular word-processing packages include Word and WordPerfect. More and more applications software manufacturers are producing **suites** of software, which combine a word processor program and spreadsheet program, and usually include a database management program, a presentation package, an e-mail package, as well as a World Wide Web browser package. Suites provide many advantages, including the fact that the programs tend to use the same basic instruction sets; the programs are designed to make it easy to move data from one suite program to another; and files within a suite's programs can be linked, so that updates to data or text are automatically recorded in all linked files.

Applications software is designed to work on top of a particular OS. "On top of" here means that the application depends on the OS, such as MS-DOS or OS/2 in order to run. For example, DOS loads an application and executes it. The application cannot run or even load itself without DOS, much like a document cannot be edited without a word processor program. DOS stays in control of the application the entire time the application is running. The application passes certain functions to DOS, such as reading from a CD-ROM or printing.

In general an application written to work with one OS will not necessarily work with another. An application written to run on DOS does not work on a Macintosh system. There are, however, some exceptions. For instance, OS/2 is written so that any application designed to work with DOS also works with OS/2, an excellent selling point for OS/2. However, to take full advantage of an operating system's power and an applications software's power, you should strive to buy applications software written specifically for the OS that you are using.

Applications software comes written on floppy disks or on CD-ROMs and is usually **installed** on a hard drive. Installing a software package usually is very easy. You typically just insert the first disk of a set of floppies or a CD-ROM, and then type a command, such as A:INSTALL or D:SETUP at the DOS prompt. If you are working in Windows 95, click the **Start** button, click **Run**, and then follow the directions on the screen. We discuss software installation in Chapter 11.

How Software Works

Those who support PCs need to understand how the hardware, the applications software, and the OS interact. Recall that when you first turn on a computer, the computer starts or boots itself, and that in the final stages of the startup process, the computer passes control to the OS. After the OS completes its own startup procedures, it passes control to the user, through a command interface.

For example, if DOS is your OS, the DOS prompt displays basic information and gives you the opportunity to enter some command for the OS to perform.

It is common for computers to provide a DOS prompt that looks like this when the machine is first turned on.

    c:\>

This prompt is usually called the C prompt. The letter C designates the hard drive. The DOS prompt C:\ (see Figure 1-18) means that the OS was copied from this drive C and root directory when the machine was first turned on. As part of the startup process, drive C then becomes the default drive and directory, sometimes called the **current** drive and directory. We define the **default drive** and **directory** as the drive and directory that DOS automatically uses to save and retrieve files. Sometimes the OS is copied from a floppy disk rather than the hard drive. In this case, the default drive and directory will be A:\ or B:\, and the command prompt will be A:\> or B:\>. A machine usually has at least two drives. The colon following the letter identifies the letter as the name of a drive, and the backslash identifies the directory on the hard drive as the root or main directory. The > symbol is the prompt symbol that DOS uses to say, "Enter your command here."

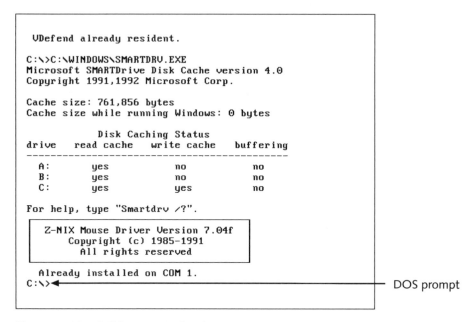

Figure 1-18   DOS prompt after booting

When a hard drive is first formatted for use by an OS, the format procedure creates a single directory on the drive. A **directory** is a table on a disk that contains a list of files that are stored on the disk. When a hard drive is first formatted, the **root directory** (that is, the first directory on a drive) is the only directory that is created. This directory is written in DOS command lines as a single backslash (\) with no other directory name following. In the preceding DOS prompt, the backslash indicates this root directory. After the drive is initially formatted, you can create other directories for file lists. These directories are given names and are listed in the root directory. These directories can, in turn, have other directories listed in them. These other directories are sometimes called **subdirectories** or **child directories**. Any directory can have files and/or other directories listed in it. By creating different directories on a hard drive, you can organize your program files and data files by placing programs in one directory and files created by those programs in a second directory. This organization is comparable to keeping paper records in separate folders. The drive and a list of directories pointing to a file is called a **path** when used in a DOS command. For instance, if the text file MYFILE.TXT is stored in the DATA directory under the WP directory on the hard drive, the path to MYFILE.TXT is written as C:\WP\DATA\MYFILE.TXT. To see the contents of the text file, MYFILE.TXT, from any DOS prompt, we use the TYPE command like this:

```
TYPE C:\WP\DATA\MYFILE.TXT
```

The TYPE command looks first on drive C. It then looks in the directory on drive C named WP. Next it looks for a directory in the \WP directory named DATA. DOS expects to find the file inside this subdirectory. It is appropriate to say that MYFILE.TXT is located in the path C:\WP\DATA. If the file is located anywhere else on the hard drive, DOS will not find it, because we have given it only this one path to the file.

The first example presented below of how software works describes the execution of a legacy DOS application. **Legacy** here refers to software written for operating systems before the most current one, Windows 95. Look at WordPerfect for DOS as an example. At the DOS prompt, when you type a single group of letters with no spaces, DOS assumes that you want to execute a program stored in a program file having the filename that you just typed. DOS attempts first to find the program file by that name, copies the file into RAM, and then it executes the program. In the case of WordPerfect, you would type the letters WP when the OS displayed the DOS prompt:

```
C:\>WP
```

Finding the program file.   A program file executed at the DOS prompt can have one of three file extensions: .COM, .EXE, or .BAT. Therefore, in this example, DOS looks for a file with one of these names: WP.COM, WP.EXE, or WP.BAT.

The first place DOS looks is in the default drive and directory; in this case, the root directory of the hard drive. If the A:\> prompt was displayed when you typed WP, then DOS would look in the root directory of drive A for the program file. DOS looks for the files in the following order: first WP.COM, then WP.EXE, and finally WP.BAT. DOS executes the first one it finds.

If DOS doesn't find any of these files, it stops looking and displays the error message,

```
Bad command or file not found
```

unless you have previously given DOS a list of paths in which to look for executable program files. You give this list of drives and directories to DOS using the PATH command. You can cause the PATH command to be executed automatically during the booting process by storing the command in the AUTOEXEC.BAT file (to be discussed next). However, you can execute the PATH command at any time after booting. The last PATH command you execute overrides any previous one. To see the list of paths that are presently active, type PATH at the DOS prompt, and then press **Enter**. To enter a new list of paths, type the PATH command followed by each path name, separating one path from the next by a semicolon, as shown in Figure 1-19.

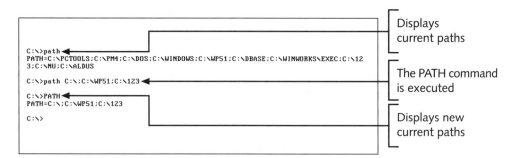

```
C:\>path
PATH=C:\PCTOOLS;C:\PM4;C:\DOS;C:\WINDOWS;C:\WP51;C:\DBASE;C:\WINWORKS\EXEC;C:\12
3;C:\NU;C:\ALDUS

C:\>path C:\;C:\WP51;C:\123

C:\>PATH
PATH=C:\;C:\WP51;C:\123

C:\>
```

Displays
current paths

The PATH command
is executed

Displays new
current paths

Figure 1-19   The PATH command

In Figure 1-19, the first PATH command displays the list of active paths. The second PATH command changes this list, giving DOS three directories in which to look to find executable files:

- Hard drive and root directory

- Hard drive and directory named \WP51

- Hard drive and directory named \123

The last PATH command in Figure 1-19 again displays the list of active paths. In summary, DOS searches for executable program files using the following rules:

1. If no path is given before the filename, DOS looks in the current directory.

2. If no path is given, and the file is not in the current directory, DOS looks in the paths given to it by the last PATH command executed.

3. If there is a path given in front of the filename in the command line, DOS looks in that path.

4. If there is a path given, but the file is not found in that path, DOS looks in the paths given to it by the last PATH command executed.

When you tell DOS to execute a program, you also can include the path to that program file as part of the command line. For example, if the WP.EXE file is stored in the directory \WP51, you can execute the program by typing the following:

```
C:\> \WP51\WP
```

Here you are telling DOS that the name of the program file is WP and its location is in the directory \WP51. DOS assumes that the directory \WP51 is on the hard drive rather than in drive A or B because C is the current default drive. Using this method, the directory that contains WordPerfect need not be the default directory nor do you need the \WP51 path in the PATH command line in the AUTOEXEC.BAT file. DOS used Rule 3 in the rules listed above for finding a program file.

Another way that you can tell DOS where the program is located is to make the directory containing the program file the current default directory by using the **change directory**, or **cd**, command. For example, you can use the following two commands to execute WordPerfect:

```
C:\> CD \WP51
C:\WP51> WP
```

The CD command directs DOS to make the directory \WP51 the default directory. This default directory appears as part of the DOS prompt. The next command executes the WordPerfect program stored in this directory. Because \WP51 is now the default directory, unless you direct WordPerfect otherwise, documents are saved to and retrieved from the \WP51 directory.

From this discussion, you can see that when you tell DOS to execute a program, DOS is unable to find that program unless you do one of the following:

- Include the path to the program file in the PATH command in AUTOEXEC.BAT

- Make the directory that contains the program file the default directory using the CD command

- Include the path to the program file in the command line to execute the program

Copying the program into memory.   Recall that once DOS finds the program file, it copies the file into memory (RAM) in a location that DOS chooses (see Figure 1-20). DOS cannot execute a program directly from the hard drive or from floppy disks; it can only execute a program stored in memory. After it copies the program into memory, DOS goes to the first address in memory occupied by the program to receive its first instruction. If the program requests some memory for its data (and most will), DOS decides which memory addresses to give the program (usually the memory after the program).

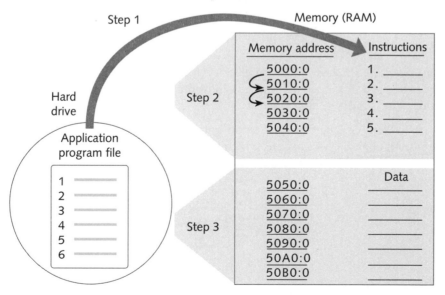

Figure 1-20   Applications software is stored in files but executed from memory

If the program wants to write or read data to and from memory, DOS manages these tasks. If the program needs to print, display something on the screen, read or write to the hard drive or a floppy disk, DOS does the work and returns to the applications software when finished. In other words, DOS is the "software behind the software" doing the utility-type tasks for the application.

An operating environment

Windows 3.x and Windows 95 offer improvements over DOS as described earlier in the overview. Windows 3.x supports applications software by providing an operating environment that offers features that DOS does not have, such as a graphic user interface (GUI), a pseudo multitasking environment, print management, and other enhancements. Windows 3.x serves as a middle layer between applications software and DOS, enhancing the abilities of the OS. It can be difficult to draw the line between DOS and Windows—where the OS ends and the operating environment begins. In fact, Windows 3.x acts like an OS much of the time, as it often bypasses DOS and interacts with the hardware directly. Windows 95, by contrast, is a complete OS. It's the marriage of DOS and Windows 3.11 into a blended whole containing some software components from DOS, some components from Windows 3.x, and some altogether new components unique to Windows 95.

Windows serves as a middle layer of software between the applications software and DOS. After Windows 3.x begins execution, an applications software program is loaded into memory. The applications software communicates with Windows, which, in turn, communicates with DOS or performs the OS task itself. For example, suppose the software requests data from a floppy disk. Windows receives the request and passes it to DOS, which passes it to System BIOS, which then reads the data and passes the data back up the line to the software that initially requested it.

When errors occur, the application can detect the error and display its own error message, or the operating environment software or the OS can detect the error and display the error message. When working with software, it is important for you to determine which software program found the error, because this information indicates which operation caused it.

Figures 1-21 and 1-22 show two examples of errors. In Figure 1-21, the error is caused by an attempt to access a disk drive that did not contain a disk. In this case, the error was detected by WordPad in Windows 95.

In Figure 1-22, the same error of attempting to access a missing disk occurred while using the Paintbrush applications software, which runs under Windows 3.1. The error, in this case, was detected by the Windows operating environment.

Figure 1-21   Disk error in Windows 95

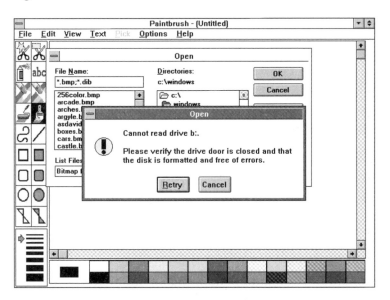

Figure 1-22   Windows error while using Paintbrush

Applications Software using Windows 3.x

You can execute applications software from Windows by one of several methods. In Windows 3.x, one way to execute software is by using an icon in a program group within Program Manager. When you double-click the icon, a command line assigned to the icon executes the program. To see what this command line contains, single-click the icon, and then choose Properties on the File menu of Program Manager. A dialog box of properties appears in which you can read the contents of the command line.

For example, the properties box for Microsoft Word for Windows in Figure 1-23 shows the command line to be as follows:

```
C:\MSOFFICE\WINWORD\WINWORD.EXE
```

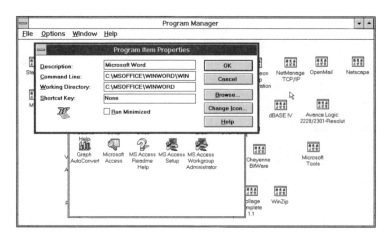

Figure 1-23 Properties of a program item in Windows 3.x

The entire command line is not visible in the box. You must click in the command line box and then use your arrow right key [→] to scroll the contents of the box to the left. This appears to be a DOS command line. If you are at the C prompt and type this same command line,

```
C:\>   C:\MSOFFICE\WINWORD\WINWORD.EXE
```

the following error message appears:

```
This program requires Windows.
```

DOS is telling you that the program will not work unless it is run in the Windows operating environment. However, if you add WIN to the front of the command line, the command does work from the DOS C prompt. In this case, the command looks like this:

```
C:\>   WIN C:\MSOFFICE\WINWORD\WINWORD.EXE
```

Note that the command WIN alone executes Windows 3.1. By following the WIN command with the command to execute WINWORD, DOS loads Windows and then executes Microsoft Word. You can take this command line one step further. If you have a document that was created by Microsoft Word, in a directory named \DATA, you can have Word automatically load this document after Word is executed. The command at the DOS C prompt looks like this:

```
C:\>   WIN C:\MSOFFICE\WINWORD\WINWORD.EXE \DATA\MYLETTER.DOC
```

This command tells DOS to execute Windows. Windows then executes Microsoft Word, which then loads the document MYLETTER.DOC.

A similar sequence of events occurs if you use File Manager in Windows 3.1 to open a document. In Figure 1-24, note that the MYLETTER.DOC file is selected. If you double-click the filename, Word for Windows is executed and the MYLETTER document loads. This action is called **launching** a document. Windows 3.1 recognizes the .DOC file extension as a Microsoft Word document.

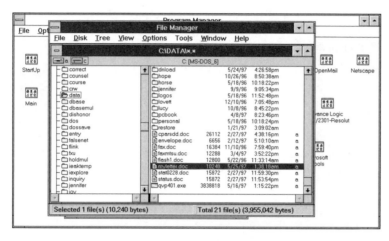

Figure 1-24   Executing a program from File Manager in Windows 3.x

Another way to execute a program from Windows is to use the Run command on the File menu in File Manager. Select **Run** on the File menu in File Manager. The Run dialog box appears, as shown in Figure 1-25. Type the following command in the Run dialog box, and then click the OK button:

    C:\MSOFFICE\WINWORD\WINWORD.EXE \DATA\MYLETTER.DOC

Word executes and the MYLETTER.DOC file loads.

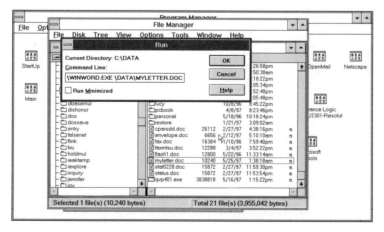

Figure 1-25   Using the Run command from File Manager in Windows 3.x

Applications Software using Windows 95

Windows 95 has a slightly different interface and methods to execute software than Windows 3.x, but the underlying events are similar. Windows 95 offers three ways to execute software. You can place a shortcut icon directly on the desktop for the applications you use often and want to get to quickly. These shortcuts contain the command line used to execute the application. Also, you can use the Run command, after clicking the Start button on the Windows 95 taskbar. Just as with the older Windows 3.11 File Manger, Windows 95 allows you to execute a program or launch an applications file by double-clicking the filename in Windows 95 Explorer.

To see the properties of a shortcut icon, right-click on the icon and select **Properties** from the drop-down menu that appears. In Figure 1-26, the properties of a shortcut icon are displayed. Double-clicking the shortcut icon launches a document created in WordPad. Figure 1-27 demonstrates how to use the Run command to execute WordPad and load MYLETTER.DOC. In either case, if you double-click the document filename in Windows 95 Explorer, the same action occurs—Windows 95 loads and executes WordPad, and then WordPad loads the document file. Windows 95 provides the operating environment for WordPad in all cases.

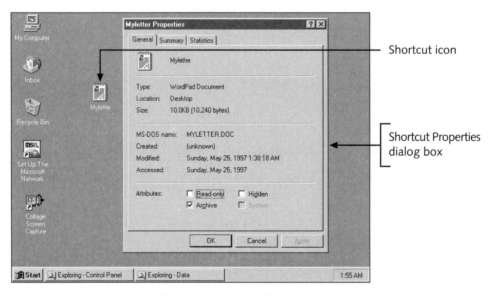

Figure 1-26   Properties of a shortcut in Windows 95

In summary, applications software is executed by either the operating environment (Windows 3.x) or the OS software (DOS). When an application is executing, you are interacting with the application. However, the applications software also is interacting with the OS software that is executing it. The OS also interacts with the hardware; although, if an operating environment such as Windows is running, it also might interact with the hardware through the device drivers for this hardware, as shown in Figure 1-28. In this example, Word is the applications software that is printing a document. Word sends the print command to

Windows 95, which in turn uses a printer device driver for a specific make of printer to communicate the print operation to the printer. Errors can occur at any point during these actions. It is important in troubleshooting software problems that you understand these software layers and the problems that can occur at each layer.

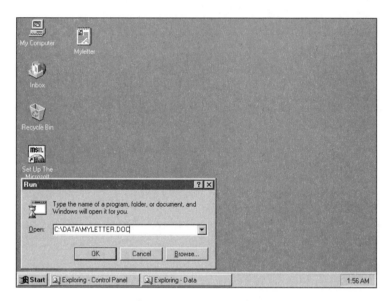

Figure 1-27   Using the Run command from the Start menu in Windows 95

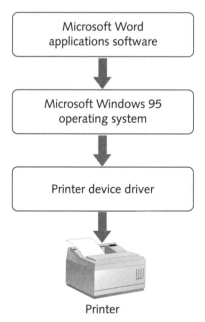

Figure 1-28   Layers of software when printing

CHAPTER SUMMARY

- A hybrid of hardware and software is a ROM BIOS microchip containing programming embedded into the chip. These chips are called firmware.

- The four most important devices outside the computer case used for input/output are the printer, monitor, mouse, and keyboard.

- A monitor is controlled from within the computer case by a video controller usually stored on a video expansion card.

- The most important component inside the computer case is the systemboard, or motherboard, which contains the most important microchip inside the case, the central processing unit (CPU), a microprocessor.

- Most primary memory inside a computer is stored on RAM chips on the systemboard, housed on small expansion cards called SIMMs.

- The three groups of logical primary memory are conventional or base memory, upper memory, and extended memory.

- Most setup information for the computer is stored on the CMOS configuration chip.

- The power supply provides the stepped-down power for all devices inside the computer case.

- Secondary storage is slower than primary storage but is permanent storage. The most common examples of secondary storage devices are the floppy disk and the hard drive.

- The OS interfaces with the computer hardware and is responsible for controlling all of the computer's resources.

- The three ways that you interface with the OS are commands, icons, and menus.

- The best-known operating systems are DOS, DOS with Windows 3.x (referring to 3.1 and 3.11, which is also called Windows for Workgroups), Windows 95, Windows NT, UNIX, OS/2, and Macintosh OS.

- When applications software is executed, the OS receives the command, finds the applications software program file, loads it from secondary storage into primary memory, and then executes each instruction from primary memory.

- Windows 3.x and Windows 95 are two IBM-compatible operating systems that provide you with a GUI (graphic user interface) and a multitasking environment that makes it possible for more than one application to be loaded at the same time.

- True multitasking is not possible using CPUs built before the Pentium.

KEY TERMS

- **BIOS (basic input/output system)** — Firmware that controls much of a computer's input/output functions, such as communication with disk drives, the printer, RAM chips, and the monitor.

- **Cards** — Adapter boards or interface cards placed into expansion slots to expand the functions of a computer, allowing it to communicate with external devices such as monitors or printers.

- **Circuit boards** — Computer components, such as the main system board or an adapter board, that have electronic circuits and chips.

- **CMOS (complementary metal oxide conductor)** — A type of chip that is powered by an on-board battery and is used to store the system configuration when the computer's power is off.

- **Coprocessor** — A chip or portion of the CPU that helps the microprocessor perform calculations and speeds up computations and data manipulations dramatically.

- **CPU (central processing unit)** — Also called a microprocessor. The heart and brain of the computer, which receives data input, processes information, and executes instructions.

- **Default Windows printer** — The printer that Windows software will use unless the user specifies another printer.

- **Device driver** — A small program that tells the computer how to communicate with an input/output device such as a printer or modem.

- **Device Manager** — A Windows 95 program that allows the user to view and set hardware configurations.

- **File** — A collection of related records or lines that can be written to disk and assigned a name (for example, a simple letter or a payroll file containing data about employees).

- **Firmware** — Software that is permanently etched onto a chip.

- **Flash ROM** — ROM that can be reprogrammed or changed without replacing chips.

- **GUI (graphical user interface)** — A user interface, such as the Windows interface, that uses graphics or icons on the screen for running programs and entering information.

- **Hardware** — The physical machinery that constitutes the computer system, such as the monitor, the keyboard, the system unit, and the printer.

- **Keyboard** — A common input device through which data and instructions may be typed into computer memory.

- **Monitor** — The most commonly used output device for displaying text and graphics on a computer.

- **Mouse** — A pointing and input device that allows the user to move the cursor around the screen and select programs with the click of a button.

- **Operating system** — Programs that control the computer's input and output operations, such as saving files and managing memory. Windows, OS/2, Mac OS, and UNIX are operating systems.

- **Peripheral devices** — Devices that are attached to the computer to enhance its capabilities, such as the monitor, printer, and mouse.

- **Pixel** — Small dots on a fine horizontal scan line that are illuminated to create an image on the monitor.

- **Port** — A physical connector at the back of a computer that allows a cable from a peripheral device, such as a printer, mouse, or modem, to be attached.

- **Power supply** — A box inside the computer case that supplies power to the system board and other installed devices. Power supplies normally provide between 5 and 12 volts DC.

- **Printer** — A peripheral output device that produces printed output to paper. Different types of printers include dot matrix, ink jet, and laser.

- **Program** — A set of step-by-step instructions to a computer. Some are burned directly into chips, while others are written in languages such as BASIC or C++.

- **Program jump** — An instruction that causes control to be sent to a memory address other than the next sequential address.

- **RAM (random access memory)** — Temporary user memory stored on chips such as SIMMs inside the computer. Information in RAM disappears when the computer's power is turned off.

- **ROM (read-only memory)** — Chips that contain programming code and cannot be erased.

- **SIMM (single in-line memory modules)** — Miniature circuit boards that are used in newer computers in place of traditional RAM chips. These mini-boards hold 8, 16, 32, or 64 MB on a single module.

- **Software** — Computer programs or instructions to perform a specific task. Software may be operating systems or application software such as a word-processing or spreadsheet program.

- **Systemboard** — The main board in the computer, also called the motherboard. The CPU, ROM chips, SIMMs, and interface cards are plugged into the system board.

- **Video card** — An interface card installed in the computer to control the monitor.

- **Video memory** — Microchips on the video card that hold the data that is being passed between the monitor and the computer. Higher moniter resolution often requires more video memory.

REVIEW QUESTIONS

1. Give three examples of hardware.

2. Give three examples of applications programs.

3. Define ROM. What functions are performed by ROM chips?

4. What does the Device Manager do? How do you launch the Device Manager?

5. What are the differences between primary and secondary storage?

6. How does Flash ROM differ from regular ROM on the systemboard?

7. Obtain the manual for a systemboard and look for a diagram of the systemboard components similar to Figure 1-4. Locate as many components from Figure 1-4 on your diagram as you can.

8. List the dictionary definitions of socket and slot. Looking at Figure 1-4, compare the two terms.

9. Describe how you would recreate the event displayed in Figure 1-22.

10. List the steps to create a shortcut icon using Windows 95.

11. Give three examples of secondary storage devices.

12. What OS (include version) does your home or lab computer use?

13. What does BIOS stand for and what does it do?

14. List three well-known operating systems.

15. Give three examples of operating systems that use GUI.

16. What might cause the error message "Bad command or file not found"?

17. What is the default directory of your home or lab computer immediately after bootup?

18. In the chapter, the concepts of primary storage and secondary storage are introduced. In Figure 1-10, a program was moved from secondary storage to primary storage before it could be executed. Based on this figure and concept, why do you think a hard drive is called secondary storage and memory is called primary storage?

19. Using Windows 95, access the Control Panel. List all the icons under the Control Panel sorted into two groups: Controls software and Controls hardware.

20. Complete the following table. Refer to Appendix D as necessary.

Type of memory	Beginning memory address in hex	Ending memory address in hex	Beginning memory address as a decimal number	Ending memory address as a decimal number	Ending memory address in decimal kilobytes
Conventional or base memory	0	9FFFF			
Upper memory area	A0000	FFFFF			
Extended memory	100000	N/A		N/A	N/A

PROJECTS

OBSERVING THE BOOT PROCESS AND HARDWARE COMPONENTS

1. Carefully watch your computer screen during the boot process (press **Pause** if necessary), and record which CPU is used by your home or lab computer.

2. As the computer boots, memory is counted. Observe the memory count and record the amount of memory detected. What number system is used to count this memory?

3. Open the printer icon in the Windows Control Panel and find out which is the default Windows printer for your home or lab computer.

4. Look at the back (or the front if the ports are located there) of your home or lab computer and make a drawing. Label on the drawing the purpose of each port and connection you see. If you are not sure what the purpose of the port is, label the port "unknown port." In later chapters, the purposes of these unknown ports will become clear.

USING MICROSOFT DIAGNOSTICS WITH WINDOWS 3.X

Windows offers the Microsoft Diagnostics command. This utility examines your system, displaying useful information about ports, devices, memory, etc. If you have Windows 3.0 or later, you can use it to survey your system. No applications should be running. From the DOS prompt, execute this command:

```
C:\> MSD
```

1

You should see a screen similar to that in Figure 1-29.

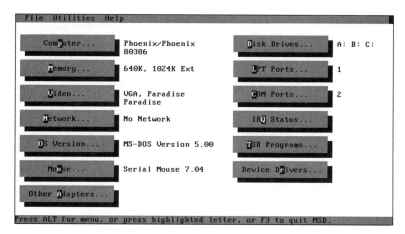

Figure 1-29 MSD opening screen

Browse carefully through all the menu options of this interesting utility and answer the following questions about your system:

a. List the following or print the appropriate MSD screen:

Manufacturer, version number, and date of your System BIOS, video BIOS, and mouse device driver.

b. What kind of video card is installed?

Use the information in Appendix D, The Hexadecimal Number System and Memory Addressing, to answer these:

c. How much memory is currently installed on this PC?

d. Look under TSR programs (a terminate and stay resident program, a program currently stored in memory but not running, will be covered in a later chapter) for the MSD.EXE program that you are executing. What is the hex address of the beginning of this program? Convert the hex address to a decimal address.

e. What version of DOS are you running?

USING MSD WITH WINDOWS 95

The MSD utility comes with Windows 95 but is not loaded automatically with the software. You must copy it from the Windows 95 CD to your hard drive. Also, when you execute MSD from a DOS session under Windows 95, inaccurate information displays. Therefore, make sure to run MSD from a DOS prompt without the Windows 95 desktop running in the background.

To run MSD from Windows 95, first boot your computer, and then press the F8 key when you see the message, "Starting Windows 95" on the screen. The Windows 95 startup menu appears. Choose option 6, which reads "Command prompt only." You then see a C prompt. Type MSD to execute the MSD utility. Answer these questions.

1. What version of Windows 95 are you running?
2. What version of DOS are you running?
3. What CPU do you have?

When you are finished, exit the MSD utility. (You return to the C: prompt.) To load the rest of Windows 95, type WIN, and then press **Enter** at the C prompt.

USING THE DEVICE MANAGER

Windows 95 provides a much more powerful tool than MSD called the Device Manager. From it you can view and print your hardware configuration. To access the Device Manager, follow these steps.

1. Click the **Start** button on the taskbar, click **Settings**, and then click **Control Panel**.
2. When the Control Panel window appears, double-click the **System** icon.
3. In the Systems Properties dialog box, click the **Device Manager** tab.

The opening menu of the Device Manager appears as shown in Figure 1-30. You can select an item from the list and then click Properties to view information about that item, or you can view the Properties by double-clicking the item. When you click the + sign to the left of an item, a list of the installed devices for that item appears beneath the item.

Answer these questions about your computer.

1. Does your computer have a network card installed? If so, what is the name of the card?
2. What are the three settings that can be changed under Device Manager?
3. What are all the hardware devices that Device Manager recognizes as present?

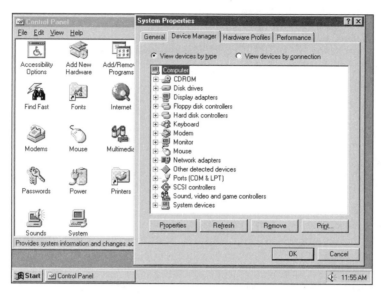

Figure 1-30 The Device Manager in Windows 95

Use Windows 95 Shareware to Examine a Computer

This exercise requires access to the Internet.

Good PC support people are always good investigators. The Internet offers a wealth of resources to those who take the time to search, download, and investigate the possible uses of software available there. This exercise is designed to help you learn to be such an investigator. Follow these directions to download a shareware utility to diagnose Windows 95 or Windows 3.x problems and print a report from the downloaded software of the hardware and software on your computer.

1. Access the Internet and go to this address:

   http://www.zdnet.com

2. Search for "SANDRA". (Don't enter the quotes.) SANDRA stands for System Analyzer Diagnostic and Reporting Assistant and offers information about the hardware and software on your computer.

3. Follow the steps on the screen to download the file SANDRA.ZIP to your PC. You can then disconnect from the Internet.

4. Uncompress SANDRA.ZIP by double-clicking the filename and then extracting SETUP.EXE with its components.

5. Run the setup program, SETUP.EXE, which creates a new program in your Program Group.

6. Run the program SiSoft Sandra and the screen shown in Figure 1-31 appears. You can execute each of the icons in turn by double-clicking them, or you can create a composite report of the results of each selection. Answer these questions:

   a. What is the model and speed of your CPU?

   b. What version of Windows 95 are you using?

   c. What icons are not available to you because your copy of SANDRA is not registered?

You will use SANDRA again in later chapters, so don't erase her! By the way, try to find SANDRA through www.shareware.com and www.sisoft.com. Is the program available through these avenues as well?

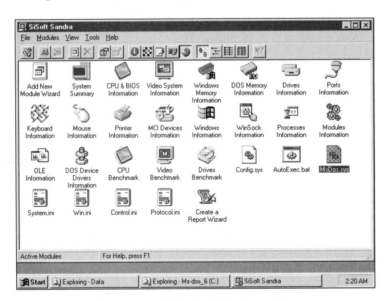

Figure 1-31   Shareware utility for Windows 95

HOW SOFTWARE AND HARDWARE WORK TOGETHER

In Chapter 1, we surveyed the hardware components of a computer and looked at different kinds of software including operating systems, applications software, and the Windows environment that often links the two. In this chapter, we focus on computer processes. When a computer is first turned on, the process of the hardware and software interacting to bring the PC to readiness is controlled by a startup program stored on a ROM BIOS chip on the systemboard and involves almost every one of a computer's hardware components. When you first turn the system on, the CPU turns control to the ROM BIOS Startup Program, which performs a hardware diagnostic test called POST (power-on self test) and then searches for an OS, loads it, and turns control over to it. The OS in turn takes control of all hardware resources and then turns to control and manage the applications software as well. In this chapter, we delve deep into each of these processes (including the interaction among layers of software introduced in Chapter 1) as we examine the way in which requests for resources are passed from applications software to the OS to hardware and back again. We study two operating systems to see how they control computer resources—DOS with Windows 3.x and Windows 95.

**IN THIS CHAPTER
YOU WILL LEARN:**

- HOW SOFTWARE MANAGES HARDWARE RESOURCES
- WHAT HAPPENS WHEN YOU FIRST TURN ON A COMPUTER SO THAT BOTH THE HARDWARE AND THE SOFTWARE ARE POISED TO FOLLOW YOUR DIRECTIONS
- WHAT HAPPENS WHEN YOU START THE EXECUTION OF APPLICATIONS SOFTWARE SO THAT THE SOFTWARE IS READY TO WORK
- PRACTICAL AND EASY WAYS TO PROTECT HARDWARE AND SOFTWARE

The overview of how computers work presented in this chapter and Chapter 1 would be incomplete if we omitted a discussion of one of the most fundamental tasks of managing computer resources: protecting data, software, and hardware from the most common hazards. This chapter ends with a section describing how to make and use backups, how to protect a computer from hazardous electricity, and the practical precautions to take when troubleshooting a computer problem.

How Software Manages Hardware Resources

Computer hardware without software is about as useless as a car without a driver. The hardware sits and waits for instructions from the CPU, which in turn waits for instructions from software. The OS is the control center for coordinating all these interactions, although sometimes instead of relating directly to the hardware, the OS uses programs—such as BIOS programs or device drivers—designed to interface with hardware. This brings yet one more layer of software into our discussions. Before the OS can manage the hardware, it must know what hardware resources are available. Information about the hardware components present in a system is communicated to the OS through configuration or setup information.

Figure 2-1 takes the car analogy introduced above a little further. Just as hardware is analogous to a car, similarly, the BIOS Startup Program is like a mechanic who prepares the car for a trip by thoroughly checking critical systems. When the car is in acceptable condition, the mechanic turns the car over to a chauffeur who does some additional minor checking of resources, such as determining the amount of gas in the car and whether the brakes work. Now all is ready to begin. The combination of software programs—applications software, the OS, the BIOS, and device drivers—is like the chauffeur, who in addition to keeping an eye on the status of the car, knows how to operate and direct the vehicle. Carrying the analogy a bit further, the computer's CPU is like the steering wheel, where the BIOS software controls the hardware via the CPU, just as the chauffeur controls the car via the steering wheel. But, remember that the chauffeur will only go where his passenger—who is analogous to a computer user—tells him to go. Thus, the various players work together: the mechanic/BIOS Startup Program checking the car/hardware to make sure it is ready to be used; the passenger/user providing specific instructions to the chauffeur/software on what to do or where to go; and the chauffeur/software interacting directly with the steering wheel/CPU, which controls the various underlying mechanisms that make the car/computer work as intended.

The processes that occur when a computer is started are extremely important in assuring that it will operate as desired.

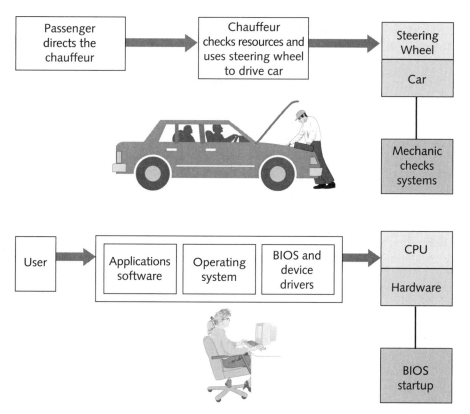

Figure 2-1   A user interacts with a computer much as a passenger interacts with a chauffeured car

You can identify four distinct steps or stages that occur when a computer starts up and the user takes control. They are as follows:

Step 1: The ROM BIOS Startup program surveys hardware resources and needs (see Figure 2-2).   The ROM BIOS Startup Program begins the startup process by reading configuration information stored in DIP switches and jumpers (which are discussed below) and the CMOS chip and comparing that information to the hardware present—the CPU, video card, disk drive, and hard drive. (Remember from Chapter 1 that the CMOS chip is the systemboard chip that holds configuration and setup information.) Some of the hardware devices have on-board BIOSs of their own to which startup BIOS assigns memory addresses. Startup BIOS also receives requests for resources from these devices and assigns resources to them.

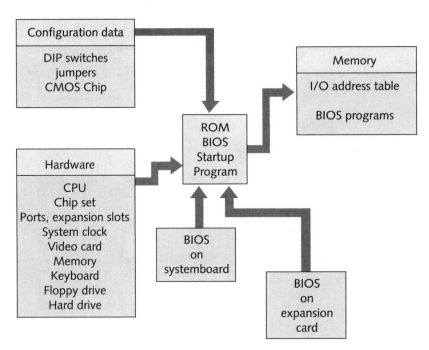

Figure 2-2   First of four major steps at startup: BIOS surveys hardware resources and needs

Step 2: The ROM BIOS Startup Program searches for and loads an OS (see Figure 2-3).   Configuration information on the CMOS chip tells Startup BIOS where to look for the OS. The BIOS turns to that device, reads the beginning files of the OS, copies them into memory, and then turns control over to the OS.

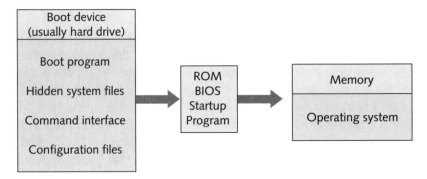

Figure 2-3   Second of four major steps at startup: BIOS searches for and loads an OS

Step 3: The OS configures the system and completes its own loading (see Figure 2-4).

The OS checks some of the same things that Startup BIOS checked, such as available memory and whether that memory is reliable. Additionally, the OS continues beyond that by loading the software to control a mouse, a CD-ROM, a scanner, and other peripheral devices. These devices generally have programs to manage them, called device drivers, stored on the hard drive.

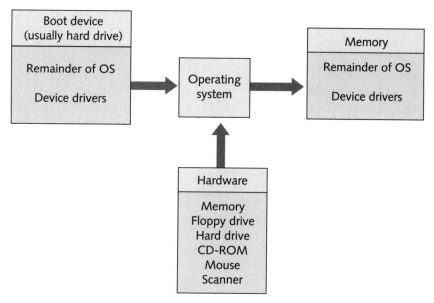

Figure 2-4   Third of four major steps at startup: The OS configures the system and completes its own load

Step 4: The user executes applications software (see Figure 2-5).

When you tell the OS to execute an application, the OS first must find the applications software on the hard drive, CD-ROM, or other secondary storage device, copy the software into memory, and then turn control over to it. Finally, you can command the applications software, which makes requests to the OS which, in turn, uses the resources stored in memory (including the System BIOS and the device drivers) to interface with and control the hardware. Your trip has begun!

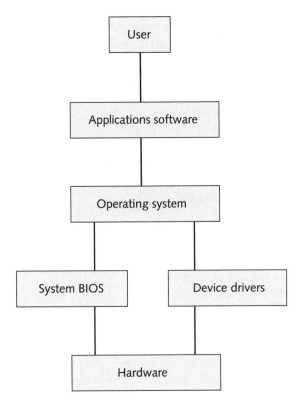

Figure 2-5   Four major steps at startup Step 4: The user executes applications software

The text now carefully examines each of the components involved in the processes just listed, and then addresses the processes themselves.

CONFIGURATION DATA AND HOW IT IS STORED

During booting, the Startup BIOS and OS must determine what hardware is present. This information is called **configuration data**, **setup data**, or simply **setup**, and it is stored in the computer in one of these devices: DIP switches, CMOS setup chips, or jumpers, described below.

Setup Data Stored by DIP Switches

Older computers typically store setup data using DIP switches on the systemboard, as shown in Figure 2-6. A **DIP** (dual in-line package) **switch** is a switch that has an ON position and an OFF position. ON represents binary 1 and OFF represents binary 0. If you add or remove equipment, you can communicate that to the computer by changing a DIP switch setting. Using DIP switches is somewhat inconvenient because you must remove the computer case

2

cover in order to access the switches to make any changes. When you change a DIP switch setting, use a sharp instrument, such as a ball-point pen, to push the switch. Don't use a graphite pencil because graphite conducts electricity. Pieces of graphite dropped into the switch can damage the switch.

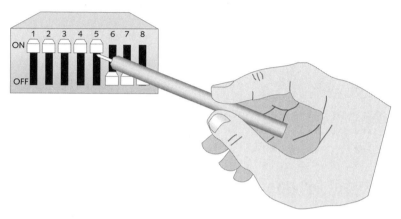

Figure 2-6 DIP switches store setup data on older machines

Setup Data Stored on a CMOS Chip

Most configuration data in newer computers is stored in a CMOS microchip that is battery powered (see Figure 2-7). The advantage of using a CMOS chip over other types of chips is that CMOSs require very little electricity to hold data. A small trickle of electricity from a nearby battery enables the CMOS chip to hold the data even while the main power to the computer is off.

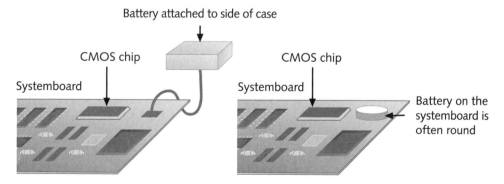

Figure 2-7 The battery that powers the CMOS chip may be on the systemboard or attached nearby

On older computers (mostly IBM 286 PCs built in the 1980s), changes are made to the CMOS setup data using a setup program stored on a floppy disk. One major disadvantage of this method (besides the chance that you might lose or misplace the disk) is that the disk drive must be working in order to change the setup. An advantage of this method is that you can't change the setup unintentionally.

On newer computers, you usually change the data stored in the CMOS chip by accessing the setup program stored in ROM BIOS. You access the program by pressing some combination of keys during the booting process. A message such as the following usually appears on the screen:

```
Press DEL to change Setup
```

or

```
Press F8 for Setup.
```

When you do so, a setup screen appears with menus and help features that is often very user friendly. When you exit the program, you have the choice to exit without saving your changes or to exit and save your changes to the CMOS chip.

Setup Data Stored by Jumpers

Most computers hold additional configuration information by using jumpers on the systemboard (see Figure 2-8). A jumper consists of two pins sticking up side by side with a cover over the two pins making a connection. The two pins and the connection together serve as electrical connectors on the systemboard. If the pins are not connected with a cover, the setting is considered OFF. If the cover is present, the setting is ON. The presence of cache memory is a typical setting that is communicated to the computer by jumpers. Jumpers also are used to communicate the type and speed of the CPU to the system or to disable a feature on the systemboard such as a mouse port. You change the jumper setting by removing the computer case, finding the correct jumper, and then either placing a metal cover over the jumper or removing the cover already there.

Passwords Stored on CMOS

Access to a computer can be controlled using **startup passwords**, sometimes called **power-on passwords**. During booting or startup, the computer asks for a password. If you do not enter the password correctly, the booting process is terminated. The password is stored on the CMOS chip and is changed by accessing the setup screen. Many computers also provide a jumper near the CMOS chip that, when set to "on," causes the computer to "forget" any changes that have been made to default settings stored in CMOS. By jumping these pins, you can disable a password.

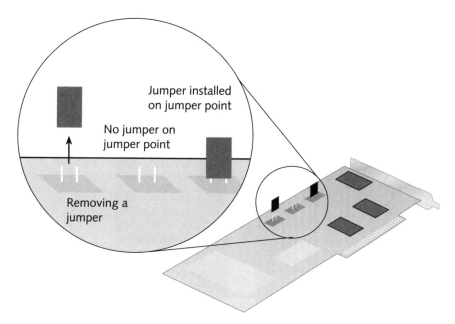

Figure 2-8   Jumpers on an add-on card

SAVING AND RESTORING SETUP INFORMATION IN CMOS

There are several utility software programs that you can use to back up setup information to a disk to be used to recover lost setup information. In this chapter, we introduce one, Norton Utilities, a popular PC utility software. Setup information on a PC can be lost if the battery dies or is replaced. Information also can be lost when errors occur on the systemboard. Possible errors and events that might indicate that setup information is lost are:

- The battery is discharged. An early indication of a weak battery is that the PC loses the correct date and time when turned off.

- Message at startup says, "Hardware information is lost." This error can be caused by a dead battery or a poorly connected battery.

- The battery has been replaced. After the battery is replaced, restore the CMOS settings using a rescue disk.

Follow the steps below to create a rescue disk using Norton Utilities for Windows 95. (Other uses of this software are found in later chapters.)

1. To save setup information to disk:

    a. Select **Start**, **Programs**, **Norton Utilities**. The list of utilities included with the software appears, as shown in Figure 2-9. Select **Rescue Disk**.

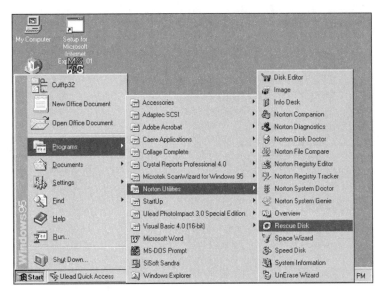

Figure 2-9   Norton Utilities lists a suite of utility programs

b. The Norton Utilities Rescue Disk window opens, as shown in Figure 2-10. To see the list of items that Norton Utilities will save to the set of rescue disks, click **Options**, shown in Figure 2-11. There are items in the list that we will discuss in future chapters and some have already been introduced. For now, notice the item, CMOS Information, that will be saved to disk. Make sure that **Rescue** is checked to be included in the list, then click **OK** to return to the opening window.

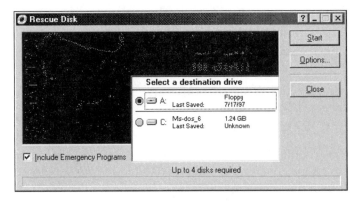

Figure 2-10   Creating a set of rescue disks using Norton Utilities

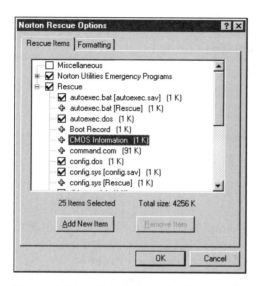

Figure 2-11   List of items to be stored on the rescue disks

    c. Check that the appropriate disk drive is selected as the destination drive, and then click **Start** to begin the process.

    d. Norton Utilities prompts you to insert the first disk, as shown in Figure 2-12.

    e. When the information is saved to disk, the process ends and you are prompted to properly label and store the disk(s), as shown in Figure 2-13.

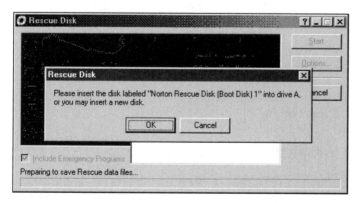

Figure 2-12   Rescue disk utility prompts you to insert the first disk

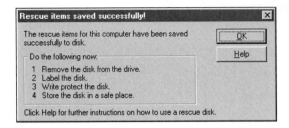

Figure 2-13 Properly label and store the rescue disks

2. To use a rescue disk to restore setup information when it is lost:

   a. Insert the disk labeled rescue disk 1, which is a bootable disk, into the disk drive, and then turn the PC off and back on. This disk boots to drive A and provides an A prompt.

   b. At the A prompt, type **RESCUE**, and then press **Enter**.

   c. Select **CMOS Information** from the items to restore, and then press **Alt R** to begin the process. Follow the instructions on screen.

   d. Remove the rescue disk from the drive and reboot. CMOS information should now be restored. Return the rescue disks to a safe place.

ROM BIOS

We next look at the firmware that reads and uses the configuration information and then passes it on to the OS. ROM BIOS is a group of programs permanently stored on a ROM chip or chips on the systemboard that manages the most fundamental communications between software and hardware. The two functions of ROM BIOS are to:

- Gather configuration information and initialize the computer when it is first turned on

- Provide software to communicate directly with various hardware components when the OS is functioning

Configuring and Initializing the Computer

When you turn on the power to a PC, the CPU begins the process of initialization by turning to the ROM BIOS for instructions. The BIOS runs a series of complex programs called the power-on self test (POST), which performs several tasks including the following:

- Testing the CPU itself

- Testing RAM

- Inventorying the hardware devices installed on the computer and comparing that inventory to configuration information

- Configuring disk drives, hard drives, keyboard, monitor, and ports

- Configuring other devices installed on the PC, such as a CD-ROM or sound card
- Assigning resources to computer hardware devices in preparation for the OS to complete and coordinate these assignments
- Setting up hardware devices to go into "sleep mode" to conserve electricity
- Running CMOS Setup if requested
- Loading into memory and turning control to the OS

Later in the chapter you will carefully examine each step in the POST process, and then look at two operating systems and their start-up processes.

Providing BIOS Services

ROM BIOS on the systemboard includes the BIOS Startup Program (see Figure 2-2) that is used only when the PC first boots. However, there are also portions of ROM BIOS programming that are stored in memory and used to support hardware devices when you run applications programs. Recall, this is sometimes called System BIOS. In Figure 2-2, System BIOS is labeled "BIOS on systemboard." For example, the keyboard is controlled by a BIOS program stored on the systemboard that is copied into memory by the ROM BIOS Startup Program. In this figure you see ROM BIOS playing two roles. First, the Startup BIOS is in control, configuring the system. The keyboard BIOS is copied from the ROM BIOS chip on the systemboard into memory and is later used in its second role, to service the keyboard. The Startup BIOS is no longer used after it turns control over to the OS, but other System BIOS programs continue to be used during computer operations.

While some of the System BIOS services are provided by the one or two ROM BIOS chips on the systemboard, other System BIOS services are provided by chips on a supporting circuit board. This portion of System BIOS is called **on-board BIOS**. An example of on-board BIOS is the software on a video card. The BIOS on the video card is part of the total BIOS services for the entire system. When the computer is first turned on, the BIOS on the systemboard and the BIOS on the video card cooperate to provide part of the total BIOS services for the system. (Also, recall that rather than being controlled by BIOS programs, hardware is sometimes managed by device drivers, which are programs stored as files on the hard drive.)

When the CPU needs to display something on the monitor screen, it depends on the video BIOS to instruct the monitor. The CPU knows where to find the BIOS software for the monitor because its location is determined during the booting process. When you press a key on the keyboard, the CPU is told that the "keyboard needs attention" and also interprets the data from the keyboard. The BIOS programs to do all this are assigned memory addresses and are matched up with the correct peripheral device during the booting process. These programs are permanently stored on ROM BIOS chips on the systemboard and supporting circuit boards.

For example, sometimes a disk drive is controlled by a System BIOS program that is a part of ROM BIOS on the systemboard. During the booting process, Startup BIOS assigns memory addresses to the System BIOS program that controls the disk drive. This program takes control and initializes the disk drive. During the operation of the PC, when an application must read from or write to a disk, the request is passed to the OS which, in turn, passes the request to the System BIOS program that controls the disk drive.

Flash ROM

Recall from Chapter 1 that **Flash ROM** is a type of memory chip that permanently retains programming code without being electrically charged, but can also be overwritten by new code. With Flash ROM, you can upgrade ROM without having to install a new ROM BIOS chip, which is the more difficult and more expensive ROM update procedure. You can upgrade BIOS in Flash ROM by overwriting existing BIOS code with new BIOS code stored on disk or downloaded from the Internet. As you add new devices to your system, you can continue to easily and inexpensively update ROM BIOS to manage these devices. Chapter 3 contains more information about Flash ROM.

DEVICE DRIVERS

Recall that some hardware devices do not have dedicated BIOS programs stored directly in ROM BIOS chips on the systemboard or on supporting circuit cards. Instead, these devices are controlled by device drivers. An example of this kind of device is a mouse; its driver is stored on the hard drive in a file named something like MOUSE.COM or MOUSE.SYS. During the booting process, the program is copied into memory and the mouse is controlled from this program in memory.

The major difference between System BIOS and device drivers is the location in which they are stored when the computer is turned off. System BIOS is permanently stored on ROM chips and device drivers are stored as files on a hard drive. However, during the booting process, both of these programs are assigned memory addresses and are later used by the OS to control a hardware device. Either way, these programs are a part of the bottom layer of software that directly relates to computer hardware, as shown in Figure 2-5.

INTERRUPT REQUEST NUMBER (IRQ)

When a hardware device needs the CPU to do something, such as when the keyboard needs a keystroke to be processed, the device passes a number, called an **interrupt request number** or **IRQ**, to the CPU. This signals to the CPU that the device has a request that needs processing. (This process of a hardware device needing attention from the CPU is often referred to as "needing servicing.") During the boot process, a unique IRQ is assigned to each hardware device that requires one, and uniquely identifies that device as well as the software that controls it.

A device requires an IRQ if it can initiate an action or provide input to the computer. Of course, the IRQ is simply a number, and the CPU needs instructions on what to do, which it finds using the **I/O address table** (also called the **interrupt vector table** or the **vector table**), where I/O stands for input/output. The I/O address table correlates each IRQ with the memory address that holds the start of the program the CPU needs to process the request from the device. Remember that during the boot process, each System BIOS program and device driver is assigned memory and the memory address of the start of each program is stored in the I/O address table at that time. So, the CPU searches the vector table for the IRQ it receives, looks up the memory address where the program it needs starts, and goes to that address to execute the right software to process the request.

Some devices that are assigned IRQs include the disk drive, the mouse, and the keyboard. The CPU uses an IRQ to identify the peripheral and find the software that controls it. In Figure 2-14 we see the hardware and software layers involved in managing a mouse. When we move the mouse or click one of its buttons, the mouse sends the IRQ to the CPU and writes the data to a special area of the I/O address table to be read later by the request handler. (A request handler is the System BIOS program or device driver that handles the I/O request.) When the CPU receives the IRQ, it turns to the I/O table for the location of the device driver, and in turn to the device driver to obtain instructions on how to interpret the data received. The mouse driver reads the data and interprets and sends the data on to the OS which in turn sends the data to the applications software currently running.

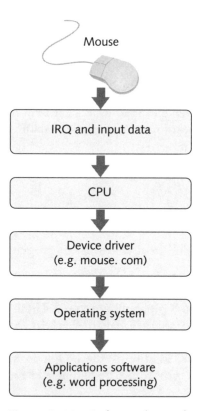

Figure 2-14   Software layers for operating a mouse

MEMORY USED BY BIOS AND DEVICE DRIVERS

To review, once the CPU receives an IRQ, it can process the request for hardware services as soon as it can access the instructions that manage the hardware, which, as you remember, are stored in either System BIOS programs or device driver files. To retrieve an instruction, the CPU turns to the appropriate memory address to first read the instruction into its internal memory and then to execute it. Sometimes the BIOS programs are copied into RAM because reading from RAM chips is generally faster than reading from ROM chips. The process of copying programs from ROM to RAM for execution is called **shadowing ROM** or just **shadow RAM**. It doesn't really matter whether the ROM programs are executed directly from the ROM chips or copied to RAM and executed from there; each line of instruction is assigned the same memory address in both places.

THE I/O ADDRESS TABLE

Recall that the memory addresses assigned to device drivers and System BIOS programs are stored in the I/O address table. This table is located at the very bottom of the memory addresses (low numbers), sometimes referred to as **I/O addresses**.

For example, when the IRQ for the mouse signals the CPU for service, the CPU looks in the I/O address table for the addresses in either conventional memory or upper memory where the device driver or System BIOS program that services the mouse is located. Device drivers must first be copied to RAM because they are stored on the hard drive and cannot be executed from there. Device driver files are copied to RAM and assigned memory addresses during the booting process. These driver files may be loaded into conventional memory or upper memory. (Recall that conventional memory is the first 640K of memory addresses; upper memory is the next 384K of addresses.)

Both System BIOS and device drivers require two different entries in memory as follows (see Figure 2-15):

- An entry in the I/O address table, which correlates device drivers and System BIOS programs with their starting addresses in memory
- A block of memory addresses that contains the driver or BIOS program

In summary, as shown in the figure, the I/O address table—a block of memory locations near the bottom of memory (low memory addresses)—is the region of memory where the beginning addresses of the device drivers and BIOS programs are stored. Think of the I/O address table as a mailbox containing the number of another mailbox. Each IRQ is associated with a certain memory location in the I/O address table. When the IRQ is received, the CPU uses this value to determine which memory location in the I/O address table holds the location of the device driver or BIOS. It then turns to this beginning address location to retrieve the program to process the request.

2

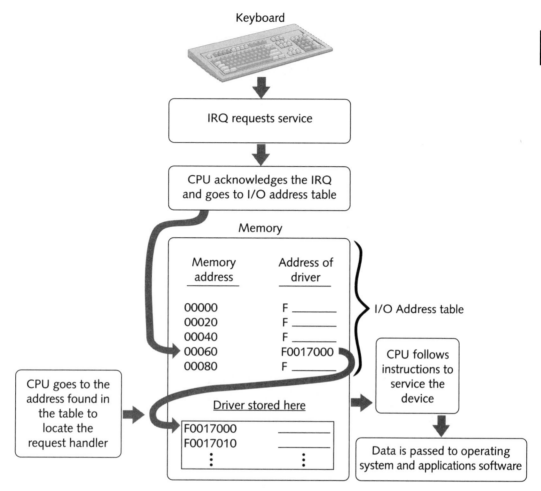

Figure 2-15   How the CPU uses the I/O address table to handle a keyboard request

SUMMARIZING HOW BIOS AND DEVICE DRIVERS WORK

Looking back at Figure 2-2 we see that the ROM BIOS Startup Program organizes hardware, configuration information, and BIOS information, storing vital information in the I/O address table in preparation for the OS to take over. In Figure 2-4, the OS continues the process of initialization by loading device drivers into memory. All this takes place before the first applications software is executed, much like the mechanic and chauffeur prepare the car before the passenger arrives. It's important to separate the BIOS used to initialize the system from the BIOS stored in memory and referred to in the I/O address table that is used later to manage hardware devices.

One of the most important procedures in the BIOS Startup Program is POST (power-on self test). During POST, when an expansion card such as the video controller card (sometimes called the **display adapter**) is accessed, the BIOS permanently stored on ROM chips on the card tells the computer that BIOS software is present on the card. POST assigns this BIOS software addresses in memory. The area of memory most often used for BIOS programs working under DOS and Windows 95 is upper memory, the range of memory addresses from 640K to 1024K. Recall that the location of the program is stored in the I/O address table, which will later be accessed by an IRQ request.

Also recall that during the execution of an applications program, a device that needs to interrupt the CPU for servicing is assigned a number called an IRQ. The CPU uses this IRQ to identify which peripheral device needs servicing. This interrupt request number is associated with an address in the I/O address table that allows the CPU to locate the System BIOS Program for the peripheral device. For the keyboard shown in Figure 2-15, for example, the process works like this:

1. You press a key on the keyboard
2. The keyboard controller sends its assigned IRQ to the CPU, thus saying, "I need attention"
3. The CPU sees the IRQ and turns its attention to servicing it
4. The CPU uses the IRQ to point to a row in the I/O address table assigned to that IRQ
5. From the I/O address table, the CPU locates the memory addresses in which the instructions to service the keyboard are stored
6. The CPU follows the instructions stored at these upper memory addresses to process the keystroke

Sometimes data from the device is temporarily stored in the I/O address table together with the locating address of the device driver or ROM BIOS needed to service the device.

The same action happens when data is read from a disk. The disk drive sends the data along with the correct IRQ for the drive to the CPU. The disk drive instructions used by the CPU are stored in System BIOS. The data is handed over to the OS, which can pass it along to an application.

Video monitors do not require an IRQ. Monitors only receive data from the CPU and never send data back to the CPU, so they never need to interrupt the CPU for servicing. (The exceptions are touch screen monitors, which serve as an input device as well as an output device). However, monitors are similar to other I/O devices, such as the mouse and keyboard, in that they have software to control them that must be accessed by the CPU when the CPU wants to use the monitor. Monitors are controlled by video cards; software to control monitors, also a part of BIOS, is found on the video card together with some video RAM that holds data being passed to the monitor.

2

A conflict can occur if more than one device is assigned the same IRQ or I/O address during POST. These conflicts are resolved on older expansion cards by changing DIP switches or jumper settings. This change causes the card to request an alternative IRQ or I/O address. For example, if a scanner card and a network card both request IRQ 10, then there is a conflict. Startup BIOS or the OS cannot write the memory address of the network driver in the same I/O address location associated with IRQ 10 if the memory address of the scanner driver is already written there. If this were to happen, and the scanner asked for service by sending IRQ 10 to the CPU, the CPU would respond with a network driver. In this case, probably neither the scanner nor the network card would work. If you encounter a conflict, check both cards. Most likely one of them has a jumper that you can set so that the card requests an IRQ other than 10.

With newer cards, called Plug-and-Play cards, instead of having to set DIP switches and jumpers to identify information about hardware and its configuration, the Startup BIOS automatically chooses the resources (such as IRQs or I/O addresses) that are assigned to the card. Because the BIOS can select the resources, conflicts are easily resolved using Plug-and-Play cards. Of course, the BIOS must be the kind that manages Plug-and-Play devices and is called **Plug-and-Play BIOS**. The OS must also be Plug-and-Play (PnP).

Plug-and-Play operating systems like Windows 95 can set IRQ or I/O addresses. Conflicts can occur that make the cards inoperable if DIP switches or jumpers on the cards are set to select a certain resource, but Windows or BIOS does not have the resource available.

DMA CONTROLLER CHIP

So far, you have seen that during startup, hardware devices are assigned IRQs and I/O addresses, and have blocks of memory assigned to their System BIOS programs or device drivers. Another resource a device might request from the system is a **DMA** (**direct memory access**) channel. A chip on the systemboard contains the DMA logic. The DMA chip provides channels that a device can use for fast access when sending data to memory. The DMA chip does this by bypassing the CPU. Some devices, such as a hard drive, are designed to use these channels and others, like the mouse, are not. Those that use the channels might be able to use only a certain channel, say channel 3, and no other. Or, the BIOS might have the option of changing a DMA channel number to avoid conflicts with other devices. Conflicts occur when more than one device uses the same channel.

SUMMARY OF COMPUTER RESOURCES REQUIRED BY HARDWARE

Table 2-1 summarizes the computer resources used by hardware.

Table 2-1   Computer resources used by hardware

Computer Resource	Purpose
IRQ	A number that identifies to the CPU the device needing service and its priority
I/O address	Location in lower part of memory where the memory address to the BIOS or device driver is stored; sometimes contains data
Upper memory address	Location of the device driver or BIOS
DMA channel	Channel by which data can pass from the device to memory bypassing the CPU

In summary, peripheral devices require some of the system resources in order to operate. Most devices require one IRQ, although some require more than one and some require none. The IRQ points to an entry in the I/O address table that tells the CPU at what address to find BIOS or device drivers. Some devices require a DMA channel.

These resources are assigned to the device during the booting process. Think of the process as a dialog that might go something like this: The startup BIOS recognizes that a hardware device is present. The BIOS asks the device, "What resources do you need?" The device says, "I need this IRQ and that I/O address and these addresses in upper memory for my BIOS." More cooperative Plug-and-Play devices simply say, "I need one IRQ, some I/O addresses, and this many upper memory addresses for my BIOS. Please tell me the resources I can use."

A device must be the sole owner of these resources. Problems occur when more than one device attempts to use the same resource.

A peripheral device's on-board BIOS can request certain memory addresses either in the I/O address table for its I/O addresses or in upper memory for its BIOS software addresses. Some cards are built so that only these addresses work. When two controller cards require the same memory addresses, **memory conflicts** occur. Memory conflicts can often be resolved if the BIOS or I/O addresses for a peripheral device can be assigned an alternative memory address. This can be done by setting switches on the controller card or allowing BIOS to make new assignments internally. Chapter 9 explains how to solve memory conflicts.

THE BOOTING PROCESS

Thus far, Chapter 2 has discussed some of the processes that go on inside a computer when it is turned on, also called **hard booting**. As you can see when you first turn on your computer, much happens before you are allowed to enter your first command. It is necessary that you understand the processes in order to troubleshoot both hardware and software problems. This section contains a step-by-step description of the booting process.

Booting comes from the phrase "lifting yourself up by your bootstraps," and refers to the computer bringing itself up to an operable state without user interference. Recall that power-on self test or POST is the part of the startup process by which the hardware checks itself before loading software. Booting includes POST, loading an OS, and the initial functions of the OS that occur before the user enters a command. Booting refers to either a "soft boot" or "hard boot." A **hard boot** involves turning on the power initially with the on/off switch. A **soft boot** involves pressing the reset button or pressing these three keys at the same time: Ctrl, Alt, and Del. A hard boot is more stressful on your machine than a soft boot, because of the initial power surge through the equipment. Pressing the reset button starts the booting process at an earlier point than does the Ctrl-Alt-Del method and is, therefore, a little slower. We divide the discussion of booting into four parts: First we describe POST, then loading the OS, what happens when the OS initializes itself in order to be poised for our first instruction, and finally loading and executing an application.

 Avoid turning off the power switch and immediately turning it back on without a pause because you can damage the machine. Always use a soft boot method to restart unless neither soft boot method works. If you must power down, wait a few seconds before turning the power back on.

POWER-ON SELF TEST OR POST, STEP BY STEP

Recall that when you first turn on your machine, the CPU looks for instructions in the ROM BIOS Startup Program. The first process executed is POST, which first checks that the CPU is working. The CPU then sends signals over the system bus checking various chips, ports, and expansion slots. It then checks the system clock making sure timing is working properly. Because the CPU has not yet checked the video system, errors encountered up to this point are communicated to you by a beeping sound. Short and long beeps indicate an error. Appendix A lists some of these error codes and their meanings. Next, POST checks the video controller card, sometimes called the display adapter. (Note that POST does not check to see if a monitor is present or working.) After the video controller passes inspection, POST can use the monitor to display its progress. POST then checks RAM by writing and reading data. A running count of RAM is displayed on the monitor during this phase.

Next, the keyboard is checked, and if you press any keys at this point, an error occurs. Secondary storage, including disk and hard drives, is checked. The hardware that POST finds is checked against the data stored in CMOS chips, jumpers, and/or DIP switches to determine that they agree.

Booting with MS-DOS

Once POST is complete, the next step is to load an OS. We use DOS for our first OS example. The BIOS Startup Program stored in ROM first looks for a disk in drive A (the setup on some computers can change this to drive C). If a disk is present, the program expects enough DOS to be on this disk to load the OS and give control to it. If the disk is present, but does not contain DOS, the ROM program displays the following error message:

```
Non system disk or disk error, replace and press any key
```

If there is no disk in the drive, the BIOS Startup Program moves on to the hard drive looking for an OS. The program looks for a master boot program in the hard drive, which, in turn, loads and executes the DOS boot record. The ROM Startup Program is terminated.

The boot record program is very short; it loads just two hidden files, which make up part of DOS, into memory. (A **hidden file** is a file not displayed in the directory list.) The boot record program knows the filenames, which are usually (but not always) named IO.SYS and MSDOS.SYS. The IO.SYS file contains more BIOS software. MSDOS.SYS contains software to manage files, run applications software, and interface with hardware. Once these two files are loaded into memory, the boot record program is no longer needed, and control turns to a program stored in MSDOS.SYS. This program looks on the hard drive for a file named CONFIG.SYS. CONFIG.SYS is the first OS file that you as a user, can change. This configuration file contains commands that tell DOS how many files it can open at any one time (FILES=) and how many file buffers to create (BUFFERS=). Also in CONFIG.SYS are the commands to load device drivers (DEVICE=) as well as other information. (Remember a driver is a program that instructs the computer how to communicate with and manage a peripheral device such as a modem or scanner.) An example of a typical command in CONFIG.SYS is the following:

```
DEVICE=C:\SCANGAL\SCANNER.SYS
```

This command line tells DOS to look in a directory named \SCANGAL on drive C for a file named SCANNER.SYS, copy it into memory, and save it there until some application requests to use a scanner. The SCANNER.SYS program tells DOS how to communicate with that scanner. Several drivers can be loaded into memory from commands in CONFIG.SYS. DOS puts these programs in memory wherever it chooses. However, a program can request that it be put in a certain memory location.

After CONFIG.SYS is executed, MSDOS.SYS looks for another DOS file named COMMAND.COM. This file consists of three parts: more BIOS code, programs for internal DOS commands such as COPY and DIR, and a short program that looks for another file named AUTOEXEC.BAT.

The filename **AUTOEXEC.BAT** stands for **automatically executed batch** program. The file holds a list of basic DOS commands that are executed automatically each time DOS is loaded. The following two commands (or similar prompt and Path commands) are typically in the AUTOEXEC.BAT file:

```
PROMPT $P$G
PATH C:\;C:\WINDOWS;C:\WP51;C:\DBASE;C:\123
```

The PROMPT command tells DOS to display the current directory name and the current drive name as part of the prompt. Without the prompt command, your prompt looks like this: C>. With the prompt command it might look like C:\WP51> where the WP51 tells you which directory is current.

Recall that you learned about the PATH command in Chapter 1. The PATH command shown above lists four paths separated by semicolons. This command directs DOS to look into five different directories for program files. Recall that without the benefit of the PATH command, you execute applications programs in one of two ways: go to the directory containing the application by using the CD (change directory) command, or include the path with the name of the executable program file when you execute the software. Sometimes during the installation of a software package, the installation process automatically adds a new path to the existing PATH command in AUTOEXEC.BAT telling DOS where the new application can be found.

Another typical use of AUTOEXEC.BAT is to load TSRs. A **TSR** is a "terminate and stay resident" program that is loaded into memory but not immediately executed. The program later executes when some "hot" key is pressed or some special action of the hardware occurs, such as moving the mouse. An example of a TSR is a screen capture program. The program is loaded by entering the following command in AUTOEXEC.BAT

```
C:\CAPTURE\SAVEIT
```

In this example, SAVEIT is the name of the program in the directory \CAPTURE. The hot key to activate this program is the Print Screen key. Later, when you are using any applications software and you press the Print Screen key, instead of the screen actually printing under DOS as it normally would, the SAVEIT program saves a copy of the screen to a graphics file or offers you other options. When you exit the screen capture program, control returns to the application where you continue working until you press Print Screen to evoke the TSR again.

COMPLETION OF THE BOOT PROCESS

The boot process is completed after AUTOEXEC.BAT has finished executing. At this point, COMMAND.COM is the program in charge, providing you with a command prompt and waiting for your command. On the other hand, if a program was executed from AUTOEXEC.BAT then it might ask you for a command.

In a Windows environment, it is common to include in the AUTOEXEC.BAT the following command to execute Windows each time the computer is booted:

```
C:\WINDOWS\WIN
```

The file that is executed above is WIN.COM found in the C:\WINDOWS directory. Windows software loads just like other software running under DOS. The program is first loaded into memory and then executed. When it executes, WIN.COM looks for several configuration files that contain user and environmental settings, such as the size of the screen display font, the desktop colors used by the monitor, or the speed of the mouse (see Table 2-2).

These configuration files, sometimes called initialization files, or .INI files, are listed in the table below and are usually stored in the same directory as WIN.COM. These files are discussed in more detail in Chapter 11.

Table 2-2   Windows Configuration Files

Windows Configuration File	General Purpose of the File
SYSTEM.INI	Contains hardware settings and multitasking options for Windows
PROGMAN.INI	Contains information about Program Manager groups
WIN.INI	Contains information about user settings including printer, fonts, file associations, and settings made by applications
CONTROL.INI	Contains information about the user's desktop including color selections, wallpaper, and screen saver options
MOUSE.INI	Contains settings for the mouse

Editing AUTOEXEC.BAT and CONFIG.SYS

You can change the contents of CONFIG.SYS and AUTOEXEC.BAT with any text editor. DOS provides EDIT, a full-screen text editor.

There is a risk in changing AUTOEXEC.BAT. If you make a mistake, your computer can stall during the boot process making it impossible to use without rebooting. Because of this risk, never change AUTOEXEC.BAT without first making a bootable disk that you can use if your AUTOEXEC.BAT file on the hard drive fails.

To make a bootable disk and a backup copy of AUTOEXEC.BAT, use this procedure:

1. From the DOS prompt, type:

   `C:\> FORMAT A:/S`

   The command will erase any files currently on the disk in drive A and the /S command copies the two DOS hidden files and COMMAND.COM to the disk in drive A.

2. If your computer shows either drive A or B as the default drive, make drive C the default as follows:

   `A:\> C:`

3. If the default directory is not the root directory, make it so as follows:

   `C:\WINDOWS> CD\`

   `C:\>`

   No matter what the default directory was (in this example, it was \WINDOWS), the backslash (\) in the prompt indicates that the root is now the default.

4. Backup the current copy of AUTOEXEC.BAT to the hard disk:

```
C:\> COPY AUTOEXEC.BAT AUTOEXEC.BK
```

or to a disk in drive A as follows:

```
C:\> COPY AUTOEXEC.BAT A:
```

5. Edit the file on drive C as follows:

```
C:\> EDIT AUTOEXEC.BAT
```

Your screen should be similar to that shown in Figure 2-16. Follow the directions on the screen to use and exit the editor.

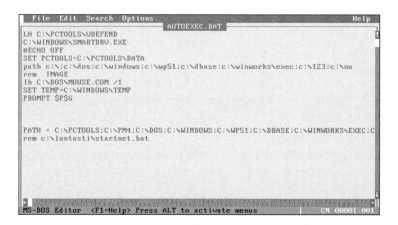

Figure 2-16 Edit AUTOEXEC.BAT

You must remove the disk from drive A and reboot your computer (using Ctl-Alt-Del) to execute the new AUTOEXEC.BAT file on your hard drive. If the computer stalls during the boot, place the bootable disk in drive A and then reboot. Remember that if the disk does not have a copy of AUTOEXEC.BAT on it, you will not have an active PATH command.

Do not use word processing software, such as WordPerfect, to edit AUTOEXEC.BAT, unless you use the ASCII text mode because word processing applications place control characters in their document files that prevent DOS from interpreting the AUTOEXEC.BAT file correctly.

Today, most computers allow you to step through each line of the CONFIG.SYS and AUTOEXEC.BAT files if you press the F8 function key as soon as the "Starting MS-DOS" message appears. This feature can be a very helpful debugging tool.

BOOTING WITH WINDOWS 95

Recall that if a computer takes full advantages of the Windows 95 OS, its BIOS is Plug-and-Play BIOS, meaning that BIOS configures the Plug-and-Play devices before it loads Windows 95. A Plug-and-Play device allows BIOS to select the device's computer resources, such as an IRQ, I/O address, and DMA channels. BIOS then turns this information over to Windows 95 when it loads. The process is described below:

1. When you boot the machine, POST occurs just as it does for BIOS that is not Plug-and-Play.

2. The Plug-and-Play BIOS begins by examining the devices on the system and determining which ones are Plug-and-Play compliant. BIOS first enables the devices that are not Plug-and-Play and then tries to make the Plug-and-Play devices use the leftover resources.

3. BIOS looks for a device containing the OS and loads Windows 95, making information about the current allocation of resources available to the OS.

4. Just as with DOS, the master boot record executes the boot record on the hard drive, which looks for the initial hidden file of Windows 95 called IO.SYS.

5. Again, just as with DOS, IO.SYS loads and looks for a CONFIG.SYS file. If found, the CONFIG.SYS file executes. The CONFIG.SYS file is not required for Windows 95. Many of its functions have been eliminated and are incorporated into Windows 95, but you can use CONFIG.SYS to load a device driver if you choose.

6. After CONFIG.SYS is complete, IO.SYS looks for MSDOS.SYS. The role of MSDOS.SYS in Windows 95 is much different from its role in DOS. In Windows 95, MSDOS.SYS is a hidden text file containing only a few lines of instructions. It follows a format similar to the .INI files of Windows 3.x. Typical lines at the beginning of MSDOS.SYS might look like those shown in Figure 2-17. The functions of the first few MSDOS.SYS entries are listed in Table 2-3.

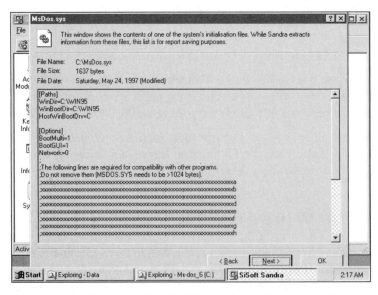

Figure 2-17   Sample MSDOS.SYS file from Windows 95

Table 2-3   Entries in the MSDOS.SYS File

Entry	Description
WinDir=	Location of the Windows 95 directory
WinBootDir=	Location of the Windows 95 startup files
HostWinBootDrv=	Drive that is the Windows boot drive
BootGUI=	When BootGUI=1, automatic graphical startup into Windows 95 is enabled When BootGUI=0, the system boots to a command prompt

7. Next, COMMAND.COM loads just as with DOS. COMMAND.COM is used to provide a command interface for users and to execute an AUTOEXEC.BAT file if it is present.

8. If AUTOEXEC.BAT is found, it now executes.

9. The heart of Windows 95 now loads, providing a desktop from which you can execute applications software. Further details regarding booting with Windows 95 are covered in Chapter 11.

You can see from this description of loading Windows 95 that there are still many DOS functions present. In fact, by using the BootGUI entry in MSDOS.SYS, it is possible to backtrack from a Windows 95 installation to the underlying DOS 7.0, which comes with Windows 95.

PROTECTING DATA, SOFTWARE, AND HARDWARE

Although someone responsible for a computer must understand its operations to solve problems that can occur during use, another objective in maintaining a well-functioning system is to protect the data, software programs, and hardware from harm. Despite your best efforts, data is sometimes lost, software stops functioning correctly, and hardware fails. By taking a few practical measures, however, you can avoid some of the common causes of loss. Here are some practical guidelines that all computer users should follow. However, it is usually the computer support person who is called upon to save the day if something is lost. As a computer support person, you should take the time to train yourself and your users about preventive maintenance and practical precautions.

KEEPING RESCUE DISKS

A rescue disk, which allows you to boot a computer, is essential for every computer. You will learn later in the book about other software that should go on a bootable disk; but at the least, a bootable disk should contain enough software to load the OS. A rescue disk can be created for DOS and Windows 3.x, using File Manager under Windows. Then copy the AUTOEXEC.BAT and CONFIG.SYS files from the root directory of your hard drive to the disk.

For Windows 95, use Explorer to create a rescue disk. If you load Windows 95 from a CD-ROM, be sure to include a DEVICE= line in a CONFIG.SYS file to load the driver for the CD-ROM. A typical line might look like this:

```
DEVICE=C:\CDSYS\SLCD /D:MSCD001
```

In either case, test the disk to make sure it works. To do this, insert the disk in the drive, hard boot, and verify that your OS does load. For Windows 95, verify that you can access your CD-ROM. More details about rescue disks are included in later chapters.

BACKUPS

How valuable is your data? How valuable is your software? In many cases, the most valuable component on the desktop is not the hardware or the software, but the data. Think about each computer you support. What would happen if the hard drive failed? Now create back-ups to prepare for just that situation.

Your backup policy depends on what you are backing up. If you use your PC to interface with a server, for example, and all data is stored on the server and not on the PC, then obviously, you will only be backing up software. (The person responsible for the server would back up the data.) If you keep original software disks and CD-ROMs in a safe place, and if you have multiple copies of them, you might decide not to back up the software. In this case, if a hard drive fails, your chore would be to reload several software packages.

However, if you maintain a large database on the hard drive of your PC, you need to seriously consider a sophisticated backup method. Suppose this database is quite large and is edited daily, several times a day. If this database is lost, so are thousands of labor hours. Plan for the worst case! A good tape backup system is probably in order. Maintain 5 or 10 tapes, where a complete backup of the database is made each night.

Even if the hard drive contains only a few important word processing files, make backups. Never keep an important file on only one media. Make a duplicate copy to a disk, to a file server, or to tape backup. Consider keeping some of your backups in an off-site location.

When protecting your data, the best plan is to back up. Plan that one day the primary media you are using for this data will fail. Know the steps you will take when that happens and prepare for it.

DOCUMENTATION

Make sure to keep the documentation that goes with your hardware and software. Suppose someone decides to "tinker" with a PC for which you are responsible and changes a jumper on the systemboard, but no longer remembers which jumper he or she changed. The computer no longer works and the documentation for the board is now invaluable. If documentation is lost or misplaced, a simple job of reading the settings for each jumper and checking them on the board can become a long and tedious research task. Keep the documentation well-labeled in a safe place. If you have several computers to maintain, you might consider a filing system for each computer. Another method is to tape a cardboard folder to the inside top of the computer case and safely tuck the hardware documentation here. This works well if you are responsible for several computers spread over a wide area.

WRITTEN OR ELECTRONIC RECORD OF SETUP

Remember that CMOS settings can be lost. Most computers today have several standard and advanced settings that, if lost, might be difficult to reconstruct. When you first become responsible for a computer, enter the setup and make a disk backup of setup or write down each setting on paper. Include the standard and advanced settings. Keep this disk or paper with the other hardware documentation for this computer. Some computers allow you to print the setup screen using the Print Screen key. You might try that before making a written record. If you are using a laser printer, after you have pressed Print Screen, you might have to exit the setup screen and command the printer to eject the paper.

A much better approach is to use Nuts & Bolts, Norton Utilities, or some other similar utility software, to make a rescue disk that contains the setup information.

DAMAGE FROM ELECTRICITY

Computers and data can be destroyed by two kinds of electricity—static electricity known as **ESD** (**electrical static discharge**) and power spikes, including lightning. There are many practical things you can do to protect from both.

ESD is most dangerous when the case of the computer is off. Never touch the inside of a computer without first taking precautions to protect the hardware from static electricity. Make sure both you and the computer are grounded before you touch anything inside. *Never* touch the inside of the computer when the computer is turned on. The Introduction to this book presents more extensive instructions on how to protect your computer when you work on it. Be sure to read this material before starting to work on your computer.

There are several devices on the market to protect the computer against electrical surges and lightning. These devices are discussed in Chapter 10.

CHAPTER SUMMARY

- POST and the booting process are important concepts in understanding how computers work.

- The ROM BIOS Startup Program (known as BIOS startup) prepares the system by inventorying hardware devices and the resources they require including I/O addresses, IRQs, DMA channels, and memory addresses for their BIOS.

- Hardware configuration information used by startup BIOS is stored by jumpers, DIP switches, and CMOS setup.

- Loading the OS includes loading information from the boot program, hidden system files, the command interface, and OS configuration files including CONFIG.SYS and AUTOEXEC.BAT in DOS and MSDOS.SYS in Windows 95.

- An input device uses an IRQ (an interrupt request number) to communicate to the CPU a need to be serviced.

- ROM BIOS includes BIOS startup programs as well as system BIOS used to manage common hardware devices.

- Total BIOS services to the hardware and OS are provided by BIOS on the systemboard and on expansion cards for individual devices.

- A device driver is software stored on the hard drive used to manage a hardware device that is loaded into memory during the boot process.

- An IRQ identifies a device to the CPU and points to an entry in the I/O address table that contains the location in memory of the software to handle the request from the device that initiated the IRQ.

- Device drivers are often stored in the upper memory area.

- A DMA channel is a direct path a device can use to pass information to memory and bypass the CPU. The device, such as a hard drive, requires a specific DMA channel that cannot conflict with the channels assigned to other devices.

- DOS begins loading with a boot program, two hidden files, CONFIG.SYS, then COMMAND.COM, and lastly AUTOEXEC.BAT.

- A TSR is a "terminate and stay resident" program that loads into memory and remains dormant until its services are requested.

- The five Windows 3.x configuration files are SYSTEM.INI, PROGMAN.INI, WIN.INI, CONTROL.INI, and MOUSE.INI, where .INI stands for initialization file.

- Make a rescue disk containing enough of the OS to boot your PC in the event the hard drive OS fails.

- Keep backups of data and software, and protect the documentation for a PC system.

- Keep a record of CMOS settings.

2

KEY TERMS

- **AUTOEXEC.BAT** — One startup file on an MS-DOS computer. It tells the computer what commands or programs to execute automatically after bootup.

- **Back up, Backup** — To make a second copy of important files or data. Backups can be made by saving a file with a different name or by copying files to a different disk or to a tape drive.

- **Configuration data** — Also called setup. Information about the computer's hardware, such as what type of hard drive, or monitor is present, along with other detailed settings.

- **DIP switch (dual in-line packet switch)** — A switch that has only two settings, and can be used to set configurations such as modem COM ports or printer setup.

- **Display adapter** — Another name for a video controller card.

- **DMA (direct memory access) controller chip** — A chip that resides on the systemboard and provides channels that a device may use to send data directly to memory, bypassing the CPU.

- **ESD (electrostatic discharge)** — Another name for static electricity, which can damage chips.

- **Interrupt vector table** — See **I/O address table**

- **I/O address table** — A table that stores the memory addresses assigned to I/O devices conrolled by the System BIOS or device drivers. Also called **interrupt vector table** or **vector table**.

- **IRQ (interrupt request number)** — A number that is assigned to a device and is used to signal the CPU for servicing (for example, the normal IRQ for a COM1 is IRQ 4).

- **Memory conflict** — A problem that occurs when two programs attempt to use the same memory address at the same time. This may cause the computer to "hang."

- **On-board BIOS** — Basic input/output system services found on a supporting circuit board such as a controller card.

- **Plug-and-Play** — A set of standards used by both hardware and software so devices are automatically recognized by computers.

- **POST (power-on self test)** — A self-diagnostic program used to perform a simple test of the CPU, RAM, and various I/O devices. The POST is performed when the computer is first turned on.

- **Shadow RAM, Shadowing ROM** — ROM programming code copied into RAM to speed up the system operation, because of the faster access speed of RAM.

- **Slot** — A socket on the systemboard into which adapter boards or interface cards can be installed.

- **System BIOS** — Basic input/output system chip(s) residing on the systemboard that control(s) normal I/O to such areas as system memory and video display.

- **TSR (terminate and stay resident)** — A program that is loaded into memory but is not immediately executed, such as a screen saver or a memory-resident anti-virus program.

- **Vector table** — See **I/O address table**.

REVIEW QUESTIONS

1. List three methods that a computer can use to store setup data.
2. Compare and contrast jumpers and DIP switches.
3. Specifically, how do you enter CMOS on your home or lab computer? (*Hint*: Carefully watch the screen as the computer boots or consult your PC's manual.)
4. Give step-by-step instructions to enter a CMOS/system password on your home or lab computer.
5. List five functions performed by POST.
6. List three devices controlled by BIOS.
7. What type of information is stored in Flash ROM?
8. During the boot process, what is the step after POST?
9. List the two hidden boot files that make up part of DOS.
10. What does the CONFIG.SYS command "DEVICE =" do?
11. What file is immediately processed after CONFIG.SYS?
12. In Windows 3.x, what does the file SYSTEM.INI do?
13. In Windows 3.x, what does the file WIN.INI do?
14. Where are SYSTEM.INI and WIN.INI usually stored on a hard drive?
15. What program is commonly used to edit files like CONFIG.SYS and AUTOEXEC.BAT?
16. List the command lines in your CONFIG.SYS file for your home or lab computer.
17. List the command lines in your AUTOEXEC.BAT file for your home or lab computer.
18. What does the /S in "FORMAT A:/S" do?
19. Give two ways to prevent system damage by static discharge.
20. Describe how a jumper is set to on or off.

PROJECTS

OBSERVING THE BOOT PROCESS

1. Use an operational computer. If your computer has a reset button, press it, and then watch what happens. If your computer does not have a reset button, turn it off, wait a few seconds, and then turn it back on. Write down every beep, light on/off, and message on the screen that you notice. Compare your notes to others to verify that you are not overlooking something.

2

2. Unplug the keyboard and repeat the steps in number 1 above. Write down what happens that is different.

3. Plug the keyboard back in, unplug the monitor, and repeat number 1 again. After you reboot, plug the monitor in. Did the computer know the monitor was missing?

4. Put a disk that does not contain DOS in drive A and press the **Reset** button. If you do not have a Reset button, press **Ctrl-Alt-Del** together to soft boot. Write down what you observe.

5. Print the AUTOEXEC.BAT and CONFIG.SYS files stored on the hard drive. Use one of the following methods, not print screen.

   `C:\> TYPE filename.ext>PRN` or `C:\> PRINT filename.ext`

6. Make a bootable disk using either of two DOS commands:

   If the disk is already formatted, but has no files stored on it, use this command:

   `C:\>SYS A:`

   To format the disk and also make it bootable, use this command:

   `C:\>FORMAT A:/S`

   Your disk should now contain a boot record, the two hidden files, and COMMAND.COM. Compare the bytes available on the disk to a disk that is not bootable. Calculate how many bytes must be in the two hidden files.

7. Test your bootable disk by inserting it in drive A and doing a soft boot. What prompt do you see on the screen?

8. At the DOS prompt, enter this prompt command:

   `PROMPT $P_____$G`

   where the space between P and $ can be used to customize the DOS command prompt.

   What prompt did you get? By examining the prompt, guess what $P in the command line accomplishes and what $G accomplishes. Test your theory by changing the PROMPT command, leaving first $P and then $G out of the command line.

9. Using EDIT, create an AUTOEXEC.BAT file on your bootable disk. Create a PROMPT command to include your first name. Test the command by booting from this disk.

10. Without the appropriate PATH command in your active AUTOEXEC.BAT file, you cannot execute software stored on drive C from the A prompt. Test this theory by trying to execute some applications software that you know is stored on your hard drive. For example, if you have WordPerfect on your hard drive, try to execute the software at the A prompt by using the following command:

    `A:\> WP`

    What error did you get? Why?

UNDERSTANDING SYSTEM.INI UNDER WINDOWS 3.1

1. Using Windows 3.x, follow these steps to look at the contents of the startup files for Windows.

   a. Access **File Manager**.

   b. Make a backup copy of SYSTEM.INI by copying it to a different directory.

   c. On the File menu, select the **Run** command.

   d. In the Command Line box, type **SYSEDIT**, and then click **OK**.

   This opens four startup files for DOS and Windows: CONFIG.SYS, AUTOEXEC.BAT, WIN.INI, and SYSTEM.INI.

2. Close all the windows except SYSTEM.INI.

   Note that a semicolon at the beginning of a command line in SYSTEM.INI disables that command making it a comment or remark line. The contents of the SYSTEM.INI file are explained in a documentation file stored in the Windows directory.

3. Leave the SYSTEM.INI file on the screen. Go back to File Manager and find this file in the Windows directory: SYSINI.WRI or SYSINI.TXT. Double-click the filename so that the appropriate editor displays its contents.

4. Using the on-line documentation, explain the meaning of the "SHELL=" command in SYSTEM.INI.

5. Revise your SYSTEM.INI file so that File Manager loads initially instead of Program Manager. Do this by putting a semicolon in front of the command line and typing a new version of the command line below the old line. This method retains the old command line so you can easily return to it later.

6. Exit and reenter Windows to test your change.

7. Restore SYSTEM.INI to its original settings and then close the file.

OBSERVING THE BOOT PROCESS USING WINDOWS 95

Hard boot your PC. When you see the message, "Starting Windows 95," press **F8**. Write down what happens when you execute each menu choice by booting several times.

CREATING A STARTUP DISK USING WINDOWS 95

Use a startup disk in Windows 95 whenever you have trouble with the OS. Doing this allows you to boot from drive A. Follow these steps to create the disk:

1. Open **Control Panel**.
2. Double-click **Add/Remove Programs**.
3. Click the **Startup Disk** tab.
4. Click **Create Disk**.

After you have created the startup disk, test it by rebooting the computer with the disk still in the drive.

USING SHAREWARE FROM THE INTERNET

Refer to the Projects at the end of Chapter 1 for directions on how to download from the Internet the shareware utility, SANDRA (System Analyzer Diagnostic and Report Assistant). Find the answers to the following questions using SANDRA and then print a report containing all the answers.

1. What is the name of the device driver file used to manage the serial ports under Windows?
2. What IRQ is your mouse using? What is the name of the mouse driver file?
3. How much conventional or base memory is free at this time?
4. What is the average access time to your hard drive?
5. If you are using Windows 95, what is the current value of the BootMulti option found in the MSDOS.SYS file? What is the purpose of the BootMulti option?

USING THE DEVICE MANAGER

Windows 95 provides a much more powerful tool than Microsoft Diagnostics (MSD) called the Device Manager. From it you can view and print your hardware configuration. To access the Device Manager, follow these steps:

1. Click **Start** on the Taskbar, point to **Settings**, and then click **Control Panel**.
2. When the Control Panel window opens, double-click the **System** icon.
3. Click the **Device Manager** tab.

The Device Manager menu appears. You can select an item and then click Properties to view information about that item, or you can view the Properties by double-clicking the item. When you click the **+** sign to the left of an item, the installed devices for that item are listed underneath the item.

Complete the following:

1. What is the filename and path of the device driver that is used to manage your printer port LPT1?

2. List the IRQs available on your computer from 0 to 15.

USING MSD

Access MSD as you did in Chapter 1 with your home or lab computer and then answer the following questions. You can print the appropriate screen in MSD showing the answers.

1. What is the IRQ assigned to the mouse?

2. What, if any, is the COM port used by the mouse?

3. What IRQ is assigned to the disk drive?

4. What is the I/O or port address used by COM 1?

5. IRQ 2 points to or "cascades" to a higher IRQ. Which IRQ does it point to?

USING NORTON UTILITIES TO SAVE SETUP INFORMATION

Using Norton Utilities, create a rescue disk containing setup information following the directions given in the chapter. After the rescue disk is created, execute the RESCUE program on the boot disk and print the opening screen.

USING NUTS & BOLTS TO SAVE SETUP INFORMATION

Following the directions in the Preface, install Nuts & Bolts to your hard drive from the CD-ROM accompanying this book. Then follow these directions to create a rescue disk that contains a record of setup information.

1. Click on **Start**, **Programs**, **Nuts & Bolts**. From the list of Nuts & Bolts utilities that are displayed, select **Rescue Disk**.

2. The 'Welcome to Rescue Disk' screen displays. Click **Next** to continue.

3. From the next screen that displays, you can choose to format the disk that will become your rescue disk or plan to use a previously formatted disk.

4. Click **Next**. Nuts & Bolts prompts you to insert the disk in drive A and creates the rescue disk. Click **Finish** when the process is complete.

5. Look at the list of files on the rescue disk. Which file do you suspect contains a backup of CMOS information?

6. To use this bootable rescue disk, insert the disk in drive A and reboot. Then follow the directions on the screen.

2

THE SYSTEMBOARD

Chapters 1 and 2 surveyed the hardware and software that make up a personal computer and described how they work together to create a functioning computer system. In this chapter, we begin the detailed process of examining how the different components of a computer work in near-perfect harmony and with accuracy. Our starting point is the systemboard, the central site of computer logic circuitry and the location of the most important microchip in the computer, the CPU.

To understand the ideas presented in this chapter, you should (1) know what the following terms mean: bit, byte, kilobyte, and hexidecimal number, and (2) be sufficiently familiar with the hexadecimal number system to read memory addresses written in hex. Appendix D describes bits, bytes, and hex numbers used to address memory locations. If this is unfamiliar territory for you, turn to Appendix D before reading on.

IN THIS CHAPTER
YOU WILL LEARN:

- WHAT PHYSICAL COMPONENTS ARE ON THE SYSTEMBOARD
- HOW THE SYSTEMBOARD TRANSPORTS DATA, FOLLOWS PROGRAMMING LOGIC, AND COORDINATES THE TIMING AND EXECUTION OF EACH PROCESSING TASK
- HOW TO SELECT SYSTEMBOARDS AND CPUs FOR YOUR SYSTEM
- HOW TO UPGRADE SOME COMPONENTS ON A SYSTEMBOARD

TYPES OF SYSTEMBOARDS

The main components on a systemboard are the following:

- A CPU and its accompanying chip set
- A real-time clock
- ROM BIOS
- A CMOS configuration chip and its battery
- RAM
- RAM cache
- A system bus with expansion slots
- Jumpers
- Ports that come directly off the board
- Power supply connections

This chapter describes each of the above. But first let's look at the systemboard itself as a component. Figure 3-1 shows a systemboard as it would look if you purchased it with no components added.

When you buy a systemboard, your selection determines the:

- CPU type and speed
- Chip set on the board
- Memory cache type and size
- Types and number of expansion slots: ISA, EISA, VESA local bus, PCI
- Type of memory: parity or non-parity, EDO, SDRAM, SIMMs, or DIMMs
- Maximum amount of memory you can put on the board and the incremental amounts by which memory can be upgraded
- Type of case you can use
- ROM BIOS, which is usually already installed
- System's ability to use Plug-and-Play ROM BIOS and/or Flash ROM
- Type of keyboard connector
- Presence or absence of different types of proprietary video and/or proprietary local bus slots
- Presence or absence of IDE adapters and SCSI controller
- Presence or absence of COM ports, LPT ports, and mouse port

Selecting the systemboard is, therefore, a very important decision when you purchase a computer or assemble one from parts because the systemboard determines so many of your computer's features.

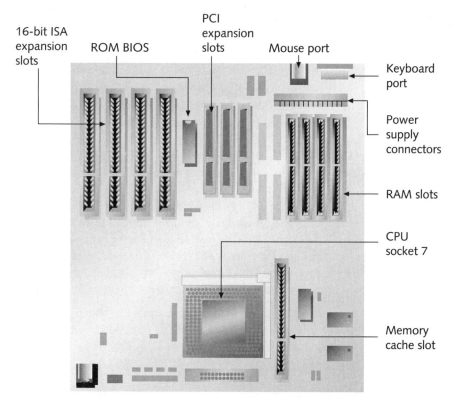

Figure 3-1   A Pentium systemboard with no components added

Depending on which applications and peripheral devices you plan to use with the computer, you can take one of three different approaches to selecting a systemboard. The first option is to select the board that provides the most room for expansion so you can upgrade and exchange components and add on devices easily. A second approach is to select the board that best suits the needs of the present configuration of this computer knowing that when you need to upgrade, you will likely switch to new technology and a new systemboard altogether. The middle ground between these two alternatives is to select a systemboard that meets your present needs with moderate room for expansion.

Some questions to ask when selecting a systemboard are:

- Is the systemboard designed so that long expansion cards don't get in the way of the CPU or other important devices you might want to access?

- How many different CPUs can the systemboard support—just those manufactured by Intel or also those made by Intel's competitors?

- What bus speeds does the board support?

- Will the systemboard support a **universal serial bus** port (a newer faster version of the serial port)?

- What is the warranty on the board?

- How extensive and user-friendly is the documentation?

- How much support does the manufacturer supply for the board?

- Does the board use many embedded devices?

Sometimes a systemboard contains a component that is more commonly offered as a separate device. (If the component is found on the board, it's called an **embedded component**.) One example is an IDE (Integrated Device Electronics) adapter used to connect an IDE hard drive to the system. The adapter and the IDE connector might be on the systemboard or the adapter might be on a card placed in an expansion slot. Another component that can either be delivered as a part of a systemboard or purchased separately is video support. The video port might be on the systemboard or might require a video card. The cost of a systemboard with an embedded component is usually less than the combined cost of a systemboard without the component and an expansion card. Be cautious about choosing a board that leans too far in the proprietary direction if you plan to expand later. A proprietary design using many embedded devices does not lend itself well to using add-on devices from other manufacturers. For example, if you plan to add a more powerful video card in the near future, you might not want to choose a systemboard that contains a video on-board.

If you have an embedded component, make sure you can disable the component so that you have the option of using another external component if needed. Most often, disabling a component on the systemboard is done through jumpers on the board.

Table 3-1 lists some manufacturers of systemboards for 486 CPUs, Pentiums, and their clones and their Web addresses.

Table 3-1   Major Manufacturers of Systemboards

Manufacturer	Product	Web Address
Acer America Corp	Pentium boards	www.acer.com
American Megatrends	486, Pentium boards	www.megatrends.com
ASUS	486, Pentium boards	www.asus.com
First International Computer, Inc.	486, Pentium boards	www.fica.com
Giga-Byte Technology, Co.	Pentium boards	www.giga-byte.com
Intel Corporation	Pentium boards	www.intel.com
Micronics Computers	Pentium boards	www.micronics.com
Ocean Office Automation, Ltd.	486, Pentium boards	www.ocean-usa.com
Supermicro Computers, Inc.	Pentium boards	www.supermicro.com
Tyan Computer	Pentium boards	www.tyan.com

THE CPU AND THE CHIP SET

3

IBM and IBM–compatible computers manufactured today use a microprocessor chip made by Intel or one of its competitors. When identifying the CPU on the systemboard, the most common model numbers for the Intel family of chips are 8088, 8086, 80286, 386, 486, and the Pentium. We mention the first three chips for historical interest and include the 386 in our discussions only because you occasionally still see one around. However, you should be familiar with the 486 and Pentium family of chips and know what you can expect from a computer whose CPU uses those chips. The following attributes are used to rate CPUs:

1. **CPU speed measured in megahertz.** Remember from Chapter 1 that the systemboard contains a system clock that keeps the beat for all systemboard activities. The more frequently the clock beats per second the faster the CPU can execute instructions. We use units called megahertz to measure clock speeds. One **megahertz** (MHz) is equal to 1,000,000 beats or cycles of the clock per second where a cycle is the smallest unit of processing the CPU can execute. The first CPU used in an IBM PC was the 8088, which worked at about 4.77 MHz or 4,770,000 clock beats per second. An average speed for a CPU today is about 166 MHz or 166,000,000 beats in a second. In less than a minute this processor beats more times than your heart beats in a lifetime!

2. **Efficiency of the programming code.** Permanently built into the CPU chip are numerous programs that accomplish fundamental operations, such as how to compare two numbers or how to add two numbers. Less efficient CPUs require more steps to perform these simple operations than more efficient CPUs.

3. **Word size, sometimes called the internal data path size.** Word size is the largest number of bits the CPU can process in one operation. Word size ranges from 16 bits (2 bytes) to 64 bits (8 bytes).

4. **Data path.** The data path, sometimes called the external data path size, is the largest number of bits that can be transported into the CPU. The size of the data path is the same as the bus size, or the number of bits that can be transported along the bus at one time. (The data path ranges from 8 bits to 32 bits.) The word size need not be as large as the data path size; some CPUs can receive more bits than they can process at one time.

5. **Maximum number of memory addresses.** A computer case has room for a lot of memory physically housed within the case, but a CPU has only a fixed range of addresses that it can assign to this physical memory. How many memory addresses the CPU can assign limits the amount of physical memory chips that can be used effectively by a computer. The minimum number of memory addresses a CPU can use is one megabyte, (where each byte of memory is assigned a single address). Recall that one megabyte is equal to 1024 kilobytes, which is equal to 1024×1024 bytes, or 1,048,576 memory addresses. The maximum number of memory addresses is 4096 megabytes, which is equal to 4 gigabytes.

6. **The amount of memory included with the CPU**. Some chips have storage for instructions and data built right inside the chip housing. This is called internal cache, primary cache, level 1, or L1 cache.

7. **Multiprocessing ability**. Some chips are really two processors in one and can do more than one thing at a time.

8. **Special functionality**. An example of this is the Pentium MMX chip, which is designed to manage multimedia devices efficiently.

Of the eight criteria listed above, the three most popular ways of measuring CPU power, until Intel manufactured the Pentium series of chips, were speed measured in megahertz and word size and data path size measured in bits. Our criteria for measuring the power of a CPU have changed since the introduction of the Pentium. The word size and path size are no longer key qualities. We currently are more interested in clock speed, bus speed, internal cache, and, especially, the intended functionality of the chip such as ability to handle graphics well (MMX technology).

THE EARLIER INTEL CPUs

Table 3-2 lists specifications for some early CPUs made by Intel. Until the introduction of Pentium chips and their clones, most chips were rated by the criteria listed in this table. Because so many of these chips are still in use, you should be familiar with their differences and features.

Table 3-2   Comparing the Power of the Earlier Intel CPUs

Model (chronological order)	Approximate Maximum Speed (MHz)	Word Size (bits)	Path Size (bits)	Memory Addresses (MB)
80386DX	40	32	32	4096
80386SX	20	32	16	16
486DX	60	32	32	4096
486SX	25	32	32	4096
First Pentium	60	32 × 2	64	4096

Looking at the first two rows of Table 3-2, note that the 80386SX chip had a smaller path size than the 80386DX although it was developed later. At the time Intel first manufactured the 80386DX, systemboard manufacturers could produce at a reasonable cost a systemboard with a path size of only 16 bits or 2 bytes. Therefore the systemboard manufacturers did not use the first 80386DX chips. In response to this, Intel produced the cheaper 80386SX chip, which accommodated the smaller path size, to keep the cost of the system more reasonable for personal computer users. The 80386SX chip used an internal 32-bit word size but an external 16-bit path size. Internal refers to operations inside the CPU and external refers to operations outside the CPU, such as on the bus. The smaller path size accounts for the slower speed of the 80386SX chip as compared to the 80386DX chip (S stands for single and D for double).

About that same time, computer users dropped the 80 in front of the model number and called a chip the "386 chip" rather than the "80386 chip." You might hear the same Intel microprocessor referred to as the 80386, the i386, or simply the 386 chip. Or, you might hear references to the 80486, the i486, or the 486 chip. The newest CPU, the Pentium, dropped the 80 prefix and numbering system altogether. Although not an official name, some call the Pentium chip the 586 chip. The name Pentium comes from the word *pente*, the Greek word for five, which Intel chose after a legal battle Intel had with two competitors, AMD and Cyrix. AMD and Cyrix won rights to continue using the X86 chip names.

Some CPU microchips are designed to work hand-in-hand with a secondary microchip processor called a coprocessor. The coprocessor performs calculations for the CPU at a faster speed than the CPU. The coprocessor for the 80386 chip is the 80387. The 486DX has the coprocessor built into the CPU housing. The 486SX has the coprocessor portion of the chip disabled. Software must be written to make use of a coprocessor. Most software today assumes you have a 486DX or Pentium chip and writes its code to take advantage of the assumed coprocessor capability.

There's an interesting story about the 486 family of chips. The 486 chip is built to contain both the CPU as well as the coprocessor in the same chip housing. However, when the chip was manufactured, the coprocessor portions of some chips did not pass final inspection. After these defective chips began to accumulate, Intel disabled the coprocessor portion of these defective chips and marketed the chip as a less powerful version of the 486 chip. And with that decision, they created the 486DX and 486SX chips. The 486DX chip is the original 486 chip with a working coprocessor; the 486SX chip has a disabled coprocessor. Both chips use a 32-bit bus.

If you own a 486SX computer, you can buy a coprocessor for it, assuming you want to continue to invest in this older technology. The coprocessor, labeled the 487SX, has the internal design of the 486DX. A systemboard using a 486SX CPU, with a slot for a coprocessor, is really accommodating a replacement CPU. When you install the 487SX in the open slot, the original 486SX CPU is disabled, and the new CPU takes over.

Table 3-2 lists the earlier CPUs chronologically by their introduction in the marketplace. The CPUs are labeled as 80386SX-16, 80486DX2-50, or use a similar convention. The number at the end of the model number, 16 or 50 in our examples, refers to the speed of the CPU in megahertz. The 2 following the 486DX CPU indicates that the chip can work in overdrive mode, which doubles the clock speed to increase the overall speed of the computer. (On some older computers, doubling the clock speed was called **turbo mode** and was accomplished by pressing a button on the computer case.) Sometimes, systemboards and CPUs that work in this overdrive mode overheat, and heat sinks and/or fans must be mounted on top of the CPU.

For notebook computers, the CPU model number often has an L in it, as in 486SL-20. The L indicates that this microchip is a 486SX that requires a lower voltage than the regular SX. The 20 indicates that the speed is 20 megahertz.

THE PENTIUM AND ITS COMPETITORS

The latest CPU microchips by Intel are the Pentium series of chips. The Pentium series are true 64-bit chips, meaning both the data path and word size are 64 bits. In addition, a Pentium chip has two arithmetic logic units, meaning that it can perform two calculations at the same time; it is therefore a true multiprocessor. To compare the Pentium family of chips and the Pentium competitors, you need some background on bus speed, clock speed, and memory cache.

The **bus speed** is the speed at which the data on the systemboard is moving, and it greatly affects the overall performance of the computer, as you will see later in this chapter. The CPU **clock speed** is the speed at which the CPU is operating internally. If the CPU operates at 150 MHz internally, but 75 MHz externally, the CPU clock speed is 150 MHz and the bus speed is 75 MHz. The CPU is operating at twice the speed of the bus. This factor is called the **multiplier**. If you multiply the bus speed by the multiplier, you get the CPU clock speed.

Bus speed × multiplier = clock speed

We'll discuss the multiplier further when we discuss buses later in the chapter, but for the purposes of evaluating the performance of CPUs, you need to know that the speed of the CPU is determined by multiplying the bus speed by a factor of 1.5, 2, 2.5 or some other number.

A **memory cache** on the systemboard is a small amount of RAM that is much faster than the rest of RAM. Both programming code and data can be stored temporarily in this faster memory. The size of the cache a CPU can support is a measure of its performance, especially during intense calculations.

Table 3-3 lists the four types of Pentium chips on the market today and the Deschutes, the temporary code name of the next expected Intel chip. Each one is discussed below.

Table 3-3   The Intel Pentium Family of Chips

Processor	Current Clock Speeds	MMX	Primary Cache
Classic Pentium	100, 120,133,150, 166, 200	No	16K
Pentium MMX	150, 166, 200	Yes	32K
Pentium Pro	166, 180, 200	No	16K
Pentium II	166, 180, 200, 266, 300	Yes	32K
Deschutes	Expecting 300, 333, 400	Yes	Unknown

Classic Pentium

The first Pentium chip was introduced in March 1993, and has now become affectionately known as the "Classic Pentium." Intel resolved early problems with this first Pentium. The lower cost of the Classic Pentium as compared to other Pentium chips makes it a wise choice for some applications. Intel plans to discontinue manufacturing this older chip; it might no longer be available by time you are reading this book.

Pentium MMX

The Pentium MMX (Multimedia Extension) targets the home market and performs well with games and multimedia software, speeding up graphical applications (Figure 3-2).

Figure 3-2   The Intel Pentium MMX

Pentium Pro

Intel recommends the Pentium Pro for applications that rely heavily on large and fast access to cache memory. Engineering applications, such as problems in computational fluid dynamics, that require intense calculations need this high-speed performance. The Pentium Pro is designed for workstations focusing on heavy computations rather than on servers or on throughput of large quantities of data. The Pentium Pro does not perform well with older 16-bit applications software written for DOS or Windows 3.x.

Pentium II

Currently the highest performing Intel processor, the Pentium II is the best choice for a powerful business computer using graphics applications such as 3D graphic manipulation, CAD (computer-aided design), multimedia presentations with graphics, motion video, and sound. The Pentium II is designed for graphics-intensive workstations and servers.

The Pentium Competitors

Intel's two primary competitors are AMD and Cyrix. Table 3-4 lists two chips that are comparable to the Classic Pentium.

Table 3-4   Cyrix and AMD Competitors of the Classic Pentium

Processor	Current Clock Speeds (MHz)	Bus Speeds (MHz)	Multiplier	Internal or Primary Cache
Cyrix 6x86 or M1	150	75	2	16K
AMD K5	75, 90, 100, 116.66	50, 60, 66	1.5 or 1.75	24K

The AMD K5 (Figure 3-3) offers an unusual assortment of clock speeds and bus speeds. The Cyrix 6x86 (Figure 3-4) contends with and exceeds the Classic Pentium in many respects. However, one disadvantage of the Cyrix 6x86 is that it uses a bus speed of 75 MHz, which is not supported by the Intel PCI standard for the PCI bus speed. Therefore, if you use this Cyrix chip, you must use a systemboard that contains supporting chips other than the popular Intel brands or use an unsupported bus speed for these systemboards that use the Intel chip sets.

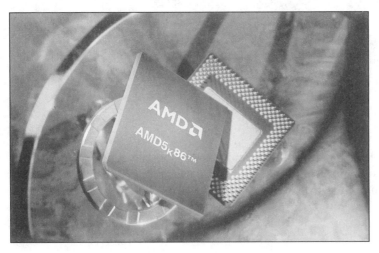

Figure 3-3   The AMD K5

The 6x86 chip has had problems with overheating, although this has been solved by the newer Cyrix 6x86L. (The "L" stands for low voltage.) If you're shopping for this chip, make sure you get the 6x86L rather than the 6x86.

Table 3-5 shows the performance ratings of two competitors of the Pentium chips using MMX technology.

Figure 3-4   The Cyrix 6x86 or M1 CPU

Table 3-5   Cyrix and AMD Competitors of the Advanced Pentiums

Processor	Current Clock Speeds (MHz)	Bus Speeds (MHz)	Multiplier	MMX	Internal or Primary Cache
Cyrix M2	187.5, 225	75	2.5, 3	Yes	64K
AMD K6	166, 200, 233	66	2.5, 3, 3.5	Yes	64K

The AMD K6 uses MMX technology and competes with the Pentium II. In early performance tests, the K6 was faster than the Pentium II in normal business applications. Both the AMD K6 and the Cyrix M2 offer an exceptionally large primary cache.

CPUs That Use RISC Technology

Another trend in chip design is RISC (reduced instruction set computer) technology. RISC chips are challenging the monopoly in the chip market held by CISC (complex instruction set computer) chips. (CISC is the name given to traditional chip design.) Most Intel chips use the CISC technology to maintain compatibility with older systems and software, although the Pentium II uses a combination of both technologies. Both the K5 and K6 by AMD use the RISC technology. The difference between the RISC and CISC technologies is the number of instructions (called the **instruction set**) contained directly on the CPU chip itself. With RISC technology, the CPU is limited to a very simple instruction set that can execute in a single clock cycle. Most CPU manufacturers have a version of RISC chip. Sun Microsystems has the SPARC chip, Digital Equipment Corporation (DEC) has the MIPS and Alpha, and IBM Corporation has the RS 6000.

One advantage that RISC chips have over CISC chips is that, because they have only a small number of operating instructions to perform, they can process much faster where few complex calculations are required. This feature makes RISC chips ideal for video or telecommunications applications. They are also easier and cheaper to manufacture.

CPU Cooling Fans

Because a CPU generates so much heat, a computer system uses a cooling fan to keep the temperature below the Intel maximum allowed limit of 185° F (see Figure 3-5). Good CPU cooling fans can maintain the temperature at 90 to 110° F. Use cooling fans to prevent system errors and to prolong the life of the CPU.

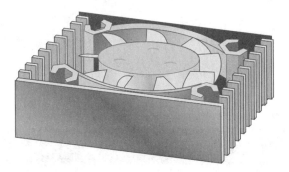

Figure 3-5   CPU cooling fan

The cooling fan usually fits on top of the CPU with a wire or plastic clip. A cream-like thermal compound made of silicon is placed between the fan and the CPU. This compound draws heat from the CPU and passes it to the fan. The thermal compound transmits heat better than air and makes the connection between the fan and the CPU airtight. The fan is equipped with a power connector that connects to one of the power cables coming from the power supply.

Some newer CPUs generate so much heat that they need extra cooling. The chips might have a heat sink attached to them and a large fan attached on top of the sink or to the side of the case blowing over the heat sink. A **heat sink** is a clip-on device that mounts on top of the CPU. Fingers or fins at the base of the heat sink pull the heat away from the CPU.

Some systemboards feature a power connection on the systemboard for the cooling fan that sounds an alarm if the fan stops working. Because the fan is a mechanical device, it is more likely to fail than the electronic devices inside the case. To protect the expensive CPU, you can purchase a heat sensor for a few dollars. The sensor plugs into a power connection coming from the power supply and is mounted on the side of the case. It sounds an alarm when the inside of the case gets too hot.

CPU Slots and Sockets

Presently there are three types of connectors for the CPU on the systemboard (see Table 3-6).

Table 3-6   Connectors for the CPU

Connector Name	Used by CPU	Description
Socket 7	Pentium MMX, Classic Pentium, AMD K5, AMD K6	Square design
Socket 8	Pentium Pro	Slightly rectangular and larger than a Socket 7
Slot 1	Pentium II	Rectangular and looks like a small expansion slot

The Pentium II stands up on its end and fits into Slot 1 much like an expansion card, although the CPU is completely contained within a black housing (see Figure 3-6). You can attach a heat sink or cooling fan to the side of the Pentium II case. Socket 7 and Socket 8 support the traditional look for CPUs—square or slightly rectangular with many connectors. The heat sink or fan clips to the top of the CPU.

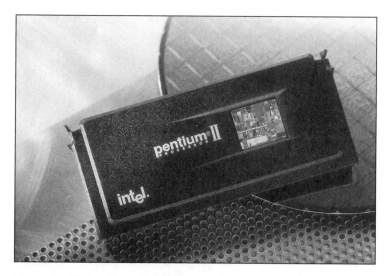

Figure 3-6   Pentium II CPU

Most Socket 7 and Socket 8 connectors offer a special ZIF (zero insertion force) feature. A ZIF socket has a small lever on the side of the socket that lifts the CPU up and out of the socket (see Figure 3-7). You can remove the CPU and replace it with another if necessary. Push the lever down. Move the CPU into its pin connectors with equal force over the entire housing.

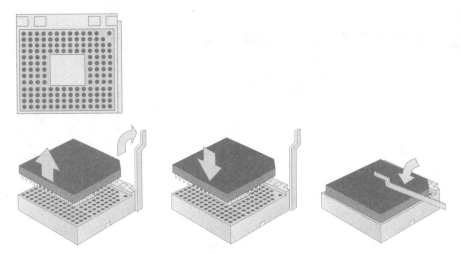

Figure 3-7   The ZIF socket

CPU Voltage Regulator

Different CPUs require different amounts of voltage on the systemboard. Some CPUs require one voltage amount for I/O operations and another amount for core operations. Those that require two different voltages are called **dual voltage CPUs**. The others are called **single voltage CPUs**. A CPU voltage regulator controls the amount of voltage on the systemboard. The voltage type selections are made by jumper settings.

Figure 3-8 shows sample documentation of CPU voltage selections for a particular systemboard. Notice that two jumpers called JP16 located near Socket 7 on the board accomplish the voltage selection. For single voltage, for the Pentium, Cyrix 6x86, or AMD K5, both jumpers are open. Dual voltage used by the Pentium MMX, Cyrix M2, and AMD K6 is selected by opening or closing the two jumpers according to the diagram. Follow the recommendations for your CPU when selecting the voltages from the chart.

THE CHIP SET

A **chip set** is a set of chips on the systemboard that collectively controls the memory cache, external buses, and some peripherals. Intel makes the most popular chip sets, which are listed in Table 3-7.

The Triton II chip set is considered the best for Pentium boards. (Some say the H in the model number stands for high quality.) The Triton II set supports up to 512 MB of RAM. You can sometimes see as many as 6 to 8 SIMM sockets on an HX systemboard. The Triton III or 430VX chip set has one advantage over the HX: it supports up to 64 MB of SDRAM on 168-pin DIMMs. (SDRAM and DIMMs are discussed later in this chapter in the section on RAM). The latest Triton series of chip sets is the 430TX, which replaces the VX and MX, becoming the first chip set by Intel used in both desktop PCs and notebooks.

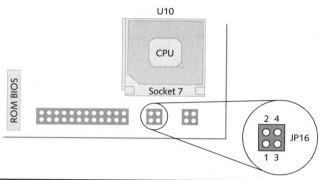

Figure 3-8   CPU voltage regulator

CPU TYPE	JP16	CPU Voltage	
		CORE	I/O
Single Voltage INTEL P54C/CQS/CT Cyrix 6x86 AMD K5	2 ○ ○ 4 1 ○ ○ 3 open	3.5V	3.5V
Dual Voltage INTEL P55C/MMX Cyrix 6x86L/M2 AMD K6	2 ○ ○ 4 1 ○ ○ 3 open	2.8V	3.4V
	2 ● ○ 4 1 ● ○ 3 1-2 closed, 3-4 open	2.9V	3.4V
	2 ○ ● 4 1 ○ ● 3 1-2 open, 3-4 closed	3.2V	3.4V

Table 3-7   The Intel Chip Set Family

Common Name	Model Number	Comments
Triton I	430FX	The oldest chip set, no longer produced
Triton II	430HX	High performance, supports dual CPUs
Triton III	430VX	Value chip set, supports SDRAM
	430MX	Used for notebooks (M=mobile)
	430TX	Supports SDRAM, ultra DMA; replaces the VX and MX
Natoma	440FX	Supports Pentium Pro and Pentium II
Orion	450GX, KX	Supports Pentium Pro

Chip sets must operate at the speed of the bus to which they are connected. Intel does not officially support any bus speed above 66 MHz for its chip sets even though the bus might go faster than that. The reason is that the PCI bus standard developed by Intel, and discussed later in this chapter, allows a bus speed of only 33 MHz. For speeds other than 66 MHz, you must turn to other manufacturers or use an unsupported bus speed with the Intel chip set. One example of where this limitation becomes a problem is with the Cyrix 6x86 or M1 CPU. The Cyrix chip uses a 75 MHz bus speed and cannot use the popular Intel Triton FX or HX chip set without an unsupported bus speed. Therefore, if you use this Cyrix chip, you must use a chip set other than the popular Intel brand or use an unsupported bus speed for the Intel Triton boards.

Manufacturers of chip sets include the following:

- Intel, Inc.

- AMD, Inc.

- Cyrix, Inc.

- Silicon Integrated Systems Corp. (known as SiS)

- Standard Microsystems Corp.

- United Microelectronics Corp.

- VIA Technology, Inc.

- VLSI Technology, Inc.

Chip Sets that Compete with Intel

VIA and AMD have combined efforts to produce a chip set to compete with the latest Intel chip set, the 430TX. Their chip set is known as either the VIA Apollo VP2/97 or the AMD-640. Features of this chip set are listed below.

- Supports dual processors

- Supports up to 512 MB of system RAM, which can be cached

- Supports pipeline burst cache

- Supports SDRAM

- Has a built-in system clock, mouse, and keyboard controller

SiS produces the Genesis and Trinity line of chip sets. SiS makes many chip sets with built-in video controllers, including a type of controller that doesn't need video RAM.

Currently, Intel dominates the chip set market for several reasons. First, Intel has a huge investment in research and development. This research support enabled Intel engineers to invent the PCI bus and the universal serial bus. Intel is currently working on a new bus, the AGP, Advanced Graphics Bus. The major advantage that Intel has over other chip set manufacturers is that they know more about their Intel CPUs than anyone else, and the chip sets are therefore more compatible with the Pentium family of CPUs. Also, Intel does not claim to support the Cyrix and AMD CPUs, and this might be the reason that Intel does not support bus speeds above 66 MHz. However, the Intel chip sets do run at the higher bus speeds of 75 or 83 MHz so that you can run the Cyrix CPU with these chip sets.

Intel's strongest competitors for chip sets are VIA and SiS, both of which support the higher bus speeds of the Cyrix chips.

3

ROM BIOS

Recall that ROM chips are also located on the systemboard. They're easy to spot because they are larger than most chips and often have a shiny plastic label on them. On the label is the manufacturer's name, the date of manufacture, and the serial number of the chip. This information is important when you are trying to precisely identify the chip, such as when selecting the correct upgrade for the chip.

Recall that BIOS (basic input/output system) software as well as the programs that boot the system are stored on ROM chips. During the boot process, some BIOS code and tables are loaded from ROM into the first 1K of RAM. This information remains in RAM to enable the operating system to communicate with input/output devices. Some BIOS code uses the memory addresses just below 1024K in the top portion of upper memory. (See Appendix D for an explanation of this address range.) Instructions stored in this area of memory are called **System BIOS** or **Motherboard BIOS**. ROM chips can be exchanged, but in the past you couldn't write to them. The chips are usually socketed in, not soldered, for easy exchange. Recall from Chapter 1 that a newer kind of ROM, called Flash ROM, is becoming increasingly popular because it allows upgraded versions of the BIOS to be written to it without having to physically replace the chip.

The most well-known and dependable ROM code is written by Phoenix Software, Award Software, and American Megatrends Inc. (AMI). When selecting a PC clone, make sure to check who wrote the ROM BIOS code. If you select code written by one of these companies, your ROM BIOS will be compatible with most software. An easy way to identify the name of the BIOS manufacturer without having to remove the case cover is to watch the boot process. The name of the BIOS manufacturer appears at the beginning of the boot process.

Not only must the BIOS code be compatible with the rest of the system, but System BIOS might need certain capabilities to operate newer software and hardware. Questions about BIOS that you must answer include the following:

- Does the BIOS support Plug-and-Play?
- Does the BIOS support larger hard drives?
- Is the BIOS chip a Flash ROM chip?

Before we look at the alternatives, let's first examine the locations of the BIOS code and the way the total BIOS in your system functions. The ROM BIOS chip contains only a portion of the total BIOS code needed to interface with all the hardware components in the system. Understanding that BIOS programs can come from several sources helps in solving memory problems and other problems that arise from resource conflicts that will be considered in future chapters.

THE TOTAL BIOS IN YOUR SYSTEM

Some expansion cards, such as a LAN board or a video controller board, also have ROM chips on them. The operating system uses the programs stored on these ROM chips to communicate with the peripheral devices. During the boot process, the expansion card tells the startup program the memory addresses that it requires to access its ROM code, usually in the upper memory area between 640K and 1024K. The ROM code from these boards becomes part of the total BIOS that the OS uses to communicate with peripherals. Usually these boards reserve certain addresses of upper memory for their exclusive use. Problems referred to as hardware configuration conflicts can occur if two boards request the same addresses in upper memory. We address these hardware conflicts and offer possible solutions when we study managing memory in Chapter 9.

Figure 3-9 shows how the programming code from various ROM BIOS chips is mapped onto the memory addresses managed by the CPU. Remember from Chapter 2 that RAM is viewed logically as a series of memory addresses that can be assigned to physical memory devices, such as a SIMM on the systemboard, a ROM BIOS chip on the systemboard, or a ROM chip on a network card. After booting is complete, most, if not all, of the BIOS on the system has declared that it exists and has requested some memory addresses. Sometimes the request is for a specific range of addresses and sometimes the request is for just a certain number of addresses. In Figure 3-9, each of the three memory devices has been assigned a different address in upper memory.

Remember from Chapter 2 that if the programming code from the ROM BIOS chips is also copied into RAM, this is called shadowing ROM or sometimes Shadow RAM. The terms indicate that RAM is shadowing ROM code. In the setup of your computer, you usually have the choice of whether to shadow System BIOS. For DOS and Windows 95, accept the default value for this option.

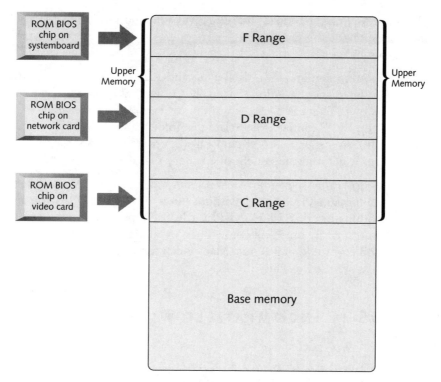

Figure 3-9   Total System and component BIOS assigned memory addresses

Plug-and-Play BIOS

Recall from Chapter 2 that Plug-and-Play (PnP) is a term that applies to both the Windows 95 OS and to some ROM BIOS. It means that rather than having you reset DIP switches and jumpers, the OS and/or the BIOS automatically configures hardware devices to reduce or eliminate conflicting requests for such system resources as I/O addresses, IRQs, DMA channels, or upper memory addresses. Windows 95 Plug-and-Play assigns these resources to a device only if the device allows it. For example, if an older sound card requires a certain group of upper memory addresses that are hard coded into its on-board BIOS, there's nothing that Windows 95 Plug-and-Play can do about that. (**Hard coded** is computer jargon for something being coded so that it cannot be changed.) Plug-and-Play simply tries to work around the problem as best it can. If two non–Plug-and-Play hardware devices require the same resource and their BIOS does not provide for accepting a substitute, these two devices cannot coexist on the same PC.

Newer devices that are Plug-and-Play-compliant are more cooperative. At startup, they simply request to work and then wait for the OS to assign the resources they need. Windows 95 tries to do that whether or not the system BIOS is Plug-and-Play BIOS. Plug-and-Play BIOS does some of the up-front work for Windows 95 like an efficient secretary organizes a boss's work for the day. At startup, it's the Startup BIOS that examines the hardware devices present, takes inventory, and then loads the OS. Part of the job of Plug-and-Play BIOS is to collect information about the devices and the resources they require and later work with Windows 95 to assign the resources.

ESCD (extended system configuration data) Plug-and-Play BIOS goes even further creating a list of all the things you have done manually to the configuration that Plug-and-Play does not do on its own. This ESCD list is written to the BIOS chip so that the next time you boot, the Startup BIOS can faithfully relate that information to Windows 95. The BIOS chip for ESCD BIOS is a special RAM chip called Permanent RAM or PRAM that can hold data written to it without the benefit of a battery that the CMOS setup chip requires.

Most ROM BIOS made after the end of 1994 is Plug-and-Play. Windows 95 can use most—but not all—of its Plug-and-Play abilities without Plug-and-Play BIOS. If you are buying a new PC, accept nothing less than Plug-and-Play BIOS. As more and more devices become Plug-and-Play-compliant, the time will come when installing a new device on a PC will be just as error-free and easy to do as it is on a Mac, which for years has known about and used the same concepts as are used in Plug-and-Play.

WHEN BIOS IS INCOMPATIBLE WITH HARDWARE OR SOFTWARE

BIOS is a hybrid of two worlds. It's technically both hardware and software—it's really the intersection point of the two—and must communicate with both well, as shown in Figure 3-10. When hardware and software change, BIOS might need to change too. In the past, most users upgraded BIOS because new hardware was incompatible with it. Sometimes, however, you need to upgrade BIOS to accommodate new software, such as Plug-and-Play.

Ages and ages ago (at least 3 years), when a new device became available, such as the 3½-inch floppy disk drive, your PC sometimes could not use the new device until you upgraded the BIOS. You did that by replacing the old BIOS chip with a new chip that supported the new device. Now, however, it's much easier. First, remember that most of today's new devices are not supported by the System BIOS at all, but by device drivers that are software programs installed on the hard drive as an add-on part of the OS. But, if some new feature does require an upgrade to BIOS, you can do that with Flash ROM. Installing a larger hard drive is an example of a hardware upgrade that might require a BIOS upgrade because it is incompatible with the existing BIOS. Older BIOS supports only those hard drives with a 504 MB capacity. If you have this problem—large drive, old BIOS—you can solve it in one of two ways. Either upgrade BIOS or use special software designed to get around the problem. Often the device manufacturer supplies the software.

3

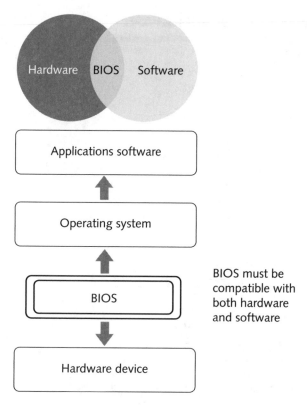

Figure 3-10   BIOS as the software/hardware interface

FLASH ROM

Technically speaking, Flash ROM is called EEPROM (electronically erasable programmable read-only memory), which means you can change the programming on the chip through software on your PC. The updated programming will be retained—even when you turn off your PC for long periods of time—until you change it again. Flash ROM allows you to upgrade system BIOS without having to replace the ROM chip.

As more devices become Plug-and-Play-compliant, Plug-and-Play BIOS will become more sophisticated. Expect to upgrade to Plug-and-Play BIOS over time. Additionally, makers of BIOS code are likely to change BIOS frequently because it is so easy for them to provide the upgrade on the Internet. You can get upgraded BIOS code from manufacturers' Web sites or disks or from third-party BIOS resellers' Web sites or disks.

Figure 3-11 shows a sample Web site for Flash ROM BIOS upgrades. See the Web site of the manufacturer of your BIOS for more information.

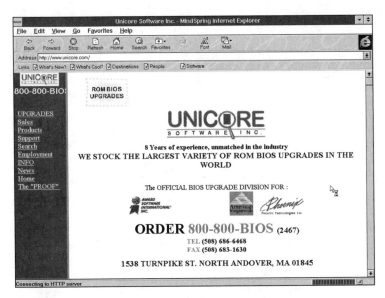

Figure 3-11   Web site for Flash ROM BIOS upgrades

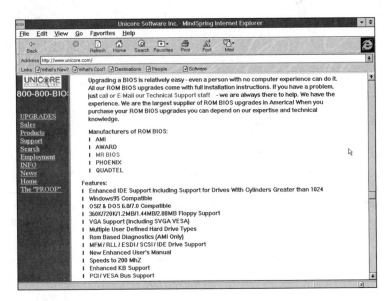

Figure 3-11   (continued)

To upgrade Flash ROM, follow the directions that came with your systemboard and the upgrade software itself. Generally, you will perform these tasks:

- Set a jumper on the systemboard telling the BIOS what to expect
- Copy the upgrade software to a bootable disk
- Boot from the disk and follow the menu options to upgrade the BIOS
- Reset the jumper, reboot the system, and verify that all is working

Be *very careful* that you upgrade the BIOS with the correct upgrade. Upgrading with the wrong file could make your system BIOS totally useless. If you're not sure that you're using the correct upgrade, *don't guess*. Check with the technical support for your BIOS before moving forward. Before you call technical support, have the information that is written on the BIOS chip label available.

RAM (RANDOM ACCESS MEMORY)

Chapter 9 discusses how to manage RAM, but for now we present the essentials of where and what RAM is and how it is used. In older machines, RAM existed as individual chips socketed to the systemboard in banks or rows of nine chips. Each bank held one byte by storing one bit in each chip with the ninth chip holding a **parity** bit (see Figure 3-12). On older PCs the parity chip was separated a little from the other eight chips. (Parity, discussed below in more detail, refers to an error-checking procedure whereby either every byte has an even number of ones or every byte has an odd number of ones. The use of a parity bit means that every byte occupies nine rather than eight bits.)

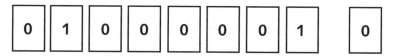

Figure 3-12   Eight chips and parity chip showing the letter A in ASCII with even parity

DYNAMIC MEMORY

There are two types of RAM: **dynamic RAM (DRAM)** and **static RAM (SRAM)**. Dynamic RAM chips hold data for a very short time; static RAM chips hold data until the power is turned off. Because DRAM is much less expensive than SRAM, most of the RAM on the systemboard is DRAM. DRAM comes in two types: parity and nonparity. Some newer computers have eliminated parity checking to cut down the cost of memory. The systemboard supports either parity or nonparity DRAM.

Parity is a method of testing the integrity of the bits stored in RAM or some secondary media, or testing the integrity of bits sent over a communication device. When data is written to RAM, the computer calculates how many ON bits (binary 1) there are in the 8 bits of a byte. If the computer uses odd parity, it makes the ninth or parity bit either a 1 or a 0 to make the number of 1s odd. Using even parity, the computer makes the parity bit a 1 or 0 to make the number of 1s in the 9 bits even.

Later, when the byte is read back, the computer checks the odd or even state. If the number of bits is not an odd number for odd parity or an even number for even parity, a **parity error** occurs. A parity error always causes the system to halt. On the screen you see the error message "Parity Error 1" or "Parity Error 2" or a similar error message about parity. Parity Error 1 is a parity error on the systemboard; Parity Error 2 is a parity error on a memory expansion board. Parity errors can be caused by RAM chips that have become undependable and that are unable to hold data reliably. Sometimes this happens when the chips overheat or power falters. If the parity errors continue to occur, you can use diagnostic software to identify the chip that is causing the parity error so that you can replace it. In older systems, when RAM was stored as individual chips, sometimes the faulty chip could be spotted by determining which chip felt warmer to the touch than the others after the computer had been running for some time.

Later, computers were made to hold RAM on a group of chips stored in a single physical unit as **SIMM**s (single in-line memory module). A SIMM is a miniboard that stores an entire bank or banks of RAM. A SIMM can have several chips with 30 or 72 pins on the edge connector of the tiny board. RAM is then upgraded or changed by unplugging and plugging in SIMMs, which are much easier to work with than single chips. You will learn to upgrade memory using SIMMs in Chapter 9. RAM chips or SIMMs are located either on the systemboard or on memory expansion cards. SIMMs hold from 4 MB to 32 MB of RAM on one board.

Some PCs can accommodate **DIMM**s (dual in-line memory module), which have 168 pins on the edge connector of the board. A DIMM can hold from 8 MB to 128 MB of RAM on a single board. Figure 3-13 shows a SIMM and DIMM module.

EDO (extended data output) **memory** is a RAM module that works about 20 percent faster than conventional RAM. Most RAM modules sold today on new computers are EDO memory. The systemboard must be able to support EDO memory. An EDO SIMM or DIMM looks about the same as a standard SIMM or DIMM module.

Dynamic RAM chips do not hold their data very long and must be refreshed about every 3.86 milliseconds. To **refresh** RAM means that the computer must rewrite the data to the chip. Refreshing RAM is done by the DMA (dynamic memory access) chip (discussed later in this chapter) or sometimes by circuitry on the systemboard other than the DMA chip.

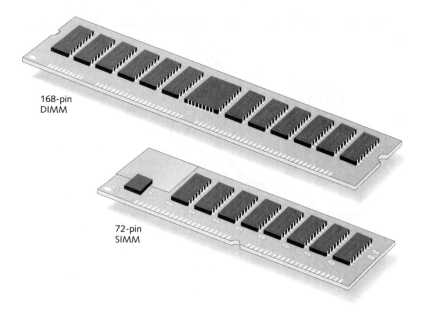

Figure 3-13   Types of RAM modules

STATIC CACHE MEMORY

Because static RAM chips are expensive, many computers substitute less expensive dynamic RAM chips, but they use some static RAM chips to speed up data access. Refreshing RAM takes time. DRAM is slower than SRAM, so data is often cached to the static RAM. A smart RAM cache holds data or programming code that is used often or anticipated next in static RAM. In this way the CPU has the instructions it needs ready and waiting without having to refresh RAM. Most cache memory on today's systemboards uses pipeline burst technology and is called **pipeline burst cache**. This type of cache is slightly slower but less expensive than other types. More on this in Chapter 9.

Levels of Cache

The hardware that caches or copies the contents of dynamic RAM into static RAM is called the **cache controller**. The cache controller on older computers was on a separate chip on the systemboard; but today, the cache controller is built into the CPU chip together with some static cache memory. Cache memory that is contained inside the CPU housing is called **internal cache**, **primary cache**, or **level 1 cache**. In technical documentation or instructions, primary cache is most often referred to as **L1 cache**. Review Table 3-3 for a listing of the amount of primary cache on each of the Pentium chips. **External cache** or **level 2 cache** is static memory stored on the systemboard that is not part of the CPU. It is most often called **L2 cache**. The standard size for L2 caches in today's computers is about 256K, although 512K will most likely be the norm in the near future.

WAIT STATES

A wait state isn't a systemboard component, but it is an idea that you need to understand in the overall performance of a computer system. A **wait state** occurs when the CPU must wait for some other component to catch up, such as a read or write to slower dynamic RAM. To allow time for the slow operation, the CPU is told to maintain a wait state by CMOS setup information. If normally the CPU can do something in two clock beats, it is told to take an extra clock beat for a total of three clock beats. It works for two beats and then waits one beat, which makes for a 50 percent slowdown in speed. Wait states are incorporated as needed to slow down the CPU so that the rest of the systemboard activity can keep up. Unfortunately, almost no computer nowadays can boast an absolute zero wait state. Look at the advanced setup screen of your computer to see which wait states the CPU has been given. There are several wait states displayed on the screen so that the CPU knows how many clock beats to remain inactive while some other piece of hardware does a task. As you will probably see on your advanced setup screen, some hardware devices require more waiting than others.

BUSES AND EXPANSION SLOTS

Remember that in addition to being a set of hardware lines connecting components of a computer to each other, a **bus** is also a communication standard, an agreement about how to pass data from one device to another. Chips and circuits are designed so that data is passed to and fro in a way that all devices and chips have agreed to; all abide by the same standards.

The computer industry is continually improving hardware performance. Over the past few years, several manufacturers have introduced new buses trying to establish a standard that will be accepted by the industry. In the early 1980s, IBM blazed the trail with the 8-bit data path ISA (Industry Standard Architecture) bus, later revising it to the 16-bit data path bus to keep up with the demand for wider data path sizes. In 1987, IBM introduced the first 32-bit bus, the MCA (Microchannel Architecture) bus, and competitors followed with the 32-bit EISA (Extended Industry Standard Architecture) bus. More recently, the 32-bit local bus and its many variations have become popular. Accommodating the Pentium chip, the newest systemboards offer a 64-bit Pentium local bus and a 32-bit PCI bus. Although other bus standards exist in the marketplace, we limit our discussion to these six popular and historically significant buses.

WHAT THE SYSTEM BUS DOES

Look on the bottom of the systemboard and you will see a maze of circuits. These embedded wires are carrying four kinds of cargo.

- **Electrical power**. Chips on the systemboard require power to function. These chips tap into the system bus's power lines and draw what they need.

- **Control signals**. Some of the wires on the system bus carry control signals that coordinate all the activity on the board.

- **Memory addresses**. The memory addresses are passed from one component to another as these components transmit data or instructions from one to another. The number of wires that make up the memory address lines of the bus determines how large a number the memory address can be. The number of wires thus limits the amount of memory the bus can address.

- **Data**. Data is passed over the system bus in a group of wires just as the memory addresses are. The number of lines in the bus used to pass data determines how much data can be passed in parallel. The number of lines depends on the type of CPU and determines the number of bits in the data path. (Remember that a **data path** is that part of the bus on which the data travels and can be 8, 16, 32, or 64 bits wide.)

Most often when comparing buses, users focus on the width of the data path and the overall bus speed. But you also should consider the type of expansion slot the bus allows. The number of fingers on the edge connector of the expansion card and the length of the edge connector are determined by the bus that controls that expansion slot. These finger connections on the expansion card allow for the flow of electrical power, control signals, memory addresses, and data.

THE FIRST ISA BUS

Used on the first IBM 8088 PCs in the early 1980s, the ISA bus had an 8-bit data path. This means that 8 bits travel abreast over the circuits on the systemboard. When you look at the systemboard, you can see the green lines embedded into the board where these bits travel, but you certainly can't see the eight lanes of traffic contained in each path or line. However, when the systemboard interfaces with other boards, the data path width becomes quite obvious. Look at the expansion slots on an 8088 systemboard in Figure 3-14 and the expansion card designed to fit in one of those slots. If you count the gold fingers on one side of the expansion card's edge connector that fits into the slot, you get 31. There are also 31 gold fingers on the other side of the edge connector of the expansion card for a total of 62 lines over which the systemboard and the circuit board can communicate. Of these 62 lines, 8 are used to pass data. Expansion slots on a computer with this ISA bus type are called "8-bit" slots. This systemboard can use almost any expansion card that has an 8-bit ISA edge connector, called an 8-bit card. Although you don't see 8088 PCs any longer, you do find, even on new computers, 8-bit expansion cards that use the ISA bus slot. These cards are often used for serial devices such as a mouse or modem.

You can most easily determine the kind of buses on a systemboard by examining the expansion slots. Many systemboards have more than one type of expansion slot on the board to accommodate different types of expansion cards.

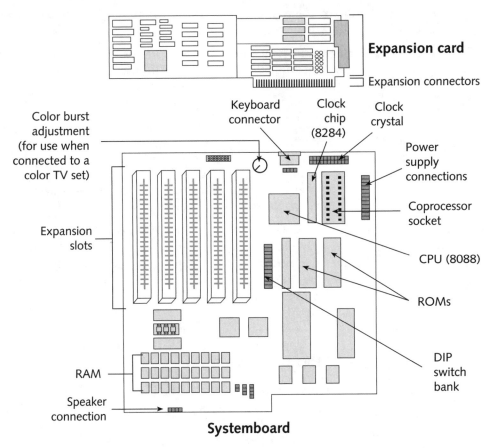

Figure 3-14   The ISA bus on the early 8088XT systemboard with an 8-bit expansion card

THE SECOND ISA BUS

IBM revised the ISA bus to have a 16-bit path size. The IBM AT personal computer used this bus and the 80286 chip, which is why the 16-bit bus is sometimes called the AT bus. IBM wanted this bus to be backward compatible with the older 8-bit ISA bus so that the older 8-bit circuit boards would fit into the newer AT computers. To maintain compatibility, IBM kept the old 62-line slot connector and added another slot connector beside it to provide the extra 8 bits. Slots with both connectors are called 16-bit slots. The AT-type machines usually had some 8-bit slots and some 16-bit slots (see Figure 3-15). The reason for this slot configuration is that some old 8-bit boards had a "skirt" that extended down and back on the circuit board, making it physically impossible to plug an 8-bit board with a skirt into a 16-bit connector. However, 8-bit boards work when plugged into the 16-bit slot.

3

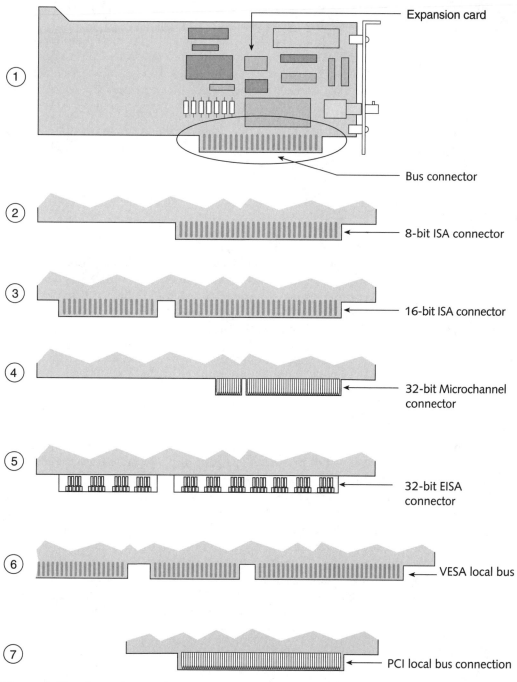

Figure 3-15   Seven bus connections on expansion cards

MICROCHANNEL ARCHITECTURE (MCA) BUS

With the introduction of the line of PS/2 computers in 1987, IBM introduced the first 32-bit bus for personal computers, the MCA bus. IBM did not intend the MCA bus to be compatible with ISA buses. Circuit boards used in older IBM computers could not be used in the PS/2 line. (The PS/2 Models 25 and 30 still, however, used the older ISA bus.)

IBM chose to patent the bus so that other companies could not economically manufacture and market it. IBM intended to control a subset of the bus market with MCA. In response, Compaq and eight other companies (named the "Gang of Nine") joined to design and build a competing bus, the EISA bus.

THE EISA BUS

Designed to compete with the MCA bus, the EISA bus (pronounced 'ease-sa'), has a 32-bit data path. The bus is compatible with older ISA buses so that expansion boards having 8-bit or 16-bit data paths work on the EISA bus. The speed of the EISA bus is about 20 MHz. To accommodate a 16-bit or 8-bit ISA circuit board, the 32-bit EISA has two slots that have the same width as 16-bit ISA slots. However, the EISA bus slots are deeper than 16-bit slots. All 32-bit circuit boards have longer fingers on the edge connectors that go deep into the EISA slot. A 16-bit circuit board reaches only part way down the slot. Various bus connections are shown in Figure 3-15.

LOCAL BUSES

A local bus is a second bus on a systemboard that already has an ISA bus or an EISA bus. Local buses are designed to provide a data path that is separate from the normal bus for the fast movement of data from a video or memory card directly to the CPU. A local bus is usually a 32-bit bus running at the same clock speed as the CPU. The bus often has a proprietary design created by the manufacturer who made the systemboard. Figure 3-16 shows that the local 32-bit bus slot is much longer than the 16-bit ISA slot. This local bus slot was designed to accommodate a memory expansion card. In an attempt to create a standard for local 32-bit buses, many manufacturers endorse the VESA (Video Electronics Standard Association) VL-bus. Many systemboards offer the VESA local bus for video and memory circuit boards. The expansion slot for a VESA local bus includes the 16 bits for the ISA slot plus an added extension with another 116 pins (see Figure 3-17).

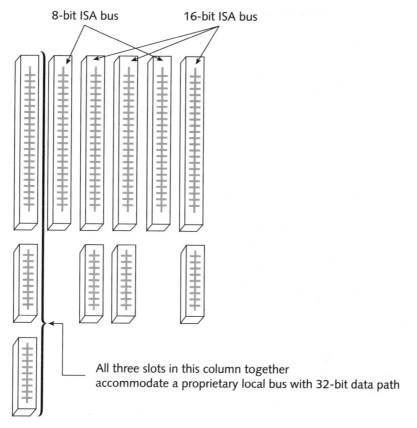

Figure 3-16   Three kinds of bus connections on the same board

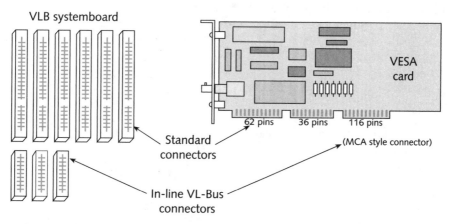

Figure 3-17   VESA local bus expansion slot

PCI Bus

Another local bus, the PCI local bus (peripheral component interconnect bus) is now the standard local bus not only with Pentium CPUs but with RISC CPUs as well. It has a 32-bit data path and runs at a speed of 33 MHz. One advantage of the PCI local bus is that devices connected to it can run at one speed while the CPU runs at a different speed. Devices connected to the VESA bus must run at the same clock speed as the CPU, which forces the CPU to endure frequent wait states. The PCI bus expansion slots are shorter than ISA slots (see Figure 3-18).

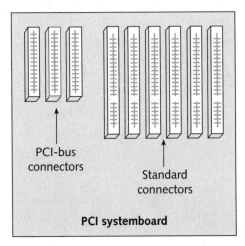

PCI-bus connectors

Standard connectors

PCI systemboard

Figure 3-18 PCI bus expansion slots

The primary intent of a local bus is to provide direct access to the CPU for a few fast devices, such as memory and video, that can run at near the same speed as the CPU. The PCI bus is not a true local bus because it serves a slightly different function for the CPU than a regular local bus does. The PCI bus interfaces with the I/O bus and the CPU, serving as the go-between for the two, controlling the input and output to the I/O bus as well as connecting the local PCI devices to the CPU. As you can see in Figure 3-19, the CPU is isolated from the ISA bus by the PCI bus. The connection between the two is the PCI bridge. The bridge allows the PCI bus to control the traffic not only from its own local devices but also from the ISA bus.

The true local bus in the Pentium system is represented by the box at the top of Figure 3-19. The CPU communicates with the external cache and main RAM on the *most-local* bus of the system, which has a 64-bit data path and runs at twice the speed of the PCI bus.

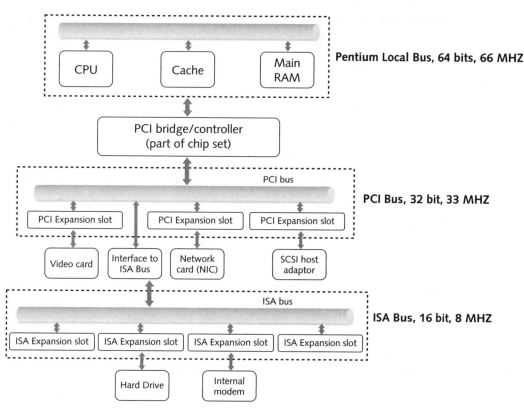

Figure 3-19   The PCI bus

In Figure 3-19, the SCSI (Small Computer System Interface) host adapter (discussed at length later in the book), a network interface card (NIC), and a video card are all connected to the PCI bus. The PCI bridge/controller accesses the local bus where the CPU and memory are allowed to run at top speed without interference or wait states. If the CPU wants to send data to the video card, for example, it dumps it on the PCI bridge/controller at top speed. The controller puts the data in its own buffer or temporary memory storage and then writes it to video at a pace slower than the local bus. The bridge/controller eliminates interference with the local bus. Figure 3-19 also shows the interface from the PCI bus to the ISA bus. This interface is a significant feature that distinguishes the PCI bus from other buses. The PCI bus was not designed to replace the traditional system bus but to support it. The ISA bus in the diagram passes data through the interface to the PCI bus, which in turn passes the data on to the local bus, to the CPU, and to memory.

The PCI bus also supports bus mastering. A **bus master** is an intelligent device (i.e., it has a microprocessor installed that manages the device) that, when attached to the PCI bus, can gain access to memory and other devices on the bus without interrupting the action of the CPU. The CPU and the bus mastering devices can run concurrently and independently of each other.

Because of the effective design of the PCI bus, the throughput performance or the data transfer rate per second is 132 MB. **Throughput performance** or **data throughput** is a measure of the actual data transmitted by the bus, not including error-checking bits or redundant data. There are plans for a 66-MHz PCI bus that will run at about 264 MB/sec with a 64-bit data path.

Notice that although the PCI bus runs much faster than the ISA bus, the hard drive is connected to the ISA bus with a hard drive adapter card in the ISA slot (see Figure 3-19). An improved configuration for this system would attach the hard drive directly on the PCI bus with a different adapter card so that it could work on the PCI bus.

Carefully planning the configuration of a system can pay off in performance. Most PCs have only three, sometimes four, PCI expansion slots. The video needs to stay on the PCI bus for speed and, in most cases, so does the network card. What's on the SCSI host adapter card? If it is a device like a scanner that's not used often, then it is a good candidate to be moved to the ISA slot. Better still, what about a SCSI hard drive that works directly from the PCI bus along with the scanner? More about this in the next chapter.

Bus Comparisons and Bus Speeds

Table 3-8 compares the buses discussed in this section. Neither the VL-bus nor the PCI bus are designed to replace the ISA or EISA bus but to complement them. On a Pentium system it is not unusual to find both the VL-bus and the PCI bus to allow for compatibility with existing VESA cards. Because the PCI bus does not normally support slow I/O devices, you almost always find a PCI bus coexisting with an ISA bus on the same systemboard.

Table 3-8 Bus Comparisons

	ISA	EISA	VL-Bus	PCI
Data path width in bits	8 or 16	32	32	32 or 64
Data bus speed in MHz	5.33 or 8.33	8.33	33	33 or 66
Data throughput in MB/sec	5.33 or 8.33	33	132	132 or 264
Maximum number of slots	8	8	2	4
Bus masters supported	No	Yes	Yes	Yes
Parity checking	No	No	No	Yes

3

How Bus Speed Affects Overall Performance

As stated earlier, the speed of the CPU is determined by multiplying the bus speed by a factor such as 1.5, 2, 2.5, or 3 (see Tables 3-4 and 3-5). In this case, the bus speed is referring to the local bus speed, which is 66 MHz in Figure 3-19. The PCI bus is running at half that speed and the ISA bus is running at only about 8 MHz. Each device on the particular bus is transferring data at that bus's rate. In Figure 3-19, the hard drive is on the ISA bus and is running only at 8 MHz, while the CPU is running at a multiple of 66 MHz. Intel recommends and supports a speed of 33 MHz; but the bus can run at a faster speed, and many manufacturers of systemboards allow you to use higher speeds. Although you can sometimes improve the performance of a computer by increasing the bus speed, use this method with caution. Bus speeds above the recommended speed might not always perform well, causing errors or causing the system to hang. Use the recommended speeds of the manufacturer for the best results especially when the data and/or the applications running are business-critical.

There are two ways you can change the speed of a computer:

1. Change the speed of the local bus (bus that connects the CPU to RAM), which, according to Intel recommendations, should normally be 60 or 66 MHz. Whatever the local bus speed is, the PCI bus is half of that.

2. Change the multiplier that determines the speed of the CPU. The choices for the multiplier normally are 1.5, 2, 2.5, 3, and 3.5.

Studies have shown that when the multiplier is large, the overall performance of the system is not as good as when the multiplier is small. This is a reasonable result because you are interested in the overall speed of the computer, which includes the CPU and the buses, not just the speed of the CPU.

Figure 3-20 shows a sample of the documentation of a Pentium systemboard. The documentation offers two choices for bus speed, which is set by Jumper 2. The CPU speed is set with Jumper 13, which is really two jumpers. Pins 1 and 2 make one jumper and pins 3 and 4 make the other jumper in the jumper bank labeled Jumper 13. The range for the Pentium CPU speed is 90 MHz to 233 MHz. Pentium chips sometimes are rated with different speeds according to the tests they pass as they leave the assembly line.

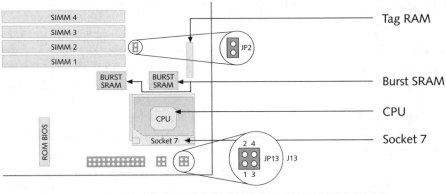

CPU Speed	Bus Clock & Multiplier	JP2	JP13 (1-2)	JP13 (3-4)
90MHz	60MHz × 1.5	closed	open	open
100MHz	66MHz × 1.5	open	open	open
120MHz	60MHz × 2	closed	closed	open
133MHz	66MHz × 2	open	closed	open
150MHz	60MHz × 2.5	closed	closed	closed
166MHz	66MHz × 2.5	open	closed	closed
200MHz	66MHz × 3	open	open	closed
233MHz	66MHz × 3.5	open	open	open

Setting	Description
JP2 closed	Bus Clock = 60MHz
JP2 open	Bus Clock = 66MHz
JP13(1-2) open & JP13(Pin 3-4) open	Multiplier = 1.5
JP13(1-2) closed & JP13(3-4) open	Multiplier = 2
JP13(1-2) closed & JP13(3-4) closed	Multiplier = 2.5
JP13(1-2) open & JP13(3-4) closed	Multiplier = 3
JP13(1-2) open & JP13(3-4) open	Multiplier = 3.5 (for 233 MHz)

Figure 3-20   Setting the CPU and bus speeds

UNIVERSAL SERIAL BUS

The universal serial bus or USB was developed by Intel and is intended to be used by low-volume I/O devices, such as modems, joysticks, touchpads, trackballs, and mice. A device must be rated as a USB device and conform to the standards set by the USB Implementers Forum, which includes Intel, Compaq, IBM, Microsoft, and NEC. A USB device must be Plug-and-Play. Windows 95 and NT both support the universal serial bus and its devices, although there are, as yet, not too many USB devices on the market.

ON-BOARD PORTS

Many systemboards contain a keyboard port and a mouse port. In addition, a parallel printer port and a serial port also might be located directly on the systemboard. Few systemboards contain more ports than these, but some do have a video port and video controller on board.

You don't have to replace the entire systemboard if one port fails. Most systemboards contain jumpers or DIP switches that can tell the CPU to disable one of these ports and look to expansion cards for the ports instead. These ports can also be disabled through CMOS setup.

When buying a new computer or systemboard, look for the ability to disable ports, floppy drive connectors, or hard drive connectors coming directly from the systemboard by changing the hardware configuration. You easily can tell if external ports are directly connected to the systemboard without opening the case; the ports are lined up along the bottom of the computer case, as shown in Figure 3-21. To discover if the floppy drive and hard drive controllers are on the systemboard, you must either open the case or read the documentation.

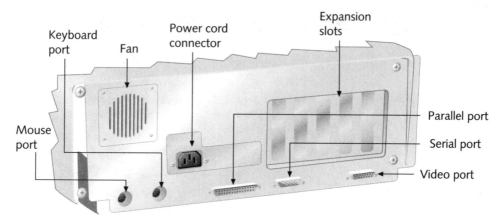

Figure 3-21   Ports along the bottom of the computer case usually are coming directly off the systemboard

HARDWARE CONFIGURATION

Recall that hardware configuration information communicates to the CPU what hardware components are present in the system and how they are set up to interface with the CPU. Hardware configuration is described by information such as how much memory is available, the kind of monitor present, and whether disk drives, hard drives, modems, serial ports, and the like are connected. Remember that during POST, BIOS looks to the system configuration information to determine the equipment it should expect to find and how that equipment interfaces with the CPU. The CPU uses this information later to process data and instructions. Configuration information is provided on the systemboard in three different ways as discussed in Chapter 2—DIP switches, jumpers, and CMOS. In this chapter, we focus on the CMOS setup information.

Setup Stored on a CMOS Chip

Computers today store most configuration information on one CMOS chip that retains the data even when the computer is turned off. (There are actually many CMOS chips on a systemboard used for various purposes.) A battery near the CMOS chip provides enough electricity to enable the chip to maintain its data. If the battery is disconnected or fails, setup information is lost. Password information is also a part of the computer's setup that is stored in CMOS. The program to change the setup information is now stored in ROM but once was on a disk that came with the computer.

Some of the settings in CMOS are listed in Table 3-9.

Table 3-9   CMOS Settings and Their Purpose

Category	Setting	Description
Standard CMOS Setup	Date and time	Use to set system date and time.
	Primary display	Use to tell POST and DOS (but not Windows) the type of video being used.
	Keyboard	Use to tell system if keyboard is installed or not installed. Useful if the computer is used as a print or file server and you don't want someone changing settings.
	Hard disk type	Use to record size and mapping of the drive.
	Floppy disk type	Choices are usually 3½ inch and 5¼ inch.
Advanced CMOS Setup	Above 1 MB memory test	Use to disable POST check of this memory to speed up booting. The OS will check this memory anyway.
	Memory parity error check	If you have a parity systemboard, use to enable parity checking to ensure that memory is correct.
	Numeric processor test	Enabled unless you have an old 386 or 486SX computer.
	System boot sequence	Use to establish the drive the system turns to first to look for an OS. Normally drive C, then A.
	External cache memory	Use to enable if you have L2 cache. A frequent error in setup is to have cache but not use it because it's disabled here.
	Internal cache memory	Normally enabled; disable only for old 386 computers.
	Password checking option	Use to establish a startup password. Use this only if you really have a problem with someone using your PC who can't be trusted.
	Video ROM shadow C000, 16K	For DOS and Windows 95, shadowing video ROM is recommended because ROM runs slower than RAM.

Table 3-9   CMOS Settings and Their Purpose (continued)

Category	Setting	Description
	System ROM shadow F000, 64K	Enabling shadow system ROM is recommended.
	IDE Multi-block mode	Enables a hard drive to read or write several sectors at a time. Dependent on the kind of hard drive you have.
	Boot sector virus protection	Gives a warning when something is being written to the boot sector of the hard drive. Can be a nuisance if your software is designed to write to the boot sector regularly.
Advanced Chip Set Setup	AT bus clock selection	Gives the number by which the CPU speed is divided to get the ISA or EISA bus speed.
	ISA bus speed	Gives the number by which the PCI bus speed is divided to get the ISA bus speed.
	Bus mode	Can be set to synchronous or asynchronous modes. In synchronous mode, the bus uses the CPU clock. In asynchronous mode its own AT bus clock is used.
	AT cycle wait state	The number of wait states the CPU must endure while it interfaces with a device on the ISA or EISA bus. Increase this if an old and slow ISA card is not working well.
	Memory read wait state	Number of wait states the CPU must endure while reading from RAM.
	Memory write wait state	Number of wait states the CPU must endure while writing to RAM.
	Cache read option	Sometimes called "cache read hit burst." The number of clock beats needed to load four 32-bit words into the CPU's internal cache. 4-1-1-1 is the usual choice.
	Fast cache read/write	Refers to external cache. Enable it if you have two banks of cache, 64K or 256K.
	Cache wait state	Refers to external cache. The number of wait states the CPU must use while accessing cache.

INTERRUPT REQUEST NUMBER (IRQ)

Recall that an interrupt request is a method by which peripherals tell the CPU they need servicing, that is that they either have some data ready for processing or they are ready to receive more data. The interrupt controller chip on the systemboard handles the hardware interrupt signals. Remember that each peripheral is assigned an interrupt number called an IRQ number. When the CPU receives the IRQ number, the CPU uses it to identify an address in the I/O address table.

The **I/O address table**, which is sometimes called the **interrupt descriptor table**, is an area at the beginning of RAM from 0000 to 03FFh (the table can take up more room if needed). Earlier PCs used a 4-byte table, called the **interrupt vector table**, which contained only the location in memory of the program that services the device issuing the interrupt. Beginning with 286 computers, the interrupt vector table was expanded to hold not only the memory address of the program that services the device, but also the addresses of data passed between the CPU and the device, as well as the commands (called tasks) communicated to the device. Most I/O address table entries are 8 bytes long.

Also recall from Chapter 2 that the I/O address table serves as the place where the CPU and the device communicate and it functions like a drop box or pick-up desk. Each device is assigned a range of I/O addresses that can be used by only a single device. If two devices try to share the same address, conflicts arise. The ROM BIOS for a device requests an I/O address during the boot process. If two devices use the same I/O address, they cannot be installed on the same computer, unless one of the devices can be assigned an alternative address by changing the device configuration through jumpers, DIP switches, or CMOS on the device's controller card.

The program that services the device is called the **interrupt handler**. This program can be (1) a device driver stored in RAM, (2) part of system BIOS, or (3) part of ROM BIOS stored on the device controller. During booting, the I/O address range is assigned to a device, and in part of those I/O addresses the location of the interrupt handler is stored in a coded format.

The I/O addresses in the I/O address table can be accessed by the OS to store data or tasks passed between the CPU and the device. An interrupt or IRQ can prompt the CPU to service a device, receive data, or perform other operations.

Consider this example of a device using an IRQ to get service from the CPU, described in nontechnical terms:

- The CPU is printing a word processing document. As the document is printing, the user presses a key on the keyboard. The keyboard sends an IRQ to the CPU requesting service.

- The CPU receives the IRQ and stops the printing. Before the CPU turns its attention to the keyboard, it records all the information that it needs to resume the print job where it left off. This print job information is stored in a **stack** or place in memory where information about suspended jobs is kept.

- The CPU handles the keyboard IRQ by accessing the I/O addresses assigned to that IRQ. In this address is stored the memory address of the keyboard BIOS. The CPU reads the address, then turns to that address, and executes the program located there. The program (interrupt handler) processes the keystroke and then returns an interrupt completed message to the CPU.

- The CPU returns to the stack, retrieves the information about the print job, and continues printing.

An interrupt can be one of three different kinds: (1) hardware interrupts initiated by hardware devices, (2) software interrupts initiated by programs, and (3) exception interrupts initiated by the CPU itself. Exception interrupts usually are caused by errors that the CPU senses, such as division by zero or a parity error.

The printer interrupt is by default IRQ 7. However, not all operating systems use interrupts to communicate with the printer. Some, like DOS, ignore IRQ 7 and communicate to the printer by another method called polling. **Polling** means that DOS asks or polls the printer for a response whenever it wants to send data. DOS initiates communication and does not wait until the printer returns an IRQ 7.

Table 3-10 lists the default IRQ numbers and I/O address ranges for some common devices. IRQs 9–12 and 14–15 are available for whatever system needs you have, such as a network card or a second hard drive.

Table 3-10   Interrupt Request Numbers and I/O Addresses for Devices

IRQ	I/O Address	Device
0	040-05F	System timer
1	060	Keyboard controller
2	0A0	Access to IRQs above 7
3	2F8-2FF	COM2 and COM4
4	3F8-3FF	COM1 and COM3
5	1F0-1F8	Sound/parallel port 2 (LPT2)
6	3F0-3F7	Floppy drive controller
7	278-27F	Printer parallel port (LPT1:)
8	070-07F	System clock
9-10		Available
11		SCSI/available
12		Systemboard mouse
13	0F8-0FF	Math coprocessor
14		IDE hard drive
15		Secondary IDE hard drive/available

As was discussed in Chapter 2, when you are responsible for a computer, keep a record of the maintenance done on the computer as well as configuration information about that machine printed or on disk. In this notebook, dedicate a page to record the IRQ and I/O address assignments for the machine. When you decide to add a new device, the IRQs available for the device are at your fingertips if you keep the notebook up-to-date.

Conflicts with interrupts arise when two peripherals have been assigned the same IRQ. For example, because DOS does not use IRQ 7 to communicate with the printer, many older LAN cards are configured to use IRQ 7. However, Windows does use IRQ 7 to communicate with the printer. Therefore, if you are using Windows with a LAN card that uses IRQ 7, a conflict arises. You usually can solve these conflicts by changing the IRQ for the LAN card. Usually the card has a DIP switch or jumper that can change the IRQ.

In this situation, if you are using Windows 95, the Plug-and-Play feature might not help you because the older LAN card is not Plug-and-Play. Even with Windows 95, you might still need to assign the IRQ manually by setting the DIP switch on the board and informing Windows 95 of what you have done. Details are in Chapter 11.

DMA Controller

As explained above, the **DMA** (direct memory access) **controller** on a systemboard is part of the chip set and provides faster memory access because it handles the movement of data in and out of RAM without involving the CPU. The DMA chip is also responsible for dynamic memory refreshing that we discussed earlier. A DMA chip traditionally offers four channels: 0, 1, 2, and 3. Channel 0 is used for dynamic memory refresh; channel 2 is used for a floppy disk drive controller, and channel 3 is used for a hard disk controller. That leaves channel 1 available for some other device to write directly to RAM, bypassing the CPU. Some computers have two DMA logical chips, making a total of 8 channels for input to RAM.

Conflicts with DMA channels can occur. When adding a second hard drive, CD-ROM drive, or floppy disk drive, check which DMA channel the device uses if you suspect a conflict. The documentation for the device should give you the information you need. During the installation, you probably can change the DMA default channel using a DIP switch or jumper if there is a conflict. This example demonstrates how important it is to safeguard your documentation. Again, if the new device is Plug-and-Play, Windows 95 does the work for you.

Power Supply Connections

Lastly, the systemboard contains connections to receive power. Two connections are found on the edge of the systemboard for the power supply. Voltages are sometimes written on the systemboard for each pin. Voltages for most systemboards are +5v, −5v, +12v, and −12v. Power supplies will be covered in detail in Chapter 10.

CHAPTER SUMMARY

- The systemboard is the most complicated of all the components inside the computer. It contains the CPU and accompanying chip set, the real-time clock, ROM BIOS, CMOS configuration chip, RAM, RAM cache, system bus, expansion slots, jumpers, ports, and power supply connections. The systemboard you select determines both the capabilities and limitations of your system.

- The most important component on the systemboard is the CPU, or central processing unit. The CPU is the microprocessor at the heart of a PC system, where almost all operations must ultimately be processed. The CPU is rated according to its speed, efficiency of programming code, word size, data path size, maximum memory addresses, size of internal cache, multiprocessing abilities, and special functionalities. Earlier Intel CPUs include the 80386DX, 80386SX, 80486DX, and 80486SX. The latest family of Intel CPUs is the Pentium family, including the Classic Pentium, Pentium MMX, Pentium Pro, and Pentium II. AMD and Cyrix are Intel's chief competitors for the CPU market. CPUs can use either RISC or CISC technology or a combination of the two.

- Newer CPUs require extra cooling, which can be accomplished with a CPU cooling fan located on top of or near the CPU.

- The three common CPU sockets today are Socket 7, Socket 8, and Slot 1 (which is really more of an expansion slot than a socket).

- Because some CPUs require one voltage for internal core operations and another voltage for external I/O operations, systemboards might have a voltage regulator on board.

- Some components can be built into the systemboard, in which case they are called on-board components, or they can be attached to the system in some other way such as on an expansion card.

- ROM chips contain the programming code to manage POST and System BIOS and to change the CMOS settings. The setup or CMOS chip holds configuration information.

- Bus speeds on the systemboard are a function of CPU speed.

- A chip set is a group of chips on the systemboard that supports the CPU. Intel is the most popular manufacturer of chip sets.

- The total BIOS of a system includes the ROM BIOS on the system board as well as BIOS on expansion cards. Plug-and-Play BIOS is designed to work in harmony with Windows 95 to resolve resource conflicts by expansion cards and other devices. Flash ROM allows the ROM BIOS to be upgraded without having to change the ROM chip.

- RAM can be either parity or nonparity memory. Dynamic RAM (DRAM) is slower than static RAM (SRAM) because dynamic RAM must be refreshed. RAM usually comes packaged as a SIMM or DIMM memory module. Two kinds of static RAM cache for the slower DRAM are internal and external cache, sometimes called level 1 and level 2 cache.

- The system bus is a path on the systemboard that carries electricity, control signals, memory addresses, and data to different components on the board. The bus can be 16, 32, or 64 bits wide. The first ISA bus had an 8-bit data path. The second ISA bus had a 16-bit data path. Some well-known buses are the 16-bit ISA bus, 32-bit MCA and EISA buses, and the two local buses, the VESA bus and PCI bus. A local bus is designed to allow fast devices quicker and more direct access to the CPU than that allowed by other buses. The VESA local bus is a standard designed by the Video Electronics Standard Association. The PCI bus was designed for the Pentium and has a 32-bit data path. To gain the maximum overall computer performance, the multiplier relating the bus speed to the CPU speed should be small.

- Expansion slots can be located on the systemboard, but they are sometimes stacked vertically in the computer case on a second board devoted to that purpose.

- An IRQ is a method that allows a device to signal the CPU requesting attention.

- The I/O address table is a group of memory addresses in the lower area of memory containing the addresses of the interrupt handlers, which is another name for the device driver or System BIOS.

- The DMA controller manages direct access to RAM as well as memory refreshing.

- Sometimes the CPU must be slowed down to accommodate slower devices by enduring wait states that cause it to wait one clock beat. Wait states often mean a significant reduction in performance.

KEY TERMS

- **Bus** — Strips of parallel wires or printed circuits used to transmit electronic signals on the system board to other devices. Most Pentium systems use a 32-bit bus.

- **Bus speed** — The speed at which the data on the systemboard is moving.

- **Cache controller** — The microchip on the system board that controls the memory cache to static RAM.

- **Chip set** — A set of chips on the system board that collectively controls the memory cache, external buses, and some peripherals.

- **Clock speed** — The speed at which the CPU operates, usually expressed in MHz. A Pentium may have a speed of 150 MHz, while a Pentium II may operate at 233 MHz.

- **Data path** — The size of a bus, such as a 32-bit-wide data path in a PCI bus.

- **DIMM (dual in-line memory module)** — A miniature circuit board that has a 64-bit path, unlike SIMMs, which have 32-bit paths. Because Pentium processors require a 64-bit path, you must install two SIMMs at a time, but you can install DIMMs one at a time.

- **Dual voltage CPU** — A CPU that requires two different voltages, one for internal processing and the other for I/O processing.

- **Dynamic RAM (DRAM)** — The most commonly used type of system memory, with access speeds ranging from 70 to 50 nanoseconds. It requires refreshing every few milliseconds.

- **EDO (extended data output) memory** — RAM that works about 20% faster than conventional RAM.

- **EISA (extended standard industry architecture) bus** — A 32-bit bus that can transfer 4 bytes at a time at a speed of about 20 MHz.

- **External cache** — Static cache memory, stored on the system board, that is not part of the CPU (also called level 2 or L2 cache).

- **Heat sink** — A piece of metal, with cooling fins, that can be attached to or mounted on an integrated chip (such as the CPU) to dissipate heat.

- **Instruction set** — The set of instructions, on the CPU chip, that the computer can perform directly (such as ADD and MOVE).

- **Internal cache** — Memory cache that is faster than external cache, and is contained inside 80486 and Pentium chips (also referred to as primary, level 1, or L1 cache).

- **Interrupt descriptor table** — Another name for the I/O address table.

- **Interrupt handler** — A program that services a device when the CPU handles an IRQ request for service. Another name for a device driver.

- **ISA bus** — An 8-bit industry standard architecture bus used on the original 8088 PC. Sixteen-bit ISA buses were designed for the 286 AT, and are still used in Pentiums for devices such as modems.

- **Level 1 cache** — *See* Internal cache.

- **Level 2 cache** — *See* External cache.

- **Local bus** — A bus connecting adapters directly to the local processor bus. On 80486 computers, it is usually a 32-bit bus running at the same clock speed as the CPU.

- **MCA (micro channel architecture) bus** — A proprietary IBM PS/2 bus, seldom seen today, with a width of 16 or 32 bits and multiple master control, which allowed for multitasking.

- **Megahertz (MHz)** — One million hertz. CPU speed is measured in MHz (for example, a Pentium II may have a speed of 233 MHz).

- **Memory cache** — A small amount of faster RAM that stores recently retrieved data, in anticipation of what the CPU will request next thus speeding up access.

- **Multiplier** — The factor by which the bus speed is multiplied to get the CPU clock speed.

- **On-board ports** — Ports that are directly on the systemboard, such as a built-in keyboard port or on-board serial port.

- **Parity** — An error-checking scheme in which a ninth, or "parity," bit is added. The value of the parity bit is set to either 0 or 1 to provide an even number of ones for even parity and an odd number of ones for odd parity.

- **Parity error** — An error that occurs when the number of 1s in the byte is not in agreement with the expected number.

- **PCI (peripheral component interconnect) bus** — A bus common on Pentium computers that runs at speeds of up to 33 MHz, with a 32-bit-wide data path.

- **Pipeline burst cache** — The most common cache on systemboards today, which is slightly slower than other types of cache, but is less expensive.

- **Plug-and-Play** — A technology in which the operating system and BIOS are designed to automatically configure new hardware devices to eliminate system resource conflicts (such as IRQ and port conflicts).

- **Polling** — A process by which the CPU checks the status of connected devices to determine if they are ready to send or receive data.

- **Primary cache** — *See* Internal cache.

- **Refresh** — The process of periodically rewriting the data on dynamic RAM.

- **RISC (reduced instruction set computer) chips** — Chips that incorporate only the most frequently used instructions, so that the computer operates faster (for example, the PowerPC uses RISC chips).

- **Single voltage CPU** — A CPU that requires one voltage for both internal and I/O operations.

- **Stack** — A place in memory where information, such as addresses of pending tasks for the CPU, is kept.

- **Static RAM (SRAM)** — RAM chips that retain information without the need for refreshing, as long as the computer's power is on. They are more expensive than traditional DRAM.

- **Turbo mode** — A means of doubling the clock speed by pressing a button on the case of some older computers. (Actually the turbo switch cuts the speed in half to run slower applications.)

- **Universal serial bus (USB)** — A bus developed by Intel Corporation, intended to be used by low-volume I/O devices such as modems, joysticks, touch pads, trackballs, and mice.

- **VESA (Video Electronics Standard Association) VL bus** — A bus used on 80486 computers for connecting 32-bit adapters directly to the local processor bus.

- **Wait state** — A clock tick in which nothing happens, used to ensure that the microprocessor isn't getting ahead of slower components. A 0-wait state is preferable to a 1-wait state.

REVIEW QUESTIONS

1. List four companies that manufacture PC microprocessors today.

2. CPU clock speeds are measured in

3. What is a typical clock speed (or range) for an 80486DX microprocessor? What is a typical clock speed (or range) for a Pentium microprocessor? What is a typical clock speed (or range) for a Pentium II microprocessor?

4. Which Intel microprocessors have coprocessors built into their CPUs?

5. Which is faster—an 80486SX or an 80486DX? Why?

6. What does the L in a 486SL chip indicate?

7. What is the main feature of MMX technology?

8. What is the significance of cache memory?

9. How big is the data path of a Pentium?

10. Which is faster, a Pentium II or a Pentium Pro?

11. List two Intel microprocessor competitors.

12. List two components that can be mounted on a CPU to help cool a hot microprocessor

13. Which type of bus is used by most serial devices?

14. In which type of socket are most Pentium and Pentium Pro CPUs placed?

15. Which type of system is designed to configure hardware devices automatically and resolve system conflicts?

16. Compare and contrast Flash ROM to RAM.

17. Compare and contrast DRAM to SRAM.

18. List four ways that you can use to change a computer's configuration.

19. Explain how parity works.

20. What would probably be the cause of a parity error?

21. What advantages do SIMM modules have over DRAM chips?

22. List three types of RAM chips and/or modules.

23. Compare and contrast parity, non-parity, and EDO memory.

24. Compare and contrast L1 and L2 cache.

25. Compare and contrast ISA, VLB, and PCI buses.

26. Draw and label five ports that you can find on the back of a typical computer.

27. List five system settings that you can store in CMOS.

28. In CMOS setup, list five features that you can change under "Chipset."

29. List three ways you can protect the inside of a computer from damage by static electricity.

30. What is the purpose of a wait state?

PROJECTS

Caution

Unless you follow proper procedures, working inside your computer can cause serious damage—to both you and your computer. To assure safety in your work setting, follow every precaution listed in the *Read This Before You Begin* section following this book's Introduction.

IMPORTANT SAFETY PRECAUTIONS

In some of these activities, you remove the cover of a computer and examine the components. Before you carry out the exercises in this chapter, carefully read the following precautions and procedures to protect yourself and the equipment. Please note that these precautions focus specifically on the activities outlined below. However, there are many risks posed by other maintenance activities, a number of which you will undertake in the course of working with this book. The Preface presents a comprehensive list of precautions that should be carefully reviewed as well.

Protect against electricity

You can actually destroy a computer chip with static electricity when you touch it, even though you might not feel a thing. More about this in Chapter 10, but for now, follow these rules to protect chips while you handle them:

1. Never touch the inside of a computer while it is turned on.
2. Never touch any component inside the computer without first grounding yourself to discharge any static electricity on your body. The best way to do this is to wear a ground bracelet or ground strap (Figure 3-22). If you don't have a ground bracelet, then leave the computer plugged in while you are working on it so that it will be grounded. For the PC to be grounded, it must have a three-prong plug and outlet, but does not need to be turned on. Touch the metal case or power supply each time before you touch any component to discharge the electricity on your body.

3

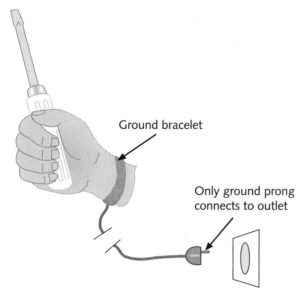

Ground bracelet

Only ground prong
connects to outlet

Figure 3-22   A ground bracelet is the best way to protect from static electricity

3. Don't work on carpet. Work on a bare floor because a carpet collects static electricity, especially in cold weather.

4. Consider both the power supply and monitor to be a "black box." Don't open either unless you are trained to understand the dangers and safety precautions for these devices. The power supply and the monitor have enough power inside them to kill you.

Other valuable rules

1. When taking boards from a PC, don't stack them. Stacking can cause components to become loose.

2. Keep screws and spacers in an orderly place, such as a cup or tray.

3. Make notes as you work so later you'll be able to backtrack.

4. In a classroom environment, after you have reassembled everything but putting the cover back on, have your instructor check your work *before* you power up.

You can learn more about additional precautions and procedures in the chapter on troubleshooting and in the Preface.

EXAMINE THE SYSTEMBOARD

1. Look at the back of your computer. Without opening the case, list the ports that you believe to be coming directly from the systemboard.

2. Now look inside the case to verify your list.

   a. Follow these directions to remove the cover:

   - Turn off the PC.

   - Unplug and move the monitor, mouse, and keyboard out of your way.

   - For a desktop case, locate and remove the screws on the back of the case. Look for the screws in each corner and one on top center as in Figure 3-23. Be careful that you don't unscrew any other screws besides these. The other screws probably are holding the power supply in place (see Figure 3-24).

   - After you've removed the cover screws, slide the cover forward and up to remove it from the case, as shown in Figure 3-25.

   - For tower cases, the screws are also on the back. Look for screws in all four corners and down the sides (see Figure 3-25). Remove the screws and then slide the cover back slightly before lifting it up to remove it.

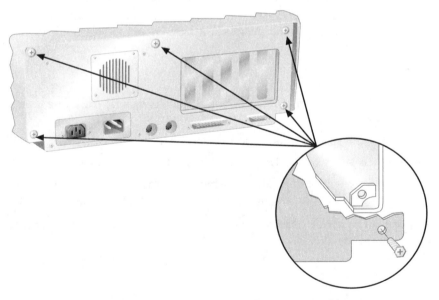

Figure 3-23   Locate the screws that hold the cover in place

3

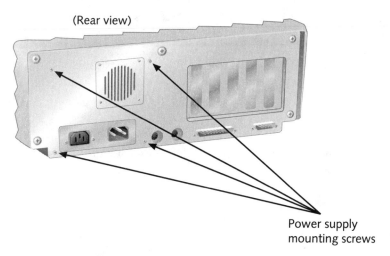

(Rear view)

Power supply
mounting screws

Figure 3-24   Power supply mounting screws

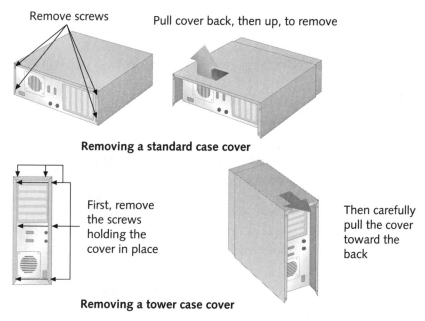

Remove screws   Pull cover back, then up, to remove

Removing a standard case cover

First, remove
the screws
holding the
cover in place

Then carefully
pull the cover
toward the
back

Removing a tower case cover

Figure 3-25   Removing the cover

b. Identify the following major components. Drawings in this and previous chapters should help.

- Power supply
- Floppy disk drive
- Hard drive
- Systemboard

List the different circuit boards in the expansion slots. Was your guess correct about which ports come from the systemboard?

3. To expose the systemboard so you can identify its parts, remove all the circuit boards following these procedures. (If you are working with a tower case, you can lay it on its side so the systemboard is on the bottom.)

a. To make reassembling easier, take notes or make a sketch of the current placement of boards and cables. You can mark a cable on a card with a marker if you like. Note the orientation of the cable on the card. Each cable for the floppy disk drive, hard drive, or CD-ROM has a color on one side of the cable called the edge color. This color marks pin 1 of the cable. On the board, pin 1 is marked either as the number 1 or 2 beside the pin or, on the back side of the board, with a square soldering pad (see Figure 3-26).

b. Remove the cables from the card. There is no need to remove the other end of the cable from its component (floppy disk drive, hard drive, or CD-ROM). Lay the cable over the top of the component or case.

c. Remove the screw holding the board to the case.

d. If you aren't wearing a ground bracelet, touch the case before you touch the board.

e. Grasp the board with both hands and remove the board by rocking the board from end to end (not side to side). Rocking the board from side to side might spread the slot opening and weaken the connection.

4. Examine the board connector for the cable. Can you identify pin 1? Lay the board aside on a flat surface.

5. You probably will be able to see most if not all the components on the systemboard now without removing anything else. Draw a diagram of the systemboard and label these parts:

- The CPU (include the prominent label on the CPU housing)
- RAM (probably SIMMs)
- Cache memory (probably one or more smaller SIMMs)

- Expansion slots (identify the slots as ISA, EISA, MCA, PCI, VLB, etc.)

- Each port coming directly from the systemboard

- Power supply connections

- ROM BIOS chip (Copy the writing on the top of the chip to paper. Identify the manufacturer, serial number, and date of manufacture of the chip.)

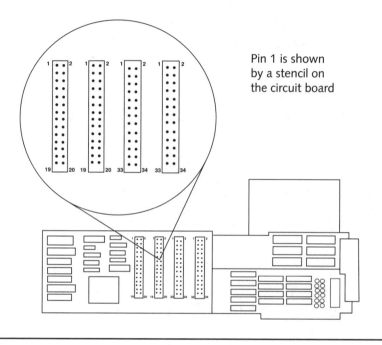

Pin 1 is shown by a stencil on the circuit board

Pin 1 is shown by square solder pads on the reverse side of the circuit board.

Figure 3-26   How to find pin 1 on an expansion card

6. Draw a rectangle on the diagram to represent each bank of jumpers on the board.

7. You can do the following activity only if you have the documentation for the systemboard: Locate the jumper or jumpers on the board that erases CMOS and/or the startup password and label it on your diagram. It is often found near the battery. Some boards might not have one.

8. You are now ready to reassemble. Reverse the disassembling activities above. Place each card in its slot (it doesn't have to be the same slot, just the same bus) and replace the screw. Don't place the video card near the power supply.

9. Replace the cables, being sure to align the colored edge with pin 1. (In some cases it might work better to connect the cable to the card before you put the card in the expansion slot.)

10. Plug in the keyboard, monitor, and mouse.

11. In a classroom environment, have the instructor check your work before you power up.

12. Turn on the power and check that the PC is working properly before you replace the cover. Don't touch the inside of the case while the power is on.

13. If all is well, turn off the PC and replace the cover and its screws. If the PC does not work, don't panic! Just go back and check each cable connection and each expansion card. You probably have not solidly seated a card in the slot. After you have double-checked, try again.

Saving and Restoring CMOS Settings

In Chapter 2, you used Nuts & Bolts to record CMOS settings to a rescue disk for later recovery. In this chapter, you use the Internet to download a shareware utility to record CMOS settings and later recover them.

1. Access the Internet and then go to this address: *www.shareware.com*. Search on "CMOS" to list the various shareware utilities available. Select and download CMOS20.ZIP. You can then exit the Internet.

2. Explode the compressed file and print the CMOS.TXT documentation file. Three utility programs are included:

   ■ CMOSSAVE.COM saves the CMOS settings to a file.

   ■ CMOSCHK.COM compares the CMOS settings to the last saved version.

   ■ CMOSREST.COM restores the CMOS settings from the file.

3. Access a DOS prompt and save the CMOS settings to a file on a floppy disk using this command:

`CMOSSAVE.COM A:\MYFILE.SAV`

4. Compare the settings stored in the file to the current CMOS settings using this command:

`CMOSCHK.COM A:\MYFILE.SAV`

The results of these commands are shown in Figure 3-27.

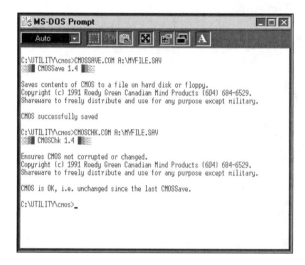

Figure 3-27   Using a shareware utility to save CMOS settings

USING A SYSTEMBOARD DIAGNOSTIC UTILITY

A well-known diagnostic utility is AMIDiag from American Megatrends, Inc. The utility is DOS-based and works under both DOS and Windows 95. You can download the utility from the Internet.

1. Access the Internet and then go to this address: *www.shareware.com*.

2. Locate the Quick Search text box and search on "amidiag" (don't enter the quotes). Download to your PC the file DIAGDEMO.ZIP. This is a shareware version of AMIDiag for PC diagnostics.

3. Leave the Internet and explode the file by double-clicking it in either Windows 3.1 or Windows 95.

4. Go to a DOS prompt and change to the directory where the demo software files are stored.

5. Execute the first program by entering this command: AMIDIAG

6. The screen shown in Figure 3-28 opens. Perform the test of processor speed. What is the detected speed?

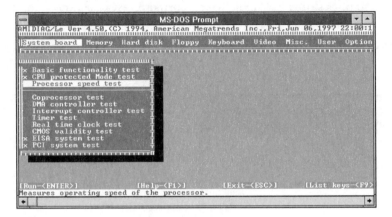

Figure 3-28   AMIDiag opening menu

7. Under the Memory menu, perform all the tests that this demonstration version of the software allows. Record any errors detected.

8. Under the Misc menu, perform the serial port test. Write down any error messages that you get. If you get an unexpected error, perform the test more than once. Do you get the same results each time?

9. Under the Options menu, ask for System Information. If you received errors in the test above, this program might lock up, and you might need to reboot. If you complete the information check successfully, write down the results.

10. Under the Systemboard menu, select the option DMA Controller Test. Why doesn't this test work?

11. Exit the program, returning to the DOS prompt.

PRACTICE ACTIVITY

Using old or defective expansion cards and systemboards, practice inserting and removing expansion cards and chips.

PRINT A SUMMARY OF YOUR SYSTEM HARDWARE

3

1. In Windows 95, right-click the **My Computer** icon.
2. On the File menu, select **Properties**.
3. Click the **Device Manager** tab.
4. View devices by type.
5. Click the **Ports** (Com & LPT) icon.
6. Click on the **Print** button.
7. Print **Selected class or device**.

UNDERSTANDING HARDWARE DOCUMENTATION

Obtain the manual for the systemboard for your PC. List at least three functions of jumpers on the board as well as the corresponding jumper numbers.

LEARN TO USE WINDOWS 95 HELP FEATURE

1. In Windows 95, click the **Start** button on the Taskbar.
2. Click **Help**.
3. Click the **Contents** tab.
4. Open **Troubleshooting**.
5. Select and print **If you have a hardware conflict**.

TROUBLESHOOT SETUP ERRORS

Change DIP switches, jumper, or CMOS configuration on a systemboard. (First make sure someone records the original settings.) Troubleshoot the system. Use this opportunity to learn to take notes as you work. List each error you encounter and what you did to work toward a solution.

RESEARCH THE MARKET

1. In a current computer magazine, find the speed and price of the fastest PC CPU on the market today.

2. In a current computer magazine, find the speed and price of the fastest PC RAM module on the market today.

OBSERVING HARDWARE CONFLICT ERRORS

Have someone set up a troubleshooting practice problem by forcing two hardware devices on a PC to use the same IRQ. Troubleshoot the problem. Take notes as you go. Describe the errors that you see and what you are doing to solve the problem.

FLOPPY DRIVES AND OTHER ESSENTIAL DEVICES

We now move from the systemboard to the first of three chapters on peripheral devices that all computer users consider essential and necessary. At least one floppy disk drive is standard equipment on all PCs, along with a keyboard and monitor. A mouse or other pointing device also is no longer considered optional (except for some PCs dedicated to a special purpose such as those found on retail sales counters). Although it has been predicted that floppy drives will be a thing of the past, their easy convenience and ready availability, the low cost of disks, and their proven usefulness and dependability have solidly implanted them in the marketplace and on every personal computer system.

In this chapter, you will examine each of the five essential hardware devices: the floppy drive, keyboard, monitor, mouse, and video card. Particular attention is paid to how data is stored on a floppy disk, how to manage that data, and how to install a floppy disk drive on a PC. You will extend the skills you acquire in working with floppy disks to hard drives in Chapters 5 and 6.

IN THIS CHAPTER YOU WILL LEARN:

- How data is stored on floppy disks
- How to use DOS and Windows commands to manage disks
- How to replace or install a disk drive
- What keyboard types and features are available
- How monitors differ in quality and performance
- How a mouse and other pointing devices work
- What monitors and video cards do and the features they offer

FLOPPY DRIVES

Just a few years ago, floppy disks came in two sizes: 5¼ inches and 3½ inches. Our emphasis is on 3½-inch disks because today, new computers are equipped with only a 3½-inch drive. However, because there are still so many computers with 5¼-inch disk drives, this section covers some details about 5¼-inch disks as well. Although they are larger, 5¼-inch disks do not hold as much data as 3½-inch disks because 5¼-inch disks do not store data as densely as 3½-inch disks. Table 4-1 summarizes the capacity of the four common types of disks. You probably won't find the 5¼-inch double-density disks very often because that technology became outdated quite some time ago. The 3½-inch extra-high-density disks also did not become as popular as was first expected. Most disks today are 3½-inch high-density and hold 1.44 MB of data.

Table 4-1   Floppy Disk Types

Type	Storage Capacity	Number of Tracks	Number of Sectors	Cluster Type
3½-inch extra-high-density	2.88 MB	80	36	2 sectors
3½-inch high-density	1.44 MB	80	18	1 sector
3½-inch double-density	720K	80	9	2 sectors
5¼-inch high-density	1.2MB	80	15	1 sector
5¼-inch double-density	360K	40	9	2 sectors

Regardless of disk size and density, the physical hardware used to access a disk looks and works much the same way. Figure 4-1 shows a floppy disk drive and connections. The data cable leaving the floppy drive goes to a controller board for the drive. The controller board is plugged into the system bus in an expansion slot. The board then communicates with the CPU, passing data back and forth from the floppy disk. Sometimes the controller is built into the systemboard so that the data cable goes directly from the drive to the systemboard. Most computers today use a combination card that allows floppy drives and hard drives to be connected to the same controller board. Sometimes these multipurpose boards also include serial and parallel ports.

The cable has the controller connection at one end and a drive connection at the other end. A second drive connection is placed somewhere in the middle of the cable to accommodate a second floppy drive. Having two drives share the same cable is a common practice for floppy drives as well as hard drives and CD-ROMs.

The power supply is the source of power for the drives, and the power flows from the power supply to the drives through the power cable. The power cable usually plugs into the back of the drive onto a board that sits on top of the drive. This board, called a **logic board**, is considered part of the drive.

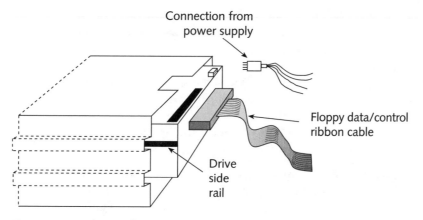

Figure 4-1   Floppy drive, data cable, and power connection

HOW DATA IS PHYSICALLY STORED ON A DISK

Floppy disks, no matter what density or size, store data in much the same way. All disks when first manufactured have nothing written on them; they are just blank sheets of magnetically coated plastic. Before data can be written on the disk, the disk must first be mapped out in concentric circles called **tracks**, and in pie-shaped wedges called **sectors**. This process of preparing the disk to receive data is called **formatting** the disk. Figure 4-2 shows a drawing of a formatted 3½-inch double-density disk. According to Table 4-1, there are 80 tracks or circles on the

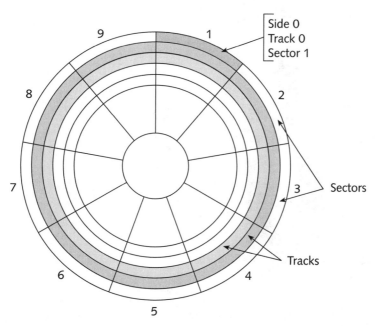

Figure 4-2   3½-inch disk showing tracks and sectors

top side of the disk and 80 more tracks on the bottom side of the disk. The tracks are numbered 0 through 79. Each side of the disk has 9 sectors, numbered 1 through 9. Even though the circles or tracks on the outside of the disk are larger than the circles closer to the center, all tracks store the same amount of data. Data is written to the tracks of the disk as bits, either a 0 or a 1. Each bit is a magnetized spot on the disk that is shaped roughly like a rectangle. Between the tracks there is a space that is not magnetized, and there is space between each spot on a track. This spacing prevents one spot from affecting the magnetism of a nearby spot. The difference between a 0 spot and a 1 spot is the orientation of the magnetization of the spot on the disk surface.

Data is written to and read from the disk via a magnetic **read/write head** mechanism in the floppy drive. Two heads are attached at the end of an actuator arm that freely moves back and forth over the surface of the disk. The arm has one read/write head above the disk and another read/write head below the disk. Moving in unison back and forth across the disk, the two heads lightly touch the surface of the disk, which is spinning at either 300 rpm (revolutions per minute) or 360 rpm depending on the type of disk. Data is written first to the bottom and then to the top of the disk beginning at the outermost circle and going in. Eraser heads on either side of the read/write head, as shown in Figure 4-3, ensure that the widths of the data tracks do not vary. As the data is written, the eraser heads immediately behind and to the sides of the write head clean up both sides of the magnetized spot making a clean track of data with no "bleeding" from the track. The magnetized area does not spread too far from the track. All tracks are then the same width, and the distance between tracks is uniform.

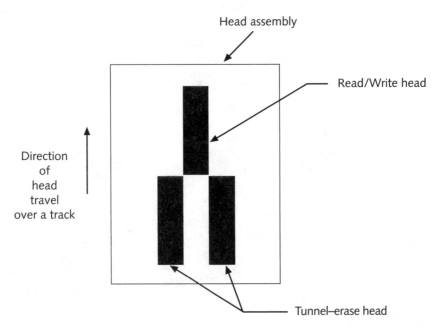

Figure 4-3   Uniform track widths are created by a floppy drive read/write head

The disk is actually a piece of Mylar similar to that used for overhead transparencies. Covering the surface of the Mylar is a layer of either cobalt oxide or iron oxide (rust) that can hold a magnetic charge. Some disks have another layer of Teflon on top to protect the oxide layer and to allow the read/write heads to move more smoothly over the surface. During formatting, the tracks are created by laying down a repeating character, the ÷ (division) symbol, which is F6 in ASCII code or 1111 0110 in binary (see Appendix C for a list of ASCII codes). The tracks are divided into sectors, and the beginning sector is marked on each track with a designated code. For 3½-inch disks, the sector address mark written on the disk during formatting marks the beginning sector. After formatting, actual data is written on the disk by overwriting the F6 patterns on the tracks.

The different disk types use varying degrees of magnetic strength when data is written to a disk or when a disk is formatted. For example, a 3½-inch high-density disk can hold more data than a double-density disk, because the data is written closer together. Data on the high-density disk is recorded at about twice the magnetic strength as data on the double-density disk. The high-density disk surface is not as sensitive to a magnetic field as the double-density is and can, therefore, handle double the strength of the fields.

Many users have discovered that the less expensive double-density disks can be formatted as high-density, and the format will work and data can be written to the disk. Beware! Don't trust that disk with important data. The surface of a double-density disk is more sensitive to the magnetic field, and eventually the magnetic spots on the disk will affect each other, corrupting the data. The life span of an incorrectly formatted disk is very short. For this reason, always format a disk using the density for which it was manufactured.

When data is read from the disk surface, the read/write head changes roles. It passes over a track on the disk, waiting for the right position on the disk to appear. When the correct sector arrives, the controller board opens a gateway, and the magnetic charge on the disk passes voltage to the read/write head. The voltage is immediately amplified and passed on to the controller board, which in turn passes the data to the system bus.

HOW DATA IS LOGICALLY STORED ON A DISK

In Figure 4-2, the part of a track that belongs to a single sector is marked; this segment of one track is also referred to as a sector. You can see that the word sector means two different things. A "sector" describes the entire pie-shaped wedge on one side of a disk, as well as the single segment of one track or circle that falls within the wedge. In most of our discussions, we use sector to mean the segment of one track, unless we specifically say that we are talking about the entire wedge. A sector, or a segment of a track, as shown in Figure 4-2, always holds 512 bytes of data. This is true for all floppy disks, no matter what the size or density. You will learn in Chapter 6 that this is also true for hard drives.

Look at a single track on the disk in Figure 4-2. Recall that there is a matching track on the bottom of the disk as well. The sector directly underneath the top sector also holds 512 bytes of data. It is written to and read from at the same time as the top sector. These two sectors together make up one cluster. A **cluster** is defined as one or more sectors that are the smallest units allocated for a file. A cluster is also the smallest unit of data that can be read from or written to a disk at one time. A file is stored on a disk in clusters. Clusters are, therefore, sometimes called **file allocation units**. On the 3½-inch double-density disk in Figure 4-2, there are 9 sectors to each track and 80 tracks on one side of the disk and 80 more tracks on the other side. The top side has 80×9 or 720 sectors and so does the bottom. Because there are two sectors to a cluster, there are a total of 720 clusters. Each cluster holds 512 bytes $\times 2 = 1,024$ bytes of data. There are, therefore, $1,024 \times 720 = 737,280$ bytes of storage space on one of these disks. Divide this number by 1,024 bytes per kilobyte and you see the storage capacity is 720 kilobytes.

Looking back at Table 4-1, you see that a 3½-inch high-density disk has 80 tracks and 18 sectors per track on each side. There are 80 tracks $\times 18$ or 1,440 sectors on each side. With this type of disk, there is only one sector per cluster, making $1,440 \times 2$ sides or 2,880 clusters on the disk. Because each cluster holds only 512 bytes (one sector) of data, this type of disk has $2,880 \times 512 = 1,474,560$ bytes of data. Divide this number by 1,024 to convert bytes to kilobytes. The storage capacity of this disk is 1,440 kilobytes. Divide by 1,000 to convert kilobytes to megabytes and the storage is then written as 1.44 MB.[1]

THE FORMATTING PROCESS

The formatting of all disks is similar, no matter what size or density. During formatting the Windows 95 or DOS FORMAT command performs the following steps:

- Creates the tracks and sectors by writing tracks as a series of F6s and, as necessary, writing the sector address mark to identify the beginning sector on a track
- Creates the master boot record (discussed below)
- Creates two copies of the file allocation table (FAT) (discussed in detail below)
- Creates the root directory

Later in this chapter you will learn how the formatting process can be altered by adding options to the formatting process. Without added options, the OS performs the steps listed above, which are described in detail next.

Creating the Tracks and Sectors

The FORMAT command is a DOS and Windows 95 command that prepares a disk for use. The first step in the formatting process erases any data that already has been written to the disk. In its simplest form, without adding any parameters, the FORMAT command always erases any data on a previously used disk, overwriting the data with the F6 character.

---

[1] There is a discrepancy in the computer industry regarding the definition of a megabyte. Sometimes 1 megabyte = 1,000 kilobytes; at other times, we use the relationship of 1 megabyte = 1,024 kilobytes.

The Master Boot Record

During formatting, DOS or Windows 95 prepares the disk so that it can be written to or read from. There is no difference in the way DOS and Windows 95 prepare disk before writing files to it. For the purposes of this discussion, you might find it easier to think of Windows 95 as simply DOS 7.

The software to access the information stored on a floppy disk is partly ROM BIOS code and partly the OS. The **master boot record** or **MBR**, sometimes called the **DOS boot record**, contains the information that DOS later uses when it reads from the disk. The MBR holds information about whether the disk was formatted and exactly how it was formatted, including which version of DOS or Windows 95 was used. This master boot record contains a uniform layout for all versions of DOS and Windows 95 and is always located at the beginning of the disk at track 0, sector 1 (bottom of the disk, outermost track). This uniformity allows any version of DOS or Windows 95 to read any disk. The master boot record contains, among other things, the information listed in Table 4-2. When an OS accesses a disk, the MBR provides the ground rules based on the information in Table 4-2; the OS then knows how to expect the data to be logically stored on the disk. A floppy disk has only one boot record, but a hard drive has at least two. On a floppy disk, the master boot record and the DOS boot record are the same record. On a hard drive, they are two different records, each with a different purpose. More about this in the next chapter.

Table 4-2   Contents of the Master Boot Record

Bytes per sector
Sectors per cluster
Number of FATs
Size of the root directory
Number of sectors
Medium descriptor byte
Size of the FAT
Sectors per track
Number of heads (always 2)
Number of hidden sectors
Program to load the OS

The ninth item in the table is the number of heads. A head refers to the read/write head that is a part of the physical components of the drive. Because the disk always has only one top and one bottom and a read/write head assigned to each, the number of heads is always two. The last item in Table 4-2 is the program that loads either DOS or Windows 95. Some disks are bootable, meaning that they contain enough DOS to load the OS — whatever it may be — into memory and to boot to the A prompt or B prompt, depending on the drive in which the disk is inserted. In Chapter 1, you learned that to make a disk bootable, certain parts of the OS must be present. For DOS, this is two hidden files and COMMAND.COM. These files can be loaded on the disk when it is formatted, or they can be loaded with the DOS SYS command. When Windows 95 creates a system disk, it copies COMMAND.COM and two hidden files, IO.SYS and MSDOS.SYS, to the disk to make the disk bootable.

All master boot records, however, are the same whether or not the disk is bootable. When the PC is looking for a bootable disk during POST, if a disk is in the drive, the program stored in the master boot record is executed. This program loads the startup files of the OS. The boot record contains the names of the two hidden files. For example, for IBM DOS 3.3, the filenames of the hidden files are IBMBIO.COM and IBMDOS.COM. The program looks for these two files on the disk. If it does not find them, a message appears, such as the following:

```
Non-system disk or disk error...Replace and strike any key
when ready...Disk boot failure.
```

POST terminates until the user intervenes. Only the program in the master boot record can determine if the disk is bootable.

The File Allocation Table (FAT)

The next item that the FORMAT command writes to the disk is two copies of the **file allocation table (FAT)**. The FAT contains the location of files on the disk. It basically is a one-column table; the length of each entry in the column is 12 bits. The FAT lists how each cluster or file allocation unit on the disk is currently being used. (Remember that a cluster is the smallest unit of disk space allocated to a file.) A file can be contained in one or more clusters. The clusters need not be contiguous on the disk. In the FAT, some clusters might be marked as bad clusters (the 12 bits to mark a bad cluster are FF7h). These bits can be entered in the FAT when the disk is formatted or added later with the DOS RECOVER command. An extra copy of the FAT is kept immediately following the first. If the first is damaged, sometimes you can recover your data and files by using the second copy.

Figure 4-4 shows an example of a FAT. In this example, the file contains 1,798 bytes. The file is stored beginning in cluster 4, then cluster 5, cluster 450, and cluster 451. Because this file is not stored in consecutive clusters, it is called a **fragmented file**. The beginning cluster number and the size of the file in bytes are stored in the root directory of this disk. The disk is a 3½-inch high-density disk, which has clusters equal to 1 sector or 512 bytes. Because the file is 1,798 bytes, this file requires 4 whole clusters or 2,048 bytes of disk space. The first FAT entry for the file tells you that the file starts in cluster 4. The cluster 4 table entry contains 005, which points to the table entry for cluster 5. Remember that all disks have 12 bits for each FAT entry. The bits are used to store 3 hex digits of 4 bits each. The location for cluster 5 has the hex numerals 1C2, which are equal to 450 in decimal. Looking to cluster 450, you see the hex numerals 1C3, which point to cluster 451 (1C3 in hex = 451 in decimal). At cluster 451 you see FFF, which marks the end of the file. These four FAT entries are called a cluster chain. The **cluster chain** determines all cluster locations for a file on a disk.

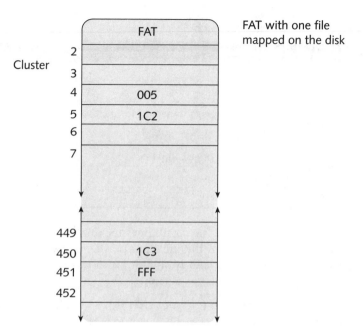

Figure 4-4   FAT with one file mapped on the disk

The Root Directory

After creating the file allocation tables, the formatting process sets up the root directory. Recall that the root directory or main directory is a table listing all the files that are assigned to this table. The root directory contains a fixed number of rows to accommodate a predetermined number of files and subdirectories; the number of available rows is dependent upon the disk type. The number of root directory entries for the four common disk types is listed in Table 4–3.

Table 4-3   Root Directory Entries for Disk Types

Disk Type	Number of Root Directory Entries
5¼-inch double-density	112
5¼-inch high-density	224
3½-inch double-density	112
3½-inch high-density	224

The root directory will later contain information about each file and subdirectory stored in it. Table 4–4 lists how the 32 bytes making up each entry in the root directory are used.

Table 4-4 Root Directory Information for Each File

Root Directory Bytes	Usage
8	Name of file
3	File extension
1	Attribute byte (special meaning for each bit)
2	Time of creation or last update
2	Date of creation or last update
2	Starting cluster number in binary
4	Size of file in binary

Notice that only the root directory contains the starting cluster number. To find out what other clusters are used to store the file, look in the file allocation table. By dividing the size of the file by the number of bytes per cluster and rounding up to the nearest whole number, you can determine how many clusters the file occupies.

Also note that there is no place for the period (often referred to as "dot") that we normally see between the filename and the file extension in DOS command lines. The period is not stored in directories but is only used in DOS command lines to indicate where the filename ends and the file extension begins. For the long filenames in Windows 95, more room in the directory is required. This is accomplished by using more than one entry in the FAT for a single file, enough to accommodate the length of the filename. Both the long filename and the DOS version short filename are stored in the directory.

Time and date of creation or last update are stored in a coded form that is converted to a recognizable form when displayed on the screen. The date and time is taken from the system date and time. For DOS, these are determined by the DOS DATE and TIME commands. For Windows 95, the date and time are changed in the Control Panel. The earliest possible date allowed for both is 1/1/1980.

The file attributes are used for various purposes. The 1 byte is broken into bits; each bit has a specific meaning. The first two bits are not used. The meanings of the other 6 bits are listed in Table 4-5, beginning with the leftmost bit in the byte and moving to the right. There are several Windows 95 and DOS commands that use and can change the file attributes. We cover many of them later in this chapter.

The root directory and all subdirectories contain the same information about each file. The root directory is the only directory that is limited by the number of entries. Subdirectories can have as many entries as disk space allows. Because long filenames require more room in a directory than short filenames, assigning long filenames reduces the number of files that can be stored in the root directory.

Table 4-5   File Attributes for each Bit in the Directory Attribute Byte (Reading from Left to Right Across the Byte)

Bit	Description	Bit=0	Bit=1
1, 2	Not used		
3	Archive bit	Not to be archived	To be archived
4	Directory status	File	Subdirectory
5	Volume label	Not volume label	Is volume label
6	System file	Not system file	Is system file
7	Hidden file	Not hidden	Hidden
8	Read-only file	Read/write	Read-only

In summary, for DOS, the FORMAT command writes tracks and sectors on the disk, and creates a master boot record, an empty file allocation table, and an empty root directory. If you include the /S option in the FORMAT line, you add the two hidden files and COMMAND.COM that together make a disk bootable. The three files are referenced in the FAT and in the root directory. The two hidden files have their file attribute bit 7, the hidden bit, set to 1 (read-only). When you make a Windows 95 rescue disk, the two hidden files and COMMAND.COM are copied to the disk to make the disk bootable.

USING DOS TO MANAGE A FLOPPY DISK

We now look at several DOS commands that you can use to manage a floppy disk. DOS commands are divided into two groups according to how the command is made available to DOS. **Internal DOS commands** are part of the COMMAND.COM program and don't require COMMAND.COM to find and load another program file. **External DOS commands** are stored as separate program files in the DOS directory. COMMAND.COM must search for and load these program files before the command can be executed. For more information about these and other DOS commands, type HELP followed by the command name at a DOS prompt, or type the command name followed by /? (slash and a question mark).

FORMAT drive: /U /V /S /Q /F:size Command

The external FORMAT command prepares a disk for use. If the drive is not specified, the command uses the default drive. The options for the FORMAT command are outlined in Table 4-6.

Table 4-6   FORMAT Command Options

FORMAT Command Options	Description
/V	Allows you to enter a volume label only once when formatting several disks. The same volume label is used for all disks. A volume label displays at the top of the directory list to help you identify the disk.
/S	Stores the system files on the disk after formatting. Writes the two hidden files and COMMAND.COM to the disk making the disk bootable.
/Q	Recreates the root directory and FATs if you want to quickly format a previously formatted disk that is in good condition. /Q does not read or write to any other part of the disk.
/F:size	Specifies the size of a floppy disk. If the size is not specified, the default for that drive is used. The common values for size are: /F:360 is 360K, double-density 5¼-inch disk /F:1.2 is 1.2 MB, high-density 5¼-inch disk /F:720 is 720 K, double-density 3½-inch disk /F:1.44 is 1.44 MB, high-density 3½-inch disk
/U	Allows for an unconditional format of the drive, which does a more thorough job of formatting the drive by erasing all data on the drive. Use this option when you have been getting read/write errors on the drive.

LABEL Command

The LABEL command changes the volume label or electronic name on a disk. The volume label is stored at the beginning of the root directory and also in the master boot record. The label is displayed at the top of the directory list that is produced by the DIR command. The label can be up to 11 characters long and can contain spaces.

CHKDSK drive: /F /V Command

The CHKDSK command creates a status report of a disk, and it can repair lost clusters in the FAT. If you do not specify a drive, DOS uses the default drive.

The CHKDSK command examines the directory, looking at the starting cluster number and the size of each file, and compares that information to the FAT. It checks that the FAT contains the correct number of entries for each file and that there is an end-of-file marker at the end of the chain. If the CHKDSK command finds entries in the FAT that don't belong to a chain, or if an entry in the FAT is in more than one chain, CHKDSK reports lost allocation units or cross-linked chains.

Do not use the CHKDSK command on a hard drive if files are currently open by other programs, such as Windows or network software. The command will mistake these open files as being lost clusters or lost file allocation units.

The /F option tells the CHKDSK command to fix lost clusters, converting them to files that are stored in the root directory under the name FILE0000.CHK (or a higher number). Never use the /F option when other programs might have open files that the command will "fix." The /V option displays a list of files as it checks the directory and the FAT.

4

SCANDISK [drive:] /FRAGMENT /UNDO /CHECKONLY /SURFACE Command

SCANDISK is a DOS utility that is an improvement over CHKDSK. SCANDISK checks for lost and cross-linked clusters as well as defragments the drive and does a surface scan for bad sectors. (Defragmentation is the process of rewriting sections of files so they are on contiguous sectors on a disk.) If you don't specify a drive, SCANDISK scans the current drive for errors. Options of the SCANDISK command are as follows:

- Use the /FRAGMENT option to defragment files on the drive.
- Use /UNDO to undo the last changes that SCANDISK made.
- Use /CHECKONLY to list the errors that SCANDISK finds without making any changes.
- Use /SURFACE to scan the drive for bad sectors.

There is a SCANDISK.INI file in the DOS directory that you can use to customize the SCANDISK utility. This file is handy for initiating a scan from the AUTOEXEC.BAT file every time you boot.

DEL or ERASE Command

The DEL or ERASE command erases files or groups of files.

For example, to erase all the files in the A:\DOCS directory, use the following command:

```
C:\> ERASE A:\DOCS\*.*
```

To erase all the files in the current default directory, use the following command:

```
A:\DOCS> DEL *.*
```

To erase all files in the current directory that have no file extension, use the following command:

```
A:\DOCS> DEL *.
```

To erase the file named MYFILE.TXT, use the following command:

```
A:\> DEL MYFILE.TXT
```

The UNDELETE command attempts to recover files that have been deleted and is discussed in the section below.

UNDELETE Command

Following are some variations of the UNDELETE command, which can be used to try to recover deleted files.

To list the files that can be undeleted without actually undeleting them, use the following command:

```
A:\UNDELETE /list
```

To recover deleted files without prompting for confirmation on each file, use the following command:

```
A:\UNDELETE /all
```

RECOVER Command

The RECOVER command attempts to recover a file from damaged sectors on a disk. Always specify the drive, path, and filename of the file you want to recover with the RECOVER command. If you have several files that need recovering, use the command on one file at a time.

To recover the file named MYFILE.TXT, use the following command:

```
A:\RECOVER A:\DOCS\MYFILE.TXT
```

Whatever portion of the file that the RECOVER command can read is stored in the root directory and named A:FILE0000.REC (or a higher number). Copy this file to another disk before trying to recover the second file.

The RECOVER command might mark clusters as bad in the FAT. Don't use this command without first making a DISKCOPY of the disk if possible (described below). Data that might have been saved by other methods can sometimes be destroyed by the RECOVER command.

DISKCOPY Command

The DISKCOPY command makes an exact duplicate (sector by sector) of one disk (called the source disk) to another disk of the same size and type (called the target disk).

To duplicate a disk using only a single drive, use the following command:

```
C:\DISKCOPY A: A:
```

DOS prompts you as many times as necessary to insert the source disk and then insert the target disk to make the exact copy. Data is copied from one disk to the other byte by byte including any hidden files, bad sectors, fragmented files, or other contents; everything gets copied as is. For this reason, the copy can be bad if the source disk has some bad sectors. DISKCOPY ignores sectors marked as bad in the FAT and copies to them anyway. The DISKCOPY command copies formatting information so that the target disk does not need to be formatted before executing the copy.

COPY Command

The COPY command copies a single file or group of files. The original files are not altered. When using the COPY command, use the following:

To copy a file from one drive to another, use the following command:

```
A:\COPY drive:\path\filename.ext drive:\path\filename.ext
```

The drive, path, and filename of the original source file immediately follows the COPY command, and the drive, path, and filename of the destination file follows the source filename. If you do not specify the filename of the copy, DOS assigns the original name of the file. If you omit the drive or path of the source or the destination, then DOS uses the current default drive and path.

To copy the file MYFILE.TXT from the root directory of drive C to drive A, use the following command:

```
C:\>COPY MYFILE.TXT A:
```

Because there is no drive or path indicated before the filename MYFILE.TXT, DOS uses the default drive and path.

To copy all files in the C:\DOCS directory to the disk in drive A, use the following command:

```
C:\>COPY C:\DOCS\*.* A:
```

To make a backup file named SYSTEM.BAK of the SYSTEM.INI file in the \WINDOWS directory of the hard drive, use the following command:

```
C:\WINDOWS> COPY SYSTEM.INI SYSTEM.BAK
```

If you use the COPY command to duplicate multiple files, the files are assigned the names of the original files. When duplicating multiple files, no filename can be listed in the destination portion of the command line.

XCOPY /M Command

The XCOPY command is more powerful than the COPY command. It follows the same general command-source-destination format of the COPY command, but it offers several more options, as outlined next.

Use the /S option with the XCOPY command to copy all files in the directory \DOCS as well as all subdirectories under \DOCS and their files to the disk in drive A. Use the following command:

```
C:\XCOPY C:\DOCS\*.* A: /S
```

To copy all files from the directory C:\DOCS created or modified after the specified date written in the form mm/dd/yy, use the following command:

```
C:\XCOPY C:\DOCS\*.* A: /d:03/14/95
```

4

DELTREE

This command deletes the directory tree beginning with the subdirectory you specify including all subdirectories and all files in all subdirectories. Use it with caution!

```
C:\DELTREE [drive:]path
```

USING WINDOWS 3.X TO MANAGE A FLOPPY DRIVE

Windows 3.x allows you to use many of the same commands you use with DOS. Most of these commands are available from File Manager.

Format a Disk

To format a disk from File Manager, click the **Disk** menu, then click **Format Disk.** The dialog box shown in Figure 4-5 opens. Click the **Capacity** list arrow to display a list of the different disk types available for that drive. In the example, the choices are 1.44 MB (high-density) and 720K (double-density) for a 3½-inch disk. Using options, you can enter a volume label and choose to make the disk bootable, or do a quick format. Remember that a Quick format does not create track and sector markings on the disk, so it takes less time. Use the Quick format to quickly erase all files and subdirectories on a disk.

Other Disk Commands in the File Manager Menu

Figure 4-6 shows the entire drop-down Disk menu in File Manager. Four menu options are explained in Table 4-7.

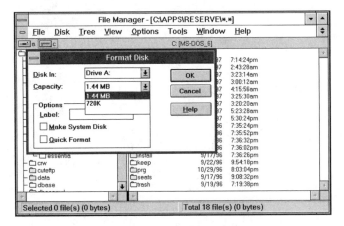

Figure 4-5 Format a disk from File Manager

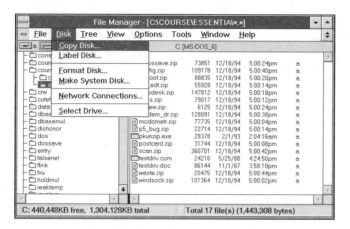

Figure 4-6   Disk menu in File Manager

Table 4-7   Four Disk Menu Options under File Manager

Disk Menu Option	Description
Copy Disk	Same as the DOS DISKCOPY command.
Label Disk	Puts a volume label on a disk.
Make System Disk	Copies the system files to a disk to make the disk bootable.
Select Drive	Selects the drive to be displayed in a File Manager drive window. This selection can also be made by clicking the drive icon below the title bar of the window.

Also notice the Network Connections option on the menu. This option is not standard in Microsoft Windows but rather was placed there by software other than Windows 3.1. Software applications sometimes add their own options to Windows menus.

The File Menu of File Manager

Figure 4-7 shows the drop-down File menu in File Manager. Table 4-8 describes the function of five of the commands. The Move, Copy, and Delete commands apply to one file or a group of files. To select a group of adjacent files on the file list in File Manager, click the first file to select it, scroll to the last file in the list, hold down the Shift key, and then click the last filename. This action selects all files between the first name and the last name in the list. To select files at random through the list, hold down the Ctrl key while clicking on the filenames.

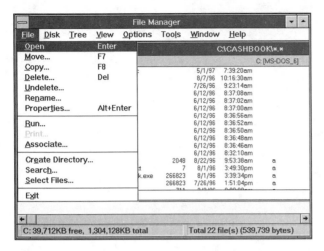

Figure 4-7 File menu in File Manager

Table 4-8 Five File Menu Options Under File Manager

File Menu Options Under File Manager	Description
Move	Moves a file or group of files from one directory to another. You can also drag the group of files from one directory to another if they are on the same drive.
Copy	Copies a file or group of files. You can also drag the group of selected files to a new location on another drive. To copy files from one directory on a drive to another directory on the same drive, hold down the Ctrl key while you drag.
Delete	Deletes a file or group of selected files. (You can also press the Delete key to delete selected files.)
Rename	Changes the name of a single file.
Properties	Displays the properties of a file. Part of the information displayed is that contained in the attribute byte for that file.

USING WINDOWS 95 TO MANAGE A FLOPPY DRIVE

Windows 95 performs similar functions to those available with DOS and Windows 3.x. A few are covered here.

Format a Disk and Make a System Disk

To format a disk, follow these steps.

- Click the **Start** button on the Taskbar, point to **Programs,** and then click **Windows Explorer**. Right-click either drive A or drive B. The menu in Figure 4-8 appears.

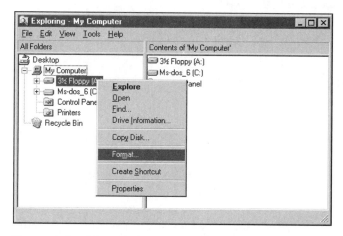

Figure 4-8   Menu to manage a floppy disk

- Click **Format** on the menu. The dialog box shown in Figure 4-9 opens. Notice that you have three format choices: a Quick format (does not remark the tracks), a full Format, or an option to copy just the system files to the disk (same as SYS command in DOS).
- Select the appropriate options to either format the disk or make the disk bootable.

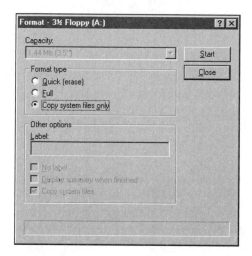

Figure 4-9   Format a disk in Microsoft Windows 95

Disk Copy Command

If you select **Copy Disk** from the menu in Figure 4-8, a dialog box opens, as shown in Figure 4-10, where the disk listed under "Copy from" is the source disk and the disk listed under "Copy to" is the destination disk. Click **Start** to copy the disk.

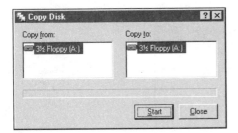

Figure 4-10   Copying a disk

The Windows 95 Rescue Disk

When you create a Windows 95 rescue disk, the disk is formatted and system files are copied to the disk just as when you make a bootable system disk as described above. In addition to the files needed to boot in Windows 95, the files listed in Table 4-9 might be copied to the rescue disk, depending on the version of Windows 95 producing the disk. The table also describes the purpose of each file.

EXCHANGING AND INSTALLING A FLOPPY DRIVE

In this section we address problems that can occur with a floppy drive and its support system, how to replace the drive and controller card, and how to add an additional floppy drive to a computer system. When a floppy drive cannot read a disk, the problem might have many causes. We cover several in detail.

Many computers today come with one 3½-inch drive and a hard drive. The machine might have one or two empty bays for a second floppy drive or for a CD-ROM drive. If you don't have an extra bay and want to add another drive, you can attach an external drive that comes in its own case and has its own power supply.

When a Floppy Drive Doesn't Work

Floppy drives are now so inexpensive that it is impractical to repair one. Once you've determined that the drive itself has a problem, simply open the case, remove the problem drive, and replace it with a new one. This procedure takes no more than 30 minutes assuming, of course, you don't damage or loosen something else in the process and create a new troubleshooting opportunity.

Table 4-9   Rescue Disk Files Created in Windows 95

File	Purpose
IO.SYS	Used to boot DOS
MSDOS.SYS	Startup configuration information
COMMAND.COM	Provides a DOS prompt
ATTRIB.EXE	Changes the attributes of a file
CHKDSK.EXE	Determines the status of a disk and repairs
EDIT.COM	DOS Editor
EDIT.HLP	Help for EDIT.COM
FC.EXE	Compares files
FDISK.EXE	Used to partition a hard drive
FORMAT.EXE	Formats a disk or hard drive
MEM.EXE	Displays information about memory
MORE.COM	Paginates the results of a command on screen
MSCDEX.EXE	CD-ROM driver
MSD.EXE	System diagnostics utility
SCANDISK.EXE	Checks and repairs hard drives
SCANDISK.INI	Initial parameters for SCANDISK.EXE
SETVER.EXE	Sets the DOS version for some programs
SYS.COM	Makes a disk or hard drive bootable
XCOPY.EXE	Copy utility

4

Drive Testing Software

To determine if a drive is damaged or not takes only a short time if you have the proper software tools to work with. You have the opportunity to work with diagnostic software called Nuts & Bolts, as well as MicroSystems Development Technologies, Inc.'s TestDrive at the end of the chapter. The explanation of drive testing in this section will help you solve drive problems and give you some insight as to how floppy drives work. Working with diagnostic software, you can test these criteria:

- **Azimuth skew:** Does the drive head align itself well with the tracks or is it at a tangent (see Figure 4-11)?

- **Hub centering:** Does the disk wobble as it turns or does it turn in a perfect circle?

- **Hysteresis:** Can the drive find a track regardless of the direction from which it approaches the track?

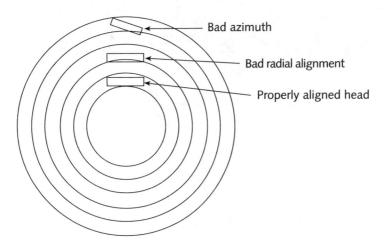

Figure 4-11 Alignment of floppy drive heads

- **Radial alignment:** Is the drive head centered correctly on the track or is it too far to the left or the right (see Figure 4–11)?

- **Rotational speed:** Does the drive turn the floppy at the proper speed?

- **Sensitivity:** How far from the data must the head be before it can read the data?

Over time, floppy drives can slowly shift out of alignment. A symptom of this problem is that a disk written by one drive cannot be read by another drive. To check thoroughly for these kinds of problems, the testing software must have a disk that it can use as its standard to measure the drive against. The software determines how the drive reads the data from a disk that it knows to be written perfectly. These disks are known as **digital diagnostic disks** or **DDD** and can be purchased at computer stores. The TestDrive software for Activity 5 uses a DDD for several of its tests. We ask you to do only those tests that don't require the DDD disk.

Sometimes a problem with the floppy drive arises during POST when BIOS displays an error message. Error messages in the 600 range occur when the floppy drive did not pass the POST test. These problems can be caused by the power supply, the drive, or the controller board.

Even if POST finds no errors, you might still have a problem. If you put a disk in the faulty drive and issue a command to access the disk, an error message such as the following might appear on the screen:

```
General failure reading drive A, Abort, Retry, Fail?
```

Or, perhaps nothing happens and the computer simply stops working. The problem might come from several sources including the following:

- The application you are currently running is pointing to a different drive

- DOS or Windows 95 may have just encountered an unrelated error that has locked up the system

- The System BIOS or CMOS setup is not correctly configured

- The disk in the drive is not formatted

- The floppy drive is bad

- The shuttle window on the floppy disk is not able to open fully

- The floppy drive controller card is loose in the expansion slot or has a bad chip

- The cable from the controller card to the drive is damaged or poorly connected

- The power supply is bad

- The power supply cable to the drive is loose or disconnected

- The command just issued has a mistake or is the wrong command

- The drive latch is not closed or the disk is inserted incorrectly

You might discover more items to add to this list. I once helped someone with a drive error. We took the 3½-inch disk out of the drive and opened the shuttle window (the spring-loaded metal cover that opens to reveal the disk inside the plastic housing) to find a blade of grass on the disk surface. We removed the grass, and the disk worked perfectly. She then remembered that she had dropped the disk in the grass. When you have any computer trouble, check the simple things first. Here are a few suggestions for solving drive problems:

- Remove the disk. Does the shuttle window move freely? Do you see any dirt, hair, or blades of grass on the disk's Mylar surface? Does the disk spin freely inside the housing cover? Some new disks simply need a little loosening up. Put the disk back in the drive and try to access it again.

- Does the light on the correct drive go on? Maybe you are trying to access drive B, but the disk is in drive A.

- Does another disk work in the drive? If so, the problem is probably caused by the disk, not the drive. There is an exception to this statement. The drive might be out of alignment. If it is, the drive will be unable to read a disk that it did not format, although it might read a disk that it formatted with its own alignment. To test this possibility, try several disks, and note whether the drive reads only those disks that it has recently formatted. If so, then you might have identified the problem, and you probably will want to replace the drive.

- Does the drive light come on at all? If not, then the problem might be with the software or the hardware. Try to access the disk with other software. Can DOS access the drive with a simple DIR A: command? Can File Manager or Windows Explorer access the disk? How about using the CHKDSK A: command? If the light doesn't come on even then, consider the problem might be with the power to the drive or the hardware connections inside the case. Does the other drive work? If both lights refuse to come on, consider the power supply or the floppy drive controller card as the source of your problem.

- Has this drive been used recently? Perhaps the system setup has lost CMOS data. The system might think it has a 720 K drive when it really has a 1.44 MB drive. Access setup and check the drive specifications.

- Reboot the machine and try again. Many problems with computers disappear with a simple reboot. If a soft boot doesn't do it, try a hard boot.

- Try cleaning the drive's read/write heads. Use a head cleaning kit that includes a paper disk and a cleaning solution. Follow the directions that come with the kit. You can purchase a kit at any store that sells computer supplies.

- If the drive still refuses to work with any disk and any software, then you must dig deeper. Inside the case, the hardware that can cause this problem is the drive itself, the data cable from the controller card to the drive, the power supply, the power cable, or the systemboard. To find the culprit, replace each hardware component with a known good component, one component at a time, until the problem goes away. It is helpful to have access to another working computer from which you can borrow parts.

- Turn off the computer and open the computer case. Check every connection from the systemboard to the drive. Check the power cable connection. Remove the controller card. If the second drive works, there is a chance (but not a guarantee) that the problem is not the card or its connection. Using a clean white eraser, erase and clean the edge connector and reseat the board.

- Take the power cable from the second working floppy drive and put it on the nonworking one to eliminate the power cable as the problem.

- Replace the data cable and try the drive again. Exchange the controller card. If that does not work, exchange the drive itself and try again.

- If the drive still does not work, suspect the systemboard or the ROM BIOS on the systemboard.

Some Common Error Messages and Their Meanings

Here are some common floppy disk error messages and explanations of what they mean.

```
Non-system disk or disk error. Replace and strike any key
when ready.
```

This message says that you are booting from a disk that does not have the OS on it. Remove the disk from the drive and press any key. The computer bypasses the floppy drive and loads the OS from the hard drive. If you really did intend to boot from the floppy drive, to boot DOS, the disk you are using should have been formatted with the /S option, or you should have used the SYS command to place the two hidden DOS system files on the disk together with COMMAND.COM. These three files are necessary to load DOS. To boot from a rescue disk in Windows 95, create the rescue disk from the Control Panel. Double-click **Add/Remove Programs**, click the **Startup Disk** tab, and then click **Create Disk**.

If you had no disk in a drive, then you can assume that some of your critical OS files are missing from the hard drive. In this case, boot from a bootable floppy disk or rescue disk, and check whether the files have been erased accidentally from your hard drive.

```
Invalid or missing COMMAND.COM
```

This error appears when DOS is loading and the two hidden files are present, but COMMAND.COM is not present or is corrupt. Boot from a bootable disk that has COMMAND.COM and then copy the file to the disk that you want to be bootable.

Incorrect DOS version

This message appears when you try to use a DOS command such as FORMAT or BACKUP. These commands are called external commands in DOS, because they require a program to execute that is not part of COMMAND.COM. DOS contains a number of programs that reside on the hard drive in a directory named \DOS or, in the case of Windows 95, in a directory named \WINDOWS\COMMAND. Two of these programs are FORMAT.COM and ATTRIB.EXE. When you type the FORMAT or ATTRIB command, you are really executing these programs. DOS knows which version of DOS created each of these programs, and the error message is telling you that the FORMAT or ATTRIB program that you are using does not belong to the version of DOS that you presently have loaded.

Invalid Drive Specification

You are trying to access a drive that the OS does not know is available. For example, the error might appear under this situation: During booting, an error message appears indicating that BIOS cannot access the hard drive. You boot from a floppy disk in drive A and get an A prompt. You then try to access drive C from the A prompt, and you get the above message. DOS or Windows 95 is telling you that it can't find drive C because it failed the test during POST. As far as the OS is concerned, the hard drive does not exist.

Not ready reading drive A:, Abort, Retry, Fail?

This message means the disk in drive A is not readable. Maybe the disk is missing or is inserted incorrectly. The disk might have a bad boot record, errors in the FAT, or bad sectors. Try using Norton Utilities or PC Tools to examine the disk for corruption.

General failure reading drive A:, Abort, Retry, Fail?

This message means the disk is badly corrupted or not yet formatted. Sometimes this error means that the floppy drive is bad. Try another disk. If you determine the problem is the disk and not the drive, the disk is probably unusable. A bad master boot record sometimes gives this message.

Track 0 bad, disk not usable

This message typically occurs when you are trying to format a disk using the wrong disk type. Check your FORMAT command. Most manufacturers write the disk type on the disk. If you have a 3½-inch disk, you can tell if you are using a high-density or double-density disk by the see-through holes at the corners of the disk. The high-density disk has holes on two corners; the double-density has a hole on only one corner. Don't try to format a disk using the wrong density.

Write-protect error writing drive A:

The disk is write-protected and the application is trying to write to it. To write to a 3½-inch disk, the write-protect window must be closed, meaning that the switch must be toward the center of the disk so that you cannot see through the write-protect hole. To write to a 5¼-inch disk, the write-protect notch must be uncovered.

REPLACING A FLOPPY DRIVE

Replacing a disk drive is easy; here are the steps.

1. Check that the computer and other peripherals are working. Can you boot to the hard drive or another floppy drive? You should know where your starting point is.

2. Turn off the computer and remove the cover.

3. Unplug the data cable and power cable from the old drive. Unscrew and dismount the drive.

4. Slide the new drive into the bay. Reconnect the data cable and power cable.

5. Turn the computer on and check the setup. Test the drive. Turn the computer off and replace the cover.

Now let's look at each step in detail.

Check that the computer and other peripherals are working.   Can you boot to the hard drive or another floppy drive? You should know where your starting point is. Imagine yourself in the following situation. You are asked to install a floppy disk drive in a computer. You remove the cover, install the drive, and turn on the PC. Nothing happens. No power, no lights, nothing. Or perhaps the PC does not boot successfully giving errors during POST that appear to have nothing to do with your newly installed floppy drive. Now you don't know if you created the problem or if it existed before you started. That is why you check the computer before you begin and make sure you know what's working and not working. The extra time is well worth it if you face a situation like this.

Here is a suggestion for a quick system check of a PC before you start to work:

- Turn on the computer and verify that it boots to the OS with no errors.

- For DOS systems with Windows 3.x, enter Windows 3.x to be sure it works well.

- Using Windows 3.x or Windows 95, open a program and perform a task from the program.

- Get a directory listing of files on a floppy disk and a CD-ROM.

- For DOS with Windows 3.x, exit Windows and run the CHKDSK command.

- For Windows 95, do a ScanDisk.

Turn off the computer and remove the cover.   As you learned in Chapter 3, guard the computer against static electricity by leaving the PC plugged in, using a ground bracelet, working on a hard floor (not on carpet), and grounding yourself before you touch any components inside the case. *Never* touch anything inside the case while the power is on.

Recall that to remove the cover of a desktop case, locate and remove the screws on the back of the case. Look for the screws in each corner and one on top center as in Figure 4–12. Be careful that you don't unscrew screws other than these or you might inadvertently remove the screws holding the power supply in place (see Figure 4-13). After you've removed the cover screws, slide the cover forward and up to remove it from the case, as in Figure 4-14.

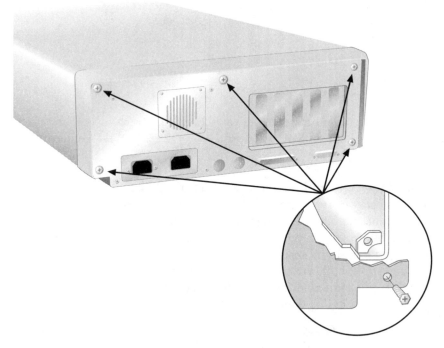

Figure 4-12   Locate the screws that hold the cover in place

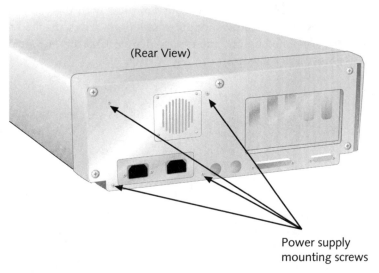

Figure 4-13   Power supply mounting screws

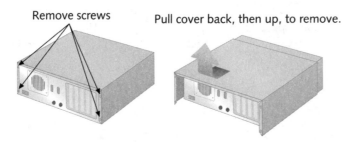

Remove screws   Pull cover back, then up, to remove.

Figure 4-14   Remove the cover

The screws are also on the back of tower cases. Look for screws in all four corners and down the sides. Remove them and then slide the cover back slightly before lifting it aside to remove it.

Unplug the data cable and power cable from the old drive.   Unscrew and dismount the drive. The data cable might go to an adapter card or directly to the systemboard. Before removing the cable, note that the cable has a color or stripe down one side. This edge color marks this side of the cable as pin 1. Look on the board to which the cable is attached. Verify that pin 1 or pin 2 is clearly marked as shown in Figure 4-15, and that the colored edge is aligned with pin 1 on both the controller card and the drive. Sometimes pin 1 on the floppy drive is marked and sometimes the drive housing is constructed so that the cable built for the drive inserts in only one direction. Note the position of pin 1 on the drive.

Look at the cable connecting drive A to the floppy drive controller card. There is a twist in the cable. This twist reverses these leads in the cable causing the addresses for this cable to be different from the addresses for the cable that doesn't have the twist. The cable with the twist is attached to drive A (see Figure 4-16). This drive is always the one that the OS looks to first for a bootable disk. By switching the cable with the twist with the cable without the twist, you exchange drives A and B. Some computers have both drives attached to the same cable. In this case, the drive attached behind the twist is drive A, and the one attached before the twist is drive B. Remove the cable from the floppy drive.

4

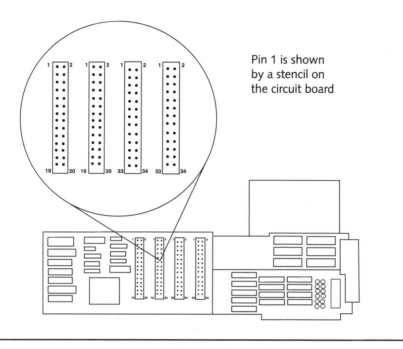

Pin 1 is shown
by a stencil on
the circuit board

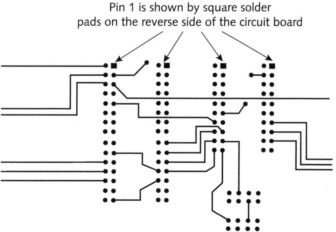

Pin 1 is shown by square solder
pads on the reverse side of the circuit board

Figure 4-15   How to find pin 1 on a circuit board

The power supply cable is a four-pronged cable that attaches to the back of the drive as in
Figure 4-17. The cable can be difficult to remove at times as the connection is very secure.
Be careful not to apply so much pressure that you break off the corner of the logic board.
Steady the board with one hand while you dislodge the power cable with the other.

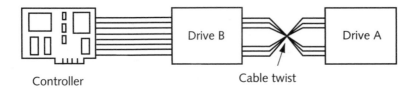

Typical PC floppy cable

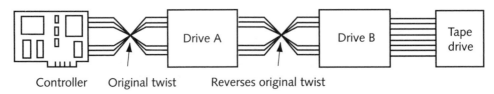

Figure 4-16   Twist in cable indentifies drive A

Remove the floppy drive next. Some drives have one or two screws on each side of the drive attaching the drive to the drive bay. After you remove the screws, the drive usually slides to the front and out of the case. Sometimes there is a catch underneath the drive that you must lift up as you slide the drive forward. Be careful not to remove screws that hold the circuit card on top of the drive to the drive housing; all this should stay intact.

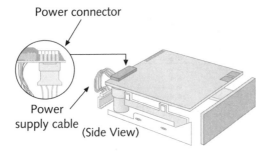

Figure 4-17   Power supply connection on the back of the drive

Slide the new drive into the bay. Reconnect the data cable and power cable. If the new drive is too narrow to fit snuggly into the bay, you can buy an adapter kit with extensions for narrow drives so that they reach the sides of the bay. Screw the drive down with the same screws used on the old drive. You might have difficulty reaching the screw hole on the back of the drive if it is against the side of the case. Make sure the drive is anchored so that it cannot slide forward or backward or up or down even if the case is turned on its side (as many users will do).

When you reconnect the data cable, make sure that the colored edge of the cable is connected to the pin 1 side of the connection as shown in Figure 4-18. Most connections on floppy drives are oriented the same way, so this one probably has the same orientation as the old drive. The power cable goes into the power connection only one way, so you can't go wrong here.

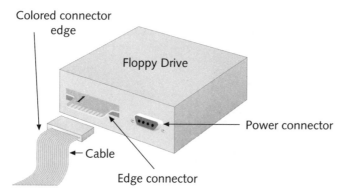

Figure 4-18   Connect colored edge of cable to pin 1

Turn the computer on and check the setup.   Test the drive. Replace the cover. Double-check all connections and turn on the computer. If you changed disk types, you must inform CMOS setup by accessing setup and changing the drive type. Test the drive by formatting a disk or doing a DISKCOPY. If you determine that all is well, replace the cover and you're done.

Note that you can run the computer while the cover is off. If the drive doesn't work, then it's much easier to turn off the computer, check connections, and try again. Just make certain that you don't touch anything while the computer is on. Leaving the computer on while you disconnect a cable and connect it again is very dangerous for the PC and will probably damage something.

Adding a New Drive

Adding a new drive is no problem if you have an empty bay, an extra power cable, and an extra connection on the floppy drive controller card. Slide the drive into the bay, screw it down, connect the cable and power cable, change setup, and you're done.

Let's consider the problems that might occur. If you don't have an extra power cable, you can use a "Y" splitter on the power cable for the existing floppy drive to provide the power connection. Most computers have only a single floppy drive cable with two connectors on it, one at the end of the cable and one in the middle.

In either case, look for the twist in the cable shown in Figure 4-19. The drive that is installed between the controller card and the twist is drive A. Drive B is the drive that is not between the twist and the controller card. Most computers are set up to boot from either drive C or drive A at startup. Therefore, it is important that you install the cable with the twist on the drive that you want to boot from when you are not booting from the hard drive.

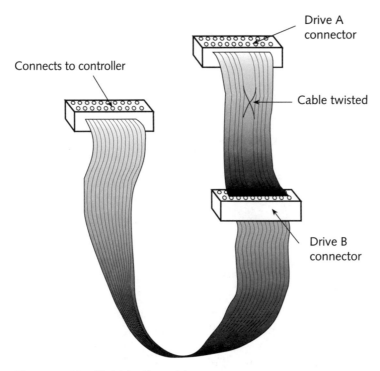

Drive A
connector

Connects to controller

Cable twisted

Drive B
connector

Figure 4-19   Twist in the cable

In most cases, you also want to orient the drives so that drive A is on the left or on the top and drive B is on the right or on the bottom. The computer really doesn't care where the drives are located; it's looking only for the twist in the cable. It is easier for you to have them placed this way. If you have an A and B drive, you can exchange the drives to be B and A simply by exchanging the data cables.

If you have a damaged floppy disk, there is much you can do to recover most, if not all, the data on the disk, especially when you understand how the data is stored and have the right tools for the job. These techniques are covered in Chapter 6.

KEYBOARDS

Computer keyboards have been criticized by users who work with them for hours at a time because they can cause a type of repetitive stress injury (RSI) known as carpal tunnel syndrome (CTS). CTS results from keeping the wrists in an unnatural position and having to execute the same motions (such as pressing keys on a keyboard) over prolonged periods of time.

You can help prevent carpal tunnel syndrome by keeping your elbows at the same level as the keyboard and keeping your wrists straight and higher than your fingers. I've found that a keyboard drawer that slides out from under a desk surface is much more comfortable because the keyboard is low enough for me to keep a correct position. If I'm working at a desk with no keyboard drawer, I sometimes type with the keyboard in my lap to relieve the pressure on my arms and shoulders.

Keyboards have either a traditional straight design or a newer ergonomic design shown in Figure 4-20. The word ergonomic means designed for safe and comfortable interaction between humans and machines. The ergonomically safer keyboard is designed to keep your wrists high and straight. Some users find it comfortable and others do not. Figure 4-21 demonstrates the correct position of hands and arms at the keyboard. Keyboards also differ in the feel of the keys as you type. Some people prefer more resistance than others, and some like more sound as the keys make contact. A keyboard might have a raised bar or circle on the F and J keys to help your fingers find the home keys as you type. Another feature is the depth of the ledge at the top of the keyboard that holds pencils, etc. Some keyboards have a mouse port on the back of the keyboard, and there are specialized keyboards with trackballs or magnetic scanners for scanning credit cards in retail stores.

4

Figure 4-20   An ergonomic keyboard

Keyboard manufacturers use one of two common technologies in the way the keys make contact: foil contact or metal contact. With a foil contact keyboard, when you press a key, two layers of foil make contact and close a circuit. A small spring just under the keycap raises the key again after it is released.

Metal contact keyboards are more expensive, heavier, and generally provide a different touch to the fingers than foil keyboards. Made by IBM and AT&T, as well as other companies, the metal contact keyboards add an extra feel of quality that is noticeable to most users. When a key is pressed, two metal plates make contact, and a spring is again used to raise the key once it is released.

Figure 4-21   Keep wrists high, straight, and supported while
at the keyboard

Keyboard Connectors

Keyboards come with one of two kinds of cable connectors. The larger connector (called a DIN connector from the German words meaning German national connector) uses five pins and the smaller connector (commonly called a PS/2 connector) uses six pins. Only four pins of each of these connectors are actually used. Table 4-10 shows the pin outs (position and meaning of each pin) for both connector types. If the keyboard you are using has a different connector than the keyboard port on your computer, use a keyboard connector adapter like the one shown in Figure 4-22.

Table 4-10   Pin Outs for Keyboard Connectors

Description	6-Pin Connector	5-Pin Connector
Keyboard data	1	2
Not used	2	3
Ground	3	4
Current (+5 volts)	4	5
Keyboard clock	5	1
Not used	6	–

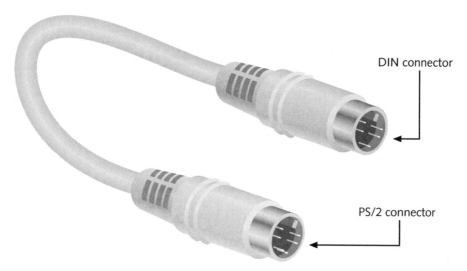

DIN connector

PS/2 connector

4

Figure 4-22   Keyboard adaptor

Regardless of the type of connection or the construction of the keyboard, when a key is pressed, the same logical progression occurs. When a key is pressed, a code is produced called the **make code**. Releasing the key produces the **break code**. A chip in the keyboard processes these codes to produce a scan code that is sent to the CPU. The chip determines the location of the key pressed and sends that location together with the IRQ to the CPU. The **scan code** is temporarily stored in the I/O address table. The keyboard driver, which is most often stored in the System BIOS, converts the scan code to the character assigned to that code based on the keyboard driver selected. The different drivers available to interpret scan codes vary by language.

COMPUTER VIDEO

The primary output device of a computer is the monitor. The two necessary components for video output are the video controller and the monitor itself.

MONITORS

The common types of monitors today are rated by screen size, resolution, refresh rate, and interlace features. There are still many older VGA (Video Graphics Adapter) monitors in use, but most sold today meet the standards for Super VGA. Monitors use either the older CRT (cathode ray tube) technology used in television sets or the new LCD (liquid crystal display) technology used in notebook PCs.

Most monitors use CRT technology, in which the filaments at the back of the cathode tube shoot a beam of electrons to the screen at the front of the tube, as illustrated in Figure 4-23. Plates on the top, bottom, and sides of the tube control the direction of the beam. The beam is directed by these plates to start at the top of the screen, move from left to right to make one line and then move down to the next line, again moving from left to right. As the beam moves vertically down the screen, it builds the displayed image. The control grid in front of the filaments controls what goes on the screen when the beam hits that portion of the line or a single dot on the screen by turning the beam on and off and selecting the correct combination of colors. Special phosphors placed on the back of the monitor screen light up when hit and produce colors. The grid controls which one of three electron guns are fired, each gun targeting a different color (red, green, or blue) positioned on the back of the screen.

When comparing and rating monitors consider the features discussed next.

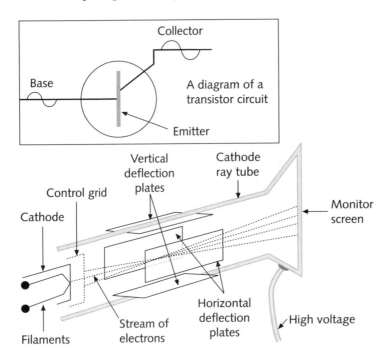

Figure 4-23   How a CRT monitor works

Screen Size

Common sizes of monitor screens are 14-inch, 15-inch, 17-inch, and 21-inch. There are special monitors for Macintosh computers designed for page layouts that are sized for legal-sized paper. The larger the screen size, the more expensive the monitor. The monitor I'm now using is advertised as having a 17-inch screen. The actual dimensions of the lighted screen are 9½ inches by 11½ inches. Its diagonal measurement is 15 inches.

Refresh Rate

The **refresh rate**, or vertical scan rate, is the time it takes for the electronic beam to fill the screen with lines from top to bottom. Refresh rates differ among monitors. The Video Electronics Standards Association (VESA) has set a minimum refresh rate standard of 70 Hz, or 70 complete vertical refreshes per second, as one requirement of Super VGA monitors.

Interlaced or Non-interlaced

Interlaced monitors draw a screen by making two passes. On the first pass, the electronic beam strikes only the even lines and on the second pass the beam strikes only the odd lines. The result is that a monitor can have a slow refresh rate and the overall effect is less noticeable than it would be if the beam hit all lines for each pass. Interlaced monitors generally have slightly more flicker than **non-interlaced monitors**, which always draw the entire screen on each pass. Buy a non-interlaced monitor if you plan to spend long hours staring at the monitor. Your eyes will benefit.

Dot Pitch

The **dot pitch** is the distance between each spot or dot on the screen that the electronic beam hits. Remember that there are three beams building the screen, one for each of three colors (red, green, and blue). Each composite location on the screen is really made up of three dots. The distance between these triads is the dot pitch. The smaller the pitch the sharper the image. A dot pitch of .28 mm or .25 mm gives the best results and costs more, although less expensive monitors can have a dot pitch of .35 mm or .38 mm.

Resolution

Resolution is a measure of how many spots on the screen are addressable by software. Each addressable location is called a **pixel** (for picture element). Because resolution depends on software, the resolution must be supported by the video controller card and the software you are using must make use of the resolution capabilities of the monitor. The standard for most software packages is 800 by 600 pixels, although many monitors offer a resolution of 1024 by 768 pixels. The resolution is set in Windows from the Control Panel and requires a driver specific for that resolution. Higher resolution usually requires more video RAM.

Multiscan Monitor

Multiscan monitors offer a variety of vertical and horizontal refresh rates. They cost more but are much more versatile than other monitors.

Green Monitor

A green monitor meets the EPA Energy Star program and uses 100 to 150 watts of electricity. When the screen saver is on, the monitor should use no more than 30 watts of electricity.

Video Controller Cards

Recall that the video controller card is the interface between the monitor and the computer. These cards are sometimes called graphic adapters, video boards, graphics cards, or display cards. Sometimes the video controller is integrated into the systemboard. If you are buying a systemboard with this integrated video controller, check that you can disable the controller on the systemboard if it needs replacement or gives you trouble. You can then install a video card and bypass the controller on the systemboard.

The two main features to look for in a video card are the bus it uses and the amount of video RAM.

The Bus Used by the Card

Pentium systemboards provide a 32-bit or 64-bit PCI bus for video. Older boards use a VESA local bus (VL-bus) for video, a proprietary local bus, or a 16-bit ISA bus. If you play computer games or use extensive graphics software, like that for CAD or desktop publishing, invest in a fast video card that uses a fast bus.

A **proprietary device** is a device made by a manufacturer specifically to interact with its other devices and is generally not easily interchanged with devices made by other manufacturers. Many older 486 PCs had proprietary 32-bit video buses that accommodated video cards made specifically for that brand of systemboard.

Memory on the Card

Data is temporarily stored in memory on a video card called video RAM, as it is passed from the systemboard to the monitor. The types of memory on a video card are DRAM and VRAM. DRAM is the same type of memory as that found on the systemboard. VRAM is faster than DRAM and more expensive. Plan on a minimum of 1 MB of video RAM or more if you want more color and higher resolution.

Large numbers of colors and high-resolution settings require more VRAM. For example, standard 640 by 480 VGA resolution requires 512 KB of VRAM on the video card. A Super VGA resolution of 1024 by 768 with 256 colors might require 1 MB of VRAM. The same resolution requires at least 2 MB of VRAM if the number of colors is more than 16,000.

POINTING DEVICES

A device that allows you to move a pointer around on the screen and perform functions such as executing (clicking) on a command button in applications software is called a pointing device. Common pointing devices are the mouse, the trackball, and touchpads (see Figure 4-24).

Figure 4-24   The most common pointing devices: a mouse, a trackball, and a touchpad

Inside a mouse is a ball that moves freely as you drag the mouse around on a surface. As shown in Figure 4-25, two or more rollers on the sides of the ball housing turn as the ball rolls against them. Each roller turns a wheel. The turning of the wheel is sensed by a small light beam as the wheel "chops" the light beam when it turns. The chops in the light beams are interpreted as mouse movement and are sent to the CPU. One of two rollers tracks the x-axis (horizontal) movement of the mouse and a second roller tracks the y-axis (vertical) movement. A mouse can have two or three buttons. Software must be programmed to use these buttons; few software packages use the third or center button. Almost all applications use the left button. Windows 95 has made great use of the right button.

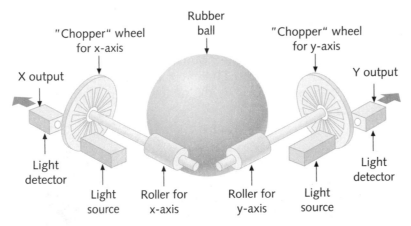

Figure 4-25   How a mouse works

A mouse is connected to the computer by one of three methods.

- By using the serial port (the mouse is then called a **serial mouse**)

- By using a dedicated round mouse port coming directly from the systemboard (**systemboard mouse** or **PS/2–compatible mouse**)

- By using a mouse **bus card** that provides this same round mouse port (**bus mouse**) as discussed above

The advantages and disadvantages of each connection type are based mainly on the resources they require because all three produce the same results; that is, the mouse port type is "transparent to the user."

The systemboard mouse is the first choice for most users. The port on the systemboard does not take up any resources that other devices might need. If you are buying a new mouse that you plan to plug into the systemboard port, don't buy a bus mouse unless the systemboard documentation states you can use a bus mouse. The systemboard port and the bus port are identical, but a bus mouse might not work on the systemboard port. Check with the systemboard manufacturer if you are not sure. A systemboard port will most likely use IRQ 12, and the I/O addresses will be 60h and 64h. If you have a systemboard port, use it. If it becomes damaged, then you can switch to a serial port or bus port.

The serial mouse requires a serial port and an IRQ for that port. Most people prefer a bus mouse over a serial port mouse because they can assign the serial ports to other peripheral devices. A bus mouse can use a bus card if the systemboard does not have a mouse port. The bus card usually allows you to select the IRQ and I/O address settings using jumpers on the card.

A track ball is really an upside down mouse. You move the ball on top to turn rollers that turn a wheel that is sensed by a light beam. Touchpads allow you to duplicate the mouse function, moving the pointer by applying light pressure with one finger somewhere on a pad that senses the x, y movement. Some touchpads allow you to double-click by tapping the touchpad's surface. Buttons on the touchpad serve the same function as mouse buttons. Use touchpads or trackballs where surface space is limited because they remain stationary when you use them. Trackballs are popular on notebook computers.

CLEANING THE MOUSE

The rollers inside the mouse housing collect dirt and dust and occasionally need cleaning. Remove the cover to the mouse ball from the bottom of the mouse. The cover usually comes off with a simple press and shift or turn motion. Clean the rollers with a cotton swab dipped in a very small amount of liquid soap.

4

CHAPTER SUMMARY

- The essential input/output devices on a computer are a floppy drive, a keyboard, a monitor, and a pointing device.

- Floppy disks are popular because they are cheap, convenient, and are now considered a standard device.

- Data is stored on floppy disks in concentric circles called tracks or cylinders. Each track is divided into sectors. Each sector holds 512 bytes of data.

- Different types of floppy disks vary according to the organization of tracks and sectors, the density at which data can be stored, and the intensity of the magnetic spot on the magnetized plastic surface of the disk.

- The smallest unit of space allocated to a file is called a cluster. On 3½-inch high-density disks, 1 cluster is the same as 1 sector, which is 512 bytes.

- When a disk is formatted for use, the formatting process creates tracks and sectors and places a master boot record, file allocation table (FAT), and root directory on the disk.

- Two hidden files and COMMAND.COM must be written on a disk for it to be a system or bootable disk.

- DOS, Windows 3.x, and Windows 95 all offer similar commands to manage files on a floppy disk.

- Installing a floppy disk drive in a PC involves firmly anchoring the drive in the bay, installing the controller card, connecting the data cable and power cable, and informing CMOS setup of the new drive.

- The computer distinguishes drive A from drive B by a twist in the data cable. The drive that gets the twist is drive A.

- Keyboards are most often selected for user comfort.

- Keyboard connectors can have either 5 or 6 pins. Adapters can easily be used to convert one connector type to the other to accommodate a keyboard using a different connector.

- A video subsystem includes a monitor and a video card controlling it.

- CRT (cathode-ray tube) monitors are rated according to several criteria including screen size, refresh rate, dot pitch, multiscan feature, energy conservation, resolution, and whether they use an interlaced or non-interlaced approach to refreshing the display.

- Features of video cards include the amount of VRAM on the card and which bus is used by the card.

- Most software programs require a pointing device. The most popular is the mouse. Trackballs are common on notebook computers, and touchpads are also used.

KEY TERMS

- **Break code** — A code produced when a computer keyboard is released. *See* Make code.

- **Bus mouse** — A mouse that plugs into a bus adapter card and has a round, 9-pin mini-DIN connector.

- **CHKDSK command** — A command that initiates checking of disk and RAM memory and displays possible problems (for example, CHKDSK C: is used to check drive C).

- **Cluster** — One or more sectors that constitute the smallest unit of space on a disk for storing data (also referred to as a file allocation unit). Files are written to a disk as groups of whole clusters.

- **Cluster chain** — A series of clusters used to hold a single file.

- **COPY command** — A command that copies files from one location to another (for example, COPY FILE.EXT A: is used to copy the file named FILE.EXT to the disk in drive A).

- **DEL command** — A command that deletes files (for example, DEL A:FILE.EXT deletes the file named FILE.EXT from drive A).

- **DELTREE command** — A command used to delete a directory, all its subdirectories, and all files within it (for example, DELTREE DIRNAME deletes the directory named DIRNAME and everything in it).

- **Directory** — A DOS table that contains file information such as name, size, time, and date of last modification, and the cluster numbers of the file's beginning location.

- **DISKCOPY command** — A command that copies the entire contents of one disk to another disk of the same type, while formatting the destination disk so that the two will be identical (for example, DISKCOPY A: A:).

- **ERASE command** — Another name for the DEL command.

- **File allocation table (FAT)** — A table on a disk that tracks the clusters used to contain a file.

- **File allocation units** — *See* Cluster.

- **Formatting (a floppy drive)** — To prepare a new floppy disk for use by placing tracks or cylinders on its surface to store information (for example, FORMAT A:). Old disks can be reformatted, but all data on them will be lost.

- **Fragmented file** — Files that have been written to different portions of the disk so that they are not in contiguous clusters.

- **Green monitor** — A monitor that is designed to conserve energy by using different techniques.

- **Make code** — A code produced by pressing a computer keyboard. *See* Break code.

- **Master boot record (MBR) (of a floppy drive)** — The record written near the beginning of a floppy disk, containing information about the disk as well as the startup operating system programs.

- **Multiscan monitor** — A monitor that can work within a range of frequencies, and thus can work with different standards and video adapters. It offers a variety of refresh rates.

- **Pixel** — Small dots on a fine horizontal scan line that are illuminated to create an image on the monitor.

- **RECOVER command** — A command that recovers files that were lost because of a corrupted file allocation table.

- **Rescue disk** — A DOS disk that can be used to start up a computer when the hard drive fails to boot. It must contain the system files IO.SYS, MSDOS.SYS, and COMMAND.COM, as well as diagnostic DOS programs to solve the boot problem.

- **Root directory** — The main directory on a disk (often represented as C:\ on a hard drive), which typically contains other directories, such as Windows and MSOffice.

- **Serial mouse** — A mouse that uses a serial port and has a female 9-pin DB-9 plug.

- **System board mouse** — A mouse that plugs into a round mouse port on the system board.

- **UNDELETE command** — A command that retrieves previously deleted files, provided that their locations have not been written over.

- **Video controller card** — A card installed in the computer to control the monitor.

- **XCOPY command** — A faster external DOS COPY program that can copy subdirectories(/S) (for example, XCOPY *.* A:/S).

REVIEW QUESTIONS

1. Use a calculator (or pencil and paper) to compute 2 to the 10th power (the exact size of a kilobyte). Use a calculator (or pencil and paper) to compute 2 to the 20th power (the exact size of a megabyte). Use a calculator (or pencil and paper) to compute 2 to the 30th power (the exact size of a gigabyte).

2. Assuming there are 512 bytes per sector, calculate the storage capacity for a floppy drive with the following: 1) 80 tracks and 18 sectors; 2) 40 tracks and 9 sectors.

3. How many root directory entries can be made on a 3½-inch high-density disk?

4. What is a cluster?

5. What three files must be on a floppy disk to make it bootable?

6. Give the complete DOS command to make a bootable floppy disk.

7. What is a file called that is not stored in consecutive clusters?

8. What DOS command checks both disk and RAM?

9. Give the complete DOS command to fix lost clusters.

10. What DOS command can be used to unerase a deleted file?

11. Give the complete DOS COPY command to make a second copy of AUTOEXEC.BAT called AUTOEXEC.JAN.

12. List the steps in Windows 95 to format a new system floppy disk using Windows Explorer.

13. List the steps to create a Windows 95 startup disk. (For help, click the **Start** button, **Help**, **Find** tab, and **Startup**.)

14. List all the files that are placed automatically on the startup disk.

15. What is the purpose of the file MSCDEX.EXE?

16. What is the purpose of the file MSD.EXE?

17. Why is EDIT.COM helpful to have on a startup or rescue disk?

18. List three physical components that you should check if a floppy drive does not work.

19. What might cause the error message: "General failure reading drive A, Abort, Retry, Fail?"

20. What does the SYS command do?

21. What would you check if your floppy drive light does not go on?

22. Give several reasons that might cause a computer not to read a disk in drive A.

23. How can you verify that a floppy drive data cable is correctly connected?

24. List the steps you would take to add a new drive B to a computer.

25. Give three strategies you can use to prevent carpal tunnel syndrome.

26. What is the smaller five-pin keyboard connector called?

27. What is a refresh rate?

28. Which is better, a smaller or larger dot pitch? Why?

29. When in Windows, what are three possible monitor resolution settings?

30. How is a bus mouse different from a serial mouse?

Projects

4

Unless you follow proper procedures, working inside your computer can cause serious damage—to both you and your computer. To assure safety in your work setting, follow every precaution listed in the *Read This Before You Begin* section following this book's Introduction.

FLOPPY DRIVE TROUBLESHOOTING AND INSTALLATIONS

1. Use a PC with A and B drives. Reverse the drives so that drive A is B and drive B is the new A. Test by booting from the new drive A. When you are finished, return the drives to their original assignments to avoid confusing other users.

2. Use a PC with only a drive A. First, verify that you can boot from drive A with a bootable disk. Then turn off the computer and open the case and examine the data cable to drive A. Look for the twist in the cable. Verify that the cable is connected to the drive so that the twist is in line. Change the cable so that there is no twist between the drive and the controller. Turn on the PC and try to boot from drive A again. Describe what happens. After you are finished, turn off the computer and restore the cable to its original position.

3. Reverse the orientation of the floppy drive cable connection to the floppy drive controller so that the edge connector is not aligned with pin 1. Boot the PC. Describe the problem as a user would describe it. Turn off the computer and restore the cable to the correct orientation.

4. In a lab setting, practice installing a floppy disk drive in a PC by working with a partner. Turn off the computer and remove a floppy drive from your PC and replace it with the floppy drive from your partner's PC.

5. Does the ROM BIOS for your computer support an extra-high-density 3½-inch disk drive? List the drive types it does support. (*Hint*: See your setup screen.)

6. Change the drive type in CMOS setup for one of the floppy drives on your PC to make it incorrect. (Make sure you don't change the hard drive type accidentally.) Reboot. What error did you see? Now correct the setting and reboot to make sure all components work again.

USING NUTS & BOLTS TO EXAMINE A FLOPPY DISK

Using the Nuts & Bolts utility on the accompanying CD, follow these directions to examine a floppy disk.

1. In Windows 95, click **Start**, **Programs**, **Nuts & Bolts**, and select **Discover Pro** from the list of utilities.
2. Click on the **Drives** tab. While the Drives tab is displayed, click on **Advanced**.
3. On the left side of the Discover Pro Advanced window, click on **drive A**. Print the Discover Pro report of the disk in drive A.

USING DIAGNOSTIC SOFTWARE

There is a diagnostic program called TestDrive from MicroSystems Development for examining and diagnosing problems with floppy drives and floppy disks. You can find a demo version on the Web that you can download from the company's site:

www.msd.com/diags/

When you download or copy the zipped file to your PC, explode it, and then do the following. (Most of the options on the TestDrive menu require that you have a DDD disk, but you can perform a few tests without one.)

Execute the TestDrive software by double-clicking the file **TESTDRIVE.COM** in Windows Explorer or File Manager. The menu shown in Figure 4-26 appears. Select the option to perform the Write/Read test. The warning box shown in Figure 4-27 appears. Perform the test with a disk that has nonessential data on it that can be erased. While the test is running, answer these questions.

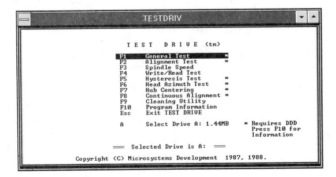

Figure 4-26   TestDrive main menu

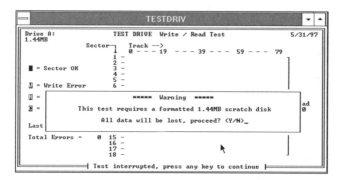

Figure 4-27   TestDrive's Write/Read Test

1. In what order is the disk tested—heads, tracks, or sectors?

2. Did you get any errors? If so, where?

3. If you got a significant number of errors, try another disk. Do you see a pattern of errors when moving from one disk to another?

WORKING WITH A MONITOR

1. For Windows 3.x, follow these directions to test different resolutions and font sizes on your monitor:

   - Make a backup copy of System.ini that you can use if you choose a display type that is incompatible with your monitor.

   - Using Windows 3.x, go to the **Control Panel** and display a list of the different resolutions available for your monitor and its drivers. Write down the current selection.

   - Try each resolution and font size available in the list.

   - If you make a mistake and select a resolution or a driver that is not compatible with your monitor, follow these directions to fix the problem.

     - Exit Windows and access the DOS prompt. Restore the System.ini file from the copy you made earlier.

     - If you did not make the backup and you made a mistake, you can still recover. From the C prompt, go to the Windows directory and type the SETUP command as follows:

       ```
       C:\WINDOWS>   SETUP
       ```

Select **VGA** as the display choice and then exit setup. Now go back to the **Control Panel** and change the setting to the one you wrote down before you started. If you didn't write down the setting, then you need to promise yourself that you'll be more careful next time! Keep trying one until you find out where your starting point was.

2. Using Windows 95, list the steps to change the monitor resolution. If you make a mistake when changing the monitor resolution, Windows 95 is much better about not allowing you to lock up your video than is Windows 3.x.

   ■ Double-click the **Display** icon in the Windows **Control Panel** and practice changing the background, screen saver, and appearance. If you are not using your own computer, make sure to restore each setting after making changes.

   ■ Pretend you have made a mistake and selected a combination of foreground and background colors that makes it impossible to read the screen. Solve the problem by booting Windows 95 into safe mode. Correct the problem and then reboot.

3. Windows 95 offers many new 32-bit video drivers for most video cards. When Windows 95 is first installed, it selects the driver for you based on the video card it detects. To see a list of available video drivers, follow these procedures:

   ■ Right-click the **desktop**, click **Properties** on the menu to open the Display Properties dialog box.

   ■ Click the **Settings** tab, which is shown in Figure 4-28. This is a "smart dialog box." The choices available depend on the resources you have on your computer.

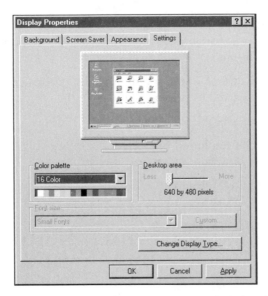

Figure 4-28   The Display Properties dialog box

- Change the resolution by using the sliding bar under **Desktop area**. The changes are immediate; you don't have to exit and re-enter Windows as you did in Windows 3.x. Make a change and then make the change permanent. You can go back and adjust later if you like.

4. To see a list of video drivers follow these steps:

   - Click the **Change Display Type** button on the **Settings** sheet to open the Change Display Type dialog box.

   - Click the **Change** button in the **Adapter Type** area. Note that you can choose between these two options.

   - Show compatible devices

   - Show all devices

   - Select each option above and note the differences in the lists. Write down the compatible models for the video manufacturer on the left side of the box.

5. Work with a partner who is using a different computer. Unplug the monitor in the computer lab or classroom, loosen or disconnect the computer monitor cable, and/or turn the contrast and brightness all the way down while your partner does something similar to his/her PC. Trade PCs and troubleshoot the problems.

6. Turn the PC off, remove the case and loosen the video card. Turn the PC back on and write down the problem as a user would describe it. Turn off the PC, reseat the card, and verify that all is working.

7. Insert a defective monitor adapter card provided by your instructor into a system. Describe the problem in writing, as a user would describe it.

TROUBLESHOOTING SKILLS

1. Create a bootable system disk in Windows 95. Boot from the disk. What version of the OS are you using? How can you enter Windows 95 from here?

2. Cause DOS to give you the error "Incorrect DOS version."

3. Troubleshoot keyboards that have been rigged with switched keys or loose cable connections.

4. Disassemble and clean a used or dirty keyboard (a chip puller is often an excellent key remover). Watch out for springs.

5. Remove a mouse ball. Using soap and water, clean the mouse ball. Using a toothpick, clean any debris from its rollers (do not use a knife!). Reassemble.

INTRODUCTION TO HARD DRIVES

In this chapter, Chapter Four's discussion of floppy disks and disk drives is extended to hard drives. You can apply much of what you learned about the way floppy disks hold and manage data to hard drives. Just like a floppy disk, a hard drive has a file allocation table (FAT) and root directory, and data is stored on the hard drive on tracks that are divided into sectors, each of which contains 512 bytes. Also, many Windows and DOS commands that manage files on a disk apply to hard drives. Because of its size and versatility, a hard drive has more complicated methods of formatting and maintaining data.

This chapter introduces hard drive basics and explains how to manage a healthy, previously installed hard drive. Different types of hard drives use different technologies, come in different sizes, and vary in their functionality. Hard drive options are described and removable drives are discussed. Chapter 6 continues our discussion of hard drives, examining installation, troubleshooting, and data recovery.

IN THIS CHAPTER
YOU WILL LEARN:

- How data is stored on a hard drive
- How to use DOS and Windows commands to manage data on a hard drive
- How to identify the various types of hard drives and understand the advantages of each
- How to manage a hard drive to get the best performance
- How to compare different removable drives

How a Hard Drive Is Physically Organized to Hold Data

Hard drives used in today's microcomputers have their origin in the hard drives of early mainframe computers of the 1970s. These drives consisted of large platters or disks that were much larger and thicker than phonograph records. Several platters were stacked together with enough room to allow read/write heads to move back and forth between the platters. All heads moved in unison while the platters spun at a fast speed. Applications programmers of the 1970s wrote their programs so that data was spaced evenly over the disks, so that the heads moved as little as possible while reading or writing a file. In today's systems, there are several layers of software between data stored on a drive or disk and the applications software that might be reading its data from or writing its data to the drive, so applications programmers do not need to concern themselves with how data is stored on a hard drive.

Hard drive structure and function has not changed, however. Modern hard drives have two or more platters that are stacked together and spin in unison. Read/write heads are controlled by an actuator and move in unison back and forth across the disk surfaces as the disks rotate on a spindle (see Figure 5-1). There are several types of hard drives for PCs, all using a magnetic medium; the data on all of them is stored in tracks and sectors. Just as with disks, data files are addressed on the hard drive in clusters made up of one or more sectors.

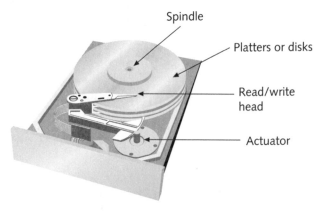

Spindle

Platters or disks

Read/write head

Actuator

Figure 5-1   Inside a hard drive case

Figure 5-2 shows a hard drive with four platters. All eight sides of these four platters are used to store data, although on some hard drives the top side of the first platter just holds information used to track the data and manage the disk. Each side or surface of one platter is called a **head**. The drive in Figure 5-2 has eight heads. Each head is divided into tracks and sectors. The eight tracks shown in Figure 5-2, all of which are the same distance from the center of the platters, together make up one cylinder. A cylinder is made up of eight tracks, one on each head, that have the same radius. If a disk has 300 tracks per head, then it also has that same number of cylinders.

5

Eight tracks (one
on each head)
make one cylinder

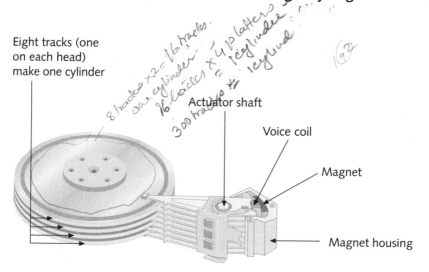

Figure 5-2   A hard drive with four platters

Data is written to the drive beginning at the outermost track, just as with disks. The entire first cylinder is filled before the read/write heads move inward and begin filling the second cylinder. Recall that the tracks closer to the center of a platter are smaller, but have to store the same amount of data as the larger tracks toward the outside of a platter. At some point as the heads move toward the center of the drive and the tracks get smaller and smaller, the read/write heads have to adjust the way they write data so that sectors store a consistent number of bytes, even if they are different physical sizes. Two methods can be used to adjust for the smaller tracks: write precompensation and reduced write current.

Write precompensation speeds up the writing of data to the drive as the tracks become smaller near the center of the platters. If a hard drive uses write precompensation, it indicates at what track or cylinder the precompensation begins. Appendix B shows that some drives don't use this method. Some tables list the write precompensation as the total number of cylinders for the drive type. Interpret this to mean that precompensation is not used.

Reduced write current means just what it says. At some cylinder near the center of the platter, the read/write heads reduce the current used to place magnetized spots on the disk because the spots are getting closer and closer together. Reduced write current is not as common as write precompensation.

HOW A HARD DRIVE IS LOGICALLY ORGANIZED TO HOLD DATA

As previously explained, hard drives contain circular platters that physically store formatting information and data in concentric circles called tracks, with each track divided into segments called sectors and with data near the center of the platter written closer together than data near the outer tracks. However, the OS reading and writing this data sees the organization of the hard drive differently. The OS is interested not only in how the data is stored physically, but also how it is stored logically. To the OS, data is stored in a long list of groups of sectors known as clusters. The BIOS managing the hard drive interfaces between the OS looking at its sequential list of clusters and the hard drive with its heads and cylinders. How the data is organized from the logical view of the OS and how the data is converted from the physical view to the logical view is discussed next.

HOW THE OS VIEWS DATA

Both DOS and Windows 95 store data in files, each of which is stored in a group of clusters. So, both operating systems view data on a hard drive as a long list of clusters that are organized into files. Each file is allocated a group of whole clusters and cannot share a cluster with another file. The OS uses two tables to keep track of which clusters are being used for a particular file together with other information about the file such as the filename, the length of the file, or whether the file is read-only or a hidden file. This high-level view of the file is all the OS needs to know. The physical location of the file is tracked by the BIOS or device driver managing the hard drive. Figure 5-3 shows the two tables, the file allocation table (FAT) and the directory, as the vehicles of exchange between the OS and the hard drive BIOS. The OS uses only one FAT for an entire logical drive but may have more than one directory on the drive. The main directory always present on a drive is called the root directory, but the root directory can have directories within it, called subdirectories in DOS or folders in Windows 95.

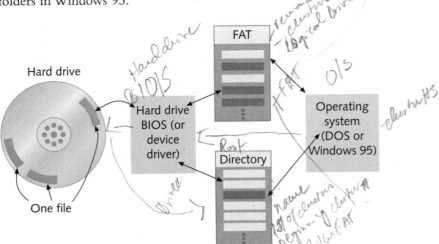

Figure 5-3 How the operating system views the hard drive when managing a file

Think of the OS as having a long list of clusters with which to work that it can use to store its files. In the directory, the OS stores the name of a file and the number of the first cluster allocated to that file together with other information about the file. The FAT is then used by the OS to track the remaining clusters allocated to the file. The OS knows only the cluster numbers that it has assigned to a file but has no idea where on the drive these clusters are physically located. When the OS requests BIOS to retrieve a file from the hard drive, the BIOS uses the directory to determine the beginning cluster number and the FAT to determine the remaining clusters to read. The BIOS knows where on the drive these clusters are physically located from the initial setup information about the drive and from the BIOS programming that addresses these clusters.

PHYSICAL DRIVES AND LOGICAL DRIVES

You might have a 1 GB hard drive that you recognize as only a single physical drive. But an OS can divide this single physical drive into more than one logical drive, which is called **partitioning the drive**. A **logical drive** is a portion of a hard drive that an OS views and manages as an individual drive. For example, a hard drive might be divided into three logical drives: drive C, drive D, and drive E, as shown in Figure 5-4. For a 1 GB drive, drive C might contain 500 MB, drive D might be allocated 300 MB, and drive E might be allocated 200 MB to account for the entire physical drive capacity. The information about the logical divisions within a physical drive is stored in the **partition table** at the beginning of the drive. One or more logical drives, sometimes called **partitions** or **volumes**, can be contained in a single partition. Even if the physical drive contains only a single logical drive, the drive must still be partitioned (in this case into only one logical drive), because the partition table is an important piece of information used by the hard drive BIOS. The partition table must be created when the drive is first installed. This is done with the DOS or Windows 95 FDISK command. Chapter 6 describes partitioning a hard drive in more detail.

When the drive is partitioned, the OS by default assigns a drive letter to the first partition. If there is only one logical drive assigned, and this is the first hard drive installed in the system, this one drive is called drive C. FDISK first creates a partition and then creates logical drives within the partition. FDISK assigns each logical drive a drive letter and creates a boot record, a FAT, and a root directory for each logical drive. For each partition, the FDISK program assigns a drive letter to the logical partition and creates a boot record, a FAT, and a root directory for that partition. The OS treats each logical partition as a logical hard drive. As far as DOS or Windows 95 is concerned, a physical drive divided into three logical drives, C, D, and E, is equivalent to three separate physical drives. The reason for this is that the OS manages a logical drive from the same high-level view whether it is a part of a physical drive or an entire physical drive: each includes a FAT, one or more directories, and files that the OS tracks by using these tables.

We now turn our attention to the directories the operating system maintains as well as the operating system's view of data stored in sectors and grouped into clusters, information that is used by the FAT. As we do so, however, we'll also relate the operating system's logical view to the translation of this information by BIOS into sectors physically located on the tracks and heads of the drive.

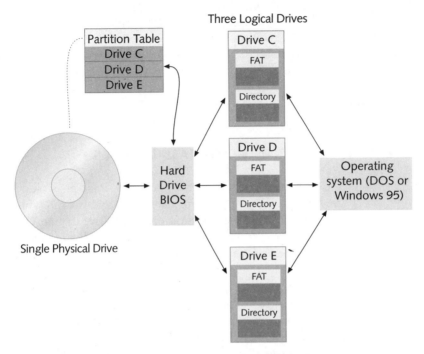

Figure 5-4   A single physical drive can be viewed by the operating system as one or more logical drives.

DRIVE CAPACITY

How much data can be stored on a hard drive? Recall that the OS views the data as groups of sectors of 512 bytes each. The number of sectors present on the drive determines the drive capacity. Each surface or platter on a hard drive is divided into tracks and sectors. All sectors in a track hold 512 bytes regardless of the radius of the track. Using this information, you can calculate the storage capacity of a drive. The table in Appendix B, "Hard Drive Types," lists the drive types first established by IBM and later added to by other companies. A computer's BIOS supports several drives from this list. For older hard drives having capacities under 528 MB, look at the specifications for the drive types in CMOS setup for the size drive you have. Because some drives are not on the list, most System BIOS programs permit a user-defined hard drive type. When you choose a user-defined drive type, you must tell the setup the number of heads, tracks, and sectors that the drive has as well as some other information, so that System BIOS knows how to address the drive. Most hard drives today are larger than 528 MB, and therefore require the user-defined hard drive type.

Notice in Appendix B that most earlier and smaller drives have 17 sectors per track. Later in the list are a few drives that have 26 sectors per track (see types 33, 34, and 37). Most drives today have more than 26 sectors per track. Even though the calculations below might seem to apply to ancient history with respect to hard drive capacity, the concepts and calculations apply to today's modern drives in the same fashion.

Now you will calculate the storage capacity of drive type 12 in Appendix B. The following table contains the information needed to calculate capacity:

Type	Number of Tracks	Number of Heads	Number of Sectors/Track
12	855	7	17

When you see an odd number of heads, you know that the first head is not used for data. The drive listed with seven heads really has eight surfaces or four platters, with the top surface of the top platter used to record the layout information for the entire drive. You calculate the capacity of the drive as follows:

855 tracks × 17 sectors/track × 512 bytes/sector = 7,441,920 bytes

There are 7,441,920 bytes on one surface or head of the drive. Therefore, the drive capacity is as follows:

7,441,920 bytes/head × 7 heads = 52,093,440 bytes

To convert bytes to kilobytes, divide by 1,024 as follows:

52,093,440 bytes × 1 K/1,024 bytes = 50,872.5 K

To convert kilobytes to megabytes, divide by 1,000 as follows:[1]

50,872.5 K × 1MB/1,024 K = 49.68 MB capacity

Let's work through one more example, for drive type 37. From Appendix B, the specifications are as follows:

Type	Number of Tracks	Number of Heads	Number of Sectors/Track
37	1,024	5	26

The capacity of this drive is calculated as follows:

1,024 tracks × 26 sectors/track × 512 bytes/sector × 5 heads = 68,157,440 bytes

68,157,440 bytes / 1,024 / 1,000 = 65 MB

Translation Methods

Later in the chapter we discuss the different hard drive technologies used in earlier years as well as those used today. In order to discuss the special problems introduced by large-capacity drives, however, it is necessary to introduce here a special concept used in hard drive technology, called translation. **Translation** converts or translates the addressing of sectors when the hard drive addressing system does not conform to what the System BIOS expects. For instance, if

---

[1] For hard drive capacity, some tables use the relation 1 MB = 1,000 K and others use 1 MB = 1,024 K. There are no standards; in fact, sometimes both relationships may be used in the same table to calculate drive capacity. A close look at Appendix B demonstrates the lack of consistency.

System BIOS expects a fixed number of sectors per track, but a hard drive has a variable number of sectors per track, then translation is used so that the System BIOS can access the hard drive correctly. **Translation methods** are used by some BIOS other than System BIOS (such as that on a hard drive controller) or it is used by software.

Translation is required under the following circumstances:

- When a drive uses zone bit recording
- On large-capacity drives

Translation for zone bit recording.   **Zone bit recording** is used in some drive technologies, such as IDE. While older hard drives (MFM and RLL) and all floppy disks use a constant number of sectors for all tracks on the drive (see Figure 5-5), zone bit recording does not use the same number of sectors per track throughout the drive. Figure 5-6 shows an example of zone bit recording where the number of sectors per track near the outer edge of the disk is greater than that near the center of the disk. Because the OS and the System BIOS expect the number of sectors per track to remain constant, either the hard drive BIOS or software must make a conversion, or translation, so the System BIOS can function. This translation presents the System BIOS with addresses that are consistent with what the BIOS expects. Different translation methods for handling zone bit recording are discussed later in the chapter.

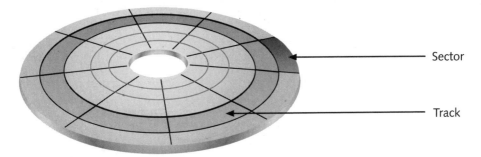

Figure 5-5   Floppy drives and older hard drives use a constant number of sectors per track

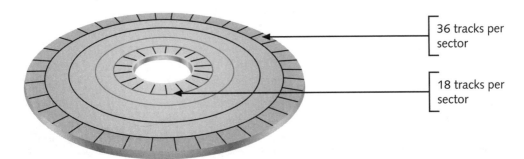

Figure 5-6   Zone bit recording can have more sectors per track as the tracks get larger

Translation for larger capacity drives.   Translation is needed for System BIOS to manage large-capacity hard drives. System BIOS was originally written to manage hard drives with a maximum capacity as follows:

- 1024 cylinders
- 16 heads
- 63 sectors/track and a constant number of sectors per track
- 512 bytes per sector

Following the calculations discussed above, the maximum size hard drive that traditional System BIOS can support is 528 MB, with only about 504 MB of this space available for data. Translation methods for large-capacity drives are used to circumvent this limitation and are introduced next. Of the limitations listed above, only the number of bytes per sector has remained as a set standard. All other limitations are exceeded by most new drives sold today.

Large-capacity Drives

Hard drives today for most PCs range from 1 GB to 2.5 GB in storage capacity, where GB stands for gigabyte and is $1,000 \times 1$ MB or 1,000 MB of storage, sometimes referred to as gig. Looking back at the above examples of calculating drive capacity for drive types 12 and 37, the number of tracks or cylinders is 855 on type 12 and 1,024 on type 37. Standard BIOS programs that access hard drive data assume that the number of cylinders on a drive never exceeds 1,024 and the program is written according to that assumption. Drives that exceed 1,024 cylinders and storage space of 528 MB are called **large-capacity drives**. A newer BIOS has since been written to accommodate the large-capacity drive and is called **enhanced BIOS**. Before you purchase a large-capacity hard drive for an older PC, look at the settings in CMOS to find out what size drive your BIOS will support. BIOS supports a hard drive in one of three ways:

- CHS (cylinders, heads, sectors) or normal mode
- "Large mode"
- Enhanced BIOS or LBA (logical block address) mode

CHS or Normal Mode.   **CHS** stands for cylinders, heads, sectors. It is the traditional method used by BIOS to read and write to hard drives by addressing the correct cylinder, head, and sector, and it requires no translation. This method is limited to 1024 cylinders, 16 heads, and 63 sectors per track, which means it works with a maximum hard drive capacity of 504 MB.

"Large Mode."   **"Large mode"** supports drives that range in capacity from 504 MB up to 1 GB. "Large mode" is a **"translation" method**, meaning that the location of the data on the hard drive is remapped to conform to the 504 MB barrier before the address information is passed on to the OS. A CMOS setting for this mode often reads either "large mode" or "translation".

Enhanced BIOS or LBA Mode.   **LBA** stands for **logical block addressing** and is a translation method that works somewhat like the FAT discussed in Chapter 4. Although the hard drive is really laid out in concentric circles on heads, this translation method—like all translation methods—masks that information from the OS by sending the OS an LBA number where each LBA is correlated with a particular cylinder, head, and sector number. For instance, an LBA equal to 0 means cylinder 0, head 0, and sector 1. So, the OS views the drive as a long linear list of LBAs and the hard drive BIOS translates each LBA number in the list to cylinder, track, and sector in a similar fashion to the FAT's translation of the linear list of clusters that the OS views into a location on the disk.

To know if your BIOS supports LBA mode for drives larger than 504 MB, look for CMOS settings like LBA, Mode, or Translation. Enable the setting for your large-capacity drive.

When BIOS Does Not Support Large-Capacity Drives.   If you want to install a large-capacity drive on a PC whose BIOS does not support it, you have the following choices:

- Upgrade the BIOS
- Upgrade the entire systemboard
- Use software that interfaces between the older BIOS and the large-capacity drive

Most large-capacity drives come with software on a disk designed to perform the translation between the older BIOS and the large-capacity drive. I have a 1.2 GB hard drive that came with a disk labeled Max-Blast Disk Manager 7.04. To use this software, I booted from the disk and followed the instructions on the screen. Doing this created a small partition or logical drive on the hard drive that stores the software to manage my new large drive for my older BIOS.

Some hard drives come with the disk manager software already installed on the drive. For a drive manufactured by Maxtor, the disk manager software is found in a directory called \MAX in a 112 MB partition that BIOS recognizes as drive C. The rest of the drive is assigned to other partitions or logical drives such as drive D or drive E.

If you upgrade BIOS, remember that the new BIOS must relate correctly to the chip set on the systemboard. Follow the recommendations of the systemboard manufacturer when selecting a BIOS upgrade.

Moving the Hard Drive or Changing BIOS.   When you move a large-capacity drive from one computer to another, there is a risk of losing the data. If you are using large mode on one computer and move the hard drive to a computer that is using LBA mode, you might lose access to the data on the hard drive. Also, the translation methods for LBA mode might not be the same from one BIOS to another. For this reason, back up the data on the drive before you move it. If the BIOS on the new computer does not allow you to access the data on the drive, you can partition and format the drive anew. (This procedure is explained in Chapter 6.) The data on the drive might be lost, but the drive will be available for the new PC.

If you have formatted and stored data on the hard drive using one mode and then enter setup and change to a different mode, you also might lose access to the data on the drive.

Returning to the correct mode might not solve the problem because changing modes can destroy data. To recover access to the hard drive, repartition and reformat the drive using the correct mode. You will regain access to the drive although the data will be lost. So don't change options in setup unless you are very sure of what you are doing.

THE FILE ALLOCATION TABLE (FAT)

As explained above, the OS manages files stored on a hard drive using a file allocation table or FAT. The FAT contains one entry for each cluster on the hard drive. A file is stored physically on a hard drive in one or more clusters. For DOS and Windows 3.1, each entry in a FAT for most hard drives is 16 bits or a convenient 2 bytes. Reading a FAT with whole-byte entries is much easier than reading a FAT for disks where each entry is 1½ bytes or 12 bits.

As with floppy disks, each entry in a hard drive FAT tracks the use of one cluster. The number of sectors per cluster varies from one hard drive to another. Use the CHKDSK command to display the size of one cluster. There is another way to determine the size of a cluster with a simple test. First, use the DIR command and note how much space is available on your hard drive. Then, create a text file containing only a single character. Using the DIR command again, note how much disk space is available and compare the two values, before and after a single one-character file is written to the disk. The difference in the two values is the size of one cluster, which is the smallest amount that can be allocated to a file. In the FAT entries discussed below, we are using a hard drive that has one cluster equal to four sectors. A cluster is, therefore, 512 bytes/sector × 4 sectors/cluster or 2,048 bytes.

Figure 5-7 shows a sample FAT with the clusters for two files recorded in the table. The first file uses 17 clusters and begins with cluster 2 and continues to cluster 18. The second file begins with cluster 19 and ends with cluster 37. Each cluster contains the number of the next cluster used by the file except the last cluster in the file, which contains an end-of-file marker.

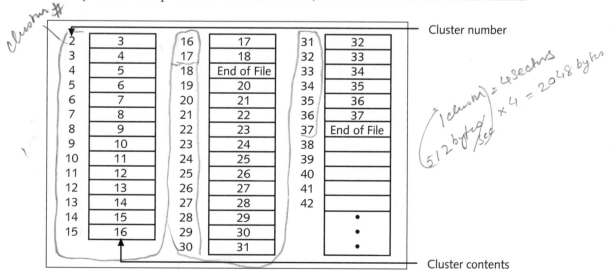

Figure 5-7   FAT showing two files

Behind the Scenes Technology: FAT

This section explains how the FAT actually appears on the hard drive. This technical discussion is optional. You can skip it and proceed to the section on the virtual file allocation table. However, if you are interested in gaining a better understanding of the information in FAT, read on.

Using DEBUG.   The DOS and Windows 95 DEBUG utility is a tool that displays for you the hex values of the FAT as well as other areas of the hard drive. This information appears exactly as it is written to the drive. You can also use higher-level utility software such as Norton Utilities or PC Tools to view FAT information in an easier-to-read format. If you understand the layout of the FAT at this hex level, later when you use Nuts & Bolts, Norton, or PC Tools to recover a damaged FAT you will have a significant edge over others who merely know how to use the software.

Using DEBUG is not difficult if you grasp one concept: DEBUG is an editor. It is just like any other editor except that it displays and works with hex values rather than filenames or numbers or other familiar terminology. For instance, when you use Notepad to open a file and edit it, these events occur: The file is "opened" by copying it from the hard drive or disk into memory. Notepad displays the contents of memory to you and allows you to edit what is in memory. When you "save" the file, Notepad copies the contents of memory back to the floppy disk or hard drive. DEBUG performs similar functions, but the commands are written differently. DEBUG works beyond the concept of a file, looking directly at the bits stored in sectors on the hard drive, converting them to hex before displaying them. DEBUG "opens" a sector by copying the sector from the disk or hard drive into memory and then displaying the contents of memory. You must tell DEBUG which sector to read from the drive and which memory addresses to copy the sector into. You can display and edit the contents of these memory addresses and then command DEBUG to copy the contents of memory back to the drive, which is similar to the "save" concept in Notepad.

The advantages of using DEBUG are that (1) you circumvent the limitation placed on you by the OS and software applications, which only let you view files; and with DEBUG, you can look at any sector on the hard drive or disk regardless of its function; and (2) by viewing critical sectors that are used to organize the data on a hard drive, you gain knowledge invaluable to you when using Nuts & Bolts, Norton Utilities, and PC Tools to recover the data on a damaged hard drive or floppy disk.

Table 5-1 compares the functions of Notepad and DEBUG to further help you become comfortable with this interesting tool.

Table 5-1   Notepad and DEBUG are both Editors

Notepad Function	DEBUG Function	Description
Open a file (use the **File**, **Open** command)	Copy a sector from disk to specified memory addresses. (Use the **L** or **Load** command.)	Gives you a "snapshot" of data written on a disk.
Display contents of file now stored in memory (Notepad does this automatically).	Display the contents of the memory addresses above. (Use the **D** or **Dump** command.)	Displays contents of memory.
Edit a file	Change the contents of memory. (Use the **E** or **Enter** command.)	Changes the data displayed that is stored in memory but does not change the data on the disk.
Save or close a file. (Use the **File**, **Save** or **File**, **Close** command.)	Write the contents of memory back to the disk. (Use the **W** or **Write** command.)	Writes data from memory to disk.

Viewing the FAT with DEBUG.   Figure 5-8 is a screenshot of the beginning of a 16-bit FAT for a hard drive created using DEBUG. The FAT contains the same two files that are in the FAT in Figure 5-7. Compare the two figures as you read this section and notice precisely what the FAT looks like to BIOS and the OS. The memory dump displayed in Figure 5-8 was created using the DEBUG utility with these commands:

Command	Description
`C:\>DEBUG`	Execute DOS DEBUG.
`-L9000:0 2 1 1`	Load into memory addresses beginning with 9000:0 from drive 2 (drive C) beginning with sector 1 and reading 1 sector.
`-D9000:0`	Dump the contents of memory beginning at 9000:0.

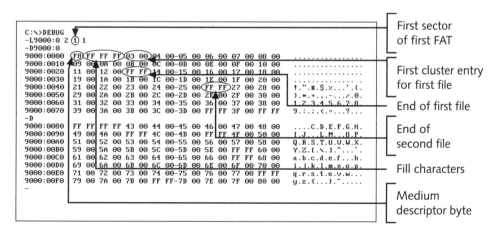

Figure 5-8   Beginning of a FAT on a hard drive

Here is what the data in the dump means. The first byte in Figure 5-8 is F8, the byte that identifies what medium a hard drive is made of. The next three bytes are FF FF FF, which indicate the beginning of the FAT. Each of the following entries in the FAT uses two bytes. The next few bytes describe the location of the first file on the disk, which begins at cluster 2. The entry for cluster 2 is 03 00. Because the contents of memory are written from right to left, you must reverse the order of the two bytes to read the cluster number. Thus, you read the 03 00 entry as 00 03, which means that the next cluster used by this file is cluster 3. The file occupies 17 clusters, ending at cluster 12h with FF FF, which indicates the end of the file. The clusters used, then, are numbered 2 through 12 (hex) or 2 through 18 (decimal). This file occupies 2,048 bytes/cluster × 17 clusters or 34,816 bytes of disk space. In a later section, we look at the file's entries in the root directory.

In Figure 5-8 the next file begins at cluster 13h and continues through cluster 25h. A quick count shows that this second file occupies 19 clusters, which equal 2,048 bytes/cluster × 19 clusters or 38,912 bytes of disk space.

The FAT begins at sector 1. This particular hard drive has 1,024 cylinders, 17 sectors per track, and 12 heads. (To find out how many cylinders, sectors per track, and heads your hard drive has so that you can make similar calculations, see your CMOS setup.) How many individual sectors and how many clusters are there, and how long is the FAT in the example discussed here? You calculate as follows:

1,024 tracks × 17 sectors/track × 12 heads = 208,896 sectors

208,896 sectors / 4 sectors per cluster = 52,224 clusters

This hard drive can accommodate only 52,224 files and subdirectories, which equal the total number of clusters. Each cluster has a 2-byte entry in the FAT, making the size of the FAT as follows:

52,224 FAT entries × 2 bytes/FAT entry = 104,448 bytes

104,448 bytes / 512 bytes per sector = 204 sectors

A hard drive keeps two copies of the FAT, just as disks do, so you can expect the second copy of the FAT to begin at sector 205. Use DEBUG to verify your calculation. To use the Load command in DEBUG, you must convert 205 to hex, which is cdh. You can use these commands to display the second copy of the FAT shown in Figure 5-9.

```
C:\>DEBUG-L9000:0 2 cd 1
```

Execute DEBUG. Load into memory beginning with memory address 9000:0 the contents of disk 2 (drive C) beginning with sector cdh and continuing for 1 sector.

```
-D9000:0
```

Dump the contents of memory beginning with 9000:0.

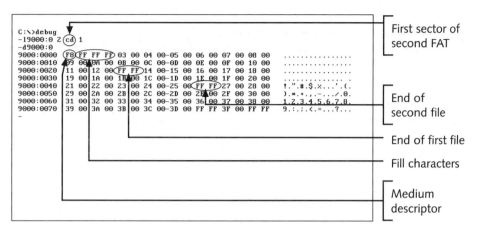

Figure 5-9   Second copy of FAT

The Virtual File Allocation Table (VFAT)

Windows 95 features a special version of the FAT called VFAT or virtual file allocation that helps Windows 95 accommodate long filenames. In Windows for Workgroups, VFAT is called 32-bit file access. In Windows 95, it supports filenames up to 256 characters. As you learned in Chapter 4, the filename and extension are stored in the root directory or a subdirectory list. Each entry in the directory is 32 bytes long, and each 32-byte entry is called a **block**. Long filenames require more than one block in the directory. When the OS allocates additional blocks for the long filenames, it stores the information in the VFAT. The VFAT records how many blocks are allocated for each file listed in the directory.

The VFAT is really a variation of the original DOS 16-bit FAT. It's a *virtualized* 32-bit FAT, meaning that it's not a *real* 32-bit FAT. A reserved area of the FAT keeps directory block information for long filenames. Some DOS-based disk utility programs can damage the VFAT entries that refer to the directory block information. Even a simple DEL command under OS/2 for a FAT entry can leave the extra blocks in the directory used to hold the long filename unavailable for later use. The Windows 95 SCANDISK utility can recover these unreleased blocks in the directory and the references to them in the VFAT.

THE ROOT DIRECTORY

The layout of the root directory is the same for hard drives as for floppy disks, discussed in Chapter 4. For convenience, the layout of a directory entry is repeated in Table 5-2. Note that there are 10 unused bytes between the attribute byte and the time-of-creation bytes. The total number of bytes for each file is 32.

Table 5-2   Root Directory Information for Each File

Bytes	Description
8	Name of file
3	File extension
1	Attribute byte (special meaning for each bit)
10	Unused
2	Time of creation or last update
2	Date of creation or last update
2	Starting cluster number in binary
4	Size of file in binary

The time and date are stored as integers according to these accepted calculations:

- time = $2048 \times$ hours + $32 \times$ minutes + seconds/2
- date = $512 \times$ (year − 1980) + $32 \times$ month + day

The attribute byte has a special meaning for each bit, as listed in Table 5-3.

Table 5-3   File Attributes as Listed in the Directory Attribute Byte
(Reading from left to right across the byte)

Bit	Description	Bit = 0	Bit = 1
1, 2	Not used		
3	Archive bit	Not to be archived	To be archived
4	Directory status	File	Subdirectory
5	Volume label	Not volume label	Is volume label
6	System file	Not system file	Is system file
7	Hidden file	Not hidden	Hidden
8	Read-only file	Read/write	Read-only

The OS creates the root directory when it formats the drive, and this directory has a fixed number of entries. The number of entries in a subdirectory, however, is not limited. The fixed length of the root directory for current versions of DOS and Windows is 512 entries; early versions of DOS allowed fewer entries in the root directory. Note, however, that the OS manuals recommend that you keep only about 150 entries in any one directory. Any more slows access to the directory. The number of entries in the root directory is stored in the boot record of the hard drive. Using long filenames reduces the number of files that can be stored in this fixed number of entries in the root directory because the long filenames require more than one entry in the directory.

Behind the Scenes Technology: The Root Directory

The root directory is written on a hard drive immediately after the second copy of the FAT. For the hard drive FAT shown in Figure 5-9, the second copy of the FAT ends at sector 408, and the root directory begins at sector 409, which is 199h. The dump of the beginning of a root directory is shown in Figure 5-10. You saw in Figure 5-8 that the first file on this hard drive occupies 34,816 bytes of disk space and begins at cluster 2. The second file on the hard drive begins at cluster 13h and occupies 38,912 bytes of disk space. You would expect this information to be confirmed by entries in the root directory. Looking at Figure 5-10, you can see that the entries for the first two files are as shown in Table 5-4.

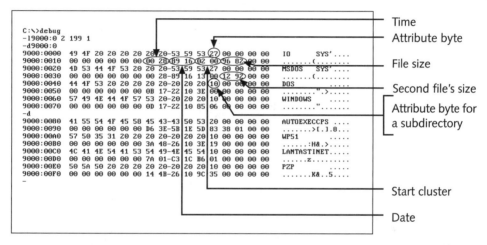

Figure 5-10   A root directory

Table 5-4   Example of Directory Entries for First Two Files in Root Directory

	File 1	File 2
Filename	IO	MSDOS
File extension	SYS	SYS
Attribute byte	27=0010 0111	27=0010 0111
Time	00 28	00 28
Date	89 16	89 16
Starting cluster number	00 02	00 13
Size of file	96 82	12 92

The hard drive is loaded with DOS and Windows 3.1. Not surprisingly, then, the first two files stored on this disk are the two DOS hidden files used to boot DOS. The attribute byte is interpreted as it was for floppy disks (see Chapter 4). In Table 5-3 you can, therefore, deduce that the two files are system files that are not to be archived, and that they are hidden, read-only files.

According to what you saw in the directory entry, the first file begins at cluster 2, and its size is written as 96 82. First reverse the bytes and then convert the hex number to decimal. The calculations for the hex number 8,296 are as follows:

$$8 \times 4,096 \ = \ 32,768$$

$$2 \times 256 \ = \ 512$$

$$9 \times 16 \ = \ 144$$

$$6 \times 1 \ = \ 6$$

TOTAL: 33,430

You saw from the directory entry that this file occupies 17 clusters x 2,048 bytes/cluster or 34,816 bytes of disk space. The unused part of the last cluster is the wasted space. The second file shows a size of 9,212h bytes, which is 37,394 in decimal. The file requires 19 clusters or 38,912 bytes of space.

Some entries in the root directory are subdirectories rather than files. The third entry in Figure 5-10 is the \DOS subdirectory. Note that the attribute byte for this entry is 10h or 0001 0000 in binary. Table 5-3 shows that having the fourth bit on and all other bits off indicates a subdirectory entry. The starting cluster number for this entry is 00 3E, which is the beginning of the directory table for the \DOS subdirectory. It would be interesting to dump this sector of the hard drive and read this directory. Also note that the size of the file is zero for a subdirectory entry because DOS does not use this information.

You have seen that the root directory begins at logical sector 409. Where does it end and where do data files begin? To calculate this, you need to know that there is room for 512 entries or blocks and that each entry is 32 bytes long. The root directory, then, occupies 512 entries × 32 bytes/entry = 16,384 bytes. To convert bytes to sectors, you divide 16,384 by 512 and see that the root directory is exactly 32 sectors long. Adding that to the starting sector 409, you find that the root directory ends at the 440th sector and the data files begin at sector 441. In the FAT, sector 441 is named cluster 2. Therefore, to read a cluster number in the FAT table and to convert this number to a logical sector number on the hard drive you must use the following conversion expression, where 4 is the number of sectors in one cluster:

(cluster number − 2) × 4 + 441 = sector number

Examining the information at the beginning of a hard drive can be tedious, but knowledge is power. You will see in Chapter 6, that when you recover data from a damaged hard drive, skills learned here will make your work much easier.

USING DOS TO MANAGE A HARD DRIVE

The DOS commands you use to manage a hard drive are described in this section, along with examples of how to use them. For more extensive discussions, see the *DOS User's Guide and Reference Manual*, or at the DOS prompt type HELP followed by the name of the command. After discussing the DOS commands, we describe these same functions in Windows 3.x and Windows 95.

MKDIR [DRIVE:]PATH OR MD [DRIVE:]PATH COMMAND

The MKDIR (abbreviated MD) command creates a subdirectory entry in a directory. You have seen what happens behind the scenes when this command is executed, which is that DOS creates an entry in the subdirectory of the directory table. Think of a subdirectory as a list within a list, much like the hierarchy of an outline or a company organizational chart. In an outline, there are major categories and under some of these major categories more detailed subordinate items are listed. Parent directories are equivalent to the major categories. These parent directories can have subordinate directories or subdirectories listed within them. When you move to these subdirectories, you see another list. This list too can have subdirectories.

You can use subdirectories to organize and categorize files. Long lists of unrelated items are tedious and difficult to manage. Putting related files under a single subdirectory heading simplifies your work. Because it is confusing to have more than one software package in the same directory, put each software package in its own subdirectory. Data that is created by a software package should not be put in the same directory as the software itself, for several reasons. If you are creating, copying, or deleting data files, you are less likely to erase or overwrite a software file if the data is in a different directory. Also, there is no question later about which files are data files and which are software files.

Another reason to keep data in one directory and the software in another is that it makes backing up easier. As soon as you have installed a software package and confirmed that it is working properly, back up the entire directory containing the software to disk or tape. This one backup of the software is all that's necessary unless you make a change to the software. The data, however, needs backing up as soon as you have several hours invested in it. If the data changes often, make regular backups. How often depends on how much data is changed and when it is changed. If the data is in its own directory, you can easily back up just that directory instead of having to back up the software with the data.

It's good practice to create a data directory as an entry in the software directory that manages that data. The software directory is called the **parent directory**, and the data directory is called a **child directory**. Just as with outlines, you commonly say that the child directory is "under" or subordinate to the parent directory. When viewing the directory structure, it is easy, then, to see which data files belong to which software.

MKDIR Syntax and Some Examples

When using the MKDIR command, you need not specify the drive if the drive is the current default drive, and you need not specify the parent directory if it is the current default directory. To create a directory named \GAME on drive C, for example, use this command:

```
MKDIR C:\GAME
```

The backslash indicates the directory is under the root directory. To create a directory named CHESS under the \GAME directory, use this command:

MKDIR C:\GAME\CHESS

DOS requires that the parent directory GAME must already exist before it can create the child directory CHESS.

Figure 5-11 shows the result of the DIR command on the directory \GAME. Note the two initial entries in the directory table, the . (dot) and the .. (dot, dot) entries. These two entries are created by the MKDIR command when DOS initially sets up the directory. You cannot edit these entries with normal DOS commands, and they must remain in the directory for the directory's lifetime. The . entry points to the subdirectory itself, and the .. entry points to the parent directory; in this case, the root directory.

```
C:\>DIR \GAME /P

 Volume in drive C has no label
 Volume Serial Number is 0F52-09FC
 Directory of C:\GAME

 .              <DIR>      02-18-93    4:50a
 ..             <DIR>      02-18-93    4:50a
 CHESS          <DIR>      02-18-93    4:50a
 NUKE           <DIR>      02-18-93    4:51a
 PENTE          <DIR>      02-18-93    4:52a
 NETRIS         <DIR>      02-18-93    4:54a
 BEYOND         <DIR>      02-18-93    4:54a
        7 file(s)             0 bytes
                       9273344 bytes free

C:\>
```

Figure 5-11 DIR of the \GAME directory

Behind the Scenes Technology: Subdirectories

In Figure 5-12 you see the DEBUG dump of the \GAME directory table. Note that the . and .. entries look just like file and subdirectory entries. Both show 10 or 0001 0000 as their attribute byte, indicating they are subdirectory entries rather than files. The starting cluster number of the . entry is 00 41, which is equal to 65 decimal. This byte marks the beginning of this directory table. The same 00 41 cluster number is found in the root directory as the starting cluster number of the \GAME directory. To use the DEBUG command to create the screen in Figure 5-12, you need to locate this directory table. Convert the cluster number in decimal to the logical sector number according to the formula explained earlier:

$(65 - 2) \times 4 + 441 = 693$ (decimal) = 2B5 (hex)

The DEBUG commands used to view the subdirectory table in Figure 5-12 then look like this:

-L9000:0 2 2B5 1

-D9000:0

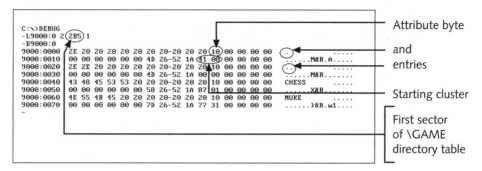

Figure 5-12 Dump of subdirectory table C:\GAME

CHDIR [DRIVE:]PATH OR CD [DRIVE:]PATH OR CD..

The CHDIR (abbreviated CD) command changes the current default directory. In its easiest-to-follow form, you simply state the drive and the entire path that you want to be current:

```
CD C:\GAME\CHESS
```

If you have previously issued the PROMPT PG command, either from the DOS prompt or from the AUTOEXEC.BAT file, the DOS prompt looks like this:

```
C:\GAME\CHESS>
```

To move from a child directory to its parent directory, use the .. variation of the command:

```
C:\GAME\CHESS> CD..
```

```
C:\GAME>
```

Remember that .. always means the parent directory. You can move from a parent directory to one of its child directories simply by stating the name of the child directory:

```
C:\GAME> CD CHESS
```

```
C:\GAME\CHESS>
```

Do not put a backslash in front of the child directory name; doing so tells DOS to go to a directory named CHESS that is directly under the root directory.

RMDIR [DRIVE:]PATH OR RD [DRIVE:]PATH

The RMDIR command (abbreviated RD) removes a subdirectory. Before you can use the RMDIR command, three things must be true:

- The directory must contain no files.
- The directory must contain no subdirectories.
- The directory must not be the current directory.

The . and .. entries are, however, still in a directory ready for removal. For example, to remove the \GAME directory in the above example, the CHESS directory must first be removed:

```
C:\> RMDIR C:\GAME\CHESS
```

Or, if the \GAME directory is the current directory, use this command:

```
C:\GAME> RD CHESS
```

Once you remove the CHESS directory, you can remove the \GAME directory. You must first leave the \GAME directory like this:

```
C:\GAME>CD..
C:\> RD \GAME
```

DELTREE [DRIVE:][PATH]

Remember that the DELTREE command deletes a directory and all the subdirectories under it along with any files they contain. Use with caution! For example, to delete the GAME directory along with the ..\CHESS directory and the files in both, use this command:

```
DELTREE \GAME
```

TREE [DRIVE:][PATH] [/F] [/A]

The TREE command displays the directory structure of a hard drive or disk. If you do not specify a drive or path, the TREE command displays the directory structure of the current drive and current directory. The command displays the structure in graphic form unless you include the /A option, which specifies text format. The /F option has the TREE command include the names of the files in a directory as well as the directory name.

For example, to display the subdirectory structure of the \WINDOWS directory with files also listed, one screen at a time, use this command:

```
C:\> TREE \WINDOWS /F | MORE
```

The |MORE option at the end of the command line causes the output of the command to be displayed one screen at a time rather than continuously scrolled.

To send the output to printer, use this command:

```
C:\> TREE \WINDOWS /F > PRN
```

ATTRIB

The ATTRIB command displays or changes the read-only, archive, system, and hidden attributes assigned to files. To display the attributes of the file MYFILE.TXT, use this command:

```
ATTRIB MYFILE.TXT
```

To hide the file, use this command:

```
ATTRIB +H MYFILE.TXT
```

To unhide the file, use this command:

```
ATTRIB -H MYFILE.TXT
```

To make the file a read-only file, use this command:

```
ATTRIB +R MYFILE.TXT
```

To remove the read-only status of the file, use this command:

```
ATTRIB -R MYFILE.TXT
```

To turn the archive bit on, use this command:

```
ATTRIB +A MYFILE.TXT
```

To turn the archive bit off, use this command:

```
ATTRIB -A MYFILE.TXT
```

MIRROR

The MIRROR command is an older DOS 5 command that still serves a very useful purpose, that of saving the partition table information to disk. To save partition table information to a disk, use this command:

```
MIRROR /PARTN
```

The MIRROR command was not included with DOS 6. If you are upgrading from DOS 5 to DOS 6, you may want to keep the command file for MIRROR in your DOS directory after the upgrade.

UNFORMAT

The UNFORMAT command not only reverses the effect of an accidental format, but also repairs a damaged partition table if the table has previously been saved with the MIRROR /PARTN command.

To unformat a disk, use this command:

```
UNFORMAT C:
```

To repair a damaged partition table if the table has previously been saved to a disk, use this command:

```
UNFORMAT /PARTN
```

PATH

As discussed in Chapter 2, the PATH command lists where DOS and Windows 3.x should look to find executable program files. This command is discussed here again to make the list of commands more complete. A sample PATH command is

```
PATH C:\;C:\DOS;C:\WINDOWS;C:\UTILITY
```

Each path is separated from the next with a semicolon. You should put the most-used paths at the beginning of the line because the OS searches the paths listed in the PATH command line from the left to right. The PATH command goes in the AUTOEXEC.BAT file.

USING BATCH FILES

Suppose you have a list of DOS commands that you want to execute several times. Perhaps you have some data files to distribute to several PCs in your office, and, having no LAN, you must walk from one PC to another doing the same job over and over. A solution is to store the list of commands in a batch file on disk and then execute the batch file at each PC. DOS and Windows require that the batch file have a .BAT file extension. For example, store these five DOS commands on a disk in a file named MYLOAD.BAT:

```
C:
MD\UTILITY
MD\UTILITY\TOOLS
CD\TOOLS
COPY A:\TOOLS\*.*
```

From the C prompt, you execute the batch file, just as with other program files, by entering the name of the file with or without the file extension:

```
A:\>MYLOAD
```

All the commands listed in the file will execute beginning at the top of the list. Look at any good book on DOS to find examples of the very useful ways you can elaborate on batch files, including adding user menus. AUTOEXEC.BAT is an example of a batch file.

USING WINDOWS 3.x TO MANAGE A HARD DRIVE

File Manager performs most hard drive management tasks for Windows 3.x. File Manager presents the tree structure of a hard drive, a floppy disk, or a CD-ROM. When you first enter

File Manager, you will probably see only the directories directly under the root directory. To see their subdirectories, single- or double-click the directory name.

Go to **File Manager** and click the **File** menu, which is displayed in Figure 5-13. The instructions that follow allow you to perform the same tasks discussed above for the DOS OS.

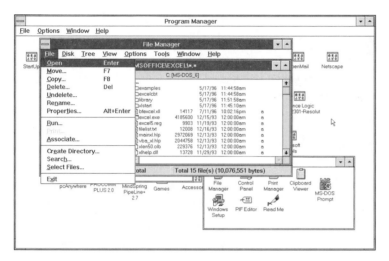

Figure 5-13   File menu in File Manager of Windows 3.1

Create Directory

To create a new directory under the File menu of File Manager (the equivalent of using the MD command in DOS), choose **Create Directory**. The dots at the end of a menu option indicate that more choices follow. Enter the name of the directory following the same rules you learned for DOS. For example, to create a directory under the \Games directory named Chess, first click the **\Games** directory to make it the current directory. Select **Create Directory** from the File menu. The dialog box in Figure 5-14 displays. Enter the name of the subdirectory, **Chess**, and click **OK**. C:\Games\Chess is created as shown in Figure 5-15.

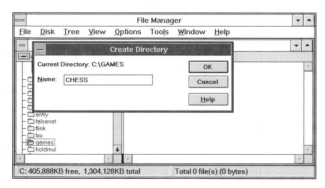

Figure 5-14   Creating a directory in Windows 3.1

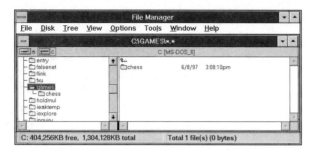

Figure 5-15 A new directory called chess is created under \GAMES

If you put a backslash in front of the word Chess in the dialog box, Windows ignores the current directory information and creates the directory Chess directly under the root directory.

Delete a Directory

To delete a directory, click the name of the directory in File Manager and then press the delete key. The dialog box in Figure 5-16 displays asking you to confirm the deletion. Click **OK** to delete the directory. Windows also deletes the files in the directory as well as any subdirectories under this directory along with their files.

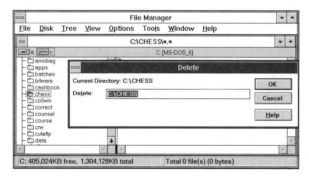

Figure 5-16 Deleting a directory

File Properties

The File Properties option in File Manager is similar to the DOS ATTRIB command. To display the properties of a file, first click the filename to select the file; go to the File menu and select **Properties**. The dialog box shown in Figure 5-17 displays. This dialog box shows you what the file attributes are and also allows you to change them. Click **OK** to save your changes or **Cancel** to exit without saving your changes.

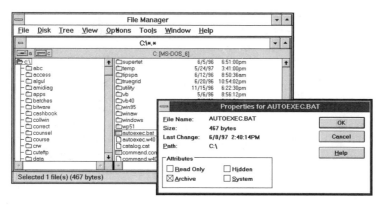

Figure 5-17   The properties of a file

The PATH Command and Batch Files

The PATH command is used by both DOS and Windows. Windows, like DOS, can also use batch files. Create a batch file with any text editor and then execute it by double-clicking the filename in File Manager.

USING WINDOWS 95 TO MANAGE A HARD DRIVE

Windows 95 Explorer is the primary tool for managing the files on your hard drive. Windows 95 calls a directory or subdirectory a **folder**. Open Explorer in Windows 95 (click **Start**, **Programs**, **Windows Explorer**, or right click **My Computer** and select **Explorer** from the menu) and follow the directions below to manage files and folders on your hard drive.

Create a New Folder

Select the folder you want to be the parent folder by clicking the folder name. For example, to create a folder named Chess under the folder named Games, first click the **Games** folder. Then click the **File** menu. Select **New** from the menu. Then select **Folder** from the submenu that displays as in Figure 5-18. The new folder will be created under Games, but its name will be New Folder. Click the folder name to open the text box and change the name of the folder. Change the name from New Folder to Chess as in Figure 5-19.

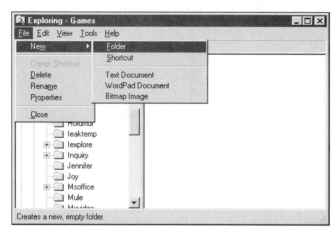

Figure 5-18   Create a new folder

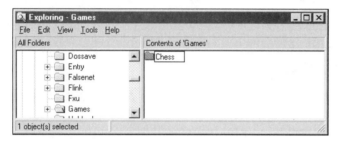

Figure 5-19   Edit the new folder's name

Delete a Folder

From Explorer, right click the folder and select **Delete** from the menu that appears. A confirmation dialog box like the one in Figure 5-20 asks you if you are sure you want to delete the folder. If you respond **Yes**, the folder and all of its contents, including subfolders, will be sent to the Recycle Bin. Empty the Recycle Bin to free your disk space.

File Properties

To access file properties in Windows 95, from the Explorer, right click a file and select **Properties** from the menu that appears. The Properties window appears as shown in Figure 5-21. Windows 95 identifies the file type primarily by the file extension. From the Properties window, you can change the attributes of the file.

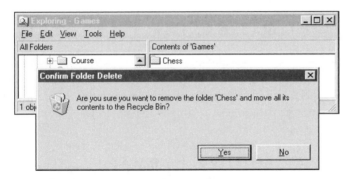

Figure 5-20   Delete a folder in Windows 95

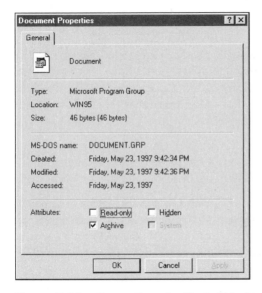

Figure 5-21   Properties of a file in Windows 95

The PATH Command and Batch Files

The PATH command in Windows 95 works just as it does with DOS and Windows 3.x. If you have an AUTOEXEC.BAT file in your root directory when Windows 95 starts, it reads the PATH command stored in that file. You can also store DOS commands in batch files and execute them from Windows 95 by double-clicking the filename of the batch file in Explorer.

Windows 95 uses a default path of C:\Windows; C:\Windows\Command if you don't have an AUTOEXEC.BAT file.

FORMATTING AND OPTIMIZING THE HARD DRIVE

In the first part of this chapter, you saw how data is stored on a drive from the perspective of the OS, which sees the drive as a long list of 512-byte sectors. This section will delve more deeply into drive technology, looking at how a drive is formatted, the different ways data is stored, and some ways to optimize data access.

LOW-LEVEL FORMAT AND OS FORMAT

Hard drives must be formatted twice. The low-level format lays the track and sector markings on the disk and the OS format puts the boot record, FAT, and root directory on the disk. With floppy disk drives, this is all done in a single format operation. With hard drives, the low-level format needs to be done before the OS can access the drive.

In Chapter 4, you saw that disks are simply blank sheets of coated Mylar until they are formatted by the OS. The formatted disk must be used by only one OS: the OS that formatted it. If Windows 95 formats the disk, for example, other operating systems like UNIX cannot make sense of the data the disk contains. For disks, this limitation is not serious because the disks can be exchanged easily and are inexpensive.

Often you will want to have more than one OS on a hard drive. One way to accomplish this is to create different hard drive partitions. One of the partitions, usually the first one, is designated the boot partition. System BIOS boots from this designated partition after POST.

Once the hard drive is divided into partitions, each OS can format its own partition, setting up a file management system. For example, if a hard drive has two partitions, one of them may be drive C and the other drive D. Each partition has its own OS boot record, two copies of its FAT, and a root directory, just like a disk. As far as the OS is concerned, drive C and drive D might as well be two different physical drives.

Formatting a hard drive is more complicated than formatting floppy disks. With floppy disks, there is only a single operation: use the DOS FORMAT command or the Windows equivalent which creates tracks and sectors, a boot record, FATs, and a root directory.

With hard drives, formatting requires three steps. They are:

- Low-level format, which physically formats the hard drive and creates the tracks and sectors. (With some technology, this is done at the factory.)

- Partitioning the hard drive. Even if only one partition is used, this step is still required. The FDISK program of Windows 95 or DOS sets up a partition table at the beginning of the hard drive. This table lists how many partitions are on the drive and their locations, and which partition is the boot partition.

- High-level format done by either DOS or Windows 95. This creates the DOS boot record, the root directory, and the FATs for each partition on the hard drive. With disk drives the high-level format also creates the tracks and sectors, but with hard drives this has already been done by the low-level format. Each partition must be formatted by an OS.

We look more closely at each of these steps in Chapter 6, which covers installing hard drives. The three steps are introduced here because low-level formatting differs from one hard drive to another.

FRAGMENTATION

Fragmentation is the undesirable placement of an individual file in several locations on the drive in a way that increases data access time. When a hard drive is new and freshly formatted, the OS writes files to the drive beginning with cluster 2, placing the data in consecutive clusters. Each new file begins with the next available cluster. Later, after a file has been deleted, the OS writes a new file to the drive, beginning with the first available cluster in the FAT. If the OS encounters used clusters as it is writing the file, it simply skips these clusters and picks up with the next available one. In this way, after many files have been deleted and added to the drive, files become fragmented. Fragmentation is caused by files being written to drive in more than one group of contiguous clusters. The clusters that make up a file are together called a **chain**. For a well-used hard drive, it is possible to have a file stored in clusters at 20, 30, 40, or more locations. Fragmentation is undesirable because (1) when DOS has to access many different locations on the drive to read a file, access time slows down, and (2) if the file should become corrupted, recovering a fragmented file is more complicated than recovering a file in one continuous chain.

For these reasons, one routine maintenance task for a hard drive is to periodically defragment the drive. For DOS, the simplest way to do this is to use DOS 6+ DEFRAG or a utility software package, such as Norton Utilities, PC Tools, or Nuts & Bolts that reads the files on your drive and rearranges the clusters so that all files are written into contiguous chains. If you have utility software that does this, running it every six months or so is a good maintenance plan. To see how badly a drive is fragmented, use Norton or PC Tools to view your FAT. Norton highlights the clusters for each file in a different color so you can easily identify all the clusters that belong to a single file. By moving your cursor over the FAT, you can easily see whether or not your drive is badly fragmented.

For Windows 95, the **Defragmenter** utility is also available. Choose **Start**, then **Programs**, then **Accessories**, then **System Tools**. The menu in Figure 5-22 display. (The other menu items, ScanDisk and DriveSpace, will be discussed next.) Click **Disk Defragmenter** and select the drive from the dialog box that displays. A status box displays (see Figure 5-23) to let you know just how fragmented the disk is and asks you if you want to continue. When the operation is complete, the message in Figure 5-24 displays; click **Yes** to exit.

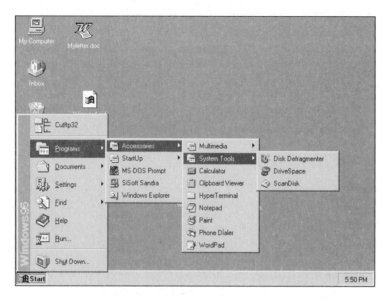

Figure 5-22   Windows 95 disk utilities

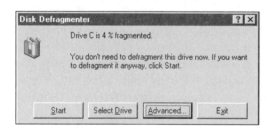

Figure 5-23   Defragmenter's status box

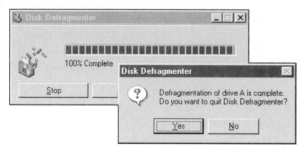

Figure 5-24   Disk Defragmenter results

CROSS-LINKED AND LOST CLUSTERS

As you learned in Chapter 4, the directory on either a disk or hard drive holds the number of the first cluster in the file. The FAT or VFAT holds the map to each cluster in a file (see Figure 4-4). Occasionally, the mapping in the FAT becomes corrupted, resulting either in lost clusters or in cross-linked clusters, as shown in Figure 5-25. Here file 3 has lost direction and is pointing to a cluster chain that belongs to File 4. Clusters 28–30 are called **cross-linked clusters** because more than one file points to them and clusters 14–16 and 27 are called **lost clusters** because no file in the FAT or VFAT points to them.

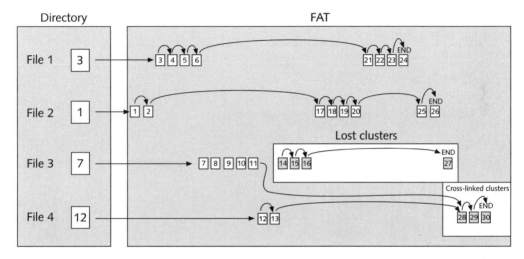

Figure 5-25   Lost and cross-linked clusters

To repair cross-linked and lost clusters, use the ScanDisk utility in either DOS or Windows 95. For DOS, enter the command **SCANDISK** from the DOS prompt. The screen in Figure 5-26 displays. When the program finishes scanning the disk, it returns you to a DOS prompt.

For Windows 95, click **Start**, then **Programs**, then **Accessories**, then **System Tools**, then **ScanDisk** as in Figure 5-22. The ScanDisk utility first asks which drive you want to scan and then begins the scan. Errors are reported as in Figure 5-27 and results display as in Figure 5-28.

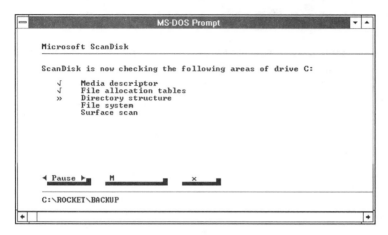

Figure 5-26 SCANDISK for DOS

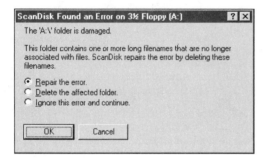

Figure 5-27 ScanDisk reports errors

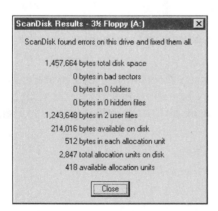

Figure 5-28 ScanDisk results

DISK COMPRESSION

Disk compression software can help meet the ever-increasing demands for more space on hard drives to hold bigger and better software. Software packages requiring 40 to 80 MB of hard drive space were unheard of three or four years ago but are now common. The sizes of hard drives have increased proportionately. Even so, we often seek ways to cram more onto near-full hard drives.

What Is Disk Compression?

5

Disk compression software works by (1) storing data on your hard drive in one big file and managing the writing of data and programs to that file, and by (2) rewriting the data in files in a mathematically coded format that uses less space. Most disk compression programs, such as Stacker and DOS DriveSpace, combine these two methods.

Disk Compression in DOS and Windows 3.x

With DOS and Windows 3.x, the first method listed above uses a device driver loaded in the CONFIG.SYS file. The driver treats all the hard drive space as one big file called the host file. When DOS tries to write files to the hard drive, it passes these files to the driver, which does the actual writing. The driver keeps track of where the files are located on the drive. Normally with DOS the smallest allocation unit for a file is 1 cluster, which can be as large as 8 sectors or 4,096 bytes, so that even files physically smaller than one cluster still occupy a full 4096 bytes. With a disk compression driver, the smallest allocation unit is one sector or 512 bytes, and sometimes this is even reduced to one-half sector or 256 bytes. The driver is free to place as many as 8 small files into the 4,096-byte cluster space that DOS would use for one small file. This method of disk compression can be very effective if the drive contains many small files. If most files on the drive exceed 4,096 bytes, there may be little gain.

The second method of disk compression for hard drives listed above takes its idea from file compression software like PK ZIP. File compression has been around for quite some time. It compresses one or more files into one small file for easy exporting to other systems. The file compression program looks for repeating characters in the data and eliminates the repetition by indicating how many times a character should be written instead of writing the character that many times. The program also writes characters that do not require an entire 8 bits using only the bits that the character needs. Most ASCII characters only use 7 of the 8 bits (see Appendix C). File compression software uses the eighth bit for something else. By making use of every bit and by eliminating repeating characters, data can be compressed to as little as 65% of its original space.

All this sounds very good. An older 500 MB hard drive can magically hold 700 MB of data and software with just one more driver in your CONFIG.SYS file. Caution, however, is in order. Remember that the compression software is putting all your software and data into a single file. Occasionally, one or two files on a hard drive or disk become corrupted. As long as this involves only a single file and happens rarely, you can deal with the loss by recovering the file from a backup, borrowing a fresh copy from a friend, or even reconstructing the file entirely. But with data compression, that one file is everything on your hard drive. All your eggs are truly in one basket!

You also have the added complexity of having one more layer of software manipulating your data. If this driver is incompatible with some application you happen to be using one day, the results could be disastrous. Also, because of this added complexity, disk access time is slowed down.

In summary, disk compression does save hard drive space, but you need to carefully consider the risks involved. If you do choose to use disk compression, keep good backups of both the data and the software. If the data and software on your drive are especially valuable, you may want to invest in a larger hard drive.

Disk Compression in Windows 95

A **compressed drive** is really not a drive at all; it's a file. Figure 5-29 shows the two parts of a compressed drive. The **host drive**, in this case drive H, is not compressed and is usually a very small partition on the drive, generally under 2 MB. The host drive contains a special file called a **CVF** (**compressed volume file**). The CVF holds everything on drive C, compressed into just one file.

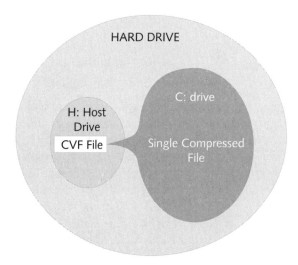

Figure 5-29   A compressed drive

Although there are several disk compression software applications on the market, Windows 95 offers its own, called **DriveSpace**. Others are STAC Electronics Stacker and DoubleSpace, both of which are supported by Windows 95. DoubleSpace is also available under Windows 3.x. DriveSpace is used in the example here.

DriveSpace does the following things to compress a drive.

- Assign a different drive letter to the hard drive, such as H
- Compress the entire contents of the hard drive into a single file on drive H
- Set up the drive so that Windows 95 and other applications view this compressed file as drive C
- Configure Windows 95 so that each time it boots the DriveSpace drive will load and manage the compressed drive

Follow these steps to compress a drive in Windows 95 using DriveSpace: Click **Start**, then **Programs**, then **Accessories**, then **System Tools**, as shown in Figure 5-22. Click **DriveSpace** to display the dialog box in Figure 5-30. Drive A is used as the example here, but drive C gives similar results. Select drive A by clicking on it and then choose **Compress** from the Drive menu. The dialog box in Figure 5-31 displays, showing how much space would be created by compressing the drive. Click **Options** and the Compression Options box in Figure 5-32 displays. Note that you can allow extra space on drive H that will not be compressed. Click **OK** to return to the box in Figure 5-31. Click **Start** to begin compression. The box in Figure 5-33 displays as the drive is being compressed.

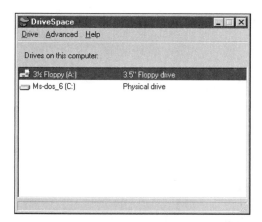

Figure 5-30   Selecting drive using DriveSpace for Windows 95

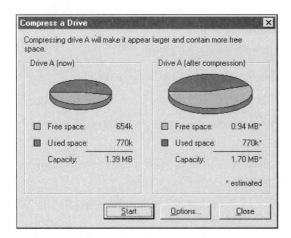

Figure 5-31   Drive compression predictions

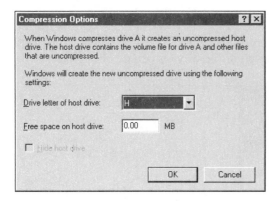

Figure 5-32   Drive compression options

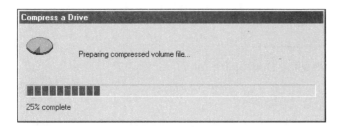

Figure 5-33   Drive compression in progress

After the drive is compressed, there will be two logical drives on the disk: the host drive H containing the compressed CVF file and the compressed drive A (see Figure 5-34). The host drive H contains a ReadThis.txt file (see Figure 5-35) that explains how to mount a compressed drive. This mounting is done automatically for a hard drive when Windows 95 loads. Compare Figures 5–31 and 5–36, which show the results of compressing two drives of the same size: one that was initially empty (Figure 5–36) and one that initially contained data (Figure 5–31). The resulting drive space for an empty disk is 2.65 MB, but the drive that started with data on it had a resulting drive space of 1.70 MB after compression. To get the most resources out of compression, begin with a relatively free hard drive.

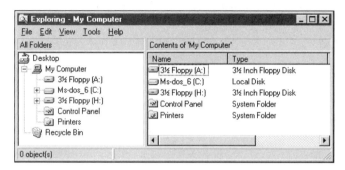

Figure 5-34   After compression, a 3½-inch disk is now two logical drives A and H

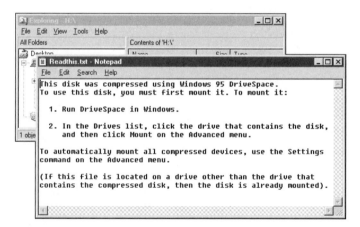

Figure 5-35   Readthis.txt file on host drive

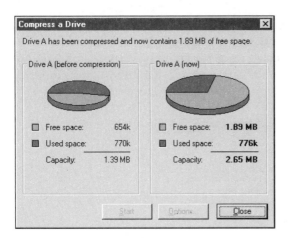

Figure 5-36   An empty 3½-inch disk yields more space
than a partially filled disk

A drive can be uncompressed from the DriveSpace Drive menu if you first delete enough files so that the amount of data on the drive does not exceed the uncompressed capacity. If you compress a disk, the driver to manage the compressed drive is loaded only when Windows 95 senses that a compressed floppy disk is being read. After the hard drive is uncompressed, Windows 95 no longer automatically loads the mounting driver.

DISK CACHING

A **disk cache** is a temporary storage area in RAM for data being read from or written to a hard drive. The idea behind a cache on a hard drive can be explained as follows:

The CPU asks for data from a hard drive. The hard drive controller sends instructions to the drive to read the data and then sends it to the CPU. The CPU requests more data, quite often data that immediately follows the previously read data on the hard drive. The controller reads the requested data from the drive and sends it to the CPU. Without a cache, each CPU request is handled with a read to the hard drive, as indicated in the top part of Figure 5-37.

With a hard drive cache, the cache software handles the requests for data as seen in the lower part of Figure 5-37. The cache program reads ahead of the CPU requests by guessing what data the CPU will request next. Since most data that the CPU requests is in consecutive areas on the drive, the cache program guesses correctly most of the time. The program stores the read-ahead data in memory (RAM). When the CPU requests the next group of data, if the cache program guessed right the program can send that data to the CPU from memory without having to go back to the hard drive. Some cache software caches entire tracks at a time; others cache groups of sectors.

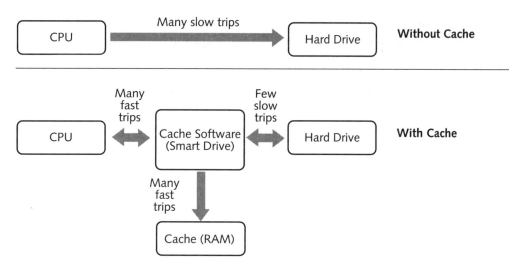

Figure 5-37   A CPU asking a hard drive for data without cache (upper part) and with cache (lower part)

Hardware Cache and Software Cache.   The two kinds of hard drive caches are the hardware cache and the software cache. Some hard drive controllers have a **hardware cache** built right into the controller circuit board. The BIOS on the controller contains the cache program and RAM chips on the controller hold the cache.

A **software cache** is a cache program that is stored on the hard drive like other software and is loaded into memory as a TSR, usually when a computer is booted. The software cache program uses system RAM to hold the cache. Most often this RAM is in extended or expanded memory. (Extended and expanded memory are discussed in Chapter 9.)

Disk Cache in DOS and Windows 3.x. SMARTDrive is the software that manages the hard drive cache that comes with Windows software and DOS. With DOS 6+, SMARTDrive is executed as a TSR from the AUTOEXEC.BAT file. With earlier versions of DOS, SMARTDrive worked as a device driver and was loaded from the CONFIG.SYS file with the DEVICE= command line. SMARTDrive caches data both being read from and written to the hard drive and also caches data being read from disks.

Other popular kinds of cache software for DOS and Windows 3.x are:

- Norton Cache, included in Norton Utilities
- PC Cache, included in PC Tools
- Mace Cache, included in Mace Utilities
- Super PC-Kwik Cache from Multisoft

DOS Buffers.   Several years ago, before hard drive caching, buffers were used to speed up disk access. A **buffer** is an area in memory where data waiting to be read or written is temporarily stored. Disk caches do a better job of speeding up disk access than buffers, but many software packages today still require that DOS maintain buffers. To specify how many buffers DOS should maintain, use the BUFFERS= command in the CONFIG.SYS file. The only reason to use buffers today is to satisfy the requirements of software that still uses them. See the software documentation for the recommended number of buffers.

Hardware Cache versus Software Cache.   Hardware caches have the cache program on the controller BIOS and do not use any conventional memory to hold the program. Software caches load their cache program into memory and, if they are not managed well, they may use some conventional memory that might be needed by your applications. Another difference is that hardware caches store the cache itself in RAM chips on the controller rather than using system memory as software caches do.

Since the hardware cache is on the controller board, data moves from the controller over the system bus to the CPU. A software cache is faster because data is stored in system RAM and moves to the CPU from system RAM that is directly on the systemboard. With Pentium computers, the PCI bus from RAM to the CPU is much faster than the bus that data coming from the controller must ride.

One other disadvantage of a hardware cache is that it is a permanent part of the hard drive controller, and today's hard drives have the controller built into the drive housing. If a faster software cache becomes available, upgrading software stored on your hard drive is a viable option, but exchanging hard drives to upgrade to a faster hardware cache is impractical.

When buying a new hard drive with controller, look for whether it includes hardware caches as an option. A controller with its own hardware cache is slightly more expensive than one without a cache.

VCACHE in Windows 95

Windows 95 has a built-in 32-bit software cache called Vcache. Vcache is automatically loaded by Windows 95 without entries in CONFIG.SYS or AUTOEXEC.BAT. VCACHE doesn't take up conventional memory or upper memory space the way SMARTDrive does and it does a much better job of caching. Also, you don't need to tell Vcache how much memory to allocate to disk caching as you do with SmartDrive; Vcache allocates the amount of memory it uses based on available memory and disk activity.

In speaking of disk caching, don't confuse a disk cache with a memory cache. Memory caching is caching slow memory (DRAM) into fast memory (SRAM). Disk caching is caching slow secondary storage (hard drive) into faster primary storage (RAM).

Using DOS under Windows 95 to Manage a Hard Drive

A word of caution: using some DOS commands on a hard drive that uses Windows 95 as the OS may cause damage to a hard drive's file structure. With a Windows 95 upgrade, some of these dangerous commands are erased from the \DOS directory on the hard drive. You will find DOS commands that come with Windows 95 stored in the \Windows\Command directory. Here are the ones to avoid:

- Don't use disk utility software that does not know about VFAT or long filenames, including older versions of Norton Utilities and Central Point PC Tools.

- Don't use FDISK, FORMAT C:, SYS C:, and CHKDSK while in a DOS session within Windows 95. Some of these functions are covered in the next chapter and will, however, be useful to you when you learn what they do and how they do it.

- Don't use software to optimize or defragment your hard drive that does not know about long filenames; look for the Windows 95 compatibility message on the package.

- Don't run hard drive cache programs unless they are written especially for Windows 95. Remember that Windows 95 has it own built-in caching software.

- Don't use the older DOS backup programs like BACKUP or MSBACKUP because the long filename information might not be saved during the backup.

Hard Drive Technology

When shopping for a hard drive, you will discover several different technologies to choose from. Older hard drives, a few of which are still in use though somewhat difficult to find on the market, can be either MFM or RLL types. The most popular kind of hard drive technology today is IDE technology, primarily because of the price, size, and ease of installation. A variation of IDE technology is SCSI, which combines an IDE drive with an especially fast I/O bus with its own bus controller.

In addition to the standard internal hard drives in a PC, removable drives are becoming more and more popular. These come in both magnetic media similar to the IDE drives and optical media similar to CD-ROM. The following sections discuss how IDE, SCSI, and removable drives work; MFM and RLL drives are covered for historical reasons only, to help you understand the basics behind today's drive technology.

Hardware Components

As was described earlier, a hard drive consists of two or more platters spinning inside an airtight housing with read/write heads that move back and forth across the platters. The drive fits into a bay inside the computer case and is securely attached to the bay with supports or braces and screws. This helps prevent the drive from being jarred while the disk is spinning and the heads are very close to the disk surfaces.

The drive requires a **controller board** filled with ROM programming to instruct the heads how, where, and when to move across the platters and how to write and read data. In IDE and SCSI drives, a controller is mounted on top of the drive and is an integral part of it. Older RLL and MFM drives had the controller board as a separate, large expansion card connected to the drive with two cables. The controller board of IDE drives communicates with the systemboard by way of a small adapter card that serves as a simple pass-through for the data and instructions. Sometimes the adapter card is an on-board systemboard component with a connector for the hard drive right on the systemboard.

IDE Technology

Figure 5-38 shows a hardware subsystem including an **IDE** (**Integrated Device Electronics**) hard drive and its adapter card. In addition to the connection for the cable, the hard drive has a connection for the power cord from the power supply.

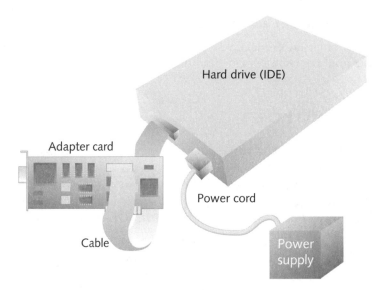

Figure 5-38   A PC's hard drive subsystem

The controller for the hard drive is inside the drive housing (hence the term Integrated Device Electronics). This arrangement makes it possible for the controller and the hard drive to work in ways that are quite different from MFM and RLL technology to low-level format the drive and store data. The controller mounted directly on the drive case communicates with the system bus by means of an **adapter card**. An adapter card is a card that merely receives data from the hard drive controller and passes it along to the system bus. An adapter card does little else but pass data along, and is, therefore, inexpensive. The controller and the adapter card are connected with a single 40-pin cable.

IDE drives are fast becoming the most popular drives on the market today, because of their large capacity, ease of installation, and competitive price. Although IDE technology is an innovative improvement over MFM and RLL type hard drives, it also introduces some new limitations. To understand how IDE technology differs from other drive technologies, the details of how drives are low-level formatted must be examined.

Sectors Per Track.   The MFM and RLL technologies use either 17 or 26 sectors per track over the entire drive platter. The larger tracks near the outside of the platter contain the same number of bytes as the smaller tracks near the center of the platter. This arrangement makes the formatting of a drive and later accessing data simpler, but it wastes drive space. The number of bytes that a track can hold is determined by the centermost track, and all other tracks are forced to follow this restriction.

One major improvement with IDE technology is that the formatting of IDE drives eliminates this restriction. The number of sectors per track on an IDE drive is not the same throughout the platter. In this new formatting system, called zone bit recording (Figure 5-6), tracks near the center have the smallest number of sectors per track, and the number of sectors increases as the tracks get larger. In other words, each track on an IDE drive is designed to have the optimum number of sectors appropriate to the size of the track. What makes this arrangement possible, however, is one fact that has not changed: there are still 512 bytes per sector for every sector on the drive. If it wasn't for this, DOS and Windows 95 would have a difficult time indeed communicating with this drive!

Communication with the OS is an important issue with IDE drives. With older drives that used consistent sectors per track communication was no problem. But because with IDE drives the OS cannot keep up with the location of the sectors on each track, the IDE controller manages the communication to its own drive for the OS. Windows 95 or DOS, in effect, cannot communicate directly with the drive and depends on the controller to handle any requests for read or write operations.

Low-Level Formatting.   In addition to the day-to-day read/write operations that are now delegated to the controller, the initial low-level formatting of the drive also is an issue. Standard low-level format programs, such as the one that resides in System BIOS, assume a consistent number of sectors per track over the entire drive. Commercial hard drive utility programs, such as Norton, SpinRite, and Disk Manager, also make this same assumption. For an IDE drive, however, such an assumption is a major catastrophe. Formatting an IDE drive in this way would probably permanently destroy the drive unless the drive controller were smart enough to ignore the command.

Because of the unique way that an IDE drive is formatted and data is accessed, you must use a controller specific to the IDE drive. IDE drives thus have their controller built directly on top of the drive housing. The controller and the drive are permanently attached to one another. The IDE drive is formatted before it leaves the factory, and the controller alone manages access to the drive.

Because IDE drives are low-level formatted by the manufacturer, they cannot be low-level formatted as part of preventive maintenance the way older drives can be. The track and sector markings on the drive created at the factory are normally expected to last for the life of the drive. For this reason IDE drives are often referred to as disposable drives. When the track and sector markings fade, as they eventually do, you just throw the drive away and buy a new one!

However, improvements for the IDE drive are becoming more commonplace. Some better-known IDE drive manufacturers are offering a low-level format program specific to their drives. If an IDE drive continues to give "Bad Sector or Sector Not Found" errors or even becomes totally unusable, ask the manufacturer for a program to perform a low-level format of the drive. Sometimes these programs are only distributed by the manufacturer to dealers, resellers, or certified service centers.

It's risky to low-level format an IDE drive using a format program other than one provided by the manufacturer, although some have tried and succeeded. Probably more drives have been permanently destroyed than saved by taking this risk, however. IDE drives last several years without a refresher low-level format. By that time, you're probably ready to upgrade to a larger drive anyway.

Adapter Card.   If the controller for an IDE drive is mounted on the drive housing, how does the controller communicate with the system bus? By way of an adapter card. An IDE adapter card is a small, inexpensive card that enables the controller card to access the system bus. The small card fits into an expansion slot on the systemboard and is connected to the controller on the hard drive by a single cable. The adapter card does little else than pass data and commands back and forth. Most adapter cards have a two-line wire that plugs into a light on the front of the computer case; you know that the hard drive is being accessed when the adapter card makes the light go on.

In summary, IDE drives have their controller card mounted directly on top of the drive. DOS does not communicate with the drive directly as is the case with older technology. DOS and Windows 95 pass their requests to a controller, which is responsible for keeping up with where and how data is stored on a drive. As far as the OS is concerned, an IDE drive is simply a very long list of logical sectors, each 512 bytes long. The OS doesn't care where on the drive these sectors are located since that information is maintained by the controller. Setup for IDE drives is very simple; the most important fact that setup and the OS need to know is how many sectors there are on the drive. It is important not to overestimate the number of sectors. You don't want DOS or Windows 95 requesting use of a sector that does not exist. However, you can tell setup that you have fewer sectors than are actually present. If you do, some sectors will remain unused. Finally, although you skip the low-level formatting when you install an IDE drive, you must partition the drive and give it an OS or high-level format the same as with other drives.

Enhanced IDE (EIDE) Technology

IDE drives follow the standard AT interface known as ATA (AT attachment interface).[2] These IDE drives translate the sector coordinates to the coordinates expected by DOS and BIOS, but are still limited to the 528 MB ceiling on BIOS because they follow the ATA standard that most BIOS at that time also followed. To break this 528 MB limitation, a new standard was developed called ATA-2, which is used by the **Enhanced IDE** (**EIDE**) drives. The ATA standard only allowed up to two devices on the same controller and they both had to be hard drives. The ATA-2 standard allows for up to four devices on the same controller, and these devices may be hard drives, CD-ROMs, or tape drives as well as other devices. The ATA standard assumed that the number of tracks or cylinders would not exceed 1,024, a limitation ATA-2 does not have. Enhanced IDE drives, accordingly, can hold more than 528 MB of data, can have more than 1,024 tracks or cylinders, and can have more than two devices on a single controller.

The most common method that EIDE drives use to exceed the 528 MB limit is logical block addressing (discussed in Chapter 3) rather than the traditional CHS (cylinders, heads, sectors) method. With LBA, DOS and BIOS see a drive only as a list of sectors, each with a 28-bit address. With 28-bit addressing, you can have as many as 268 million sectors of 512 bytes each, which allows for a maximum disk capacity of about 128 GB. Refer to Chapter 3 for setup options that support LBA mode.

There are two other standards for hard drive technology. EIDE technology can also follow the ATAPI standard or a competing standard known as Fast-ATA, which is based on the ATA-2 standard.

SCSI Technology

SCSI (pronounced scuzzy) stands for **Small Computer Systems Interface** and is a standard for communication to the system bus. SCSI is somewhat like a small LAN inside a computer. More accurately, SCSI is a kind of bus. The SCSI bus is a closed system that can contain, and be used by, up to eight devices. The gateway from this bus to the system bus is an adapter card inserted into an expansion slot on the systemboard. The adapter card, called the **host adapter**, is responsible for managing all the devices on the SCSI bus. When one of these devices must communicate with the system bus, the data passes through the host adapter, the gateway or bridge to the system bus. Think of the SCSI subsystem as the CPU outsourcing the I/O activity on the SCSI bus to the microprocessor on the host adapter. In fact, I have my own acronym for SCSI: smart CPU out-sourcing I/O.

The host adapter is responsible for keeping up with the interchange between the devices on the SCSI bus and the system bus. SCSI technology has the added advantage that two devices on the SCSI bus can pass data back and forth across the SCSI bus without ever having to go through the CPU. This method of data transmission provides a convenient way to back up a SCSI hard drive to a tape drive on the same host adapter without involving the CPU in the activity.

---

[2]   AT originally stood for advanced technology and refers to one of the early IBM PCs of the 1980s. The XT came before the AT PC. Sometimes you still hear the term XT/AT compatible or AT standard, which means the technology follows the standard established by this early AT PC.

One SCSI bus can link up to eight devices or sixteen devices, including the host adapter. The maximum number of devices the SCSI bus can support depends on the type of SCSI being used. Each device on the bus is assigned a number from zero to seven called the **SCSI ID** or the **LUN** (**logical unit number**) using DIP switches, dials on the device, or software settings. Cables connect the devices physically in a straight chain. The devices can be either internal or external, and the host adapter can be at either end of the chain or somewhere in the middle.

A SCSI device such as a hard drive, tape drive, or CD-ROM interfaces with the host adapter rather than directly with the CPU. The technology of a SCSI device can be the same as the technology of a similar device that is not SCSI, with the added functionality of being able to use the SCSI bus and communicate with the host adapter. A device is a SCSI device not because of the technology of the device but because of the bus it uses.

Just as with IDE drives, a SCSI hard drive has its controller mounted directly on the drive and can have a variable number of sectors per track, and therefore should not be low-level formatted after leaving the factory. In fact, some SCSI drives are IDE drives. What makes a SCSI hard drive a SCSI drive is not the drive technology itself but the way data is passed over a SCSI bus to the host adapter and on to the system bus. Technically, a SCSI drive can simply be an IDE drive with one more chip on the controller card on top of the drive and a different kind of data connection designed to fit the SCSI standard. The SCSI chip, called the **SCSI bus adapter chip** (**SBAC**), controls the transfer of data over the SCSI bus.

Figure 5-39 illustrates this concept of SCSI as a bus. On the left side, the CPU communicates with the hard drive controller that is contained in the hard drive case through the system bus. On the right side, the CPU communicates over the system bus to the SCSI host adapter, which communicates over the SCSI bus to the SCSI adapter in the hard drive case. The SCSI adapter in the hard drive case communicates to the hard drive controller, which, in turn, communicates with the hard drive.

Some SCSI devices, including hard drives, have the SCSI host adapter built directly into the device itself. Hard drives require a simple adapter card to communicate with the system bus, much like regular IDE drives do. These devices are called **embedded SCSI** devices and, because the host adapter technology resides on the drive logic board, can only have the one device on the SCSI bus. Other SCSI devices on this computer are altogether separate from this SCSI bus system. Embedded SCSI devices often don't conform to standard SCSI specifications, because they do not accommodate any other SCSI device. They are the only device on such a SCSI system.

Because there are several variations of the SCSI bus, when you buy a new SCSI device, you must be sure that it is compatible with the SCSI bus you already have. If the SCSI device is not compatible, you also must buy a new host adapter card for the device. You can have more than one SCSI bus system with their individual host adapters on the same computer, but this is more costly because you must buy a host adapter for each SCSI system. The different SCSI bus systems available today are SCSI-1, SCSI-2, wide SCSI, and ultra SCSI.

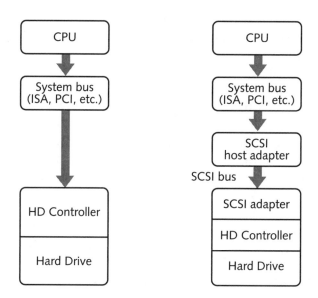

Figure 5-39 SCSI hard drives communicate with the CPU
through the SCSI host adapter

SCSI-1. The oldest SCSI bus standard, established in 1986 by the American National
Standards Institute (ANSI), SCSI-1 is a set of specifications or standards for all manufacturers to adhere to in order that devices can be more easily interchanged. SCSI-1 requires an
8-bit parallel bus with optional parity checking. Devices are strung together in a single daisy
chain. Cables use 50-pin connections as shown in Figure 5-40. The device on each end of
the chain must have an electrical resistor in place to terminate the electrical power moving
through the cable. This resistor is called the **terminating resistor**. On devices developed
after SCSI-1, software terminated resistance, making installation much simpler. Up to eight
devices including the host adapter can be on the chain.

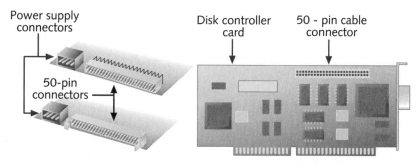

Figure 5-40 SCSI 50-pin connectors

SCSI-2.   SCSI-2 improved the SCSI-1 bus. SCSI-2 requires parity checking and the methods of terminating resistance for the devices at the end of the chain are improved to make installation easier. There are several variations of SCSI-2. SCSI-2 can support up to eight devices on a chain including the host adapter.

Wide SCSI.   This version of SCSI-2 requires a 16-bit or 32-bit data path. Wide SCSI uses different cables with 68-pin connections instead of the normal 8-bit SCSI. The 32-bit wide SCSI is rarely available. When you see a wide SCSI drive advertised that does not specify the size of the data path, assume it has a 16-bit bus. Wide SCSI can support up to 16 devices including the host adapter.

Ultra SCSI.   Sometimes called Fast-20 or Fast SCSI, or SCSI-3, the Ultra SCSI bus offers 20 MB/sec burst transfers across 8-bit paths and 40 MB/sec burst transfers across wide 16-bit paths. **Burst transfer** describes the way data is transferred across the bus. In this method, one packet immediately follows the next without waiting for clock beats and/or addressing information. Burst transfer can, in effect, saturate the bus with data, making for more efficient use of the bus and, therefore, faster transfer of data. Ultra SCSI is backward compatible with SCSI-1 and SCSI-2. Eight-bit Ultra SCSI can support up to eight devices on the chain including the host adapter. Sixteen-bit Ultra SCSI can support up to 16 devices.

One advantage of Ultra SCSI is that it supports **SCSI configuration automatically** (**SCAM**), which follows the Plug-and-Play standard. SCAM makes installations of SCSI devices much easier, assuming that the device is SCAM compatible.

Ultra SCSI offers a serial SCSI bus in addition to the traditional parallel SCSI bus. Bits travel across a serial bus in single file, rather than moving in 8-bit, 16-bit, or 32-bit groups as in a parallel bus. The advantage of a serial bus is that the cables can be longer and are not as expensive as cables for a parallel bus.

A sample configuration of a SCSI subsystem is shown in Figure 5-41. Note that you can mix SCSI-1, SCSI-2, and Ultra SCSI on the same subsystem. Also note that the only connection this subsystem has to the overall computer system and the CPU is through the host adapter. You can see from the diagram why some people compare a SCSI system to a miniature LAN inside a computer, or why SCSI can be described as out-sourcing for the CPU.

Other Variations of SCSI Hardware and Software

In addition to the differences in SCSI standards, there are other components of SCSI that vary. Some of these are termination, device drivers, and host adapters.

Termination.   There are several ways to terminate electrical power at the end of the daisy chain. **Termination** prevents an echo effect of command signals at the end of the chain that causes interference of the data transmission. There are several ways to terminate power:

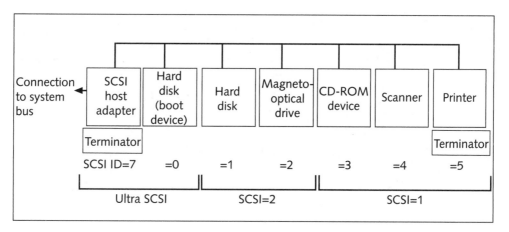

Figure 5-41 Sample SCSI configuration

- The host adapter can have a switch setting that activates or deactivates a terminating resistor on the card, depending on whether or not the adapter is at one end of the chain.

- A device can have either a single SCSI connection requiring that the device be placed at the end of the chain, or the device can have two connections, where one connection ties the device into the chain and the other connection can tie a second device onto the chain or it may terminate the chain. The chain can be terminated by placing an external terminator on the connection. This external terminator serves as the terminating resistor (see Figure 5-42).

- The device at the end of the chain can also be terminated by a resistor that is physically mounted on the device in a specially designated socket.

- Some devices have built-in terminators that you can turn on or off with a jumper setting on the device.

- Termination can be controlled by software.

There are several types of terminators, some more reliable than others. The three kinds of terminators available are passive terminators, active terminators, and forced perfect terminators. Forced perfect terminators are more expensive and more reliable than the other two.

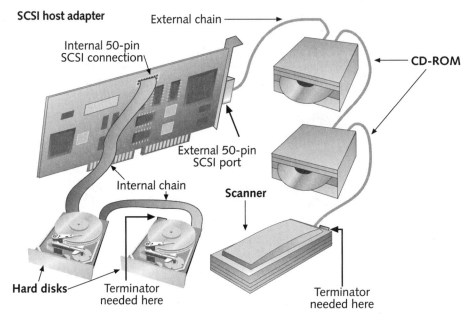

Figure 5-42   SCSI subsystem showing terminators at each end of the cable

When buying terminating resistor hardware and cables for a SCSI bus (see Figure 5-43), get high-quality products even if they cost a little more. The added reliability and enhanced data integrity are worth the extra money.

Device Drivers.   Device drivers are needed to enable DOS or another OS to communicate with a host adapter. Although many drivers are available, it is best to use the drivers recommended by or provided by the host adapter vendor. Two popular drivers are the **Advanced SCSI Programming Interface** (**ASPI**) and **Common Access Method** (**CAM**). ASPI is probably the more popular of the two.

No SCSI device drivers are included with Window 3.1 or DOS. SCSI hardware manufacturers write their own drivers and include it with the device. The driver is loaded in the CONFIG.SYS file just as other drivers are. Its DEVICE= command must appear in the CONFIG.SYS file before any device drivers for a SCSI device. For example, if you have a SCSI CD-ROM driver whose device driver must be installed in CONFIG.SYS, you must place the command for this driver after the one that installs the host adapter driver. The installation instructions for the CD-ROM drive will offer similar instructions and will give you the specific command. Windows 95 has built-in support for SCSI devices.

Many computers have some SCSI interface software already present in their System BIOS, enough, in fact, to allow a SCSI hard drive to be the boot device of the system. The System BIOS can access the SCSI drive, execute the load program in the drive's master boot record, and load the SCSI device drivers stored on the hard drive into memory. If there are two hard drives in a system, one being an IDE and one a SCSI, the IDE drive must always be the boot device. This is because the systemboard BIOS takes precedence over the BIOS on the SCSI host adapter.

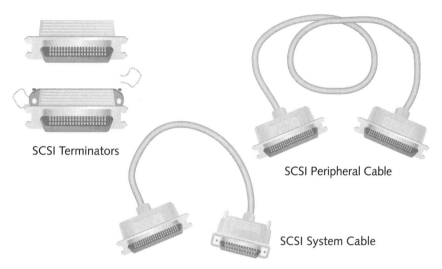

SCSI Terminators

SCSI Peripheral Cable

SCSI System Cable

Figure 5-43 SCSI cables and terminators

Host Adapter Issues. An important issue when you install a SCSI bus system for the first time is the sophistication of the host adapter. More expensive host adapters are often easier to install because the installation software does more of the work for the installer and offers more help than does less expensive adapter software. When buying a host adapter, compare the installation procedures for each adapter and also look for options, such as a built-in disk drive controller, software-controlled termination, and configuration BIOS built into the adapter's ROM.

A SCSI host adapter controller has a BIOS that loads into memory addresses on the PC and controls the operation of the SCSI bus. This SCSI controller uses a DMA channel, an I/O address, and memory addresses in upper memory. You must install a SCSI device carefully to avoid resource conflicts with devices that are not on the SCSI subsystem.

In summary, to understand SCSI hard drive technology think of it as a SCSI bus system—a closed bus system that can include several devices as well as the host adapter that acts as the bridge to the system bus. SCSI drives are usually faster than IDE drives but also more expensive. When buying SCSI drives, know if the host adapter is built into the drive (embedded SCSI), or if you must purchase it separately. When installing a new SCSI system, be aware of the many variations of SCSI and buy compatible components.

Even though the installation of a SCSI system may sound complicated and requires many decisions about what components to buy, the installation instructions for SCSI devices and host adapters are usually very thorough and well-written. By carefully following all instructions, SCSI installations can be smooth and problem free.

Comparing SCSI Hard Drives and EIDE Hard Drives

These are the issues to consider when choosing between using an EIDE hard drive and a SCSI hard drive:

- A SCSI hard drive with its supporting host adaptor and cable costs more than an EIDE hard drive with its supporting adaptor card.

- A SCSI subsystem provides faster data transfer than an EIDE drive, although a SCSI bus is the source of the performance rather than the hard drive technology.

- A SCSI bus supports multitasking, allowing the CPU to request data from more than one SCSI device at the same time, whereas when the CPU requests data from an EIDE drive on an ISA bus it can only process data from one I/O device at a time. The CPU must wait until the ISA bus and EIDE drive have completed the request before it can tackle another task. With SCSI, the CPU can perform another I/O task while waiting for the SCSI bus to complete the first request. (The CPU outsources this request for data to SCSI so it can busy itself with other "core business functions.")

- A good SCSI host adapter allows you to connect other devices to it, such as a printer, scanner, or tape drive.

- If you have two IDE drives on the same adapter, only one of them can be busy at any one time. With SCSI, two or more devices can operate simultaneously. If one of your IDE devices is a CD-ROM, the hard drive must wait for the CD-ROM to complete a task before it can work again. If you plan to transfer a lot of data from CD-ROM to hard drive, this is a good reason to choose SCSI.

In summary, SCSI is more expensive than EIDE but gives you better performance.

Chapter 6 covers installation of SCSI devices in detail, but here are some tips to make SCSI installations easy:

- Keep the controller from conflicting with other devices when using system resources.

- Keep SCSI IDs unique.

- Provide for proper termination.

Removable Drives

Not long ago there were few good choices for removable drives. They were expensive, awkward, proprietary, and many had low volume. That's now changing as standards are emerging. Costs are decreasing, and several manufacturers offer improved removable drives with attractive features. This section looks at some of the advantages of removable drives and their various technologies, and surveys some of the products available.

WHY USE A REMOVABLE DRIVE?

A removable drive is more expensive than a stationary internal hard drive. But it does offer some advantages. Table 5-5 identifies some reasons to use removable drives:

Table 5-5   Reasons to Add Removable Drives to Your System

Advantage of a Removable Drive	Description
Unlimited capacity	Because you can remove one hard disk and place a new one in the drive, there are no data storage limits.
Multi-user applications	In a business office, several users often share the same computer. If you require your own database or large files, as in desktop publishing or CAD/CAM applications, the removable drive can allow you to have your own hard drive capacity.
Transportability	Databases, software, and files can follow you from computer to computer. This is especially useful when you work on systems with weak WAN or LAN support.
Data Security	Removable drives support data privacy. Simply remove the drive and place it under lock and key.
Virus protection	When downloading software or data to a removable drive, a possible virus will be contained to this drive. You can then scan this one drive prior to transporting data to other drives.
Organization	Removable drives permit data to easily be organized by volumes. This is especially useful for organizing several large projects.
Back up	When using a removable drive to back up data from the internal fixed hard drive, you can use fast random access to locate data or files; tape drives use sequential access, which is much slower.
Fault tolerance	If the computer stops working, it's easy to simply remove the drive and take it to another computer.
Internet servers	If removable drives are used for Internet services, each category can be stored on one removable drive. When you want to update that category, you can do the updating on another computer and then do an easy swap with the removable drive on the Internet server.

5

REMOVABLE DRIVE TECHNOLOGIES

Table 5-6 summarizes how removable drives all fall into three categories of technology, according to their method of data storage:

Table 5-6   Removable Drive Types

Removable Drive Type	Description
Magnetic media drives	Removable drives can use a magnetic medium similar to that used by fixed drives and floppy disks. The Jaz drive and the smaller Zip drive by Iomega are examples of magnetic media drives.
Optical hard drives (sometimes called magneto-optical or MO drives)	These use similar technology to CD-ROMs, giving them increased capacity over magnetic drives. One example of an optical hard drive is the 4.6 GB Apex by Pinnacle.
Phase-dual (PD) or phase change (PC) drives	A better technological implementation of optical hard drives, the PD drives can also read CD-ROMs. PD drives are available from Panasonic, Plasmon Data, Disctec, and Toray. Panasonic is the OEM (original equipment manufacturer).

AVAILABLE PRODUCTS

Before considering specific products, here are some typical features to look for when you're selecting a removable hard drive:

- Auto-eject cartridge mechanism (even if the power is off)
- Good door seal (prevents dust buildup)
- High drop height
- Audible feedback features
- Ability to automatically drop into sleep mode when not in use (for external drives)
- Ability to systematically clean the media
- Availability of write protect options
- Availability of a convenient method of changing the SCSI ID (for SCSI drives)
- Inclusion of the host adaptor in the cost of the drive (for SCSI drives)
- Presence of a port on the drive for the printer plug (for drives that use a parallel port)
- Value of half-life of the media (how long will the data be there?)
- Speed
- Plug-and-Play compliance

- Compatibility with other drives using the same technology (can you use disks from other manufacturers on this drive?)

- Cost of the drive and the disks

- Warranty and quality of service department and technical support

- Quality of documentation—is it easy to read and thorough?

A couple of terms in this list need explanation. The **drop height** is the height from which the manufacturer says you can drop the drive without making the drive unusable. The Iomega Zip drive has a drop height of eight feet, whereas the Iomega Jaz has a drop height of only three feet. Optical and PD drives have a drop height of only 30 inches, but this applies only to the casing. The optical disk inside the casing is usually undamaged when dropped from this and greater heights.

The **half-life** of the disk is the time it takes for the magnetic strength of the data to weaken to half of its strength. Magnetic media, including traditional hard drives and floppy disks, have a half-life of five to seven years, but optical media including the PD drives have a half-life of 30 years.

Plug-and-Play compliant means that the drive can interface with Plug-and-Play BIOS and with Windows 95 installations without the need to set switches and jumpers manually. Most of the SCSI drives are Plug-and-Play. Other drives may or may not have this feature.

Several manufacturers offer different versions of removable drives using one of the technologies described earlier. These new drives are competitors to traditional 3½-inch floppy disks, but because of their ubiquity and low cost floppy disks are surely here to stay for some time.

High-capacity Disk Drives

The Iomega 3½-inch Zip drive stores 100 MB of data on each of its disks. The Zip drive external model costs under $175 and disks are under $20. The external Zip drive plugs into a SCSI port. The drive and disk look very much like a traditional disk drive and disk. If you choose to include a Zip drive on a new PC, don't eliminate your traditional floppy disk drive. For today's technology, consider the Zip drive an add-on, not a replacement for the standard 3½-inch disk drive.

Hard Disk Removable Drives

The Iomega Jaz drive is one example of a magnetic media removable drive that stores 1 GB of data on each removeable disk. The external model uses a SCSI port and costs around $450. The internal model has a SCSI interface and costs about $350. A removable disk costs under $100. Iomega advertises that you can back up 1 GB of data from your fixed hard drive to the Jaz drive in as little as five minutes.

SyQuest Technology offers the SyJet drive with a 1.5 GB capacity. The internal drive costs around $350. The SyJet offers both a parallel port and a SCSI port version. One nice feature of the SyJet parallel port drive is that you can easily carry it around with you. (It weighs less than a notebook computer and takes up a lot less space.) You can plug it into almost any computer's parallel port for quick and convenient access to data, but data access is limited to the parallel port speed.

SyQuest also offers the EZFlyer 230 with 216 MB of storage space and costing about $300 for the external unit. The EZFlyer also comes in 420 MB and 800 MB versions. Another manufacturer, Nomai, offers a 540 MB removable disk hard drive.

Magneto-Optical Drives

One example of a magneto-optical drive is the Fujitsu DynaMO 230 Parallel Port drive. It has a storage capacity of about 230 MB and complies with the ISO standard. This means that the disks can be read by most other optical drives. Expect the speed of any parallel port drive, including this one, to be slower than that of SCSI drives.

Another example of an MO drive is the Olympus PowerMO 230, which has 216 MB of storage space and uses a faster SCSI interface. The SCSI card bundled with the drive is not Plug-and-Play-compliant. When installing this drive, you must manually set the switches on the card to match those on your Windows 95 Device Manager.

Phase-Dual Optical Drives

One advantage of phase-dual (PD) optical drives is that they serve as a CD-ROM reader (though with a slower speed) as well as a read/write PD drive. Some examples of PD drives are the Plasmon PD/CD2000e and the Toray PC Phasewriter Dual, both of which have a 633 MB capacity. The Disctec PD RoadRunner Express has a 650 MB capacity and offers both a SCSI and parallel port interface. PD disks look like CD-ROMs in a disk housing (see Figure 5-44). Almost all PD drives are Plug-and-Play compliant.

Figure 5-44   Phase dual optical drive and disk

Installing a Removable Drive

These are the general steps to follow when installing an external removable drive:

1. Identify the connectors. Many removable drives use either the parallel port or a SCSI port for connection. A parallel drive has a 25-pin connector for the cable to the 25-pin parallel port on the back of the PC and another 25-pin connector for the printer cable. A SCSI drive has a 50-pin or 68-pin connector on the drive for the cable to the PC and another connector for the next SCSI device on the external SCSI bus.

2. For a parallel device, turn off your PC and connect the parallel cable from the drive to the parallel port on the PC. If you have a printer, connect the printer cable to the printer port on the drive. Go to Step 5.

3. For a SCSI device, if you already have a SCSI host adapter installed, connect the SCSI cable to the drive and the SCSI port off the host adapter. If you have a new host adapter, open the case and insert the SCSI host adapter card in an expansion slot and then connect the SCSI cable.

4. For a SCSI drive, set the drive's SCSI ID. You might also need to set the host adapter to recognize an external device. See the documentation for the host adapter.

5. Check all your connections and plug the AC power cord for the drive into a wall socket.

6. Turn on your PC and install the software. See the installations procedures in the documentation that came with the removable drive. Most often, the software is on an accompanying disk.

7. If you have problems, turn everything off and check all connections. Power up and try again.

5

Chapter Summary

- Hard drive capacity is determined by the number of heads, tracks, and sectors on the disk, each sector holding 512 bytes of data.

- System BIOS and software can use CHS, large mode, or LBA mode to manage a hard drive. The size of the drive normally determines which mode is used.

- Some older systemboard BIOS does not support larger capacity drives. You can solve the problem by upgrading BIOS, upgrading the systemboard, or using software designed to interface between the drive and the BIOS.

- The FAT or file allocation table lists all clusters on the hard drive and how each is allocated.

- A directory on a hard drive holds the information about each file stored on the drive. The main directory created when the drive is first formatted is called the root directory.

- Commands to manage a hard drive include those to create and remove directories, change the attributes on a file, and list paths where the OS can look to find software. DOS, Windows 3.x, and Windows 95 all offer commands or menu options to perform these tasks.

- Some ways to optimize drive space and access speed are to reduce fragmentation, to compress the drive, and to use disk caching.

- Older hard drives use either MFM or RLL technology. Most hard drives for PCs today use IDE technology. SCSI hard drives refer more to the bus used by the drive than the technology of the drive.

- There are several variations of SCSI buses and bus devices including SCSI-1, SCSI-2, Wide SCSI, and Ultra SCSI.

- Every SCSI bus subsystem requires a host adapter with a SCSI controller and SCSI IDs assigned to each device including the host adapter.

- Each end of the SCSI bus must have a terminating resistor, which can be either hardware or software.

- There are three technologies used by removable drives: magnetic media, optical or magneto-optical, and phase dual.

- Removable drives vary considerably in cost per KB of storage, drop height, half-life of the data, interfaces to the CPU, and other features.

- External removable drives use either a parallel port or a SCSI port to interface with the CPU.

KEY TERMS

- **Adapter card** — Also called an interface card. A small circuit board inserted in an expansion slot and used to communicate between the system bus and a peripheral device.

- **Advanced SCSI programming interface** (**ASPI**) — A popular device driver that enables operating systems to communicate with a SCSI host adapter. (The "A" originally stood for Adaptec.)

- **ATTRIB command** — A DOS command that can display file attributes and even lock files so that they are "read-only" and cannot be modified (for example, ATTRIB +R FILENAME).

- **Batch file** — A text file containing a series of DOS instructions to the computer, telling it to perform a specific task (for example, AUTOEXEC.BAT, which contains a series of startup commands).

- **Buffer** — A temporary memory area where data is kept before being written to a hard drive or sent to a printer, thus reducing the number of writes to the devices.

- **Burst transfer** — A means of sending data across the bus, with one packet immediately following the next, without waiting for clock beats and/or addressing of the information being sent.

- **CD or CHDIR command** — A DOS command to change directories (for example, CD\WINDOWS would change the directory to the Windows directory, and CD\ would return to the Root directory).

- **Chain** — A group of clusters used to hold a single file.

- **CHS (cylinders, heads, sectors)** — The traditional method by which BIOS reads and writes to hard drives by addressing the correct cylinder, head, and sector.

- **Common access method (CAM)** — A standard adapter driver used by SCSI.

- **Compressed drive** — A drive whose format has been reorganized in order to store more data. A compressed drive is really not a drive at all; it's actually a type of file, typically with a host drive called H.

- **Controller board** — An adapter board used to interface between a computer and a device such as a disk drive.

- **Cross-linked clusters** — Errors caused when files appear to share the same disk space, according to the file allocation table.

- **Data compression** — Reducing the size of files by various techniques such as using a shortcut code to represent repeated data.

- **Defragment** — To "optimize" or rewrite a file to a disk in one contiguous chain of clusters, thus speeding up data retrieval.

- **DELTREE command** — A DOS command used to delete a directory, its files, all its subdirectories, and all files within the subdirectories (for example, DELTREE DIRNAME will delete the directory named DIRNAME and everything in it).

- **Device driver** — A small program that tells the computer how to communicate with an input/output device such as a printer or modem.

- **Disk cache** — A method whereby recently retrieved data and adjacent data are read into memory in advance, anticipating the next CPU request.

- **Disk compression** — Compressing data on a hard drive to allow more data to be written to the drive.

- **DriveSpace** — A utility that compresses files so that they take up less space on a disk drive, creating a single large file on the disk to hold all the compressed files.

- **Drop height** — The height that a manufacturer states its drive can be dropped without making the drive unusable.

- **Embedded SCSI devices** — Devices that contain their own host adapter, whereby the SCSI interface is built into the device.

- **Enhanced BIOS** — A newer BIOS that has been written to accommodate larger-capacity gigabyte drives.

- **Enhanced IDE technology** — A newer drive standard that allows systems to recognize drives larger than 528 MB and to handle up to four devices on the same controller.

- **Folder** — A Windows directory for a collection of related files (for instance, a person may find it convenient to create a MYDATA directory, or folder, in which to store personal files).

- **Fragmentation** — The distribution of data files, such that they are stored in noncontiguous clusters.

- **Gigabyte** — Approximately 1 billion bytes of data (actually 2 to the 30th power, or 1,073,741,824 bytes).

- **Half-life** — The time it takes for a medium storing data to weaken to half of its strength. Magnetic media, including traditional hard drives and floppy disks, have a half-life of five to seven years.

- **Hard disk removable drives** — High-capacity drives, such as Zip or Jaz drives, that have disks that can be removed like floppy disks.

- **Hardware cache** — A disk cache that is contained in RAM chips built right on the disk controller.

- **Host adapter** — The circuit board that controls a SCSI bus that supports as many as eight separate devices, one of which is a host adapter that controls communication with the PC.

- **Host drive** — Typically drive H on a compressed drive. *See* Compressed drive.

- **Integrated Device Electronics** (**IDE**) — A hard drive whose disk controller is integrated into the drive, eliminating the need for a signal cable and thus increasing speed, as well as reducing price.

- **Large mode** — A format that supports hard drives that range from 504 MB to 1 GB, mapping the data to conform to the 504 MB barrier before the address information is passed to the operating system.

- **Logical block addressing** (**LBA**) — A method in which the operating system views the drive as one long linear list of LBAs, permitting larger drive sizes (LBA 0 is cylinder 0, head 0, and sector 1).

- **Logical unit number** (**LUN**) — A number from 0 to 7 (also called the SCSI ID) assigned to each SCSI device attached to a daisy chain.

- **Lost clusters** — Lost file fragments that, according to the file allocation table, contain data that does not belong to any file. In DOS, the command CHKDSK/F can free these fragments.

- **Magneto-optical** (**MO**) **drives** — Removable, rewritable, high-capacity drives that combine magnetic and optical disk technology.

- **MD or MKDIR command** — A command used to create a directory on a drive (for example, MD C:\MYDATA).

- **MIRROR command** — An old DOS command that saves information about deleted files as they are deleted. This information can be used later by the UNDELETE command to recover a deleted file. The command can be used to save the partition table to a floppy disk.

- **Normal mode** — The traditional method by which the BIOS reads and writes to hard drives by addressing the correct cylinder, head, and sector. *See* CHS.

- **PATH command** — A command that tells DOS and Windows where to look for executable files (for example, the PATH command in an AUTOEXEC.BAT file might be C:\DOS;C:\WINDOWS).

- **Phase-dual or PD optical drives** — A type of optical hard drive that is rewritable and may store several gigabytes of data, yet can also read traditional CD-ROMs.

- **PnP or Plug-and-Play** — A technology that allows a new device to be connected and automatically recognized by the system. The new device, system BIOS, and OS can all be PnP.

- **RD or RMDIR command** — A DOS command to remove an unwanted Directory (for example, RD C:\OLDDIR). You must delete all files in the directory to be removed, prior to using this command.

- **Reduced write current** — A method whereby less current is used to write data to tracks near the center of the disk, where the bits are closer together.

- **Removable drives** — High-capacity drives, such as Zip or Jaz drives, that have disks that can be removed like floppy disks.

- **Root directory** — The main directory on the computer (often represented as C:\on a hard drive), which typically contains other directories, such as Windows and MSOffice.

- **SCAM (SCSI configuration automatically)** — A method that follows the Plug-and-Play standard, to make installations of SCSI devices much easier, assuming that the device is SCAM compatible.

- **SCSI (small computer system interface)** — A faster system-level interface with a host adapter and a bus that can daisy-chain as many as seven other devices.

- **SCSI-1** — The oldest SCSI bus standard, established in 1986, which requires an 8-bit parallel bus with optional parity checking.

- **SCSI-2** — An improved version of SCSI-1 with several new features and options added. Although compatible, the additional features found in SCSI-2 will be ignored by SCSI-1 devices.

- **SCSI bus adapter chip** — The chip mounted on the logic board of a hard drive that allows the drive to be a part of a SCSI bus system.

- **SCSI ID** — *See* Logical unit number.

- **SMARTDrive** — A hard drive cache program that comes with Windows 3.x and DOS that can be executed as a TSR from the AUTOEXEC.BAT file (for example, DEVICE=SMARTDRV.SYSCACHE-SIZE#).

5

- **Software cache** — Cache controlled by software where the cache is stored in RAM.

- **Terminating resistor** — The resistor added at the end of a SCSI chain to dampen the voltage at the end of the chain. *See* Termination.

- **Termination** — A process necessary to prevent an echo effect of power at the end of the chain resulting in interference of the data transmission. *See* Terminating resistor.

- **TREE command** — A DOS command that shows the disk directories in a graphical layout similar to a family tree (for example, TREE/F shows every filename in all branches of the tree).

- **Ultra-SCSI** — Also called Fast-20 or Fast SCSI. A technology that offers 20 MB/sec burst transfers across 8-bit paths and 40 MB/sec burst transfers across wide 16-bit paths.

- **UNFORMAT command** — A DOS command that performs recovery from an accidental FORMAT, and may also repair a damaged partition table if the partition table was previously saved with MIRROR/PARTN.

- **VCACHE** — A built-in Windows 95 32-bit software cache that doesn't take up conventional memory space or upper memory space, as SmartDrive does.

- **Virtual file allocation table (VFAT)** — A variation of the original DOS 16-bit FAT that allows for long file names.

- **Wide SCSI** — A type of SCSI that allows for 16- to 32-bit parallel data transfer. It has not become a standard in the PC environment.

- **Write precompensation** — A method where data is written faster to the tracks that are near the center of a disk.

REVIEW QUESTIONS

1. Describe how each of the following are related to each other: Platters, heads, cylinders, sectors, and clusters.

2. Given that there are 512 bytes per sector, calculate the hard drive storage for the following:

| heads: 32 | tracks (cylinders): 1024 | sectors/track: 63 |

3. Compare and contrast how CHS (normal mode) and LBA mode manage a hard drive. How can you determine if your hard drive uses LBA mode?

4. What does the acronym FAT stand for and what is the purpose of a FAT?

5. What three files must be in the root directory in order for a drive to be bootable?

6. List two files that are typically hidden.

7. Give a complete DOS prompt command to create a directory called DATA on drive C.

8. Give a complete DOS prompt command to change to a directory called DATA on drive C.

9. How is the command DELTREE different from the command DEL?

10. Give a complete DOS command line to make the file Resume.doc read-only.

11. List all of the DOS commands that would be included in a DOS batch file that would copy all of the files stored in C:\DATA\HOMEWORK to drive A.

12. List the steps to create a new subfolder under the DATA directory in a Windows 95 system.

13. In Windows 95, how would you examine the file properties of the file Resume.doc?

14. What causes a file to be fragmented?

15. In Windows 95, what steps would you use to defragment a file?

16. Typically, what new drive letter is created when a disk is compressed on a non-network drive?

17. What are the disadvantages of compressing a drive?

18. Why does the use of cache memory speed up a computer?

19. What is the storage capacity limit of a normal IDE hard drive? What is the storage capacity limit of a normal EIDE hard drive?

20. List three differences between SCSI and IDE drives.

21. What is a terminating resistor? List three different termination methods.

22. What is a host adapter?

23. List two different technologies for removable drives. List two different brands and models of removable drives.

24. What is a PD drive? Contrast a PD drive with a Jaz drive.

25. What hardware port are most external drives usually attached to?

PROJECTS

USING NUTS & BOLTS TO MANAGE A HARD DRIVE

1. Use the Nuts & Bolts Disk Tune utility to defragment your hard drive. Click Start, Programs, Nuts & Bolts, and Disk Tune. Select the drive to defragment and click Next. When the visual presentation of your hard drive displays, answer these questions:

   a. What is the first cluster number that Nuts & Bolts is accessing to defragment?

   b. What is the last cluster number on your hard drive?

   c. Name at least one file on your hard drive that is fragmented.

   d. Name at least one file on your hard drive that is not fragmented.

5

EXAMINE A HARD DRIVE'S BIOS SETTINGS

1. From the CMOS setup information on your computer, calculate the capacity of the drive. Show your method of calculation.
2. Write down or print all the CMOS settings that apply to your hard drive. Explain each setting that you are able to.

EXAMINE THE FIRST ENTRIES AT THE BEGINNING OF A HARD DRIVE

(Refer to the optional "Behind the Scenes Technology" sections before tackling this project.)

1. Print out the OS boot record of your hard drive. On the printout, label each item in the record and explain it.
2. Print out the beginning of the first FAT on your hard drive (see Figure 5-6). (*Hint:* Use DEBUG and PrintScreen.)
3. Calculate the memory location of the beginning of the second copy of the FAT. Show your method of calculation.
4. Calculate the memory location of the beginning of the root directory. Show your method of calculation.
5. Get a printout of the beginning of the root directory of your hard drive. Identify the first five entries in the root directory and the number of clusters in each entry that make up a file. For each of the five entries, explain the meaning of each ON bit in the attribute byte.

USING DOS AND WINDOWS 3.x TO MANAGE A HARD DRIVE

1. Print the contents of SCANDISK.INI in the \DOS directory of your hard drive. SCANDISK.INI contains settings that SCANDISK for DOS reads and uses when it executes. The Windows 95 version of ScanDisk does not use these settings.
2. What is the setting that allows SCANDISK to delete the contents of a lost cluster without prompting you first?
3. From the INI file information, can SCANDISK repair a damaged boot sector of a compressed drive?
4. Run **SCANDISK** from a DOS prompt. What errors did it find?

5. From a DOS prompt, type **HELP DEFRAG**. What are the cautions listed concerning when not to use DEFRAG?

6. Following the directions from the Help utility, defragment a disk or hard drive using the DEFRAG utility.

7. From a DOS prompt, type **HELP SMARTDRV** and then print the help information about the SmartDrive utility.

8. Look in either the CONFIG.SYS or AUTOEXEC.BAT file of your computer for the SmartDrive command. It should be in one or the other of the two files but not both. Using your printout, explain each option used in the command line.

USING WINDOWS 95 TO MANAGE A HARD DRIVE

1. Using the chapter example of Windows 95 DriveSpace, practice disk compression by compressing a disk. Use a newly formatted disk and a disk about half full of data. Compare the results of the two compressions.

2. With your instructor's permission, use the Defragmenter utility to defragment the hard drive of your computer. Don't use this utility if your disk has been compressed by a utility program other than Windows 95. If you haven't used Windows 95 to compress the drive, look at the documentation for your compression software to see if it offers a defragmenter utility, and use that to defragment the drive.

3. If you are not using add-on utility software to compress your hard drive, use Windows 95 ScanDisk to repair any cross-linked or lost clusters on the drive. If you are using utility software other than Windows 95 to compress your hard drive, use that software utility to scan for cross-linked or lost clusters.

4. Create a file on an empty disk with a long filename. Using DEBUG, display the root directory entries for this file. What are the two filenames in the root directory?

COMPARING THE DATA STORAGE COST OF DEVICES

Research the market (using, for example, *Computer Shopper*) and fill in the following table to compare the storage costs of different secondary storage devices.

Type of Device	High capacity disk	Removable magnetic hard drive	Optical drive	Phase-dual drive
1. Manufacturer				
2. Model				
3. Capacity				
4. Price of drive and first disk				
5. Cost per KB of drive and first disk				
6. Price of additional disk				
7. Cost per KB of additional disk				

RECOVER A FILE

Using a word processor, create and save a short document under the name Test.del. Using Windows Explorer, delete the newly created document. Open the **Recycle Bin**, and select **File**, **Restore** to undelete the file Test.del.

PRACTICING DOS

Perform the following procedures and commands. For a dot matrix printer, adjust the paper in the printer to start exactly at the top of the page. If possible, attempt to complete all steps on one page only. Use the section on "Using DOS to Manage a Hard Drive" as a reference.

1. Cold boot the computer. Go to the DOS prompt.
2. List the directory of drive C in wide format.
3. FORMAT a new system disk in drive A (Use your last name for the volume label.)
4. Switch to drive A. (Look for the A:\> prompt.) List the directory of the newly formatted disk.

5. Switch back to drive C. (Look for the C:\> prompt.)

6. Use the COPY command and the wildcard (*) to copy all files in the root directory to your disk in drive A.

7. Display the current DATE on the monitor.

8. Perform a SCANDISK of drive A.

9. Switch to Drive A. (Be sure the A:\> prompt appears.)

10. ERASE all .COM files from the disk in drive A.

11. List the directory of drive A.

12. Print the screen contents. Turn the printer Off Line (tap the Online button to make the Online light go off). Use the Line Feed or Form Feed button to eject the rest of the page from the printer.

5

HARD DRIVE INSTALLATION AND SUPPORT

This chapter extends Chapter 5's discussion of hard drives to explain how to install a new hard drive and how to use software utility packages to help manage a hard drive. The chapter addresses what to do when a hard drive fails, data is lost, or a drive shows clear signs of impending disaster. You will learn how important it is to keep good backups of software and data stored on your hard drive as well as backups of the partition table, boot record, the root directory, and the FAT. No amount of experience replacing a defective hard drive can substitute for good backups. The data itself is often the most valuable thing inside your computer case.

IN THIS CHAPTER
YOU WILL LEARN:

- HOW TO INSTALL A HARD DRIVE
- ABOUT HARD DRIVE DIAGNOSTIC SOFTWARE
- ABOUT METHODS OF RECOVERING LOST DATA ON HARD DRIVES
- ABOUT HARD DRIVE TROUBLESHOOTING SKILLS

INSTALLING A HARD DRIVE

Hard drive installation is much easier than it was a few years ago. Drives today come already low-level formatted and optimum interleave has already been established. (**Interleave** is a method to speed up data access.) A few years ago, when MFM and RLL drives were popular, you purchased a controller that conformed to the type of drive you had. You then needed to low-level format the drive using either a format program stored in the controller BIOS or some other utility software such as SpinRite. As you did the low-level format, the software would examine your drive and recommend the optimum interleave, and if you wanted, the software would automatically change the interleave to the optimum value. As was explained in the last chapter, today's IDE and SCSI drives are low-level formatted at the factory. Now you should low-level format a hard drive only as a last resort, using a specific low-level format program recommended by the manufacturer to refurbish a failing drive. This chapter will focus on today's IDE and SCSI hard drives

Installation of IDE and SCSI hard drives includes:

- Installing the hardware and setting jumpers and DIP switches
- Informing CMOS setup of the new IDE drive
- Creating one or more partitions on the drive
- High-level formatting the drive partitions
- Installing the OS and other software

PHYSICAL INSTALLATION OF A HARD DRIVE

For an IDE drive installation, you need the drive, an adapter card, a data cable, and perhaps a kit to make the drive fit into a much larger bay. To install a SCSI drive, you need the drive, a cable compatible with the host adapter you are using, possibly an external terminator if the drive is on the end of the daisy chain, a host adapter if you don't already have one, and a kit to make the drive fit the bay. First an IDE drive installation is considered and then a SCSI drive installation.

The first step in any installation is to take some precautions. First, make sure that you have a good bootable disk or Windows 95 rescue disk; test it to make sure it works. Just in case you lose setup in the process, make sure you have a record of your setup screen and the advanced setup screen either written out or to a disk. You should always have these records on hand for a computer that you are responsible for. The next step requires some self-discipline. Before you take anything apart, carefully read all the documentation for the drive and the adapter card, as well as any part of your PC documentation that covers hard drive installation. Look for problems you have not considered, such as IRQ or DMA conflicts if this is a second hard drive for your system. Is your computer limited as to System BIOS? Also check the setup of your computer. Does it accommodate the size and type of hard drive you want to install?

If you plan to use a user-defined type (where you must enter the drive specifications), will your PC accept the values you want? You should find answers to these questions in your PC documentation. If you discover that your PC does not accommodate the large-capacity drive you have, consider changing your ROM BIOS before changing the drive. Or, you could opt to keep the large-capacity drive and not use all of it. Just define it as a smaller drive type.

Make sure that you can picture in your mind the entire installation. If you have any questions, find answers to them before you begin. Either keep reading until you locate the answer, call technical support, or ask a knowledgeable friend. It is better to discover that what you are installing will not work on your computer before you begin. This avoids hours of frustration and a disabled computer. You can't always anticipate every problem, but at least you can know that you made your best effort to understand everything in advance. What you learn in thorough preparation pays off every time!

Having read the documentation for the hard drive, you should understand the meaning of each DIP switch or jumper on the drive. It is now time to set the jumpers and DIP switches. Usually the settings are already correct for an IDE drive to be used as the master drive. Before you change any setting, write down the original ones. Thus, if things go wrong you can always revert back to the original settings and begin again.

While the settings on the drive can be DIP switches, most settings are jumpers. Each drive type can have a different jumper configuration. See the documentation for explanations if they are not written on the drive near the bank of jumpers. A typical arrangement is shown in Figure 6-1. The three choices for jumper settings for this drive are listed in Table 6-1.

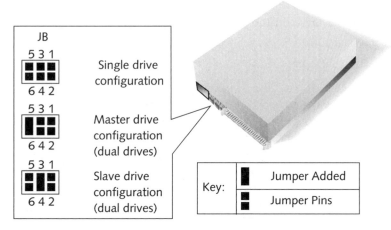

Figure 6-1   Jumper settings on a hard drive and their meaning

Your hard drive might or might not have the first configuration as an option, but it should have a way of indicating if the drive will or will not be the master or boot device. If you are installing a hard drive and do not have the documentation for the drive, you can usually go to the drive manufacturer's Web site to find out what the jumper settings mean as well as other information normally found in the documentation for the drive. One end-of-chapter activity gives you a good example of this.

Table 6-1   Jumper Settings on a Hard Drive

Configuration	Description
Single drive configuration	This is the only hard drive.
Master drive configuration	This is the first of two drives; it is the boot device.
Slave drive configuration	This is the second drive for the system and will not be used as the boot device.

The next step is to prepare a large, well-lit place to work. Set out your tools, the documentation, the new hardware, and your notebook. Remember the basic rules concerning static electricity. Ground yourself and the computer. It's a good idea to not work on carpet in the winter, when there's a lot of static electricity. Some added precautions for working with hard drives are:

- Handle the drive carefully.

- Do not touch any exposed circuitry or chips.

- Prevent other people from touching any exposed microchips on the drive.

- When you first take the drive out of the static-protective package, touch the package containing the drive to a screw holding an expansion card or cover or to a metal part of the computer case for at least two seconds. This will drain the static electricity from the package and your body.

- If you must set the drive down outside the static-protective package, place it component-side up on top of the static-protective package on a flat surface.

- Do not place the drive on the computer case cover or a metal table.

Verify the state of the computer before you turn it off. Know where your starting point is. Does everything work that's supposed to work?

Turn the computer off but leave it plugged in so that it is well grounded. Unplug the monitor and move it to one side. Remove the computer case. Decide which expansion slot you will use for the adapter card. Don't use the one nearest the power supply unless it's your only choice; heat can shorten the life of any card. Check that the cable you are using reaches from the drive to the card. If it doesn't, you may need to use a different expansion slot. Next check that the wire that controls the drive light on the front of the computer case reaches to the front of the case or to wherever the connection for the wire is on the systemboard. My experience has been that this wire often does not reach as far as it should. Either get a new wire or just don't use the drive light. Check that you have a power cord from the power supply that is available.

Next look at the drive bay that you will use for the drive. You must be able to securely mount the drive in the bay; there should be no free movement of the drive once it is screwed down. Line up the drive and bay screw holes and make sure everything will fit. If the bay is too large for the drive, a universal bay kit will enable you to securely fit the drive into the bay. These kits are inexpensive and should create a tailor-made fit. In Figure 6-2 you can see how the universal bay kit adapter works. The adapter spans the distance between the sides of the drive and the bay.

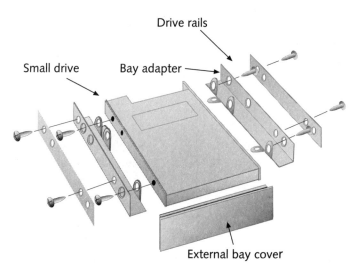

Figure 6-2   Using a universal bay kit to make the drive fit the bay

You don't want the drive to be stressed with any torque. For example, you don't want to force a drive into a space that is too small for it. Also, placing two screws in diagonal positions across the drive can place pressure diagonally on the drive.

For tower cases, the drive can be positioned either horizontally or vertically. There can be external bays that require a bay cover in the front of the tower or internal bays that don't involve the front of the tower (see Figure 6-3).

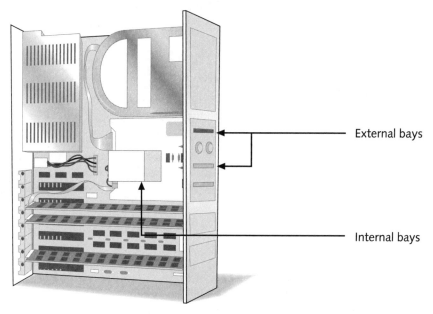

Figure 6-3   A tower case may have internal or external bays

Be careful that screws are not too long so that you don't screw too far into the drive housing and damage the drive itself. After checking the position of the drive and determining how screws are placed, mount the drive in the bay. You might want to connect the data cable and power cord to the drive before or after you screw it down, depending on how accessible the connections are.

Once the drive is in place, insert the adapter card in the expansion slot, being careful not to touch the gold contact fingers on the edge connectors. Use one screw to secure the card to the case at the expansion slot. Don't eliminate this screw: without it cards can work themselves loose over time. Be certain you place the card securely in the slot. The most common error beginners make is not getting the card properly seated (see Figure 6-4).

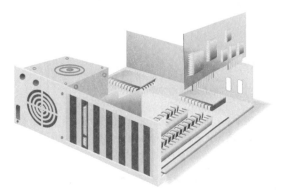

Figure 6-4   Place the adapter card in an expansion slot

Connect the cable, making certain pin 1 and the edge color on the cable are aligned correctly at both ends of the cable. Connect a power cord to the drive. The cord only goes into the connection one way, so you can't go wrong here.

Connect the wire from the card to the drive light on the front of the case, and the hardware installation is done. If you reverse the polarity of the LED wire to the drive light at the front of the case the light will not work. Unless the screw holes in the drive do not align with the screw holes in the bay, or there is some other unusual situation, physical installations go rather quickly.

Before you replace the computer case, plug in the monitor and turn on the computer. Verify that your System BIOS can find the drive before you replace the cover. If you have a problem it will most likely involve a loose cable or adapter card. Here are some things to do and check in this case:

- Turn off the computer and monitor before you do anything inside the case.
- Remove and reattach all drive cables. Check for correct pin 1 orientation.
- Remove and reseat the adapter card.
- Place the adapter card in a different slot.

- Check the jumper or DIP switch settings.

- Inspect the drive for damage such as bent pins on the connection for the cable.

- Check the cable for frayed edges or other damage.

- Check the installation manual for things you might have overlooked. Look for a section about system setup and carefully follow all directions that apply.

INFORMING SETUP OF THE NEW DRIVE

If this drive is the master drive on your computer, you need to boot the computer from a disk. You are now ready to use setup to tell CMOS the hard drive type you are installing. Your computer will probably display a list of hard drive types from which to choose and perhaps offer the option of selecting a user-defined type as well. Follow the directions on your setup screen to scroll through the list of drives the BIOS supports. The list will look similar to the one in Appendix B. The documentation that came with the hard drive tells you which type to choose, and it also tells you the number of heads and cylinders. The head and cylinder information is often written on the top of the drive housing. If your computer does not offer an exact match, you can enter your own values under the user-defined type.

If your computer does not offer an exact match or a user-defined type, you can improvise. You must choose the correct number of heads, but you can select a number of cylinders that is smaller than the number of cylinders the drive actually has. Choosing fewer cylinders causes some cylinders on your drive to remain unused. Choose the number of cylinders closest to the number you actually have without going over.

After you have identified the drive type, save the information to CMOS and reboot your computer from the disk drive to the A prompt. You are now ready to partition the drive.

If you get an error at POST when you reboot, turn off the computer and check the drive and card connections. Check the setup to make sure you have chosen the correct drive type.

BIOS Issues for Large-Capacity Drives

If your drive capacity exceeds 504 MB, BIOS needs to be set with LBA mode active. If BIOS does not support LBA mode, you have these choices:

- Upgrade BIOS or your entire systemboard

- Use an advanced EIDE adapter card that supports LBA mode without software or BIOS settings.

- Use software drivers stored on the hard drive that support LBA mode. Most hard drives come with a disk containing this software. If the disk is not included, check the hard drive manufacturer's Web site and download the software.

BIOS That Is Auto-Detecting

Newer BIOS and hard drives provide for auto-detection. When asked, you can allow the BIOS to determine the drive type for you. For this to work both the BIOS and the hard drive must be built to communicate this information.

MAKING PARTITIONS

After the hard drive is physically installed, the next step is to partition the drive. The partition table is written at the very beginning of the drive and contains information about the size of each partition on the drive and which partition contains the OS that the PC boots. The partitions on the IDE drive are created by the DOS and Windows 95 FDISK utility. For DOS or for Windows 95 upgrades (Windows 95 upgrades must find some DOS on the hard drive before it will install), insert DOS disk 1 in drive A and reboot the computer. FDISK is automatically executed by the install procedure. The FDISK opening menu is shown in Figure 6-5. Select option 1 first to create the partition. The menu in Figure 6-6 appears. Use option 1 to create the primary DOS partition. If you plan to install Windows 95 later, be sure this partition is at least 32 MB, preferably more. The remainder of the hard drive can be an extended DOS partition, using option 2. This extended partition can be divided into logical DOS drives using option 3 on the menu.

With versions of DOS before 5.0, put the disk that contains the FDISK program in the drive and execute FDISK from the A prompt. The program prompts you for the number of partitions you want to create. Make the first partition the active partition. In DOS terms, the active partition is the partition that is used to boot DOS. The active partition will most likely be drive C. If you have other DOS partitions on the same drive, they are called extended partitions by DOS and will be drive D, drive E, and so on. If you are using DOS 3.3 or earlier, you cannot have a partition that is larger than 32 MB.

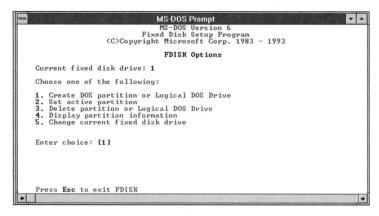

Figure 6-5   Fixed Disk Setup Program (FDISK) menu

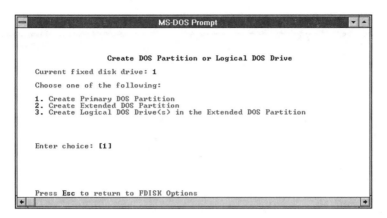

Figure 6-6 FDISK menu to create partitions and logical drives

The non-upgrade version of Windows 95 also begins with DOS. The software comes with a DOS bootable disk. Boot from the disk, which prompts you to partition the drive, format it, and provide enough DOS on the hard drive to install Windows 95.

When the hard drive is partitioned with FDISK (using any version of DOS or of the Windows 95 DOS boot disk), the utility also creates a partition table. The partition table is stored at the very beginning or first physical sector of the hard drive on head 0, track 0, sector 1. Table 6-2 lists the contents of the partition table. Don't confuse the first physical sector of the hard drive with sector 1 as DOS or Windows 95 knows it. The OS's sector 1 comes after the physical sector 1.

The partition table is exactly 512 bytes long and is sometimes called the **master boot sector**. As you can see, the table allows for only four partitions. During POST, the partition table program, sometimes called the **master boot record**, executes, checking the integrity of the partition table itself. If it finds any corruption, it refuses to continue execution, and the disk is unusable. If the table entries are valid, this program looks in the table to determine which partition is the active partition, and it executes the boot program in the boot record of that partition.

Table 6-2 Hard Drive Partition Table

Item	Bytes Used	Description
1	446 bytes	Program that calls the boot program on the DOS boot record
2	16-bytes total	Description of first partition
	1 byte	Is this the bootable partition? (Yes=90h, No=00h)
	3 bytes	Beginning location of partition
	1 byte	System indicator; possible values are:
		0=Not a DOS partition 1=DOS with a 12-bit FAT 4=DOS with a 16-bit FAT 5=Not the first partition 6=Partition larger than 32 MB
	3 bytes	Ending location of partition
	4 bytes	First sector of the partition relative to the beginning of the disk
	4 bytes	Number of sectors in the partition
3	16 bytes	Describes second partition using same format as first partition
4	16 bytes	Describes third partition using same format as first partition
5	16 bytes	Describes fourth partition using same format as first partition
6	4 bytes	Signature of the partition table, always AA55

As shown in Figure 6-7, you can display partition table information by choosing option 4 of FDISK. This function is a useful tool in diagnosing hard drive problems. If the partition table is damaged, FDISK displays an error message.

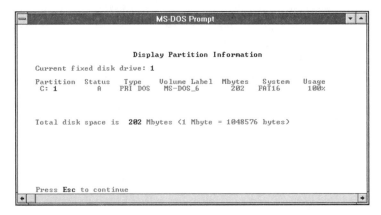

Figure 6-7 FDISK displays partition information

Why Use More Than One Partition

Some people prefer to use more than one partition or logical drive to organize their hard drives, especially if they plan to have Windows 3.x and Windows 95 on the same drive. Another reason to use more than one partition is that the cluster size of the partition is partly determined by how large the partition is. You may choose to use more than one partition so that your clusters will be smaller. Smaller clusters increase the efficiency of your hard drive space, especially if you store many small files on the drive.

There is a limitation of 2 GB for a single DOS partition, so if your drive has more than a 2 GB capacity you must create more than one partition.

6

OS OR HIGH-LEVEL FORMAT

A low-level format writes sector and track markings to the drive. Then the drive is partitioned using the FDISK utility. The next step in preparing the drive for use is to high-level format the drive.

Each partition or logical drive within a partition must be individually formatted by an OS. This is called the high-level format or the OS format. The Windows 95 or DOS format writes the **boot record** in the first sector of each partition. This boot record is sometimes called the **DOS boot record (DBR)** or **volume boot record**. DOS or Windows 95 identifies this sector as sector 0 for each "drive" or partition. Following the boot record, the OS creates two copies of the FAT as well as the root directory, just as it does on disks. When the OS creates the FAT, the FORMAT program scans the track and sector markings that were created by the low-level format of the drive. If the low-level format encounters bad or unusable sectors, it marks these sectors so that the FORMAT program can recognize them as bad. FORMAT marks them in the FAT as bad sectors. The FFF7 entry in the FAT marks an entire cluster as bad so that the drive will not use these areas.

If you include the /S option in the FORMAT command, the program also writes the two hidden files and COMMAND.COM to the drive. The hard drive is now bootable. If you are using a DOS 5 or later installation disk, the install procedure also creates the \DOS directory and copies the rest of the DOS software to that directory. If you are using an earlier version of DOS, you must create the \DOS directory yourself and copy the files to it using the COPY command. You should also create an AUTOEXEC.BAT file and a CONFIG.SYS file. The commands in these two files are discussed in Chapter 1.

INSTALLING SOFTWARE

You are now ready to install Windows 3.x or Windows 95. If you are using the non-upgrade version of Windows 95, the DOS bootable disk has put enough DOS on the hard drive to allow you to boot from the drive. Nowhere is it so clear that Windows 95 still uses this

DOS 7.0 core as when you are preparing a hard drive for Windows 95. DOS 7.0 has created the partition, the FAT, and the root directory in preparation for Windows 95.

If you are installing Windows 95 from a CD-ROM, the CD-ROM driver needs to be installed next. CD-ROM installation is covered in more detail in Chapter 8, but you can generally load the CD-ROM drivers onto the hard drive using the disk that comes with the CD-ROM drive.

After your new hard drive is bootable and you have installed either Windows 3.x or Windows 95, you are ready to load the applications software, a subject that is addressed in later chapters. Once your drive has software completely loaded and working, there's no better time to make a complete backup of the entire drive to tape with utility software designed for that purpose. Also, for Windows 3.x and DOS, make a bootable disk that contains all the files in the root directory of the drive. This disk will be your emergency disk if you have trouble with the drive later. For Windows 95, make a rescue disk as discussed in Chapter 2.

Saving the Partition Table to Disk

If you have DOS 5, Norton Utilities, Nuts & Bolts, PC Tools, or other similar software, create a "rescue" disk to recover from a corrupted partition table. How to save the partition table using Norton Utilities, Nuts & Bolts, and PC Tools is covered when each software program is introduced in the next section. To use DOS to make a copy of the partition table, follow these directions:

1. Locate the DOS 5 MIRROR command, which creates a file on a disk that contains a copy of the partition table. If you are using a later version of DOS or Windows 95 that does not include the MIRROR command, you might have to do some searching to find it. Once you locate a copy of the older DOS 5, be sure to save the MIRROR command for future use.

2. Use the MIRROR command to save the partition table. The command line is:

```
C:\> MIRROR /PARTN
```

The DOS UNFORMAT command restores the partition table from the disk. Details were given in Chapter 5.

WHEN THINGS GO WRONG

Sometimes trouble will crop up during the installation process. Keeping a cool head, thinking things carefully through a second, third, and fourth time, and using all available resources will most likely get you out of any mess. Installing a hard drive is not difficult unless you have an unusually complex situation.

For example, your first hard drive installation should not involve installing a second SCSI drive into a system that has two SCSI host adapters. Nor should you install a second drive into a system that uses a disk controller for one drive on the systemboard and an adapter card in an expansion slot for the other. If a complicated installation is necessary and you have never installed a hard drive, consider asking for some expert help! Know your limitations. Start with the simple and build your way up. Using what you have learned in this chapter and in Chapter 5, you should be able to install a single IDE drive in a PC or a second slave drive using the same adapter card and cable as the master drive. After mastering that, tackle something more complicated.

Here are some errors that might occur during a hard drive installation, their causes, and what to do about them. This list has been compiled from experience! Everyone makes mistakes when learning something new, and you probably will, too. You can then add your own experiences to this list.

1. The IDE adapter card and IDE hard drive were physically installed. The machine was turned on and the setup was told what drive was present. When the machine was rebooted from a disk, the following error message was displayed:

   `Hard drive not found.`

   Even though the hard drive is not yet bootable, POST should be able to find it. We turned off the machine, checked all cables, and discovered the data cable from the card to the drive was not tightly connected. We reseated the cable and rebooted. POST found the drive.

2. We got to the same point as in the previous situation except that we had replaced the cover on the computer case. When we rebooted from a disk, POST beeped three times and stopped.

   Diagnostics during POST are often communicated by beeps if the tests take place before POST has checked video and made it available to display the messages. Three beeps on most computers signal a memory error. We turned the computer off and checked the memory SIMMs on the systemboard. A SIMM positioned at the edge of the systemboard next to the cover had accidentally been bumped as we replaced the cover. We reseated the SIMM and booted from a disk again, this time with the cover still off. The error disappeared.

3. The card and drive were physically installed and the computer was turned back on. The following error was displayed:

   `No boot device available.`

   We forgot to insert a bootable disk. We put the disk in the drive and rebooted the machine.

4. We physically installed the card and drive, inserted a disk in the disk drive and rebooted. The following error message was displayed:

   `Configuration/CMOS error. Run setup.`

   This error message is normal. POST did not find the hard drive it was expecting. The next step is to run setup.

5. We physically installed the card and drive and tried to reboot from a disk. The error message 601 displayed on the screen. Any error message in the 600 range refers to the disk. Since the case cover was still off, we looked at the connections and discovered that the power cord to the disk drive was not connected. (It had been disconnected earlier to expose the hard drive bay underneath.) We turned off the machine and plugged the cable in. The error message went away.

6. The hard drive just did not physically fit in the bay. The screw holes did not line up. We got a bay kit, but it just didn't seem to work.

   We took a break, went to lunch, and came back to make a fresh start. We asked others to help who could view the brackets, holes, and screws from a fresh perspective. It didn't take long to discover correct alignment for the brackets in the bay.

7. We physically installed a drive and card after changing DIP switch settings on the drive. We booted up, changed setup, and rebooted. The following error message was displayed:

   `Hard drive not present.`

   We rechecked all physical connections and found everything OK. After checking the DIP switch settings, we realized we had set the settings as if this was the second drive of a two-drive system when this was the only drive. Changing the DIP switches back to their original state was the solution. In this case, as in most cases, the DIP switches were already set correctly at the factory.

   One last caution. When things are not going well, you can tense up and make mistakes more easily. But there's one very costly error that you want to be certain to avoid. If you're trying to boot without success, be sure to turn off the machine before doing anything inside. A friend was in this situation once. After trying and retrying to boot for some time, he got frustrated and careless. He plugged the power cord into the drive without turning the PC off. Smoke went up and everything went dead. The next thing he learned was how to replace a power supply!

Calling Technical Support

To make calls to technical support more effective, have as much of the following information as you can available before you call. This includes:

- Drive model and description
- Manufacturer and model of your computer
- Exact wording of error message, if you've gotten one
- Description of the problem
- Hardware and software configuration for your system

INSTALLING A SCSI DRIVE

When you install a SCSI drive, make sure that your host adapter and the cables you are using are compatible with the SCSI hard drive. The vendor can help you here. Read the documentation for both the SCSI host adapter and the hard drive before beginning; most SCSI documentation is well-written and thorough. In addition to the procedure already discussed for IDE hard drives, a SCSI installation requires that you configure the SCSI host adapter and the SCSI hard drive so they can communicate with each other. This is done as follows:

1. **Set SCSI IDs.** Set the ID for each device on the SCSI bus. The host adapter documentation will probably explain that the host adapter must be set to ID 7. If the hard drive will be the boot device for the system, its ID must be 0. The second hard drive ID is usually 1.

2. **Disable or Enable Disk Drive and Hard Drive Controllers.** If the host adapter has a built-in disk drive controller that you are not using, the controller must be disabled with jumper or DIP switches or from the SCSI software setup program. The host adapter documentation will explain how to do this. Incidentally, if you are not using a hard drive or disk drive controller on your systemboard, you must disable these controllers by setting jumpers or DIP switches on the systemboard. See the documentation for your systemboard.

3. **Terminating Resistors.** Devices on both ends of the bus must have terminating resistors enabled so that the voltages to these devices do not spike. The documentation will advise you to use terminating resistors that plug into a socket on the board or device, or to use terminating resistor connections where the cable plugs into the device. Some host adapters have jumper or DIP switches that enable or disable resistors on the card. Again, the documentation will be specific.

4. **CMOS Setup for a SCSI System.** After you have physically installed the SCSI host and drive, you must tell setup that the SCSI system is present. Remember that for SCSI devices, the computer does not communicate with the hard drive directly but interfaces with the SCSI host adapter. To use a SCSI hard drive, some computers require that you tell setup that no hard drive is present. The SCSI host provides that information to the computer by way of a device driver in CONFIG.SYS. Sometimes, the computer setup will have the choice of a SCSI hard drive type. That's all it needs to know, and the SCSI host adapter takes over from there. To recognize a SCSI drive, some computers require that the drive type be set to 1 in setup.

5. **SCSI Device Drivers.** A SCSI bus system on a computer using DOS requires a SCSI device driver to be loaded in the CONFIG.SYS file of the bootable drive. Windows 95 offers its own SCSI driver, although if the host adapter documentation recommends you use the adapter's driver instead, then do so. As was described in Chapter 5, the two better-known device drivers for SCSI systems are ASPI and CAM. After the physical installation and changing CMOS setup, the next step in any hard drive installation is to boot from a disk. For SCSI hard drives, that is the boot device. The hard drive package will include a bootable disk that

loads the device driver to access the SCSI system. In addition to the files necessary to boot to a DOS prompt, for a SCSI installation the disk has a CONFIG.SYS file that contains the DEVICE= line to load the SCSI driver. In addition to the CONFIG.SYS file, the file containing the driver program must also be on the disk. (It's a good idea to have more than one bootable disk available. If you have problems, you can boot from the one that doesn't have the SCSI driver on it.) After you have partitioned and DOS-formatted the drive, the installation disk will put this same device driver on your hard drive.

The procedure has more steps if the SCSI drive is installed on the same computer with an IDE drive. For this installation, the IDE drive must be the boot drive and the SCSI drive must be the secondary drive. Because the SCSI bus does not contain the boot device, you must communicate the location of the boot drive to the SCSI host adapter. Again, the documentation for the host adapter will explain how to do this. It may tell you to disable the SCSI host adapter BIOS and drive the SCSI bus (no pun intended) with a device driver loaded in the CONFIG.SYS file of the bootable non-SCSI hard drive.

If you have a CD-ROM drive or other device on the SCSI bus, its device drivers may need to be installed in CONFIG.SYS for the device to operate. Place the DEVICE= command for any SCSI device after the DEVICE= command that loads the SCSI host device driver.

A SCSI hard drive installation is a little more complicated than an ordinary IDE installation, but by having a SCSI bus on your system you are ready to add other SCSI devices to this bus, such as a CD-ROM drive or a cassette tape for backups.

MULTIPLE OPERATING SYSTEMS

You can install DOS with Windows 3.1 and Windows 95 on the same hard drive so that you can use software made for each operating environment within its native OS. To do this, follow these general procedures:

1. Install DOS 6.x on your hard drive, using the DOS setup disk to partition and format the drive. DOS installs itself in a directory named \DOS.

2. Install Windows 3.x. By default, it installs itself in the \WINDOWS directory.

3. Because Windows 95 deletes some DOS utility programs, back up your \DOS directory to a different directory using this command:

   ```
   XCOPY C:\DOS\*.* C:\DOSSAVE\*.* /e
   ```

4. Install Windows 95. When asked for the directory name, chose a directory name that is different from the directory in which Windows 3.x is installed, such as \WIN95.

5. Edit the Windows 95 system file, MSDOS.SYS, in the root directory to allow for a dual boot by making the MSDOS.SYS so that it is not hidden, not read-only, and not a system file, using this command:

   ```
   ATTRIB -R -H -S C:\MSDOS.SYS
   ```

6. Now open MSDOS.SYS with any text editor, such as EDIT, and in the [OPTIONS] section, add this line:

```
BootMulti=1
```

This setting allows for a multi-boot. Save the file.

7. Reboot your PC. The PC normally boots to Windows 95. If you want to boot to DOS and Windows 3.x, press F8 when you see the message that Windows 95 is starting to stop the process. A menu displays. Choose the option that says a previous version of MS-DOS.

Windows 95 saves DOS files under different names when it is installed. When you reboot to the previous version of MS-DOS, Windows 95 renames the files for DOS back to the names that DOS will expect. Table 6-3 lists the renamed files.

6

Table 6-3   DOS and Windows 95 Files That Get Renamed by Windows 95

Name when Windows 95 is Active	Name when DOS is Active	This File Belongs To
AUTOEXEC.BAT	AUTOEXEC.W40	Windows 95
AUTOEXEC.DOS	AUTOEXEC.BAT	DOS
COMMAND.COM	COMMAND.W40	Windows 95
COMMAND.DOS	COMMAND.COM	DOS
CONFIG.SYS	CONFIG.W40	Windows 95
CONFIG.DOS	CONFIG.SYS	DOS
IO.SYS	WINBOOT.SYS	Windows 95
IO.DOS	IO.SYS	DOS
MSDOS.SYS	MSDOS.W40	Windows 95
MSDOS.DOS	MSDOS.SYS	DOS

UTILITY SOFTWARE

This section examines three popular utility software programs: Nuts & Bolts (which is included on a CD-ROM with this book) Norton Utilities, and PC Tools. Each of the following descriptions tells you what to expect from the software with regard to recovery from a hard drive failure; they do not, however, provide a complete listing of all the software's functions. You can find detailed instructions for performing the operations discussed here in the documentation for the software.

NORTON UTILITIES

Norton Utilities offers several easy-to-use tools to recover data, resurrect a damaged hard drive, enhance hard drive speed and performance, and provide security. Figure 6-8 shows all the programs available under the Norton Utility software. Following is an overview of each of the Norton Utility programs with reference to three main functions: prevention of damage, recovery from damage, and increased system performance.

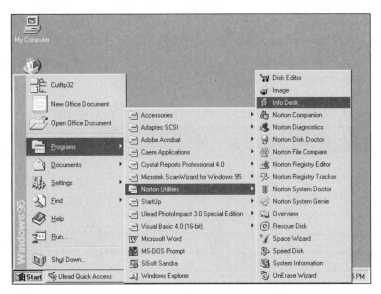

Figure 6-8   The programs of Norton Utilities

Prevention

Preparing in advance for problems that may occur later is the key to making the best use of Norton Utilities. Four programs that help you do that are Norton System Doctor, Norton Protection, Rescue Disk, and Image.

Norton System Doctor.   Norton System Doctor detects potential disk and system problems and scans for viruses. By default it runs in the background at all times and informs you when it encounters a problem. You determine when Norton System Doctor should react to certain problems and what it should do about them. You can configure it to check the integrity of your hard drive routinely and to automatically open Norton Disk Doctor if it encounters a problem. Figure 6-9 shows some sample alarms produced by Norton System Doctor while running in the background.

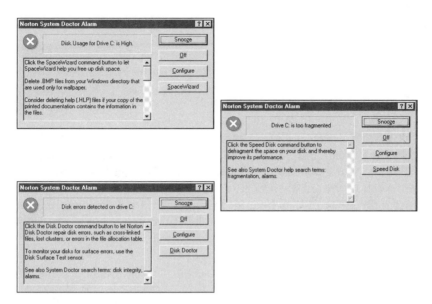

Figure 6-9   Examples of Norton System Doctor alarms

Norton Protection.   Norton Protection adds an extra layer of protection to the Windows 95 Recycle Bin.

Rescue Disk.   Norton Utilities allows you to create a rescue disk set that you can use to recover from hard drive disasters. Once they are created, you can use them to:

- Format a hard drive
- Make a bootable disk
- Partition your hard drive using FDISK
- Recover erased files
- Recover accidentally formatted disks or heavily damaged disks including a damaged partition table and boot record
- Recover damaged files using Disk Editor
- Recover your CMOS setup
- Troubleshoot hardware conflicts using Norton Diagnostics

Norton System Doctor can be configured to alert you whenever the rescue disk information becomes out of date.

Image.   Image creates a snapshot of disk information including the boot record, FAT, and root directory information. You can configure Image to record this data each time you boot.

Recovery

Norton Utilities offers five programs to help in recovering data and setup information and repairing damaged areas of the hard drive and disks. They are Norton Disk Doctor, UnErase Wizard, Norton Registry Tracker, Norton File Compare, and a DOS program called Disk Editor.

Norton Disk Doctor. Norton Disk Doctor (NDD) automatically repairs many hard disk and disk problems without your intervention. If you ask it to, it creates a backup of the disk before it makes any changes (called the Undo feature). Norton Disk Doctor examines and makes some repairs to the partition table, the DOS boot record, the FAT, directories, and files. It also scans the entire disk looking for inconsistencies and diagnoses the disk problems for you, giving you a printed report of the results. If the disk is physically damaged, NDD can mark bad clusters in the FAT so they are not reused. However, Norton Disk Doctor is not a cure-all; some problems are beyond its capabilities.

UnErase Wizard. UnErase Wizard offers added functionality to the Windows 95 Recycle Bin to help recover erased files.

Norton Registry Tracker. Norton Registry Tracker monitors changes to the Windows 95 registry and allows you to backtrack changes to the registry.

Norton File Compare. Norton File Compare compares data files as well as Windows 95 registry and INI files.

Disk Editor. Disk Editor is a powerful tool for editing any part of a disk or hard drive including the partition table, directory entries, DOS boot record, and FAT. Disk Editor can freely access any portion of the disk. You can reconstruct files manually sector by sector, and Disk Editor can sometimes read a disk that DOS or Windows 95 refuses to read. Using Disk Editor requires an understanding of how data is stored on a disk as explained in Chapters 4 and 5.

Performance

The four programs designed to improve overall system performance are Norton System Genie, Norton Registry Editor, Speed Disk, and Space Wizard.

Norton System Genie. Norton System Genie allows you to change the way Windows 95 starts up, looks and feels, handles files, and runs applications software.

Norton Registry Editor. Norton Registry Editor is an alternative to the Windows 95 registry editor offering improved user interface and functionality.

Speed Disk. Speed Disk is an enhanced disk defragmenter that also allows you to affect the order in which files and folders are written to a disk.

The Help Features of Norton Utilities

Norton Utilities offers several ways to access its help features. One method is the direct access to Info Desk. Click **Start**, **Programs**, **Norton Utilities**, **Info Desk** to call up the Info Desk window as shown in Figure 6-10. The Index tab works very much like the index of a book: type some characters or a word, and items appear that you can choose to display or print.

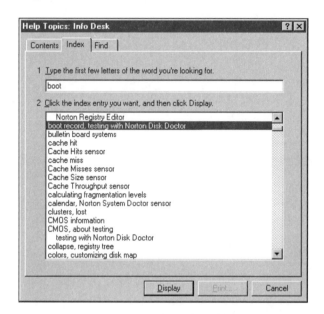

Figure 6-10   One Norton Help Utility – The Info Desk

Another way to access the Norton help features is from the utility programs themselves. For example, if you select **Rescue Disk** from the program list in Figure 6-8 to create a new rescue disk set, the Rescue Disk screen appears. From that window, if you click on the Options button, the Norton Rescue Options window displays as in Figure 6-11. The third item in the list on the rescue disk is Rescue. To find out more about this item, right click the item. The dialog box in Figure 6-12 displays. Select **What's This** for information about the item; select **How To** for step-by-step procedures involving this item; and select **Info Desk** for a direct link to the Info Desk and its information about this item. You can also click the **?** in the title bar of each window for general information about the window.

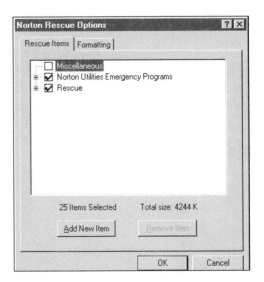

Figure 6-11   Norton Rescue Disk Options

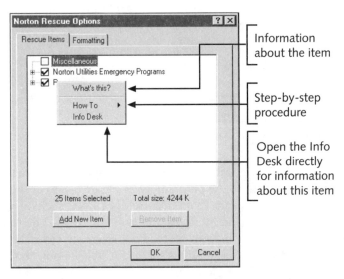

Figure 6-12   To find out more about a Norton Rescue Option,
Right click on the item

Creating and Viewing Contents of Norton Utilities Rescue Disk Set

To view the contents and create a set of rescue disks that contain, among other things, a backup of the hard drive partition table and boot records, follow these directions: Click **Start**, **Programs**, **Norton Utilities**, **Rescue Disk**. When the Rescue Disk opening screen appears, click **Options** (Figure 6-11). Click the + sign to the left of an item to see the list under that item. For example, to see a list of files that will be included on the rescue disks, click the + sign to the left of Rescue. Figure 6-13 shows part of the list. Note that the Boot Record is in the list. Further down in the list the partition table would also be listed. From the options screen, you can choose to include or exclude certain items from the list. When finished, return to the previous screen by clicking **OK**.

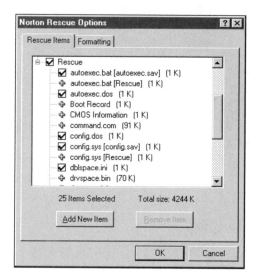

Figure 6-13   Files and information on the Norton Rescue Disk

NUTS & BOLTS

Nuts & Bolts by Helix Software Co. is made up of four suites: Repair and Recover, Clean and Optimize, Prevent and Protect, and Secure and Manage. This somewhat limited discussion of recovering from a hard drive failure looks at only one of the four utilities included in the Repair and Recover utility package. The programs in the Repair and Recover segment of the software are as follows:

- **Disk Minder** diagnoses and repairs hard drive problems including the partition table, boot record, FAT, files, and directories.

- **Image** creates an image of critical disk information, which is written to a file on the hard drive to be used later if the disk is corrupted.

- **Rescue Disk** creates a disk from which you can boot and begin the recovery process if you can't start the system from the hard drive.

- **Discover Pro** displays information about hardware and software and lets you run diagnostics and benchmark tests.

Figure 6-14 shows the main menu of Nuts & Bolts together with WinGuage, part of the Prevents and Protects feature, which constantly monitors the system for potential problems (including applications software crashes) before they occur. Following is a look at three utilities useful in repairing hard drive errors.

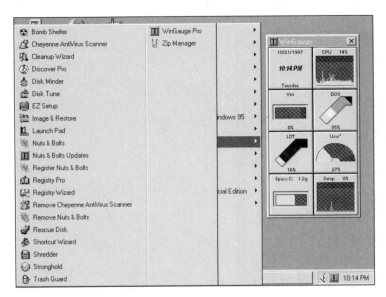

Figure 6-14 Nuts & Bolts main menu together with WinGauge that monitors system resources

Disk Minder

From the main menu of Nuts & Bolts shown in Figure 6-14, click on **Disk Minder** to access this feature of the software. Figure 6-15 displays the opening screen. Click on **Properties** to display the box in Figure 6-16 showing the options that Disk Minder will check. Disk Minder includes the functionality of ScanDisk plus additional features and is faster than ScanDisk. Disk Minder can check and correct problems with the partition table, boot sector, FAT, disk compression structure, directories, filenames, file dates and times, and clusters.

This version of Disk Minder is run under Windows 95 or Windows 3.x, but Disk Minder for DOS is also included in the software in the event you cannot boot from the hard drive. Look for directions below under the section "Rescue Disk." After you have recovered the hard drive so that you can boot from it again, use Disk Minder for Windows to complete the recovery process.

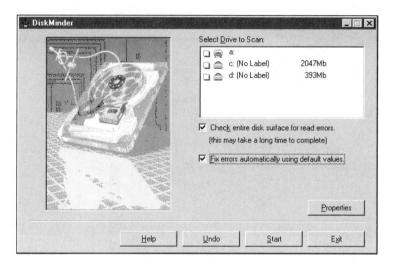

Figure 6-15   Nuts & Bolts Disk Minder opening dialog box

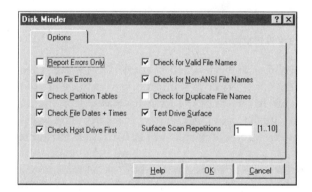

Figure 6-16   Nuts & Bolts Disk Minder will check these things
                  on a disk

Image

Select **Image** from the buttons in Figure 6–14 to access this utility, which creates a snapshot of critical sectors of the hard drive and stores this information on the hard drive in a .DAT file. You can set Image so that it takes this snapshot each time you boot. In the event of a hard drive crash or destruction caused by a virus or other catastrophe, use Image to restore the directories and FAT to the place they were when the last snapshot was taken. Use Image frequently so that your snapshot will be current if it is needed. When you select Image from the Nuts & Bolts main menu, the Image dialog box displays. Click **Properties** to see the dialog box in Figure 6–17. From this Image Properties dialog box, you can choose to have Image take a snapshot of the hard drive every time the PC is booted.

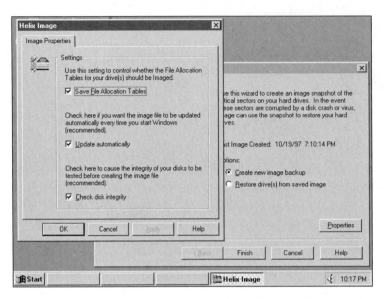

Figure 6-17 Image Properties shows how to have Nuts & Bolts take a snapshot of critical areas of the hard drive each time Windows is loaded

Figure 6-18 shows the dialog box that appears when you select "Restore drive from saved image" from the Image dialog box. Click **Next** to select the hard drive; you are then given a list of all snapshot images that Image has made of the hard drive, as seen in Figure 6-19. Note that these files have been created in the root directory of the hard drive. Click **Next** and Figure 6-20 displays, allowing you to select which areas of the hard drive to restore. You would not want to select the file allocation tables if many changes have been made to the file structure on the hard drive since the last snapshot was made. Use Disk Minder instead. However, the master boot sector and the partitions table information should not have changed since the drive was last partitioned and formatted or drive compression was implemented. Click **Finish** to restore the selected areas of the drive. The Image restore process can also be implemented from the Nuts & Bolts rescue disk. Nuts & Bolts writes the Image snapshot file to the drive in such a way that it can read the file even from a drive that is severely damaged.

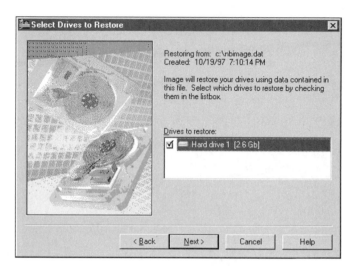

Figure 6-18   Restoring a hard drive from the Image snapshot

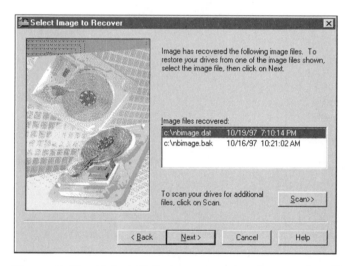

Figure 6-19   Nuts & Bolts Image creates the snapshot files in
the root directory of the hard drive

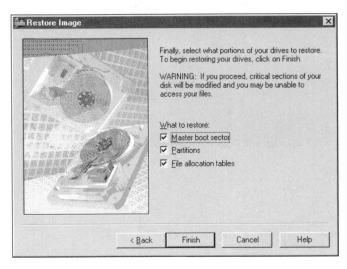

Figure 6-20   What Nuts & Bolts Image can restore on a damaged
hard drive

Rescue Disk

Create a rescue disk from the Nuts & Bolts main menu to be used in the event you cannot boot from the hard drive. When the opening dialog box of the Rescue Disk utility
displays, click on **Advanced** to see the files that the utility will write to the disk as seen in
Figure 6-21. You can add other files to the list or remove files from the list. Click **OK** to
return to the opening dialog box and click **Next** to complete the process.

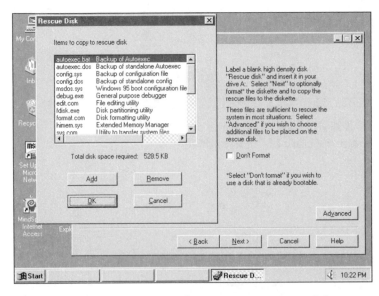

Figure 6-21   Items Nuts & Bolts stores on a rescue disk

When you cannot boot from the hard drive, boot from the rescue disk. After booting, the screen in Figure 6-22 automatically displays asking if the rescue disk was created on your system or on another PC. If the rescue disk was not created on your current PC, Nuts & Bolts can still be effective in recovering the drive. In either case, Nuts & Bolts will examine the drive and then display the menu in Figure 6-23. From this you can use the DOS versions of Disk Minder, Image/Restore, and SysRecover to repair the drive.

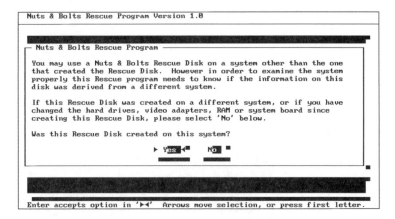

Figure 6-22   Using the Nuts & Bolts rescue disk

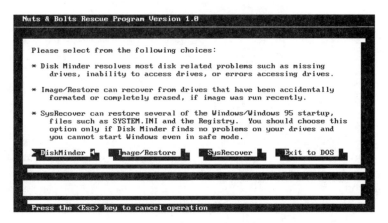

Figure 6-23   Utilities available on the Nuts & Bolts rescue disk

PC TOOLS

PC Tools is a collection of data recovery and utility software as well as a desktop manager. Though it offers many features, the ones listed below are only those that apply to this discussion of hard drives:

- The program diagnoses a hard drive or disk, informing you of damage that it finds, recommending and asking permission to repair the damage. The repair process is reversible.

- The program allows you to create a recovery disk containing the partition table, boot record, and setup information. You are given the opportunity to create the recovery disk during the installation of PC Tools or you can create the disk after installation using this command:

  ```
  C:\PCTOOLS> INSTALL /RD
  ```

- The program includes a virus scan utility, a disk cache, and defragment utilities.

- The program can do a nondestructive low-level format.

- The program includes a powerful hex editor that allows you to edit files without disturbing header records or footer records that contain special information about the file used by the applications software that created it.

- The program offers UNDELETE and UNFORMAT utilities and a backup utility.

AN OUNCE OF PREVENTION

Taking good care of your hard drive is not difficult, but it does require a little time. Before beginning a discussion of hard drive troubleshooting and data recovery, here are some precautions you can take to protect your data and software as well as the drive itself.

- **Make Backups and Keep Them Current.** It's worth saying again: keep backups. Never trust a computer; it'll let you down. Make a backup of your hard drive partition table, boot record, and CMOS setup. Whenever you install a new software package, back it up to disks or tape. Keep data files in directories separate from the software to make backing up data easier. Back up the data as often as every four hours of data entry. Rotate the backup disks or tapes by keeping the last two or three most recent backups.

- **Defragment Files and Scan the Hard Drive Occasionally.** A fragmented hard drive increases access time, and reading and writing files wears out the drive. If you are trying to salvage a damaged file, it is much more difficult to recover a fragmented file than one stored in contiguous clusters. Regularly scan your hard drive for lost or cross-linked clusters.

- **Don't Smoke Around Your Hard Drive.** To a read/write head, a particle of smoke on a hard drive platter is like a boulder with a 10-foot circumference in the highway. Hard drives are not airtight. One study showed that smoking near a computer reduced the average life span of a hard drive by 25%.

- **Don't Leave the PC Turned Off for Weeks or Months at a Time.** Once my daughter left her PC turned off for an entire summer. At the beginning of the new school term, the PC would not boot. We discovered the master boot record had become corrupted. PCs are like cars in this respect: long spans of inactivity can cause problems.

- **High Humidity Can Be Dangerous for Hard Drives.** High humidity is not good for hard drives. I once worked in a basement with PCs and hard drives failed much too often. After installing dehumidifiers, the hard drives became more reliable.

6

DATA RECOVERY

This section focuses on recovering data and configuration information on a disk or hard drive. Nuts & Bolts, Norton Utilities, and PC Tools are all discussed. An optional section, "Behind the Scenes Technology: Data Recovery," is included if you desire to better understand what is actually stored on the drive and what these programs do to recover and repair these areas of the drive.

RETURNING TO FLOPPY DISKS

Floppy disks are inexpensive and less risky to use than a hard drive when learning new skills. This section returns to earlier discussions in Chapter 4 on using floppy disks and on how to recover data from a damaged one. You can easily apply data recovery skills practiced on floppy disks to hard disks.

Damaged Boot Record

Begin at the beginning, with the disk's boot record. If you try to read a disk, you might have a bad boot record if you get the error message:

```
Unable to read drive A:   Abort, Retry, Fail.
```

Here are some methods to restore the damaged area of the disk. If the boot record is not the problem, none of these methods does any further damage to the disk (although they won't help either).

The primary tools for disk troubleshooting and repair in this chapter are Nuts & Bolts and Norton Utilities. The discussion of the Windows 95 version of Norton Utilities below refers to Version 2.0, although other versions offer the same or similar functionality. The intent here is not to review all the features Norton Utilities offers, but simply to view and demonstrate some techniques to repair the disk and hard drive problems discussed below.

Contents of the Boot Record. Table 6-4 shows the complete record layout for the boot record. The medium descriptor byte tells the OS what type of disk this is. The values of this descriptor byte are given in Table 6-5.

Table 6-4 Layout of Boot Record

Description	Number of Bytes
Machine code	11
Bytes per sector	2
Sectors per cluster	1
Reserved	2
Number of FATs	1
Number of root directory entries	2
Number of logical sectors	2
Medium descriptor byte	1
Sectors per FAT	2
Sectors per track	2
Heads	2
Number of hidden sectors	2
Program to load DOS	Remainder of the sector

Table 6-5 Disk Type and Descriptor Byte

Disk Type	Descriptor Byte
3½-inch double-density floppy disk, 720 K	F9
3½-inch high-density floppy disk, 1.44 MB	F0
Hard Disk	F8

Depending on the utility program you are using, you might or might not be able to read the boot record directly. Later in this chapter there is an optional section using DEBUG, where you can see each entry in the table as it is written to the disk.

If the boot record on a disk is damaged, you might get an error message such as "Invalid media type", "Non-DOS disk", or "Unable to read from Drive A" when you first try to read from the disk. In any of these cases, if the boot record is damaged the most practical approach is to simply recover any data on the disk and then reformat the disk.

Recovering from a Damaged Disk. If a disk cannot be read by DOS or Windows, perform a DISKCOPY to copy the data on the disk to another disk. From the command prompt, the command is:

```
DISKCOPY A: A:
```

You will be instructed to insert first the source disk and then the destination disk until all the data is copied to a new disk. If the data is intact, you should be able to read it from the new disk.

Using Norton Utilities to Examine the Boot Record. To examine the contents of a boot record on a disk using Norton Utilities, follow these directions:

1. Access Norton Utilities Disk Editor. One way is to click **Start**, **Programs**, **Norton**, **Disk Editor**. Since Disk Editor is a DOS program, Windows 95 will be unloaded and Norton will load Disk Editor from a DOS prompt. When you exit Disk Editor, Norton returns you to Windows 95.

2. From the opening screen of Disk Editor, choose the Object menu by pressing **ALT-O**.

3. Select **A: 3½-inch disk** and select **OK**. Since you won't have the use of the mouse, use the Tab key to move to the correct option and then press **Enter**.

4. Select the Object menu by pressing **ALT-O**.

5. Select **Boot Record** from the menu.

6. The contents of the Boot Record display. Compare the results to Table 6-4.

You can also repair a boot record if you know the data that appears in Norton Disk Doctor to be incorrect. This activity can be good practice for making repairs to a hard drive boot record.

Behind the Scenes Technology: Data Recovery. This section is optional; in it you are given the opportunity to use DEBUG to closely examine the contents of a boot record as it is written to a disk.

Many good data recovery software products are available today that can recover data automatically, and you don't have to understand exactly what is going on behind the scenes to use them. If you do want a more hands-on sense of the process, however, this section describes how to interpret what's written on the disk, how a disk becomes damaged, and a manual method of data recovery that gives you the most control over what is happening. This approach is not always the best or fastest way to recover lost data, but it is certainly the most reliable. The reasons for using the not-too-friendly DOS and Windows 95 DEBUG utility are (1) everyone who has DOS or Windows 95 on his or her computer has DEBUG, and (2) with DEBUG you can see and learn at the "grass roots" level what is written on a disk. Learning about data recovery using DEBUG provides the strong technical insight that you need to use more user-friendly utility software, such as Nuts & Bolts, Norton, and PC Tools, and to be confident that you understand how it works. The better you understand how data is constructed on the disk and exactly what problems can arise, the better your chances of recovering lost or damaged data.

The first topic addressed below is the use of DEBUG to examine a good boot record. To use DEBUG you need to understand the hexadecimal number system and how memory is addressed in microcomputers by using the segment address followed by a colon and the offset. Appendix D includes these topics. If you have not already done so, read this appendix before proceeding. Follow these steps:

To begin, reboot your computer with only the essential software loaded so that memory is relatively free. This makes it easier to find some unused part of memory to use as a "scratch pad" as you work.

Create a bootable disk using the following command or use Windows 95 Explorer to create a system disk:

```
FORMAT A:/S
```

Figure 6-24 shows the result of formatting a disk using Windows 95. From the figure, you can see that there are 512 bytes in each allocation unit or cluster, which means there is one sector in each cluster. Also, there are 2,847 clusters or sectors on the disk.

Insert the bootable floppy disk in drive A and either soft boot or hard boot your computer. By booting from a floppy disk, little software is loaded into memory.

Examine the boot record.

You are now at the A prompt. Go to the C prompt by typing C:.

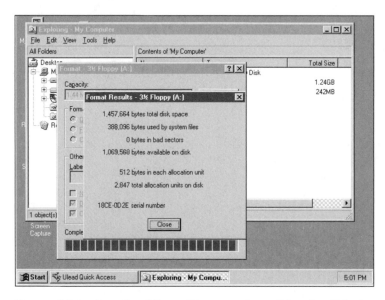

Figure 6-24   Results of formatting a system disk using Windows 95

Execute DEBUG. The DEBUG program should be stored in the \DOS directory of your hard drive for DOS and the \WINDOWS\COMMAND directory for Windows 95. The paths should be:

```
\DOS\DEBUG
```

or

```
WINDOWS\COMMAND\DEBUG
```

Look for an area of memory where you can store the boot record. Use the DUMP command to search for an unused area of memory. You need enough memory for 512 bytes or one sector of the disk. Near the top of conventional memory is a good place to look for some empty area to use as a "scratch pad." Try the memory location 5000:0. If you find data there, keep looking until you find an empty area of memory. Enter this dump command:

```
-d5000:0
```

You should now see 128 bytes of memory beginning with the location 5000:0. When you press **d** followed by no parameters, DEBUG gives you the contents of the next 128 bytes of memory. In Figure 6-25, you see that memory is clean (i.e., contains no data) from 5000:0000 through 5000:00FF. That equals 256 bytes. Because a sector on a 3½-inch high-density disk is 512 bytes, issue the DUMP command twice more to make sure that a total of 512 bytes of memory are unused:

```
-d

-d
```

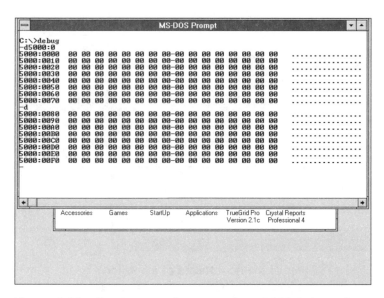

Figure 6-25   Empty area of memory from 5000:0 through
5000:00FF (two dump commands)

You now know that copying the boot record into this area of memory will not overwrite something important. If your dump displays data in memory at this location, try some other area until you find 512 free bytes.

Load the boot record into memory. Use this command:

```
-L5000:0 0 0 1
```

The command line is interpreted as follows:

L5000:0 Load into the area of memory beginning at location 5000:0

0 From the disk in drive A (drive B is 1 and drive C is 2)

0 Begin with sector 0

1 Load 1 sector

Look at the contents of memory using the DUMP command:

```
-d5000:0
```

Follow this with three more **d** commands to see the entire 512-byte sector. Figure 6-26 shows the first 128 bytes of the boot record of a 3½-inch disk formatted with DOS. Figure 6-27 shows the beginning of the boot record for the same size disk formatted with Windows 95 for comparison. Note that most of the data cannot be interpreted by the editor on the right side of the screen. This section is converting the hex numbers to their ASCII representation as described in Appendix C; most of this data is not ASCII code and, therefore, makes no sense when converted to ASCII.

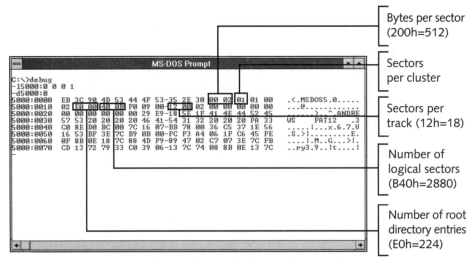

Figure 6-26   The first 128 bytes of the boot record of a 3½-inch floppy disk formatted with DOS

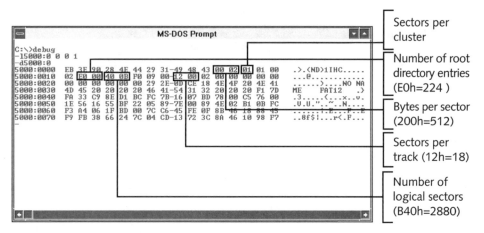

Sectors per cluster

Number of root directory entries (E0h=224)

Bytes per sector (200h=512)

Sectors per track (12h=18)

Number of logical sectors (B40h=2880)

Figure 6-27   The first 128 bytes of the boot record of a 3¹/₂-inch floppy disk formatted with Windows 95

The figure labels highlight some interesting entries at the beginning of the record. Table 6–4 shows the complete record layout for the boot record. The medium descriptor byte tells DOS what type of disk this is. The values of this descriptor byte are shown in Table 6–5.

The program code that loads DOS starts at location 5000:0200. In the last 128 bytes of the record shown in Figure 6-28, you can see that the message that prints if this program does not find the hidden files that it needs to load DOS is as follows:

> Non-System disk or disk error...Replace and press any key when ready...

At the bottom of the record are the names of the files that it is searching for, in this case IO.SYS and MSDOS.COM. Continue to use the DUMP command until you can see all of these entries. Figure 6-29 shows a similar presentation of this message for a Windows 95 disk.

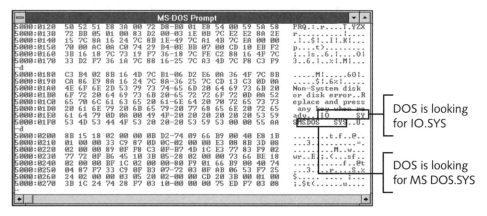

DOS is looking for IO.SYS

DOS is looking for MS DOS.SYS

Figure 6-28   "Non-system disk" message for a DOS disk

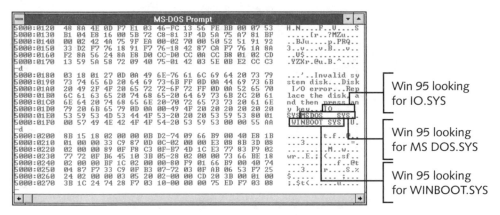

Figure 6-29 "Invalid System Disk" message for a Windows 95 disk

To repair a damaged boot record using DEBUG, follow this procedure:

- Find or make a disk of the same size and density as the damaged disk.
- Using the procedure above, load this good boot record into memory.
- Copy the good boot record from memory to the damaged disk using this command:

```
-W5000:0 0 0 1
```

The command line is interpreted as:

W5000:0	Write beginning with the data located at memory address 5000:0
0	Write to drive A (B=1 and C=2)
0	Write to sector 0
1	Fill one sector

Using Nuts & Bolts. Nuts & Bolts offers an easy method of examining and restoring a disk. Disk Minder discussed earlier in the chapter examines all areas of the disk including the boot sector, FAT, files and directories, lost clusters, and the disk surface. Nuts & Bolts will automatically make repairs, only report problems, or make repairs as you give it permission.

To use Nuts & Bolts to examine and repair a disk, follow these directions:

For Windows 95, click on **Start**, **Run**, **Programs**, **Nuts & Bolts**, **Disk Minder**. The Disk Minder opening screen appears as in Figure 6-15.

Select **drive A** and click **Properties** to select the items you want Disk Minder to check. When finished, return to the opening screen by clicking on OK.

Click **Start** to begin the process. Disk Minder examines and repairs the items you selected.

Using PC Tools. PC Tools offers an easy method of restoring a boot record. The example below uses Version 7 for DOS. Other versions give similar results.

For this version of PC Tools, use the chosen utility program by executing the program from the C prompt. The DISKFIX program is the one you want:

```
C:\> \PCTOOLS\DISKFIX
```

Choose **Repair a Disk** (see Figure 6-30). This option is similar to Norton's Disk Doctor and Nuts & Bolts' Disk Minder. It scans the disk for errors, makes suggestions, and asks permission to repair the disk. If the boot record is badly corrupted, instead of creating a working boot record for the disk from which you can boot, DISKFIX writes a boot record that only displays on the screen the message that this is not a bootable disk. However, the disk data is accessible after this substitute boot record is created.

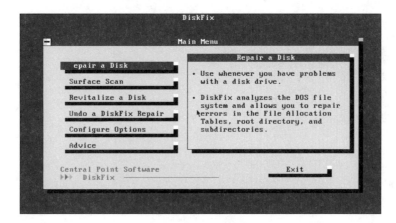

Figure 6-30   PC Tools DISKFIX opening menu

Damaged File Allocation Table

One message generated by a disk with a damaged file allocation table is:

```
Sector not found reading drive A, Abort, Retry, Ignore,
Fail?
```

Sometimes, however, there is no error message; files or directories are simply missing. Norton Utilities, Nuts & Bolts, and PC Tools can all be used to recover from a corrupted FAT.

Norton Utilities The two Norton Utilities programs that might be helpful in repairing a damaged FAT as well as other areas of the disk are Norton Disk Doctor and Disk Editor. Norton Disk Doctor does not require you to understand much of what the program is examining on or doing to the disk. Disk Editor gives you more control, but this also means you must understand what you are doing as you make decisions and edit critical areas of the disk yourself.

Norton Disk Doctor. Norton Disk Doctor offers an automated way to examine a disk or hard drive and to reconstruct it where the programs deem necessary. Norton Disk Doctor might be able to reconstruct a boot record, either copy of the FAT, a directory, and even files. In some situations it is an easy fix for a damaged disk.

To access Norton Disk Doctor, click **Start**, **Programs**, **Norton**, **Norton Disk Doctor**. Select the disk drive from the list of drives and click **Diagnose** to begin the process, which is shown in Figure 6-31. Norton Disk Doctor examines and might repair the boot record, FAT, directories, and files on the disk.

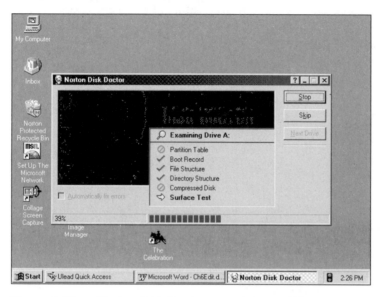

Figure 6-31   Norton Disk Doctor examining a disk

Norton Disk Editor. Norton Disk Editor can automatically repair a damaged disk, including damage to the FAT, or you can make changes directly to either copy of the FAT and to the directory. As you move the cursor over the FAT entries, all the entries for one file change color so they are easy to find and edit.

Disk Editor allows you, for example, to take a damaged disk that has a fragmented file that you want to recover, and copy the file sector by sector to another disk. Disk Editor will create a new file on the second disk and append one sector from the damaged disk after another to that new file.

The time to learn how to use Disk Editor is not when you need it but before you need it. Start with a disk that has several files, and examine the root directory, the FAT, and the files themselves. Practice data recovery by copying a file one sector at a time to a new disk. Also, learn to recover data on a hard drive by first practicing with disks. The activities at the end of the chapter will help you gain experience by working with disks.

For a truly damaged disk with important data on it, be sure to make a copy of the disk before you start working with it. Try Windows 95 Copy Disk or DOS DISKCOPY first. If they will not copy your disk, try Norton's UNDO feature before you begin editing the disk.

Nuts & Bolts. Use Disk Minder to recover a corrupted FAT on either a disk or hard drive. The process is automatic but does give you the option to choose what to repair and what to leave as is. Under the Disk Minder Properties box shown in Figure 6-16, select **FAT**.

PC Tools. PC Tools offers DISKFIX, which scans and diagnoses a disk, making suggestions and repairing the boot record, the FAT, root directory, and files. The process is automatic and does not require you to understand what is happening. You have little control over the outcome, so make a backup first. PC Tools also offers PCSHELL. Under the FILE menu in PCSHELL is a hex editor that allows you to repair damaged files manually.

Behind the Scenes Technology: How FAT is Written and Used. This optional section is designed to help you understand how the FAT is written to a disk and how it is used. This will allow you to better use Norton Disk Editor or similar editors to recover data from a disk and ultimately from a hard drive. The discussion below uses DEBUG as a tool to demonstrate what these editors are really doing. Using DEBUG to recover data from a disk is not very practical, but DEBUG is a useful learning tool. The discussion first takes a look at some healthy FATs. Figure 6-32 shows a FAT of a freshly formatted disk using Windows 95 that does not contain system files; this is the emptiest FAT possible. The same results can be obtained using DOS to format the disk.

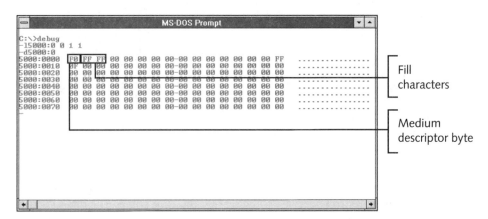

Figure 6-32   Empty FAT

The FAT in Figure 6-32 can be produced using this procedure:

1. Format a 3½-inch high-density floppy disk using Windows 95 Explorer.

2. Load the first copy of the FAT into an empty area of memory. Use the following command:

```
C:\>\WINDOWS\COMMAND\DEBUG-L5000:0 1 1 1
```

An explanation of the command line is as follows:

L5000:0	Load data into memory addresses beginning at 5000:0.
0	Load from the disk in Drive A (A=0, B=1, C=2).
1	Begin the load with sector 1.
1	Load one sector.

Remember that the boot record is located at sector 0, and the FAT begins at sector 1. Looking at Figure 6-32, you see that the first byte is the medium descriptor byte, which tells DOS what kind of disk is being used. The next two bytes are called fill characters and are always FF FF. The rest of the FAT is empty.

Next WordPad is used to create a file on this disk and save the file as a DOS text file using the choices given in the WordPad Save As command. Name the file MYFILE.TXT and put in it the five characters "HAPPY". Figure 6-33 shows the result of the DOS DIR command and the newly dumped FAT. Note first in Figure 6-33 the difference in the number of free bytes on the disk and the number of free bytes before you created the five-character file:

$$1,457,664 \text{ bytes} - 1,457,152 \text{ bytes} = 512 \text{ bytes}$$

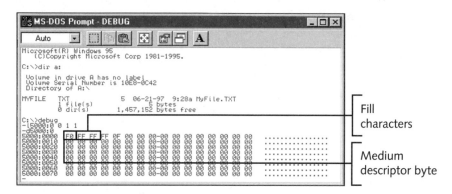

Figure 6-33   Directory of disk showing MYFILE.TXT followed by a DEBUG dump displaying FAT with five-character file

The five-character or five-byte file took up 512 bytes of disk space! Disk space is wasted because one file allocation unit or one cluster on this disk equals 512 bytes. Compare the FAT in Figure 6-33 with the one in Figure 6-32. Note that two bytes are now altered, and read

    FF 0F

Before you begin interpreting these two bytes, three facts need to be pointed out:

- All disks have 12-bit file allocation tables, and each entry in the table is 12 bits long. These 12 bits equal 1.5 bytes.
- Entries in a file allocation table are written in reverse order. In other words, if you label two bytes 1 and 2 in the FAT, you read the bytes as 2 and 1 when

reading the FAT entry. In Figure 6-33, you read the second byte first, so the bytes are read 0F FF.

- The end of a file in the FAT is written as all 12 bits filled with 1s. This record (1111 1111 1111) is converted to FFF in hex, which is what you see in the FAT entry.

- Clusters are numbered in the FAT beginning with cluster 2. Cluster 2 in a FAT entry is really not physically the second cluster on the disk, because the boot record, the two copies of the FAT, and the directory table all come before the data files. Windows 95 and DOS both number the clusters allocated for data beginning with 2.

Now back to Figure 6-33. You know that your file only takes up one cluster or one sector, and you would expect that to mean only one entry in the FAT. You interpret the first two bytes in reverse order as 0F FF. One entry is 12 bits or 1.5 bytes long, and the end of a file is identified with FFF. You see then that this file has the one entry FFF.

Next, you copy to the disk a second file named Long Word File.DOC that uses a long file name and contains 4,608 characters or bytes. Examining the result of the CHKDSK command in Figure 6-34, you see the short DOS version of the filename and see that the number of clusters or sectors required by this second file is:

4608 bytes/512 bytes per cluster = 9 clusters

Figure 6-34   Disk with two files

Since you can't allocate partial clusters, if the number of clusters had been a fractional number you would have rounded up to the nearest whole cluster; this file however requires exactly nine clusters. Adding one cluster for your our original file, you get a total of 10 clusters used on the disk. Figure 6-35 shows a dump of the FAT with the two files stored on the disk. Since the FAT entries are 1.5 bytes long, you will first divide these bytes into groups of three bytes apiece. Each group of three bytes contains two FAT entries and can be interpreted as follows:

```
AB CD EF = DAB EFC
```

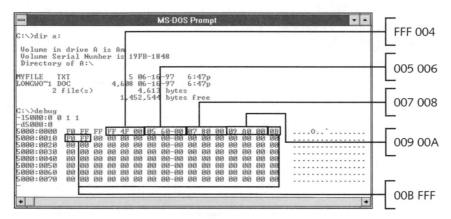

Figure 6-35   Dump of the FAT showing two files

AB CD EF represents two FAT entries of 1½ bytes each. The first entry is AB and half of the next entry, CD. However, since the entries are written reversed, the part of the CD entry that belongs to the first FAT entry is the D, not the C. Also, the first entry is written going from byte two (CD) to byte one (AB) so that the entry is DAB. Similarly, the second entry begins with the EF and ends with C.

For example, say the first three bytes are FF 4F 00. We reverse these bytes and read them as FFF 004. The first entry marks the end of the first file, which is one cluster long. The second entry points to cluster 4. Remember that DOS begins with 2 when counting clusters. These two entries contain the pointers for cluster 2 and cluster 3. Cluster 3, the first cluster of Long Word File.DOC, tells DOS to continue on to cluster 4 to find more of Long Word File.DOC. Reading from Figure 6-35, you see that cluster 4 points to 5, 5 points to 6, 6 points to 7, 7 points to 8, 8 points to 9, 9 points to A, A points to B, and B marks the end of the file with FFF.

Restoring a Damaged FAT Using DEBUG.   With a great deal of patience, you could read a disk sector by sector marking the beginning and ending of a file, calculate the FAT entries, and reconstruct a damaged FAT by editing it using DEBUG. To do this (besides needing tons of patience), you only need one more DEBUG command, the E or ENTER command, which allows you to change the contents of memory. You can load a damaged FAT into memory, make the necessary changes with the ENTER command, and write the corrected FAT back to the disk.

For example, suppose you decide to limit the file Long Word File.DOC to three clusters. You want to put the FFF at the FAT table entry 5 so that only clusters 3, 4, and 5 are allocated to the file. The command is:

```
-E5000:0007
```

DEBUG responds with 5000:0007 60.

Whatever you now type replaces the 60 currently at this location. You respond with 5000:0007 60.F0 (typing only the F0).

Pressing the spacebar, you can continue to enter new data that replaces whatever is stored in memory from this location forward. Therefore, instead of only typing F0, you can correct both bytes like this:

```
5000:0007 60.F05000:0008 00.FF
```

In the first line, everything up to the first period was displayed. You typed F0 and one space. DEBUG responded with the contents of the next byte, which was 00 followed by a period. You then typed FF and pressed **Enter**, which changed the second byte and terminated the command.

In the last step, you write the altered FAT to disk with this command:

```
-W5000:0 1 1 1
```

The command causes the one sector to be written to sector 1 of the A drive disk.

There is only one problem. Windows 95 or DOS is expecting a file that is 4,608 bytes long, but you only have given it three clusters, which is not enough. There is one last thing to do; you must alter the root directory to change the size of the file so that the OS will expect to find three clusters when reading the file. Editing a directory table is coming up.

Second Copy of the FAT. Recall that Windows 95 and DOS keep a second copy of the FAT immediately following the first copy. Without utility software, this second copy is not available to you if the first copy is damaged. You can look at the second copy of the FAT on a 3½-inch high-density disk with this DEBUG command:

```
-L5000:0 0 A 1
```

The second FAT begins with sector A in hex or 10 in decimal. The first FAT began at sector 1. A quick calculation tells you that the first FAT requires nine sectors or 512 bytes/sector × 9 sectors = 4,608 bytes. You see this must be so because this disk has 80 tracks/head × 18 sectors/track × 2 heads/disk or 2,880 sectors (see Table 4-1). Because one sector equals one cluster, the FAT has 2,880 entries. Since each entry is 1.5 bytes long the FAT contains 4,320 bytes, which is equal to 8.44 sectors. Hence, your nine sectors for one FAT are all accounted for. If you're reconstructing a FAT using DEBUG, don't forget to alter the second FAT as well as the first.

Even more important, maybe the second FAT isn't damaged. Load it into memory and see. If it isn't damaged, write it to the disk into the first FAT's location and your disk is restored.

Using Norton Disk Editor to View a FAT. Viewing a FAT with Norton Disk Editor gives you a clear picture of how a data file is written to a disk. The FAT can also be used to recover a corrupted file, because you can locate each cluster of the file and copy the data, cluster by cluster, to a new disk.

One way to access the Disk Editor is to click **Start**, **Programs**, **Norton**, **Disk Edito**r. Windows 95 will unload and Disk Editor will be loaded from DOS. Another way to load Disk Editor is to type DISKEDIT at the command prompt. Norton Utilities puts a copy of DISKEDIT.EXE on the rescue disks and it's also located on the Emergency Disks that come as a part of the software.

From the opening menu, select the **Object** menu (**ALT-O**) and select the **A: 3½ Floppy** as the object. Click **OK**.

Select the **Object** menu again; this time select **1ˢᵀ FAT** from the Object menu. The FAT displays as a table of entries, each entry representing one cluster on the disk as shown in Figure 6-36. Look at the bottom of the screen for the cluster in the FAT that you are currently pointing to. The entry in that cluster location will either be <EOF> to mark the end of the file or the pointer to the next cluster in the file.

```
                              Disk Editor
 Object   Edit  Link  View  Info  Tools  Help
    708     709    710     711     712     713     714     715
    716     717    718     719     720     721     722     723
    724     725    726     727     728     729     730     731
    732     733    734     735     736     737     738     739
    740     741    742     743     744     745     746     747
    748     749    750     751     752     753     754     755
    756     757    758     759     760   <EOF>   <EOF>   <EOF>
  <EOF>   <EOF>  <EOF>   <EOF>     768     769     770   <EOF>
    772     773    774     775     776     777     778     779
    780     781    782     783     784     785     786     787
    788     789    790     791     792     793     794     795
    796     797    798     799     800     801     802     803
    804     805    806     807     808     809     810     811
  <EOF>     813    814     815     816     817     818     819
    820     821    822     823     824     825     826     827
    828     829    830     831     832     833     834     835
    836     837    838     839     840     841     842     843
    844     845    846     847     848     849     850     851
    852     853    854     855     856     857     858     859
    860     861    862     863     864     865     866     867
    868     869    870     871     872     873     874     875
 FAT (1st Copy)                                      Sector 3
 A:\MSDOS.B4                              Cluster 767, hex 2FF
```

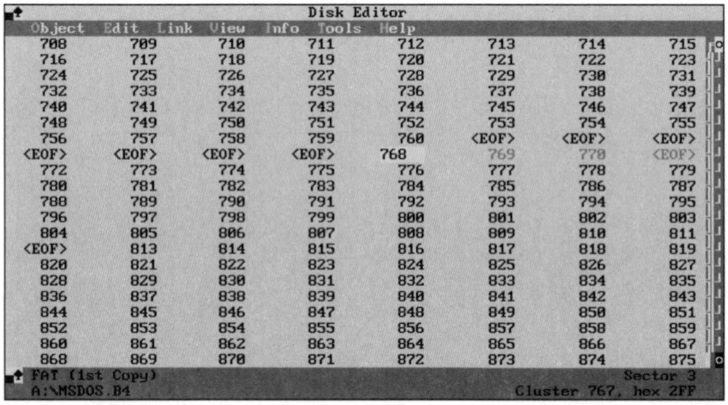

Figure 6-36 Norton Utilities Disk Editor in FAT view

Damaged Root Directory. Next in order on the disk is the root directory. The root directory contains information about each file and all the subdirectories stored in the root directory. Table 6-6 lists the 32 bytes that make up each entry in the root directory and how they are used, and Table 6-7 lists the meaning of each bit of the attribute byte.

Table 6-6 Root Directory Information for Each File

Bytes	Description
8	Name of file
3	File extension
1	Attribute byte (special meaning for each bit)
2	Time of creation or last update
2	Date of creation of last update
2	Starting cluster number in binary
4	Size of file in binary

Table 6-7 File Attributes in the Directory Attribute Byte (reading from left to right across the byte)

Bit	Description	Bit=0	Bit=1
1,2	Not used		
3	Archive bit	Not to be archived	To be archived
4	Directory status	File	Subdirectory
5	Volume label	Not volume label	Is volume label
6	System file	Not system file	Is system file
7	Hidden file	Not hidden	Hidden
8	Read-only file	Read/write	Read only

To view a directory using Norton Utilities, load **Norton Disk Editor** and choose **Directory** from the Object menu. You will be given a list of directories on the currently selected drive. Select a directory from the list of directories and the following information will be displayed in a table for each entry in the directory:

- File or subdirectory name
- File extension
- Attribute byte information
- Date
- Time
- Beginning cluster number
- Size

Behind the Scenes Technology: Directory Repair. This optional section gives you an in-depth look at the entries in a directory to help you understand that happens when a utility like Norton Utilities repairs a directory. You can also use this information to help in the recovery of a corrupted file using Norton Disk Editor.

On the 3½-inch high-density disk used as in the example below, the directory begins at sector 13h. Remember that the second copy of the FAT began at sector A and was nine sectors long. Thus, it ends at sector A + 8 or 12 in hex (10 + 8 = 18 in decimal), and the root directory begins with sector 13h. Figure 6-37 is a memory dump of the root directory of the disk with the two files, MYFILE.TXT and Long Word File.DOC. The root directory was first loaded into memory using this DEBUG command:

```
-L5000:0  0  13  1
```

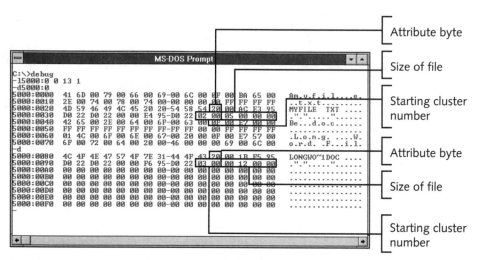

Figure 6-37 Memory dump of a root directory containing two files

The layout of the root directory was listed previously in Tables 6-6 and 6-7. The first 32 bytes of the root directory contain the volume label of the disk. Each entry after that is also 32 bytes long for DOS and longer for Windows 95 when using long filenames. The extra information for the long filename is listed in the root directory before the 32 bytes used by both DOS and Windows 95 for each file entry.

Look at the entries for MYFILE.TXT and Long Word File.DOC in Figure 6-37. The attribute byte, starting cluster number, and size of the file are labeled for each of the two files listed in this root directory. The second file has a long filename together with its short DOS filename. The size of the file Long Word File.DOC is stored in 4 bytes at the end of the 32-bit entry of the file that follows the long filename information (see addresses 5000:0080 of the dump). These four bytes read:

```
00 12 00 00
```

To interpret them, you must read in reverse order like this:

```
00 00 12 00
```

You can then convert the hex 1200 to decimal, which is 4,608, the size of the file.

In Figure 6-37, the attribute byte for this file is at memory location 5000:008B. The byte reads 20 in hex. Converting 20h to binary so that you can read each bit, you take each hex number and convert it to binary like this:

```
2 in hex = 0010 in binary and 0 in hex = 0000 in binary,
therefore the byte is 0010 0000
```

Looking back at Table 6-7, you can interpret each of these eight bits, reading from left to right, in the following way:

- 0   Not used
- 0   Not used
- 1   To be archived
- 0   A file, not a directory
- 0   A normal directory entry, not a volume label
- 0   A normal file, not a system file (like IO.SYS)
- 0   Not hidden
- 0   Read/write file, not read-only

By understanding how to interpret each item in the directory entry, you can reconstruct a damaged directory table if you need to. Again, you may never use DEBUG to repair a directory because utility software is so much easier to use, but the purpose of using it here is to learn exactly how entries are written to the directory so you can understand what these utilities are doing for you. Norton Utilities Disk Editor or PC Tools Disk Editor make reading and writing to directories very easy to do. Each converts the entries to decimal for display, accepts your decimal entry, and converts it to hex and binary before writing it to the disk.

Damaged Files

A data file or program file can be damaged on a disk and the directory and FAT OS might show no errors. When this happens, some of the data from a file can usually be recovered using OS commands, Nuts & Bolts, Norton Disk Editor, or PC Tools Disk Editor. The basic idea for all these tools is to create a new file on another disk or on the hard drive containing all the sectors from the original file that can be read from the damaged disk or hard drive. Most often some of these sectors are so damaged that they cannot be read; you have to edit the newly created file to replace the missing data. The discussion below first covers what can be done with Windows 95 or DOS commands and then looks at procedures that Norton Utilities, Nuts & Bolts, and PC Tools offer.

Using Windows 95 and DOS to Recover Files. How successful an OS is in recovering data depends on how badly damaged the file is. A few examples of how data commonly gets damaged and see what can be done to recover it are discussed below. If a file has been accidentally erased, or the disk or hard drive is otherwise damaged, remember these two things: (1) don't write anything to the disk or hard drive, because you may overwrite data that might otherwise be recovered; and (2) if you are recovering data from a disk, use DISKCOPY in DOS or, for Windows 95, use Copy Disk in Explorer to make a copy of the disk before you do anything else. If Copy Disk or DISKCOPY doesn't work, try copying the disk with Norton Utilities or PC Tools.

Lost Allocation Units. A disk can lose allocation units or lose clusters if a program cannot properly close a file that it has opened. For example, if you boot your computer while an application is running (not a good thing to do for this very reason), the application won't have the opportunity to close a file and may lose clusters. Another way clusters are lost is to remove a floppy disk from a drive while the drive light is still on (also not a good thing to do).

Lost clusters make up a chain of clusters that are not incorporated into a file. The CHKDSK and SCANDISK commands take this chain of clusters, turn it into a file with the name FILE0000.CHK, and store the file in the root directory. To use this utility in DOS to access lost clusters, use the command with the /F option like this:

```
C:\> CHKDSK A:/F
```

Often the file created can be used by the application that it belongs to, although you might have to change the file extension so the application will recognize the file.

For Windows 95, use the ScanDisk utility described in Chapter 5 to accomplish the same results.

Bad Sectors. If a disk contains some bad sectors, the COPY command can sometimes recover the remaining file data that is located in the good sectors. For example, if you have a disk in drive A that has bad sectors, and a file named DOCUMENT.DOC is unreadable by an application, for DOS try this command:

```
C:\TEMP> COPY A:DOCUMENT.DOC
```

Choose the **Ignore** option by pressing I when the following message appears:

```
Unable to read from Drive A: Abort, Retry, Ignore
```

DOS ignores that bad sector and moves on to the next sector. You should be able to copy at least part of the file on the disk.

For Windows, use the COPY command from File Manager in Windows 3.x or Explorer in Windows 95.

Use the RECOVER command only on one file at a time. Don't use it at all unless you have made a backup copy of the disk or you have no other option. Sometimes the RECOVER command actually destroys data that might have been recovered by some other method. As with CHKDSK, the file created by RECOVER might need to be renamed so that its application recognizes it.

Erased File. With DOS, if the file has been erased by the DOS DEL or ERASE command, it can sometimes be recovered. DOS 5.x offers the UNERASE or UNDELETE command that recovers some erased files. When DOS deletes a file from a disk or hard drive, it does so as follows:

- The first character of the filename in the root directory is overwritten with the character s, which has the hex value E5.

- All entries in the FAT for this file are replaced with 00s.

When you issue the DOS UNDELETE command, DOS looks for an entry in the root directory matching the filename and replaces the first character of the filename in the root directory. From the root directory, DOS can read the starting cluster of the file and the size of the file. If the file is not too fragmented and the disk is otherwise healthy, DOS can locate the sectors belonging to the file and reconstruct the FAT.

When you delete a file using Windows 95, this OS handles floppy disk files differently from hard drive files. Floppy disk files are treated just as DOS treats a file when it is deleted; there's no Recycle Bin. Windows 95 offers no tools to undelete a file from a floppy disk. However, for a hard drive, the file is moved to the Recycle Bin and stays there until you purge it. The file information is still retained in the FAT and the file takes up space on the hard drive. You can recover the file simply by dragging it from the Recycle Bin to a new location. If the file has been deleted from the Recycle Bin, you might still be able to recover the file by using the DOS UNDELETE command. This command is not included with Windows 95 so you must look for it in your older DOS 5.x or DOS 6.x directory. To undelete a file from Windows 95 using DOS UNDELETE, follow this procedure

1. From the Windows 95 Start menu choose **Shut Down**, and then choose **Restart the computer in MS–DOS mode**.

2. At the DOS prompt, type **LOCK**, which makes the FAT and directories available for DOS utilities without allowing other applications to access it.

3. Undelete the file using the DOS UNDELETE command. Don't forget to include the path in the command line as necessary.

4. Type **UNLOCK** to release the file system to applications.

5. Type **EXIT** to relaunch Windows 95.

Using Utility Software to Recover Files.   Norton Utilities, Nuts & Bolts, and PC Tools offer user-friendly ways to recover files. Norton Disk Doctor might be able to do the work (and the thinking) for you if you choose to let it. You have more control, however, with Disk Editor.

There are two approaches to using Disk Editor to recover a file. One is to copy the file, sector by sector, to another disk or hard drive. You can locate the file by looking in the root directory for the starting cluster number and the size of the file. From the file size and the size of one cluster, calculate the number of clusters the file uses. Next, go to the FAT and look for the entries beginning with the first cluster in the file. The Disk Editor in FAT view is shown in Figure 6-36. If the FAT has been erased (for example, when the file was accidentally deleted), the FAT is virtually useless. However, clusters currently in use in the FAT can be eliminated as possible locations for the file, unless, of course, the file was overwritten after the deletion occurred. Write down or print all the information that you can get from the FAT.

Next go to the disk data area and read the disk as single sectors. Use the list from the FAT to locate the data. You will need to know what you're looking for. Try to get the latest printout of the file if one exists. If there is no printout, you will at least need to know what the data looks like so that you will recognize it when you see it. With the Disk Editor, create a file on another disk and copy one sector after another to the new file, appending each sector to the file.

The second approach to using Disk Editor is to edit the root directory and FAT entries on the damaged disk to point to that area on the disk that is undamaged. Suppose, for example, you discover that only a few clusters of a 128-cluster file are damaged. The file begins at cluster 150. You can read the file cluster by cluster using Disk Editor until you get to cluster 221. Good data picks up again at cluster 229. Here's what you do:

1. Edit the root directory of the original file, changing the size of the file to the number of bytes of the original file less the number of bytes in the damaged clusters. You will need to know the number of bytes in one cluster for this disk.

2. Change the FAT entry at 220 to point to 229, not 221. Do the same for the second copy of the FAT.

3. Having altered the directory and FATs so that they do not read the damaged sectors, immediately copy the file to a new disk.

You can actually create files on a disk using the above method. By using a disk editor or DEBUG (a disk editor is much easier), you can add a new entry to the root directory and edit the two FATs to point to all the sectors on the disk you need for the file. The new file now exists! This method works well if you have a damaged data area of the disk but the root directory and FATs are still somewhat intact.

An Ounce of Prevention. Make backups! Instruct users whom you support to always make at least two copies of important data. If one copy goes bad, instruct them to be careful not to do anything to the only good copy before making a backup of it. Keeping extra copies of data disks is the best insurance against lost data. Always be careful never to remove disks from a drive while the drive light is on. Follow the exit procedure in an application so that you close files properly. Store disks away from heat, magnetic fields, and heavy dirt and dust.

Occasionally, copy all files from one disk to another, so that you have a newly copied disk that is not fragmented. (Don't use DISKCOPY; it just makes an exact copy of the disk, fragments and all.) You can also use DEFRAG command to do the job for you. Disks that are not badly fragmented are faster to read and write to and, if data is damaged, are easier to recover.

SUMMARY OF DISK DATA RECOVERY

Disks of different sizes and densities format data much the same way. All disks have a boot record, file allocation table, and root directory. DOS and Windows 95 offer the tools to manage the data on a disk and DOS can recover lost data if the disk is not too badly damaged. Utility software can sometimes read a disk too damaged for the OS, because the software does not use the OS or System BIOS to read and write to the disk. When trying to recover data from a disk, if possible, make a backup of the disk first. As always, keeping a second copy of important data on more than one disk is good practice.

HARD DRIVE TROUBLESHOOTING AND DATA RECOVERY

We have now laid the foundation for a thorough understanding of how data is stored on hard drives, how DOS and utility software can access and sometimes repair damaged data, and what you can do to protect against data loss. This section applies the knowledge and skills learned to help you become more effective when you are responsible for maintaining and recovering damaged data on hard drives.

PROBLEMS WITH HARD DRIVES

6

Problems with hard drives can be caused by either hardware or software. Problems can also be categorized as those that prevent the hard drive from booting and those that prevent the data from being accessed. Hardware and software causes of hard drive problems can be summarized as follows:

1. Hardware Problems

   - Problems with the hard drive controller, power supply, data cable, BIOS or setup—that is, with the supporting firmware and hardware needed to access the drive

   - Damage to the drive mechanism or physical damage to the disk surface where the partition table, boot record, directories, FAT, or the data itself are stored

2. Software Problems

   - Corrupted OS files

   - Corrupted partition table, boot record, or root directory making all data on the hard drive inaccessible

   - Corruption of the area of the FAT that points to the data, the data's directory table, or the sector markings where the data is located

   - Corruption of the data itself

   - Data or access to it destroyed by a virus

SETTING PRIORITIES BEFORE YOU START

If a hard drive is not functioning and data is not accessible, setting priorities will help to focus your work. For most users, the data is the first priority unless they have a very recent backup. The software can also be a priority if it is not backed up. Reloading software from the original installation disks or CD-ROM can be very time-consuming, especially if the configuration is difficult or you have written software macros or scripts that are not backed up.

If you have good backups of both the data and software, the hardware might be your priority. It could be expensive to replace and down time can also be costly. The point is, when trouble arises, determine your main priority and start by focusing on that.

It's important that you are aware of what resources are available to help you resolve a problem. Documentation lists error messages and their meanings. Technical support for the ROM BIOS, hardware, and software can give you a better understanding of the meaning of an error message, or it can provide general support in diagnosing a problem. Most technical support is available during working hours by telephone. Check your documentation for telephone numbers.

An experienced computer troubleshooter once said, "The people who solve computer problems do it by trying something and making phone calls, trying something else and making more phone calls, and so on, until the problem is solved." There's a lot a truth in that statement.

Remember one last thing. After making a reasonable and diligent effort to resolve a problem, getting the problem fixed could become more important than your resolving it yourself. There comes a time when you might need to turn the problem over to a more experienced technician.

RESOLVING HARD DRIVE PROBLEMS

Hardware problems usually show up at POST, unless there is physical damage to an area of the hard drive that is not accessed during POST. Hardware problems often make the hard drive totally inaccessible.

In the "Projects" section below, you will have the opportunity to display the error messages that you get at POST when your computer cannot find a working adapter card or hard drive, or it does not find the drive that it was expecting. Recall that before the video system has been tested, errors encountered at POST are communicated to us by beep codes. After ROM BIOS has access to video, error messages appear on the screen. The hard drive and its components are accessed after the video. Any problem with the hard drive will be communicated by error messages on the screen. Some possible error messages at POST are listed below. Any error message in the 1700s generally means fixed disk errors if they follow the standard conventions established by IBM. Error messages for your machine might not list the numeric code, or the message could be stated differently depending on who wrote your ROM BIOS code.

Fixed disk or hard disk error messages in numeric code range from 17xx to 104xx. Some examples are:

- Fixed disk error
- Hard drive error
- Fixed disk POST failed
- Fixed disk adapter or drive error

Check that the controller board or adapter is securely seated. Clean the edge connectors. Check the cabling and power supply. Perhaps the hard drive mechanism is damaged. Check setup.

SCSI adapter errors in numeric code might have the following forms: 096xxxx, 112xxxx, 113xxxx, 206xxxx, 208xxxx, 210xxxx, or 1999xxxx. Check the SCSI adapter card, cables, and power supply to the drive. Check DIP switches and terminators.

If you have disconnected and cleaned the edge connectors, reseated all boards and cables, and checked setup and still get the same error message, the next step is to ask these questions:

When did the hard drive last work? What has happened in the meantime? Perhaps a new device was installed and is conflicting with the hard drive's resources; equipment was just moved or badly jarred; there was a power outage or a thunderstorm; new software was installed or changes were made to the drive configuration or software setup; another user accessed the drive; the machine was turned off for an extended time; and so on. If you can answer "yes" to any of these questions, assume first that the problem is caused by what recently happened. The recent event is guilty until proven innocent.

What does work? Can you boot from a disk? If so, can you access the hard drive from the A prompt? Are there other error messages at POST indicating the problem is not confined to the hard drive alone? What other systems on the computer that are not directly dependent on the hard drive are not working?

If the problem is isolated just to the hard drive system and no recent event can be blamed for the hard drive failure, your next course of action is to replace one component at a time with a known good component until the system works.

Sometimes older drives refuse to spin at POST. Drives that are having trouble spinning often whine at startup for several months before they finally refuse to spin altogether. If your drive whines loudly when you first turn on the computer, never turn the computer off. One of the worst things you can do for a drive that is having difficulty starting up is to leave the computer turned off for an extended period of time. Some drives, just like old cars, will refuse to start if they are left unused for a long time.

Do not trust valuable data to a drive that is having this kind of trouble. Plan to replace the drive soon. In the meantime, make frequent backups and leave the power on.

A true hard drive crash might occur when the read/write heads crash against the disk surface, damaging either the heads or the disk surface or both. If the head mechanism is damaged, the drive and its data are probably a total loss. If the first tracks that contain the partition table, boot record, FAT, or root directory are damaged, the drive could be inaccessible even though the data might be unharmed.

Here's a trick that might work for a hard drive whose head mechanism is intact but whose first few tracks are damaged. Find a working hard drive that has the same partition table information as the bad drive. With the computer case off, place the good drive on top of the bad drive housing, and connect a spare power cord and the data cable from the adapter to the good drive. Leave a power cord connected to the bad drive. Boot from a disk. No error message should show at POST. Access the good drive by entering C: at the A prompt. The C prompt should show on the monitor screen.

Without turning off the power, gently remove the data cable from the good drive and place it on the bad drive. Do not disturb the power cords on either drive or touch chips on the drive logic boards. Immediately copy the data you need from the bad drive to floppy disks using the DOS COPY command. If the area of the drive where the data is stored, the FAT, and the directory are not damaged, this method should work. If the FAT is damaged, you might need to read sectors instead of files to retrieve the data using either DEBUG (repeating the LOAD and WRITE commands for all sectors) or utility software.

For a hard drive to be accessible by DOS or Windows 95, these items, in the order they are accessed, must be intact:

- The partition table
- The boot record
- The FAT
- The root directory

In order for the hard drive to be bootable, in addition to these items the following must be intact:

1. For DOS
   - The two DOS hidden files
   - COMMAND.COM
   - CONFIG.SYS and AUTOEXEC.BAT (these are optional)
2. For Windows 95
   - The two Windows 95 hidden files
   - COMMAND.COM
   - CONFIG.SYS and AUTOEXEC.BAT (optional)
   - VMM32.VXD and several files that it uses to load the desktop

Windows 95 does not require a desktop to load just enough of the OS to attain a command prompt. If you press F8 during the process of loading Windows 95, you can then choose the command prompt. Doing this gives you the C prompt provided by COMMAND.COM and prevents VMM32.VXD from loading.

The hard drive does not have to be bootable to access the data. You can always boot from a disk and then access drive C. After Windows 95 or DOS accesses the drive, in order for the OS to access the data these items must be intact:

- The directory in which the files are located

- The sector information where the files are located

- The beginning of the file, sometimes called the header information, and the end of the file, called the end-of-file marker

- The data itself

Looking back at the preceeding three lists, you see that there are several opportunities for failure. To recover lost data due to a software problem, you must first determine which item in the three lists is corrupted. Then you must either repair the item or bypass it to recover the data.

PREPARING FOR DISASTER

As discussed earlier, Norton Utilities offers Image, a utility program that makes a copy of important hard drive information including the boot record, FAT, and root directory. You can configure your PC to execute Image each time you boot. Norton System Doctor can also track when you have made the last image and prompt you to make another when the information becomes outdated. Figure 6-38 shows the Options for Image window where you can select to start Image automatically each time Windows starts and also to create an Image backup file in case the first copy of Image is corrupted.

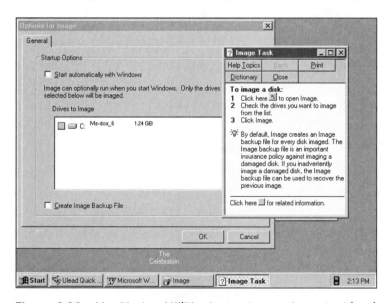

Figure 6-38   Use Norton Utilities Image to save important hard drive information

To create the Image file Image.dat, which is stored as a read-only file in the root directory, click **Start**, **Programs**, **Norton**, **Image**, and **Start** from the Image window.

Later, when hard drive problems arise, several of the Norton Utilities programs will be able to look for the Image.dat file and use it to recover the information it keeps. Earlier in the chapter, directions were given to create a set of rescue disks which contain a copy of the partition table, boot record, and OS startup files.

DAMAGED PARTITION TABLE OR BOOT RECORD

If the hard drive and its supporting hardware pass the POST tests done by the System BIOS, BIOS looks to load an OS from the hard drive if no disk is in drive A. Even if the OS is loaded from a floppy disk, the partition table and the boot record must be intact for the OS to access the hard drive. The FAT and root directory must be readable for the OS to read data stored on the drive.

BIOS first reads the master boot program at the beginning of the partition table information on the hard drive. If the partition table is damaged, the error message is as follows:

```
Invalid drive or drive specification.
```

In this case, you should still be able to boot from a floppy disk. When you get to the A prompt and try to access the hard drive by entering C:, you will get the same error.

If you suspect the partition table is corrupted, use the FDISK command discussed in Chapter 5 to display the partition table information. The FDISK command will give an error when trying to display the information if the table is corrupted.

Restoring the partition table is impossible if the track is physically damaged. However, if you have previously saved the partition table and there is no physical damage, the process is simple. In Chapter 5, you saw that the partition table can be saved to a disk using PC Tools, Norton Utilities, Nuts & Bolts, or the DOS 5 MIRROR command. If you have not saved this information, but you have another hard drive with a matching partition table, try saving the table from the good drive and writing it to the bad drive. Sometimes the UNFORMAT command will allow this and sometimes not.

If you have saved the information using the DOS MIRROR command, restore the partition table with this command:

```
UNFORMAT /PARTN
```

The command prompts you for the disk containing the file PARTNSAV.FIL, and it restores the partition table and boot records for all partitions on the drive.

Also, to recover the FAT, directories, and files, this variation of the UNFORMAT command sometimes gives results:

```
UNFORMAT /U
```

Norton Disk Doctor, Nuts & Bolts Disk Minder, and PC Tools DISKFIX also can repair a damaged partition table. You must have the utility software on floppy disks and execute the program from the disks. If you have made a set of rescue disks with Nuts & Bolts, PC Tools, or Norton Utilities, use these disks to restore the partition table. With Nuts & Bolts and Norton Utilities, if you have not made a set of rescue disks try the Emergency Disks, which can sometimes correct the problem.

Don't use FDISK to make a new partition table, because it will also overwrite the first few sectors on the hard drive that contain the FAT. Part of the partition information can be recovered using FDISK with the /MBR parameter. Sometimes the following error message is displayed:

```
Invalid Drive or Drive Specification,
```

After booting from a floppy disk to restore the boot program in the partition table (called the master boot record), which is at the very beginning of the partition table information, try this command:

```
A> FDISK /MBR
```

Oftentimes, this command solves the problem. Note that the /MBR option is not documented in the DOS or Windows 95 manuals. The FDISK program must be stored on the A disk; keep a copy of it on an emergency bootable disk for just this purpose.

You can, however, start all over by repartitioning and reformatting the drive. Even though the first few tracks are damaged, you might still be able to recover part of the storage space on the drive. The partition table is written on the very first sector of the hard drive and this sector must be accessible. After that, you can skip as many sectors as you need to by making a non-DOS or non-Windows 95 partition at the beginning of the drive. This partition will never be used. Make the second partition, which will be the first DOS or Windows 95 partition, the bootable partition. All this is done using the FDISK command available in either DOS or Windows 95.

Don't perform a low-level format on an IDE or SCSI drive unless the drive is otherwise unusable. Use the low-level format program recommended by the manufacturer, and follow its instructions. Call the drive manufacturer's technical support to find out how to get this program or check the manufacturer's Web site for details.

If the boot record is damaged, the best solution is to recover it from the backup copy you made when you first became responsible for the PC. If you did not make the backup, try Norton Utilities Disk Doctor, or Nuts & Bolts Disk Minder. Figure 6-39 shows help information from Norton Utilities about testing the boot record. A floppy disk has only one boot record, but a hard drive has one master boot record in the partition table area and a boot record at the beginning of each partition on the drive.

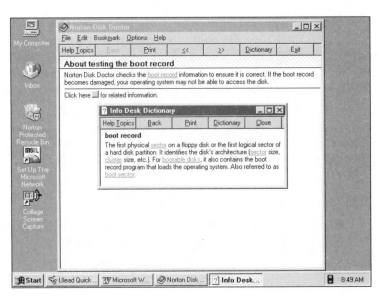

Figure 6-39   Help from Norton Utilities about testing the boot record

Norton Disk Doctor will test and repair the damaged boot record if it can. The Norton Utilities Rescue Disk will simply refresh the boot record with the backup copy on the disk. To use Norton Disk Doctor, click **Start**, **Program**, **Norton**, and **Norton Disk Doctor**. Select the hard drive from the list of drives displayed on the first screen of the program and click **Diagnose**. Figure 6-40 displays as Norton Disk Doctor tests the entire drive including the boot record. If it discovers errors to the boot record or other areas of the disk, it asks for permission to repair the damage or repairs it without asking permission, depending on how you have set the program options. Figure 6-41 displays the test results. When you click **Details** on this screen you are given the opportunity to print a detailed report of the test and any corrections made.

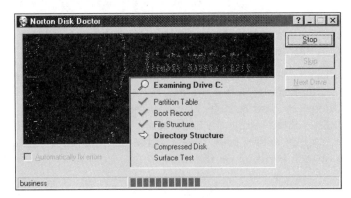

Figure 6-40   Norton Disk Doctor examining a hard drive

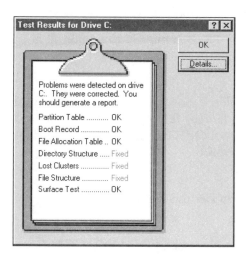

Figure 6-41   Norton Disk Doctor displays test results for drive C

DAMAGED FAT OR ROOT DIRECTORY

The partition table and boot record are easily backed up to disk; they will not change unless the drive is repartitioned or reformatted. Always back them up as soon as you can after you buy a new computer or become responsible for a working one.

Unlike the partition table and boot record, the FAT and the root directory change often and are more difficult to back up. Nuts & Bolts Disk Minder, Norton Disk Doctor, and PC Tools DISKFIX provide tools to repair a damaged FAT or root directory. Their degree of success is dependent on the degree of damage to the tables.

If the physical areas of the FAT and root directory are damaged and you cannot repair them, you can still read data from the hard drive by reading sectors instead of files. With Norton Disk Editor, read one sector at a time and write each to a disk.

CORRUPTED SYSTEM FILES

If the two OS hidden files are missing or corrupted, you should see the following error message:

```
Non-system disk or disk error...
```

for DOS or

```
Invalid system disk...
```

for Windows 95. When this happens, first boot from a floppy disk, then access drive C, and begin looking for the problem. Use the ATTRIB command to unhide all files in the root directory, as follows:

```
C:\> ATTRIB -H *.*
```

You should see the two exposed hidden files if they are there. If they are missing or corrupted, you can use the COPY command to copy them from a disk to the hard drive root directory. (Unhide them on the disk first so COPY can find them.) Once they are on the hard drive, hide them again with this command:

```
C:\> ATTRIB +H IO.SYS
```

Substitute another filename as necessary. You can also use this command:

```
A:\> SYS C:
```

The SYS command copies the two hidden files and COMMAND.COM from the disk to the hard drive.

COMMAND.COM must be in the root directory. If COMMAND.COM is missing, you should get the following error message:

```
Command file not found
```

or something similar. You will probably find a spare copy in the \DOS directory or \WINDOWS\COMMAND, or you can copy it from your bootable disk.

CONFIG.SYS and AUTOEXEC.BAT sometime give error messages when changes are made to them or they accidentally get erased. Keep a backup of these files so that you do not have to remember all the commands listed in them if you have to rebuild.

To prevent a user from accidentally erasing COMMAND.COM, CONFIG.SYS, and AUTOEXEC.BAT, you might want to hide these files using the ATTRIB command in DOS or the Properties sheet in Windows 95. You also can make them read-only files using this version of ATTRIB:

```
ATTRIB +R COMMAND.COM
```

CORRUPTED SECTOR AND TRACK MARKINGS

The first few bits of each sector are labels that the hard drive BIOS must read before it reads any data in that sector. The data might be perfectly fine, but, if the sector markings are faded, BIOS will not read the sector. DOS will give you the following error message:

```
Bad Sector or Sector Not Found.
```

Nuts & Bolts, Norton Utilities, or PC Tools might be able to read the sector. Try them first. If one of them can read the data, copy the data to a disk and have the utility mark the cluster as bad in the FAT so it will not be used again. If the drive continues to report bad sectors, it needs to be low-level formatted. Only the low-level format will refresh these sector bits.

There are two kinds of low-level formats: a nondestructive and a destructive format. The nondestructive format does not destroy the data. It copies the data on one track to another area of the drive, rewrites the sector bits on that track, and then copies the data back to the track.

A destructive low-level format completely ignores old format information and starts all over again, writing track and sector markings to the drive and overwriting all data. The advantages of using a destructive format are that it's faster and it does a better job of determining bad sectors and marking them than a nondestructive format. If you have a choice, choose the destructive format.

Remember that it is dangerous to low-level format an IDE drive because the track and sector locations can be specific to this drive. Only use a low-level format program recommended by the drive manufacturer.

6

CORRUPTED DATA AND PROGRAM FILES

Data and program files can become corrupted for many reasons, ranging from power spikes to user error. If the corrupted file is a program file, the simplest solution might be to reinstall the software or recover the file from a previous backup.

To restore a data file that is not backed up, you have several choices:

- Nuts & Bolts, Norton Utilities, or PC Tools might be able to recover the file for you.

- Try to use DOS or Windows 95 to copy the file to disk. Press I for Ignore when an error message appears ending with the question "Abort, Retry, or Ignore?" That part of the file is skipped and the OS picks up with the next readable part.

- Try CHKDSK or ScanDisk. If the program that produced the file was interrupted before it could write the end-of-file marker, this is the best choice for recovery. These programs create a file in the root directory named FILE0000.CHK that might contain all the data.

- You can reconstruct the file yourself using a disk editor. This procedure is the same as the procedure discussed earlier for recovering data from a disk.

Many applications place header information (called the file header) about a file at the beginning of the file. This data follows a different format than the rest of the file and is needed for the application to identify the file and its contents. If the file header is lost or corrupted and an application needs that header to read the file, you can sometimes recover the contents by treating the file as an ASCII text file. Most applications allow a text file to be imported into the application, after which it can be converted into the application's format. Read your application's documentation to learn how to import a text file.

VIRUS PROBLEMS

If you suspect a virus could be your problem, use a virus scan program to scan memory and your hard drive for an active or inactive virus.

SUMMARY OF HARD DRIVE TROUBLESHOOTING

Making good backups is the most important thing you can do to prepare for a hard drive failure. Once the failure happens, approach the problem by first establishing the priorities that will determine your course of action. If you have valuable data on the drive that is not backed up, proceed with caution. If you have accidentally deleted an important data file, don't write anything to the hard drive until you have recovered the data. A file written to a sub-directory different from the one that contained the erased file can still overwrite data. Windows 95 and DOS write files to the next available sector regardless of subdirectory.

If you plan to use Nuts & Bolts, PC Tools, or Norton Utilities to recover a file, but they are not installed on your hard drive, don't install them; you may overwrite the data. You can execute these utility programs from a floppy disk.

HARD DRIVE TROUBLESHOOTING GUIDELINES

Begin troubleshooting by interviewing the user, being sure to include the following questions:

1. Was the computer recently moved?
2. Was any new hardware recently installed?
3. Was any new software recently installed?
4. Was any software recently reconfigured or upgraded?
5. Has the computer had a history of similar problems?

There are a number of ways hard drives can malfunction, including the ones discussed below.

HARD DRIVE DOES NOT BOOT

If the hard drives does not boot, proceed as follows:

- Confirm that both the monitor and computer switches are turned on.
- Try using a bootable disk, then log on to drive C. If you have a Windows 95 rescue disk, you can use SCANDISK, CHKDSK, or FDISK to examine the system.
- If the PC will not boot from the boot disk, verify that the boot disk is good. Try using it in a different computer. To protect against viruses, write-protect the boot disk first.
- Check to be sure the power cable and disk controller cable connections are good.

If the drive still does not boot, it is suggested that you perform the following procedures in order:

- Reconnect or swap the drive data cable.
- Reseat or exchange the drive adapter card.

- Exchange the hard drive.

A bad power supply or a bad systemboard also might cause a disk boot failure. If the problem is solved by exchanging one of the above modules, you still must reinstall the old module to verify that the problem was not caused by a bad connection.

Damaged, missing, or mismatched system files (COMMAND.COM, IO.SYS, MSDOS.SYS) can keep a hard disk from booting. You can see if they are of the same version by typing DIR/AH. This will show the hidden system files and their dates. If COMMAND.COM and the hidden files have different dates, then they are usually mixed and incompatible versions. You can replace the three system files using the following steps:

- Boot a Rescue or system DOS disk from drive A (make sure you are using the same DOS version).

- Restore hidden system files on drive C (A:\>SYS C:)

- Older versions of DOS require you to copy COMMAND.COM separately. You can restore COMMAND.COM by typing:

  `A:\>COPY COMMAND.COM C:`

- Run SCANDISK

- Run a current version of an anti-virus program.

DRIVE RETRIEVES AND SAVES DATA SLOWLY

If the drive retrieves and saves data slowly, proceed as follows:

- This might be caused by fragmented files that have been updated, modified, and spread over different portions of the disk. Run DEFRAG to rewrite fragmented files to contiguous sectors.

- Verify that the hard disk drivers are properly installed.

COMPUTER WILL NOT RECOGNIZE A NEWLY INSTALLED HARD DRIVE

If the computer will not recognize a newly installed hard drive, proceed as follows:

- Does the manual state that you must first do a "low-level" format or run a Disk Manager? IDE drives are already low-level formatted. Older drives require the user to perform this routine.

- Has the FDISK utility been successfully run? Choose "Display Partition Information" from the FDISK menu to verify the status.

- FORMAT C:/S is the last required "format" step. Has this been done?

- Has the CMOS setup been correctly configured?

- Are there any drivers to install?

- Are there any DIP switches or jumpers that must be set?

- Has the data cable been properly connected? Verify that the cable stripes are connected to pin 1 on the edge connectors of both the card and cable.

- Call the drive manufacturer if the above steps are not productive.

CHAPTER SUMMARY

- Installing a hard drive includes setting jumpers or DIP switches on the drive, physically installing the adapter card, cable, and drive, changing CMOS setup, partitioning, formatting, and installing software on the drive.

- Hard drives can be installed as the master drive, slave drive, or only drive on the system.

- Protect the drive and the PC against static electricity during installation.

- Large capacity hard drives must have LBA mode set in CMOS setup or use software or a special EIDE adapter card in order for System BIOS to support the drive.

- Some BIOS can autodetect the presence of a hard drive if the drive is designed to give this information to BIOS.

- A drive can have one primary partition and one extended partition that can be subdivided into logical drive partitions.

- Use more than one partition to optimize the cluster size, handle drives greater than 2 GB, or to improve the organization of the software on the drive.

- The OS or high-level format creates the FATs, root directory, and boot record on the drive and marks any clusters bad in the FAT that the low-level format had previously identified.

- Windows 95 upgrade requires that DOS be previously installed on the drive.

- You can make a backup of the partition table with the MIRROR command, Nuts & Bolts, PC Tools, or Norton Utilities.

- Installing a SCSI drive involves installing the host adapter, terminating resisters, setting SCSI IDs, and configuring the SCSI system to consider whether the drive is the boot device or not.

- Windows 95 and DOS with Windows 3.x can be installed on the same hard drive, and you can boot to either OS.

- High humidity, smoking near the PC, and leaving the PC turned off for long periods of time can damage a hard drive.

- Utility software such as Nuts & Bolts, PC Tools, and Norton Utilities, can sometimes be used to quickly recover lost hard drive information and data without extensive knowledge or an understanding of the problem.

- Sometimes the second copy of the FAT on a hard drive can be used when the first copy becomes corrupted.

- ScanDisk and CHKDSK can be used to recover lost allocation units caused by files not being properly closed by the application creating them.

- When data is lost on a hard drive, don't write anything to the drive if you intend to try to recover the data.

- Low-level formats should be used as a last resort to restore an unreliable IDE hard drive. Only use the low-level format program recommended by the drive manufacturer.

KEY TERMS

- **Auto-detecting BIOS** — A feature on newer system BIOS and hard drives that provides for auto-detection when identifying and configuring a new drive in the CMOS setup.

- **Corrupted files** — Data and program files that are damaged for any of a variety of reasons, ranging from power spikes to user error.

- **DEBUG utility** — A DOS utility that shows exactly what is written to a file or memory, using the hexadecimal numbering system to display memory addresses and data.

- **Disk editor** — A powerful tool for editing any part of a disk, including the partition table, directory entries, DOS boot record, and FAT.

- **High-level format** — Formatting performed by means of the DOS or Windows 95 FORMAT program (for example, FORMAT C:/S).

- **Interleave** — To write data in nonconsecutive sectors around a track, so that time is not wasted waiting for the disk to make a full revolution before the next sector is read.

- **Lost allocation units** — *See* Lost clusters.

- **Lost clusters** — File fragments that, according to the file allocation table, contain data that does not belong to any file (in DOS, the command CHKDSK/F can free these fragments).

- **Low-level format** — A process, usually performed at the factory, that electronically creates the hard drive cylinders and tests for bad spots on the disk surface.

- **Operating system format** — *See* High-level format.

- **Partition table** — A table written at the very beginning of a hard drive, which describes the number and location of all partitions, and identifies the boot partition.

- **SCSI bus** — A faster bus standard used for peripheral devices tied together in a daisy chain.

- **Utility software** — Software packages, such as Nuts & Bolts, Norton Utilities, or PC Tools that provide the means for data recovery and repair, virus detection, and the creation of backups.

REVIEW QUESTIONS

1. List three types of information that CMOS setup stores concerning hard drives.
2. List the steps you need to follow to partition a hard drive.
3. Why might a user create more than one partition?
4. How would you configure a drive as a slave drive?
5. List and describe all of the wires and/or cables that are used when physically installing a hard drive.
6. How would you determine which side of the data cable is connected to pin 1?
7. List three of the menu options on the FDISK utility.
8. List the steps to install Windows 95 on a new hard drive.
9. Compare and contrast IDE and SCSI adapter cards.
10. List three files that FORMAT C:/S will place on a hard drive.
11. In what sector is the master boot record of a hard drive located?
12. How could you restore a damaged boot record?
13. What DOS/Windows utility can be used to defragment a drive?
14. What could cause a lost cluster?
15. How is a bad sector different from a lost cluster?
16. How can you unerase a file in DOS?
17. How can you unerase a file in Windows 95?
18. What conditions might prevent a file from being unerased?
19. List three ways to back up the file RESUME.DOC.
20. List three precautions that can be used to protect a valuable disk from damage or loss.
21. List three physical components to check or examine if a hard drive does not boot.
22. List and describe three DOS utilities that can be used to examine or solve hard drive problems.
23. List two third-party software packages that can be used to solve hard drive problems.
24. Compare and contrast LOW LEVEL FORMAT, FDISK, and FORMAT C:/S

PROJECTS

Unless you follow the proper procedures, working inside your computer can cause serious damage—to both you and your computer. To assure safety in your work setting, follow every precaution listed in the *Read This Before You Begin* section following this book's Introduction.

PREPARING FOR HARD DRIVE HARDWARE PROBLEMS

1. Boot your PC and make certain that it is working properly. Make sure you have a bootable disk available in case you need it. Turn off your computer, remove the computer case, and loosen the adapter card to your hard drive. Turn the computer back on. Write down the message that you get.

2. Turn the computer off and reseat the card. Disconnect the data cable and turn the computer back on. Write down the error that you get.

3. Turn off the computer and reconnect the data cable. Disconnect the power supply cord to the hard drive. Turn the computer on. Write down the error that you get.

4. Turn off the computer, reconnect the power cord, and turn on the computer. Rename COMMAND.COM in the root directory of your hard drive and reboot. Write down the error that you get. Reboot from the bootable floppy and rename the file on the hard drive back to COMMAND.COM. Reboot again to make certain that all is well.

5. Access setup, write down the hard drive type and parameters you have, change the type, and reboot. Write down the errors you get. Access setup, restore the drive type to the correct value, and reboot.

6. For DOS, add the following files to the rescue disk that you created in the Chapter 2 "Projects."

   - FDISK.EXE (to display partition information and to refurbish the master boot record with the command FDISK/MBR)

   - FORMAT.COM

   - SYS.COM

   - A copy of the partition table of your hard drive (use the DOS MIRROR command or some other utility software)

   - DEBUG.EXE (to examine the hard drive)

   - EDIT.COM (to create a new AUTOEXEC.BAT and other files)

   - QBASIC.EXE (a program that EDIT.COM needs to work if you have an older version of DOS)

   - Your current AUTOEXEC.BAT and CONFIG.SYS files if you have them on the hard drive

7. For Windows 95, get a listing of all the files that Windows 95 puts on a rescue disk that it creates. Explain as far as you can the purpose of each file.

DATA RECOVERY

The following exercises are designed to help you practice working with the tools used to recover data from floppy disks and hard drives.

   a. The volume label is stored in two places on a floppy disk: the boot record and the root directory. Use a floppy disk that does not contain important information. To practice editing skills and to test your knowledge of a floppy disk layout, change the volume label of a floppy disk using either DEBUG, Norton Utilities, or PC Tools disk editors.

   b. Work with a partner on this problem. Separately alter an entry in the FAT of a file on a floppy disk using Nuts & Bolts, DEBUG, Norton Utilities, or PC Tools. Don't tell your partner which file is damaged or what you did to the FAT. Exchange disks. Use DEBUG, Norton Utilities, Nuts & Bolts, or PC Tools to repair the damaged FAT. Don't practice this exercise on a hard drive!

   c. Use a healthy floppy disk that has at least one file stored on it. Edit the directory entry and the two FATs and divide the file into two files. Both files should be readable. Document or text files are better here than database or spreadsheet files that have header information.

   d. Use a healthy floppy disk that is full of document or text files. Take a straight pin and make a small hole in the disk. Recover as much of the data on the disk as you can. When you're finished with this exercise, throw the disk away!

   e. If a floppy disk has a damaged cover, it is still possible to recover the data on the disk. Cut the cover so you can remove the disk without damaging it. Sacrifice a good disk by cutting a slit carefully in the end of the cover and inserting the disk.

THE PARTITION TABLE

Using Nuts & Bolts, Norton Utilities, PC Tools, or some other disk management software, get a printout of the partition table of your hard drive. On the printout, label each item in the table and explain it.

RESEARCH USING THE INTERNET

Pretend you plan to install a 340 MB Quantum LPS 340AT hard drive as a second drive on a PC. You want the drive to be the slave drive and know that you must change the jumper settings as they currently stand. There are three jumpers on the drive labeled DS, SP, and CS.

From the description of the jumpers, you don't know how to set the jumpers so the drive is the slave. The documentation is not available. What do you do?

The best solution is to use the Internet to access the drive manufacturer's Web site for this information. In this case, the site is www.quantum.com. Use this example or some other example given by your instructor to determine the correct settings for the jumpers.

RECOVERING DATA FROM A FLOPPY DISK

Use a floppy disk that contains data, but not important data that you cannot afford to loose. If you have Norton Utilities, use the Disk Editor to alter the contents of the boot record on the disk so that the disk cannot be read by your OS. Recover the data on the disk.

USING WINDOWS 95 HELP

Using the Windows 95 **Start** button, **Help**, **Contents** tab, and **Troubleshooting** option, list specifically what to do if:

1. You run out of memory
2. You have trouble starting Windows

TROUBLESHOOTING A HARD DRIVE PROBLEM OVER THE PHONE

A friend calls you to say that her hard drive does not work. She is using Windows 95 and has a rescue disk. Over the phone, walk her through the process of booting from the rescue disk and use the utilities on the rescue disk to examine the hard drive. List the utilities on the rescue disk that you plan to use in the order that you would use them and write down for each utility what you would do with it.

In a lab environment, you can simulate this phone call by sitting with your back to a user sitting at a PC. Talk the user through the process without turning around and looking at the PC screen.

HARD DRIVE TROUBLESHOOTING

You have a virus scan program installed on your PC that executes each time you boot. The message it gives when it executes is "Unable to read boot record on drive C:". Is this the Master Boot Record or the DOS Boot Record? What can you do to restore this information on the drive?

USING NUTS & BOLTS

Using Nuts & Bolts utility software, make a snapshot image of the critical hard drive areas using Image. Create a Nuts & Bolts rescue disk. Boot from the rescue disk. Use the DOS version of Disk Minder on the rescue disk to check the partition table for errors. Display the summary information from Disk Minder. Print the summary information screen.

From a DOS command prompt, delete a file on your hard drive that is expendable. Use Nuts & Bolts to recover the deleted file.

PREPARING FOR DISASTER

Using the Windows 95 Explorer, format a bootable system disk in drive A, and copy the following files from C:\WINDOWS\COMMAND to the new disk:

ATTRIB, CHKDSK, EDIT, FDISK, FORMAT, MEM, MSCDEX, SCANDISK

Create a directory and store a backup of critical Windows 95 startup files in it. Follow these directions.

1. On drive C, create a new folder called WIN-BAK.INI.
2. In the C:\WINDOWS folder highlight all of the .INI files.
3. Copy them by tapping CTRL C.
4. Click the WIN-BAK.INI directory, then paste the copied .INI files into WIN-BAK.INI by tapping CTRL V.
5. Using Explorer, set the View, Options to "Show all files".
6. Copy C:\WINDOWS\SYSTEM.DAT to C:\WIN-BAK.INI (do not drag!).
7. Copy C:\WINDOWS\USER.DAT to C:\WIN-BAK.INI (do not drag!).

TROUBLESHOOTING FUNDAMENTALS

This chapter addresses some common sense guidelines to solving computer problems. The first section covers defensive procedures that make computer problems easier to cope with. Such measures, which include backing up hardware and software, write protecting applications disks, and keeping records and documentation, minimize the losses a user experiences if hardware or software fail. They also reduce the time it takes to get a system running again. The remainder of the chapter suggests ways to resolve problems when they arise. In trying to solve a computer problem, you want to avoid making the situation worse by damaging either hardware, software, valuable data, or yourself. Before describing specific hardware or software problems, the chapter outlines some practical precautions to always follow when troubleshooting computer problems. The chapter goes on to discuss what troubleshooting tools are essential and to discuss the various sources of system problems. You will learn how to identify each source, and consider some general guidelines in dealing with these problems. In the end-of-chapter projects, you will have the opportunity to disassemble a microcomputer and reassemble it to help further develop troubleshooting skills.

IN THIS CHAPTER,
YOU WILL LEARN:

- How to protect yourself, the hardware, and the software while solving computer problems

- What tools are needed to support personal computers

- How to isolate computer problems and devise a course of action

- The importance of good record-keeping

- How to take a computer apart and put it back together

TROUBLESHOOTING PERSPECTIVES

There are several perspectives a person might have as a PC troubleshooter. You might have a problem to solve on your own PC, or you might be solving a problem for someone else as a friend, a coworker, or a PC technician. As a PC technician, there are four different job functions you might be performing:

- **A PC support technician** working on site who closely interacts with users and is responsible on an ongoing basis for the PCs he or she maintains

- A **PC service technician** who goes to a customer site in response to a service call and, if possible, repairs a PC on site

- A **bench technician** who might or might not interact with the person who actually uses the PC being repaired and is not permanently responsible for this PC

- A **help desk technician** providing telephone support

The PC support technician is the only one of the four listed above who is responsible for the PC before the trouble occurs and, therefore, has the opportunity to prepare for a problem by keeping good records and maintaining backups (or teaching the user how to do so).

A PC service technician is usually not responsible for the ongoing maintenance of a PC, but usually has the opportunity to interact with the user of the computer.

The bench technician is probably not working at the same site where the PC is kept. He or she may have the benefit of interviewing the user to get information about the problem, or might simply be presented with a PC to repair without being able to call the user to ask a question.

The help desk technician, who does not have physical access to the PC is at the greatest disadvantage of the four. He or she is limited to interacting with the user over the phone and must obviously use different tools and approaches than the technician at the PC.

In this chapter, the primary emphasis is on the first job function listed, that of a PC support technician who is free to interact with the user and has overall responsibility for the welfare of the PCs he or she maintains and repairs. However, the special needs and perspectives of the service technician, the bench technician, and the help desk technician are also addressed.

PROTECT YOURSELF, THE HARDWARE, AND THE SOFTWARE

Please remember that every time you work on your PC, you run the risk of hurting yourself, the hardware, and the software. However, there are precautions you can take to protect all three and they are extremely important to remember. They are summarized here, but before you start trouble-shooting, please read the detailed precautions in the *Read This Before You Begin* section of the preface of this book. Remember that you can compound a problem, causing even more damage, by carelessly not following these safety precautions.

Don't open your computer's case until you read this warning. Removing, replacing, and modifying pieces of hardware inside your computer without following the necessary precautions can cause you and your computer serious damage. The most common risk to a computer is posed by the discharge of static electricity, which can destroy circuit boards and chips. However, accessing the insides of the power supply or monitor can pose serious safety risks to you as well. These dangers can be avoided. To assure safety in your work setting, follow every precaution listed in the *Read This Before You Begin* section following this book's Introduction.

The most common threat to hardware is electrostatic discharge (ESD), commonly known as static electricity. Damage by ESD can cause a catastrophic failure, which can destroy components, or can cause an upset failure that produces unpredictable malfunctions of components, which are often difficult to detect or diagnose.

The three best protections against ESD as you work on a computer are a ground strap, a ground mat, and static shielding bags. A **ground strap**, sometimes called a ground bracelet or a static strap (see Figure 7-1), is worn on your wrist and is grounded to a ground mat, computer case, or a ground prong of a wall outlet. A **ground mat** (see Figure 7-2) often comes equipped with a cord to plug into the ground prong of the wall outlet and a snap on the mat to which you can snap the end of your ground strap. New components come shipped in **static shielding bags**. Save the bags to store other devices not currently installed on your PC.

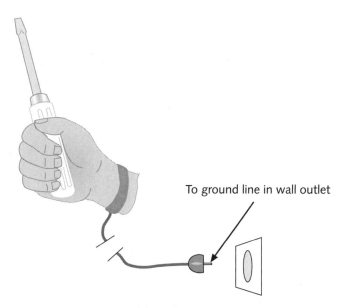

To ground line in wall outlet

Figure 7-1   A ground bracelet protects against ESD

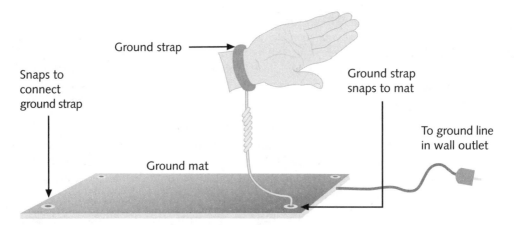

Snaps to
connect
ground strap

Ground strap

Ground strap
snaps to mat

To ground line
in wall outlet

Ground mat

Figure 7-2   Ground mat and ground strap

Here is a brief summary of some tips on how to further protect disks and other hardware as you work, as described in the Preface to this book:

- Don't touch chips or edge connectors on boards unless absolutely necessary
- Don't stack boards
- Don't touch chips with a magnetized screwdriver
- Don't use a graphite pencil to change DIP switch settings
- Don't put cards on top of or next to the monitor
- When laying components down, lay them on a grounded mat or static shielding bag
- Always turn off the PC before moving it (for even a few inches) to protect the hard drive
- When working inside a monitor, be careful to *not* ground yourself
- When unpacking hardware or software, remove the packing tape from the work area as soon as possible
- Don't place a PC on the floor where it might get kicked
- Keep disks away from magnetic fields, heat, and extreme cold
- Don't open a disk's shuttle window or touch the surface of a disk

TOOLS TO HELP SUPPORT PERSONAL COMPUTERS

There are many tools to help diagnose and repair computer problems. Your choice depends on the amount of money you can spend and the level of support you are providing for PCs. Here is a list of the essential tools and the convenient ones:

- Flat-head screwdriver
- Phillips-head screwdriver
- Torque screwdriver
- Tweezers for picking pieces of paper or dropped screws from tight places
- A chip extractor to remove chips (To pry up the chip a simple screwdriver is usually more effective, however.)
- Extractor, a spring-loaded device that looks like a hypodermic needle (When you push down on the top, three wire prongs come out that can be used to pick up a fallen screw where hands and fingers can't reach.)

All the above tools can be purchased together in a handy PC tool kit. The following tools might not be considered essential, but they are very convenient:

- Multimeter to check the power supply output (this will be discussed in Chapter 10)
- Needle-nose pliers for holding things in place while you screw (especially those pesky nuts on cable connectors)
- Flashlight to see inside dark places of the PC case
- Ground bracelet and/or ground mat
- Small cups or bags to help keep screws organized as you work
- Pen and paper for taking notes
- Bootable rescue disks
- Virus detection software on disks
- Diagnostic cards and diagnostic software
- Utility software

Keep your tools in a tool box designated for that purpose. If you put the disks and hardware tools in the same box, don't include a magnetized screwdriver and be sure to keep the disks inside a plastic case. Make sure the diagnostic and utility software you use is recommended for the hardware and software you are working with.

7

BOOTABLE DISK FOR DOS

For DOS, make a bootable disk using the same version of DOS that is on your hard drive. Use this command:

```
C:\> FORMAT A:/S
```

The /S option tells DOS to copy to the disk the files needed to load DOS from this disk. On the disk will be a small boot record that identifies the layout of the disk and the names of the two DOS hidden files. This command also puts the two hidden files and COMMAND.COM on the disk.

It's important that the boot disk has the same version of DOS that is on your hard drive. By being consistent with versions, once you're booted you can use some of DOS loaded from the disk and some DOS program files on the hard drive without DOS displaying error messages about using different versions of DOS. Use the VER command at the DOS prompt to display the current version of DOS.

You can also add some DOS utility commands to the disk so that it can serve as a rescue disk if needed. In addition to the boot files, copy these files to the disk:

- ATTRIB.EXE
- CHKDSK.EXE
- EDIT.COM (which may also require QBASIC.EXE if you are using an older version of DOS)
- FDISK.EXE
- FORMAT.COM
- MSCDEX.EXE
- SCANDISK.EXE
- SYS.COM
- DEFRAG.EXE
- HIMEM.SYS
- UNDELETE.EXE

RESCUE DISK FOR WINDOWS 95

For Windows 95, make a rescue disk as discussed in Chapter 2. In Chapter 8 you will learn to also put on this rescue disk the files needed to allow access to the CD-ROM without depending on the hard drive.

POST DIAGNOSTIC CARDS

Diagnostic cards are designed to discover and report computer errors and conflicts at POST. One example is POSTcard V3 by Unicore Software, Inc. Another is Post Code Master by MSD, Inc. Diagnostic cards can communicate an error to you by displaying a number on the card. Web sites for these manufacturers are:

- MSD   www.msd.com
- Unicore Software   www.unicore.com

DIAGNOSTIC SOFTWARE

There are many diagnostic software programs on the market designed for various purposes. If the software rates itself as being at the professional level, it generally assumes greater technical expertise and also provides more features than does end-user or novice-level software. Diagnostic software is generally used to identify hardware problems. The most effective diagnostic software does not use the OS to run from because the OS may sometimes mask a hardware problem. Here are a few examples of diagnostic software.

PC-Technician by Windsor Technologies, Inc.

This professional-level PC diagnostic software loads and operates without using the OS because it has its own proprietary OS built in. Results are thus unaltered by any errors in the OS on the PC. Other DOS- and Windows-based diagnostic software can sometimes give incorrect information.

PC-Technician is capable of relocating itself during memory testing so that it can successfully test all of main memory.

PC-Technician bypasses standard ROM BIOS when translation mode is used by the system so that the diagnostic software communicates directly with the hard drive controller.

PC-Technician performs over 200 tests including testing main memory, extended memory, expanded memory, hard drives, disk drives, video display, video cards, serial and parallel ports, and keyboards.

PC-Technician comes with test plugs (called loop-back plugs) used to test parallel and serial ports by looping data out of and back to the port (called a loop-back test). These loop-back tests determine that hardware ports are working.

There is a downloadable version of this software called TuffTEST-Pro. See the company Web site www.windsortech.com.

PC-Diagnosys by Windsor Technologies, Inc.

This software is designed for the less-experienced PC support/service person and the end-user. It contains some of the same features of PC-Technician discussed above, but at a much lower cost. It's very easy to use and includes its own proprietary OS so that the OS on the PC will not mask results.

Tests include main memory, extended memory, hard drives, disk drives, video display, video cards, and serial and parallel ports.

WINProbe 4 by Quarterdeck Corp.

WINProbe focuses on identifying hardware problems including those on the hard drive. It provides over 50 tests and information screens.

The company Web site is www.qdeck.com.

UTILITY SOFTWARE FOR UPDATES AND FIXES

Utility software is primarily designed to repair and/or maintain the software on a PC and requires the OS to work. Some utility software uses Internet access to download software patches and updates. Examples include the following:

First Aid 97 by CyberMedia

First Aid 97 surveys and repairs problems with Windows 95 including non-working Windows 95 Shortcuts. It can connect to the Internet to update older versions of device drivers and Windows 95 system files. It does not update applications software.

The company Web site is www.cybermedia.com.

Oil Change by CyberMedia

Oil Change is designed to keep PC software including drivers and applications up-to-date. Oil Change scans the system, creating an inventory of software and drivers. It then connects to the Cybermedia database on the Internet, checks for new versions, and fixes and automatically downloads and installs the updates.

WebPatch by NetSync

WebPatch is free to Internet users. Vendors who want to provide updates for their software pay to maintain this Web site. It downloads only the files of the software that need updating rather than the entire package.

The product Web site is www.webpatch.com.

PC Handyman by Symantec

PC Handyman fixes common Windows 95 system and driver problems. It includes a CD-ROM of video clips that provide help resolving problems and installing hardware.

The company Web site is www.symantec.com.

GENERAL PURPOSE UTILITY SOFTWARE

General purpose utility software can be used to manage a hard drive, monitor system resources, recover lost data, and secure a system. Popular choices include Norton Utilities, Check It, Nuts & Bolts, and PC Tools.

Norton Utilities by Symantec

Norton Utilities by Symantec is a general purpose, user-friendly utility software that provides a variety of functions including recovering data from a hard drive; it was discussed in some detail in Chapter 6.

The company Web site is www.symantec.com.

Nuts & Bolts by Helix Software

Nuts & Bolts by Helix Software Co., which is included on a CD-ROM with this book, is a comprehensive package of utilities including data recovery, security, system monitoring, and hard drive clean-up. Nuts & Bolts was also introduced in Chapter 6.

The company Web site is www.helixsoftware.com.

Check It Diagnostic Kit by Touchstone Software

Check It by Touchstone is a general-purpose software and hardware utility product that includes hard drive testing, performance testing, port testing (loop-back plugs are included), setup, and testing for resource conflicts.

The product Web site is www.checkit.com.

PC Tools

PC Tools was produced by Central Point Software, who sold the product to Symantec. It is a general-purpose utility software package including hard drive recovery and software diagnosis. The product is still used by many companies.

The Symantec Web site is www.symantec.com.

HANDLING VIRUSES

When troubleshooting PCs that show symptoms of either hardware or software problems, consider a virus as the source of the problem. If you suspect a virus may be involved, use a virus scan program to scan memory and your hard drive for an active or inactive virus. DOS 6.x offers the virus scan utility that is part of the Central Point antivirus software sometimes sold with PC Tools. An antivirus program searches hard drives and disks and informs you of the presence of a virus and asks permission before deleting it. For Windows, the utility is under the Microsoft Tools group. DOS 6.x also offers VSAFE, a TSR that constantly monitors for virus activity. You can load it from AUTOEXEC.BAT if you want it to run every time you boot.

Any antivirus software is no better than the kinds of viruses it knows to detect and erase. When choosing such software, look for features like free updates from the company Web site or other online service so that you can easily keep the software up-to-date in order to be protected against new and different viruses as they arise. Some other antivirus software programs on the market include the following:

- F-Protect (F-PROT) is rated as a quality antivirus product with excellent scanning and removal ability.

- McAfee ViruScan (SCAN) is probably the best-known antivirus software product.

- Norton Anti-Virus (NAV) is popular because of its ease of use and graphical interface.

- Central Point Anti-Virus (CPAV) is another well-known product.

Viruses can hide in an executable file like COMMAND.COM or in any other program. They also can hide in the DOS boot record or the partition table load program and are also commonly found in macros of word-processing files. They can lie dormant for an extended time and, once active, can do mild or deadly damage. Viruses are usually transmitted by disks that contain program code or by program files downloaded from the Internet.

Some things that you can do to reduce the threat of viruses are:

- Write-protect original software disks and backup copies.

- Boot from your hard disk or a write-protected disk only.

- Don't download from a bulletin board or always use a virus scan program when you do.

- Use a scan utility such as Microsoft's Anti-virus or McAfee's SCAN on a regular or even daily basis.

Some warning signs that a virus is present are:

- A program takes longer than normal to load.

- Disk access times seem excessive for simple tasks.

- Unusual error messages occur regularly.

- Less memory than usual is available.

- Files disappear mysteriously.

- There is a noticeable reduction in disk space.

- Executable files have changed size.

- The access lights on hard drives and floppy drives turn on when there should not be any activity on that device.

When working on a PC, be careful to not transmit a virus from your own bootable disk. Make a practice of scanning your boot disk for viruses before using it to troubleshoot another PC.

HOW TO ISOLATE COMPUTER PROBLEMS AND DEVISE A COURSE OF ACTION

When a computer doesn't work and you're responsible for fixing it, you should generally approach the problem first as an investigator and discoverer, always being very careful not to compound the problem through your own actions. If the problem seems difficult to you, see it as an opportunity to learn something new. Ask questions until you understand the source of the problem. Once you understand this, you're almost done because, most likely, the solution will then be evident. Take the attitude that you can understand the problem and solve it no matter how deeply you have to dig, and you probably will.

HANDLING AN EMERGENCY

In an emergency, protect the data and software by carefully considering your options before acting, by not assuming data is lost even when hard drive and floppy drive errors occur, and by taking practical precautions to protect software and OS files. Decide what your first priority is. For example, the first priority might be to recover data that is lost or it might be to get the PC back up and running as soon as possible. Consult the user for his or her advice when practical.

Don't Assume the Worst

When it's an emergency situation and your only copy of data is on a hard drive and the hard drive is not working, don't assume the data is lost. Much can be done to recover your data, as you learned in Chapter 6, but one important point is worth repeating. If you want to recover lost data on a hard drive, don't write anything to that hard drive; you might write on top of your lost data, eliminating all chances of recovery.

In an Emergency, Carefully Consider Your Options

When a computer stops working, if there is data still in memory that has not been saved or if there is data or software on the hard drive that is not backed up, look and think carefully before you leap! A wrong move can be costly. The very best advice is don't hurry. Carefully plan your moves. Read the documentation if you're not sure what to do, and don't hesitate to ask for help. Don't simply try something hoping it will work—unless you've run out of more intelligent alternatives!

For example, suppose a user calls who has been working on a word-processing document and has not saved his work for several hours. (Just thinking about that made me just save mine!) When he finally tried to save, he got a message similar to: "Unable to write to drive C:". The beginning of the call is not the time to remind him to save his work every 10 or 15 minutes, although you need to explain that to him when things are a little calmer. Be sensitive to his situation and his fears. Remember that you could have made similar if not worse mistakes. But what to do first? Carefully think through the alternatives and don't rush. Why can't the software write to drive C? Is the disk full, or is he writing to the root directory, which already has its limit of files? Is there something wrong with the filename or path he entered? If he can't write to drive C, can he write to drive A? What does the documentation say about problems with saving files? Who can you turn to for help? A logical approach to this problem is:

- Have the user read the error message to you in full and write it down if you don't understand it.

- Look up the error message in your online help for the software. Don't have the user do this as it might cause the file to be lost if there are other system errors happening.

- Have the user tell you each keystroke that is entered as he or she attempts to save the file.

- If you suspect a problem with the hard drive, try to save to a floppy disk.

- If you suspect a problem with the filename or extension, use a different filename. Try not using a file extension or a period following the filename. Let the software do that.

- Try to save to a different floppy disk that you know is formatted. Is the disk write-protected?

- Ask if there are two floppy drives and check that the disk is in the correct one.

- If the file cannot be saved after trying several methods, can the document be printed? A hard copy is better than nothing.

- Don't give up and tell the user to just reboot unless you have first asked for help from your own support.

Keeping a cool head, thinking things through, and getting help may save his data if it can be saved. The point is you may only have one chance to make a right move; just be sure your first effort is your best effort.

FUNDAMENTAL RULES

Here are a few fundamental rules for PC troubleshooting that I've found work for me.

- **Approach the problem systematically**. Most problems with computers are simple, such as a loose cable or circuit board. Computers are logical through and through. Whatever the problem, it's also very logical. Start at the beginning and walk your way through the situation in a thorough, careful way. This one rule is worth its weight in gold. Remember it and apply it every time. If you don't find the explanation to the problem after one systematic, logical walk-through, then repeat the entire process. Check and double-check to find the step you overlooked the first time.

- **Don't overlook the obvious**. Ask simple questions. Is the computer plugged in? Is it turned on? Is the monitor plugged in? Most problems are so simple that we overlook them because we expect the problem to be difficult. Don't let the complexity of computers fool you. Most problems are simple and easy to fix. Really, they are!

- **Check the simple things first**. It is more effective to first check the components that are easiest to replace. For example, if the video does not work, the problem may be with the monitor or the video card. When faced with the decision of which one to replace first, choose the easy route: replace the monitor before you replace the video card.

- **Make no assumptions**. This rule is the hardest one to follow, because there is a tendency to trust anything in writing and assume that people are telling you exactly what happened. But documentation is sometimes wrong and people don't always describe events exactly as they occurred, so do your own investigating. For example, if the user tells you that the system boots up with no error messages, but his or her software still doesn't work, boot for yourself. You never know what that user might have overlooked.

- **Become a researcher**. This rule is the most fun. When a computer problem arises that you can't easily solve, be as tenacious as a bulldog. Read, make phone calls, ask questions, read, make phone calls, and ask questions. Take advantage of every available resource including online help, the Internet, documentation, technical support, and books such as this one. What you learn will be yours to take to the next problem. This is the real joy of computer troubleshooting. If you're good at it, you're always learning something new.

- **Write things down**. Keep good notes as you're working. They'll help you think more clearly. Draw diagrams. Make lists. Write down clearly and precisely what you're learning. Later, when the entire problem gets "cold," these notes will be invaluable.

- **Reboot and start over**. This is an important rule. Fresh starts are good for us and uncover events or steps that might have been overlooked. Take a break; get away from the problem. Begin again.

- **Divide and conquer.** This rule is the most powerful. Isolate the problem. In the overall system of hardware and software, remove first one hardware and software component after another until the problem is isolated to a small subsystem of the whole system. You will learn many methods of applying this rule in this book. For starters, here are a few. Remove any memory-resident programs (TSRs) to eliminate them as the problem. Boot from a disk to eliminate the OS and startup files on the hard drive as the problem. Remove any unnecessary hardware devices, such as a scanner card, internal modem, and even the hard drive. Once down to only the essentials, start exchanging components you know are good for those you suspect may be bad until the problem goes away.

Eliminate the Unnecessary

This rule is worth emphasizing. When you're not certain if the problem is a software problem or a hardware problem, apply this rule. Boot from a disk that you know is good and that has a minimal OS configuration (i.e., no CONFIG.SYS or AUTOEXEC.BAT files). By doing so you have eliminated all the applications software loaded at start-up on the PC, all the TSRs loaded at start-up, and much of the OS, especially in Windows 95. If the problem goes away, you can deduce that the problem is with (a) the software on the PC or (b) the hard drive and/or its subsystem that is used as the boot device.

If you suspect the problem is caused by faulty hardware, eliminate any unnecessary hardware devices. If the PC still boots with errors, disconnect the network card, the CD-ROM, the mouse, and maybe even the hard drive. You don't need to remove the CD-ROM or hard drive from the bays inside the case. Simply disconnect the data cable and the power cable. For the network card, remove the card from its expansion slot. Remember to place it on an anti-static bag or grounded mat—not on top of the power supply or case. If the problem goes away, you know one or more of these devices is causing the problem. Replace one at a time until the problem returns. Remember the problem might be a resource conflict. If the network card worked well until the CD-ROM was reconnected, and now they both won't work, try the CD-ROM without the network card. If the CD-ROM now works, you most likely have a resource conflict.

Trade Good for Suspected Bad

When diagnosing hardware problems, this method serves you well if you can draw from a group of parts that you know work correctly. Suppose the monitor does not work; it appears dead. The parts of the video subsystem are the video card, the power cord to the monitor, the cord from the monitor to the PC case, and the monitor itself. Also, don't forget that the video card is inserted into an expansion slot on the systemboard and the monitor depends on electrical power. Suspect each of these five components to be bad. Trade the monitor for a monitor that you know works. If the monitor still doesn't work, trade the power cord, trade the cord to the PC video port, move the video card to a new slot, trade the video card. When you're trading a good component for a suspected bad one, work methodically by eliminating one component at a time. Don't trade the video card and the monitor and then turn on the PC to determine if they work. It's possible that both the card and the monitor are bad, but first assume only one component is bad before you consider whether multiple components need trading.

In this situation, suppose you keep trading components in the video subsystem until you have no more variations. Next take this entire subsystem, video card, cords, and monitor to a PC that you know works, and plug each of them in to see if they work. If they do, you have isolated the problem to the PC, not the video. Now turn your attention back to the PC—the systemboard, the software settings within the OS, the video driver, etc. Knowing that the video subsystem works on the good PC gives you a valuable tool to work with. Compare the video driver on the good PC to the one on the bad PC. Make certain the CMOS settings, software settings, etc., are the same.

DEVISING A COURSE OF ACTION

7

Problems with computers originate with the user, the software, the computer, or the peripheral devices. We survey all of these briefly, and offer some general guidelines and places to look for the causes of problems.

Interacting with the User

Ask the user to explain to you in detail exactly what happened when the computer stopped working. What procedure was taking place at the time? What had just happened? What recent changes did the user make? When did the computer Last work? What has happened in the meantime? What error messages did the user see? Re-create the circumstances when the computer stopped as best you can, and in as much detail as you can. Make no assumptions. All users make simple mistakes and then overlook what was done. If you realize that the problem was caused by the user's mistake, take the time to explain the proper procedures so the user understands what went wrong and what to do next time.

Use diplomacy and good manners when you work with a user to solve a problem. For example, if you suspect that the user dropped the PC, don't ask "Did you drop the PC?" but rather put the question in a less accusatory manner: "Could the PC have been dropped?" If you're standing beside a user who asked for your help who is sitting in front of the PC, don't assume you can take over the keyboard or mouse without permission. Also, if the user is present, ask permission before you make a software or hardware change, even if the user has just given you permission to interact with the PC.

When working at the user's desk, consider yourself a "guest" and follow these general guidelines:

- Don't "talk down" to or patronize the user.
- Don't take over the mouse or keyboard from the user without permission.
- Don't use the phone without permission.

- Don't pile your belongings and tools on top of the user's papers, books, etc.

- Accept personal inconvenience to accommodate the user's urgent business needs. For example, if the user gets an important call while you are working, step out of the way so he or she can handle it.

Whether or not you are at the user's desk, you should generally follow these guidelines when working with the user:

- Don't take drastic action like formatting the hard drive before you ask the user about important data on the hard drive that may not be backed up.

- Provide the user with alternatives where appropriate before you make decisions affecting him or her.

- Protect the confidentiality of data on the PC such as business financial information.

- Don't disparage the user's choice of computer hardware or software.

- If you have made a mistake or must pass the problem on to someone with more expertise, be honest.

In some PC support situations, it is appropriate to consider yourself as a support to the user as well as a support to the PC. Your goals may include educating the user as well as repairing his or her computer. In this kind of situation, if you want the user to learn something from a problem he or she caused, don't fix the problem yourself unless the user asks you to. Explain how to fix the problem and walk him or her through the process if necessary. It takes a little longer this way, but is more productive in the end because the user learns more and is less likely to repeat the mistake.

Here are some helpful questions to ask the user when you are first trying to discover what the problem is:

- When did the problem start?

- Were there any error messages or unusual displays on the screen?

- What programs or software were you using?

- Did you move your computer system recently?

- Has there been a recent thunderstorm or electrical problem?

- Have you made any hardware changes?

- Did you recently install any new software?

- Did you recently change any software configuration setups?

- Has someone else been using your computer recently?

The goal is to gain as much information from the user as you can before you begin investigating the hardware and the software.

Problems with the Software

Suppose the computer boots with no errors, and all but one software package on this computer work correctly. When you try to load the problem software package, however, you get an error message and the software terminates. If this is the case, you can probably conclude that the software caused the error. Ask yourself these questions: Has this software ever worked? If it has not, then try installing it again. Maybe wrong information was given during the installation. Be sure you check the requirements for the software. Maybe you don't have enough memory or space on your hard drive to create the necessary working files.

When was the last time the software worked? What happened differently then? Did you get an error message that at the time did not seem significant? What has happened to your computer since the software last worked? Have you added more software or changed the hardware configuration?

Consider reinstalling the software even if it has worked in the past. Maybe a program file has become corrupted. Before you do that, however, ask yourself: If I reinstall it will I erase data that this software has placed on my hard drive? If you're not sure, back up the data. Maybe you can just copy the data to another directory while you reinstall the program. If the installation does erase the data in the original directory, you can copy one file and then another back to the original directory. If the problem reoccurs, then you've found the corrupted data file that caused the problem.

Software often uses configuration files and scripting files that are specific to a particular PC or user. If you reinstall the software, most likely you will lose the configuration information. Either save the configuration files before you begin or print the contents of the files. See the documentation of the software for the names and location of the configuration files (a file extension of .CFG is common). Consider that the problem with the software might be a corrupted configuration file.

If this particular software package doesn't work and everything else does, the problem might still not be with the software. One user could not get a software package to work on his machine after many installation attempts. The video displayed only a blank screen. All other software worked properly on his computer. He had purchased his computer one year earlier. It was shipped as a complete system directly from the manufacturer and was equipped with a super VGA color monitor. During the software installation, the user correctly told the software to interface with a super VGA video card. After many phone calls to technical support for both the software and hardware companies, the problem was finally identified. The manufacturer had mistakenly sent him a computer with a super VGA monitor but a VGA (not super VGA) video card. All the other software packages interfaced with the VGA card with no problems, but this one was more discriminating.

This is a case where Nuts & Bolts, Norton Utilities, or similar utility software could have helped. These utilities can display system hardware information and tell you what type of video card you have.

Software problems might be caused by other software. Windows 3.x and Windows 95 both use files stored in the \WINDOWS\SYSTEM directory to support software files for many software applications as well as Windows. These files can have extensions of .DLL, .OCX,

.OCA, .VBX, etc. The most common are the DLL (Dynamic Link Libraries) files. These files perform tasks for many software packages such as displaying and managing a dialog box on screen. When you install an application, the installation program may write a DLL to the \WINDOWS\SYSTEM directory and overwrite an earlier version of the DLL used by another application. The original application may have problems because it cannot use the new DLL. If the software being investigated started to have problems after you installed another software program, the problem may well be the DLL it is unsuccessfully trying to use. Chapter 11 discusses solving DLL problems and similar difficulties created by "bad neighbor" software.

Problems with the Keyboard, Monitor, and Printer

If the peripheral devices, such as the keyboard, monitor, or printer, don't work, ask questions like these: Does the device work in situations other than the current one? Perhaps the problem is with the applications software interfacing with the device rather than the device itself. Has the device ever worked? Will another device work in this same situation? Exchange the keyboard or monitor for one you know works. If the good device now fails to work, you can then eliminate the original device as the source of the problem. The problem must be the software, the cable, the computer, or the user. Check all connections and exchange cables.

Intermittent Problems

Intermittent problems can make troubleshooting challenging. The trick in diagnosing problems that come and go is to look for the patterns or clues as to when the problems appear. If the problem is such that you or the user can't reproduce the problem at will, ask the user to keep a log of when the problems occur and exactly what messages appeared on the screen. Show the user how to get a printed screen of the error messages when they appear. Here's the method:

- For simple DOS systems, the PrintScreen key directs the displayed screen to the printer.

- In Windows, the PrintScreen key copies the displayed screen to the Clipboard.

- Launch the Paint software accessory program and paste the contents of the Clipboard into the document. You might need to use the Zoom Out command on the document first. You can then print the document with the displayed screen using Paint. You can also paste the contents of the Clipboard into a document created by a word-processing application such as Word.

TROUBLESHOOTING GUIDELINES: PERIPHERAL DEVICES

This section contains troubleshooting guidelines for the keyboard, monitor, printer, and PC. Troubleshooting the PC is divided into two basic categories: the PC does or does not boot. There are many other troubleshooting guidelines found in this book, but here is a collection of the most common problems and what to do about them.

TROUBLESHOOTING KEYBOARD PROBLEMS

Often dirt, food, or drink in the keyboard causes one or more keys to stick or not work properly. These and other keyboard problems are described next and what you can do to correct them is explained.

Because of the low cost of keyboards, if a keyboard does not work, the solution is most often to replace it. However, there are a few simple things you can do to repair one that is not working.

A few keys don't work

Remove the cap on the bad key with a chip extractor. Spray contact cleaner into the key well. Repeatedly depress the contact in order to clear it out. Don't use rubbing alcohol to clean the key well as it can leave a residue on the contact.

If this method of cleaning solves the problem, then clean the adjacent keys as well.

The keyboard does not work at all

Is the cable plugged in? PC keyboard cables may become loose or disconnected.

If the cable connection is good and the keyboard still does not work, swap the keyboard with another keyboard of the same type that you know is in good condition to verify that the problem is in the keyboard and not in the computer.

If the problem is in the keyboard, check the cable. If possible, swap the cable with a known good one, perhaps from an old discarded keyboard. Sometimes a wire in a PC keyboard cable becomes pinched or broken. Most cables can be easily separated and detatched from the keyboard by removing the few screws that hold the keyboard case together, then simply unplugging the cable. Be careful as you work; don't allow the key caps to fall out!

In Chapter 10 you will learn how to use a multimeter to test a cable. This test is called a continuity test.

If the problem is not the cable, try replacing the keyboard with a new one.

Connect the keyboard that is not working with the current PC to another computer that works properly. If the keyboard proves to be good, connect a keyboard that you know is good to the original computer. If that keyboard now doesn't work, then the problem must be with the computer.

On the systemboard, the two chips that affect the keyboard functions are the keyboard chip and the ROM BIOS chip. You might choose to swap each of these chips on the systemboard. Otherwise the entire systemboard might have to be replaced.

Key continues to repeat after being released

The problem might be a dirty contact. Some debris may have conductive properties, short the gap between the contacts, and therefore cause the key to repeat. Try cleaning the key switch with contact cleaner.

Very high humidity and excess moisture will sometimes short key switch contacts and cause keys to repeat because water is an electrical conductor. The problem will usually resolve itself once the humidity level returns to normal. You can hasten the drying process by using a fan (not a hot hair dryer) to blow air at the keyboard.

Keys produce the wrong characters

This problem is usually caused by a bad chip. PC keyboards actually have a processor mounted on the logic board inside the keyboard. Try swapping the keyboard for one you know is good. It the problem goes away, replace the keyboard.

TROUBLESHOOTING MONITOR PROBLEMS

For monitors, as well as other devices, do the easy things first. There are hardware and software adjustments you can make. Remember the "trade good for suspected bad" method. Many monitor problems are caused by poor cable connections or bad contrast/brightness adjustments. Also check if the monitor is still under warranty. Remember that many warranties are voided if an unauthorized individual works on the system. Typical monitor problems and how to troubleshoot them are described next:

Power light (LED) does not go on, no picture

Is the monitor plugged in?

Verify that the wall outlet works by plugging in a lamp, radio, etc.

If the monitor power cord is plugged into a power strip or surge protector, verify that the power strip is turned on and that the monitor is also turned on.

If the monitor power cord is plugged into the back of the computer, verify that the connection is tight and the computer is turned on.

A blown fuse could be the problem. How to check for a blown fuse is covered in Chapter 10.

Power LED light is on, no picture on power up

Check the contrast adjustment. If there's no change, then leave it at a middle setting.

Check the brightness adjustment. If there's no change, then leave it at a middle setting.

Is the cable connected securely to the computer?

If the monitor-to-computer cable detaches from the monitor, exchange it for a cable you know is good or check the cable for continuity (Chapter 10).

If this solves the problem, reattach the old cable to verify that the problem was not simply a bad connection.

Confirm that the proper system configuration has been set up. Some older systemboards have a jumper or DIP switch that can be used to select the monitor type.

Trade for a different monitor of the same type. For example, trade a color SVGA with another color SVGA.

Test the monitor that isn't working on a computer that works with another monitor.

Test a monitor you know is good on the computer you suspect to be bad. It is very important to do both this and the previous step to keep from being fooled. If you think the monitor is bad, make sure that it also fails to work on a good computer.

Check the CMOS settings or software configuration on the computer.

Trade a good video card for the video card you suspect is bad.

Test the video card you think is bad on a computer that works. Test a video card you know is good on the computer that you suspect may be bad. Whenever possible, try to do both.

If the video card has some socketed chips that appear dirty or corroded, consider removing them and trying to clean the pins. You can use a clean pencil eraser to do this. Normally, however, if the problem is a bad video card the most cost-effective measure is to replace the card.

Test the RAM on the systemboard. (To be discussed later in this chapter.)

Trade the systemboard for one you know is good. Sometimes, though rarely, a peripheral chip on the systemboard of the computer can cause the problem.

Power on, but monitor displays the wrong characters

Wrong characters are usually not the result of a bad monitor but of a problem with the video card. Trade the video card for one you know is good.

Exchange the systemboard. Sometimes a bad chip, ROM or RAM, on the systemboard will display the wrong characters on the monitor.

Monitor flickers and/or has wavy lines

Check the cable. Monitor flicker can be caused by poor cable connections.

Check if something in the office is causing a high amount of electrical noise. For example, you might be able to stop a flicker by moving the office fan to a different outlet. Bad fluorescent lights or large speakers have also been known to produce interference. Two monitors placed very close together can also cause problems.

If the vertical scan frequency (the refresh rate at which the screen is drawn) is below 60 Hz, a screen flicker may appear. Most new monitors do not have this problem if the ideal refresh rate is selected, and purchasing a new monitor may be the only cure for older systems.

Before making a purchase, verify that the new monitor will solve the problem.

Check the Control Panel, Display, Settings to see if a high resolution (greater than 800 × 600 with more than 256 colors) is selected. Consider these issues:

1. The video card might not support this resolution/color setting.

2. There might not be enough video RAM; 2 MB may be required.

3. The added (socketed) video RAM might be of a different speed than the soldered memory.

Does the monitor have a degauss button to eliminate accumulated or stray magnetic fields? If so, press it.

No graphics display or the screen goes blank when loading certain programs

A special graphic or video accelerator card is not present or is defective.

Software is not configured to do graphics or the software does not recognize the installed graphics card.

The video card might not support this resolution and/or color setting.

There might not be enough video RAM; 2MB might be required.

The added (socketed) video RAM might be of a different speed than the soldered memory.

The wrong adapter/display type is selected. Start Windows 95 from Safe Mode to reset display. (How to do this is explained later in this discussion.)

Screen goes blank 30 seconds or one minute after the keyboard is left untouched

A Green systemboard (Green systemboards follow energy-saving standards) used with an Energy Saver monitor can be configured to go into a Standby or Doze Mode after a period of inactivity. This might be the case if the monitor resumes after tapping a key or moving the mouse. Doze times can be set for as short a period as 20 seconds to as long as one hour. The power LED light normally changes color from green to orange to indicate Doze Mode. Monitors and video cards using these energy-saving features are addressed in Chapter 10.

You might be able to change the doze features by entering the CMOS menu and looking for an option such as Power Management, or in Windows 95 by going to the Control Panel and selecting **Display**, **Screen Saver**.

Some monitors have a Power Save switch on the back of system. This might not be switched to your desired setting.

Poor quality color display

Read the documentation for the monitor to learn how to use the color-adjusting buttons on the outside of the monitor to fine-tune the color.

Exchange video cards.

Add more video RAM; 2 MB or 4 MB might be required for higher resolutions.

Check if there is a fan or large speaker (speakers have large magnets) or another monitor nearby that could be causing interference.

Picture out of focus or out of adjustment

Check the adjustment knobs on the control panel on the outside of the monitor.

There are adjustments inside the monitor that might solve the problem. If you have not been trained to work inside the monitor, take the monitor to a service center for adjustments.

Crackling sound

An accumulation of dirt or dust inside the unit might be the cause. Someone trained to work on the inside of the monitor can vacuum the inside.

To configure or change monitor settings and drivers in Windows 95

Insert the video driver disk in drive A.

From the Start menu choose **Run**.

Type **A:Setup** and click **OK** (or choose **Browse** if the driver has a setup program with a different name).

To change the Video Driver configuration

Select the **Display** icon from the Control Panel.

Select the **Settings** tab to change the color palette, resolution (for example, 800 × 600 to 1024 × 768), or change the driver for the video card or monitor type. Click on **Change Display Type** from the Settings tab to show the Change Display Type window (see Figure 7–3). From this window, you can change the video card or the monitor type.

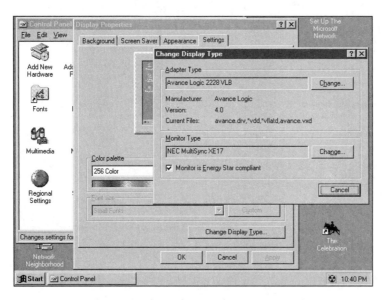

Figure 7-3   Changing the video card type in Windows 95

If you increase the resolution, the Windows icons and desktop text become smaller. Consequently you might want to select Large Fonts under the Settings tab and increase the Desktop Icon size found under the Appearance tab.

Returning to standard VGA settings

When the display settings don't work, you should return to standard VGA settings as follows:

In Windows 3.x, go to the DOS prompt.

Change to the Windows directory (CD\WINDOWS).

Type **SETUP.**

Change the display type to VGA, 640 × 480, which almost always works. This common video driver is most likely already installed with Windows 95.

For Windows 95, reboot the system and tap the **F8** function key after the first beep.

When the Microsoft Windows 95 Startup Menu displays, select **Safe Mode** to boot up with minimal configurations and standard VGA display mode.

Select the **Display** icon from the Control Panel and reset to the correct video configuration.

TROUBLESHOOTING PRINTER PROBLEMS

When troubleshooting printer problems, first determine that the problem is truly with the printer. The problem might be the computer hardware communicating with the printer, the applications software using the printer, the printer driver, the printer cable, or the printer. Ask these questions and try these things:

Is the printer turned on and is the printer online?

Is the correct printer selected as the default printer?

Can another applications software program other than the program currently running use the printer?

Is the printer using the correct driver? Does the driver need updating? Is the driver correctly installed?

Can you move the printer to another computer and print from it? Will another printer work on this computer?

Once you are convinced that the problem is not with the computer hardware or software, but is indeed a problem with the printer itself, you are ready for the following troubleshooting guide.

Laser Printer Problems

The printer documentation can be very helpful and most often contains a phone number to technical support for the printer manufacturer. A good test for a printer is to print the manufacturer's test page from the PC, not just directly from the printer. For example, for an HP Laser Jet III, access the **Control Panel** and double-click on **Printers**. The printer control appears. Right-click on the printer you want to test and the drop down menu displays as in Figure 7-4. Select the **Properties** option. The Properties box displays as in Figure 7-5. Click on **Print Test Page** to send a test page to the printer.

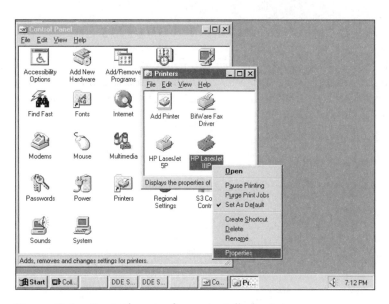

Figure 7-4   Control menu for an installed printer

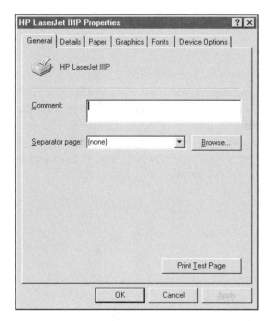

Figure 7-5   The Properties box for an installed printer allows you to print a
test page

Printer never leaves warm-up mode. The warming up message should disappear as soon as
the printer establishes communication with the PC. If this doesn't happen, try the following:

Turn the printer off and disconnect the cable.

Turn on the printer. If it now displays to a Ready message, the problem is communication.

Verify the cable is connected to the correct printer port, not a serial port.

Verify that data to the installed printer is being sent to the parallel port. For example, access the Properties box of the installed printer as described above. Verify that the print is being sent to LPT1: as shown in Figure 7-6.

Replace the cable.

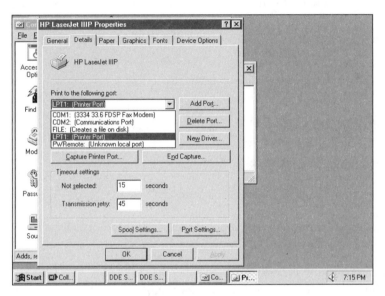

Figure 7-6 Verify that print data is being sent to the parallel port

A Paper Out message displays. Remove the paper tray. Be sure there is paper in the tray. Carefully replace the tray, being certain the tray is fully inserted in the slot.

Check the lever mechanism that falls into a slot on the tray when no paper is present. Is it jammed or bent?

A Toner Low message displays or print is irregular or light. Remove the toner cartridge from the printer, tap the cartridge to redistribute the toner supply, and replace it in the printer. Don't shake the cartridge too hard, to avoid flying toner. This is really just a temporary fix for a cartridge low on toner. Eventually the user must put a new toner cartridge in the printer. Extreme humidity may cause the toner to clump in the cartridge and give the same error message.

A Paper Jam message displays. If paper is jammed inside the printer, follow the directions in the printer documentation to remove the paper. Don't jerk the paper from the printer mechanism but with care pull evenly on the paper.

If there is no jammed paper, then remove the tray and check the metal plate at the bottom of the tray. Can it move up and down freely? If not, replace the tray.

When you insert the tray in the printer, does the printer lift the plate as the tray is inserted? If not, the lift mechanism might need repairing.

One or more white streaks appear in the print. Remove the toner cartridge, tap it to redistribute the toner supply, and replace the cartridge. Check the printer manual for specific directions as to what part might need replacing if this problem occurs.

Print appears speckled. Try replacing the cartridge. If the problem continues, the power supply assembly might be damaged.

Printed images are distorted. Check for debris that might be interfering with the printer operation.

Replace the toner cartridge.

Dot Matrix Printer Problems

Here is a troubleshooting guide for dot matrix printers:

Print quality is poor. Begin with the ribbon. Does it advance normally while the carriage moves back and forth? Replace the ribbon.

If the ribbon still does not advance properly, check the printer's advance mechanism.

Adjust the print head spacing. There is usually a lever adjustment that can alter the distance between the print head and plate.

Check the print head for dirt. Make sure it's not hot before you touch it. If there is a buildup, wipe off each wire with a cotton swab dipped in alcohol or contact cleaner.

Printer self-test works, but printing from a computer application does not work. To perform a printer self-test, see the printer documentation. This test ensures that the printer itself is functioning correctly, and that the problem is communication from the PC.

Check cable connections. Is the printer online?

Print head moves back and forth, but nothing prints. Check the ribbon. Is it installed correctly between the plate and print head?

Does the ribbon advance properly?

Ink Jet Printers

Here is a troubleshooting guide for ink jet printers:

Print quality is poor.   Is the correct paper for ink jet printers being used?

Is the ink supply low or is there a partially clogged nozzle?

Remove and re-install the cartridge.

Follow the printer's documentation to clean each nozzle.

In the Printer Setup dialog box, click the Media/Quality tab, then change the Print Quality selection. Try different settings with sample prints.

Is the print head too close to or too far from the paper?

If you are printing on transparencies, try changing the fill pattern in your application.

Printing is intermittent or absent.   Is the ink supply low?

Are nozzles clogged?

Replace the ink cartridges or replenish the ink supply.

PROBLEMS WITH THE COMPUTER

Problems with a computer that is not working can be divided into two major categories: the computer boots or it does not boot. Begin by asking the initial questions listed earlier in this chapter to learn as much as you can from the user. Next, determine your starting point. Before trying to solve the problem, know for certain that the problem is what the user says it is. If the computer does not boot, carefully note where in the boot process it fails. If the computer does boot to an OS, before changing anything or taking anything apart, verify what does and what doesn't work, preferably in the presence of the user.

When the Computer Does Not Boot

Chapter 2 examined the boot process in detail because it gives many clues to help diagnose a problem. If the computer does not successfully boot, consider the questions, possible sources of problems, and suggestions on how to approach the situation, all outlined below for different sets of circumstances.

Blank screen.   In this case, the PC appears "dead." Are there any burnt parts or odors? Any loose cable connections?

Is the computer plugged in?

Are *all* the switches turned on? Computer? Monitor? Surge Protector? Uninterruptible Power Supply? Separate circuit breaker?

Is the wall outlet (or surge protector) good?

If the fan is not running, turn off the computer, open the case, and check the connections to the power supply. Are they secure? Are all cards securely seated?

Check the voltage output from the power supply. (How to do this is covered in Chapter 10.)

Remove all nonessential expansion cards (modem, sound card, mouse) one at a time. Verify that they are not drawing too much power and pulling the system down.

It is possible that the expansion cards are all good, but the power supply is not capable of supplying enough current for all the add-on boards.

It could be that there are too many cards and the computer is overheating. The temperature inside the case should not exceed 113° F.

Excessive dust insulates components and causes them to overheat. Vacuum the entire unit, especially the power supply's fan vent.

Test the power supply output with a multimeter. (You will learn how in Chapter 10.)

Trade the power supply for another you know is good. Be certain to follow the black-to-black rule when attaching the power cords to the systemboard.

Is there strong magnetic or electrical interference? Sometimes an old monitor will emit too much static and EMF (electro-magnetic force), and bring a whole system down.

If the fan is running, reseat or trade the CPU, BIOS, or RAM. A POST code diagnostic card is a great help at this point.

Sometimes a dead computer can be fixed by simply disassembling it and reseating cables, adapter cards, socketed chips, and SIMMs. Bad connections and corrosion are common problems.

Check jumpers, DIP switches, and CMOS settings.

Is the system in a Doze or Sleep Mode? Many Green systems can be programmed through CMOS to suspend the monitor or even the drive if the keyboard and/or CPU have been inactive for a few minutes. Pressing any key will usually cause operations to resume exactly where the user left off.

If the battery is dead, or dying, it may cause problems. Sometimes, after a long holiday, a weak battery will cause the CMOS to forget its configuration.

Use a POST code diagnostic card to check systemboard components.

Exchange the systemboard.

The computer does not recognize all installed RAM or SIMMs.   Are CMOS settings correct?

Run a diagnostic software such as PC-Technician to test memory.

Are RAM or SIMM modules properly seated?

Look for bent pins or chips installed the wrong way on cache memory. Look for loose SIMM modules.

Place your fingers on the individual chips. Sometimes a bad chip may be noticeably hotter than the other chips.

Make sure the RAM or SIMMs have a correct or consistent part number. For example, if there are four installed SIMMs, they usually must be the same size (in megabytes) and same speed (in nanoseconds).

Trade SIMMs one at a time. For example, if the system only recognizes six out of eight megabytes of RAM, swap the last two SIMM modules. Did the amount of recognized RAM change? You might be able to solve the problem just by reseating the modules. Use SIMM modules with the same part number. Chapter 9 has more information about choosing the correct SIMMs for a systemboard.

Sometimes a problem can result from a bad socket or a broken **trace** (a fine printed wire or circuit) on the systemboard. If this is the case, you might have to replace the entire systemboard.

Error messages appear when booting.   When a PC boots, one beep indicates all is well after POST. If you hear more than one beep, look up the beep code in Appendix A. Error messages on the screen indicate that video is working. Look up the error message in Appendix A if the message on the screen is not clear.

Try a hard boot. A soft boot might not do the trick, because TSRs are not always "kicked out" of RAM with a soft boot.

Boot from a floppy disk. You should boot to an A prompt. If you are successful, the problem is in the hard drive subsystem and/or the software on the drive.

Can you access the hard drive from the A prompt?

If you can get a C prompt, then the problem is in the software that is used on the hard drive to boot, including the partition table, master boot record, OS hidden files, and command interface files. See Chapter 6 for help diagnosing hard drive problems.

Run diagnostic software to test for hard drive hardware problems.

Check all connections and reseat all boards.

Reduce the system to essentials. Remove any unnecessary hardware such as expansion cards and then try to boot again.

Substitute good hardware components for suspected bad ones. Be cautious here. A friend once had a computer that would not boot. He replaced the hard drive and the hard drive controller card with no change. He replaced the systemboard next. The computer booted up with no problem; he was delighted until it failed again. Later he discovered that a faulty power supply had damaged his original systemboard. When he traded the bad one for a good one, the new systemboard also got zapped! Check the voltage coming from the power supply before putting in a new systemboard!

Start over as many times as you need. Get away from the problem and give yourself a fresh start. Ask someone to help.

Keep notes and, when the problem is solved, write down exactly what you did to fix it. Be careful to write down any configuration changes you made, and make a new copy of your bootable disk if you changed the files in the root directory.

7

Windows 95 does not load correctly.   Learn to use the Windows 95 Startup Menu, which is described in other chapters and which has the options displayed in Figure 7-7. Try Safe Mode first. If that doesn't work, use the step-by-step confirmation to identify the command causing the problem. Use the Logged option and examine the BOOTLOG.TXT file created. Try booting to just the command prompt. If none of these work, boot from the Windows 95 rescue disk or try booting from a rescue disk created by a utility software such as Nuts & Bolts or Norton Utilities.

1.	Normal
2.	Logged (\BOOTLOG.TXT)
3.	Safe Mode
4.	Safe Mode with network support
5.	Step-by-step confirmation
6.	Command prompt only
7.	Safe Mode command prompt only
8.	Previous version of MS-DOS
	Enter a Choice: 1

Figure 7-7   Windows 95 Startup Menu

Problems after the Computer Boots

Either hardware or software can cause problems that occur after the computer boots.

If you suspect the software, try diagnostic software like Nuts & Bolts, ScanDisk, or Norton Utilities before reloading the software package. See Chapter 11 for more suggestions in diagnosing software problems.

If you suspect the hardware, first isolate the problem by removing devices and trading good components for suspected bad ones. Be aware the problem might be a resource conflict.

Check the voltage output from the power supply with a multimeter (to be covered in Chapter 10).

Check jumpers, DIP switches, and CMOS settings for the devices.

Suspect a corrupted device driver. Reinstall the driver.

Suspect the applications software using the device. Try another application or reinstall the software.

WHEN A PC IS YOUR PERMANENT RESPONSIBILITY

When a PC is your permanent responsibility, either as the user of the PC or as the ongoing support person for it and the user, much can be done to prepare for future troubleshooting situations. This section describes these tasks and procedures.

Accurate records of the configuration data on a PC, the hardware, the software, and the data are essential to effective troubleshooting. Make these records or teach the user to make them when all is well. Keep documentation on hardware and software in an easy-to-find location. Prepare a bootable disk that contains copies of the necessary startup files on the hard drive specific to this PC. Organize the hard drive to keep the number of files in the root directory to a minimum.

ORGANIZE THE HARD DRIVE ROOT DIRECTORY

In the root directory, keep only startup files for your system and necessary initialization files for the software. These files may include AUTOEXEC.BAT, CONFIG.SYS, and COMMAND.COM and the hidden files, MSDOS.SYS and IO.SYS. See Table 6-3 in Chapter 6.

Software applications or files containing data don't belong in the root directory, although these applications will sometimes put initialization files in the root directory to be used when they first load. Keep applications software and their data in separate directories. For example, if you find a long list of WordPerfect document files in the root directory, create a directory for these documents. One logical place to put this documents directory is under the WordPerfect directory. Create the documents directory as a child to the WordPerfect directory that the document files belong to. Another method is to create a directory under the root directory named \Data and create subdirectories under this directory for each type of data file. For example, WordPerfect documents could go into \Data\WP and Microsoft Excel spreadsheet files in \Data\Excel.

The easiest way to do this in Windows 3.x is to use Windows File Manager. Create the new directory, select the files, and drag them from the root directory to the new directory. This action moves the files from one location to another; if you want to copy them, hold down the CTRL key while you drag.

Filenames and file extensions can help identify files that applications software puts in the root directory to initialize itself. For example, PRODIGY.BAT is a DOS batch file that the Prodigy software uses to execute. Other software packages often use .BAT files for this same purpose. Other file extensions to look for as initialization files are .INI, .BIN, and .DAT. If you are not sure of the purpose of one of these files, leave it in the root directory. Some software packages might not work if their file isn't in the root directory. Also, it is common to find a mouse driver file, such as MOUSE.SYS, in the root directory. Don't move it unless you understand how to edit the CONFIG.SYS file to assign a path to this driver file.

In general, there should be only a few utility-type files in the root directory on your hard drive. Remember to avoid storing data files or applications software in the root directory. Keep the number of files in the root directory to a minimum.

CREATE A BOOT OR RESCUE DISK

After you have cleaned up the root directory, make a bootable system disk for DOS, and for Windows 95 make a rescue disk as discussed in Chapter 2. Copy to this disk all files in the root directory of the hard drive. In Chapter 8, for Windows 95, you will learn to also put on this rescue disk the files necessary to allow access to the CD-ROM without depending on the hard drive.

Test your bootable disk to make sure that it works; label it with the computer model, date, and OS version; and keep it available at the PC. If you add a new file to your root directory, copy it to this disk as well. If you edit your AUTOEXEC.BAT file or CONFIG.SYS, don't forget to update your bootable disk, too.

If you accidentally erase the files in the drive C root directory, you can boot up from drive A and restore the files to the hard drive from this disk.

DOCUMENTATION

When you first set up a new computer, start a record book about this computer using either a file on disk or a notebook dedicated to this machine. In this notebook or file, record any changes in setup data as well as any problems or maintenance that you do on this computer. Be diligent in keeping this notebook up-to-date, as it will be invaluable in diagnosing problems and upgrading the equipment. Keep a printed or handwritten record of all setup data for this machine, and store this with the hardware and software documentation.

If you are not the primary user of the computer, you might want to keep the hardware documentation separate from the computer itself. Label the documentation so that you can easily identify that it belongs to this computer. Some support people tape a large envelope inside the computer case that contains important documentation and records specific to that computer. Keep the software reference manuals in a location that is convenient for users.

RECORD OF SETUP DATA

Keep a record of the setup screen showing hard drive type, drive configuration, and so on. Use a CMOS save program similar to the one discussed in Chapter 3, or use Nuts & Bolts, Norton Utilities, or similar utility software to save the setup data to a floppy disk. This information should be stored on a floppy disk along with the software necessary to use it. Label the disk with the PC type, date, and any information needed to use the disk. Put the disk in a safe place.

If you don't have access to software to save setup, use the print screen key to print the setup screens. If the print screen key does not work while viewing setup on the PC, carefully copy down all settings on paper. On many machines there is an advanced CMOS setup screen. Copy that screen as well, even though you might never expect to change these advanced settings yourself. CMOS can lose these settings, and you will want to be able to reconstruct them when necessary. Also keep a record of DIP switch settings and jumper settings on the systemboard. You can record these settings the first time you remove the cover of the machine. At the very least, record the settings before you change them! Keep all this information in your notebook.

When installing expansion cards, write down in your notebook information about the card and keep the documentation that came with it in your notebook. If you must change jumper settings or DIP switches on the card, be certain to write down the original settings before you change anything. When the card is configured correctly, write down the correct settings in your notebook or on the documentation for the card. It is unlikely that a user will accidentally change these settings and then ask you to fix them, but you never know!

PRACTICAL PRECAUTIONS TO PROTECT SOFTWARE AND DATA

7

If software files become corrupted, the most thorough approach is to restore the software from backups or to reinstall the software. To avoid both of these time-consuming tasks, here are a few suggestions:

- Before you install a new software package, back up the configuration files for DOS and Windows 3.x or make a backup of the Windows 95 registry and the Windows 95 configuration files.

- Because many software packages overwrite files in the \Windows\SYSTEM directory during installation, if you have the hard drive space, back up this entire directory before you begin an installation.

- Don't compress your hard drive, because compressed drives are more likely to become corrupted than those that are not compressed.

- Don't store data files in the same directory as the software, because there will be less chance of accidentally deleting or overwriting a software file.

At the very least, before beginning an installation, create a folder for the Windows 95 files that are likely to be altered during an application installation and back up these files to that folder. Figure 7-8 shows an example of such a folder, named WIN-INI.BAK. Store in this folder these files: WIN.INI, SYSTEM.INI, USER.DAT, and SYSTEM.DAT. The last two files make up the Windows 95 registry, which is discussed in Chapter 11.

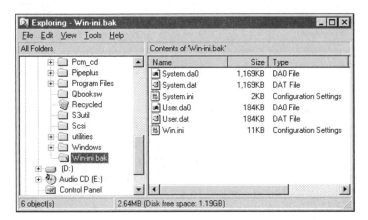

Figure 7-8   Backup Windows 95 files that are likely to be altered during an installation

BACKUP OF ORIGINAL SOFTWARE

Many software packages today come stored on CD-ROM, which cannot be backed up easily. If you request a copy of the software on floppy disks, this can serve as your backup. If the software only comes on disk, most software copyright agreements allow the user to make a backup copy of the original disks. The copyright most likely does not allow you to distribute these backup copies to friends, but you can keep your copy in a safe place in the event something happens to the originals. Many installation procedures that come with software suggest that you make backup copies and then use the copy for the installation rather than using the original. To make an exact duplicate of a disk, use the Copy Disk command in Windows 95 or Windows 3.x or the DISKCOPY command in DOS.

BACKUP OF DATA ON THE HARD DRIVE

Don't expect the worst but prepare for it! If important data is kept on the hard drive, back up that data on a regular basis to tape (using utility software designed for that purpose), to removable hard drives, to floppy disks, or to a company file server. The procedures and methods to keep good backups are beyond the scope of this chapter, but the principle needs stating: Don't keep important data on only one media.

CHAPTER SUMMARY

- Keep a bootable disk containing the root directory files of your system.

- Keep backups of hard drive data and software.

- Protect documentation by keeping it in a safe place.

- Keep a written record of CMOS setup or save it on disk.

- While you are working on a computer, protect the computer and its components against ESD.

- Tools for solving computer problems include a repair kit, bootable disk, and diagnostic hardware and software.

- Two important rules when troubleshooting are to eliminate unnecessary hardware and software and to trade components you know are good for those you suspect may be bad.

- Learn to ask the user good questions (using good manners and diplomacy) that help you understand the history behind the problem.

- One good method of solving intermittent problems is to keep a log of when they occur.

- Troubleshooting keyboards, monitors, and printers should follow the general guidelines listed in the chapter.

- Problems with computers can be divided into two groups: the computer boots or it does not boot.

- Diagnostic cards give error codes based on POST errors.

- Diagnostic software performs many tests on a PC. Some of these software programs use their own proprietary operating systems.

- Utility software can update and repair device drivers and applications. Some utility software downloads these updates from the Internet.

KEY TERMS

- **Bootable disk** — For DOS, a floppy disk that can upload the operating system files necessary for computer startup. It must have the two hidden system files IO.SYS and MSDOS.SYS, and also COMMAND.COM.

- **Diagnostic cards** — Adapter cards designed to discover and report computer errors and conflicts at POST time (before the computer boots up), often by displaying a number on the card.

- **Diagnostic software** — Utility programs that help troubleshoot computer systems. Some DOS diagnostic utilities are CHKDSK and SCANDISK. PC Technician is an example of a third-party diagnostic program.

- **Documentation** — Manuals, tutorials, and help files that provide information that a user needs in order to use a computer system or software application.

- **Electrostatic discharge (ESD)** — Another name for static electricity, which can damage chips and destroy system boards, even though it might not be felt or seen with the naked eye.

- **Power-on self test (POST)** — A built-in self-diagnostic used to do a simple test of the CPU, RAM, and various I/O devices. The POST is performed when the computer is first turned on.

- **Static electricity** — *See* Electrostatic discharge.

- **Utility software** — Software packages, such as Nuts & Bolts, Norton Utilities, PC Tools, and SpinRite II, that perform data recovery, disk repair, and virus detection, and create backups.

- **Video driver** — A program that tells the computer how to effectively communicate with the video adapter card and monitor. It is often found on a floppy disk that is shipped with the card.

REVIEW QUESTIONS

TROUBLESHOOTING HARDWARE AND SOFTWARE

1. What files are placed on a disk after using the command FORMAT A:/S?

2. In Windows, to copy a file to a new directory, what key do you hold down while dragging the file?

3. List the files stored in the root directory of your home or lab computer.

4. What is ESD and how can you protect against it?

5. Why are magnetized screwdrivers dangerous around computer equipment?

6. List three things to do if you get the message "Unable to write to C:".

7. List five ways to "eliminate the unnecessary" when troubleshooting a system.

8. Using the rule "trade good for suspected bad," describe how to easily troubleshoot a video problem.

9. Give five possible questions that should be asked of a user who is experiencing computer problems.

10. What are DLL files and why could they cause problems?

11. What is the best way to document intermittent problems?

12. Describe the process of cleaning a dirty keyboard.

13. Starting with the easiest procedures first, list five things to check if a monitor does not display a picture.

14. Give three things that may cause monitor flicker.

15. What is the value of installing additional video RAM?

16. Starting with the easiest procedures first, list five things to check if your printer does not print.

17. What can you do to temporarily solve streaking or light printing on a laser printer?

18. Starting with the easiest procedures first, list five things to check if your PC does not boot.

19. Give three things to check if your PC does not recognize all of the installed memory.

20. What is the rule to follow when connecting the power supply leads (P8 and P9) to the systemboard?

21. Using the Windows Control Panel or the Windows 95 My Computer, System Properties, Device Manager, determine what specific controller (and/or driver) is used for your home or lab monitor?

22. Using the Windows Control Panel or the Windows 95 My Computer, System Properties, Device Manager, what specific controller (and/or driver) is used for your home or lab printer?

23. Using the Windows Control Panel or the Windows 95 My Computer, System Properties, Device Manager, what specific controller (and/or driver) is used for your home or lab hard drive?

24. Using the Windows Control Panel or the Windows 95 My Computer, System Properties, Device Manager, what specific controller (and/or driver) is used for your home or lab modem?

25. Using the Windows Control Panel or the Windows 95 My Computer, System Properties, Device Manager, what specific controller (and/or driver) is used for your home or lab CD-ROM?

INTERACTING WITH THE USER

26. As a help desk technician, what are some good "detective" questions to ask if the user calls to say, "My PC won't boot."

27. A user calls your help desk complaining that the printer does not work. The printer power light is on, but the PC cannot send a print job to it. What questions do you ask?

28. With the printer problem in Question 27, you suspect the cable is not correctly connected. List the directions to walk the user through checking the printer cable connections.

29. You are a support technician working at a user site. A user has just erased all the files in the root directory of a PC using DOS and Windows 3.1. Describe how you handle the situation.

30. Rob, a PC service technician, has been called on site to repair a PC. He has not spoken directly with the user, but he knows the floor of the building where the user, Lisa, works and can look for her name on her cubicle. The following is a description of his actions. Create a table with 2 columns. List in one column the mistakes he made and in the next column the correct action he should have taken.

Rob's company promised that a service technician would come sometime during the next business day after the call was received. Rob was given the name and address of the user and the problem, which was stated as "PC will not boot." Rob arrived the following day at about 10:00 A.M. He found Lisa's cubicle but she was not present. Since Lisa was not present, Rob decided not to disturb the papers all over her desk, so he lay his notebooks and tools on top of her work.

Rob tried to boot the PC and it gave errors indicating a corrupted FAT on the hard drive. He successfully booted from a disk and was able to access a C prompt. A DIR command returned a mostly unreadable list of files and subdirectories in the root directory. Next Rob used Norton Utilities to try to recover the files and directories but was unable to do so. He began to suspect a virus had caused the problem, so ran a virus scan program that did not find the suspected virus.

He made a call to his technical support to ask for suggestions. Technical support suggested that he try partitioning and formatting the hard drive to remove any possible viruses and recover the hard drive. Rob partitioned and formatted the hard drive and was on the phone with technical support and in the process of reloading Windows 95 from the company's file server when Lisa arrived.

Lisa took one look at her PC and gasped. She caught her breath and asked where her data is. Rob replies, "A virus destroyed your hard drive. I had to reformat."

Lisa tried to explain the importance of the destroyed data. Rob replied, "Guess you'll learn to make backups now." Lisa left to find her manager.

PROJECTS

⚠ **Caution** Unless you follow the proper procedures, working inside your computer can cause serious damage—to both you and your computer. To assure safety in your work setting, follow every precaution listed in the *Read This Before You Begin* section following this book's Introduction.

USING SOME NUTS & BOLTS DIAGNOSTIC TESTS

Follow these directions to perform a series of diagnostic tests on your computer using Nuts & Bolts.

7

1. In Windows 95, click **Start**, **Programs**, **Nuts & Bolts**, and select **Discover Pro**.
2. From the Discover Pro main screen, select the **Diagnostics** tab.
3. Although you can perform the five diagnostics tests listed from this screen, to have more control over the tests, click the **Advanced** button on the bottom of the screen.
4. Select the hard drive test by clicking on the **HD Diag** button on the left side of the screen. Select the hard drive from the list of drives on the right side. Click **Start** to perform the test. Print the results of the test by clicking **Print**.
5. Perform and print the results of each of the remaining four diagnostic tests.

USING THE WINDOWS CONTROL PANEL

1. Using the Windows Control Panel, set up your monitor to Low power, Standby, or Doze Mode.
2. Using the Windows Control Panel, record the current Video Driver and video resolution settings. Then change the Video Driver to Standard VGA with a 640 × 480 resolution. Reboot the computer and change the video resolution back to the original settings.
3. Using the Windows Control Panel, add a new printer (choose from any on the printer list). When done, remove the printer driver, then check to confirm that the correct printer is set as the default.
4. Log on to the Internet and download one of the diagnostic utilities mentioned earlier in the chapter. Use it to test your home or lab computer.

TAKE A COMPUTER APART AND PUT IT BACK TOGETHER

Follow these general guidelines to take a computer apart and put it back together:

1. Put the computer on a table with plenty of room. Have a plastic bag or cup available to keep screws from being lost. When reassembling the PC, use the same group of screws in the same group of holes. (This is especially important with the hard drive. Screws that are too long can puncture the hard drive housing.) You'll need a Phillips head screwdriver and a flat-head screwdriver, paper, and pencil.

2. Leave the computer plugged in so that it's grounded. If your computer uses CMOS for setup, print out all settings or save them to a floppy disk. Make a bootable disk if you don't already have one. Turn the computer off.

3. Remove the monitor from the top of the case. Unplug and remove the mouse and keyboard.

4. Remove the case cover. For some computers, the case slides to the front; others lift off the top. After you set the top aside, ground yourself by touching the computer case to discharge any static electricity on your body.

5. Draw a diagram of all cable connections, DIP switch settings, and jumper settings. You might need the cable connection diagram to help you reassemble. You will not change any DIP switch settings or jumper settings, but accidents do happen. Be prepared. If you like, use a felt tip marker to mark across a cable connection, board placement, systemboard orientation, speaker connection, brackets, and so on, so that you can simply line up the marks when you reassemble.

6. Before removing the cables, note that each cable has a color or stripe down one side. This edge color marks this side of the cable as pin 1. Look on the board or drive that the cable is attached to. You should see that pin 1 or pin 2 is clearly marked. Verify that the edge color is aligned with pin 1 as shown in Figure 7-9. Look at the cable used to connect drive A to the floppy drive controller card. There is a twist in the cable. This twist reverses these leads in the cable, causing the addresses for this cable to be different from the addresses for the cable that doesn't have the twist. The connector with the twist is attached to drive A (see Figure 7-10). Remove the cables to the floppy drives and the hard drives. Remove the power supply cords from the drives.

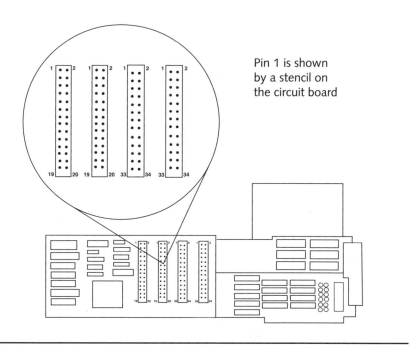

Pin 1 is shown
by a stencil on
the circuit board

7

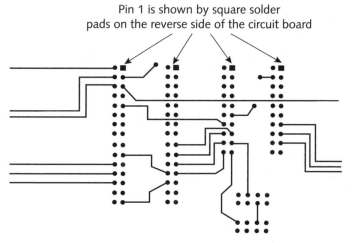

Pin 1 is shown by square solder
pads on the reverse side of the circuit board

Figure 7-9   How to find pin 1 on an expansion card

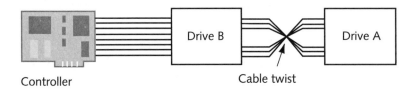

Controller   Cable twist

Typical PC floppy cable

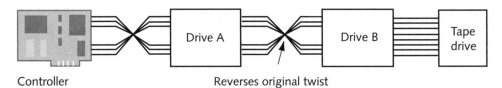

Controller   Reverses original twist

Figure 7-10   Twist in cable indentifies drive A

7. Remove the expansion cards. There is usually a single screw holding each card to the back of the case. Remove the screws first, and place them in your cup or bag. When removing a card, don't rock the card from side to side because you can spread the card's slot, making connections more difficult. Don't rock the card from back to front. Don't put your fingers on the edge connectors or touch a chip. Don't stack the cards on top of one another. Lift the card straight up from the slot.

8. Remove the floppy drives next. Some drives have one or two screws on each side of the drive attaching the drive to the drive bay. After you remove the screws, the drive usually slides to the front and out of the case. Sometimes there is a catch underneath the drive that you must lift up as you slide the drive forward. Be careful not to remove screws that hold the circuit card on top of the drive to the drive housing. The whole unit should stay intact.

9. Remove the hard drive next. Look for the screws that hold the drive to the bay. Be careful to remove only these screws, not the screws that hold the drive together. Handle the drive with care.

10. You might need to remove the power supply before exposing the systemboard. Unplug the two power supply lines to the systemboard. Carefully note which line is labeled P8 and which is labeled P9. You will want to be certain that you don't switch these two lines when reconnecting them, since this would cause the wrong voltage to flow in the circuits on the systemboard and can destroy the board. Fortunately, most connections today only allow you to place the lines in the correct order, which is *always* black leads on P8 next to black leads on P9. Remember, "black to black." Look for screws that attach the power supply to the computer case as shown in Figure 7-11. Be careful not to remove any screws that hold the power supply housing together. You do not want to take the housing apart. After you have removed the screws, the power supply still might not be free. Sometimes it is attached to the case on the underside by recessed slots. Turn the case over and look on the bottom for these slots. If they are present, determine in which direction you need to slide the power supply to free it from the case.

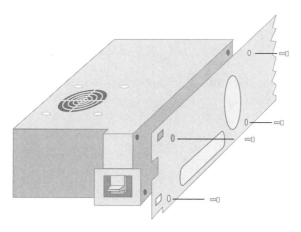

Figure 7-11   Removing the power supply mounting screws

7

11. The systemboard is now the last thing to be removed. It probably has spacers keeping it from resting directly on the bottom of the computer case. Carefully pop off these spacers and/or remove the three or four screws that hold the board to the case.

12. Now that the computer is fully disassembled, reassemble it in reverse order: first the systemboard, then the power supply, the hard drive, the floppy drives, the expansion cards, and the cables. Refer to your diagrams and marks on the cables as needed.

13. Before replacing the computer case, plug in the monitor and keyboard and have your instructor inspect your work. Do one last visual inspection before turning on the power. Then turn on the power and make sure everything works. If the computer doesn't work the first time, don't panic. You probably have not connected something snugly enough. Turn off the power and double check all cards, cables, and power cords. Refer to your drawings and make sure that all cables are attached correctly. If the machine still doesn't work, it's possible you loosened a chip on a board as you were working. Use a screwdriver or your fingers and firmly but carefully push down all four corners of every chip on the systemboard. As you work, be certain to turn off the power before touching the inside of the machine. Once the machine is working, replace the cover and you're done.

PRACTICE MAKES PERFECT

Repeat the previous project using a different model computer. You should feel comfortable disassembling and reassembling a computer before you leave this exercise.

USING THE HELP FEATURE IN WINDOWS 95

Research the Help feature in Windows 95. From the **Start** button, choose **Help**. Figure 7-12 displays showing the **Index** tab selected. Type the first few letters of the word you want to search on and then click the index entry you want. Click **Display**. Figure 7-13 displays the **Find** tab. Type the word to find, click on one of the topics listed, and select **Display**.

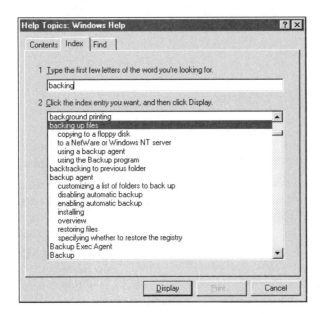

Figure 7-12   The Windows 95 Help Index sheet

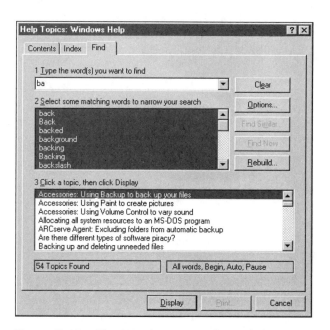

Figure 7-13   The Windows 95 Help Find sheet

Using the Help tool, list the steps for making a backup of the \Windows\System folder to disk.

List the steps to restore the \Windows\System folder from disk.

USING THE HELP FEATURE IN WINDOWS 95 FOR MONITOR PROBLEMS

Research the Help feature in Windows 95. From the **Start** button, choose **Help**.

Under the **Find** tab enter the words **Monitor** or **Troubleshooting**. Print the section for troubleshooting monitor problems.

TROUBLESHOOTING A MODEM PROBLEM

An external modem is connected to a PC. When you attempt to use the modem, the error message is "Modem not found." There is a working PC and external modem nearby. List the steps to determine if the problem is with the PC, the modem, or the modem cable. Why can you assume the problem is not with the phone line?

TROUBLESHOOTING A BOOT PROBLEM

Edit the CONFIG.SYS file on your PC. If you are using an installation of Windows 95 which does not use a CONFIG.SYS file, then create one. Enter a command line in the file that you know will cause an error. Boot the PC. Press F8 during the boot and walk through the boot process to demonstrate how this procedure can be used to diagnose a problem with startup files.

Correct the command line in CONFIG.SYS and boot again walking through each command in the boot process.

DEVELOPING HELP DESK SKILLS

Work with a partner who will play the role of the user. Sit with your back to the user, who is in front of the PC. Troubleshoot the problem and talk the user through to a solution. Abide by these rules:

1. A third person has previously created an error on the PC so that the PC does not boot successfully. Neither you nor your partner knows what the third person did.

2. The user pretends not to have technical insight but is good at following directions and will answer any nontechnical questions.

3. Don't turn around to look at the screen.

4. Practice professional mannerisms and speech.

5. As you work, keep a log of the "phone call to the help desk," recording in the log the major steps toward diagnosing and correcting the problem.

6. When the problem is resolved, have the third person create a different problem that causes the PC not to boot correctly and exchange roles with your partner.

ADJUSTING A MONITOR

Using the documentation that accompanies a monitor, learn to adjust the monitor using the buttons on the monitor. In a class situation, demonstrate your skills to the class and answer any questions others may have.

CUSTOMIZING A PERSONAL COMPUTER SYSTEM WITH PERIPHERAL EQUIPMENT

In Chapter 4, you learned to install a floppy disk drive by mounting the drive inside the case and connecting the data cable and power cord. You then only needed to tell setup that the floppy drive was present. The BIOS that manages a floppy drive is part of the system BIOS. You did not need to install a device driver or other software to manage the floppy disk drive. The programs that manage other peripheral devices, however, are not part of the standard system BIOS, so installation includes a new task. You first install the hardware device and then install the device driver or other software that manages the device.

This chapter focuses on the many nonstandard devices that turn a general-purpose microcomputer into a customized tool able to perform a specialized function. Adding a scanner, a sound card, a modem, a CD-ROM drive, or some other add-on, can turn a computer into a unique machine designed for a specialized task. In this chapter, you will learn common rules and guidelines that make it easier to add these peripherals to a computer. For example, the techniques for adding a scanner to your computer system can easily be transferred to the task of adding a modem. You will also learn that the guidelines for one scanner work well for other brands of scanner. This chapter does not include every detail for adding every device on the market to your computer, but after reading it you will understand the installation guidelines that apply to each device, and we will cover the details of adding several sample devices.

**IN THIS CHAPTER
YOU WILL LEARN:**

- ABOUT PERIPHERAL DEVICES AND SOFTWARE THAT CAN ENHANCE COMPUTER SYSTEMS TO MAKE THEM SPECIALIZED TOOLS

- HOW TO USE STANDARD RESOURCES ON A COMPUTER SYSTEM TO INSTALL ADD-ON DEVICES

- HOW TO RESOLVE RESOURCE CONFLICTS

- HOW TO INSTALL A NEW DEVICE ON A COMPUTER

THE RIGHT TOOLS FOR THE JOB

Most computer systems today come with the essentials for home and office already installed. Every user needs an operating system, and most people rely on a word processor to write letters and prepare documents. A paint program is useful for constructing a diagram or chart. Another software program many users consider essential is spreadsheet software, such as Excel or Lotus 1-2-3, for organizing financial information. Database software, such as Fox Pro or Access, manages large volumes of data. All these software packages require or recommend they be run on no more than the standard hardware that comes with most systems: a floppy drive, a hard drive, a color monitor, a mouse, and a printer.

Computer systems can be expanded to become specialized systems for power-packed applications. Two popular special-purpose applications for microcomputers are desktop publishing and multimedia presentations. This section looks at the hardware and software requirements for each.

Before you purchase a new computer system or a peripheral, research your purchase. Computer hardware and software change frequently, and choices and price ranges abound. Some of your best resources are other satisfied users, trade magazines, retailers, books, the Internet, and computer service centers.

Trade magazines, such as *PC Computing*, *PC World*, *Home PC*, *Computer Shopper*, *PC Novice*, *PC Magazine*, and *PC Today*, offer a wealth of valuable information. Stop by a library and search for feature articles that review and rate the most popular devices. These reviews usually include excellent explanations describing how these devices work and listing the features needed by most people. You will also find articles reviewing and rating the applications software packages that utilize the devices.

Use the Internet to research by visiting the Web sites of magazines and manufacturers to learn about products and how they are rated. For example, try these magazine Web sites:

Home PC	www.homepc.com
Computer Shopper	www.cshopper.com
PC Magazine	www.pcmag.com
PC World	www.pcworld.com
PC Computing	www.pccomputing.com

DESKTOP-PUBLISHING DEVICES

One of the most popular uses of microcomputers today is desktop publishing. What once was done by graphic designers, typesetters, and print shops can now be accomplished on a microcomputer by a single user. The purpose of desktop publishing is to produce a camera-ready printout or file of a document, ready for the print shop to reproduce. Newsletters, business cards, advertising flyers, and yearly financial reports are but a few applications suitable for desktop-publishing. Typically, the minimum software and hardware requirements for an adequate desktop-publishing system include:

- A 486DX computer or higher with a hard drive and a minimum of 8 MB of RAM, a mouse, and a color monitor

- A word-processing software package

- A scanner (see Figure 8-1) and related software

- A laser printer

- A graphics software package to create and/or edit graphics

- A page composition software package, such as the one in Figure 8-2, to bring together all the individual elements of text, graphics, and scanned images into an easy-to-read and visually appealing finished document

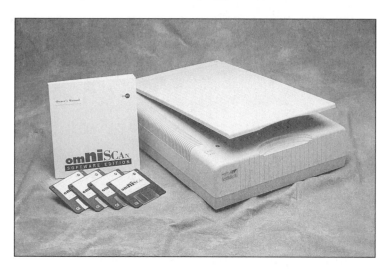

Figure 8-1   Flat-bed scanner

Figure 8-2   A page composition software package

If your budget is limited, spend money on the computer itself rather than the peripherals. A computer system is no faster than the CPU, no matter how sophisticated the peripherals. A laser printer is an expensive item; you can use an ink jet or dot matrix printer for rough drafts and then take your work on disk to another system with a laser printer. By postponing the purchase of the laser printer, you may be able to afford a faster Pentium processor or more memory on the systemboard. The speed and reliability of the computer are invaluable.

MULTIMEDIA DEVICES

A multimedia presentation is a presentation that might include text, graphics, sound, full-motion video, and still video. Chalkboard and 35-mm slide presentations are fast giving way to sophisticated combinations of sound, video, text, and graphics emitted from a complex computer system.

Multimedia devices and software make large demands on computer resources and require vast amounts of hard drive space and memory. For example, full-motion video can occupy as much as 25 MB of storage space per second of video. When considering a multimedia computer system that requires a large investment, look for devices and software that follow the industry standards.

In an attempt to establish some guidelines for a mushrooming multimedia market, the industry has established the Multimedia Marketing Council and the MPC (Multimedia Personal Computer) guidelines (discussed in Chapter 4). When buying multimedia devices, make sure they meet or exceed the MPC Standard Level 3. The minimum requirements for a multi-media computer system capable of producing an appealing sight-and-sound presentation are:

- 75 MHz Pentium or higher
- 8 MB of RAM
- 540 MB hard drive or larger
- CD-ROM drive
- 16-bit digital sound card with wavetable and MIDI playback
- Speakers measured and tested at 3 watts/channel
- MPEG1 hardware or software for video playback

The ability to use CD-ROMs provides a potentially endless library of text, video, and sometimes sound for presentations. CD-ROM drives can be mounted internally or externally. Some CD-ROM drives are portable and can plug into a bidirectional parallel port on your computer.

A sound card records sound, saves it to a file on your hard drive, and plays back sound. Some cards give you the ability to mix and edit sound, and even to edit the sound using standard music score notation. Sound cards have ports for external stereo speakers and microphone input. Some play CD audio by way of a cable connecting the CD to the sound card. For good quality sound you will definitely need external speakers and perhaps an amplifier. Sound cards are either 8-bit or 16-bit. Sound can be saved to a file in either FM or MIDI format. MIDI provides the best musical sound quality.

An NTSC (National Television Standards Committee) **video capturing card** is another multimedia option. With this card, you can capture input from a camcorder or directly from TV. Video can be saved as motion clips or stills. When comparing prices and quality of NTSC cards, look for a feature called **genlock**, which refers to the ability of the card to capture a video as a single complete frame, rather than a sampling of what might be partial frames. This feature makes for better quality stills and makes editing easier and smoother. However, genlock significantly increases the price of the card.

Authoring software, such as Authorware, coordinates sound, graphics, text, still video, full-motion video, and photos into one continuous show or presentation.

You often need special equipment for a large-scale presentation that requires a computer, because it is inconvenient for a group to gather around a single PC monitor. One way to display your presentation to a group is to project it using an overhead projector. The projector has an LCD panel on top of the projector surface, which connects to the video port of the PC and becomes the PC's monitor. There is more sophisticated hardware for large-scale presentations, but the overhead projector with the LCD panel is relatively inexpensive and works well with groups of up to 25 people.

BITS ARE STILL BITS

This section introduces several peripheral devices: the scanner, CD-ROM, sound card, and video-capturing card. Just as with the first electronic digital computer, each device represents data as a series of 0s and 1s. When working with these devices, keep this basic fact in mind along with a few other basics that haven't changed.

A black-and-white scanner sends a light beam across an image and reads that image as a series of black and white dots. Each dot is represented as a 1 or 0, and is stored in a file called a **bit map file**. A sound card captures sound, converts each segment of the sound into a series of 0s and 1s, and stores these in a MIDI file that can later be interpreted once again as sound. A video-capturing card captures a segment of video and converts it to—you guessed it—a series of 1s and 0s, when it is stored in a file. Each device reduces sound, video, or pictures to digital or numeric data that is always stored on a computer medium as bits. The common denominator of all the data on these storage devices is bits.

Another uniform quality is that each device transfers its data over the same bus to the CPU; the CPU processes the data in the same way. Each device may require an IRQ, a DMA channel, an I/O address, and room in upper memory for its BIOS. All their basic computing needs are the same. When working with these devices, don't be intimidated by their complexity. Installation still involves meeting these basic needs.

BASIC PRINCIPLES

When adding new peripherals to a computer, consider these fundamental principles.

- The peripheral is a hardware device that is controlled by software. You must install both the hardware and the software.

- The software might exist at different levels. For example, a device could require driver software that interfaces directly with the hardware device and an applications software package that interfaces with the driver. You must install all levels of software.

- More than one peripheral device might attempt to use the same computer resources. This conflict could disable a device or cause it to hang up. Possible conflicts arise when more than one device attempts to use:

  - The same IRQ
  - The same DMA channel
  - The same I/O addresses
  - The same upper memory addresses

In earlier chapters, the IRQ was defined as an interrupt request number that is assigned to a device. When the device needs attention, it passes this number to the CPU. The CPU relates the IRQ to an address in the lower part of memory called the I/O address table, where it has stored the address of the request handler, the program that handles the request. It is common for these request handlers, called device drivers or BIOS, to be assigned memory addresses in the upper part of memory between 640 K and 1024 K. In addition to containing the location of the request handler, the I/O address table might also contain data that the device is passing to the CPU. The DMA channels are direct paths from the device to the CPU, used to speed up data access by bypassing. The channel number is assigned to the device during the startup process.

Peripheral devices need (in addition to the standard computer resources you already expect to be present) the hardware device itself, the firmware, the device driver, and the applications software. To demonstrate these principles, the installation of a typical hardware device, a modem, will be examined. Installing the device, the device driver, and the software will be discussed, and how these principles apply to other devices, such as the mouse or a scanner will also be explained.

HARDWARE

Consider a hardware device such as a modem. You know that a modem provides a way to connect one computer to another, as a network. There are many kinds of modems and networks. Some modems use normal telephone lines for communication, whereas others use dedicated circuits. Internal modems are expansion cards that are installed inside the computer case; they provide one, usually two, telephone line sockets that connect a telephone line directly into the back of the computer. External modems are contained in their own case with their own power supply. The external modem is connected to the computer by a cable that plugs into the back of the computer case, usually to a serial port. The telephone line then plugs into the back of the modem. In either case, the modem converts the computer's bits to a form that can be communicated over telephone lines and other circuits.

Most often internal devices are less expensive than external devices, because external devices have the additional expense of the power supply and case. Internal devices also offer the added advantage of not taking up desk space, and they have all cables and cords neatly tucked away. An advantage of external devices is that they can be moved easily from one computer to another. In the case of a modem, the external device provides added security.

If you've ever shopped for a peripheral device, such as a modem or a sound card, you know what a large variety of features and prices today's market offers. Research pays. First, know your own computer system. For a start, know which CPU, system bus, and local bus you have, and how much memory and what size hard drive your system currently has. Know which OS you have and what version it is (for example, DOS 6.22 or Windows 3.11). Determine how much space is available on your hard drive, and how many expansion slots and what kinds of slots are free in your computer.

In addition to a basic knowledge of your system, you might need some technical information. For example, most computers have a power supply that well exceeds the requirements of the standard system, making it possible to add internal devices without exceeding the total wattage that can be supplied by the power supply. However, if your computer is old (for computers, that's over five years), and you're adding more than one internal device, the power supply could limit your choices. If you install more internal devices than the power supply can handle, you might need to upgrade it as well.

Unless you are using Plug-and-Play-compliant devices and a Plug-and-Play OS, it also might be important to know what IRQs, I/O addresses, DMA channels, and upper memory addresses your present devices use. Recall that a notebook dedicated to your PC, which was discussed in Chapter 7, should have records of each device and the present settings of the device.

Generally, if you buy the device and other accompanying hardware (such as the interface board and cables) from the same source, they will more likely be compatible.

FIRMWARE

A peripheral device may require several levels of software to make it work. The most fundamental software needed is stored on ROM chips inside the device or on the interface board. This software is called **firmware** because the programming on these chips cannot be changed (unless you replace a chip). All devices have firmware residing on the device in ROM chips. Some devices also contain some memory to temporarily store data moving through the device. This memory is called RAM and should not be confused with system RAM, discussed in Chapter 3. Sometimes it is necessary to interface with the firmware to set a parameter, such as the IRQ number. If the device and your system are Plug-and-Play, you will not need to change the resource parameters of the device. If you are not using Plug-and-Play, you can set a parameter of the firmware by changing a DIP switch or jumper setting. However, for some sophisticated devices, you can interface with the firmware using programs provided by the manufacturer, which present a chip setup screen similar to the systemboard CMOS setup screen. The documentation for the device should tell you what parameters can be changed and how to communicate those changes to the firmware.

The DIP switches and jumpers are normally set by the manufacturer in the most commonly used default settings. Don't change a DIP switch or jumper on a device without (1) writing down the original settings so you can always backtrack, and (2) carefully reading the documentation.

Why change a firmware or other parameter? The most common reason is to prevent a conflict in the assignment of computer resources. If you buy a second modem to install on your computer, and both modems are using the same IRQ by default, you might be able to instruct the new modem to use an alternate IRQ by changing a DIP switch on the modem, like the DIP switch in Figure 8-3. Making this change tells the firmware on the modem to use the alternate IRQ.

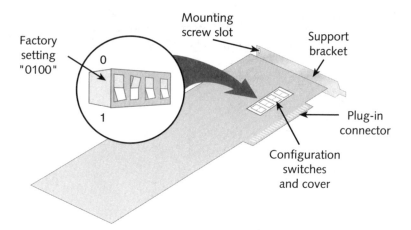

Figure 8-3 DIP switch on an internal modem

8

DEVICE DRIVERS

The second level of software for a hardware device is a device driver. Recall that a device driver is the software that communicates directly with the device. Device drivers usually are TSRs that are normally loaded from the file CONFIG.SYS at startup for DOS and are loaded automatically by Windows 95 at startup after the device is installed. A common device driver is the mouse driver. For example, the file MOUSE.SYS is loaded in the CONFIG.SYS file with this command:

```
DEVICE=C:\UTIL\MOUSE.SYS
```

The DEVICE= command in CONFIG.SYS tells DOS that the program file is a TSR needed to drive a device. The program file MOUSE.SYS is found in the \UTIL directory on hard drive C. Sometimes the device driver needs some parameters listed at the end of the command line. For example, a device driver can direct a serial port mouse to use COM 2 instead of the default, COM 1, by adding a parameter to the end of the command line:

```
DEVICE=C:\UTIL\MOUSE.SYS /C2
```

See your documentation to find out what parameters can be used on the command line for a device driver.

For Windows 95, the device driver is installed at the time the hardware device is installed, and then automatically executes each time Windows 95 starts. You can view and change current device drivers from the Control Panel. Click **Start**, **Settings**, **Control Panel** to see the Control Panel in Figure 8-4. For example, to view the current video driver selected, double-click **Display**, choose the **Settings** tab and then **Change Display Type**. The Change Display Type sheet displays as in Figure 8-5. Under Adapter Type, click **Change**. The

Select Device dialog box displays (Figure 8-6). Click **Show all devices** to see a list of all video drivers supplied with Windows 95. If your video card manufacturer and type of card are not listed, you can enter your own. Click **Have Disk** to provide your own new driver.

Figure 8-4   Windows 95 Control Panel

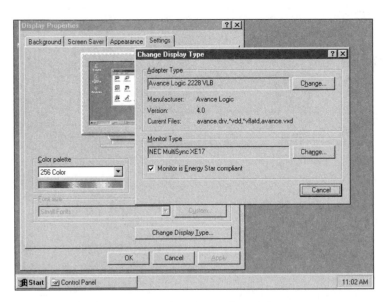

Figure 8-5   The current video driver for a PC

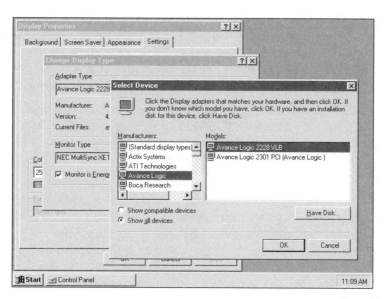

Figure 8-6   Windows 95 video drivers

Most often the device driver comes as part of the hardware package. When you buy a mouse or a video card, a disk is enclosed that contains the driver. Normally you use the driver that comes with the device, rather than substituting another, although occasionally you may need to upgrade the driver as the manufacturer provides newer and better drivers for the device.

 When you upgrade to DOS with Windows, Windows 95 or Windows NT, and if your video card is not in the list for which Windows 95 or Windows NT provides drivers, the solution may be to use the Internet to locate a new 32-bit driver for your video card. One of the projects at the end of this chapter will show you how.

APPLICATIONS SOFTWARE

The next level of software is the applications software that uses the device. For example, an applications software package, such as Word for Windows, uses the mouse. In Word, you can use the mouse to access windows and move the cursor. When an application uses the mouse, the mouse communicates with the application by way of the device driver.

When you install applications software, you might need to provide some information about hardware devices it uses. For example, ProComm is a communications software package that can communicate with a modem. If an internal modem is configured to use COM 2 by a DIP switch on the modem, ProComm must also be told to look for the modem on COM 2. If the modem is communicating on COM 2, and ProComm is communicating on COM 1, ProComm will not find the modem. On the setup screen in ProComm, the user may choose COM 2 as the communication port.

Not all devices use serial ports to communicate with the CPU. For instance, an expansion card for a bus mouse must be installed inside the computer case to provide the mouse port. No matter how the mouse is installed, once the mouse and its driver are in place, any applications software package that uses a mouse should be able to use this mouse. However, the software might not take advantage of all functions of the mouse, such as the third mouse button.

There are exceptions to the last point. I once used a computer that contained one application that required a serial port mouse and another application that required a bus mouse. There were two mice installed on this computer, one for each application. These kinds of limitations by applications software would hardly be tolerated today.

A scanner is another example of a hardware add-on. Scanners come in a variety of sizes and shapes from hand-held to large flat-bed scanners (see Figure 8-1). However, installation is about the same for all scanners. A scanner is an external device residing outside the computer case. It uses an expansion card installed inside the case to interface with the systemboard. When you buy a scanner, you are buying (1) the scanner, (2) the expansion card that interfaces with the computer, (3) the cable to connect the scanner to its expansion card, (4) the device driver on disk, and (5), very importantly, the documentation. Installation includes installing the expansion card in one of the expansion slots on the systemboard, plugging in the scanner itself, and installing the driver.

For DOS and Windows 3.x, installing the driver probably means executing a setup program from floppy disk or CD-ROM that will copy the driver file to the hard drive and add the DEVICE= command to CONFIG.SYS. For Windows 95, the setup program is executed from the Start, Run command and installs the device driver automatically. After the device driver has been installed in Windows 95, the next step is to use the Control Panel and Add New Hardware option. A comprehensive example of these procedures used to install a scanner is given at the end of this chapter.

When you purchase a scanner, if all the components described above are not included (sometimes they are, and sometimes they are not), then you must purchase them separately. Some scanners interface with the systemboard by way of a general purpose SCSI host adapter card.

However, you still need applications software to use the scanner, for example, Scangal for Windows. You install the Scangal software like any other application package, and then you are ready to scan something. The driver and the scanner expansion card are specific for each brand and model of scanner; however, the applications software does not have as narrow an application. Any application package that uses a scanner should work with most scanners. In fact, you might have several applications that use the same hardware device.

USING PORTS AND EXPANSION SLOTS FOR ADD-ON DEVICES

Devices may be plugged directly into a serial or parallel port, or they might use an expansion card plugged into an expansion slot. Some devices use a peripheral bus, called a SCSI bus, that interfaces with the system bus through a SCSI expansion card called the host adapter. Many notebook computers use a special bus slot called a PC Card slot or a PCMCIA slot. The text below addresses the specific details of these kinds of installations.

USING SERIAL PORTS

All computers have a minimum of one or two serial ports and one parallel port. These ports can be identified by (1) counting the pins and (2) determining if the port is male or female. Figure 8-7 shows the ports on the back of a typical general purpose I/O card that has one 9-pin serial and one 25-pin parallel port on the card itself and an adjacent connector bracket that provides a 25-pin serial port and a game port. These ports are sometimes called DB-9 and DB-25 connectors. DB stands for data bus and refers to the number of pins on the connector.

Serial ports are almost always male ports, and parallel ports are almost always female ports. Earlier computers provided two serial ports labeled COM1 and COM2. COM1 was assigned IRQ 4, and COM2 was assigned IRQ 3. Later, two more serial ports were added, labeled COM3 and COM4. However, they share IRQs with COM1 and COM2, making it impossible to use more than two serial ports without switching some default IRQ assignments. See Table 8-1 for a list of ports and IRQs. The I/O addresses in the table are the memory addresses of the I/O Address Table where the address of the request handler is stored. The numbers are written in hex. For a discussion of hex memory addressing, see Appendix D.

Serial ports were originally intended for input and output devices, and parallel ports were intended for printers. In Figure 8-7, the serial ports can be configured for COM1, COM2, COM3, or COM4. Parallel ports can be configured as LPT1:, LPT2:, or LPT3:

A serial port conforms to the standard interface called RS-232c (stands for Reference Standard 232 revision c) and is sometimes called the **RS-232** port. This interface standard originally called for 25 pins, but since microcomputers only use 9 of those pins, a modified, 9-pin port was often installed by the manufacturer. Today some computers have a 9-pin serial port, and some have a 25-pin serial port, or both. Both ports work the same way. The 25-pin port uses only 9 pins; the other pins are unused.

8

Table 8-1   Default Port Assignments on Many Computers

Port	IRQ	Type	I/O Address
COM1	IRQ 4	Serial	03F8
COM2	IRQ 3	Serial	02F8
COM3	IRQ 4	Serial	03E8
COM4	IRQ 3	Serial	02E8
LPT1:	IRQ 7	Parallel	0378
LPT2:	IRQ 5	Parallel	0278

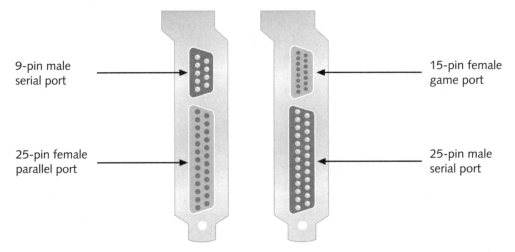

Figure 8-7   Serial, parallel, and game ports

Figure 8-7 shows a typical configuration that might be found on a PC: two serial ports, one parallel port, and a game port. The two serial ports are both male; one is 9-pin and the other is 25-pin, in order to accommodate devices that use one or the other number of pins. Typically, the 9-pin serial port would be configured as COM 1, and the 25-pin serial port would be configured as COM 2, although this might not always be so. To know for sure, open the case and look for the cables leading from these ports, which should connect to connections on the systemboard or I/O card labeled COM 1 and COM 2. Possibly the ports come directly off an I/O card, which, in this case, should have the ports labeled somewhere on the card.

Serial 25-pin ports are often found on modems. You can buy adapters that convert 9-pin ports to 25-pin ports, and vice versa, to accommodate a cable you already have.

One of the 9 pins on a serial port transmits data in a sequence of bits, and a second pin receives data sequentially. The other 7 pins are used to establish the communications protocol. A **protocol** is a set of agreed-upon rules for communication that is established before data is actually passed from one device to another. The protocol for using the 9 pins on the port is given in Table 8-2. The table describes the functions of the pins of a serial port connection to a modem that is connected to another remote modem and computer. External modems sometimes use lights on the front panel to indicate the state of these pins. The labels on these modem lights are listed in the last column.

Table 8-2   9-Pin and 25-Pin Serial Port Specifications

Pin Number for 9-Pin	Pin Number for 25-Pin	Pin Use	Description	LED Light
1	8	Carrier detect	Connection with remote is made	CD
2	3	Receive data	Receiving data	RD or RXD
3	2	Transmit data	Sending data	SD or TXD
4	20	Data terminal ready	Modem hears its computer	TR or DTR
5	7	Signal ground	Not used with PCs	
6	6	Data set ready	Modem is able to talk	MR
7	4	Request to send	Computer wants to talk	RTS
8	5	Clear to send	Modem is ready to talk	CTS
9	22	Ring indicator	Someone is calling	

The table is included not so much to explain the use of each pin, as to show that more than just data is sent across a line. Also, when using serial ports, one of the devices is called the DTE (Data Terminal Equipment), and the other device is called the DCE (Data Communications Equipment). For example, for a modem, the modem is called the DCE and the computer to which it is installed is called the DTE.

Null Modem Connection

When two DTE devices, such as two computers, are connected, software can transmit data between the two DTE devices over a special cable called a **null modem cable** or a **modem eliminator** without the need for modems. The cable is not a standard serial cable, but has several wires cross-connected in order to simulate modem communication. For example, based on the 9-pin specifications in Table 8-2, a 9-pin null modem cable would connect pin 2 on one end of the cable to pin 3 on the other end of the cable with a single wire, so that the sending data on one end is the receiving data on the other end of the cable. Similarly, pin 3 would be connected to pin 2 on the other end of the cable, so that the received data on one end is the sent data on the other end. Crossing pins 2 and 3 allows data to be sent from one computer and received by the other. Standard modem software can often be used to transmit data, but because there are no actual modems in the connection, very fast transfer with high accuracy is possible.

Table 8-3 describes the pins connected and crossed for a 25-pin null modem cable. Figure 8-8 shows the same information as a picture.

Table 8-3   Pin Connections for a 25-Pin Null Modem Cable

Pin on one end is	Connected to the pin on the other end	so that:
2	3	Data sent by one computer is received by the other.
3	2	Data received by one computer is sent by the other.
6	20	One end says to the other end, "I'm able to talk."
20	6	One end hears the other end say, "I'm able to talk."
4	5	One end says to the other, "I'm ready to talk."
5	4	One end hears the other say, "I'm ready to talk."
7	7	Both ends are grounded.

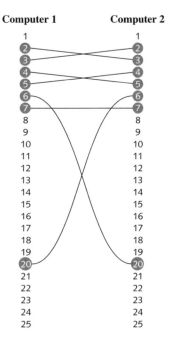

Figure 8-8   Wire connections on a 25-pin null modem cable used to transmit data from one computer to another

The UART Chip

Serial ports are controlled by a chip called the **UART chip** (universal asynchronous receiver/transmitter chip). This chip controls all 9 pins of a serial port, establishes the communications protocol to be used, and converts parallel data bits coming to it from the system bus into serial bits for transmission. It also converts incoming serial data bits it receives into the parallel form needed by the system bus. The first UART chip was the 8250, and the next version was called the 16450 chip. The 16550 version of the UART chip contains a **FIFO buffer** (first-in-first-out buffer) that solves the problem of lost data that sometimes occurs with the 16450 UART. Also, look for the A in the chip identification (16550A) to indicate an improved version of the 16550 chip. Some computers don't actually have the physical chip on the board, but the UART logic is contained in another chip. However, in all cases, utility software can tell you what is present.

Many inexpensive I/O cards and some systemboards that have on-board serial ports still use the 16450 UART, which can be the cause of lost data and slow transmission. The 16550 UART requires a driver that makes use of the FIFO buffer. Windows 95 uses this faster driver, but if you are using DOS or Windows 3.x, check the driver being used and upgrade if necessary. There is a program called 16550.EXE, which tells the UART to turn on the FIFO buffer. If the driver or the communications software is not using the capabilities of the faster 16550 UART, then you can run this program to evoke the buffering.

This driver for the UART 16550 is built into Windows 95. To verify that you are using the driver, click **Start**, **Settings**, **Control Panel**. Double-click **System** and choose the **Device Manager** tab. Select **View devices by connection**. Click one of the communications ports, for example **COM1**, and then click **Properties**. Figure 8-9 displays. Note that the drop-down box is opened to display the bits per second or baud rate of the port, which is currently set at 9600. Don't expect the port rate to exceed this value unless you are using the 16550A UART chip with buffering. Click **Advanced**, and the screen in Figure 8-10 displays, showing the Advanced Port Settings. Note that **Use FIFO buffers** is checked. The standard FIFO buffer is 16 bytes long, which is indicated by the high range for the buffer size. Newer UART chips exceed this buffer size, so you should expect an improved version of the Windows 95 serial port driver to follow shortly.

One example of a newer UART chip by Texas Instruments has a 64-byte buffer. Another example by Lava Link, Inc., called the 16650, increases speed by (1) using a faster clock speed, (2) increasing the buffer size, and (3) improving flow control.

Also, some UART chips are Plug-and-Play-compliant. These UART chips provide an interface with Plug-and-Play ROM so that autoconfiguration can be done at startup. Texas Instruments now offers Plug-and-Play-compliant UART chips. The Web sites of these two manufacturers are www.lavalink.com and www.ti.com

If you are losing data when using an external modem, look first for the kind of UART chip the serial port is using. You might need to upgrade to the 16550 or 16650 chip. Internal modems have their own UART chip on the card, or other chips that simulate the UART interface. If the UART logic is integrated into other chips, they most likely cannot be changed.

8

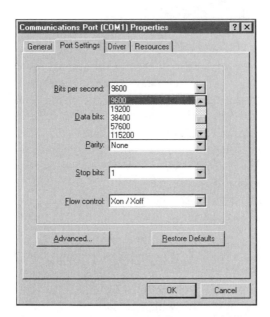

Figure 8-9   Properties of COM1 serial port in Windows 95

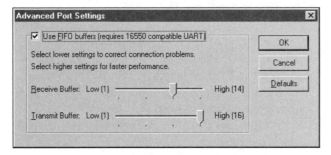

Figure 8-10   Windows 95 Advanced Port Settings for COM1 serial port, indicating
FIFO option

To determine what kind of UART chip you have, use MSD.EXE. From the main menu of
MSD, choose the **COM port** option. MSD displays information about each serial or COM
port, including the UART chip used. However, if you execute MSD while Windows is
running, the information can be deceiving. For example, Figure 8-11 shows the results of the
MSD report taken while Windows was not running. Figure 8-12 is an MSD report from the
same computer while Windows was running. Compare the results. With Windows running,
the COM1 serial port shows the UART chip being the older 8250 chip. In fact, the UART
chip on this general-purpose I/O card is the 16550AF chip, which, when Windows is running, is correctly reported for COM2 because COM2 *is* in use but is incorrectly reported
for COM1 because COM1 is *not* in use. For this computer, a serial port mouse is using
COM2. Because COM2 is in use, Windows correctly recognizes the UART chip and MSD
is able to pick up the correct information.

```
Microsoft Diagnostics version 2.00 7/05/97 9:35am Page 1

------------------- COM Ports -------------------
                            COM1:   COM2: COM3: COM4:
                            -----   ----- ----- -----
Port Address                03F8H   02F8H  N/A   N/A
Baud Rate                    1200    2400
Parity                       None    None
Data Bits                       7       8
Stop Bits                       1       1
Carrier Detect  (CD)           No      No
Ring Indicator  (RI)           No      No
Data Set Ready  (DSR)          No      No
Clear To Send  (CTS)           No      No
UART Chip Used            16550AF  16550AF
```

Figure 8-11   MSD COM port report from DOS prompt without Windows

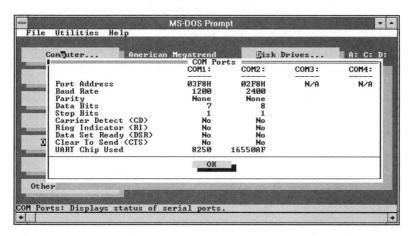

Figure 8-12   MSD COM port report from DOS prompt with Windows 3.1 running

Another interesting fact about this particular computer is that the documentation that came with the I/O card stated that the UART chip is a 16450 UART. Here's a case where the manufacturer updated the product but not the documentation that came with the product.

Resources Used by Serial Ports

Table 8-1 listed the I/O addresses for standard serial and parallel ports. Remember from earlier chapters that an IRQ points to a memory address in the Interrupt Vector Table or I/O Address Table. This table resides at the very beginning of the memory addresses and has memory address 0. You normally need not be concerned with an I/O address conflict if the IRQs for the two devices don't conflict, especially for the first 16 IRQs. However, it is interesting to see which I/O address is assigned to a particular port. You can view I/O addresses using the DOS or Windows MSD command or from Device Manager of Windows 95.

In summary, serial ports are used for various input/output data transfers, including data transferred over modems, to mice, to printers, and to other computers. Serial ports follow the RS-232c industry standard for communication. Each port is assigned a unique IRQ listed in Table 8-1 and a unique I/O address. The UART chip controlling the port determines the speed of the port.

USING PARALLEL PORTS

Parallel ports transmit data in parallel, 8 bits at a time. If the data is transmitted in parallel over a very long cable, the integrity of the data is sometimes lost because bits may separate from the byte they belong to. Because of this limitation, parallel cables should never be longer than about 15 feet to insure data integrity.

Parallel ports were originally intended to be used only for printers. However, some parallel ports are now used for input as well as other output of data. These parallel ports, called bidirectional parallel ports, are often used for fast transmission of data over short distances. One common use is to download and upload data from a PC to a laptop. Some external CD-ROM drives use a bidirectional parallel port to transmit and receive data. The MPC Standards Levels 1, 2, and 3 for multimedia computer systems all require that a PC have a bidirectional parallel port. If an existing parallel port can be used to install a peripheral device, installation is very simple. Just plug the device into the port and load the software. To accommodate a second parallel port, configure the port as LPT2:. An example of this will be described in the next section.

The uses of the pin connections for a 25-pin parallel port are listed in Table 8-4.

EXAMINING A GENERAL-PURPOSE I/O CARD

Figure 8-13 shows an example of a general-purpose I/O card that includes an adapter offering one floppy drive connection that can handle two floppy drives with a two-connection cable. The cable has a connection for this card at one end, a connection for one floppy drive in the middle of the cable, and a connection for another floppy drive at the other end of the cable. There is also an IDE adapter on the card supplying one IDE hard drive connector (labeled the IDE HDD connector), which can accommodate two hard drives with a two-connection cable. Directly on the back of the card is one 9-pin male serial port and one 25 pin female bidirectional parallel port (see Figure 8-7). There are short cables connecting to an adjacent bracket that contains a 15-pin female game port and a 25-pin male serial port (see Figure 8-14).

Table 8-4   25-Pin Parallel Port Pin Connections

Pin	Input or Output from PC	Description
1	Output	Strobe
2	Output	Data bit 0
3	Output	Data bit 1
4	Output	Data bit 2
5	Output	Data bit 3
6	Output	Data bit 4
7	Output	Data bit 5
8	Output	Data bit 6
9	Output	Data bit 7
10	Input	Acknowledge
11	Input	Busy
12	Input	Out of paper
13	Input	Select
14	Output	Auto feed
15	Input	Printer error
16	Output	Initialize printer
17	Output	Select input
18	Input	Ground for bit 0
19	Input	Ground for bit 1
20	Input	Ground for bit 2
21	Input	Ground for bit 3
22	Input	Ground for bit 4
23	Input	Ground for bit 5
24	Input	Ground for bit 6
25	Input	Ground for bit 7

8

There is also an internal game port connector. This card costs about $25–30, and is not Plug-and-Play-compliant. It comes with one 40-pin IDE hard drive cable, one 34-pin floppy drive cable, and a user's manual.

There are four banks of jumpers on the card, which allow us to configure the card's ports. To know which jumper controls a particular setting, you would read the documentation for the card.

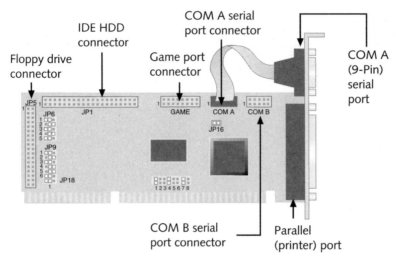

Figure 8-13   General-purpose I/O card

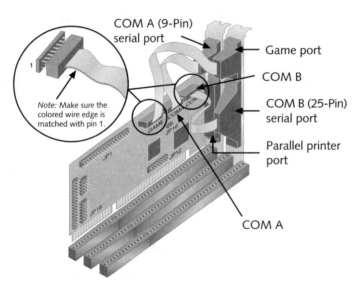

Figure 8-14   Installing a general-purpose I/O card

Table 8-5   Settings Controlled by Jumpers on a Typical, General-Purpose I/O Card

Item	Jumper controls
Hard drive controller	Enable or disable Choose a primary or secondary DMA channel Choose IRQ14 or IRQ15
Floppy drive controller	Enable or disable Reverse drives A and B without switching the data cable Choose a primary or secondary DMA channel
Serial Port A	Enable or disable Choose COM1, COM3, or COM4 Choose IRQ3, IRQ4, or IRQ5
Serial Port B	Enable or disable Choose COM2, COM3, or COM4 Choose IRQ3, IRQ4, or IRQ5
Game port	Enable or disable
Parallel port	Enable or disable Choose I/O port address of 3BCh, 378h, or 278h Choose IRQ5 or IRQ7

In Table 8-5, the I/O port addresses listed in the last row, second column, are memory addresses in the I/O address table and are written in the hex number system. The h following the number (for example, 278h) indicates that the number is written in hex. Relate these I/O port addresses back to those shown in Table 8-1.

In Table 8-5, note that the parallel port gives a choice of I/O port addresses but not a choice of LPT1:, LPT2:, or LPT3:. The parallel port is assigned by the BIOS according to the I/O port address. The parallel port with the highest I/O address (3BCh) will be LPT1:. The next will automatically become LPT2:, and the port with the lowest I/O address will be LPT3:. The default I/O address for this card is 278h, which will be LPT1 if there are no other parallel ports on the system. If there is another I/O card or a parallel port on the systemboard, be certain that its address is not set to 278h. Depending on the setting of the I/O address of the other parallel port, this parallel port set to 278h may be configured as LPT1 or LPT2 by the system. Figure 8-14 shows the card inserted in an expansion slot with the cables connected to all four external ports.

RESOLVING RESOURCE CONFLICTS

As you can easily see, given the settings available on this card, it is possible to have more than one resource conflict when installing a new device. Plug-and-Play solves many of these conflicts and is discussed later in this chapter, but there are tools you can use to determine what resources are available and how to allocate them if you are not working with a fully Plug-and-Play-compliant system.

To find out what resources are presently used by your system, for DOS and Windows 3.1, use the MSD diagnostics software discussed earlier. Figure 8-15 shows the results of displaying the IRQ settings. However, in the report in Figure 8-15, IRQs 10, 11, and 12 all have Reserved status. IRQ 11 and 12 are available, but on this computer, IRQ 10 is being used by a SCSI host adapter. MSD does not always tell all. Depend on the list of IRQs in the notebook that you keep on each PC you are managing.

For Windows 95, click **Start**, **Setting**, **Control Panel**, **System**, **Device Manager**. Click **Computer** and then **Properties**. Select the **View Resources** tab. Figure 8-16 displays, showing the IRQs currently in use. Note that IRQ 11 is available to be used by a new device.

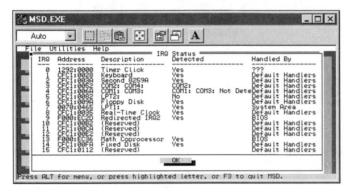

Figure 8-15   MSD report of IRQ settings

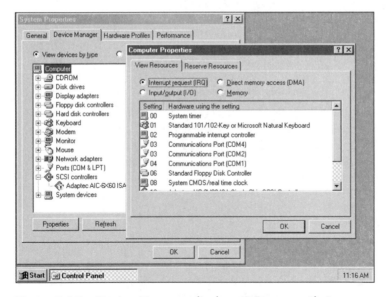

Figure 8-16   Device Manager displays IRQs currently in use

Select **Input/output (I/O)** to display a list of I/O addresses currently in use (see Figure 8-17). Note that LPT1 is currently assigned the I/O address of 0378h.

Select **Memory** to display the current upper memory addresses in use by devices (see Figure 8-18). The A, B, and C range of upper memory addresses are normally reserved for video. The F range is reserved for system BIOS. Not all the memory addresses actually in use are listed on this screen, only those that are directly requested by a working hardware device.

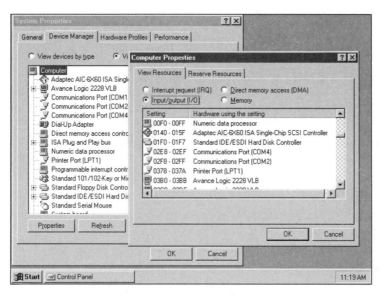

Figure 8-17 I/O port addresses currently in use

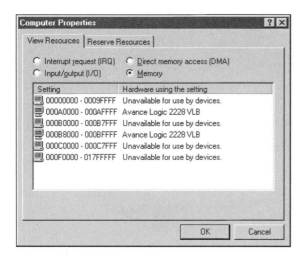

Figure 8-18 Upper memory addresses used by devices

NOTEBOOK COMPUTERS AND THE PC CARD SLOTS

Many notebook computers contain special bus expansion slots called **PC Card slots**, formally called **PCMCIA slots**. There are currently three standards for these slots developed by the PCMCIA organization (Personal Computer Memory Card International Association), and a fourth standard is being developed. Once intended only for memory cards, these PC Card slots can now be used by many devices, including modems, network cards, CD-ROMs, sound cards, and hard disks. Some docking station PCs also have a PC Card slot, so that the device you can use with your notebook can also be attached to the docking station. (A **docking station** is a special PC that is designed to connect to a notebook PC for downloading and uploading data.)

The three standards are named Type I, Type II, and Type III. Generally, the thicker the PC card, the higher the standard. A thick hard drive card might need a Type III slot, but a thin modem card might only need a Type II slot. The PC Card is about the size of a credit card, but thicker, and inserts into the PC Card slot. Type I cards can be up to 3.3-mm thick and are primarily used by adding additional RAM to a notebook PC. Type II cards can be up to 5.5-mm thick and are often used by modem cards. Type III cards can be up to 10.5-mm thick, which is large enough to accommodate a portable disk drive.

The PC Card might contain a data cable to an external device, or it might be self-contained. For example, in Figure 8-19, for a PC Card modem, the modem is the card. Insert the card in the PC Card slot and connect the telephone line to the modem PC Card. For a CD-ROM, the PC Card is the interface between the notebook PC and the CD-ROM external drive. Insert the PC Card in the PC Card slot. The data cable from the PC Card connects to the external CD-ROM drive, which has its own power supply that must be connected into a wall outlet.

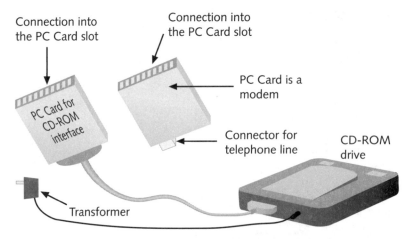

Figure 8-19   Two examples of PC cards, one self-contained (the modem), the other connected to an external device (the CD ROM)

One feature to look for in PC Card slots is **hot swapping**, which allows you to remove one card and insert another without powering down the PC. For example, if you are currently using a modem in the PC Card slot and want to switch to the CD-ROM, first turn off the modem card by using the PC Card object in the Windows 95 Control Panel. Then remove the modem card and insert the CD-ROM card with the attached external CD-ROM drive.

When buying a notebook PC, look for both Type II and Type III PC Card slots. Often one of each is included.

SCSI DEVICES

Installing a SCSI device is normally accomplished in one of three ways:

- Install the SCSI device using a simplified version of a SCSI host adapter designed to accommodate one or two devices. These adapters often come bundled in the SCSI device package.
- Install the SCSI device on an existing or new host adapter designed to handle several devices.
- Install a SCSI CD-ROM using the SCSI connection that is provided by many sound cards.

Matching the Host Adapter to the SCSI Devices It Supports

When selecting a SCSI host adapter or when determining if an existing host adapter will work with a new SCSI device, consider the issues described below.

Same SCSI Standard.   In Chapter 5, you saw that there are several SCSI standards, including SCSI-1, SCSI-2, SCSI-3, Fast SCSI, and Wide SCSI. SCSI-1, SCSI-2, and Fast SCSI use a 50-pin connection. Wide SCSI and SCSI-3 use a 68-pin connection. Your device should match the host adapter according to the number of pins on the connections.

The Host Adapter Must Be Made for the Correct Expansion Slot.   The host adapter must fit the expansion slot you plan to use. SCSI host adapters are made for 8-bit ISA, 16-bit ISA, 16-bit MCA, 32-bit MCA, 32-bit EISA, VL-Bus, and PCI. For a Pentium systemboard, you probably can choose either a 16-bit ISA host adapter or a PCI host adapter. Choose the 32-bit PCI bus for faster data transfer rate, or the 64-bit PCI bus if it is available.

Bus Mastering.   Choose a host adapter that uses bus mastering, discussed in Chapter 3, if your system bus supports it. For PCI buses that do support bus mastering, you have the added advantage that, when bus mastering is used, the SCSI host adapter does not require a DMA channel.

8

A Host Adapter that Supports Several SCSI Standards.   A host adapter that supports both 50-pin connections and 68-pin connections allows you to choose a variety of devices without having to purchase a second host adapter.

Device Driver Standard.   Select a host adapter that supports one of the two leading driver standards for SCSI, either the ASPI or the CAM standard. These two standards are the best known in the industry. ASPI, a standard developed by Adaptec, a leading SCSI manufacturer, is probably the better known of the two. ASPI (Advanced SCSI Programming Interface) or CAM (Common Access Method) describes the standard for the way the host adapter communicates with the SCSI device driver that interfaces with the SCSI device. The ASPI or CAM standard has nothing to do with the SCSI-1, SCSI-2, or SCSI-3 types, but rather with the way the drivers are written. Be sure that the host adapter and all the device drivers meet the same standard. As shown in Figure 8-20, the ASPI or CAM standard also affects the way the host adapter relates to the operating system. For Windows 95, the SCSI driver is built-in, but many host adapters provide their own host adapter drivers to be used by Windows 95, and by DOS with Windows 3.x. The manufacturer of the host adapter usually provides the SCSI driver on floppy disk or CD-ROM.

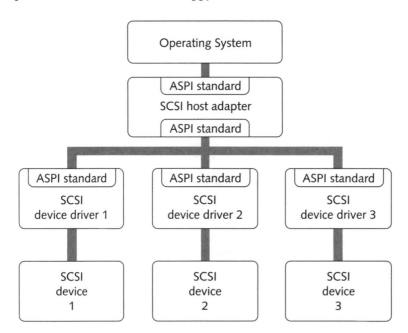

Figure 8-20   A SCSI device driver standard affects the interaction of the host adapter with the device drivers and the OS

Single-Ended and Differential SCSI.   Select a host adapter that matches the devices according to electronic signaling method. The two choices are **single-ended** SCSI devices and **differential** SCSI devices. Single-ended devices use only half the number of wires in the cable that differential devices do, but they do not work if the total length of the cables exceeds six meters. Differential devices can work if the total length of the cables does not exceed 25 meters. Don't mix the two types of devices on the same SCSI system or use a host adapter that does not match. You can damage the devices if you do.

SCAM Compliant. **SCAM** (SCSI Configuration AutoMatically or SCSI Configuration AutoMagically, depending on the literature you're reading) is a method by which SCSI devices and the host adapter can be Plug-and-Play-compliant. SCAM-compliant host adapters and devices can assign SCSI IDs dynamically at startup. For SCAM devices, you do not need to set the IDs on the device. Most SCSI devices currently in use are not SCAM-compliant, and you will need to set the unique ID on the device by jumpers, rotary dials, or other methods.

There are two levels of SCAM. Level 1 requires that the devices, but not the host adapter, can be assigned an ID at startup by software. Level 2 requires that the host adapter, as well as the devices, can be assigned an ID at startup by software. SCSI-2 devices must be SCAM-compliant to carry the logo "Designed for Windows 95."

A Sample Host Adapter for a Single Device

In the first example below, a typical host adapter designed to be used by only a single device is the Adaptec AVA-1502AE ISA-to-SCSI host adapter. It has one external 25-pin SCSI connection and is shown in Figure 8-21. The card is set to have SCSI ID 7. Termination is automatically supplied since it will always be at one end of the SCSI chain. The card only supports a single-ended device, hence the 25-pin connection; it uses only 25 of the 50 pins of the SCSI cable.

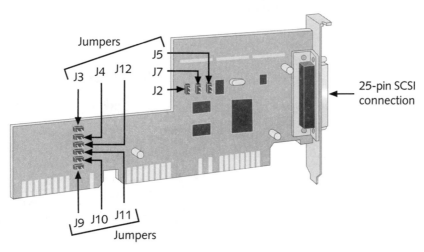

Figure 8-21 SCSI host adapter for one single-ended device

The jumpers on the card control these things:

- Enable or disable the connection
- I/O port address can be 140h or 340h
- SCSI parity checking is enabled or disabled
- IRQ can be set at 9, 10, 11, or 12

Follow these general steps to install this host adapter:

- Determine which IRQ is available on your PC.
- Set the jumpers on the card.
- Install the card in an ISA expansion slot.
- Install the host adapter driver that is supplied by Adaptec on floppy disk or CD-ROM.
- Tell the operating system to recognize the host adapter.

For DOS, use MSD to determine which IRQ is available. When you install the driver from a floppy disk, the entries are made in the CONFIG.SYS file for you, so the last step above is omitted.

For Windows 95, use the Device Manager to list the IRQs currently in use, and select one not listed. To tell Windows 95 to recognize the host adapter, click **Start**, **Settings**, **Control Panel**, **Add New Hardware**. Select **Yes** when you see the prompt, "Do you want Windows to search for your new hardware?"

To verify that the host adapter is correctly installed, click **Start**, **Settings**, **Control Panel**, and double-click **System**. Select the **Device Manager**. Double-click **SCSI controllers**. The Adaptec host adapter should display as shown in Figure 8-22.

After you have installed the host adapter, you are ready to install the external SCSI device. For example, if the device is a SCSI scanner, follow these directions:

- Install the software to run the scanner, which will include the scanner driver.
- Plug the SCSI cable into the host adapter port.
- Plug the other end of the cable into the scanner.
- Set the SCSI ID on the scanner.
- Connect the scanner's power cord to a wall outlet and turn the scanner on.
- Restart your PC and test the scanner.

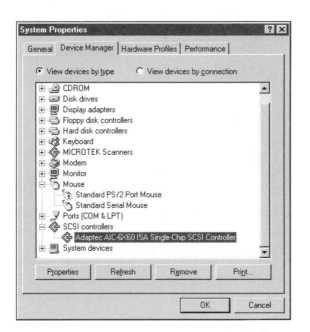

Figure 8-22 Device Manager displays the newly installed host adapter

CD-ROM Drives

Of the multimedia components discussed in this chapter, one that is growing in popularity is the CD-ROM. The technology of a CD-ROM drive is different from that of a hard drive, even though both are designed to hold data. Using technology that allows them to hold much larger volumes of data, CD-ROMs can accommodate the large space requirements of video and sound files.

CD-ROM drives are read-only devices. Data is written to the disc only once, because the surface of the disc is actually embedded with the data. Figure 8-23 shows a CD-ROM surface that is laid out as one continuous spiral of sectors of equal length that hold equal amounts of data. The surface of a CD-ROM stores data as pits and lands. **Lands** are raised areas, and **pits** are recessed areas on the surface, each representing either a 1 or a 0, respectively. The bits are read by the drive with a laser beam that distinguishes between a pit and a land by the amount of deflection or scattering that occurs when the light beam hits the surface.

Figure 8-23   The spiral layout of sectors on a CD-ROM surface

There is a small motor with an actuator arm that moves the laser beam to whatever sector on the track is to be read. If the disc were spinning at a constant speed, the speed near the center of the disc would be greater than the speed at the outer edge. To create the effect of **constant linear velocity (CLV)**, the CD-ROM drive uses a mechanism that alters the speed of the spinning disc so that, when the laser beam is near the center of the disc, it is over a sector for the same amount of time as it is when it is reading a sector near the outer edge. As the laser reads data near the center of the disc, the disc slows down, but it speeds up when the laser beam moves to the outer edge.

The transfer rate of the first CD-ROM drives was about 150 K per second of data, with the rpm (revolutions per minute) set to 200 when the laser was near the center of the disc. This transfer rate was about right for audio CDs. To allow video and motion to be displayed in a smooth manner without a choppy effect, the speed of the drives was increased to double speed (150 K per sec × 2), quad speed (150 K per sec × 4), and so on. It is not uncommon now to see CD-ROM drives with speeds at 20 times the audio speeds. Audio CDs must still drop the speed down to the original speed of 200 rpm and a transfer rate of 150 K per second.

When you choose a CD-ROM drive, look for the **multi-session** feature that allows data to be written to the disc in more than one session. You can purchase the disc only partially filled and later have other data added to the data already on the disc. A multi-session CD-ROM drive can read the disk both before and after new data has been written to it.

More expensive CD-ROM drives have a feature that requires placing the CDs in a caddie before putting the caddie in the drive. Other drives only provide a tray. You must remove the CD from the plastic or cardboard case and place it in the tray, increasing the likelihood that you will scratch the CD, put fingerprints on it, or otherwise damage the underside of the CD where data is stored. The caddies eliminate these risks. If your CD-ROM drive uses a caddie, you can buy several of them and permanently store the CDs in their own caddies, and you will never have to directly handle the CDs again.

Some CD-ROM drives have power-saving features controlled by the device driver. For example, when the drive waits for a command for more than five minutes, it enters Power Save Mode, causing the spindle motor to stop. The restart is automatic when the drive receives a command.

CD-ROM drives can interface with the systemboard in one of five ways. The drive can:

- Use an IDE interface; it can share an IDE adapter card and/or cable with a hard drive

- Use a SCSI interface using a SCSI host adapter

- Use a SCSI interface with the connection housed on a sound card

- Use a proprietary expansion card that works only with CD-ROMs from a particular manufacturer

- Use a proprietary connection on a sound card

CD-ROM drives might be Plug-and-Play-compliant. These drives allow a system to avoid resource conflicts. Look for "Ready for Windows 95" on the box.

Installing a CD-ROM drive is easy, especially when the adapter is already present. If you are using a SCSI CD-ROM, install the host adapter or sound card first, and then install the drive. If you are using a proprietary adapter, install both at the same time. If you are using an existing IDE adapter card, simply install the CD-ROM drive using an existing connection on the card or an extra connection on the hard drive data cable.

Figure 8-24 shows the front of a typical SCSI CD-ROM drive, and Figure 8-25 shows the rear view where the power cord, data cable, sound cord, and ground connector attach. Also note that there is an "audio out" connection that supports a direct connection to a sound card. The jumper pins on the CD-ROM can control these things:

- The SCSI ID for the drive

- Enable or disable SCSI parity checking

- Enable or disable the built-in SCSI terminator on the drive

The example shown is a SCSI CD-ROM drive. However, for IDE CD-ROM drives, expect to find jumpers that can set the drive as either the slave drive or the master drive in the IDE subsystem.

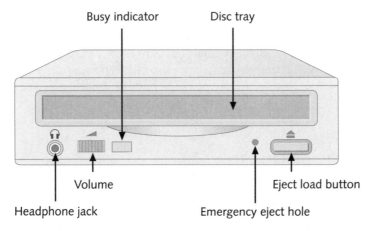

Figure 8-24 Front view of a typical SCSI CD-ROM drive

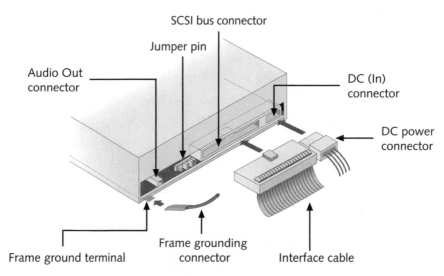

Figure 8-25   Rear view of a typical SCSI CD-ROM showing drive connections

CARING FOR **CD-ROM** DRIVES

Most problems with CD-ROMs are caused by dust, fingerprints, scratches, defects on the surface of the CD, or random electrical noise. Don't use a CD-ROM drive if it is standing vertically, such as when someone turns a desktop PC case on its side to save desktop space. If a CD gets stuck in the drive, there is an emergency eject hole that may enable you to remove it. Insert an instrument such as a straightened paper clip into the hole to manually eject the tray. Turn off the power to the PC first.

Use these precautions when handling CDs:

- Hold the CD by the edge; do not touch the bright side of the disc where data is stored.
- To remove dust or fingerprints, use a clean, soft, dry cloth.
- Do not write on, or paste paper to, the surface of the CD. Don't paste any labels to the top of the CD, as this can imbalance the CD and cause the drive to vibrate.
- Do not subject the CD to heat.
- Do not use cleaners, alcohol, and the like on the CD.
- Do not make the center hole larger.
- Do not bend the CD.
- Do not drop the CD or subject it to shock.

Installing a CD-ROM Drive

The documentation that comes with a CD-ROM drive is your best installation guide, but here are a few general guidelines. The CD-ROM will become another drive on your system, such as drive D or E. After it is installed, you access it just like any other drive by typing **D:** or **E:** at the DOS prompt, or by accessing the drive through Explorer in Windows 95. The major differences are (1) the CD-ROM drive is read-only—you cannot write to it; (2) it holds a lot more data than hard drives; and (3) it is a little slower to access than hard drives.

Install the Interface Card

To prepare for a CD-ROM installation, if you are using a SCSI host adapter or a sound card, install the card first with its drivers before you begin the CD-ROM installation.

For an IDE CD-ROM, there will probably be a jumper on the rear of the drive, allowing you to designate the drive as the slave drive or master drive. If you already have a hard drive connected to this IDE adapter, set the hard drive as the master drive and the CD-ROM as the slave drive. You might have the choice of using a second IDE connector on the card or on the systemboard, or a second connector on the hard drive cable. If this is the case, choose to use two cables, having the hard drive connected to the adapter, and the CD-ROM connected to the adapter on a separate connection. This way, the hard drive's performance and speed are not affected by the slower CD-ROM drive.

If the CD-ROM is the only drive connected to the IDE adapter, set the CD-ROM as the master drive.

Install the Drive

Some systems use rails on the drive to slide it into the bay. The rails should come with your computer, and you can screw them into the sides of the drive. If you have them, screw the rails in place and slide the drive into the bay. If you have no rails, then put two screws on each side of the drive, tightening the screws without overtightening them. You don't want the drive to be loose so that it can shift in the bay. If necessary, buy a mounting kit to extend the sides of the drive so that it will fit into the bay and be securely attached.

Connect the Cables and Cords

Find an extra four-prong power cord and plug it into the drive. For IDE drives, connect the 40-pin cable to the IDE adapter and the drive, being careful to follow the Pin 1 rule: match the edge color on the cable to Pin 1 on both the adapter card and the drive.

Some CD-ROM drives come with an audio cord that attaches the interface card to a sound card. The sound card then receives sound input directly from the CD-ROM. Attach the audio cord if you have a sound card. Don't make the mistake of attaching a miniature power

8

cord designed for a 3½-inch disk drive coming from the power supply to the audio input connector on the sound card. The connections appear to fit, but you'll probably destroy the drive by doing so.

Some drives have a ground connection, with one end of the ground cable attached to the computer case. Follow the directions included with the drive.

Verify Power to the Drive

Check all connections, and turn on the power. Press the eject button on the front of the drive. If it works, then you know power is getting to the drive.

Install the Device Driver for DOS

To operate in a DOS environment, a CD-ROM needs a device driver that is loaded from the CONFIG.SYS file. The driver interfaces with the drive and a program called the Microsoft CD-ROM extension for DOS (MSCDEX.EXE), which must be loaded from AUTOEXEC.BAT. Both of these programs will come on floppy disk with the CD-ROM drive. The disk also should contain an installation program. Run the installation program on the disk. It copies the files to the hard drive and edits both the CONFIG.SYS and the AUTOEXEC.BAT files. Restart the computer so that the changes will take effect. If there are problems accessing the drive after you have restarted, check the items listed under Troubleshooting Tips for a CD-ROM Installation.

Install the Device Driver for Windows 95

Windows 95 supports CD-ROM drives without add-on drivers. Click **Start**, **Settings**, **Control Panel**, and double-click **Add New Hardware**. Select **Yes** when you are asked, "Do you want Windows to search for your new hardware?" Complete the installation by following the directions on the Add New Hardware sheet.

Test the Drive

The drive is now ready to use. Press the eject button to open the drive shelf, and place a CD in the drive. Since data on CDs is written only on the bottom, be careful to protect it. You can now access the CD with the DIR D: command. (The actual drive letter assigned to the drive will be the next available letter.)

If you have a problem reading the CD, verify that the CD is placed in the tray label-side-up, and that the format is compatible with your drive. Try another CD—the CD may be defective or scratched.

Update Your Windows 95 Rescue Disk to Include Access to the CD-ROM

The rescue disks you created in earlier chapters to start the system in the event of a hard drive failure need to include access to the CD-ROM drive. Because Windows 95 is normally loaded from CD-ROM, update the AUTOEXEC.BAT and CONFIG.SYS files on the rescue disk to access the CD-ROM drive if the hard drive fails.

Include on your rescue disk the command lines from the AUTOEXEC.BAT and CONFIG.SYS files that are on your hard drive, but with references to drive A instead of drive C in the paths, or simply eliminate the paths altogether, which forces DOS or Windows 95 to use files on the disk that it is booting from. Copy all files that these two command lines refer to onto the disk.

For example, on a rescue or boot disk designed to access the CD-ROM drive without depending on any files or commands on the hard drive, the CONFIG.SYS file might contain this command:

```
DEVICE = SLCD.SYS /D:MSCD001
```

The AUTOEXEC.BAT file might contain this command line:

```
MSCDEX.EXE /D:MSCD001 /L:E /M:8
```

The files that would need to be copied to this disk for these two commands to work are MSCDEX.EXE and SLCD.SYS.

If your hard drive fails and you start up from your rescue disk, once the CD-ROM drivers are loaded and the CD is recognized, you will be able to install or reinstall Windows 95 from CD. To do this, insert the Win 95 CD into the CD-ROM drive, and from the D: (or E:) prompt type **Setup** and then press **Enter**. Once Windows 95 is installed, it will often ignore existing CONFIG.SYS lines (turning them into comment lines by adding REM to the beginning of the line) and handle the CD-ROM drivers through its own configuration routines and registry.

Troubleshooting Tips for a CD-ROM DOS Installation

The specific command lines placed in CONFIG.SYS and AUTOEXEC.BAT are partially dependent on the brand and model of CD-ROM being installed, but below is one example that demonstrates what you might expect the CD-ROM installation program to put in these two files. In the CONFIG.SYS file, the following is a possible command line:

```
DEVICE = C:\CDSYS\SLCD.SYS /D:MSCD001
```

The C:\CD.SYS is the directory for the drive-specific CD-ROM files. (Notice the backslash, \, indicating a directory path.) SLCD.SYS is actually the system device file for the particular CD installed. The CD device file might be called WCD.SYS or MTMCDAI.SYS instead. The /D: means "load the Microsoft Driver," in this case the standard MSCD001. (Notice the slash, /, indicating a command switch.)

The AUTOEXEC.BAT file is often modified with a new line that looks like:

```
C:\DOS\MSCDEX.EXE /D:MSCD001 /L:D /M:8
```

MSCDEX.EXE loads the Microsoft CD driver using the standard MSCD001. The optional /L:D indicates that the CD ROM is drive D. The optional /M is used to increase the number of memory buffers.

The Error Message "Invalid Drive Specification" Appears While the System Is Starting Up.

Check that there are no errors in the command lines in the CONFIG.SYS or AUTOEXEC.BAT files according to the documentation that came with the CD-ROM. Did you get an error message during startup, such as "Bad Command" or "File Not Found"?

Turn off the computer and reseat the adapter card and check cable connections.

The MSCDEX.EXE program might not be loaded. Sometimes when an installation program edits the CONFIG.SYS or AUTOEXEC.BAT files, the command is added too late in the file. For example, if AUTOEXEC.BAT has a command to execute Windows (C:\WINDOWS\WIN or some similar command), and the command to load the CD-ROM program occurs after this Windows command, the command will not execute. If this is the case, move the command up near the beginning of the AUTOEXEC.BAT file.

You might be using a version of the MSCDEX.EXE program that is different from the version that comes with DOS. If you have DOS 6+, use the version of MSCDEX.EXE that is in the \DOS directory. Change the path to the command in AUTOEXEC.BAT. For example, if the command line looks like this:

```
C:\CDROM\MSCDEX /D:MSCD001 /M:10
```

change it to read:

```
C:\DOS\MSCDEX /D:MSCD001 /M:10
```

For an explanation of the parameters in the command line, see your DOS or CD-ROM manual.

The Install Process Is Terminated with the Message "MSCDEX.EXE Not Found."

MSCDEX.EXE must be copied onto the hard drive. Put it in the \DOS directory, then restart the install process. Sometimes MSCDEX is placed in the Windows directory, and sometimes a copy is put in the newly created CD-ROM directory.

The Error Message "Not Enough Drive Letters" Appears During the Startup Process.

By default, DOS only allows five logical drive letters (A through E). If you have used these up, then you must tell DOS to accept more drive letters with the LASTDRIVE line in CONFIG.SYS. The line can look like this:

```
LASTDRIVE=Z
```

Conflict Errors Exist. These will appear during startup as error messages, or they will cause some other device to fail to operate. The IRQ and I/O address of your CD-ROM should be in the documentation. If not, call the manufacturer's technical support for this information.

Troubleshooting Guidelines for CD-ROM Operation

Follow these guidelines to deal with problems you may encounter when trying to use a CD-ROM.

Computer Does Not Recognize CD (No D: Prompt). Consider the following configurations:

1. When using DOS, does the CONFIG.SYS file contain a CD device command line?
2. Does the AUTOEXEC.BAT file call MSCDEX.EXE? Is MSCDEX.EXE placed in the correct directory? (A correct Windows 95 installation will not need to have MSCDEX.EXE in the AUTOEXEC.BAT file.)
3. Is MSCDEX.EXE on the hard drive?
4. For Windows 95, has the CD-ROM driver been installed?
5. Check to see if another device is using the same port settings or IRQ number. See Control Panel, System Icon, Device Manager.

Check the following connections:

1. Is the power cable attached to the CD-ROM?
2. Is the data cable attached to the CD-ROM and to the controller?
3. Is the stripe on the data cable correctly aligned to Pin 1? (Look for an arrow or small 1 printed on the drive. For a best guess, Pin 1 is usually next to the power connector.)
4. Is the correct master/slave jumper set? For example, if both the hard drive and the CD-ROM drive are hooked up to the same ribbon cable, one must be set to master (the one attached to the end connector) and the other set to slave (the one attached to the middle connector).

No Sound. Is the sound cable attached between the CD-ROM and the analog audio connector on the sound card?

Are the speakers turned on?

Is the speaker volume turned down?

Are the speakers plugged into the line "Out" or the "Spkr" port of the sound card?

Is the transformer for the speaker plugged into an electrical outlet on one end and into the speakers on the other end?

Is the volume control for Windows turned down? (To check, click **Start**, **Programs**, **Accessories**, **Multimedia**, **Volume Control**.)

Does the sound card have a "diagnose" file on the install disk?

Reinstall the sound card drivers.

Is another device using the same I/O addresses or IRQ number?

To check for a bad connection, turn off the computer and remove and re-install the sound card.

Replace the sound card with one you know is good.

WHEN DEVICE INSTALLATIONS CREATE PROBLEMS

Suppose you install a new sound card and it does not work. If you also discover that your network card has stopped communicating, it is likely that there is a conflict of resources between the two devices. It's important to realize that there might be other reasons neither device is working, such as a poorly seated circuit card or a loose cable. Check all connections carefully before proceeding. You might also remove the sound card, and check that your network is working. You can then conclude that you most probably have a conflict.

The place to begin to diagnose a conflict is with the documentation. Read everything carefully, looking for what has been discussed earlier in this chapter. What IRQ, I/O address, DMA channel, or upper memory addresses is the device being installed using? What does your network card use? Compare the two, and you will discover your conflict. The fix might be easy, or it might be impossible if neither board offers alternatives. Fortunately, most devices today offer alternate choices for these settings. Again, read the documentation for directions. Plug-and-Play devices make this process much easier, but many devices today are still not Plug-and-Play-compliant.

CHAPTER SUMMARY

- To harness the full power of today's microcomputer, you can add some peripheral devices that turn a basic microcomputer into a machine capable of producing camera-ready copy, multimedia presentations, and the like.

- Adding new devices to a computer requires installing both hardware and software, and resolving possible resource conflicts.

- The trend in new and better devices is not only toward more speed and functionality, but also toward ease of use and ease of installation.

- Trade magazines, retail stores, and the Internet are sources for learning about new hardware devices and the applications software that use them.

- The minimum hardware configuration required to successfully run a desktop publishing system includes a 486DX computer with at least 8 MB of RAM, a mouse, a color monitor, a scanner and related software, a laser printer, and a graphics software package to create and/or edit graphics.

- When buying a computer system, put your money into the computer itself before the peripheral devices.

- The Multimedia Marketing Council standardizes multimedia requirements according to their MPC Standard Levels 1, 2, and 3.

- Authoring software is used to put together a complete multimedia presentation including video and sound.

- Most hardware devices require similar resources from a computer, including an IRQ, DMA channel, I/O addresses, and some upper memory addresses to contain their device drivers.

- Most computers provide two serial ports and one parallel port to be used for a variety of devices.

- A null modem connection is used to connect two computers using their serial ports and a cable, but no modems.

- The UART chip controls serial ports.

- Because data bits in parallel might sometimes lose their relationship with the byte they represent, parallel cables should not exceed 15 feet in length.

- Many general-purpose I/O cards provide serial and parallel ports as well as IDE adapters.

- Notebook computers sometimes have a PC Card slot, formally called the PCMCIA slot, which can support a variety of hardware devices.

- When selecting a SCSI host adapter, consider the bus slot the adapter will use, the device driver standard used by the host adapter, single-ended versus differential SCSI, SCAM compliance, and whether or not the host offers bus mastering.

- Some inexpensive SCSI host adapters are sold bundled with hardware devices that only support one or two SCSI devices.

- CD-ROMs are read-only devices in which data is physically embedded into the surface of the disc.

- The speed of a CD-ROM slows down as the laser beam moves from the outside to the inside of the disc.

- CD-ROM drives might have an IDE or SCSI interface, or they might connect to the system bus through a proprietary expansion card or use a connection on a sound card.

- Data is only written to the bottom of a CD-ROM, which should be protected from damage.

8

KEY TERMS

- **Applications software** — Programs that perform specific tasks, such as word processing, database management, or mathematical calculations (for example, Word, FileMaker, and Excel).

- **Authoring software** — Software that allows the user to incorporate text, sound, graphics, photos, animations, and video into one continuous show (for example, Authorware).

- **Bit-map file** — A type of graphics file in which the image is written as a series of 0s and 1s. These files have the extension .BMP and can be loaded into paint programs to be edited and printed.

- **Constant linear velocity (CLV)** — A CD-ROM format in which the spacing of data is consistent on the CD, but the speed of the disc varies depending on whether the drive is reading near the center or the edge of the disc.

- **Desktop publishing** — Production of professional-quality, camera-ready output using a microcomputer for tasks once done by graphic designers, typesetters, and print shops.

- **Differential SCSI device** — A device (with a cable up to 75 feet long) that sends signals through a pair of wires and is less vulnerable to noise than single-ended SCSI devices. *See* Single-ended SCSI devices.

- **Docking station** — A special PC that is designed to connect to a portable or notebook computer for downloading and uploading data and for sharing local peripheral devices.

- **FIFO (first-in first-out)** — A method of storing and retrieving data from a table or stack, whereby the first element stored is the first one retrieved.

- **Firmware** — The programs stored permanently on ROM chips. An example of firmware, which cannot be changed, is the instructions on circuit board ROM chips that dictate how to control the board.

- **FIFO buffer** — A buffer on a 16550 UART chip that solves the problem of lost data, which sometimes occurred with the older 16450 UART chips.

- **Genlock** — A standard for video-capturing cards that refers to the ability of the card to capture a single unique frame of video, rather than "sampling" pieces of adjoining frames.

- **Hot swapping** — The ability of a PC or notebook computer to use a device such as a PC Card that is inserted while the computer is running without the PC needing to be rebooted.

- **I/O card** — A card that often contains serial, parallel, and game ports on the same adapter board providing input/output interface with the CPU.

- **Lands** — Microscopic flat areas on the surface of a compact disc that separate pits. Lands and pits are used to represent data as either a 0 or a 1.

- **Modem-eliminator** — A technique that allows two data terminal equipment (DTE) devices to communicate by means of a null modem cable in which the transmit and receive wires are cross-connected and no modems are necessary.

- **Multimedia** — A type of computer presentation that combines text, graphics, animations, photos, sound, and/or full-motion video.

- **Multisession** — A feature that allows data to be read (or written) on a CD during more than one session. This is important if the disc was only partially filled during the first write.

- **NTSC (National Television Standards Committee)** — An organization that sets standards for such devices as video-capturing cards.

- **Null modem cable** — *See* Modem-eliminator.

- **Parallel port** — A female port on the computer that can transmit data in parallel, 8 bits at a time, that is usually used with a printer. The DOS names for parallel ports are LPT1 and LPT2.

- **PC card** — Also called PCMCIA card. A credit-card-sized adapter card that can be slid into a slot in the side of many notebook computers and is used for connecting to modems, networks, and CD-ROM drives.

- **PC card slot** — Also called a PCMCIA card slot. An expansion slot on a notebook computer, into which a PC card is inserted.

- **PCMCIA (Personal Computer Memory Card International Association) card** — *See* PC card.

- **PCMCIA card slot** — *See* PC card slot.

- **Pits** — Recessed areas on the surface of a compact disc separating lands or flat areas. Lands and pits represent data as either a 0 or a 1.

- **SCAM (SCSI configuration automatically)** — A method in which SCSI devices and the host adapter are Plug-and-Play-compliant, and the user does not need to manually set the ID on the device.

- **Serial ports** — Male ports on the computer used for transmitting data serially, one bit at a time. They are commonly used for modems and mice, and in DOS are called COM1 or COM2.

- **Single-ended SCSI device** — A SCSI device that uses half the number of wires in the cable that a differential devices uses, and is limited in the cable length.

- **UART (universal asynchronous receiver/transmitter) chip** — A chip that controls serial ports. It sets protocol and converts parallel data bits received from the system bus into serial bits.

- **Video-capturing card** — A multimedia card that can capture input video and convert the frames into motion files or still clips that can be stored on disk.

8

REVIEW QUESTIONS

1. What are the minimum requirements for a multimedia computer system capable of producing an appealing sight-and-sound presentation?
2. Define and describe genlock.
3. What conflicts might disable a device or cause it to hang?
4. What should you do before changing a DIP switch, jumper, or CMOS setting?
5. How can you instruct the new modem to use an alternate IRQ?
6. In Windows 95, how can you view and change current device drivers?
7. What is the typical I/O address and IRQ for COM1?
8. What is the typical I/O address and IRQ for LPT1?
9. What does RS-232c refer to?
10. How many pins are in a typical serial mouse port?
11. How many pins are in a typical parallel printer port?
12. List three "protocol" settings.
13. What is a null modem cable and what is it often used for?
14. What is a UART chip?
15. What does the DOS utility MSD do?
16. Normally, what is the length limitation for parallel cables?
17. What is a PCMCIA slot or PC Card slot?
18. List three types of settings that may be controlled by adapter card jumpers.
19. What are pits and lands?
20. When can a SCSI hard drive be the startup device for a system?

PROJECTS

Unless you follow the proper procedures, working inside your computer can cause serious damage—to both you and your computer. To assure safety in your work setting, follow every precaution listed in the *Read This Before You Begin* section following this book's Introduction.

RESEARCH HARDWARE AND SOFTWARE ON YOUR COMPUTER

Know the computers for which you are responsible. Gather the documentation for your computer and/or use the Nuts & Bolts software on the accompanying CD-ROM and fill in the following chart. Copy the chart and put it in a notebook that is kept for this computer.

To use Nuts & Bolts to gather information about your computer, click on **Start**, **Programs**, **Nuts & Bolts**, and **Discover Pro**.

Computer Fact Sheet

Location of computer: _____

Owner: _____

Date purchased: _____

Warranty expires: _____

Size and speed of CPU: _____

RAM present: _____

Type of monitor: _____

Type of video card: _____

Hard drive type: _____

Hard drive size: _____

Disk drive A size: _____

Disk drive B size: _____

8

Software Installed:

Name	Version	Installed By	Date
1.			
2.			
3.			
4.			
5.			

Other Devices:

Name of Device	IRQ	I/O Address	DMA Channel	Device Driver Filename
1. Serial port 1				
2. Serial port 2				
3. Parallel port				
4. Mouse				
5. Modem				
6. CD-ROM drive				
7.				
8.				

INSTALL A DEVICE

Install a device on a computer. If you are working in a classroom environment, you can simulate an installation by moving a device from one computer to another.

RESEARCH A COMPUTER AD

Pick a current magazine ad for a complete, working computer system including computer, monitor, keyboard, and software together with extra devices such as a mouse or printer. Write a four- to eight-page report describing and explaining the details in this ad. This exercise will give you a good opportunity to learn about the latest offerings on the market as well as current pricing.

COMPARE TWO COMPUTER ADS

Find two computer ads for computer systems containing the same processor. Compare the two ads. Include in your comparison the different features offered and the weaknesses and strengths of each system.

SEARCH THE INTERNET FOR A VIDEO DRIVER

You have a 486DX computer with a VESA local bus video card by Avance Logic, Inc. You upgrade your DOS 6.22 and Windows 3.1 operating systems to Windows 95. When you install the video, you discover that Windows 95 does not support Avance Logic video drivers. You temporarily substitute a standard super VGA driver so you can complete the installation, but you notice that the video and color are not as clear as you think they should be. How do you resolve the problem? Follow these steps to a solution.

1. On the Internet, find the Web site for Avance Logic, Inc. Here's where some educated guessing can be effective. Try www.avance.com.

2. Look for drivers for Windows 95. Your video card is labeled Avance Logic 2228. After a little searching, you arrive at the screen shown in Figure 8-26.

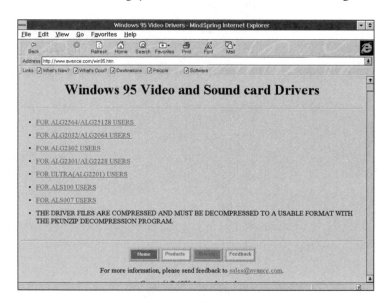

Figure 8-26   Video driver for Windows 95

3. Download and explode the file labeled For alg2301/alg2228 users.

4. Print the Readme.txt file that lists the instructions to use to install the new device driver in Windows 95. If you follow the instructions, don't apply the driver unless you really do have this particular video card.

PREPARE FOR A WINDOWS 95 CRASH

Suppose you have Windows 95 stored on a CD-ROM and you don't have the disk copy. Your hard drive fails, or for some other reason Windows 95 on your hard drive will not load. How do you recover Windows 95 from the CD-ROM if the only way to access the CD is through Windows 95 on the hard drive? Prepare a recovery disk with which you can do these things:

a. Boot from the disk to a command prompt

b. Access the CD-ROM drive without using the hard drive

Include on the disk AUTOEXEC.BAT and CONFIG.SYS files that make no reference to drive C. As resources, use the current AUTOEXEC.BAT and CONFIG.SYS files on the hard drive and the documentation to the CD-ROM drive.

PLAN THE DESIGN OF A 9-PIN NULL MODEM CABLE

Draw a chart similar to Table 8-3 showing the pin outs (functions of each pin) for a 9-pin null modem cable.

ADDITIONAL ACTIVITIES

1. On your home or lab computer, find out what IRQ is used for the CD-ROM.
2. Play a music CD with the Windows CD Player.
3. Change Windows sounds through the Control Panel Sounds icon.
4. Record a voice message using the Sound Recorder.
5. Set up one of the following troubleshooting practice problems and have a fellow student discover the problem and the solution.

    a. Speaker cables disconnected

    b. Speaker turned off

    c. Speaker cable plugged into the wrong jack

    d. Volume turned all the way down

    e. MSCDEX.EXE not called in AUTOEXEC.BAT file

    f. MSCDEX.EXE not on drive

6. Use the Hardware Wizard to remove the CD-ROM drivers, and then reinstall the CD-ROM.

CHAPTER NINE

UNDERSTANDING AND MANAGING MEMORY

In the last few chapters secondary storage, including floppy disk drives, hard drives, and other peripheral devices has been discussed. In this chapter your attention is turned back to the systemboard and expansion boards. You will learn how the operating system uses the memory located on these boards, and how to manage this memory to meet the needs of the software you are using. You will also learn how to upgrade the RAM on your computer. Before turning to these topics, you will look at the physical memory to see where it is located, and what kinds of memory chips and modules are found in a computer.

**IN THIS CHAPTER
YOU WILL LEARN:**

- THE TYPES OF PHYSICAL MEMORY HOUSED ON THE SYSTEMBOARD AND EXPANSION BOARDS

- HOW MEMORY IS USED BY DOS AND WINDOWS 95

- HOW TO MANAGE MEMORY USING DOS, WINDOWS 3.x, AND WINDOWS 95

- HOW TO UPGRADE THE MEMORY IN YOUR COMPUTER

PHYSICAL MEMORY

Recall that computer memory is divided into two categories: ROM and RAM. ROM, or read-only memory, consists of memory chips that contain programs that are acid-burned into the chips at the factory. The programs on a ROM chip (sometimes called firmware) are permanent; they cannot be changed. On EEPROM (electrically erasable programmable ROM) chips, a higher voltage is applied to one of the pins to erase its previous memory before the new instruction set or data is electronically written. EPROM (erasable programmable ROM) chips have a special window that allows the current memory contents to be erased with a special ultraviolet light so that the chip can be reprogrammed. Many BIOS chips are EPROM chips. They are seen on the systemboard with shiny tape covering the window. However, for the discussions in this chapter, you will consider the EEPROM, EPROM, and ROM chips to all provide BIOS that is not erasable during normal PC operations.

When you purchased your computer, it contained several ROM chips on the systemboard and some on the expansion boards. These ROM chips contain the programming that the computer uses to start up (boot itself) and to do routine, utility operations, such as reading from and writing to hardware devices and performing basic data manipulation. As was discussed in earlier chapters, the ROM chips on the systemboard contain much of the BIOS for your computer. BIOS is a set of programs that do the basic input/output chores. The OS, Windows 95 or DOS, calls on the BIOS programs to interact with input/output devices as they are needed.

The BIOS stored in the ROM chips on your systemboard is called System BIOS (see Figure 9-1). Expansion boards also can have ROM chips that provide the programming that drives the devices that they control. For example, a network card contains ROM chips that provide the programming to communicate with the network, and video cards contain ROM chips that hold the programming that controls the monitor.

Recall that the second kind of computer memory is RAM, random access memory. RAM chips are either (1) socketed or soldered directly on the systemboard, or (2) housed on little miniboards, called SIMMs (single in-line memory modules) or DIMMs (dual in-line memory modules), that plug directly into the systemboard (examples are shown in Figure 9-2).

SRAM, DRAM, AND MEMORY CACHING

RAM is volatile: when you turn your computer off, all the data in RAM is lost. Remember that one RAM chip, called the CMOS setup chip, doesn't lose its data, because it has its own battery that powers it when the machine is turned off. RAM is used to store both data and programs so that the CPU can execute the programs and process the data.

The RAM chips on the systemboard are usually called primary memory. Circuit boards also might contain RAM chips that hold data that is being processed. For example, a video card might have RAM chips that hold data just before it is displayed on the monitor. These chips are called video RAM or VRAM.

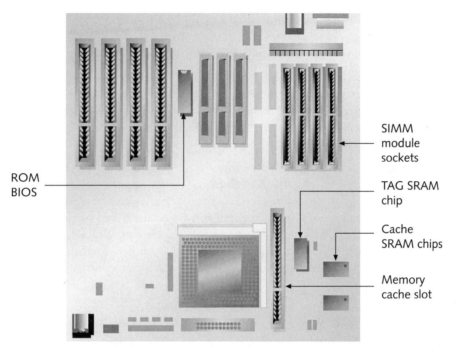

Figure 9-1 Memory on a systemboard

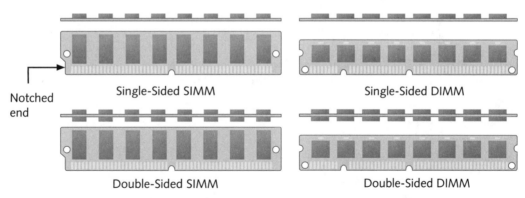

Figure 9-2 RAM on the systemboard is stored on SIMMS and DIMMS

RAM chips come in two kinds: **static RAM**, written SRAM and pronounced S-RAM (two words), and **dynamic RAM**, written DRAM and pronounced D-RAM (two words). Static RAM is not as volatile as dynamic RAM. Here, the word static means "doesn't lose or change its value." When the power to either SRAM or DRAM goes off, all data stored is lost. When something is written to static RAM, it is not lost as long as there is power to the chip. However, dynamic RAM does not keep the data written to it very long even with an uninterrupted supply of power. Data written to DRAM chips is lost after about 4 milliseconds. Thus D-RAM data must be rewritten before that time is up. This means that the CPU must use some of its time to refresh dynamic memory. Dynamic memory refresh is partly accomplished by the DMA controller discussed in previous chapters. Thus, part of your computer's resources must be devoted to refreshing DRAM every 4 milliseconds or so.

Static RAM does not need to be refreshed. Because the computer's resources do not refresh SRAM, data and programs stored in SRAM are accessed faster than those stored in DRAM. SRAM chips are more expensive than DRAM chips, which is why all RAM is not made up of SRAM chips. As a compromise, most computers have a little SRAM on the systemboard and a lot of DRAM.

Memory caching is a method used to store data or programs in SRAM for quick retrieval. Memory caching requires some SRAM chips and a cache controller to control the caching. When memory caching is used, the cache controller tries to anticipate what data or programming code the CPU will request next, and copies that data or programming code to the SRAM chips. Then, if the cache guessed correctly, it can satisfy the CPU request from SRAM without having to access the slower DRAM. Under normal conditions, memory caching guesses right more than 90% of the time and is an effective way of speeding up memory access.

On older 386 computers, the cache controller was located on a single chip labeled the 385 chip, but 486 and later CPUs have the cache controller chip embedded in the CPU chip housed together with some static RAM. This SRAM is called an internal cache, level 1 cache, or L1 cache, and is found in all 486 CPUs and higher. A systemboard, however, can have additional static RAM, called an external cache, level 2 cache, or L2 cache.

How much SRAM on a systemboard is enough without being prohibitively expensive? On most computers 256K of SRAM is considered the minimum, and many systemboards come with 256K already on the board, with additional banks for another 256K. The second 256K of cache does not improve performance nearly as much as the first 256K does. More than 512K of cache does not offer a significant improvement in access time.

MEMORY ON THE SYSTEMBOARD

ROM chips are usually socketed onto the systemboard. Occasionally, you will have to replace a ROM chip either because the ROM chip has gone bad or because the ROM programming is outdated and you must upgrade ROM. The chips can be removed easily, and a new ROM chip can be popped into the socket. Static RAM chips are sometimes soldered directly on the systemboard and sometimes located on SIMMs, but dynamic RAM is most often housed on SIMMs or DIMMs, discussed in Chapter 3.

SIMM and DIMM Modules

SIMMs commonly come in sizes of 4 MB to 64 MB with 30 or 72 pins on the SIMM module edge connector. A SIMM might have three or more chips, but this doesn't affect the amount of memory that the SIMM can hold. SIMMs are also rated by speed, measured in nanoseconds. A nanosecond (abbreviated ns) is one billionth of a second. Common SIMM speeds are 60, 70, or 80 ns. This speed is a measure of access time, the time it takes for the CPU to receive a value in response to a request. Access time includes the time it takes to refresh the chips. An access time of 60 ns is faster than an access time of 70 ns. Therefore, the smaller the speed rating, the faster the chip. DIMMs have 168 pins on the edge connector of the board and hold from 8 MB to 128 MB of RAM.

What to Look for When Buying Memory Chips and Modules

Memory chips and memory modules are sold at different speeds, with or without parity (a method to verify data), and with different features. Chips can be high-grade, low-grade, remanufactured, or used. The occurence of frequent **General Protection Fault (GPF)** errors in Windows, application errors, and errors that cause the system to hang can be caused by poor-quality memory chips. It pays to know the quality and type of memory you are buying. The following are some guidelines to follow to assure you are purchasing high-quality memory chips.

Memory Speed. The documentation for a systemboard states what speed of memory to use on the board and is usually written as something like this: "Use 70 ns or faster." In this example, 60 ns will work on this board, but 80-ns memory will cause problems. It is possible, but not recommended, to mix the speed of memory modules on a systemboard, but don't mix the speeds within a single memory bank. More will be said about this later in the chapter.

Memory Parity. Some systemboards support parity memory, and some only use nonparity memory. On a SIMM, if there is an odd number of chips, most likely the SIMM is parity memory; an even number of chips usually indicates nonparity memory. As discussed in Chapter 3, parity memory validates the integrity of the data stored in RAM by counting the number of even or odd bits set to 1 that are stored in RAM, and by setting a parity bit either to make the number of 1-bits even (called even parity) or to make the number of 1s odd (called odd parity). When the data is read, the number of 1s is counted. If parity is even but the number of 1s is odd (or vice versa), then a parity error occurs, and the CPU will stop processing this data.

Most manufacturers of PC systemboards today use nonparity memory to save space and processing time and therefore money. Some of the issues surrounding memory parity are discussed next.

Fake Parity. A **parity generator chip**, sometimes called a **fake parity chip**, or **logic parity**, is designed to simulate parity checking so that you can use less expensive nonparity memory modules on a systemboard that is expecting parity memory. For example, a SIMM module often has nine chips. Eight of these chips each holds one of the 8 bits that make up one byte, while the ninth chip holds the parity bit and checks parity when data is read from the module. With fake parity, this ninth chip simply always sends the positive parity check signal without holding or checking parity information.

If a systemboard is using fake parity when it is expecting parity memory, it will continue to operate even if it receives corrupted data, which might result in corrupted data being sent to the application using it. There are two ways to determine if the SIMM you have contains true parity or fake parity. BP, VT, GSM, or MPEC will appear as part of the chip ID on a fake parity chip. Another approach is to use diagnostic software specifically designed to test for fake parity. Some manufacturers advertise fake parity chips at reduced prices as alternatives to parity SIMMs. However, other manufacturers may sell the fake parity SIMMs as parity memory.

EDO and FPM Memory. EDO (extended data output) memory is an improvement over earlier FPM (fast page mode) memory. EDO memory is faster because it allows the memory controller to eliminate the 10-ns delay in the time that it would normally wait before it issues the next memory address. When no memory cache is present, computer performance increases 10% to 20% when using EDO memory instead of FPM memory. However, if 256K of cache is used, the increased performance from FPM to EDO memory is only 1% to 2%. EDO memory does not cost significantly more than FPM memory, but your systemboard must be able to support it. Check your systemboard documentation or CMOS setup to determine if you should use EDO memory. If your systemboard does not support EDO memory, you can still use it, but it will not increase system performance. EDO memory is used on SIMMs, DIMMs, and video memory, and is often used to provide on-board RAM on various expansion boards.

Flash Memory. Flash memory acts more like secondary storage than like other types of memory, because it does not lose its data when the power is turned off. Flash memory is different from a hard drive in that a hard drive holds its data as a magnetized area on a platter, whereas flash memory holds its data electronically. Also, flash memory provides much faster data access than a hard drive does, because a hard drive is a mechanical device and flash memory is an electronic device. Another difference is that flash memory is much more expensive than hard drive storage.

Flash memory is used on notebook computers and is often found on PC Cards (PCMCIA). Flash ROM is one example of the use of this kind of memory on a systemboard. Flash memory is also used to hold picture data in digital cameras.

Synchronous DRAM or SDRAM Modules. Synchronous DRAM modules are about 50% more expensive than SIMM modules. SDRAM modules operate at various speeds, depending on the bus speed, whereas a SIMM module only operates at a single speed.

Tin or Gold Leads. Memory modules and the banks that hold them might be made of either tin or gold. On a systemboard the connectors inside the memory slots are made of either tin or gold, as are the edge connectors on the memory modules. You should match tin leads to tin connectors and gold leads to gold connectors to prevent a chemical reaction between the two different metals, which can cause corrosion. Corrosion can result in intermittent memory errors and can even cause the PC to be unable to boot.

Choosing the Correct Size Module. Not all sizes of memory modules will fit on any one computer. Use the right number of SIMM or DIMM modules with the right size memory on each module to fit the memory banks on your systemboard. There will be more information about this later in the chapter.

Remanufactured and Used Modules. Stamped on each chip of a SIMM or DIMM module is a chip ID that identifies, along with other things, the date the chip was manufactured. Look for the date in the YYWW format, where YY is the year the chip was made and WW is the week of that year. For example, 9809 indicates a chip made in the ninth week of 1998. If you see date stamps on a SIMM or DIMM chip that are older than one year, chances are that these chips are used memory. If only some of the chips are old, but some are new, the module is probably remanufactured. When buying memory modules, look for ones on which all chips have dates that are relatively close together and less than a year old.

Re-marked Chips. New chips have a protective coating, which gives them a polished, reflective-looking surface. If the surface of the chip is dull or matted, or you can scratch the markings off with a fingernail or knife, suspect that the chip has been re-marked. Re-marked chips are chips that have been used and returned to the factory, marked again, and sent out.

Varieties of SRAM Memory

SRAM memory can be installed on a systemboard as individual chips or as a module. SRAM is installed in increments of 64 KB, 128 KB, 256 KB, or 512 KB. See the documentation for the systemboard to determine which amounts of cache the board supports and what kind of memory to buy. SRAM comes as either synchronous SRAM or asynchronous SRAM (explained below). Synchronous SRAM is more expensive and about 30% faster than asynchronous SRAM.

Synchronous and Asynchronous SRAM. All RAM sends data and control signals over the system bus. The methods used to coordinate how and when data and control signals are sent and read differ with various kinds of memory. **Synchronous SRAM** requires a clock signal to validate its control signals. This enables the cache memory to run in step with the CPU. Synchronous SRAM can be either burst or pipelined burst SRAM. Burst SRAM is more expensive than pipelined burst SRAM and only slightly faster. Burst SRAM uses the concept that data is sent as a two-step process: the data address is sent, and then the data itself is sent. **Burst SRAM** sends a burst of data without sending all the addresses of the data, only the first address. Burst allows a large amount of data to be sent without interruption. **Pipelined burst** uses more clock cycles per transfer, as does the burst without pipelining, but it does not significantly slow down the process and is desirable because of the reduced cost.

Asynchronous SRAM does not work in step with the CPU clock speed. It must look up the address sent to it by the CPU and return the data within one clock cycle, which makes it able to process less data in one request and results in overall slower memory access.

To understand the difference between asynchronous and synchronous memory, think of this analogy. Children are jumping rope with a long rope, and one child on each end turns the rope. A child who cannot keep in step with the turning rope can only run through on a single pass, and must come back around to make another pass through. A child who can keep in step with the rope can run into the center and jump for quite a while, until he or she is tired and runs out. Which child can perform the most rope-jumping cycles in a given amount of time? The answer is: the one who can keep in step with the rope. Similarly, synchronous memory can retrieve data faster than asynchronous memory can.

Single Chips and COAST. SRAM comes as either single chips or as chips on a module called **COAST (Cache On A STick)**. Figure 9-3 shows both types. Only COAST is available for pipelined burst synchronous SRAM. A systemboard might be designed to support both asynchronous and synchronous SRAM, but not at the same time. See the documentation for the systemboard to determine which kinds of SRAM the board can support, and then look to see what kind of SRAM is already present on the board, before you buy new SRAM. You might need to replace the existing SRAM on the board in order to upgrade to a larger or faster cache.

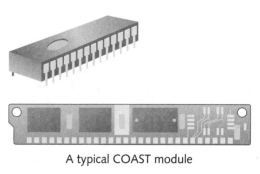

A typical COAST module

Figure 9-3   Single SRAM chip and a COAST module

MEMORY ON EXPANSION BOARDS

Expansion boards can contain both ROM chips and RAM chips. The ROM chips hold the programming for the expansion board, and the RAM chips hold the data that the board is processing. A good example is a video card with video RAM on-board. Video BIOS for the card, stored on ROM chips, processes the data from the CPU and presents it to the monitor. Data is written to the video RAM on the card by the CPU and read from the video RAM by the video BIOS.

HOW MEMORY IS USED BY DOS AND WINDOWS 95

You have just looked at the many different ways memory can be physically installed on the systemboard and expansion boards. The text now addresses the logical organization of memory, which is primarily the function of the OS. The following discussion will focus on how the OS categorizes memory, accesses memory, and uses memory.

Windows 95 uses the same memory organization techniques as the older DOS OS, although Windows 95 has improved the methods of optimizing and allocating this memory, so that most of the DOS limitations are transparent to Windows 95 applications. In contrast, Windows NT takes a totally different approach to the way it organizes memory. Windows NT memory concepts and methods are covered later in this chapter.

The subject of memory management under DOS and Windows 95 can be quite complicated, because the methods have changed as microcomputers have evolved over the past 14 years or so. Like an old house that has been added to and remodeled several times, the present-day design is not as efficient as that of a brand new house. Decisions made by IBM and Microsoft in the early 1980s still significantly affect how memory is used today. Before the limitations caused by early decisions are explained, a few concepts will be introduced.

9

PHYSICAL MEMORY AND MEMORY ADDRESSES

There is a significant difference between the terms "memory" and "memory address." **Memory** is physical microchips that can hold data and programming. It is located on the systemboard or on expansion boards as single chips or modules. Memory can be either ROM or RAM. A **memory address** is a number that the CPU assigns to physical memory to keep track of the memory that it can access. A CPU has a limited number of memory addresses that it can assign to physical memory.

Some physical memory only works when it is assigned a particular address, say a hexadecimal number like C80000. This address is part of its ROM programming; no other address works for it. An example of this kind of memory is a ROM chip on an older video card. Some memory, usually ROM chips on expansion boards, must be assigned one of two—or sometimes three—different addresses. You make the choice by setting jumpers or DIP switches on the board or, in more recent cases, you make the choice when you run an installation program for the board. Most new boards don't have this restriction. Their ROM code can be assigned any values chosen by the OS and/or System BIOS. Plug-and-Play cards are required to use whatever memory addresses are assigned to them.

Most memory, however, doesn't have to be assigned a specific address. The system is free to assign any address it chooses to this physical memory. RAM on the systemboard is an example of memory that can be assigned any address that the CPU chooses. Sometimes the CPU has memory addresses that it cannot assign to any physical memory, because of the limitations of the CPU, the OS, or the applications software. It is possible to have a situation in which plenty of addresses and plenty of memory are available, but the addresses and the memory are useless because the CPU cannot assign the unused addresses to the unused memory.

Another concept that is important to understand is that both RAM and ROM must be assigned memory addresses in order for the CPU to access this memory. System BIOS stored on ROM chips on the systemboard must be assigned addresses by the CPU so that the CPU can access that programming. The assigning of addresses to both RAM and ROM occurs during booting (see Figure 9-4), and is sometimes called **memory mapping**. In Figure 9-4, the memory addresses available to the CPU are listed on the left, and the physical RAM and ROM needing these addresses are on the right. These RAM and ROM chips and modules are located on the systemboard, a video card, and a network card in this example.

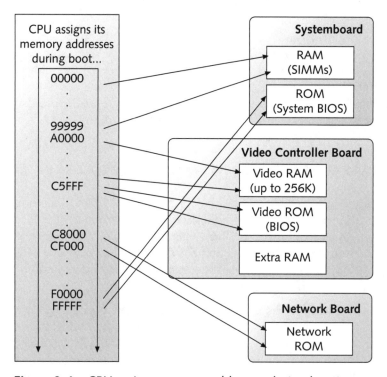

Figure 9-4   CPU assigns memory addresses during booting

Programming stored on ROM chips is not usually copied into RAM, despite what many people believe. It is simply assigned memory addresses by the CPU. These ROM programs become part of the total memory available to the CPU, and do not use up part of total RAM. The addresses assigned to ROM may be used up, however. The RAM memory is still available to be assigned other addresses. Shadowing ROM, which will be discussed later in this chapter, is an exception because the programs stored on ROM are copied to RAM when this ROM is shadowed.

The final concept discussed here is related to the complexity of DOS and Windows 95 memory management. The limitations of using memory in this OS environment are caused not so much by DOS or Windows 95, but by applications written for them using the standards presented to the industry when DOS was first introduced. DOS (and the applications written for it in the 1980s that are still used today) incorporated assumptions that continue to affect memory management. Compared to other operating systems, memory management in DOS and Windows 95 is handicapped because DOS has existed longer than most other operating systems. Therefore, DOS must maintain compatibility with software that has been around for a long time. Also, Microsoft made the commitment with Windows 95 that it, too, would be compatible with older software written for DOS and Windows 3.x using DOS. Probably the greatest limitation of DOS today is this commitment to maintain backward compatibility with older software and hardware.

AREAS OF THE MEMORY MAP

With these concepts in mind, you will now examine several types of memory that the OS manages. To get a clear picture of this memory, consider the memory map shown in Figure 9-5. The first 640K of memory addresses are called **conventional memory** or **base memory**. The memory addresses from 640K up to 1024K are called **upper memory**. Memory above 1024K is called **extended memory**. The first 64K of extended memory are called the **high memory area**. Memory that is accessed in 16K segments, or pages, by way of a window in upper memory is called **expanded memory**. The text will now discuss each kind of memory in detail.

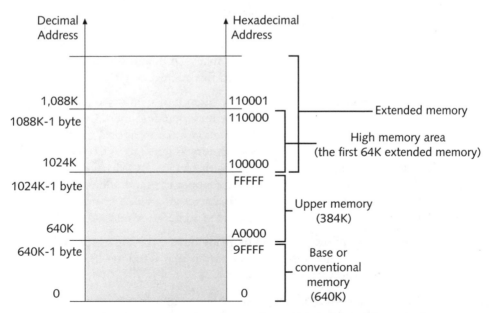

Figure 9-5   Memory map showing the starting and ending addresses of conventional, upper, and extended memories including the high memory area

Conventional Memory

In the early 1980s, when IBM and Microsoft were designing the original PCs, they decided to make 640K of memory addresses available to the user. These 640K of addresses were intended to hold the OS, the applications software, and the data being processed. At that time, 640K of memory addresses were many times more than enough to handle all the applications available. It was assumed that 640K would be plenty to do the job. Today, 640K of memory addresses are inadequate for the following reasons:

- Many applications are very large programs, requiring a considerable number of memory addresses to hold the programs as well as the data.

- Often more than one application is run at a time, each of which requires its own memory area for the program and data. Also, sometimes computers in a network serve more than one user at a time. In the early 1980s, a PC was expected to be used by a single user, operating one application at a time.

- Software is expected to provide a user-friendly graphical user interface or GUI. Graphical user interfaces provide icons, graphics, and windows on a screen, all of which require large amounts of memory.

The problem caused by restricting the number of memory addresses available to the user to only 640K could have been easily solved by simply providing more addresses to the user in future versions of DOS. However, another decision made at the same time ruled this out. The next group of memory addresses, the 384K above conventional memory, called upper memory, were assigned to utility operations for the system. The system requires memory addresses in order to communicate with peripherals. The programs (BIOS on the expansion boards) and data are assigned memory addresses in this upper memory area. For example, the video BIOS and its data are placed in the very first part of upper memory, the area from 640K to 768K. All video ROM written for DOS-based computers assumes that these programs and data are stored in this area. Also, many DOS and Windows 95 applications interact directly with video ROM and RAM in this address range.

Programs almost always expect data to be written into memory directly above the addresses for the program itself, an important fact for understanding memory management. Thus, if a program begins storing its data above its location in conventional memory, eventually it will "hit the ceiling," the beginning of upper memory assigned to video ROM. The major reason that there is a 640K limit for applications is that video ROM begins at 640K. If DOS and Windows 95 allowed applications into these upper memory addresses, all DOS-compatible video ROM would need to be rewritten, many existing video boards would be obsolete, and many DOS applications that access these video addresses would not work.

Later, a reference to this concept will be made during the discussion of how Windows NT uses memory, because this is the primary reason that Windows NT is not backward compatible with older hardware and software.

Applications under DOS and Windows 95 are simply boxed in within the first 640K of addresses. Also, because the OS, BIOS, and TSRs use some conventional memory, not all the

640K of memory is available to applications. Several methods have been proposed and used to expand the 640K limit. These methods involve either freeing up more conventional memory or providing memory outside of conventional memory. The ultimate objective is to provide more memory addresses to applications programs and their data.

Upper Memory

The memory map in Figure 9-5 shows that the memory addresses from 640K up to (but not including) 1024K are called upper memory. In the hexadecimal number system (see Appendix D for an explanation of this system), upper memory begins at A0000 and goes through FFFFF. Video ROM and RAM are stored in the first part of upper memory, hex A0000 through CFFFF (the A, B, and C areas of memory.) BIOS programs for other expansion boards are assigned memory addresses in the remaining portions of upper memory. BIOS on the systemboard (called System BIOS) is assigned the top part of upper memory from F0000 through FFFFF (known as the F area of upper memory). Upper memory often has unassigned addresses, depending on which boards are present in the system. **Memory management** involves gaining access to these unused addresses in upper memory and using them to store device drivers and TSRs.

Figure 9-6 shows that video memory addresses fall between A0000 and CFFFF. For VGA and Super VGA video, the A and B areas are used to hold data being sent to the video card, and the C area is used for the video BIOS.

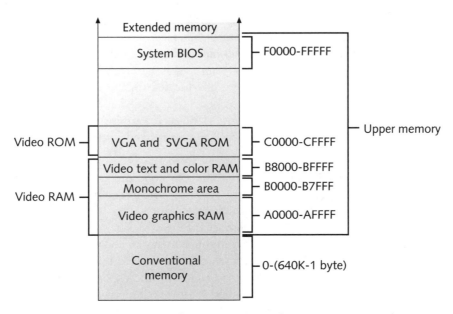

Figure 9-6   Memory map of upper memory showing starting and finishing addresses and video ROM assignments

Extended Memory and the High Memory Area

Memory above 1 MB is called extended memory. The first 64K of extended memory are called the **high memory area**. This high memory area exists because a bug in the programming for the older 286 CPU (the first CPU to use extended memory) produced this small pocket of unused memory addresses. Beginning with DOS 5, the OS capitalized on this bug by storing portions of itself in the high memory area, thus freeing some conventional memory where DOS had been stored. This method of storing part of DOS in the high memory area is called "loading DOS high." You will see how to do this later in the chapter.

Extended memory is actually managed by the OS as a device that is controlled by a device driver. To access extended memory, you need the device driver (called a memory manager) that controls it, and you must use applications that have been written to use the extended memory. DOS 5+ and Windows 3+ both offer memory management software that you will learn to use later in the chapter, and Windows 95 has automated the process. The amount of extended memory you can have on your computer is limited by the size of the CPU. Extended memory addresses can be assigned to memory that is housed on the systemboard or on expansion boards.

Expanded Memory

Few of today's applications software programs use expanded memory, but it is included in our discussion because occasionally you see an older program that needs it, and also because of the similarity between expanded memory and the Windows NT memory model. Figure 9-7 shows that **expanded memory** is memory that falls outside of the linear addressing of memory. **Linear addressing** means that all memory is assigned addresses beginning with 1, and counting up. Expanded memory breaks out of this pattern. When first introduced in the 1980s, expanded memory was always physically located on the memory expansion boards that contained the ROM BIOS that managed it. Expanded memory was made available through a small window called a page frame. A **page frame** is 64K of upper memory that is projected onto expanded memory in 16K segments called pages. It works as follows.

The system requests some expanded memory from the memory manager. The memory manager selects some expanded memory on the expanded memory card, say 32K of it, and assigns 32K of the 64K of upper memory addresses to this memory. The system now has actual physical memory assigned to the memory addresses in upper memory. The expanded memory manager keeps track of what memory on the card is being used, so that, on the next request for expanded memory, it will assign upper memory addresses to a different 32K of physical memory on the card. The same memory addresses in upper memory may be used over and over to access different memory addresses on the expansion board. These 64K of memory addresses may access several hundred kilobytes of physical memory during a single session. The 64K of upper memory addresses become the window that is moved around, over the expanded memory, thus gaining access to it. Applications software must be written in a way that makes use of this expanded memory.

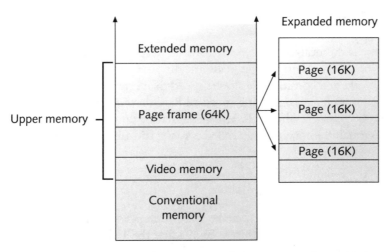

Figure 9-7   Expanded memory map showing page frame and pages

Expanded memory was developed by the Lotus Corporation in conjunction with Intel and Microsoft, because version 2.0 of Lotus 1-2-3 needed more memory. Other applications also make use of expanded memory. The term LIM (Lotus, Intel, Microsoft) memory is sometimes used for expanded memory. Incidentally, later versions of Lotus 1-2-3 don't use expanded memory, but instead use extended memory. Expanded memory is also sometimes called EMS memory (expanded memory specifications).

At one time, in order to have expanded memory for an application that required it, you would install an expanded memory card on your computer. There is, however, an alternative to an expanded memory card. Windows and DOS extended memory manager for 386 CPUs and later CPUs can emulate expanded memory by taking some extended memory and making the application believe that this extended memory is really expanded memory. You can then make either extended memory or emulated expanded memory available to your software, depending on which kind of memory the software requires.

SHADOW RAM OR SHADOWING ROM

Shadowing ROM is a method that copies the System BIOS into RAM (which is then called Shadow RAM) on the systemboard. This RAM on the systemboard is then assigned the memory addresses that would have been assigned to the ROM code. Shadow RAM sometimes speeds up a computer, because RAM chips on the systemboard can be accessed faster than ROM chips on the systemboard. Shadow RAM can usually be disabled in the CMOS setup.

Sometimes older hardware devices and software did not work well with Shadow RAM, and it needed to be disabled. Today, if your computer offers Shadow RAM in CMOS setup, use it, because most of the problems with Shadow RAM have been eliminated with newer devices and updated software.

VIRTUAL MEMORY

Virtual memory is the utilization of some hard drive space such that it acts like memory. The purpose of virtual memory is to increase the amount of memory available. Of course, virtual memory works at a considerably slower speed than real memory, and some hard drive space is used. For example, in comparing speeds, a hard drive may have a data access time of 10 ms (10/1,000,000 second), whereas RAM speed may be 60 ns (60/1,000,000,000 second). Windows stores virtual memory in a file called a **swap file**, discussed later in the chapter.

RAM DRIVES

Creating a **RAM drive** is a method that makes part of memory act like a hard drive. A RAM drive is just the opposite of virtual memory. By loading the TSR that creates a RAM drive, you can make your computer appear to have a second hard drive, say, drive D. This drive D is really an area of memory set aside to act like a drive. A RAM drive was once useful to hold software that had to be loaded many times. Since software is so large today, RAM drives have become impractical. However, RAM drives still have value in a few instances, as you will see later. Since a RAM drive is not a real drive, but memory, nothing is really saved when data is stored to a RAM drive. Data written to a RAM drive is no safer than data still in RAM. Therefore, do not use a RAM drive to "store" data.

Another purpose for a RAM drive is to store programs. Programs are permanently stored on the real hard drive, drive C. On startup, the programs are copied to the RAM drive, drive D. When you are ready to execute the program, the program is loaded from drive D (one part of memory) to another part of memory, where it is executed. (Remember that programs can't be executed from a hard drive, even if the hard drive is not a drive at all, but a RAM drive.) Loading the program from the RAM drive is faster than loading the program from the hard drive, because it is faster to copy from memory to memory than from hard drive to memory.

The only gain in speed is in the loading process. Once the software is loaded, the RAM drive is no longer used. In this case, you gain speed from using a RAM drive if you load software many times in one session, that is, if you go in and out of software packages many times during a session.

With DOS and Windows 3.x, you create a RAM drive by using a DEVICE= command in the CONFIG.SYS file:

```
DEVICE=C:\DOS\RAMDRIVE.SYS 1024
```

The program that produces the RAM drive, RAMDRIVE.SYS, is stored on drive C in the \DOS directory. The 1024 in the command line tells DOS to create a RAM drive that contains 1024K of space. The RAMDRIVE program assigns the next available letter to the drive. Suppose you have a floppy disk drive and a hard drive, which are drives A and C respectively. The RAM drive then becomes drive D and is used just like any other drive in the system.

Summary of How Memory is Managed

In this section, the different kinds of memory and the ways this memory can be used were introduced. Memory management makes the greatest amount of conventional memory available to an application. During the boot process, after ROM and RAM from expansion boards acquire upper memory addresses, any unused addresses in upper memory are used to hold TSRs and device drivers. Also, applications must be able to access extended and expanded memory. The next section will look at the details of how DOS, Windows 3.x, and Windows 95 manage memory effectively.

Managing Memory with DOS or Windows 3.x

Version 3.0 of Windows introduced new memory management software. Newer versions of this memory management software were released with DOS 5.0 and later versions of both DOS and Windows. The TSRs that manage memory above 640K, HIMEM.SYS and EMM386.EXE, are loaded and utilized from the CONFIG.SYS and AUTOEXEC.BAT files at startup. The program file HIMEM.SYS is the device driver for memory above 640K. The program file EMM386.EXE contains the software that loads user TSRs and device drivers into upper memory and makes extended memory emulate expanded memory for those applications that utilize expanded memory. Each in turn will be covered and some examples will be given of how each is used.

Using HIMEM.SYS

HIMEM.SYS is loaded into your system from the CONFIG.SYS file. Recall that the CONFIG.SYS file is executed during booting and loads device drivers that control devices into memory. The CONFIG.SYS file is executed, and drivers are loaded into memory before COMMAND.COM is executed and, in turn, executes AUTOEXEC.BAT. AUTOEXEC.BAT is the DOS batch file that is automatically executed each time you boot the computer. It contains a list of DOS commands that are executed by COMMAND.COM. TSRs can be executed from AUTOEXEC.BAT. Remember that a TSR is a terminate and stay resident program that is loaded into memory and lies dormant until executed by some later action, such as pressing a "hot" key.

HIMEM.SYS is considered a device driver because it manages the device, which in this case, is memory. It is executed by the DEVICE= command in CONFIG.SYS. Figure 9-8 shows an example of a very simple CONFIG.SYS file.

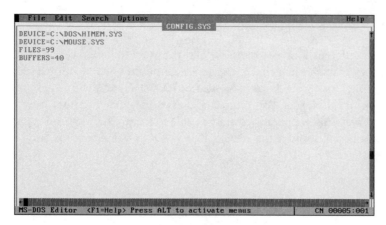

Figure 9-8 CONFIG.SYS set to use memory above 640K

In Figure 9-8, you are shown use of the EDIT command, which provides a full-screen text editor that can be used to create and/or edit a file. To access the CONFIG.SYS file, at a DOS prompt or a Run dialog box in Windows 3.x, enter this command:

```
EDIT C:\CONFIG.SYS
```

To exit from the editor, press the **ALT** key to activate the menus, and choose **EXIT** from the File menu. You will be asked if you want to save the changes that you have made. Respond **YES** to exit the editor with changes saved. After making changes to the CONFIG.SYS file, boot the computer to activate these changes.

The last two lines in Figure 9-8 are usually found in a CONFIG.SYS file. The command FILES=99 tells DOS how many files it can have open at one time. The command BUFFERS=40 tells DOS how many buffers to maintain to transfer data to and from secondary storage devices. A **buffer** is an area of memory that serves as a holding area for incoming or outgoing data. When writing data to a device, DOS fills the holding area with data. When the area is full, DOS writes all the data at once to the device. When reading data, DOS reads enough data from the device to fill the holding area, or buffer, and uses that data up before going back for more. Buffers reduce the need for DOS to return again and again to the device for data; DOS only needs to access the device every now and then for data. Using buffers to speed up reading and writing data is largely outdated nowadays. A more effective method, disk caching, which was described in Chapter 5, is more common. However, many software packages still use buffers, and so DOS must provide these buffers. The more files and buffers that are open, the less free memory is available, so limit the number of buffers to the smallest value that will still accommodate the DOS applications.

The first line in the CONFIG.SYS file is the one that loads the driver HIMEM.SYS into memory. HIMEM.SYS makes memory above 640K available to your applications as extended memory. Remember that you must be using applications software that can utilize extended memory.

The first line in the CONFIG.SYS file also contains the path that tells DOS where to find HIMEM.SYS. The path C:\DOS\ indicates that HIMEM.SYS is stored on drive C in the directory named \DOS. If you are using the Windows version of HIMEM.SYS, your command line looks like this:

```
DEVICE=C:\WINDOWS\HIMEM.SYS
```

You should use the latest version of HIMEM.SYS that you have. Look in the \DOS or \WINDOWS directory, and use the one that is the latest update.

The second line in the CONFIG.SYS file, DEVICE=C:\MOUSE.SYS, tells DOS to load a device driver into memory. The driver that controls a mouse is stored in the file named MOUSE.SYS on drive C in the root directory. The mouse software is a TSR that is loaded into conventional memory; it does not execute until you use the mouse.

USING EMM386.EXE

In DOS and Windows, EMM386.EXE utilizes the memory addresses in upper memory and also emulates expanded memory. To provide the maximum amount of conventional memory to applications, store as many programs as possible in upper memory, using upper memory blocks. To see which programs are loaded into conventional memory and which programs are loaded into upper memory, use a variation of the MEM command with the /C option. Also include the |MORE option to page the results to your screen. Figure 9-9 was produced using this command:

```
MEM /C |MORE
```

In Figure 9-9, the first column shows the programs currently loaded in memory. The second column shows the total amount of memory used by each program. The columns labeled Conventional and Upper Memory show the amount of memory being used by each program in each of these categories. This PC is not making use of upper memory for any of its programs. At the bottom of the screen is the total amount of free conventional memory (578,448 bytes) that is available to new programs to be loaded. Making this value as high as possible is the subject of this section.

```
─                                MS-DOS Prompt                          ▼ ▲
Modules using memory below 1 MB:

 Name        Total      =    Conventional    +    Upper Memory
─────────────────────────────────────────────────────────────────
 MSDOS      15,565  (15K)     15,565  (15K)          0  (0K)
 SETVER        480   (0K)        480   (0K)          0  (0K)
 HIMEM       1,168   (1K)      1,168   (1K)          0  (0K)
 COMMAND     2,928   (3K)      2,928   (3K)          0  (0K)
 win386      6,704   (7K)      6,704   (7K)          0  (0K)
 SMARTDRV   27,488  (27K)     27,488  (27K)          0  (0K)
 WIN         1,520   (1K)      1,520   (1K)          0  (0K)
 SHARE      17,904  (17K)     17,904  (17K)          0  (0K)
 COMMAND     3,056   (3K)      3,056   (3K)          0  (0K)
 Free      578,448 (565K)    578,448 (565K)          0  (0K)

Memory Summary:

 Type of Memory      Total    =    Used    +    Free
─────────────────────────────────────────────────────
 Conventional       655,360        76,912      578,448
 Upper                    0             0            0
 Reserved           131,072       131,072            0
── More ──
┌─┐                                                                   ┌─┐
└┘                                                                    └┘
```

Figure 9-9 MEM report with /C option on a PC not using upper memory

Creating and Using Upper Memory Blocks

Figure 9-10 shows an example of a CONFIG.SYS file that is set to use upper memory addresses. The first line loads the HIMEM.SYS driver. The second line loads the EMM386.EXE file on drive C in the \DOS directory. EMM386.EXE assigns addresses in upper memory to memory made available by the HIMEM.SYS driver. The NOEMS switch at the end of the command line says to DOS, "Do not create any simulated expanded memory." The command to load EMM386.EXE must appear after the command to load HIMEM.SYS in the CONFIG.SYS file.

The command DOS=HIGH,UMB serves two purposes. The one command line can be broken into two commands like this:

        DOS=HIGH

        DOS=UMB

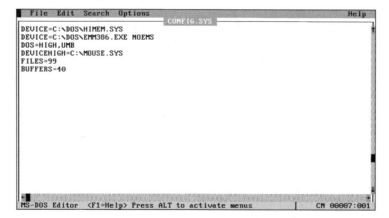

Figure 9-10 CONFIG.SYS set to use upper memory

The DOS=HIGH portion tells DOS to load part of DOS into the high memory area. Remember that the high memory area is the first 64K of extended memory. This memory is usually unused unless we choose to store part of DOS in it with this command line. Including this command in CONFIG.SYS frees some conventional memory that would have been used by DOS. Storing DOS in this high memory area is sometimes called "loading DOS high."

The second part of the command, DOS=UMB, creates upper memory blocks. An **upper memory block (UMB)** is a group of consecutive memory addresses in the upper memory area that is assigned physical memory. DOS identifies blocks that are not being used by expansion boards, and the memory manager makes these blocks available for use. This command, DOS=UMB, enables DOS to access these upper memory blocks. UMBs are put to use in three ways:

- Using the DEVICEHIGH= command in CONFIG.SYS
- Using the LOADHIGH command in AUTOEXEC.BAT
- Using the LOADHIGH command at the DOS prompt

The next line in the CONFIG.SYS file in Figure 9-10 uses a UMB. The command DEVICEHIGH=C:\MOUSE.SYS tells DOS to load the mouse device driver into one of the upper memory blocks created and made available by the previous three lines. DOS loads a driver into the largest unused upper memory block. This process of loading a TSR into upper memory addresses is called **loading high**.

9

Loading Device Drivers High

Using the DEVICEHIGH= command in CONFIG.SYS, rather than the DEVICE= command, causes the TSR to load high. DOS stores these drivers in UMBs using the largest UMB first, then the next largest, and so on until all are loaded. Therefore, to make sure there is enough room to hold them all in upper memory, order the DEVICEHIGH= command lines in CONFIG.SYS so that the largest drivers are loaded first. To determine the size of a driver, begin by simply looking at the size of the file. However, other factors also affect the size of a UMB needed for a driver.

A device driver needs some space immediately above it to hold its data. In addition, sometimes when the program first executes, it requires some extra room to initialize itself. This space may be released later, but it is still required in order to execute the driver. The largest amount of memory that a driver needs to initialize itself and to hold its data is called the maximum size or the **load size**. It is almost always a little larger than the size of the program file. Since you don't always accurately predict what this maximum size will be, you can understand why a device driver might fail to load into upper memory even when the UMB is larger than the file size. If you include the DEVICEHIGH= command in CONFIG.SYS, but later discover that the device driver is still in conventional memory and did not load high, DOS did not find a UMB large enough for it.

You can determine the amount of memory a device driver allocates for itself and its data by using an option to the DOS MEM command:

```
MEM /M filename
```

The filename is the name of the device driver without the file extension. Later, this chapter will examine methods to determine just where in upper memory a driver is loaded, and what to do if things go wrong.

Loading TSRs High

All device drivers are TSRs, but not all TSRs are device drivers. You can load TSRs that are not device drivers into upper memory either from AUTOEXEC.BAT or from the DOS prompt. In either case, the command is LOADHIGH followed by the path and name of the program file.

For example, suppose that you want to print some screen captures like the screen capture that was used to produce Figure 9-10. While using DOS, you can press the Printscreen key to get a printout of the screen; while using Windows 3.x, use the Printscreen key to copy the contents of a screen into the clipboard, and print it using an applications software program such as Paint Brush. Sometimes the printout, however, looks very rough, is hard to read, and cannot easily be saved to a file. The screen capture in Figure 9-10 was created and printed with a software package called Pizazz Plus. Pizazz Plus is a TSR. It is loaded into memory by typing C:\PZP\PZP at the C prompt. This command tells DOS the name of the program file, PZP, and the path to it, drive C, \PZP directory. The program loads into conventional memory and immediately returns to the C prompt. It does not execute at the time it is loaded; it remains dormant until you press the Printscreen key.

You can then execute any software package and work until you are ready to use the screen capture software. When you have a screen ready to print, press the **Printscreen** key, the hot key for this TSR. Rather than printing the screen, the Printscreen key brings up the Pizazz menu, and you can save the screen to a file for printing later. When you exit from the Pizazz menu, DOS returns you to the software you are executing, and you pick up where you left off.

The Pizazz program needs conventional memory, and a problem arises when you are running other software that requires a lot of conventional memory. The software might not run at all, might run unacceptably slowly, or might give errors. You can solve this problem by storing the Pizazz program in upper memory. You do this by using the following command at the C prompt:

```
C:\> LOADHIGH C:\PZP\PZP
```

The command line can be shortened by replacing LOADHIGH with the shorter version, LH:

```
C:\>LH C:\PZP/PZP
```

The program is loaded into the largest UMB available and does not use up more precious conventional memory. Note that before the LOADHIGH command will work, these three lines must be added to CONFIG.SYS and executed by booting the computer:

```
DEVICE=C:\DOS\HIMEM.SYS

DEVICE=C:\DOS\EMM386.EXE NOEMS

DOS=UMB
```

If you intend to use the Pizazz software often, you can make it load into upper memory every time you boot the computer. To do this, the previous LH line is included in the AUTOEXEC.BAT file without any changes.

Figure 9-11 shows an AUTOEXEC.BAT file that loads the Pizazz software every time the computer boots. Note that the path to the PZP program must be included in the last command line, because \PZP is not included in the earlier PATH command.

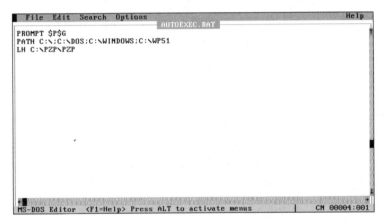

Figure 9-11   AUTOEXEC.BAT loading a TSR high

When TSRs are loaded high, two things can go wrong. Either the TSR might not work from upper memory, causing problems during execution, or there might not be enough room in upper memory for the program and its data. If the program causes the computer to hang when you attempt to run it, or if it simply refuses to work correctly, remove it from upper memory.

Simulating Expanded Memory

You can use HIMEM.SYS together with EMM386.EXE to simulate expanded memory. Some extended memory that is being managed by this memory management software can be allocated to "act" like expanded memory for software that requires it.

In Figure 9-12, the parameter 1024 RAM replaces the NOEMS parameter of Figure 9-10. By adding this parameter, you still have upper memory blocks available, but you also have told DOS to make 1024K of extended memory simulate expanded memory. Use this parameter when you are running software that can use expanded memory, instead of installing an expanded memory card. Consult the manual for the software that will use the expanded memory, in order to determine how much simulated expanded memory to allocate. Memory that simulates expanded memory is no longer available for extended memory applications.

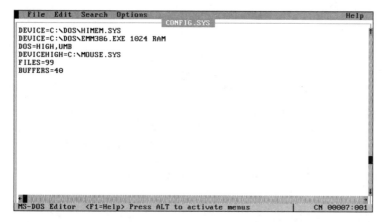

```
  File  Edit  Search  Options                                    Help
                            CONFIG.SYS
DEVICE=C:\DOS\HIMEM.SYS
DEVICE=C:\DOS\EMM386.EXE 1024 RAM
DOS=HIGH,UMB
DEVICEHIGH=C:\MOUSE.SYS
FILES=99
BUFFERS=40




MS-DOS Editor   <F1=Help> Press ALT to activate menus          CN 00007:001
```

Figure 9-12   CONFIG.SYS set to simulate expanded memory

Memory Reports Using the MEM Command

The DOS MEM command with the appropriate parameters shows exactly where in upper memory the UMBs are located, and what software has been assigned addresses in upper memory. In its simplest form, the MEM command looks like Figure 9-13. You will look at several examples of memory reports at different stages of memory management.

```
                          MS-DOS Prompt

C:\>mem

Memory Type         Total  =  Used  +  Free
--------------      -----     -----    -----
Conventional         640K      75K     565K
Upper                  0K       0K       0K
Reserved             128K     128K       0K
Extended (XMS)     3,328K   2,304K   1,024K
                   ------   ------   ------
Total memory       4,096K   2,507K   1,589K

Total under 1 MB     640K      75K     565K

Total Expanded (EMS)            1,024K (1,048,576 bytes)
Free Expanded (EMS)             1,024K (1,048,576 bytes)

Largest executable program size    565K (578,432 bytes)
Largest free upper memory block      0K     (0 bytes)
MS-DOS is resident in the high memory area.

C:\>
```

Figure 9-13   MEM report without UMBs available

In Figure 9-13, upper memory blocks are not being used, and the total memory under 1 MB is reported to be only 640K. In Figure 9-9, you saw the same PC with no changes to memory management. The MEM command in Figure 9-9 includes the /C option:

```
MEM /C |MORE
```

which shows a more complete report. You see several programs using conventional memory, and no use being made of the upper memory area.

To get a printed version of this report, use this command:

```
C:\> MEM/ C >PRN
```

You can read the report one screen at a time using this command:

```
C:\> MEM/ C   MORE
```

In Figure 9-14, you can see how this upper memory area is helping to free some conventional memory after you have added the commands to CONFIG.SYS and AUTOEXEC.BAT to make use of upper memory. In Figure 9-15, the EMM386.EXE program was loaded from CONFIG.SYS, as in Figure 9-10, and two TRSs, SMARTDRV.EXE and SHARE.EXE, were loaded high from AUTOEXEC.BAT. Note that upper memory is now recognized by the system.

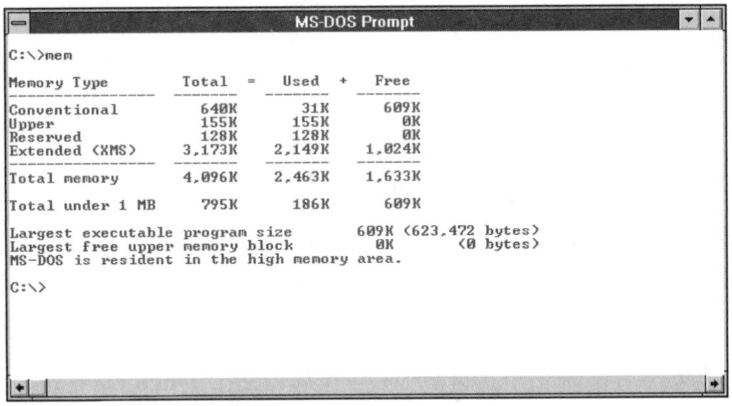

9

```
C:\>mem

Memory Type        Total   =   Used  +   Free
--------------     ------      ------    ------
Conventional        640K         31K      609K
Upper               155K        155K        0K
Reserved            128K        128K        0K
Extended (XMS)    3,173K      2,149K    1,024K
--------------     ------      ------    ------
Total memory      4,096K      2,463K    1,633K

Total under 1 MB    795K        186K      609K

Largest executable program size       609K (623,472 bytes)
Largest free upper memory block         0K      (0 bytes)
MS-DOS is resident in the high memory area.

C:\>
```

Figure 9-14   MEM report on a PC using upper memory

```
┌─────────────────────────── MS-DOS Prompt ──────────────────── ▼ ▲ ┐
│                                                                    │
│ Modules using memory below 1 MB:                                   │
│                                                                    │
│ Name         Total       =   Conventional   +  Upper Memory        │
│ ───────────────────────────────────────────────────────────       │
│ MSDOS       15,581  (15K)    15,581  (15K)       0     (0K)         │
│ SETVER         480   (0K)       480   (0K)       0     (0K)         │
│ HIMEM        1,168   (1K)     1,168   (1K)       0     (0K)         │
│ EMM386       3,120   (3K)     3,120   (3K)       0     (0K)         │
│ COMMAND      2,928   (3K)     2,928   (3K)       0     (0K)         │
│ win386     117,088 (114K)     3,920   (4K)  113,168  (111K)         │
│ WIN          1,520   (1K)     1,520   (1K)       0     (0K)         │
│ COMMAND      3,056   (3K)     3,056   (3K)       0     (0K)         │
│ SMARTDRV    27,488  (27K)         0   (0K)   27,488   (27K)         │
│ SHARE       17,904  (17K)         0   (0K)   17,904   (17K)         │
│ Free       623,488 (609K)   623,488 (609K)       0     (0K)         │
│                                                                    │
│ Memory Summary:                                                    │
│                                                                    │
│ Type of Memory      Total   =   Used    +   Free                   │
│ ───────────────────────────────────────────────────               │
│ Conventional       655,360      31,872     623,488                 │
│ Upper              158,560     158,560           0                 │
│ -- More --                                                         │
│ ◄                                                              ►   │
└────────────────────────────────────────────────────────────────────┘
```

Figure 9-15   MEM/C report on a PC using upper memory

Compare the amount of extended memory available in Figure 9-9 to that in Figure 9-15. You see that the amount of extended memory was reduced when upper memory increased, but total memory remained the same at 4,096K. This is because the amount of physical memory remains the same. What changes is the way DOS allocates memory addresses to this fixed amount of physical memory.

In comparing Figure 9-9 with Figure 9-15, you see some interesting differences. EMM386 is requiring some memory in Figure 9-15, but was not used in Figure 9-9 since it had been omitted from CONFIG.SYS commands. Total conventional memory available for software increased from 578,448 in Figure 9-9 to 623,488 in Figure 9-15.

Also note the way WIN386 is using memory in both figures. In Figure 9-9, 6,704 bytes were being used when no upper memory blocks were available, but in Figure 9-15, WIN386 is using 117,088 bytes of memory. To see how this memory is being allocated, you use this command:

```
MEM /M WIN386
```

Figure 9-16 shows the results. Notice that all the upper memory area used by WIN386 is being used to store its data. WIN386 is managing virtual memory for Windows and is able to decide to use upper memory area if it is available.

Using MemMaker with DOS 6+

DOS 6.0 and later versions offer an automatic way to manage upper and extended memory. MemMaker edits your CONFIG.SYS and AUTOEXEC.BAT files for you, placing the same commands in these files that were just discussed. It might edit an existing EMM386.EXE command line and change DEVICE= commands to DEVICEHIGH= commands. If it determines that a TSR loaded from AUTOEXEC.BAT can be loaded high, it adds the LH parameter to the beginning of the command line.

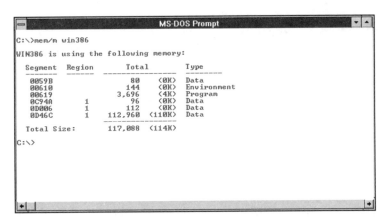

Figure 9-16   How WIN386 is using memory

To execute MemMaker, type **MEMMAKER** at the C prompt. MemMaker will ask you some questions about your system and then tell you that it is ready to reboot. During the boot process MemMaker monitors the loading of device drivers and other TSRs. After the boot process is complete, it makes some calculations to decide the best way to configure memory, and then edits the CONFIG.SYS and AUTOEXEC.BAT files. Sometimes it will edit the Windows SYSTEM.INI file. Again, it will ask you to reboot the machine. After this reboot, it will ask if you saw any error messages during the boot process, and if your machine appears to be working well. If you say "Yes," then MemMaker is finished.

MemMaker saves the original files before it edits them. AUTOEXEC.BAT is saved as AUTOEXEC.UMB, CONFIG.SYS is saved as CONFIG.UMB, and SYSTEM.INI is saved as SYSTEM.UMB. To return to these original files, type this command:

```
C:\> MEMMAKER /UNDO
```

The original copies of AUTOEXEC.BAT, CONFIG.SYS, and SYSTEM.INI will be restored. Also, MemMaker offers a custom configuration. During this configuration, it will ask you what kind of video you are using. If you are not using a monochrome monitor, then it will use the B range of memory addresses for upper memory blocks.

If you have DOS 6+, you might want to compare your computer's performance before and after MemMaker has configured memory. Save the original CONFIG.SYS and AUTOEXEC.BAT files yourself, and compare the original and edited versions after MemMaker is finished. You might see some settings you might like to change in MemMaker's edited files; if so, you can make changes to the edited files yourself. It might take several iterations of MemMaker to completely optimize memory.

MANAGING MEMORY WITH WINDOWS 3.X

Because Windows 3.x runs as an operating environment on top of DOS, DOS performs most of the core memory management. However, Windows 3.x has some memory management functions of its own. A few of them are discussed next.

SWAP FILES AND VIRTUAL MEMORY

Swapping is the method of freeing some memory by moving data temporarily to the hard drive into files called **swap files**. Most applications software programs use some form of swapping. There are three ways that Windows 3.x uses swap files.

- Temporary files
- Applications swap files
- Swap files used to create virtual memory

Temporary files

Used by applications software programs, these files are created at will by Windows applications and may or may not be deleted when the application is unloaded. The files are created in the directory specified by the TEMP variable in AUTOEXEC.BAT.

The SET command assigns a value to a **system variable,** which is a variable that has been given a name and a value and then becomes available to the OS, Windows, and to the applications software program. In AUTOEXEC.BAT, if the command is written:

```
SET TEMP=C:\WINDOWS\TEMP
```

interpret this command to mean that (1) the name of the system variable is TEMP, and (2) the value assigned to TEMP is "C:\WINDOWS\TEMP." Windows and applications software later use the value as the path they will use to store their temporary files.

Applications Swap Files

Windows 3.x is able to provide a multitasking environment where more than one applications software program can run at a time, because Windows 3.x can temporarily move data in and out of memory into these applications swap files. Inactive applications and their data can be moved to a swap file in the TEMP directory so that Windows can give resources to the currently active application. Do not delete these swap files in the TEMP directory while Windows is running, because an application that is currently loaded and waiting in the background might be dependent on them.

Swap Files Used to Create Virtual Memory

Windows 3.x can run in two modes: standard mode and 386 enhanced mode. Standard mode was used on older computers before the 386 PC became available. Windows 3.x today most often runs in 386 enhanced mode, requiring that HIMEM.SYS be executed from the CONFIG.SYS file before Windows can load. In 386 enhanced mode, Windows can provide virtual memory through swap files. The virtual memory can be contained in either a temporary swap file named WIN386.SWP or in a permanent swap file named 386SPART.PAR. Both files are hidden system files on the hard drive and should not be deleted. The files are stored in the root directory of the same drive that holds SYSTEM.INI, although you can change the location by an entry in SYSTEM.INI.

Optimizing Windows with the Swap File.   You can change the size and type of the virtual memory swap file and affect the overall performance of Windows. If Windows cannot find enough space on the hard drive, it might not be able to create a swap file at all. If this is the case, Windows performance decreases significantly. For Windows 3.x, the optimum choice for a swap file is a permanent swap file set to the size that best matches the amount of RAM on the system.

You want to make the swap file large enough so that Windows does not slow down because of a memory shortage, but not so large as to cause Windows to use the swap file when it could have been using faster RAM. If you have less than 8 MB of RAM, use a large swap file, but no more than two or three times the size of memory. If you have 24–32 MB of RAM or more, decrease the proportional size of the swap file to about the same number of megabites as the RAM you have. By decreasing the size of the swap file, you encourage Windows to use the memory rather than the swap file.

 Because the swap file is stored on secondary storage, virtual memory is slower than the real memory in RAM. Because Windows sometimes uses the swap file even when it has RAM available, here's a trick that might speed up a system: Put the swap file on a RAM drive. By so doing, you prevent the system from slowing down when Windows uses the hard drive for virtual memory.

There are two reasons a swap file should be a permanent swap file rather than a temporary one. A permanent swap file is always made up of contiguous clusters of memory, whereas a temporary swap file can become fragmented over time, increasing access time. The time it takes to increase and decrease the size of the temporary swap file also slows down access time. One disadvantage of using a permanent swap file is that the storage space devoted to the swap file is not available for other applications, even when Windows is not running.

How to Change the Swap File. First determine what kind of swap file you have and, if it's a permanent file, determine what size it is. If you need to change the swap file from temporary to permanent, make some preparations before making the changes. Follow these directions to change the type and size of the swap file.

1. To view the type and size of the swap file on your PC, open the **Main** group of Program Manager and open **Control Panel**.

2. Double-click **386 Enhanced program** and then click **Virtual Memory**. The Virtual Memory dialog box appears, as in Figure 9-17.

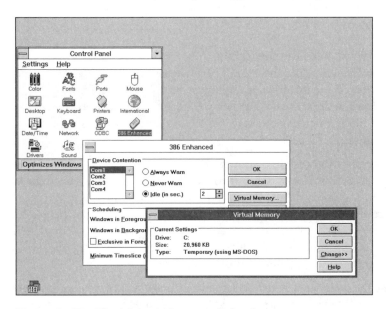

Figure 9-17   The Virtual Memory dialog box

3. If the swap file is temporary and you want to make it permanent, first exit this dialog box and then defragment your hard drive to make the most space available for the permanent swap file.

4. Return to the Virtual Memory dialog box and click **Change** to change the settings. The dialog box shown in Figure 9-18 displays, giving you the option to change the swap file to a permanent one, and also showing what Windows recommends as the file size. Also note that you can change the drive where the swap file will be stored. Click **OK** to make the change.

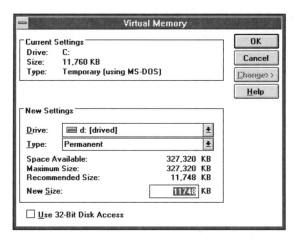

Figure 9-18   Settings to convert the swap file from temporary to permanent

Figure 9-19   Creating a permanent swap file

9

5. The screen in Figure 9-19 then appears telling you that the change was made. You are then instructed to allow Windows to reboot the PC to make the change permanent.

6. If you access the Virtual Memory dialog box with a permanent swap file as the current type, Windows recommends that you leave the file as type Permanent. This is the case in Figure 9-20, where the current setting is Permanent and the recommended new setting is also Permanent.

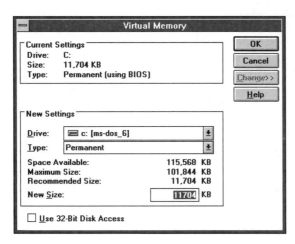

Figure 9-20   Windows recommends that the swap file remain permanent

MANAGING MEMORY WITH WINDOWS 95

Memory management has not changed fundamentally with Windows 95; memory is still organized as conventional, upper, extended, and expanded. However, Windows 95 has made some improvements in the allocation of this memory and in the automation of the process that make it easier for us to manage memory. One of the major improvements takes us to a new level of 32-bit protected mode drivers. These 32-bit drivers are automatically loaded into extended memory (not conventional or upper memory) when Windows 95 loads, thus eliminating the need for DEVICE= entries in CONFIG.SYS.

Software written with 32-bit code is generally faster and takes up more memory than older software written in 16-bit code. Windows 95 offers many drivers written in 32-bit code that can replace older 16-bit drivers written for DOS. DOS 16-bit drivers run in **real mode**, a processing mode in which programs can access memory addresses of other programs. For Windows 95 to use older 16-bit drivers, it must provide a DOS real mode environment for these drivers to operate in, by using entries in CONFIG.SYS and AUTOEXEC.BAT files that normally are not needed with Windows 95. In **protected mode**, the OS limits the program to its own memory addresses and does not allow it access to another program's memory area. New 32-bit drivers are sometimes called **virtual device drivers** or **VxD drivers**; they have .VXD or .386 file extensions and operate in this protected mode.

Another improvement in Windows 95 is that it frees up more of conventional and upper memory, because it no longer uses SMARTDRV.EXE or SHARE.EXE, two TSRs that required a lot of memory below 1 MB. SMARTDRV.EXE, a 16-bit driver to manage disk caching, was replaced by 32-bit disk caching that is built into Windows 95. The 16-bit SHARE.EXE was replaced by the 32-bit VSHARE.386, a part of VMM32.EXE that is automatically loaded when Windows 95 starts.

If you are fortunate enough to be using all 32-bit drivers and applications in a Windows 95 environment, memory management requires no work on your part. Just let Windows 95 automate the process for you. However, if you are running older 16-bit applications under Windows 95, you might need to provide some of the same memory management aids needed by DOS. Windows 95 does not need AUTOEXEC.BAT or CONFIG.SYS files to run. However, if these files are present when Windows 95 boots, Windows 95 processes them just as DOS did.

During the boot process, HIMEM.SYS is automatically loaded by IO.SYS. Without it, Windows 95 will not load. However, if you need to use CONFIG.SYS entries that include EMM386.EXE, then you must include the entry for HIMEM.SYS as well, because IO.SYS does not load HIMEM.SYS until after CONFIG.SYS is completed. For EMM386.EXE to load, it must find HIMEM.SYS already loaded. If you need to load a 16-bit device driver into a UMB, then you must have a CONFIG.SYS file with these lines in it:

```
DEVICE=HIMEM.SYS
DEVICE=EMM386.EXE NOEMS
DOS=HIGH,UMB
```

However, if you are using all 32-bit drivers, you don't even need the CONFIG.SYS file. Windows 95 is much improved because it uses 32-bit drivers and software, but it is also backward compatible with 16-bit drivers and software that were written for DOS and Windows 3.x. When you are using these older programs, you have the same kinds of memory problems and require the same solutions as you did with DOS. All the commands for CONFIG.SYS and AUTOEXEC.BAT and the MEM command discussed earlier apply under Windows 95 using 16-bit drivers and older 16-bit software.

The file extension might help you to figure out whether you are using a 16-bit driver or a 32-bit driver to support a hardware device, but there is one way you can know for certain. Windows 3.x and DOS do not support 32-bit drivers, so if the driver works under DOS, you are using a 16-bit driver.

During the Windows 95 installation, Windows 95 setup tries to substitute 32-bit drivers for all 16-bit drivers it finds in use, and, if it can, to eliminate the CONFIG.SYS file altogether. However, if it can't substitute a 32-bit driver for the older 16-bit driver present, it puts (or keeps) the proper lines in the CONFIG.SYS file and sets itself up to use the older driver. More about this in Chapter 11.

When running DOS applications under Windows 95, a DOS-like environment must be provided to the application. For example, to provide a DOS environment for the DOS program EDIT.COM on a PC running Windows 95, go to Explorer and find the file EDIT.COM in the \Windows\Command directory. Right-click on the filename and select **Properties** from the drop-down menu that appears. Figure 9-21 displays, showing the Properties sheet for a DOS application. The entries on this sheet make up the **PIF (program information file)** for this application, which describes the environment the DOS program uses. Click on the **Memory** tab, and Figure 9-22 appears, listing the memory options available. From the Memory tab, you can specify how much conventional, expanded, and extended memory will be made available to the application, or leave the settings at Auto, which allows the application to use whatever is available. The last entry on the tab is MS-DOS protected mode (DPMI) memory. This entry assigns the amount of protected-mode memory allowed the application. If you check Protected in the Conventional memory frame, the OS will protect memory used by the system from the application.

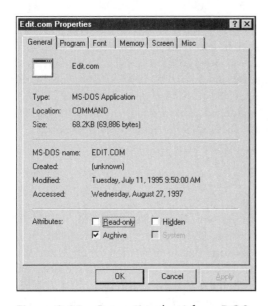

Figure 9-21 Properties sheet for a DOS application

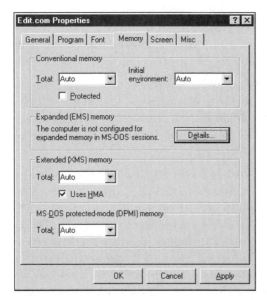

Figure 9-22 Setting up memory for a DOS application running under Windows 95

Many DOS applications run with the default Auto settings with no problems. However, sometimes a DOS application has a problem with being given too much memory. Limit the amount of memory given the application using the Properties sheet shown in Figure 9-22.

WINDOWS 95 SWAP FILE

Windows 95 automates the managing of virtual memory for you. Although you can override the automation, there is little reason to do so. To see what options Windows 95 offers, click **Start**, **Settings**, **Control Panel**, then select **System** and select the **Performance** tab. A window similar to Figure 9-23 appears. Click **Virtual Memory**, and the dialog box in Figure 9-24 displays. Unless you have a very good reason to do otherwise, check **Let Windows manage my virtual memory settings**.

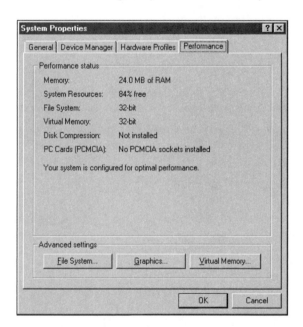

Figure 9-23   System Properties Performance box in Windows 95

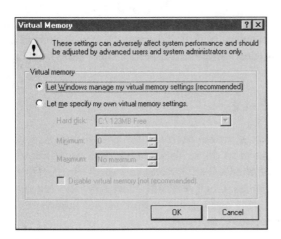

Figure 9-24   Options for managing virtual memory
in Windows 95

THE ULTIMATE SOLUTION: WINDOWS NT

Memory managment under Windows NT, compared to memory management under DOS and Windows 95, is like traveling on a freeway rather than an obstacle course. The memory mapping for Windows NT is one continuous, linear, 32-bit address space that allows each program and driver using Windows NT access to any part of this memory. Obstacles, out of the way!

Although it is not the intent of this chapter to delve too deeply into managing Windows NT memory, because of the complexity of dealing with conventional, upper, extended, and expanded memory, you can appreciate the ultimate solution to memory management on PCs—Windows NT.

The Windows NT memory management model is shown in Figure 9-25. Earlier in the chapter it was explained that expanded memory is accessed, by page frames, from upper memory and mapped onto the expanded memory card. The application thought it had addresses in upper memory stored in RAM on the systemboard, when it really had only a window from upper memory mapped onto memory on the expansion board. You can compare this process to the memory management model for Windows NT.

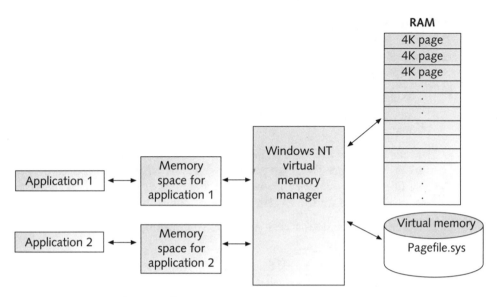

Figure 9-25 Windows NT memory management

Figure 9-25 shows the object-oriented approach to memory management. The application or device driver only says, "I want memory." It has no right to say which physical memory or which memory addresses it wants, or even the range of addresses that it wants to fall within. It can only say to Windows NT, "I want memory." Windows NT uses its Virtual Memory Manager to interface between the application or driver and the physical and virtual memory that it controls. Memory is allocated in 4K segments called **pages**. Applications and devices that are written for Windows NT only know how many pages they have. The virtual manager takes care of the rest. It is free to store these pages in RAM or on the hard drive in the swap file named Pagefile.sys. The only time an application would ever expect to run out of memory is when Pagefile.sys and RAM are full. Memory is only limited by the amount of physical memory available and the number of memory addresses that Windows NT can use, which is 4 GB.

With Windows NT, struggles with "out of memory" errors should be a thing of the past.

MEMORY TROUBLESHOOTING GUIDELINES

This section describes what to do when things go wrong with memory management, and how to prevent potential errors.

When a TSR Will Not Load High. Sometimes after instructing DOS to load a TSR high, using a MEM report will show you that the load high instruction did not work. You included the DEVICE=HIMEM.SYS, the DEVICE=EMM386.EXE, and the DOS=UMB command lines in the CONFIG.SYS file, and you attempted to load a TSR high, using either the DEVICEHIGH= command in CONFIG.SYS or the LOADHIGH command in AUTOEXEC.BAT. But, when you get a MEM/C report, you discover that the TSR is still in conventional memory. Probably, the problem is either that the TSR did not have enough space in the UMB assigned to it, or that there were no more UMBs available for it. Do these things:

1. Check that all command lines in CONFIG.SYS and AUTOEXEC.BAT are correct.

2. Make sure that the DEVICEHIGH= commands in CONFIG.SYS are ordered so that the larger TSRs are placed first, in the larger UMBs. Still, they might not all fit in upper memory. By putting the largest ones possible in upper memory, you have freed up the largest amount of conventional memory possible.

3. MEMMAKER does a very good job of choosing the best order of loading TSRs. Try it.

4. Some TSRs do not work from upper memory, so test them before assuming that all is well.

When Devices Do Not Work or the System Hangs. When DOS creates a UMB, DOS might "think" that no expansion board is using these memory addresses, when in fact they are being used by a card. If a TSR is loaded into this UMB, a memory conflict occurs. A memory conflict occurs when more than one program or their data have been assigned the same memory addresses. Memory conflicts can cause programs or devices to give errors, or can cause the computer to "lock up" and refuse to function.

There are two kinds of memory conflicts that cause a device to stop working or cause the system to hang:

1. Two expansion boards are using the same upper memory addresses

2. DOS has created and is using a UMB in the same memory addresses used by an expansion board

Two Expansion Boards Using the Same Upper Memory Addresses. You have a scanner card installed to drive your scanner, and it works well. But when you install a network card in this computer, the scanner refuses to work, and the network does not work properly. It is likely that both the network card and the scanner card are using the same upper memory addresses. Consider the following approaches:

1. Some expansion boards have DIP switches or jumpers that allow you to substitute one set of memory addresses for another.

2. You might change the memory addresses by adding a parameter to the command line that loads the device driver for the expansion board.

3. When two devices use the same memory addresses, you can often change one to an alternate set of memory addresses. If neither device accepts an alternate address, then you cannot install the two devices on the same computer. To find out which memory addresses are assigned to the devices, whether an alternate set of memory addresses is available, and how to access it, consult the documentation for the device or the software that drives the device. It is very important to keep the hardware and software documentation in a place where you can find it. Without the documentation, your only recourse is to call technical support for the software or hardware.

 When reading the documentation, you will find that most addresses are given in hex rather than decimal form. (See Appendix D for an explanation of the hex number system.) Sometimes the memory addresses are written without the last hexadecimal numeral. For example, if the documentation says that the device uses C800 through CFFF, interpret this to mean that the upper memory address range is C8000 through CFFFF. Once you have discovered that the two devices use the same memory addresses, find out if one can use alternate addresses. If so, your problem is solved.

When UMBs and Expansion Boards Conflict. When DOS creates a UMB, it assigns memory addresses that it "thinks" are not being used by devices. However, some devices don't tell DOS what memory addresses they are using until the device is activated after booting. This delay causes DOS to think that the memory addresses assigned to a device are available, and DOS creates and loads a TSR into the UMB. If this conflict happens, the system might hang, the TSR might not work properly, and/or the device might not work properly. Try the following approach:

1. Read the documentation that came with the device to find out which memory addresses it is using. With this information, you can change the EMM386.EXE so that this range of addresses is not used.

2. Use the Exclude option to the EMM386.EXE command line. The last numeral in the hex address is not included in the command line. For example, suppose you read from the documentation that came with the device that it uses addresses CC000–CFFFF. To exclude these addresses from the addresses used by UMBs, use this command line:

```
DEVICE=C:\DOS\EMM386.EXE NOEMS X = CC00 - CFFF
```

3. Reboot your computer to activate the change. The memory conflict problem should then be solved.

Problems with Plug-and-Play are covered in Chapter 11.

9

UPGRADING MEMORY

Upgrading memory means to add more RAM to a computer. Many computers, when first purchased, have empty slots on the systemboard, allowing you to add SIMMs to increase the amount of RAM. If all the slots are full, sometimes you can take out small-capacity SIMMs and replace them with larger-capacity SIMMs. When you add more memory to your computer, ask yourself these questions:

- How much memory do I need?

- How much memory can my computer physically accommodate?

- What increments of memory does my systemboard support?

- How much additional memory is cost effective?

- What kind of memory can fit on my systemboard?

- What memory is compatible with the memory I already have installed?

With the demands today's software places on memory, the answer to the first question is probably, "All I can get." Windows 95 needs from 24 MB to 32 MB of memory. The minimum requirement is 8 MB, although performance will be slow with this little memory because the system is forced to write working files to the slower hard drive as virtual memory instead of using the much faster RAM.

Adding more than 32 MB of memory to improve a slow-performing PC will probably not help. Perhaps what you might really need is a more powerful CPU, or a faster hard drive or systemboard.

HOW MUCH MEMORY CAN FIT ON THE SYSTEMBOARD?

To determine how much memory your computer can physically hold, read the documentation that comes with your computer. For example, one manual for a 486 computer explains that the systemboard can support up to 32 MB of memory, but there are only nine possible memory configurations. A table that describes these configurations might look like Table 9-1.

Table 9-1 shows that this systemboard has two banks. A **bank** is a location on the systemboard that contains slots for memory modules. On this systemboard, each bank can hold 256K, 1 MB, or 4 MB of memory. The first bank always has some memory in it, but the second bank might or might not contain memory. This computer, which is typical of many older 486 boards, uses SIMMs on the systemboard. Recall that a SIMM is a small miniboard that contains memory chips. The SIMMs are inserted into the slots in a bank. This computer can support these sizes: 256K, 1 MB, and 4 MB.

Table 9-1 Memory Configuration of a 486 Systemboard

SIMM Size in Bank 1	SIMM Size in Bank 2	Total RAM on Systemboard
256K	0	1 MB
256K	256K	2 MB
1 MB	0	4 MB
1 MB	256K	5 MB
1 MB	1MB	8 MB
4 MB	0	16 MB
4 MB	256K	17 MB
4 MB	1MB	20 MB
4 MB	4MB	32 MB

To determine how many slots are in one bank, you must know the computer's bus size. This 486 computer uses a 32-bit bus. When bits travel down a circuit on the systemboard to the bank to be stored in RAM, they are moving 32 bits abreast. The bank must receive 32 bits at a time to work with this bus. This systemboard uses 30-pin SIMMs. Each 30-pin SIMM receives one 8-bit byte at a time. Figure 9-26 shows that the 32-bit bus directs 8 bits to each of four SIMMs in the bank. The bank must contain four SIMMs to receive these 32 bits. Since each SIMM receives an equal part of the 4 bytes traveling down the circuit, all SIMMs within one bank must store the same amount of bytes.

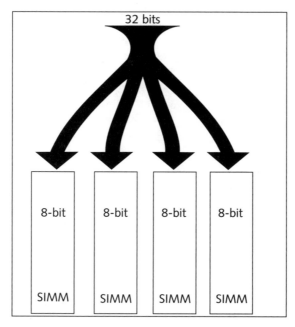

Figure 9-26 One bank on a 486 systemboard that uses a 32-bit bus and 8-bit, 30-pin SIMMs

In Table 9-1, you see in the first row of the table that bank 1 contains 256K SIMMs, and bank 2 is empty. Bank 1 contains four slots, each of which must contain a SIMM in order to accommodate the 32-bit bus. Hence, the amount of memory is 4 $\times$ 256K or 1 MB of memory. In the second row of the table, each bank contains four 256K SIMMs for a total of 2 MB of memory: (4 $\times$ 256K) + (4 $\times$ 256K) = 2 MB.

Notice that in the fourth row of the table, bank 1 contains 1-MB SIMMs, and bank 2 contains 256K SIMMs for a total of 5 MB of memory on the systemboard (calculations are left to the reader). The four SIMMs in a bank must be the same size, but the SIMMs can vary in size from one bank to another.

Our second example of a systemboard is one used by a Pentium, and it supports up to 128 MB of RAM. It has four SIMM sockets divided into two banks. Bank 0 holds SIMMs 1 and 2, and bank 1 holds SIMMs 3 and 4 (see Figure 9-27). Memory can be installed using 4-MB, 8-MB, and 16-MB SIMMs using either 72-pin EDO or EPM modules, which must have at least 70 ns speed.

Remember from Chapter 3 that the Pentium local bus between RAM and the CPU is 64 bits wide (see Figure 3-19). Most SIMM modules sold today accommodate a 32-bit data path so two SIMMs must be paired together to receive data from the 64-bit Pentium local bus. One bank of memory on the Pentium systemboard must contain two 32-bit SIMMs. The other bank does not need to be filled, but, if it is used, both of the two SIMMs must be present in that second bank. Pentium systemboards that use DIMM modules use only one socket to a bank since a DIMM module accommodates a data path of 64 bits. As you study Figure 9-27, remember that this is the Pentium local bus connecting the CPU and RAM, not the PCI bus, which is only 32 bits wide.

Table 9-2 shows half of the memory configurations supported by a Pentium systemboard using SIMMs. The other half is in a project at the end of this chapter with calculations left to the reader.

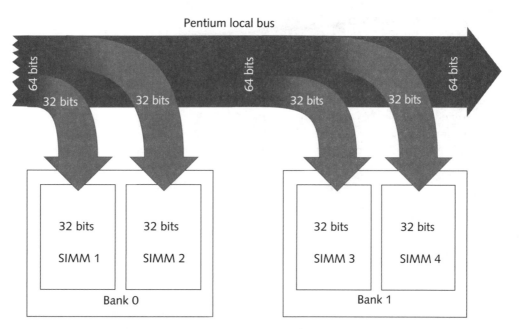

Figure 9-27   A Pentium local bus is 64 bits wide and requires two 32-bit SIMMs to accommodate the bus width. Each 64-bit bank can be used independently of the other.

9

Table 9-2   Memory Configuration for a Pentium Systemboard

SIMM Size in Bank 0	SIMM Size in Bank 1	Total Memory
4 MB	0	8 MB
4 MB	4 MB	16 MB
4 MB	8 MB	24 MB
4 MB	16 MB	40 MB
4 MB	32 MB	72 MB
8 MB	0	16 MB
8 MB	4 MB	24 MB
8 MB	8 MB	32 MB
8 MB	16 MB	48 MB
8 MB	32 MB	80 MB
16 MB	0	32 MB
16 MB	4 MB	40 MB
16 MB	8 MB	48 MB

Selecting Memory Types

When you are placing memory on the systemboard, match the type of memory to the systemboard requirements. For example, for the Pentium systemboard just discussed, the documentation says that you must use 72-pin SIMMs, which can be either EDO or FPM modules. The speed must be at least 70 ns. Avoid mixing speeds on the same systemboard. If you use a SIMM having one speed in one bank and a SIMM having another speed in the other bank, your computer will only work as fast as the slower bank. Always put the slower SIMMs in the first bank. However, to ensure the most reliable results, use the same speed of SIMMs in all banks and also buy the same brand of SIMMs.

READING ADS ABOUT MEMORY MODULES

Figure 9-28 shows a typical memory module ad listing 72-pin SIMMs, 30-pin SIMMs, and 168-pin SDRAM DIMMs. When you are selecting memory, the number of pins, the speed, the size, and the type of module are all important. The first column shows the total amount of memory on each module. For example, the first entry shows a 4 MB 72-pin SIMM. The third column gives the speed and tells whether or not the module is EDO memory. The second column tells what type of module is present, and from the type, the size of the module can be calculated.

1-800-555-0000

MACKRO TIME INC. 57353 Sevok Drive
Suite #601. Westlake. OH 59044
Sales: *Mon-Fri: 9 a.m. to 7 p.m.*
Sat: 10 a.m. to 5 p.m. EST
Phone: 612-459-0469 Fax: 612-495-5640
TECH SUPPORT HOURS:
Mon-Fri: 10 a.m. to 5 p.m. 612-495-6479

72-Pin SIMMS

4MB	1x32	60ns		$25
4MB	1x32	60ns	EDO	$26
4MB	1x36	60ns		$35
8MB	2x32	60ns		$44
8MB	2x32	60ns	EDO	$45
8MB	2x36	60ns		$59
16MB	4x32	60ns		$87
16MB	4x32	60ns	EDO	$89
16MB	4x36	60ns		$99
32MB	8x32	60ns		$168
32MB	8x32	60ns	EDO	$169
32MB	8x36	60ns		$195
64MB	16x32	60ns		$429
64MB	16x32	60ns	EDO	CALL
64MB	16x36	60ns		$469

30-Pin SIMMS

1MB	1x3	60ns	$11
1MB	1x9	60ns	$24
4MB	4x3	60ns	$29
4MB	4x9	60ns	$42

168-Pin SDRAM

16MB	SDRAM	12ns	$149
32MB	SDRAM	12ns/10ns	$269/289
64MB	SDRAM	12ns	CALL

Figure 9-28   Typical ad for memory modules

The second column indicates the type of chip. For example, the first row is 1 $\times$ 32 and is read "one by thirty-two." The number to the right of the $\times$ (for example, the 32 in 1 $\times$ 32) can tell us if the module is parity or nonparity. All 72-pin SIMMs accommodate a 32-bit data path and have either 32 or 36 as this last number. The 32 indicates nonparity memory, and the 36 indicates parity memory. For nonparity memory, there are 8 bits in a functioning byte (32 = 4 $\times$ 8), and in parity memory there are 9 bits in a functioning byte (36 = 4 $\times$ 9). For 30-pin SIMMs that accommodate an 8-bit data path, the number to the right of the $\times$ in the ad is either 3 or 9. For these modules, an odd number indicates parity and is the number of chips on the module. The 3 says that there are 3 chips on the module: the first chip holds 4 bits, the second chip holds 4 bits, and the third chip holds the parity bit. The 9 to the right of the $\times$ indicates 9 chips on the module, 8 chips holding the byte, with the ninth chip holding the parity bit.

In most cases, you can multiply the number on the left by the number on the right, and then divide the answer by 8 or 9, depending on parity, to determine the size of the module. This method fails when the type reads 1 $\times$ 3. You must just remember that with 30-pin SIMMs you must translate the 3 to 9 before you multiply.

For DIMMs, the size of the module is given, and the type is simply listed as SDRAM together with the speed.

INSTALLING MEMORY

When installing SIMMs or DIMMs, remember to protect the chips against static electricity. Turn the power off, but leave the computer's power cord plugged in to ground the box. Remove the cover to the case. Handle memory modules with care. Ground yourself before unpacking or picking up a card. Don't stack cards, because you can loosen a chip. Usually modules pop easily into place and are secured by spring catches on both ends. Look for the notch on one side of the SIMM module that orients the module in the slot. The module slides into the slot at an angle, as shown in Figure 9-29. Place each module securely in its slot. Turn on the PC and watch the amount of memory being counted by POST during the boot process. If all the memory you expect does not count up correctly, remove and reseat each module carefully. To remove a module, release the latches on both sides of the module and gently rotate the module out of the socket at a 45-degree angle.

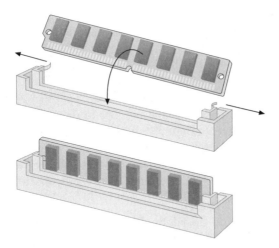

Figure 9-29 Installing a SIMM module

For DIMM modules, as shown in Figure 9-30, small latches on either side of the slot hold the module in place. Look for the edge connector breaks on the DIMM module to orient it into the slot. Insert the module straight down into the slot just as you would an expansion card.

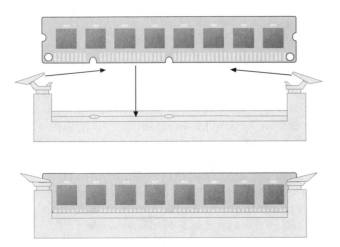

Figure 9-30 Installing a DIMM module

Most often, placing the memory on the systemboard is all that is necessary for installation. When the computer powers up, it counts the memory present without any further instruction. For some computers, you must tell the setup how much memory is present. Read the instructions that come with your computer to determine what yours requires.

Chapter Summary

- Memory can be viewed as both physical memory installed on the systemboard and expansion boards and as logical memory managed by the OS.

- Two kinds of physical memory are RAM and ROM.

- System BIOS is stored on ROM chips on the systemboard. In addition, expansion boards sometimes have ROM chips on them, holding BIOS programming to manage the device.

- Two kinds of memory modules are SIMMs and DIMMs.

- There are two kinds of RAM: SRAM and DRAM. SRAM is faster because it holds data as long as power is available to the chip. DRAM loses the data after a very short time and must be refreshed.

- SRAM is used in a memory cache, which speeds up the overall computer performance by temporarily holding data and programming that may possibly be used by the CPU in the near future.

- When buying memory modules, match speed, parity checking, and type of memory to your systemboard requirements and to the memory chips already on the board.

- The two types of memory used today are EDO and FPM memory. EDO is faster and only slightly more expensive than FPM, but the systemboard must support this type of memory to make use of its increased speed.

- Flash memory holds data permanently until it is overwritten, and is commonly used on Flash ROM chips and memory cards for notebook computers.

- Synchronous DRAM is a faster kind of memory than the less expensive asynchronous DRAM found on SIMMs.

- When buying memory, only use gold edge connectors on memory modules that will be inserted in slots containing gold connections, and only use tin connectors in tin slots.

- When buying memory, beware of remanufactured and re-marked memory chips.

- SRAM comes as either synchronous or asynchronous memory. Synchronous is faster and slightly more expensive than asynchronous memory.

- Synchronous SRAM can come as either burst or pipelined burst memory.

- COAST is a cache memory module holding pipelined burst SRAM chips.

- Logical memory is divided into conventional memory, upper memory, and extended memory, according to the memory addresses assigned to it.

- In order for ROM or RAM physical memory to be used by the computer, memory addresses must be assigned to it.

- Upper memory is traditionally used to hold BIOS and device drivers. Drivers for video normally fill the A, B, and C range of upper memory addresses.

- The beginning of extended memory is called the high memory area and can hold a portion of DOS.

- Expanded memory is located on an expansion board and is accessed by page frames given upper memory addresses.

- Windows can emulate expanded memory, taking some of RAM and presenting it to applications software as expanded memory.

- The practice of copying BIOS from slower ROM chips to faster RAM chips for processing is called shadowing ROM. The area of RAM holding the BIOS is called shadow RAM.

- Virtual memory is space on the hard drive that is used by the OS as pseudo-memory.

- A RAM drive is space in memory that is used as a pseudo-hard-drive.

- DOS and Windows 95 use the device driver HIMEM.SYS to manage extended memory.

- DOS uses EMM386.EXE to make more efficient use of upper memory addresses and to emulate expanded memory.

- An upper memory block is a group of upper memory addresses made available to TSRs.

- Storing device drivers and TSRs into upper memory is called loading high.

- DOS can load device drivers into upper memory blocks by using the DEVICEHIGH command in CONFIG.SYS.

- DOS can load a TSR high by the LOADHIGH command in AUTOEXEC.BAT.

- MEMMAKER is a utility that can help in managing upper memory addresses.

- A swap file is the file on the hard drive that is used to create virtual memory for the OS.

- Windows NT uses an approach to memory management that is altogether different from that of DOS and Windows 95. Conventional, upper, and extended memory concepts do not exist in Windows NT.

- Memory modules must be installed on a systemboard in the slots of a memory bank according to the rules specified in the systemboard documentation. There are a fixed number of memory configurations that a board supports.

KEY TERMS

- **Asynchronous SRAM** — Static RAM that does not work in step with the CPU clock and is, therefore, slower than synchronous SRAM.

- **Bank** — An area on the systemboard that contains slots for memory modules (typically labeled bank 0, 1, 2, and 3).

- **Buffer** — A temporary memory area where data is kept before being written to a drive or sent to a printer, thus reducing the number of writes needed when devices communicate at different speeds.

- **Burst SRAM** — Memory that is more expensive and slightly faster than pipelined burst SRAM. Data is sent as a two-step process; the data address is sent, and then the data itself is sent without interruption.

- **COAST (cache on a stick)** — Chips on a module available for pipelined burst synchronous SRAM.

- **DIMM (dual in-line memory modules)** — Sixty-four-bit miniboards. Because Pentium processors require a 64-bit path, the user must install two 32-bit SIMMs at a time, but DIMMs can be installed one at a time.

- **Dynamic RAM (DRAM)** — Common system memory with access speeds ranging from 70 to 50 nanoseconds, requiring refreshing every few milliseconds.

- **EDO (extended data output) memory** — A type of RAM that may be 10-20% faster than conventional RAM because it eliminates the delay before it issues the next memory address.

- **EEPROM (electrically erasable programmable ROM) chip** — A type of chip in which higher voltage may be applied to one of the pins to erase its previous memory before a new instruction set is electronically written.

- **EMM386.EXE** — A DOS utility that provides both emulated expanded memory (EMS) and upper memory blocks (UMBs).

- **EPROM (erasable programmable ROM) chip** — A type of chip with a special window that allows the current memory contents to be erased with special ultraviolet light so that the chip can be reprogrammed. Many BIOS chips are EPROMs.

- **Expanded memory (EMS)** — Memory outside of the conventional 640K and the extended 1024K range that is accessed in 16K segments, or pages, by way of a window to upper memory.

- **Extended memory** — Memory above the initial 1024 KB, or 1 MB, area.

- **Fake parity chip** — A parity chip generator designed to simulate parity checking so that the user can use less expensive nonparity memory modules on a systemboard that expects parity memory.

- **Flash memory** — A type of RAM that can electronically hold memory even when the power is off.

- **Flash ROM** — ROM that can be reprogrammed or changed.

- **FPM (fast page mode) memory** — An earlier memory mode used before the introduction of EDO memory.

- **General Protection Fault (GPF) error** — A Windows error that occurs when a program attempts to access a memory address that is not available or is no longer assigned to it.

9

- **High memory area (HMA)** — The first 64K of extended memory. The method of storing part of DOS in the high memory area is called loading DOS high.

- **HIMEM.SYS** — A utility that helps manage device drivers in the high memory area. It is often executed by the line DEVICE = C:\DOS\HIMEM.SYS in a Windows 3.x CONFIG.SYS file.

- **Load size** — The largest amount of memory that a driver needs to initialize itself and to hold its data. It is almost always a little larger than the size of the program file.

- **Loading high** — The process of loading a driver or TSR into upper memory.

- **Logic parity** — A fake parity chip designed to simulate parity checking so that the user can use less expensive nonparity memory modules on a systemboard that expects parity memory. *See* Fake parity chip.

- **MEM command** — A DOS utility used to display how programs and drivers are using conventional, upper, and extended memory (an example of memory command is: MEM/C/P).

- **MemMaker** — A DOS utility that can increase the amount of conventional memory available to DOS-based software applications, by loading drivers and TRSs into upper memory.

- **Memory caching** — Using a small amount of faster RAM to store recently retrieved data, in anticipation of what the CPU will next request, thus speeding up access.

- **Memory management** — The process of increasing available conventional memory, required by DOS-based programs, accomplished by loading device drivers and TSRs into upper memory.

- **Memory mapping** — Assigning addresses to both RAM and ROM during the boot process.

- **Nonparity memory** — Slightly less expensive, 8-bit memory without error checking, used on Macs and recently in DOS PCs. A SIMM part number with a 32 in it (4 × 8 bits) is nonparity.

- **Page** — Memory allocated in 4K or 16K segments within a page frame.

- **Page frame** — A 64K upper memory area divided into four equal-sized pages through which the memory manager swaps data.

- **Parity generator chip** — A fake parity chip designed to simulate parity checking so that the user can use less expensive nonparity memory modules on a systemboard that expects parity memory. *See* Fake parity chip.

- **Parity memory** — Nine-bit memory in which the 9th bit is used for error checking. A SIMM part number with a 36 in it (4 × 9 bits) is nonparity. Older DOS PCs almost always use parity chips.

- **Pipelined burst SRAM** — A less expensive SRAM that uses more clock cycles per transfer than nonpipelining burst, but does not significantly slow down the process.

- **Program Information File (PIF)** — A file used by Windows 3.x to describe the environment for a DOS program to use.

- **Protected mode** — The mode in which the operating system limits a program to its own memory addresses and does not allow it access to another program's memory area.

- **RAM drive** — A RAM area configured as a virtual hard drive, such as drive D, so that frequently used programs can be accessed faster. It is the opposite of virtual memory.

- **Real mode** — A CPU processing mode where the CPU can access only 1 MB of memory and programs have direct access to memory addresses.

- **Re-marked chips** — Chips that have been used and returned to the factory, marked again, and sent out. The surface of the chips may be dull or scratched.

- **Shadow RAM** or **shadowing ROM** — The process of copying ROM programming code into RAM to speed up the system operation, because of the faster access speed of RAM.

- **Static RAM (SRAM)** — RAM chips that retain information without the need for refreshing as long as the power is on. They are more expensive but less volatile than traditional DRAM.

- **Swapping** — A method of freeing some memory by moving a "page" of data temporarily to a swap file on the hard drive; it can later be copied from disk back into memory.

- **Synchronous DRAM** — Modules that are more expensive than SIMM modules and can operate at various speeds, depending on the bus speed, whereas SIMMs only operate at a single speed.

- **Synchronous SRAM** — SRAM that is faster and more expensive than asynchronous SRAM. It requires a clock signal to validate its control signals, enabling the cache to run in step with the CPU.

- **System variable** — A variable that has been given a name and a value; it is available to the operating system, Windows, and applications software programs.

- **Temp directory** — A location to which inactive applications and data can be moved as a swap file, while Windows continues to process current active applications. (Avoid deleting TEMP swap while Windows is running.)

- **Temporary file** — A file that is created by Windows applications, to save temporary data, and may or may not be deleted when the application is unloaded.

- **TSR (terminate and stay resident)** — A program that is loaded into memory but is not immediately executed, such as a screen saver or a memory-resident antivirus program.

- **Upper memory** — The memory addresses from 640K up to 1024K, originally reserved for device drivers and TSRs.

- **Upper memory block (UMB)** — A group of consecutive memory addresses in RAM from 640K to 1 MB that can be used by device drivers and TSRs.

9

- **Virtual device driver (VDD)** or **VxD drivers** — A 32-bit device driver running in protected mode used to emulate a 16-bit DOS device driver.

- **Virtual memory** — Hard disk space used when a system starts to run low on RAM. Because hard drives are much slower than RAM access, virtual memory is relatively slow.

REVIEW QUESTIONS

1. How is a ROM chip different from a RAM chip?
2. What is the function of BIOS chips?
3. Define and contrast DRAM, SRAM, VRAM, SIMM, DIMM.
4. How does cache memory speed up computer processing?
5. Which type of RAM is usually used for cache memory?
6. How is L1 cache different from L2 cache?
7. How much cache is used on a typical systemboard?
8. What units are used to measure the speed of SIMM memory?
9. What is EDO memory, and why is it slightly faster than conventional parity and non-parity memory?
10. Define pipelined burst and compare to other burst memory.
11. Why would you want to free up conventional memory in order to speed up computer processing?
12. What area of memory does most video BIOS use?
13. Contrast extended memory and expanded memory.
14. What is an advantage of using Shadow RAM?
15. Define virtual memory and discuss its speed relative to RAM.
16. What does the CONFIG.SYS command LOADHIGH do?
17. What does the CONFIG.SYS command DEVICEHIGH do?
18. What does the DOS utility MEMMAKER do?
19. What conditions could cause Windows to be unable to create a swap file?
20. Using your home or lab computer, answer the following questions:
    a. How much RAM is on the systemboard?
    b. How much virtual memory is used?
    c. Is the virtual memory permanent or temporary?

PROJECTS

> Unless you follow the proper procedures, working inside your computer can cause serious damage—to both you and your computer. To assure safety in your work setting, follow every precaution listed in the *Read This Before You Begin* section following this book's Introduction.

USING NUTS & BOLTS TO EXAMINE MEMORY

Use the Nuts & Bolts utility, Discover Pro, to answer the following questions about the memory on your PC. Using Windows 95, click **Start**, **Programs**, **Nuts & Bolts**, and select **Discover Pro** from the list of Nuts & Bolts utilities. From Discover Pro, select **System** and then **Advanced**. Select the **BIOS/CMOS** icon in the Advanced section.

9

1. What memory addresses are currently being used by your computer to hold System BIOS?

2. Are any System BIOS programs being shadowed into RAM?

3. What is the memory address of the I/O address table where the keyboard buffer is located?

4. Convert this keyboard buffer address to decimal (see Appendix D).

From Discover Pro, select **Memory** and then **Advanced** to answer these questions.

5. What memory addresses are currently assigned to video?

6. What memory addresses in upper memory are available for UMBs?

HELP DESK SUPPORT

1. A friend calls who is sitting at his computer and asks you to help him determine how much RAM he has on his systemboard. Step him through the process. List at least two different ways to find the answer. He is using Windows 3.1 with DOS 6.22.

2. Answer question 1 above, assuming that your friend is using Windows 95.

3. A customer calls who has Norton Utilities on her PC. She has an applications software program installed, and she wants to know whether it is a 16-bit or 32-bit application. Unfortunately, she does not have the documentation for the software available. Help her to find the answer to her question.

PLANNING AND PRICING MEMORY

Read the documentation and look at the systemboard of your computer. What is the maximum amount of memory the banks on your systemboard can accommodate? How much memory do they now hold? Look in a computer catalog, such as *Computer Shopper*, and determine how much it costs to fill the banks to full capacity. Don't forget to match the speed of the SIMMs already installed, and plan to use only the size SIMMs your computer can accommodate.

USING UPPER MEMORY

Does your computer make the best use of upper memory? Get a printout of the files CONFIG.SYS and AUTOEXEC.BAT and the results of the MEM/C command. Study the printouts to determine any improvements that could free more conventional memory for applications.

INSTALLING A TSR

DOSKEY is a very handy TSR. When it is installed, you can retrieve previously issued DOS commands by pressing the Up Arrow key. See your DOS manual for other uses of DOSKEY. To install DOSKEY at the C prompt, use this command:

```
C:\>DOSKEY
```

To install DOSKEY so that it is available every time your computer boots up, you must include the command in your AUTOEXEC.BAT file. Installing DOSKEY in upper memory so that it does not use any conventional memory requires that you create upper memory blocks. List the commands in CONFIG.SYS and AUTOEXEC.BAT to install DOSKEY in upper memory.

UPGRADING MEMORY

To practice installing additional memory in a computer in a classroom environment, remove the SIMMs from one computer and place them in another computer. Boot the second computer and check that it counts up the additional memory. When finished, return the borrowed SIMMs to the original computer.

USING MSD TO VIEW MEMORY

Access MSD, and then access its view of memory on your computer. Get a printout of the MSD memory report.

HOW MEMORY IS ALLOCATED

Use the /M option on the MEM command to list the ways in which three TSRs currently installed in the memory of your computer are using this memory. For example, for a mouse driver named MOUSE.SYS currently installed, type this command:

```
MEM/M MOUSE
```

USING MEMMAKER

On a PC using DOS and Windows 3.x that does not provide access to upper memory, print a MEM report similar to Figure 9-13. Use MemMaker to create the commands necessary at bootup to manage memory effectively. Print a new MEM report to verify the improvement. Print copies of the AUTOEXEC.BAT and CONFIG.SYS files before and after using MemMaker.

TROUBLESHOOTING MEMORY

Loosen a memory module on a systemboard and boot the PC. What error do you get? Don't forget to follow rules to protect the PC against ESD as you work.

PLAN MEMORY INSTALLATION

Fill out the following table, referring back to Table 9-2 in the text.

9

Memory Configuration for a Pentium Systemboard

Bank 0	Bank 1	Total Memory
16 MB	16 MB	64 MB
16 MB	32 MB	
32 MB		64 MB
	4 MB	72 MB
32 MB	8 MB	
32 MB	16 MB	
	32 MB	128 MB
0		8 MB
0	8 MB	
	16 MB	32 MB
0		64 MB

Assume that this systemboard is using EDO, 60-ns, 72-pin SIMMs and currently has 32 MB of memory in Bank 1. Find and make a copy of a memory module ad. Mark in the ad the memory module that is needed by this systemboard to upgrade to 64 MB. How many modules are needed, and what is the total cost?

ELECTRICITY AND POWER SUPPLIES

Earlier chapters covered most hardware components of the computer except the power supply, which supplies the power to all other components inside the computer case. To competently test the power supply and to use a voltmeter, you need a basic understanding of electricity. This chapter begins by discussing how to measure electricity, and the form in which it comes to you as house current. The chapter then addresses the power supply, how to measure its output and how to change a defective power supply. Lastly, the chapter considers backup power sources so that you will understand what to look for when buying one to protect your computer system from electrical variations and outages.

**IN THIS CHAPTER
YOU WILL LEARN:**

- How electricity is measured
- How to measure the voltage output of the power supply
- How to change a power supply
- How a computer system can be protected from damaging changes in electrical power

INTRODUCTION TO BASIC ELECTRICITY

Electricity is used every day, and is missed terribly when it's cut off. Nearly everyone in modern society depends on it, but few really understand it. To most people, volts, ohms, watts, and amps are vague, ambiguous words that simply mean electricity. If these terms are mysterious to you, they will become clear in this section as electricity is discussed in non-technical language, using simple analogies.

Electricity is energy; water is matter. However, the two have enough in common that some analogies can be made. Consider Figure 10-1. The water system shown in Part (a) is closed, that is, the amount of water in the system remains the same because no water enters and no water leaves the system. The pump lifts up the water against the force of gravity, and as the water is released from the pump, water pressure is high. The water seeks a path of least resistance and falls down because of gravity. When it gets to ground level, the water pressure decreases. As the water seeks a lower level, some of its energy is converted to another form of energy by the water wheel.

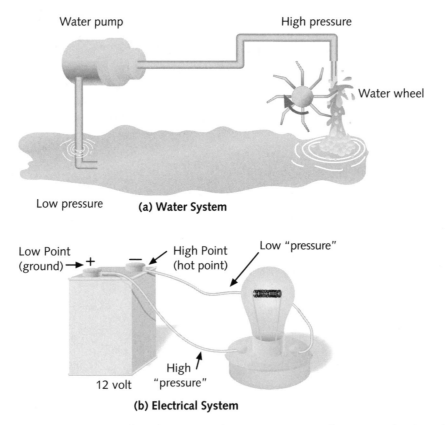

Figure 10-1   Two closed systems: a) Water system with pump, wheel, and pool: b) Electrical system with battery and light bulb

The electrical system in Part (b) is similar in several respects. Think of electricity as a stream of tiny charged particles (electrons) that flow like water. The water pump produces pressure in the system and causes the water to seek a place of rest as gravity pulls on it. A battery produces electrical pressure in the closed system by creating a difference of positive and negative charges, causing the flow of electrons to seek a place of rest. Electrons are negatively charged and are attracted to positively charged particles or atoms. As the water flows through the system, some of its force is harnessed by the water wheel and is converted to a form of energy, motion. As the electrons flow in the closed electrical system, some of the force of the moving electrons is harnessed by the light bulb and converted to another form of energy, light.

VOLTAGE

Next consider how to measure the water flow. Water pressure is sometimes measured in pounds per square inch (psi). If you measure the water pressure of the water directly above the water wheel, and then measured the water pressure just as the water lands in the pool, you would find that the water pressure above the wheel is greater than the water pressure below it.

Now consider the electrical system. If you measure the electrical pressure on one side of the light bulb and compare it to the electrical pressure on the other side of the bulb, you see a difference in pressure. The electrical force that drives the electrons through the system is the potential difference in electrical pressure between two points, and is called **voltage**, which is measured in units called **volts**.

In Figure 10-2, the leads of a **voltmeter**, a device for measuring electrical voltage, are placed on either side of a light bulb that is consuming some electrical power. You can measure the difference between the "pressure" on one side of the device and the "pressure" on the other side. This difference in pressure is the voltage in the closed system.

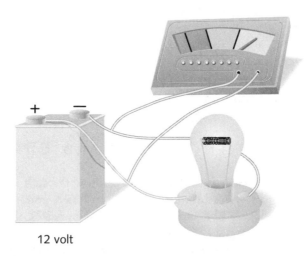

12 volt

Figure 10-2 A voltmeter measuring the voltage across a bulb and a battery

AMPS

Look back at Figure 10-1. The amount of water in the system does not change. If you measure the amount of water flowing in the pipe leading to the pump, that amount is the same as the amount of water flow, or current, flowing from the water wheel into the pool. No matter where in the system you measure, the current is constant. The water pressure changes at different points in the system, but the amount of water in the system is constant.

To measure water current, you pick one point in the system and measure the volume of water that passes through that point. Water current is sometimes measured in gallons per minute.

In the electrical system, the analogy still holds. If you measure the number of electrons, or electrical current, at any point in the system, you get the same value. The current is constant throughout the entire system. Electrical current is measured in **amperes**, abbreviated **amps**. Figure 10-3 shows the measuring device called an **ammeter**, which measures electrical current in amps. You place the ammeter in the path of the electrical flow so that the electrons must flow through the ammeter.

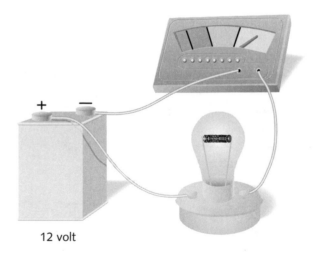

+   −

12 volt

Figure 10-3 Battery and bulb circuit with ammeter in line

THE RELATIONSHIP BETWEEN VOLTAGE AND CURRENT

Refer again to the water system. To increase the volume of water flow through the system, you increase the difference in water pressures between the low and high points (which is referred to as the pressure differential). As the pressure differential increases, the current increases, and as the water pressure differential decreases, the current decreases. Another way of saying this is: there is a direct relationship between pressure differential and current. The same relationship exists for the electrical system. As the electrical "pressure" differential or voltage increases, the current increases; as the voltage decreases, the current decreases. There is a direct relationship between voltage and current.

OHMS

Suppose you are working your pump in the water system to full capacity. If you still want to increase the overall power of your water system, you can use either larger pipes or a lighter water wheel. A large pipe offers less resistance to the flow of water than a small pipe. A lighter or more easily turned water wheel offers less resistance than a heavier, hard-to-turn wheel. As resistance decreases, current increases. As resistance increases (smaller pipes or a heavier wheel), current decreases.

Resistance in an electrical system is a property that opposes the flow of electricity. As the electrical resistance increases, the current decreases. As the resistance decreases, the current increases. When there is more resistance to the flow of electricity, the flow of electrons decreases, and the electrical energy changes to heat energy. Wires too small to contain the flow of electricity through them, just like water pipes, offer too much resistance to the flow. The result is overheating. Electrical resistance is measured in **ohms**.

Resistors are devices used in electrical circuits to resist the flow of electricity. (Sorry, I couldn't resist saying that!) Resistors control the flow of electricity in a circuit much as small pipes can control the flow of water.

RELATIONSHIPS AMONG VOLTAGE, CURRENT, AND RESISTANCE

There is a *direct* relationship between voltage and current. This means that when voltage increases, current increases. There is an *inverse* relationship between resistance, on the one hand, and voltage and current on the other. This means that as resistance increases, current and voltage decrease. As resistance decreases, current and voltage increase. This last statement is known as Ohm's Law. There is a similar statement that defines the relationship among the units of measure—volts, amps, and ohms. One volt drives a current of one amp through a resistance of one ohm.

WATTAGE

A discussion of electricity would not be complete without covering one last measure of electricity. **Wattage** is a measure of the total amount of power that is needed to operate an electrical device. When thinking of the water system, you recognize that the amount of water power in the system used to turn the water wheel is not just a measure of the water pressure that forces current through the system. The amount of power is also related to the amount of water available to flow. For a given water pressure, you have more power with more water flow and less power with less water flow. A lot of power results when you have a lot of pressure and a lot of current.

As with the water system, electrical power increases both as voltage increases and as current increases. Wattage, measured in **watts**, is calculated by multiplying volts by amps in a system.

The following table recaps this discussion of the measures of electricity.

In summary, electricity is energy that can be measured in various ways. The example of a battery and light bulb used in this section is a simple example that applies to the most complex electrical systems.

Table 10-1   The Measures of Electricity

Unit	Definition	An Example as Applied to a Computer
Volts	A measure of electrical "pressure" differential. Volts are measured by finding the potential difference between the pressures on either side of an electrical device in the system.	A PC power supply usually supplies four separate voltages: +12 V, -12 V, +5 V, -5 V.
Amps	Abbreviated as A (for example, 1.5 A). A measure of electrical current. Amps are measured by placing an ammeter in the flow of current.	A 17-inch monitor requires less than 2 A to operate. A small laser printer uses about 2 A. A CD-ROM drive uses about 1 A.
Ohms	A measure of resistance to electricity. Devices are rated according to how much resistance they offer to electrical current. The ohm rating of a resistor or other electrical device is often written somewhere on the device. The symbol for ohm is Ω.	A resistance of less than 20 ohms indicates that current can flow in typical computer cables and wires. This is called continuity.
Watts	A measure of electrical power. Watts are calculated by multiplying volts by amps. Watts measure the total electrical power needed to operate a device.	A computer power supply is rated at about 200 watts.

MEASURING THE VOLTAGE OF A POWER SUPPLY

Electricity can be either AC, alternating current, or DC, direct current. **Alternating current (AC)** is current that cycles back and forth rather than traveling in only one direction. AC current is the kind that travels over electrical lines to our homes and workplaces. Alternating current can be forced to travel great distances by decreasing current and increasing voltage. When it reaches its destination, the voltage can be decreased and the current increased to make it more suitable for driving our electrical devices. House current is about 110 volts of AC current.

Direct current (DC) travels in only one direction and is the type of current required by a computer. House current is alternating current (AC), which travels in two directions. A **rectifier** is a device that converts alternating current to direct current. A **transformer** is a device that changes the ratio of current to voltage. A computer power supply changes and conditions the house electrical current in several ways, functioning as both a transformer and a rectifier (see Figure 10-4). It steps down the voltage from the 110-volt house current to 5 and 12 volts, and changes incoming alternating current to direct current, which the computer and its peripherals require. The monitor, however, receives the full 110 volts of AC current.

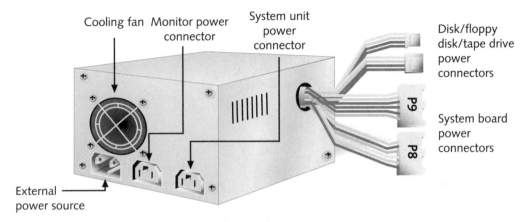

Figure 10-4 Power supply with connections

Recall that direct current flows in only one direction. An electrical circuit has a positive side and a negative side, which dictates the direction the current flows. For a PC, a line may be either +5 or –5 volts in one circuit, or +12 or –12 volts in another circuit, depending on whether the circuit is on the far or near end of the power output. There are several circuits coming from the power supply. To determine that a power supply is working properly, measure all the circuit voltages going to the systemboard and the power to each device. Measure the voltage with all connections in place and the computer turned on. How to do this is explained below.

USING A MULTIMETER

A voltmeter measures voltage in volts, and an ammeter measures electrical current in amps. Figure 10-5 shows a **multimeter**, which can be used as either a voltmeter or an ammeter, or can measure resistance or continuity (the presence of a complete circuit), depending on a dial or function switch setting. A multimeter is sometimes called a **DVM** (digital voltage meter). Less expensive DVMs commonly measure voltage, resistance, and continuity, but not amps. For the specific details of how to use your multimeter, consult the manual. This will explain what you can measure with a multimeter and how to use one.

A multimeter can provide either a digital or an analog display. A digital display shows the readings as digits displayed on an LCD (liquid crystal display) panel. An analog display shows the readings as a needle moving across a scale of values. Multimeters are sometimes small, portable, battery-powered units. Larger ones are designed to sit on a countertop and are powered by the wall outlet.

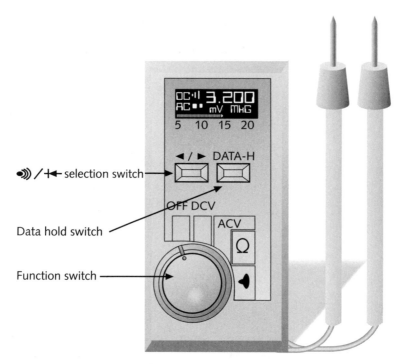

Figure 10-5 A digital multimeter

When you use a multimeter, you must tell it three things before you begin: (1) what you want it to measure (voltage, current, or resistance), (2) whether the current is AC or DC, and (3) what range of values it should expect. If you are measuring the voltage output from a wall outlet (110–120 V), the range should be much higher than when measuring the voltage output of a computer power supply (3–12 V). Setting the range higher assures you that the meter will be able to handle a large input without pegging the needle (exceeding the highest value that the meter is designed to measure) or damaging the meter. Setting the range lower assures you that the measure will be as accurate as you need. Most meters do not allow a very large voltage or current into the meter when the range is set low, in order to protect the meter. Some multimeters are **autorange meters**, which sense the quantity of input and set the range accordingly.

A meter comes with two test probes. One is usually red and the other black. You attach the red probe at the positive (+) jack on the meter and the black probe at the negative (–) jack. The red probe is attached to the high, or hot, point in the current (high pressure), and the black probe is attached to the low point, or ground, in the current. Just as with the closed water system, an electrical circuit has a high point (hot) and a low point (ground). The ground measures no electrical pressure or voltage, and the hot point measures a higher pressure or voltage in the circuit. The voltage is the difference between these two measures.

To measure voltage, place the black probe at the ground point and the red probe at the hot point, without disconnecting anything in the circuit and with the power on. For example, to measure voltage using the multimeter in Figure 10-5, turn the function switch to DCV for DC Voltage measurement. This meter is autoranging, so this is all that needs to be set. With the power on, place the two probes in position and read the voltage from the LCD panel. The DATA-H switch (data hold) allows you to freeze the displayed reading.

To measure current in amps, as in Figure 10-3, the multimeter itself must be part of the circuit. Disconnect the circuit at some point so that you can connect the multimeter in line to get a measure in amps. Not all multimeters can measure amps.

A multimeter can also be used to measure continuity, the continuous lack of resistance between two points, which indicates a closed connection between the two points. This measurement is taken with no electricity present in the circuit.

For example, if you want to know that pin 2 on one end of a serial cable is connected to pin 3 on the other end of the cable, without the cable being connected to anything, set the multimeter to measure continuity. (See the documentation for the multimeter to determine how to do this.) Put one probe on pin 2 at one end of the cable and the other probe on pin 3 at the other end. If the two pins connect, the multimeter will indicate this with a reading on the LCD panel, or a buzzer will sound (see the documentation). In this situation, you might find that the probe is too large to extend into the pin hole of the female connection of the cable. A straightened small paper clip works well here to extend the probe. However, be very careful not to use a paper clip that is too thick and might widen the size of the pin hole, which can later prevent a good connection for that pin hole.

The multimeter in Figure 10-5 measures continuity when the function switch is set to the continuity test position (rightmost choice in the diagram). A buzzer sounds when the circuit has less than 20 ohms resistance, and the measured resistance displays. Measurements below 20 ohms indicate continuity.

How to Measure the Voltage of a Power Supply

To determine that a power supply is working properly, measure the voltage of each circuit supported by the power supply. First open the computer case and identify all power cords coming from the power supply, as in Figure 10-6. Look for the two cords from the power supply to the systemboard and other power cords to the drives. Some power cords to the drives may not be used. Follow the directions described in the next section to measure the voltage of the power supply output to the systemboard (see Figure 10-7).

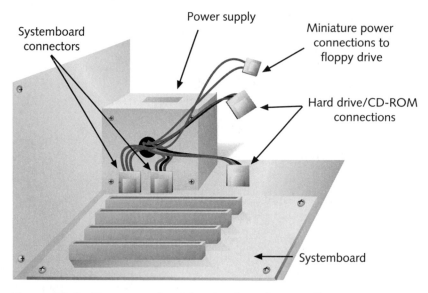

Figure 10-6   Power supply and systemboard connections

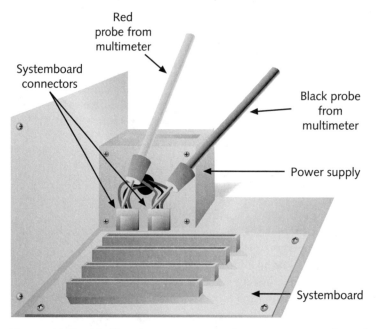

Figure 10-7   Multimeter measuring voltage on a systemboard

Testing the Power Output to the Systemboard

The computer must be turned on to test the power supply output. Be very careful not to touch any chips or disturb any circuit boards as you work. The voltage output from the power supply is no more than 14 volts, which is not enough to seriously hurt you if you accidentally touch a hot probe. However, you can damage the computer if you are not careful.

You can hurt yourself if you accidentally create a short circuit from the power supply to ground through the probe. A **short circuit**, often simply called a **short**, is a side circuit of very low resistance connecting two points in an electric circuit of higher resistance, so that most of the current is diverted through this side circuit. If you touch the probe to the hot circuit and also to ground, the current will be diverted away from the computer circuit and through the probe to ground. This short might be enough to cause a spark or to melt the probe, which can happen if you allow the two probes to touch each other while one of them is attached to the hot circuit and the other is attached to ground.

Because of the danger of touching a hot probe to a ground probe, you might prefer not to put the black probe into a ground lead that is too close to the hot probe. Instead, when the directions say to place the black probe on a lead that is very close to the hot probe, you can use a black wire lead on an unused power supply connection meant for a hard drive. The idea is that the black probe always be placed on a ground or black lead.

A ground lead is always considered at ground, no matter which ground lead you use for that purpose on the PC. The ground leads for P8 and P9 are the four black center leads 5, 6, 7, and 8. The ground leads for a hard drive power connection are the two black center leads, 2 and 3.

1. Remove the cover of the computer. Often the voltage range for each connection is written on the top of the power supply. The two power connections to the systemboard are often labeled P8 and P9. Figure 10-8 shows a close-up of the two connections, P8 and P9, coming from the power supply to the systemboard. Each of the two connections has six leads, for a total of 12 leads. Of these 12, four are ground connections, and lead 1 is a "power good" pin, used to indicate that the systemboard is receiving power. A common arrangement for these 12 leads is listed in Table 10-2.

2. Set the multimeter to measure voltage, DC current in a range of 20 volts. Insert the black probe into the – jack and the red probe into the + jack of the meter.

3. Turn on the multimeter, and turn on the computer.

4. To measure the +12-volt circuit and all four ground leads:

   ■ Place the red probe on lead 3. The probe is shaped like a needle (alligator clips don't work too well here); insert the needle down into the lead housing as far as you can. Place the black probe on lead 5. The acceptable range is +8.5 to +12.6 volts.

10

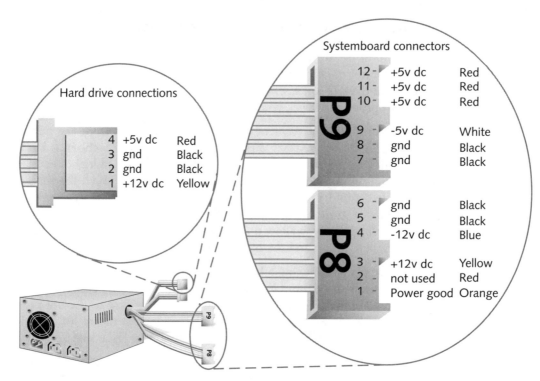

Figure 10-8 Power supply connections

- Place the red probe on lead 3, and place the black probe on lead 6. The acceptable range is +8.5 to +12.6 volts.

- Place the red probe on lead 3, and place the black probe on lead 7. The acceptable range is +8.5 to +12.6 volts.

- Place the red probe on lead 3, and place the black probe on lead 8. The acceptable range is +8.5 to +12.6 volts.

5. To measure the –12-volt circuit, place the red probe on lead 4, and place the black probe on any ground lead or on the computer case, which is also grounded. The acceptable range is –8.5 to –12.6 volts.

6. To measure the –5-volt circuit, place the red probe on lead 9, and place the black probe on any ground. The acceptable range is –4.5 to –5.4 volts.

7. To measure the three +5-volt circuits:

- Place the red probe on lead 10, and place the black probe on any ground. The acceptable range is +2.4 to +5.2 volts.

- Place the red probe on lead 11, and place the black probe on any ground. The acceptable range is +2.4 to +5.2 volts.

- Place the red probe on lead 12, and place the black probe on any ground. The acceptable range is +2.4 to +5.2 volts.

8. Replace the cover.

Table 10-2   Twelve Leads to the Systemboard from the Power Supply

Connection	Lead	Description	Acceptable Range
P8	1	"Power Good"	
	2	Not used	
	3	+12 volts	+8.5 to +12.6 volts
	4	–12 volts	–8.5 to –12.6 volts
	5	Black ground	
	6	Black ground	
P9	7	Black ground	
	8	Black ground	
	9	–5 volts	–4.5 to –5.4 volts
	10	+5 volts	+2.4 to +5.2 volts
	11	+5 volts	+2.4 to +5.2 volts
	12	+5 volts	+2.4 to +5.2 volts

Testing the Power Output to a Floppy or Hard Drive

The power cords to the floppy disk drive, hard drive, and CD-ROM drive all supply the same voltage: one +5-volt circuit and one +12-volt circuit. The power connection to any drive uses four leads; the two outside connections are hot, and the two inside connections are ground (see Figure 10-8). The power connection to a 3.5-inch floppy disk drive is usually a miniature connection, as shown in Figure 10-6. Follow these steps to measure the voltage to any drive:

1. With the drive plugged in, turn the computer on.

2. Set the multimeter as described above.

3. Place the red probe on lead 1 shown in Figure 10-8, and place the black probe on the lead next to it (lead 2), which is ground. The acceptable range is +11.5 to +12.6 volts.

4. Place the red probe on the lead 4, and place the black probe on the lead next to it (lead 3). The acceptable range is +4.8 to +5.2 volts.

You may choose to alter the method you use to ground the black probe. In step 4 above, the red probe and black probe are very close to each other. You may choose to keep them farther apart by placing the black probe in a ground lead of an unused hard drive connection.

10

EXCHANGING THE POWER SUPPLY

If you assemble a PC from parts, most often you purchase a computer case with the power supply already installed in it. However, you might need to exchange the present power supply because it is damaged, or because you need to upgrade to one with more power. In this section, you will learn how to detect a faulty power supply and how to exchange one.

POWER SUPPLY TROUBLESHOOTING GUIDELINES

If any of the following symptoms appear, the problem might be with the power supply or the house current to the PC.

- The computer stops or hangs for no reason. Sometimes it might even reboot itself
- Memory errors appear occasionally
- Data is written incorrectly to the hard drive
- The keyboard stops working at odd times
- The systemboard fails or is damaged
- The power supply overheats and becomes hot to the touch

The symptoms of electrical power problems might be caused by a brownout (reduced current) of the house current or by a faulty power supply. If you suspect that the house current could be low, check the other devices that are using the same circuit. A copy machine, laser printer, or other heavy equipment might be drawing too much power. Remove the other devices from the same house circuit.

If this doesn't correct the problem, check the power supply by measuring the voltage output or by exchanging it for one you know is good.

Install an electrical conditioner to monitor and condition the voltage to the PC. Conditioners are discussed later in the chapter.

The fan on the power supply stops working.   The problem might be a faulty power supply or could be caused by a short somewhere else in the system drawing too much power. Don't operate the PC with the fan not working. Computers without cooling fans can quickly overheat and damage chips.

Turn the power off and remove all power cord connections to all components, including P8, P9, and all power cords to drives. Turn the power back on. If the fan comes on, the problem is with one of the systems you disconnected, not with the power supply or its fan.

Turn the power off and reconnect the power cords to the drives. If the fan comes on, you can eliminate the drives as the problem. If the fan does not come on, try one drive after another until you identify the drive with the short.

If the drives are not the problem, suspect the systemboard subsystem. With the power off, reconnect all power cords to the drives.

Turn the power off and remove the power to the systemboard by disconnecting P8 and P9. Turn the power back on.

If the fan comes back on, the problem is probably not the power supply, but a short in one of the components powered by P8 and P9. The power to the systemboard also powers interface cards.

Remove all interface cards and reconnect P8 and P9.

If the fan still works, the problem is with one of the interface cards. If the fan does not work, the problem is with the systemboard or something still connected to it.

A short through the systemboard might be caused by allowing the connections on the bottom of the systemboard to accidentally make improper contact with the chassis, which can cause serious damage to the systemboard. Check for missing standoffs, the problem that most often causes these improper connections.

Shorts in the circuits on the systemboard might also cause the problem. Look for damage on the bottom side of the systemboard. These circuits are coated with plastic, and quite often damage is difficult to spot.

Frayed wires on cable connections can also cause shorts. Disconnect hard drive cables connected directly to the systemboard. Power up with P8 and P9 connected, but all cables disconnected from the systemboard. If the fan comes on, the problem is with one of the systems you disconnected.

 Never replace a damaged systemboard with a good one without first testing the power supply. You don't want to subject another good board to possible damage.

UPGRADING THE POWER SUPPLY

If you are installing a hard drive or CD-ROM drive and are concerned that the power supply might not be adequate, test it after you finish the installation. Make both the new drive and the floppy drive work at the same time by copying files from one to the other. If the new drive and the floppy drive each work independently, but data errors occur when both are working at the same time, suspect a lack of electrical power.

If you prefer a more technical approach, you can estimate how much total wattage your system needs by calculating the watts for each circuit and adding them together. Wattage is calculated as volts × amps. The power supply is rated in watts, and it should be rated about 50% higher than total wattage needs. In most cases, however, the computer's power supply is more than adequate if you add only one or two new devices.

Power supplies can be purchased separately, but often come with the computer case. Power supplies for microcomputers range in power from 200 watts for a small desktop computer system to 600 watts for a tower floor model that uses a large amount of multimedia or other power-hungry devices.

INSTALLING A NEW POWER SUPPLY

If you suspect that the power supply is faulty, either because of the measured voltage output or because one of the symptoms listed earlier appears, most often the solution is to replace it with a new power supply, rather than to have it repaired. You can determine if the power supply really is the problem by turning off the PC, opening the computer case, and setting the new power supply on top of the old one. Disconnect the old power supply's cords and plug the PC devices into the new power supply. Turn on the PC and verify that the problem is solved before you go to the trouble of removing the old power supply and replacing it with a new one.

If the new power supply is needed, follow these procedures:

1. Turn off the power.

2. Remove all external power cables from the power supply connections.

3. Remove the cover.

4. Disconnect all power cords from the power supply to other devices.

5. Determine just which components must be removed before the power supply can be safely removed from the case. You might need to remove the hard drive, several cards, or the CD-ROM. In some cases, the systemboard may even need to be removed.

6. Remove all the components necessary to get to the power supply. Remember to protect the components from static electricity, as described in Chapter 7.

7. Unscrew the screws on the back of the computer case that hold the power supply to the case.

8. Look on the bottom of the case for slots that are holding the power supply in position. Often the power supply must be shifted in one direction to free it from the slots.

9. Remove the power supply.

10. Place the new power supply into position, sliding it into the slots used by the old power supply.

11. Replace the power supply screws.

12. Replace all other components.

13. Before replacing the case cover, connect the power cords, turn on the PC, and verify that all is working.

14. Test the voltage output of the new power supply and verify that it falls within acceptable ranges.

15. Turn off the PC and replace the cover.

ENERGY STAR COMPUTERS (THE GREEN STAR)

Energy Star computers and peripherals have the U.S. Green Star, which indicates that they satisfy the requirements of the U.S. Environmental Protection Agency (EPA). Such devices are designed to decrease the overall consumption of electricity in the U.S., in order to protect and preserve our natural resources. The standards, sometimes called the **Green Standards**, generally mean that the computer or the device has a standby program that causes the device to go into sleep mode when it is not being used. During **sleep mode**, the device must use no more then 30 watts of power. Devices that can carry the Green Star are computers, monitors, printers, copiers, and fax machines.

Office equipment is among the fastest growing source of electrical load in industrialized nations. Much of this electricity is wasted as computers and other equipment are often left on overnight. Because Energy Star devices go into sleep mode when they are unused, there is an overall energy savings of about 50%.

10

ENERGY STAR PCs

For computer systems, there exist three power management methods:

- Advanced Power Management (APM), championed by Intel and Microsoft
- AT Attachment (ATA) for IDE drives
- Display Power Management Signaling (DPMS) standards for monitors and video cards

The Energy Star features of a PC can sometimes be enabled and adjusted in CMOS setup. The features are designed to work in incremental steps, depending on how long the PC is idle. Look for the kinds of features in setup described next. For a particular setup screen, these listed features might not be available, setup might include additional features, or the features might be labeled differently.

Green Timer on the Systemboard

This setting is the number of minutes of inactivity before the CPU will go into sleep mode. You can enable or disable the setting and select the number of minutes to sleep mode.

Doze Time

Doze time is the time before the system will reduce 80% of its power consumption. This is accomplished in different ways by different systems. For example, for one Pentium systemboard BIOS, in doze mode, the system speed changes from turbo speed to slow speed.

Standby Time

The time before the system will reduce 92% of its power consumption is **Standby time**. For example, a system might accomplish this by changing the system speed from turbo to slow and suspending the video signal.

Suspend Time

The time before the system will reduce 99% of its power consumption is **Suspend time**. The way this reduction is accomplished might be different for different systems. The CPU clock might be stopped, in addition to suspending the video signal. After entering suspend mode, the system needs a warm-up time so that the CPU, monitor, and other components can reach full activity.

Hard Drive Standby Time

This is the amount of time before a hard drive will shut down.

Figure 10-9 shows the main menu of the CMOS setup for Award BIOS for a Pentium systemboard. Select the Power Management Setup option to see these settings. Figure 10-10 shows the Power Management Setup screen with default settings. Note that, by default, the power management features are all disabled. In Figure 10-10, the Power Management feature is disabled. Other settings offered are User Defined, Optimize, Test/Demo, and Disable. The Wake-Up Events listed are the items that can be enabled in order to return the system to full power. The Power Down Activity list shows the items that prevent any power management features from being enabled when these events happen.

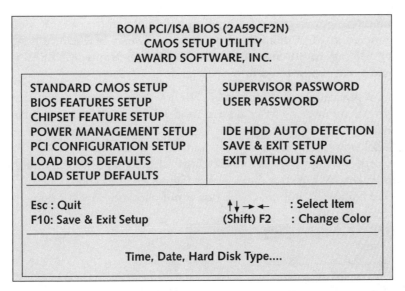

Figure 10-9   Main menu for Award BIOS for a Pentium systemboard

```
            ROM PCI/ISA BIOS (2A59CF2N)
            POWER MANAGEMENT SETUP
               AWARD SOFTWARE, INC

Power Management    :Disable    IRQ3 (COM 2)          :OFF
PM Control by APM   :No         IRQ4 (COM 1)          :OFF
Video Off Method    :V/H SYNC+Blank  IRQ5 (LPT 2)     :OFF
                                IRQ6 (Floppy Disk)    :OFF
Doze Mode           :Disable    IRQ7 (LPT 1)          :OFF
Standby Mode        :Disable    IRQ8 (RTC Alarm)      :OFF
Suspend Mode        :Disable    IRQ9 (IRQ2 Redir)     :OFF
HDD Power Down      :Disable    IRQ10 (Reserved)      :OFF
                                IRQ11 (Reserved)      :OFF
IRQ3(Wake-up Event) :OFF        IRQ12 (PS/2 Mouse)    :OFF
IRQ4(Wake-up Event) :OFF        IRQ13 (Coprocessor)   :OFF
IRQ8(Wake-up Event) :OFF        IRQ14 (Hard Disk)     :OFF
IRQ12(Wake-up Event) :OFF       IRQ15 (Reserved)      :OFF
   ** Power Down Activity **    ESC: Quit    ▲▼►◄ :Select Item
COM Ports Accessed  :OFF        F1 :Help       PU/PD/+/–:Modify
LPT Ports Accessed  :OFF        F5 :Old Values    (Shift) F2: Color
Drive Ports Accessed :OFF       F6 : Load BIOS Defaults
                                F7 : Load Setup Defaults
```

Figure 10-10   A Power Management setup screen showing power management features

ENERGY STAR MONITORS

Most computers and monitors sold today are Energy Star compliant. To know if your computer is Energy Star compliant, look for the green Energy Star logo onscreen when the PC is booting.

In order for a monitor's power-saving feature to function, the video card or computer must also support this function. Most monitors that follow the Energy Star standards adhere to the **Display Power Management Signaling (DPMS)** specifications by VESA, which allow for the video card and monitor to go into sleep mode simultaneously.

When a monitor is installed using Windows 95, Windows 95 might recognize that the monitor is an Energy Star monitor by its brand and model. To see if Windows 95 has identified a monitor as Energy Star compliant, select the **Display Properties** window. One way to do this is to right-click anywhere on the desktop and select **Properties** from the menu. From the Display Properties window, select the **Settings** tab, and then select **Change Display Type**. The Change Display Type box displays as in Figure 10-11. If you know that your monitor is Energy Star compliant and the check box is not checked, check it now.

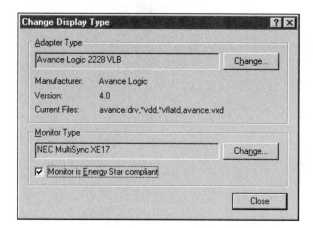

Figure 10-11   Windows 95 Setting for an Energy Star monitor

 Problems might occur if CMOS is turning off the monitor because of power management settings, and Windows 95 is also turning off the monitor. If the system hangs when you try to get the monitor going again, try disabling one or the other.

To apply the Energy Star features of your monitor, select the **Screen Saver** tab and Figure 10-12 will display. You can set the Low-power standby to activate after a selected number of minutes. This feature causes your Energy Star monitor to go into sleep mode. Some monitors have an additional feature that allows the PC to shut off the monitor after a selected number of minutes of inactivity. Read the documentation that comes with the monitor to learn what features a monitor has and how to use them.

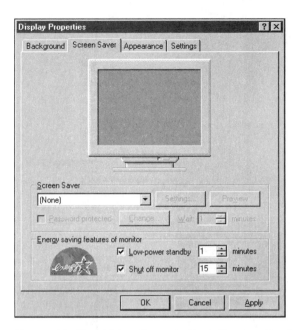

Figure 10-12   Using the monitor's Energy Star features

10

SURGE PROTECTION AND BATTERY BACKUP

There is a wide range of devices on the market that filter the AC input to computers and their peripherals and that provide backup power when the AC current fails. These devices fall into three general categories: surge suppressors, power conditioners, and uninterruptible power supplies (UPSs). On all these devices, look for the UL (Underwriters' Laboratory) logo that ensures that the device has been tested by this agency, a provider of product safety certification.

Before you look at these devices that protect computers against overvoltage, know that one simple way to help prevent damage from heavy spikes of power, such as lightning, is to tie knots in power cords. This method offers no guaranteed protection, but it is a simple technique that has proven to help lessen a damaging spike.

SURGE SUPPRESSORS

A **surge suppressor**, also called a **surge protector**, provides a row of power outlets and an on/off switch that protects equipment from overvoltages on AC power lines and telephone lines. Surge suppressors can come as power strips, as seen in Figure 10-13 (but not all power strips have surge protection), wall-mounted units that plug into AC outlets, or consoles designed to sit on a desk top (Figure 10-14) with the monitor placed on top. Some provide an RJ-11 telephone jack to protect modems and fax machines from spikes.

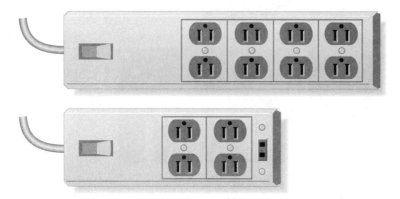

Figure 10-13   A surge suppressor can protect a device against overvoltage or spikes

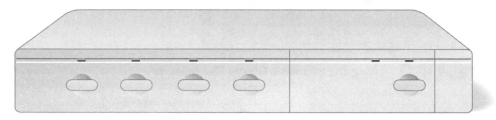

Figure 10-14   A surge suppressor might be designed to sit underneath the monitor on the desktop

Surge suppressors are not always reliable, and once the fuse is blown, a surge suppressor no longer protects from a power surge. It continues to provide power without warning you that the protection is lost. The performance of a surge suppressor as protection against spikes is measured in two ways, let-through voltage and joules.

The maximum voltage that is allowed through the suppressor to the device being protected is called the **let-through**. Less is better. The better units are expected to let through under 330 volts. Less expensive suppressors let through 400 volts or more.

The degree of protection can be measured in **joules**, a measure of energy taking into account both voltage and current over a one-second interval. More is better. Look for devices that offer at least 240 joules of protection.

A surge suppressor might be a shunt type that absorbs the surge or might be a series type that blocks the surge from flowing, or it might be a combination of the two. The shunt-type suppressor is measured by a term called **clamping voltage**, which describes the let-through voltage.

When buying a surge suppressor, look for those that guarantee reimbursement for equipment destroyed while the surge suppressor is in use. Avoid surge suppressors that don't guarantee against damage from lightning.

Data Line Protectors

Data line protectors serve the same function for the telephone line to your modem that a surge suppressor does for the electrical lines. Telephone lines carry a small current of electricity and need to be protected against spikes, just as electrical lines do. The let-through rating for a data line protector for a phone line should be no more than 260 volts.

MEASURING POWER RANGES OF DEVICES

The next two types of protective devices are power conditioners and uninterruptible power supplies, both of which condition (alter so as to provide continuity) the power passing through them. They provide a degree of protection against spikes (temporary surges of voltage) and raise the voltage when it drops during brownouts (temporary reductions of voltage). Both types of devices are measured by the load they support in watts, volt-amperes (**VA**), or kilovolt-amperes (**kVA**).

To determine how much VA is required to support your system, multiply the amperage of each component by 120 volts and then add up the VA for all components. For example, a 17-inch monitor has 1.9 A written on the back of the monitor, which means 1.9 amps. Multiply that value times 120 volts and you see that 228 VA is required. A Pentium PC with a 17-inch monitor and tape backup system requires about 500 VA of support.

10

POWER CONDITIONERS

In addition to providing protection against spikes, **power conditioners** also regulate, or condition, the power, providing continuous voltage during brownouts. These voltage regulators, sometimes called **line conditioners**, can come as small desktop units (see Figure 10-15) costing in the range of $200 to $300 for 600 VA of support.

Figure 10-15   A power conditioner can protect a device against overvoltage (spikes) and provide continuous voltage during brownouts.

Low-cost line conditioners use a stepped transformer to adjust the output voltage. Higher-priced models use a **ferroresonant regulator**, which contains a magnetic coil that can retain a charge of power to be used to raise the voltage during a brownout.

These electricity filters are a good investment if the AC current in your community suffers from excessive spikes and brownouts. However, if the device is rated under 1 kVA, it will probably only provide corrections for brownouts, and not spikes. Line conditioners, like surge suppressors, provide no protection against a total blackout.

UNINTERRUPTIBLE POWER SUPPLY

The **UPS** (**uninterruptible power supply**) is a device designed to provide a backup power supply in the event that the AC current fails completely. It also offers some filtering of the AC current. A UPS device is designed as either a standby device, an in-line device, or a line-interactive device (which combines features of the first two). Among these three devices, there are several variations on the market whose prices vary widely.

A common UPS device is a rather heavy box that plugs into an AC outlet and provides one or more outlets for the computer and its peripherals (See Figure 10-16). It has an on/off switch, requires no maintenance, and is very simple to install.

Uninterruptible
power supply

Figure 10-16 Uninterruptible power supply (UPS)

Prices increase dramatically depending on the features offered. A UPS device is rated according to the amount of power it can provide in VAs during a complete blackout, and the length of time it can sustain that power. Most UPSs for microcomputer systems only claim to provide backup power for about 15 minutes, only enough time to save any work in progress and to do an orderly shutdown. The high cost of a UPS prohibits greater power.

Standby and in-line UPSs differ in the circuit the devices use as the primary circuit, and in the way they function when the AC power fails. A **standby UPS** switches circuits from the AC circuit to the battery-powered circuit. In contrast, the **in-line UPS** continually provides power through the battery-powered circuit and therefore requires no switching, which assures continuous power.

The Standby UPS

Figure 10-17 shows how UPSs work. The solid line represents the primary circuit by which electricity normally flows. The dashed line represents the secondary circuit that is used when the AC current fails. For the standby UPS, the primary circuit is the house AC current circuit with an in-line surge suppressor and filter. A relatively small amount of the current flows to the secondary circuit to keep the battery charged in case it is ever needed. When the AC current fails, the UPS switches from the primary to the secondary circuit and the battery provides the power, which is converted from DC to AC before it leaves the UPS.

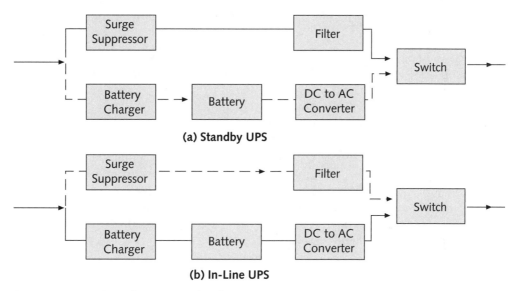

(a) Standby UPS

(b) In-Line UPS

Figure 10-17   Standby UPS and in-line UPS

The switching time (the time it takes for the UPS to switch from the AC circuit to the battery-charged circuit) caused problems for earlier computers, even causing the PC to reboot. Today, however, computer power supplies are better designed and able to keep the computer running during the fraction of a second it takes to switch the power in the UPS. One variation on a stand-by UPS uses a ferroresonant regulator that delivers power to the circuit during the switching time, to virtually eliminate any interruption of power.

Other variations of this type of UPS reduce the cost by eliminating the filter. The purpose of the filter is to condition the AC current, reducing the effect of brownouts and spikes. These electricity filters or line conditioners must be purchased separately.

The In-Line UPS

In Figure 10-17, notice that the in-line UPS uses the battery-powered circuit as the primary circuit, instead of the AC circuit. The AC circuit is only used if the battery-powered circuit registers any error conditions caused by failure of some component in the circuit. These conditions are not related to spikes, brownouts, or blackouts of the AC current, but rather to the performance of the components.

When the AC current fails, no switching is needed since the primary circuit continues to be the battery-powered circuit. The only thing that is lost is the battery recharging. These UPS devices are sometimes called true UPSs because they truly do provide uninterruptible power.

The in-line UPS also provides more line conditioning than does the standby UPS, and, because of the clean, constant 120-volt current it produces, it can extend the life of computer equipment. Because the in-line UPS converts the AC power to battery power in DC and then back to AC power, the in-line design is sometimes referred to as **double conversion**. Because the battery is in constant use, the in-line UPS battery tends to wear out sooner than does the standby UPS battery.

The in-line UPS is more expensive than the standby UPS; one less-expensive variation eliminates the secondary circuit altogether, leaving the battery-charged circuit with no backup.

THE LINE-INTERACTIVE UPS

The line-interactive UPS is a variation of the standby UPS that shortens the switching time by always keeping the inverter working, so that there is no charging-up time for the inverter. An inverter is a device that converts DC to AC. However, during regular operation, the inverter filters the electricity and charges the battery by converting AC to DC (technically, it is operating as a rectifier at this time and not as an inverter). If the power fails, the inverter switches roles and begins to convert the battery's DC to AC. The delay for the inverter to switch roles is shorter than the delay for a standby UPS that must start up the inverter.

The line-interactive UPS also offers good line conditioning because there is an automatic voltage regulator called the **buck-boost** feature. During spikes in electrical power, the regulator decreases (in other words bucks) the voltage, and it boosts it during brownouts. The boost feature means that the line-interactive UPS does not need to draw on battery power to respond to a brownout, as does the true standby UPS.

The Intelligent UPS

Some UPSs can be controlled by software from a computer to allow for additional functionality. For example, from the front panel of some UPSs you can check for a weak battery. If the UPS is an **intelligent UPS**, you can perform the same function from the utility software installed on your computer. In order for a UPS to accommodate this feature, it must have a serial port connection to the PC and a microprocessor on board. Some of the things this utility software and an intelligent UPS can do are:

- Diagnose the UPS
- Check for a weak battery
- Monitor the quality of electricity received

- During a blackout, monitor the percentage of load the UPS is carrying
- Automatically schedule the weak-battery test or UPS diagnostic test
- Send an alarm to workstations on a network to prepare for a shutdown
- Close down all servers protected by the UPS during a blackout
- Provide pager notification to a facilities manager if the power goes out during a weekend
- After a shutdown, allow for startup from a remote location over phone lines

When Buying a UPS

The power supplies in most computers can operate over a wide range of electrical voltage input, but operating the computer under these conditions for extended periods of time can shorten the life not only of the power supply, but of the computer as well. Power protection devices offer these benefits.

- Conditions the line accounting for both brownouts and spikes
- Provides backup power during a blackout
- Protects against very high spikes that could damage the equipment

When you purchase a UPS, cost often drives the decision about how much and what kind of protection you buy. However, do not buy an in-line UPS that runs at full capacity. A battery charger operating at full capacity produces heat, which can reduce the life of the battery. The UPS rating should exceed your total VA or wattage output by at least 25%. Also be aware of the degree of line conditioning that the UPS provides. Consider the warranty and service policies as well as the guarantee the UPS manufacturer gives for the equipment the UPS protects.

CHAPTER SUMMARY

- Electricity is measured in voltage, which is a measure of electrical pressure in a system.
- Electrical current is measured in amps, and electrical resistance is measured in ohms. One volt drives a current of one amp through a resistance of one ohm.
- Wattage is a measure of electrical power. Wattage is calculated by multiplying volts by amps in a system.
- Microcomputers require DC current, which is converted from AC current by the power supply inside the computer case.
- The power supply is technically a transformer and rectifier rather than a supplier of power.
- A multimeter is a device that can measure volts, amps, ohms, and continuity in an electrical system.

- Before replacing a damaged systemboard in a PC, first measure the output of the power supply to make sure that it did not cause the damage.

- A faulty power supply can cause memory errors, data errors, system hangs, or reboots, and it can damage a systemboard or other component.

- The U.S. Environmental Protection Agency has established Energy Star standards for electronic devices, to reduce energy consumption.

- Devices that are Energy Star compliant go into a sleep mode in which they use less than 30 watts of power.

- PCs that are Energy Star compliant often have CMOS settings that affect the Energy Star options available on the PC.

- Devices that control the electricity to a computer include surge suppressors, line conditioners, and UPSs.

- A surge suppressor protects a computer against damaging spikes in the electrical voltage.

- Line conditioners level out the AC current to reduce brownouts and spikes.

- A UPS provides enough power to perform an orderly shutdown during a blackout.

- There are two kinds of UPSs: the true UPS, called the in-line UPS, (or, sometimes, the on-line UPS) and the standby UPS.

- The in-line UPS is the more expensive, because it provides continuous power. The standby UPS must switch from one circuit to another when a blackout begins.

- An intelligent UPS can be controlled and managed from utility software at a remote computer, or from a computer connected to the UPS through a serial cable.

- Data line protectors are small surge suppressors designed to protect modems from spikes on telephone lines.

Key Terms

- **Alternating current (AC)** — Current that cycles back and forth rather than traveling in only one direction. Normally between 110 and 115 AC volts are supplied from a standard wall outlet.

- **Ammeter** — A meter that measures electrical current in amps.

- **Ampere (A)** — A unit of measurement for electrical current. One volt across a resistance of one ohm will produce a flow of one amp.

- **Autorange meter** — A multimeter that senses the quantity of input and sets the range accordingly.

- **Buck-boost regulator** — A line-interactive UPS that offers good line conditioning and has an automatic voltage regulator that decreases ("bucks") the voltage during electrical spikes and boosts it during sags.

- **Clamping voltage** — The maximum voltage allowed through a surge suppressor, such as 175 or 330 volts.

- **Continuity** — A continuous, unbroken path for the flow of electricity. A "continuity test" can determine whether or not internal wiring is still intact.

- **Data line protectors** — Surge protectors designed to work with the telephone line to a modem.

- **Direct current (DC)** — Current that travels in only one direction (the type of electricity provided by batteries). Computer power supplies transform AC current to low DC current.

- **Display power management signaling (DPMS)** — Energy Star standard specifications that allow for the video card and monitor to go into sleep mode simultaneously. *See* Energy Star systems.

- **Double conversion** — The process by which the in-line UPS converts the AC power to battery power in DC form and then back to AC power.

- **Doze time** — The time before an Energy Star or "Green" system will reduce 80% of its activity.

- **Energy Star systems** — "Green" systems that satisfy the EPA requirements to decrease the overall consumption of electricity. *See* Green standards.

- **Ferroresonant regulator** — A UPS device that contains a magnetic coil that can retain a power charge that can be used during a brownout to raise the voltage at switching time.

- **Green Standards** — Standards that mean that a computer or device can go into sleep or doze mode when not in use, thus saving energy and helping the environment.

- **Hard drive standby time** — The amount of time before a hard drive will shut down to conserve energy.

- **In-line UPS** — A UPS that continually provides power through a battery-powered circuit, and, because it requires no switching, ensures continuous power to the user.

- **Intelligent UPS** — A UPS connected to a computer by way of a serial cable so that software on the computer can monitor and control the UPS.

- **Joule** — A measure of energy equal to the work done when a current of one ampere is passed through a resistance of one ohm for one second.

- **Let-through** — The maximum voltage allowed through a surge suppresser to the device being protected.

- **Line conditioners** — Devices that regulate, or condition the power, providing continuous voltage during brownouts and spikes.

- **Line-interactive UPS** — A variation of a standby UPS that shortens switching time by always keeping the inverter from AC to DC working, so that there is no charge-up time for the inverter.

10

- **Multimeter** — Either a voltmeter or an ammeter that can also measure resistance in ohms or as continuity, depending on a switch setting.

- **Ohms** — The standard unit of measurement for electrical resistance. Resistors are rated in ohms.

- **Power conditioners** — Line conditioners that regulate, or condition, the power, providing continuous voltage during brownouts.

- **Resistance** — The degree to which a device opposes or resists the flow of electricity. As the electrical resistance increases, the current decreases. (*See* Ohms and Resistor.)

- **Resistor** — An electronic device that resists or opposes the flow of electricity. A resistor can be used to reduce the amount of electricity being supplied to an electronic component.

- **Sleep mode** — A mode used in many "Green" systems that allows them to be configured through CMOS to suspend the monitor or even the drive if the keyboard and/or CPU have been inactive for a set number of minutes. *See* Green standards.

- **Standby time** — The time before a "Green" system will reduce 92% of its activity. *See* Green standards.

- **Standby UPS** — A UPS that quickly switches from an AC power source to a battery-powered source during a brownout or outage.

- **Surge suppressor** — A device or power strip designed to protect electronic equipment from power surges and spikes.

- **Suspend time** — The time before the system will reduce 99% of its activity. After this time, the system needs a warm-up time so that the CPU, monitor, and hard drive can reach full activity.

- **Transformer** — A device that converts AC to DC or DC to AC current. A computer power supply is basically a transformer.

- **UPS (uninterruptible power supply)** — A device designed to provide a backup power supply during a power failure. Basically, a UPS is a battery backup system with an ultrafast sensing device.

- **Volt** — A measure of electrical pressure differential. A computer power supply usually provides four separate voltages: +12V, -12V, +5V, and -5V.

- **Voltage** — Electrical differential that causes current to flow, measured in volts. (*See* Volts.)

- **Voltmeter** — A device for measuring electrical voltage.

- **Watts** — The unit used to measure power. A typical computer may use a power supply that provides 200 watts.

REVIEW QUESTIONS

1. What is the measure of electrical pressure called?

2. What is the unit of measure for voltage? What device is used to measure voltage?

3. What is the measure of electrical current called?

4. What is the unit of measure of electrical current? What device is used to measure electrical current?

5. Define electrical resistance.

6. What is the unit of measure of electrical resistance? What device is used to measure electrical resistance?

7. What electronic devices can be placed in an electronic circuit to reduce the flow or current of electricity?

8. What is the measure of electrical power called?

9. Define alternating current.

10. Where is alternating current usually found? What voltage is typically supplied in AC systems?

11. Define direct current.

12. What types of devices usually use direct current? What voltage is typically supplied in DC systems?

13. What is a transformer?

14. Where is a transformer usually found in a PC?

15. What is a multimeter?

16. On a multimeter, how is a digital display different from an analog display?

17. What is continuity?

18. What type of situations may indicate problems with a PC electrical power supply?

19. How many cable connectors are attached to a typical PC power supply? What are they typically used for?

20. What voltage is supplied by a typical PC power supply?

21. How many watts are supplied by a typical PC power supply?

22. Define and describe sleep mode.

23. What is a spike?

24. What are some of the features to consider when buying a surge protector?

25. What is a UPS? What are some of the features to consider when buying a UPS?

26. How is a brownout different from a blackout?

PROJECTS

ENERGY STAR FEATURES ON A PC

Write down each of the power management and Energy Star features that can be set through CMOS on your home or lab computer.

PRICE AND VALUE COMPARISONS

At your local computer vendor(s), compare the prices and ratings of two different surge suppressors.

PC POWER SUPPLY FACTS

Remove the cover from your home or lab PC and answer the following questions:

1. How many watts are supplied by your power supply? (It is usually printed on the label on the top of the power supply.)
2. How many cables are supplied by your power supply?
3. Where does each cable lead?
4. Is there a switch on the back of the power supply that can be set for 220 volts (Europe) or 110 volts (U.S.)?

BUILD A CIRCUIT TO TURN ON A LIGHT

1. From the following components, build a circuit to turn on a light.
   - An AC light bulb or LED (*Note*: An LED has polarity—it must be connected with the negative and positive terminals in the correct positions.)
   - A double-A battery (*Note*: A 9-volt battery can cause some bulbs to blow up.)
   - A switch (A knife switch or even a DIP switch will work.)
   - Three pieces of wire to connect the light, the switch, and the battery
2. Add a second battery to the circuit and record the results.

3. Add a resistor to the circuit and record the results.

4. Place an extra wire in the middle of the circuit running from the battery to the switch (thus making a short) and record the results.

MEASURE THE OUTPUT OF YOUR POWER SUPPLY

Measure the power output to the systemboard of your computer and to the floppy drive. Fill in the following chart:

Systemboard

Red Lead	Black Lead	Voltage Measure
3	5	
3	6	
3	7	
3	8	
4	ground	
9	ground	
10	ground	
11	ground	
12	ground	

Floppy Drive

Red Lead	Black Lead	Voltage Measure
1	2	
4	3	

RESEARCH THE MARKET FOR A UPS FOR YOUR COMPUTER SYSTEM

For a computer system you have access to, determine how much wattage output a UPS should have in the event of a total blackout, and estimate how long the UPS should sustain the power. Research the market and report on the features and prices of a standby UPS and an in-line UPS. Include the following information in your report:

- Wattage supported

- Length of time the power is sustained during total blackout

- Line conditioning features

- AC backup present or not present for the in-line UPS

- Ferroresonant transformer present or not present

- Surge suppressor present or not present

- Number of power outlets on the box and other features

- Written guarantees

- Brand name, model, vendor, and price of the device

USING A MULTIMETER IN TROUBLESHOOTING

A user comes to you with a problem. He has a cable that connects the serial port of his computer to a serial printer. He needs to order more of the same cables, but he does not know whether this cable is a regular serial cable or a specialized cable made specifically for this printer. One connector on the cable is 9-pin and the other connector is 25-pin. Use a multimeter measuring continuity to answer these questions.

1. Is this a regular serial cable? (*Hint*: use your pin out results of the project at the end of Chapter 8 and verify with a multimeter that your expectations are correct.)

2. If this is not a regular serial cable, but a specialized cable, give the user the pin outs necessary to order new custom-made cables.

SUPPORTING WINDOWS 3.X AND WINDOWS 95

Supporting Windows requires a general knowledge of how hardware works and a detailed knowledge of how Windows and other types of software work. Having a conceptual understanding of how Windows works to manage memory, other hardware devices, and applications software helps in troubleshooting and problem solving.

Windows 95 has its roots in DOS and Windows 3.x. Many of the techniques used to troubleshoot and solve Windows 95 problems work equally well with DOS and Windows 3.x. However, each OS has its unique features, and you must study each separately. This chapter will first look at Windows 3.x and how to solve software problems in this operating environment. The chapter will then turn to Windows 95, addressing the similarities and differences between the two. There are many diagnostic software programs available to help solve Windows problems. Several will be used in this chapter.

IN THIS CHAPTER
YOU WILL LEARN:

- About Windows installations and customizing the Windows environment
- How to install and resolve problems with applications software
- How to manage Windows resources including memory and hard drives
- About ways to optimize Windows performance
- About the Windows registry and how to repair a corrupted registry
- How to use some diagnostic software
- About Plug-and-Play and how to troubleshoot Plug-and-Play problems

SUPPORTING WINDOWS 3.1 AND WINDOWS 3.11

Figure 11-1 shows a comparison of revenue received for plant operations OS licenses in 1996. Even though Windows 95 and Windows NT are the most popular operating systems being purchased today for single-user PCs, many computers still use DOS and Windows 3.x. This section covers installation problems, problems with applications software in a Windows 3.x environment, and troubleshooting and optimizing Windows 3.x. Remember that in this book Windows 3.x refers to Windows, Windows 3.11 (Windows for WorkGroups) and Windows 3.1.

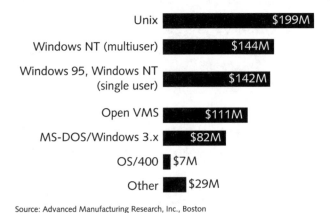

Source: Advanced Manufacturing Research, Inc., Boston

Figure 11-1   1996 plant operations license revenue by operating system

WINDOWS 3.X CONFIGURATION AND APPLICATION INFORMATION

When applications software is installed under Windows 3.x, the software installation program passes information about itself to Windows. Windows, in turn, stores this configuration information in what are called configuration or initialization files (with .ini extensions) and in the registry database, Reg.dat. Windows 3.x also stores configuration information about the hardware devices it has access to, about decisions it and you made during the installation of Windows, and about any changes you make to the Windows environment. If the information in these .ini files or in the registry becomes lost or corrupted, many aspects of the system can be affected, including the applications software, the way Windows uses its hardware resources, and the Windows environment and settings. This section will discuss the contents of the .ini files and the registry, and what to do to repair a corrupted registry.

Configuration Files

An **initialization file** with an .ini file extension is a file used by Windows or applications software to store configuration information needed when Windows or an application is first loaded. Earlier versions of Windows stored all configuration information in only one .ini file, Win.ini. Later releases of Windows used other .ini files, and the most recent versions of Windows move information previously stored in .ini files to the registry, which is discussed next. Table 11-1 lists Windows .ini files.

Table 11-1   Windows .ini files

.ini File	Contents
Win.ini	Characteristics of Windows, customized settings
System.ini	Customized settings, hardware configuration information
Control.ini	Information that can be changed from the Control Panel, including colors, wallpaper, and printer configuration
Progman.ini	Information about the icons in Program Manager and security restrictions
Winfile.ini	Settings and characteristics of File Manager
Filename.ini	Many applications software programs have an .ini file in the Windows directory containing startup information about the application.

11

Files with a .ini extension are organized by sections, which are each given a name. Within a section, values are assigned to variables using this format:

```
[SECTION NAME]

KEYNAME=value
```

Any value to the right of the Keyname becomes available to Windows or an applications software program reading the file, much like the SET command in Autoexec.bat that assigns a value to a system variable.

Ini files are only read when Windows or an application using them starts up. If you change a Windows .ini file, you must restart Windows for the change to take effect. If you change an applications software .ini file, you must restart the software for the change to take effect.

It's a good practice to back up the .ini files before you install new software or make changes to the Windows setup. For example, the name of the display driver is kept in System.ini. Before you try a new display driver, copy System.ini to another directory. If the change causes Windows to be unable to use the monitor correctly, you can exit Windows, restore the old version of System.ini to the Windows directory, and restart Windows, to return you to the old settings.

Ini files are ASCII text files, meaning that you can edit them with any text editor, such as Notepad. The best way to change the contents of an .ini file, however, is to make the changes using Windows Program Manager, Control Panel, Windows Setup, and other tools provided by Windows. Changes made in the menus of Program Manager are recorded in Progman.ini. Changes made from the Control Panel are recorded in Control.ini. File Manager changes are recorded in Winfile.ini. Windows Setup changes and Printer Setup changes are recorded in either Win.ini or System.ini. Most applications software programs have a setup icon in their program group in Program Manager that is designed to make changes to the application's .ini file.

System Configuration Editor (Sysedit) is the tool provided by Windows to view and manually edit .ini files as well as to edit Autoexec.bat and Config.sys. From either Program Manager or File Manager, select **File, Run**. In the Run dialog box, type **Sysedit** and click **OK**. The System Configuration Editor window displays, showing four files ready to edit, Config.sys, Autoexec.bat, System.ini, and Win.ini. In Figure 11-2, Win.ini is displayed. The section name [Extensions] is shown together with several lines in that section. This section is used by Windows to associate a file extension with an application. Note in Figure 11-2 that .txt file extensions are associated with Notepad.exe. You can verify this setting by going to File Manager and selecting a file with a .txt extension by single-clicking the file. With the .txt file selected, choose **File, Associate** from the File Manager menu. The Associate dialog box in Figure 11-3 displays, and you can see that files with the .txt extension are associated with Notepad.exe. Here is an example of a Windows setting that was set in File Manager and retained in Win.ini. (Later in the chapter, you will see that associations are also kept in the Windows registry.)

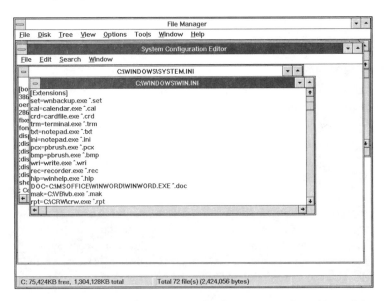

Figure 11-2 Using the System Configuration Editor (Sysedit)

Figure 11-3   The .txt file extension is associated with Notepad.exe

You can change a line in an .ini file into a comment line by putting a semicolon at the beginning of the line. **Comment lines** are ignored by Windows and other software and are only used to document the file. Sometimes a semicolon is placed in front of a line as a troubleshooting technique to see if temporarily disabling that line solves a problem.

Here's another example of how comments can be helpful. Windows records the current video driver filename in System.ini, and changes are made under the Windows Setup icon of the Control Panel. Suppose you want to try a new video driver that you don't know will work. To prepare for a problem with video after you make the change, edit the System.ini file. Make a copy of the line "display.drv =" in the [boot] section of System.ini, which identifies the video driver file to Windows. Then put a semicolon in front of the line, to make the copy of the line a comment. Save changes and exit the editor. Next, go into the Control Panel, Windows setup, and change setup to the new video driver. Windows records this change by editing the display.drv line to contain the new driver filename, overwriting the older filename. Restart Windows to see the change take effect. If Windows does not provide good video with the new driver, you can exit Windows and get to a DOS prompt. Edit the System.ini file. Put a semicolon in front of the display.drv line that contains the video driver filename that caused the problem, and remove the semicolon from the first display.drv line, which you saved earlier.

Figure 11-4 shows a sample of System.ini where there are two display.drv lines. One is a comment and the other is not. Also note in Figure 11-4 that when Central Point Software made a change to System.ini during its installation, it politely saved the earlier value of the line that it changed (the mouse line), as a comment line, and added its own comment indicating what happened.

The maximum file size of .ini files is 64K, although files greater than 32K can give some applications software problems. If you notice that the Win.ini file size exceeds 32K, you can reinstall Windows, which rebuilds the file, or, if you are aware of entries in the file that no longer apply to your system, you can manually edit the file and delete these lines. If you are not absolutely sure that a line is no longer needed, place a semicolon in front of the line, so that it can be easily retrieved if necessary.

11

```
[boot]
386grabber=ALVGA.3GR
oemfonts.fon=8514OEM.FON
286grabber=VGACOLOR.2GR
fixedfon.fon=8514FIX.FON
fonts.fon=8514SYS.FON
display.drv=V631P.DRV
;display.drv=avga800.drv
shell=progman.exe
; Central Point Software Commute requires the following line
replaced:
;  mouse.drv=mouse.drv
mouse.drv=commmou.drv
```

Figure 11-4   Using comment lines in the System.ini file

Before reinstalling Windows 3.x, upgrading Windows, or installing a new application, back up all .ini files to a different directory or to a disk.

The Windows 3.x Registry

Beginning in 1994, versions of Windows 3.x began to store some configuration information in a **registration database** named Reg.dat, which is found in the Windows directory. During the installation of applications software, entries are made to Reg.dat. You can use the Registration Info Editor, Regedit.exe, to view and modify the registry. From either File Manager or Program Manager, choose **File, Run** and enter **Regedit** in the Run dialog box. The editor loads Reg.dat and displays a list of applications it has registered, as shown in Figure 11-5. The most common reasons for an application to record an entry in the Windows 3.x registry are for object linking to other applications and for dynamic data exchange.

Object linking is a method by which you can be in one application and execute a command on an object created by another application, which causes the application that created the object to load. An example of object linking is accessing a picture file created in PaintBrush and embedding it in a Word document. Double-click on the picture, and PaintBrush loads, allowing you to edit the picture file using its parent application. For this to work, both applications must have information recorded in the registry.

Dynamic data exchange allows one application to communicate with another and share data. File associations are also kept in the registry.

Setup.reg is an ASCII text file that contains the same entries as Reg.dat. Figure 11-6 shows some of the contents of this file.

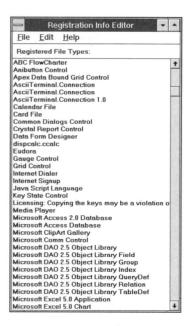

Figure 11-5   Windows 3.x Registration Info Editor (Regedit.exe)

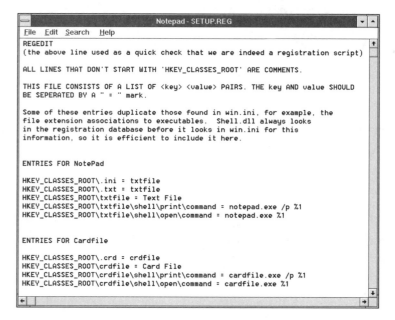

Figure 11-6   Setup.reg contains a text version of the Windows
Reg.dat file

Errors that occur in applications that are not correctly registered generate messages such as "Object not found". You might get this error message if you try to insert a new object into an application, and the parent application of the object is not found in the Insert Object dialog box.

Many applications register themselves during installation. Other applications rebuild their entries every time the application starts. If you suspect that an application is not correctly registered, because of an error message, as described above, you can register the application yourself. If there is a file in the applications directory with a .reg file extension, simply double-click the filename to register the application.

In the \Tools\PSS directory on the Microsoft Visual BASIC 4.0 CD-ROM, there is a utility named Regsvr.exe that registers applications. Copy this utility program to your hard drive or to a disk to quickly and easily register applications. To use it, from either Program Manager or File Manager, select **File, Run**. In the Run dialog box, type **Regsvr** together with its path and the name of the file you want to register, and click **OK**. A message displays that the file was correctly registered. For example, to register the data access object file Da02516.dll, use this command:

```
\UTILITY\REGSVR.EXE   \WINDOWS\SYSTEM\DAO2516.DLL
```

Regsvr.exe is a handy utility program to keep, in case you need to rebuild a corrupted registry.

Corrupted Registry. The Reg.dat file might become corrupted. One of the following errors might indicate a corrupted registry.

- File Manager will not open or print the selected file.

- File associations in File Manager are lost.

- During the installation of software, the setup program gives an error message relating to the registry.

- An application gives the error message that an OLE server initialization failed. (Object linking and embedding capabilities of Windows allow applications to share files.)

- An application gives the error message that the Windows registration database is not valid.

- The Reg.dat file size exceeds 65,000 bytes.

When you get one of these errors, try rebuilding the registry by following these steps:

1. Back up the Reg.dat file to another directory or under another name.

2. From Program Manager or File Manager, choose **File, Run**. From the Run dialog box, enter this command:

```
REGEDIT /U C:\WINDOWS\SYSTEM\SETUP.REG
```

This command rebuilds the registry as it was when you first installed Windows.

3. Look in File Manager in the \Windows\system directory for Reg.dat. If you don't see it, then exit and restart Windows. The file should then be present.

4. Because many file associations are now lost, do the following. From File Manager, select the **Reg.dat** file and choose **File, Associate** from the menu. Associate the file with Regedit.exe.

5. Do the same for a file with the .reg file extension, to associate these file types with Regedit.exe.

6. Exit and restart Windows.

7. Register all applications that have a .reg file in their directories by doing the following. From the File menu in File Manager, choose **Search**. Search for *.reg files from the C:\ directory and all subdirectories. Run every .reg file you find by double-clicking on the filename from File Manager.

WINDOWS 3.X INSTALLATIONS

The Windows 3.x setup utility is easy to use, and the instructions are clear. However, the following tips might help avoid installation problems.

Before the Installation

Before installing Windows 3.x, prepare your hard drive by running CHKDSK/F to recover lost clusters, deleting these .CHK files created by CHKDSK, and running DEFRAG to defragment your hard drive. These DOS commands were discussed in Chapters 5 and 6. Not only does the defragmenting improve overall hard drive performance, but you might be able to increase the size of your swap file.

To ensure that you can backtrack to an earlier version of Windows, save to a disk Autoexec.bat and Config.sys files found in the root directory and all the .ini files and .grp files in the \Windows directory. Files with the .grp file extension are **group files** that contain information about a program group displayed in Program Manager. If you have problems with the installation, you can reinstall the original version of Windows and copy the .ini files and .grp files back to the \Windows directory to fully recover from the problem installation.

Preparing for a Clean Boot.   Check the Config.sys and Autoexec.bat files for potential problems. Before you install Windows, configure your memory with the methods discussed in Chapter 9, using Memmaker, or enter the commands manually into these two files. Optimizing memory before installing Windows allows Windows to edit correctly configured Autoexec.bat and Config.sys files. If there are TSRs such as QEMM386 (a memory manager by Quarterdeck) loaded from Config.sys or Autoexec.bat, you might have no problem with them running during the installation. However, if problems arise, comment these lines to temporarily disable them during the installation. After the installation, you can activate them again. To comment a line in either Autoexec.bat or Config.sys, type **REM** at the beginning of the command line. The line becomes a **Comment line** or **Remark line** and is ignored by the OS.

Installing Windows on a Compressed Drive.   Windows can be installed on a drive that has previously been compressed. However, the swap file and temporary files should be written to an uncompressed logical drive, usually the drive that contains the host drive. If the host drive is not large enough to hold these files, check the software used to compress the drive, to see if you can increase the size of the host drive.

11

Setup Options

Place the Windows 3.x setup disk 1 in the floppy drive and type **A:\Setup** at the DOS prompt. The Setup program loads. At the beginning of the Windows installation, you are given two choices, the Express Setup and the Custom Setup.

Express Setup.   The Express Setup makes more decisions for you than does the Custom Setup. The Express Setup automatically updates the Autoexec.bat and Config.sys files. Windows installs itself in the C:\Windows directory without giving you the opportunity to select a different directory. If there is not enough room on drive C to install Windows, it looks for other drives on the system with enough space. If it cannot find enough room, a limited version of Windows is installed. If there is a previous version of Windows on the system, printer driver information is carried forward into the new installation. The Express Setup also searches your system for applications and automatically creates Program Groups and icons for those that it finds.

Custom Setup.   The Custom Setup provides more opportunity for you to customize the Windows environment. Custom Setup allows you to select the drive and directory where Windows will be installed, select desktop options such as the wallpaper, and select accessories that you want installed. Custom Setup allows you to change the hardware it has detected, and shows you the changes it plans to make to Autoexec.bat and Config.sys files. You can edit any changes to these files during the installation. You have control over the printers that Custom Setup installs and over the applications that it places in Program Manager.

Reinstalling Windows.   After Windows has been used for some time and several software installations and uninstalls have been done, it is not uncommon to encounter problems under Windows that might affect software running under it. Reinstalling Windows might resolve a problem with an applications software program. During the installation, if Windows detects that a previous version of Windows is installed, you are given the opportunity to install the software on top of the existing software, in the same directory. When you make this choice, previous Windows settings and printer drivers are retained. If Windows detects that older printer drivers need to be replaced with newer versions, it will do so.

 If applications software using Windows begins to generate an unusual number of errors, one thing you can do toward resolving the problem is to reinstall Windows.

Problems During the Installation.   Here are some things that might go wrong during Windows installation and advice on what to do about them.

Setup continues to ask for the same installation disk.   Remove the disk from the floppy drive and verify that you have the correct disk. The shuttle windows on new disks sometimes stick; open and close the shuttle window several times and try the disk again. It's possible that the disk could be defective. In that case, you will need to obtain a replacement disk from the retailer or manufacturer.

Setup does not list the hardware you have on your system.   Check the documentation for your hardware to see if you can substitute an alternate brand and model. For example, if the printer you have is not listed in the printer list that Windows supports, the documentation for the printer probably offers an alternate printer that uses a driver compatible with your printer.

Sometimes applications software has trouble with the alternate printer driver, so the long-range fix is to obtain a Windows driver from the manufacturer for your printer. Also, the documentation for your hardware might not offer an alternative. Windows driver programs for the hardware are usually found on a disk that is shipped with the printer, or you can obtain them from the hardware manufacturer (ask for a Windows-compatible driver) or download many from the Microsoft support Web site, www.microsoft.com or from the manufacturer's Web site.

You don't have enough hard drive space for the installation.   Did you erase lost clusters and defragment the drive before the installation? Look for temporary files or applications software that you no longer use that can be deleted. Run the Custom Setup and choose to not install the accessories, including wallpaper, when given the opportunity. You can later add some of them to Windows if you have the space.

Setup hangs during the installation.   Most likely, Setup is having trouble detecting the hardware present. Reboot to DOS. Add the /I option to the Setup command line like this:

```
C:\>   A:SETUP /I
```

The I option runs a Custom Setup that bypasses the search for hardware. With this option, you are required to select the hardware manually. See the documentation for the hardware for answers to the questions that Setup asks about the hardware.

Another possible source of trouble is a virus. Run a virus scan program on the hard drive from the DOS prompt.

Windows will not boot after the installation is complete.   Boot to the DOS C prompt. Change directories to the Windows directory and enter Setup at the DOS prompt like this:

```
C:\WINDOWS>   SETUP
```

Check the hardware installed and make changes as necessary.

Check the Config.sys and Autoexec.bat files for TSRs and comment these lines out to make the cleanest boot possible.

After the installation, the mouse does not work in Windows.   Verify that the mouse works in DOS before you load Windows. Load the mouse driver in either the Config.sys or Autoexec.bat file. For example, to load the driver for a Microsoft-compatible mouse, use one of these two methods:

Use this command in the Config.sys file:

```
DEVICE=\DOS\MOUSE.SYS
```

Use this command in the Autoexec.bat file:

```
\DOS\MOUSE.COM
```

Boot to the DOS prompt and test the mouse. Try to edit a file using Edit.com. If the mouse driver loaded correctly, you should have the use of the mouse in this editor. If the mouse still does not work, you are probably using the wrong driver for the type of mouse you have. Most often a mouse comes with a disk containing the driver file for the mouse. Try the driver on this disk.

After you have the mouse working in DOS, try loading Windows again.

After the Installation Is Complete

After the installation is completed, to ensure optimum performance, check that you are using the latest version of Himem.sys, Emm386.exe, and Smartdrv.exe. Versions of all three files should be in your DOS directory and in the Windows directory. Check the date stamp on each file and determine which directory holds the most recent version of each. Edit the Config.sys file and Autoexec.bat file so that the paths to these three TSRs point to the file with the most recent date.

At the end of the Windows installation, you have the opportunity to read the documentation files. These five files are located in the Windows directory and can be read at any time with Windows Write. Double-click the filename from File Manager to open, read, and/or print each file. The five files are:

- Readme.wri   Updates to the User Manual
- Printers.wri   Information about setting up printers
- Networks.wri   Information about Windows on a network
- Sysini.wri   Detailed information about the System.ini file
- Winini.wri   Detailed information about the Win.ini file

CONFLICTS AND PROBLEMS WITH APPLICATIONS SOFTWARE IN A WINDOWS ENVIRONMENT

This section addresses software conflicts, memory errors, other Windows error messages caused by applications software, and problems installing applications software.

Installing Applications Software

Generally, installing applications software is easy and presents few problems. The steps listed below summarize the software installation process. Of course, the documentation for the software is your best source for instructions on installing any package.

Check Available Resources.   Check your computer resources to make sure you have (1) enough space on your hard drive, (2) the minimum requirements for memory, and (3) the proper CPU and video monitor—and that you can fulfill any other requirement of the particular software program. The minimum requirements for the software should be listed in the installation manual. Remember that you should not completely fill the hard drive with software and data.

 Allow a minimum of 10 MB of unused hard drive space for working temporary files used by applications.

Protect the Original Software.   If you are using a CD-ROM for the software installation, be careful not to scratch or mar the shiny surface as you work. When the CD-ROM is not in the drive, place it in its original case. For floppy disks, write-protect the original disks before you begin the installation. After the installation is complete, put the original disks or CD-ROM in a safe place.

Back up Your System Configuration Files.   Many software packages will want to edit Config.sys, Autoexec.bat, Win.sys, Program.ini, and/or System.ini files during the installation. Before you begin the installation, make backup copies of all of these files so that you can backtrack if you choose.

Install the Software.   From Program Manager or File Manager, select **File, Run**. Type the drive and name of the installation program, for example, A:Install or D:Setup. The installation program loads and begins execution. If the installation program asks you a question you cannot answer, you can always abandon the installation and try again later.

Most software will ask you for a serial number unique to your copy of the software. This serial number might be written on the CD-ROM or on the first floppy disk or might be stamped on the documentation. If the number is not printed on the floppy disk or CD-ROM, but on the documentation, write the serial number on the floppy disk or CD case, so that you will still have it if the documentation is later lost. Copyright agreements often allow you to install the software on only one computer at a time. This serial number identifies the copy of the software that you have installed on this machine.

You might be asked if you want to perform full, default, custom, or partial installation. If you have plenty of hard drive space, a full installation lets you see all that the software has to offer. You can always delete what you don't want later. Most packages today store the modules in separate subdirectories. For example, a tutorial may be installed in one directory under the parent directory that contains the main module, and sample files may be stored under a child directory. You can most often easily identify these directories by their names. Delete their contents if you need the hard drive space.

If you are short on drive space, you can eliminate portions of the software, only choosing what is recommended for a partial installation. For example, if you are already familiar with the software, consider eliminating the tutorials and samples.

11

Test the Software. If you are not familiar with the software, read the documentation and look for a tutorial or help utility. Most software comes with sample files that can help you learn to use the software. For example, Adobe PageMaker comes with several sample documents that demonstrate what PageMaker can do.

When you are learning to use a new package, one good approach is to "copy the best". For example, if you're learning to use Microsoft Excel, find a good example of a spreadsheet that you like and think you might use, and reproduce it yourself. If you're learning to use PageMaker, duplicate a professional-looking document. You will not only learn the details of the package, but also will gain experience making a professional-looking document.

What Can Go Wrong. Listed next are some problems that might occur during an installation and suggestions about solving them.

Windows does not allow software to be installed. There might have been some restrictions placed on Windows to prevent software from being installed or uninstalled by the user. Look in the Progman.ini file for a section labeled [Restrictions]. These restrictions can prevent program groups from being added and deleted from Program Manager. Among other restrictions, look for the line "EditLevel=". Any EditLevel above 0 can hamper a program installation.

There is not enough hard drive space. Most installation programs will check the hard drive space before they begin. You should also check the hard drive space yourself before the installation. During the installation, insufficient hard drive space might trigger the error message "Insufficient disk space." After the installation, the program or some other program might refuse to run because the hard drive does not have enough space for it to open temporary working files.

The software is installed, but when you first execute it, it tells you that an environmental variable is not defined. Software installation programs often add a SET command to your Autoexec.bat file. This command might look something like this:

```
SET MYPATH=C:\VERT
```

Later the software will use the environmental variable MYPATH in the program. If the installation program placed the SET command too late in the Autoexec.bat file, an error will occur. Suppose the file looks like this:

```
WIN
```

```
SET MYPATH=C:\VERT
```

The first line (WIN) tells DOS to execute the Windows software. The SET command will not be executed until you exit Windows. If the program you installed runs under Windows, the variable MYPATH will not be defined for the program, and an error will occur. The solution is to move the SET command in front of the WIN command in the Autoexec.bat file. Incidentally, some software installation programs use the SET command to append a line to the PATH command without editing the existing PATH command line itself. It works like this:

```
SET PATH=%PATH%;C:\VERT
```

This SET command works because PATH is to DOS its own environmental variable. The variable PATH is here defined to be the old PATH plus the new appended directory C:\Vert.

The problem is unknown; the software just does not work after the installation. Wrong configuration information might have been given to the installation program. If you suspect that this is the problem, begin again, giving the correct information.

Try reinstalling the software and carefully watching for error messages. Before you begin again, use the uninstall program that comes with the software. Sometimes this program is on the CD-ROM for the software, and sometimes it is listed in the program group of Program Manager. If there is no uninstall program, use a third-party uninstaller, or erase all files that the installation program copied to the hard drive and remove the directories it created. Look in Autoexec.bat and Config.sys files for errors. Restore the original Autoexec.bat, Config.sys, Win.ini, Progman.ini, and System.ini, and begin at the beginning of the installation process. One of the disks might be corrupted, or the installation program might not have been able to perform some task, such as creating a new directory. You might have overlooked an error message the first time. If you are still having problems, try to execute some portion of the software such as the HELP utility. Look for information about installation requirements. Consult your documentation and technical support for the software.

After the installation is complete and the software is working, update your backup copies of Autoexec.bat, Config.sys, System.ini, Win.ini, and Progman.ini so that they, too, reflect the changes that the applications software made to these configuration files.

Problems with Software Conflicts

Suppose you have Microsoft Word installed correctly on your PC; it has worked well for some time. You install several new applications software programs, and, after the installations, Word begins to give you problems. Icons that once were displayed correctly now display as black objects, or, whenever you exit Word, Windows displays a General Protection Fault error message. You attempt to correct the problem by reinstalling Word, but the problem does not go away. What happened to Word when you installed the other software that cannot be repaired by reinstalling Word?

The answer is found in the directory \Windows\system. Take a look at this directory as shown in Figure 11-7. The directory holds files that are used by Windows and other applications software programs. Several programs can use the same files found in this directory. The most common type of file found here has a **.dll** extension, which stands for **dynamic link library**. These library files contain various programming routines that are used by many application programs to perform such common tasks as opening a database file or displaying a dialog box on the screen. Windows comes with many of these .dll files already installed, but when you install an applications program, it might place other .dlls in the \Windows\system directory or it might update an existing copy of a .dll file with a later version.

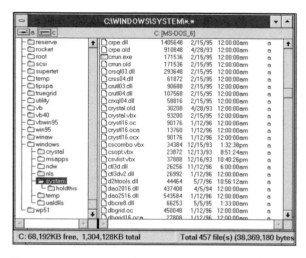

Figure 11-7   Some files in the \Windows\system directory

During the installation, the setup program compares the date stamp on its version of the .dll to the date stamp of the .dll already in \Windows.system. If the setup program determines that its version of the .dll is more recent than the file already present, it may put its own version in the directory. Most installations don't save previous copies of a .dll that it updates; the new application program simply overwrites the file with its own version without informing you of what it's doing.

Problems arise when an application already installed on the PC uses a .dll that has been updated by the new software, and the new .dll is not compatible with the older software or the new .dll is corrupted. Reinstalling the older software does not help because it too is only updating the .dll if it finds that the .dll file in the \Windows\sytem directory has an older date than the date of its version of the .dll.

Finding the .dll that is causing the problem can be like looking for the proverbial needle in a haystack. Looking at Figure 11-7, you see that there are 457 files in this \Windows\system directory. It's not uncommon for a small applications software program to install as many as 50 files in this commonly shared directory. Furthermore, when you uninstall an applications software program, the uninstall program does not (and should not) erase the .dlls in this shared directory. Over time the directory can get quite large, just as the one in Figure 11-7 has.

Solutions to problems with applications software trying to share .dlls and other files in this directory involve taking more control over the installation process and knowing how to use some utility software to help diagnose software problems. Here are some steps to take to avoid and address software conflicts.

Back up the \Windows\system Directory.   If you have the room on your hard drive, you can back up the entire \Windows\system directory before you install new software. After the software is installed, if another program has problems, the older .dlls will be available to you. Perhaps the new software can use an older .dll, and your problem will have a solution.

However, how do you determine which .dll is causing the problem? First, you must know which .dlls were changed by the new software, and you must know which of these .dlls the old software uses. After that, it's usually a matter of replacing each one in turn until the problem goes away. Things can get even more complicated because .dlls sometimes work as groups. For example, you must keep the four or five files in the OLE group together as a group; exchanging only one file in the group causes an error.

Monitor the Files Being Updated During the Installation Process.   Know what files an applications software setup program has written to the \Windows\system directory, or to any directory for that matter, and know the changes made to the Windows .ini files. Two examples of tools you can use to do this are Norton Utilities and a shareware program called In Control. This section looks at how In Control works.

In Control by Neil Rubenking was first published in the September 1995 issue of *PC Magazine*. Two versions, In Control 2 for Windows 3.x and In Control 3 for Windows 95 and NT are available on the Web site www.zdnet.com. Search for PC Magazine and PC Utilities. Download the shareware and read the documentation that is included in the compressed file. In Control works two ways. First, you can take a snapshot of the Windows directory before you perform an installation and then take another snapshot after. The report produced by In Control tells you what changes. The second way you can use the software is to run it while an installation is in progress. After the installation is complete, In Control produces a report of what happened to the entire hard drive, including the Windows directory and the .ini files.

The following example shows how to generate a report using In Control after it monitors an installation. First, execute In Control; Figure 11-8 shows the opening screen.

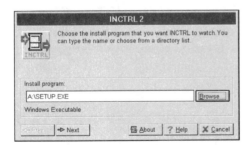

Figure 11-8   In Control 2 opening screen

Enter the path and name of the installation program you want In Control to monitor. In this example, the installation is of a memory manager software program (Moremem) that is being installed from a floppy disk. Enter **A:\SETUP.EXE** and click **Next**. The screen after that asks for the name of the software being installed, which will later be included in the report title. The screen after that asks for the location and name of the report, as in Figure 11-9.

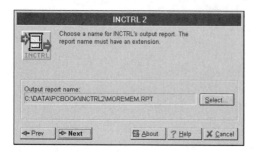

Figure 11-9   In Control 2 saves the report to a file

The next screen, in Figure 11-10, displays the information you have just given it.

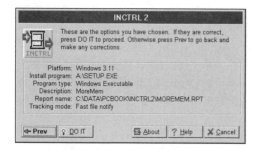

Figure 11-10   In Control 2 summary of options selected

When you click **DO IT**, In Control executes the setup program and monitors the process. In Figure 11-11, the installation of the memory manager, MoreMem, is proceeding normally.

As shown in Figure 11-12, after the installation is complete, In Control tells us that 22 files and directories have been added. The complete report is shown in Figure 11-13.

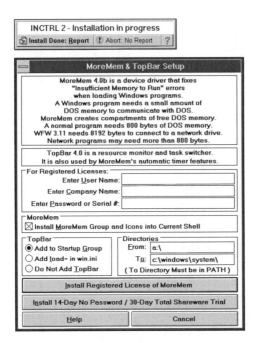

Figure 11-11   In Control 2 monitors an installation

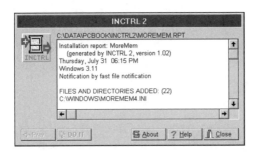

Figure 11-12   In Control 2 reports installation is completed

```
Installation report: MoreMem
     (generated by INCTRL 2, version 1.02)
Thursday, July 31   06:15 PM
Windows 3.11
Notification by fast file notification

FILES AND DIRECTORIES ADDED: (22)
C:\WINDOWS\MOREMEM4.INI
C:\WINDOWS\TEMP\~SPL3E31.TMP
C:\WINDOWS\TEMP\~SPL3D4A.TMP
C:\WINDOWS\TEMP\~MF3D4A.TMP
C:\WINDOWS\SYSTEM.M00
C:\WINDOWS\SYSTEM\TOPBAR4.EXE
C:\WINDOWS\SYSTEM\MEMPOP4.EXE
C:\WINDOWS\SYSTEM\MEMICON4.EXE
C:\WINDOWS\SYSTEM\MOREMEM4.DRV
C:\WINDOWS\SYSTEM\MOREMEM4.HLP
C:\WINDOWS\SYSTEM\MOREMEM4.DOC
C:\WINDOWS\SYSTEM\MM4-US.DOC
C:\WINDOWS\SYSTEM\MOREMEM4.RTF
C:\WINDOWS\SYSTEM\MEMORDER.WRI
C:\WINDOWS\SYSTEM\MEMORDER.TXT
C:\WINDOWS\GRIMOREM.GRP
C:\WINDOWS\TEMP\~SPL3307.TMP
C:\WINDOWS\TEMP\~SPL3151.TMP
C:\WINDOWS\TEMP\~MF360E.TMP
C:\WINDOWS\TEMP\~MF360E.TMP

FILES AND DIRECTORIES DELETED: (3)
C:\WINDOWS\TEMP\~SPL0702.TMP
C:\WINDOWS\TEMP\~SPL0A17.TMP
C:\WINDOWS\TEMP\~MF0A17.TMP

CHANGES MADE TO SYSTEM.INI...
KEYS ADDED TO SYSTEM.INI: (1)
[drivers]MoreMem4=moremem4.drv   ◄──────────[ Driver added

KEYS CHANGED IN SYSTEM.INI: (1)
[boot]drivers=C:\QEMM\FREEMEG.DLL C:\QEMM\RSRCMGR.DLL
mmsystem.dll to moremem4.drv c:\qemm\freemeg.dll c:\qemm\
rsrcmgr.dll mmsystem.dll

NO CHANGES MADE TO WIN.INI...
```

Figure 11-13   In Control report of an installation

Notice in Figure 11-13 that a driver has been added to the System.ini file. This memory manager software runs as a TSR under Windows to save conventional and upper memory by putting into extended memory the .dlls that an application loads into memory. This particular software places several files in the \Windows\system directory. Even though they are not .dlls, from this example, you can see exactly what the software does to the system directory.

Later, if a problem arises with another applications software, by comparing the In Control reports of the two programs, you can identify shared files, thereby narrowing down the possible problem files to a select few. Also, if you ever want to uninstall MoreMem, this report tells you exactly which files to delete from \Windows\system to save drive space and which entries in System.ini you can remove.

In Control does not tell you if a file written to the hard drive has replaced an existing file of the same name. To know that, you must save a copy of \Windows\system before the installation and use the report to search for overwritten files.

An excellent practice is to run In Control each time you install software and keep the report with the software documentation as a record of what happened when the software was first installed.

Know What .dlls an Application Uses. When an application is first loaded, and later as different events happen (for example, a database is read or a dialog box displays on the screen) while the application is running, the application loads and unloads .dlls into memory. You can monitor this process with a Microsoft utility called DLL Unloader available from the Microsoft Web site. Windows developers use DLL Unloader to manage .dlls as they write them. Figure 11-14 shows an example of DLL Unloader running. It displays all drivers and .dlls currently loaded in memory. Select one by clicking it, then click **Info** for the name and complete path to the file. Don't click Unload, because this might cause problems for software currently running.

11

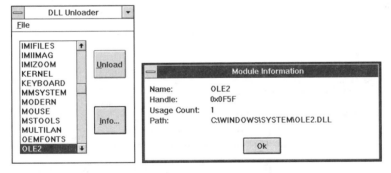

Figure 11-14   DLL Unloader.exe displays all .dlls currently in memory

Run DLL Unloader while an application program is loaded. For example, if an applications software program is giving problems, use DLL Unloader to list the .dlls that might be corrupted. If the software works successfully on one PC, but generates errors on another PC, run DLL Unloader on the good PC. At the point where the software hangs on the other PC, look for a .dll that is loaded at that time. If you discover one, you probably have identified the file causing the problem.

Unloader can be a very useful utility to help identify a .dll that was overwritten by another software installation and is causing problems for the current software. However, Unloader might not tell the entire story. Sometimes when software loads a .dll, it first reads initialization information from another file in the \Windows\system directory, which might be causing the problem. The file is used by the software but is not listed by DLL Unloader.

Also, when you get a Windows error message on the screen, if the dialog box offers a Details command button, click on the button for more information. Sometimes the name of the .dll causing the problem is listed.

How Windows 3.x Manages Memory

One of the primary resources Windows uses is memory. Windows organizes memory into heaps. A **heap** is a programming term that refers to an area of memory that is set aside for programs to use for their data. When a program is first loaded, Windows takes part of memory from the heap and assigns it to this program. When the program terminates, the program returns the memory to the heap managed by Windows.

Memory Heaps

The five memory heaps maintained by Windows are listed in Table 11-2.

Table 11-2   Windows memory heaps

Memory Heap	Contents
System heap	Memory including virtual memory that is available for Windows to assign to programs and their data, and to use for system overhead
GDI heap	Memory used for graphical items such as fonts, icons, mouse pointer objects, etc.
Menu heap	Memory that holds menus and their associated data
Text string heap	Memory that holds Windows text
User heap	Memory that holds information about the desktop, including open and minimized windows and dialog boxes

The amount of memory assigned to any one heap is limited by both Windows 3.x and Windows 95 because of the DOS limitations placed on them, but Windows NT can have heaps with unlimited amounts of memory. The system heap and the GDI heap in Windows 3.x and Windows 95 are the ones most often used to full capacity, resulting in "Out of Memory" error messages. If a program fails to release its memory back to the heap as it terminates, the system can run out of memory. These problems are called **memory leaks** and are addressed later in the chapter.

Problems with Memory

Problems with memory include memory errors and insufficient memory to run an application program. Memory errors in Windows are most often called **GPFs, General Protection**

Fault messages, and are caused by an application program attempting to use memory addresses that have not been allotted to it. You can often solve problems of insufficient memory by applying some general guidelines to conserve memory under Windows. Both problems are discussed in this section with some recommended solutions.

Memory Errors.   With the early PCs of the 1980s, DOS operated totally in real mode. Real mode is a processing mode whereby a program can have access to any area of memory. Real mode memory addressing is not controlled by the OS. In those days, it was assumed that one PC would be running only one program controlled by one user. OS designers gave little thought to allowing for a multitasking environment. The 80286 CPU introduced a new processing mode called protected mode. In protected mode, the OS controls the memory addresses that a program can access. When a program attempts to access a memory address that has not been assigned to it, an error occurs. When this error occurs in Windows, Windows displays the message "Program name caused a General Protection Fault in module..." This message is more commonly known as a GPF. Sometimes, Windows can recover from a GPF by simply closing down the program that caused the error. For more serious errors, the entire Windows environment might hang, and the only recourse is to reboot.

GPF error messages were originally intended to indicate only errors with applications misusing memory. However, over time the scope of GPF errors has increased to generally mean that an error has occurred with the software that might or might not pertain to memory.

If you get a GPF while running software, note what was happening just before the GPF occurred, what other software was loaded at the time, and what, if any, unusual conditions existed at the time. This information will be helpful in identifying the source of the problem. If you notice that a GPF consistently happens during the same event when you are using an application program, suspect a program bug. Call technical support for the software and ask for a possible fix. Gather as much information as possible about the problem before you call. Printed screens can be very useful in these situations. If you can reproduce the problem at will, especially while technical support is on the phone, you are more likely to find a solution.

If the software in question is made by Microsoft, log onto the www.microsoft.com Web site and search for the software and the errors. For example, if a GPF consistently occurs while you are using Microsoft Word, enter the query "GPF and Microsoft Word" in the search box.

Insufficient Memory.   Problems with insufficient memory are caused by the limited size of the five memory heaps more than by the total amount of RAM installed on the systemboard. Windows 3.x uses memory heaps that are a fixed size and do not increase even when much more RAM is installed. The same basic problem also exists with Windows 95. Both of these operating environments have limitations on the amount of RAM they can utilize successfully. Again, look to Windows NT as the ultimate solution because the memory heaps in that OS are not as limited in size. However, for Windows 3.x and Windows 95, there are still some things you can do to better manage memory used by application programs in these environments.

11

Nuts & Bolts offers two tools to monitor system resources including memory. WinGauge Pro monitors system resources, virtual memory, swap file requests, and drive space, and Discover Pro monitors memory use down to the individual application level.

Another tool to help monitor an application's use of memory is WindSock, freeware by Chris Hewitt, available from the shareware Web site, www.shareware.com. Download the compressed file, uncompress it, and read the documentation files for a quick explanation of how to use the software. WindSock, shown in Figure 11-15 with the Options dialog box open, displays the percentage of memory available from the five Windows 3.x heaps. You can choose to display the percentages as a bar graph, digital values, or a line graph. WindSock runs as a TSR and can be helpful in determining which applications are using large amounts of the memory heaps.

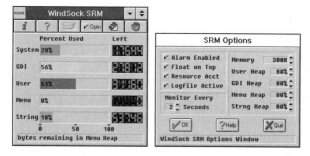

Figure 11-15   WindSock monitors Windows memory usage

For example, Figure 11-15 shows that 56% of the GDI memory heap is in use. An application program is loaded, and then Figure 11-16 shows the increase in memory usage. Note that the GDI heap usage jumped from 56% to 92%. If you now load one more application program that also requires a portion of the GDI heap, a memory error occurs, as shown in Figure 11-17 when an attempt was made to open Word. You see from the error message that Word displays that the insufficient memory problem is with a display operation that requires some GDI memory. When Word is running without the other application program loaded, only 38% of the GDI heap is being used, but the two programs together exceed the GDI heap resource.

Figure 11-16   WindSock shows a large amount of the GDI
memory heap being used

Figure 11-17   Insufficient memory when loading Microsoft Word

 By knowing which application programs use large portions of a heap, you can avoid exceeding the memory heap available by only running these programs when no other applications programs are loaded.

When watching WindSock monitor memory resources, it's interesting to see that a program that is minimized on the desktop (click the **Minimize** button in the upper right corner of the screen) uses no less memory than one open in a full window. In fact, occasionally you see that when you minimize an application program, its memory usage actually increases.

Memory Leaks.   Memory leaks are caused by an application program not releasing the memory addresses assigned to it when it unloads. Memory leaks cause the memory heaps to have less and less memory available for new application programs being loaded. If you notice that you have memory problems after you have loaded and unloaded several programs or the same program several times, suspect a memory leak. Once you have identified the software causing the leak, go to the software manufacturer and request a fix or patch. An upgrade of the software might be available that has solved the memory leak problem.

WindSock can be helpful in determining which application program does not release memory when it is unloaded. From the Options dialog box in WindSock shown in Figure 11-15, check the box **Logfile Active**. A log file is created in the same directory containing the WindSock executable file. Figure 11-18 shows a sample of this log file. WindSock records in the file the percentage and the amount of each heap used and when applications are loaded and unloaded. In Figure 11-18, Notepad.exe is loaded and then unloaded. Note in the String Heap column that 15% of the heap was available before NotePad was loaded, but only 14% was available after it was unloaded. You might suspect that NotePad did not correctly release the missing 1%. What you see here is not proof that Notepad has a memory leak, because you don't know what else might have been happening while Notepad was in use. Perhaps another applications program was minimized or maximized while NotePad was running.

11

```
WindSock SRM 3.10 Log File
Time        Memory      GDI          User         Menu          String      GDI
                        Heap         Heap         Heap          Heap        Acct
21:55:58    26% 6208    48% 29649    44% 27019    0% 635707431   15% 9354   636
New Tasks: NOTEPAD
21:56:00    26% 6208    48% 29665    44% 27019    0% 635707431   15% 9354   636
21:56:02    26% 6208    48% 29629    44% 27019    0% 635707431   15% 9354   634
21:56:04    26% 6208    48% 29655    44% 27019    0% 635707431   15% 9354   635
21:56:06    26% 6208    48% 29645    44% 27019    0% 635707431   15% 9354   634
21:56:09    26% 6208    48% 29659    44% 27053    0% 635707431   15% 9354   634
21:56:11    26% 6190    59% 36581    43% 26907    0% 635707431   14% 8792   630
End Tasks: NOTEPAD
21:56:13    26% 6190    59% 36605    43% 26907    0% 635707431   14% 8792   630
21:56:15    26% 6199    51% 31551    44% 27067    0% 635707431   14% 8792   643
```

Figure 11-18   WindSock log file can monitor possible memory leaks

Also, a better indication of a memory leak is the second column of the report, which is labeled Memory and is monitoring the System heap, the memory assigned to the program, and its data. Watch the WindSock report during several loads and unloads of an application program; if the System heap loses memory consistently, then you have most likely identified a memory leak. The program is not returning memory resources back to the system when it unloads.

OPTIMIZING WINDOWS 3.x

Listed here are several tips to help conserve Windows resources, including memory and drive space.

- Don't use wallpaper because it takes up part of the GDI heap. Also photos in the background require much of a GDI heap.

- Don't use screen savers. Newer SVGA monitors don't need them as older ones did. These are TSRs that require memory. Use pale shades for background colors.

- Reduce the number of colors used by the video.

- Reduce the number of fonts in Control Panel, fonts. Don't delete the fonts file, but don't list them as fonts available for Windows, because these fonts are loaded into memory at Windows startup.

- From Control Panel, Printers, check the box that says Use Print Manager for Each Printer. This option buffers print jobs and can help prevent out-of-memory errors when printing.

- Use a hard drive software cache. Most often, this means SmartDrive in Windows 3.x.

- Reduce the number in the "BUFFERS=" line in Config.sys. Use a small value such as BUFFERS=15, unless you are running older DOS applications that require a larger value.

- Run an optimizing utility once a week to defragment your hard drive. You can use Windows ScanDisk and Defrag, Nuts & Bolts offers DiskMinder and Disk Tune, and Norton Utilities offers SpeedDisk.

- Use a permanent swap file. See Chapter 9 for the recommended sizes.

- Keep things simple. Don't run unnecessary TSRs. Keep your desktop as clear as possible. When you're finished with an application program, close it instead of minimizing it.

SUPPORTING WINDOWS 95

Before delving into the details of supporting Windows 95, it is important to better understand the fundamental ways in which Windows 95 differs from DOS and Windows 3.1, the variety of software and hardware compatibility problems, and the nature of Windows NT. The chapter will then turn to ways to support Windows 95 including installation, memory management, hard disk management, and general troubleshooting.

HOW WINDOWS 95 DIFFERS FROM WINDOWS 3.X AND DOS

Windows 95 is an OS that bridges two worlds. In Figure 11-19, you see that Windows 3.x and DOS constitute a 16-bit world with memory management centered around conventional, upper, and extended memory limitations. Windows 95, as you have seen throughout several chapters, still has a DOS-based core, still uses many 16-bit programs, and must manage base, upper, and extended memory in fundamentally the same way as does DOS. However, Windows 95 introduces 32-bit programming, the concept of virtual machines that protect computer resources from offending programs, memory paging, networking, and many other features available in Windows NT. Windows 95 claims to be completely backward compatible with older software and hardware designed to work in a DOS and Windows 3.x environment. Windows NT is the break with the past. It does not claim total backward compatibility, because it is a freshly designed OS with new ways of managing software and hardware resources. Software written for DOS or Windows 3.x might not work in Windows NT because the methods and rules have changed. New software for Windows NT must comply with these new standards. Hardware must also be compatible with the new way this OS manages it.

11

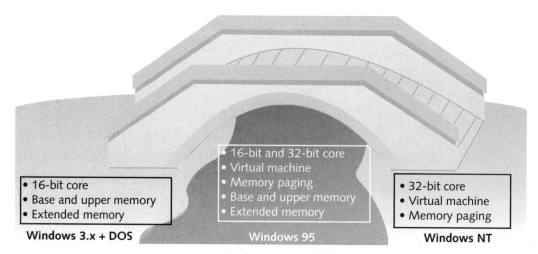

Figure 11-19   Windows 95 is the bridge from DOS to Windows NT

16-Bit and 32-Bit Programming.   DOS is a 16-bit OS. All portions of the OS are written using 16-bit code, and DOS will only support 16-bit drivers and 16-bit application programs. Windows 95 contains some 16-bit code and some 32-bit code. Programs written in 32-bit code require more memory and are generally faster than programs written in 16-bit code. The programming that supports VFAT in Windows 95 is written with 32-bit code. Windows for Workgroups 3.11 also used this 32-bit code to support the 32-bit FAT, but generally speaking Windows 3.x is a 16-bit program and only supports 16-bit application programs.

Windows 95 is a hybrid between 16-bit and 32-bit code. Although Windows 95 supports 16-bit device drivers, the preference is to use the 32-bit drivers supplied with Windows 95, for two main reasons. They are generally much faster, and 32-bit drivers can be stored in extended memory, releasing more of the first MB of memory to application programs. In contrast, 16-bit drivers must be stored in conventional or upper memory. When Windows 95 is installed over DOS, it searches for these 16-bit drivers and replaces them with the 32-bit drivers if it can.

Figure 11-20 shows the three core portions of the Windows 95 OS, which are the kernel, the user, and the GDI programs. The purposes of each of the three components are listed in Table 11-3. In Figure 11-20, you can see that the basic Windows 95 core component, the kernel, uses mostly 32-bit code. The 16-bit code is only retained as entry points into the kernel from 16-bit application programs. The user portion uses mostly 16-bit code, primarily because it uses less memory than the 32-bit equivalent and does not have a need for significant speed. The GDI core uses a mix of 16-bit and 32-bit code in order to maintain compatibility with 16-bit application programs.

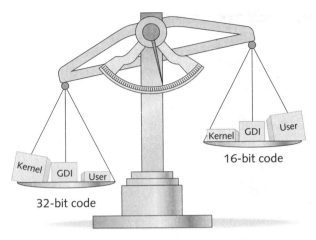

Figure 11-20   Windows 95 uses some 32-bit and some 16-bit
code in its three core components

Nuts & Bolts Discover Pro Memory tab shown in Figure 11-21 gives an excellent presentation of how memory resources are being allocated as well as a list of 16-bit and 32-bit programs and their uses of memory. As shown in Figure 11-21, click the Advanced button to see a full break-down of how each Windows heap is being utilized as well as several other interesting presentations of memory use.

Table 11-3   Core components of Windows 95

Component Name	Main Files Holding the Component	Functions
Kernel	Kernel32.dll	Handles the basic OS functions such as managing memory, file I/O, loading and executing programs
User	User32.dll, User.exe	Controls the mouse, keyboard, ports, and the desktop, including position of windows, icons, and dialog boxes
GDI	GDI32.dll, GDI.exe	Draws screens, graphics, lines, and print

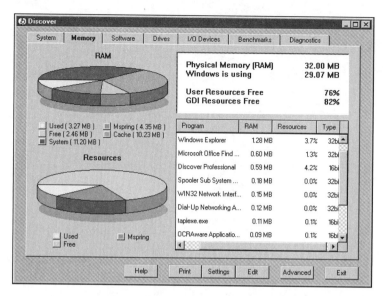

Figure 11-21 Nuts and Bolts Discover Pro shows available User and GDI resources and how applications are using them

Virtual Machines. Another important difference between Windows 95 and DOS with Windows 3.x is that Windows 95 makes use of the concept of virtual machines. Think of **virtual machines** (VM) as several logical machines within one physical machine, as represented in Figure 11-22, similar in concept to several logical drives within one physical hard drive.

In Figure 11-22, the System Virtual Machine can support 32-bit and 16-bit Windows application programs, but DOS programs are put aside into their own virtual machines. Remember that DOS programs don't take into account the sharing of resources. A DOS program expects to directly control the hardware of the entire PC, memory included. If a DOS program begins to use memory addresses not assigned to it, errors occur in a multi-tasking environment. Windows 95 solves this problem by providing the DOS program with its own logical machine. In effect, the application program says, "I want all of memory and all of this and all of that." Windows 95 says, "OK, here they are," and gives the program its own PC, including all the virtual memory addresses it wants from 0 to 4 GB as well as its own virtual hardware! As far as the DOS program is concerned, it can go anywhere and do anything within its own PC. That's a virtual machine! The DOS application program does not try to communicate with another application program or access the data of another program, because it thinks there are no other programs—it controls its entire world, and it's the only program in it.

One important result of running DOS programs in their individual virtual machines is that, when a program makes an error, the virtual machine it is using hangs, but the rest of the actual PC is isolated from the problem.

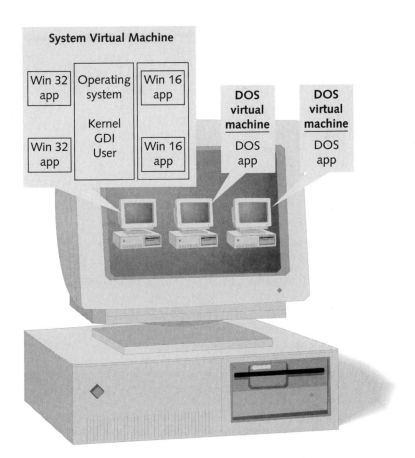

Figure 11-22   Windows 95 uses the virtual machine concept

Windows 16-bit applications programs offer a slightly different challenge to Windows 95. These programs make some of the same mistakes that DOS programs do and can cause the system to hang. However, they also sometimes expect to be able to access other programs and their data. The 16-bit Windows programs don't expect to control the hardware directly, and are content to route their requests to Windows. Windows 95 places these programs within the system VM because they communicate with hardware through the OS, but Windows 95 puts these programs together in their own memory space so they can share memory addresses.

The result of this arrangement is that, when a 16-bit Windows program causes an error, it can disturb other 16-bit programs, causing them to fail, but it does not disturb DOS programs in their own VM or 32-bit programs that don't share their virtual memory addresses.

Memory Paging. How does Windows 95 provide virtual memory addresses to DOS and 16-bit Windows application programs? By **memory paging**, which provides virtual memory addresses to programs and is managed by the **Virtual Memory Manager**. Look at Figure 11-23. In the top diagram, you see Windows 3.x with the memory model you have observed in earlier chapters. Applications programs in Windows 3.x share the memory addresses that have been assigned to either the physical or virtual memory of a system. For example, in Figure 11-23, there are 64 MB of memory addresses available. Perhaps half of these addresses are assigned to physical RAM stored on SIMMs and the other half of the addresses are virtual memory contained in the swap file on the hard drive. In this case, there is only one set of memory addresses, and all applications programs must share these addresses.

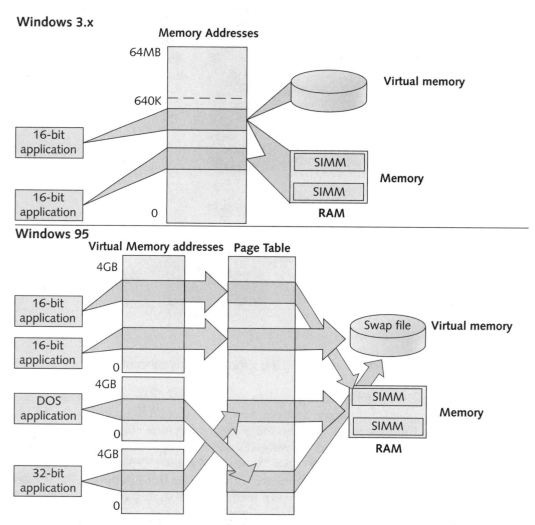

Figure 11-23   How Windows 95 manages memory differently than does Windows 3.x

As you can see, in the lower part of Figure 11-23, Windows 95 not only has virtual memory stored in a swap file, but also provides virtual memory addresses to application programs. In Figure 11-23, there are three sets of virtual memory addresses. Each set can contain 0 to 4 GBs of addresses. The top set is being used by two 16-bit programs. The second set of virtual addresses is being used by a single DOS program, and a third set of addresses is being used by a 32-bit program. This agrees with Figure 11-22. Each VM for DOS has a set of virtual memory addresses. The 16-bit Windows programs share a single set of virtual memory addresses, and each 32-bit program has its own individual set of addresses.

In Figure 11-23, all these virtual addresses map onto the page table, which in turn maps onto either physical memory (RAM) or virtual memory on the hard drive (swap file). Obviously, not all virtual memory addresses in Windows 95 have physical or virtual memory assigned to them. These virtual addresses remain unassigned until an applications program uses them.

In Windows 95, the Virtual Memory Manager controls the page table, moving 4K pages in and out of physical RAM. If a program requests memory that the memory manager knows is stored on the swap file, the manager generates a **page fault**, which causes the manager to go to the drive to return the data from the swap file to RAM. This action is called a **page-in**. If RAM is full, the manager takes a page and moves it to the swap file, which is called a **page-out**.

If RAM is full much of the time, the Virtual Memory Manager might spend excessive time moving pages in and out of RAM, which can cause a decrease in overall system performance and excessive hard drive use. This situation is sometimes called **disk thrashing** and can cause premature hard drive failure. Symptoms of excessive memory paging are:

- Very high CPU use
- Very slow system response
- Constant hard drive use

The solution is to leave fewer application programs open at the same time or to install more RAM.

Having covered the differences between Windows 95 and Windows 3.x with DOS, the chapter now turns to installing and customizing Windows 95.

11

INSTALLING AND CUSTOMIZING WINDOWS 95

Before describing steps for installing Windows 95 and what can go wrong, the text below will first look at what Windows 95 is doing behind the scenes as installation progresses. To begin installation, insert the Windows 95 CD-ROM in the CD-ROM drive and type **D:Setup** or begin with the Windows 95 setup floppy disk 1. Insert the disk in the drive and type **A:Setup**.

Windows 95 Setup begins installation in real mode and then later converts to protected mode. During real mode, it runs ScanDisk, checks for existing Windows software, performs several system checks, loads the extended memory driver, looks for existing TSRs, and starts Windows if it is not already started. This Windows logo screen is the first thing the user normally sees during the installation. Setup then switches to protected mode.

Setup creates the registry, getting it ready to contain the hardware information, and then searches for hardware. It loads its own drivers for the detected hardware, or, if it cannot detect the hardware, requests the drivers from the user. The drivers are copied to the hard drive.

Up to this point, if Setup fails and you reboot the PC, you boot into DOS. Next Setup alters the boot records on the hard drive to point to the Windows 95 file, Io.sys, rather than to the DOS hidden files. Now, if Setup fails and you reboot, you reboot into Windows 95.

During a normal installation, the PC reboots and Windows 95 is loaded. Some initial startup programs are run to set the time zone and to change existing application programs to Windows 95. Depending on the hardware present, the PC may reboot again to load new drivers.

During the installation, Setup is recording information into log files. The Detection Log (Detlog.txt) keeps a record of hardware detected. If the system fails to respond during the hardware detection phase, an entry is recorded in Detcrash.log.

For example, if Setup suspects that a network card is present, because it sees a network driver installed in Config.sys, it records in Detlog.txt that it is about to look for the card. If it successfully finds the card, it records the success in Detlog.txt. However, if an error occurs while Setup is searching for the card, an entry is made in the Detcrash.log file.

Setup is also recording information in Setuplog.txt, so it records that it is attempting to detect a network card. If the system crashes, restart by using the power on/power off method so that the ISA bus is fully initialized, which does not always happen during a soft boot.

During the boot-up process, Setup looks at Detcrash.log and Setuplog.txt to determine what it was trying to do at the time of the crash. It skips that step and goes on to the next step, so that it doesn't make the same mistake twice.

Even though Setup might crash several times during the installation process, progress is still being made. By reading the contents of the log files, Setup is able to skip those steps that caused a problem and move forward. Be careful not to delete the log files during the installation process, especially if you've just experienced a crash.

Customizing the Desktop

After the installation is complete, adding shortcuts to the desktop and having Windows 95 automatically load software at startup can make the environment more user-friendly. A **shortcut** on the desktop is an icon that points to a program that can be executed. The user double-clicks on the icon to load the software. A shortcut can be created in several ways. One way is to use the Properties option on the Taskbar. Right-click on the Taskbar and select **Properties** from the menu that appears (see Figure 11-24). The Taskbar Properties sheet appears (see Figure 11-25).

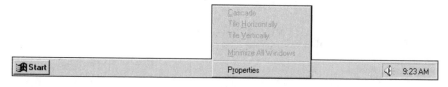

Figure 11-24 To customize the desktop, use the Properties sheet of the Windows 95 Taskbar

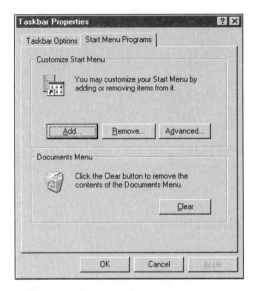

Figure 11-25   The Taskbar Properties sheet of Windows 95

Select the **Start Menu Programs** tab. Click on **Add** to add a new icon to the desktop. Figure 11-26 displays.

11

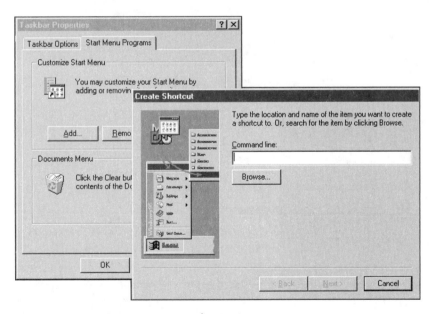

Figure 11-26   Creating a new shortcut

Enter the command line for the new shortcut or click on **Browse** to select the program from the list of programs installed. After you have made your selection, click on **Next**. Figure 11-27 displays to allow you to select where to put the shortcut.

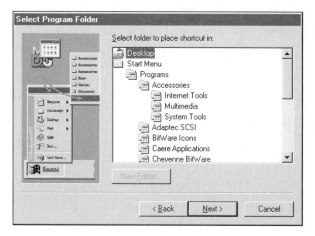

Figure 11-27   A shortcut can be added to the desktop or the Start menu

Select **Desktop** to place the shortcut on the desktop. Click **Next** and Figure 11-28 displays, asking for the title that will appear underneath the shortcut icon.

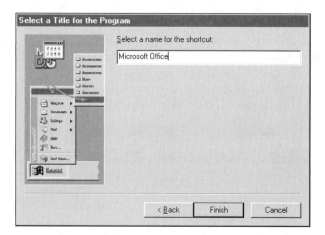

Figure 11-28   Enter a title for the new shortcut

Enter the title and click **Finish**. The new shortcut displays on the desktop as in Figure 11-29.

To add a shortcut to the Start menu, from Figure 11-27, scroll down the list to see a list of folders to select from. Select the folder where you want the shortcut to appear in the Start menu. If you want the program to load whenever Windows 95 starts, put its shortcut in the StartUp folder, as in Figure 11-30.

Figure 11-29   New shortcut created

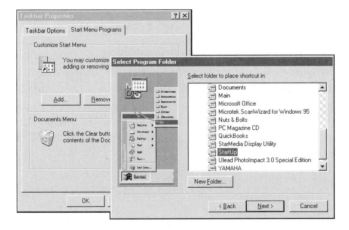

Figure 11-30   To have the program execute each time
Windows starts, place the shortcut in the
StartUp folder

Click **Next** and enter the title of the shortcut that will appear in the Start menu. Click
Finish to complete the process. You can see the new shortcut added to the Start menu in
Figure 11-31. All items in the StartUp folder are automatically executed when Windows 95
starts.

11

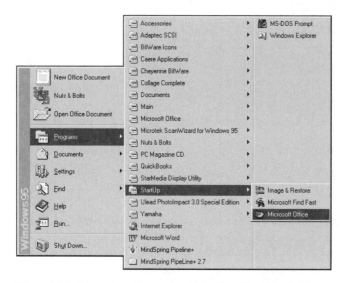

Figure 11-31 New item placed in the StartUp folder

Customizing the Installation with MSDOS.SYS

In the following discussions concerning Windows 95 installations, the contents of the text file MSDOS.SYS play a significant role. Remember from earlier chapters that this file is a text file used by Windows 95 to set different options for the OS. You can edit the file using EDIT.COM or some other text editor. The file is a hidden, read-only, system file so before you can edit it, you must first use the ATTRIB command to make the file available for editing. Also, make a backup copy of the file in case you want to revert back to the form it was in before the changes were made.

Follow these steps to change the options in MSDOS.SYS:

- Go to a DOS command prompt.

- Go to the root directory of your hard drive by typing:

  `CD\`

- Make the file available for editing by typing:

  `ATTRIB -R -H -S MSDOS.SYS`

- Make a backup copy of the file by typing:

  `COPY MSDOS.SYS MSDOS.BK`

- Use EDIT.COM to edit the file by typing:

  `EDIT MSDOS.SYS`

- Save the file and return it to a hidden, read-only, system file by typing:

  `ATTRIB +R +H +S MSDOS.SYS`

Table 11-4 lists each entry in the file and its purpose. You can refer back to this table as you read about the different options available when installing and configuring Windows 95.

Table 11-4   Contents of the MSDOS.SYS File Options section

Command Line Variable Name	Purpose of the Values Assigned to the Variable
BootMulti	0= (Default) Boot only to Windows 95 1= Allows for a dual boot
BootWin	1= (Default) Boot to Windows 95 0= Boot to previous version of DOS
BootGUI	1= (Default) Boot to Windows 95 with the graphic user interface 0= Boot only to the command prompt for DOS 7.0 (Autoexec.bat and Config.sys will be executed, and you will be in real-mode DOS.)
BootMenu	0= (Default) Don't display the Startup Menu 1= Display the Startup Menu
BootMenuDefault	1 through 8 = The value selected from the Startup Menu by Default (Normally this value should be 1.)
BootMenuDelay	n= Number of seconds delay before the default value in the Startup Menu is automatically selected
BootKeys	1= (Default) The function keys work during the boot process (F4, F5, F6, F8, Shift F5, Ctrl F5, Shift F8) 0= Disable the function keys during the boot process (This option can be used to help secure a workstation.)
BootDelay	n= Number of seconds the boot process waits (when it displays the message "Starting Windows 95") for the user to press F8 to get the Startup Menu (Default is 2 seconds.)
Logo	1= (Default) Display the Windows 95 logo screen 0= Leave the screen in text mode (You can change the logo screen to be another .bmp file. The Windows 95 logo file is stored in Logo.sys in the root directory. Rename it and name a new .bmp file to Logo.sys to customize this startup screen.)
Drvspace	1= (Default) Load Drvspace.bin, used for disk compression, if it is present 0= Don't load Drvspace.bin
DoubleBuffer	1= (Default) When you have a SCSI drive, enables double buffering for the drive (see the drive documentation) 0 = Don't use double buffering for the SCSI drive
Network	1= If network components are installed, include the option, "Safe mode with network support" in the Startup Menu 0= Don't include the option in the Startup Menu (This will normally be set to 0 if the PC has no network components installed. The Startup Menu will be renumbered from this point forward in the menu.)
BootFailSafe	1= (Default) Include Safe mode in the Startup Menu 0= Don't include Safe mode in the Startup Menu

11

Table 11-4   Contents of the MSDOS.SYS File Options section (continued)

Command Line Variable Name	Purpose of the Values Assigned to the Variable
BootWarn	1= (Default) Display the warning message when Windows 95 boots into Safe mode 0= Don't display the warning message
LoadTop	1= (Default) Load COMMAND.COM at the top of conventional memory 0= Don't load COMMAND.COM at the top of conventional memory (Use this option when there is a memory conflict with this area of memory.)

Figure 11-32 shows a sample MSDOS.SYS file. The lines containing x's at the bottom of the file are used to ensure that the file size is compatible with other programs.

```
[Paths]
WinDir=C:\WIN95
WinBootDir=C:\WIN95
HostWinBootDrv=C

[Options]
BootMulti=1
BootGUI=1
BootMenu=1
Network=0
;
;The following lines are required for compatibility with other programs.
;Do not remove them (MSDOS.SYS needs to be >1024 bytes).
;xxxxxxxxxxxxxxxxxxxxxxxxxxxxxxxxxxxxxxxxxxxxxxxxxxxxxxxxxxxxxxxxa
;xxxxxxxxxxxxxxxxxxxxxxxxxxxxxxxxxxxxxxxxxxxxxxxxxxxxxxxxxxxxxxxxb
;xxxxxxxxxxxxxxxxxxxxxxxxxxxxxxxxxxxxxxxxxxxxxxxxxxxxxxxxxxxxxxxxc
;xxxxxxxxxxxxxxxxxxxxxxxxxxxxxxxxxxxxxxxxxxxxxxxxxxxxxxxxxxxxxxxxd
;xxxxxxxxxxxxxxxxxxxxxxxxxxxxxxxxxxxxxxxxxxxxxxxxxxxxxxxxxxxxxxxxe
;xxxxxxxxxxxxxxxxxxxxxxxxxxxxxxxxxxxxxxxxxxxxxxxxxxxxxxxxxxxxxxxxf
;xxxxxxxxxxxxxxxxxxxxxxxxxxxxxxxxxxxxxxxxxxxxxxxxxxxxxxxxxxxxxxxxg
;xxxxxxxxxxxxxxxxxxxxxxxxxxxxxxxxxxxxxxxxxxxxxxxxxxxxxxxxxxxxxxxxh
;xxxxxxxxxxxxxxxxxxxxxxxxxxxxxxxxxxxxxxxxxxxxxxxxxxxxxxxxxxxxxxxxi
;xxxxxxxxxxxxxxxxxxxxxxxxxxxxxxxxxxxxxxxxxxxxxxxxxxxxxxxxxxxxxxxxj
;xxxxxxxxxxxxxxxxxxxxxxxxxxxxxxxxxxxxxxxxxxxxxxxxxxxxxxxxxxxxxxxxk
;xxxxxxxxxxxxxxxxxxxxxxxxxxxxxxxxxxxxxxxxxxxxxxxxxxxxxxxxxxxxxxxxl
;xxxxxxxxxxxxxxxxxxxxxxxxxxxxxxxxxxxxxxxxxxxxxxxxxxxxxxxxxxxxxxxxm
;xxxxxxxxxxxxxxxxxxxxxxxxxxxxxxxxxxxxxxxxxxxxxxxxxxxxxxxxxxxxxxxxn
;xxxxxxxxxxxxxxxxxxxxxxxxxxxxxxxxxxxxxxxxxxxxxxxxxxxxxxxxxxxxxxxxo
;xxxxxxxxxxxxxxxxxxxxxxxxxxxxxxxxxxxxxxxxxxxxxxxxxxxxxxxxxxxxxxxxp
;xxxxxxxxxxxxxxxxxxxxxxxxxxxxxxxxxxxxxxxxxxxxxxxxxxxxxxxxxxxxxxxxq
;xxxxxxxxxxxxxxxxxxxxxxxxxxxxxxxxxxxxxxxxxxxxxxxxxxxxxxxxxxxxxxxxr
;xxxxxxxxxxxxxxxxxxxxxxxxxxxxxxxxxxxxxxxxxxxxxxxxxxxxxxxxxxxxxxxxs
```

Figure 11-32   A sample MSDOS.SYS file

Installing Windows 95 Over DOS and Windows 3.x

If DOS and Windows 3.x exist on the PC prior to installing Windows 95, you have the choice of installing Windows 95 over DOS and Windows 3.x or installing Windows 95 in a separate directory from Windows 3.x so that you can still run 16-bit programs under Windows 3.x.

The advantages of overwriting Windows 3.x and DOS are:

- Less hard drive space is used.

- Windows 95 Setup copies information about existing application programs from the .ini files of Windows 3.x into the Windows 95 registry, eliminating the need for you to install the existing programs into Windows 95.

- These programs are added to the Start menu of Windows 95.

- Existing programs can find their .dlls in the same Windows\system folder as they did with Windows 3.x.

The advantages of installing Windows 95 in a separate directory are:

- You can create a dual boot and run the PC with either Windows 3.x or Windows 95.

- The Windows\system folder of Windows 95 is not cluttered with old, outdated .dlls that current programs no longer use. In effect, you get a "fresh start."

If you install Windows 95 in a separate directory, you must then reinstall each application program that you want to run under Windows 95, so that it gets information into the Windows 95 registry, its programs are listed under the Start menu, and its .dlls and other supporting files are copied to the Windows\system folder.

Dual Boot Between Windows 95 and DOS with Windows 3.x

You can install DOS with Windows 3.1 and Windows 95 on the same hard drive, so that you can use software made for each operating environment within its native OS. To do this, follow these general procedures.

1. Because Windows 95 deletes some DOS utility programs, back up your \DOS directory to a different directory, like this:

   ```
   XCOPY C:\DOS\*.* C:\DOSSAVE\*.*
   ```

2. Install Windows 95. When asked for the directory name, chose something different from the one Windows 3.x is installed in such as \WIN95.

3. Edit the Windows 95 system file, MSDOS.SYS, to allow for a dual boot by adding these two lines in the [Options] section:

   BootMulti=1   (allows for a dual boot)

   BootMenu=1   (displays the Startup Menu)

4. Restore your \DOS directory, which was partially deleted during the installation:

```
COPY C:\DOSSAVE\*.* C:\DOS
```

5. Reboot your PC. When the Startup Menu displays, you can choose between Normal, which boots into Window 95, or a Previous Version of MS-DOS.

Windows 95 saves DOS files under different names when it is installed. When you reboot to the previous version of MS-DOS, Windows 95 renames the files for DOS back to the names that DOS will expect. Here's the list.

Table 11-5   DOS and Windows 95 files that get renamed by Windows 95

Name When Windows 95 Is Active	Name When DOS Is Active	This File Belongs to:
AUTOEXEC.BAT	AUTOEXEC.W40	Windows 95
AUTOEXEC.DOS	AUTOEXEC.BAT	DOS
COMMAND.COM	COMMAND.W40	Windows 95
COMMAND.DOS	COMMAND.COM	DOS
CONFIG.SYS	CONFIG.W40	Windows 95
CONFIG.DOS	CONFIG.SYS	DOS
IO.SYS	WINBOOT.SYS	Windows 95
IO.DOS	IO.SYS	DOS
MSDOS.SYS	MSDOS.W40	Windows 95
MSDOS.DOS	MSDOS.SYS	DOS

If you don't want to see the Startup Menu each time you boot, omit the BootWin line from the MSDOS.SYS file. The PC will automatically boot to Windows 95. When you see the "Starting Windows 95" message on the screen, press the F8 key which causes the Startup Menu to appear. You can then boot to DOS and Windows 3.x. Select the option that reads "Previous Version of MS-DOS." It will be number 7 or number 8 on the menu, depending on whether or not the network support option is present.

Microsoft Windows 95 Startup Menu

If you have set up your PC for a dual boot as described above, the following menu always displays when you boot. The time the menu stays on the screen is determined by a setting in MSDOS.SYS. However, you can get this menu at any time by pressing F8 when the message "Starting Windows 95" displays during the boot process. The Microsoft Windows 95 Startup Menu options are:

1. Normal

2. Logged(\BOOTLOG.TXT)

3. Safe mode

4. Safe mode with network support

5. Step-by-step confirmation

6. Command prompt only

7. Safe mode command prompt only

8. Previous version of MS-DOS

Enter a choice: 1

What to expect when you select each option on the menu is described next.

Normal. If BootGUI=1, then this option starts Windows 95. If BootGUI=0, then this option will boot to the DOS 7.0 prompt. Either way, the commands in Autoexec.bat and Config.sys are executed.

Logged (\BOOTLOG.TXT). This option is the same as choosing Normal, except that Windows 95 tracks the load and startup activities and logs them to this file. This file can be a helpful tool when troubleshooting.

Safe mode. On the Startup Menu listed above, Safe mode is an option. Safe mode starts Windows 95 with a minimum and default configuration to give you an opportunity to correct an error in the configuration. For example, if you selected a video driver that is incompatible with your system, when Windows 95 starts, it detects the problem and enters Safe mode with a standard VGA driver selected. You can then go to Device Manager, select the correct driver, and restart Windows.

From the Startup Menu, you can choose to enter Safe mode yourself if you know of a problem you want to correct. For example, if you had previously selected a group of background and foreground colors that makes it impossible to read the screens, you can reboot and choose Safe mode. Safe mode gives you the standard color scheme along with the VGA mode. Go to Display Properties, make the necessary corrections, and reboot.

In Safe mode, the commands in Autoexec.bat and Config.sys are not executed. You can also go to Safe mode by pressing F5 when the message "Starting Windows 95" displays.

Safe mode with Network Support. This option allows access to the network when booting into Safe mode. It is useful if Windows 95 is stored on a network server and you need to download changes to your PC in Safe mode.

Step-by-Step Confirmation. The option asks for confirmation before executing each command in Io.sys, Config.sys, and Autoexec.bat. You can accomplish the same thing by pressing Shift-F8 when the message "Starting Windows 95" displays.

Command Prompt Only. This option executes the contents of Autoexec.bat and Config.sys, but doesn't start Windows 95. You will be given a DOS prompt. Type **WIN** to load Windows 95.

11

Safe mode Command Prompt Only.   This option does not execute the commands in Autoexec.bat or Config.sys. You will be given a DOS prompt.

Previous Version of MS-DOS.   This option loads a previous version of DOS if one is present. You can get the same results by pressing F4 when the message "Starting Windows 95" displays.

PLUG-AND-PLAY AND HARDWARE INSTALLATIONS

Plug-and-Play (PnP) is a set of design specifications for both hardware and software that work toward effortless hardware installations. For a system to be truly Plug-and-Play, it must meet three criteria:

- The System BIOS must be PnP.
- All hardware devices and expansion cards must be PnP-compliant.
- The OS must be Windows 95 or another OS that supports PnP.

If all these things are true and you have the latest 32-bit drivers, hardware installation should be very easy and is only a matter of installing the new hardware device, turning on the PC, and perhaps providing the 32-bit driver, if it is not included with Windows 95. During the boot process, Windows 95 surveys the devices and their needs for resources and allocates resources to each device. Windows 95 is free to assign these resources to the devices and avoids assigning the same resource to two devices. For PnP to work, each device in the system must be able to use whatever resources the OS assigns to it.

How Plug-and-Play Works

A Plug-and-Play OS like Windows 95 provides two main services: resource management and runtime configuration. **Resource management** occurs at startup as system resources are allocated to devices. **Runtime configuration** is an ongoing process that monitors any changes in system devices, such as the removal of a PC Card on a notebook or docking and undocking a notebook to and from a docking station. The BIOS must be able to recognize these changes during OS runtime (any time the OS is running) and communicate them to the OS.

Windows 95 uses four components in implementing PnP architecture:

- The **configuration manager** controls the configuration process of all devices and communicates these configurations to the devices.
- The **hardware tree** is a database built each time Windows 95 starts up that contains a list of installed components and the resources they use.
- The **bus enumerator** locates all devices on a particular bus and inventories the resource requirements for these devices.
- The **resource arbitrator** decides which resources get assigned to which devices.

When Windows 95 is started, if the systemboard BIOS is PnP, the configuration manager starts the PnP process by receiving the list of devices from the BIOS. If the BIOS is not PnP, the bus enumerator for each bus on the system provides the information to the configuration manager. The manager oversees the process of assigning resources by loading one device driver after another for each installed device, and instructing the driver to wait until resources have been assigned to it.

The manager performs a process of examining and reexamining required resources until it determines an acceptable configuration of all resources and devices. For example, for ISA devices, according to the PnP standards, each device has a unique 72-bit ID derived from the manufacturer ID, a product ID, and a serial number. Each ISA device competes for resources, and the device with the largest-value ID is assigned resources first. The bus enumerator manages this process and receives the resource assignments from the configuration manager. The configuration manager interacts with the resource arbitrator, allowing the arbitrator to determine what resources are assigned, and then receives that information from the arbitrator, passing it on to the bus enumerator.

The bus enumerators collectively build the hardware tree, which is stored in memory. Information to build the hardware tree comes from the configuration at the current moment as well as from information kept in the registry about devices that have been installed, including what device drivers are used to operate the device and user-defined settings for the device. The hardware tree is built each time Windows 95 is started, and is dynamically changed as hardware is plugged and unplugged while the system is running.

11

Plug-and-Play BIOS

As discussed in previous chapters, BIOS that is PnP-compliant gathers resource configuration information prior to loading Windows 95, presenting to Windows 95 details it can use to complete the process. Systemboards manufactured after 1994 most likely contain PnP BIOS. PnP BIOS can also be ESCD BIOS. ESCD (extended system configuration data) BIOS creates a list of configuration changes that you have manually made and stores that list on the BIOS chip. Even if the hard drive crashes or you must reload Windows 95, the configuration changes are still available from the BIOS when it goes through the boot process and presents the information to Windows 95 at start-up.

To know if your BIOS is PnP, look for a message about the BIOS type on the startup screen. Information about the BIOS might also be displayed on the CMOS setup screen. Use MSD and choose Computer from the menu to get information about your BIOS. The documentation for the systemboard should also say whether or not the BIOS is PnP.

If the BIOS is not Plug-and-Play, you can still use Plug-and-Play Windows 95 software for hardware devices that are Plug-and-Play. However, you might need to manually configure the hardware, or, in some cases, disable the Plug-and-Play features of the interface card.

Hardware Device Installations

Windows 95 provides better support during the installation of new hardware devices than does Windows 3.x. If the computer system is completely PnP-compliant, installations are automated and go very smoothly. However, with older hardware devices and older drivers, problems can occur that must be resolved manually.

This section looks at three sources of problems with hardware installations and what to do about them. Table 11-6 summarizes these problems and their solutions. A device or expansion card that is not PnP is called a **legacy** (handed down from the past) device. Legacy devices are not able to have their resources assigned to them by PnP. If the device driver is an older 16-bit driver, there might be a problem with Windows 95 installing and using the driver. Also, Windows 95 might or might not have a built-in driver for the device. Each problem and how to address it is discussed below.

Table 11-6   Hardware device installation problems and solutions

Source of the Problem	Nature of the Problem	Solution to the Problem
Unsupported devices	Windows 95 does not have a built-in device driver designed for the device	Provide a device driver from the manufacturer or use a substitute
16-bit drivers	Windows 95 has trouble initially recognizing and installing the driver	First, install the driver using DOS or Windows 3.x
Legacy cards	Can cause a conflict of resources between two devices (IRQ, I/O addresses, upper memory addresses)	Change the DIP switches or jumpers on the card to use different resources

Unsupported Devices.   New hardware devices are installed from the Control Panel under Add New Hardware. Windows 95 uses the Add New Hardware Wizard to recognize the device, install the correct driver, and allocate the correct resources to the device. The following are general directions to use if Windows 95 does not recognize the device you are installing. After physically plugging in or installing the device, turn on the PC and go to the Control Panel and choose **Add New Hardware**. When the options in Figure 11-33 display, answer **Yes** to allow Windows to search for the device, and then click **Next**.

If Windows 95 locates a new device and recognizes it to be PnP, as shown in Figure 11-34, simply click **Next** and the work is done.

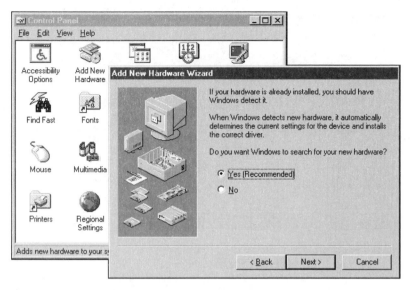

Figure 11-33   Add New Hardware Wizard

Figure 11-34   If Windows 95 recognizes the new
device it can complete the installation
with no help

If Windows 95 detects the device and recognizes that it is not PnP, it suggests resources that
can be assigned to the device, as seen in Figure 11-35. It's left up to you to manually
configure the device to use the suggested resources or to select other resources.

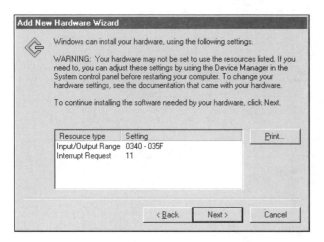

Figure 11-35 If the new device is not PnP, Windows 95 suggests the resources for a legacy device to use

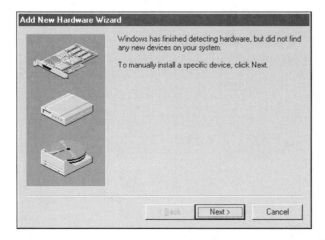

Figure 11-36 The new device is not detected or recognized by Windows 95

However, if Windows 95 cannot detect a new device, it will ask for your help, as shown in Figure 11-36. When you click **Next**, a list of devices displays, as shown in Figure 11-37. Select the device and click **Next**. The list of supported manufacturers and models for that device type displays. For example, Figure 11-38 shows a list of CD-ROM controllers. You can select a manufacturer and model from the list, but if your device is not listed, then the device is not supported by Windows 95, and you have two choices.

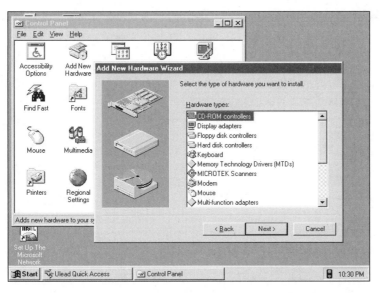

Figure 11-37   When Windows 95 cannot recognize the new
hardware, you must select the device

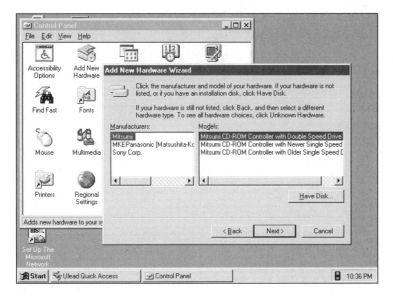

Figure 11-38   List of manufacturers and models of supported
CD-ROM controllers

You can choose a substitute or generic choice for the device, or you can use a driver from a
floppy disk or CD-ROM that is provided by the manufacturer of your device. To select a substitute device from the list, look in the documentation for the device to learn which device
you can choose from the list of Windows 95 devices that can be substituted for this one.

If you have a driver supplied by your manufacturer, click **Have Disk** and provide the disk or CD-ROM with the driver.

Problems with 16-Bit Drivers.   When you supply a device driver to Windows 95 for an unsupported device, Windows 95 will copy one or more device driver files to the hard drive and make the appropriate entries in the registry so that it will load the driver each time it starts up. If the driver is a 16-bit driver, it will also make the appropriate entries in the Autoexec.bat and Config.sys files. If Windows 95 has problems locating and installing a 16-bit driver, then you again have three choices. You can contact the manufacturer of the device for an updated driver, you can ask them to recommend a substitute driver, or you can install the driver using DOS or Windows 3.x. If the device driver has an install program, run the install program under either DOS or Windows 3.x, depending on what the install program requires. It makes the correct entries in the Autoexec.bat and Config.sys files and copies the driver files to the hard drive. You should then be able to install the device in Windows 95 with no problems.

Problems with Legacy Cards.   When you are installing Windows 95 onto a PC that has previously worked well with DOS and Windows 3.1, legacy cards will not normally be a problem because the conflict of resources will usually have already been resolved when the cards were first installed.

Another problem arises if the device is a legacy device and requests resources that conflict with another legacy device already installed. You then must intervene and change the jumpers or DIP switches on one of the devices to force it to use a different resource.

During the installation, Windows 95 might inform you that there is a resource conflict, or the device might simply not work. To see a list of installed devices and information about a problem, use Device Manager. Go to the Control Panel, choose **System**, and select the **Device Manager** tab. The list of devices displays, as seen in Figure 11-39. A + beside the device name indicates that you can click on the device for a list of manufacturers and models installed. An X through the device name indicates that the device has been disabled. A yellow exclamation point indicates a problem. To see a better explanation of the problem, click the device and select **Properties**. The Device Properties box displays, which can give you helpful information about solving the problem.

For more information from Windows 95 on how to resolve a problem, click **Start**, click **Help**, and double-click **Troubleshooting**. The information displayed includes suggestions that can lead you to a solution. For example, in Figure 11-40, the Hardware Troubleshooter suggests that you check to see that the device is not listed twice in Device Manager. If this were the case, you would have to remove the second occurrence of the device.

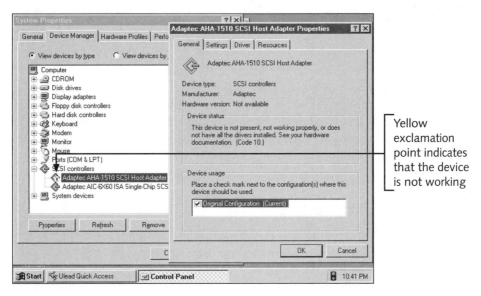

Figure 11-39   The Properties box of an installed device that is
not working

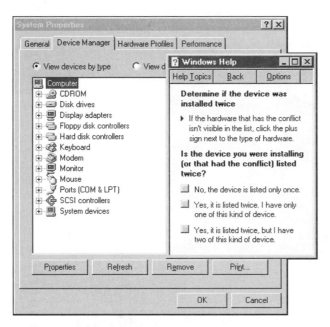

Figure 11-40   Troubleshooter making a suggestion toward
resolving a hardware conflict

11

THE WINDOWS 95 REGISTRY

The Windows 95 registry is intended to replace the many .ini files that Windows and Windows software used under Windows 3.x. Organizing the information contained in these older .ini files is accomplished by using a hierarchical database with a tree-like, top-to-bottom design. All kinds of information are stored in the registry, including system configuration, user settings, Device Manager information, applications software settings, hardware settings, and so on. In this section you will examine how the registry is organized, what kinds of information are in the registry, how and why you might edit the registry, and how to recover from a corrupted registry.

How the Registry Is Organized

Figure 11-41 shows a portion of a Windows 3.1 System.ini file. Notice that there are section names in square brackets, key names on the left of the equal signs, and values assigned to these key names on the right of the equal signs. The Windows 95 registry takes on a similar design but enhances it by allowing for keys to cascade to several levels on the tree. Figure 11-42 shows a portion of a Windows 95 registry. Consider names on the left side of the screen as similar to section names in System.ini; these names are called **keys** by Windows 95. On the right side of the screen are value names such as ScreenSaveTime, and to the right of each name is the **value data** assigned to that name, such as "60." The value names, called **values** by Windows 95, are similar to the key names in System.ini, and the value data are similar to the values assigned to key names in System.ini.

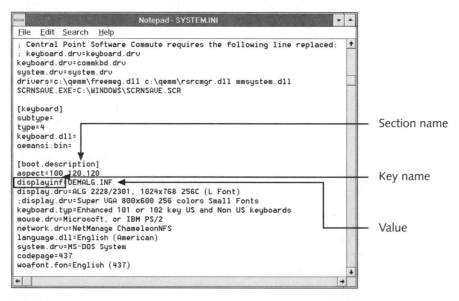

Figure 11-41 System.ini entries contain section names, key words, and values

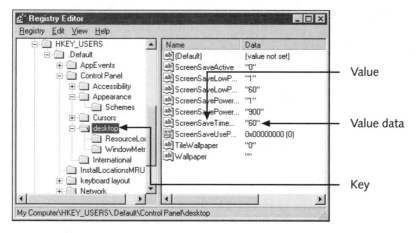

Figure 11-42   Structure of the Windows 95 registry

The registry is organized into six major keys or branches of the registry tree, which are listed in Table 11-7. The registry is contained in two files, System.dat and User.dat, located in the Windows directory as hidden, read-only, system files, although the information forms only a single database.

Table 11-7   Six major branches or keys of the Windows 95 registry

Key	Description
HKEY_CLASSES_ROOT	Contains information about file associations and OLE data (This branch of the tree is a mirror of HKEY_LOCAL_MACHINE\Software\Classes.)
HKEY_USERS	Includes user preferences, including desktop configuration and network connections
HKEY_CURRENT_USER	If there is only one user of the system, this is a duplicate of HKEY_USERS, but for a multi-user system, this key contains information about the current user preferences.
HKEY_LOCAL_MACHINE	Contains information about hardware and installed software
HKEY_CURRENT_CONFIG	Contains the same information in HKEY_LOCAL_MACHINE\Config and has information about printers and display fonts
HKEY_DYN_DATA	Keeps information about Windows performance and Plug-and-Play information

Recovering from a Corrupted Registry

Windows 95 maintains a backup copy of the two registry files called System.da0 and User.da0. Each time Windows boots successfully, it makes a backup copy of these two files. If Windows 95 has trouble loading and must start in Safe mode, it does not back up the registry files.

If Windows 95 does not find a System.dat when it starts, it automatically replaces it with the backup System.da0. If both System.dat and User.dat are missing, or the "WinDir=" command is missing in MSDOS.SYS, Windows 95 tells you that the registry files are missing and starts in Safe mode. It then displays the Registry Problem dialog box. Click the **Restore From Backup** and **Restart** buttons. The registry files are restored from System.da0 and User.da0. If these files are also missing, the registry cannot be restored. You can either restore the files from your own backups or run Windows 95 Setup. There is one other option. Look for the file System.1st in the root directory of the hard drive. This is the System.dat file created when Windows 95 was first installed. In an emergency, you can revert back to this file.

Nuts & Bolts Registry Wizard can back up and restore the registry, clean the registry of unneeded data, search for and repair registry orphans (registry entries that refer to files that have moved or no longer exist), and tune up and optimize the registry for better performance. Click **Start**, **Programs**, **Nuts & Bolts**, and select **Registry Wizard** from the list of Nuts & Bolts utilities. Figure 11-43 shows the opening screen of the Registry Wizard. The best time to use the Registry Wizard is before the problem occurs by making a backup of the registry before installing new software or hardware, making significant system configuration changes, and before editing the registry.

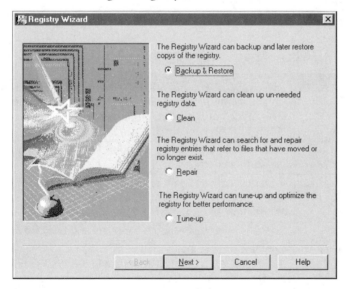

Figure 11-43　Nuts and Bolts Registry Wizard can back up, restore, clean, repair, and optimize the Windows 95 registry

Modifying the Registry

When you make a change in the Control Panel or Device Manager or many other places in Windows 95, such as installing software, you modify the registry. This is by far the best way to modify the registry. For most users, this is the only way they will ever change the registry. Make a practice of backing up the System.dat and User.dat files before you install new software or make major changes to Windows 95, because the registry is critical and will be edited during the process.

However, there are rare occasions when you might need to manually edit the registry. One example is when you have accidentally deleted the device driver for a hardware device, but Device Manager says that the device is still installed. Another example is when the wrong software starts when Windows 95 is loaded. Both these problems can be corrected by manually editing the registry.

Editing the Registry.   The first step in editing the registry is to back up the two files, System.dat and User.dat. Sometimes the files are small enough to fit on floppy disks and can be copied using Explorer. If the files are too large to copy to floppy disk, copy them to a different folder on the hard drive or use compression software such as PKZIP to copy them to floppy disks. The following directions use Windows 95 Regedit to edit the registry. Utility software, including Nuts & Bolts and Norton Utilities, has a registry editor that allows for backing up the registry before entering the editor so that reverting back to the version before editing is easy.

After backing up the registry files, the next step is to use Regedit.exe located in the Windows folder. You can use Explorer to locate the file, then double-click it, or click on **Start**, **Run**, and type **Regedit** in the Run dialog box. When you do, Figure 11-44 displays. Open one branch on the tree by clicking on the + sign to the left of the key, and close the branch by clicking on the – sign.

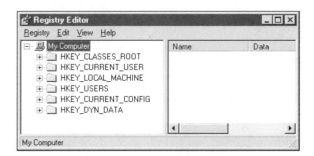

Figure 11-44   The six major keys or branches of the registry
seen in the Registry Editor

To search for an entry in the registry, click **Edit**, **Find**. The Find dialog box displays as in the screen in Figure 11-45, which is ready to find the text, "software," in the registry. Enter the key, the value, or the value data and click **Find Next**. You can choose to search keys, values, and/or value data by clicking on the check boxes in the dialog box.

For example, suppose the wrong programs start when you load Windows 95. First try to correct the problem without editing the registry. Using Explorer, open the Windows folder and then double-click the **Start Menu** folder. Delete any items that you don't want to start when you load Windows. If this does not correct the problem, the problem might be caused by a wrong entry recorded in the registry. Try editing the registry.

First locate the Shell Folders, which will be in the following branch:
HKEY_CURRENT_USER\Software\Microsoft\Windows\CurrentVersion\Explorer\Shell Folders

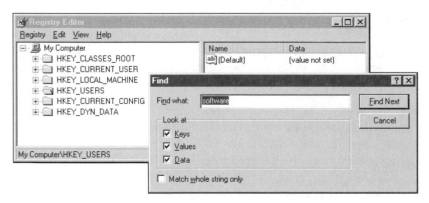

Figure 11-45   Searching for entries in the registry

Search for these keys and subkeys one at a time. (Search for HKEY_CURRENT_USER. After you have located it, search for Software, and continue through the list until you come to Shell Folders.)

The value name "Startup=" in the Shell Folders subkey should be "C:\Windows\Start Menu\Programs\Startup." If the data is incorrect, click **Startup** and select **Modify** from the drop-down menu that displays. Figure 11-46 shows the Editing dialog box that displays. Change the value data and click **OK**.

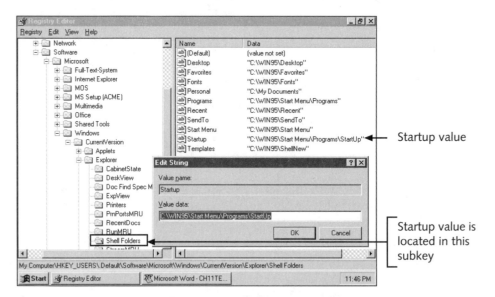

Figure 11-46   Editing an entry in the registry using Regedit.exe

Tracking Changes During an Installation

Two utilities that can track changes to not only the Windows 95 registry but also to .ini files and folders are a shareware program, In Control 3, and Norton Utilities Registry Tracker.

To use Norton Utilities Registry Tracker, click **Start**, **Programs**, **Norton Utilities**, **Norton Registry Tracker**, as shown in Figure 11-47. Figure 11-48 shows the Norton Registry Tracker main windows. When the utility first loads, it takes an Activation Snapshot of the system, which it will later use as the baseline to determine if future snapshots have detected any changes.

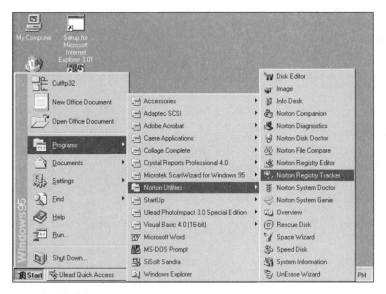

Figure 11-47   Finding Norton Utilities Registry Tracker

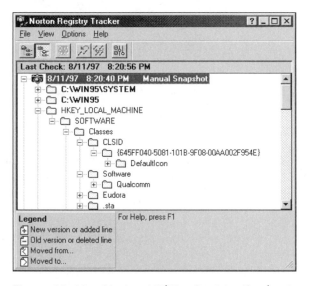

Figure 11-48   Norton Utilities Registry Tracker tracks changes to the Windows 95 registry

With the Norton Registry Tracker, you can first choose what it is you want to track and then take a snapshot of the system. Next install the software and then take another snapshot. Compare the two snapshots to see what the installation did to those things you chose to track.

To change the items tracked, click **Options**, **Settings** from the Norton Registry Tracker menu. The Tracker Settings screen displays as in Figure 11-49. Select the tab **Registry Keys** to see a list of keys to be tracked. Norton Registry Tracker tracks the two keys and their subkeys, HKEY_LOCAL_MACHINE and HKEY_USERS, because these keys contain the first copy of changes made when software is installed and user settings are changed. In Figure 11-49, the camera and the check mark beside the SOFTWARE subkey indicate that changes to it are to be tracked. If you want to track other keys, select the key and click **Track Key** or **Track Subkey**. Under the Folders tab you can choose which folders to track. By default, the Windows folder and the Windows/System folder are tracked. Under text files, Autoexec.bat, Config.sys, and the . ini files are tracked. Return to the main window by clicking **OK**.

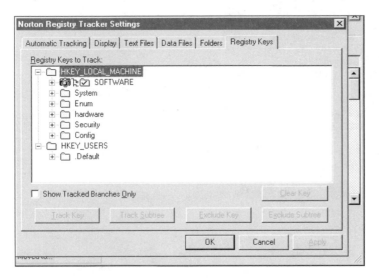

Figure 11-49   Select what you want Norton Registry Tracker to track during an installation

To take a snapshot, select **File**, **New Snapshot**. Figure 11-50 displays, asking you to name the snapshot. Enter the name and click **OK**. The snapshot is made and compares the things being tracked to the original activation snapshot made when the utility was first loaded. In the snapshot, changed items are color-coded.

Take a snapshot before the installation, perform the installation, and take another snapshot after the installation. The Norton Registry Tracker can then provide a side-by-side view of the two snapshots to make comparisons easy. Always using Norton Registry Tracker in this way is a good practice whenever installing software.

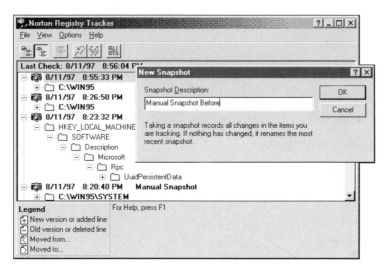

Figure 11-50   Naming the new snapshot

11

MICROSOFT SUPPORT ON THE INTERNET

When working with Microsoft products, including Windows 3.x and Windows 95, the Microsoft Web site can be a valuable source of information, software utilities and enhancements, and troubleshooting guidelines. For Microsoft Technical Support Knowledge Base, access this Web site:

www.microsoft.com/kb

Figure 11-51 shows the beginning query screen for this Web site. Follow the steps to research specific or general topics for the Microsoft products. For example, if you want to learn more about how to optimize Windows 95, choose **Windows 95** in Step 1 of Figure 11-51 and enter **optimize** as the key phrase to search for. Click **Begin Search**. A list of related articles displays. Double-click the article to display it.

Figure 11-51 Microsoft Technical Support Web site

CHAPTER SUMMARY

- Windows NT and Windows 95 are the most popular operating systems for new single-user PCs, although DOS and Windows 3.x are still being sold and supported.

- Windows 3.x stores most configuration information in .ini files. Some is stored in the registry.

- Files with a .ini extension are organized into sections, key names, and values and can be edited using a text editor.

- Lines in .ini files that begin with a semicolon are comments and ignored by the OS.

- Windows 3.x uses the registry, Reg.dat, to store information about file associations, OLE information, and data about applications software supporting programs.

- Before installing Windows 3.x, clean the hard drive by removing lost clusters, defragment the drive, and back up the Autoexec.bat and Config.sys files.

- If Windows 3.x setup hangs during installation, most likely the problem is with recognizing hardware devices. Use the /I option in the Setup command line.

- Documentation files in Windows generally have a .wri file extension.

- Applications software conflicts can occur if more than one application program uses the same .dll file stored in the Windows/system directory.

- Utility software can track changes to the Windows/system directory and changes to Windows .ini files and the registry during software installation.

- Windows manages memory using five categories of memory called heaps.

- PCs can operate in either real mode or protected mode. Real mode allows a program more control of the PC by allowing access to all areas of memory. Protected mode limits programs to certain areas of memory.

- A General Protection Fault (GPF) error at one time always meant a memory violation by software, but now can mean many different software errors.

- Windows application programs can give insufficient memory errors because a portion of a memory heap is not available, even though all of physical RAM is not entirely used yet.

- A memory leak is caused when an applications software program does not release a group of memory addresses back to the heap when it unloads.

- Windows 3.x is mostly a 16-bit application, whereas Windows 95 is a mixture of 16-bit and 32-bit code.

- The core components of Windows 95 are the kernel, the user, and the GDI processes.

- Windows 95, as well as Windows NT, uses the virtual machine concept to protect against program faults from other software currently running.

- Memory paging is a Windows 95 method of allocating a different set of memory addresses to different virtual machines.

- Windows 95 can be customized by entries in the MSDOS.SYS file.

- Windows 95 and Windows 3.x can coexist on the same PC; this is called a dual boot.

- Press F8 when Windows 95 is loading to view and use the Windows 95 Startup Menu, which can be helpful in troubleshooting Windows problems.

- Plug-and-Play (PnP) is a group of architectural standards designed to automate the installation of new hardware devices to PCs.

- In order for a PC to be completely Plug-and-Play-compliant, the System BIOS, all hardware devices, and the OS must be Plug-and-Play.

- The four components of the OS portion of Plug-and-Play are the configuration manager, the hardware tree, the bus enumerators, and the resource arbitrator.

- A legacy card is an expansion card that is not PnP and must be manually configured.

- Windows 95 uses 32-bit drivers stored in extended memory, although it does support older 16-bit drivers stored in the first MB of memory.

- Windows 95 loads older 16-bit drivers from either Config.sys or Autoexec.bat.

- The Windows 95 registry keeps information that was previously kept in Windows 3.x .ini files.

- The Windows 95 registry uses six major branches or keys.

11

KEY TERMS

- **Bus enumerator** — A component of Windows 95 Plug-and-Play that locates all devices on a particular bus and inventories the resource requirements for these devices.

- **Comment lines** — Documentation lines that are ignored by DOS. A Rem in front of a line will comment out an Autoexec command. A semicolon will turn an .ini file line into a comment.

- **Configuration manager** — A component of Windows 95 Plug-and-Play that controls the configuration process of all devices and communicates these configurations to the devices.

- **Disk thrashing** — A condition that results when the hard drive is excessively used for virtual memory because RAM is full. It dramatically slows down processing and can cause premature hard drive failure.

- **Dual boot** — The ability to boot using two or more different operating systems, such as Windows NT and Windows 95. However, programs cannot be shared between Windows NT and the other OS.

- **Group files** — Windows 3.x files with the .grp file extension that contain information about a program group of Program Manager.

- **Hardware tree** — A database built each time Windows 95 starts up that contains a list of installed components and the resources they use.

- **Heap** — A memory block set aside for a program's data. If the heap fills up, an "Out of memory" error might occur, even if there is plenty of regular RAM left, especially in 16-bit applications.

- **Initialization files** — Configuration information files for Windows. Win.ini and System.ini are the two most important Windows 3.x initialization files.

- **Keys** — Section names of the Windows 95 registry.

- **Legacy** — An older device or adapter card that does not support Plug-and-Play, and might have to be manually configured through jumpers or DIP switches.

- **Memory leak** — A problem caused when an application does not release the memory addresses assigned to it when it unloads, causing the memory heaps to have less and less memory for new applications.

- **Memory paging** — In Windows 95, swapping blocks of RAM memory to an area of the hard drive to serve as virtual memory when RAM memory is low.

- **MSDOS.SYS** — A read-only, hidden MS-DOS system file that must be on the boot disk for a system to boot successfully.

- **Page fault** — A program interrupt that occurs when an application requests data or instructions stored in virtual memory.

- **Page-in** — The process in which the memory manager goes to the hard drive to return the data from a swap file to RAM.

- **Page-out** — The process in which, when RAM is full, the memory manager takes a page and moves it to the swap file.

- **Plug-and-Play (PnP)** — In Windows 95, a set of design specifications that allows a new device to be connected, and then automatically recognized by the system. The device, system BIOS, and OS can all be PnP.

- **Plug-and-Play BIOS** — Basic input/output system for Plug-and-Play devices that are designed to be automatically recognized by the computer when they are installed.

- **Protected mode** — A mode used by 80286 and newer systems that can address more than 1 MB of memory. It controls memory addresses that a program can access. (Windows 95 runs in protected mode.)

- **Real mode** — A mode used by the original 8088 systems whereby a program can access any area of memory, and the addressing is not controlled by the operating system. It can only access 1 MB of memory.

- **Registration database** — A database used to store Windows 3.x configuration information. You can use REGEDIT to look at REG.DAT, which displays a list of applications that Windows has registered.

- **Resource arbitrator** — A PnP component that decides which resources are assigned to which devices.

- **Resource management** — The process of allocating resources to devices at startup.

- **Runtime configuration** — A PnP ongoing process that monitors changes in system devices, such as the removal of a PC Card on a notebook computer or the docking of a notebook computer to a docking station.

- **Safe mode** — The mode in which Windows 95 is loaded with minimum configuration and drivers in order to allow the correction of system errors. To enter Safe Mode, press F5 or F8 when "Starting Windows 95" is displayed.

- **Value data** — In Windows 95, the name and value of a setting in the registry.

- **Virtual machines (VM)** — Multiple logical machines created within one physical machine by Windows, allowing applications to make serious errors within one logical machine without disturbing other programs and parts of the system.

- **Virtual memory manager** — A Windows 95 program that controls the page table, swapping 4K pages in and out of physical RAM to and from the hard drive.

- **Windows Custom Setup** — A setup feature that allows user customization of such things as directory locations, wallpaper settings, font selections, and many other features.

- **Windows Express Setup** — A setup feature that automatically installs Windows in the most commonly used fashion.

11

REVIEW QUESTIONS

1. What are .ini files?

2. What do the files Win.ini and System.ini do?

3. List two programs that can be used to edit .ini files.

4. How can you turn a line in an .ini file into a comment line, so that it will be ignored later?

5. How can you turn a line in an Autoexec.bat or Config.sys file into a comment line, so that it will be ignored later?

6. What does the file Regedit do? How do you run Regedit?

7. List the steps to correct the problem if Windows does not load or hangs after installation.

8. List the steps to correct the problem if Windows setup cannot find a driver for your hardware.

9. What does .dll stand for? What is the function of .dll files?

10. List five memory heaps maintained by Windows.

11. What is a GPF? What is the most common cause of GPF errors?

12. What is protected mode?

13. What is memory paging? What is excessive memory paging? What can be the consequences of excessive memory paging?

14. What is meant by dual boot? List the steps to set up a dual boot system so that the system automatically boots to Windows 3.x instead of Windows 95.

15. What boot options are contained in the file Msdos.sys?

16. What function key can you press during startup to see the Windows 95 Startup Menu?

17. List five options that are listed in the Windows 95 Startup Menu.

18. How can the file Bootlog.txt be helpful in troubleshooting?

19. What is the Safe mode? When would you enter the Safe mode?

20. What is Plug-and-Play?

21. What three things must be true for a system to be truly Plug-and-Play?

22. What is a legacy device? How are legacy devices typically configured?

23. After physically installing a new device in a Windows 95 system, what might have to be done to tell Windows that it is installed?

24. List and briefly describe the six major keys of the Windows 95 registry.

25. When you make a change in Control Panel or Device Manager or many other places in Windows, such as installing software, what are you modifying?

PROJECTS

EXAMINE YOUR PC

1. List all of the .ini files stored in your home or lab computer's Windows directory.

2. Print out your home or lab computer's System.ini file and identify each hardware component that is referenced.

3. In a Windows 95 system, click the **Start** button, then **Run: Edit C:\Msdos.sys**. Then select **File**, **Print** and print the contents of this file.

4. Follow these steps to list Windows troubleshooting tools:

   a. Click the Windows 95 **Start** button.

   b. Choose the **Settings** option.

   c. Select the **Control Panel**.

   d. List at least six Control Panel utilities that can be used to configure and resolve hardware problems.

WINDOWS 95 START MENU

As soon as your computer displays the message "Starting Windows 95" during the boot process, press the F8 function key. Select **Logged(\Bootlog.txt)**. When done, open the file named Bootlog.txt and print out its contents. Shut down Windows, reboot the computer, and press F8 again. Select the **Safe mode** option and note the differences in the screen appearance. Shut down Windows, reboot the computer, and press F8 again. This time choose the **Step-by-step Confirmation** option. Write down each command that executes.

11

BACKING UP CRITICAL WINDOWS 95 FILES

Keep a copy of critical Windows 95 files in a separate directory. Each time you install or uninstall hardware or software, redo the backup.

1. Using Windows 95 Explorer, create a new folder called Win-bak.ini.

2. In the C:\Windows folder highlight the System.ini and Win.ini files. Copy them by pressing **Ctrl C**.

3. Click the **Win-bak.ini** directory, then paste the copied .ini files into the Win-bak.ini by pressing **Ctrl V**.

4. Using Explorer, set the View, Options to **Show all files**.

5. Copy C:\Windows\system.dat to C:\ Win-bak.ini (do not drag!).

6. Copy C:\Windows\user.dat to C:\ Win-bak.ini (do not drag!).

MONITOR A SOFTWARE INSTALLATION

Using utility software such as In Control or Norton Utilities, monitor the installation of an applications software package. Install the software following the installation instructions documented with the software. Does the software allow you to customize the environment? What files are used to store the custom configuration? By looking at the date and time stamp on files, how can you guess which files contain custom setup information for this installation of the application?

DOWNLOAD A UTILITY FROM THE INTERNET

Download WindSock from the Web site www.shareware.com. Using Windows 3.x, compare the memory used with and without desktop wallpaper. Print screens showing the comparisons.

TRACK CHANGES TO THE WINDOWS 95 REGISTRY

Use Norton Utilities or In Control 3 to track the changes to the Windows 95 registry while installing an applications software package.

CUSTOMIZING A DUAL BOOT

You have your PC set for a dual boot between DOS with Windows 3.1 and Windows 95. You boot to your previous version of DOS and decide to make a change to the Windows 95 Msdos.sys file. What is the current name of the file? List the steps to edit the file. Verify that your answers are correct by changing the BootMenu option in Msdos.sys. Be certain to first back up the file.

USE THE CONTROL PANEL TO TEST YOUR MODEM

1. Click the Windows 95 **Start** button.

2. Choose the **Settings** option.

3. Select the **Control Panel**.

4. Double-click the **Modems** icon.

5. Choose the **Diagnostics** tab.

6. Select the appropriate COM port and click the **More Info** button to verify that an OK message is displayed.

7. Click the **Help** button and list at least four things that the Modem Troubleshooter will help solve.

MOUSE TROUBLESHOOTING

Assume that your friend is having a difficult time finding and following the mouse pointer on his new laptop computer. Enter Control Panel and list the steps that you would use to make the mouse pointer easier to see. Test your steps on your home or lab computer.

CUSTOMIZING WINDOWS 95

Change the Windows 95 logo screen to another .bmp file at startup.

USING NUTS & BOLTS TO VIEW THE WINDOWS 95 REGISTRY

Nuts & Bolts offers a powerful editor for the Windows 95 registry. Use it here to save the registry to a text file (called exporting a registry file) for easy and safe viewing. This text file can later be edited and then imported back into the registry. Registry text files are also convenient for transporting portions of a registry from one PC to another. In this example, you export the mouse options set in Control Panel to a registry file and view the text file.

1. Using Windows 95, click **Start**, **Programs**, **Nuts & Bolts**, and select **Registry Pro** from the Nuts & Bolts utilities.

2. Click on **Search**, **Find** and search for the text "mousekeys." The occurrences of mousekeys will display in the key list at the bottom of the editor. Double-click on the **HKEY_CURRENT_USER** occurrence of mousekeys. This key should now display in the editor view window.

3. On the left side of the editor window, you can view the value names and their values for the mouse. Click on **File**, **Export Registry File** to save this key to a text file. In the Save As dialog box that displays, enter the path and filename for the file. For example, to save the file to a folder named Data, using MouseSave as the filename, enter **\Data\MouseSave** and click **Save**. The editor will assign a .reg file extension to the file.

11

4. Leaving the Registry pro editor still on screen, use any text editor or word processor to open the file MouseSave.reg. Print the contents of this text file and compare them to the MouseKeys key values showing in Registry Pro.

5. Exit Registry Pro.

USING NUTS & BOLTS WIZARD

Use the Registry Wizard of Nuts & Bolts to first make a backup of the registry and then perform the clean, repair, and tune-up procedures shown in Figure 11-52.

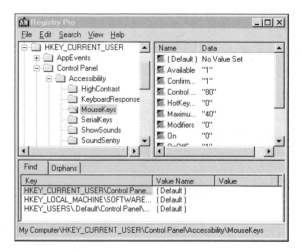

Figure 11-52   Nuts and Bolts offers a powerful registry editor, Registry Pro

1. Back up the registry.

2. Clean the registry of the Recent Docs List. Verify the clean was successful by clicking on **Start**, **Documents**.

3. Repair the registry. Allow the Registry Wizard to search for and fix any orphan entries (entries without associated files) in the registry that it can. How many orphans did it fix?

4. Tune-up the registry. From the Registry Wizard opening screen, select **Tune-up**. Print the Registry Wizard screen showing the values or write down the size of the System.dat and User.dat files before and after the tune up.

CHAPTER TWELVE

UNDERSTANDING AND SUPPORTING WINDOWS NT WORKSTATION

This chapter covers an introduction to Windows NT Workstation (the NT stands for new technology) including basic architecture, installation, maintenance, and troubleshooting. There are two versions of Windows NT: Windows NT Workstation and Windows NT Server. Windows NT Workstation can be used on a standalone PC or can be used as the operating system on a workstation connected to a network. Windows NT Server, which is not covered in this book, can do the same, as well as provide a domain environment on a network. (A **domain** is a group of computers joined together over a network that share a common database controlling security to each PC on the network.) Windows NT Workstation, as well as Windows NT Server, is architecturally built more like the UNIX OS than like other Windows operating systems, such as DOS with Windows 3.x and Windows 95. Windows NT is designed with a strong emphasis on room for expandability, primarily accomplished by its modular approach to dealing with applications and hardware. Windows NT is also intended to port to several non-Intel-based platforms, provide a high level of security, performance, and reliability, and offer strong networking features.

IN THIS CHAPTER
YOU WILL LEARN:

- ABOUT THE WINDOWS NT ENVIRONMENT AND ITS ARCHITECTURE
- ABOUT THE STRENGTHS AND WEAKNESSES OF WINDOWS NT
- HOW TO EVALUATE WHEN WINDOWS NT IS THE BEST CHOICE FOR A PC OS
- HOW TO INSTALL AND CUSTOMIZE WINDOWS NT
- HOW TO SET UP A WINDOWS NT ENVIRONMENT FOR A DOS OR WINDOWS 3.X APPLICATION
- HOW TO USE SOME WINDOWS NT TROUBLESHOOTING TECHNIQUES AND TOOLS

In this chapter, Windows NT Workstation is often compared to Windows 95, on the assumption that you are familiar with the latter OS, so that you can make an informed decision when choosing between the two. However, sometimes the comparisons are difficult to make because the two operating systems are so fundamentally different. It would be much easier to compare Windows NT to UNIX, particularly when talking about performance, reliability, and networking features. However, UNIX is not a viable choice for a PC operating system, so, for the purposes of these discussions, it will not be considered. Furthermore, to fully appreciate the strengths of Windows NT, you would need to go beyond the scope of this chapter into the depths of the networking arena.

WINDOWS NT VS. WINDOWS 95

Table 12-1 summarizes some comparative points between Windows NT and Windows 95, which will be addressed in this section. For instance, although Windows 95 and Windows NT Workstation have many features in common, including a common user interface, common utilities such as Internet Explorer and Microsoft Messaging, and common features such as system policies, user profiles, and hardware profiles, the two operating systems differ dramatically in underlying architecture and structure. Windows NT Workstation offers higher performance and higher reliability and security than does Windows 95. On the other hand, Windows 95 has less demanding hardware requirements, offers broad application and device compatibility, and works well on notebook PCs because of better power management features and Plug-and-Play.

The key to appreciating what Windows NT offers over Windows 95 is in the platforms and settings that Windows NT targets. Windows NT is designed to satisfy the needs of powerful workstations networked together in a corporate environment, whereas Windows 95 dominates the home market and is used on low-end PCs where applications software using multimedia devices and ease of installation are more of an issue than network security and high-end performance.

You learned from the last chapter that Windows 95 has evolved from DOS and Windows 3.x and that, while it might require greater resources, Windows 95 can run on the same basic hardware and run the same software as its predecessors. This ability is referred to as maintaining **backward compatibility**. This is not true, however, of Windows NT, which places more extensive requirements on both hardware and software and has functionality that differs from that of Windows 95 and its predecessors. Windows NT makes the break with the past by not claiming to be 100% backward compatible with older hardware and software, thereby allowing Windows NT to offer more power and functionality.

In comparing Windows 95 to Windows NT, there are two important points to remember: first, if Windows NT is installed on a PC that is not as powerful as the type of computer Windows NT was designed to run on, Windows NT will not perform as well as Windows 95 would, on the same PC. However, on a powerful workstation PC with a configuration recommended for Windows NT, Windows NT will perform faster and better than Windows 95. The second important point is that Windows NT is not one more evolution of DOS, Windows 3.x, and Windows 95. In fact, the opposite is true. Windows NT was developed before Windows 95. Windows 95 was built as a bridge between the old (DOS with Windows 3.x) and the new (Windows NT). The remainder of this section will highlight and expand on several of the differences between Windows NT and Windows 95.

Table 12-1   Comparing Windows NT to Windows 95

Feature	Windows 95	Windows NT
Hardware requirements	Low, requiring a 486 PC with 8–16 MB of RAM	High, requiring a Pentium with 16–32 MB RAM
Hardware compatibility	Supports most legacy devices	Supports most current devices, but does not claim backward compatibility with legacy devices
Software compatibility	Fully backward compatible with older DOS and Windows 3.x applications	No support for any application that attempts to access hardware directly
Installation	Offers Plug-and-Play	Does not offer Plug-and-Play and offers less device driver support
Power management	Built-in power management for laptops	None
Performance	Offers multitasking for 32-bit and 16-bit applications	Also offers multitasking for 32-bit and 16-bit applications. Has significantly better performance on systems with at least 32 MB of RAM
Reliability and stability	Much better than Windows 3.x	Very high reliability and stability; all applications run in protected memory space
Security	Allows violation of the logon process controlled from a server	Very high security down to the file level

12

FEATURES OF WINDOWS NT

Windows NT Workstation includes the following features:

- **Desktop performance**. Supports a powerful multitasking environment and supports multiple microprocessors for true multitasking
- **Hardware profiles**. Can maintain different hardware profiles for different hardware configurations on the same PC

- **Internet Explorer**. Provides a built-in Web browser (Internet Explorer)
- **Peer Web Services**. Provides a personal Web server
- **Security**. Provides security for individual files, folders, and other resources. User access to a PC's resources can be controlled by user IDs and passwords on the standalone PC or managed from a network controller.
- **OS Stability**. Protective processing prevents applications from causing errors in other applications or in Windows NT itself.

Many of these same features, including the Internet Explorer, hardware profiles, and user access, are available from Windows 95 as well. Windows 95 allows more hardware devices to be used than does Windows NT, has a simpler installation process, and supports power management features and Plug-and-Play better than does Windows NT. Windows NT has higher performance, including faster speed on high-end PCs, higher reliability, and better security than does Windows 95. The minimum hardware requirements for Windows NT on an IBM-compatible PC are listed below. However, even though Windows NT does run on this minimum hardware configuration, remember that, in order to experience the full benefits of Windows NT, a powerful high-end PC is needed.

- 486DX, 33 MHz or better CPU
- 12 MB of RAM (16 MB is recommended)
- 120 MB of hard disk space

While the minimum requirements listed above reference IBM-compatible machines, Windows NT can run on computers other than those that are IBM-compatible. The interface and functionality are the same from one CPU to the next; the main difference is in the layer (which is a part of Windows NT) between the OS and the hardware, called the **hardware abstraction layer** or **HAL**. The CPUs supported by Windows NT are listed below. This chapter focuses only on the Intel-based CPUs of IBM-compatible machines.

- Intel 486DX, 33-MHz-based processor or Intel Pentium-based processor
- MIPS R4x00-based processor
- Digital Alpha AXP-based processor

The Windows NT CD-ROM contains three installation directories to choose from, one for each of these three types of processors. Each of these three directories contains a different version of HAL, sometimes referred to as the core of the OS designed to interact with the CPU type. HAL is discussed at greater length later in this chapter.

Hardware Supported by Windows NT

Many hardware devices are not supported by Windows NT. For this reason, before you decide to upgrade a PC to Windows NT, first determine if all components on your PC will work under Windows NT. For instance, a network card, modem, video card, and the like, might need to be replaced before Windows NT will work. To determine if hardware components are supported by Windows NT, see the **hardware compatibility list** (**HCL**) for Windows NT, which comes with the software. The latest copy is available on the Microsoft Web site at www.microsoft.com/hwtest. On the list, which can be searched by hardware category and/or company name, are all hardware devices supported by Windows NT. For instance, Figure 12-1 shows the partial results of a search for modems compatible with Windows NT 4.0. If a device is not on the list, ask the manufacturer if there is a driver specifically for Windows NT (not just Windows 95). If no driver exists, this device will not work under Windows NT.

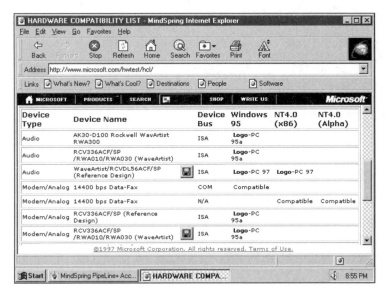

Figure 12-1   Some modems compatible with Windows NT from the HCL

The Windows NT Desktop Is Similar to Windows 95

Beginning with Windows NT 4.0, the Windows NT desktop took on a similar look and feel to Windows 95. Figure 12-2 shows the Windows NT desktop with the Start menu and Control Panel showing, both of which work just as they do in Windows 95, although some Control Panel icons are different. Shortcuts are created the same way as in Windows 95, and the Taskbar works the same, too.

Beginning with Something Familiar: Windows NT Command Prompt

Another similarity between Windows NT and Windows 95 is the command prompt that allows the user to enter DOS-like commands. To access the command prompt, click **Start**, **Programs**, and **Command Prompt** (as in Figure 12-2). The Command Prompt window will appear, as in Figure 12-3. From the command prompt, DOS commands can be entered. There is a difference between the DOS prompt under Windows 95 and under Windows NT. In Windows 95, the DOS prompt is actually accessing a version of DOS (Windows 95 uses

COMMAND.COM at startup). Windows NT, however, provides a DOS command interface primarily as a convenience for those wanting to use familiar DOS commands. There are
no DOS programs underlying and running under Windows NT.

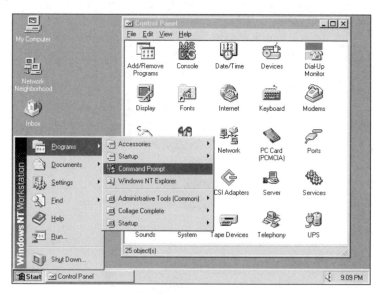

Figure 12-2   The Windows NT desktop is similar to that of Windows 95

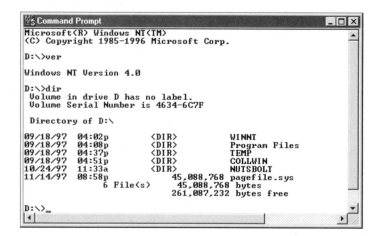

Figure 12-3   The Windows NT command prompt uses DOS-like commands

As a side note, notice in Figure 12-2 that the Control Panel for Windows NT
contains an icon, MSDOS, which is labeled Console. Click on the **Console** icon
to change the properties of the DOS command window. The Console Windows
Properties sheet appears, which allows you to customize the Command Prompt
window (see Figure 12-4). If you prefer to use the familiar command prompt
often, you can create a shortcut to it by dragging this icon to the desktop.

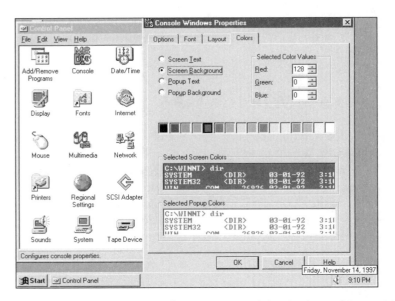

Figure 12-4   Customizing the properties of the Command Prompt Window

CHOOSING BETWEEN WINDOWS 95 AND WINDOWS NT

When choosing between using Windows 95 or Windows NT as your PC OS, consider the following:

- Does Windows NT support all the hardware devices on your PC? (Check the hardware compatibility list.)

- Is the PC powerful and big enough to support Windows NT? (See the hardware requirements listed earlier in the chapter, and then allow extra resources for your applications.)

- Will the software you intend to use on the PC work better under Windows 95 or Windows NT? Running older DOS and Windows 16-bit applications might be a problem in a Windows NT environment. Verify that your current, older software works under Windows NT before making the investment, or plan to replace the current software with 32-bit versions. Be aware, however, that some 32-bit programs written for Windows 95 might not work under Windows NT because of differences in the API calls. (An **API** is an advanced program interface, which is a method by which one program calls another program to perform a task.)

- Is price a factor? Windows NT costs more than Windows 95.

Windows NT is faster on high-end PCs, more secure, more efficient, and more fail-safe than Windows 95. So if you can answer "yes" to each of the questions above, Windows NT

12

Workstation might be your first choice. If the hardware is not powerful enough or compatible with Windows NT, or the software is not compatible, then Windows 95 is probably the best choice.

UPGRADING FROM WINDOWS 95 TO WINDOWS NT

Because Windows NT differs so fundamentally from Windows 95, there is no automatic upgrade path from Windows 95 to Windows NT. When you change a PC from Windows 95 to Windows NT, Windows NT can be installed in a different folder. No system settings in Windows 95 will be transferred to Windows NT. After Windows NT is installed, each application must be reinstalled on the PC under Windows NT. Windows NT can be present as the only OS on a PC or it can be installed on the same PC as Windows 95. This method of having two operating systems on the same PC is called a **dual boot** and is discussed later in this chapter.

Registries

The most important reason that Windows 95 cannot be easily upgraded to Windows NT is that their registries differ. (Remember that a registry is a database containing all configuration information for the OS.) The Windows 95 registry is not compatible with the Windows NT registry, so it is difficult to transfer information from one to the other. There is no such problem when upgrading from Windows 3.x to Windows NT because Windows NT can read the .ini files in Windows 3.x and transfer that information to the Windows NT registry. Again, you must realize that Windows NT is not to be viewed as the next stepping stone beyond Windows 95, but viewed as a new road altogether.

A Choice of File Systems

Windows NT can work with two types of file systems, the FAT (file allocation table) file system, which is used by Windows 95 and its predecessors, and the Windows NT file system (NTFS), which works only with Windows NT. A **file system** is the method used by the OS to manage the data on a drive. The FAT file system is backward compatible with DOS and Windows 95 and uses less overhead than NTFS. The NTFS file system, on the other hand, is more fail-safe, provides more security, and is more efficient with large hard drives. Below, you will see how these two file systems are built and then explore what to consider when choosing between the two.

The FAT file system includes four components, the boot record, the FAT, directories, and data files. Most FAT tables are made with 16-bit entries including the VFAT table of Windows 95. (Sometimes the Windows 95 file system is built with a true 32-bit FAT called FAT32.)

The NTFS file system is built with 64-bit entries and has as its core component the **master file table (MFT)**. Entries in the MFT are ordered alphabetically by filename in order to speed up a search for a file listed in the table. Each cluster on the hard drive can range from 512 bytes on smaller disks to 4K on larger disks. Clusters are numbered sequentially by **logical cluster numbers (LCN)** from the beginning to the end of the disk.

As seen in Figure 12-5, the MFT contains information about each file, including header information (abbreviated H in Microsoft documentation), standard information (SI) about the file (including date and time data), filename (FN), security information about the file called the security descriptor (SD), and data in one record or row of the MFT. The data area in the MFT record is 2K in size for small hard drives, but can be larger for larger hard drives. For small files, if the data can fit into the 2K area, the file, including its data, is fully contained within the MFT.

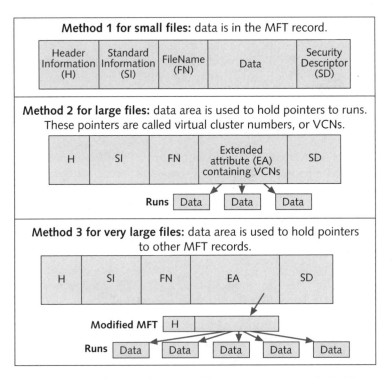

Figure 12-5   The Windows NT file system Master File Table uses three methods to store files, depending on the file size

If the file is moderately large and the data does not fit into the MFT, the data area in the MFT becomes an extended attribute (EA) of the file, which points to the location of the data. The data itself is moved outside the table to clusters called **runs**. The record in the MFT for this moderately large file contains pointers to these runs. Each data run, or cluster, assigned to the file is assigned a 64-bit **virtual cluster number** (**VCN**). The MFT maps the VCNs for the file onto the LCNs (logical cluster numbers) for the drive. This mapping is stored in the area of the MFT record that would have contained the data if the file had been small enough.

If the file is so large that the pointers to all the VCNs cannot be contained in one MFT record, then additional MFT records are used. The first MFT record is called the **base file record** and holds the location of the other MFT records for this file.

Advantages of NTFS and FAT.   When choosing between the NTFS file system and the FAT file system, consider these advantages, which NTFS offers over the FAT:

- The NTFS file system is a recoverable file system. NTFS retains copies of its critical file system data and automatically recovers a failed file system using this information the first time the disk is accessed after a file system failure.

- The NTFS file system offers increased security over the FAT file system. Security is provided for each file, and auditing information about access to files is more complete.

- The NTFS file system supports mirroring drives, meaning that two copies of data can be kept on two different drives to protect against permanent data loss in case of a hard drive crash. This feature makes the NTFS file system an important alternative for file servers.

- The NTFS file system uses smaller cluster sizes than does the FAT, making more efficient use of hard drive space when small files are used.

- The NTFS file system supports large-volume drives. NTFS uses 64–bit cluster numbers, whereas FAT uses either 16–bit or 32–bit cluster numbers. Because the number of bits assigned to hold each cluster number is so large, the cluster number itself can be a large number, and the table can accommodate very large drives with many clusters. NTFS is overall a more effective file system for drives over 1 GB and offers more robust drive compression, allowing compression of individual folders and files.

The advantages of the FAT file system are:

- The FAT file system has less overhead than the NTFS file system and, therefore, works best for hard drives that are less than 500 MB in size.

- The FAT file system is compatible with other operating systems. If you plan to use either DOS or Windows 95 on the same hard drive as Windows NT, use the FAT file system so that DOS and Windows 95 can access files used by Windows NT.

- In the event of a serious problem with Windows NT, if you are using FAT on the active partition of the drive, you can boot the PC from a disk, using DOS, and gain access to the drive.

You can choose to have Windows NT use the NTFS file system by reformatting the hard drive for NTFS (remember reformatting will erase all data on the hard drive) or by using Windows NT to partition a drive so that one partition of the drive uses the FAT format and the other uses the NTFS format. Windows NT also allows logical drives to be formatted with either the FAT or NTFS file system on the same extended partition.

Hard Drive Partitions

Windows NT assigns two different functions to hard drive partitions (see Figure 12-6). The **system partition**, normally drive C, is the **active partition** of the hard drive. This is the partition that contains the boot record (often called the DOS boot record) that Startup BIOS and then the master boot program in the boot sector look to for the boot program as the first step in turning the PC over to an OS. The other partition, called the **boot partition**, is the partition where the Windows NT operating system is stored. The system partition and the boot partition can be the same partition, or they can be separate partitions. Both can be formatted with either the FAT or NTFS file system. However, only Windows NT can read files formatted with the NTFS file system. If it is intended that other OSs access this hard drive, then the FAT file system must be used for the partition that another OS accesses.

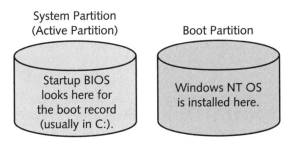

System Partition
(Active Partition)   Boot Partition

Startup BIOS
looks here for   Windows NT OS
the boot record   is installed here.
(usually in C:).

Figure 12-6   Two types of hard drive partitions

Don't be confused by the terminology here. It is really true that, according to Windows NT terminology, the Windows NT OS is on the boot partition, and the boot record is on the system partition, even though that might sound backward. The PC boots from the system partition and loads the Windows NT operating system from the boot partition.

WINDOWS NT AND A DUAL BOOT

Remember that it is possible for Windows NT to coexist on the same PC with either Windows 95 or DOS. To set up Windows NT for a dual boot so that it can boot either Windows NT or Windows 95, or can boot either Windows NT or DOS, the system partition must not be NTFS, but must be FAT, so that Windows 95 or DOS can read it. Windows NT resides on the boot partition, which can also be formatted for the FAT file system and can even be the same partition. However, Windows NT could reside on a second partition, say drive D. Drive D can be either FAT or NTFS. If drive D is NTFS, then Windows 95 cannot read any data stored on that drive. If drive D is a FAT partition, then either OS can read data from either drive.

After both operating systems are installed, a startup menu appears, asking which OS to boot (similar to the menu provided when Windows 95 and DOS are on the same PC). The disadvantage of a dual boot of DOS or Windows 95 with Windows NT is that applications software cannot be shared between the two OSs. Instead, the software must be installed twice, once for each OS.

12

THE WINDOWS NT ENVIRONMENT AND ARCHITECTURE

Understanding the Windows NT environment and architecture begins with understanding the goals and objectives of Windows NT. This section begins by examining some of the objectives of Windows NT, which helps explain why Windows NT works the way it does. Following that discussion is an examination of how Windows NT accomplishes these objectives.

THE GOALS OF WINDOWS NT

Windows NT had its beginnings when IBM and Microsoft collaborated in building OS/2. While IBM took over OS/2, Microsoft redesigned and added to the original and called the new OS Windows NT. Windows NT has many of the same objectives as UNIX and is considered the primary competitor to UNIX in the client/server industry. Because Windows NT also functions on a LAN, it is also considered a competitor of NetWare software by Novell, which is popular for managing LANs. Finally, Windows NT competes for some of the standalone PC market, contending with Windows 95. For an OS to contend for so many markets, its objectives must, by nature, be many, including the following:

- **Room to Grow.** Windows NT has been planned and designed for expandability, so it can more easily accommodate new hardware and software in the future. The main way that NT does this is by using a modular approach to performing tasks. For example, remember from earlier discussions of the limitations of DOS that one way that DOS is limited in allowing an application more memory addresses is that real-mode DOS drivers can access memory addresses directly without going through DOS, and thereby can "box in" an application in the first 640K of memory addresses. (Remember from Chapter 9, that memory beginning just above 640K could not be allocated to applications.) Windows NT never allows this "boxing in" to happen. Applications are required to pass their requests to NT, which processes them. Because of this layer of protection between software and hardware, when hardware requirements change, only Windows NT must change; the application is insulated from the change. (However, a disadvantage to this approach is that, when new hardware devices come on the market, Windows NT must provide the interface to the driver before any application operating under Windows NT can make use of it.)

- **Portability to Different Platforms**. Because of the Windows NT modular approach, it easily ports to different platforms or hardware configurations, including different CPU technologies. Remember that the Windows NT installation CD-ROM comes with three directories ready to accommodate three different CPU technologies. Windows NT is able to do this by isolating parts of the OS from other parts in a modular fashion. The part of the OS that interacts with the hardware is the HAL (hardware abstraction layer), which is available in different versions, each designed to address the specifics of a particular CPU technology. HAL is the only part of the OS that has to change when platforms change. The other components of the OS need not be changed when the platform changes.

- **Compatibility with Other OSs and Legacy Software**. Because Windows NT had its beginnings in OS/2, Microsoft is committed to Windows NT being compatible with software written for OS/2. As long as DOS applications don't attempt to access resources directly, they too can run under Windows NT. Windows 3.x 16-bit applications can run under Windows NT in a virtual machine environment similar to a Windows 95 virtual machine (discussed at greater length below). Windows NT also supports POSIX (Portable OS Interface) based on UNIX, a set of standards adopted by the federal government in order to better ensure that OSs and software can more easily port from one platform to another.

- **Security**. Windows NT provides security similar to that found on UNIX systems, which is greater than that found in Windows 95. Windows NT security allows for: (1) the requirement that a user have a logon ID and password to gain access to the PC, (2) security between users on the same PC, so that one user can block another user from data or software, (3) auditing trails to identify security breaches, and (4) memory protection between different applications loaded at the same time.

- **Performance and Reliability**. Although no OS is faultproof, Windows NT provides a much more stable environment than do many OSs, including Windows 95. Windows NT is less likely to hang or "lock up" than are other PC OSs. If an application stalls, other applications also loaded are less likely to be affected. When using powerful workstations, Windows NT outperforms Windows 3.x and Windows 95 when running applications written for Windows NT, as well as when running applications written for Windows 3.x, Windows 95, and DOS.

12

THE MODULAR CONCEPT OF WINDOWS NT

Here's an analogy to help you understand the modular concept of Windows NT. The idea is to isolate one process from another so that a change in one process has the least effect possible on the other processes. Consider the self-serve restaurant in Figure 12-7. In the process illustrated in Figure 12-7a, customers arrive for breakfast, walk to the back of the restaurant, stand over the cook, tell him what they want for breakfast, wait for him to cook it, take it back to a table, and eat. Customers are responsible for getting their own drinks, silverware, and the like. What is the flaw in this design? There are many, but concentrate on only one at this time. Suppose someone in the kitchen moves the silverware or installs a new and different drink-dispensing machine. How many people have to learn a new process in order for the system to continue working? Every customer. This process is nonmodular and clearly does not minimize the effect that a change in one part of the process has on other parts of the process.

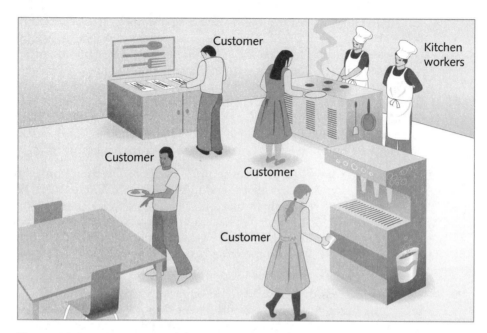

Figure 12-7a   In a nonmodular restaurant model, every customer is responsible for many of the steps in the process

Figure 12-7b   In a partially modular restaurant model, customers are isolated from some processes

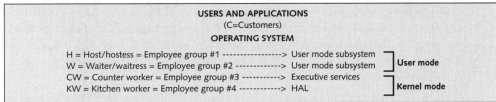

Figure 12-7c In a highly modular restaurant model, employees are grouped by function, and customers interact only with one group of employees. Employee groups are analogous to different parts of the Windows NT operating system.

12

Now consider Figure 12-7b. A counter has been added, and customers are not allowed behind this counter. They come to the counter and tell others in the kitchen what they want to eat, and someone in the kitchen brings the food, drink, and silverware to them at the counter. Things work a little better now. When processes change in the kitchen, only employees who work in the kitchen must be retrained. However, there is still a flaw in the efficiency of this design. Every kitchen worker must know how to cook, how to make drinks, and where the silverware is located. This model introduces some benefits of a modular design, but still has flaws.

Figure 12-7c further refines the process, and our restaurant is now a full-service, highly modular affair. Employees are divided into four groups, each with a different function. The first group of employees—the hosts and hostesses, waiters and waitresses—relates to the customers, greeting them at the door, showing them their seats, taking orders, and serving food. The waiters and waitresses serve as an interface between customers and counter workers (the second group). The counter workers stand between the kitchen counter and the customer counter, and in their area are the drink machines and the silverware. The waiters and waitresses pass food requests to the counter workers, who pass the requests to the third group, the kitchen workers, who now only prepare the food. When the food is passed back to the counter workers, these workers gather up drinks, silverware, and food and pass them on to the waiters and waitresses, who serve the customers. This model uses a more highly modular arrangement that provides the benefits of separating processes from each other, even though the overhead (the additional resources needed to implement the new model) is higher than in the other models.

What are the advantages of the last model? If the drink machine is upgraded, only the counter workers must be retrained. If the oven or stove in the kitchen is replaced with an altogether new electronic unit, only the kitchen workers change their methods. The counter workers are unaffected. The waiters and waitresses don't need to know how to communicate with the cook, but can focus on customer service. The customer is isolated from the entire process. In comparing Figures 12-7a and 12-7c, on first appearance it looks as though the process has only been complicated. New workers are required, and customers now have to wait to be seated. A new layer of complexity is added, and two counters are required. However, on closer examination, you see that the advantages of the new system outweigh its disadvantages and overhead. Not only can equipment be easily upgraded without having to retrain so many people or reorient customers to the new procedures, but the integrity of the operation is enhanced: because the processes have been separated from each other, they can now be more easily controlled. Standards and procedures can be more easily applied to each segment of the process because fewer people are involved. With fewer people involved at each step in the operation, confusion is reduced, and the overall efficiency of the operation improves. In summary, the three main reasons to use the highly modular model rather than the nonmodular model are as follows:

- To make upgrades of equipment easier. (Some employees and all customers are unaffected.)
- To increase the overall efficiency of the operation. (Each process involves fewer people than in the other models.)
- To better ensure the integrity of processes. (Standards are more easily enforced.)

The process of running the restaurant can be viewed as analogous to the way Windows NT and earlier OSs run a computer: Customers can be viewed as a combination of users and applications software; employees can be viewed as the OS; the stove, drink machine, silverware stand, and the like can be viewed as the hardware; and the cook can be viewed as those parts of the OS that relate directly to hardware, system BIOS, and device drivers. The process illustrated in Figure 12-7a is most analogous to DOS, where applications were allowed "behind the counter" to interact directly with BIOS and device drivers, and even to perform some of their own operations with hardware, rather than necessarily turning to the OS to perform hardware operations. For example, in DOS, an applications program written to address specific hardware configurations might depend on video BIOS always being found at certain memory addresses, and the program could access that BIOS directly.

The process illustrated in Figure 12-7b is most analogous to a model of the Windows 95 OS, where the customers (the applications) are isolated from some of the interaction with hardware, but not all. Notice, for instance, that the silverware stand is still available for customer use, just as similarly, in Windows 95, a 16-bit program could interact directly with video memory and other resources.

The process illustrated in Figure 12-7c is most analogous to a model of the Windows NT OS, which includes an additional layer between the applications (customers) and hardware (the restaurant equipment): applications (customers) are almost completely isolated from interaction with hardware (restaurant equipment). In fact, Windows NT processing is divided into two core components called user mode and kernel mode. **User mode** is a nonprivileged processor mode in which programs have only limited access to system information and can only access hardware through other OS services. **Kernel mode** is a privileged processor mode in which programs have extensive access to system information and hardware.

In the Windows NT analogy, the customers represent users and applications. The user mode includes the hosts and waiters. The kernel mode is a combination of the counter workers and the kitchen workers. The kernel mode is made up of two main parts: HAL (which is like the kitchen workers) and a part called **executive services** (which is like the counter workers). Applications in user mode have no access to hardware resources. In kernel mode, executive services has limited access to hardware resources, but the HAL primarily interacts with hardware.

Windows NT was designed to easily port to different hardware platforms. In the analogy, you see how this is possible. Because only the kernel mode is actually interacting with hardware, it is the only part that needs to be changed when Windows NT moves from one hardware platform to another. For instance, if there is a major change in hardware (analogous to a new stove in the kitchen), only the HAL must change. Minor hardware changes might cause changes in executive services. When hardware changes are made, the user mode requires little or no change. When hardware improves, even though applications have these new resources available to them, they are not responsible for knowing how to interface with these resources.

By limiting access to the hardware mainly to the HAL, system integrity is increased because more control is possible. With this isolation, an application cannot cause a system to hang by making illegal demands on hardware. Overall performance is increased because the HAL and executive services can operate independently of the slower, less efficient applications using them.

On the other hand, it is easy to see why Windows NT requires a much more robust system than does Windows 95 or DOS. The increased overhead of this OS only benefits you when hardware and applications software are hefty enough to take advantage of the more powerful OS.

User Mode

In the restaurant analogy in Figure 12-7c, the purpose of the hosts and waiters is to interface with the customers. The purpose of the user mode is to interface with the user and with applications; what you view when running Windows NT is primarily running in user mode. The user mode is made up of subsystems all working together to serve the user and applications. The Explorer is one example of a program that runs in user mode. The Windows NT logon screen is another example. This logon screen provides security much as a host or hostess would do at a restaurant.

User mode is a set of modules that runs processes within Windows NT that interact with applications and with the user directly. Windows NT facilitates this interaction by creating different modules (called **subsystems**) that are responsible for specific aspects of interaction with applications and users. Figure 12-8 shows the user mode and kernel mode together with their core functions. The **user mode** is built as a group of subsystems, of which the Win32 subsystem is the most important because it manages all 32-bit programs and provides the user interface (for example, the Explorer). (Remember from Chapter 11 that 32-bit programs are programs written for protected mode using 32-bit code.) The security subsystem provides logon to the system and other security functions, including privileges for file access. Other subsystems might or might not be running.

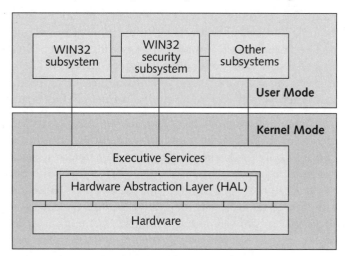

Figure 12-8   User mode and kernel mode in Windows NT

There are two kinds of user mode subsystems, which are defined by their functions (see Figure 12-9). **Environment subsystems** provide an environment for an application to run in; consider an environment subsystem a **virtual machine** because it provides a total and complete environment for an application, and, in effect, places the application in "its own little world." The second group of subsystems is the **integral subsystems**, which are used to provide services to the rest of the system. An example is the security subsystem serving other subsystems by handling the security for files and folders.

All environment subsystems must relate to the executive services by way of the Win32 subsystem, which is itself an environment subsystem. Figure 12-9 shows how various programs that run under Windows NT interact with subsystems. For instance, each DOS application resides in its own **NT virtual DOS machine (NTVDM)**, an environment where a DOS application can only interface with this one subsystem. Think of an NTVDM as the DOS application's "own little world," one in which the program running in this isolated system can only interact with the system itself, but cannot relate to anything outside the system. All the 16-bit Windows 3.x applications reside in one NTVDM called a **Win 16 on Win 32 (WOW)** environment. Within the WOW, these 16-bit applications can communicate with one another, and they can communicate with the WOW, but that's as far as their world goes. Because Windows 3.x is itself a DOS application, it must reside in an NTVDM. Figure 12-9 shows three 16-bit Windows 3.x applications residing in a WOW that resides in one NTVDM. Because DOS applications expect to run as the only application on a PC, each has its own NTVDM.

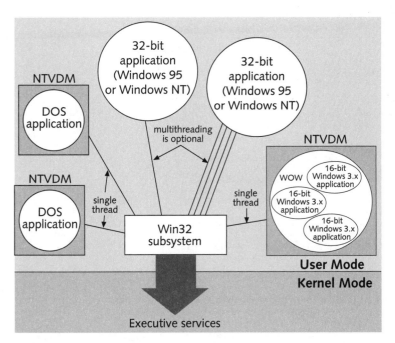

Figure 12-9 Environment subsystems in Windows NT user mode include NTVDMs for DOS and Windows 3.x applications and optional multithreading for 32-bit applications

You can see in Figure 12-9 that 32-bit applications do not require an NTVDM and can relate to the Win32 subsystem directly, because they are written to run in protected mode. The figure shows that 32-bit applications can also use a single line of communication (called **single threading**) with the Win 32 subsystem or can use a multiple line of interface (called **multithreading**) with the Win32 subsystem, depending upon what the application requests. An example of multithreading is when an application requests that the subsystem read a large file from the hard drive while performing a print job at the same time. Single threading happens when the application is not expecting both processes to be performed at the same time, but simply passes one request followed by another.

Kernel Mode

Remember that the kernel mode of Windows NT includes executive services and the HAL, which interface more directly with the hardware than does the user mode. Figure 12-10 expands the information from Figure 12-8 to show several of the components of the executive services portion of the kernel mode. Most interaction with the hardware is done by executive services passing the request to the HAL. However, from the diagram, you see that executive services includes device drivers, which have direct access to the hardware and do not require interaction with the HAL.

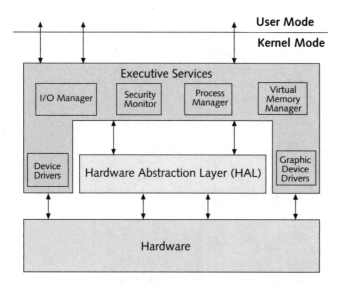

Figure 12-10 Components in the Windows NT kernel mode relate to subsystems in user mode and relate to hardware

Only kernel mode components can access hardware. For example, in DOS, applications are allowed to access hardware resources directly, or they can use an API call to ask DOS to perform the task. In Windows NT, if a DOS application tried to directly access the printer port LPT1 address in the I/O address table, Windows NT would shut down the DOS application. But, if the DOS application tried to access the printer by passing a DOS API call to the Windows NT NTVDM, it would be allowed to proceed. In Windows NT, applications cannot directly access disk space, use IRQs, or perform any other direct interaction with the hardware, as they can do in DOS or Windows 95.

Windows NT Memory Model

An excellent example of how the user mode subsystems, executive services, and the HAL all cooperate and work together is memory management. Windows NT provides memory addresses to an application by way of the user mode subsystem. When an application makes a request to the subsystem to write data to some of these addresses, the subsystem turns to the executive services for this service. The component within executive services that manages memory (the virtual memory manager) is responsible for coordinating the interface between the subsystem and the HAL. This executive service presents the request to the HAL, which is responsible for the actual writing of the data to memory and responds back to the executive service when finished. The executive service then reports back to the subsystem, which, in turn, reports back to the application.

Chapter 9 introduced the Windows NT memory model, which is shown in Figure 12-11. In Figure 12-10, you saw that the virtual memory manager is part of the executive services of the kernel mode. This memory manager interfaces with physical memory in RAM and virtual memory on the hard drive (contained in the Pagefile.sys file) by way of the HAL. Each 32-bit application and NTVDM is assigned its own memory address space, which the virtual memory manager maps onto physical and/or virtual memory. You can say that the NTVDM and the 32-bit applications are using memory addresses that the virtual memory manager maps onto either physical or virtual memory. By this method, an application cannot hang the system by storing information in memory that another application or the OS is trying to read, since the application cannot directly access memory.

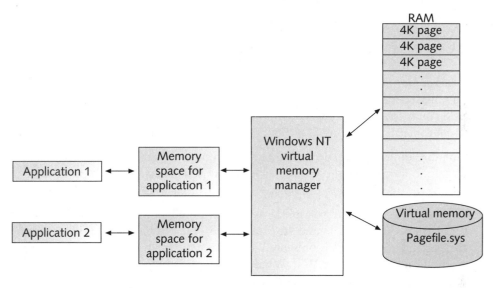

Figure 12-11   Windows NT memory management

As you can see from Figure 12-9, three 16-bit applications share the same virtual DOS machine inside a WOW. Therefore, the virtual memory manager would have all three 16-bit applications in the WOW share what is considered one virtual address space. These 16-bit applications are responsible for managing their memory addresses among themselves, in such a way that they do not write to each others' memory addresses and cause another application to hang. The 16-bit applications are sharing memory address space so that they can pass information back and forth through these addresses, such as when a spreadsheet passes a graph to a word processor. It is possible, however, to set a Windows 16-bit application into its own unique NTVDM apart from other 16-bit Windows applications to allow it to have full access to all resources in the NTVDM. However, in doing so, the application is isolated from other 16-bit applications and cannot share information.

PROCESSES AND THREADS

Windows NT is a multithreaded OS, which allows for more powerful programming so that applications can request and process more than one event to the CPU at the same time. Understanding processes and threads is important to grasping the full power of Windows NT.

Remember from earlier in the book that a program is a file sitting on secondary storage or ROM BIOS that contains a set of instructions to perform one or more functions. A **process** is a program or group of programs that is running together with the system resources assigned to it such as memory addresses, environmental variables, and other resources. There can be more than one process running for the same program at the same time. For example, in Figure 12-9, each NTVDM and each 32-bit application is a process. There are three NTVDM processes running, even though all three originated from a single NTVDM program stored on the hard drive. The NTVDM process that contains the WOW has at least three (actually more) programs sharing one process. A **thread** is a single task that the process requests from the kernel, such as the task of printing a file. An NTVDM process can only manage one thread at a time. It passes one task to the kernel and must wait for its completion before passing another task. A 32-bit application written for either Windows 95 or Windows NT can pass more than one thread to the kernel at the same time, which is called multithreading. For example, the application might have one thread performing a print job while it continues with another thread to read a file. An application must be specifically written to manage multithreading. As indicated in Figure 12-9, some 32-bit applications only use a single thread, while others use multithreading.

Multithreading improves performance. If a computer system contains more than one CPU, the kernel mode manages the threads in such a way that one thread is passed to one CPU and another thread is passed to the other CPU, which makes for a true multitasking environment.

Here is an excellent comparison between the potential performance of Windows NT and Windows 95. Compare Figure 12-9 to Figure 11.21 of Chapter 11, where the Windows 95 virtual machine concept is presented. In Windows 95, all 32-bit and 16-bit applications run in a single virtual machine. With Windows NT, a 32-bit application is not only released from having to share resources with other applications in the Windows 95 virtual machine, but also can use multithreading so that it can make simultaneous requests to the CPU. However, even though you can see the potential for more robust performance under Windows NT, unless the hardware can handle these requests for resources, the advantage is lost, and, if the hardware is very limited, the overhead of Windows NT actually slows down performance.

VIRTUAL DOS MACHINE CONCEPT

Remember that a virtual DOS machine isolates an application from the rest of the system by providing the entire DOS-like environment to the application. Because a common challenge that arises when a system is running Windows NT is having to run 16-bit applications in a Windows NT environment, NTVDMs are explained in more detail below. A Windows NT virtual DOS machine is made up of four main components:

- Ntvdm.exe, which emulates a DOS environment

- Ntio.sys, which performs the same function as does DOS's IO.SYS

- Ntdos.sys, which performs the same function as does DOS's MSDOS.SYS

- An instruction execution unit, which is only required for RISC-based computers, because DOS applications expect to work on an Intel-based CPU.

As you can see from the four components listed above, all the basics of DOS are present in an NTVDM. In addition to these basics, the NTVDM provides **virtual device drivers (VDD)** to emulate the DOS device drivers for the mouse, keyboard, printer, and serial ports.

In order for a WOW to run within an NTVDM, the following components are also running within this one NTVDM process:

- Wowexe.exe, which emulates the Windows 3.x environment
- Wow32.dll, which emulates the DLL layers of Windows 3.x, which enhance 16-bit applications
- Krnl386.exe, User.exe, and Gdi.exe, which emulate the corresponding three core programs in Windows 3.x

When Windows NT is loaded, a single NTVDM starts, which is then ready to run any 16-bit Windows applications that are loaded. One limitation of a WOW is that there is no communication between a 16-bit application running in the WOW and a 32-bit application or process running outside the WOW. It can become a difficult chore for these two applications to communicate, and it might be impossible. (For example, if you are using a 32-bit word processor and have a graph on a spreadsheet that is a 16-bit application, it might be impossible for the spreadsheet to pass the graph to the word processor.) How to set up an NTVDM is covered later in this chapter.

WINDOWS NT NETWORKING

One of the main reasons Windows NT is chosen as an OS is because of its strong networking features. Remember that there are two versions of Windows NT: Windows NT Workstation and Windows NT Server. In a general PC environment, a workstation is a desktop PC that both accesses a network and works as a standalone PC. In the most general sense, a server is a computer that contains data and software that are commonly shared by workstations on the network. A server on the network is generally not also a workstation. Even though it may have a keyboard and monitor connected to it, these are generally only used by a network administrator to administer and monitor the network; the server is solely dedicated to serving the network.

All the functionality offered by Windows NT Workstation is available with Windows NT Server. The primary difference between Windows NT Workstation and Windows NT Server is that Windows NT Server offers the additional functionality of administering and monitoring the network from this centralized location. However, both Windows NT Workstation and Windows NT Server can be configured to work as one node in a workgroup or as one node on a domain, as explained below.

When a group of computers is connected to share resources, you have the choice between configuring these computers as a network using the workgroup model or using the domain model. Resources including data, software, and printers can be shared using either model. The difference between the two is how the network is administered, either from each individual PC (in a workgroup) or from a centralized location (in a domain).

12

Also, as you read the following information about workgroups and domains, remember that the group of computers, which can be either a workgroup or domain, is a logical group, not a geographical group of computers. A workgroup of computers may be in a single building, or it may include PCs in other cities. Distance makes no difference as long as there is networked connectivity either over phone lines or by other means. PCs are grouped together for the purpose of sharing resources, not necessarily because they are geographically near one another. For example, a sales staff might need to share a marketing database, and the accounting staff of a company might need to share a journals database. The sales staff is spread over several cities and so is the accounting staff. Members of the sales staff make up the sales workgroup, and members of the accounting staff make up the accounting workgroup, so each user can share resources within the appropriate chosen group.

When you implement Windows NT Workstation, it is often necessary to set up users in a workgroup with other PCs using Windows NT or Windows 95 and to configure the PC to be a member of a domain controlled by a Windows NT server. Understanding the concepts of workgroups and domains and how they are managed is the first step in learning how to support them.

Using Workgroups and Domains

A **workgroup** is a logical group of computers and users that share resources (Figure 12-12), where the control of administration, resources, and security is distributed throughout the network. Every computer has its own directory database of user accounts and security policies. Each computer in a workgroup manages the accounts on that computer for other users and computers that want to access information on it. If you are a member of a workgroup and want to allow another user on another PC to access files on your PC, you must establish an account for that user. The information about that account is kept only on your PC.

A workgroup can be made up of computers that use either Windows NT Workstation or Windows NT Server. However, PCs that have Windows NT Server installed must be configured as standalone units. A workgroup does not require a Windows NT server to be present. There is no centralized account management or security.

A Windows NT **domain** is a group of networked computers that share a centralized directory database of user account information and security for the entire set of computers. In Figure 12-13 you see the possible different components of a Windows NT domain. The **primary domain controller** (**PDC**) stores and controls a database of (1) user accounts, (2) group accounts, and (3) computer accounts. This database is called the **directory database** or the **security accounts manager** (**SAM**) database.

The directory database can be updated by an administrator logged onto any workstation or server on the domain by accessing the PDC from the remote computer, but there can be only one PDC on the domain. One or more read-only backup copies of the directory database can be kept on other computers. Each computer with a backup of the directory database is called a **backup domain controller** (**BDC**). A system can be set up so that whenever the database on the PDC is updated, copies are written to each BDC. In Figure 12-13, there are two BDCs, each keeping a copy of the directory database. A BDC is read-only and is used only to authenticate users as they log on. Workstations on the domain are in the lower part of Figure 12-13. As indicated, the three types of OSs supported by the domain for workstations are Windows NT Server configured as a standalone server (which cannot function as a domain controller), Windows NT Workstation, and Windows 95.

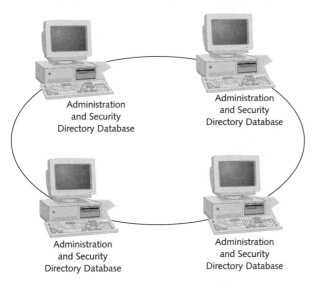

Figure 12-12   A Windows NT workgroup

12

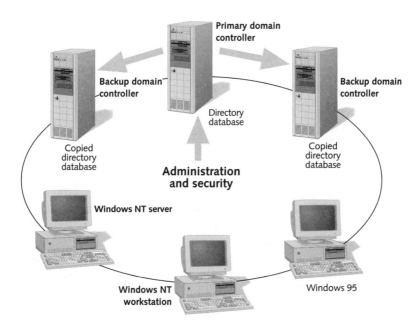

Figure 12-13   A Windows NT domain

User Accounts

User accounts are used on PCs to control who has access to what programs, files, and other resources on a PC or network. With DOS and Windows 95, there is no all-encompassing security to the PC except the power-on password, which is a function of the ROM BIOS rather than the OS. Windows NT, however, provides this all-encompassing security to the PC. In order for a user to gain access to a computer, the user must have a **user account** on that computer, which, in a workgroup, must be set up on each computer, or, in a domain, can be set up from the centralized domain server. During the Windows NT installation, an **administrator account** is always created. An administrator has rights and permissions to all computer software and hardware resources.

 If the file system for the active partition of a PC is FAT, it is possible to boot from a DOS boot disk and bypass the Windows NT security logon. When you use the NTFS file system, booting from a DOS boot disk is not possible. Use the NTFS file system if you want a high level of security. You can still boot the PC from Windows NT boot disks, but the Windows NT logon is required.

When Windows NT first boots, a logon is necessary before anyone can use the OS. The logon screen displays when you press the **Ctrl**, **Alt**, **and Del** keys together. (Remember that these keystrokes in the DOS and Windows 95 environment are used to soft boot. This different use of the same three keys is another example of the differences between Windows NT and these other two OSs.) To log on, enter a User Name and Password and click **OK**. Windows NT tracks which user is logged onto the system and grants rights and permissions to the user according to the group the user is assigned to or uses specific permissions granted this user.

Administering a Network.   Permissions granted to a user and the OS environment that the user has are controlled by the administrator. An administrator can assign a user to a group and assign restrictions and rights to the group that, in turn, apply to all users in the group, or an administrator can assign individual restrictions and rights to a user. A **profile** is a special file with a .usr file extension that contains information about which desktop configuration, sound, color, and resources should be made available to a particular user. The administrator can modify a user profile or group profile to control the types of changes a user can make to his or her environment, including the ability to install or configure software or hardware.

In a typical office environment, many PCs are supported by a single administrator who is responsible for maintaining and supporting the PCs' software and hardware. An administrator usually controls what the user can do through the user profile, most commonly giving users just enough rights and permissions to perform their jobs, but not so much as to alter hardware or software settings. Thus, users may be denied the ability to set an environmental variable, install a printer, install software, or do any other chores that change the PC software or hardware environment. In many office environments, gone are the days when employees could bring that favorite screensaver or game to work and install it on their PC.

Using Windows NT Server, an administrator can set profiles for an entire network of workstations from his or her PC, and can allow users to move from PC to PC with their profiles following them. These users are known to Windows NT as **roaming users**.

Creating a User Account.   User accounts are created and managed by the User Manager portion of Windows NT. Follow these directions to set up a new user account.

1. Click on **Start**, **Programs**, **Administrative Tools**, and then select **User Manager** (see Figure 12-14). The User Manager screen displays. The default user accounts, those that NT sets up as part of installation, are an administrator account and one guest account.

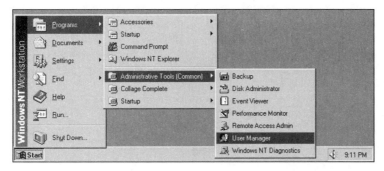

Figure 12-14   The User Manager under Administrative Tools of Windows NT can be used to add a new user

2. To create a new user account, click on the **User** menu and select **New User**. The New User dialog box displays (see Figure 12-15).

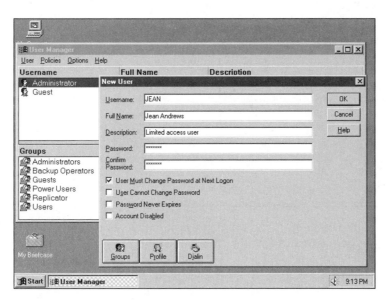

Figure 12-15   Use the New User dialog box to provide information about a user

3. Enter the information requested about the user. When logging on, the user will enter the Username and Password. Notice in Figure 12-15 that the option has been selected that requires the user to change his/her password at the next logon.

4. Click on the **Groups** icon at the bottom of the dialog box, and the Group Memberships dialog box displays (see Figure 12-16), showing that in this example the new user JEAN is a member of the Users group, the default choice unless the administrator changes it. The available groups that a user is *not* a member of are listed on the right. The group with the most rights is the Administrators group. The administrator can assign rights to an entire group that apply to all users in that group. Click **OK** to return to the New User box.

5. From the New User box, click on **Dialin**, and the Dialin Information dialog box displays (see Figure 12-17).

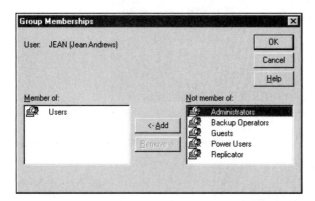

Figure 12-16   Assigning a group membership to a user

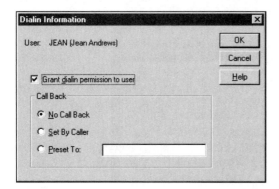

Figure 12-17   Use the Dialin Information dialog box to give a new user permission to dial in to this workstation

6. Check the **Grant dialin permission to user** box, to allow the user to access this workstation from a remote PC, using a modem.

7. Click **OK** to return to the New User box.

Remember that the administrator can control the rights of this user by assigning the user to a group that has certain rights, or by assigning a unique profile to this user.

8. Click **Profile** in Figure 12-15 and enter the path and name of a profile file to apply to this individual user. Click **OK** when done.

9. From the New User dialog box, click **OK** to complete the task of adding a new user to the workstation.

To verify that the new account works correctly, log off the system as the administrator and log back on as the new user. To log off, press the **Ctrl**, **Alt**, and **Del** keys together. The Windows NT Security box displays (see Figure 12-18). Click **Logoff**. The Windows NT logo screen displays, and no more activity is allowed at this PC until a user logs on. Press the **Ctrl**, **Alt**, and **Del** keys together again to display the logon screen. Enter the new Username and Password to access the PC under this new user account.

Figure 12-18   Log off the computer using the security box

In order to demonstrate one way in which Windows NT distinguishes between the permissions of different users, access the User Manager window again. Click **Start**, **Programs**, **Administrative Tools**, and **User Manager**. The User menu displayed in Figure 12-19 shows the limited access for this user account. Remember that in the administrator account, the User menu showed all options in dark type, giving the Administrator access to any of them. Notice that now the New User option is grayed out, so that this user is not allowed to add a new user to the workstation.

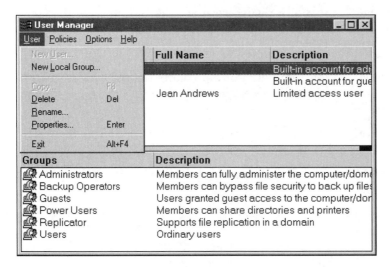

Figure 12-19   Windows NT controls access to options by "graying out" options to users who have not been assigned rights to them

INSTALLING AND CUSTOMIZING WINDOWS NT

This section gives the step-by-step process to install Windows NT. In the following example, you will install Windows NT on a second partition on the hard drive, assuming that Windows 95 is already installed on the first partition.

PREPARING FOR THE INSTALLATION

Before beginning the installation of Windows NT or upgrading from DOS or Windows 95 to Windows NT, you need to make some preparations.

Hardware Compatibility

To determine if your hardware can support Windows NT, begin by searching the HCL (hardware compatibility list) to determine whether or not your PC qualifies for Windows NT. If a device on your system is not on the HCL, contact the manufacturer for a Windows NT driver. (Remember that if no driver exists, you will not be able to use the device with Windows NT.) Be sure you have enough hard drive space. Windows NT requires 120 MB of drive space to install itself and more if the cluster size is large. A floppy drive and CD-ROM are required. For computers without a CD-ROM drive, Windows NT can be installed from a server over a network.

If you are using an Intel-based computer, there is a way that you can have software from Microsoft examine your PC to determine if the PC qualifies for Windows NT. The NT

Hardware Qualifier found on the Windows NT installation CD-ROM can be copied to a disk. After you have copied the utility to the disk, boot from the disk, and the utility will examine your system to determine if all hardware present qualifies for NT. Use the following directions to use the NT Hardware Qualifier:

1. Insert a bootable disk in drive A.

2. From Windows 95 Explorer or Windows 3.x File Manager, access the Windows NT CD-ROM and execute the program: \SUPPORT\HQTOOL\MakeDisk.bat. Windows NT will then create the Hardware Qualifier disk.

3. Boot from the newly created disk. The following message will be displayed on your screen:

   `Preparing the NTHQ`

   You can watch as NT tells you it is creating a RAM drive and copying files to it. Next a screen will display informing you that the report the utility generates will take several minutes and will be written to the disk and saved as NTHQ.TXT.

4. Print the report.

Figure 12-20 contains a portion of a sample report from the NTHQ. Note that the two devices listed at the top were not found in the NTHQ. To determine if the devices will work with Windows NT, check the latest HCL on the Microsoft Web site or contact the manufacturer of each device.

12

```
Adapter Description: CIRRUS LOGIN PnP V34 MODEM
Adapter Device ID: CIR1000
Listed in Hardware Compatibility List: Not found-check the latest HCL

Adapter Description: OPL3-SAX Sound Board
Adapter Device ID: YMH0024
Listed in Hardware Compatibility List: Not found-check the latest HCL

Adapter Description: S3 Inc. 801/928/964
Listed in Hardware Compatibility List: Yes

Adapter Description: Adaptec AHA-1522
Listed in Hardware Compatibility List: Yes

Adapter Description: Sound Blaster Adapter or compatibles
Listed in Hardware Compatibility List: Yes

Adapter Description: Joystick/game port
Listed in Hardware Compatibility List: Yes
```

Figure 12-20   Sample report from the NT Hardware Qualifier

Choosing the Right File System

When you install Windows NT, you must consider a number of criteria before choosing which of the two available file systems you want, FAT or NTFS. If you plan to have a dual boot on your PC with either DOS or Windows 95, use the FAT file system. If you need a high level of security, remember that NTFS offers a higher level of security, including security features unavailable with FAT. If Windows NT is the only OS on the hard drive and security is an issue, then use NTFS. RISC-based computers must use FAT for the active partition.

STEP-BY-STEP INSTALLATION

Below is a discussion of how to install Windows NT, both as a second OS on a system that already has Windows 95, and as the first OS on a system.

Installing Windows NT as a Second OS

The discussion below describes an installation of Windows NT as a second OS under the following conditions:

- Windows NT is being installed on an Intel-based PC.
- The installation will use a dual boot.
- The PC has a 2.4 GB hard drive.
- The drive has one partition already created: drive C is 2 GB. The remainder of the drive is unpartitioned.
- Windows 95 is installed on drive C, the active partition.
- Windows NT will be installed on the presently unpartitioned space, which will become drive D.
- Drive C will be the system partition, and drive D will be the boot partition for Windows NT (see Figure 12-6).

The following is a step-by-step description of the installation process to add Windows NT to a PC that already has Windows 95 installed.

1. Insert the Windows NT installation CD-ROM in the CD-ROM drive and reboot the PC. The Windows NT opening screen program executes, displaying the message

   `To set up Windows NT now, press ENTER.`

   Press **Enter**. (Another method to begin setup is to execute Winnt.exe in the \I386 directory of the CD-ROM for Intel-based PCs.)

2. The program Winnt.exe executes. A dialog box appears (Figure 12-21) asking for the location of the installation files. For Intel-based computers, choose the \I386 directory. If hard drive space is plentiful, you can copy the contents of the \I386

directory and its subdirectories to the hard drive and perform the installation from there, which is faster because access to the hard drive is faster than access to the CD-ROM. If the computer is connected to a network, the contents of the \I386 directory can be copied to the network server, and the Winnt.exe program can be executed from the server to install Windows NT on the PC if certain conditions exist. (Installations from servers are not covered in this chapter.)

12

Figure 12-21   The first dialog box of the Windows NT Setup program asking for the location of the installation files

3. Confirm the location of the installation files and press **Enter**. If setup can recognize the presence of the formatted hard drive, it copies files from the CD-ROM to the hard drive.

4. Next the licensing agreement appears. Press **F8** to indicate your agreement and continue.

5. Setup then examines the computer to determine what hardware and software components are present. In the example described at the beginning of this section, the following information displays:

```
2442 MB Disk 0 at Id 0 on bus 0 on atapi

C: FAT              2047 MB

Unpartitioned space    394 MB
```

Select the space in which to install Windows NT. Choose the **Unpartitioned Space** and press **Enter** to continue.

6. Setup responds with this information:

```
You have asked Setup to create a new partition on 2442 MB
disk 0 at Id 0 on bus 0 on atapi.
```

```
The minimum size for the new partition is 4 MB
The maximum size for the new partition is 394 MB
Create partition of size (in MB):
```

Respond by entering **394**, the maximum possible size for the partition, and press **Enter**.

7. Setup creates the new partition and then displays the following:

```
To install Windows NT on the highlighted partition or
unpartitioned space, press ENTER:

C: FAT                 2047 MB

D: new (unformatted)   394 MB
```

Select the unformatted drive D by highlighting it and press **Enter**.

8. Setup displays the following:

```
The partition you have chosen is newly created and thus
unformatted. Setup will now format the partition.

Select a file system for the partition from the list below:

Format the partition using the FAT file system

Format the partition using the NTFS file system
```

Select the FAT file system and press **Enter**.

9. After the formatting is completed, Setup asks for this information:

```
Setup installs Windows NT files onto your hard disk. Choose
the location where you want those files to be installed.
\WINNT
```

The default choice is to install Windows NT in the \Winnt directory. Accept the default by pressing **Enter**.

10. Setup now asks for permission to examine the hard drive for corruption. You can either allow it by pressing **Enter** or skip this examination by pressing **Esc**.

11. Next, Setup tells you that it is copying files to the hard drive. After the copying is complete, the following displays:

```
Press ENTER to restart your computer.
```

```
When your computer restarts, Setup will continue.
```

12. Up to this point in the installation, all screens appeared to be DOS-like with little graphic user interface and no use of the mouse. When the PC reboots, you are using a true Windows GUI. The opening screen lists the three steps that Windows NT performs to complete the installation:

```
1) Gathering information about your computer

2) Installing Windows NT networking

3) Finishing Setup
```

The first item in the list is highlighted. Using the mouse, click **Next** to continue the installation.

13. Setup offers four options:

    * `Typical`

    * `Portable`

    * `Compact`

    * `Custom`

    Select **Typical** and click **Next** to continue.

14. Setup requests a name and the name of your organization. Provide them.

15. You are then asked to enter the CD key that identifies the copy of Windows NT being installed. Provide that.

16. Setup then requests a computer name. You are told that the name must be 15 characters or less and must be unique for your network. This computer name will later be used to identify this computer on a network. Enter the name and click **Next**.

17. Remember that every Windows NT workstation has an administrator account by default. Next Setup asks for the password for this account:

    `Administrator Account`

    `Password:`

    `Confirm Password:`

    Administrators have full privileges on the workstation. Users have fewer privileges depending on what the administrator assigns them. If other users, who will not have administrator privileges will be using this workstation, or if you are concerned about security at this PC, enter a password. If you are the sole user of this PC and security is not an issue, you do not need to enter a password. Just press **Enter**.

18. Setup then gives you the option to create an **emergency repair disk (ERD)** (discussed later in the chapter). Select **Yes** to create the emergency repair disk, and then click **Next** to continue.

19. Setup then gives you the option to choose what components to install. Since you can later easily install components not installed during the installation, choose **Install the most common components**.

20. Setup then returns to the opening Windows NT setup screen (see Step 12) and continues with Installing Windows NT networking.

21. The choices presented are:

    * `Do not connect this computer to a network at this time`

    * `This computer will participate on a network, either:`

        * `Wired to the network (ISDN adapter or network adapter)`

        * `Connected remotely to the network using a modem`

> Choose **Do not connect the computer to a network at this time**, and click **Next** to continue.

22. Setup returns to the opening screen (see Step 12) and continues with Finish Setup. You are asked to select the date and time from the Date/Time Properties Sheet.

23. Setup automatically detects the correct display adapter. You can change any options on the Display Properties Sheet.

24. Setup requests that you insert a blank disk labeled emergency repair disk. Insert a blank disk. Setup creates the repair disk.

25. You are instructed to remove the CD and disk from the drives and restart the PC. When the PC reboots, because there are two OSs present, a startup menu (called the **boot loader menu**) displays giving you the choice between Windows NT Workstation Version 4.0 and Microsoft Windows (Windows 95). Select Windows NT Workstation, and it then loads.

Installing Windows NT as the First OS on the Hard Drive

If Windows NT is installed on a hard drive that does not have an OS already installed on it, the procedures are slightly different. Windows NT comes with three disks that contain a simplified version of Windows NT, enough to boot a PC and access the CD-ROM so that it can continue the installation from the CD-ROM as described above.

Insert setup disk 1 into the floppy drive and boot the PC. You will be asked to insert disk 2, followed by disk 3. After Windows NT has loaded these three disks, it can access the CD-ROM, and installation continues from the CD. The program on the CD that is executed at that point is Winnt.exe. There is a faster version of Winnt.exe on the CD-ROM that can be used instead of Winnt.exe, named Winnt32.exe. This program can be run only after Windows NT has already been installed the first time and is used to upgrade from an older version of NT to a new version or to reinstall a corrupted version.

The three setup disks can later be used to boot the PC in the event that files on the hard drive become corrupted. You can also create a new set of bootable disks. How to do this is discussed later in the chapter.

Installing a Local Printer

After the Windows NT installation is complete, one of the first things you will want to do is install a printer. Follow these step-by-step directions:

1. Click **Start**, **Settings**, and then select **Printers**. The Printers screen displays.

2. Double-click on **Add Printer**. The Add Printer Wizard displays as in Figure 12-22. If this is a local printer operating off the PC's printer port, then select **My Computer** and click **Next**.

3. A list of ports displays. Select **LPT1**: and click **Next**.

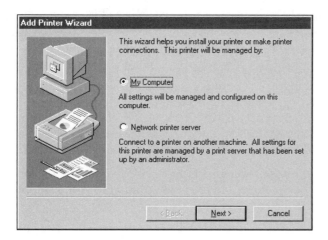

Figure 12-22 The Add Printer Wizard

4. A list of manufacturers and printer models displays (see Figure 12-23). Select first the manufacturer and then the model from the list. If your printer is not listed, and you have the printer driver for Windows NT on disk or CD-ROM, click **Have Disk**. Drivers designed for Windows 95 might or might not work. If you select a manufacturer and model from the Windows NT list, Windows NT will ask for the location of the \I386 directory where it can find the driver files. Insert the Windows NT CD-ROM and, if necessary, change the path to the files in the dialog box that displays.

To eliminate the need to have the CD-ROM readily available to install this and other devices, you can copy the entire contents of the \I386 directory and its subdirectories from the CD to your hard drive or to a server on your network.

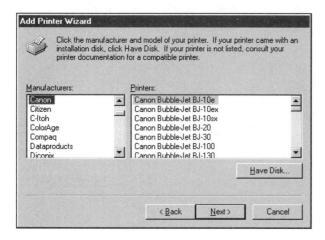

Figure 12-23 Select the manufacturer and model of your printer

5. Next you will be asked for the printer name, which will later appear in the list of available printers. Windows NT provides the default name of this printer, but you can type anything meaningful to you here. Click **Next** to continue.

6. Next, the Add Printer Wizard asks if this printer will be shared with others on a network. If you click Shared, you must enter a name for the printer, which must be unique from other printers on the network. If the printer is to be shared, select from the list of operating systems displayed all OSs of PCs on the network that will use the printer. More than one OS can be selected. If the printer is only to be used by your PC, then click **Not Shared** and click **Next** to continue.

7. You are then given the opportunity to print a test page, which you should do. Select **Yes** to print the test page, and then click **Finish** to complete the installation. Close the Printer screen.

SUPPORTING WINDOWS NT AND APPLICATIONS

Comprehensive coverage of Windows NT administration is beyond the scope of this book, but you will look at a few common procedures that apply to supporting a standalone NT PC using both 16-bit and 32-bit applications. How the boot process works and how to troubleshoot problems during booting will also be covered.

THE WINDOWS NT BOOT PROCESS

Understanding the boot process and making changes to it are paramount to supporting Windows NT. When a PC is first turned on, the boot load menu asks you to select an OS. You can control this menu from the System Properties box of the Control Panel. Click **Start**, **Settings**, **Control Panel**. The Control Panel shown in Figure 12-24 allows you to configure Windows NT, add hardware devices and software, and configure the environment for applications.

Double-click on the **System** icon. The System Properties box displays. Click on the **Startup/Shutdown** tab (see Figure 12-25). From the Startup drop-down list, select the OS that you want to start by default. Select the number of seconds to wait before the system chooses the default option. Also from this sheet, you can choose what you want the system to do when an error occurs that prevents Windows NT from loading (called a **fatal system error**). If you choose "Write an event to the system log," you can view this information under the event viewer. Debugging information written to the memory dump file can later be used by Microsoft support persons in diagnosing problems with booting.

When you make changes and click OK, you are told that the system must reboot before the changes take effect.

Figure 12-24   The Windows NT Control Panel

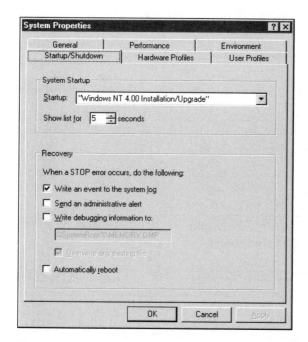

Figure 12-25   System Properties box showing Startup/Shutdown tab

12

What Happens During the Boot Sequence

The following is a look behind the scenes with a description of each step in the boot process. As you read, refer to Table 12-2 for an outline of the boot sequence for Intel-based computers.

Table 12-2   Steps in the Intel-based CPU boot process

Description	Step
POST (power-on self-test) is executed.	1. Performed by startup BIOS
MBR (master boot record) is loaded, and the master boot program within the MBR is run. (The master boot program is at the very beginning of the hard drive as part of the partition table information. The program searches for and loads the OS boot record of the active partition.)	2. Performed by startup BIOS
Boot sector from active partition is loaded, and program in this boot sector is run.	3. Performed by MBR program
Ntldr (NT Loader) file is loaded and run. (The Ntldr file is the initially executed Windows NT OS file and is similar to Io.sys in Windows 3.x.)	4. Performed by boot sector program
Processor is changed from real mode, in which all programs have full access to the entire system, to flat memory mode, in which 32-bit code can be executed.	5. Performed by Windows NT loader
Minifile system drivers (described below) are started so files can be read.	6. Performed by Windows NT loader
Read Boot.ini file and build the boot loader menu described in the file. (This menu is discussed later in 1 the chapter.)	7. Performed by Windows NT loader
If user chooses Windows NT, then run Ntdetect.com to detect hardware present; otherwise, run Bootsect.dos.	8. Performed by Windows NT loader
Ntldr loads information from the registry about device drivers and loads them. Also loads the Hal.dll and Ntoskrnl.exe.	9. Performed by Windows NT loader
Ntldr passes control to Ntoskrnl.exe; load is complete.	10. Last step performed by the loader

BIOS Executes POST.   First, Startup BIOS performs POST, which happens just as it would regardless of the OS present. After POST, BIOS turns to the hard drive to load an OS. In earlier chapters, you saw that BIOS looks for the partition information at the beginning of the hard drive.

BIOS Executes the MBR Program.   The first thing in the partition information that BIOS needs is the MBR (master boot record) containing the master boot program. Remember from earlier chapters that the master boot program is the very first thing written in the first sector of a hard drive. The master boot program is followed by the partition table itself, and both are stored in the master boot sector. BIOS executes this master boot program, which examines the partition table, looking for the location of the active partition on the drive, and then turns to the first sector of the active partition to find and load the program in the boot sector of that active partition. So far in the boot process, nothing is different between Windows NT and other OSs.

The MBR Program Executes the OS Boot Program.   Remember that when DOS or Windows 95 boots, the DOS boot sector contains the name of the initial OS load program, Io.sys. When Windows NT is installed, it edits this boot sector of the active partition, instructing it to load the Windows NT program Ntldr at startup, instead of Io.sys.

The Boot Program Executes Ntldr.   With the execution of Ntldr, Windows NT then starts its boot sequence. This program is responsible for loading Windows NT and performing several chores to complete the load. It then passes off control to the OS.

Ntldr Changes the Processor Mode and Loads a File System.   Up to this point, the CPU has been processing in real mode; every program had complete access to system resources. Ntldr is a 32-bit program and begins by changing the CPU mode from real mode to a 32-bit mode called **32-bit flat memory mode** in order to run its 32-bit code. Next a temporary, simplified file system called the **minifile system** is started so that Ntldr can read files from either a FAT or an NTFS file system.

Ntldr Reads and Loads the Boot Loader Menu.   Ntldr then is able to read the Boot.ini file, a hidden text file that contains information needed to build the boot loader menu discussed earlier. The menu displays, and the user can make a selection or, after the preset time expires, the default selection is used.

Ntldr Uses Ntdetect.com.   If Ntldr is to load Windows NT as the OS, the Ntldr runs the program Ntdetect.com, which checks the hardware devices present and passes the information back to Ntldr. This information will later be used to update the Windows NT registry concerning the last-known good hardware profile used (discussed later in the chapter).

Ntldr Loads the OS and Device Drivers.   Ntldr then loads Ntoskrnl.exe, Hal.dll, and the System hive, a portion of the Windows NT registry that includes hardware information that is now used to load the proper device drivers for the hardware present.

Ntldr Passes Control to Ntoskrnl.exe.   Ntldr then passes control to Ntoskrnl.exe, and the boot sequence is complete.

If an Operating System Other Than Windows NT Is Chosen.   If a selection was made from the boot loader menu to load an OS other than Windows NT, such as DOS or Windows 95, Ntldr does not complete the remaining chores to load Windows NT, but loads and passes control to the program Bootsect.dos, which is responsible for loading the other OS.

12

The Bootsect.dos file contains information from the partition table for this particular hard drive and cannot be copied from another PC.

The files needed to successfully boot Windows NT are listed in Table 12-3. (In the table, references to *winnt_root* follow Microsoft documentation conventions and mean the name of the directory where Windows NT is stored, which is \\Winnt by default.)

Table 12-3   Files needed to successfully boot Windows NT

File	Location
Ntldr	Root directory of the system partition (usually C:\\)
Boot.ini	Root directory of the system partition (usually C:\\)
Bootsect.dos	Root directory of the system partition (usually C:\\)
Ntdetect.com	Root directory of the system partition (usually C:\\)
Ntbootdd.sys*	Root directory of the system partition (usually C:\\)
Ktoskrnl.exe	*winnt_root*\\system32 directory of the boot partition
Ntoskrnl.exe	*winnt_root*\\system32 directory of the boot partition
Hal.dll	*winnt_root*\\system32 directory of the boot partition
System	*winnt_root*\\system32\\config of the boot partition
Device drivers	*winnt_root*\\system32\\drivers of the boot partition

* Ntbootdd.sys is only used with a SCSI boot device.

Troubleshooting the Boot Process

Windows NT offers several tools and methods to aid in troubleshooting and fixing problems that happen during the boot process. For instance, each time the OS boots and the first logon is made with no errors, the OS saves a copy of the hardware configuration from the registry, which is called the **Last Known Good** configuration. The next time the PC boots, if an error occurs, the Last Known Good configuration can be used. Windows NT also offers a set of boot disks and an emergency rescue disk. If the emergency rescue disk has been kept up to date, it can be invaluable in solving boot problems. This section discusses how to use all three of these tools in troubleshooting the boot process.

Last Known Good Configuration.   During the boot process, after the initial logon, if the boot is successful, information about the current configuration stored in the registry is saved in a special part of the registry called Last Known Good. The key in the registry that contains this information is:

```
HKEY_LOCAL_MACHINE\HARDWARE
```

When Windows NT is loaded during the boot process, if errors are encountered, the Last Known Good configuration can be used. If a problem during boot is encountered, from the

Windows NT menu that displays, select the Last Known Good configuration. For example, if you install a new device driver, restart Windows NT, and the system hangs, by using the Last Known Good configuration, you can revert back to the configuration before the device driver was installed.

Because the configuration information is not saved to the Last Known Good area until after the logon, if you are having trouble with the boot, don't attempt to log on. Doing so will cause the Last Known Good to be replaced by the current configuration, which might have errors.

For example, if you have installed a new video driver and you restart Windows, but the screen is very difficult to read, don't log on. Instead, press the reset button to reboot the PC. When given the choice, select Last Known Good from the startup menu.

To prevent hard drive corruption, if you are having problems booting Windows NT, wait for all disk activity to stop before pressing the reset button or turning off the PC, especially if you are using the FAT file system.

If you accidentally disable a critical device, Windows NT will make the decision to revert to the Last Known Good for you. You will not be provided a menu choice.

Reverting to the Last Known Good causes any changes made to the hardware configuration since the Last Known Good was saved to be lost. Therefore, it is wise to make one change at a time to the hardware configuration and reboot after each change, so that, if problems during booting are encountered, only the most recent change is lost.

Windows NT Boot Disks.   With Windows 95 and DOS, any single disk could be formatted as a boot disk or system disk. Windows NT is different. It requires three disks to hold enough of Windows NT to boot. However, formatting a disk to just hold data or software is still done using Explorer.

When a disk is formatted by Windows NT, the boot sector is written to boot the Ntldr program instead of the two DOS programs, as DOS and Windows 95 do. To format a disk, use Windows NT Explorer. Right-click on the **3½ Floppy (A:)** line in Explorer and choose **Format** from the drop-down menu. Figure 12-26 displays.

The only file system available for a disk is FAT. Note in the figure that there is no option to make the disk a system disk or boot disk. If you try to boot from a disk that has been formatted by Windows NT, this error message displays:

```
BOOT: Couldn't find NTLDR
Please insert another disk
```

Creating boot disks is done by a different method. Remember that Windows NT comes with a set of three disks that are initially used to boot the machine before the installation continues from the CD-ROM. After the OS is installed, these disks can also be used in an emergency situation to boot the OS. These three disks come with Windows NT, but you can make extra sets. The set of boot disks is the same no matter what PC you are using. There is no special information on the disks about your system.

12

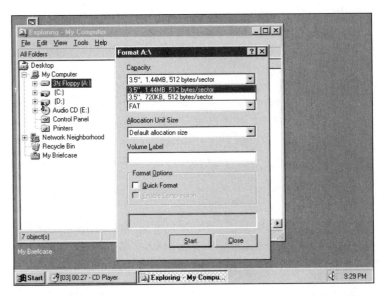

Figure 12-26 Windows NT dialog box used to format a disk

If the original three disks to boot Windows NT become corrupted or are lost, you can make extra copies using either Winnt32.exe or. Winnt.exe. It is not necessary that you be on the PC on which you intend to use the disks in order to make them, since the disks don't contain unique information for a PC. If you are running Windows NT, use Winnt32.exe to create the three disks, but if you are running another OS, such as DOS or Windows 95, use Winnt.exe to create the disks. Proceed as follows to create boot disks using Windows NT:

1. Click on **Start, Run** and enter the path and name of the program with the /OX option, which says to only create the set of three disks without performing a complete installation. Note the E:\I386\winnt32.exe/ox entry in the run window of Figure 12-27, which shows the command line from within Windows NT used to create the disks when drive E contains the Windows NT installation CD.

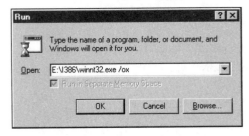

Figure 12-27 Using Winnt32.exe to create a set of boot disks

2. The program asks for the location of the installation files. In this example, you would enter E:\i386. You are then prompted to insert three disks. The program creates the disks beginning with disk 3.

If the PC later cannot boot Windows NT from the hard drive, these three disks can be used to load Windows NT. After Windows NT is loaded, use the emergency repair disk to restore critical system files to their state at the time the last update was made to the emergency repair disk.

The Windows NT Emergency Repair Disk. A fourth important disk is the emergency repair disk (ERD), which does contain information unique to your OS and hard drive. You are given the opportunity to create the disk during installation. Always select to create this disk because it is your record of critical information about your system that can be used to fix a problem with the OS.

The ERD is, in effect, a backup of the Windows NT registry on your hard drive, which contains all the configuration information of Windows NT. In addition, information that is used to build a NTVDM to run DOS applications is also included on the disk. The files on the ERD are listed in Table 12-4. More about each file is covered later in the chapter when the registry is discussed. Files stored on the ERD are also written to the hard drive during the installation process. Using Explorer, you can see the files listed in the *winnt_root*\repair folder.

Table 12-4 Files on the emergency repair disk

File	Description
Setup.log	A read-only, hidden system file that is used to verify the files installed on a system
System._	A compressed file containing part of the registry
Sam._	A compressed file containing the security accounts manager (SAM) from the registry
Security._	A compressed file containing security information from the registry.
Software._	A compressed file containing software information from the registry
Default._	A compressed copy of the Default hive of the registry
Config.nt	The Windows NT version of CONFIG.SYS used for creating a virtual DOS machine (NTVDM)
Autoexec.nt	The Windows NT version of autoexec.bat used for creating a virtual DOS machine
Ntuser.da_	A compressed copy of \winnt_root\profiles\defaultuser\ntuser.dat

12

After the installation, you can create a new ERD or update the current one by using the Rdisk.exe utility in the */winnt_root*/system32 folder. You should update the disk any time you make any major changes to the system configuration. To use the Rdisk.exe utility, click **Start**, **Run**, and then either use Browse or enter the path to the utility. Add the /S option so that the utility will also update the SAM, Default, and Security files of the registry.

If Windows NT is stored on drive D, the command line is:

```
D:\WINNT\System32\rdisk.exe /s
```

Files are first updated to the *\winnt_root*\repair directory, and then you are given the opportunity to create a new ERD.

Using the Boot Disks and ERD to Recover from Failed Boot.

If you cannot recover Windows NT from the last-known good hardware profile, the next step is to boot from the set of three boot disks that come with the Windows NT CD-ROM or that you made using either Winnt.exe or Winnt32.exe. The Windows NT programs on these disks may also request that you provide the ERD. Insert the first boot disk and reboot. You will be prompted to insert disk 2, followed by disk 3. The Setup menu in Figure 12-28 then displays.

```
Windows NT Workstation Setup

Welcome to Setup.
The Setup program for the Microsoft(R) Windows NT(TM) OS version 4.0
prepares Windows NT to run on your computer.

        *To learn more about Windows NT Setup before continuing, press F1
        *To set up Windows NT now, press ENTER
        *To repair a damaged Windows NT version 4.0 installation, press R
        *To quit Setup without installing Windows NT, press F3
```

Figure 12-28   Windows NT Workstation Setup menu

Select the option to repair a damaged installation by pressing **R**. When you press R, the following list of optional tasks displays:

```
(X) Inspect registry files

(X) Inspect startup environment

(X) Verify Windows NT system files

(X) Inspect boot sector

Continue (perform selected tasks)
```

Table 12-5 summarizes the purpose of each task on the Repair menu.

Table 12-5   The purpose of each task on the Repair menu

Repair Menu Option	Description
Inspect registry files	This task prompts you before you replace each registry file stored on the ERD. Any changes to security and SAM are lost, and they revert to the state they were in at system installation. Changes to software and system are restored to the last update made to the ERD.
Inspect startup environment	Inspects the Boot.ini file and edits it so that Windows NT is added as an option if it is not already present
Verify Windows NT system files	Identifies and offers to replace files that have been altered from the original files on the Windows NT CD-ROM. Includes verifying files needed to boot.
Inspect boot sector	Verifies that the boot sector on the active partition has the reference to Ntldr and puts it there if needed. This action can correct the problem caused by someone using the DOS.SYS command that changes the boot sector to reference a DOS file instead of Ntldr.

By default, all optional tasks listed above are selected. You can choose not to perform a task by highlighting it and pressing **Enter**, which removes the selection mark X. After you have selected your options, highlight **Continue** and press **Enter**.

Files are copied from the boot disks as needed to repair the startup environment. Some of the options listed above use the ERD. You are asked if you have the disk; if you answer positively, you will be asked to insert the disk. For example, boot sector information used to perform the task "Inspect boot sector" is included in the files on the ERD. Setup asks for the disk and restores the boot sector from the information on the disk.

Table 12-6 lists some error messages that might display during the boot process when critical files are missing or corrupted. In all cases listed in the table, the solution is to boot from the boot disks and provide the CD-ROM or ERD when requested by the setup program.

Table 12-6   Some Windows NT errors at startup

Missing or Corrupted File	Error Message
Ntldr	BOOT: Couldn't find NTLDR. Please insert another disk.
Ntdetect.com	NTDETECT V1.0 Checking Hardware.... NTDETECT failed
Ntoskrnl.exe	Windows NT could not start because the following file is missing or corrupt: \winnt_root\system32\ntoskrnl.exe Please re-install a copy of the above file
Bootsect.dos	I/O Error accessing boot sector file multi(0) disk (0) rdisk (0) partition (1):\bootsect.dos

12

MANAGING LEGACY SOFTWARE IN THE WINDOWS NT ENVIRONMENT

Even though it would be nice if all software running under Windows NT were written in the newer 32-bit code used by Windows 95 and Windows NT, this doesn't always happen. As you recall from the discussion above, Windows NT makes provisions for running DOS applications by creating a separate NTVDM for each application, so that each program can run in its native environment. Windows 16-bit applications can run in individual NTVDMs, or several 16-bit Windows applications can run in the same NTVDM so they can share resources. How to do this is discussed next.

Customizing an NTVDM for a DOS Application

To prepare to run a DOS application with Windows NT, first create a shortcut to the DOS application. For example, a quick and easy way to place a shortcut on the desktop is to use Explorer. From Explorer, click on the executable filename and press and drag the filename to the desktop. A shortcut is immediately created. You can edit the name of the shortcut on the desktop by clicking inside the name area, which creates an insertion point in the text.

Next edit the Properties of the shortcut. Right-click on the shortcut icon. A drop-down menu displays, as in Figure 12-29. Select **Properties** from the menu. From the Properties sheet, click on the **Program** tab. Click on **Windows NT**, and the Windows NT PIF Settings dialog box displays (see Figure 12-30). Notice the names of the Autoexec and Config files. They are Autoexec.nt and Config.nt in the *winnt_root*\system32 folder. From this dialog box, you can edit the names and locations of these files. Click **OK** to return to the DOS Properties sheet.

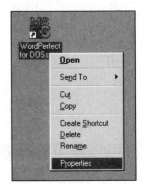

Figure 12-29   Right-click on a shortcut icon to see the icon's drop-down menu

Each DOS application can have individual initialization files, but by default, they all use these two, Autoexec.nt and Config.nt. You can edit the contents of these two files and put any DOS command compatible with DOS 5.0 in them. These commands will be executed when the NTVDM is first loaded.

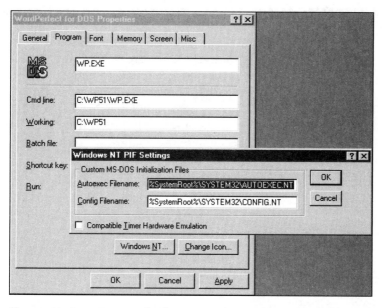

Figure 12-30   Setting the location of initialization files for a DOS application

To configure memory for a DOS application to run under Windows NT, click on the **Memory** tab (see Figure 12-31). In most cases, you should leave the conventional memory at Auto to allow Windows NT to make the selection.

12

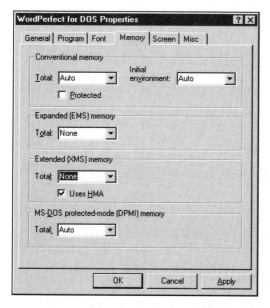

Figure 12-31   The memory sheet of the DOS Properties box

Customizing an NTVDM for 16-bit Windows Applications

As with customizing Windows NT for DOS applications, the first step in customizing Windows NT for 16-bit Windows applications is to create a shortcut for the application. After the shortcut is created, right-click on the **shortcut** and choose **Properties** from the drop-down menu. The Windows Properties box displays. Select the **Shortcut** tab (see Figure 12-32). To run the application in its own individual NTVDM, check **Run** in Separate Memory Space. If you are running a 16-bit application from the Start menu, as in Figure 12-33, when Windows NT recognizes the application to be a 16-bit application, it makes the check box available so that you can choose to run the application in its own memory address space. The box is grayed out if the application is a 32-bit or DOS application.

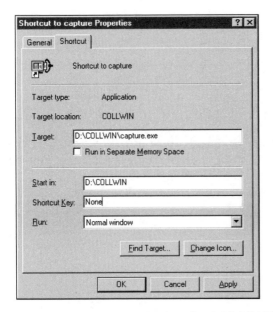

Figure 12-32 Properties box for a 16-bit Windows application

Figure 12-33 Windows NT allows a 16-bit application to run in a separate memory space

Reasons Why Applications Might Not Work with Windows NT

The following is a list of reasons why applications might not work with Windows NT, which will display errors instead.

- DOS applications that try to access hardware directly are shut down by Windows NT when the illegal attempt is made.

- A 16-bit Windows application that uses virtual device drivers (VxD) will fail because the virtual device drivers attempt to access hardware directly.

- A 32-bit application that was developed on a different hardware platform than the current PC might not run under Windows NT.

- Some OS/2 applications are not compatible with Windows NT.

THE WINDOWS NT REGISTRY

The Windows NT registry is a hierarchical database containing all the hardware, software, device drivers, network protocols, and user configuration information needed by the OS and applications. Many components depend on the registry for information about hardware, software, users, security, and much more. The Windows NT registry provides a secure and stable location for configuration information about these entities. Table 12-7 lists ways in which some components use the registry.

The registry is a hierarchical database that follows an upside-down tree structure similar to that used by folders and subfolders. In the next section, you will look at how the registry is organized, how to view the contents of the registry, how to back up and recover the registry, and how Windows NT makes changes to the registry.

12

HOW THE REGISTRY IS ORGANIZED

When studying how the registry is organized, keep in mind that there are two ways to look at this organization, the physical organization and the logical organization.

Table 12-7   Components that use the Windows NT registry

Component	Description
Setup programs for devices and applications	Setup programs can record configuration in the registry and query the registry for information needed to install drivers and applications.
User profiles that are maintained and used by the OS	Windows NT maintains a profile for each user that determines the user's environment. User profiles are kept in files, but, when a user logs on, the profile information is written to the registry, where changes are recorded, and then later written back to the user profile file. The OS uses this profile to control user settings and other configuration information specific to this user.
When Ntldr is loading the OS	During the boot process, Ntdetect.com surveys hardware devices present and records that information in the registry. Ntldr reads from the registry information about device drivers to load and initialize, including the order in which to load them.
Device drivers	Device drivers both read and write configuration information in the registry each time they load. The drivers read hardware configuration information from the registry to determine the proper way to load.
Hardware profiles	Windows NT can maintain more than one set of hardware configuration information for one PC, called **hardware profiles**. The data is kept in the registry. An example of a PC that has more than one hardware profile is a PC that is also a docking station. Two hardware profiles describe the PC, one docked and the other undocked. This information is kept in the registry.
Application programs	Many application programs read the registry for information about the location of files the program uses and various other parameters that were once stored in .ini files under Windows 3.x and Windows 95.

Logical Organization of the Registry

Logically, the registry is a hierarchical database, meaning that the organization looks like a tree similar to that shown in Figure 12-34. The registry is a tree with five branches called **keys** or **subtrees**, which are categories of information stored in the registry. The five keys, or subtrees, are named in the figure. Each key is made up of several **subkeys** that may also have subkeys under them. Subkeys lead to **values**. Each value has a name and data assigned to it. Data in the registry is always stored at the lowest level of the tree, in values.

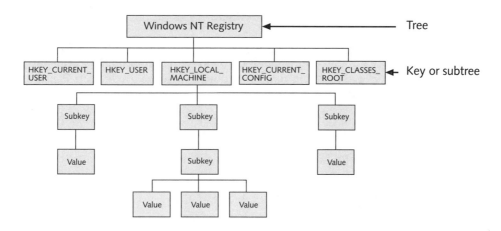

Figure 12-34   The Windows NT registry is logically organized in an upside-down tree structure of keys, subkeys, and values

The logical organization of the registry can be seen in Figure 12-35, showing the Windows NT Registry Editor. When you first open the editor, the editor shows the subtree level as five cascading windows, one for each subtree. The first window in the figure shows the HKEY_CURRENT_USER subtree and a list of the subkeys in this subtree. Notice in the figure that some subkeys have + signs in the icon. A + sign indicates that this subkey has subkeys under it. Later in the chapter you will see how to move down these subkeys to the lowest level of the tree where the values are stored.

12

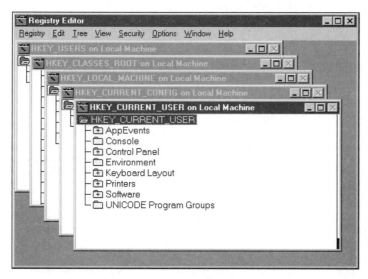

Figure 12-35   The five subtrees of the Windows NT registry

Physical Organization of the Registry

The physical organization of the registry is quite different from the logical organization. Physically, the registry is stored in five files called **hives**. There is not a one-to-one relationship between the subtrees and these five files, even though there are five of each. Figure 12-36 shows the way the subtrees are stored in hives, summarized as follows:

- HKEY_LOCAL_MACHINE is contained in four hives, the SAM hive, the Security hive, the Software hive, and the System hive.

- HKEY_CURRENT_CONFIG data is kept in two hives, the Software hive and the System hive.

- The information in HKEY_CLASSES_ROOT is contained in the Software hive.

- HKEY_USER data is kept in the Default hive.

- HKEY_CURRENT_USER data is contained in a portion of the Default hive.

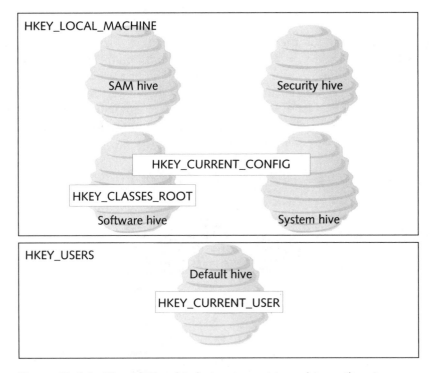

Figure 12-36   The relationship between registry subtrees (keys) and hives

From Figure 12-36, you can also see that physically, some subtrees use data that is contained in other subtrees. For instance, the HKEY_CURRENT_USER data is a subset of the data in the HKEY_USER key. HKEY_CURRENT_CONFIG and HKEY_CLASSES_ROOT subtrees use data that is contained in the HKEY_LOCAL_MACHINE subtree. However, don't let this physical relationship cloud your view of the logical relationship among these subtrees. Even though data is shared among the different subtrees, logically speaking, none of the five subtrees is considered subordinate to any other.

The registry hives are stored in the *winnt_root*\system32\config folder as a group of files (see Figure 12-37). In a physical sense, each hive is a file. Each hive is backed up with a log file and a backup file, which are stored in the *winnt_root*\system32\config folder.

In addition, registry information about each user who has ever logged on to this workstation (which is temporarily kept in the HKEY_CURRENT_USER subtree while the user is logged on) is also permanently stored in a file in the *winnt_root*\profiles folder in a subfolder with the same name as the Username stored in a file called Ntuser.dat. For example, for the Username JEAN, the path and name to the file is:

```
C:\WINNT\Profiles\JEAN\Ntuser.dat
```

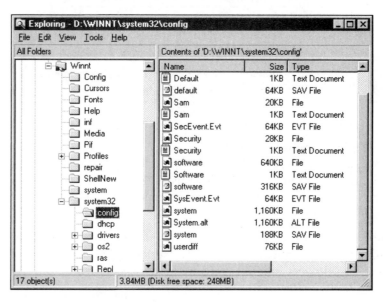

Figure 12-37   The registry is stored in *winnt_root*\system32\config folder

A Closer Look at Subkeys and Values

And now back to the logical organization of the registry. The five subtrees of the registry, displayed in Figure 12-35, are listed in Table 12-8 together with their primary functions. As you might notice from the table, the HKEY_LOCAL_MACHINE subtree is the supporting mainstay key of the registry.

Table 12-8   The five subtrees of the Windows NT registry

Subtree (Main Keys)	Primary Function
HKEY_CURRENT_USER	Contains information about the currently logged-on user. Similar information about each user who has ever logged on to this workstation is also kept in a folder with the same name as the Username stored in a file called Ntuser.dat.
HKEY_CLASSES_ROOT	Contains information about software and the way software is configured. This key points to data stored in HKEY_LOCAL_MACHINE.
HKEY_CURRENT_CONFIG	Contains information about the active hardware configuration, which is extracted from the data stored in the HKEY_LOCAL_MACHINE subkeys called SOFTWARE and SYSTEM.
HKEY_USERS	Contains only two subkeys: information used to build the logon screen and the ID of the currently logged-on user.
HKEY_LOCAL_MACHINE	This key contains all configuration data about the computer, including information about device drivers and devices used at startup. The information in this key does not change when different users are logged on.

We next use the Registry Editor to view the registry so that we can get a close look at registry values. Even though the Registry Editor allows you to make changes to the registry, this should only be done as a last resort, and usually only when you are instructed to do so by a network administrator or Microsoft technical support. *Never* make changes to the registry without first creating a current ERD.

Figure 12-38 shows a view of the registry all the way down to the value level. The figure was produced using the Registry Editor, Regedt32.exe, located in the *winnt_root*\system32 folder. Double-click on the filename in Explorer or use this command from the Start, Run dialog box to access the Registry Editor.

winnt_root\System32\regedt32.exe

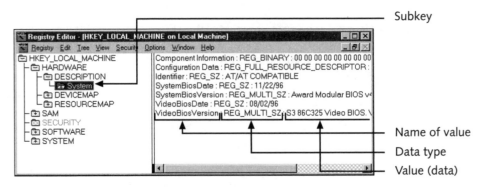

Figure 12-38   Registry Editor showing subkeys and values

When you don't plan to make changes to the registry, set the editor to read-only mode to avoid making changes unintentionally. For example, follow these directions to view the HKEY_LOCAL_MACHINE portion of the registry.

1. Select the **Options** menu and check **Read Only Mode** to avoid making changes unintentionally.

2. Reduce to icons all subtree windows except HKEY_LOCAL_MACHINE.

3. Maximize the HKEY_LOCAL_MACHINE window. The HKEY_LOCAL_MACHINE key has four subkeys. The hardware subkey is the only one that does not relate to a hive. This key is built each time Windows NT is loaded from information gathered during the boot. (As you work with the Registry Editor, double-click on a yellow folder on the left side of the screen to expand the folder, and double-click on it again to reduce it.)

4. Double-click on **Hardware**, then **Description**, then **System**. Figure 12-38 shows the results of this action; you can now see values within the system sub-key on the right side of the Registry Editor screen. Each entry of a value includes a name, a data type, and the value itself, which is sometimes called the **configuration parameter**. The value name is listed first, followed by the data type of the value, followed by the value itself.

5. If you ever need to edit a value, you can do so by double-clicking on the value, and the edit box will appear. You can make changes and click **OK** to record the changes. Because you are in Read-Only mode, if you double-click on a value now, a warning displays saying that your changes will not be saved.

6. Exit the editor by clicking on the **Registry** menu and choosing **Exit**.

MAKING CHANGES TO THE REGISTRY

Windows NT makes most of its changes to the registry through the Control Panel. Although you can edit the registry directly using Registry Editor, this should not be your first choice unless it is your only option. Use the Control Panel instead. The Control Panel controls hardware devices and software as well as many user preferences, which are then saved to the registry. The Windows NT Control Panel (see Figure 12-24) looks and works in a similar way to that of Windows 95. Covered next are two examples of changes made from the Control Panel that are recorded in the registry: installing software and installing a new hardware device.

Installing Software

Software is installed from the Control Panel under the Add/Remove Programs icon. Installation works very much the same way as under Windows 95. Access the Control Panel by clicking **Start**, **Settings**, **Control Panel**. From the Control Panel, double-click on the **Add/Remove Programs** icon. The Add/Remove Program Properties box displays. Any software that installs with a Setup.exe or Install.exe program can be installed using this box. Click on **Install**, and the dialog box requests the location of the setup program.

12

To add new components to Windows NT that were not installed when Windows NT was originally installed, click on the **Windows NT Setup** tab of the Add/Remove Programs Properties box. You will see a list of all of the Windows NT components. From this list, you can select to install new components or to uninstall components that are already installed.

Installing Hardware Devices

Windows NT builds its list of available hardware devices each time it is booted. This list is not permanently kept in the registry. However, when a new hardware device is installed, device driver information is kept in the registry. New hardware devices are installed from the Control Panel. The example of installing a sound card is used because it is typical of the installation of many hardware devices.

1. To install a sound card, access the **Control Panel** and double-click on the **Multimedia** icon. The Multimedia Properties box displays.

2. Click on the **Devices** tab to see a list of multimedia devices.

3. Select **Audio Devices** and click on the **Add** button. The Add dialog box displays. You can either select a device driver from the list or click on **Unlisted** or **Updated Driver** to install your own device driver from disk or CD-ROM.

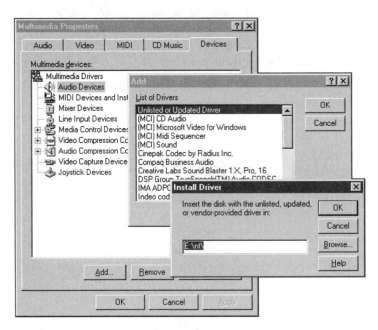

Figure 12-39   When installing a device driver, you can use a driver provided by Windows NT or one from the device vendor

4. If you choose to install your own driver, click on **Unlisted or Updated Driver**. The Install Drive dialog box displays asking for the location of the driver. As the

example shown in Figure 12-39 shows, the vendor-provided driver is selected. On the CD-ROM that comes with the sound card, versions of the driver are located in several directories, one for each OS supported.

5. In this CD, the location for the driver is E:\nt\. Enter the path and click **OK** to continue the installation. If Windows NT already has the driver you are installing, the OS gives you the choice to use the driver provided by the vendor or the Windows NT driver.

6. The driver is copied to the hard drive, and then the hardware setup dialog box displays, as seen in Figure 12-40. The suggested I/O address, IRQ, and DMA channel are selected, but you can change these values if you are aware of a conflict. Otherwise, leave the values as suggested and click **OK** to complete the installation.

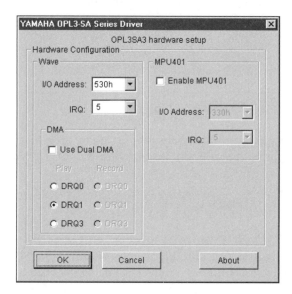

Figure 12-40   Windows NT suggests a hardware setup for the new device

7. The Windows NT registry is then updated, and you are asked to restart the PC in order for the changes to the registry to take effect.

8. Install the CD Player component of Windows NT to use the new sound card. As with many devices, software is necessary to use the sound card. The next step is to go to the Add/Remove Programs icon of the Control Panel and install the CD Player component of Windows NT in order to use the sound card to play audio CDs. This installation window works just as with Windows 95.

This example is typical of many hardware installations. The Control Panel was used to install the device driver and you saw how Windows NT suggests the hardware setup resources to use.

Next time the PC boots, the registry communicates to the Ntldr program to load the sound card device driver. As the driver loads, it looks to the registry for the list of resources that it will use.

The software to use the CD player is also installed from the Control Panel. This information is now kept in the registry to be used each time the OS loads. The OS uses this registry information to provide the CD Player option under Start, Accessories, Multimedia.

BACKING UP THE REGISTRY

In the last example, several changes were made to the Windows NT registry, as you installed both new hardware and software, which are typical of many installations. Before making significant changes to the registry, such as installing software or hardware, and before editing the registry, make a backup of the registry. To back up the registry, use Rdisk.exe, discussed earlier in the chapter, to create an ERD, which also makes a copy of the registry files to the *winnt_root*\repair folder.

WINDOWS NT DIAGNOSTIC TOOLS

Windows NT provides several diagnostic tools to help support users, the OS, and applications, and to help with troubleshooting. Three tools are introduced: the Task Manager, the Event Viewer, and Windows NT Diagnostics.

THE TASK MANAGER

The Task Manager is a new tool that was first introduced with Windows NT 4.0. It allows you to monitor processes and applications running on the PC, and to start and stop them. It also displays performance measurements including processor time, main memory and virtual memory size, and number of threads to help in diagnosing problems with poor performance. To access the Task Manager, right-click on the **Taskbar** and select **Task Manager** from the drop-down menu that appears. Click on the **Applications** tab to display a list of applications currently running. For instance, in Figure 12-41, two applications are running. This window is actively monitoring all tasks as they are started and stopped by other means than the Task Manager. However, you can end a task, switch from one task to another, and start a new task from this sheet.

Figure 12-41   The Task Manager lists applications currently running

Click on the **Processes** tab to see a list of current processes (see Figure 12-42). In the figure, it is interesting to see that there are two programs subordinate to the Ntvdm.exe process, which provides a NTVDM. Capture.exe is a 16-bit, Windows 3.1 application that requires a WOW to run in an NTVDM. The Wowexe.exe provides the WOW.

12

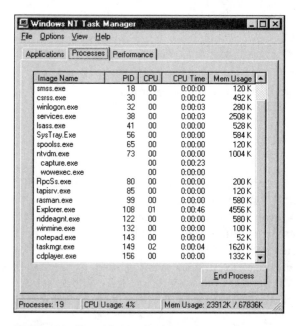

Figure 12-42   The Task Manager tracks current processes and how they are using system resources

From this sheet, you can monitor CPU time and memory used by the process, you can end the process by clicking on End Process, and you can visually see how some programs are related to others within a process.

Click on the **Performance** tab to see a graphical representation of how system resources are being used. CPU usage and memory usage are graphed, and other statistics are displayed at the bottom of the sheet. In Figure 12-43, the sudden jump in CPU usage shown in the graph was caused when a print job with graphics (this screen capture) was sent to the printer. Use the task manager to end applications that have locked up, to monitor processes and applications that are draining computer resources, and to search for potential problems with memory and the CPU.

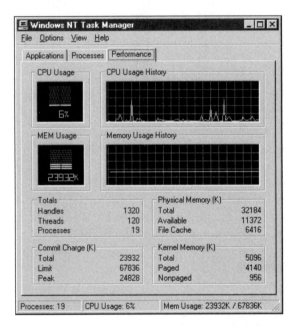

Figure 12-43   The Task Manager monitors system performance

THE EVENT VIEWER

One of the most important uses of the Event Viewer is to view a log that Windows NT created because of a failed event. Most information can be found here to help resolve the failed event. Access the Event Viewer by clicking on **Start**, **Programs**, **Administrative Tools**, and selecting **Event Viewer** from the menu list. The Event Viewer tracks events as they are performed by the applications, the OS, services, or processes, and by user actions. When an attempted action causes a problem, this event, as well as significant successful events, is recorded in the Event Viewer. In Figure 12-44, a failed event is indicated by a stop sign in front of the event line; the eighth event in the log failed. Near the bottom of the list, a possible future problem with an event is indicated by an exclamation point. Events marked with the letter "i" indicate that the event completed successfully. To see the details of an event, double-click on the event line in the log. For example, to see a description of the problem for the event that failed, double-click on that line. The details for the failed event of Figure 12-44 are shown in Figure 12-45.

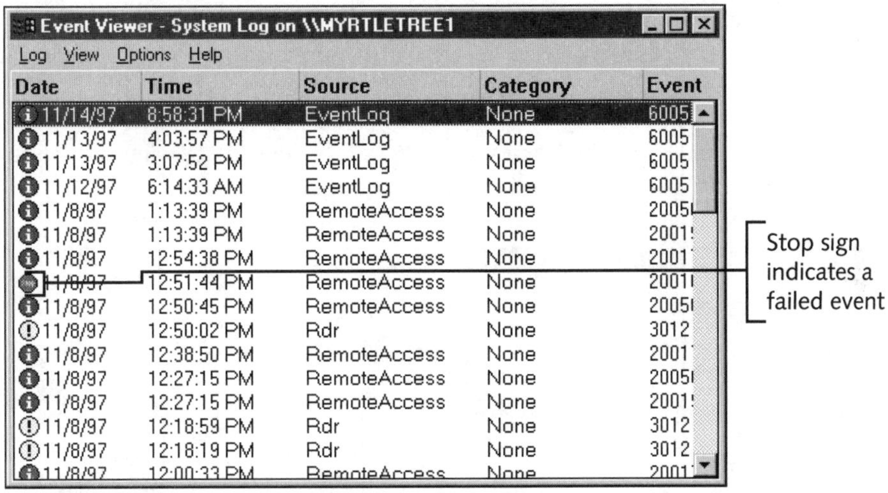

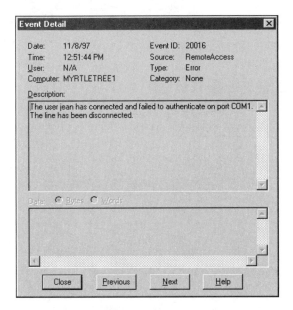

Figure 12-44   The Event Viewer tracks failed events and many successful ones

12

Figure 12-45   The details of a failed event

WINDOWS NT DIAGNOSTIC

The Windows NT Diagnostic utility is a graphical view of the Windows NT registry showing hardware and OS data, which can be used to resolve conflicts, diagnose failed hardware, view information about drivers and services that are loaded, and much more. The utility is located in the Administrative Tools group. Click on **Start**, **Programs**, **Administrative Tools**, and select **Windows NT Diagnostics**. Information cannot be updated using this utility, but it is a convenient way to view the information. For example, click on the **Resources** tab to see a list of different resources. By using the buttons at the bottom of this sheet, you can see a list of IRQs (see Figure 12-46), I/O ports, DMA channels, memory, and devices in use. Browsing through the Windows NT Diagnostic tabs allows you to see a thorough overview of the hardware and OS configurations.

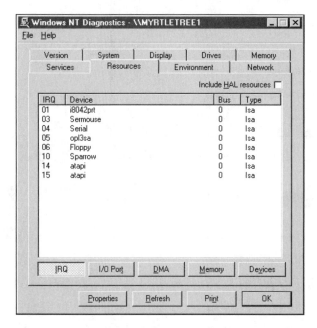

Figure 12-46   The Windows NT Diagnostics utility shows information from the registry

CHAPTER SUMMARY

- Windows NT comes in two versions, Windows NT Workstation and Windows NT Server.

- Both versions can operate on standalone PCs or on a network, but Windows NT Server can also operate as a controller in a network domain.

- Windows NT does not claim to be fully backward compatible with legacy hardware and software as does Windows 95.

- Windows NT requires at least a 486DX Intel-based CPU, 12 MB of RAM, and 120 MB of hard drive space.

- Windows NT is written for different CPU technologies. The installation information for three different CPU types is contained on the CD-ROM.

- The hardware compatibility list (HCL) is maintained by Microsoft and is a list of devices that, according to Microsoft, are compatible with Windows NT.

- Windows NT and Windows 95 have a similar desktop; many functions look and act the same way.

- Windows NT can operate using two different file systems: FAT and NTFS. NTFS offers more security and power than does FAT, but FAT is backward compatible with older OSs.

- A PC can be configured to dual boot between Windows NT and either DOS or Windows 95.

- Windows NT works on different platforms and with different software because of its modular approach to interfacing with both.

- The two operating modes of Windows NT are user mode and kernel mode. Kernel mode is further divided into two components: executive services and the hardware abstraction layer (HAL).

- A process is a unique instance of a program running together with the program resources and other programs it may use.

- An NTVDM provides a DOS-like environment for DOS and Windows 3.x applications.

- Windows 3.x 16-bit applications run in a WOW.

- A workgroup is a group of computers and users sharing resources. Each computer maintains a list of users and their rights on that particular PC.

- A domain is a group of computers and users that is managed by a centralized controlling database on a computer called the primary domain controller (PDC).

- Of all Windows NT accounts, the administrator account has the most privileges and rights and can create new user accounts and assign them rights.

- The NT Hardware Qualifier is on the Windows NT CD-ROM and can be used to survey the hardware devices on a PC to determine if they qualify to run under the Windows NT OS.

- Four disks are important to recover from a failed Windows NT boot. Three disks are required to boot Windows NT, and an emergency repair disk (ERD) can be prepared to recover critical system files on the hard drive.

- The Windows NT registry is a database containing all the hardware, software, and user configuration information on the PC. The registry is stored in five files called hives.

12

- Windows NT makes most changes to the registry when you change the system configuration from the Control Panel.

- Three diagnostic utilities included with Windows NT are the Event Viewer, Windows NT Diagnostics, and the Task Manager.

KEY TERMS

- **32-bit flat memory mode** — A protected processing mode for the CPU that can process programs written in 32-bit code. NT is a full 32-bit OS.

- **Administrator account** — An account that grants to the administrator(s) rights and permissions to all hardware and software resources such as the right to add, delete, and change accounts and to change hardware configurations.

- **Backup domain controller (BDC)** — A computer on a network that holds a read-only copy of the SAM (Security Accounts Manager) database.

- **Boot loader menu** — A startup menu that gives the user the choice between Windows NT Workstation Version 4.0 and another OS such as Windows 95.

- **Boot partition** — The hard drive partition where the Windows NT operating system is stored. The system partition and the boot partition may be different partitions.

- **Configuration parameter** — Another name for the value names and values of the registry; information in the Windows registry.

- **Domain** — A logical group of networked computers, such as those on a college campus, that share a centralized directory database of user account information and security for the entire domain.

- **Dual boot** — The ability to boot using two different operating systems such as Windows NT and Windows 95. Note that programs cannot be shared between Windows NT and the other OS.

- **Environment subsystems** — A user-mode process in which a subsystem runs an application in its own private memory address space as a virtual machine. (Compare to integral subsystems.)

- **Event Viewer** — A utility that tracks and logs events as they are performed by the applications, processes, or user actions. Accessed by: clicking Start, Programs, Administrative Tools, and then selecting Event Viewer.

- **Executive Services** — In Windows NT, a subsystem running in kernel mode that interfaces between the user mode and HAL.

- **Fatal system error** — An error that prevents Windows NT from loading. An example is a damaged registry.

- **Hardware abstraction layer (HAL)** — The low-level part of Windows NT, written specifically for each CPU technology, so that only the HAL must change when platform components change.

- **Hardware compatibility list (HCL)** — The list of all computers and peripheral devices that have been tested and are officially supported by Windows NT. (*See* www. microsoft.com/hwtest)

- **Hardware profiles** — Configuration information about memory, CPU, and OS, for a PC. A PC may have more than one profile. For example, a docking station PC may have two profiles, one with and one without the notebook PC docked.

- **Hive** — A physical segment of the NT registry that is stored in a disk file.

- **Integral subsystems** — Processes used to provide services to the rest of the system and the applications the system supports. (Compare to environment subsystems.)

- **Kernel mode** — A Windows NT "privileged" processing mode that has access to hardware components.

- **Minifile system** — A simplified file system that is started so that Ntldr (NT Loader) can read files from either a FAT or an NTFS file system.

- **Multithreading** — The ability to pass more than one function (thread) to the kernel at the same time, such as when one thread is performing a print job while another reads a file.

- **NT Hardware Qualifier** — This utility, found on the NT installation CD-ROM, examines your system to determine if all hardware present qualifies for NT.

- **Ntldr (NT Loader)** — Ntldr is the OS loader used on Intel systems.

- **NT virtual DOS machine (NTVDM)** — An emulated environment in which a 16-bit DOS application or a Windows 3.x application resides within Windows NT with its own memory space or WOW (Win 16 application on a Win 32 platform). (*See* WOW.)

12

- **Portable operating system interface (POSIX)** — A set of standards adopted to allow operating systems (such as UNIX and NT) and their applications to port from one platform to another.

- **Primary domain controller (PDC)** — The computer that controls the directory database of user accounts, group accounts, and computer accounts on a domain.

- **Process** — An executing instance of a program together with the program resources. There can be more than one process running for a program at the same time. One process for a program happens each time the program is loaded into memory or executed.

- **Roaming users** — Users who can move from PC to PC within a network, with their profiles following them.

- **SAM (security accounts manager)** — A portion of the Windows NT registry that manages the account database that contains accounts, policies, and other pertinent information about the domain.

- **Subtree** — One of five main keys that make up the Windows NT registry. Examples are HKEY_CURRENT_USER and HKEY_LOCAL_MACHINE.

- **System partition** — The active partition of the hard drive containing the boot record and the specific files required to load Windows NT.

- **User account** — The information, stored in the SAM database, that defines an NT user, including user name, password, memberships, and rights.

- **User mode** — Provides an interface between an application and an OS, and only has access to hardware resources through the code running in kernel mode.

- **User profile** — A personal profile about the user kept in the NT registry, which enables the user's desktop settings and other operating parameters to be retained from one session to another.

- **Virtual device drivers (VDD)** — Programs that emulate the DOS device drivers for hardware devices as provided by NTVDM.

- **Windows NT file system (NTFS)** — A file system first introduced with Windows NT that provides improved security, disk storage, file compression, and long filenames.

- **Windows NT registry** — A database containing all configuration information, including the user profile and hardware settings. The NT registry is not compatible with the Windows 95 registry.

- **Workgroup** — A logical group of computers and users in which administration, resources, and security are distributed throughout the network, without centralized management or security.

- **WOW (Win 16 on Win 32)** — A group of programs provided by Windows NT to create a virtual DOS environment that emulates a 16-bit Windows environment, protecting the rest of the NT OS from 16-bit applications.

REVIEW QUESTIONS

1. Which is more backward compatible: Windows 95 or Windows NT?
2. Which version of Windows is designed to run on computers other than IBM-compatibles: Windows 95 or Windows NT?
3. List five ways in which Windows 95 and Windows NT are identical.
4. List five ways in which Windows 95 and Windows NT are different.
5. Do 16-bit applications work better under Windows 95 or Windows NT?
6. What two types of file systems are used by Windows NT?
7. Is it possible for Windows NT to coexist on the same PC with either Windows 95 or DOS?
8. In a dual boot, dual OS Windows NT environment, will a new application have to be installed only one time, or twice (once for each OS)?
9. Which OS is less likely to hang or lock up, Windows 95 or Windows NT?
10. How is the kernel mode different from the user mode?

11. List and describe some of the techniques used by Windows NT to speed up processing.

12. How are workgroups different from domains?

13. What should you check before beginning the installation of Windows NT or upgrading from DOS?

14. What type of information is stored in HKEY_LOCAL_MACHINE\HARDWARE?

15. During the Windows NT boot process, if the boot is successful, information about the current configuration stored in the registry is saved as what?

16. Why is it wise to only make one change at a time to hardware configuration?

17. What do you do if you cannot recover Windows NT from the Last Known Good hardware information?

18. How can you create a shortcut to a DOS application in Windows NT?

19. List three reasons why applications might not work with Windows NT.

20. A software developer comes to you with a problem. She has been asked to convert software that she has written for Windows 95 to Windows NT. The software consists of two 16-bit programs that work equally well under Windows 3.x and Windows 95. She was able to convert one of the programs to a 32-bit version, but had to leave the other program in 16-bit code. Both programs run at the same time and share data in memory. However, when she runs the two programs under Windows NT, the 32-bit program cannot read data written to memory by the 16-bit program. Why not? What should she do so that the two programs can work under Windows NT?

12

PROJECTS

USING THE CONTROL PANEL

1. Shut down and restart Windows NT and observe the number of seconds that the boot loader program waits until Windows NT is loaded. Key in the number of seconds to wait so that the number of seconds is doubled. Verify that the change is made, by rebooting. When you have verified the change, return the number of seconds to the original value.

2. Check under the Accessories and Games sections of Windows NT and install a new game or accessory that is not currently installed. Verify that the program is installed.

3. Change the colors in the Display Properties box and verify the changes.

TROUBLESHOOTING THE BOOT PROCESS

Prepare a copy of the three Windows NT setup disks and an emergency rescue disk, and then reproduce one of the errors listed in Table 12-6. Use the disks to recover from the error.

EDITING THE WINDOWS NT REGISTRY

Be sure you have an updated copy of the three boot disks and the emergency repair disk before editing the registry. Insert a CD-ROM that has autorun and verify that autorun is working. Then make a change to the registry to disable autorun from a CD-ROM by editing this subkey:

```
HKEY_LOCAL_MACHINE\System\CurrentControlSet\Services\CdRom\
Autorun = 0.
```

USE THE INTERNET FOR PROBLEM SOLVING

Access the www.microsoft.com Web site for Windows NT Workstation support. Print one example of a frequently asked question and its answer.

USING THE WINDOWS NT DIAGNOSTIC UTILITY

1. Using Windows NT Diagnostics, print out information about memory for your PC.

2. List the IRQs currently not used by your system.

3. List the DMA channels that are currently being used and explain how each is used.

WINDOWS NT AND 16-BIT APPLICATIONS

Try running a DOS utility such as MSD or SANDRA (from Chapter 1) under Windows NT. What error message do you get? Why?

MULTIMEDIA TECHNOLOGY

The sights and sounds generated by microcomputers are constantly improving, challenging us to make new, imaginative uses of technologies that reach far beyond traditional data processing. The ability of PCs to create output in such a vast array of media—audio, video, and animation, as well as text and graphics—has turned PCs into multimedia machines. From video conferencing for the executive to teaching the alphabet to four-year-olds, the multimedia computer offers much to take advantage of. This chapter examines some of the older and newer multimedia devices, what they can do, how they work, and how to support them. Supporting video and printers is of paramount importance to the PC support technician, and these issues are also addressed in more detail in this chapter than was done earlier in the book.

The goal of multimedia technology is to produce the most lifelike representations for audio, video, and animation. Computers store data digitally, and ultimately only as two numbers, 0 and 1. In contrast, images and sounds are continuous analog signals made up of an infinite number of variations. The challenge of multimedia technology is to bridge these two worlds—the computer with only two values, and images and sounds with an infinite number of values. The key to doing this is twofold: reduce this infinite number of values down to a finite few, and record as many as needed to reproduce an approximation of the original sight or sound without overloading the capacity of the computer to hold data.

IN THIS CHAPTER
YOU WILL LEARN:

- ABOUT THE FUNDAMENTALS OF MULTIMEDIA TECHNOLOGY
- ABOUT THE MINIMUM REQUIREMENTS FOR A MULTIMEDIA PC
- ABOUT STANDARD AND NEW FEATURES OF VIDEO CARDS AND MONITORS
- HOW TO SUPPORT PRINTERS
- ABOUT THE FEATURES OF SEVERAL MULTIMEDIA DEVICES

When studying multimedia technology, look for these two features: large amounts of storage capacity and the ability of a computer to handle this large volume, including sophisticated methods of sampling sight and sound used to turn continuous analog signals into digital, non-continuous data. Also, as you study, look for the attempts of the industry to standardize these features so that software and hardware are as interchangeable as possible, considering the fast-changing technology that manufacturers must contend with.

MULTIMEDIA ON A PC

A multimedia PC presents information using more than one medium, such as animated or motion video, stereo sound, digital photographs, and so on, often with the goal of more closely simulating a lifelike experience through a PC. Multimedia has traditionally targeted the home market, with games and more games at the top of the list of software that uses multimedia. Alternatively, the business market has, in the past, taken the direction of more powerful computing power, networking, and remote management of PCs.

Most software today that uses multimedia still targets the home market, although a trend is beginning to emerge whereby business computers are using multimedia for applications such as business presentations, video conferencing, and computer-based training (CBT).

In the evolution of computers, hardware must improve in advance of the software designed to use it. A good example of this is the MMX (multimedia extensions) technology used with the Intel MMX Pentium CPU. Now that the hardware technology is here, more software is becoming available to use the technology. In the future, you can expect continuing improvements in multimedia hardware, which will continue to lead to the development of new software. In general, expect multimedia to become more realistic in presentation (remembering that the goal is to make a computer presentation appear more lifelike) and directed toward the business market as well as the home market.

Evidence of this inroad into the business market is the Pentium Pro CPU, which is marketed as a business CPU. The Pentium Pro debuted in 1995 and did not have MMX technology included, even though Intel had the technology at the time. In 1998, the Pentium Pro will have MMX technology—a strong indication of the future advances of multimedia into the business market.

WHY MULTIMEDIA?

The goal of multimedia on computers is to produce as high a quality of sound, graphics, or moving images as possible. In the case of reproducing music, it is multimedia's goal to recreate sound as close to the original as possible. In the case of graphics, be they full-motion video, animation, photographs, or quality graphics, it is multimedia's goal to produce lifelike (highresolution) quality. Before you study multimedia technology, examine for a moment the special challenge confronting multimedia technology: reproducing something that is inherently analog (or continuously changing, as discussed below) such as sights and sounds, on a PC, which is digital (and in the purest sense, binary, which means that continuous changes are not possible, only changes from one state to another).

The word "analog" comes from the same word as "analogous," and means "the same." "Digital" comes from the Latin word *digitus*, which means a finger or toe. "Digital" originates from our ten counting digits. As you recall, all communication must be converted into binary digits (or bits) before storage in a computer. And because a computer is binary, it is digital. Thus, sound and images must be converted to counting numbers, which are then converted to bits, before storage in a PC.

Figure 13-1 illustrates the difference between using digital communication to describe the shape of a loading ramp (which is analog) and the shape of a staircase (which is digital). Understanding the distinction between analog and digital signals is essential to grasping the challenges facing multimedia technology. A loading ramp is essentially analog, and a staircase is essentially digital. Figure 13-1 shows that it is easy to measure the height of each step of the staircase. It is not so easy to measure the overall height of the loading ramp, because there is a continuous and gradual change of height over the entire ramp. You can measure the height of each end of the ramp, but to measure the height of the ramp at any one point on the ramp, you are forced to take only a sample height. Choosing a series of representative points on the ramp and measuring the heights at those points is called **sampling**. With this approach, you can approximate the shape of the ramp.

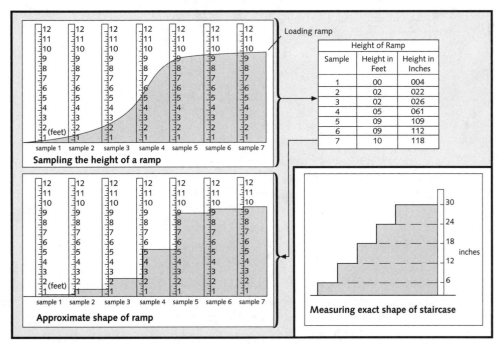

Figure 13-1 Expressing analog phenomena in digital terms is a challenge of multimedia

Now look at the sound wave in Figure 13-2. In order to record and store this sound wave in a PC so that you can have the PC later reproduce it as closely to its original analog nature as possible, you must record the sound wave as numbers—that is, digitize the analog wave—since your PC can only store data that way. To digitize the wave, first select how many samples you want to take (how frequently you will take a sample), how accurate your measurements will be, and how you will store these numbers. Later, you must have a reverse process in place to retrieve these numbers and use them to reproduce a sound wave as close to the original as possible.

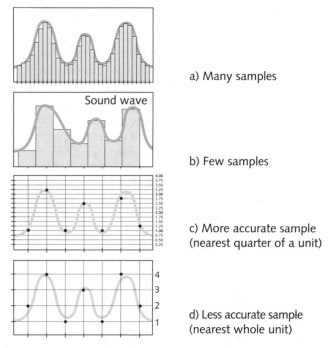

a) Many samples

b) Few samples

c) More accurate sample
(nearest quarter of a unit)

d) Less accurate sample
(nearest whole unit)

Figure 13-2   Sampling a sound wave

When digitizing the sound wave to produce the best possible reproduction, the more samples taken over a given period of time and the more accurate each measurement, the more accurate will be the later representation of the sound. However, there is a trade-off between the quality of the reproduced sound and the ability of a system to effectively process highly accurate measurements and dedicate enough storage space to accommodate all the data. The trade-off between quality of reproduction and use of resources is important in the multimedia world and drives many purchasing decisions.

Look back at Figure 13-1. In order to measure the height of the loading ramp, first decide how many samples to take and how accurate each sample needs to be. For example, if you measure the height to the nearest foot, you need to store only a two-digit number in the table of heights, because the highest point of the ramp is only 10 feet. The range of sampling values in feet is 0, 1, 2, 3, 4, 5, 6, 7, 8, 9, and 10. If you choose to be more accurate, say to the nearest inch, then the range of sampling values increases to 0, 1, 2, 3, 4...144 inches, and the table must now hold three digits to store one number, which translates into a 50% increase in storage space to obtain greater accuracy. The number of samples and the accuracy of each sample determine the amount of storage needed to hold the values. And the amount of storage needed to hold each measurement is called the **sample size**. However, there are techniques that can be used to compress the data in the table. You need a compression method that does not lose too much information, and you need a method to later decompress the values when you are ready to use them.

The impact of increasing the accuracy of measuring the loading ramp can be applied to multimedia applications in computers as well. The accuracy of the ramp measurement (feet vs inches) affects the size of the number needed in the table as well as the storage space needed (two digits are needed to hold values in feet, three digits to hold values in inches). Computers use bits instead of digits. Twelve feet in binary is stored as 1100 (4 bits), but 120 inches is stored as 1111000 (7 bits) in binary. Since bits are stored in most multimedia files in groups sized as multiples of two, measurements in feet would require 4-bit values, but measurements in inches would require 8-bit values, which creates a 100% increase in the storage requirement to gain added accuracy. In this chapter, look for the size in bits of the numeric values being stored as an indication of the accuracy of the data and the storage requirement.

In the two examples discussed above, the process is not very complicated and the calculations are extremely easy. You just do the same thing many times, which is called "repetitive looping." However, especially with the sound wave sampling, you can see that the volume of data kept can get quite large when many samples are taken over a period of time. Multimedia data processing follows this model of repetitive looping and high input/output volume.

As you study the remainder of the chapter, the method of measuring the height of a loading ramp, storing these values in a list, and using them to approximately duplicate the ramp in digital terms can be applied quite often. Look for different methods of sampling, digitizing samples, compressing numbers, decompressing them later, and finally reproducing the original analog entity, be it sight or sound.

13

MULTIMEDIA PC REQUIREMENTS

Standards are everywhere, enhancing and strengthening consistency, stability, and progress in all areas of life, and standards for computers are no exception. Standardizing the requirements of multimedia PCs and devices better ensures that different hardware and software components will be interchangeable and compatible with one another. This provides manufacturers with a general direction for setting goals, provides buyers with some guidelines by which to make decisions, and provides the PC support person with a more informed knowledge base for anticipating what supporting multimedia PCs might entail.

The standards for multimedia PCs were written by the Multimedia PC Marketing Council, Inc. and are known as the **MPC** (Multimedia PC) standards or, more officially, as the **MPC Specifications**. Here is one good example of how these standards can work to your advantage. You want to purchase a CD-ROM drive from one vendor and a sound card from another. You know that there is an audio wire that connects the CD-ROM drive to the sound card so that sound can be piped directly from the CD-ROM to the sound card without involving the CPU. You are also aware that there are many variations of audio wires, each having a different type of connector. Since the MPC standards specify what kind of connection the audio wire uses, if both the CD-ROM and the sound card vendors state that their products meet the MPC standard, you are assured that the audio wire provided with one device will connect properly to the other device.

THE MPC SPECIFICATIONS

The MPC standards are the results of discussions and debates throughout the industry and are designed with two goals in mind: to help the manufacturers of hardware and software and to help the consumer. By creating a set of written and agreed-upon standards, manufacturers have a strong incentive to develop and invest in these standardized technologies, and the consumer has some guidelines when purchasing multimedia PCs, devices, and software. In order for both of these goals to be met, the standards must stay abreast of new developments and challenge the industry to achieve excellence and progress.

Three levels of MPC standards have been published. The most recent level of standards was introduced in February 1996, and is known as the Multimedia PC Level 3 (MPC3) Specifications. As some of the more important items in these standards are listed, you will notice that many of them appear to require outdated technology. However, the standards can also serve as a guideline for the development of new devices, and they are also used by different manufacturers to ensure that their devices are compatible with one another.

MPC3 Specifications

The multimedia standards cover both software and hardware. The list below, although not comprehensive, includes the most common features to look for on multimedia PCs, software, and devices. As the standards are described, you will notice many new terms for this interesting technology. As the specifications are listed, any new term not already introduced in the book is explained.

Processors.   Remember from Chapter 3 that a CPU that processes multimedia data is best designed to handle large volumes of throughput over intense calculations. The processor or CPU, in order to be MPC3-level-compliant, must pass the MPC3 test suite, which measures the performance of a processor against one of the following:

- A 75 MHz Pentium CPU with no external cache and with hardware-assisted MPEG1 ability (which means part of the logic to handle MPEG1, described below, is contained within the CPU itself).

- A 100 MHz Pentium CPU with 256 kB of external cache and MPEG software.

The CPU does not need to exactly match either of these two configurations, but the performance of the CPU must at least be comparable.

MPEG is an international standard for data compression for motion pictures. Developed by the **Moving Pictures Experts Group** (**MPEG**), it tracks movement from one frame to the next, and only stores what changes, rather than compressing individual frames. MPEG is a type of lossy compression. **Lossy compression** methods work by dropping unnecessary data, hence the idea of the loss of data or "lossy" compression. MPEG compression can yield a compression ratio of 100:1 for full-motion video (30 frames per second or 30 fps).

RAM.   A multimedia application storing a sound file or a motion picture file requires a large amount of secondary storage to hold the large volume of data inherent to these types of files. When these files are processed, large amounts of speedy RAM are also important. The minimum multimedia requirement for RAM is 8 MB with 100 MB/second read and write time. Most multimedia PCs today have much more than 8 MB of RAM.

Floppy Drive.   A 3.5-inch, 1.44 MB floppy drive is required on a PC, but is optional for laptops. Always consider a floppy drive to be essential equipment on any PC.

Hard Drive.   Huge amounts of secondary storage are important for multimedia because sound and video files are so large. The minimum unformatted capacity for a hard drive is 540 MB with at least 500 MB of usable capacity excluding overhead. The performance of the hard drive must also meet the following requirements:

- No more than 40% CPU utilization during a 1.5 MB/second sustained transfer rate under Windows 3.x or DOS, and no more than 7% CPU utilization under Windows 95 or Windows NT

- Average seek time less than 12 ms when performing input/output activity randomly accessing the entire drive

CD-ROM Drive.   CD-ROMs must meet the following criteria:

- Data must be transferred to the host system in block sizes of 2048, 2336, and/or 2352 bytes, as appropriate for each CD format.

- The driver must not use CPU cycles except when the host system makes a request for data.

- The CD-ROM drive must be capable of reading CD audio discs and must comply with the Microsoft MSCDEX version 2.2 or equivalent driver standard.

- The CD-ROM drive must use read-ahead buffering and have on-board buffers.

- A sustained data transfer rate must be at least 550 KB/second.

- The average access time must be less than 250 ms for 4× speed computed while randomly reading data over the entire CD. (Remember from earlier chapters that 4×, also called quad speed, refers to CD-ROM speed, and is a comparative measure of seek time and data transfer scale, such that 4× is twice as fast as 2×, and so on.)

- For laptops, the average access time must be less than 400 ms for a 4× mode CD-ROM.

13

Video.   Multimedia software probably puts more demand on video than on any other subsystem of a computer. Multimedia video standards are designed to accommodate graphics, animation, and motion video at fast enough speeds to produce a smooth video presentation:

- Graphics performance standards require direct access to the frame buffers for the graphics subsystem with a resolution of 352 × 240 at 30 fps or 352 × 288 at 25 fps at 15 bits/pixel scaling (scaling is defined below).
- The video controller card must be PCI 2.0 compliant.
- The system must write to the memory on the video card using less than 14 PCI clock beats per every 32 bytes of data, while writing at a rate of 10 MB/second.
- Video playback to the monitor must have direct access to the **frame buffers** (the area of memory on a video controller that is used to store the data to be displayed on the screen), using the same resolution described for writing to video. The video controller and the monitor must support DPMS Power Management.
- The video controller must also support color space conversion and interpolative scaling.

Interpolative scaling is a method used to produce a more realistic-looking image when a small video window is enlarged to full-screen size. Without interpolative scaling, when the image is enlarged, each pixel is simply duplicated to fill the empty space as the image is enlarged. Interpolative scaling adds a range of pixels calculated to fill the spaces with a progression of color that produces smoother-looking lines and a gradual transition of color. Figure 13-3 demonstrates how a line made up of four black pixels is expanded to fill twice the space with and without interpolative scaling.

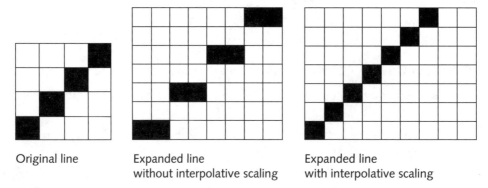

Original line   Expanded line   Expanded line
                             without interpolative scaling   with interpolative scaling

Figure 13-3   Interpolative scaling improves enlarged images

Color space conversion is a method of converting the way color is stored in files to a format that a video card can use to communicate the color to a monitor. Color space conversion must always be done on the PC; the issue is whether it will be done by the CPU or the video card.

Color space conversion can be done either by the CPU before the video data is sent to the video controller or it can be done by the video controller after the data is received. Most animation is stored in **YUV** color space (Y = brightness, U = color or hue, and V = intensity or saturation), but screen display is stored in **RGB** color space (R = red, G = green, B= blue).

RGB data transmits over the system bus at a slower rate than does YUV data. If the CPU must first convert RGB to YUV before sending it to the video controller, the CPU processing time for the video data and the time required to send slower RGB data are both greater. Video controllers that do their own color space conversion contribute to an overall faster system.

User Input.   There is nothing surprising about the standards for a keyboard and a mouse. A standard 101-key or greater keyboard that uses either a PS/2 style, DIN, or universal serial bus (USB) connector is required. See Chapter 4 for more about these connectors. A mouse with two or more buttons is required, and at least one communications port must remain free after the mouse is installed.

Input/Output.   A controller for the serial port and parallel port is required. As discussed in Chapter 8, this controller may be located on the systemboard or on an I/O card. The serial port controller must use 16550AF UART technology or better. Either an IBM-style analog or digital joystick or a USB port is required. One **MIDI (musical instrument digital interface**, pronounced "middy") port must provide support for both input and output.

MIDI is a standard for transmitting and storing sound in electronic devices, including computers. MIDI controllers (sound cards) convert sound into bits according to the MIDI standards. These MIDI files are stored on hard drives and later converted back to sound by the same controller. Sound travels as an analog signal; MIDI devices and computers convert and store that data as digital signals (see Figure 13-4). While an analog signal can take on any value over a continuous range, remember that bits can be only one of two values, 0 or 1.

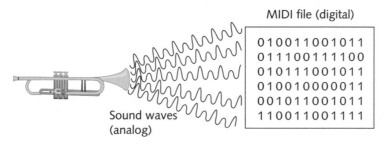

Figure 13-4   Sound has analog properties, but MIDI files store sound digitaly

The MIDI standard is supported by most synthesizers, so sounds created on one synthesizer can be played by another. Computers with a MIDI interface can receive sound created by a MIDI synthesizer and then manipulate the data in MIDI files to produce new sounds. The MIDI standards include storing sound data, such as a note's pitch, length, and volume, and can include attack and delay times.

Sound Card.   Sound is easy to produce on a computer; every computer comes equipped with a speaker that beeps during startup. However, quality sound is a challenge for multimedia technology and is primarily a function of the number of samples taken of a sound and the number of values that are used to measure and store the sound.

Remember that converting sound from analog to digital storage is done by first sampling the sound and then digitizing it. Sampling and digitizing the sound is done by a method called **pulse code modulation** (**PCM**). It follows that the opposite technology—which converts analog to digital—is also needed, and it is done by a **digital to analog converter** or **DAC**. The DAC technology on a sound card converts digital sound files back into analog sound just before output to the speakers.

One method of compressing and later decompressing sound files, as well as other large files such as video files, is called **CODEC** (**COder/DECoder**). CODEC compression does not drop any data and is, therefore, called **lossless compression** as compared to lossy compression.

A **wave table** is a method of more accurately synthesizing sound than the earlier FM (frequency modulation) method. With the **FM method** of synthesizing sound, sound is reproduced by making a mathematical approximation of the musical sound wave. Using the wavetable method, a sample of the actual musical sound made by the original instrument is stored and used to synthesize the sought-after sound. This table of stored sample sounds is called the wave table, and a group of samples for each instrument is called a **voice**. How all this works is described later in the chapter.

MPC3 requires that a sound card must support 8- or 16-bit DAC samples with PCM encoding CODEC samples at a rate of 8.0, 11.025, 16.0, 22.05, and 44.1 kHz sample rates with stereo channels. Sound data must be buffered from ISA to PCI by DMA transfers. Internal wavetable synthesizer capability with 16 simultaneous melody voices and six simultaneous percussive voices is required. Audio output from the CD-ROM to the sound card must be direct, bypassing the CPU with volume control that can be accomplished through either hardware or software.

Speakers.   If external speakers are included with a full system, at least two speakers are required, and either the hardware or software must have volume control.

Communications.   The system must provide inbound and outbound call control and comply with **Telephony Application Programming Interface** (**TAPI**), a standard jointly developed by Intel and Microsoft, used by Windows to connect a PC to telephone services. TAPI is a type of API (application programming interface) that Windows can call when it needs to make a telephone connection. **Telephony** is a term describing the technology of converting sound to signals that can travel over telephone lines (the technology of telephones). TAPI is discussed in greater detail in Chapter 15.

Operating System.   The operating system must be Windows 3.11 with DOS 6.0 or better.

MPC1 and MPC2 Specifications

Because many multimedia devices still sold today advertise that they adhere to the MPC Level 1 or Level 2 standards, these standards are outlined in Table 13-1.

Table 13-1   MPC1 and MPC2 specifications

Device	MPC Level 1 Standard	MPC Level 2 Standard
CPU	386-25 MHz	486-25 MHz
RAM	2 MB RAM	4 MB RAM
Video card	640 × 380 with 256 colors VGA card	800 × 600 with 65,535 colors SVGA
Hard drive	30 MB	160 MB
CD-ROM drive	Single-speed (150 Kb/sec) without consuming more than 40% CPU bandwidth in the process	Double-speed
Sound card	8-bit DAC, linear PCM sampling with 22.05 and 11.025 kHz sampling rate, microphone input, direct audio connection to CD-ROM	16-bit DAC, linear PCM sampling with 44.1, 22.05, and 11.025 kHz sampling rate, DMA buffered transfer, microphone input
Mouse	Two-button mouse	Two-button mouse
Ports	Serial port, parallel port, MIDI I/O port, headphones or speakers	Serial port, parallel port, MIDI I/O port, headphones or speakers

WHAT CPU MMX TECHNOLOGY DOES FOR MULTIMEDIA

The MMX Pentium processor by Intel was designed with multimedia applications in mind. Multimedia software tends to use input/output operations more than it performs complex computations. MMX technology was designed to speed up the repetitive looping of multimedia software needed to manage the high-volume input/output of graphics, motion video, animation, and sound. MMX technology added three new architectural enhancements to the Pentium, all designed to speed up the repetitive looping of multimedia.

13

- **New Instructions.** Intel added 57 new instructions to the CPU logic, all designed to handle the parallel, repetitive processing found in multimedia operations.

- **SIMD Process.** A process called **single instruction multiple data** (**SIMD**) was added that allows the CPU to execute a single instruction on multiple pieces of data rather than having to repetitively loop back to the previous instruction many times.

- **Increased Cache.** Intel increased the size of the internal cache to 32K on the processor, reducing the number of times the CPU must access slower, off-chip memory for information.

Taking Advantage of MMX Technology

For the MMX technology to affect the performance of multimedia devices and software to its full extent, the multimedia software must be written to take advantage of MMX enhancements. Look on the software package for the "Intel MMX" symbol to know that the software is using the MMX technology. In the future, more multimedia software will be written to take advantage of MMX technology; however, the software should also be backward compatible with older CPUs.

VIDEO CARDS AND MONITORS

The quality of a video subsystem of a computer system is rated according to how it affects overall system performance, video quality (including resolution and color), power-saving features, and ease of use and installation. Because the video controller is separated from the core system functions, manufacturers can use a variety of techniques to improve performance without being overly concerned with compatibility with functions on the systemboard. An example of this flexibility is seen in the many different ways memory is managed on a video controller. This section will look at the features available on video cards, especially video memory, and revisit features available on monitors that were discussed in previous chapters.

VIDEO CARDS

Remember that a video card is an expansion card responsible for receiving data and instructions from the CPU, processing the data, and sending it on to the monitor. Four basic steps happen on the video card, as seen in Figure 13-5.

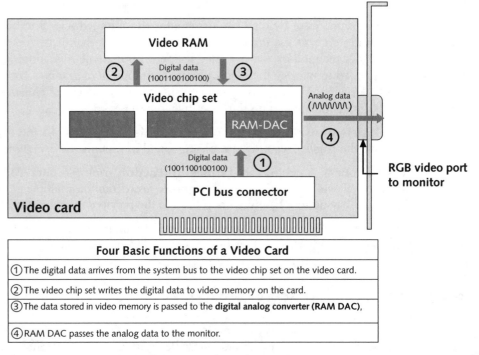

Four Basic Functions of a Video Card
① The digital data arrives from the system bus to the video chip set on the video card.
② The video chip set writes the digital data to video memory on the card.
③ The data stored in video memory is passed to the **digital analog converter (RAM DAC)**,
④ RAM DAC passes the analog data to the monitor.

Figure 13-5   Four basic functions of a video card

The RAM DAC technology may be housed on a single RAM DAC chip on the video card or may be embedded in the video chip set. RAM DAC actually includes three digital-to-analog converters, one for each of the monitor's three color guns: red, green, and blue (RGB).

Since 1995, video cards have been designed to use only the PCI bus. Older video cards were made to run on VESA local buses, ISA buses, and EISA buses. The PCI bus can have a bus data path of 32 bits, although 64-bit PCI buses are now available. The speed of the PCI bus is partly determined by the systemboard chip set and CPU. If the CPU uses MMX technology, it will also boost video performance significantly.

On the video card itself, performance is affected by the chip set, memory, and the RAM DAC as well as the bus speed and size. One method to improve performance is to allow both the video chip set and the RAM DAC (both the input and the output processes) to access video memory at the same time. This method, called **dual porting**, requires a special kind of video RAM discussed later in this section. Another method of increasing performance is to place a processor on the video card, making the card a **graphics accelerator**.

The bus external to the video card is the PCI bus, but there is also an internal video bus on the card itself. The volume of data that can travel on the bus is called **bandwidth**. Current video buses use a data path that may be 32 bits, 64 bits, 128 bits, or even 256 bits wide. The effective bandwidth of the bus is partly determined by the width of the data path and by how much memory is on the card.

Graphics Accelerators

One of the more important advances made in video cards in recent years has been the introduction of graphics accelerators. A graphics accelerator is a type of video card that has its own processor to boost performance. With the demands that graphics applications make in the multimedia environment, graphics accelerators have become not just an enhancement, but a common necessity.

The processor on a graphics accelerator card is similar to a CPU, but specifically designed to manage video and graphics. Some features included on a graphics accelerator are MPEG decoding, 3D graphics, dual porting, color space conversion, interpolated scaling, EPA Green PC support, and applications support for popular high-intensity graphics software such as AutoCAD, Ventura Publisher, Windows 95, and Windows NT.

Video Memory

Older video cards do not have memory on them, but with the heavy demands placed on video today, video memory is a necessity in order to handle the large volume of data generated by increased resolution and color. Video memory is stored on video cards as memory chips. The first video cards to have memory all used DRAM chips, but now there are several technologies for video memory chips. This section discusses how much video memory is needed and what kinds of video memory chips can be used on a card to obtain the best possible performance.

How Much Video Memory Is Needed?   The amount of data received by a video card from the CPU for each frame (or screen) of data is determined by the screen resolution, measured in pixels, and the number of colors, which is called the **color depth**, measured in bits. The more data required to generate a single screen of data, the more memory is required to hold that data. Recall that this memory is called the frame buffer. There are other needs for memory on the video card besides the frame buffer, including the memory used by some cards to store font or other graphical information. Aside from these other uses of memory, Table 13-2 shows the amount of memory needed to hold the frame buffer, which is determined by the screen resolution and number of colors.

Table 13-2   Video RAM required for different video resolutions and color depths

Video Resolution	4-bit color depth (16 colors)	8-bit color depth (256 colors)	16-bit color depth (65,000 colors)	24-bit, true color (16.7 million colors)
640 × 480	512K	512K	1 MB	2 MB
800 × 600	512K	1 MB	2 MB	2 MB
1,024 × 768	1 MB	1 MB	2 MB	4 MB
1,152 × 1,024	1 MB	2 MB	2 MB	4 MB
1,280 × 1,024	1 MB	2 MB	4 MB	4 MB
1,600 × 1,200	2 MB	2 MB	4 MB	8 MB

Color depth is directly related to the number of bits used to compose one pixel and can be 4, 8, 16, or 24 bits per pixel. Remember that the larger the number of bits allocated to storing each piece of data, the more accurate the value can be; in like manner, the greater the number of bits allocated to store the value of pixel color, the greater the number of color shades you can use and color depth you can have.

To determine the number of colors that can be represented by these number of bits, use the number of bits as the power (exponent) of the number 2. For example, to calculate the number of colors represented by 4 bits per pixel, raise 2 to the 4th power, which equals 16 colors. (Note that the largest 4-bit number is 1111, which equals 15 in decimal. If you include 0, then the number of values that can be stored in a 4-bit number is 16.) A color depth of 24 bits per pixel equals 2 to the 24th power or 16.7 million colors.

To determine the amount of RAM needed for one frame buffer, multiply the number of bits per pixel times the number of pixels on the screen, giving the total number of bits per screen. Divide the number of bits by 8 to determine the number of bytes of RAM needed for the buffer.

For example, for a screen resolution of 1,024 × 768 and 256 colors, Table 13-2 shows the amount of RAM required to be 1 MB. The way that number is derived is illustrated below:

- The number of pixels for one frame buffer: 1,024 × 768 = 786,432 pixels
- For 256 colors, you need an 8-bit color depth or 8 bits per pixel. (Remember that 1111 1111 in binary equals 255 in decimal, which, along with the value zero, provides 256 options.)

- Number of bits for one frame buffer: 786,432 pixels × 8 bits/pixel = 6,291,456 bits

- Number of bytes of memory needed: 6,291,456 bits/8 bits per byte = 786,432 bytes

- Since RAM comes as either 512K, 1 MB, 2 MB or 4 MB increments, you must have 1 MB of video RAM to accommodate the frame buffer of 786,432 bytes.

Another factor that determines how much video memory is required is the bus width on the card. Just as with systemboards, the RAM configuration on the card must conform to the bus width so that data can move from the bus to the card. A normal 1 MB memory chip on a video card has a bus width of 32 bits. In Figure 13-6, because each 1 MB video RAM chip is 32 bits wide, you can see why 2 MB of memory is needed if the video bus is 64 bits wide. In fact, this bit width of the video chip is the reason that a video card that has a 64-bit bus width and only 1 MB of installed memory is so slow. If your video card uses a 64-bit bus, be sure to install at least 2 MB of RAM.

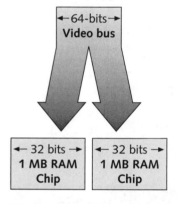

Figure 13-6 Video bus with 64-bit width addressing two 1 MB memory chips with 32-bit widths

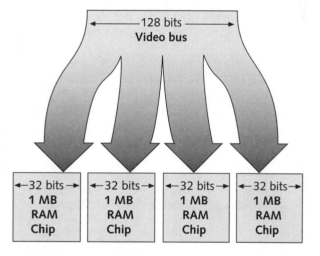

Figure 13-7 128-bit video bus addressing 4 MB of video memory

In Figure 13-7, 4 MB of RAM is required to make the most efficient use of the 128-bit video bus width. Some manufacturers of video chip sets have developed a method to use a 128-bit bus with less than 4 MB of memory. For example, the Tseng Labs ET6000 chip set uses a special kind of video RAM called **Multibank DRAM** (**MDRAM**) that is able to use the full 128-bit bus path without requiring the full 4 MB of RAM.

Types of Video Memory.   You have already been introduced to several different versions of video memory: Dual-ported memory, one type of which is sometimes called **video RAM** or **VRAM**, is designed so that video memory can be accessed by both the input and output processes at the same time. MDRAM memory chips are designed so that the full width of the video bus can be used with fewer memory chips than needed to provide the full bus width access to RAM. Three other types of memory chips designed to improve performance of video cards are: WRAM, SGRAM, and 3D RAM.

SGRAM (synchronous graphics RAM) is similar to SDRAM, discussed in Chapter 9, but designed specifically for video card processing. SGRAM, like SDRAM, can synchronize itself with the CPU bus clock, which makes the memory faster. SGRAM also uses other methods to increase overall performance for graphics-intensive processing.

WRAM (Window RAM) is another type of dual-ported RAM, but is faster and less expensive than VRAM. WRAM was named more for its ability to manage full-motion video than for its ability to speed up Microsoft Windows video processing. WRAM's increase in speed is primarily due to its own internal bus on the chip, which has a data path that is 256 bits wide.

Some video processing involves simulating 3D graphics; **3D RAM** was designed specifically to improve this performance. Much of the logic of 3D processing is embedded on the chip itself. A graphics card chip set normally calculates which pixel of a 3D graphic is to be displayed, based on whether or not the pixel is behind other pixels and, therefore, out of sight in a 3D graphic. After the pixel is drawn and a calculation is made as to whether or not the pixel is seen, if the pixel is not to be displayed, the chip set writes it back to memory to be used later. With 3D RAM, the chip set simply passes the data to the 3D RAM chip that draws the pixel and decides whether or not to display it without involving the chip set.

CHOOSING THE RIGHT MONITOR

How a monitor works and what features are available on monitors were discussed in Chapter 4. These features are summarized in Table 13-3.

Table 13-3   Some features of a monitor

Monitor Characteristic	Description
Screen size	Screens are usually described as 14 inch, 16 inch, 17 inch, 21 inch, or larger. This screen size usually refers to the diagonal length of the lighted area, although the measurement is not particularly accurate. The actual diagonal is usually shorter than the advertised measurement.
Refresh rate	Refresh rate, or vertical scan rate, is the time it takes for an electronic beam to fill a video screen with lines from top to bottom. A Super VGA monitor must have a minimum refresh rate of 70 Hz or 70 times per second.
Interlaced	Rather than drawing the entire screen on every pass, interlaced monitors only refresh half the screen on every pass: the first pass draws the odd lines and the second pass draws even lines. Compared to noninterlaced monitors, interlaced monitors do not provide the same quality for the same refresh rate, although, because of interlacing, the overall effect is less noticeable.

Table 13-3 Some features of a monitor (continued)

Monitor Characteristic	Description
Dot pitch	Dot pitch is the distance between adjacent dots on the screen. The smaller the dot pitch, the higher the quality of the image. A high-quality monitor should have a dot pitch of no more than .28 mm.
Resolution	A measure of how many spots, or pixels, on the screen are addressable by software. The video controller card as well as the monitor must be capable of supporting the chosen resolution. A common resolution is 800 by 600. Resolutions are set from Control Panel in Windows.
Multiscan	Monitors that offer a variety of refresh rates are called **multiscan** monitors. Multiscan monitors can support different video cards, whereas **fixed frequency** monitors only support a single refresh rate.
Green monitor	A green monitor supports the EPA Energy Star program. When a screen saver is on, the monitor should use no more than 30 watts of electricity.

The screen size of a monitor is the one feature that most affects price. Figure 13-8 shows the sales of monitors by size, projected into 1999. The 15-inch monitor is the most popular, and the small screen, 14-inch monitor is losing popularity as most users are opting for larger screens.

When matching a monitor to a video card, a good rule of thumb is to match a low-end video card to a small, 14-inch monitor, a midrange video card to a 15-inch monitor, and a high-end video card to a 17-inch or larger monitor to get the best performance from both devices. However, you may prefer to compare the different features of the video card to the monitor, such as the resolutions supported, the refresh rate, and the bandwidth.

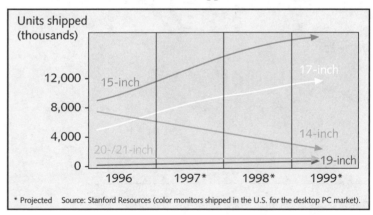

Figure 13-8 The market for larger screen monitors has grown

There is some debate about the danger of monitors giving off **ELF** (**extremely low frequency**) emissions of magnetic fields. Standards to control ELF emissions are Sweden's MPR II standard and the TCO '95 standards. The TCO '95 standards also include guidelines for energy consumption, screen flicker, and luminance. Most monitors manufactured today comply with the MPR II standard, and very few comply with the more stringent TCO '95 standards.

DEVICES SUPPORTING MULTIMEDIA

This section looks at three popular multimedia devices: sound cards, digital cameras, and the Digital Video Disc (DVD).

SOUND CARDS

A sound card is an expansion card that enables a computer to input, manipulate, and output sound. As explained above, the critical factor in the performance of a sound card is the accuracy of the samples as determined by the number of bits used to hold each sample value. This number of bits is called the **sample size**. Sound cards have connections for a microphone and speakers. Nearly all sound cards support MIDI, the industry standard for storing sound electronically. Also, sound cards may be Sound Blaster compatible, which means that they can understand the commands sent to them that have been written for a Sound Blaster card, which is generally considered the standard for PC sound cards (see Figure 13-9).

Figure 13-9   A Sound Blaster sound card

Sample Rate and Size

Remember that sound is analog and computers are digital, and that systems need a way to convert from one to the other. Remember that a sound card uses an **analog-to-digital converter** (**A/D** or **ADC**) to convert sound into digital values that can be stored on hard drives. This process, sometimes called sampling, is done by the PCM (pulse code modulation) method. The analog sound is converted to analog voltage by a microphone and is passed to the sound card.

The sampling rate of a sound card (the number of samples taken of the analog signal over a period of time) is usually expressed as samples (cycles) per second or **hertz**. One thousand hertz (one kilohertz) is written as kHz. Remember that a low sampling rate provides a less accurate representation of the sound than does a high sampling rate. Our ears detect up to about 22,000 samples per second or hertz. The sampling rate of music CDs is 44,100 Hz or 44.1 kHz. When recording sound on a PC, the sampling rate is controlled by the software.

As explained above, sample size is the amount of space used to store a single sample measurement. The larger the sample size, the more accurate the sampling will be. The number of values used to measure sound is determined by the number of bits allocated to hold each number. If 8 bits are used to hold one number, then the sample range can be from –128 to 128. This is because 1111 1111 in binary equals 255 in decimal, which, together with zero, equals 256 values. Samples of sound are considered to be both positive and negative numbers, so the range is –128 to 128 rather than 0 to 255. However, if 16 bits are used to hold the range of numbers, then the sample range increases dramatically because 1111 1111 1111 1111 in binary is 65,535 in decimal, meaning that the sample size can be –32,768 to 32,768, or a total of 65,536 values.

An 8-bit sound card uses 8 bits to store a sample value, or uses a 256 sample size range. A 16-bit sound card has a sample size of 65,536. Sound cards typically use 8- or 16-bit sample sizes with a sampling rate from 4,000 to 44,000 samples per second. For quality sound, use a 16-bit sound card. Samples may also be recorded on a single channel (mono) or on two channels (stereo).

Don't confuse the sample size of 8 bits or 16 bits with the ISA bus size that the sound card uses to attach to the systemboard. A sound card may use an 8-bit sample size but a 16-bit ISA bus. When you hear someone talk about an 8-bit sound card, they are speaking of the sample size, not the bus size.

Digital-to-Analog Conversion

Sound cards use two methods to convert digitally stored sound into real analog sound: FM (frequency modulation) synthesis and wavetable synthesis. The difference between the two is that FM synthesis creates a sound by artificially creating a wave that is close to the sound wave produced by the instrument. For example, the sound of a trumpet would be produced by imitating the sound wave produced by the trumpet through a series of mathematical calculations. Wavetable synthesis produces the sound by using a sample recording of the real instrument. Wavetable synthesis produces better sound than does FM synthesis, but is also more expensive.

Storing Sound Files

Sound cards also have two methods to store sound in files: MIDI with .MID file extensions, which was discussed earlier, and sampled files, which Microsoft calls WAV files (pronounced, and stands for, "wave"). Most game music is stored in MIDI files, but most multimedia sound is stored in WAV files, so look for a sound card that can handle both as well as music CDs.

Sound Playback

In order for sound to be played back using a sound card, speakers are needed. There are two differences between the speakers used for other sound equipment and the speakers used for computers. Speakers made for computers have built-in amplifiers and extra shielding to protect the monitor from the magnetic fields around regular speakers.

 If you plan to put speakers close to a monitor, be certain that they are shielded. Speakers that are not shielded first cause the monitor to display strange colors, and can eventually do permanent damage to the monitor. Also, setting floppy disks on top of unshielded speakers can damage the data on the disks.

Installing a Sound Card and Software

Most sound cards come with a device driver as well as all the software needed for normal use, such as applications software to play music CDs. The installation of a sample sound card is described below. The sample card used is a low-cost sound card, costing around $30, that uses the Yamaha OPL3 chip. The card complies with the MPC Level 1 standard for sound cards. It comes with a CD-ROM and some short explanations on the CD cover. Several versions, in several languages, of the complete installation and user guide are stored as documents on the CD. This sound card has an on-board adapter to support a CD-ROM drive, but the installation does not use the adapter. The card also has a connection to connect the sound output from the CD-ROM drive directly to the sound card—which *will* be used.

The three main steps in the installation of a sound card are to install the card itself in an empty 16-bit ISA slot on the systemboard, install the driver under Windows 95, and then install the applications stored on the sound card's CD.

 Unless you follow proper procedures, working inside your computer can cause serious damage—to both you and your computer. To assure safety in your work setting, follow every precaution listed in the *Read This Before You Begin* section following this book's Introduction.

Installing a Sound Card.   Follow these steps to install a sound card:

- Turn the PC off, remove the cover, and locate an empty expansion slot for the card. Since this installation uses the connecting wire from the sound card to the CD-ROM drive, place the sound card near enough to the CD-ROM drive so that the wire can reach between them.
- Attach the wire to the sound card (see Figure 13-10) and to the CD-ROM drive.
- Remove the cover from the slot opening at the rear of the PC case and place the card into the slot, making sure that the card is seated firmly. Use the screw taken from the slot cover to secure the card to the back of the PC case.
- Check again that both ends of the wire are still securely connected, and replace the case cover.
- Plug in the speakers to the ports at the back of the sound card and turn on the PC. The speakers may or may not require their own power source.

Figure 13-10 Connect the wire to the sound card that will make the direct audio connection from the CD

Installing the Sound Card Driver.   Once the card is installed, the device driver must be installed. When Windows 95 starts, it detects that new hardware is present. The New Hardware Found dialog box displays, saying that it has discovered the OPL3-SAx Sound Board. Follow these steps to install the sound card driver:

- The New Hardware Wizard gives you these two options for installing the driver for the board:

  - Windows default driver

  - Driver from disk provided by hardware manufacturer

- Select the option to install from the disk provided by the manufacturer. The Install From Disk dialog box displays, asking for the location of the driver files.

- Insert the CD-ROM disc into the drive and enter the drive letter (for instance, D:) and the directory on the drive that the OS should use. The directories to choose from are NT, OS2, Win31, and Win95.

- Enter D:\Win95 in the dialog box, and then click **OK**. The sound card driver will be installed.

After the installation is complete, Windows 95 continues to load. After you have entered Windows 95, verify that the device and the driver are correctly installed in Windows 95 by using the Device Manager.

- Click on **Start, Settings, Control Panel**, and then double-click on **System**.

- Select the **Device Manager** tab. Figure 13-11 shows the list of installed devices. Look for two entries under Sound, video and game controllers (YAMAHA OPL3-SAx GamePort and YAMAHA OPL3-SAx Sound System) to be sure the driver has been installed.

13

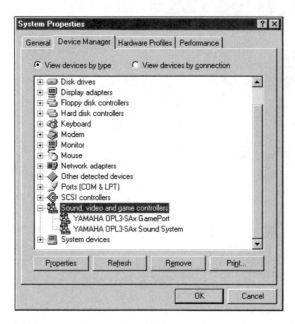

Figure 13-11   Device Manager shows the sound card installed

Using Sound with Windows 95.   Windows 95 offers some support for sound, such as playing a music CD or a WAV file or providing sound when performing certain Windows functions (such as starting an application or exiting Windows). This section will look at these features first and then move on to the sound applications included with the sound card CD.

To configure the Windows 95 sound system to use the new sound card, first determine that sound control is installed under the Windows 95 Multimedia section, and then test the sound using Windows 95:

- Click **Start, Settings, Control Panel**, and then double-click on **Add/Remove Programs**.

- Click on the **Windows Setup** tab. From this tab, shown in Figure 13-12, you can install components of Windows 95 that were not installed at the original installation.

- Click on **Multimedia**, and then click on **Details** to see the five components of the Windows 95 multimedia support, which are shown in Figure 13-13. Installed components are checked.

- If Multimedia audio—including Volume Control, Media Player, and Sound Recorder—is not installed, then install it now. Select the files by clicking inside the check box.

- Click **Apply** to install these components. You may be asked to insert the Windows 95 CD or floppy disks.

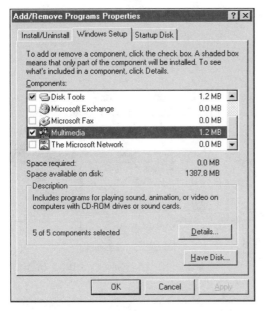

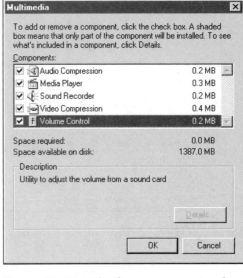

Figure 13-12   Windows 95 offers multimedia support

Figure 13-13   The five components of Windows 95 multimedia support

To test the sound, access the Multimedia group of Windows 95:

- Click on **Start, Program, Accessories, Multimedia**. Figure 13-14 shows the three selections under Multimedia.

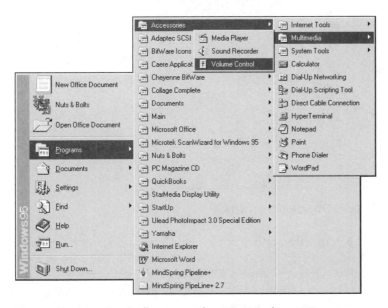

Figure 13-14   Controlling sound using Windows 95

- To play a music CD, click on **Media Player**. The Media Player dialog box displays, as in Figure 13-15.

- Select **Device**. From the Device drop-down list in Figure 13-16, select **CD Audio**, and then click on the **Play** button.

- To adjust the volume of the sound card, select **Volume Control** from the Multimedia menu of Figure 13-14. The Volume Control dialog box in Figure 13–17 displays. Adjust the volume and close the dialog box when finished.

Figure 13-15   Playing a music CD with Windows 95

Figure 13-16   Select a type of sound to play

- A handy way to adjust the volume is to have Windows keep the volume control on the taskbar. To do this, use the Multimedia control in Control Panel: Click on **Start, Settings, Control Panel** and then double-click on **Multimedia**, and then click on the **Audio** tab of the Multimedia window (see Figure 13-18). Check **Show volume control on the taskbar**.

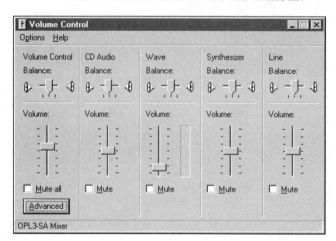

Figure 13-17   Windows 95 volume control

- Also on the Multimedia control of Control Panel, you can see the resources that the sound card is using: Click on the **Advanced** tab to see a list of multimedia devices installed. Open the **Audio Devices** group, and then click on the sound card in the group (see Figure 13-19). Click on **Properties** for a complete list of resources used by the card (see Figure 13-20).

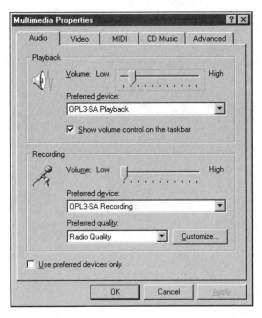

Figure 13-18 Windows 95 multimedia audio selection includes the option to put volume control on the taskbar

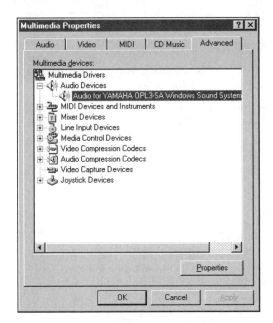

Figure 13-19 A list of multimedia devices installed under Windows 95

13

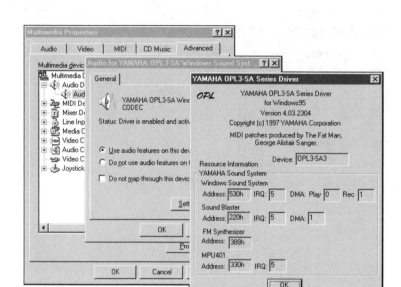

Figure 13-20   Resources used by the sound card installed under
Windows 95

Recording Sound.   In addition to being able to play sound, a multimedia system must be
able to record it, for which you need a microphone. You can attach a microphone to the
MIC port on the back of the sound card to record sound. Windows 95 saves sound files in
the WAV file format. To record sound using Windows 95, follow these steps:

■ Click on **Start, Programs, Accessories, Multimedia, Sound Recorder**.
  Figure 13-21 shows the Sound Recorder dialog box.

■ Click on the **Record** button (the red dot on the right side of the dialog box) to
  record. Sound enters the microphone and moves as an analog signal to the sound
  card, which samples and digitizes it before passing it on to the CPU by way of
  the system bus.

■ Click the **Stop** button when finished recording. Under the Edit menu of the dialog box, select **Audio Properties** to view the Audio Properties window in
  Figure 13-22.

■ Under **Recording**, you can click on the drop-down list of **Preferred quality** to
  select a sound quality: Click on the **Customize** button to display the Customize
  dialog box shown in Figure 13-23. From it you can select the sampling rate and
  choose between mono and stereo sound. Click **File** and **Save As** to save the
  sound file for later use.

Figure 13-21   Recording Sound
using Windows 95

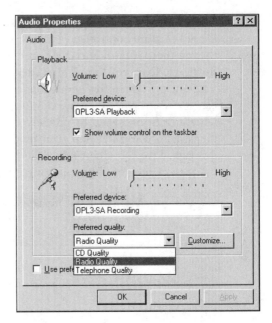

Figure 13-22   Choosing the sound quality

13

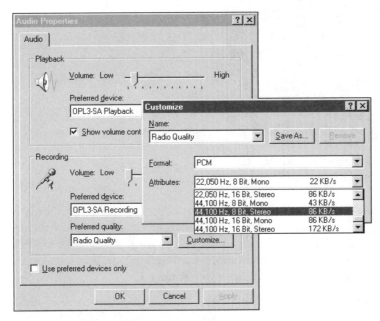

Figure 13-23   Customizing Windows 95 recorded sound

Controlling Windows 95 Sounds.   When certain events occur, Windows 95 will play sounds that are controlled by the Sounds control of the Windows 95 Control Panel. To customize these sounds and the times at which they occur, access Control Panel (click **Start, Settings, Control Panel**), and then double-click on the **Sounds** icon. Items listed that have a horn icon beside the item cause a sound. The sound for this item is defined in the Name list. For example, in Figure 13-24, for the event Exit Windows, the sound will be The Microsoft Sound.wav. To preview the sound, click on the **Play** button to the right of the filename. You can develop your own customized choices of sounds for chosen events using this box. Save the scheme as a file using the Save As option at the bottom of the box, and use it to create a multimedia sound experience when working with Windows 95!

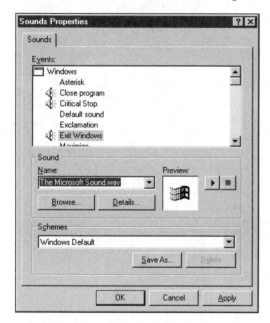

Figure 13-24   Controlling sound events
under Windows 95

Installing the Sound Application Software.   In addition to the driver already installed, the sound card CD includes a number of applications that offer more enhanced features and ability to manipulate sound than does Windows 95. For instance, a brief instruction on the CD cover instructs the user to install the applications software while in Windows by executing the install program Winstall.exe in the Appl directory on the CD:

- Go to Windows 95 Explorer and double-click on the filename. The dialog box displays, as in Figure 13-25, asking if you want to install the Yamaha application.

- Click **OK**. After installation, the Yamaha group is found in the Programs group of the Start menu, as shown in Figure 13-26.

Figure 13-25   Sound cards often come with additional sound application software

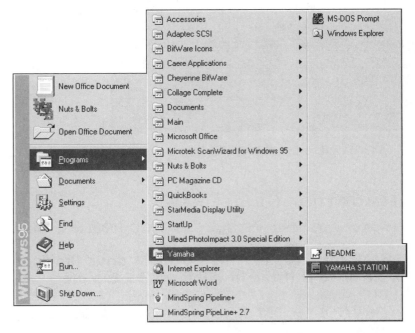

Figure 13-26   Sound applications software installed

The Yamaha Station, which is the user interface to the applications, looks like Figure 13-27 and offers many more options and features than does the Windows 95 Media Player. From Figure 13-27, it is easy to see that this card supports all three types of sound files: Wave, MIDI, and music CDs. The documentation to use the software is stored in a documents file on the CD.

13

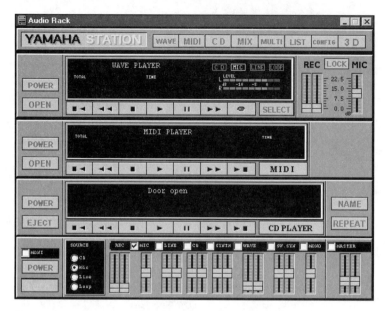

Figure 13-27   Sound card software Audio Rack

TROUBLESHOOTING GUIDELINES

This section covers some troubleshooting guidelines for CD-ROM drives and sound cards.

Computer does not recognize the CD-ROM drive (no D: prompt in DOS, or no drive D listed in Windows 95 Explorer)

1. For a DOS system, does the CONFIG.SYS file contain a CD device command line?
2. Does the AUTOEXEC.BAT file call Mscdex.exe? Is Mscdex.exe placed in the right directory?
3. Is Mscdex.exe missing?
4. Has the CD-ROM drive been installed?
5. Is another device using the same port settings or IRQ number? For Windows 95, see Control Panel, System, Device Manager.
6. Suspect a boot virus. Run a virus scan program.
7. Is the power cable attached to the CD-ROM drive?
8. Is the data cable attached to the CD-ROM drive and to the controller?
9. Is the edge color on the CD-ROM data cable correctly aligned to pin 1 on the drive and the controller?
10. Is the master/slave jumper set correctly? If both the hard drive and the CD-ROM drive are hooked up on the same ribbon cable, one must be assigned the master (the one attached to the end connector) and the other set to slave (middle connector).

There is no sound

1. Is the audio wire attached between the CD-ROM drive and the audio connector on the sound card?
2. Are the speakers turned on?
3. Is the speaker volume turned down?
4. Are the speakers plugged into the line "Out" or "Spkr" port of the sound card?
5. Is the transformer for the speaker plugged into an electrical outlet on one end and into the speakers on the other end?
6. Is the volume control for Windows turned down? (Click **Start**, **Programs**, **Accessories**, **Multimedia**, **Volume Control**.)
7. Does the sound card have a "diagnose" file on the install disk? If so, run the program.
8. Reinstall the sound card driver.
9. Is another device using the same port settings or IRQ number?
10. Remove the sound card from the expansion slot and reseat it. Try a different expansion slot.
11. Install a sound card you know is good, to see if that solves the problem.

DIGITAL CAMERAS

A recent introduction to multimedia, with markets in both business and home computing, is the digital camera, which is becoming more popular as quality improves and price decreases (see Figure 13-28). Digital photography opens up new possibilities for pictures, such as incorporating them into presentations, Web pages, and e-mail without first scanning hard copy. In digital photography, a camera view is essentially scanned, and then recorded in bits and bytes, rather than re-created photo-optically on paper, as with traditional photography.

13

Figure 13-28   Digital camera

To use a digital camera, first select the resolution and the compression level, frame the picture using the camera's viewfinder or LCD screen, then shoot. Expect a five- to eight-second delay in the shot. The image will be digitized and recorded as a file, which can then be transferred to your PC. TWAIN (Technology Without An Interesting Name) format is a standard format used by both digital cameras and PCs for transferring the image. Transfer the image to your computer's hard drive using a serial cable supplied with the camera, a parallel cable, or some external disk medium such as a flash RAM card. From the PC, use the camera's image-editing software or another program such as Adobe Photoshop to view and touch up the picture. The picture file, which is usually in JPEG (**Joint Photographic Experts Group**) format, can then be imported into documents. **JPEG** is a common lossy compression standard for storing photos.

Most digital cameras also have a video-out port so that you can attach the camera to any TV using a serial cable. You can then display pictures on TV or copy them to videotape.

Digital camera technology works much like scanner technology, except that it is much faster. It essentially scans the field of image set by the picture taker, and translates the light signals into digital values, which can be stored as a file and viewed with the appropriate software to interpret the stored values.

The image sensing may be done by two kinds of technology: infrared sensor or charge-coupled device (CCD). The image sensor captures light reflected off the subject and converts that light to a serial stream of small DC voltages. The image sensor is made up of three sensors, each filtering a different color (red, green, or blue). Figure 13-29 shows the process a digital camera uses to create a picture. The figure shows only one channel of the three channels used (one channel for each color). The image sensor captures the light and converts it into voltage signals that will become pixels. These signals move through the DC restore or DC clamping stage and then on to the gain stage, where the signals are amplified and buffered. Next, the signals enter the ADC (analog-to-digital converter), where they are digitized. The digital pixels are then processed by the image processor and sent on to storage through the I/O process. The controller in the diagram controls all processing of the digital signals.

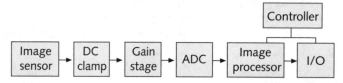

Figure 13-29 The signal chain used by a digital camera

Since digital cameras are used away from the PC and are only connected to the PC through a serial cable, no installation of hardware is necessary. If the camera uses a device such as a CompactFlash card to store the pictures, a drive capable of reading from the card must be installed on the PC.

DIGITAL VIDEO DISC (DVD)

With multimedia, the ability to store massive amounts of data is paramount to the technology's success. The goal of storing a full-length movie on a single computerized, inexpensive storage medium has been met by more than one technology, one of the most promising of which is digital video disc (DVD) technology (see Figure 13-30). There appears to be a consensus on the DVD standard in the industry, so this one technology may become the ultimate replacement for the CD-ROM. It takes up to seven CDs to store a full-length movie and only one DVD disc.

Remember that another contender to replace the CD-ROM is the phase dual drives discussed in Chapter 5. These drives are rewritable optical CD drives. Phase dual drives (known as PD drives) can also play CD-ROMs and audio CDs.

Figure 13-30   A DVD device

How Does DVD Work?

Both DVD and CD-ROM technologies use patterns of tiny pits on the surface of a disc to represent data, which is then readable by a laser beam. Because DVD uses a shorter wavelength laser, it can read smaller, more densely packed pits, which increases a disc's capacity. In addition, there is a second layer added to DVD discs, an opaque layer that also holds data, which almost doubles the capacity of a disc.

Just as important as the DVD disc drive itself is the MPEG-2 controller card that accompanies it. This PCI controller card decodes the MPEG video stored on the DVD disc and separates the sound data from the video data. Figure 13-31 shows the flow of data through the PC coming from a DVD device. The DVD drive is attached to the systemboard by way of a SCSI controller that enables the data to bypass the CPU and to be routed directly to the MPEG-2 decoder card. The MPEG-2 decoder separates the video data from the sound data, sending the video data to the video controller card and the sound data to a DAC on the card that directs the analog sound signal to the speakers.

13

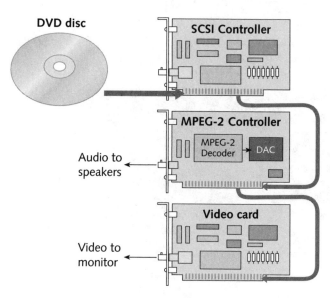

Figure 13-31   How a PC uses DVD data

SUPPORTING PRINTERS

In Chapter 7, the fundamentals of supporting printers were covered. This section takes a closer look at two of the more popular printers for multimedia applications, the laser printer and the ink-jet printer.

LASER PRINTERS

Laser printers range from the small, personal desktop size to huge network printers capable of handling large volumes of printing on a continuous basis. Figure 13-32 shows an example of a typical laser printer for a desktop computer system, the Hewlett-Packard LaserJet 5L.

Laser printers require the interaction of mechanical, electrical, and optical technologies to work. Understanding how they work helps us to understand why safety precautions that are stated in laser printer user manuals are necessary, and is also helpful for supporting and servicing the printer. This section covers how laser printers work and offers some tips on how to support them.

How a Laser Printer Works

Figure 13-33 shows the six progressive steps of laser printing. Four of these steps use the components that undergo the most wear in the process, which are contained within the removable cartridge. The last two steps are performed outside the cartridge. Laser printers work by

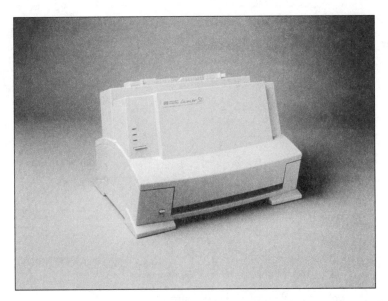

Figure 13-32   The HP LaserJet 5L desktop laser printer

placing toner on an electrically charged rotating drum and then depositing the toner on paper as the paper moves through the system at the same speed the drum is turning. Follow the step-by-step procedures of laser printing below while you refer to Figure 13-33:

1. *Cleaning.* The drum is cleaned of any residual toner and electrical charge.

2. *Conditioning.* The drum is conditioned to contain a high electrical charge.

3. *Writing.* A laser beam is used to discharge the high charge down to a lower charge, only in those places where toner is to go.

4. *Developing.* Toner is placed onto the drum where the charge has been reduced.

5. *Transferring.* A strong electrical charge draws the toner off the drum onto the paper. This is the first step that takes place outside the cartridge.

6. *Fusing.* Heat and pressure are used to fuse the toner to the paper.

Note that Figure 13-33 shows only a cross-section of the drum, mechanisms, and paper. Remember, as you visualize the process, that the drum is as wide as a sheet of paper. The mirror, blades, and rollers in the drawing are also as wide as paper. First note the location of the removable cartridge in the drawing, the photosensitive drum inside the cartridge turning in a clockwise direction, and the path of the paper, which moves from right to left through the drawing.

13

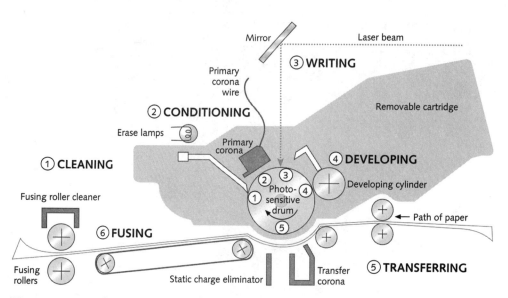

Figure 13-33 The six progressive steps of laser printing

Step 1: Cleaning.   Figure 13-34 shows a clear view of the cleaning step. First a sweeper strip cleans the drum of any residual toner, which is swept out away from the drum by a sweeping blade. A cleaning blade completes the physical cleaning of the drum. Next the drum is cleaned of any electrical charge by erase lamps (located in the hinged top cover of the printer), which light the surface of the drum to neutralize any electrical charge left on the drum.

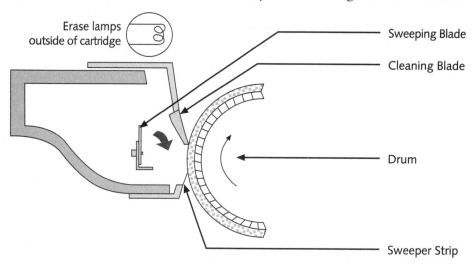

Figure 13-34   The cleaning step cleans the drum of toner and electrical charge

Step 2: Conditioning.   The conditioning step puts a uniform electrical charge of −600 V on the drive. The charge is put there by a primary corona wire, which is charged by a high-voltage power supply assembly. The primary corona in Figure 13-33 is between the primary corona wire and the drum, and regulates the charge on the drum, ensuring that it is a uniform −600 V.

Step 3: Writing. In the writing step, the uniform charge that was applied in Step 2 is discharged only where you want the printer to print. This is done by controlling mirrors to reflect laser beams onto the drum in a pattern that recreates the image desired. This is the first step in which data from the computer must be transmitted to the printer. Figure 13-35 shows the process: Data from the PC is received by the formatter (1) and passed on to the DC controller (2) that controls the laser unit (3). The laser beam is initiated and directed toward the octagonal mirror called the **scanning mirror**. The scanning mirror (4) is turned by the scanning motor in a clockwise direction. There are eight mirrors on the eight sides of the scanning mirror. As the mirror turns, the laser beam is directed in a sweeping motion that can cover the entire length of the drum. The laser beam is reflected off the scanning mirror and is focused by the focusing lens (5) and sent on to the mirror (6), which is also shown in Figure 13-33. The mirror deflects the laser beam to a slit in the removable cartridge and on to the drum (7).

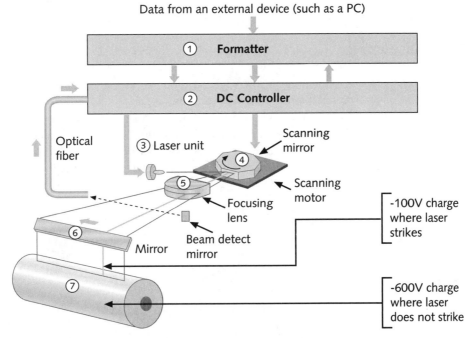

Figure 13-35 The writing step, done by an invisible laser beam, mirrors, and motors, causes a discharge on the drum where the image will be

The speed of the motor turning the drum and the speed of the scanning motor turning the scanning mirror are synchronized so that the laser beam completes one pass, or scanline, across the drum and returns to the beginning of the drum (right side of the drum in Figure 13-35) to begin a new pass. For a 300 dots per inch (dpi) printer, the beam makes 300 passes for every one inch of the drum circumference. The laser beam is turned on and off continually as it makes a single pass down the length of the drum, so that dots are written along the drum on every pass. For a 300 dpi printer, 300 dots will be written along the drum for every inch of linear pass. The 300 dots per inch down this single pass, along with 300 passes per inch of drum circumference, together accomplish the resolution of 300 × 300 dots per square inch of many desktop laser printers.

Where the laser beam strikes the surface of the drum, the drum discharges from its conditioned charge of -600 V down to -100 V where toner will be placed on the drum. Toner will not stick to the highly-charged areas of the drum.

To synchronize the output of data to the scanline, before the beam begins across the scanline of the drum, the **beam detect mirror** detects the initial presence of the laser beam by reflecting the beam to an optical fiber. The light travels along the optical fiber to the DC Controller, where it is converted to an electrical signal that is used to synchronize the data output. The signal is also used to diagnose problems with the laser or scanning motor.

When the writing process is complete, the area on the drum surface that is the image that will be created by the printing process contains a -100 V charge that will be used in the developing stage to transmit toner to the drum surface.

Step 4: Developing.   Figure 13-36 shows the developing step, in which toner is applied by the developing cylinder to the discharged areas of the drum. Toner transfers from the cylinder to the drum as the two rotate very close together. The cylinder is kept coated with a layer of toner, made of black resin bonded to iron, which is similar to the toner used in photocopy machines. The toner is held on the cylinder surface by its attraction to a magnet inside the cylinder. (A **toner cavity** keeps the cylinder supplied with toner.) A **control blade** prevents too much toner from sticking to the cylinder surface. The toner on the cylinder surface takes on a negative charge because the surface is connected to a DC power supply called the DC bias.

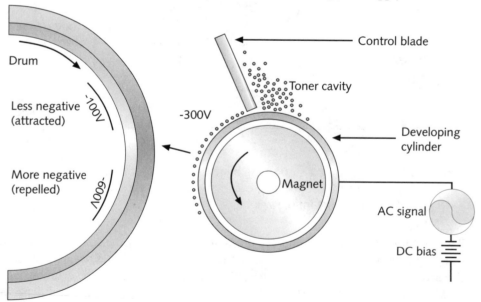

Figure 13-36   In the developing step, charged toner is deposited onto the drum surface

The negatively charged toner is less negative than the –100V on the drum surface but more negative than the –600V surface. Because of this fact, the toner is attracted to the less negative drum surface just as though the surface were positive. The toner is repelled from the drum surface that is more negative than it is. The result is that toner sticks to the drum where the laser beam has hit and is repelled from the area where the laser beam did not hit.

When you adjust the print density control of the laser printer, the result of this adjustment is that the DC bias charge is reduced or increased. When more charge is applied, more toner is attracted to the cylinder, which results in a denser print. Less charge results in a less dense print.

Step 5: Transferring.   In the transferring step, the transfer corona (shown in Figure 13–33) produces a positive charge on the paper that pulls the toner from the drum onto the paper that is passing between the transfer corona and the drum. The static charge eliminator (refer again to Figure 13-33) weakens the positive charge on the paper and the negative charge on the drum so that the paper does not adhere to the drum, which it would otherwise do because of the difference in charge between the two. The stiffness of the paper and the small radius of the drum also help to cause the paper to move away from the drum and toward the fusing rollers. If very thin paper is used in a laser printer, the paper can wrap around the drum, which is why printer manuals usually instruct you to use only paper designated for laser printers.

Step 6: Fusing.   The fusing step causes the toner to bond with the paper. Up to this point, the toner is merely sitting on the paper. The fusing rollers apply both pressure and heat to the paper. The toner melts, and the rollers press the toner into the paper. The temperature of the rollers is monitored by the printer. If the temperature exceeds an allowed maximum value (410° F for some printers), the printer shuts down.

INK-JET PRINTERS

Ink-jet printers don't normally provide the quality resolution of laser printers, but are popular because of their small size and their ability to inexpensively print color. Ink-jet printers work by spraying ionized ink (which means that it has an electrical charge) at a sheet of paper. Plates carrying a magnetic charge direct the path of ink onto the paper to form the desired shapes. Ink-jet printers tend to smudge on inexpensive paper, and they are slower than laser printers. Figure 13-37 shows one example of an ink-jet printer.

IMPROVING PRINTER PERFORMANCE

The speed of a small, desktop printer is dependent on the speed of the computer as well as that of the printer. If the printer is very slow, upgrading the computer's memory or the CPU may help. For a laser printer, if the bottom portion of a page does not print, the problem is that there is not enough memory, either on the PC or the printer. Upgrading memory on either the PC or the printer may solve the problem.

13

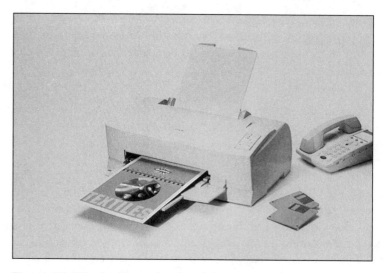

Figure 13-37   An example of an ink-jet printer

Many businesses use a switch box (sometimes called a T-switch) to share one printer between two computers. A printer cable connects to the printer port of each computer. The two cables connect to the switch box. A third cable connects from the switch box to the printer. A switch on the front of the box controls which computer has access to the printer. Switch boxes were built with older dot matrix printers in mind. They are not recommended for ink-jet or laser printers that use a bidirectional parallel cable.

CHAPTER SUMMARY

- Multimedia PCs and devices are often measured against the MPC specifications developed by the Multimedia PC Marketing Council, Inc.
- There are three published MPC standards known as Level 1, Level 2, and Level 3.
- MPEG is a lossy compression method for files storing full-motion video, where lossy compression refers to compressing data by eliminating some of the data.
- A frame buffer is the area of memory on a video card used to store one full screen of data.
- Interpolative scaling produces a more realistic-looking image on a screen when images are enlarged.
- Video cards that perform their own color space conversion are generally faster than those that require the CPU to do the conversion.
- MIDI is a standard for the transmitting and storage of synthesized sound and is used by many sound cards.
- A sound card uses a sampling method to convert analog sound to digital, which is called pulse code modulation or PCM.

- Two methods of synthesizing sound are FM and wavetable. The wavetable method is more expensive and more accurate than FM.
- The MMX Pentium chip improves the speed of processing graphics, video, and sound using improved methods of handling high-volume repetition during I/O operations.
- In order to take full advantage of MMX technology, software must be written to use its specific capabilities.
- A video card receives data from a system bus, stores it in memory on the card, converts it to an analog signal suitable for a monitor, and transmits it to the monitor.
- A graphics accelerator is a video card with an on-board processor that significantly speeds up the card.
- The amount of memory on a video card is determined by the size of the frame buffer and the size of the on-board video bus.
- The size of the frame buffer is determined by the amount of data it must hold to draw a full screen on the monitor. The amount of data is determined by the screen resolution and the number of colors.
- Memory on the video card can be dual-ported, which means that it is capable of handling input at the same time that it is handling output.
- SGRAM video memory is synchronous memory similar to SDRAM, but better able to manage graphic data.
- Window RAM (WRAM) increases the speed of a video card with a very wide data path of 256 bits.
- To optimize your use of a combination of monitors and video cards, match a low–end monitor to a low-end video card and a high-end monitor to a high-end video card.
- The six stages that a laser printer uses to print are: cleaning, conditioning, writing, developing, transferring, and fusing.
- Of the six stages of laser printing, the first four are performed inside the removable toner cartridge.
- Ink-jet printers print by shooting ionized ink at a sheet of paper.
- Installing a sound card includes physically installing the card, then installing the sound card driver and sound applications software. Windows 95 supports multimedia sound without using other applications software, but applications that usually come with sound cards enhance the ability to control various sound features.
- Digital cameras use light sensors to detect light and convert it to a digital signal stored in JPEG format.
- A DVD disc can store a full-length movie and uses an accompanying MPEG decoder card to decode the video before passing it on to the video card for display.

KEY TERMS

- **3D RAM** — Special video RAM designed to improve 3D graphics simulation.
- **Analog-to-digital converter (A/D or ADC)** — A component on a sound card that samples and converts analog sound into digital values that can be stored on hard drives.

13

- **Bandwidth** — The range of frequencies that a communications cable or channel can carry. In general use, the term refers to the volume of data that can travel on a bus or over a cable.

- **Beam detect mirror** — Detects the initial presence of a laser printer's laser beam by reflecting the beam to an optical fiber.

- **CODEC (COder/DECoder)** — A method of compressing and later decompressing sound, animation, and video files. MPEG is a common example.

- **Color depth** — The number of possible colors used by the monitor. Determines the number of bits used to compose one pixel. One of two characteristics (the other is screen resolution) that determine the amount of data sent to the video card to build one screen.

- **Color space conversion** — Converting images to RGB values before they are displayed. Processing is faster if the video card does the conversion instead of the CPU.

- **Control blade** — A laser printer component that prevents too much toner from sticking to the cylinder surface.

- **DAC (digital-to-analog converter)** — A component that converts digital data back into analog signals just before output from the computer. For example, DAC technology is used to convert digital sound to analog sound just before playback to the speakers.

- **Digital video disc (DVD)** — A faster, larger CD-ROM format that can read older CDs, store over 4 gigabytes of data, and hold full-length motion picture videos.

- **Dual ported** — When the video chip set (input) and the RAM DAC (output) can access video memory at the same time. A special kind of video RAM is required.

- **ELF (extremely low frequency)** — Very low-frequency monitor emission of magnetic fields. ELF guidelines are established to ensure that computers are safe and energy efficient.

- **Fixed frequency** — Monitors that only support a single refresh rate. Compare to multiscan monitors, which support different video cards and different refresh rates.

- **FM (frequency modulation) method** — A method of synthesizing sound by making a mathematical approximation of the musical sound wave. MIDI may use FM synthesis or wavetable synthesis.

- **Frame buffer** — An area of memory on a video controller that is used to store the data to be displayed on the screen.

- **Graphics accelerator** — A type of video card that has an on-board processor that can substantially increase speed and boost graphical and video performance.

- **Hertz (Hz)** — Unit of measurement for frequency, calculated in terms of vibrations, or cycles, per second. For example, a Pentium CPU may have a speed of 233 MHz (megahertz). For 16-bit stereo sound, 44,100 Hz is used.

- **Interpolative scaling** — A method used to fill in the gaps in an image to produce a more realistic-looking display when a small video window is enlarged to full-screen size.

- **JPEG (Joint Photographic Experts Group)** — A "lossy" graphical compression scheme that allows the user to control the amount of data that is averaged and sacrificed as file size is reduced. It is a common Internet file format. See Lossy compression.

- **Lossless compression** — A method that substitutes special characters for repeating patterns without image degradation. A substitution table is used to restore the compressed image to its original form.

- **Lossy compression** — A method that drops unnecessary data, but with image and sound loss. JPEG allows the user to control the amount of loss, which is inversely related to the image size.

- **MMX (Multimedia Extensions) technology** — A variation of the Pentium processor designed to manage and speed up high-volume input/output needed for graphics, motion video, animation, and sound.

- **MPC (Multimedia Personal Computer) specifications** — The minimum standards created by Microsoft and a consortium of hardware manufacturers for multimedia PCs.

- **MPEG (Moving Pictures Experts Group)** — A processing-intensive standard for data compression for motion pictures that tracks movement from one frame to the next, and only stores the new data that has changed.

- **Multibank DRAM (MDRAM)** — A special kind of RAM that is able to use a full 128-bit bus path without requiring the full 4 MB of RAM.

- **Musical Instrument Digital Interface (MIDI)** — Pronounced "middy," a standard for transmitting sound from musical devices, such as electronic keyboards, to computers where it can be digitally stored.

- **Pulse code modulation (PCM)** — A method of sampling sound in a reduced, digitized format, by recording differences between successive digital samples instead of their full values.

- **Sample size** — Refers to samples taken when converting a signal from analog to digital. Sample size is a measure of the amount of storage allocated to storing a single measurement of a single sample. The larger the sample size, the more accurate the value and the larger the file sizes needed to store the data.

- **Sampling** — Part of the process of converting sound or video from analog to digital format, whereby a sound wave or image is measured at uniform time intervals and saved as a series of smaller representative blocks. (*See* Sampling rate.)

- **Sampling rate** — The rate of samples taken of an analog signal over a period of time, usually expressed as samples per second or Hertz. For example, 44,100 Hz is the sampling rate used for 16-bit stereo.

- **Scanning mirror** — A component of a laser printer. An octagonal mirror that can be directed in a sweeping motion to cover the entire length of a laser printer drum.

- **SGRAM (synchronous graphics RAM)** — Memory designed specifically for the video card processing that can synchronize itself with the CPU bus clock.

- **Single instruction multiple data (SIMD)** — An MMX process that allows the CPU to execute a single instruction simultaneously on multiple pieces of data rather than by repetitive looping.

- **Telephony** — A term describing the technology of converting sound to signals that can travel over telephone lines.

- **Telephony Application Programming Interface (TAPI)** — A standard developed by Intel and Microsoft that can be used by 32-bit Windows 95 communications programs for communicating over phone lines.

- **Toner cavity** — A container in a laser printer that is filled with toner. The black resin toner is used to form the printed image on paper.

13

- **Video memory** — RAM chips on video cards that temporarily hold data coming from the CPU and going to the monitor.
- **Video RAM** or **VRAM** — RAM on video cards that allows simultaneous access from both the input and output processes.
- **Wavetable** — A table of stored sample sounds used to synthesize sound by reconstructing the sound from digital data using actual samples of sounds from real instruments.
- **WRAM (window RAM)** — Dual-ported video RAM that is faster and less expensive than VRAM. It has its own internal bus on the chip, with a data path that is 256 bits wide.
- **YUV** — A scheme of determining color by specifying brightness or luminance (Y), the color or hue (U), and the intensity or saturation (V).

REVIEW QUESTIONS

1. What type of compression can MPEG provide? How does it accomplish this?
2. Typically, how many frames per second are displayed with MPEG?
3. What term refers to the standard interface for computers to electronic sound devices, such as musical keyboards?
4. What sound card technology converts digital sound files back into analog signals just before output to the speakers?
5. How does MMX technology improve multimedia applications?
6. How do graphics accelerators increase video speed?
7. How much video RAM is required to produce a resolution of 800 × 600 with 65,000 colors?
8. Give three examples of monitor screen sizes. How are monitor screen sizes measured?
9. Which is faster and easier to view, an interlaced monitor or a noninterlaced monitor? Why?
10. List three common monitor resolution settings.
11. What type of monitor can offer a variety of refresh rates?
12. What are some of the features found in a "green" monitor?
13. What is the sampling rate (in Hz) of music CDs?
14. What are the two most common file extensions for sound files?
15. What effect could unshielded or very large speakers have on monitors if they are placed too close to the computer system?
16. What will happen if Windows 95 detects that a new sound card has been installed?
17. What would be a quick, short test to see if a sound card was successfully installed?
18. List four things to check if sound does not play after a sound card and CD-ROM are installed.
19. How can you adjust the sound volume in Windows?
20. List several common file extensions used with graphics files.
21. What size frame buffer is needed on a video card to hold the data for 1,280 × 1,024 screen resolution and 65,000 colors?
22. How much video memory should there be on the card in Question 21?

23. For each of the following pairs, state which item is analog and which is digital:
    a. Text stored on a floppy disc, handwritten note
    b. MIDI file, sound
    c. Monitor display, video memory
    d. A loading ramp, a flight of stairs
    e. A serial cable, a telephone line
24. What is the sample size of a sound card that meets the MPC1 specifications?
25. What is the sample size of a sound card that meets the MPC2 specifications?

PROJECTS

SOUND WHEN STARTING WINDOWS 95

1. Load the Windows Sound Recorder: click **Start**, **Programs**, **Accessories**, **Multimedia**, **Sound Recorder**.
2. Connect a microphone to the MIC jack on the sound card at the back of the computer.
3. Press the **Record** button and record a greeting message such as "Welcome to my computer."
4. Click on **File**, **Save as**, and then save the file as "Greeting" in the directory of \Windows\Start Menu\Programs\Startup.
5. Reboot the computer and your greeting should automatically play.

COMPARING SOUND QUALITY

1. Load the Windows Sound Recorder: click **Start**, **Programs**, **Accessories**, **Multimedia**, **Sound Recorder**.
2. Insert a music CD in the CD-ROM drive.
3. Press **record** in the sound recorder window and record a 15-second sound clip.
4. Click on **File**, **Save As** and save it as "SoundEx."
5. Open **Windows Explorer**, find "**Sound Ex**," and note its file extension and also its file size.
6. Click on **Edit**, choose **Audio Properties**. Press the **Customize** button and change the Attributes from a value such as 44,100 Hz, 16-bit, Stereo to 8,000 Hz, 8-bit, Mono. Save the file with a different name. Compare both the sound quality and file sizes of the two saved files.

WINDOWS 95 SOUND PROPERTIES

Using a PC with a sound card and speakers, create your own customized Windows 95 sound scheme using at least six events and four different sounds. Save the sound scheme file to a floppy disk. Take the file to another PC and install the sound scheme there.

13

USING NUTS & BOLTS TO EXAMINE MULTIMEDIA DEVICES

1. Using Nuts & Bolts Discover Pro, print a full description of your PC's sound, video, and printer functions. Include in the printout the amount of RAM that is stored on the video card.

2. What are the current resolution and number of colors of your monitor? Calculate the size of the frame buffer required for these settings. Compare your results to the calculation made by Nuts & Bolts under System in Discover Pro.

USING MMX TECHNOLOGY

Research the market and list five software packages that claim to use MMX technology. *Hint:* See the Intel Web site for a list of software that uses MMX. The Web site is www.intel.com.

TROUBLESHOOTING SKILLS

1. A friend calls to say that he has just purchased a new sound card and speakers to install in his PC and wants some help from you over the phone. The PC already has a CD-ROM installed. Your friend has already installed the sound card in an expansion slot and connected the audio wire to the sound card and the CD-ROM. List the steps you would guide him through to complete the installation.

2. Suppose, in the previous situation, the audio wire connection does not fit the connection on the CD-ROM. You think that if the problem is that the audio wire will not work because of a wrong fit, perhaps you can improvise to connect audio from the CD-ROM drive directly to the sound card. You notice that the CD-ROM drive has a port for a headphones connection, and the sound card has a port for audio in. How might you improvise to provide this direct connection? Check your theory using the appropriate audio wire.

3. Work with a partner. Each of you set up a problem with a PC and have the other troubleshoot the problem. Some suggestions as to what problem to set up are:
   - Speaker cables disconnected
   - Speaker turned off
   - Speaker cable plugged into the wrong jack
   - Volume turned all the way down
   - MSCDEX.EXE not called in the AUTOEXEC.BAT file for DOS
   - MSCDEX.EXE file missing

   As you troubleshoot the problem, write down the initial symptoms of the problem and the steps you take towards the solution.

PURCHASING A PC OR BUILDING YOUR OWN

This chapter presents guidelines to follow when purchasing a new PC and also presents detailed step-by-step procedures for building a PC from parts. For low-volume purchases of computers, such as for your own personal use, consider assembling a PC yourself, not necessarily to save money, but to benefit in other ways. Other choices include purchasing a brand-name PC or a clone.

In deciding between a brand-name PC, such as IBM or Compaq, and a PC built from parts without recognizable names, after-sales service and support are probably the most prominent reasons to choose a brand-name PC, even though the cost may be higher. Important reasons for choosing to build your own PC rather than buying a comparable one already assembled are the knowledge gained and the fact that you will have complete control over every part purchased to make your own customized integrated system.

**IN THIS CHAPTER
YOU WILL LEARN:**

- ABOUT SOME GUIDELINES TO USE WHEN PURCHASING A PC
- REASONS WHY YOU MIGHT CHOOSE TO ASSEMBLE A PC YOURSELF
- HOW TO ASSEMBLE A PC FROM SEPARATELY PURCHASED PARTS

SELECTING A PERSONAL COMPUTER TO MEET YOUR NEEDS

So far, this book has been chock-full of information to help you make decisions concerning which computers, peripheral devices, operating systems, and software to buy and how to manage and maintain them once they are yours. However, hardware and software are changing daily, and it's important to stay informed if you make buying decisions or give advice about these decisions. There are three alternatives from which to choose when selecting a PC: buy a brand-name PC, buy a clone, or buy parts and assemble a PC yourself, which, in effect, results in your own personally designed clone.

A **brand-name PC**, sometimes called an IBM-compatible PC, is a PC with a recognizable name such as Compaq, Packard Bell, Dell, Gateway, or IBM. A **clone** is generally understood to mean a PC that has been assembled by local companies without readily recognizable brand names and parts. (Brand-name PCs and clones once had entirely different meanings. Originally, the one and only brand-name PC was the IBM, and all other personal computers were called clones.) Brand-name and clone PCs each have advantages and disadvantages when considering warranties, service contracts, and ease of obtaining replacement and added parts. For instance, while it may seem advantageous that brand-name PCs and most clones come with some software already installed, the software is not necessarily standard, brand-name software. The pre-installed software may be any variety of shareware, unknown software, or the like, and the documentation and original installation disks for the software may not be included in the total package.

When selecting a computer system that will include both hardware and software, begin by taking a high-level view of the decisions you must make. Start by answering these questions:

- What is the intended purpose of this computer? (How will it be used?)
- What functionality do you want the computer to have (as determined by its intended purpose)?
- What hardware and software do you need to meet this functionality?
- What is your budget?
- If you determine that a clone meets your needs, do you want to assemble it yourself ?

In order to make the best possible decision, consider the first question to be the most important, and each succeeding question less important than the one before it. For example, if you intend to use the computer for playing games and accessing the Internet, the functionality required is considerably different than for a computer used for software development. Listed below are some examples of possible answers to the first question. A computer may be intended for these purposes:

- To access the Internet
- To play games

- To use software stored on a file server while connected to a LAN
- For Windows software development
- For business applications on a standalone PC or on a LAN
- For computing-intensive engineering or mathematical applications such as CAD/CAM
- To provide help-desk support with online remote control of other computers
- For multimedia presentations before large and small groups
- For use in a retail store, including cash register support
- For network administration

After you have identified the intended purpose of the computer, list the functionality required to meet the needs of the intended purpose. For example:

- If the computer is to be used for playing games, some required functionality might be:
  - Ability of the hardware to support games software
  - Excellent video and sound
  - Sophisticated input methods
- If the computer is to be used for Windows software development, required functionality might include:
  - Standard hardware and software environment that most customers using the developed software might have
  - Software development tools and hardware to support the software
  - Comfortable keyboard and mouse for long work hours
  - Removable, high-capacity storage device for easy transfer and storage of developed software
  - Reliable warranty and service to guarantee minimal "downtime"

Once the required functionality is defined, the next step—defining what hardware and software are needed—is much easier. Research what hardware and software meet the desired functions. For example, if a comfortable keyboard designed for long work hours is a required functionality, begin by researching the different types of keyboards available, and try out a few in the stores if necessary. It would be a mistake to purchase the cheapest keyboard in the store for this intended purpose. However, for game playing, an expensive, comfortable keyboard is not needed. For game playing, spend the least amount of money on a keyboard and put your resources into a sophisticated joystick.

In the last example above, the least possible amount of downtime is a required functionality. This is a required functionality for many business-use computers, and the one most important reason a business chooses a brand-name computer over a clone.

14

Brand-Name PC vs. Clone

As you have most likely noticed, brand-name PCs generally cost more than clone PCs with similar features. One reason that brand-name PCs cost more is that you are paying extra money for after-sales service. For example, an IBM personal computer comes with a three-year warranty, a 24-hour service help line with a toll-free number, and parts delivered to your place of business. A clone manufacturer may also give good service, but this may be due to the personalities of a few employees, rather than to company policies. Most likely, clone company policies will not be as liberal and all-encompassing as those of a brand-name manufacturer.

On the other hand, many brand-name manufacturers use nonstandard parts with their hardware and nonstandard approaches to setting up their systems, making their computers more **proprietary** than clones. Proprietary systems are ones that are unique to a particular vendor (or proprietor), often forcing customers to use only parts and service from that vendor. One of the most common things a brand-name manufacturer does to make its computer more proprietary is put components on the systemboard rather than use more generic expansion cards. Remember from earlier chapters that an easy way to tell if ports are coming directly off a systemboard is to look at the back of the PC. If ports are aligned horizontally on the bottom of a desktop PC or vertically down the side of the tower-case PC, these ports most likely come directly off the systemboard, making it more likely to be a proprietary-type board.

For example, a brand-name system may include video, sound, or network logic on the systemboard rather than on an expansion card. Or rather than CMOS setup being updated by a setup program in BIOS, the setup program may be stored on the hard drive. The shape and size of the computer case may be such that a standard systemboard does not fit; only the brand-name board will do. These kinds of things make upgrading and repair of brand-name PCs more difficult. You are forced to use the brand-name parts and brand-name service to maintain and/or upgrade the PC.

Selecting Software

When selecting software, go back to the required functionality that you have identified, which drives your decisions about software selection. Choose the operating system first, according to guidelines presented in Chapter 2. When choosing applications software consider these things:

- What do you want the software to do? (This will be defined by your answer to the functionality question above.)

- Is compatibility with other software or data required?

- Is training available, if you do not already have the skills needed to use the software?

- How good is the documentation?

- What are upgrade policies?

- How well-known or popular is the software? (The more popular, the more likely you'll find good training materials, previously trained people, technical support, and other compatible software and hardware.)

Caution is in order if you are buying a brand-name or clone computer that has pre-installed software that you are not familiar with. The software may not provide the functionality that you need, and may not have good documentation or reliable upgrades or support. Unless you feel that you have the skill to manage this software, you're probably better off staying with mainstream-market software. One way to identify which brand of software is the most prevalent in the industry is to browse the computer books section of a local bookstore, looking for the software that has the most "how to" books written about it. Also see trade magazines, the Internet, and your local retailer.

SELECTING HARDWARE

When selecting hardware, the two most important criteria are compatibility and functionality. Begin with the systemboard. See Chapter 3 for more information about how to select one.

- If you plan to use Windows 95 on a PC, choosing a PC that is made up of 100 percent Plug-and-Play components is of value, but not necessary. Be certain, however, that the BIOS is Plug-and-Play.

- If you intend to use the PC for multimedia applications, including games, you will want the MMX technology for the CPU and plenty of memory and drive space.

- If you plan to use the PC for heavy network use, buy a PC with plenty of processing power.

- If Internet access is important, don't skimp on the modem, and, if it's an external modem, be sure to include a high-speed serial port in your requirements.

- When selecting a computer case, keep in mind that tower cases generally offer more room than desktop units, and are easier to work with when adding new devices. Make sure the case has a reset button and, if security is an issue, a key lock in order to limit access to the inside of the case. Some cases even have a lock on the floppy drive so that booting from a floppy disk is secured in order to prevent a security breach.

14

SELECTING A TOTAL PACKAGE

When selecting a complete computer package including hardware and software, consider these things:

- Are the hardware and software compatible with those found on the general market? (For example, if you wanted to upgrade your video card or word processor, how difficult would that be?)

- What is the warranty and return or exchange policy?

- What on-site or local service is available? Do you know of anyone who has used this service, and were they satisfied?

- Is the system Energy Star compliant?

- What software comes pre-installed?

- What documentation or manuals come with the system?

- Does the systemboard allow for expansion of RAM, both DRAM and SRAM?

- What expansion slots are not being used? (Always allow for some room to grow.)

- Can features such as video on the systemboard be disabled if necessary? (Refer back to Chapter 3 for other guidelines on selecting systemboards.)

- How much does the system cost?

When considering price, keep in mind that middle-range priced PCs are most likely to be network compatible and easily expandable; they offer a broader range of support, and have had extensive testing of vendor products for reliability and compatibility. Low-end priced PCs may not have been tested for network compatibility; they offer a limited range of support, and the quality of components may not be as high.

Concerning pre-installed software, remember that sometimes unneeded software is more of a hindrance than a help, taking up needless space. For example, it is not uncommon for a brand-name computer to come with three or four applications for Internet access (for example, America Online, CompuServe, Prodigy, and Internet Explorer). Typically, only one is needed.

PREPARING TO BUILD YOUR OWN PC

Assembling your own PC takes time, skill, and research, but it can be a great learning experience. You might even want to consider it your "rite of passage" toward being a PC technician. All your needed skills to be a PC technician are tested: research, knowledge of user needs and the computer market, planning, organization, patience, confidence, problem solving, and extensive knowledge of both hardware and software.

However, if you are considering buying parts and assembling your own PC, know that you will most likely not save money by doing so. The total price of all parts usually about equals the price of a comparable clone PC that is ready-built. However, there are several good reasons why you might want to assemble your own PC. Here are a few:

- Most of us like to build things. The whole process can be quite fun.

- Knowledge is power. The knowledge and experience gained in researching the parts to buy, studying the documentation, and finally actually assembling the PC can't be overemphasized.

- When you buy all the parts and software for a PC individually, you are also getting the documentation for each hardware component. This is most likely not the case when you buy a PC already assembled. If you plan to upgrade your PC later, having this documentation available is important.

- Many ready-built PCs come with software already preloaded. You may or may not be provided with the original CDs or disks for the installation. The documentation for preloaded software may also be limited. However, when you buy each software package individually, you have the installation disks, CDs, and documentation.

- When you purchase each computer part individually, you are more likely to understand exactly what you are buying, and you can be more particular about the selection of each component. You have control over the brand and features of each component in the PC.

Here are a few reasons why you might *not* want to build your own PC:

- If you are in a rush to get a PC up and running, assembling your own is probably not a good idea, especially if you are a first-time builder. The process takes time and requires patience, and the first time you do it, you most likely will make a few mistakes that will need to be resolved.

- Individual parts may be warrantied, but if you build your own PC, there is no overall warranty on the PC. If a warranty or a service agreement is important, then look for a ready-built PC with these services included.

- Don't plan to assemble a PC for the first time unless you have access to an experienced technician or some technical service center, in the event that you encounter a problem you cannot resolve. For example, you may buy all the parts from a store that has a service center. The store may offer to assemble the PC for you for a charge ($50.00 to $75.00 is about right). If you find you cannot resolve a problem, you can always go back to the store for this service.

- Don't assemble the PC to save money, because you probably won't.

GETTING READY FOR ASSEMBLY: SELECTING PARTS

If you have decided to buy parts and assemble a PC, expect the process to take some time. The systemboard and expansion cards are full of jumper switches, connections, and ports, and the documentation must be carefully read to determine just how to configure the systemboard and all components to work together. Technicians in service centers can assemble a PC in less than an hour—but they have already assembled the same group of parts many times!

Planning the assembly of a PC is like packing for a camping trip to a remote location. You must plan for everything you will need before you begin. As you select and purchase each part, two things are important: part functionality and compatibility with other parts.

Every computer needs these essentials: systemboard, CPU, RAM, hard drive, floppy drive, case, power supply, video card, monitor, keyboard, and mouse. And, most likely, you will also want a CD-ROM drive, sound card, and modem. Make careful and informed decisions about every part you buy. Selecting each component requires revisiting your functionality, compatibility, and budget needs and determining what parts meet your criteria. Select the systemboard first, and then select the rest of the parts around this one most important component. Remember from Chapter 3 that the Intel chip set is preferred to other brands of chip sets. Also, if you want to be assured that your systemboard will be compatible with other components, the systemboard you buy should be made by Intel as well.

When selecting parts, including the systemboard, carefully examine the documentation. Look for good documentation that you can understand without struggling. When buying

14

parts for your first assembly, you should probably not use mail order. Buy from a reputable local dealer who will allow you to examine a part and look at the documentation, and who is willing and able to answer any technical questions you may have. Know the return policy of the store and the manufacturer's warranty for the part.

If you can buy the systemboard, CPU, and memory from the same dealer, who can help you determine that all three are compatible, do so to avoid later problems with compatibility. The documentation for the systemboard is quite valuable. Make sure it's readable and complete. Does the CPU need a voltage regulator, heat sink, or fan? Ask the dealer for recommendations, and read the documentation for the CPU.

After you have selected the systemboard, RAM, and CPU, select the case and accompanying power supply. Remember the two rules: the case must meet your predetermined functionality, and it must be compatible with other parts (especially the systemboard). Next, select the hard drive and other drives. Does your BIOS on the systemboard support the IDE or SCSI hard drive selected? Is there an IDE adapter on the systemboard? Are ports available for the CD-ROM drive, floppy drive, removable drive, and the like?

If the video logic is not included on the systemboard (for clone systemboards it probably will not be), select the video card next and make sure that you have a PCI slot to accommodate it. Next, select the hard drive, CD-ROM drive, and floppy drive and then the peripherals, including a mouse, keyboard, and monitor.

Getting Ready for Assembly: Final Preparations

When all parts are purchased, prepare the assembly well. Prepare a work area that is well lit and uncluttered. Read all the documentation and plan the assembly through, from beginning to end, before you start. If you have questions or are unsure how to proceed, find the answers to your concerns before you begin. For example, if you're not sure how to set the jumpers on the systemboard even after you have read the documentation, take the documentation to your technical support (dealer, service center, a knowledgeable friend) and ask for help in interpreting the settings in the documentation before you start the work.

While working, don't get careless about protecting against static electricity (and review the safety precautions at the beginning of this book). Always use the ground strap on your wrist. Work methodically and keep things organized. If you find yourself getting frustrated, take a break. Remember, you want the entire experience to be fun!

Building a Personal Computer, Step by Step

This section is a step-by-step, detailed description of building a Pentium PC from parts, with hard drive, floppy drive, CD-ROM drive, and a SCSI card to support a scanner. Depending on what you have decided you want your computer for, and what functionality and budget you are operating with, you may choose to build a slightly different PC, with a different CPU and different parts. While we do not have the space to provide instructions on the assembly of many different PCs, the example below will provide you with background and guidance, and demonstrate how to approach the task at hand.

The text describes some of the problems actually encountered during an assembly. I wish I could invite you to work beside us, reading the documentation for that jumper setting, deciding just which card should go in which slot for the best overall fit, and enjoying the pleasure of turning on the PC and seeing it boot up for the first time. However, the best I can do is invite you into the experience through this book. My hope is that you will one day have the opportunity to experience it for yourself.

> Unless you follow proper procedures, working inside your computer can cause serious damage—to both you and your computer. To assure safety in your work setting, follow every precaution listed in the *Read This Before You Begin* section following this book's Introduction.

OVERVIEW OF THE ASSEMBLY PROCESS

The research done and the parts purchased, organize everything you'll need to assemble the PC. Have the parts with the accompanying documentation and software available together with your PC tools. You'll need a safe place to work, with a ground mat and ground strap. Be careful to follow all the safety rules and precautions discussed in the preface.

Figure 14-1 shows the parts purchased for the PC before the beginning of the assembly:

- Standard monitor
- Case with power supply
- Systemboard
- SIMMs
- Video card

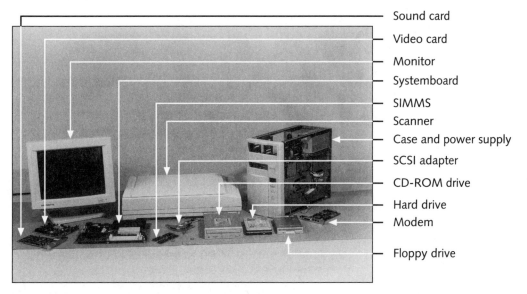

Figure 14-1   The parts of a PC before assembly

- Hard drive
- Floppy drive
- CD-ROM drive
- Sound card
- Modem
- SCSI host adapter (to interface with a scanner)
- Mouse and keyboard (not shown in Figure)

The general steps to assemble the PC are as follows:

1. Set the jumpers on the systemboard
2. Install the CPU and CPU fan
3. Install RAM on the systemboard
4. Verify that the systemboard is working by performing a memory test
5. Install the systemboard in the computer case
6. Connect the serial and parallel ports to the systemboard
7. Install the floppy drive
8. Install the hard drive
9. Install the CD-ROM drive
10. Install the sound card
11. Install the modem
12. Install the SCSI host adapter
13. Install the speaker
14. Install the video card
15. Connect essential peripherals
16. Set CMOS and install the operating system
17. Install the case cover
18. Connect the scanner

STEP 1: SETTING THE JUMPERS ON THE SYSTEMBOARD

This section describes how to set jumpers on the systemboard to configure hardware; the jumpers and their functions are listed in Table 14-1. Figure 14-2 shows a diagram of the systemboard with the main parts identified. When doing an installation, read the systemboard documentation carefully, looking for the type of information in the table, and set the jumpers according to the hardware you will be installing, which may differ from what appears here. For example, although this systemboard does not require that a jumper be set to indicate what type of CPU is installed, many systemboards do have a jumper for this purpose.

Table 14-1   Jumper settings on the systemboard

Jumper Groups on the Systemboard	Description
JP 8 and JP 9	Controls CPU bus clock selection
JP 11	CPU core to bus clock ratio selection
JP 13	Controls CPU voltage selection
JP 14	CMOS RAM clearance (clears CMOS settings)
JP 30, JP 31, and JP 33	Cache size selection

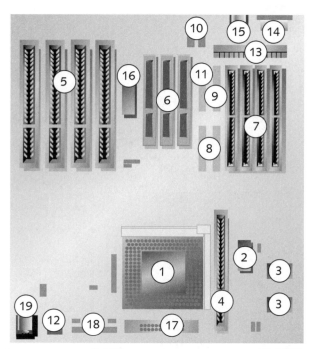

14

1. CPU socket
2. TAG SRAM chip
3. Cache SRAM chips
4. Cache slot
5. ISA expansion slots
6. PCI expansion slots
7. SIMM module sockets

8. IDE connectors
9. Floppy drive connector
10. Serial port connectors
11. Parallel port connector
12. IR port connector
13. Power connector
14. Keyboard connector

15. PS/2 mouse header
16. BIOS ROM
17. VRM header
18. Front panel connector
19. Battery (CR2032 Lithium)

Figure 14-2   Systemboard layout

One of the most time-consuming steps of assembling a PC is setting the jumpers on the sys-temboard—or rather studying the systemboard documentation to learn how to set the jumpers. (Once you know how to set them, doing so is quick and easy.) The documentation for the systemboard used here is really very good. Every jumper is clearly marked, and the settings for the jumper are clearly explained. That is not always the case.

First, locate the jumper groups on the systemboard. Figure 14-3 shows the diagram of the systemboard with the jumpers clearly marked, and Table 14-1 lists the five major jumper groups and what they control. Each jumper group will be discussed in turn to determine what they do and what settings they should have. As each jumper set in the documentation is examined, one setting for each jumper group will be marked as a default setting. Normally this is the setting that the factory uses. If you want to use the default setting, check to see that the jumper is set as indicated, because sometimes the factory sets the jumpers differently from what is listed in the documentation as the default.

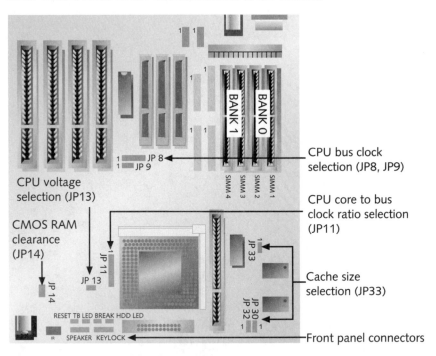

Figure 14-3   Systemboard jumper locations

Also, occasionally the wrong documentation will be shipped with a systemboard, or the doc-umentation will have an error. After power-up, if you have problems because the system is incorrectly sensing your systemboard configuration, double-check your settings. If you don't find an error, suspect the problem may be with the documentation. If your systemboard manufacturer has a Web site, check it for the latest information about jumper settings.

Jumpers are set to the closed position by placing a small cap across a pair of pins. An open jumper has no cap across the pair. If you want to set the jumper to open, you can place the unused cap on one of the two pins, so as to make it easy to find later when you might want to use it. This is called "parking" the jumper. Take out your systemboard and documentation and set the following jumpers:

CPU Bus Clock Selection: JP 8 and JP 9

The CPU bus clock selection jumpers determine the speed of the CPU bus. They, together with the jumper that sets the CPU core to bus clock ratio (JP 11), determine the overall speed of the PC. Figure 14-4 shows the four different configurations for these jumpers, where dark shading over two pins indicates that they are closed, and white indicates that the pins are open. (The darkened pins will always be in pairs because a jumper cap closes two pins by connecting the pair.) Generally, in documentation, expect pin 1 to be marked as a square, and other pins as circles. On the systemboard, a very small 1 is sometimes imprinted next to pin 1. The jumper numbers, in this case JP 8 and JP 9, are also imprinted on the systemboard.

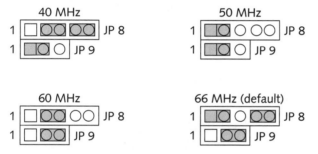

Figure 14-4   Jumper settings for CPU bus clock selection

Remember, from Chapter 3, that the Pentium local bus runs at 66 MHz (see Figure 3-19 of Chapter 3), which, as Figure 14-4 shows, is the default setting for JP 8 and JP 9 on the systemboard. This is the setting you want for all Pentium CPUs unless you know that the CPU you are installing is not rated for this fast a speed. (When making these selections, don't confuse the Pentium CPU bus speed with the CPU core speed, which is much faster, up to 300 MHz at the writing of this book.) For this assembly, proceed as follows:

- Locate the JP 8 and JP 9 jumpers on the systemboard.
- Set the jumpers according to the fourth configuration in the figure.

CPU Core to Bus Clock Ratio Selection: JP 11

The systemboard documentation here describes the different CPU core to bus clock ratios that the board supports. In the example, JP 11 determines the ratio of the CPU clock speed to the bus clock speed. There are four different configurations for this jumper with 6 pins, for multiples of 1.5, 2, 2.5, and 3, as seen in Figure 14-5. The CPU has been rated to run with a bus speed of 167 MHz, so a multiple of 2.5 is selected, which is the third configuration (167 MHz = 66 MHz × 2.5). It is possible that the system could run well at 200 MHz, even though the CPU is only rated at 167 MHz. However, the setting for the recommended speed is made, since that is the speed supported by the manufacturer. Your system may have different ratios, and your CPU may be rated for a different speed, but you can determine the ratio as we did above. For this assembly, proceed as follows:

- Locate JP 11 on the systemboard.

- Set the jumper group to the third configuration shown in Figure 14-5.

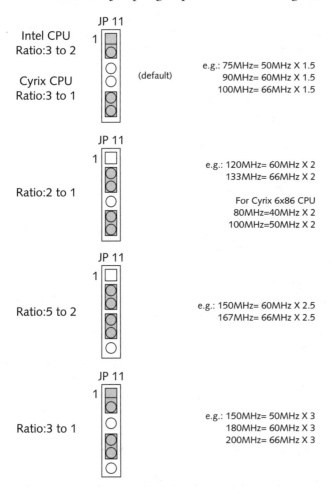

Figure 14-5   Jumper settings for CPU core to bus clock ratio selection

CPU Voltage Selection: JP 13

Jumper 13 is used to select CPU voltage. The CPU voltage selection is set according to the requirements specified for the CPU, which you should be able to find in your CPU documentation. The documentation for the systemboard tells you what voltages are supported and how to make the settings. Figure 14-6 shows that, for our system, there are two choices for the voltage: 3.3 V or a range of 3.45 V to 3.6 V, and the CPU documentation tells us that our CPU needs 3.45 V to 3.6 V. Proceed as follows:

■ Check the documentation for the CPU to determine what the voltage should be set to. In our example, the second option is required, 3.45 V to 3.6 V.

■ Find JP 13 on the systemboard and put the jumper in place.

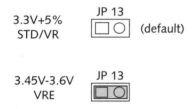

Figure 14-6   Jumper settings for CPU voltage selection

Cache Memory Selection: JP 30, JP 32, JP 33

Looking back at Figure 14-2, Items 2, 3, and 4, we see that there are three components on the systemboard that can collectively make up cache memory: one TAG SRAM chip (Item 2), two cache SRAM chips (Item 3) that are Data SRAM, and one cache slot (Item 4) that can hold a COAST module (Cache-On-A-Stick is a cache memory module). What is present in each of these locations, constituting the total cache memory on the systemboard, is made known to the BIOS by means of the following jumper group: JP 30, JP 32, and JP 33. There are three possible configurations for cache, which are shown in Figure 14-7. Option 14-7a uses the two Data SRAM chips and the one Tag SRAM chip, which altogether make 256 KB of on-board cache. The COAST slot is empty in this configuration. In option 14-7b, the Tag and Data SRAM chips are present as well as a 256 KB COAST module. In option 14-7c, the Tag and Data SRAM chips are not present, and there is one COAST module in the slot, which can be either a 256 KB or 512 KB module. In our example, we have no COAST module in the slot, but we do have the Tag and Data SRAM chips on the board, so we select the option shown in Figure 14-7a. Proceed as follows:

■ Locate JP 30, JP 32, and JP 33 on the systemboard.

■ Set the jumpers according to the option shown in Figure 14-7a.

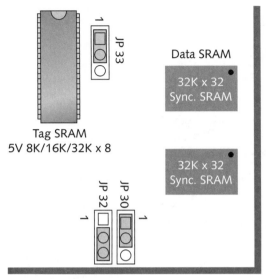

a) 256KB cache on board

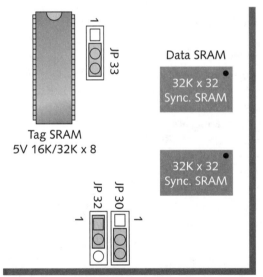

b) 256KB cache on board and 256KB cache module make a total 512KB. Note: Only cache module designed following Intel COAST specification will work in this configuration.

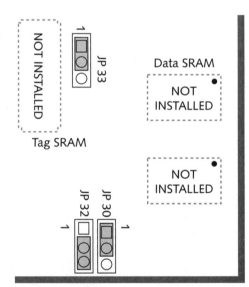

c) 256KB/512KB cache module: Neither tag SRAM nor Data SRAMs are installed

Figure 14-7 Jumper settings for cache memory selection for three different arrangements

CMOS RAM Clearance: JP 14

Closing (capping) JP 14 clears CMOS, should that ever be necessary in order to remove a forgotten password or erase improper, but forgotten, CMOS changes. We leave the jumper open (uncapped) for now. It's best to park the jumper cap on one pin.

STEP 2: INSTALLING THE CPU AND CPU FAN

After the jumpers are set, the next step is to install the CPU on the systemboard. Figure 14-8 shows the alignment of the Pentium CPU into the ZIF socket on the systemboard. The processor should seat easily with no force. Figure 14-9 shows the processor with the cooling fan already attached, ready to be seated into the ZIF socket. Proceed as follows:

- Align the blunt end of the CPU with the diagonally arranged pinholes on the corner of the socket, and seat the processor. When you do this, pay attention to the 1 that is usually printed on the systemboard at this corner to help orient the processor in the slot.

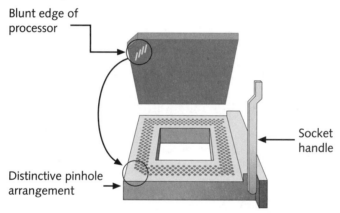

Figure 14-8   ZIF socket and the Pentium CPU

14

Figure 14-9   CPU with cooling fan ready to be inserted into the ZIF socket

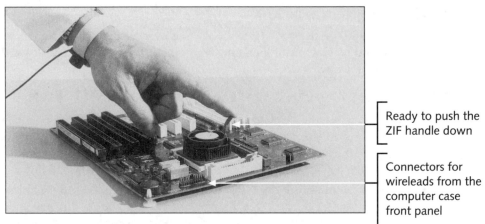

Ready to push the
ZIF handle down

Connectors for
wireleads from the
computer case
front panel

Figure 14-10   Close the ZIF socket handle to complete the
seating of the processor

- Push the ZIF handle down to secure the processor in place, as seen in Figure 14-10.

When the CPU for this computer was purchased, the cooling fan had already been sealed to the processor. Sometimes this will not have already been done. In this case, you will need to seat the processor first, and then place **thermal grease** on top of the processor, followed by the cooling fan and the cooling fan clip. If this is the case, proceed as follows:

- After the processor is in place and the ZIF handle is pushed down, apply a thin, even layer of thermal grease to the top of the processor, using a thermal grease applicator such as the one in Figure 14-11. It is very important not to use too much thermal grease, as it is difficult to remove and very messy.

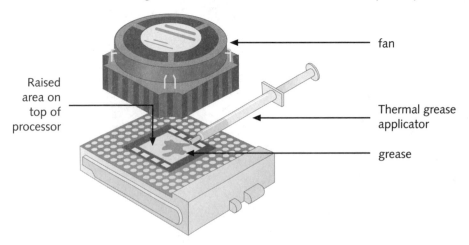

fan

Raised
area on
top of
processor

Thermal grease
applicator

grease

Figure 14-11   Apply the thermal grease with the applicator to the top of the processor

- Next firmly press the cooling fan heat sink onto the thermal grease until you feel the heat sink contact the metal of the processor.

- Wipe off any excess thermal grease.

Figure 14-12 shows the last step to secure the cooling fan to the processor. The cooling fan we will use comes packaged with a cooling fan clip.

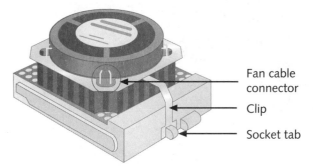

Fan cable connector

Clip

Socket tab

Figure 14-12   The cooling fan is secured to the processor with a clip

Proceed as follows:

- Slip the yoke of the clip under the fan cable connector to encircle the fan housing. The ends of the clip slip over small tabs on the socket of the systemboard.

- After the cooling fan is secured to the CPU, attach the power wire from the cooling fan to one of the power connections coming from the power supply. The wire connection is keyed so that it will only attach in one orientation to the power cord. The wire is made of two wires, one black, the other red. The black wire is ground, and the red wire is +12 V.

Some CPUs come with a large heat sink on top of the CPU housing instead of a cooling fan. Some consider a heat sink more reliable because a cooling fan may fail. Heat sinks do not require a wire connection to the power supply.

Figure 14-13 shows the systemboard with jumpers set and CPU installed. Compare this photograph with the diagram in Figure 14-2. Item 17 in Figure 14-2 is labeled VRM Header. This is the **voltage regulator module** (**VRM**) socket, which is used to support other Pentium processors that require different voltages than are normally available on the systemboard. The VRM converts the system power supply voltage to the voltage required by the CPU. The Pentium we used does not need this support. Your CPU documentation will give you the details about voltage regulation.

14

Figure 14-13 Systemboard with CPU installed

STEP 3: INSTALLING RAM ON THE SYSTEMBOARD

From discussions in Chapter 9, you know how to select the right kind of RAM and the right amount for your systemboard, and you know that you should be careful to match size, manufacturer, production batch, and mode. In our example, dynamic RAM for the systemboard is 32 MB made up of two 16 MB, 72-pin EDO SIMMs. The board allows 72-pin SIMMs in sizes of 4 MB, 8 MB, 16 MB, or 32 MB, used in pairs of matching speed, size, and mode. The two modes allowed are EDO and Fast Page mode. While your system may be different, it will most likely have some combination of SIMMs or DIMMs making up RAM. For this system, proceed like this:

- As shown in Figure 14-14, insert the two SIMMs into position in the RAM sockets. When inserting SIMMs, pay attention to the correct orientation for the module, placing the notched end of the module into the matching end of the slot.

- You can then slide the SIMM module into the slot at an angle.

- When the module has gone far enough into the slot, you can easily snap it into place by pushing forward slightly on the module.

Figure 14-14   Installing a SIMM module on the systemboard

STEP 4: VERIFYING THAT THE SYSTEMBOARD IS WORKING BY PERFORMING A MEMORY TEST

Before we get too far along in the details of installation, we do a quick verification that the critical components are working. To do this test, we connect the video card and connect power to the systemboard, plug in the monitor, and turn on the PC. We should get a good memory test (before the first error occurs saying that BIOS cannot find a boot device). By getting a good memory test, we know that the BIOS, RAM, CPU, most of the systemboard, and video are all working. If any one of these components fails, there is no purpose in continuing the installation until the problem is located or the part replaced.

Preventing the Systemboard from Grounding Out

When the electricity is turned on, it's important for the systemboard to not touch anything that might cause it to ground. Inside the computer case, the systemboard is kept from touching the case by plastic spacers, or **standoffs**, that come with the case and are attached to the board and the case. For our memory test, we also don't want the board touching the grounding mat, so we install the standoffs first.

14

To understand how the standoffs will later fit onto the back of the computer case, see Figure 14-15. The white standoffs, like the one in the photo, will first be inserted into the slots on the systemboard, and then these same standoffs will be set into the slots shown in the photo. When the systemboard is installed into the case, the standoffs will slide into the narrow, lower end of the slot to help hold the board securely in place. Proceed as follows:

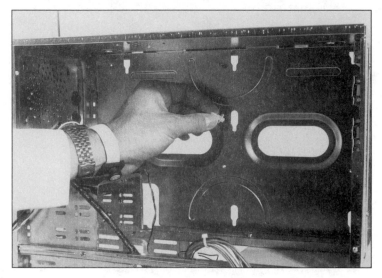

Figure 14-15   Spacers fit into slots on the computer case and on the systemboard to prevent the systemboard from grounding

- To determine in which slots to use the standoffs, align the systemboard with the case and consider the later position of the board in the case. To help orient the board to the case, remember that the expansion slots must fit up against the card slots on the back of the case.

- Insert the standoffs into the slots on the bottom of the systemboard, as in Figure 14-16.

Figure 14-16   Insert the spacers into slots on the bottom of the
systemboard

- Use as many standoffs as there are aligned slots. With this case and board, four standoffs can be used. The standoffs snap into position as you push them through the holes.

- If you need to remove a standoff to move it to a new slot, needle-nose pliers work well to squeeze the top of the standoff so that you can slide it out of the hole.

Installing the Video Card

The next step for our test is to temporarily install the video card on the systemboard. The diagram in Figure 14-17 shows the general layout of a Tseng Labs ET6000 video card, which we will use for our assembly.

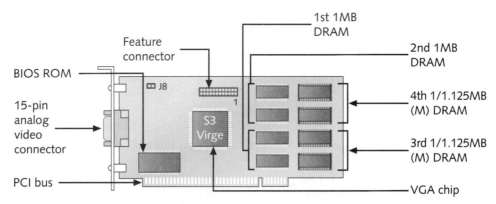

Figure 14-17   Layout of the video card

14

Two MB of DRAM is factory installed with chip sockets for another 2 MB of RAM. The video BIOS ROM chip is clearly identified on the board with a label. At the heart of the board is the S3 video chip. Proceed as follows:

- As in Figure 14-18, place the video card into position.
- When seating a card, push the card directly down into the expansion slot, as the photo illustrates.

An expansion card inserted into a systemboard that is not already installed in a case is vulnerable to damage. Be careful that you don't move the systemboard much once the card is installed, so that the card is not bent as the systemboard is moved about.

Figure 14-18 Install the video card on the systemboard so that memory can be tested before continuing with the installation

Powering Up and Watching for the POST Memory Test

In this next step, we connect the systemboard to the power supply and to the monitor, and perform POST in order to verify that critical parts are working.

- Set the systemboard near enough to the computer case so that the power cords can reach the power connections on the systemboard (see Figure 14-19).
- Connect the power cords, being certain that the power cords are in the correct slots. Connect them so that the black wires (ground) on each connection are in the center (black-to-black rule).
- Plug the video cable into the video port of the video card.
- Connect the power cords from the case and monitor to a wall outlet or surge suppressor.
- Before turning on the power, check again that all connections are secure, unused power cords are tucked safely out of harm's way, and the systemboard is not touching anything that would ground it, but is sitting firmly on the spacers, which are sitting on the ground mat.

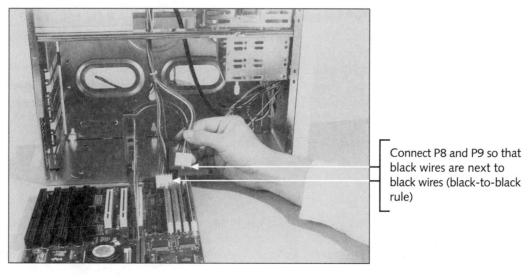

Figure 14-19   Connect the Power cords, P8 and P9, to the
                   systemboard

Connect P8 and P9 so that
black wires are next to
black wires (black-to-black
rule)

- Turn on the monitor and the PC and watch startup BIOS perform the POST
  test (see Figure 14–20).

- Look for POST to count up a full 32 MB of RAM on the monitor screen. Next,
  POST looks for hard drives and finds none, and then gives an error message when
  it also cannot detect a floppy drive or keyboard. This is all to be expected; however,
  the memory test does prove that the critical components of the system already
  installed are working, and that we can continue with the installation.

- Turn the computer and monitor off, remove the video card, and disconnect
  power cords (including the power cord from the power supply to the systemboard) before continuing the installation.

14

Figure 14-20   Memory test is successful

STEP 5: INSTALLING THE SYSTEMBOARD IN THE COMPUTER CASE

Installing the systemboard in the computer case may take more patience than installing other components. The case comes with the necessary spacers and screws, and most systemboards align well with most cases. However, sometimes the holes are difficult to align, and screws and spacers difficult to install. Proceed as follows:

- If you are using a tower case, lay it on its side so that you are installing the systemboard flat into the case, not vertically.

- After the spacers have been installed on the systemboard, insert the systemboard inside the case.

- Insert the spacers into the spacer holes in the case and move the systemboard in the correct direction so that the spacers slide into the narrow end of the slots on the case. You should feel the systemboard move snugly into position with all four spacers secure.

Securing the Systemboard to the Case

Just the spacers alone are not enough to securely hold the systemboard and prevent it from shifting when expansion cards and cables are later installed. To finish the installation, do the following:

- Locate at least three or four screw holes in both the board and the case that you can align and use to secure the board to the case in a stable, unmoving position.

- Insert the screws. Sometimes nylon washers are included to be used between the systemboard and the case or between the screw head and the systemboard.

- Don't quit until you have at least two screws tightly in position. Because a case is designed to fit more than one type of systemboard, there will be unused spacer holes as well as screw holes on the case. If you cannot locate a screw hole on the case, try tipping the case on its end so that you can see the bottom where the holes are. When finished, the systemboard should feel tightly stable and secure with no movement at all within the case.

- Replace the power cords, being very certain that P8 and P9 are oriented according to the black-to-black rule.

Figure 14-21 shows the systemboard securely attached to the case. Notice that one corner of the board had to go underneath the drive bays in the lower left corner of the photo. Two screws and one spacer that are visible are labeled in the figure. In the lower right corner of the figure, the two power cords from the power supply are attached to the systemboard.

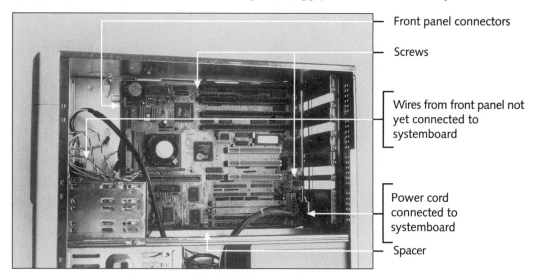

— Front panel connectors

— Screws

Wires from front panel not yet connected to systemboard

Power cord connected to systemboard

— Spacer

Figure 14-21   Systemboard is installed in the case

Attaching the Front Panel Connectors to the Systemboard

The next step to complete the installation of the systemboard is to connect the wire leads from the front panel of the case to the systemboard. You can see the front panel connectors in the diagram of Figure 14-2 as Item 18 and labeled in the photos of Figure 14-10 and Figure 14-21. The wires coming from the front panel of the case are also labeled in Figure 14-21.

There are seven connectors on the systemboard to accommodate the wires from the front panel. A diagram of these connectors is shown in Figure 14-22.

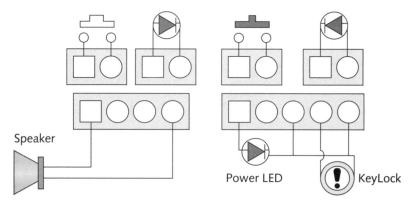

Speaker

Power LED   KeyLock

Figure 14-22   Diagram of front panel connectors on the systemboard

14

The connectors are really pins. A lead wire from the front panel may have pin holes for two, three, or four pins. The seven connectors are:

- Reset switch. Used to reboot the computer
- Turbo LED. Not used
- Break switch. Not used
- HDD LED. Light signifying that the hard drive is in use
- Key lock. For cases that have a lock-and-key access
- Speaker. Controls the speaker
- Power LED. Light indicating that power is on

The first five connectors all use a 2-pin connector. The speaker uses a 4-pin connector, and the power LED uses a 3-pin connector. A 3-pin connector similar to the power LED is shown in Figure 14-23.

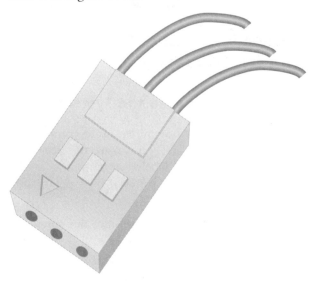

Figure 14-23   Look for the small triangle embedded on the wire lead connectors
to correctly orient the connector to the systemboard connector pins

Look for a small triangle embedded on the black connector that marks one of the outside wires that is used to orient the connector on the systemboard pins. When connecting a black connector to a lead on the systemboard, align the triangle on the connector with the pin on the systemboard that matches up with the square pin in the diagram.

The wires coming from the connector are color-coded, although the coding scheme for the wires is often not included in the computer case documentation. Some connectors have the name of the lead printed or embedded on the connector; the case we use does not have that. To know which wire lead goes to which connector on the systemboard, you must trace the wire back to its source on the front panel and often do a little guessing until you get the right lead wires connected to the right location on the systemboard. Sometimes you will not know if your guess is right until you power up and check out the reset button and LED lights on the front of the case. In general, proceed as follows:

- If the purpose of the wire lead is not written on the wire connector, then trace it back to its source to determine which lead belongs where.

- Locate the HDD LED by tracing it to the hard drive light on the front of the case. This lead causes the light to be lit when the hard drive is in use.

- Orient the lead to the pins by looking for the triangle on the lead connection and orienting it according to the diagram in Figure 14-22. Figure 14-24 shows the wire leads being connected to the systemboard connections.

Figure 14-24   Connect wire leads from the front panel of the computer case to the systemboard connections following the systemboard documentation diagrams

- The speaker lead is also easy to locate. The speaker that comes with the computer case attaches to the side of the case, and the wire from it connects to the speaker pins. In our assembly, we choose not to attach the speaker at this point to leave more room to work. The speaker will be added in one of the last steps of the assembly.

- The 3-pin lead from the power button on the front of the case is easy to spot and connect to the only 3-pin connection on the systemboard.

Our case does not have a key lock, so the key lock connection is not used. The break switch and the turbo LED, used on earlier computers, are not used.

STEP 6: CONNECTING SERIAL AND PARALLEL PORTS TO THE SYSTEMBOARD

Once again looking back at Figure 14-2, we see that the systemboard provides two serial port connectors (Item 10 in Figure 14-2) and one parallel port connector (Item 11 in Figure 14-2). Figure 14-25 shows a diagram of the serial, parallel, floppy disk, and IDE port connectors on the systemboard. Take a moment to locate these port connectors in the photo of the systemboard of Figure 14-13.

The computer case comes with a port adapter containing two serial ports with a data cable for each, which will connect to the systemboard. Figure 14-26 shows the two ports on the small adapter.

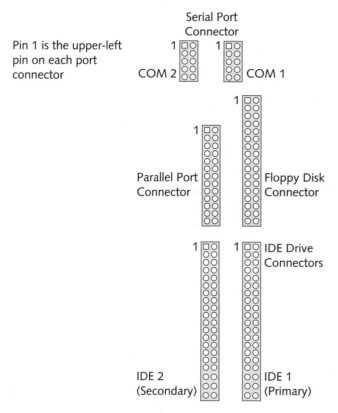

Figure 14-25   Diagram of I/O port connectors on the systemboard

Figure 14-26 Adapter with two serial ports and data cables to the systemboard

One port is a 9-pin, and the other a 25-pin connection. For this type of system, do the following:

- Look for the edge color on the cables to orient the cables to pin 1 on the systemboard connection.
- Connect the two cables to the COM 1 and COM 2 connections on the systemboard.
- Remove a plate cover from the back of the case and mount the port adapter in the empty slot, using the screw from the cover to secure the adapter.
- The parallel port adapter is connected in a similar way.

STEP 7: INSTALLING THE FLOPPY DRIVE

It's generally easier to install the floppy drive if you connect the data cable and the power cord to the rear of the drive before you slide the drive into the bay.

The floppy drive cable has two or more connections on it. Use the connection that fits your drive connection and has the twist in the cable behind the connection so that the

14

drive becomes drive A. Orient the cable so that the edge color aligns with pin 1 on the drive connection. Do the following:

- Attach the floppy drive data cable to the floppy drive connection, as in Figure 14-27.

- Connect the other end of the floppy drive cable to the floppy drive port connection on the systemboard, being careful to align the edge color on the cable to pin 1 on the systemboard connection (see Figure 14-28).

Figure 14-27   Connect the floppy drive data cable with the twist to the floppy drive

Figure 14-28   Connect the floppy drive data cable to the floppy drive connection on the systemboard

- Connect a power cord with one of the small connections for floppy drives to the drive, as in Figure 14-29. The cord can only connect in one direction.

- Slide the drive into the bay from the rear of the bay, and secure the drive to the bay with two screws on each side of the bay, as shown in Figure 14-30. Use the short screws that come with the computer case. Don't use extra long screws on any of the bays, or the screws may extend into the drives and damage a drive.

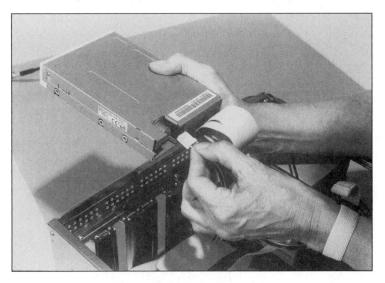

Figure 14-29   Connect a power cord to the floppy drive

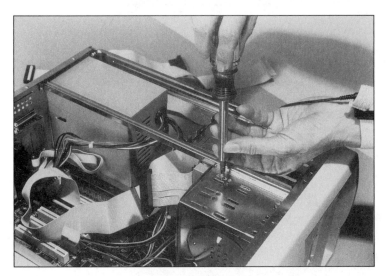

Figure 14-30   Complete the floppy drive installation by securing the drive in the bay with two screws on each side of the bay

14

STEP 8: INSTALLING THE HARD DRIVE

The next step is to install the hard drive, which in our case is a 2.4 GB Western Digital hard drive, shown in Figure 14-31. On the top of the drive housing is a diagram showing jumper settings to be used to designate the drive as single, master, or slave. In our case, we are installing this drive as a single drive on one of the two IDE controllers on the systemboard. The single drive setting does not require that any jumpers be closed. Figure 14-32 shows the rear of the hard drive where the jumper connector is sitting in a lengthwise position on the jumpers, meaning that no jumper setting is on. Jumpers on your hard drive may need to be set differently to accomplish the same configuration. Check the drive diagram or your documentation.

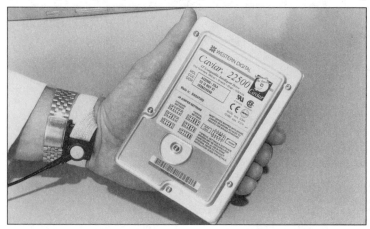

Figure 14-31   2.4 GB Western Digital hard drive with jumper settings printed on the top of the drive

In our case, do the following:

- Leave the jumper parked in this position rather than removing it so that, later, if a second drive is installed in this system, the jumper connector can be easily located.
- Connect the data cable that came with the drive to the 40-pin IDE connector on the rear of the drive as in Figure 14-33. Align the edge color on the data cable to pin 1 on the drive.

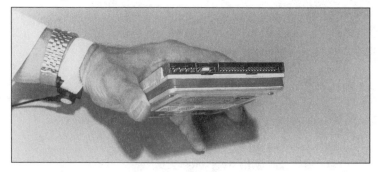

Figure 14-32   Leave the jumper connector in its factory-set position, which leaves all jumpers open

Figure 14-33   Connect the HD data cable to the hard drive,
aligning the edge color to pin 1 on the drive

- Attach the other end of the cable to the systemboard. Figure 14-34 shows this end of the IDE data cable ready to be connected to the IDE 1 (primary) controller on the systemboard. Notice that the edge color on the data cable is correctly aligned with pin 1 on the controller connection.

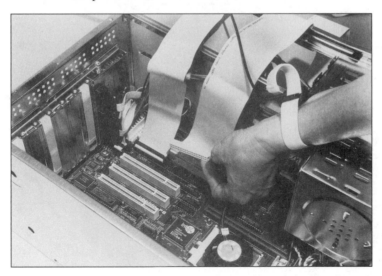

Figure 14-34   Connect the hard drive data cable to the IDE 1
primary controller on the systemboard

14

- Connect one of the power cords to the hard drive, as in Figure 14–35.
- Slide the hard drive into the rear of the bay and secure it with two short screws on both sides of the bay (see Figure 14–36).
- Snap the plastic bay cover into place on the front of the bay.

The hard drive installation is now complete.

Figure 14-35   Connect the power cord to the hard drive

Figure 14-36   Secure the hard drive in the bay with two screws on each side of the bay

STEP 9: INSTALLING THE CD-ROM DRIVE

In the next step, we install an IDE CD-ROM drive, shown in Figure 14-37. A drawing of the rear panel of the drive is shown in Figure 14-38 so that you can better read it. Moving from left to right across the drive are: first, the audio port for sound card direct connections; second, three jumpers labeled Cable Select, Slave, and Master; third, a 40-pin IDE port connection; and fourth, a connection for a power cord.

There are two IDE controller ports on the systemboard. We want to connect the CD-ROM drive to the secondary port so that it is not on the same cable with the hard drive, which would cause the slower performance of the CD-ROM drive to affect the hard drive performance. Proceed as follows:

- The factory default setting for the jumper is set to Slave, so move the jumper to the rightmost position, which is Master, since it will be the only device on the secondary ID port.

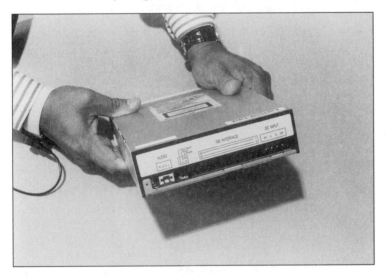

Figure 14-37 Rear panel of the IDE CD-ROM drive

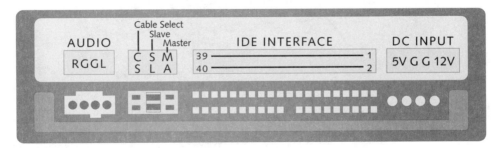

Figure 14-38 Diagram of the rear panel of the IDE CD-ROM drive

■ Looking at the location of the bay for the CD-ROM drive and the power cord, we decide to connect the data cable first (see Figure 14-39). Survey your own situation for the best approach. Slide the drive from the front of the bay partly into the bay, and then connect the power cord, as shown in Figure 14-40.

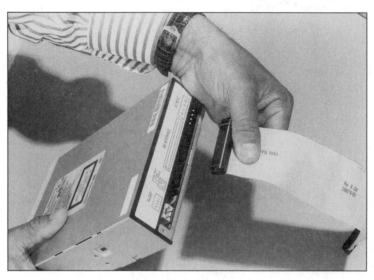

Figure 14-39 Connect a 40-pin IDE data cable to the CD-ROM drive

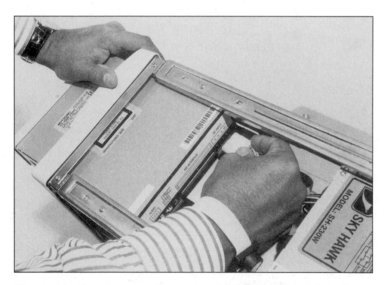

Figure 14-40 Connect the power cord to the CD-ROM drive while the drive is partway into the bay

Figure 14-41   Secure the CD-ROM drive to the bay with short screws on both sides of the bay

- Then slide the drive the rest of the way into the bay and secure it with screws on both sides of the bay, as in Figure 14-41.

The CD-ROM drive installation is now complete. The wire connecting the CD-ROM drive to the sound card will be installed after the sound card is installed.

Step 10: Installing the Sound Card

The next step is installing the sound card. Many sound cards have an IDE port connection to support a CD-ROM drive as well as a connection for an audio wire, so that sound can be piped directly from the CD-ROM drive to the sound card without using CPU resources. Our sound card has both, but we are only using the audio wire connection, and not the CD-ROM drive connection. For this arrangement, proceed as follows:

- Attach the wire to the sound card. Figure 14-42 shows the wire about to be attached.

- Install the sound card into one of the 16-bit ISA expansion slots on the system-board, and secure the card with a screw to the case, as shown in Figure 14-43.

- Attach the other end of the audio wire to the CD-ROM drive.

14

Figure 14-42   Attach the audio wire to the sound card and then to the audio connection on the CD-ROM drive

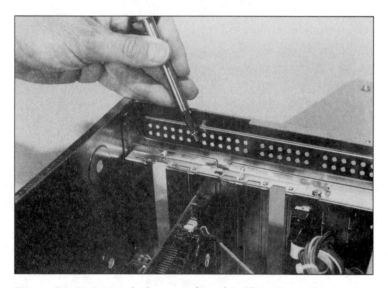

Figure 14-43   Attach the sound card to the case with a screw

STEP 11: INSTALLING THE MODEM

Our next step is to install an internal modem, as shown in the diagram in Figure 14-44. The ports on the back of the modem are shown in Figure 14-45. There are a line and a phone connector, a speaker and microphone port, and a bank of DIP switches on the back of the card. Also shown in Figure 14-44 and in Figure 14-46 are a bank of jumpers on the card itself. For some modems, the speaker and microphone ports can be used, together with software that accompanies the modem, to create a voice-quality answering machine on the PC.

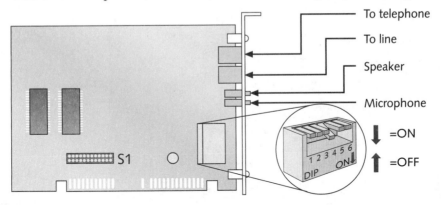

Figure 14-44   Diagram of the modem card

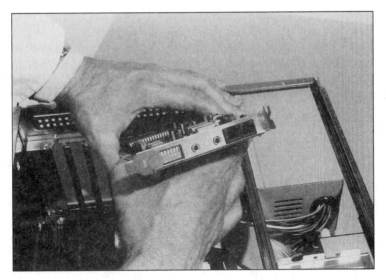

Figure 14-45   Ports and DIP switches on the back of the internal modem

14

Figure 14-46   Placing the last jumper into position on the internal modem

Whatever modem you use, the documentation should contain information such as that in the table shown in Figure 14-47, explaining the purpose of the card's DIP switches and jumpers.

	COM Port (address)	IRQ	DIP1	DIP2	DIP3	DIP4	DIP5	DIP6	S1
Non	1 (03F8)	4	ON	ON	OFF	OFF	ON	OFF	
	2 (02F8)	3	OFF	ON	OFF	ON	OFF	OFF	
PnP	3 (03E8)	5	ON	OFF	OFF	OFF	OFF	ON	Remove All Caps On S1
		4	ON	OFF	OFF	OFF	ON	OFF	
Mode	4 (02E8)	2	OFF	OFF	ON	OFF	OFF	OFF	
		3	OFF	OFF	OFF	ON	OFF	OFF	
PnP mode			OFF	OFF	OFF	OFF	OFF	OFF	Install All Caps On S1

Figure 14-47   Table of IRQ and COM port jumper and DIP switch settings

Although it may not at first be evident, the table tells you that by using a combination of DIP switches and jumpers, you can configure the modem for either Plug-and-Play or a variety of IRQ, COM ports, and I/O address settings. There is a bank of DIP switches on the outside of the card and one bank of jumpers on the card, labeled S1 in Figure 14-44. For example, in Figure 14-44, the fourth DIP switch is set to On, and all others are set to Off. Looking at Figure 14-47, we see on the right side of the figure that if you remove all the caps on all the jumpers on the card, you get the combination of jumper and DIP switch settings shown in the sixth line in the table, which, you can see in the figure is Non-Plug-and-Play Mode, COM 4, I/O address 02E8, and IRQ 3. After reviewing the modem documentation in some detail, proceed as follows:

- Because we want to use Plug-and-Play abilities, set the switches as indicated in the last row of Figure 14-47: leave all DIP switches off and install all caps on the entire bank of jumpers, as in Figure 14-46.

- After the jumpers and DIP switches are set, install the modem card in a 16-bit expansion slot on the systemboard and secure the card with a screw. Make sure, when you tighten the screw, that you don't put stress on the card alignment, which may cause it to move out of position. You may need to put a slight bend in the metal plate to align the card correctly.

The modem is now installed.

STEP 12: INSTALLING THE SCSI HOST ADAPTER

Next is the installation of a SCSI host adapter. The SCSI host adapter we use is shown in Figure 14-48 and supports only one single-ended SCSI device as evidenced by the 25-pin port on the back of the card. (Remember that differential SCSI devices use a 50-pin connection.) The card is set to use SCSI ID 7 and, since it will always be on one end of the SCSI chain, to provide termination on the SCSI bus. Figure 14-49 shows a diagram of the card with the jumpers marked. There are several jumpers on the card, which collectively make up the card configuration, including the IRQ, I/O address, SCSI parity, and SCSI disconnection.

Figure 14-48   Single-ended SCSI host adapter

14

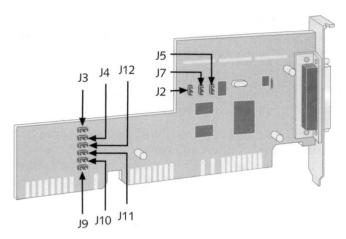

Figure 14-49   Diagram of the SCSI host adapter showing jumper
positions on the card

Figure 14-50 shows a table of jumper settings similar to that in the card documentation. After reviewing our options, we choose the default settings, which are IRQ 10, I/O address 140h, SCSI parity disabled, and SCSI disconnection disabled. When you're installing any card, don't forget to mark the selections you have made on the documentation. Later, if you want to know what settings have been chosen, you can look at the documentation rather than having to remove the case cover to see the card. Proceed as follows:

- Even though the jumpers should already be set to these settings according to the table in Figure 14-50, verify that they are set correctly on the card.

- Install the card in a 16-bit ISA expansion slot. Figure 14-51 shows the card installed.

SCSI Disconnection	J2	I/O Port Address	J5	SCSI Parity		J7
Enabled	Off	140h*	On	Enabled*		On
Disabled*	On	340h	Off	Disabled		Off

	IRQ Channel	J3	J4	J12	J11	J10	J9
On = Jumper	9	On	On	Off	Off	Off	On
Off = No Jumper	10*	Off	On	Off	Off	On	Off
	11	On	Off	Off	On	Off	Off
	12	Off	Off	On	Off	Off	Off

Figure 14-50   Table of jumper settings for the host adapter

Figure 14-51   SCSI host adapter installed

STEP 13: INSTALLING THE SPEAKER

The next step is to install the speaker, which all PCs have. Proceed as follows:

- Slide the speaker, which is included in the accessories to the case, into the tabs in the case. Figure 14-52 shows the speaker installed on the bottom of the tower case.

- Connect the wire from the speaker to the systemboard at the speaker connection shown earlier in Figure 14-22.

14

Figure 14-52   The speaker is installed on the bottom of the tower case

Step 14: Installing the Video Card

To complete the installation of components inside the computer case, reinstall the video card in one of the PCI expansion slots and secure it with a screw. Figure 14-53 shows the completed installation inside the case.

Figure 14-53   All components inside the case are installed

Step 15: Connecting Essential Peripherals

Before putting on the case cover, connect the mouse, keyboard, speakers, and monitor, and then install the operating system in order to ensure that everything inside the case is working.

Step 16: Setting CMOS and Installing the Operating System

The next step is to turn on the PC and make sure that CMOS settings accurately reflect the system. For our example, the Main Program screen of CMOS setup is shown in Figure 14-54, and the Standard CMOS Setup screen is shown in Figure 14-55.

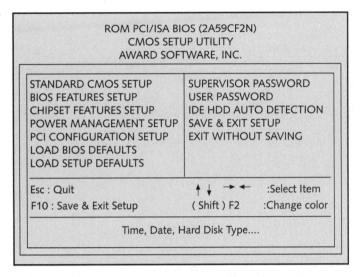

Figure 14-54 The main program screen of CMOS setup

We can set the hard drive type by either entering the values that are printed on the top of the hard drive or using the IDE HDD Auto Detection option shown in Figure 14-54 and allowing the BIOS to make the determination. Written on the top of the drive in Figure 14-31 is the following: 4960 cylinders, 16 heads, 63 tracks per sector, and 2559 MB. The CMOS supports either Normal mode, LBA mode, or Large mode. Proceed as follows:

- Turn on the PC and access Setup.
- Select the Hard Drive mode, and then choose to allow the BIOS to autodetect the drive. Because the drive has more than 1,024 cylinders, our choice is Large mode.
- Set drive A to 1.44 MB, 3.5-inch floppy disk.

14

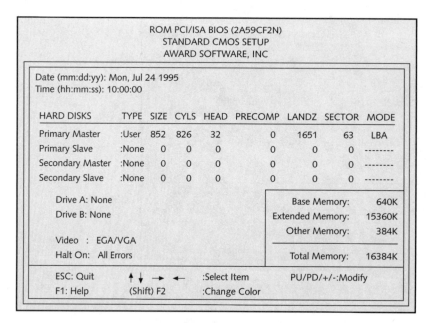

ROM PCI/ISA BIOS (2A59CF2N)
STANDARD CMOS SETUP
AWARD SOFTWARE, INC

Date (mm:dd:yy): Mon, Jul 24 1995
Time (hh:mm:ss): 10:00:00

HARD DISKS	TYPE	SIZE	CYLS	HEAD	PRECOMP	LANDZ	SECTOR	MODE
Primary Master	:User	852	826	32	0	1651	63	LBA
Primary Slave	:None	0	0	0	0	0	0	--------
Secondary Master	:None	0	0	0	0	0	0	--------
Secondary Slave	:None	0	0	0	0	0	0	--------

Drive A: None   Base Memory: 640K
Drive B: None   Extended Memory: 15360K
                                       Other Memory: 384K
Video : EGA/VGA
Halt On: All Errors   Total Memory: 16384K

ESC: Quit   ↑ ↓ → ←   :Select Item   PU/PD/+/-:Modify
F1: Help   (Shift) F2   :Change Color

Figure 14-55   Standard CMOS Setup screen

The only other change we need to make from the default settings of CMOS at this time is the boot sequence:

- From the main program menu in Figure 14-54, select BIOS Features Setup, which is shown in Figure 14-56.

- Change the Boot Sequence from C, A to A, C so that we can easily boot from a floppy disk to better control the PC while installing the OS and software.

- Save the settings and exit Setup.

- Reboot the PC with the bootable floppy disk that comes with Windows 95. If your copy of Windows 95 is an upgrade, then you will need to boot from a DOS bootable disk and load the CD-ROM drivers as discussed in Chapter 11.

- Follow the directions on the Windows 95 installation floppy disk to partition and format the hard drive and install Windows 95 from the CD-ROM drive. Be sure to make a rescue disk when given the opportunity during the installation.

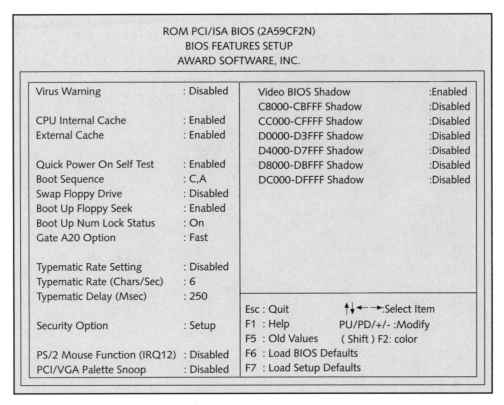

ROM PCI/ISA BIOS (2A59CF2N)
BIOS FEATURES SETUP
AWARD SOFTWARE, INC.

Virus Warning	: Disabled	Video BIOS Shadow	:Enabled
		C8000-CBFFF Shadow	:Disabled
CPU Internal Cache	: Enabled	CC000-CFFFF Shadow	:Disabled
External Cache	: Enabled	D0000-D3FFF Shadow	:Disabled
		D4000-D7FFF Shadow	:Disabled
Quick Power On Self Test	: Enabled	D8000-DBFFF Shadow	:Disabled
Boot Sequence	: C,A	DC000-DFFFF Shadow	:Disabled
Swap Floppy Drive	: Disabled		
Boot Up Floppy Seek	: Enabled		
Boot Up Num Lock Status	: On		
Gate A20 Option	: Fast		
Typematic Rate Setting	: Disabled		
Typematic Rate (Chars/Sec)	: 6		
Typematic Delay (Msec)	: 250	Esc : Quit ↑↓←→:Select Item	
		F1 : Help PU/PD/+/- :Modify	
Security Option	: Setup	F5 : Old Values (Shift) F2: color	
		F6 : Load BIOS Defaults	
PS/2 Mouse Function (IRQ12)	: Disabled	F7 : Load Setup Defaults	
PCI/VGA Palette Snoop	: Disabled		

Figure 14-56   BIOS Features Setup screen

STEP 17: INSTALLING THE CASE COVER

14

The next step is to install the case cover:

- Check that all wires and cables are tucked out of the way of the CPU fan and the edges of the case where the cover will fit. Check that all cards are well seated and that cables and wires are securely attached.

- Put the cover on as shown in Figure 14-57. Slide the top edge of the cover under the lip at the front of the case and rotate the cover into place.

- Use four screws to attach the cover to the case, as seen in Figure 14-58.

Figure 14-57   Put the cover on the case

Figure 14-58   Use screws to attach the cover to the case

STEP 18: CONNECTING THE SCANNER

The last step is to connect the scanner to the system:

- Connect the SCSI cable to the host adapter port, as seen in Figure 14-59.

- Attach the other end of the cable to the SCSI port on the back of the scanner. The terminating resistor is attached between the cable and the scanner port, as seen in Figure 14-60.

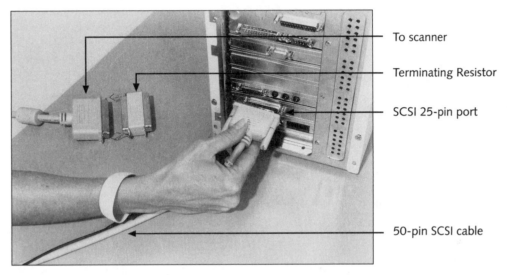

To scanner

Terminating Resistor

SCSI 25-pin port

50-pin SCSI cable

Figure 14-59   Attach the SCSI cable to the host adapter port

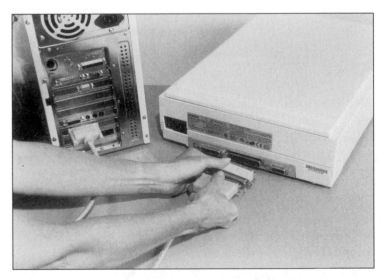

14

Figure 14-60   A terminating resistor is placed between the scanner port and the SCSI cable

FINISHING THE JOB

Figure 14-61 shows the completed system with keyboard, monitor, and mouse attached. As with almost any installation, ours was not without problems. After the hardware was all installed and we turned on the PC and installed Windows 95, we encountered one problem. The serial port mouse refused to work, even when we substituted a mouse that we knew was good. After working with the problem from several different approaches, we discovered that the small serial cable from the systemboard to the serial port was bad. We replaced the cable, and the mouse began to work. (It's very unusual for one of these small cables to be the source of the problem, and we checked many other things before we suspected the cable.)

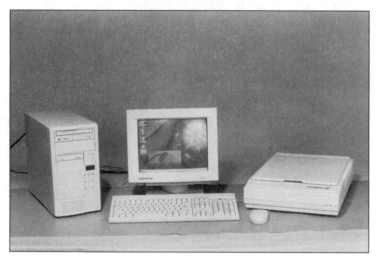

Figure 14-61   The completed system

CHAPTER SUMMARY

- The most common reason to buy a brand-name PC rather than a clone is after-sales service.

- Many brand-name PCs use proprietary designs that force you to use only that particular brand-name's parts and service when upgrading or maintaining the PC.

- Middle-range PCs offer more network capability, more expandability, more support, and more prior testing than do low-end PCs.

- Some reasons to build your own PC are the knowledge you will gain, the control you will have over the choice of individual parts, the availability of documentation and original software disks, and the satisfaction of having built the PC yourself.

- When choosing to build your own PC, be aware that the process will take time, that you will likely encounter problems along the way, that there will be no warranty on the assembled product, and that you probably will not save money.

- Plan the project of assembling a PC well. Get answers to any questions you may have on the details before you begin. Keep things organized as you work. Expect the project to be fun.

- When assembling a PC, follow this general plan:

  - Study the systemboard documentation and set all jumpers and DIP switches.

  - Verify that the systemboard, CPU, and memory are all working before installing the systemboard in the case.

  - Install the systemboard and serial and parallel ports.

  - Install the floppy drive, hard drive, and CD-ROM drive.

  - Install the sound card, modem, and any other cards present, including the video card.

  - Connect the speaker and peripherals.

  - Install the operating system and put the case cover in place.

KEY TERMS

- **Clone** — Originally, a computer that was compatible with IBM computer hardware and MS-DOS software. Today, the word clone often refers to no-name Intel and Microsoft compatibles.

- **Ground mat** — An antistatic mat designed for electronic workbenches to dissipate static electricity. It often uses a wire attached to the ground connection, in a standard electrical outlet.

- **Ground strap** — An antistatic wrist strap used to dissipate static electricity. Typically grounded by attaching an alligator clip to the computer chassis or to a nearby grounded antistatic mat.

- **Jumpers** — Small, plastic-coated conductive shorting blocks that are installed on pins on circuit boards to close or complete a circuit to configure the board. They are often labeled JP 1, JP 2, and so on.

- **PC-compatible** — A computer that uses an Intel (or compatible) processor and can run DOS and Windows.

- **PCI (peripheral component interconnect) expansion slot** — Slots found on most Pentium systemboards. They can accept 32- or 64-bit adapter cards, and allow the card to interface with the PCI bus.

- **Proprietary** — When a company has exclusive rights to manufacture and/or market a product. Proprietary computer components are typically more difficult to find and more expensive to buy.

- **Standoffs** — Small plastic spacers placed on the bottom of the main systemboard, to raise it off the chassis, so that its components will not short out on the metal case.

14

- **Thermal grease** — A special compound placed on processors to facilitate the transfer of heat from the top of the CPU to a heat sink.

- **Voltage regulator module (VRM) socket** — Converts the system power supply voltage to the voltage required by the CPU.

- **ZIF (zero insertion force) socket** — A chip socket that has a small locking lever attached to its side. If the lever is raised, the CPU can be easily lifted out of its socket.

REVIEW QUESTIONS

1. What are the advantages of buying a well-known, brand-name computer?

2. What are the advantages of buying a less-expensive PC clone?

3. List three reasons why it may be wise to build your own PC. List three reasons, other than fear, why you may not want to build your own PC.

4. When building a new computer, you may have to change jumper settings on the systemboard. List two reasons for this.

5. List three items that are typically used to cool microprocessors.

6. What rule must be followed when connecting the power supply cables to the systemboard?

7. What should you do before switching on the power of a freshly assembled system?

8. List several LED connectors that are typically attached to a systemboard.

9. What rule must be followed when attaching drive cables?

10. List five port connectors that are commonly built into most systemboards today.

11. Is floppy drive A attached to the middle cable connector or the end cable connector of the floppy drive cable?

12. The audio wire connects the _____ to the _____.

13. What will be the SCSI ID of a host adapter on the SCSI chain?

14. Where and when are SCSI terminating resistors attached?

15. Assume that you are shopping for a new personal computer. Answer the following questions to help in making the best buying decision.

    a. What is the intended purpose or purposes of the computer?

    b. What functionalities must the computer have to satisfy each intended purpose?

    c. What hardware and software components are needed to perform each function?

    d. For each hardware and software component, state one question that you want answered about the component before you make your decision.

PROJECTS

PRACTICING COMPUTER ASSEMBLY SKILLS

Work with a partner. With your partner not watching, carefully write down where every wire and cable inside your computer is connected. Disconnect all cable connections: power, drives, and LED indicators. Without your help, have your partner replace each connection. Work together with your partner to carefully inspect the connections, using your diagram as an aid. Reboot and test the computer.

PLANNING AN UPGRADE

Using a systemboard manual, write down what jumper changes must be made to upgrade a CPU or to upgrade memory cache.

TROUBLESHOOTING AN ASSEMBLY PROBLEM

After assembling the PC shown in this chapter, we found that the mouse did not work. List the steps you would take to troubleshoot the problem in the order you would do them.

14

PLANNING TO BUY PARTS FOR A PC

Price the following parts needed to build a PC:

- Systemboard for a Pentium CPU
- Pentium CPU
- 32 MB of RAM
- Hard drive with at least 2 GB of storage
- Floppy disk drive
- CD-ROM drive
- Computer case and power supply
- I/O card and IDE adapter if these components are not on the systemboard

- Video controller card
- Sound card

List the features of the systemboard, CPU, and RAM you chose.

What speed is the CD-ROM drive you selected?

Identify and price at least one other device to install inside the computer case that you would want on your own PC.

As you price each part, if you select a high-end (more expensive) part rather than a low-end (less expensive) one, list the feature on the part that caused you to plan to spend the extra money.

UPGRADING MEMORY

Looking back at the documentation in the chapter for the systemboard, what memory modules would you buy and how much would it cost to upgrade cache memory from 256K to 512K? What memory modules would you buy, and how much would it cost to upgrade RAM from the 32 MB installed to 64 MB?

COMMUNICATING OVER PHONE LINES

Most personal computers today have modems, and most often the PC support person not only has to be able to install and troubleshoot modems but is also expected to know how to support communications software. Windows 95 and Windows NT both offer services that allow you to use a modem to connect to another PC or a network without needing any additional software.

IN THIS CHAPTER YOU WILL LEARN:

- ABOUT THE BASICS OF HOW COMPUTERS COMMUNICATE WITH EACH OTHER

- ABOUT THE PROBLEMS FACED BY SYSTEMS COMMUNICATING OVER PHONE LINES

- HOW MODEMS WORK AND WHAT FEATURES AND PROTOCOLS MODEMS MAY USE

- HOW TO CONFIGURE A MODEM USING WINDOWS 95 OR WINDOWS NT

- ABOUT THE FEATURES OF DIFFERENT COMMUNICATIONS SOFTWARE PROGRAMS AND HOW TO USE TWO OF THE MORE POPULAR ONES (PROCOMM PLUS AND PCANYWHERE)

- HOW TO TROUBLESHOOT MODEM OPERATIONS

- ABOUT DIGITAL COMMUNICATION LINES, INCLUDING ISDN

Modems are almost becoming standard equipment on new PCs that target the home market because of the ever-increasing popularity of the Internet and the World Wide Web, and also because many corporations are seeing advantages to allowing their employees to telecommute. Small businesses are also increasing their use of phone lines for data communications as business use of the Internet increases. With all this attention to telecommunications, technology and software to use the technology are improving. However, there is a speed ceiling on regular phone lines that is resulting in an emphasis on the development of digital alternatives, such as ISDN, a digital replacement for regular phone lines. This chapter discusses digital lines, how they work, and what is needed on a PC to support them.

The ultimate goal of many PC home users is to use their modems and phone lines to access a network, either the Internet or a private business network. However, this chapter focuses on installing and configuring modems on phone lines, and leaves the subject of networking, including accessing the Internet, for the next chapter.

COMMUNICATIONS LAYERS

The morning paper arrives filled with all the latest news; readers quickly turn to the editorial section to see what the editors are thinking today. Seldom do they stop to think about the systems, methods, people, and equipment required for that morning paper with the interesting editorials to arrive at the door. It is generally understood that there are layers of systems in place to make it possible for this single event, and many more like it, to occur. As you look at Figure 15-1, think for a moment about the systems necessary to allow the paper to be transported to your door. News editors write the material sent to the press. There is a distribution center at the press where the papers are loaded onto trucks that carry them to distribution points in the city. Delivery persons pick them up and have their own system in place to disperse the papers.

As you read an editorial, the news editor is communicating with you even though you recognize that this communication is not directly physical (face to face) but logical or virtual (by indirect methods). Another way of saying this is that virtual communication takes place between the editor and the reader by way of physical communication, through systems that the two people may or may not be aware of. The editor is aware of the printing process and does communicate with that system, and the reader is aware of the delivery person on the bicycle and communicates with him or her. However, neither the reader nor the editor needs to be aware of, or communicate with, the other systems in the diagram.

Now think in terms of communication layers. In order to transport papers, a delivery system often depends on a supporting system to make it work. For example, the distribution department depends on the truck drivers and their trucks. The truck system is dependent on the road system. If a bridge goes out, a truck can't pass over it, the truck driver cannot perform his or her duty, the person at the distribution center cannot fill an order at a distribution point, and the morning paper does not arrive. As you study communications over phone lines, think about this analogy of transport systems being dependent on other supporting systems. This concept is often referred to as communications layers. Four communications layers in the newspaper analogy are: the editor and reader, the distribution system, the trucking system, and the road system.

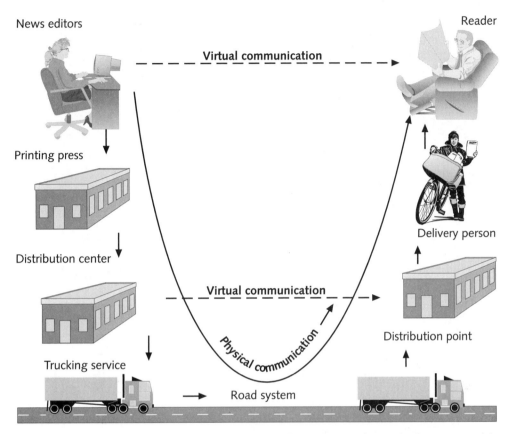

Figure 15-1   Virtual or logical communication between reader and editor is possible
because of underlying physical systems

Figure 15-2 illustrates physical communications over phone lines. One computer sends data
to its modem, which transmits that data over phone lines to a modem on the other end,
which transmits the data to a receiving computer. The figure also indicates that the mode of
communication differs at different stages in the process: PC-to-modem communication is
digital, but modem-to-modem communication is analog.

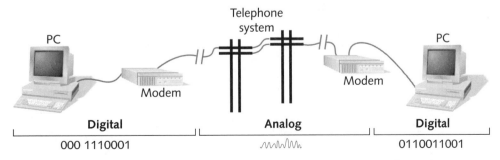

Figure 15-2   Communicating over phone lines can be viewed as physical

Even though communications over phone lines are customarily thought of as physical, this communication can also be considered virtual. Look at Figure 15-3, where two users are communicating by way of their PCs and modems. The communication between the two users is virtual and is possible because of the underlying supporting layers and systems, which are physical.

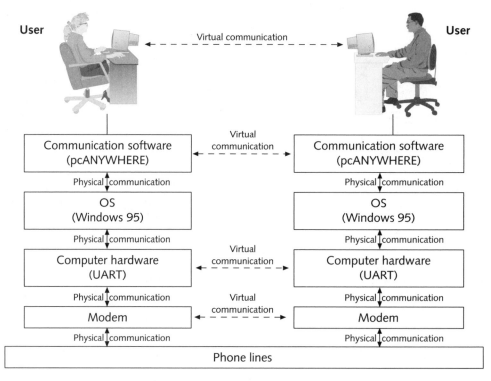

Figure 15-3 Communications over phone lines is both physical and virtual

One user enters data into his or her communications applications software, such as pcANYWHERE or ProComm Plus. The communications applications software communicates with the OS, which communicates with the computer hardware. The computer hardware communicates with a modem, which uses phone lines to send the information to a remote modem, computer hardware, OS, communications software, and finally a remote user.

In the newspaper analogy in Figure 15-1, virtual communication is taking place between reader and editor, but other underlying systems are also communicating with their counterpart systems at remote locations. For example, the distribution center receives an order for newspapers from a remote distribution point in the city, and the center fills the order, sending newspapers to the remote point. This, too, can be seen in the drawing as virtual communication.

Virtual communication at different levels of data communications also occurs. In Figure 15-3, the communications software on one end says to the communications software at the other end, "I want the such-and-such file." The remote software responds and sends the file. As you read this chapter, you will also see virtual communication taking place computer-hardware-to-computer-hardware, as well as modem-to-modem. This communication between correlating systems on corresponding layers of each side of the drawing is virtual, but communication from one layer to the next layer in the drawing is physical.

The remainder of this chapter examines each layer or level of communication shown in Figure 15-3, beginning with the modem layer and working up the diagram to computer hardware, OS, and finally communications software.

ALL ABOUT MODEMS

The modem, a device used by a PC to communicate over a phone line, is both hardware and firmware. Inside an external modem (see Figure 15-4) or on an internal modem card is firmware, on ROM chips, that contains protocol and instructions needed to format and convert data so that it can be transported over phone lines to a receiving modem on the other end. In general, modems are considered to be hardware, but it is fundamental to an understanding of communications to also consider them to be firmware.

Figure 15-4   SupraSonic external modem

Computers are digital; regular phone lines are analog. Earlier chapters discussed the difference between digital data and analog data, and Figure 15-2 shows how this concept applies to phone lines. Recall that data is stored inside a PC and communicated to a modem as binary or digital data—0s and 1s. A modem converts this binary or digital data into an analog signal (the process is called **modulation**) that can travel over a phone line, and then the modem at the receiving end converts it back to digital (this process is called **demodulation**) before passing it on to the receiving PC. The two processes of MOdulation/DEModulation lead to the name of the device: modem.

15

Recall that an analog signal is made up of an infinite number of possible values in its range of values, but a digital signal has only a finite number of values in its range of values. (Remember from Chapter 13 the analogy that compared a loading ramp and a staircase to an analog and a digital signal, respectively. The loading ramp is analog, with an infinite number of continuous heights. The staircase is digital, with a finite number of discrete heights.) Remember also that phone lines were designed to transmit sound (that is, the human voice). Sound traveling over regular phone lines is transmitted as analog signals, meaning that there are an infinite number of sound values, just as there are an infinite number of sound values in the human voice. When data is transmitted over phone lines, even though the data from a PC is inherently digital, it, too, must be converted to an analog signal in order to use telephone technology. Think of PC data as being converted from two simple states or measurements (0 and 1, or on and off) to waves (like sound waves), which have a potentially infinite number of states or measurements. Modems use different characteristics of waves to correspond with the 0s and 1s of digital communication.

HOW MODEMS ARE RATED

Two PCs communicate over phone lines by using either internal or external modems. A PC initiates a phone call by instructing its modem to make the call. The modem makes the call, and a modem on the remote end answers the call and passes this event on to its PC. The two PCs communicate with one another by using the modems as their interpreters or translators. Because information traveling over phone lines is analog in nature and data processed by a PC must be digital, the two PCs can communicate only if the modems between them are translating data from digital to analog before sending it onto the phone lines, and then translating received data back to digital before the PC sees it.

There are many ways that a modem can translate digital data into an analog signal so that a receiving modem can understand it, quality of transmission can be assured, and the best possible transmission speeds can be attained. Using Windows 95, you can view the properties of an installed modem on a PC. Many people install their modems by simply choosing settings supplied by others, or by allowing the installation program to use default selections, even though they may not understand what these modem properties mean or why certain selections, such as transmission speeds and methods of controlling data flow, are made. This section explains what each modem property means, and how it affects the modem's performance and compatibility with other modems in order to make communication possible.

Getting Started

When you first use a modem to make a dial-up call to another PC, you hear the modem making noises as the dial-up is completed. The two modems are establishing the rules of communication between them. What you hear are the sounds being sent over the phone lines as the two modems negotiate these rules. The process is called **training** or **handshaking**. There are many protocols (agreed on methods of communication) used for modems to communicate, and, in this handshaking phase, the calling modem and the receiving modem are communicating to each other the protocols and speeds they can support, and arriving at the best possible common solution. The decisions made about protocols include how to handle data compression and error checking, and methods of data transfer.

Modem Speeds

The speed at which a modem passes data over phone lines is partly determined by the transmission standard the modem is using. Modem speed is measured either in **baud rate** (named after the inventor, J.M.E. Baudot), which is the number of times a signal changes in one second, or in bits per second (bps); bps is the more common unit of measurement. For slower baud rates, only one bit can be "written" on one signal (in which case baud rate is equal to bps rate); slower modems are often measured in baud rates. For faster baud rates, more than one bit can be carried on one signal, so faster modems are measured in bps (and baud rate may differ from bps). When measuring modem speed using baud rate, the number of bps will always be equal to or a multiple of the baud rate. The most commonly rated speeds of modems in use today are 14.4 Kbps, 28.8 Kbps, 33.6 Kbps, and the newest speed in modems, 56.6 Kbps.

The maximum speed of a modem is often written into the manufacturer's name for the modem. Using Windows 95, click on **Start**, **Settings**, **Control Panel**, and double-click on **Modems**. The Modems Properties box in Figure 15-5 displays. The installed modem is labeled as a 3334 33.6 FDSP Fax Modem. The 33.6 portion of the name indicates the speed of the modem: 33.6 Kbps.

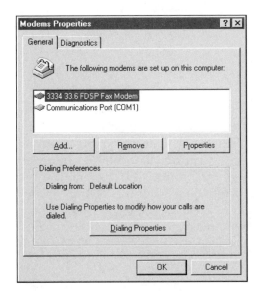

Figure 15-5 The maximum modem speed is often included in the modem name (in this case 33.6 Kbps)

The Ceiling on Modem Speeds

The limitation on modem speeds is not caused by the limits of modem technology, but rather by the nature of regular phone lines. There are limitations on the quality of audio signals that analog phone lines support, which affects transmission speed. In addition to the analog limitations there are limitations on newer digital phone lines as well. Older phone lines (before 1940) were analog from beginning to end; there were no digital components. This is not true today; regular telephone lines are always analog as they leave a customer's house or office building, but are almost always converted to a digital signal at some point in the transmission. These digital signals can then be transmitted, using sophisticated computing equipment and methods, and then converted back to analog signals at some point before traveling that last step between a local central office and the phone of the person receiving the call.

One limitation on modem speeds is the result of the method used when an analog signal is converted to a digital signal. The phone company takes a sampling of the analog signal (8,000 samples every second) and converts each sample to an 8-bit byte. Modem transmission is limited to this 8,000 bytes/second (64,000 bits/second) transmission of the digital signal. Therefore, taking into account the overhead of data transmission (bits and bytes sent with the data used to control and define transmissions), the maximum transmission rate that a modem can attain is about 56,000 bps or 56 Kbps.

In order for a modem to achieve this high a transmission rate, the conversion by the phone company from analog to digital can only take place once during the transmission. Also, if the lines in your neighborhood are multiplexed (several logical phone lines sharing a common physical line), the 56K speed cannot be attained. Also, there is often some disturbance on the line, such as a crackling noise caused by lines bumping against one another in the wind. This reduction in line quality is called a **dirty** or **noisy line**. A line that consistently produces high quality results is called a **clean line**.

Modem Standards

There are several modem standards used today that determine modem speed and protocols. Avoid a modem using a proprietary standard because it may only be able to communicate with another modem by the same manufacturer. The industry-approved standards for international communication were written by **Comité Consultatif Internationale de Télégraphie et Téléphonie (CCITT)**. In 1992, the CCITT organization was incorporated into the **International Telecommunications Union (ITU)**, an intergovernmental organization approved by the United Nations to be responsible for adopting standards governing telecommunications. You may see the standards used by modems referred to as the CCITT standards (more common) or as the ITU standards. The CCITT standards are listed in Table 15-1.

Table 15-1 Transmission standards used by modems

Standard	Applies Mainly to	Description
Bell 212A	Speed (up to 1,200 bps)	An older standard that supports 1,200 bps
CCITT V.32	Speed (up to 9,600 bps)	This standard runs at 9,600 bps, includes error checking, and can negotiate standards with other modems. V.32 uses 2,400 baud, transmits 4 bits per each baud or 9,600 bps. This standard was used for quite some time.
HST	Speed (up to 14.4 Kbps)	An older proprietary standard that supports 9,600 or 14,400 bps, created by U.S. Robotics. (U.S. Robotics also supports the CCITT standards.)
CCITT V.32bis	Speed (up to 14.4 Kbps)	This standard is an improvement over V.32 (bis means "second" in Latin), and has a speed of 14,400 bps. It transmits at 2,400 baud rate and transmits 6 bits per baud, or 14,400 bps.
CCITT V.34	Speed (up to 33.6 Kbps)	This standard transmits at 28,800 bps, or 28.8 Kbps. Optional higher speeds are 31.2 Kbps and 33.6 Kbps. This standard prevails today.
MNP Class 4	Error correction	Developed by Microcom, Inc. and called the Microcom Networking Protocol (MNP), this standard provides error detection and correction, and also automatically adjusts the speed of transmission based on the quality of the phone line. Earlier classes of MNP standards for error correction are Class 2 and Class 3.
CCITT V.42	Error correction	This is an error-correcting standard that adopted the methods used by MNP Class 4. Data that is corrupted during transmission is automatically retransmitted using this standard. A modem can use this standard for error correction and one of the standards listed above for speed.
MNP Class 5	Data compression	MNP Class 5 standard provides data compression, which can double normal transmission speeds between modems. It is common to see both MNP Class 4 and MNP Class 5 supported by a modem. They are sometimes called MNP-4 and MNP-5.
CCITT V.42bis	Data compression	An improved version of V.42 that also uses data compression. By compressing the data, overall faster throughput is attained. Many modems use the V.42bis standard for data compression and error checking and, at the same time, use the V.34 standard for data transmission protocols.
K56flex	Speed (up to 56 Kbps)	One of two current standards used to attain a speed of 56 Kbps. This standard is currently backed by Lucent Technologies and Rockwell International Corp.
x2	Speed (up to 56 Kbps)	One of two current standards that support a speed of 56 Kbps. This standard is supported by U.S. Robotics.

15

When one modem first dials up another modem, during the handshake, the two modems first attempt to establish a communications protocol or standard at the fastest speed that both can support. The receiving modem takes the lead in negotiating these protocols by offering its best solution. If the calling modem does not respond to this protocol, the receiving modem continues to offer a slower protocol until the fastest possible solution common to them both is agreed upon. Data compression and error checking protocols are also negotiated and agreed upon during the handshake, if both modems can support the same standards for these features. More details about handshaking are covered later in the chapter.

You will now look at a couple of examples. Figure 15-6 shows a table of specifications supported by the 33.6 internal modem shown in Figure 15-7, which was installed in the PC in Chapter 14. Note in Figure 15-6 the many different modulation standards (which indicate speed) that the modem can support. The fastest standard, CCITT V.34, is the standard that the modem first uses when trying to establish communication with another modem, unless specified otherwise in the modem setup.

Item	Specifications
Modulation std.:	V.34, V.32bis, V.32, V.29, V.27ter, V.22bis, V.23, V.22, V.21 ch2, V.17, Bell212/103
Compression:	V.42.bis, MNP Class 5
Error Correction:	V.42, MNP Class 2-4
Host Interface:	ISA 16 bit bus
COM ports:	1, 2, 3, 4
IRQ lines:	2, 3, 4, 5, 7*, 10*, 11*, 12*
FAX Group:	Group III
FAX Command:	Class 1
VOICE Command:	IS-101
Transmit level:	-10 dBm +/- 1 db
Sensitivity:	-43dBm
UART:	16550 compatible
Power:	.75 W max
Temperature:	0 to 55 degrees C, operating; -20 to 80 degrees C, nonoperating

Note: *IRQ7, IRQ10, IRQ11, and IRQ 12 are support for Plug-and-Play model only

Figure 15-6 Specifications for a 33.6 modem

Figure 15-7   A 33.6 bps internal modem

For example, if you want to force this modem to communicate with another modem using the Bell proprietary standard, in Windows 95, follow these directions:

1. Click on **Start**, **Settings**, **Control Panel**, and double-click on **Modems**. The Modems Properties dialog box displays, as in Figure 15-5.

2. Select the modem from the list of installed modems, and then click on **Properties**. The Properties box for the selected modem displays, as shown in Figure 15-8. Note in this figure that the maximum speed of the modem is set at 115,200 bps; this speed is not attainable over phone lines. You can, however, use this box to force the modem to transmit at a slower speed than it normally would, in order to offset problems with a dirty phone line. A noisy or dirty phone line is a line that has disturbances on it, because of a variety of reasons, that prevent clean transmission of data. Slowing down the speed of your modem may solve the problem.

15

3. Click on the **Connections** tab of the modem Properties box. Figure 15-9 shows the connection preferences that are supported by this modem. These preferences are discussed later in the chapter.

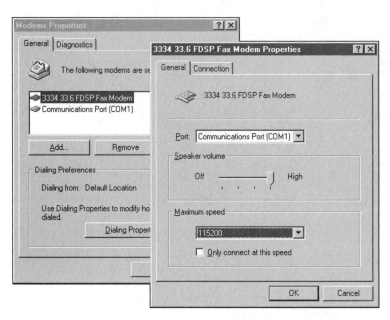

Figure 15-8 The Properties box of the selected modem

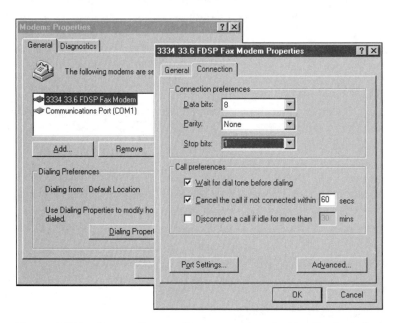

Figure 15-9 Connection preferences supported by the installed modem

4. Click on the **Advanced** button. Figure 15-10 shows the advanced connection settings, which allow you to select a modulation standard for this modem. The figure shows the drop-down list of standards. You can select Non-standard or Standard. The standard selection for this modem will cause the modem to function according to one of the CCITT modulation standards listed in Figure 15-6. If you select the Non-standard setting, this modem attempts to communicate using the Bell212/103 standard listed in Figure 15-6 under "Modulation std."

5. Leave the Modulation type set to Standard and click **Cancel** to exit the window.

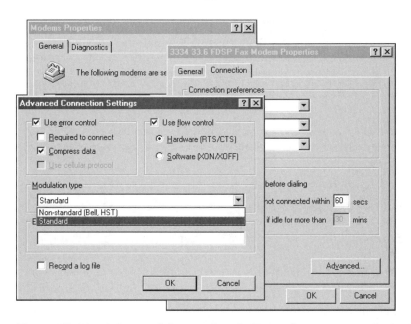

Figure 15-10   Advanced Connection Settings allows you to select a transmission standard for the installed modem

Modems with 56 Kbps Speeds

For a transmitting modem to use either the x2 or the K56flex standard for 56 Kbps transmission, the modem on the receiving end must also support this same standard; if it doesn't, then reliable communication is not possible at 56 Kbps. Because of this potential incompatibility, U.S. Robotics, Lucent Technologies, and Rockwell International have all agreed to support a third standard for 56 Kbps transmission. Both the x2 and K56flex camps intend to abandon their current standards for the new, unified standard, which will probably be published before the printing of this book. If you are purchasing a 56 Kbps modem, know what the manufacturer intends to do when the new standard is accepted. Some manufacturers are offering a free upgrade to the modem's Flash ROM when the new standard goes into effect. (Flash ROM upgrades can usually be downloaded from a manufacturer's Web site.)

15

Another concern about buying a 56 Kbps modem is that, if your phone line is too noisy, the high speed cannot be attained. 3Com, a manufacturer of modems, offers a way for you to test your phone line to determine if it qualifies, before you buy a 56 Kbps modem. With a modem using the V.34 standard, access the 3Com Web site (www.x2.usr.com/linetest1.html) and read and follow the directions to have the 3Com program analyze your line.

Data Compression

Remember the concept of communications layers presented earlier in the chapter. The next discussion focuses on the physical communication between the two layers represented by the modem and the phone lines. The modem includes the firmware (permanent programming) housed on the modem, which can perform error correction and data compression. These and other functions of data communication can be performed by either hardware (firmware on the modem) or software (programs on the PC).

When data compression is performed by a modem, it applies to all data that is transmitted by the modem. If data compression is performed by the software on the PC, it applies to single-file transfer operations. Software protocols used to compress data will be addressed later in the chapter.

Data compression done by the modem follows either the MNP-5, CCITT V.42, or V.42bis protocol. All three of these protocols also perform error correction. A modem using one of these methods of data compression must be communicating to its computer at higher speeds than it is using to communicate to the phone line. This is because the data is being compressed at the modem and, therefore, there are fewer bits to be transmitted over the phone line, assuming, of course, that few errors occur. This fact may cause the overall speed of the data transmission at the PC to appear much faster than the actual phone line transmission rate.

The compression ratio of MNP-5 is 2:1, and V.42bis can have up to a 4:1 compression ratio. MNP-5 also has more overhead in its compression methods, and sometimes, if a file is already compressed (such as a ZIP file), because of this overhead, the actual transmission time increases because of MNP-5. V.42 can determine if a file is already compressed, and therefore does not compress it a second time. If you are sending compressed files over a modem and you only have MNP-5 compression, disable MNP-5 compression to speed up data transmission.

Error Correction

As seen in Table 15-1, the standards that include error correction are MNP-4, CCITT V.42, and CCITT V.42bis. It is common for a modem to support all three standards. If a modem does support all three standards, during the handshaking process, the answering modem tries to establish an error correction protocol with the other modem by first suggesting the fastest, best standard. If the calling modem responds by accepting that standard, then it is used by both. If the calling modem does not support the suggested protocol, then the two modems negotiate to find a protocol they both can use, or simply decide not to use error correction.

Look back at Figure 15-10: the Advanced Connection Settings for the installed modem. From this box, you can click on **Use error control** to determine if the modem will be allowed to use error control if it can negotiate a protocol with the other modem. You can also specify from this window that error control is required to connect. (Click **Required to connect** under **User error control** in Figure 15-10.) If the other modem cannot use error control, then this modem will not complete the connection. Also note that data compression cannot be selected unless error control is evoked.

Error correction works by breaking data up into small packets called **frames**. The sending modem performs some calculations on a frame of data and sums these calculations into a checksum. A **checksum** is a summary calculation of data that will later be used to check or verify the accuracy of the data when received. Checksum works somewhat like a parity bit, except that it is a little more complicated and applies to more data. The checksum is attached to the data frame and they are transmitted. The receiving modem performs the same calculations and compares its answer to the checksum value received. If they do not agree, then the receiving modem requests a new transmission of the packet. This process does slow down the transmission of data, especially on dirty or noisy phone lines, but accuracy is almost 100% guaranteed.

More About Handshaking

Now that you understand several of the different protocols that must be established between two modems before they can communicate data, you can more carefully examine the handshaking process in which these protocols are agreed upon. Follow the step-by-step process of two modems performing a handshake:

1. The calling modem dials a phone number, and the phone rings at the other end.

2. The answering modem picks up. The answering modem sends a modem tone, sometimes called a **guard tone**, which the calling modem recognizes to be another modem and not a human voice, and so it does not break the connection.

3. The answering modem sends a signal that is called the **carrier**, which is unmodulated (unchanging), or a continuous tone at a set frequency, or pitch (a sound's frequency is called the pitch), depending on the speed of communication the answering modem is attempting to establish with the calling modem. This process, called **establishing carrier**, sounds like static, which you hear during handshaking.

4. The answering modem keeps sending one unmodulated carrier (or signal) after another until the calling modem responds.

5. If the calling modem responds with the same carrier, then both modems use it. If the calling modem does not respond, then the answering modem simply drops this particular carrier and tries another.

6. After carrier is established, the two modems enter the **equalization stage**, which sounds like hissing or buzzing on the line. The modems are both testing the line quality and will compensate for poor quality by changing the way they transmit.

15

7. Having established carrier and adjusted for line quality, the two modems have now agreed on a speed of data transmission between them, called the modem speed or the line speed.

8. The speakers on the modems are now turned off. Next the modems begin to talk about how data is to be transmitted. The answering modem asks if the other modem can support MNP-4, MNP-5, V.42, V.42bis, and so on. After some interchange, the methods of data transmission are agreed upon, and the handshaking is complete. The two modems can now communicate.

External modems give you the status of what is happening by turning on and off lights on the front of the modem and displaying messages on an LCD panel (called a display readout). Internal modems, of course, don't have these lights available for you to see, so communications software sometimes displays a pseudo-modem-panel on your computer screen. The modem lights were listed in Table 8.2 of Chapter 8 and are discussed in more detail later in this chapter.

When a modem is first activated, it raises (turns on) its Clear to Send (CTS) signal and, for an external modem, the CTS light also goes on. When the PC receives the CTS signal from its modem, it will turn up its Request to Send (RTS) signal in order to begin a call. For external modems, the RTS or RS light goes on.

After the handshaking explained in Step 7 above, when carrier between the two modems is established, if the modems are external modems with these status lights, each modem turns on its Carrier Detect (CD) light, which stays on as long as the modems are connected. When a communications technician sees this light, he or she will say that carrier is up. Not only does the light come on, but the CD signal transmitted to the PC over the serial port cable is also raised (turned on), letting the computer know that communication has been established, and that data can now be sent. Data transmission can be detected by looking at the external modem lights, TXD and RXD (or they may be TD and RD) for transmitting and receiving data.

If error correction or data compression is used, the communication established will most likely be synchronous over the phone line, which means that data is sent from one modem to the other as blocks of data based on timed intervals. Clocks on each modem are used to synchronize the transmissions. Asynchronous communication relies on bits being sent before and after the data to communicate when each modem should transmit. These bits are called stop bits and start bits. Asynchronous communication can also use parity checking.

MODEM FEATURES

In addition to the speed, protocols, data compression, and error correction that are used to rate a modem, there are other features. Some additional abilities you might want to look for in a modem are:

- **Caller ID** (provided that you subscribe to that service from the phone company) is supported.

- **Display readout** on external modems provides information about the status of the modem. (See Chapter 8, Table 8.2, for a list of modem lights and their meanings. The modem can also have an LCD panel for messages such as Training or Idle.)

- **Flash ROM** allows you to upgrade your modem to support future standards.

- **Plug-and-Play for Windows 95** makes modem installation automatic.

- **Voice/data capability** allows the modem to also serve as a telephone, complete with built-in speaker and microphone.

- **Auto-answer** makes it possible for the modem to receive incoming calls while you are away from the PC.

COMPUTER-HARDWARE-TO-MODEM COMMUNICATION

Looking back to the newspaper analogy (see Figure 15-2), the newspaper distribution system must coordinate its efforts with the trucking system. In data communication with computers, this coordination can be equated to the computer hardware coordinating its communication with its modem. Between the PC hardware layer and the modem layer, communication is digital. How the PC hardware and the modem communicate is the subject of this section.

Figure 15-11 shows an overview of PCs and modems communicating. The computers are classified as **data terminal equipment** (**DTE**), and the modems are called **data communications equipment** (**DCE**).

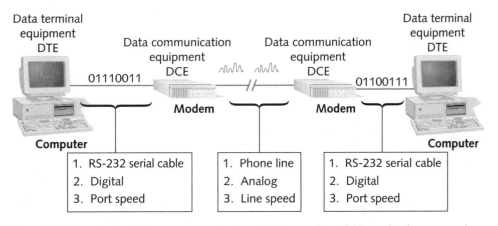

Figure 15-11   A computer communicates with a modem differently than a modem communicates with another modem

PCs don't communicate with modems in the same way that modems communicate with modems. Transmission speeds, error checking, and data format from the PC to the modem (DTE to DCE) are different than they are between a modem and another modem (DCE to DCE). Remember that a modem may be an internal or an external modem. As you study communication between DTEs and DCEs, the concepts are easier to visualize if you think of a PC and an external modem sitting beside it connected by a serial cable. However, the same concepts apply to an internal modem as to an external modem, even though the modem card and the PC are not connected by a cable.

Transmission Speed

Look back at Figure 15-8 at the modem properties for a 33.6 modem. Notice that the maximum speed that is available for this modem is 115200. This speed is given in bps, and you naturally may wonder why it is so much higher than the rated speed of the modem. The answer is that this speed is referring to the transmission speed from the PC to the modem, which may very well be this high.

Now turn back to Figures 15-8 and 15-11. The speed highlighted in Figure 15-8 refers to communication between a DTE (computer) and a DCE (modem) and is called the DTE speed, or the **port speed**, because the PC is using a serial port to communicate with the modem. The port speed (in this case 33.6 Kbps) must be significantly higher than the modem speed in order for the PC to take advantage of data compression performed by the modem.

 As a general rule, port speed should be about four times as fast as modem speed.

For example, for a 28.8 Kbps modem, set the port speed to 115.2 Kbps. The speed seen in Figure 15-8 is the port speed that is supported by this particular modem. Modem speed (sometimes called line speed) is determined by several factors, including the rated speed of the modem, line quality, and the speed of the remote modem.

The UART

The chip responsible for any communication over the serial port is the UART (universal asynchronous receiver-transmitter), sometimes called an ACIA (asynchronous communications Interface Adapter), which was first introduced in Chapter 8. The UART controls the port speed as well as other features of serial port communications. Table 15-2 summarizes the speeds of the different UARTs.

Table 15-2   Maximum port speeds of UARTs

UART	Maximum Speed	FIFO Buffering
Intel 8250, an 8-bit chip	38.4 Kbps	None
Intel 16450, a 16-bit chip	38.4 Kbps	None
Intel 16550, a 16-bit chip	115.2 Kbps	Has a 16-byte buffer
Intel 16650, a 16-bit chip	230 Kbps	Has a 32-byte buffer

Remember from Chapter 8 that the FIFO (first-in-first-out) buffer is needed by the UART chip to temporarily hold data as it is being received or transmitted. If your UART chip has a buffer, you can control its size as well as the port speed from the Modems Properties box of Windows 95. Follow these directions:

1. Click **Start**, **Settings**, **Control Panel**, and then double-click on **Modems**.

2. Select the communications port from the list and then click **Properties**. Figure 15-12 shows the COM1 Properties box. From this Properties box, you can select the port speed in Bits per second.
3. Click the **Advanced** button. The Advanced Port Settings dialog box displays, as in Figure 15-13. From this box, you can control the size of the FIFO buffer of the 16550 UART and establish whether or not the buffer is to be used.

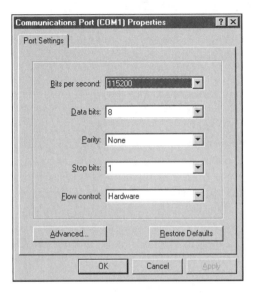

Figure 15-12   COM1 Properties box lets you control port settings, including the port speed in bits per second

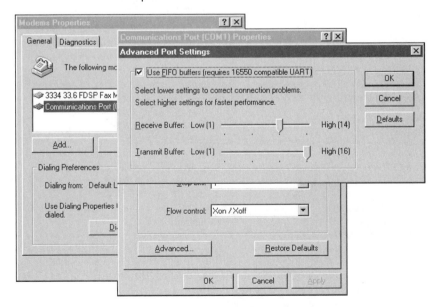

Figure 15-13   Selecting the FIFO buffer size of a 16550 UART chip

15

4. Click **OK** to exit the box.

Other settings on the Communications Port Properties box are discussed later in the chapter.

As can be seen from Table 15-2, if you have a very fast external modem with data compression, but your UART cannot support the speed, the modem cannot attain its maximum speed. The solution may be to upgrade your UART or to install an I/O controller card with a fast UART chip. Remember from Chapter 8 that you can use MSD (Microsoft Diagnostics Utility) to determine which UART you have on your PC. When reading documentation about the speed of communication over phone lines, you may see the UART or port speed referred to as the DTE speed, and the modem or line speed called the DCE speed.

The UART Chip on External and Internal Modems

Let's now consider the different ways internal and external modems use the UART. Figure 15-14 shows the differences between an external and internal configuration as applied to the UART. Almost all systemboards sold today contain either a UART or the UART logic somewhere within the chip set on the systemboard. External modems connect to a PC by way of a serial port, and therefore use the UART on the systemboard that controls this serial port. In this case, data from the systemboard travels over the serial cable to the modem in digital form, so the external modem must have a UART in it to receive the digital data. Sometimes the external modem may combine the UART logic into other chips in the modem.

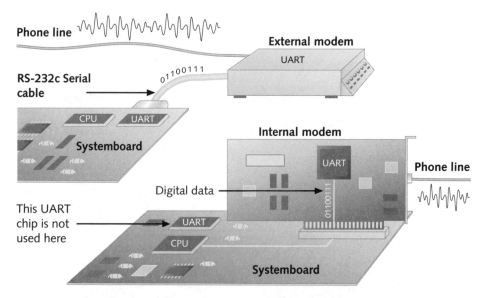

Figure 15-14 For an external modem, digital data is controlled by the UART chip on the systemboard. For an internal modem, the controlling UART chip is on the modem card

Internal modems are expansion cards that connect to the systemboard by way of an 8-bit ISA, a 16-bit ISA, or a PCI expansion slot. Internal modems have their own UART on the modem card and provide their own serial port to the computer system. This is why an internal modem must be configured to have its own COM port assigned to it for its UART to control. A typical configuration for a PC is to have COM1 assigned to the serial mouse and COM2 assigned to the internal modem. (An external modem does not need a COM port assigned to it, because it uses the existing COM port already configured on the system.) The UART on the systemboard holding the internal modem is not used by the modem, because the modem is not using the COM ports on the systemboard.

 Sometimes a COM port on a systemboard can compete for resources with the COM port on an internal modem, causing a conflict. In this case, disable the conflicting COM port on the systemboard.

The UART on an internal modem and the UART chip on a systemboard supporting an external modem basically perform the same function—controlling digital data sent from the CPU to the modem. Either of these UARTs may perform error checking and control the flow of data. In the discussions that follow about the functions of the UART chip in modem communication, the same principles apply to either an external or an internal modem. The difference is the location of the UART performing the function.

In speaking of the need to upgrade a slow UART, a slow UART chip on an internal modem has the same effect as a slow UART chip on a systemboard supporting an external modem. A UART chip on an internal modem is also controlling the speed at which data is transferred from the system bus to the modem. If this UART is not fast enough, then your only recourse is to replace the modem card.

Flow Control

There are three speeds involved when data is transmitted (see Figure 15-11): the port speed between the calling PC and its modem, the line speed between the two modems, and the port speed between the answering PC and its modem. Since each of these speeds may be different, a way is needed to stop the data from flowing when either the DTE or DCE needs to catch up. For example, if the receiving modem is receiving data faster than it can uncompress it and pass it off to its PC, it must stop the flow coming from the remote modem long enough to catch up. **Flow control** is a method of controlling the flow of data by sending a message to stop data flow. Either the receiving PC or the receiving modem can initiate a flow control message.

There are two methods of flow control: flow control over software channels called Xon/Xoff protocol and flow control over hardware channels called RTS/CTS protocol. Looking back at Figure 15-10, you can see the two choices of flow control under Connection Settings. Figure 15-15 illustrates the difference between the two methods: Software flow control uses the same methods to send the stop and start messages as are used by the software to send data. Hardware flow control uses the methods also used by the modem (hardware) to initially establish communication.

15

Software Flow Control

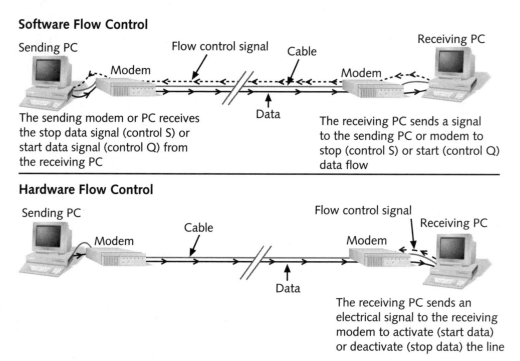

Sending PC

Flow control signal   Cable

Receiving PC

Modem

Modem

Data

The sending modem or PC receives the stop data signal (control S) or start data signal (control Q) from the receiving PC

The receiving PC sends a signal to the sending PC or modem to stop (control S) or start (control Q) data flow

Hardware Flow Control

Sending PC

Flow control signal

Cable

Receiving PC

Modem

Modem

Data

The receiving PC sends an electrical signal to the receiving modem to activate (start data) or deactivate (stop data) the line

Figure 15-15   Software flow control sends in-band software messages from the receiving PC to the sending device; hardware flow control sends out-of-band electrical signals only from the receiving PC to the receiving modem

In software flow control, the receiving device transmits a message to the sending device to pause transmission by sending a special control character within the same channel (frequency) in which data is sent. This method is called **inband signaling**. The control character to stop the data from flowing, Xoff, is Control-S, sent as an ASCII character whose ASCII value is 19. (See Appendix C for information about ASCII characters.) The Xon control character is Control-Q, or ASCII value 17, which tells the sending device to begin sending data again. This method of flow control works well as long as only ASCII data is being transmitted, but if data is being transmitted in some other coding format, the control characters themselves may be valid data and may be mistakenly included in the data stream as regular data, which will cause problems with communication. Another problem with software flow control is that data needs to be continually monitored to detect the signals, which, at the high speeds at which data is transmitted today, may not be detected in time to stop the data.

Instead of embedding signals within data, hardware flow control uses electrical signals from a PC to its modem which are not part of the data flow channel; this is called **out-of-band signaling**. Hardware flow control is a way for a PC to tell its modem to stop the other modem from sending data. When the first (receiving) modem receives the signal from its PC, it just deactivates the line between the two modems, forcing the other modem to wait. In order to understand how hardware flow control works, turn your attention back to a subject from an earlier chapter: serial port communication.

RS-232c Serial Port Communication

Remember from Chapter 8 that serial port communication on PCs follows the RS-232c standard, which specifies how information and commands travel over nine wires in the serial cable. All RS-232c serial communication is controlled by the UART chip. Hardware flow control is accomplished by the UART chip, using two of these wires: one to stop and one to start the data.

As you can see from Figure 15-15, with hardware flow control the message to stop or start data flow need only travel from the receiving PC to the receiving modem. Remember that the cable uses nine wires and can have either a DB25 (25-pin) or a DB9 (9-pin) connection at either end. Table 15-3 lists the purpose of each of these nine wires and the pin connection for both the DB9 and DB25 connectors at the computer or DTE end. (In the table, look for the acronyms for the modem lights in the third and fourth columns.) On a PC, serial port communication is asynchronous, meaning that data flow does not stay in sync with a clock. The RS-232c standard includes pin outs used to synchronize data transmission with the receive and transmit clocks, but, since PCs don't use this feature, only nine pins are used, making possible the more convenient 9-pin connection for PCs rather than always requiring a 25-pin port.

Table 15-3   RS-232c standard for serial port cable pins

Pin Number for 9-Pin Connector	Pin Number for 25-Pin Connector	Pin Use	Description	Modem Light
1	8	Carrier detect	Connection with remote is made	CD
2	3	Receive data	Receiving data	RD or RXD
3	2	Transmit data	Sending data	SD or TXD
4	20	Data terminal ready	Modem hears its computer	TR or DTR
5	7	Signal ground	Not used with PCs	
6	6	Data set ready	Modem is able to talk	MR
7	4	Request to send	Computer wants to talk	RTS
8	5	Clear to send	Modem is ready to talk	CTS
9	22	Ring indicator	Someone is calling	

15

Looking back at Figure 15-10, you can see which of the two pins in Table 15-3 is used for hardware flow control: RTS and CTS. In most cases, RTS and CTS stay on the entire time a communication session is active. Also, remember that between the two modems, carrier (indicating that the line is still open) from each modem must also stay up for communication to take place. When the receiving computer wants to stop receiving data, it drops the RTS signal. Its modem responds by dropping the CTS signal and deactivating the line. When the receiving computer is ready for more data, it raises RTS, and the receiving modem responds by raising CTS and activating the phone line. ("Dropping" and "raising" signals here are terms used by communications technicians. They mean that a signal is either stopped or started, respectively.)

Additional UART Protocols

When a UART chip from a sending device sends digital data to a sending modem, it first prepares the data to be received by the UART chip on the other end. When the receiving UART chip receives digital data from its modem, it performs some error checking based on information sent to it from the sending UART chip. Think of this process as another communication layer: UART-to-UART.

Both the sending and receiving UART chips must have determined to use the same protocol to send and receive data, for communication to take place. The five protocols for digital communication between two PCs as controlled by their UART chips are listed in Table 15-4. Figure 15-12 shows the Windows 95 screen where these protocols are set for the UART chip and its COM port. The resulting selections are known as the **port settings**.

Table 15-4   Communication protocol between two UART chips

Port Setting	Description	Common Values
Bits per second	What will be the speed of transmission in bps?	2400, 4800, 9600, 19,200, 38,400, 57,600, 115,200, 230,400, 460,800, 921,600 bps
Data bits	How many bits are to be used to send a single character of data?	7 or 8 bits
Parity	Will there be error checking, and if so, what will be its format?	Odd, Even, or None
Stop bits	What will be the code to indicate that a character (its string of bits) is starting or ending?	1, 1.5, or 2 bits
Flow control	How will the flow of data be controlled?	Xon/Xoff or Hardware

The first and last items in this table (speed and flow control) have already been discussed. This section covers the other three settings.

Data Bits.   Back when most data sent across modems was in ASCII format, the question arose: How many bits are necessary to send one ASCII character? The answer to this question was critical because the maximum number of bits needed to represent one ASCII character is 7 bits, not 8. (To understand this point, see Appendix C, and convert the largest hex value to binary.) Therefore, to transmit in ASCII really requires that only 7 bits be used per character. The choice, therefore, for character transmission is either 7 or 8 data bits. Most often today, you should choose 8 data bits unless you know that you are only transmitting in ASCII.

Parity. Parity checking in telecommunications is performed in much the same way that memory on a systemboard checks parity. When you are using 7 data bits, add an extra bit, which can be 0 or 1 to make either odd or even parity. The receiving UART chip compares the parity to its count of odd or even bits to check the data bits for errors. In most cases today, you don't want the UART chip to use parity checking. Error checking as well as error correction can be better performed by the modem.

Stop Bits. Whenever the sending UART chip is ready to send a group of data bits (a character) to the receiving UART chip, it puts one start bit in front of the data bits to indicate to the receiving UART chip that a character is starting. In most cases, the UART chip also sends one stop bit to indicate that the character is complete, although two stop bits can be selected.

INSTALLING AND CONFIGURING A MODEM

Follow these steps to install an internal modem:

1. Read the modem documentation.

2. Determine which serial port is available on your system.

3. Set any jumpers or DIP switches on the modem card. (See your documentation for details about your card. Common jumper and DIP switch settings are for COM ports, IRQ, and I/O addresses, and to indicate whether or not the card is to use Plug-and-Play.)

4. Turn off your computer and remove the case. Find an empty slot, remove the face cover, and save the screw. Mount the card firmly into the slot, and replace the screw to anchor the card.

5. Replace the cover. (Or you may choose not to replace the computer cover until you know that the modem is working.)

6. Plug the telephone line from the house into the modem. The second jack on the modem is for an optional telephone.

For an external modem, follow these steps:

1. You will need an RS–232c serial cable to connect the modem to the serial port. If the modem does not come with a cable, don't skimp on price here; buy a good quality cable. Connect the cable to the modem and to the serial port.

2. Plug the electrical cord from the modem into a 110V AC outlet.

3. Plug the telephone line from the house into the modem. The second jack on the modem is for an optional telephone.

15

Turn on your computer and follow these steps to configure the modem under the OS. Begin with Step 1 for Windows NT, with Step 12 for Windows 95, and with Step 14 for Windows 3.x.

1. For Windows NT, click **Start**, **Settings**, **Control Panel**, and then double-click on **Modem**. The Install New Modem dialog box displays, as in Figure 15-16. If you want Windows NT to detect and install the modem for you, click **Next** and go to Step 3. If you want to provide the installation disk for the modem, click **Don't detect my modem: I will select it from the list**, and proceed to Step 2.

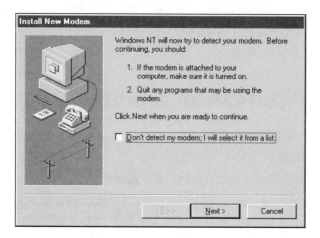

Figure 15-16   Installing a new modem

2. Either select the modem from the list of modems provided by Windows NT or, if you have an installation disk provided with the modem, click **Have Disk** and provide the location of the files. (It is typical of modem manufacturers to offer a disk with \Win95 and \NT directories on the disk to support both OSs. Select the \NT directory on the disk. In the case of the 33.6 modem used in the example in this chapter, the name of the directory on the installation disk is \NT40, indicating the version of Windows NT that the drivers support.) Go to Step 4.

3. After the modem is detected, Windows NT will request the location of the Windows NT \I386 directory—which is located on the Windows NT installation CD-ROM—from which it copies the necessary drivers. Place the CD in the drive and tell Windows NT the location of the directory (for example, D:).

4. After the modem drivers are installed, the next step is to configure the modem. Click **Start**, **Settings**, **Control Panel**, and then double-click the **Modem** icon. The modem Properties box displays, which looks and works about the same way as does Windows 95. Click on the installed modem and click **Properties**.

5. Use the properties listed below unless you have a specific reason to do otherwise (such as to compensate for a noisy phone line).

   ▪ Set the modem speed at the highest value in the drop-down list, which is the highest value supported by this modem.

   ▪ Set the port protocol at "8, No, and 1," which is a computer jargon way of saying 8 bits, no parity, and 1 stop bit.

   ▪ Use hardware flow control.

6. If you want to use Windows NT to make calls without using other software, then install Dial-Up Networking. Double-click the **My Computer** icon, and then double-click **Dial-Up Networking**. Figure 15-17 displays, and Windows NT tells you that you can now install the service.

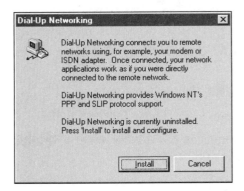

Figure 15-17   Windows NT instructs the user to install Dial-Up Networking before it can be used

7. Click **Install**.

8. Windows NT requests the location of the \I386 directory. Provide the CD-ROM and tell it the location of the directory.

9. When Windows NT asks you to select the RAS (Remote Access Service, pronounced "razz") device, select the newly installed modem and click **OK** to continue.

10. When you are asked to select the type of communication protocols that you want to use when connected, select two, NetBEUI and TCP/IP (Dial-Up Networking is covered in detail in Chapter 16).

11. Reboot the PC. The configuration is now complete for Windows NT.

15

12. For Windows 95, turn on the PC. Windows 95 Plug-and-Play will detect that a new hardware device is present. Allow the OS to identify the modem and install the drivers, or provide your own disk.

13. After the modem drivers are installed, configure the modem. Use the same method as for Windows NT. The Windows 95 installation is now complete.

14. For Windows 3.x, insert the installation disk for the modem in the floppy drive and enter A:\SETUP or A:\INSTALL from a Run dialog box. Follow the directions of the installation program to install and configure the modem. The installation program will make the appropriate entries into AUTOEXEC.BAT, CONFIG.SYS, and Windows INI files.

What can go wrong during modem installation and how to detect and resolve conflicts are covered under the Troubleshooting section later in the chapter. The last step after the modem installation is complete is to test the modem using some communications software.

An excellent software utility that can be used to test a modem is HyperTerminal, a quick and easy way to make a phone call from a Windows 95 PC. Follow these directions to test your modem:

1. Click **Start**, **Programs**, **Accessories**, **HyperTerminal**.

2. Double-click the **Hpertrm.exe** icon in the HyperTerminal folder.

3. When the Connection Description dialog box displays, enter a descriptive name for your connection and the phone number to dial.

4. Click **Dial** to make the connection. Even if you dial an out-of-service number, you can still hear your modem make the call. This confirms that your modem is installed and configured to make an outgoing call.

COMMUNICATIONS SOFTWARE

You have seen how one modem communicates with another modem and how computer hardware (a UART controlling a COM port) communicates with a modem. You have also seen how one computer's hardware communicates with another computer's hardware (UART-to-UART). Now take this process a step further up the communications layers to where hardware communicates with an OS and communications software, as shown in Figure 15-3. The UART chip is sending and receiving data only because the software on the PC is communicating with it. Two examples of communications software programs are ProComm Plus and pcANYWHERE. These two applications software programs can be used to send files back and forth between computers, control remote computers, and perform a variety of other communications tasks.

This section looks at how this and other communications software communicates with a modem (by way of a UART chip) and at how communications software on one PC communicates with the same or similar software on another PC.

SOFTWARE-TO-MODEM COMMUNICATION

In previous sections you have seen how one modem communicates with another modem, and how a PC and a modem communicate with each other, using the RS-232c standard for out-of-band signaling. Sometimes the commands that a PC needs to send to a modem cannot fit into the pin outs provided by the RS-232c standard, such as the command to make a call, or what phone number to dial. This type of information needs to be sent to a modem as characters, but the modem must distinguish between characters it is receiving from the computer that it should interpret as commands and characters that are simply being sent along as data and don't need to be interpreted.

One of the pioneers in modem communications, Hayes Microcomputer Products, developed a language for PCs to use to control modems. Hayes did not patent or copyright the language, and so most modems today are built to understand this language. Any modem that contains the logic to understand this language is said to be Hayes-compatible, and the language has become a *de facto* standard. (A **de facto standard** is a standard that does not have an official backing, but is considered a standard because of widespread use and acceptance by the industry.)

The Hayes language for modem control is called the **AT command set** because, when the modem is receiving commands, each command line is prefaced with AT for ATtention. A modem that uses this language stays in command mode at any time it is not connected to another modem. When a modem is in command mode and bits and bytes are sent to it from a PC, the modem interprets the bytes as commands to be followed, rather than as data to be sent over a phone line. It leaves command mode when it either receives an incoming call or dials out, and returns to command mode when a call is complete or a special escape sequence is sent to it by its computer.

Other manufacturers of modems have added to the Hayes AT command set, but Table 15-5 lists a few of the core AT commands that most modems understand. The commands that begin with the ampersand character (&) are part of the extended command set; the others are part of the basic command set. When a modem is in command mode, it responds to each command with OK or gives the results after performing the command. You can type a command from a communications software window to be executed immediately or enter a command from a dialog box for the modem configuration to be executed later, when the modem makes a call.

15

Table 15-5   AT commands for Hayes-compatible modems

Command	Description	Some Values and Their Meanings
+++	**Escape sequence:** Tells the modem to return to command mode. You should pause at least 1 second before you begin the sequence. After you end it, wait another second before you send another command. Don't begin this command with AT.	
On	**Go online:** Tells the modem to return to online data mode. This is the reverse command from the escape sequence above.	O0 Return online O1 Return online and retrain (perform training or handshaking again with the remote modem)
A/	**Repeat last command:** Repeat the last command performed by the modem. Don't begin the command with AT, but do follow it with Enter. Useful when redialing a busy number.	
In	**Identification:** Instructs the modem to return product identification information	I0 Return the product code I3 Return the modem ROM version
Zn	**Reset:** Instructs the modem to reset and restore the configuration to that defined at power on	Z0 Reset and return to user profile 0 Z1 Reset and return to user profile 1
&F	**Factory default:** Instructs the modem to reload the factory default profile. In most cases, use this command to reset the modem rather than the Z command.	
A	**Answer the phone:** Instructs the modem to answer the phone, transmit the answer tone, and wait for a carrier from the remote modem	
Dn	**Dial:** Tells the modem to dial a number. There are several parameters that can be added to this command. A few are listed on the right.	D5551212 Dial the given number D, Causes the dialing to pause DP Use pulse dialing DT Use tone dialing DW Wait for dial tone D& Wait for the credit card dialing tone before continuing with the remaining dial string
Hn	**Hang up:** Tells the modem to hang up	H0 Hang up H1 Hang up and enter command mode
Mn	**Speaker control:** Instructs the modem as to how it is to use its speaker	M0 Speaker always off M1 Speaker on until carrier detect M2 Speaker always on

Table 15-5   AT commands for Hayes-compatible modems (continued)

Command	Description	Some Values and Their Meanings
Ln	**Loudness:** Sets the loudness of the modem's speaker	L1 Low L2 Medium L3 High
Xn	**Response:** Tells the modem how it is to respond to a dial tone and busy signal	X0 Blind dialing; the modem does not need to hear the dial tone first and will not hear a busy signal X4 Modem must first hear the dial tone and responds to a busy signal (this is the default value)

The AT command set is used by communications software to communicate with modems. For example, when using pcANYWHERE, you can tell the software to dial up a remote computer by clicking on a button and typing a phone number to dial. The software performs this task in the background for you by sending the appropriate AT commands to the modem.

Using pcANYWHERE for Windows 3.x, follow the following procedures to establish a connection to a remote PC. (The Windows 95 version of pcANYWHERE works similarly.)

1. Double-click the **pcANYWHERE** icon in Program Manager. The pcANYWHERE opening screen displays, as in Figure 15-18.

2. Click **Call a Host PC** and select **pcANYWHERE Host via modem** from the Host PC Directory that displays. Click **Call**.

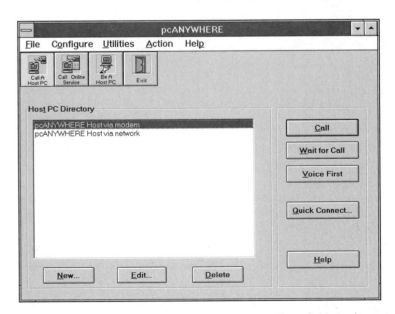

Figure 15-18   Opening screen of pcANYWHERE for Windows 3.1

3. You are then asked to enter the phone number to dial and click OK. pcANYWHERE does the rest. The Connecting dialog box displays, as in Figure 15-19, showing the dialog between the software and its modem. (Notice in the Modem Dialog box of Figure 15-19 that some of the AT command strings contain this format: Sn=number, where n is a number. These commands are setting the modem's internal registers, which are memory locations in the modem where the modem temporarily keeps configuration information. For example, the AT command S7=30 in Figure 15-19 says to store the value 30 into modem register 7. Modem register 7 is used to keep the number of seconds that the modem is to wait for a carrier from the other modem before assuming the modem is not there. The value is set to 30 seconds. For a complete listing of the modem registers and the values they support, see your modem manual.)

4. After the connection is made, pcANYWHERE creates a window on your screen that is an exact replica of the remote PC's screen.

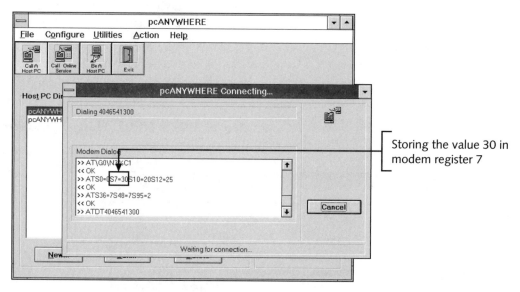

Figure 15-19 Sample dialog between the communications software and its modem shows modem registers being set

Even though most communications software controls the modem for you, some programs allow you to use the AT command set yourself to manually control your modem. One example of software that provides the user with a command mode is ProComm Plus for Windows, shown in Figure 15-20. When you first access the software, by default you enter the modem command mode. Table 15-6 shows an example of an interchange between a modem and a user.

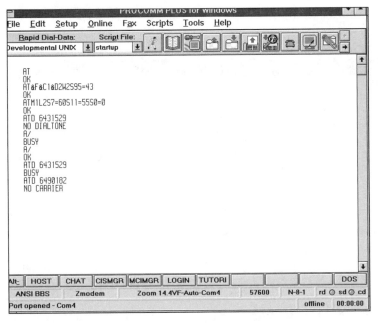

Figure 15-20   ProComm Plus for Windows in command mode allows the user to enter AT commands to manually control the modem

Table 15-6   An example of a dialog between a user and a modem

Source	Command or Response	Description
From user	ATD 5551221 [enter]	Dial the given number.
From modem	CONNECT 19200	Modem responds with the agreed-on bps. At this point, you can transfer data using a utility provided by the communications software. Then wait at least 1 second before the next command.
From user	+++	Escape sequence telling the modem to return to command mode (then pause 1 second)
From modem	OK	Modem responds by giving you the OK response.
From user	ATH0 [Enter]	Disconnect the line.
From modem	OK	Modem responds by giving you the OK response.

15

Some other AT commands and their meanings are listed in Table 15-7.

Table 15-7   Some examples of AT commands

Command	Description
ATDT 5552115	Dial the given number using tone dialing.
ATDP 5552115	Dial the given number using pulse dialing.
ATD 9,5552115	Dial 9 and pause, then dial the remaining numbers (use this method to get an outside line from a business phone).
AT &F1DT9,5552115	Restore the default factory settings. Dial using tone dialing. Pause after dialing the 9. Dial the remaining numbers.
ATM2L2	Always have the speaker on. Set loudness of speaker at medium.
ATI3	Report the modem ROM version.

SOFTWARE-TO-SOFTWARE COMMUNICATION

Even though you know that software cannot physically communicate with software on another computer without going through modems to do so, logically this fact can be masked so that there can be virtual communication between the software programs. Back to the newspaper analogy in Figure 15-1: The distribution center at the newspaper press headquarters receives a request for papers from a remote distribution point in the city. The center fills the order and responds that the newspapers are on the way. The truck and road systems are involved in this transaction, yet there is a very real sense in which the two distribution points communicate and do business at a high level where trucks and the road system supporting them are not even considered, but are transparent to the two distributors.

This concept is also true of two communications applications communicating. One application sends its data to another application, which receives the data and responds. This higher communication layer is the beginning of the software realm of data communication. There are basically two ways that software communicates with other software:

- **Remote control**: In this mode, the remote PC controls the host PC. The remote PC sends commands to the host PC. The host PC uses these commands to execute software on the host PC and passes the results of the commands back to the remote PC. This method passes commands from the remote PC to the host. The host PC cannot pass commands to the remote PC.

- **Data transfer**: In this mode, the remote PC requests data from the host PC, and the host PC sends the requested data to the remote PC. File transfer is one example of this type of communication. This method passes requests for data from the remote PC to the host. The host PC cannot request data from the remote PC.

The first method is usually slower than the second method, but offers more power to the remote PC. This section looks at an example of each type of software-to-software communication, using pcANYWHERE.

FILE TRANSFER WITH pcANYWHERE

Sharing data between two PCs is one of the most common tasks of communications software. Most communications applications provide file transfer utilities that have their own look and feel, but the basics of file transfer are the same from one utility to another. The file transfer function of pcANYWHERE for Windows 3.x (which operates identically to the file transfer of pcANYWHERE for Windows 95) is the example used below. pcANYWHERE on one computer can make a connection to another PC in one of three ways:

- A remote PC calling a host PC
- A host PC calling a remote PC
- A PC calling an online service

In the explanation below, the terminology used by pcANYWHERE is followed. The two PCs are called the host PC and the remote PC. The host follows the commands or processes requests for data from the remote PC. The first instance listed above is the example used below: a remote PC calling a host PC. If you are sitting at a PC making a call to another PC, your PC is called the remote PC, even though it is not "remote" to you, but rather is your local PC, and the other PC is called the "host" PC. The connection is made as follows:

1. Make the call to the host PC. The connection is made at the modem-to-modem level. Then a window displays on your screen that is a replica of the host PC's screen. An example is shown in Figure 15-21.

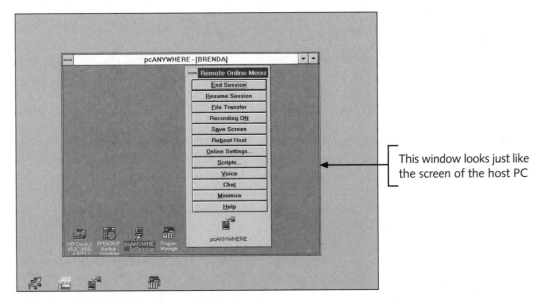

This window looks just like the screen of the host PC

Figure 15-21 pcANYWHERE provides a window on the remote PC that replicates the screen on the host PC

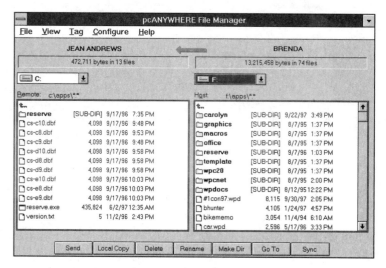

Figure 15-22   The pcANYWHERE File Transfer utility is called the pcANYWHERE File Manager

2. Select the option **File Transfer**. Figure 15-22 displays.

3. From this pcANYWHERE File Manager window, you can see your directories and files on the left side of the window (called the Remote side) and the files on the other PC on the right side of the window (called the Host side). Commands are listed at the bottom of the window. To copy a file from the Remote to the Host, select the file on the left and drag and drop it on the right side, or you can use the Send command button at the bottom of the window.

4. Exit the utility by selecting **File**, **Exit** from the menu at the top of the window.

REMOTE CONTROL WITH PCANYWHERE

One very useful tool for software communication, especially for a PC support person, is remote control. With remote control, a person sitting at one PC (called the remote) can dial up another PC (called the host) and remotely control the other PC. The user can execute software on the host PC just as though he or she were sitting at the other PC, and even reboot the host PC. Help desk personnel find this kind of control very useful when supporting a user and PC at a remote location. A person working from home or off-site can dial into his or her computer at work and perform just about any task on that PC that can be done while sitting in front of it, although the speed of response does limit how productive that work can be.

In Figure 15-21, a connection is established between the remote (this end) and the host (the other end). If the Host window shown in the figure is the active window, any mouse movement or keyboard strokes that are performed at the remote PC are passed to the host computer to be executed. If the Host window is not active, then the user is controlling his or her own computer locally.

Remote control requires that both computers have pcANYWHERE installed. When you purchase pcANYWHERE, you are purchasing two licenses, one for the remote and one for the host. ProComm Plus also offers a remote control utility with a similar licensing policy. With both applications, a PC can be set up to be either the remote or the host, but can't do both at the same time. The host serves the remote, passing data to it or performing commands it receives from the remote. The remote PC has more control over what is being done than does the host.

In order to make your computer a host computer, you must set pcANYWHERE to be a host and leave the application open and waiting for a call. To do so, follow these directions:

1. Execute pcANYWHERE. In this example, pcANYWHERE under Windows 3.1 is being used, but pcANYWHERE under Windows 95 works the same way.

2. Click **Be a Host PC**. Figure 15-23 displays.

3. If you want to require a password for the caller or limit the caller to only certain directories or drives on your PC, you can do that by clicking **Settings**.

4. After you have specified any desired settings, click **Wait for Call**. After initializing the modem, pcANYWHERE reduces itself to an icon and waits, as in Figure 15-24.

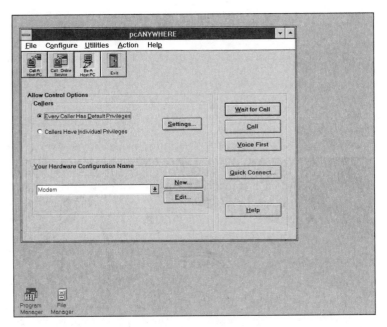

Figure 15-23   Setting up a PC to be a host using pcANYWHERE

Figure 15-24   A small desktop icon indicates that pcANYWHERE is waiting for an incoming call

5. You can use the PC in any other way while the PC is listening for a call. When a call from a remote PC is in progress, you can watch what is happening at the host end.

TROUBLESHOOTING GUIDELINES

This section provides a guide to solving problems with modems and communicating over phone lines. Some keys to troubleshooting are: determine what does work and what does not work, find out what has worked in the past that now no longer works, and establish what has changed since things last worked. Much of this can be determined by asking the user and yourself questions and by trying the simple things first. These guidelines give you some questions to ask and some things to try.

The modem does not respond.

1. Is it plugged into the phone jack?

2. Is the external modem plugged into the computer? Is the connection solid?

3. There are two jacks on a modem. Are the lines reversed?

4. Is the phone line working? Plug in a phone. Is there a dial tone?

5. Do you need to dial an extra character to get an outside line, such as 9 or 8?

6. Has the modem ever worked, or is this a new installation? If it is a new installation, check these things:

   - Is the modem set to the same COM port and IRQ that the software is set to?

   - Is another device also configured to the same COM port or IRQ that the modem is using?

   - For an internal modem, check the DIP switches and jumpers. Do they agree with the modem properties in the OS?

   - Try moving an internal modem to a different expansion slot. For an external modem using a serial port card, move the serial port card to a different slot.

   - For an external modem, use a different serial cable.

   - Did the software correctly initialize the modem? If you did not give the correct modem type to the software, it may be trying to send the wrong initialization command. Try AT&F. (Under Windows 95, click **Start**, **Settings**, **Control Panel**. Double-click **Modem**. Select the modem and click **Modem Properties**, **Connections**, **Advanced Connection Settings**. Figure 15-25 displays. Enter the AT command under Extra Settings.) Retry the modem.

   - Is the computer short on RAM or hard drive space? Try closing all other applications currently running.

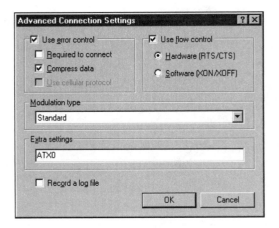

Figure 15-25   Extra settings box allows you to send extra AT commands to the modem on any call

The modem says there is no dial tone, even though you can hear it.

1. The modem may not be able to detect the dial tone even if you can hear it. Try unplugging any other equipment plugged into this same phone line, such as a Fax machine.

2. Try giving the ATX0 command before you dial. Enter the command under Advanced Settings, as in Figure 15-25.

3. Straighten your phone lines! Don't let them get all twisted and crossed up with other heavy electrical lines.

The modem dials and then says that the other end is busy, even when you know that it is not.

1. This can happen with international calls; the modem does not recognize the signal as a ring. Try giving the ATX0 command first.

2. Straighten the phone lines and remove extra equipment, as described above.

The sending modem and the receiving modem take a very long time to negotiate the connection.

1. This is probably because of a noisy phone line. Try calling again or using a different number.

2. Remove other equipment from your line. A likely suspect is a credit card machine.

3. Try turning off data compression and try again.

4. Turn off error correction and try again.

5. Try forcing your modem to use a slower speed.

15

During a connection, it sounds as if the handshaking starts all over again.

Modems normally do this if the phone line is noisy and causes much data to become corrupted; it's called **retraining**, and it sometimes can solve the problem as the modems renegotiate, compensating for the noisy line. Do the things listed above to clear your line of equipment and twisted phone lines.

File transfers are too slow.

Does your modem support data compression? Check that the modem is configured for it.

The modem loses connection at odd times or is slow.

1. Check the communications software for the speed assigned to it. Many times people set the communications software speed for the modem speed instead of for what the software is asking for, the port speed, which should be about four times the modem speed.

2. You may have a noisy phone line. Try the connection using two modems of the same brand and model. If performance is better, the problem is most likely the phone line.

3. Is the phone line from the modem to the jack too long? About 4 feet is the limit; otherwise, electromagnetic interference may be the problem.

4. Straighten the phone lines and clear the line of any extra equipment.

5. Reinstall the modem. Allow Windows 95 to detect the modem for you and install its own drivers.

The modem drops the connection and gives the NO CARRIER message.

1. Most likely the connection was first dropped by the remote modem. Is someone trying to use a phone extension on this line?

2. Disable call waiting. To do this, put *70, before the dialing number. Some communications software has a setting to disable call waiting. If not, you can put these four characters in the Extra Settings box of Advanced Connections Settings (see Figure 15-25).

3. Remove extra equipment from the line and straighten the phone lines.

Whenever the weather is bad, the connection disconnects often.

This is caused by a dirty phone line. Does your line make extra noises at these times? Remove any extra equipment and straighten the lines.

Whenever large files are downloaded, some of the data is lost.

Make sure that hardware flow control is on, and that software flow control is off, for the software, the COM port, and the modem.

The connection fails whenever large files are uploaded or downloaded.

There may be a buffer overflow. Try these things to gain better control of data flow:

1. Make sure that hardware flow control is on, and that software flow control is off, for the software, the COM port, and the modem.

2. Is the serial port speed set too high for the UART chip you have? Lower the port speed.

3. For an external modem, try a different serial port cable.

You get nothing but garbage across the connection.

1. Check the port settings. Try 8 data bits, no parity, and one stop bit (8, No, and 1).

2. Slow down the port speed.

3. Slow down the modem speed.

FASTER THAN PHONE LINES

The speed of communicating data is constantly improving. Looking back at Figure 15-3, you can see that no matter how fast communication can be between the computer and its modem, the speed between one modem and another can be no faster than the limited speed of the regular analog phone lines to which they are connected. You also learned in this chapter that phone lines most often become digital once they reach a central office of the phone company or some other centralized location. The phone company transports voice and data digitally over long distances and then converts it back to an analog signal just before it reaches the customer location, which is usually done at the customer's central office.

The problem with slow analog lines can be greatly improved by making the phone lines digital all the way from one customer to the next. This has been done for large commercial customers. One example of a digital line is called a T1 line, which carries the equivalent of 24 phone circuits and can transmit data at 1.5 million bps. Prices for T1 lines vary and are somewhere around $400 per month. These lines are sometimes installed as private circuits connecting two locations of the same company.

A less expensive version of a digital phone line has been developed that follows an accepted international standard called **integrated services digital network** or **ISDN**. An ISDN line is fully digital and consists of two channels, or phone circuits, on a single pair of wires. Each line can support speeds up to 64,000 bps. The two lines can be combined so that, effectively, data travels at 128,000 bps, which is about five times the speed of regular phone lines.

Because ISDN lines are designed for small business and home use, the two lines can support voice communication, Fax machines, and computers. The two circuits are logically two phone lines, which can each have a different phone number, although most often only one number is assigned to both lines. Because an ISDN line must have little noise on it, only a

15

single jack for the line—which initially connects to one device—is allowed at a customer location.

In order to use an ISDN line at your business or home, you must have these things:

- An ISDN line leased from the phone company

- An ISDN device on your computer (comparable to a modem for a regular phone line)

- ISDN software on your PC to manage the connection (see the Web site www.ticom.com for some examples)

If you plan to use an ISDN line to access the Internet, then, in order for you to see a performance gain, your service provider must also have an ISDN line. If you plan to use the ISDN line for telecommuting, then your place of business must also have ISDN in order for performance to improve.

The single ISDN device that connects to the ISDN line at your home can be an expansion card inside your PC or can be an external device. Figure 15-26 shows that communications software, the OS, and computer hardware relate to an ISDN device for digital phone lines just as they relate to a modem for analog phone lines (see Figure 15-3). The communications software and the OS make the distinction that they are communicating to a digital device rather

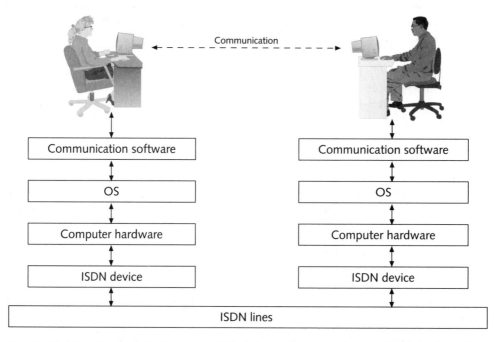

Figure 15-26   Communicating over digital phone lines requires an ISDN device rather than a modem

than to a modem. If the device is external and using the COM port on the computer system, then the UART chip controlling that COM port does not make a distinction between communicating with an ISDN device or with a modem, since all its communication is digital in either case. There are three choices as to how you can connect to ISDN:

- **Internal card**: An internal card is less expensive than the other two choices, but limits the use of the ISDN to when your computer is on.

- **External device**: An external device requires a connection to your PC. If you connect the device by way of your serial port, you have a bottleneck at the serial port; the device can communicate to your PC only as fast as the serial port speed.

- **External device and network card**: You can use an external device connected to your PC by way of a network card. The price is higher, but this solution offers the most advantages.

Figure 15-27 shows one setup for an ISDN external device. The external ISDN device can also function as a bridge between a LAN in your building and the ISDN line. (In networking, a **bridge** is a device that connects two networks so that communication can take place between them.) Every PC would then connect to the ISDN line by way of its network card, which is also its access to the LAN. Some of these external ISDN devices also supply ordinary phone jacks so that ordinary telephones can also be connected to the ISDN line without having to go through a PC in your building.

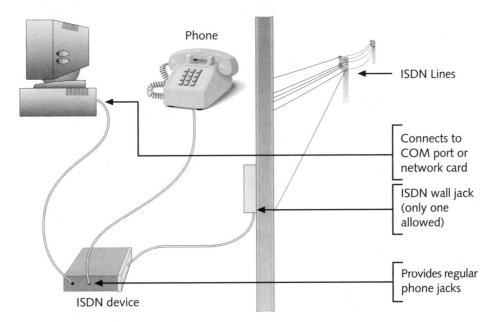

Phone

ISDN Lines

Connects to
COM port or
network card

ISDN wall jack
(only one
allowed)

Provides regular
phone jacks

ISDN device

15

Figure 15-27   An external ISDN device serves as a connection
point for PCs and telephones

The ISDN device, be it internal or external, in North America is technically an NT1 (network termination 1) device because, in order for a PC to connect to an ISDN line, an NT1 interface is required. You may hear an external NT1 called an ISDN modem or an ISDN box. An internal NT1 may be called an ISDN card or an ISDN modem. Call it a box or a card or a device, but calling it an ISDN modem is not correct! A modem converts digital to analog and analog to digital. An ISDN circuit is digital all the way. No modems are needed.

CHAPTER SUMMARY

- Communicating over phone lines involves both virtual communication and physical communication. Virtual communication takes place between counterpart layers at each end, and physical communication occurs between adjacent layers.

- A modem is a device used by a PC to convert digital data to analog signals suitable for transmission over phone lines, and to convert the data back to digital once it is transmitted.

- When two modems first connect, they must decide how data will be transmitted. This process is called training or handshaking.

- Modems can perform data compression to speed up transmission, and error correction to ensure the integrity of the data.

- The speed that data can travel over phone lines is called modem speed or line speed and is measured in baud rates of bits per second (bps).

- The limitation of modem speeds is partly determined by the analog quality of phone lines and the way data is sometimes converted to digital signals during transmissions over the phone company lines.

- Modem standards have been set by CCITT (Comité Consultatif Internationale de Télégraphie et Téléphonie), now called either CCITT standards or ITU standards.

- Modem standards include standards of speed, data compression, and error correction.

- The protocols used by modems are factory-set into the modem's firmware, but can be partially controlled by settings controlled by the operating system or communications software.

- Error correction performed by modems is done by dividing data into packets or frames and calculating a checksum on each packet. The checksum is calculated again at the receiving end. If the two checksums differ, another transmission is requested by the receiving modem.

- The handshaking between two modems can be heard as hissing sounds when the two modems first connect.

- Computers communicating through modems are called data terminal equipment (DTE). The modems are called data communications equipment (DCE).

- Overall transmission speed is partially determined by the port speed, which is the speed of the UART chip controlling the communications port used by the modem.

- Both internal and external modems use a UART chip to control the transmission of digital data from the computer.

- The method that a receiving modem or PC uses to stop and start the flow of data to it is called flow control.

- Flow control can be performed by a computer or a modem. Two methods of flow control are software flow control and hardware flow control. Hardware flow control is the preferred choice.

- Serial ports use the RS-232c standard for communication. Hardware flow control uses two of the connections in the RS-232c standard.

- The UART chip controls data transmission speed, parity checking, start and stop bits, and flow control.

- Communications software can either provide remote control to a host PC or pass data from one PC to another. Remote control is usually the slower of the two methods.

- Most communications software communicates to modems using a modem language developed by Hayes called the AT command set. Modems that use this language are said to be Hayes-compatible.

- ISDN is a faster alternative to regular analog phone lines because it is digital and provides two lines rather than only the single line provided by regular phone lines.

- In order to benefit from using ISDN technology, both the sending and receiving computers must have an ISDN connection. Each computer must use an ISDN device and ISDN software.

KEY TERMS

15

- **Analog signals** — Signals that have an infinite number of values within a range of possible values. An example is the transmission of sound, in wave format, over traditional telephone lines. Compare to Digital signal.

- **AT command set** — A set of commands used by a PC to control a modem. AT is the ATtention command, which alerts a modem to prepare to receive additional commands. For example, ATDT means attention and listen for a dial tone.

- **Baud rate** — A line speed of communication between two devices such as a computer and a printer or a modem. This speed is measured in the number of times a signal changes in one second.

- **Carrier** — A reference signal used to activate a phone line to confirm a continuous frequency; used to indicate that two computers are ready to receive or transmit data via modems.

- **Checksum** — A method of error checking of transmitted data, whereby the digits are added up and their sum compared to an expected sum.

- **Data bits** — The number of bits used to make up a transmitted character or value. PC communication will typically use 8 data bits and 1 stop bit for communicating data over phone lines.

- **Data communications equipment (DCE)** — The hardware, usually a dial-up modem, that provides the connection between a data terminal and a communication line.

- **Data terminal equipment (DTE)** — This term refers to both the computer and a remote terminal or other computer to which it is attached.

- **De facto standard** — A standard that does not have an official backing, but is considered a standard because of widespread use and acceptance by the industry.

- **Demodulation** — When digital data that has been converted to analog data is converted back to digital data. *See* Modulation.

- **Digital signal** — A signal that has only a finite number of values in the range of possible values. An example is the transmission of data over a serial cable as bits, where there are only two values: 0 and 1.

- **Error Correction** — The ability of some modems to identify transmission errors and then automatically request another transmission.

- **Flow control** — When using modems, a method of controlling the flow of data from a sending PC by having the receiving PC send a message to the sending device to stop or start data flow. Xon/Xoff is an example of a flow control protocol.

- **Frame** — A small, standardized packet of data that also includes header and trailer information as well as error-checking codes.

- **Handshaking** — When two modems begin to communicate, the initial agreement made as to how to send and receive data. It often occurs when you hear the modem making noises as the dial-up is completed.

- **Inband signaling** — In modem communication, the name of the signalling used by software flow control, which sends a message to pause transmission by sending a special control character in the same channel (or band) that data is sent in.

- **ISDN (Integrated services digital network)** — A communications standard that can carry digital data simultaneously over two channels on a single pair of wires, at about five times the speed of regular phone lines.

- **Modem** — From MOdulate/DEModulate. A device that modulates digital data from a computer to an analog format that can be sent over telephone lines, then demodulates it back into digital form.

- **Modem speed** — The speed a modem can transmit data along a phone line measured in bits per second (bps). Two communicating modems must talk at the same speed for data transmission to be successful.

- **Modulation** — Converting binary or digital data into an analog signal that can be sent over standard telephone lines.

- **Noise** — An extraneous, unwanted signal, often over an analog phone line, that can cause communication interference or transmission errors. Possible sources are fluorescent lighting, radios, TVs, or bad wiring.

- **Out-of-band signaling** — The type of signalling used by hardware flow control, which sends a message to pause transmission by using channels (or bands) not used for data.

- **Port settings** — The configuration parameters of communications devices such as COM1, COM2, or COM3, including IRQ settings.

- **Port speed** — The communication speed between a DTE (computer) and a DCE (modem). As a general rule, the port speed should be about four times as fast as the modem speed.

- **Remote control** — Controlling a computer or other device from a remote location (for example, when a person controls a computer from another computer connected by a phone line).

- **Start bit** — A bit that is used to signal the approach of data.

- **Stop bit** — A bit that is used to signal the end of a block of data.

- **UART (Universal Asynchronous receiver-transmitter chip)** — A chip that controls serial ports. It sets protocol and converts parallel data bits coming from the system bus into serial bits.

- **V.34 standard** — A communications standard that transmits at 28,800 bps and/or 33,600 bps.

REVIEW QUESTIONS

1. Briefly describe modulation and demodulation.
2. In Windows 95, how can you check your modem type and configuration?
3. When referring to a modem, what does 33.6 really mean?
4. Why is the maximum transmission rate of today's modems limited to 56.6 Kbps?
5. How is the V.34 standard different from the k56flex or x2 standard?
6. Give two ways to deal with a noisy or dirty phone line.
7. How does error correction work with modem communication?
8. What type of ports do modems use to communicate: serial or parallel?
9. What are the typical DOS names for the ports modems use to communicate?
10. As a general rule, the port speed should be about _____ times as fast as the modem speed.
11. What chip is responsible for communicating over a serial port?
12. What is the name of the physical port that is used to connect an external modem? Describe its shape and the number of pins it has.

15

13. What are pins 2 and 3 used for in a typical serial port cable?

14. What is the name of the protocol used for modem error checking?

15. List and briefly describe three modem protocols that must be correctly set for successful telecommunication.

16. In Windows 95, click on **Start**, **Help**, and then select the **Contents** Tab. Double-click on **Troubleshooting**. Double-click on **If you have trouble using your modem**. List four problems covered by the Modem Troubleshooter.

17. List three hardware reasons why a modem might not respond.

18. List three software reasons that can cause a modem not to respond.

19. What could cause you to get nothing but garbage across a modem connection?

20. For high-speed communication, what type of line is much faster than a typical telephone line?

PROJECTS

QUICK MODEM TEST

Use Windows HyperTerminal to make a call from your computer to any phone number. Describe what happens. What does this test confirm and not confirm about your modem and its setup?

DOES YOUR PHONE LINE QUALIFY FOR A 56 KBPS LINE

You must have a V.34 standard modem for this project. Determine if your phone line is clean enough to support a 56 Kbps modem. Access the 3Com Web site and follow the directions to perform the line test. Get a printed screen of your results. The Web site is www.x2.usr.com/linetest1.html.

FIND OUT ABOUT YOUR MODEM

1. Open the Control Panel: Click **Start**, **Settings**, **Control Panel**.

2. Double-click on **Modems**.

3. Click on the **Diagnostics** tab.

4. Under Port, click on the port that shows the installed modem.

5. Click on the **More Info**… button

   a. What DOS Port does the modem use?

   b. What Interrupt does the modem use?

   c. What port Address does the modem use?

   d. What UART chip is used?

   e. What is the highest possible speed supported by the UART chip?

   f. What model of modem is installed?

   g. List several types of information stored under the Command and Response headings.

6. Select the **General** tab, then click the **Dialing Properties** button. If you are using a business phone, how do you tell the computer what to do to access an outside line?

CHANGE YOUR MODEM'S CONNECTION SETTINGS

Following the directions in the troubleshooting guidelines, change your modem connection settings so that the modem speaker remains on the entire time the modem is connected, by using the ATM2 command under the Extra settings box of Advanced Connection Settings.

Make a call with this setting. After you have finished the call, remove the extra setting.

MODEM TROUBLESHOOTING

In the Advanced Connections Settings dialog box, check the box **Record a log file**. This action causes Windows 95 to create a log file named Modemlog.txt in the folder where Windows is installed. Make a phone call using the modem and then disconnect. Print the log file that is created.

15

SIMULATING MODEM PROBLEMS

Work with a partner on this project. Using a computer with an internal modem and a phone line, simulate a problem with the modem, as your partner does the same with another PC. Don't tell your partner what you did to your modem, and then exchange PCs. Troubleshoot the problem created by your partner. Here are some examples of problems to create:

- Change a jumper or DIP switch on the modem. (Don't do this without first carefully writing down the original setting.)

- Disable the COM port the modem is using.

- Uninstall the modem in the operating system.

- Loosen the modem card from its expansion slot.

- Disconnect the phone line.

- Insert the phone line in the wrong jack on the modem.

As you work to troubleshoot the problem caused by your partner, keep notes of what you discover and what you try. Begin by answering these questions:

1. Describe exactly what happens when you attempt to make a call.

2. List what you know works with the modem and the software.

3. List what you suspect the problem might be.

4. List the steps you take to correct the problem.

5. What was the source of the problem (not your partner!)?

Using Nuts & Bolts to Get Serial Port Information

Using Nuts & Bolts, access Discover Pro. From the Discover Pro main screen, click the **Diagnostic** tab, and then click **Advanced**. Select **Serial Diag** from the icons on the right side of the advanced diagnostics screen. Figure 15-28 displays. Perform the serial port test, and then print the test results. What does the term "external loopback" mean?

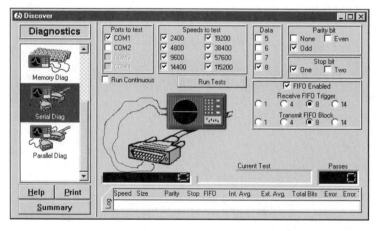

Figure 15-28 Nuts & Bolts advanced diagnostics can test a serial port

NETWORKING FUNDAMENTALS AND THE INTERNET

When studying how to manage and maintain a personal computer, you should not overlook the subject of networking, because more and more PC users are connecting to the Internet from a home PC or connecting to a LAN or WAN at their places of business. This chapter first looks at the fundamentals of the hardware and software that make up networks, and then turns to the largest network of all, the Internet, and explains how to support a PC that interfaces with the Internet.

IN THIS CHAPTER YOU WILL LEARN:

- About the typical hardware components of a network
- How several popular network architectures manage data traffic
- How data is transmitted over several interconnected networks
- About how communications layers and their protocols are used on a network
- About many of the popular Applications used on a network
- How to connect to a network using a modem and a phone line
- About the Internet and how to support PCs connected to the Internet

AN OVERVIEW OF NETWORKING

Networking is a means of connecting computers together so that they can share data, such as files and programs, and resources such as printers and modems. As with all other computer-related subjects, the subject of networking can be broken down into two categories: network hardware and network software. This section addresses both the hardware and software used by networks, with the focus on how networking relates to personal computers.

Before beginning a discussion of networking, a reminder of a couple of concepts from earlier chapters is in order. Each computer or workstation on a network is called a network station, a node, or—if the node serves special functions—a host. Data is sent over a network as bits and bytes that have been translated into electronic signals. Data is first divided into segments, each of which has a header and trailer attached. The entire unit is called a **packet**, or a **frame**. The data packets, or frames, are sent as independent units over the network. At the receiving end, the header and trailer information is removed, and the data within the packets is reassembled into contiguous data.

You can think of this process of sending data over a network as similar to that of shipping a computer to a destination. The computer is first disassembled and packed into several boxes. When the boxes all arrive, the components are unpacked and reassembled into a complete computer. Think of the computer as data, the various components as data segments, and the shipping boxes with address labels as the headers and trailers. The units (the combination of shipping boxes, labels, and computer components) are the data packets. While in transit, the computer (or data) cannot function as a computer because it has been temporarily disassembled. But once it arrives at its destination, the packing is removed, and the computer is reassembled and made ready for use.

Just as an address is information written on a shipping box, a **header** is information sent in front of data to identify for receiving protocols the data destination and the protocols that the packet is using. A **trailer** follows the data and contains information used by some protocols for error checking. For PCs, it is the job of the network card to break the data into segments and enclose each segment in headers and trailers, thus creating individual packets, and, on the receiving end, to reassemble the segments back into contiguous data. In the computer shipping analogy, think of the network card in the sending PC as the packing and shipping department and the network card in the receiving PC as the person who receives the boxes, unpacks them, and assembles the computer system.

Remember from Chapter 12 that there are two approaches to managing a network: a peer-to-peer network where each individual workstation manages its own security and resources, and a central-server network that is managed by a single server. Windows NT calls these two networks a workgroup and a domain, respectively.

TYPES OF NETWORKS

A network may be either a LAN (local area network, typically a network located in a single building or adjacent buildings, with nodes connected by cables) or a WAN (wide area network, covering a large geographical area, with nodes connected by methods other than just cables, such as microwave signals). Several networks of either type can be tied together, which is called **internetworking**.

A network design is sometimes called the network architecture, or network topology. The three most popular physical network architectures are Ethernet, Token Ring, and FDDI (Fiber Distributed Data Interface). An older type of network is ARCnet (Attached Resource Computer network), which is seldom seen today. Each type of architecture is designed to solve certain network problems, and each has its own advantages and disadvantages. What distinguishes one network architecture from another includes many details not covered in this chapter, but two basic differentiating characteristics—how computers are logically connected and how traffic is controlled on the network—are discussed here.

Ethernet

Ethernet is the most popular network topology used today. Ethernet can be configured as either a bus or a star. Figure 16-1 shows an example of each. A **bus network architecture** connects each node in a line with no centralized point of connection. A **star network architecture** uses a **hub**, a device that provides a central location through which the cables of all computers on the network are connected. The star arrangement is more popular because it is easier to wire and to maintain than is the bus arrangement, and because the failure of one node does not affect the other nodes, as is the case with the bus arrangement. In a star arrangement, some hubs are called **intelligent hubs** because they can be remotely controlled from a console using network software. Intelligent hubs can monitor a network and report errors or problems. With intelligent hubs, stations that are having problems can be remotely disabled from network access.

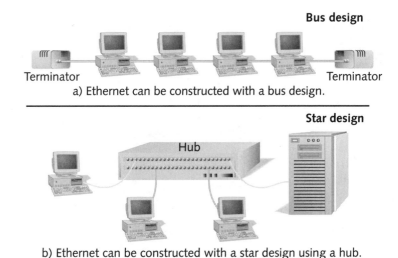

Bus design

Terminator   Terminator
a) Ethernet can be constructed with a bus design.

Star design

Hub

b) Ethernet can be constructed with a star design using a hub.

Figure 16-1   Ethernet is a simple and popular networking topology

16

An Ethernet network is a **passive network**, meaning that the networked computers, not dedicated network devices, originate the signals that manage the network. (A dedicated network device is a device, such as a hub, used solely to support a network, while other devices on the network, such as PCs, have functions other than networking.) For instance, in Figure 16-1b, the hub is not driving the signals over the network; the computers on the network are doing all the work. Ethernet works much like an old telephone party line. When someone on the party line wanted to use a phone, he or she would pick up and listen. If there was a dial tone (carrier), then the person could make a call. If someone else was talking, the person would hang up and try again later. If two people attempted to make a call at the same time, both calls would fail. They would each need to hang up and begin again. The first one back on the line would be able to make a call.

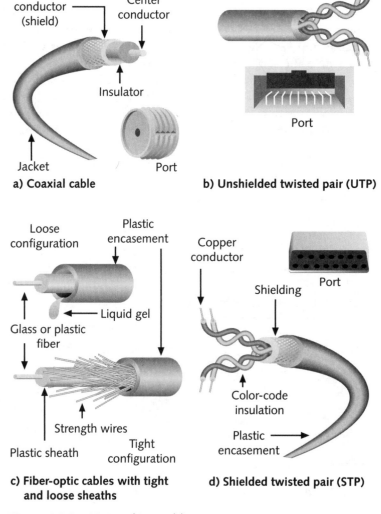

a) Coaxial cable

b) Unshielded twisted pair (UTP)

c) Fiber-optic cables with tight and loose sheaths

d) Shielded twisted pair (STP)

Figure 16-2   Networking cables

Similarly, a computer that wants to send packets over an Ethernet will first listen on the network for silence. If it hears nothing, it begins to transmit. As it transmits, it is also listening. If it hears something other than its own data being transmitted, it stops transmitting and sends out a signal that there has been a **collision**, which occurs when two computers attempt to send data at the same time. A collision can cause packets just sent to be corrupted. Each computer waits for a random amount of time and then tries to transmit again, first listening for silence. This type of network architecture is called a **contention-based** system because each computer must contend for opportunity on the network. Computers using Ethernet are said to gain access to the network using the **carrier sense multiple access with collision detection** (**CSMA/CD**) method. The name of the method suggests three characteristics of the way computers communicate on Ethernet: (1) a computer must sense that the network is free to handle its transmission (carrier sense), (2) many computers use the same network (multiple access), and (3) each computer must detect and manage collisions (collision detection).

Ethernet can use any one of four cabling systems, which are described in Table 16-1. Figure 16-2 shows an example of each of these cables.

Table 16-1   Cabling systems used by Ethernet

Cable System	Cable	Description
10Base5 (thicknet)	Thick coaxial cable	Coaxial cable is made of two conductors: a center wire and a metallic braid that surrounds the center wire. Foam insulation separates the two. The maximum segment length of thicknet is 500 meters.
10Base2 (thinnet)	Thin coaxial cable (sometimes called thinnet)	A less expensive, smaller coaxial cable than thicknet, with a maximum segment length of 185 meters. Thinnet and thicknet are sometimes used on the same Ethernet.
10BaseT (twisted-pair)	Unshielded twisted-pair (UTP) cable	Two wires, each insulated from the other and twisted together inside a plastic casing to lessen crosstalk and outside interference. (**Crosstalk** is the interference that each wire produces in the other.) There are several grades of UTP. (A lower grade of UTP not suitable for 10BaseT is often used for telephone wire.)
100BaseT (fast Ethernet)	Shielded twisted pair (STP) cable	STP costs more than UTP and thin coaxial cable, but less than thick coaxial cable and fiber-optic cable. STP is rigid and thick and has a shielding around the twisted wires to protect them from outside interference. (Sometimes a very high grade of UTP can also be used for Fast Ethernet for local connections.)
10BaseFL	Optical fiber (fiber-optic cable)	This cable uses light rather than electricity to transmit signals. A glass or plastic fiber in the center of the cable, about the same diameter as a human hair, transmits the light.

16

Because signals transmitted over long distances on a network can weaken, devices are added to amplify signals. For example, for a 10BaseT Ethernet cable, if the cable exceeds 100 meters (328 feet), amplification is required. A **repeater** is a device that amplifies the signals on a network. There are two kinds of repeaters. An **amplifier repeater** simply amplifies the incoming signal, noise and all. A **signal–regenerating repeater** "reads" the signal and then creates an exact duplicate of the original signal before sending it on.

Each of the cable systems listed in the table is limited as to the number of nodes it can support. As the number of nodes increases, performance speed and reliability can drop for the overall network. One method to prevent this kind of congestion is **segmentation**. Segmentation splits a large Ethernet into smaller segments. Each segment contains two or more computers and is connected to the other segments by a **bridge** or **router**, as shown in Figure 16-3. Stations on a single segment only need to contend with other stations on the same segment to send their packets. The bridge or router transfers packets to other segments only when it knows that the packet is addressed to a station outside its segment. All other network traffic is contained within the segment. Figure 16-3 shows an Ethernet of two segments connected by a bridge. Computers on Segment A can communicate with each other without using the bridge. However, if a computer on Segment A wants to communicate with a computer on Segment B, then the communication must go to the bridge. Don't let the two T shapes in the diagram confuse you. The Ts logically exist, but do not physically exist. If you were to wire these four PCs and one bridge together, the physical diagram could look like Figure 16-3b. More about bridges and routers later in the chapter.

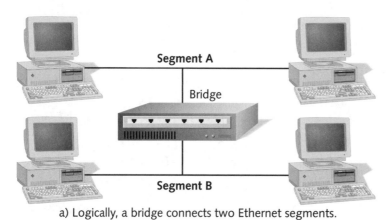

a) Logically, a bridge connects two Ethernet segments.

b) Physically, the PCs and bridge can be cabled together in this manner.

Figure 16-3   A bridge connects two Ethernet segments

Token Ring

Token Ring networking was developed by IBM and is more complex and expensive than Ethernet. It is a robust, highly reliable network, although, because of its complexity, it is more difficult to maintain than Ethernet.

Connecting Components on a Token Ring.   Token Ring is logically a ring, but stations are physically connected to the network in a star formation. Each station connects to a centralized hub called a **controlled-access unit (CAU)**, a **multistation access unit (MSAU** or sometimes just **MAU)**, or a **smart multistation access unit (SMAU)**. Figure 16-4 shows one Token Ring configuration using two IBM 8228 MSAUs. Each MSAU shown in the figure can connect eight workstations to the network, and, for this type of MSAU, there can be as many as 33 MSAUs on one Token Ring network. One MSAU can connect to another by a cable called a patch cable. The ends of the MSAU have either a Ring In (data flows into the MSAU) or Ring Out (data flows out from the MSAU) connection. The main ring includes any patch cables and the cable connecting the last MSAU Ring Out to the first MSAU Ring In. In Figure 16-4, this cable is labeled main ring cable. This main ring cable can be fiber-optic.

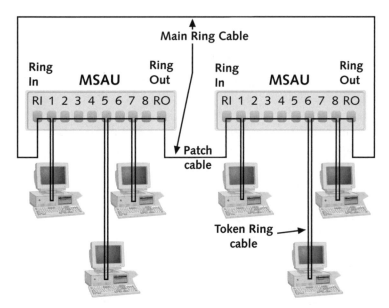

Figure 16-4 A Token Ring network uses one or more centralized hubs called multistation access units

The entire token ring, however, is made up of not only the main ring, but also the cabling to each PC on the token ring. Each workstation contains a token ring LAN card with a 9-pin connector for the Token Ring cable, which connects each workstation to an MSAU. Each Token Ring network card has a unique address, which is assigned to it during manufacturing and encoded on the card's firmware. Token Ring cables can be either UTP or STP cables that have two twisted pairs for a total of four wires in the cable.

16

Looking at Figure 16-4, you can see why a Token Ring network is said to be a physical star but a logical ring. All workstations connect to a centralized hub (in this case, two hubs strung together), but you can also follow the ring path around the entire network. The ring path in the figure goes from the first MSAU down to each PC and back again, across the patch cable to the next MSAU, from this MSAU down to each PC connected to it and back again, and finally, around the main ring cable back to the first MSAU.

Communication on a Token Ring.   Communication and traffic on a Token Ring network is controlled by a **token**, which is a small frame with a special format, that travels around the ring in only one direction. One station receives the token from the station before it on the ring, called its **nearest active upstream neighbor** (**NAUN**), and passes it on to the next station on the ring, called its **nearest active downstream neighbor** (**NADN**). As one station passes the token to the next station, it can attach data in a frame to the token. The next station receives the token together with the data frame and reads this data frame. If the frame is intended for it, it changes 2 bits in the frame to indicate that the data has been read by the intended station. It then passes the data frame on. When the token and frame are received by the station that sent the frame, it sees that the frame was successfully received and does not send the frame on again. In this case, it releases the token by passing it on to the next PC, without a data frame attached. However, if the amount of data requires more than one frame, instead of releasing the token, the PC sends the next frame with the token. In either case, the token is passed on to the next PC.

Any PC receiving a token with no data frame attached is free to attach a data frame before passing on the token. The token is busy and not released to another PC until the sending PC has received word that the data was successfully received at its destination. In other words, the only PC that should remove a data frame from behind the token is the PC that attached it in the first place.

FDDI

Fiber Distributed Data Interface (**FDDI**, pronounced "fiddy") is a ring-based network, like Token Ring, but does not require a centralized hub, making it both a logical and physical ring. FDDI provides data transfer at 100 Mbps, which is much faster than Token Ring or regular Ethernet, and a little faster than Fast Ethernet, which also runs at about 100 Mbps. At one time, FDDI used only fiber-optic cabling, but now it can run on UTP as well as on fiber-optic cable. FDDI is often used as a backbone network. A **backbone** is a network used to link several networks together. For example, several Token Rings and Ethernets can be connected using a single FDDI backbone.

FDDI uses a token-passing method to control traffic, but FDDI is more powerful and sophisticated than Token Ring. FDDI stations can pass more than one frame of data along the ring without waiting for the first frame to return. Also, once the frames are transmitted, the sending station can pass the FDDI token on to the next station to use, so that more than one station can have frames on the ring at the same time. With Token Ring, a data frame is only found traveling behind the token. With FDDI, data frames travel on the ring without the token. A PC keeps the token until it has sent out its data and then passes the token on. Possessing the token gives a PC the right to send data. A token is released (sent on) when the PC has finished transmitting.

Look at Figure 16-5, which shows a FDDI network with five stations. There are three frames of data currently on the ring, all sent from Station 1 to Station 5. The FDDI token has been passed from Station 1 to Station 2. If Station 2 is ready to send data, it can do so now even though data from Station 1 is still on the ring. Another optional feature of FDDI is multiframe dialogs. **Multiframe dialogs** allow one station to send a **limited token** to another station. With this limited token, the second station can communicate only with the first station, not with other stations on the network. This "private conversation" allows for continuous communication between two stations without interference from other stations.

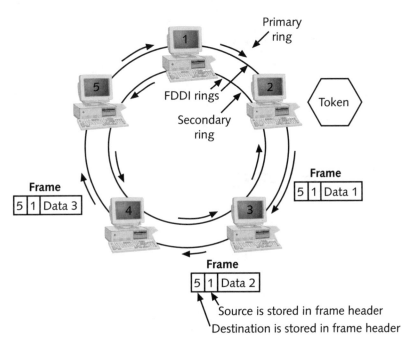

Figure 16-5   A FDDI network can have more than one frame of data on the rings. Shown here are three frames of data moving clockwise around the ring

One important strength of FDDI is dual counter-rotating rings, as seen in Figure 16-5. Instead of a single ring like the one the Token Ring uses, FDDI has two rings linking each device on the network, a primary ring and secondary ring. Data normally travels on the primary ring. However, if a break occurs on the FDDI ring, any device can switch the data to the secondary ring, which causes the data to travel in the opposite direction back around the ring, as in Figure 16-6. When the data reaches the break coming from the other direction, a station switches the data back to the primary ring, and it continues in the opposite direction again. In this way, communication continues even with a break in the FDDI ring.

Station 5 diverts the data from the secondary to primary ring

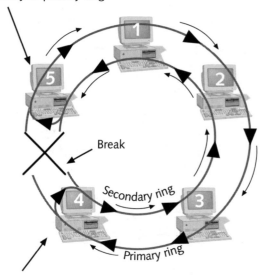

Station 4 diverts the data from the primary to the secondary ring

Figure 16-6   A break in the FDDI ring causes stations to divert data from one ring to another

Summary of Network Architecture

Table 16-2 shows a comparison and summary of the three network architectures discussed above.

Table 16-2   Comparing three network architectures

Item	Ethernet	Token Ring	FDDI
Logical topology or shape	Bus	Single ring	Dual ring
Physical topology or shape	Star or bus	Ring or star	Ring
Media	Twisted-pair, coaxial, or fiber-optic cable	Twisted-pair, fiber-optic cable	Primarily fiber-optic cable
Standard bandwidth	10 Mbps (Fast Ethernet is becoming available, which runs at 100 Mbps)	4 or 16 Mbps	100 Mbps to 200 Mbps
How token is released	Not applicable	After receive	After transmit
Maximum number of nodes	500	260	1024
Advantages	Of the three networks, Ethernet is the least expensive, simplest, and most popular solution.	Token Ring operates more reliably under heavy traffic than does Ethernet, but can be difficult to troubleshoot.	FDDI is much faster than Token Ring and regular Ethernet and faster than 100BaseT (Fast Ethernet).

NETWORKING HARDWARE

Almost all LANs and WANs today are designed using Token Ring, some form of Ethernet, or FDDI. Besides network cards in the PCs and cabling connecting them, there are other devices needed to physically construct a network. It is beyond the scope of this book to cover all the many hardware components needed to make a LAN or WAN work, but this chapter introduces a few common components: For a PC, the direct connection to a network is by way of a network interface card (NIC), sometimes called a network card or a network adapter already referenced above. Sometimes the logic normally contained on the NIC is on the systemboard, with a network port coming directly off the systemboard. This is a common practice for Compaq and Macintosh computers. Hubs are used to provide the centralized location for nodes to connect on a star network. Bridges, routers, and gateways connect one network to another, each performing a slightly different function when connecting like and unlike networks.

16

Network Interface Card (NIC)

A **network interface card** (**NIC**) plugs into a systemboard and provides a port or ports on the back of the card for connection to the network. The NIC may be designed as an Ethernet card, a Token Ring card, or a FDDI card. See Figure 16-7 for some examples of network cards. The card manages the communication and network protocol for the PC. An Ethernet card waits for silence (no data is being transmitted by another PC) before transmitting, and manages collisions. A Token Ring card waits to receive the token with no data frame attached before transmitting. A FDDI network card waits for a token before transmitting and manages the primary and secondary rings. The network card and the device drivers controlling the network card are the only components in the PC that are aware of the type of network being used. In other words, the type of network in use is transparent to the applications software using it.

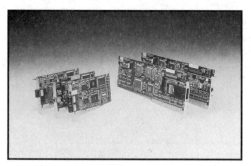

a. Ethernet

b. Token Ring

c. FDDI

Figure 16-7   Three different types of network cards:
(a) Ethernet; (b) Token Ring; and (c) FDDI

A network card sends and receives data from the system bus in parallel, and sends and receives data to and from the network in serial (Figure 16-8). Also, the network card is responsible for converting the data it is transmitting into a signal that is in a form appropriate to the network. For example, a fiber-optic FDDI card contains a laser diode that converts data to light pulses before transmission, and a twisted-pair Ethernet card converts data from the 5-volt signal used on the computer to the voltage used by twisted-pair cables. The component on the card that is responsible for this signal conversion is called the **transceiver**. It is common for an Ethernet card to contain more than one transceiver, each with a different port on the back of the card, in order to accommodate different cabling media. This type of Ethernet card is called a **combo card**.

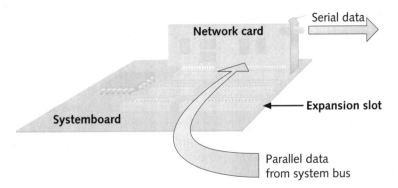

Figure 16-8   Network cards communicate with the network in serial, and with the computer in parallel

Different networks have different ways of identifying each node on the network. Ethernet and Token Ring cards have unique addresses hard-coded on the card by the manufacturer. Called **media access control** (**MAC**) addresses or **adapter addresses**, these addresses are 6-byte hex addresses unique to each card. Part of the MAC address contains the manufacturer, and part of the address is unique to each card; therefore, no two adapters should have the same MAC address.

Network cards require an IRQ, an I/O address, and, for DOS and Windows 95, upper memory addresses. Network cards may be Plug-and-Play, or they can use jumpers or DIP switches on the card to determine which resources to request. When selecting a network card, three things are important:

- The type of network you are attaching to (for example, Ethernet, Token Ring, FDDI, or a proprietary network standard)

- The type of media you are using (for example, shielded twisted-pair, coaxial, and fiber-optic cable)

- The type of system bus you are attaching the card to (for example, PCI and ISA. When selecting the system bus to use, know that FDDI is much too fast a network for an ISA bus; always use a PCI bus with FDDI cards.)

Bridges, Routers, and Gateways

Remember that when more than one network is connected, the networks form an internetwork. A large Ethernet network can be broken into smaller, more easily managed segments, and a device is needed to bridge them. When two networks use different methods of transmission, such as Ethernet and Token Ring, then a device is needed to translate between the two networks. When many networks are interconnected, a device is needed that can choose the best route over these networks.

To satisfy these requirements, bridges, routers, and gateways are used to connect networks and network segments to each other. Two main reasons for internetworking are: (1) to

16

extend the geographical area past what a single LAN can support, such as to different floors in a building or to other buildings, and (2) to decrease the amount of traffic on a single LAN by dividing the LAN into more than one network.

Bridges connect network segments. Figure 16-3 shows a bridge connecting two network segments. When a bridge receives signals from one network segment, it makes an intelligent decision as to whether to pass the signals on to the next segment, based on the destination network address. In this way, the bridge limits network traffic across it to only traffic going from one network segment to another, thus making the network more efficient. Using a bridge on a network can improve network performance if the bridge is strategically placed in the network so that most traffic remains contained on its own side of the bridge. An example of a strategic use of segmenting a network is to use a bridge to isolate a group of computers that shares the same printers or files; then, the heavy traffic of this group communicating within itself does not affect the rest of the network.

Routers connect networks and are more sophisticated than bridges. Routers are a little slower than bridges because they take the time to make more intelligent decisions about how to route packets to other networks. For example, large networks are often logically divided into many smaller separate networks, and each small network is identified by a logical network name. These smaller networks are sometimes called **subnetworks**, or **subnets**. Now each packet or frame, in addition to having a physical device address, also has a logical network or subnet address. A router can make decisions as to which neighboring network to send a packet to, based on its ultimate destination subnet address.

Routers can be computers with operating systems and special network software, or they can be other dedicated devices built by network manufacturers. Routers hold tables of network addresses, along with the best possible predetermined routes to these networks. These **router tables** can also contain the cost of sending data to a network. The cost can be expressed in one of two ways:

- **Tick count**: The time required for a packet to reach its destination. One tick equals 1/18 second.

- **Hop count**: The number of routers a packet must pass through in order to reach its destination.

The routing tables are modified every few minutes to reflect changes in the networks. When a router rebuilds its router table, on the basis of new information, the process is called **route discovery**.

A **gateway** connects networks that use different protocols. For example, gateways are used to connect a Token Ring LAN to an Ethernet, or an Ethernet to a mainframe. The gateway translates the incoming network traffic to the protocol needed by the receiving network. Gateways can even function so that a computer on one network that uses one protocol can use data from an application stored on a computer on another network that uses a different protocol. Because of the added overhead of making translations, a gateway is more expensive and slower than a router.

For example, suppose a gateway is a powerful PC that is designed to connect an Ethernet to a Token Ring network. The PC will have two network cards. One card will be an Ethernet card that belongs to the Ethernet network; the other card will be a Token Ring card that belongs to the Token Ring network. The PC is then the intersection point of the two networks, belonging to both networks.

THE OSI LAYER NETWORK MODEL

In the 1970s, when manufacturers were beginning to build networking software, firmware, and hardware to connect computers, each manufacturer developed its own standards of communication within its proprietary network design. In the early 1980s, manufacturers began to make attempts to standardize networking so that networks from different manufacturers could communicate. Two bodies that were leaders in this standardization are the International Organization for Standardization (ISO) and the Institute of Electrical and Electronics Engineers (IEEE). For example, one major effort of the IEEE was to standardize Token Ring and Ethernet protocols, which are both considered industry standards for networking at the network interface card level.

In an overall effort to identify and standardize all the levels of communication needed in networking, ISO developed a networking model called the Open Systems Interconnect (OSI) reference model, which is illustrated in Figure 16-9. This model includes all the logical levels of communication needed for one user or application to communicate with another over a network. To accomplish this overall or complete communication, seven layers, or levels, were identified. This model is developed and understood in much the same way as the model for communications over phone lines shown in Chapter 15, Figure 15.3, except that the OSI model covers strictly software and firmware, not hardware. Communication between adjacent layers is considered direct, but communication between matching layers is considered logical or virtual.

16

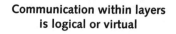

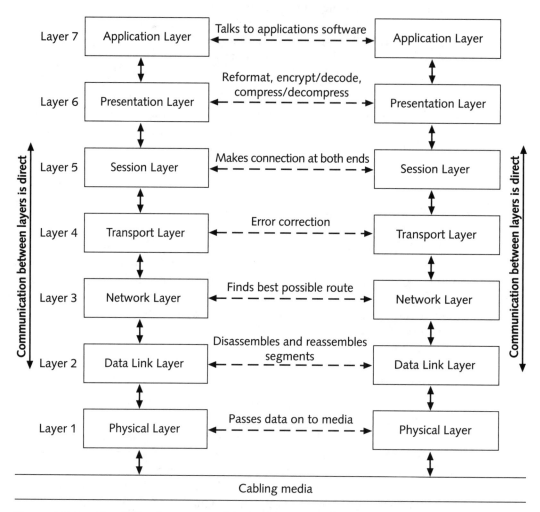

Figure 16-9   The OSI reference model identifies seven layers of network communication within software and firmware

When studying the model, remember that not all networks have a separate software or firmware layer that matches each of the seven layers. In fact, there is probably no network in use today that perfectly follows the model, but the model does serve the networking industry as a reference point for discussing different levels or layers in a network. For example, Token Ring and Ethernet each operate in the Physical layer and the Data Link layer in the model. From Figure 16-9, we see that these layers are responsible for 1) disassembling data into segments to be assigned to separate packets, 2) later reassembling packets into contiguous data, and 3) passing packets to and receiving packets from the network media or cabling.

For our discussions, it would be unproductive to try to distinguish which portion of Token Ring or Ethernet is the Data Link layer, and which portion is the Physical layer, because both are contained as firmware on the NIC. However, it is useful to talk about Token Ring and Ethernet covering these two layers and then to look for other software or firmware on the network that is managing the layers higher up in the model. For example, once you know that an Ethernet network is responsible for the bottom two layers of data transmission, then you next ask the question, "What software on the network is deciding the best possible route by which a packet will be sent in order for it to arrive at its destination?" This question is addressed by the Network layer. The answer will not be found on the firmware of the Ethernet card, because Ethernet does not encompass the Network layer of the OSI model. By referring to the OSI model, manufacturers have a structure from which to work as they develop and enhance new networking software, protocols, and designs.

Without getting too deeply into the details of the OSI model, the following provides an overview of the role each layer plays in a network, starting at the top.

Application Layer

The **Application layer** of the OSI model is responsible for interfacing with the applications software using the network. For example, suppose you are using a word processor such as Word for Windows. Word for Windows can open a document file that is stored on your hard drive (drive C), and it can just as easily open a document file stored on a file server connected to the LAN. The file server is known to the word processor as just another drive, such as drive F. You can open C:\data\MyFile.doc or F:\data\MyOtherFile.doc. When the word processor attempts to open the file on drive F, which is the file server, it communicates the request to the Application layer of the network software. The communication over the network is transparent to the application from that point forward. The file is retrieved over the network and presented to the word processor by the OSI Application layer. An example of software that handles the Application layer is NFS for Chameleon by NetManage (NFS stands for Network File Service).

Presentation Layer

The **Presentation layer** receives requests for files from the Application layer and presents the requests to the Session layer (described below). Any reformatting, compressing, or encryption of data is performed by the Presentation layer in order for the Application layer and the Session layer to communicate, for the data to be sent faster, or to secure the data.

Session Layer

The **Session layer** is responsible for establishing and maintaining a session between two networked stations or nodes. A session over a network works somewhat like a telephone call over phone lines. The caller makes a call; someone answers on the other end. After both parties know that communication is established, conversation goes in both directions until either the caller or receiver ends the phone call. The Session layer performs similar duties.

16

An attempt is made to establish a session between two nodes on a network. Both nodes acknowledge the session, and the session is usually assigned an identifying number. Either node can disconnect a session when communication in both directions is completed. Sometimes a session between two nodes on a network is called a **socket**. When a session is established, a socket is opened. A disconnected session is called a closed socket.

Transport Layer

The **Transport layer** is responsible for error checking and requests retransmission of data if errors are detected. The Transmission layer guarantees successful delivery of data.

Network Layer

The **Network layer** is responsible for finding the best possible route by which to send frames over an internetwork. The two most common protocols that make up both the Transport layer and the Network layer are **TCP/IP (Transmission Control Protocol/Internet Protocol)** and **IPX/SPX (internetwork packet exchange/sequenced packet exchange)**, which are both supported by Windows NT and Windows 95. For TCP/IP, used by the Internet, the TCP portion of the protocol is responsible for error checking, and therefore operates in the Transport layer. The IP portion of the protocol makes up the Network layer and is responsible for routing. IPX/SPX is used by NetWare by Novell, one of the most popular network operating systems for LANs. The IPX portion of the protocol is the Network layer responsible for routing, and the SPX portion of the protocol manages error checking, making it the Transport layer. These network protocols are further discussed later in the chapter.

Data Link Layer

The **Data Link layer** is responsible for receiving frames of data from the Network layer and splitting them up into segments of bits to be presented to the Physical layer for transport. When data is received from the Physical layer, the bits are reconstructed into frames to be presented to the Network layer. Token Ring and Ethernet firmware on network cards are examples of code that handles both the Data Link and Physical layers of the OSI model.

Physical Layer

The OSI **Physical layer** is not the physical network, such as cabling or network cards, but the protocol, or way, that data is transmitted over the physical media. At this level, data is nothing but indistinguishable bits. Remember that data is packaged into frames or packets before it is transmitted. This packaging of data has already occurred before this layer; the physical layer does not distinguish the frame header or trailer from the payload, or data, within the frame. The Physical layer sees all of it as just bits that need to be passed on.

Data Frames

Remember that data is segmented into frames, or packets, before transmission over a network. Each layer in the seven-layer model can add information to the beginning and ending of a data frame, or packet, to be read by the counterpart layer on the receiving workstation. At its most complex stage, a frame may look like that in Figure 16-10, in which each layer has added its identifying information to the frame. Some layers add just a header to the frame, and other layers add both a header and a trailer to the existing frame.

A single data frame

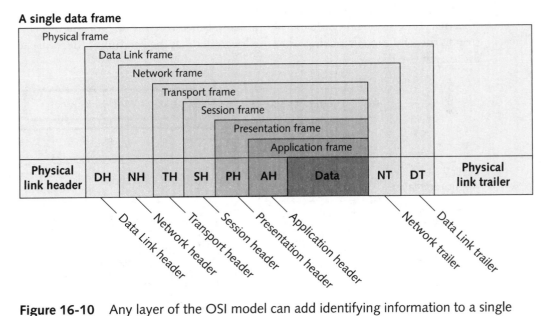

Figure 16-10   Any layer of the OSI model can add identifying information to a single data frame, either as a header or a trailer

Later, when the frame is presented to the counterpart layer on the receiving station, that layer interprets the information in the header and trailer (if present) intended for that layer, and then strips off that header and trailer information before passing the frame on to the next higher layer in the model. For frames to transmit successfully, each layer of the OSI model must communicate using the same protocol as its counterpart layer on the remote computer.

16

NETWORKING SOFTWARE OVERVIEW

Each of the seven layers in the OSI model uses different methods of communicating to its counterpart layer. These methods are called protocols. From the preceding discussion, you can see why there are many different protocols simultaneously in use when a network is working. You have seen that the two lowest layers (the Physical and Data Link layer) are controlled by the firmware on the network cards. However, most of the layers of the OSI model are controlled by the OS managing the network. The three best-known network operating systems in the PC world are the UNIX operating system, NetWare by Novell, and Microsoft Windows NT. In addition to the OS that is managing the network, third-party add-on software can be used to provide the top layers of the model. Some examples of this software are Netscape Communicator, Chameleon by NetManage, and Eudora by QUALCOMM. This section first looks at an overview of all the software components of a network and then looks in detail at several of the more popular products used at the topmost layers of the OSI model, the ones users are most accustomed to seeing and using.

A map showing how the components of a network relate to one another and to the OSI model is shown in Figure 16-11. The figure is not intended to be comprehensive. There are other user and applications services than the ones listed, and other networks than just Ethernet, Token Ring, FDDI, and phone lines. But this figure shows how real-life networks map to the OSI model, moving from the lowest level at the bottom of the figure to the highest level at the top.

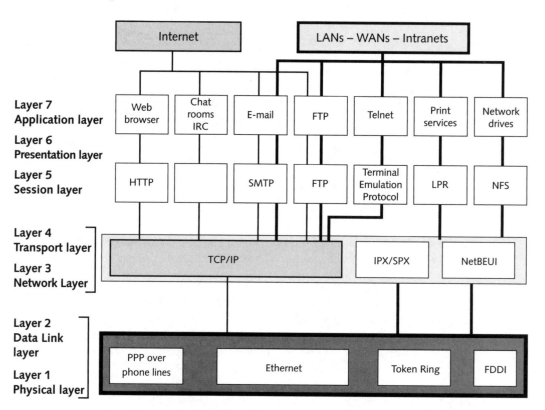

Figure 16-11 An overview of networking software showing the relationships between components

Network Protocol

The three network architectures shown in the bottom layer (Physical and Data layers) of Figure 16-11 have already been discussed: Ethernet, Token Ring, and FDDI. Also shown at the bottom layer is **PPP (Point-to-Point Protocol)** over phone lines, which is a protocol by which PCs with modems can connect to a network. The Point-to-Point Protocol is the most popular protocol for managing network transmission from one modem to another. The next level up in the figure shows the Network and Transport layers, showing TCP/IP as the protocol used by the Internet. It is also used on LANs, WANs, and intranets. (An **intranet** is a private multiple network used by a large company over a wide geographical area.) The IPX/SPX protocol is used primarily on Novell LANs. Since TCP/IP is becoming the most popular protocol at this level, Novell also supports TCP/IP as an alternate protocol. Less significant, but shown in the figure, is the **NetBEUI** protocol (**NetBIOS Extended User Interface**, pronounced "net-boo-ee"), a proprietary Microsoft protocol used only by Windows-based OSs (such as Windows for Workgroups) and limited to LANs, since it does not support routing. Other proprietary protocols that can be used at this level are XNS, DECnet, and VINES.

The higher layers in the network model shown in Figure 16-11 also use protocols to communicate with their counterpart services on the receiving node of the network. For example, when you send e-mail across a network, the e-mail is sent using **SMTP (Simple Mail Transfer Protocol)**, which operates on the Session layer. Network drives use NFS protocol, and the World Wide Web on the Internet uses **HTTP (Hypertext Transfer Protocol)**, both of which operate on the Session layer as well. Transferring files across the Internet is most often done using **FTP (File-Transfer Protocol)**. E-mail, the World Wide Web, and FTP are all discussed later in the chapter.

Network Services

At the highest level of the OSI model are the Application and Presentation levels. Users access some of these components directly, and others are designed to be interfaces between the network and applications software. Some of the more popular network applications offered at this level are listed below:

- **Web browser**: Provides primary access to the Internet
- **Chat rooms**: Provides online, interactive communication among several people on the Internet
- **E-mail**: Provides electronic mail (which consists of text files) across the Internet or other networks
- **FTP**: Provides a method of transferring files from one computer to another

16

- **Telnet**: Provides a console session from a UNIX computer to a remote computer. (In a console session, a window that looks and acts just like the UNIX OS console displays on a PC screen, giving the user the opportunity to issue UNIX commands to control the UNIX computer from the PC.)

- **Print services**: Refers to sharing printers across a network

- **Network drive**: Hard drive space on one computer on the network made available to another computer as a virtual or logical drive for the remote computer

Two Network Configurations

Using Figure 16-11 as an anchor point, recall from Chapter 12 that a network can be logically configured either as a peer-to-peer network or as a network using a dedicated server. Figure 16-12 shows an example of a peer-to-peer network. Users at each workstation can use shared printers and files on each others' computers. The services on a peer-to-peer network are most often limited to FTP, print services, and network drives. Nodes on a peer-to-peer network can communicate with any other node on the network and access files and other resources on that node, subject to security limitations. Each node is responsible for the security of its own resources.

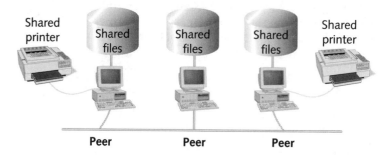

Figure 16-12 A peer-to-peer network allows all computers to share and use resources

A dedicated-server network, seen in Figure 16-13, has at least one computer, or server, on the network that serves the other computers on the network. If the server contains applications software together with data that is shared by other computers on the network (called clients, or workstations), then the network is called a client/server network. The application on the client that makes use of data stored on the server is called the **front end**. The application on the server that processes requests for data is called the **back end**.

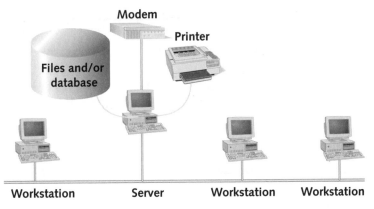

Figure 16-13 A dedicated-server network allows a server to make resources available to all workstations on the network

Dedicated-server networks can be used in one of two ways. If data is processed by the front end, and the server only holds the data, processing can be very slow because much interaction between client and server is required. In a true client/server environment, the front end passes all information that is needed to process the data to the back end, and the back end does the processing. When the back end is finished, it can pass a positive response or a calculated answer back to the client. This last method requires less network traffic and is considered to be a better use of the network.

Looking back at Figure 16-11, note that all the programs listed at the Application layer can operate on either a dedicated-server or peer-to-peer network. However, the World Wide Web, chat rooms, and e-mail always involve at least one dedicated server. A service that is not listed in the figure, but that is used in a client/server environment, is the software necessary for an application on a client to pass requests to a server, and for a server to respond with data. This type of software is called **middleware**. One popular example of middleware is Microsoft's **Open Database Connectivity** (**ODBC**) software. With ODBC, a front-end application on a client passes a request to update or query a database on the server. The ODBC back-end version of the software processes the request on the dedicated server and returns an answer to the client.

16

NETWORKING WITH WINDOWS 95 AND WINDOWS NT WORKSTATION

When you are using Windows 95 or Windows NT Workstation to connect to a network, the networking portion of the OS must be enabled, although sometimes this process is more automatic than at other times. The proper hardware must be installed, along with the device drivers to use that hardware. The device drivers and firmware on modems and network cards generally operate at the Physical and Data Link layers of the network. Windows 95 and

Windows NT handle most of the Application, Presentation, Session, Transport, and Network layers of the OSI model. Later, the chapter looks at some examples of Windows services offered at the Application, Presentation, and Session layers. One well-known example of such a service is Internet Explorer.

At the Transport and Network layers, Windows 95 and Windows NT support three different Transport and network protocols: TCP/IP, IPX/SPX, and NetBEUI. Each of these protocols is designed as an approach to one of three different methods of connecting to a network that are supported at the Data Link and Physical layers by Windows 95 and Windows NT Workstation: (1) using a network card (either Ethernet, Token Ring, or some other network design), (2) using Direct Cable Connect (uses a serial or parallel port), and (3) using Dial-Up Networking (uses a modem and phone lines). This section addresses these three methods of connecting to a network at this lowest level of networking.

DIAL-UP NETWORKING

A PC that is not directly connected to a network using a NIC and network cabling can remotely connect to it through a modem and phone lines. When Windows 95 or Windows NT Workstation operating systems make this dial-up connection to a network, the process is called **Dial-Up Networking** (**DUN**). In effect, the modem on the PC acts like a network card. After the Dial-Up connection is made, applications software on the PC relates to the network just as though it was directly connected to the network using a network card, but a network card is not needed. The modems and phone lines in between are transparent to the user, except for a noticeable reduction in speed when transferring large amounts of data, compared to the speed of a direct network connection. This section covers how to use Windows 95 and Windows NT Dial-Up Networking utilities.

How Dial-Up Networking Works

Dial-Up Networking works by using PPP (Point-to-Point Protocol) to send packets of data over phone lines. PPP packages frames that have already been prepared for network traffic, having been previously packaged in a network protocol. Figure 16-14a shows how this works. The data is presented to the network protocol, either TCP/IP, NetBEUI, or IPX/SPX, which adds its frame header and trailer information. Then the frame is presented to the line protocol, PPP, which serves as the Data Link layer in the OSI model. The frame is enclosed in the PPP header and trailer and then presented to the modem for delivery over phone lines to a modem on the receiving end.

The modem on the receiving end is connected to a PC or server that has a direct connection to the network. The receiving computer strips off the PPP header and trailer information and sends the packet on to the network still packaged in the TCP/IP protocol, or whatever other protocol the network is using. In Figure 16-14b, you can see how these two protocols act like envelopes. Data is put into a TCP/IP envelope for travel over the network. This envelope is put into a PPP envelope for travel over phone lines. When the phone line segment of the trip is completed, the PPP envelope is discarded.

PPP is sometimes called a bridging protocol or, more commonly, a **line protocol**. An earlier version of a line protocol is **Serial Line Internet Protocol** (**SLIP**), which is seldom used today.

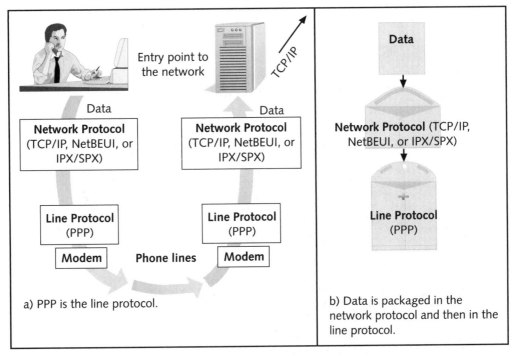

Figure 16-14   PPP allows a PC to connect to a network using a modem

Creating a Dial-Up Connection

In order to use either Windows 95 or Windows NT Workstation to communicate to a network over phone lines, Dial-Up Networking must first be installed as an OS component on your PC. After installation, you then create an icon in the Dial-Up Networking group, and then use the icon to make a connection. After the connection is made, any network service available on your network can be used if you have the software on your PC to support it. For example, a network drive is a useful method of passing files back and forth to and from the host computer or other computers on the network. However, experience says that FTP is a more reliable way to transmit files; the choice is yours. If you are using Windows 95, follow these directions to create a connection using Dial-Up Networking:

1. If Dial-Up Networking is not installed, click **Start**, **Settings**, **Control Panel**. Double-click **Add/Remove Programs**.

2. From the Add/Remove Programs window select the **Windows Setup** tab.

3. Select **Communications** and click **Details**. The right-hand window of Figure 16–15 shows the four components of the Communications group of Windows 95.

16

4. If Dial-Up Networking is not checked, check it now, and click **OK** to install the component. You will be asked for the Windows 95 CD-ROM or disks.

5. After Dial-Up Networking is installed, click **Start**, **Programs**, **Accessories**, and **Dial-Up Networking**. The Dial-Up Networking window displays as in Figure 16-16.

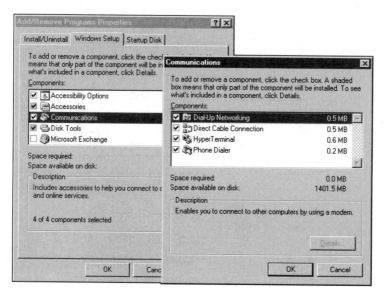

Figure 16-15 Use the Add/Remove Programs window to install Dial-up Networking

6. Double-click on **Make New Connection**. The Make New Connection dialog box appears, also shown in Figure 16-16.

7. Enter some text descriptive of the computer you will be dialing. If your modem is already installed, it will appear in the modem list. If not, see Chapter 15 about installing modems.

8. If a logon is required, either before or after you dial into the network, you can request a logon window. Click **Configure** to see the Modem Properties box shown in Figure 16-17.

9. Click the **Options** tab as in Figure 16-17. Select the option to display a terminal window either before or after dialing. Click **OK** to return to the previous screen. Click **Next** to continue.

10. In the next dialog box, type the phone number to dial, and click **Next** to continue.

11. Click **Finish** to build the icon. The icon displays in the Dial-Up Networking window.

12. Dial-Up Networking uses default values for the properties of this icon. To view these values, right-click on the icon and select **Properties** from the drop-down menu that displays.

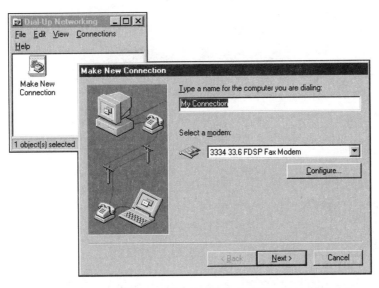

Figure 16-16   Creating a Dial-Up Networking connection icon

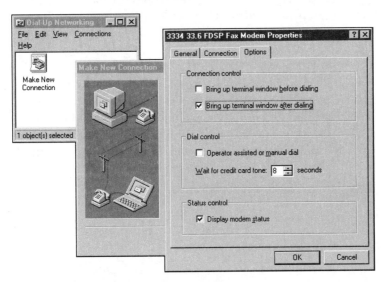

Figure 16-17   When setting up the logon interface, you can request that a terminal window be displayed before or after dialing

13. Click on **Server Type**. Figure 16-18 shows the resulting dialog box. Notice that all three network protocols are selected, meaning that the connection will support

whichever of the three the network is using. PPP for Windows 95, Windows NT 3.5, or the Internet is the selected Dial-Up Server. Click **Cancel** twice to return to the Dial-Up Networking window.

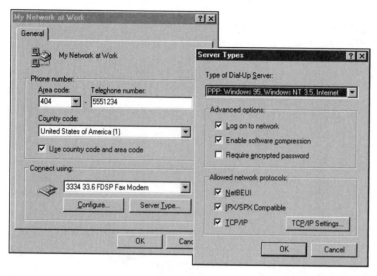

Figure 16-18   Properties of a Dial-Up icon showing server types

14. To make a connection, double-click on the icon just created, and click **Connect**. You should now hear the modem making the connection.

Dial-Up Adapter

When Windows 95 installs Dial-Up Networking, it also "installs" a Dial-Up Adapter. In terms of function, think of a Dial-Up Adapter as a pseudo-network-card, or a virtual network card, not as a real hardware device, or you can think of a Dial-Up Adapter as a modem when it is playing the role of a network card for Dial-Up Networking. After DUN is installed, go to Device Manager, and you can see your "new" Dial-Up Adapter listed under Network adapters, as in Figure 16-19. You can also see it listed as an installed network component under the list of installed components in the Network window of Control Panel.

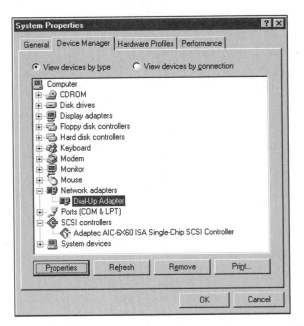

Figure 16-19   After Dial-up Networking is installed, a new
virtual network device, Dial-Up Adapter, is listed
as an installed hardware device

Client for Microsoft Networks

When Dial-Up Networking is installed, Dial-Up Adapter is automatically installed. In the same manner, Client for Microsoft Networks, shown in Figure 16-20, is automatically installed. This software layer is responsible for determining how your computer will make use of the network protocols to initiate and maintain communication. Client for Microsoft Networks is also automatically installed when you install a network card. Because it is installed automatically, you may never need to manually install this network component, but sometimes the component is accidentally removed. The PC cannot communicate over a network without this software, so part of network troubleshooting involves checking that the component is installed and adding it when it is missing.

16

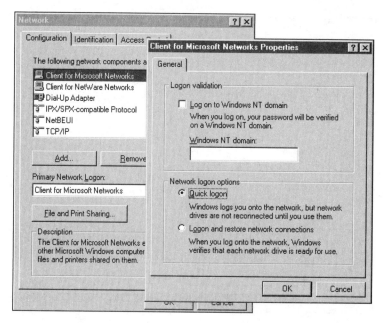

Figure 16-20   Client for Microsoft Networks is automatically installed when Dial-Up Networking is installed

Also from Figure 16-20, if you select Client for Microsoft Networks and then click Properties, its Properties box displays. If this workstation belongs to a Microsoft Windows NT domain, check **Log on to Windows NT domain** and enter the name of the Windows NT domain. For Dial-Up Networking, leave this selection unchecked. Later in the chapter, you'll see the purpose of the Network logon options of the Properties box.

DIRECT CABLE CONNECT

Windows 95 and Windows NT offer a direct cable connect service that allows you to connect two PCs using either a null modem cable (a cable that connects two PCs using their serial ports) or a parallel cable. When using Windows 95, follow these directions to use this handy utility (for example, when all you need to do is have two PCs share files or printers, and they are sitting near enough that a cable can reach between them). You can also use this method to allow a guest computer to access shared network resources that a host computer has access to.

1. If it is not already installed, install Direct Cable Connection. Click **Start**, **Settings**, **Control Panel**, and double-click on **Add/Remove Programs**.

2. Click the **Windows Setup** tab.

3. Select **Communications** and click **Details** (see Figure 16-15). Select **Direct Cable Connection** and check it if it is not already checked.

4. Once a connection is made, in order to share files and printers, the Windows 95 file-and-print-sharing component must be installed. To install this network component, click **Start**, **Settings**, **Control Panel**.

5. Double-click on the **Network** icon. Select the **Configuration** tab. If File and printer sharing for Microsoft Networks is not already installed, click **Add**.

6. Select **Service** from the list of components. Click **Add**.

7. From the list of network services, select **File and printer sharing for Microsoft Networks**, and click **OK**. You will be asked to provide the Windows 95 CD-ROM or disks and to restart your computer to complete the installation.

8. After you have installed File and Print Sharing, access Explorer. Select the drive or folder you want to share, and click **File**, **Sharing**. Select **Share** from the dialog box. A folder that is shared has a hand at the bottom of the folder's icon in Explorer.

9. To use the Direct Cable Connection, click **Start**, **Programs**, **Accessories**, and **Direct Cable Connection**. The Direct Cable Connection dialog box displays, as in Figure 16-21.

10. You must execute Direct Cable Connection on both computers. Select one computer as the host and the other computer as the guest. The host computer will listen for the guest computer. Configure the computer that is to share its resources as the host computer, and the one to use these shared resources as the guest computer. Click **Next** to continue.

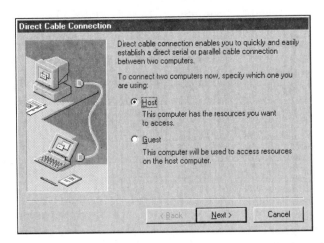

16

Figure 16-21   Direct Cable Connection is a quick and easy way to connect two computers

11. Select the port you want to use, either a serial port or a parallel port. In order to use the parallel ports, both computers must have bidirectional parallel ports. Parallel port connections require a parallel cable, and serial port connections require a null modem cable. A printer cable will not work as this parallel cable, because the connection at the printer end of the cable will not fit a PC's parallel port. Buy a parallel cable with two DB-25 male/male connections, or buy an adapter for your printer cable. Connect the cable to both computers and click **Next** to continue.

12. Click **Finish**. For the host computer, the Direct Cable Connection tells you that it is now listening for the guest computer. When you click Finish on the guest computer, it attempts to make the connection.

13. After the connection is made, use Windows Explorer on the guest computer to view the shared folders on the host computer. The guest computer can now use resources on the host computer that have been designated for sharing.

INSTALLING NETWORK ADAPTERS USING WINDOWS 95 AND WINDOWS NT

The most powerful and direct access to a network is not gained by using a dial-up connection or a direct cable connection, but is accomplished by using a network adapter, or card. A network adapter may be FDDI, Ethernet, Token Ring, or some other type of network architecture, or design. Earlier, the chapter discussed how to select a NIC and configure it. This section moves forward to the next step, installing the NIC using either Windows 95 or Windows NT.

Using Windows NT

Before purchasing a network adapter to be used with Windows NT, check the Windows NT Hardware Compatibility List to make sure that the card is supported by Windows NT. (See Chapter 12 for details of how to do this.) Follow these directions to install a network adapter under Windows NT:

1. Based on information in the card documentation, set DIP switches or jumpers on the card to configure the IRQ and I/O addresses used by the card. Physically install the card in an expansion slot.

2. Turn on the PC and go to the Network window: click **Start**, **Settings**, **Control Panel**, and double-click **Network**.

3. Click on the **Adapters** tab. From this tab you can add, remove, and change the settings of adapter cards.

4. Click **Add**. A list of NICs supported by Windows NT displays, as shown in Figure 16-22. Either select the network adapter from the list or click **Have Disk** if your adapter is not in the list and you have on disk the drivers that are designed to work under Windows NT.

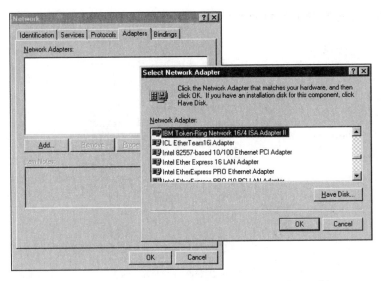

Figure 16-22   Selecting a network adapter supported by
Windows NT

5. If you selected an adapter from the list, you are asked to supply the location of
the Windows NT CD-ROM and the location of files on the CD. For example,
if your CD-ROM drive is drive E, type E:\i386.

6. Windows NT then displays a dialog box (see Figure 16-23) showing the suggested
resources to be assigned to the card. You will need to know the type of cabling
connected to the card and the IRQ and I/O address that the card is configured to
use. Click **OK** when done.

7. If Windows NT recognizes that there is more than one bus on the PC, it will
ask you to select the bus that you are using for the card (as determined by the
expansion slot you used). Click **OK** when done. The card will now be listed
under the Adapters tab as an installed card.

16

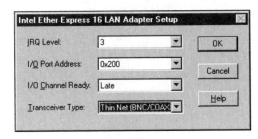

Figure 16-23   Assigning resources to a network card under
Windows NT

Using Windows 95 for Networking

Windows 95 supports Ethernet, Token Ring, and ARCnet networking cards. In most situations, Windows 95 detects a network card when the PC is first turned on, and automatically configures the card for you. However, you can configure the adapter settings yourself using the Control Panel as follows:

1. Set DIP switches or jumpers and physically install the network card in the PC. If the card is Plug-and-Play, it might or might not have jumpers or DIP switches to set.

2. Turn on the PC. Windows 95 detects the new device and configures it for you. You can check the settings by using the Control Panel: click **Start**, **Settings**, **Control Panel**, and double-click **Network**.

3. Select the **Configuration** tab. The network card should be in the list of installed network components.

4. Select the card from the list and click **Properties**. Figure 16-24 displays.

5. The IRQ and the I/O address of the card are showing. If this is not a Plug-and-Play card, and you know what the card DIP switches and jumpers are set to, you can compare those values to the values shown here. If Windows 95 did not make a correct match, you can change the settings now. From the Configuration type, select **Basic Configuration**, so that you can change the IRQ and I/O address settings. Click **OK** when done.

6. Click **OK** again to save your changes.

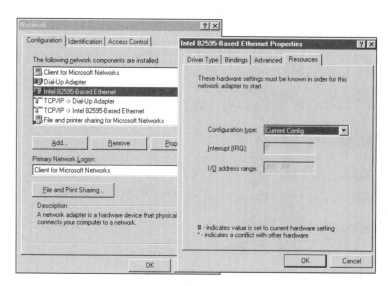

Figure 16-24 A network adapter's resources show in the properties option of the Windows 95 network window

SERVICING PCs ON A NETWORK

As a PC technician, you most likely will be asked to troubleshoot and repair a PC that is connected to a network. You will need to know how to recognize that a PC is connected to a network and how to verify that the connection is working. If the hard drive loses data or is replaced, you will need to know how to recover the network configuration that was originally on the drive. When the repair is made, you must restore the PC to the network and verify that the connection is once again working. Below are general step-by-step directions for a typical situation in which you must remove a PC from a network, make repairs, and then restore the PC to the network.

When you first arrive on-site, even though a PC may not be working, if the hard drive information is still intact, you can look on the hard drive for telltale information that the PC is network-ready. If the hard drive needs replacing or reformatting, you can save network configuration information to disk, to make restoring the PC to the network easier. Work with the network administrator in restoring the network software on the PC and configuring the network connection, if that information has been lost. Also, when the repairs are made and you are ready to test the network connection, the PC must be logged back on to the network with a valid user ID and password. The PC's end user will have that information. If he or she is not available, see the network administrator, who is also your resource for any other specific questions you may need answered about the network.

The steps to disconnect a PC from a network, repair the PC, and reconnect it to the network with the least possible disturbance of network configuration are summarized in this section:

Step 1. Verify that the PC is network-ready.

Step 2. Log off the network.

Step 3. Save the network files and parameters to disk if you think you might destroy them on the hard drive as you work.

Step 4. Disconnect the network cable and repair the PC.

Step 5. Restore the network configurations.

Step 6. Reconnect the PC to the network.

Step 7. Verify that network resources are available to the PC.

Step 1: Verify That the PC is Network-Ready

To verify that a PC is connected to a network, the simplest approach is to look for a network card on the PC with a network cable attached. However, it may be that the PC has a network card installed and is network-ready, but that the network cable is not currently attached. To verify a PC is network-ready for DOS and Windows 95, look for entries in the CONFIG.SYS and AUTOEXEC.BAT files that execute network software. Also, look in File Manager or Explorer for a network drive. (Remember that a network drive is space on a network server

16

that appears to be a logical drive on the PC.) Common drive letters for network drives are F or J. If when you double-click on the drive in File Manager or Explorer you see a list of folders available on the server for this PC, then the PC is connected to a network.

Step 2: Log Off the Network

Even though you can simply turn a PC off, and its connection to the network will eventually be terminated, a cleaner approach is to log off the network with a logoff command. If you simply reboot a PC while it is logged onto the network, the network session may not immediately be terminated. If the user attempts to log onto the network again after the reboot, the user's new session may not be allowed, since he or she still has an active session, according to the network server. Therefore, it is important to actually issue the logoff command so that the current session is properly terminated at the network server.

To log off using NetWare by Novell, Inc. (the most popular LAN for DOS and Windows 95 systems), access a command prompt and type LOGOFF. For Windows NT systems, press CTRL-ALT-DEL and choose logoff from the dialog box that displays.

Step 3: Save the Network Files and Parameters to Disk

NetWare by Novell uses entries in CONFIG.SYS and AUTOEXEC.BAT for DOS and Windows 95, to load network software and drivers and to provide a logon screen for the user to log onto the network. You will want to preserve these entries without changes in order to successfully restore the network connection after the repair. The NetWare software, by default, is located in the directory \NWCLIENT, although another directory name can be used. Expect to see four to six command lines in the AUTOEXEC.BAT file placed there by NetWare or by the network administrator, and one command line in CONFIG.SYS. The one entry in CONFIG.SYS is LASTDRIVE=Z: (or some other letter), which allows for network drive letters.

An example of a group of startup commands for NetWare that typically might be found in AUTOEXEC.BAT is shown below:

```
SET NWLANGUAGE=English
C:\NWCLIENT\LSL.COM
C:\NWCLIENT\3C5X9.COM
C:\NWCLIENT\IPXODI.COM
C:\NWCLIENT\VLM.EXE
F:\LOGIN JANDREWS
```

Look for the commands to be grouped together in AUTOEXEC.BAT, and they might be preceded by remarks indicating that they are used to load the client software. IPXODI.COM and VLM.EXE (lines 4 and 5 above) are the two main programs of the NetWare client software. The third line above loads a driver for the network card. Sometimes the command lines will include LH at the beginning of the command line, to cause the program to load into upper memory.

The last command line in the list provides a logon screen for the user. The username is included in the command line (JANDREWS in this example) so that the user only needs to enter his or her password. The username can be omitted in the command line and entered from the prompt. The F:\ at the beginning of the command line tells NetWare to access the NetWare server to run the logon program to log onto the network. Figure 16-25 shows the results of the LOGIN command without the username included. The user enters the username and password just as it is recorded on the NetWare server.

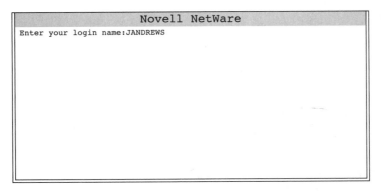

Figure 16-25 Netware provides a logon screen to log onto a
Novell LAN

Sometimes you will see the command lines listed above stored in a batch file, and the batch file referenced in AUTOEXEC.BAT. For example, a batch file named START.BAT might be in the \NWCLIENT directory, and the command C:\NWCLIENT\START in the AUTOEXEC.BAT file.

If you are planning to replace or reformat the hard drive: to preserve the network settings, when you back up all critical system files, be certain to back up the CONFIG.SYS and AUTOEXEC.BAT files, including the network commands. In addition to these two files, one important file in the \NWCLIENT directory is NET.CFG, which contains the specific configuration information for this PC. If you are having problems with the hard drive, but you have the opportunity to save just a few files, consider this one file important, because it contains information specific to this PC's network configuration.

Windows NT Workstation on a NetWare network is configured differently than is a DOS or Windows 95 workstation. There are two ways that a Windows NT workstation can be connected to a network: using the client software included with Windows NT Workstation, or using client software from Novell. If Microsoft's NT client software is used instead of Novell's, then you will see the CSNW (Client Service for NetWare) icon in the Control Panel. In either case, if the hard drive of a PC using Windows NT Workstation loses the client software installation, a network administrator must reinstall either the Windows NT Workstation Client Service for NetWare or the client software from Novell. It will not be possible to simply copy files back to the hard drive, as with DOS or Windows 95, because of the required entries in the Windows NT Registry.

16

Step 4: Disconnect the Network Cable and Repair the PC

After you have logged off the network and saved configuration information to disk, disconnect the network cable and repair the PC. If you must exchange the NIC, use an identical card with identical jumper and DIP switch settings, because the drivers on the PC are set up specifically for this card. If you are exchanging one NIC for a different type of NIC, ask the network administrator to help you reconfigure the PC for the new type of card.

Step 5: Restore the Network Configurations

Reboot the PC without reconnecting the network cable, and restore the network files and parameters, including the commands in CONFIG.SYS and AUTOEXEC.BAT, to load the network software and provide a logon screen. The network administrator may provide you with network software to reinstall, or may simply ask you to restore the \NWCLIENT directory together with the OS startup files, CONFIG.SYS and AUTOEXEC.BAT. For Windows NT, ask the network administrator to help reinstall the network software.

Step 6: Reconnect the PC to the Network

Turn the PC off and reconnect the network cable, and then turn the PC back on. When the PC boots, the network software loads, and a logon screen is provided to reestablish a network session. For NetWare, when you reboot the PC the logon screen in Figure 16-25 displays. Have the user log on to the network with his or her user ID and password, or use one provided to you by the network administrator for testing. NetWare displays a message saying that you are logged on, and then Windows is loaded.

For DOS and Windows 95, if the network software loads, but the logon screen does not appear, you can issue the LOGON command from the command prompt. Just enter the command as it appears in the AUTOEXEC.BAT file. For Windows NT, if the workstation is connected to a Microsoft network, the logon to the workstation will also log the workstation onto the network. With NetWare networks, the logon may be two different logons, one to the workstation and the other to the NetWare network, or the logon may be synchronized so that both logons occur simultaneously.

Step 7: Verify That Network Resources Are Available to the PC

To verify that all is well with the network, look in File Manager or Explorer and verify that the network drive is present. Look for drive F or drive J, or some other drive letter representing a network drive. You can find the network drive letter by looking either in AUTOEXEC.BAT at the LOGIN command, or at the contents of NET.CFG in the \NWCLIENT directory. Network drives are covered in more detail later in the chapter. For Windows NT, check Network Neighborhood for networking resources to determine if the network is functioning correctly.

PCs and the Internet

The Internet is the largest network in the world. To be more accurate, it is the largest grouping of many networks internetworked together. Looking back at Figure 16-11, you see that the software and protocols used by the Internet encompass the OSI layers from the Application layer through the Network layer. At the foundation of the Internet is TCP/IP, which operates at the OSI Transport and Network layers. TCP/IP was developed in 1969 by the U. S. Department of Defense (DOD) to provide a decentralized and fast network to connect networks. The network was originally called ARPANET (for Advanced Research Project Agency network), from which the civilian Internet evolved. DOD wanted decentralized data transfers so that communication would not be dependent on any one server or network, backbone network, or centralized geographic location in order to function. This decentralized concept means that, even if many networks fail, data will still arrive at its destination. Originally, this design was intended to protect data communications in the event of a major military attack on the United States, in which many networks might be put out of service. Another goal of decentralization was to allow any one communication to travel from source to destination through any number of different paths, or to be broken into parts that travel different paths, and come together at their single destination. Networking using TCP/IP and the software and protocols in layers above it has grown over the years and come to be known as the Internet.

The Internet is a web of interconnecting, yet independent networks. Many people confuse the Internet with the World Wide Web (WWW). Again, note in Figure 16-11 that the Web is only one service of many services that use TCP/IP and operates at the OSI Application and Presentation layers. The Web presents data to Internet users as pages—called Web pages—on computer screens. These pages of information can contain graphics and texts with links to sound files, video files, and other Web pages. The Web is only one way to communicate at the user, or Application level over the Internet. Other ways, also shown in Figure 16-11, are chat rooms, e-mail, and FTP.

From Figure 16-11, also note that the Internet is a network of networks. Underneath TCP/IP is some other protocol such as PPP, Ethernet, Token Ring, or FDDI, providing the bottom two layers of the OSI model. TCP/IP enables packets of data to traverse many networks to arrive at their destination. To understand how these packets can be routed all the way around the world is to understand TCP/IP. One way of looking at this relationship between TCP/IP and other network protocols is to consider that the Internet, using TCP/IP, makes use of these underlying networks much as a shipping department makes use of different transportation systems across the country. For example, a package is shipped first by truck, then by train, then by plane, and again by truck before arriving at its destination. In this analogy, TCP/IP is like the shipping box that encloses the contents and the mailing label that identifies the package, its sender, and its destination to all the subsystems sending it on its way.

16

HOW THE INTERNET WORKS

Figure 16-26 shows a simplified, bird's-eye view of how networks work together to send data over the Internet. A user in California accesses a server in New York by traversing many networks. Each network operates independently of all other networks but can also receive a packet from another network and send it on to a third network, while it also manages it own routine, internal traffic. Networks are connected by routers, which belong to more than one network. In Figure 16-26, Network B contains four routers: Routers 1, 2, 3, and 4. But Routers 3 and 4 also belong to Network C. Network C contains Router 8, which also belongs to the same network as the server in New York that the user wants to access.

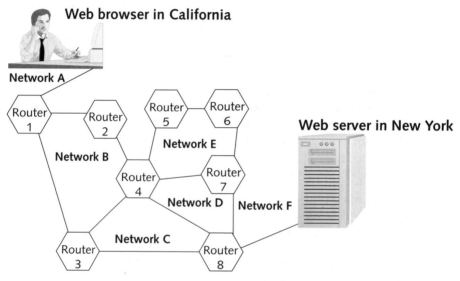

Figure 16-26   The Internet is a web of interconnecting, yet independent networks

How many paths are there on the Internet by which the user in California can access the server in New York? One path is through Router 1, then 3, then 8, and finally to the server, although there are several other possible paths in the diagram. Data going from the server to the user may travel a different path than the request for data traveling from the user to the server. In fact, if there is a lot of data divided into several packets, each packet may take a different route, and the packets may not arrive at the user's PC in the same order in which they were sent. It's up to the lower layers in the OSI model to sort it all out and reassemble the data before it's presented to the Application layer to be presented to the user.

CONNECTING TO THE INTERNET

There is a variety of ways for a PC to access the Internet. Most people access the Internet through an **Internet Service Provider (ISP)**. For a monthly fee, the service provider gives you a username and password, and an access phone number, and may include necessary software for your PC. The larger ISPs also provide online services, an infrastructure that enables subscribers to communicate with one another, to get stock quotes and news, and to use community bulletin boards. The largest ISPs that also provide online services are America Online, Microsoft Network, and CompuServe. For a listing of over 3,000 ISPs see the Web site www.thelist.internet.com.

In Figure 16-26, a router belongs to any given network because it has a network address on that network. However, a router can have more than one network address. Router 4, in the diagram, belongs to four networks (B, C, D, and E), and would, therefore, have four network addresses. On the Internet, each device that can be addressed by TCP/IP is assigned a combination address containing both the network address (identifies the network) and the host address (identifies the individual device or computer). This combo address is called an **Internet Protocol address (IP address)**. A **host** on the Internet is defined as any computer or device that can have an IP address. Therefore, in Figure 16-26, Router 4 would be assigned four IP addresses. The network portion of each IP address would correspond to each of the four networks it belongs to, and the host portion of each IP address would be unique to all other host addresses on the given network.

This section looks at the basics of the Internet, how IP addresses on the Internet are determined, how TCP/IP uses these IP addresses to route data, and the details of connecting a PC to the Internet.

IP ADDRESSES

The Internet and the UNIX operating system use Transmission Control Protocol/Internet Protocol (TCP/IP) as their network protocol. TCP/IP requires that each node on a network be assigned a unique numeric address, called an IP address. The organization that keeps track of all IP address assignments is Network Solutions, Inc. (NSI), working under an agreement with the National Science Foundation. The work is done at the **Internet Network Information Center (InterNIC)** in Menlo Park, California. When a company, college, or some other organization applies for IP addresses, InterNIC assigns a range of addresses appropriate to the number of hosts on the organization's networks. For more information about InterNIC, see its Web site, www.internic.com.

An IP address is made up of four numbers separated by periods. An IP address is 32 bits long, making each of the four numbers 8 bits. The largest possible 8-bit number is 11111111, which is equal to 255 in decimal, so the largest possible IP address is 255.255.255.255. Each

16

of the four numbers separated by periods is called an **octet** (for 8 bits) and can be any number from 0 to 255, making for a total of 4.3 billion IP addresses ($256 \times 256 \times 256 \times 256$). (However, because of the allocation scheme used to assign these addresses, not all of them are readily available for use.)

Classes of IP Addresses

IP addresses are divided into three classes—Class A, Class B, and Class C—and IP addresses are assigned according to the scheme outlined in Table 16-3. A Class A license is assigned a single number to be used in the first (leftmost) octet of the address, which becomes the network address. The other three octets on the right of the IP address can be used for host addresses that uniquely identify each host on this network. The first octet of a Class A license is a number between 0 and 126. For example, if a company is assigned 87 as its Class A network address, then 87 is used as the first octet for every host on this one network. Examples of IP addresses for hosts on this network are 87.0.0.1, 87.0.0.2, and 87.0.0.3 (the last octet does not use 0 or 255 as a value, so 87.0.0.0 would not be valid). Therefore, one Class A license can have approximately $256 \times 256 \times 254$ node addresses, or about 16 million IP addresses.

Table 16-3   Classes of IP addresses

Class	Network Octets (blanks in the IP address are used for host octets)	Total Number of Possible Networks or Licenses	Host Octets (blanks in the IP address are used for network octets)	Total number of possible IP Addresses in Each Network
A	0.___.___.___ to 126.___.___.___	127	___.0.0.1 to ___.255.255.254	16 million
B	128.0.___.___ to 191.255.___.___	16,000	___.___.0.1 to ___.___.255.254	65,000
C	192.0.0.___ to 254.255.255.___	2,000,000	___.___.___.1 to ___.___.___.254	254

A Class B license is assigned a number for each of the first two octets, leaving the last two octets for host addresses. The number of possible values for two octets is about 256×256, or about 65,000 host addresses in a single Class B license. However, the first octet of a Class B license is a number between 128 and 191, which gives about 63 different values for a Class B first octet. The second number can be between 0 and 255, so there are approximately 63×256, or about 16,000, Class B networks. For example, suppose a company is assigned 135.18 as the network address for its Class B license. The first two octets for all hosts on this network are 135.18, and the company uses the last two octets for host addresses. Examples of IP addresses on this company's Class B network are 135.18.0.1, 135.18.0.2, 135.18.0.3, and so forth.

A Class C license is assigned three octets as the network address and can have 254 host addresses. The first number of a Class C license is between 192 and 254. For example, a company is assigned a Class C license for its network with a network address of 200.80.15. Some IP addresses on this Class C network are 200.80.15.1, 200.80.15.2, and 200.80.15.3.

When a small company is assigned a Class C license, it obtains 254 IP addresses for its use. If it only has a few nodes (say, less than 25 on a network), many IP addresses go unused, which is one of the reasons that there is a shortage of IP addresses. But suppose that the company grows and now has 300 workstations on the network. It has run out of IP addresses. There are a couple of ways to solve this problem. One way is to take into account that not all of these 300 workstations need to have access to the Internet. As long as the network is a private network, if the company is using TCP/IP, the company can make up its own IP addresses. Since these nodes are isolated from the Internet, no conflicts arise. The Internet Assigned Numbers Authority (IANA) recommends that the following IP addresses be used for private networks:

- 10.0.0.0 through 10.255.255.255

- 172.16.0.0 through 172.31.255.255

- 192.168.0.0 through 192.168.255.255

When assigning these isolated IP addresses, also keep in mind that a few IP addresses are reserved for special use by TCP/IP and should not be used. They are listed in Table 16-4.

Table 16-4   Reserved IP addresses

IP Address	How It Is Used
255.255.255.255	Broadcast messages
0.0.0.0	A currently unassigned IP address
127.0.0.1	Indicates your own workstation; yourself

All IP addresses on a network must be unique. If you are using a standalone computer, it does not matter what IP address you are using (for example, when you are testing networking software on a PC that is not connected to the network, you may need to temporarily assign an IP address in order to use the software). On an isolated private network, you are free to make up your own IP addresses, although you should avoid using the reserved addresses.

Dynamically Assigned IP Addresses

Another solution for the company that now has 300 computers on its network but only 254 IP addresses is to dynamically assign IP addresses. Instead of IP addresses being permanently assigned to workstations (called **static IP addresses**), when a workstation comes online to the network, a server assigns an IP address to it to be used for the current session only (called a **dynamic IP address**). When the session is terminated, the IP address is returned to the list of available addresses. Because not all workstations are online at all times, fewer IP addresses than the total number of workstations can satisfy the needs of the network.

The server that manages these dynamically assigned IP addresses is called a **Dynamic Host Configuration Protocol** (**DHCP**) server. In this arrangement, workstations are called DHCP clients. DHCP software resides on both the client and the server to manage the

16

dynamic assignments of IP addresses. DHCP software is built into both Windows 95 and Windows NT. Many Internet service providers (ISPs) use dynamic IP addressing for their Dial-Up users.

Plans for New IP Addresses

Because of an impending shortage of IP addresses, a new scheme of IP addresses is currently being developed. Called the IP version 6 (IPv6) standard, it will use 128 bits instead of 32 bits, and will have the added advantage over current IP addressing that it can automatically assign an IP address to a network device. Current IP addresses using 32 bits have 8 bits in each octet. With the new system, each octet can have 32 bits, for a total of 128 bits for the entire address.

Domain Names

Because IP addresses are numbers and sometimes difficult to remember, and because companies might want to change their IP addresses without also changing the name that the outside world knows them by, hosts are sometimes given alphabetic—or word-based—names called **domain names**. Domain names provide a more convenient way of identifying a host than IP addresses. Domain names are an alternate way of addressing a host on the Internet, but the domain name must eventually be mapped onto the IP address of the host before the contact with the host can take place. Think of a domain name as a pseudonym or an alias; the real name of the host computer is its IP address.

Domain names are assigned by NSI under the InterNIC project and the Internet Assigned Numbers Authority (IANA). The last segment of a domain name tells you something about the host. Domain names in the United States end in .edu (for educational institution), .gov (for government institution), .com (for commercial institution), .org (for nonprofit institution), and .net (for Internet provider). There are other endings as well, including codes for countries, such as .uk for the United Kingdom. Examples of domain names are course.com, microsoft.com, and leeuniversity.edu. The enormous demand for commercial domain names, combined with a shortage of acceptable domain names, has created an ongoing controversy over new naming conventions, and over who will keep track of these names.

DOMAIN NAME RESOLUTION

There is not necessarily a fixed relationship between a domain name and an IP address. A host computer can have a certain domain name and can be connected to one network and assigned a certain IP address, and then be moved to another network and assigned a different IP address. The domain name can stay with the host while it connects to either network. It is up to a name resolution service to track the relationship between a domain name and the current IP address of the host computer.

There are two name resolution services that track relationships between domain names and IP addresses: **Domain Name System**, also called **Domain Name Service**, (**DNS**) and Microsoft's **Windows Internet Naming Service** (**WINS**). At the heart of DNS is a distributed database, which must initially be updated manually. When a new domain name is assigned, that name and its corresponding IP address are entered into a database on a top-level domain name server. When a remote computer tries to access your host by using your domain name, if that remote computer does not know the IP address currently assigned to that domain name, it queries its DNS server. If the DNS server does not have the information in its DNS database, it contacts another DNS server for that information and updates its database. This second DNS server is designated as its top-level DNS server and may contain the initial manual entry into the Internet system that relates a domain name to an IP address. The local DNS server is also informed, and then tells the remote computer the IP address of the domain name.

WINS also uses a distributed database, but WINS is mostly used for Windows networks resolving Windows 95 or Windows NT host names. WINS has an advantage over DNS in that WINS can manage name resolution when IP addresses are dynamically assigned.

THE INTERNET, NETWORKS, AND SUBNETS

The Internet is a group of networks, and networks can be divided into subnets. A map of all the subnets and networks that make up the Internet illustrates why parts of the Internet are often referred to as a web. At the foundation of this structure of networks and subnets is the protocol suite of the Internet, TCP/IP. When you understand how TCP/IP addresses networks and host computers and routes data across this maze, the task of configuring Windows 95 or Windows NT to connect to the Internet becomes much easier. This section begins by introducing the many different protocols that make up the group of protocols collectively called TCP/IP, and then discusses how TCP/IP uses the IP address system.

Routing Using TCP/IP

TCP/IP was designed to enable routing of data from one network to another over a huge geographical area and over a huge number of networks. TCP/IP uses routers to transfer packets of data, sometimes called **datagrams**, from network to network in such a way that the overall transmission makes all these networks appear to be one large network. TCP/IP is really a suite of protocols, each designed to perform a single task—such as error checking or sending error messages back to the sending host—as part of the overall stupendous task of routing packets of data around the world. TCP and IP are the two principal protocols of the suite, but there are others.

The Suite of TCP/IP Protocols.   Although TCP/IP can use more than one protocol at each OSI layer that it supports, when data is being transmitted, only one protocol at each layer is used. The choice of which protocol to use is dependent on what type of data is being transmitted and on what applications software is interfacing with the network.

Figure 16-27 shows the protocols of the TCP/IP suite supported by Windows 95 and Windows NT. The Windows Sockets protocol (sometimes called WinSock) is designed to interface with applications that rely on sockets or sessions to connect to a remote computer.

Browser software for the World Wide Web is one example of software that uses sockets. **NetBIOS over TCP/IP** (**NetBT**) is another applications protocol designed to interface with applications that rely on NetBIOS for communication. There is more information about applications protocols later in the chapter.

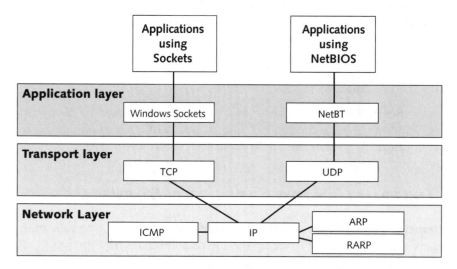

Figure 16-27   Protocols of the TCP/IP suite

There are two protocols at the Transport layer, TCP and UDP. **User Datagram Protocol** (**UDP**) is a **connectionless protocol**, meaning that it does not require a connection to send a packet and does not guarantee that the packet will arrive at its destination. UDP is used to send broadcast messages over the network when responses from each node are not required. One service at the Application layer that uses UDP is a network drive map, which uses UDP because it does its own verifying that the packets have arrived safely. (A network drive map makes space on a remote computer's hard drive look like a hard drive on the local computer.) TCP is a **connection protocol**, meaning that data is guaranteed to arrive at its destination. Most network applications use TCP rather than UDP. To understand the difference in sending data over a network with or without a connection, think of the difference between a radio broadcast and a telephone call. The radio broadcast does not require a connection at the remote end to each radio receiving the data and is, therefore, a type of connectionless communication. A telephone call requires a connection at both ends for data to be communicated, and is an example of communication with a connection.

At the Network layer, **Address Resolution Protocol** (**ARP**) translates IP addresses into physical network addresses such as Ethernet IDs or Token Ring MAC addresses. A counterpart protocol, **Reverse Address Resolution Protocol** (**RARP**) does the reverse and translates physical network addresses into IP addresses. Also at the Network layer is **Internet Control Message Protocol** (**ICMP**), which is used to transmit error messages and other control messages to hosts and routers. For example, if a router is unable to deliver a packet, it informs the sender of the failure using ICMP.

IP Addresses and Physical Addresses.   Fundamental to the design of TCP/IP is the concept of routing packets across networks by using IP addresses that relate to physical network adapter addresses. The routers of each network are responsible for routing packets from the outside networks to the hosts within their own network. These routers may or may not know the adapter address of the host but will "learn" the address the first time a packet is sent to it. Also, other routers outside the network may know the adapter addresses of hosts within this one network.

Think of IP addresses and adapter addresses as phone numbers and street addresses of houses, respectively, as seen in Figure 16-28. A house on a certain street of a city may have one phone number today, but another one tomorrow if new owners move in, or if the present owner has his or her phone number changed. However, the street and city address of this house will most likely never change.

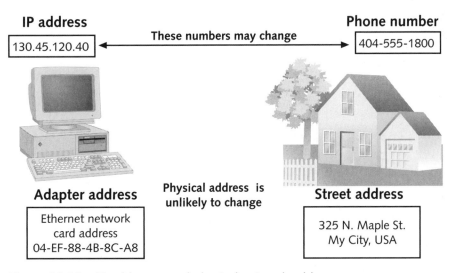

IP address
130.45.120.40

These numbers may change

Phone number
404-555-1800

Adapter address
Ethernet network
card address
04-EF-88-4B-8C-A8

**Physical address is
unlikely to change**

Street address
325 N. Maple St.
My City, USA

Figure 16-28   IP addresses and physical network addresses can be compared to phone numbers and street addresses

16

IP addresses and adapter addresses are similar to phone numbers and street addresses in this respect. An IP address is assigned to a host as a phone number is assigned to a house (no inherent relationship), and both the IP address and phone number can easily change. An adapter address is like the physical address of the host and only changes if the network adapter card is exchanged, just as the street address of a house seldom, if ever, changes. Think of the adapter address as the permanent physical network address of a host.

We can take the analogy one step further. An IP address is made up of a network and host address, just as phone numbers consist of area codes followed by seven-digit numbers. The area code generally identifies the approximate location of the house, just as the network portion of an IP address generally identifies the location of the network where the host resides.

When configuring a workstation to use TCP/IP, one step in the configuration is to associate an adapter address to an IP address. This process is called binding the adapter address to the IP address. When an IP address is bound to the adapter address, TCP/IP data that is addressed to this IP address now has a physical computer or adapter address to send the data to. (In general, the term **binding** refers to associating any OSI layer in the network to a layer just above it or just below it. For example, an Application protocol can be bound to a Transport protocol, and a Transport protocol can be bound to a Network protocol. When the two layers are bound, communication continues between them until they are unbound or released.)

How TCP/IP Routing Works.   Figure 16-29 shows an example of two networks connected by a router. The router (Computer C) belongs to both networks and has an IP address for each network. Think of it as the intersection point of the two networks.

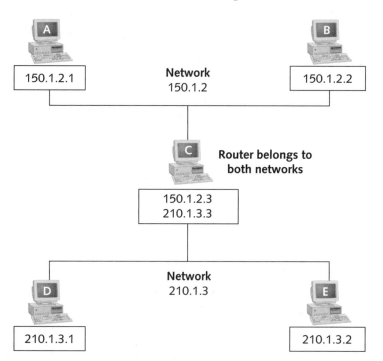

Figure 16-29   Two networks using TCP/IP connected by a router

Suppose both these networks are Ethernet, and Host A wants to send data to Host B, which is on the same network. Host A knows the IP address of Host B. It would also need to know the Ethernet address (adapter address) of Host B in order to send the packet. This is what happens:

1. Host A knows the Host B IP address and turns the job of discovering the adapter address over to ARP (Address Resolution Protocol), which looks up the IP address of Host B in its routing tables on the PC.

2. If ARP does not find the IP address of Host B in its tables, it sends out a broadcast message to the entire network (Hosts B and C in this case), containing a request for the IP address of Host B.

3. Host B recognizes its IP address and responds with its Ethernet address.

4. Host A receives the packet and updates its routing tables.

5. Host A sends its packet to Host B.

Now suppose that Host A is now ready to send a packet to Host E, which is on the other network. Here's what happens:

1. Host A looks at the IP address of Host E and recognizes that Host E does not belong to its network. (How it recognizes that is coming up.)

2. Because Host A is trying to communicate with a different network, it sends the packet to the router of its network, in this case, Host C. Host A knows the Ethernet address of its router, so it knows where to send the packet. (Host A did not attempt to broadcast for a response from Host E because it recognized that Host E would not hear the broadcast message, since it is on a different network.)

3. Host C receives the packet and looks at the destination IP address. Host C recognizes that the destination IP address is on its second network, so it sends the packet to Host E, just as Host A sent the packet to Host C. In other words, it will first look in its router table. If it doesn't find the IP address of Host E, it will send out a broadcast message to network 210.1.3.

Host C is an IP router but is also called a gateway because it serves as the connection point of two networks.

Default Gateways.   Sometimes a large network will have more than one router, as seen in Figure 16-30. The network in the upper left of the figure is 250.1.2 and has two routers (D and E), each belonging to other networks. Host E is designated as the **default gateway**, meaning that any host on this 250.1.2 network will send packets addressed to other networks to this gateway by default. The other router, Host D, is called the **alternate gateway** and will be used if communication to the default gateway fails.

Suppose Host A wants to send a packet to Host K on Network 210.1.3 in the figure. Host A does not know that the alternate gateway is a better choice, but just sends the packet to the default gateway. However, the default gateway may have routing information that Host A does not know. If so, it will send an ICMP redirect packet back to Host A telling Host A to use the alternate gateway when addressing Host K. The next time Host A attempts to send a packet to Host K, it will read from its routing table to use the alternate gateway.

16

Netmask.   Comparing the network addresses in Figure 16-30 to those of Table 16-3, you can see that networks 250.1.2 and 210.1.3 are Class C networks, and network 130.5 is a Class B network. Also remember that Host A had to determine that Host K was not on its network, but was on a foreign network. How did it know that? By comparing Host K's IP address to the network mask. A **network mask** is that part of the IP address that identifies the network rather than the host. Host A's network address is 250.1.2. Host A compared these values to the first three octets of Host K's IP address. Since they were not the same, Host A knew that Host K was on another network.

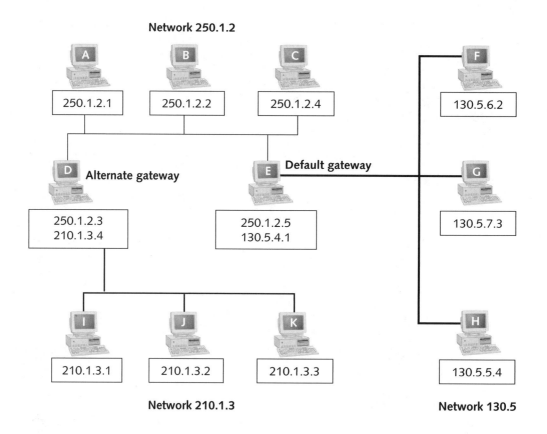

Figure 16-30   A network can have more than one router. One router of the network will
be the default gateway

The three network addresses in Figure 16–30 are 250.1.2, 210.1.3, and 130.5. Class C hosts
have a network address of three octets. Hosts on Class B networks have a network address of
only two octets.

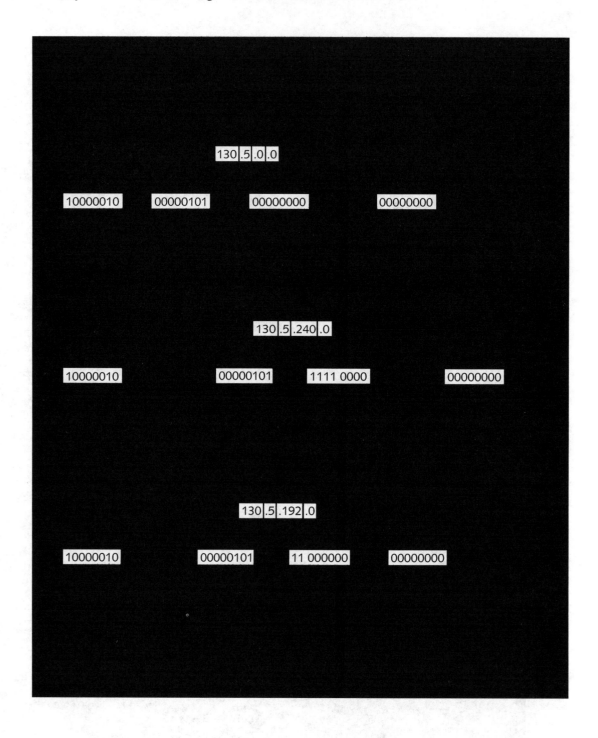

WAN Connections

It is not uncommon for a service provider to own several Class C network addresses and sub-lease or subnet them to small companies. These are called **classless addresses**. The service provider leases several IP addresses and might also provide a gateway to the Internet with an IP address to the gateway. For example, in Figure 16-32, a small organization has two networks, a Token Ring and an Ethernet. It leases IP addresses from an ISP with an ISDN direct line to an Internet gateway to the ISP. The company uses a subnet mask of 255.255.255.192 so that it can have each network on a different subnet. (In this case, the subnet portion of the host address is the first 2 bits of the fourth octet.) There is a computer that serves as a router connecting the two networks. It has an Ethernet card to connect to the Ethernet LAN. The Ethernet card is associated with or bound to the IP address 240.10.12.65. The rightmost or last octet in this IP address is 0100 0001, which is decimal 65. The first 2 bits are the subnet address, and the remaining bits are the host address. All hosts on the Ethernet use these same subnet bits.

16

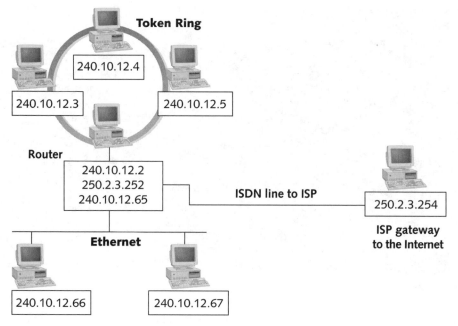

Figure 16-32 A small organization may use classless addresses with a gateway to the Internet

The router also has a Token Ring card to connect to the Token Ring network, which is associated with an IP address of 240.10.12.2, using a subnet address of 00. The subnet mask is also 255.255.255.192 for all hosts on this network. The router has one more communication card, an ISDN card to communicate with the ISP gateway to the Internet. This ISDN card uses a third IP address, 250.2.3.252, to associate with the subnet that the gateway to the Internet is on. The router, therefore, belongs to three subnets.

Using TCP/IP with Windows 95 and Windows NT

Looking back at Figure 16-30, note that any workstation on either of these three networks can be using Windows 95 or Windows NT Workstation, except for Hosts D and E. They can use either Windows NT Workstation or Windows NT Server. Routing of packets over networks can be done by **static routing** (routing tables don't automatically change and must be manually edited) or by **dynamic routing** (routing tables are automatically updated as new information about routes becomes known and is shared by one router with another). Windows NT and Windows 95 only support static routing.

TCP/IP and Windows 95.   To use TCP/IP with the networking software that comes with Windows 95, install and configure TCP/IP under the Network window of Control Panel. Follow these directions:

1. Click **Start**, **Settings**, **Control Panel**, and double-click on **Network**. Click the **Configuration** tab.

2. If TCP/IP is not already installed, click **Add** and select **Protocol** from the list of network components that can be installed. Click **Add**.

3. The Select Network Protocol dialog box appears, as seen in Figure 16-33. Select **Microsoft** from the list of manufacturers on the left. Select **TCP/IP** from the list of network protocols on the right. (Notice that NetBEUI and IPX/SPX are also choices at this point in the process.) Click **OK**. You will be asked to provide the Windows 95 CD-ROM or disks.

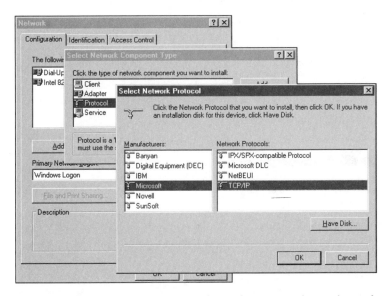

Figure 16-33   Installing TCP/IP from the Network window of the Control Panel

16

4. When you return to the Network window, notice that TCP/IP is automatically bound to the two adapters already installed: a network card (Intel 82595-Based Ethernet) and Windows Dial-Up Adapter (see Figure 16-34). Windows treats the Dial-Up Adapter just as though it were a network card. You can think of it as the software that turns your modem into a NIC.

5. The next step is to configure TCP/IP for each of the bindings listed that you will use. If you plan to use TCP/IP with the network card (so that the PC can communicate over networks other than its LAN), then click that selection in the list. In this case, select **TCP/IP –> Intel 82595-Based Ethernet** from the list in Figure 16-34. The TCP/IP Properties window displays, as in Figure 16-35.

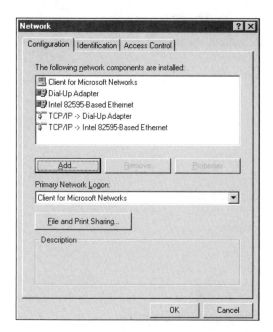

Figure 16-34 TCP/IP is automatically bound to the two network adapters already installed

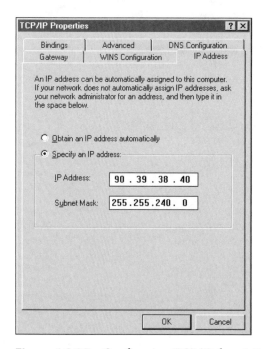

Figure 16-35 Configuring TCP/IP for static IP addressing

6. The information in this Properties window must be provided by your network administrator. For the IP Address tab, you must know if your network uses static or dynamic IP addressing. If static IP addressing is used, then click **Specify IP address** and enter the IP Address and Subnet Mask as supplied by your administrator. If dynamic IP addressing is used, click **Obtain an IP address automatically**. This will most likely be your selection when connecting to the Internet. Other tabs under this TCP/IP Properties window are discussed later in the chapter.

7. When finished, click **OK** to exit the Properties window.

Using TCP/IP with Windows NT. To use TCP/IP with Windows NT, first install and configure this protocol, and then bind it to the appropriate adapters, follow these directions:

1. Click **Start**, **Settings**, **Control Panel**, and double-click the **Network** icon. The Network window displays. Click the **Protocols** tab.

2. If TCP/IP is not already listed as an installed protocol, click **Add**. A list of network protocols supported by Windows NT will display, as in Figure 16-36.

3. Select TCP/IP Protocol from the list and then click **OK**.

4. During the installation, Windows NT asks if you plan to use a DHCP (Dynamic Host Configuration Protocol) server. If you plan to use static IP addressing, answer **No**, but if you plan to use dynamic IP addressing, as when connecting to the Internet, answer **Yes**.

5. You will be asked to provide the Windows NT CD-ROM and to point to the drive and directory of the installation files. For example, for a CD-ROM drive E, enter E:\i386.

6. Click the **Close** button at the bottom of the Network window to complete the installation.

7. You are then given the opportunity to configure TCP/IP for any network adapters that Windows NT detects are already installed. To allow you to do this, the TCP/IP Properties box displays as in Figure 16-37. Again, you must choose between static and dynamic IP addressing. If you choose static, by selecting Specify an IP address, enter the IP Address, Subnet Mask, and Default Gateway for this PC. Obtain this information from your network administrator.

16

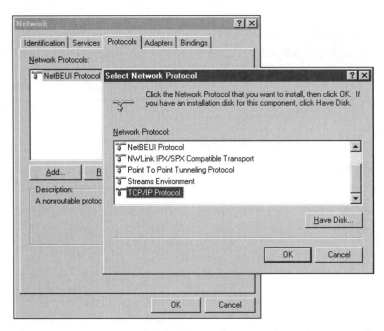

Figure 16-36 For Windows NT, install TCP/IP from the Network window of the Control Panel

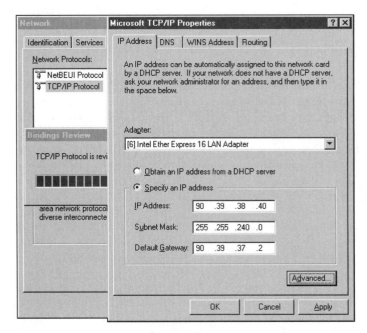

Figure 16-37 Configuring TCP/IP for Windows NT for static IP addressing

CONNECTING TO THE INTERNET

When supporting personal computers in a business environment where PCs are connected to a company LAN or corporate WAN, most network support is performed by a network administrator. However, many times a PC support person is called on to help a user connect to the Internet. In this case, you are often on your own, without the help of a network administrator. You may or may not be able to call on technical support from the Internet Service Provider. This section looks at the process of connecting a PC running either Windows 95 or Windows NT to the Internet, using Dial-Up Networking to make the connection.

Connecting to the Internet Using Windows 95

Connecting to the Internet for Web access and e-mail when using Windows 95 is a five-step process:

Step 1. Install and configure your modem.

Step 2. Set up Dial-Up Adapter under Control Panel.

Step 3. Set up Dial-Up Networking.

Step 4. For Web browsing, install Windows 95 Internet Explorer or some other software provided by your ISP, such as Netscape.

Step 5. For access to e-mail, install Windows 95 Windows Messaging (Inbox) or some other e-mail software, such as Eudora Light.

The text below describes how to do each step. Step 1 (installing and configuring a modem) is covered in Chapter 15 (see page 783). Steps 2 and 3 have been covered earlier in this chapter, but they are repeated here for completeness. Using Windows 95, follow these directions to connect to the Internet.

Step 1: Installing and Configuring a Modem.   See Chapter 15, see page 783.

Step 2: Setting up Dial-Up Adapter.   Remember that a Dial-up Adapter is Windows 95 terminology for making a modem act like a network card. The Dial-Up Adapter is automatically installed when Dial-Up Networking or Direct Cable Connection is installed. However, someone might have accidentally removed it after the installation of DUN or DCC. If necessary, you can reinstall Dial-Up Adapter from Control Panel. Also, when DUN and DCC are installed, network protocols IPX/SPX and NetBEUI are automatically installed, but not TCP/IP. You must install TCP/IP and then bind it to the Dial-Up Adapter. Follow these procedures:

1. Access the Network window of Control Panel. If Dial-Up Adapter is not listed as an installed network component, click **Add**.

2. Select **Adapter** from the list of components to install, and then click **Add**. Manufacturers and network cards that are supported by Windows 95 are listed.

16

3. Select **Microsoft** as the manufacturer on the left and **Dial-Up Adapter** from the list on the right. Click **OK**. You will be asked to provide the Windows 95 CD-ROM or disks. You will then be returned to the Network window, and Dial-Up Adapter should be listed along with IPX/SPX and NetBEUI protocols. Windows 95 installs these two protocols automatically when Dial-Up Adapter is installed.

4. To use the Internet, you need TCP/IP. Click **Add** and select **Protocol** from the list to install and click **Add**.

5. From the list of supported protocols, select **TCP/IP** and click **Add**. You will be asked for the Windows 95 CD-ROM or disks.

6. After TCP/IP is installed, you are returned to the Network window. Select **TCP/IP** and then click **Properties** to configure the protocol. The Properties dialog box displays.

7. Under the IP Address tab, select **Obtain an IP Address automatically**.

8. Under the WINS resolution tab, select **Disabled**.

9. Under the Gateway tab, no installed gateways should be listed.

10. Under the DNS Configuration tab, select **Disable DNS**.

11. Click **OK** to close the Properties box.

12. Click **OK** to close the Network window. You may be asked to reboot the PC.

Step 3: Verifying That the Client for Microsoft Networks Is Installed. When you installed either Dial-Up Networking and a modem or a network card, Windows 95 also installed Client for Microsoft Networks. You need to verify that the software is still installed.

1. Go to Control Panel and double-click on the **Network** icon.

2. If Client for Microsoft Networks is not present, click **Add** and select **Client** from the list of components to install.

3. Select **Microsoft** from the list of manufacturers.

4. There are two clients supported by Microsoft: Client for Microsoft Networks and Client for NetWare Networks for a Novell LAN. In this case, select **Client for Microsoft Networks** and click **OK**. When you return to the Network window, the client should be listed among the installed components.

Step 4: Setting up Dial-Up Networking. If Dial-Up Networking is not installed, follow the directions earlier in the chapter to install it (see page 835), then follow the directions below to create a dial-up icon for your ISP:

1. Click **Start**, **Programs**, **Accessories**, **Dial-Up Networking**. Double-click on **Make New Connection**.

2. Verify that the modem listed under **Connect using** is the correct modem installed on your PC.

3. When creating the Dial-Up Networking icon, you will need the phone number of your ISP and your user name and password.

4. Click the **Server Type** button. In this Server Type box, shown in Figure 16-38, verify that these choices are made:

   ■ Type of Dial-Up Server: PPP Windows 95, Windows NT 3.5, Internet

   ■ Advanced Options: Select Enable software compression (software compression is most likely to be enabled, but this option really depends on what the ISP is doing) and log on to the network.

   ■ Allowed Network Protocols: TCP/IP

5. Click TCP/IP Settings. The TCP/IP Settings dialog box displays, as in Figure 16-39. Verify that these settings are chosen:

   ■ Server assigned IP address

   ■ Specify name server addresses

   ■ Use IP header compression

   ■ Use default gateway on remote network

6. Enter the IP addresses of the Primary and Secondary DNS servers. This information is provided by your ISP.

7. Click **OK** two times to complete building the Dial-Up Networking connection.

8. You should now be able to dial up your ISP and see the connection complete. Once connected, however, you will not be able to use the Internet until you have installed some application-level software to access it.

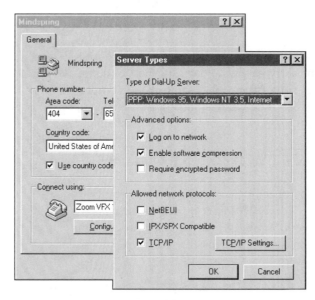

Figure 16-38   Configuring the server type for a connection to the Internet

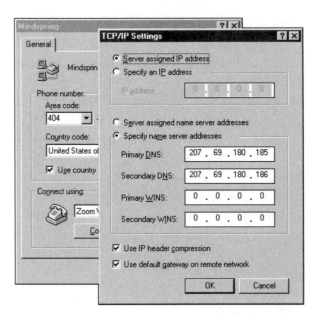

Figure 16-39   TCP/IP settings for a connection to the Internet

Installing a Web Web Browser and E-mail Software.   Most ISPs provide you with a Web browser and e-mail software, and probably will include other software as well, such as chat room software. Install this software following the directions given to you by the ISP.

If you are using Internet Explorer, after you have installed the software, you can upgrade your version with the latest Internet Explorer from Microsoft. See directions on the company's Web site, www.microsoft.com, to download the latest version. Internet Explorer is free to all who have a license to use a Windows OS.

There are many e-mail software programs available. A popular freeware is Eudora Light, which is likely to be included with the software from your ISP. You can download the latest version from the Web site www.eudora.com. After you download the compressed file, execute it by double-clicking on it from Explorer. The file will decompress and a setup program executes.

SOME EXAMPLES OF NETWORK SERVICES

Look back at Figure 16-11. The chapter began by discussing the bottom two layers in the figure (the Physical and Data Link layers). Next it turned to the next two layers in the figure, the Network and Transport layers, and discussed the most popular protocol at these layers, TCP/IP. Looking upward in the figure, note that the next layers to address are the Session, Presentation, and Application layers.

At the highest level of the OSI model is the Application layer, which interfaces with users and with applications software that uses networks. Figure 16-11 shows some of the more common services. For the Internet, there are Web browsers, chat rooms, e-mail, and FTP. For LANs, WANs, and corporate intranets, there are e-mail, FTP, Telnet, print services, and network drives. You have also learned from this chapter that other application-level software exists, such as middleware used to pass requests for data between a client PC and a network server. This section looks at several of the more common network services. Most of these services function at the top three layers of the OSI model: the Application, Presentation, and Session layers.

Also shown in Figure 16-11 are several upper-level protocols, including **Hypertext Transfer Protocol** (**HTTP**) used by the World Wide Web, File Transfer Protocol (FTP) used to transfer files, and Simple Mail Transfer Protocol (SMTP) used to transfer e-mail. For addressing services on remote computers, in addition to the domain name, sometimes the protocol is used in front of the domain name. The protocol, domain name, and a path or filename are collectively called a **universal resource locator** (**URL**). An example of a URL with the three parts labeled is shown in Figure 16-40. This URL is pointing to a Web site that uses HTTP, as seen by the protocol portion of the address. The path or filename portion of the URL includes a filename and file extension, DOCUMENT.HTML.

Figure 16-40   A universal resource locator (URL) can include protocol, domain name, and specific path and filename information

At the Application, Presentation, and Session layers of the OSI model, protocols use one of two methods to establish communication with lower level-protocols: sockets or NetBIOS. **Network Basic Input/Output System** (**NetBIOS**) is mostly used on LANs for PC-based networking, and is a network extension of the older DOS BIOS used by applications software to interact with hardware. NetBEUI (NetBIOS Extended User Interface) protocol at the Transport and Network layers was written to interface with NetBIOS working at the Session, Presentation and Application layers.

Recall that a **socket** is a virtual connection from one computer to another, such as from a PC to a server. The Session-layer protocol HTTP uses the socket method. HTTP sends a request to the server to open a socket, and the socket is assigned a number for the current session. HTTP can then refer to this number when sending a GET command to the Web server. The socket software then in turn uses TCP to segment and send the data. (See Figure 16-27, where the application using a socket is a Web browser.) Internet protocols making connections to remote computers mostly use the socket method rather than NetBIOS, although, looking back again at Figure 16-27, you can see that the TCP/IP protocol suite includes support for NetBIOS; the protocol of TCP/IP that supports NetBIOS is NetBT.

16

One more concept is needed before looking at examples of network services. For all these network services, there must be a program running on both nodes of the network for the service to work. For example, for FTP to work, FTP Client must be running at one end and FTP Server at the other. When using the World Wide Web, Web browser software must be running at one end and Web service software must be running on the other end. (The Web service will most likely be running on a more powerful computer than a desktop PC.) Also for a network drive map to work, the network drive service must be running on the host PC, and the network drive client software must be running on the client PC. Looking back at Figure 16-9, you can see this concept depicted in the diagram as the Application layer on one computer logically communicating with the Application layer on the other computer. Also, in the case of the Internet, these top-layer programs are using TCP/IP, which provides the middle layers of the OSI model.

WORLD WIDE WEB BROWSERS

Web browser software is designed to provide the interface between Web sites and PCs. A Web site resides on a server, has a domain name and a static IP address, and provides Web pages to those computers requesting them. Using the Internet, a Web browser can access the server by either the IP address or the domain name. The browser can also further identify files and folders to access by putting an extension, containing paths and filenames, on the domain name. The domain name is followed by a forward slash and the path or filename to be selected.

Communication over the Web by Web browsers consists of passing document files from the Web host site to the PC. The protocol used to request and pass these documents is HTTP.

FILE TRANSFER

A common task of communications software is file transfer, the passing of files from one computer to another. For file transfer to work, the software on both ends must be using the same protocol. The most popular way to transfer files over the Internet is with File Transfer Protocol (FTP), which is used to transfer files between two computers using the same or different operating systems. A popular use of the Internet is for companies to provide files for customers to download to their PCs, such as when new upgrades for software become available. This service is commonly provided by Windows NT or UNIX servers that provide access to files using FTP and are called FTP servers or FTP sites. These commercial FTP sites only provide the ability to download a file to your PC. However, FTP offers more power than just that. A user who has first logged onto a remote computer can use FTP utility software to copy, delete, and rename files, make directories, remove directories, and view details about files and directories.

Most communications applications provide a file transfer utility that has its own look and feel, but the basics of file transfer are the same from one utility to another. The text below discusses a couple of examples of file transfer utilities, highlighting their similarities and differences.

File Transfer from a Command Prompt

FTP can be initiated at a DOS, Windows 95, or Windows NT command prompt, assuming that a connection is established to a network or the Internet. FTP at a command prompt is a quick-and-dirty way to transfer files when the computer does not have more user-friendly FTP software installed. For example, Windows NT Workstation has FTP available at the command prompt, but a GUI version of FTP is not packaged with the OS and must be installed. The FTP DOS commands work like the dialog in Table 16-5.

Table 16-5   A sample FTP Session from a DOS command prompt

Command Entered at the DOS Command Prompt	Description
FTP	Execute the DOS FTP utility
OPEN 110.87.170.34	Open a Session with a remote computer having the given IP address
LOGIN: XXXXXX	The host computer provides a prompt to enter a user ID for the computer being accessed.
PASSWORD: XXXXXX	The host computer requests the password for that ID. Logon is then completed by the host computer.
CD /DATA	Change directory to the /DATA directory
GET YOURFILE.DAT	Copy the file YOURFILE.DAT (or whatever file you want) from the remote computer to my computer
PUT MYFILE.DAT	Copy the file MYFILE.DAT (or whatever file you want) from your computer to the remote computer
BYE	Disconnect the FTP session

File Transfer Using an Internet Service Provider

When you subscribe to an Internet service provider (ISP), the provider will most likely provide you with software for using FTP. This example looks at how to execute FTP using such a service:

1. Connect to the Internet using the procedures provided by your ISP.

2. Execute the FTP utility provided by the ISP. The FTP utility screen displays.

3. Click on **Connect** to log on to an FTP site. A Session Profile dialog box displays, such as the one in Figure 16.41.

4. Enter the Host Name, for example ftp.course.com. Enter the User ID and Password for this host computer, and then click **OK**.

5. The connection is made, and your ID and password are passed to the host. After you have been authenticated by the host computer, a screen similar to that in Figure 16-42 displays.

16

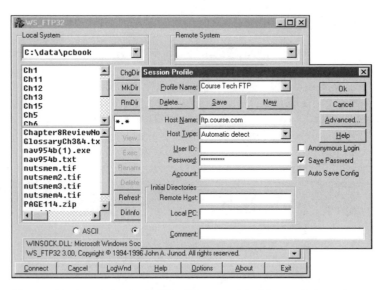

Figure 16-41 A typical FTP utility provided by an Internet
service provider

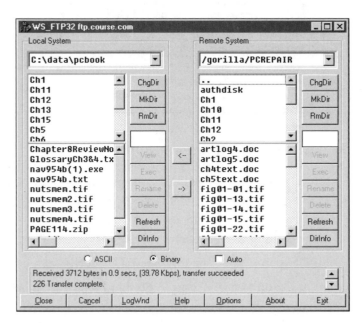

Figure 16-42 An FTP utility screen showing local and remote files

6. The files on the left belong to you, and the files on the right belong to the remote
host computer. You can drag and drop files either to or from the other computer, or
you can use the commands at the bottom of the window. Notice in Figure 16-42
the choices toward the bottom of the window: ASCII, Binary, or Auto. These

choices refer to the format that is to be used to transfer the files. Use ASCII only for text files, and use Binary for all others. If you are not sure which to use, choose **Auto**.

7. When transferring files is complete, click **Exit** to leave the utility.

Many times when you are using the Internet, a Web page will provide the ability to download a file. It is likely that this file is not being downloaded from the Web server, but the author of the Web page has programmed a link from the Web page to an FTP server. When you click on the filename on the Web page, the program controlling the page executes FTP commands to the FTP server to download the file to you. If you get an error when downloading the file this way, you can sometimes solve the problem by going directly to the company's FTP server and using an FTP utility, like the one described here, to successfully download the file or even see a list of other files that you might also like to download.

NETWORK DRIVE MAP

A network drive map is one of the most powerful and versatile methods of communicating over a network. By using network file service (NFS) software, the network drive map makes one PC appear to have a new hard drive, such as drive E that is really hard drive space on another host computer. Even if the host computer is using a different OS, such as UNIX, the drive map still functions. Using a network drive map, files and folders on a host computer are available even to network-unaware DOS applications. The path to a file simply uses the remote drive letter instead of a local drive such as drive A or drive C.

The following example connects two computers, using Dial-Up Networking. The host computer is using Windows NT, and the local computer is using Windows 95. The Windows 95 PC will map a network drive to the Windows NT PC.

Preparing a Windows NT Host Computer for a Network Drive Map

For Windows NT to allow a remote PC to dial-in, Remote Access Service (RAS) must be installed and running. The remote user must have been set up with a user ID and password, and drives and/or folders must be shared, meaning that other computers are allowed to have access to them.

Follow these directions for setting up a Windows NT PC to allow a network drive map from a remote PC that is using Windows 95:

1. Install RAS: Click **Start**, **Settings**, **Control Panel** and double-click the **Network** icon.
2. Select the **Services** tab. If Remote Access Service is not already listed as being installed, click **Add**. From the list of Network services, select **Remote Access Service** and click **OK** to install the service. You will be asked to supply the Windows NT CD-ROM and the path to the \i386 directory on the CD.

16

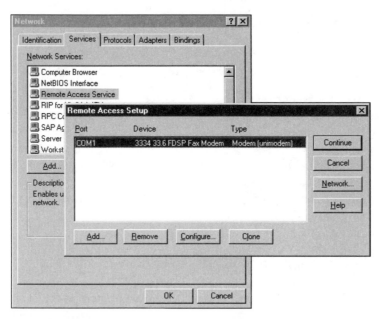

Figure 16-43   Remote Access Service allows another PC to dial
into a Windows NT PC

3. From the Network window, select **Remote Access Service** and click
   Properties. The Remote Access Setup dialog box displays, as in Figure 16-43.

4. Click **Configure**. The Configure Port Usage dialog box displays, as in Figure 16-44.
   Select **Dial out and Receive calls**. Click **OK**.

5. From the Remote Access Setup box, click **Network**. Figure 16-45 displays,
   showing the three network protocols for either dial-out or dial-in calls. For one
   PC to connect to another, NetBEUI is the most efficient choice. You can select
   only NetBEUI or leave others selected as well. Use IPX for a Novell LAN and
   TCP/IP to connect to the Internet. Click **OK** twice to return to Control Panel.

6. Once RAS is installed, it can be set to start automatically each time you boot, or
   you can start it manually. To start the RAS service, click **Start**, **Settings**, **Control
   Panel**, and double-click on **Services**. Select **Remote Access Server** and then
   click **Start**.

7. Follow instructions from Chapter 12 to set up a user ID and password from the
   User Manager. (Click **Start**, **Programs**, **Administrative Tools**, **User Manager**.)
   Be sure to grant the user the permission to dial in from a remote PC.

8. To establish which drives and/or folders you want the remote user to have access
   to, access Explorer, and then right-click on the drive or folder you want to share.
   Select **Sharing** from the drop-down menu. Select **Shared As** and give the
   resource a name, such as MarketFolder or C. The workstation is now set to
   allow a dial-in. The next time you want to allow the remote use of the PC, all
   that you must do is start RAS.

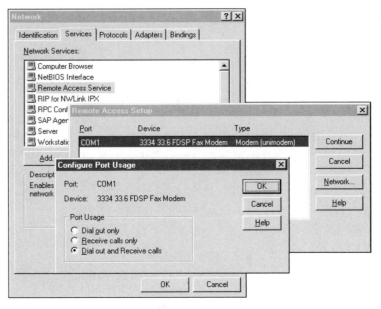

Figure 16-44   Configuring RAS under Windows NT to allow both incoming and dial-out calls

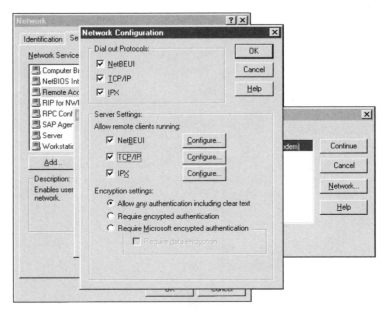

16

Figure 16-45   Windows NT RAS supports three network protocols

Mapping the Network Drive from Remote to Host Computer

In order to set up a host computer to allow a network drive map to your hard drive, or to access the network drive from a remote computer, each computer must be running network drive software. Windows NT and Windows 95 include support to map network drives to other Windows PCs. To map network drives to computers using other OSs, you must use third-party software.

The remote computer can use either a regular network connection or Dial-Up Networking to connect to the host computer. After you are connected, to map a network drive on your computer, use Explorer. Follow these directions:

1. While connected to a network, access Windows Explorer. Click on the **Tools** menu shown in Figure 16-46. Select **Map Network Drive**.

2. The Map Network Drive dialog box displays, as seen in Figure 16-47. Select a drive letter from the drop-down list.

3. Enter a path to the host computer. Use two backslashes, followed by the name of the host computer, followed by a backslash and the drive or folder to access on the host computer. For example, to access drive C on the computer named MyrtleTree1, enter \\MYRTLETREE1\C and then click **OK**.

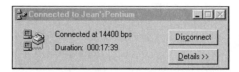

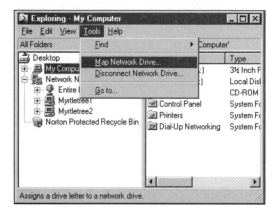

Figure 16-46   Mapping a network drive to a remote computer, using Explorer

4. Figure 16-48 shows the results of the drive map. There is a new drive E displayed in Explorer. Folders listed on the right side of the figure are on the host PC.

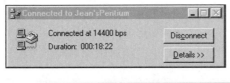

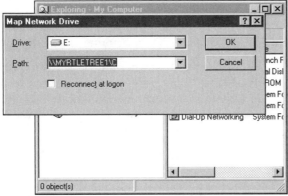

Figure 16-47   To map a network drive, enter a drive letter to use on your PC and the path to the remote computer

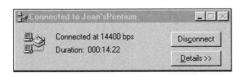

Figure 16-48   Folders listed on the right side of Explorer belong to the remote computer. This computer sees them belonging to its drive E

16

PRINT SERVICES

Print services over a network allow computers to use printers that are connected to other computers on the network or connected directly to the network. Print services under Windows 95 and Windows NT work similarly to sharing files and folders. You can share a printer much as you would share a file or folder: allow sharing, give the printer a name, and grant the right for a remote user to dial-in. For Windows NT, run RAS, and for Windows 95, run the Microsoft Plus! utility to allow dial-in. Follow these directions to allow a remote PC running Windows 95 to use a printer on a Windows NT workstation that is running RAS:

To prepare the Windows NT host computer for Network Printing, do the following:

1. On the Windows NT PC, allow print sharing: click **Start**, **Settings**, **Printers**. The Printers window displays. Right-click on the printer you want to share, and select **Sharing** from the drop-down menu that displays. The printer Properties box displays, as seen in Figure 16-49. Select **Shared** and enter a name for the printer. Click **OK** when done.

2. The Windows NT PC must be connected to a network either directly or through RAS.

To Use a Shared Printer

On the Windows 95 local PC, follow these directions to use a shared printer on another PC:

1. Connect to the host computer.

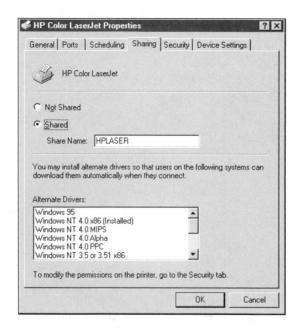

Figure 16-49   Windows NT print sharing requires that you give
                   the printer a name

2. Add a new printer: click **Start**, **Settings**, **Printers**. Double-click **Add Printer**. The Add Printer Wizard window displays.

3. In response to the question, "How is this printer attached to your computer?", select **Network printer**. Click **Next**. Figure 16-50 displays.

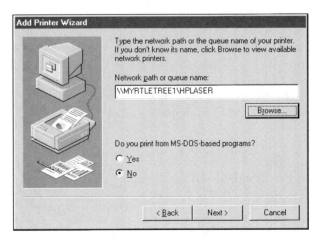

Figure 16-50   To use a network printer under Windows 95, enter the host computer name followed by the printer name

4. Enter the host computer name and printer name. Begin with two backslashes and separate the computer name from the printer name with a backslash. Click **Next**.

5. Select the printer manufacturer and then the printer model from the list of supported printers. Click **Next** when finished.

6. Enter a name for the printer. You might include in the name the location of the printer, such as 3rd Floor Laser or John's Laser. Click **Next** to continue.

7. You are then given the opportunity to print a test page, which is recommended. Click **Finish** to complete the network printer installation.

8. The network printer is now available for use.

In the above directions, if your network is using static IP addressing and you know the IP address of the host PC, you can enter the IP address of the host rather than the name of the host PC when attempting to map a network drive or gain access to a printer.

16

NETWORK TROUBLESHOOTING GUIDELINES

This section covers some guidelines to use when troubleshooting network problems.

WINDOWS 95 DIAL-UP PROBLEMS

Modem problems

When using Windows 95 Dial-Up Networking, you may experience problems with dialing into a host computer that are caused by the modem. See Chapter 15 for troubleshooting guidelines for modems.

Cannot make a connection.   Because Dial-Up Networking involves so many different components, first find out what works and what doesn't work. Find out the answers to these questions:

- Does the modem work? Compare the printout of a modemlog.txt file that was made during a successful connection at another PC to the modemlog.txt file of this PC, to identify the point in the connection at which an error occurs. (For Windows 95, to log modem events to the modemlog.txt file, double-click on **Modems** in Control Panel, then select the modem, click **Properties**, **Connection**, **Advanced**, and turn on **Recording to a log file**.)

- Are all components installed? Check for the Dial-Up Adapter and TCP/IP, and check the configuration of each.

- Check the Dial-Up Networking connection icon for errors. Is the phone number correct? Does the number need to include a 9 to get an outside line? Has a 1 been added in front of the number by mistake?

- Reboot your PC and try again.

- Try removing and reinstalling each network component. Begin with TCP/IP.

- Try dialing the number manually from a phone. Do you hear beeps on the other end?

- Try another phone number.

- Sometimes older copies of the Windows socket DLL may be interfering with the current Windows 95 socket DLL. (Windows 95 may be finding and executing the older DLL before it finds the newer one.) Search for and rename any files named WINSOCK.DLL except the one in the Windows\System directory.

You can connect, but you get the message "Unable to resolve hostname...".   This error message means that TCP/IP is not able to determine how to route a request to a host. Right-click on the **Dial-Up Networking** connection icon, select **Properties**, and check for these things:

- Under Server Type, try making the only network protocol allowed TCP/IP?

- Under TCP/IP settings, check the IP addresses of the DNS servers.

- Is **Using the default gateway** selected?

- Try *not* selecting IP header compression.

After connecting, you get the error message "Unable to establish a compatible set of network protocols".   This error is most likely to be caused by a problem with the installation and configuration of Dial-Up Networking and/or TCP/IP. Try these things:

- Verify that Dial-Up Adapter and TCP/IP are installed and configured correctly.

- Remove and reinstall TCP/IP. Be sure to reboot after the installation.

- Try putting the Windows 95 PCs in different workgroups.

- Windows 95 can write to a log file the events of PPP processing a call. Create the PPPLog.txt file on a PC that makes a successful connection, and compare it to the log file of your bad connection to see exactly when the problem began. To turn on the logging of events to the file, double-click the **Network** icon in Control Panel. Click **Dial-Up Adapter**, click **Properties**, select the **Advanced** tab and select **Record a log file**. On the Value list, click **Yes**, then click **OK**. Reboot the PC. The file PPPLog.txt is created in the Windows folder as the connection is made and used.

When you double-click on the network browser, the modem does not dial automatically.   When this occurs, right-click on the network browser icon and select **Properties** from the drop-down menu. Under the Connection tab, check **Connect to the Internet as needed**.

PROBLEMS WITH TCP/IP

Windows 95 and Windows NT offer several TCP/IP utilities that can help in troubleshooting. Some are introduced here.

Problems with TCP/IP Configuration or Suspected Network Problems

A useful diagnostic tool for either Windows 95 or Windows NT is **packet Internet groper** (**PING**), which tests connectivity. PING sends a signal to a remote PC. If the remote PC is online to the network and hears the signal, it will respond. IPConfig under Windows NT and WinIPcfg under Windows 95 test TCP/IP configuration. Try these things:

- For Windows NT, at the command prompt, enter IPconfig, or, for Windows 95, go to Explorer and double-click on **WinIPcfg** in the Windows 95 folder. If the TCP/IP configuration is correct, for static IP addressing, the IP address, subnet

16

mask, and default gateway display along with the adapter address. If DHCP is used for dynamic IP addressing and no IP address has yet been assigned, the IP address should read 0.0.0.0.

- Next try the loopback address test. Enter the command PING 127.0.0.1. This IP address refers to yourself. It should respond with a reply message from yourself. If this works, most likely TCP/IP is configured correctly.

- If you have been assigned an IP address, PING it. If you get any errors up to this point, then assume that the problem is on your PC. Check the installation and configuration of each component. Remove and reinstall each component and watch for error messages. Compare the configuration to that of a PC that is working on the same network.

- Next PING the IP address of your default gateway. If it does not respond, then the problem may be with the gateway or with the network to the gateway.

- Now try to PING the host computer you are trying to reach. If it does not respond, then the problem may be with the host computer or with the network to the computer.

- If you substitute a URL for the IP address in the PING command, and the PING works, then you can conclude that DNS works. If an IP address works, but the URL does not work, the problem lies with DNS. Try this: PING microsoft.com.

PROBLEMS WITH NETWORK PRINTERS

If you are having problems with network printers, first determine that the problem is not a physical problem with the printer. For guidelines on how to do that, see Chapters 7 and 13 and Appendix E. Problems with network printing may be caused by the printer, the network to the printer, or the computer trying to use the printer. You can isolate the problem by finding the answers to the following questions:

- Is the printer on line?

- Is the network printer on the remote PC configured correctly?

- Is the correct network printer selected on the remote PC?

- Is there enough hard disk space available on the remote PC?

- Can you print successfully from another application on the remote PC?

- Can you print successfully from the host PC using the identical application?

- Can you print to a file and then send the file to the host PC to successfully print? If this works, then the problem is with data transmission. If this does not work, then the problem is with the application or print driver on the remote PC.

- For DOS applications, you may need to exit the application before printing occurs.

CHAPTER SUMMARY

- A network can be either a LAN or a WAN. Connecting LANs and WANs together is called internetworking.

- The three most popular network architectures today are Ethernet, Token Ring, and FDDI. Each is designed to satisfy a different networking need.

- Ethernet can follow either a bus or star physical design and is the least expensive and most popular network type. Token Ring is more reliable, but more expensive and difficult to maintain. FDDI is used to fill massive networking needs over a wide area, for example, serving as the backbone network between smaller networks in a large building complex such as a large hospital.

- There are several kinds and grades of networking cables, including coaxial cable, unshielded twisted-pair (UTP) cable, shielded twisted-pair (STP) cable, and fiber-optic cable.

- Segmentation is a method of breaking a large network into smaller segments in order to control traffic over the network.

- Bridges, routers, and gateways are used to interconnect networks.

- Repeaters are used to amplify signals that are traveling a long distance on a network.

- A network interface card (NIC) prepares data for transmission by disassembling the data into data packets or frames, transmits the data over cabling media, and reassembles the data back into a contiguous stream at the receiving end.

- Each NIC has embedded on it at the factory a unique identifying 6-byte hex number called the media access control (MAC), or adapter, address. This number uniquely identifies the NIC on the network and is used by the network to physically identify the node on the network.

- The seven-layer OSI network model is used as a guideline for discussing the different protocols, software, and firmware of a network. Mapping the many different components onto the model helps in understanding how they interrelate and what function each serves for the network.

- Examples of networking software components that satisfy the bottom two layers of the OSI model (Physical and Data Link layers) are Ethernet, Token Ring, FDDI, and PPP over phone lines. Examples of protocols that work at the Network, Transport, and Session layers are TCP/IP, IPX/SPX, and NetBEUI. Software examples of the top OSI layers (Presentation and Application) are Web browsers, e-mail and chat room software, and Telnet.

- Windows 95 and Windows NT both support phone line access to networks. This OS service is called Dial-Up Networking, and it makes a modem appear to be a NIC on the network.

- Windows 95 and Windows NT also support Direct Cable Connect, a method of networking two PCs with a serial or parallel cable.

16

- The Internet is a huge interconnection of many networks. It is a decentralized method of successfully routing data over many networks that use varying protocols, software, and hardware. The principal protocol of the Internet is TCP/IP, which identifies each node on the network with an IP address that ultimately must match up with the computer's MAC address.

- An IP address has two parts: a network address identifying the network, and a host address identifying the individual PC on the network. Sometimes the network address also includes a subnet address to allow a network to be broken up into logical segments in order to control traffic within the network.

- IP addresses can be permanently assigned to PCs (called static IP addressing) or dynamically assigned. When IP addresses are dynamically assigned, a different IP address is assigned to a host each time the host goes online to the network. Servers that manage dynamic assignments of IP addresses are called DHCP (Dynamic Host Configuration Protocol) servers.

- A domain name is a convenient and user-friendly method of naming a host on a network. A domain name must ultimately be mapped to the IP address of the host before data can be routed to the host. Two services that track domain names and their corresponding IP addresses are DNS (domain name service) and WINS (Windows Internet naming service).

- TCP/IP is really a suite of protocols that satisfy differing needs of a network and include the Network, Transport, and Session layers of the OSI model.

- Once connection to the Internet is made using TCP/IP and PPP (with a modem), software at the higher layers of the OSI model is used to send and receive data over the network. Different types of Internet software access different Internet services, including Web browsing, e-mail, and FTP.

- Important networking services typically used on smaller networks are network drive maps and print services.

Key Terms

- **Adapter address** — A 6-byte hex hardware address unique to each NIC card and assigned by manufacturers. The address is often printed on the adapter. An example is 00 00 0C 08 2F 35.

- **Address Resolution Protocol (ARP)** — A method used by TCP/IP that dynamically or automatically translates IP addresses into physical network addresses such as Ethernet IDs or Token Ring MAC addresses.

- **Alternate gateway** — An alternate router that is used if the default gateway is down. *See* gateway.

- **Amplifier repeater** — A repeater that amplifies whatever it receives regardless of its source.

- **Application layer** — The layer of the OSI model responsible for interfacing with the user or application using the network.

- **Back end** — In a client/server environment, the application on the server that processes requests for data from the client.

- **Backbone** — A network used to link several networks together. For example, several Token Rings and Ethernets may be connected using a single FDDI backbone.

- **Binding** — Associating an OSI layer to a layer above it or below it.

- **Bridge** — A hardware device or box, coupled with software at the Data Link Layer, used to connect similar networks and network segments. *See* Router.

- **Bus network architecture** — A network design in which nodes are connected in line with one another, with no centralized point of contact.

- **Carrier Sense Multiple Access with Collision Detection (CSMA/CD)** — A feature used in ethernet networks whereby packets are sent after listening for a silence, and are resent if a collision is detected.

- **Classless addresses** — Class C network addresses a service provider owns and then subleases to small companies.

- **Collision** — In an ethernet network, when transmitted packets of data are sent at the same time and collide. Ethernet will first listen for silence before it transmits, and it will stop and resend if a collision occurs.

- **Connection protocol** — In networking, confirming that a good connection is made before transmitting data to the other end. To accomplish this, most network applications use TCP rather than UDP.

- **Connectionless protocol** — When UDP is used and a connection is not required before sending a packet. Consequently, there is no guarantee that the packet will arrive at its destination. An example of a UDP transmission is a broadcast to all nodes on a network.

- **Contention-based system** — A system in which each computer contends for the opportunity to transmit on the network. If there is a collision, a computer waits a random amount of time and resends.

- **Controlled-access unit (CAU)** — A centralized hub on a Token Ring network. *See* Multistation access unit.

- **Crosstalk** — The interference that one wire, in a twisted pair, may produce in the other.

- **Data Link layer** — The OSI layer that disassembles packets and reassembles data into packets.

- **Datagrams** — Packets of data that travel between networks from a sender to a receiver. A datagram typically includes an IP header, address information, a checksum, and data.

- **Default gateway** — The main gateway or unit that will send or receive packets addressed to other networks.

16

- **Dial-Up Networking** — A Windows application that allows a PC to remotely connect to a network through a phone line. A Dial-Up Network icon can be found under My Computer.

- **Domain name** — A unique, text-based name that identifies an IP (Internet address). Typically, domain names in the United States end in .edu, .gov, .com, .org, or .net. Domain names also include a country code, such as .uk for the United Kingdom.

- **Domain name system** or **domain name service (DNS)** — A database on a top-level domain name server that keeps track of assigned domain names and their corresponding IP addresses.

- **Dynamic Host Configuration Protocol (DHCP)** — The protocol of a server that manages dynamically assigned IP addresses. DHCP is supported by both Windows 95 and Windows NT.

- **Dynamic IP address** — An assigned IP address that is used for the current session only. When the session is terminated, the IP address is returned to the list of available addresses.

- **Dynamic routing** — Routing tables that are automatically updated as new information about routes becomes known and is shared by one router with another. Compare to static routing.

- **Ethernet** — The most popular network topology used today. It uses Carrier Sense Multiple Access with Collision Detection (CSMA/CD) and can be physically configured as a bus or star network.

- **FDDI (Fiber Distributed Data Interface)** — Pronounced "fiddy." A ring-based network, similar to Token Ring, that does not require a centralized hub. FDDI often uses only fiber-optic cabling.

- **Front end** — In a client/server environment, the application on the client that makes use of data stored on the server.

- **FTP (File Transfer Protocol)** — An Internet standard that provides for the transfer of files from one computer to another. FTP can be used at a command prompt, or with a GUI interface, which is available with FTP software or with a Web browser. When using a Web browser, enter the command "ftp" in the browser URL line instead of the usual "http://" used to locate a Web site.

- **FTP server** or **FTP site** — A computer that stores files that can be downloaded by FTP.

- **Gateway** — A device or process that connects networks with different protocols. *See* Bridge and Router.

- **Header** — Information sent ahead of data being transferred over a network to identify it to receiving protocols. An IP header consists of things such as header and datagram length, flags, checksum, addresses, and so on.

- **Hop count** — The number of routers a packet must pass through in a network in order to reach its destination.

- **HTTP (Hypertext Transfer Protocol)** — The common transfer protocol used by Internet browsers on the World Wide Web.

- **Hub** — A network device or box that provides a central location to connect cables.

- **Intelligent hubs** — Network hubs that can be remotely controlled at a console, using network software. These hubs can monitor a network and report errors or problems.

- **Internet** — The worldwide collection of over a million hosts that can communicate with each other using TCP/IP. The lowercase *internet* simply means multiple networks connected together.

- **Internet Control Message Protocol (ICMP)** — Part of the IP layer that is used to transmit error messages and other control messages to hosts and routers.

- **Internet Network Information Center (InterNIC)** — The central group that assigns and keeps track of all Internet IP addresses on the organizational level.

- **Internet service provider (ISP)** — A commercial group that provides a user with software for Internet access for a monthly fee. AOL, Prodigy, GTE, and CompuServe are four large ISPs.

- **Internetwork** — Two or more networks connected together, such as a LAN and a WAN joined together.

- **Intranet** — A private internet used by a large company over a fairly wide geographical area.

- **IP (Internet Protocol) address** — A 32-bit "dotted-decimal" address consisting of four numbers separated by periods used to uniquely identify a device on a network that uses TCP/IP protocols. The first numbers identify the network; the last number identifies a host. An example of an IP address is 206.96.103.114.

- **IPX/SPX** — A protocol developed and used by Novell NetWare for LANs. The IPX portion of the protocol works at the Network layer, which is responsible for routing, and the SPX portion of the protocol manages error checking at the Transport layer.

- **Limited token** — Applies to a FDDI network. A token sent that allows a receiving station to communicate only with the sending station, thus providing continuous communication between the two stations.

- **Line protocol** — A protocol used over phone lines to allow a connection to a network. Also called bridging protocol. The most popular line protocol is PPP (Point-to-Point Protocol).

- **MAC (media access control)** — An element of Data Link layer protocol that provides compatibility with the NIC used by the Physical layer. An adapter address is often called a MAC address.

- **Middleware** — Software necessary for an application on a client to pass requests to a server, and for a server to respond with data. Microsoft's **Open Database Connectivity** (**ODBC**) is an example of middleware.

16

- **Multistation access unit (MSAU or MAU)** — A centralized hub device used to connect IBM Token Ring network stations.

- **Multiframe dialog** — When a token is sent that allows a receiving station to communicate only with the sending station, thus providing continuous communication between the two stations.

- **Nearest active downstream neighbor (NADN)** — The next station to receive a token in a token ring.

- **Nearest active upstream neighbor (NAUN)** — The station that has just sent a token to the nearest active downstream neighbor in a token ring.

- **NetBEUI (NetBIOS Extended User Interface)** — A proprietary Microsoft networking protocol used only by Windows-based systems, and limited to LANs because it does not support routing.

- **NetBT** (NetBIOS over TCP/IP) — An alternative Microsoft NetBEUI component designed to interface with TCP/IP networks.

- **Network interface card (NIC)** — A network adapter board that plugs into a computer's systemboard and provides a port on the back of the card to connect a PC to a network.

- **Network layer** — The OSI layer responsible for routing packets.

- **Network mask** — That portion of an IP address that identifies the network.

- **Node** — Each computer, workstation, or device on a network.

- **Octet** — A traditional term for each of the four 8-bit numbers that make up an IP address. For example, the IP address 206.96.103.114 has four octets.

- **Open Systems Interconnect (OSI)** — A seven-layer (Application, Presentation, Session, Transport, Network, Data Link, Physical) model of communications supported by a network. Refers to software and firmware only.

- **Packet** — Network segments of data that also include header, destination addresses, and trailer information.

- **Passive network** — A network, such as Ethernet, in which the computers, not dedicated network devices, drive the signals over the network.

- **Physical layer** — The OSI layer responsible for interfacing with the network media (cabling).

- **PPP (Point-to-Point Protocol)** — A common way PCs with modems can connect to an internet. The Windows Dial-Up Networking utility, found under My Computer, uses PPP.

- **Presentation layer** — The OSI layer that compresses and decompresses data and interfaces with the Application layer and the Session layer.

- **Protocol** — A set of preestablished rules for communication. Examples of protocols are modem parity settings and the way in which header and trailer information in a data packet is formatted.

- **Repeater** — A device that amplifies weakened signals on a network.

- **Reverse Address Resolution Protocol (RARP)** — Translates the unique hardware NIC addresses into IP addresses (the reverse of ARP).

- **Route discovery** — When a router rebuilds its router tables on the basis of new information.

- **Router** — A device or box that connects networks. A router transfers a packet to other networks only when the packet is addressed to a station outside its network. The router can make intelligent decisions as to which network is the best route to use to send data to a distant network. *See* Bridge.

- **Router table** — Tables of network addresses that also include the best possible routes (regarding tick count and hop count) to these networks. *See* Tick count and Hop count.

- **Segmentation** — To split a large Ethernet into smaller segments that are connected to each other by bridges or routers. This is done to prevent congestion as the number of nodes increases.

- **Session layer** — The OSI layer that makes and manages a connection between two nodes of the network.

- **Signal-regenerating repeater** — A repeater that "reads" the signal on the network and then creates an exact duplicate of the signal, thus amplifying the signal without also amplifying unwanted noise that is mixed with the signal.

- **SLIP (Serial Line Internet Protocol)** — An early version of line protocol designed for home users connecting to the Internet. SLIP lacks reliable error checking and has mostly been replaced by PPP.

- **SMTP (Simple Mail Transfer Protocol)** — A common protocol used to send e-mail across a network.

- **Socket** — A virtual connection from one computer to another such as that between a client and a server. Higher-level protocols such as HTTP use a socket to pass data between two computers. A socket is assigned a number for the current session, which is used by the high-level protocol.

- **Star network architecture** — A network design in which nodes are connected at a centralized location.

- **Static IP addresses** — IP addresses permanently assigned to a workstation. In Windows 95, this can be done under Dial-Up Networking, Server Type, TCP/IP settings. Specify an IP address.

- **Static routing** — When routing tables do not automatically change and must be manually edited. Windows NT and Windows 95 support only static routing.

- **Subnet mask** — Defines which portion of an IP address identifies the network, and which portion identifies the host. A 1 in the mask indicates that the bit is part of the network address, and a 0 indicates that the bit is part of the host address. For example, the subnet mask 255.255.192.0, in binary, is 11111111.11111111.11000000.00000000.

16

Therefore, the network address is the first two octets and the first two bits of the third octet. The rest of the IP address refers to the host.

- **Subnetworks** or **subnets** — Divisions of a large network, consisting of smaller separate networks (to prevent congestion). Each subnetwork is assigned a logical network IP name.

- **TCP/IP (Transmission Control Protocol/Internet Protocol)** — The suite of protocols developed to support the Internet. TCP is responsible for error checking, and IP is responsible for routing.

- **Tick count** — The time required for a packet to reach its destination. One tick equals 1/18 of a second.

- **Token** — A small frame on a Token Ring network that constantly travels around the ring in only one direction. When a station seizes the token, it controls the channel until its message is sent.

- **Token ring** — A network that is logically a ring, but stations are connected to a centralized multistation access unit (MAU) in a star formation. Network communication is controlled by a token.

- **Trailer** — The part of a packet that follows the data and contains information used by some protocols for error checking.

- **Transceiver** — The bidirectional (transmitter and receiver) component on a NIC that is responsible for signal conversion and monitors for data collision.

- **Transport layer** — The OSI layer that verifies data and requests a resend when the data is corrupted.

- **URL (universal resource locator)** — A unique address that identifies the domain name, path, or filename of a World Wide Web site. Microsoft's URL address is: http://www.microsoft.com/

- **User Datagram Protocol (UDP)** — A connectionless protocol that does not require a connection to send a packet and does not guarantee that the packet arrives at its destination.

- **Windows Internet Naming Service (WINS)** — A Microsoft resolution service with a distributed database that tracks relationships between domain names and IP addresses. Compare to DNS.

REVIEW QUESTIONS

1. Describe the composition of a packet, or frame.
2. List and define two different types of networks.
3. What is the most popular network topology used today?
4. What happens if an Ethernet network detects a transmission collision?

5. List and describe three types of cables that can be used on an Ethernet network.

6. What is the function of a router in a network environment? How is a router different from a bridge?

7. Describe how data is communicated over a Token Ring network to avoid conflicts.

8. Describe the operations and design of a bus network.

9. List and briefly describe the seven network layers.

10. List and fully describe two common network protocols.

11. Use Windows Help, and describe how to set up TCP/IP in Windows.

12. Describe a client/server network.

13. Use Windows Help, and describe how to use FTP to obtain a missing driver from the Microsoft Web site.

14. List three of the largest ISPs.

15. Give an example of a Class C Internet address.

16. Who assigns Internet addresses?

17. What are the advantages of dynamically assigned IP addresses?

18. List the five main domain name extensions used in the United States.

19. What is the domain name extension for Harvard University? For Microsoft Corporation? For the White House?

20. Who assigns domain names?

21. What part of an IP address contains the subnet?

22. What is the subnet mask for Class C IP addresses on a network where 1 bit of the host address is used for the subnet address? How many subnets are possible using this arrangement?

23. Why would an organization use a WAN? What type of organization would use a WAN?

24. What utility is commonly used to "transfer" files on the Internet?

25. What is the purpose of Telnet?

16

PROJECTS

PRACTICE DIAL-UP NETWORKING SKILLS WITH WINDOWS 95

1. Open My Computer and open the Dial-Up Networking folder.

2. Double-click **Make New Connection** option.

3. Enter the name **TEST** for the name of the computer that you are dialing.

4. Enter your home phone number.

5. Click the **Finish** button to create the Test dial-up.

6. Double-click on the newly created Test dial-up icon, and confirm that it dials out correctly. Describe what happens.

USE THE PPPLOG.TXT FILE FOR TROUBLESHOOTING

Set Windows 95 so that the PPPLog.txt file is used to record events. Reboot the PC and make a good connection to the Internet, using a modem. Print the log file. This printout of a good connection can later be used to compare to a log file of a bad connection to help identify problems.

Now cause an error to occur in the dial-up connection to the Internet by setting a wrong configuration for TCP/IP (make a note of the correct configuration before you change it!). Attempt the connection. Print the log file for the bad connection and compare the two files. At what point during the connection did it fail? Restore the TCP/IP configuration to the correct value and verify that all is well.

PRACTICE TCP/IP NETWORKING SKILLS

While using TCP/IP on a network with or without Dial-Up Networking (such as while connected to the Internet), answer these questions:

1. What is your current IP address?

2. Disconnect and reconnect. Now what is your IP address?

3. Are you using dynamic or static IP addressing? How do you know?

4. What is your adapter address?

5. What is your default gateway IP address?

6. What response do you get when you PING the default gateway?

USING WINDOWS 95 HELP

Click on the **Start** button and select **Help**. Search for "Internet," and write down a step-by-step set of directions that can be used to connect to the Internet using Dial-Up Networking.

DIRECT CABLE CONNECTION

Using either a null modem cable or a parallel cable, connect two computers using Direct Cable Connection under Windows 95. After the connection is made, use Explorer on the guest computer to copy a file from the host computer. Next, reverse roles, making the host the guest computer, and the guest the host computer. Copy a file from the host to the guest computer.

DIAL-UP NETWORKING

Work with a partner on this project. You each need a PC with Windows 95 or Windows NT, a modem, and a phone line. For two computers with Windows 95, one of the PCs must have Microsoft Plus! in order to be set up to receive incoming calls. Follow the directions in the chapter to connect the two computers using Dial-Up Networking over phone lines. After the connection is made, use Explorer to share files between the two computers.

USING A NULL MODEM CABLE WITH WINDOWS NT

A null modem cable can be used by Windows NT to communicate to another PC over a serial port. Install a null modem cable as though it were a modem. In the list of supported modems, select **Standard Modem Types** as the manufacturer, and select **Dial-Up Networking Serial Cable between 2 PCs** as the modem model.

Using two Windows NT PCs and a null modem cable, install and run Dial-Up Networking to establish communication between the PCs. Map a network drive from one PC to the other.

16

BUILDING A PEER-TO-PEER NETWORK

Follow these directions to build a peer-to-peer network using network cards and a Microsoft network:

1. Obtain the following materials:
   - Two computers with Windows 95
   - Network cards for each computer
   - Cabling and connectors for the network cards

2. Install the NICs. Check the configuration in Windows 95 against the card documentation.

3. Select the client software to be **Client for Microsoft Networks**.

4. Add the service **File and Print Sharing**. Verify that File and Print Sharing is running from the Network window.

5. Share a folder or folders on the hard drive. If you have a printer connected, share the printer.

6. Reboot both PCs and verify that you are connected, by browsing the Network Neighborhood of each PC.

BACKUP NETWORK FILES

Look on a PC that is connected to a Novell NetWare LAN. What entries in the AUTOEXEC.BAT file can you identify as commands used to load network software? What directory contains the NetWare software? Print the contents of NET.CFG in this directory. What is the drive letter of the network drive used to log on to the LAN?

CHAPTER SEVENTEEN

VIRUSES, DISASTER RECOVERY, AND A MAINTENANCE PLAN THAT WORKS

When you are responsible for a computer, regular maintenance can help prevent disaster, lower repair costs, and make problems that do occur less disruptive. Two important aspects of preventive maintenance are making regular backups of hard drives and dealing with viruses. These two issues, as well as routine hardware maintenance and how to design a disaster recovery plan, are addressed in detail in this chapter.

IN THIS CHAPTER YOU WILL LEARN:

- ABOUT PREVENTIVE MAINTENANCE AND PROCEDURES DESIGNED TO PROTECT SYSTEMS

- HOW TO DEVELOP A PREVENTIVE MAINTENANCE PLAN

- HOW SYSTEMS BECOME INFECTED WITH VIRUSES AND OTHER INFESTATIONS

- HOW VIRUSES WORK, HOW TO PROTECT SYSTEMS AGAINST THEM, AND HOW TO DEAL WITH THEM ONCE THEY DO INFECT YOUR SYSTEM

- ABOUT THE STRENGTHS AND WEAKNESSES OF DIFFERENT BACKUP PROCEDURES AND SYSTEMS AND HOW TO USE DIFFERENT BACKUP SOFTWARE

- HOW TO DEVELOP A DISASTER RECOVERY PLAN

PREVENTIVE MAINTENANCE

If you are responsible for the PCs of an organization, you will want to make and implement a preventive maintenance plan to help prevent failures and reduce repair costs and downtime. In addition, you will need a disaster recovery plan to manage the situation when failures do occur. PC failures are caused by many different environmental and human factors, including heat, dust, magnetism, power supply problems, static electricity, human error (such as spilled liquids or an accidental change of setup and software configurations), and viruses. The goals of preventive maintenance are to reduce the likelihood that the events that cause PC failures will occur and to lessen the damage if and when they do occur. When designing a preventive maintenance plan, consider what you can do to help prevent each cause, and write into the plan the actions you can take. Also, think through the situation caused by each problem. What would happen to the PC, the software, the data, the user's productivity, and so on, if and when a failure occurs? What would you do in that situation? What can you do ahead of time to help make the situation less disastrous?

For example, consider the problem caused by a user accidentally changing CMOS setup. What can you do to prevent that from occurring? If it does occur, what can you do? What can you do now to prepare for that event? By answering these three questions, you might arrive at these preventive maintenance and recovery procedures: (1) Make a backup copy of setup to floppy disk. (2) Label the disk and keep it in a safe place. (3) Educate the user about the importance of not changing setup. (4) Keep a maintenance record of this PC, including the last time setup was backed up.

A PREVENTIVE MAINTENANCE PLAN

Your company may have established guidelines for PC preventive maintenance. If so, you will want to read the plan and put in place the necessary procedures to make it work. If your company does not have an established plan, make your own. Table 17-1 lists some guidelines for developing a preventive maintenance plan that may work for you.

The general idea of preventive maintenance is to do what you can to make a PC last longer and give as little trouble as possible, but you may also be responsible for ensuring that data is secure and backed up, that software copyrights are not violated, and that users are supported. When designing your preventive maintenance plan, as with all planning, first know your overall goal or goals, and design the plan accordingly. The guidelines listed in Table 17-1 address primarily the problems that prevent a PC from lasting and from performing well.

Table 17-1   Guidelines for developing a PC preventive maintenance plan

Component	Maintenance	How Often
Inside the case	■ Make sure air vents are clear. ■ Use compressed air to blow the dust out of the case. ■ Ensure that chips and expansion cards are firmly seated. ■ Clean the contacts on expansion cards.	Yearly
CMOS setup	■ Keep a backup record of setup (for example, use Nuts & Bolts rescue disk).	Whenever changes are made
Floppy drive	■ Only clean the floppy drive head when the drive does not work.	When the drive fails
Hard drive	■ Perform regular backups. ■ Automatically execute a virus scan program at startup. ■ Defragment the drive and recover lost clusters regularly. ■ Don't allow smoking around the PC. ■ Place the PC where it will not get kicked or bumped.	At least weekly At least daily Monthly
Keyboard	■ Keep the keyboard clean. ■ Keep the keyboard away from liquids.	Monthly Always
Mouse	■ Clean the mouse rollers and ball (see Chapter 7).	Monthly
Monitor	■ Clean the screen with a soft cloth.	At least monthly
Printers	■ Clean out the dust and bits of paper. ■ Clean the paper and ribbon paths with a soft cloth. ■ Don't re-ink ribbons or use recharged toner cartridges.	At least monthly
Software	■ If so directed by your employer check that only authorized software is present. ■ Regularly remove files from the recycle bin and \Temp directories. ■ Remove any temporary files in the /DOS directory.	At least monthly
Written record	■ Record all software, including version numbers and the OS installed on the PC. ■ Record all hardware components installed, including hardware settings. ■ Record when and what preventive maintenance is performed. ■ Record any repairs done to the PC.	Whenever changes are made

17

Documentation and recordkeeping are often overlooked when discussing preventive maintenance. A record of what is done to a PC is valuable when problems arise or when upgrading is under consideration. Secure all hardware documentation. Users who are not responsible for hardware may not realize the significance of a user manual for a hardware device, such as a sound card or modem, and may not be careful to protect these documents over time. You may want to file these documents together in an envelope with a log of everything you have done to the PC for regular maintenance, installations, and repairs, and a boot disk that contains a copy of CMOS setup for this PC. Consider taping the envelope to the inside of the computer case. This works especially well when you are responsible for PCs at off-site locations where you may not have assigned filing cabinet space. This information might also be kept in a notebook along with other similar notebooks at your work station. Label each notebook to identify the PC that it tracks.

In addition to the list in Table 17-1, there are some routine things you can encourage users to do on a regular basis as part of your preventive maintenance plan. To conserve hard drive space, regularly delete the files in the \TEMP directory. After installing Windows 3.x or Windows 95, remove temporary files from the \DOS directory or reinstall DOS. For Windows 95 and Windows NT, regularly empty the Recycle Bin. Routinely back up the hard drive, or you may choose to back up only directories that contain data. More information about hard drive backups appears later in the chapter. Also, when you initially set up a PC, if you are using an older version of DOS, check the SET TEMP command in the Autoexec.bat file. If it reads SET TEMP=C:\DOS, change it to read SET TEMP=C:\TEMP and create a \TEMP directory. Storing temporary files in the \DOS directory can create problems.

WHEN MOVING EQUIPMENT

When shipping a PC there is always a potential for damage caused by rough handling, exposure to water, heat, and cold, and misplaced, lost, or stolen packages. Don't ship a PC that has the only copy of valuable data on it or data that should be secured from unauthorized use. When you are preparing a PC for shipping, take extra precautions to protect the PC. Here are some general guidelines:

- Back up the hard drive onto a tape cartridge. If you don't have access to a tape cartridge, back up important system and configuration files to a floppy disk. Don't ship a PC that has the only copy of important data on the hard drive.

- Remove any floppy disks, tape cartridges, or CDs from the drives. Make sure that the tapes or disks holding the backup data are secured and protected during transit.

- Turn off the PC and all other devices.

- Disconnect the power cords from the electrical outlet and from the devices. Disconnect all external devices from the computer.

- If you think there might be a problem with later identifying which cord or cable belongs to which device or connection, label the cable connections with white tape or white labels.

- Coil up all cords and secure them with plastic ties or rubber bands.

- Pack the computer, monitor, and all devices in their original shipping cartons or similar boxes with enough packing material to protect them.

VIRUSES AND OTHER COMPUTER INFESTATIONS

A computer support person needs to know how to protect computers against computer infestations (including viruses), how to recognize them, and how to get rid of them. Understanding what infestations are, how they work, and where they hide helps technicians to deal with them successfully. A computer **infestation** is any unwanted program that is unknowingly transmitted to a computer and is designed to do varying degrees of damage to data and software. Computer infestations do not do damage to PC hardware, although, when boot sector information is destroyed on a hard drive, it can appear as though the hard drive is physically damaged. What most people refer to as viruses really fall into three categories of computer infestations: viruses, Trojan horses, and worms. As you study each type of infestation in this section, in order to distinguish among them, look for how they spread, what damage they do, and how they hide.

Because viruses are by far the most common of the three kinds of computer infestations, one of the most important defenses against computer infestations is **antivirus** (**AV**) software. This section looks at several AV programs and how to use them effectively.

UNDERSTANDING COMPUTER INFESTATIONS

There are three types of computer infestations, which are categorized by the way they transmit themselves: viruses, worms, and Trojan horses. A virus is a program that can replicate itself by attaching itself to other programs. The infected program must be executed in order for a virus to execute. When a virus executes, it may simply replicate itself, or it may also do damage by immediately performing some negative action. Also, a virus may be triggered to perform a negative action at some future point in time, such as on a particular date (for instance, Friday the 13th), or at the time some logic within the host program is activated. A virus is different from a **worm**, which is a program that spreads copies of itself throughout a network without needing a host program. A **Trojan horse** is a third type of computer infestation that, like a worm, does not need a host program to work, but is substituted for a legitimate program and cannot replicate itself. (There are exceptions to this last statement. A Trojan horse program, disguised as an automatic backup utility from the Internet, was used to create backups and replicated itself to the backups, damaging several systems on the subsequent Friday the 13th. In this case, the Trojan horse program would also be considered a virus because of its ability to replicate.) Also, sometimes problems on a PC caused by an error or bug in software can look and act very much like a virus, even when no virus is involved.

17

The most common of the three kinds of infestations are viruses. A worm is seldom seen except on a network where it becomes a problem because of overloading the network as it replicates itself. The worm does damage by its presence rather than by performing a negative action as a virus does. The worm overloads memory or hard drive space by replicating itself over and over again. Trojan horse infestations cannot replicate themselves and require human intervention to move from one location to another, and therefore they are not as common as viruses.

Where Viruses Hide

A program is called a virus because (1) it has an incubation period (does not do damage immediately); (2) it is contagious (can replicate itself); and (3) it is destructive. In order to avoid detection by antivirus software, a virus sometimes hides itself. There are four ways that a virus can hide itself. Sometimes a virus can use more than one method at the same time.

Boot Sector Virus.   A boot sector virus can hide in the program code that is part of the Master Boot Record on a hard drive or part of the boot record program that loads the OS on the active partition of the hard drive. On a floppy disk, a boot sector virus hides in the boot program of the boot sector. One of the most common ways a virus is spread is on a floppy disk that is used to boot a PC. During the boot, when the boot program is loaded into memory, so is the virus, which can then spread to other programs.

However, a floppy disk does not have to be bootable to spread a virus. All floppy disks have a Master Boot Record. If a PC is configured to first boot from drive A before drive C, then, if a floppy disk is in the drive when the PC is booted, BIOS reads the Master Boot Record on the disk. If the disk is not bootable, an error message displays, such as "Nonsystem disk or disk error." If the disk is then removed and the user presses any key, the PC will then boot from the hard drive. However, if the Master Boot Record of the floppy disk contains a boot sector virus, the virus might already have been loaded into memory. When the system boots from the hard drive, the virus is then spread to the boot sector of the hard drive.

To prevent this kind of infection, don't press a key to cause the PC to move on to the hard drive after it has already attempted to boot from the floppy disk. Also, pressing CTRL-ALT-DEL may not be enough to prevent the problem, as the loaded virus can still hide in memory. Use a cold boot, turning the PC off, removing the floppy disk, and turning the PC back on. This kind of virus infection is a good reason to configure your computer to always boot from the hard drive first, and then, if the hard drive is not bootable, to boot from the floppy drive. This boot order will normally prevent BIOS from reading a Master Boot Record of a floppy disk that is inserted during boot. The order of booting from the A and C drives is determined in CMOS setup.

Incidentally, many CMOS setups have an option that prevents writing to the boot sector of the hard drive. This does not always work against viruses, but must be turned off before trying to install Windows 95 or Windows NT, which both must write to the MBR during installation. Windows 95 does not tell you that you must turn the feature off and start the installation over until about half way through the installation.

File Viruses.   A **file virus** hides in an executable (.exe or .com) program or word processing document that contains a macro. A **macro** is a small program that is contained within a document and can be automatically executed when the document is first loaded, or can be executed later by pressing a predetermined keystroke. An example of a macro is a word-processing feature that automatically reads the system date and copies it into a document each time the document is loaded. Viruses that hide in macros of document files are called **macro viruses**.

One variation of a file virus is a virus that searches a hard drive for files with .exe file extensions and then creates another file with the same filename, but using the .com file extension. When the OS executes a program, it first looks for the program name with the .com file extension. It then finds the virus, which it executes. The virus is loaded into memory and then loads the program with the .exe extension. The virus is then free to do damage or spread itself to other programs.

A virus cannot work if it is contained in a data file with no embedded macros. Sometimes a virus will copy itself to a data file by mistake. Once the virus is there, it can no longer do any damage, since the data is not a program and, therefore, cannot be executed from memory. The only possible damage from the virus in a data file is the corrupted data caused by the virus overwriting what was already in the file.

Multipartite Viruses.   A **multipartite virus** is a combination of a boot sector virus and a file virus. It can hide in either type of program.

Cloaking Techniques

One thing a virus attempts to do is hide from antivirus (AV) software. AV software detects a virus because it has previously been programmed to search out and recognize a particular virus. AV software detects a virus that it knows exists by looking for distinguishing characteristics of the virus called the **virus signature**, which is why it is so important to keep your AV software updated.

 Antivirus software cannot detect a virus it does not know to look for. Therefore, continue to upgrade your AV software as new viruses are discovered.

There are two methods by which a virus attempts to hide from AV software: by changing its distinguishing characteristics (its signature) and by attempting to mask the fact that it is present.

Polymorphic Viruses.   A polymorphic virus changes its distinguishing characteristics as it replicates itself. Mutating in this way makes it more difficult for AV software to recognize the presence of the virus.

Encrypting Viruses.   One key symptom that AV software looks for is the ability of a program to replicate itself. A virus that is an encrypting virus can transform itself into a

17

nonreplicating program in order to avoid detection. However, it must transform itself back into a replicating program in order to spread or replicate itself. It can then be detected by AV software.

Stealth Viruses.   A stealth virus actively conceals itself, using one or more of the following techniques:

- Because AV software may detect a virus by noting the difference between a program's file size before the virus has infected it and after the virus is present, the virus alters OS information so as to mask the size of the file it is hiding in.

- The virus monitors when files are opened or closed. When it sees that the file it is hiding in is about to be opened, it temporarily removes itself from the file or substitutes a copy of the file that does not have the virus included. The virus keeps a copy of this uninfected file on the hard drive just for this purpose.

The Damage an Infestation Can Cause

Viruses, worms, and Trojan horses have not been known to physically damage a hard drive or other hardware device. The damage they do ranges from the very minor, such as displaying bugs crawling around on a screen, to major damage such as totally erasing everything written on a hard drive. The damage done by an infestation is called the payload and can be accomplished in a variety of ways. A virus may be programmed to drop its payload only in response to a triggering event such as a date, opening a certain file, or pressing a certain key. Figures 17–1 and 17–2 show the results of two harmless viruses that simply display garbage on the screen.

Figure 17-1   The harmless or benign Walker virus displays a man walking across the screen

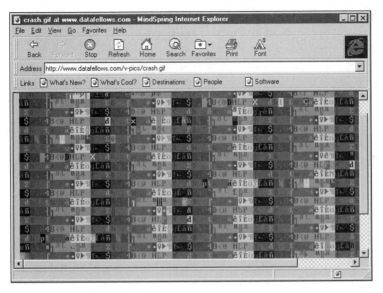

Figure 17-2   The crash virus appears to be destructive, making the screen show only garbage, but does no damage to the hard drive data

How Infestations Spread

Understanding how infestations spread is essential to understanding how to protect your computer against them. Some computers are more at risk than others, largely depending on the habits of the user. Below is a list of user activities that make a computer susceptible to infestations.

- Trading floppy disks containing program files
- Connecting the computer to an unprotected network
- Buying software from unreliable sources
- Downloading programs from the Internet
- Using floppy disks from unknown sources
- Using shared network programs
- Using used, preformatted floppy disks
- Using e-mail that automatically executes a word processor to read attached files
- Not write-protecting original program disks

How a Virus Replicates.   Once a program containing a virus is copied to your PC, the virus can spread itself only when the infected program is executed. The process is shown in Figure 17-3. Recall from earlier chapters that the first step in executing a program, whether it is stored in a program file or in a boot sector, is to load the program into memory. Viruses that are hidden in a program can then be executed from memory. A virus can either be a

memory-resident virus and stay in memory, still working, even after the host program is terminated, or a virus can be a **non-memory-resident virus**, which means that it is terminated when the host program is closed.

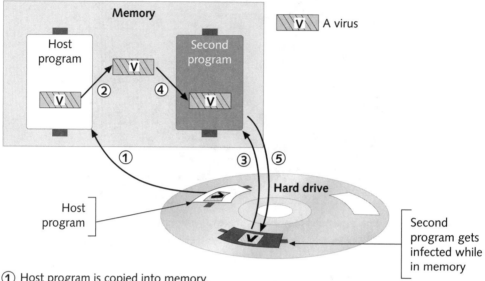

① Host program is copied into memory.

② The virus may or may not move itself to a new location in memory.

③ A second program is opened and copied into memory.

④ The virus copies itself to the second program in memory.

⑤ The newly infected second program is written back to the hard drive.

Figure 17-3 How a virus replicates

After a virus is loaded into memory, it looks for other programs that are loaded into memory. When it finds one, it copies itself into the other program in memory and then into that same program file on disk. From Figure 17-3, you can see that a virus becomes more dangerous the longer it stays loaded into memory and the more programs that are opened while it is there. For this reason, if you use a computer that has been used by other people such as in a computer lab, always reboot the computer before you begin work. Use a hard boot, not just a soft boot, to insure that all memory-resident programs (including a memory resident virus) are erased from memory.

How a Trojan Horse Gets into Your Computer. A Trojan horse is an infestation that masquerades as a legitimate program. One interesting example of a Trojan horse is the AOL4FREE program. This program originally was an illegal program that could provide unauthorized access to America Online. After the program's usefulness was blocked by AOL, a new program emerged, also calling itself AOL4FREE, which was not an online access program at all, but a destructive Trojan horse. People passed the program around, thinking that it would provide illegal access to AOL, however, if executed, it actually erased files on their hard drives.

Virus Hoaxes.   A **virus hoax** is a letter or e-mail warning about a nonexistent virus. The warning is itself a pest because it overloads network traffic. Here's an example of an e-mail message I received that is a virus hoax:

> There is a new virus going around in the last couple of days!!. DO NOT open or even look at any mail that you get that says: "Returned or Unable to Deliver." The virus will erase your whole hard drive and attach itself to your computer components and render them useless. Immediately delete any mail items that say this. AOL has indicated this is a very dangerous virus, and there is NO remedy for it at this time. Please be careful and forward to all your online friends ASAP. This is a new email virus and not a lot of people know about it; just let everyone know, so they won't be a victim. Please forward this email to your friends!!!

First of all, don't believe the part about a virus rendering computer components useless. No virus has been known to actually do physical damage to hardware, although viruses can cause a PC to be useless by destroying programs or data. Second, don't believe the part that says the virus will be activated just because you open an e-mail message. An e-mail message is text, not a program, and a virus can't hide there. (It can, however, hide in word-processing documents containing macros that are attached to an e-mail message.) And third, don't be gullible and take the bait by forwarding the message to someone else. The potential damage a hoax like this can do is to overload an e-mail system with useless traffic, which is the real intent of the hoax. When I received this e-mail, there were over a hundred names on the distribution list.

PROTECTING AGAINST COMPUTER INFESTATIONS

There is much you can do to protect your computer against viruses and other infestations. Your first line of defense is to regularly make backups and use virus scan software. After that, use wisdom when managing programs. Here are some general guidelines:

- Buy antivirus software and set your computer to automatically run the AV program at startup.

- Keep the AV software current by periodically downloading upgrades from the Internet.

- Set a virus scan program to automatically scan word-processor documents as they are opened.

- Establish and faithfully execute a plan to make scheduled backups of your hard drive to protect against damage that can be done by a virus or a Trojan horse.

- Only buy software from reputable vendors, to avoid a Trojan horse or a virus.

- Don't trade program files on floppy disks.

- Don't use floppy disks from unknown sources.

- Download software from the Internet sparingly, and then scan program files for viruses before executing them.

17

- Never use pirated software.

- Avoid using shared network programs such as Java or ActiveX programs on the Internet.

- Format floppy disks before first use.

- Write-protect original program disks.

- In a business environment, adopt strict company policies against using unauthorized software.

- If you find a computer already on, which others have used before you, reboot the computer before you use it.

- Set your computer CMOS settings to boot from drive C, then drive A.

- Turn on antivirus protection for your MBR in the CMOS settings, if available.

Virus Symptoms

Know what to expect when a virus is replicating itself or dropping its payload. Here are some warnings that might suggest that a virus is at work:

- A program takes longer than normal to load.

- The number and length of disk accesses seem excessive for simple tasks.

- Unusual error messages occur regularly.

- Less memory than usual is available.

- Files mysteriously disappear or appear.

- Strange graphics display on your computer monitor, or the computer makes strange noises.

- There is a noticeable reduction in disk space.

- The system is unable to recognize the hard drive when you have booted from a floppy disk.

- The system is unable to recognize the CD-ROM drive, although it has worked earlier.

- Executable files have changed size.

- The access lights on the hard drive and floppy drive turn on when there should not be any activity on that device. (However, sometimes an OS will perform routine maintenance on the drive when the system has been inactive for a while.)

- Files constantly get corrupted.

- Strange or bizarre error messages display.

- DOS error messages display about the FAT or partition table.
- The hard drive boots but hangs up before getting a DOS prompt or Windows 95 safe boot.
- File extensions or file attributes change without reason.
- A message displays from the virus scanner software.
- The number of bad sectors on the hard drive continues to increase.
- The DOS MEM command reveals strange TSRs loaded into memory.

What to Do When You Suspect a Virus

If you suspect that a virus is present, run a virus scan program to detect and delete the virus. If the antivirus software is not already installed, you can still use it. Consult the documentation for the software. In many cases, the installation process will detect the virus and eliminate it before continuing the installation. However, know that a virus may still be present even if AV software does not detect it. This can occur because the virus was not one that the AV software knew to look for, or because it successfully hid from the AV program. If the AV software found nothing, but you still suspect a virus, get the latest upgrade of your AV software and try it, or try another AV program.

Protecting Against Viruses

Antivirus software cannot prevent a Trojan horse program from being copied to your computer, tell you that an e-mail message is a hoax, or force you to use wisdom in handling software. However, aside from preventing a virus from entering your system, antivirus software is your best line of defense against a virus. Some of the better-known antivirus software is listed in Table 17-2.

Table 17-2　Antivirus software

Antivirus Software	Web Site
Norton AntiVirus by Symantec Corporation	www.symantec.com
Dr. Solomon's Software	www.drsolomon.com
McAfee Virus Scan by McAfee Associates, Inc.	www.mcafee.com
EliaShim's ViruSafe	www.eliashim.com
PC-cillin II by Touchstone Software	www.checkit.com
Cheyenne AntiVirus Scanner (a version is included on the CD-ROM with this book)	www.cheyenne.com
F-PROT Antivirus by Command Software Systems	www.commandcom.com

17

When selecting antivirus software, look for these features:

- Ability to download new software upgrades from the Internet so that, as new viruses occur, your software knows about them

- Ability to automatically execute at startup

- Ability to detect macros in word-processing documents as the document is loaded by the word processor

- Ability to automatically monitor files being downloaded from the Internet

Using Antivirus Software

Antivirus software can work at different times to scan your hard drive or a floppy disk for viruses. Most AV software can be configured to run each time your PC is booted to scan the entire hard drive for viruses. In addition, look for features that include the ability to scan files as they are downloaded from the Internet or a network, and the ability to scan documents for macro viruses each time a document is opened by a word processor. The AV software should scan both files and boot sectors of hard drives and disks. A version of Cheyenne AntiVirus software is included with Nuts & Bolts on the CD-ROM accompanying this book. Using this software, follow these directions to scan a floppy disk for viruses:

1. For Windows 95, click **Start**, **Programs**, **Nuts & Bolts**, **Cheyenne AntiVirus Scanner**.

2. In the Scanning box, enter the drive, drive and path, or the drive, path, and file-name that you want the software to scan. To scan a floppy disk, insert the disk in the drive and enter **A:**.

3. Click **Advanced** to see what options are available. Figure 17-4 displays. Under the Options tab, check that both the boot sector and files are selected as objects to scan.

4. Click on the **File Types** tab. Figure 17-5 displays. Verify that **All Files** is selected. (The one other choice is Executable Files Only.) Verify that compressed files will also be scanned. Click **OK** to return to the opening screen.

5. Execute the scan by clicking **Start**. Any viruses that are detected will be listed in the box at the bottom of the screen.

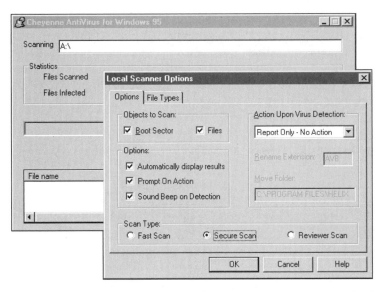

Figure 17-4   Set the Cheyenne AntiVirus software to scan both boot sectors and files

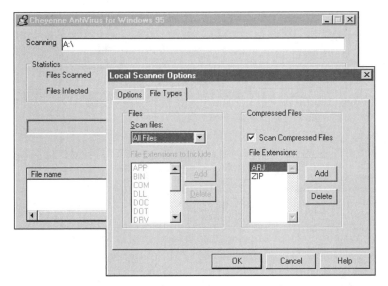

Figure 17-5   Set the Cheyenne AntiVirus software to scan all files, including compressed files

ALL ABOUT BACKUPS AND FAULT TOLERANCE

There's nothing like a rousing discussion of computer viruses to make a PC support person appreciate hard drive backups and other methods of protecting data. With data and software, a good rule of thumb is: if you can't get along without it, back it up. This section covers the hardware and software needed to make backups of data and software from a hard drive. Windows 95 and Windows NT both offer backup tools, which are also covered in this section. Another feature of preventive maintenance is to make hard drives more fault tolerant. Several methods to do this are collectively called **RAID**. The term first stood for **redundant array of inexpensive disks**, but has recently been updated to mean **redundant array of independent disks**. The different methods of RAID are also discussed in this section.

BACKUP HARDWARE

The most popular hardware device used to make backups of a hard drive on a standalone personal computer is a tape drive. Tape drives have drive capacities anywhere from several hundred kilobytes to several gigabytes and come in several types and formats. Although tape drives don't require that you use special backup software to manage them, most likely you will want to invest in specialized backup software to make backups as efficient and effortless as possible. This section covers both tape drives and the software that manages them. Other devices that can be used to back up a hard drive are removable drives, including Zip and Jaz drives, and read-write CDs. However, tape drives still remain the most popular method primarily because of their lower cost.

In a business environment, if a PC is connected to a file server, it is generally more practical to back up data from the hard drive to the file server and not back up the software. If the software becomes corrupted, it can quickly be reinstalled from the installation files kept on the file server. Data on both the PC and the file server may become corrupted. However, the file server will most likely have its own automated backup utility in place, that backs up to either tape or a larger mainframe computer.

Tape Drives

Tape drives (Figure 17-6) are an inexpensive way of backing up an entire hard drive or portions of it. The advantages of using tape drives for this procedure are that they are more convenient than floppy disks or other types of removable disks and that they are relatively inexpensive. The one biggest disadvantage of using tape drives is that data is stored on tape by **sequential access**, meaning that, in order to read data from anywhere on the tape, you must start at the beginning of the tape and read until you come to the sought-after data. This sequential access makes it slow and inconvenient to use tapes for general-purpose storage of data (other than backups) and to recover individual files from full tapes. Even though tape drives still remain the most popular medium for systematic backups, new media such as read-writable CDs or Jaz drives are becoming acceptable for PC backups because they can be used for other purposes as well, and because of recent price reductions.

Figure 17-6   A tape drive system

There is a variety of standards and types of tape drives and tapes. Several of the more common are described below.

How a Tape Drive Interfaces with a Computer.   A tape drive can be an external device or an internal device. The external device costs more but provides the advantage that it can be used by more than one computer. A tape drive can interface with a computer in these ways:

- An external tape drive can use the parallel port (see Figure 17-7) with an optional pass-through to the printer (so that the drive and the printer can use the same parallel port).

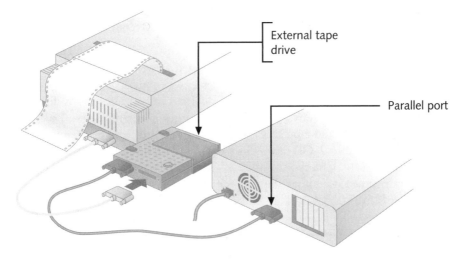

External tape drive

Parallel port

17

Figure 17-7   An external tape drive can use the parallel port for input/output, with an optional pass-through to the printer

- An external or internal drive can use the SCSI bus. This method works well if the tape drive and the hard drive are on the same SCSI bus, which contains the data pass-through just to the SCSI system.

- An external or internal drive can use its own proprietary controller card.

- An external or internal drive can use the floppy drive controller.

The Tapes Used by a Tape Drive.   Tape drives accommodate one of two kinds of tapes: Full-sized **data cartridges** are 4 × 6 × ⅜ inches in size, and the smaller **minicartridges**, like the one in Figure 17-8, are 3¼ × 2½ × ⅜ inches. Minicartridges are the more popular of the two because their drives can fit into a standard 5½-inch drive bay of a PC case.

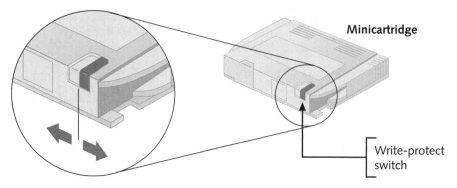

Minicartridge

Write-protect switch

Figure 17-8   Minicartridge for a tape drive has a write-protect switch

The technology used by tape drives to write to tapes is similar to that used by floppy drives (see Chapter 4). There is a FAT at the beginning of the tape tracking the location of data and bad sectors on the tape. The tape must be formatted before data can be written to it. Many tapes come preformatted from the factory. Buy these tapes to save the time needed to format the tape.

Standards for writing data to tapes have not developed as well as consumers would like, making it necessary to carefully match tapes to tape drives when purchasing and using them. Several standards exist, which have been promoted by different organizations as well as by individual manufacturers. Figure 17-9 shows two tables, each from a different tape drive manufacturer, showing the tape formats and tape types that are supported by one of their tape drives. Figure 17-9a shows that the Ditto 2-GB drive can write using only the Ditto 2-GB method, but can read tapes using a variety of methods. Figure 17-9b shows that the Eagle(TM) TR-3 tape minicartridge tape drive can use either the QIC-3010 or QIC-3020 format and five tape types. Note that these drives are also likely to be able to read other formats that are compatible with these formats.

Capacity	Tape format	Tape Type	Read	Write
2GB	Ditto 2GB	Ditto 2GB	YES	YES
2GB	QIC-3020 Travan	TR-3	YES	NO
2GB	QIC-3020 Wide	3020XLF	YES	NO
2GB	QIC-3020	3020XL	YES	NO
2GB	QIC-80 Travan	TR-1	YES	NO
2GB	QIC-80 Wide	5122	YES	NO
2GB	QIC-80XL	2120XL	YES	NO
2GB	QIC-80	2080 or 2120	YES	NO
2GB	Irwin 40 and 80	2000	YES	NO

a) Tape compatibility for the Ditto 2GB tape drive

Tape format	Tape types				
	Travan TR-3	QIC Wide	MC 3000XL	TR-3 EXtra	MC 3020 EXtra
QIC-3020*	3.2 GB	1.7 GB	1.4 GB	4.4 GB	3.2 GB
QIC-3020	1.6 GB	850 GB	680 MB	2.2 GB	1.6 GB
QIC-3010*	1.6 GB	840 MB	680 MB	2.2 GB	1.6 GB
QIC-3010	800 MB	420 MB	340 MB	1.1 GB	800 MB

*Using software compression with an assumed 2:1 compression ratio.

b) Minicartridge capacities obtained by the Eagle TR-3 tape drive using five different tape types

Figure 17-9   Tables from two tape drive manufacturers indicate the multitude of formats used when reading and writing to tapes

Tape Formats and Tape Types.   One of the first efforts to standardize the way data is written to tape was established around 1983 by a group of manufacturers who formed Quarter-Inch Cartridge Drive Standards, Inc., sometimes called the **Quarter-Inch Committee** or quarter-inch cartridge (**QIC**). There have been many QIC standards developed, but only a few are in use today. 3M developed a standard, called Travan, based on the QIC format. Travan is a standard that has been backed by many of the industry leaders in tape drive manufacturing. There are different levels of Travan standards, called TR-1 through TR-4, each based on a different QIC standard.

Looking at the third column of Figure 17-9a, showing tape types, and at the column headings of Figure 17-9b, you can see that there are several types of tapes available. Although most manufacturers suggest that you use a tape cartridge made by them for their drive, tape drives often support a variety of tape types. Even though a tape drive may use a minicartridge rather than a data cartridge, not all minicartridge tapes can be used in any one drive. Consult the tape drive's user guide to find out which tape type you can use with the drive. Minicartridge tape drives use more than one type of tape drive mechanism, and more than one density is used to write data to the tape, just as there is more than one density for floppy disks. Also, some tape drives don't format tapes, meaning that you must buy preformatted tapes.

17

Troubleshooting Guide for Tape Drives

The following are some general guidelines for solving problems with tape drives.

A minicartridge does not work

1. If you are trying to write data, verify that the minicartridge is write-enabled.
2. Are you inserting the minicartridge correctly? Check the user guide.
3. Check that you are using the correct type of minicartridge. See the user guide.
4. Is the minicartridge formatted? The format is done by the software and can take an hour or more.
5. Retension the tape. Use the backup software to do this. Some tape drives require this and others do not. **Retensioning** fast forwards and rewinds the tape to eliminate loose spots on the tape.
6. Take the minicartridge out and reboot. Try the minicartridge again.
7. Try using a new minicartridge. The old one may have worn out.
8. Just as with floppy disks, if the tape was removed from the drive while the drive light was still on, the data being written at that time may not be readable.

Data transfer is slow

1. Does the tape software have an option for optimizing speed or data compression? Try turning one, and then the other, off and on.
2. Some tape drives can use an optional accelerator card to speed up data transfer. See the tape drive user guide.
3. Try a new minicartridge.
4. If the tape drive can do so, completely erase the tape and reformat it. Be sure that the tape drive has the ability to perform this procedure before you tell the software to do it.
5. If you have installed an accelerator card, verify that the card is connected to the tape drive.
6. Check that there is enough memory for the software to run.

The drive does not work after the installation

1. Check that pin 1 is oriented correctly to the data cable at both ends.
2. Check for a resource conflict. The tape drive normally requires an IRQ, DMA channel, and I/O address.
3. For DOS, check the entries in CONFIG.SYS and AUTOEXEC.BAT.

The drive fails intermittently or gives errors

1. The tape might be worn out. Try a new tape.
2. Clean the read/write head of the tape drive. See the tape drive user guide for directions.

3. For an external tape drive, move the drive as far as you can from the monitor and computer case.

4. Reformat the tape.

5. Retension the tape.

6. Verify that you are using the correct tape type and tape format.

BACKUP METHODS

When backing up to tapes, several backup methods can be used to reuse tapes and to make the backup process more efficient. The child, parent, and grandparent method is a plan for reusing tapes. Full, incremental, and differential backups are methods used to speed up the backup process, and scheduled backups are done so that backing up data causes the least inconvenience to users. Selective backups only back up data that changes often on the hard drive. By selecting only certain critical folders on the drive to back up, the backup routine goes much faster and recovery of lost data is much easier.

The Child, Parent, and Grandparent Method

When you become responsible for performing routine backups of hard drives, one of the first things you must do is devise a backup plan or procedure. One common plan for backing up data, called the **child, parent, grandparent method**, makes it easier to reuse tapes. This method is explained in Table 17-3. Put the plan in writing and keep a log of backups performed.

Table 17-3   The child, parent, grandparent backup method

Name of Backup	How Often Performed	Storage Location	Description
Child backup	Daily	On-site	Keep four daily backup tapes and rotate them each week. Label the four tapes Monday, Tuesday, Wednesday, and Thursday. A Friday daily (child) backup is not made, because on Friday you'll make the parent backup.
Parent backup	Weekly	Off-site	Perform the weekly backup on Friday. Keep five weekly backup tapes, one for each Friday of the month, and rotate them each month. Label the tapes Friday 1, Friday 2, Friday 3, Friday 4, and Friday 5.
Grandparent backup	Monthly	Off-site, in a fireproof vault	Perform the monthly backup on the last Friday of the month. Keep 12 tapes, one for each month. Rotate them each year. Label the tapes January, February, and so on.

17

Full, Incremental, and Differential Backups

Some backup methods are designed to make backing up more efficient, by not performing a complete backup of all data each time a backup is done. A **full backup** does just that: all data on the hard drive is backed up. An **incremental backup** backs up only files that have changed or files that have been newly created since the last backup, whether that backup is itself an incremental or full backup. **Differential backups** back up files that have changed or have been created since the last full backup.

Begin by performing a full backup. The next time you make a backup, if you select incremental as your backup method, only files that have changed or been created since the full backup are backed up. The second time you perform an incremental backup, only the files that have changed or been created since the last incremental backup are backed up.

For example, using the child, parent, grandparent method, a full backup can be performed each Friday. Monday through Thursday backups can be incremental backups. The advantage of this method is that incremental backups are faster and require less tape space than full backups. The disadvantage of this method is that, when data must be recovered, you must begin with the last full backup and work your way forward through each incremental backup up to the time that the data was lost. This process can be time-consuming. If you use incremental backups, plan to make a full backup at least every sixth or seventh incremental backup. The Windows 95 and Windows NT backup utilities support incremental backups.

If you use the differential backup method with the child, parent, grandparent method, create a full backup on Fridays. On Monday, do a differential backup. All files that have changed since Friday are backed up. On Tuesday, a differential backup also backs up all files that have changed since Friday (the full backup). Differential backups don't consider whether or not other differential backups have been performed, but compare data only to the last full backup, which is how differential backups and incremental backups differ. The advantage of differential backups over incremental ones is that, if you need to recover data, you only need to recover from the last full backup and the last differential backup. Differential backups are not supported by Windows 95, but are supported by Windows NT.

Scheduling Backups

Backups can be performed interactively or can be scheduled. Interactive backups are done by the user sitting at the computer. A scheduled backup is scheduled to be automatically performed by software when the computer is commonly not in use, such as during the middle of the night. Scheduled backups are supported by Windows NT. How to schedule an automatic backup is covered later in the chapter.

BACKUP SOFTWARE

Most tape drives come with some backup software. You can also purchase third-party backup software or use Windows 95 or Windows NT for backing up your hard drive. As you learn about backup software, bear in mind that the software only backs up files that are not currently in use, so close all files before performing a backup.

Windows 95 Backup Utility

Windows 95 offers a backup utility that includes support for backup to both floppy disks and tape drives. Table 17-4 lists the tape drives that are supported by the utility and those that are not. You can still use the drives and tapes listed on the right side of the table with Windows 95, but you must use some third-party backup software with them.

Table 17-4 Tape drives supported and not supported by Windows 95 Backup

Supported by Windows 95 Backup	Not Supported by Windows 95 Backup
QIC 40, 80, and 3010 drives made by these companies and using a primary floppy drive controller: Colorado Memory Systems, Iomega, Wangtek	Drives connected to a secondary floppy drive controller or to an accelerator card
Colorado Memory Systems QIC 40, 80, and 3010 tape drives connected through a parallel port	Archive drives
	Irwin drives
	Mountain drives
	QIC Wide tapes
	QIC 3020 drives
	SCSI tape drives
	Travan drives
	Summit drives

If the Windows 95 Backup component is not installed under Windows 95, you can install it as follows:

1. Click **Start**, **Settings**, **Control Panel**, and double-click on **Add/Remove Programs**.

2. Click on the **Windows Setup** tab.

3. Under **Disk Tools**, select **Backup**. Click **OK** and then click **Apply** to install the component. You will be asked to supply the original Windows 95 floppy disks or CD so that the OS can complete the installation.

With the Windows 95 backup utility, you can back up files, folders, or an entire hard drive by following these directions:

1. Click **Start**, **Programs**, **Accessories**, **System Tools**, and **Backup**. The Welcome to Microsoft Backup screen displays, as in Figure 17-11, with a dialog box telling you that it has automatically created a file set for a **full system backup** of the

17

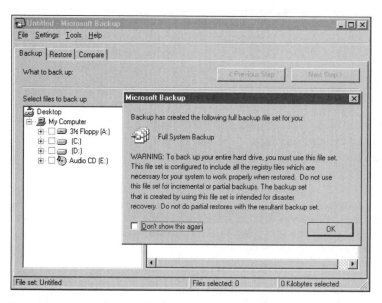

Figure 17-10   The Windows 95 Backup utility automatically builds a file set to back up the entire hard drive

entire hard drive (which consists of logical drives C and D in the figure and includes all system files, including the Windows 95 registry). Click **OK** to continue.

2. In order to complete the full system backup of the entire hard drive, including the Windows 95 registry and all other system files, do the following: with the Backup tab selected, click **File**, **Open File Set**. The list of file sets displays. If this is the first time you have used the backup utility, only the Full System Backup set is listed. Select it and then click **Open**.

3. The backup utility will now build a complete list of all files on all logical drives of the hard drive. Notice in Figure 17-10 that there is an empty white box to the left of the drive name. When the list is complete, all boxes for all folders on the hard drive will be checked, indicating that they will each be backed up. Click **Next Step** to create the full system backup.

4. To back up only certain folders, files, or logical drives, don't open the full system backup set, but rather select the drives, folders, or files by checking the boxes to the left of their names. (For example, to back up the logical drive C, check the box to the left of C:.) Also, to show a list of all folders under the root, click the box with the + sign in it, to open the drive list. For instance, to select all files in the \Colldos folder of drive C (see Figure 17-11), check the empty box to the left of the folder name. Figure 17-11 shows that all files listed in the folder on the right side of the screen are automatically checked. Backup indicates that only parts of a folder or drive are selected for backup by placing a check in the box and making the box background gray.

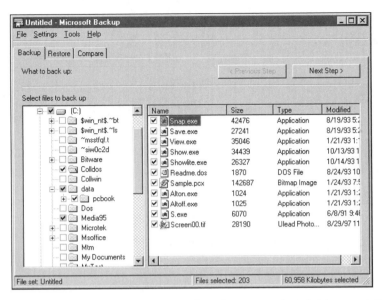

Figure 17-11 Windows 95 Backup lets you select folders and files to back up

5. Click **Next Step** to continue. Backup will provide a list of devices to which it can write the backups. An installed tape drive that it can support will be included in the list as well as hard drives and floppy drives.

6. Select the device to hold the backup. You can select a hard drive or a folder on the drive to be used for the backup.

7. Click **Start Backup** to begin the process. You will be asked to enter a Backup Set Label, which will later be used in the list of file sets available for restoration. A progress report displays on the screen as the backup is performed.

In order to recover files, folders, or the entire hard drive from backup using the Windows 95 Backup utility, follow these directions:

1. From the Backup utility, click the **Restore** tab.

2. Click the medium to restore from under the **Restore from** list. A list of backup labels on that disk or tape displays.

3. Select the backup you want to use from the list and click **Next Step**.

4. A **backup set** displays, which is a list of all the files and folders backed up in this set. Sometimes this list is called a **backup catalog**.

5. Check the entire backup set, or you can select individual files or folders you want to restore. Then click **Start Restore** to continue.

17

Windows 95 Backup offers the following features that can be set under the Backup Settings menu:

- Back up only files and folders that have been altered during a selected time interval
- Back up only files with certain file extensions
- Use a full backup or use an incremental backup of only files that have changed since the last full backup
- Use data compression
- Verify backup by automatically comparing files when the backup is finished
- Format tapes when needed
- Always erase or don't erase tapes before backing up
- Always erase or don't erase floppy disks before backing up

Using the Windows NT Backup Utility

With the Windows NT Backup utility, you can either perform backups manually or schedule unattended backups when no one is using the system. In this section, you learn how to use the Backup utility and how to schedule a backup using Windows NT.

Recall from earlier chapters that an OS tracks an archive attribute for each file it stores. This archive attribute indicates to the OS whether or not the file has been backed up since it was last changed. Windows NT also maintains this archive attribute when creating and changing files, and uses it to tell when a file needs backing up. When a file is first created, the archive attribute is set so that a backup command will know that the file needs backing up. After the backup is complete, in most cases, the Backup utility sets the archive attribute to indicate that a current backup exists. The next time the file is changed, the archive backup is reset to indicate that a backup is needed.

Manual Backup. The Windows NT Backup utility looks and works about the same way as Windows 95 Backup. However, Windows NT Backup does not support backup to floppy disk. (To back up to floppy disks using Windows NT, use the Windows NT BACKUP or XCOPY command from the command prompt.) Follow these directions to back up to tape:

1. Click **Start**, **Programs**, **Administrative Tools**, and **Backup**. The Backup utility opening screen displays, as in Figure 17-12.

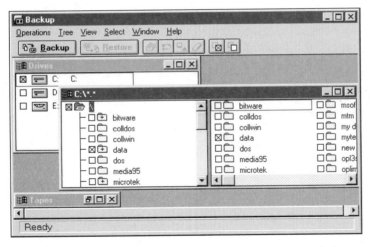

Figure 17-12 Windows NT backup utility works similarly to Windows 95 Backup

2. Select the drives, folders, and files to back up by clicking in the empty boxes to the left of the name.

3. Click **Backup**. The Backup Information dialog box displays. Using this dialog box, enter the following information about the backup:

   ■ Enter a descriptive tape name.

   ■ Choose to verify the data after backup.

   ■ Choose to back up the Windows NT Registry.

   ■ Choose to use data compression on the tape.

   ■ Choose whether to append new data to existing data on the tape or to over-write existing data.

   ■ Enter a description of the backup set.

   ■ Choose to create a log of backup information containing either summary or full detail information. The path and filename of the log file are required.

   ■ Choose the type of backup. The types of backups that you can choose from are:

      ■ **Normal:** A full backup that sets the archive attributes of all files and folders it backs up, to indicate that there is a current backup

      ■ **Copy:** A full backup that does not change the archive attributes of files and folders, so that incremental and differential backups don't "sense" this backup

      ■ **Incremental:** Backs up all files and folders that have changed (as determined by the archive attribute) since the last backup, excluding the copy backups, which don't affect the archive attributes

      ■ **Differential:** Backs up all files and folders that have changed since the last full backup (as determined by the archive attribute), excluding the copy backups

17

- **Daily copy:** Backs up all files and folders that have changed during that day, but does not change the archive attributes of files and folders, so that incremental and differential backups don't "sense" this backup

4. Click **OK** to start the backup. The backup reports its progress on-screen as it works.

From the list of backup types above, you can see that there are several approaches you can take to making backups using Windows NT. These and other options are used by other backup applications and operating systems as well. Listed below are four possible plans for backing up data. There are others as well.

1. Make a full backup weekly, followed by incremental backups daily.

2. Make a full backup weekly, followed by differential backups daily.

3. Make daily copies each day.

4. Make a full backup monthly and make daily copies each day.

Your choice of backup plans depends on several things, including the following:

- How are folders and files used?

- How volatile is the data?

- Is the ability to restore from backup required for auditing purposes?

- How valuable is the data?

Scheduled Backups Using Windows NT.   Using scheduled backups helps the PC user because the backup process can be scheduled so that it happens when files are not currently open or when computer resources are needed for other activities. Scheduling also helps by making the backup procedure happen automatically, without someone initiating it every time. Windows 95 can schedule events using the Microsoft Plus! for Windows 95 System Agent. When the Microsoft Plus! for Windows 95 add-on software is first installed, System Agent is added to System Tools under Accessories. It can be used to schedule ScanDisk, Disk Defragmenter, and Backup to help prevent and protect against hard drive failures.

Windows NT also allows you to schedule processes at predetermined times and dates. The AT command (AT is the word *at*) is included with Windows NT Workstation and is used from the command prompt to schedule a task, and WinAT, contained in the Windows NT Resource Kit, schedules tasks using a GUI interface. The first step toward using either AT or WinAT is to install the Scheduler service, if it is not already installed, under Windows NT. After the service is installed, it can be used to schedule backups, and other events, to happen in the future. The Windows NT NTBACKUP command is used as the scheduled command within the AT command, in order to schedule a backup. The NTBACKUP command is covered later in this section.

Installing the Schedule Service.   Remember from Chapter 12 that a service is a background process that can be evoked by OS commands and applications. Follow these steps to activate the Windows NT Scheduler service:

1. Click **Start**, **Settings**, **Control Panel**. Double-click on **Services**.

2. From the Services window, select **Schedule**. If the Startup entry is not listed as Automatic (meaning that the Scheduler is already installed), click **Startup**. Figure 17-13 displays.

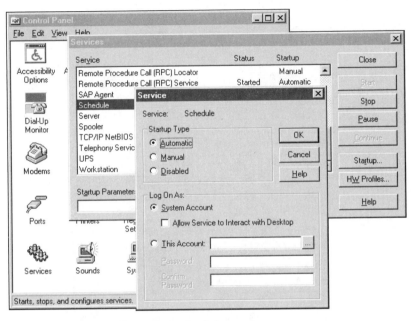

Figure 17-13   Installing the Schedule service

3. Select the **Startup Type** to be **Automatic**, and select **System Account** under **Log On As**. The Automatic option means that the Scheduler will start up each time Windows NT is loaded. When the System Account is selected, no user needs to be logged on for the Scheduler to work.

4. Click **OK** to return to the Services window. Click **Start** to start the Scheduler. A message should display, saying that the Scheduler started successfully.

5. Click **Close** to close the Services window. The service is now running and will automatically start each time the OS is loaded. You can now use the AT command to schedule an event.

The AT Command.   From the Windows NT command prompt, the AT command schedules a program to run at a later time and date. Scheduled commands are stored in the Windows NT Registry and are made active each time Windows NT loads. You must have administrator rights in order to use the command. The syntax of the AT command is shown in Table 17-5. The two forms of the command are listed at the top of the table, and descriptions of each parameter in the command line are found in the table.

17

Table 17-5   Explanation of parameters in Windows NT for two AT commands used to schedule tasks for a later date and time

Windows NT AT Commands Used to Schedule Tasks:[1]
AT [\\computername] [[id] [/DELETE [/YES]]
AT [\\computername] time [/INTERACTIVE] [/EVERY:date[,...] | /NEXT:date[,...]] "command"

Command Parameter	Description
\\computername	The name of a remote computer that the command is applied to. If omitted, then the local computer is used.
id	An identification number that is automatically assigned by Windows NT to a scheduled command when the command is first scheduled.
/DELETE	Deletes the identified command. If the ID is omitted, all scheduled commands are deleted. For example, AT /DELETE deletes all scheduled commands.
/YES	Provides the confirmation of the deletion without waiting for the user to respond. The DELETE option requires a YES to confirm the deletion. If the parameter is left off the command line, then you must manually confirm the deletion.
time	The time that the event is scheduled to occur. Use the format 00:00am, 00:00pm or use military time, omitting the am and pm.
/INTERACTIVE	Allows the process to interact with the user. If this is not included, then the process does not show on the user desktop.
/EVERY: date,...	Specifies what day of week or day of month the process is scheduled for. For day of week, use Su, M, T, W, Th, F, S. For day of month, use a number from 1 to 31. For example, to perform the process on the 1st and 15th day of the month: /EVERY:1,15. If /EVERY is omitted, the current day is assumed.
/NEXT:date,...	Specifies the next date that the process is to be performed. Use either day of week or day of month. For example, to perform the command on the following Sunday: /NEXT:Su. If /NEXT is omitted, the current day is assumed.
"command"	The command that you are scheduling. Recall from earlier chapters that a command at a command prompt is really the name of an executable file or program. In addition to the filename, the command line can also contain parameters that are passed to the program being executed. The command that is scheduled by the AT command can use any executable file ending with an .EXE, .COM, .BAT, or .CMD file extension. .CMD files are Windows NT batch files. Enclose the command in quotation marks so that you can include command line parameters. Include the path to the executable file.
AT with no parameters	Displays currently scheduled events. Use the AT command with no parameters to see a list of commands currently scheduled.

[1] This and other commands are presented using customary syntax for commands. Words in uppercase are used as they are. Words in lowercase must have a value substituted in their places. When a parameter is enclosed in brackets [ ], it is optional; ellipses (...) indicate that more than one occurrence of the parameter is allowed.

Two examples of how to schedule commands are shown below:

To schedule a COPY command next Monday at 1:00 pm, use this AT command:

```
AT 1:00pm /NEXT:M "COPY MyFile1.txt MyFile2.txt"
```

The AT command contains the time parameter and the /NEXT parameter. The command to be scheduled is included in quotation marks.

To schedule a batch file to execute every weekday at midnight, use this command:

```
AT 00:00 /EVERY:M,T,W,Th,F "C:\MyFolder\MyBatch.CMD"
```

The time for midnight is 00:00. The /EVERY parameter lists every weekday. The batch file, MyBatch.CMD, can contain any number of commands. Using a batch file in the command line greatly improves the power of the AT command, since the batch file can contain many commands which are, in effect, all scheduled.

Scheduling a Backup Using NTBackup.

The Windows NT command NTBackup performs backups from the command prompt, giving the exact same results as the Backup utility under Administrative Tools. The syntax of this command and the explanation of each command parameter are shown in Table 17-6.

Some examples of the NTBACKUP command are listed below.

- To back up the entire drive C, including the Registry, use:

```
NTBACKUP backup C: /b /t normal
```

- To back up the files and folders in the C:\data folder that have changed today, use:

```
NTBACKUP backup C:\data /t daily
```

- To include a log file of the exceptions or errors that occurred during the backup, use:

```
NTBACKUP backup C:\data /t daily /l
     "C:\WinBack\Backup.log" /e
```

You put the AT and NTBACKUP commands together to schedule a backup. Here is an example of scheduling a daily backup of the C:\data directory on the hard drive every weekday at 12:50 pm.

```
AT 12:50pm /EVERY:M,T,W,Th,F "ntbackup backup C:\data /t
daily"
```

If the command line becomes too long, or if you want to perform other chores than just the backup, such as first deleting any old log files, put the commands in a batch file and execute the batch file using the AT command.

When scheduling backups to be performed when people are not present, be sure that a tape is in the drive and ready to go, and that the tape is long enough to contain the entire backup, because no one will be present to exchange it.

17

Table 17-6   Explanation of parameters of the NTBackup command

NTBACKUP command:[1]
NTBACKUP operation path [/a] [/v] [/r] [/d "text"] [/b] [/hc:{on	off}] [t {option}][/l "filename"][/e]

Command Parameter	Description
Operation	Substitute either BACKUP (perform the backup) or EJECT (eject the tape).
path	The path or paths to files and folders to back up
/a	/a causes the data to be appended to data already on the tape. If /a is omitted, the existing data is overwritten.
/v	Verifies that the write operation is done with no errors
/r	Restricts access to the tape
/d "text"	The description of the backup contents
/b	Says to back up the registry. If /b is not included, the registry is not backed up.
/hc:on or /hc:off	Use data compression
/t option	Specifies the type of backup. Use one of the following: /t normal /t incremental /t daily /t copy /t differential
/l filename	Record to a log file. Include the path to the log file in the filename. The log file tracks what happens during the backup procedure.
/e	Only include exceptions in the log file

[1] This and other commands are presented using customary syntax for commands. Words in uppercase are used as they are. Words in lowercase must have a value substituted in their places. When a parameter is enclosed in brackets [ ], it is optional; ellipses (...) indicate that more than one occurrence of the parameter is allowed.

Managing and Maintaining Tapes

Backup software, including Windows 95 and Windows NT, offers commands to help you manage tapes used for backups. Some of the commands available and what they do are listed below:

- **Erase Tape:** This command erases all data on the tape. Sometimes there is a Quick Erase option that only erases the header information on the tape. A full erase can take several hours.

- **Retension Tape:** This command fast forwards to the end of the tape and then rewinds the tape to eliminate loose spots on the tape. Some tapes don't require retensioning, so the command may not be available when the software knows that this type of tape is present.

- **Format Tape:** This command formats the tape. The backup software only makes this command available if it knows that the type of tape present can be formatted.

- **Eject Tape:** This command ejects the tape cartridge from the tape drive.

- **Catalog:** This command lists a description of the backup, including a list of folders and files backed up. Use this command when searching for individual items to restore from the tape.

RAID

Besides maintaining a good backup, another method of protecting data is to continuously write two copies of the data, each to a different hard drive. This method is most often used on high-end, high-cost file servers, but occasionally there can be situations in which it is appropriate for a single-user workstation.

Collectively, these several methods, used to improve performance and/or automatically recover from a failure, are called RAID (redundant array of independent disks). There are several levels of RAID, but this section discusses only the three most commonly used (Table 17-7). Only the first level is financially practical for a standalone workstation.

Table 17-7 The three most common RAID levels

RAID Level and Common Name	Intended Purpose	Description
RAID 0: Disk striping without parity (Striping refers to writing data across more than one physical drive.)	Increases performance and volume capacity	Data is written to two or more hard drives. The set of drives is treated as a single volume (a single virtual drive). Because more than one drive is doing the work, performance improves.
RAID 1: Disk mirroring or disk duplexing	Provides fault tolerance	Data is written twice, once to each of two drives. Disk mirroring uses only a single HD adapter. Disk duplexing uses two adapters, one for each drive.
RAID 5: Disk striping with parity	Increases performance and volume capacity and provides fault tolerance	Data is written to two or more drives, but parity information is also written to a third or additional drive so that, if one drive fails, the other drives can re-create the data stored on the failed drive.

17

RAID Level 0 increases the logical drive capacity by treating two drives as a single logical drive, but it does not offer a way to recover from a failure (an important feature of **fault tolerance**). RAID 0 is one method of **disk striping**, a method in which more than one hard drive is treated as a single volume. For an array of two hard drives, some data is written to one hard drive and some to the other; both drives make up one logical drive or volume, and data is only written once. RAID 0 is supported by Windows NT Workstation.

RAID Level 1 is designed to protect data from a hard drive failure by writing the data twice, once to each of two drives. One type of RAID Level 1 is called **disk mirroring**, in which the two hard drives both use the same adapter card.

The advantages of RAID 1 disk mirroring are:

- If either drive fails, the data is still safe on the other drive.
- Disk reads are speeded up because the adapter has two places to read from.

The disadvantages of RAID 1 are:

- Having two hard drives in the same computer is more expensive.
- Because the data is written twice, hard drive capacity is, in effect, cut in half.
- Disk writes are slowed down because the data must be written twice.

One weakness in drive mirroring is that both hard drives are using the same adapter. If the adapter fails, then neither hard drive is accessible. An improvement of disk mirroring, also considered RAID 1, is **duplexing**, in which each hard drive has its own adapter card. The initial cost is higher, but you are now protected from possibly losing the data on both drives if one adapter fails. Disk mirroring or duplexing may be appropriate for a workstation if the data is considered valuable enough to merit the added expense, and backup to a server on a network is not possible.

Because Windows NT Workstation does not support RAID 1, in order to use RAID 1 on a workstation, the two hard drives must be managed by firmware on the controllers rather than by the OS. This adds to the hardware expense because of the higher cost of controllers that contain this firmware. Windows NT Server does support RAID 1 and RAID 5.

RAID 5, or disk striping with parity, is an interesting variation of RAID 0 combined with RAID 1, in which fault tolerance and drive capacity are both improved. RAID 5 requires at least three hard drives. In Figure 17-14, RAID 5 is depicted using four hard drives grouped as one virtual hard drive. When any data is written to this one "virtual hard drive," the data is divided into three segments. Each segment is written to one of the first three drives, and parity information about the three segments is written to the fourth drive.

If one of the four drives fails—and it doesn't matter which one fails—the data can be recovered from the other three drives. How this is done is described in the bottom part of the figure. Using any two segments and the parity information, the three segments can be recreated, or, if the parity drive fails, the three segments are still safely stored on the first three drives.

To understand how data is recovered using parity information, consider this simple example. Suppose you have three numbers stored on three different drives. If you store the sum of the three numbers on the fourth, or parity drive, it is possible to use the information you have to calculate any one number that might later be missing. For example, if the three numbers are 1, 2, and 6, you would store their sum (9) on the parity drive. If the first number is lost, it can be calculated from the sum and the other two numbers.

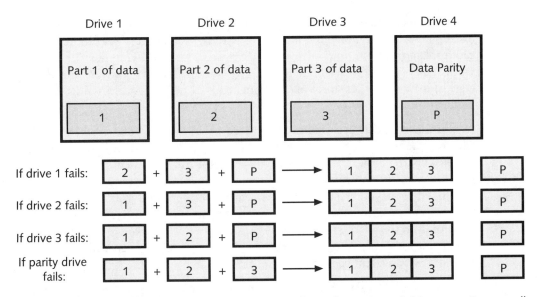

Figure 17-14   RAID 5, disk striping with parity, allows for increased drive capacity as well
as fault tolerance: Any one drive can fail and data can still be re-created.

When a drive fails, the failed drive is replaced with a new drive. When using Windows NT
Server, you can then go to the Disk Administrator of the Administrator Tools and execute a
Regenerate command. Windows NT does the rest by recreating the data to the new drive.
The action is very automatic, and you can still use the computer for other operations while
regenerating is taking place.

For file servers using RAID 5 that must stay up and work continuously, it may be practical to
use hardware that allows for hard drive **hot swapping**, which means that one hard drive can
be removed and another hard drive inserted without powering down the computer. However,
hard drives that can be hot swapped cost significantly more than do regular hard drives.

PLANNING FOR DISASTER RECOVERY

The time to prepare for a disaster is before it occurs. If no preparation has been made, when
the inevitable disaster does occur, the damage will most likely be greater than if plans had
been made and followed. Consider the hard drive on your PC at this moment. Suppose it
suddenly stopped working and all information on the drive was lost. What would be the
impact? Are you prepared for this event? Backups are important, but knowing how to use
them to recover lost data is equally important. Also important is knowing when the backup
was made and what you must do to recover information entered since the last backup. Here's
where careful recordkeeping can pay off.

When you perform a backup for the first time or set up a scheduled backup, verify that the
backup tape or disks can be used to successfully recover the data if that becomes necessary.

17

This is a very important step in preparing to recover lost data. After you have created a backup tape, erase a file on the hard drive, and use the recovery procedures to verify that you can recreate the file from the backup. Not only are you verifying that the tape or floppy disk works, but you are also verifying the effectiveness of recovery software and your own knowledge of how to use it. After you are convinced that the recovery works, document how to perform the recovery.

As you make regular backups, keep a record of this activity. Use a notebook that contains a table of scheduled backups. Include in the table the folders or drives backed up, the date of the backup, the type of backup, and the name of the tape used. You can check them off as you do them. This table will become invaluable if you need to recover data that was lost days or weeks before you discover that it needs to be recovered. You can also make a complete log to a log file each time you back up, and print this log file, keeping it on file. However, you may find this method too time-consuming to do on a daily basis. Even though the software is automatically recording events to the log file, the backup will take longer because of the extra writing, and printing the file later will also consume time.

Periodically, perform a full restoration of a hard drive that you back up. Use the tape made from a full backup and a different hard drive. Restore the first hard drive to the new hard drive and compare the results.

CHAPTER SUMMARY

- PC failures are caused by many different environmental and human factors, including heat, dust, magnetism, power supply problems, static electricity, spilled liquids, viruses, and human error.
- The goals of preventive maintenance are to make PCs last longer and work better, protect data and software, and reduce the cost of repairs.
- A PC preventive maintenance plan includes blowing dust from the inside of the computer case, cleaning the contacts on expansion cards, keeping a record of setup, backing up the hard drive, and cleaning the mouse, monitor, and keyboard.
- Protecting software and hardware documentation is an important preventive maintenance chore.
- Never ship a PC when the only copy of important data is on its hard drive.
- Computer infestations include viruses, Trojan horses, and worms, which are categorized by the way they are transmitted.
- Antivirus software is your best defense against the damage caused by viruses.
- Viruses can hide in program files, boot sectors, and documents that contain macros.
- Viruses attempt to cloak themselves from antivirus software by changing their distinguishing characteristics and attempting to mask the fact that they are present.
- Some viruses are relatively harmless, only displaying garbage on the computer screen. Others can be so destructive as to erase everything on a hard drive, including partition table information.

- Steps you can take to prevent viruses from infesting your computer include not trading floppy disks, only buying software from reliable sources, not downloading programs from the Internet, and only using networks with caution.

- A virus hoax is intended to overload network traffic. It does its work by tricking people into forwarding e-mail messages about viruses.

- To protect against damage by viruses, use antivirus software and back up your hard drive regularly.

- Tape drives are the most common hardware devices used to back up a hard drive. There are many variations of tape types and formats.

- RAID (redundant array of independent disks) is used to mirror data stored on a hard disk and to increase hard drive capacity by making more than one hard drive work as a single virtual drive.

- The child, parent, grandparent method of backing up data is used to reuse tapes according to a straightforward and easy-to-follow plan.

- Using a full backup, followed by incremental or differential backups, speeds up the time it takes to make a backup.

- Scheduled backups are designed to be performed when no one is using the computer.

- Windows 95 and Windows NT each include a Backup utility that can be used with tape drives. In addition, Windows 95 Backup can use floppy disks.

- Windows NT allows backups to be scheduled for a later date and time.

- When planning for recovering from a disaster, keep careful records of backups and periodically test your backup method to assure that you can successfully recover lost data. Have a disaster recovery plan in writing.

KEY TERMS

- **Anti-Virus (AV) software** — Utility programs that prevent infection, or scan a system to detect and remove viruses. Norton AntiVirus and McAfee Associates Virus Scan are two popular AV packages.

- **Backup catalog** — A backup set that displays a list of the files and folders previously backed up. See backup set.

- **Backup set** — The name for the set of files you backed up. For example, perhaps only the C:\data and C:\mail directories were backed up. DATA and MAIL might be used as the backup set names.

- **Boot sector virus** — An infectious program that can replace the boot program with a modified, infected version of the boot command utilities, often causing boot and data retrieval problems.

- **Child, parent, grandparent backup method** — A plan for backing up and reusing tapes or removable disks by rotating them each week (child), month (parent), and year (grandparent).

- **.CMD files** — Windows NT batch files that contain a list of commands to be executed as a group.

17

- **Copy backup** — A full backup that does not change the archive attributes of files and folders, so that incremental and differential backups don't "sense" this backup.

- **Daily copy backup** — Backs up all files that have changed during a day, but does not change the archive attributes of files; in this way, incremental and differential backups don't "sense" the backup.

- **Data cartridge** — A type of tape medium typically used for backups. Full-sized data cartridges are 4 × 6 × ⅝ inches in size. A minicartridge is only 3¼ × 2½ × ⅝ inches.

- **Differential backup** — Backs up only files that have changed or have been created since the last *full* backup. When recovering data, only two backups are needed: the full backup and the last differential backup.

- **Disk duplexing** — An improvement of disk mirroring, whereby redundant data is written to two or more drives, and each hard drive has its own adapter card. This provides greater protection than disk mirroring.

- **Disk mirroring** — A strategy whereby the same data is written to two hard drives in a computer, to safeguard against hard drive failure. Disk mirroring uses only a single adapter for two drives.

- **Disk striping** — Treating multiple hard drives as a single volume. Data is written across the multiple drives in small segments, in order to increase performance and logical disk volume, and, when parity is also used, to provide fault tolerance. RAID 5 is disk striping with an additional drive for parity.

- **Encrypting virus** — A type of virus that transforms itself into a nonreplicating program in order to avoid detection. It transforms itself back into a replicating program in order to spread.

- **Fault tolerance** — The degree to which a system can tolerate failures. Adding redundant components, such as disk mirroring or disk duplexing, is a way to build in fault tolerance.

- **File virus** — A virus that inserts virus code into an executable program and can spread whenever that program is accessed.

- **Full backup** — A complete backup, whereby all of the files on the hard drive are backed up each time the backup procedure is performed. It is the safest backup method, but it takes the most time.

- **Hot swapping** — A system feature, desirable in file servers, whereby a hard drive can be removed and exchanged without powering down a computer.

- **Incremental backup** — A time-saving backup method that only backs up files changed or newly created since the last full *or* incremental backup. Multiple incremental backups might be required when recovering lost data.

- **Infestation** — Any unwanted program that is unknowingly transmitted to a computer and is designed to do varying degrees of damage to data and software. There are a number of different types of infestations, including viruses, Trojan Horses, Worms, and time bombs, among others.

- **Macro** — A small sequence of commands, contained within a document, that can be automatically executed when the document is loaded, or executed later by pressing a predetermined keystroke.

- **Macro virus** — A virus that can hide in the macros of a document file. Typically, viruses do not reside in data or document files.

- **Memory-resident virus** — A virus that can stay lurking in memory, even after its host program is terminated.

- **Minicartridge** — A tape drive cartridge that is only 3¼ × 2½ × ⅜ inches. It is small enough to allow two drives to fit into a standard 5½-inch drive bay of a PC case.

- **Multipartite virus** — A combination of a boot sector virus and a file virus. It can hide in either type of program.

- **Non-memory-resident virus** — A virus that is terminated when the host program is closed. Compare to memory-resident virus.

- **Normal backup** — A full backup that sets the archive attributes of all files and folders it backs up so that later backups can sense that a current backup exists.

- **Polymorphic virus** — A type of virus that changes its distinguishing characteristics as it replicates itself. Mutating in this way makes it more difficult for AV software to recognize the presence of the virus.

- **Quarter-Inch Committee** or **quarter-inch cartridge (QIC)** — A name of a standardized method used to write data to tape. Backups made with the Windows 95 System Tools Backup utility have a .QIC extension.

- **RAID (redundant array of inexpensive disks or redundant array of independent disks)** — Several methods of configuring multiple hard drives to store data to increase logical volume size and improve performance, and so that if one hard drive fails, the data is still available from another hard drive.

- **Retension** — A tape maintenance procedure that fast forwards and then rewinds the tape to eliminate loose spots on the tape.

- **Sequential access** — A method of data access used by tape drives whereby data is written or read sequentially from the beginning to the end of the tape or until the desired data is found.

- **Stealth virus** — A virus that actively conceals itself by temporarily removing itself from an infected file that is about to be examined, and then hiding a copy of itself elsewhere on the drive.

- **Trojan horse** — A type of infestation that hides or disguises itself as a useful program, yet is designed to cause damage at a later time.

- **Virus** — A program that often has an incubation period, is infectious, and is intended to cause damage. A virus program might destroy data and programs or damage a disk drive's boot sector.

- **Virus signature** — The distinguishing characteristics or patterns of a particular virus. Typically, AV signature updates for new viruses can be downloaded monthly from the Internet.

- **Worm** — An infestation designed to copy itself repeatedly to memory, on drive space, or on a network until little memory or disk space remains.

17

REVIEW QUESTIONS

1. List one or two preventive maintenance measures that can be taken to help protect each of the following: computer case, CMOS setup, floppy drive, hard drive, keyboard, mouse, printer, and software.
2. List three things that should be done before moving or shipping a computer.
3. List and describe three different types of viruses.
4. List three ways to "catch" a virus.
5. List three ways to prevent a virus.
6. List three symptoms or problems that may indicate that a virus is present.
7. List three things to check if a tape drive fails to work properly.
8. How is disk mirroring different from disk duplexing?
9. When one hard drive can be removed and another hard drive inserted without powering down a computer, this is called _____.
10. Clearly explain how the child, parent, grandparent method works as a plan for reusing tapes.
11. How are differential backups different from full backups, and what are the advantages of each?
12. How are differential backups different from incremental backups, and what are the advantages of each?
13. Why would you want to "retension" a backup tape?
14. What are two reasons why you would want to schedule a hard drive backup to occur during the night?
15. Why is it important to verify that your disaster recovery plan works and to put it in writing?

PROJECTS

CREATING A PREVENTIVE MAINTENANCE AND DISASTER RECOVERY PLAN

Assume that you are a PC technician responsible for all of the 30 to 35 PCs of a small organization. The PCs are networked to a file server that is backed up each evening. There is presently no individual power protection or line conditioning for any PC. Although some users make backups of data on their PC to tape drives or Zip drives, there is no company procedure in place to back up data or software on PCs. Your supervisor has asked you to submit a preventive maintenance and disaster recovery plan for these PCs and to estimate the amount of time you will spend each month for the next 12 months on preventive maintenance. She has also asked you to submit a suggested PC data backup plan for all users to follow, which will become a company policy. Do the following to create these plans and estimate your time.

1. List the possible causes of PC failures.

2. Using the list above, list what you can do to prevent these problems from occurring. Break the list down into two categories: what you plan to do one time for each PC or user, and what you plan to do on a routine or as-needed basis.

3. For each PC, estimate the amount of time you will need to implement the one-time-only plan and the amount of time you will need each year for the ongoing maintenance.

4. Based on your answers to Question 3, how much time do you plan to spend, on the average, each month for the next 12 months on preventive maintenance?

5. In response to the request for a recommended company policy to back up PC data, write a policy for users to follow to back up data on their PCs. Since all PCs are networked to the file server, suggest that company policy be that data on a PC should be backed up to the file server, where it will be backed up nightly in case of a file server failure. Write the backup policy and instructions on how to use it.

USING THE INTERNET TO LEARN ABOUT VIRUSES

The classic source of information about viruses on the Web is Data Fellows. Go to the Web site www.datafellows.com/vir-info/, shown in Figure 17-15, for information about viruses; the viruses are listed in alphabetical order with complete descriptions, including any known source of the virus. Print a description of three viruses from this Web site:

1. One virus that destroys data on a hard drive

2. One harmless virus that only displays garbage on the screen

3. One virus that hides in a boot sector

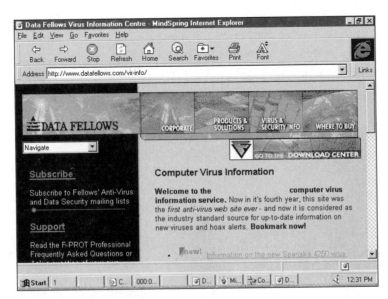

Figure 17-15   For complete virus information, see the Data Fellows Web site

DOWNLOAD LATEST UPDATE OF AV SOFTWARE

If you own antivirus software, download the latest antivirus definition list from the Internet. For example, for Norton AntiVirus, follow these directions:

1. Log on to the AV site:

   www.symantec.com/avcenter/download.html

2. Answer the required questions, such as:

   Product: NAV for Windows 95

   Language: English, US

   Operating Environment: Windows 95

3. Then follow the directions to download the latest update and signature list for the particular version of your AV software.

4. While online, see if the site offers any information on virus hoaxes. Create a list of hoaxes available on the site.

USING WINDOWS NT AT AND NTBACKUP COMMANDS

1. Using the AT command, schedule a command to copy the contents of one folder on the hard drive to a floppy disk. Since NTBackup does not back up to a floppy, use either the XCOPY or BACKUP command. Schedule the command to perform each weekday at 6:00 pm. However, you may want to test the command by first scheduling it to perform a minute or two past your current time. If the command does not work, check the Event Viewer for errors.

2. Execute the NTBackup command from the Windows NT command prompt, to back up a folder to tape. Use a full backup of the folder, and record errors to a log file.

3. Use the AT and the NTBackup commands to schedule a backup of the folder above.

USING NUTS & BOLTS, CHEYENNE ANTIVIRUS SCANNER

Using the Cheyenne AntiVirus Scanner, scan a floppy disk for viruses.

RESEARCH THE MARKET FOR A TAPE DRIVE

Fill in the following table for two tape drives that you might consider purchasing, in order to evaluate the two drives. Which drive seems more appropriate for a standalone PC that is used heavily for data entry and needs data backed up daily? Why?

	Tape Drive 1	Tape Drive 2
Product Name		
Manufacturer		
Price		
Accelerator (yes/no/optional)		
Software included		
Type (internal/external)		
Warranty (1 year/2 years/lifetime)		
Tape formats supported		
Maximum capacity (also indicate the tape format required to meet this maximum capacity. Example: 4.4 GB using QIC-3020)		
Types of cartridges supported		

17

USING WINDOWS 95 TO BACK UP FILES AND FOLDERS

This exercise is designed to give you practice using Windows 95 Backup and to show you how the Backup utility manages several situations.

Part I

  1. Using Windows Explorer, create a folder called BACKTEST on a hard drive.

2. Use Explorer to find a .BAT file, and copy it to the new folder. Copy two other files to the BACKTEST folder. Make a subfolder called SUBFOLDER in BACKTEST and copy a fourth file to C:\BACKTEST\SUBFOLDER.

3. Right-click on the .BAT file and rename it Overwrite.txt. Right-click on the second file and rename it Delete.txt. Rename the third file NoChange.txt. The fourth file can be left alone for now. Use Explorer and write down the file sizes before the backup.

4. Click **Start**, **Programs**, **Accessories**, **System Tools**, and **Backup**.

5. Use the directions provided in this book to back up the folder Backtest to a floppy disk. Use Explorer and compare the backup file size to the original file sizes. How are they different?

6. Delete the file **Delete.txt**. Edit and change the contents of the file Overwrite.txt. Make no changes to the file NoChange.txt. Delete **SUBFOLDER**.

7. Using Windows 95 Backup, restore the files from the backup to their original folder.

   a. What did Backup do with the Delete.txt file?

   b. What did Backup do with the Overwrite.txt file?

   c. What did Backup do with the NoChange.txt file?

   d. What did Backup do with the missing SUBFOLDER and missing file?

   e. What is the name of the backup file on the floppy disk?

   f. What are the name and path to the error log created by Backup?

   g. Print the error log.

Part II

8. Use Windows Explorer to copy the BACKTEST folder to a second floppy disk.

9. Delete all the files in the BACKTEST folder on the hard drive.

10. Use Windows Explorer to copy the three files back to the BACKTEST.

11. Once again, delete the files in the BACKTEST folder on the hard drive.

12. Open the Recycle Bin and restore the three files back to the BACKTEST folder by highlighting the selected files and using the File, Restore option. Did they return to the correct folder?

13. Once again, delete the files in the BACKTEST folder on the hard drive.

14. Again highlight the three files in the Recycle Bin, but this time choose **File**, **Delete**. Can you still restore the files?

CHAPTER EIGHTEEN

THE PROFESSIONAL PC TECHNICIAN

As a professional PC technician, you will want to manage your professional career by staying abreast of new technology and striving for top certifications in the profession. In addition, you will want to maintain excellent customer relationships and professionalism, and seek opportunities for joining professional organizations. Earlier, in Chapter 7, "Troubleshooting Fundamentals," you learned how to work with customers while trying to solve a problem, whether at the customer's site or over the phone. The chapter discussed what types of questions to ask, how to pose them, and how to maintain good customer relations as you work. This chapter builds on that information and also addresses other topics that will help establish you as a professional in your chosen field.

As you know, PC technicians provide service to customers over the phone, in person on-site, and sometimes in a shop where they may have little customer contact. While there are challenges specific to each setting, almost all of the recommendations made in this chapter apply across the board. After all, even if your company is contracted to provide on-site service, you most likely will try to help solve problems first by phone. And even if you work in a shop, you may get calls from customers with questions or complaints. So, you should focus on polishing all the skills needed in all the service settings in which you may find yourself.

IN THIS CHAPTER YOU WILL LEARN:

- How to make and keep excellent customer relationships
- Tips for maintaining a successful help-desk
- About organizations and certifications for the PC technician
- About software copyrights and software piracy
- How to stay abreast of new technology

WHAT CUSTOMERS WANT

Probably the most significant indication that a PC technician is doing a good job is that his or her customers are consistently satisfied. The paramount principle to follow in order to have satisfied customers is simple: provide service and treat customers as you would want to be served and treated in a similar situation. Think about situations in which you have been dependent on service technicians for help. Some probably helped you quickly, some may have needed a bit more time, and in some situations, the technician may have had to turn to someone else to help you. Many factors probably affected your level of satisfaction, but there is probably one underlying characteristic that made the difference between being satisfied or not: if you truly believed that the person did his or her very best for you in your situation, you were much more likely to be satisfied with his or her performance. The right attitude from a service technician can be the deciding factor between satisfied and dissatisfied customers.

Those people who are personally committed to doing their very best in each and every situation tend to be the successful ones. If you have not already done so, make the personal commitment right now to always give your best in your profession; this one decision can catapult you to success.

Part of giving your best is to be prepared, both technically and nontechnically. Being prepared includes knowing what the customer wants, identifying what customers look for, what they don't like, and what they expect from a PC technician.

Your customers may be "internal" (you both work for the same company) or "external" (your customers come to you or your company for service). Customers may be highly technical or technically naive, represent a large company or simply own a home PC, be prompt or slow at paying their bills, want only the best or be searching for bargain service, be friendly and easy to work with or demanding and condescending. In each and every one of these situations, the key to success is always the same: give your best and don't allow circumstances or personalities to affect your personal commitment to excellence.

We've all heard, "If a job's worth doing, it's worth doing well." A disgruntled coworker once told me, "I'll do the job, but don't expect me to give my best. It just won't happen." Think of the worst situation you could be in with a customer—a situation that would cause you to take the same attitude as my disheartened coworker. I'm sure, if given a few moments, anyone could come up with a situation that justifies this kind of response. Now that you've pictured that situation, see yourself doing your very best in it, not because of the situation or people involved, but because of *you* and *your* personal commitment to excellence. See the difference? A person's professional (or unprofessional) response should have nothing to do with specific circumstances and everything to do with the person. Incorporate this principle into your work, and you'll be an asset to your organization, personally successful, and favored in your profession.

NOT JUST TECHNICAL PROFICIENCY

Up to this point, this book has emphasized your becoming a competent PC technician; the value of this cannot be overemphasized. However, all customers, be they technical or non-technical, want more from you than just technical proficiency. Listed below are things that matter, things that distinguish one competent technician from another in the eyes of the customer. Specific ways to reinforce these qualities in your service are discussed later under "Learning to Be a Better Communicator."

Positive and Helpful Attitude

A positive and helpful attitude goes a long way toward establishing good customer relationships. A friendly disposition and positive outlook is appreciated by customers. Smile. Don't belittle your customer's choice of hardware or software. Don't complain. Give compliments and say good things when you can. Be empathic; put yourself in the customer's situation and respect his or her needs. Express your concern for the situation, especially when you are the bearer of bad news. And, remember, a brief but heartfelt apology for whatever complaint a customer might have can go a long way toward taking care of the customer, and can allow you to move forward to actually helping him or her as quickly as possible.

Dependability

Customers appreciate those who do what they say they'll do. If you promise to be back at 10:00 the next morning, be back at 10:00 the next morning. If something happens beyond your control that prevents you from keeping your appointment, never, never ignore your promise. Call, apologize, let the customer know what happened, and reschedule your appointment.

Be Customer-Focused

When you're working with or talking with a customer, focus on him or her. Don't be distracted. Listen; take notes if appropriate. Make it your job to satisfy this person—not just your organization, your boss, your bank account, or the customer's boss. It may not always be possible to give customers exactly what they ask for, especially when a customer is not paying the bill directly, but try your best.

Credibility

Convey confidence to your customers. Being credible certainly means being technically competent and knowing how to do your job well, but there's another important aspect of credibility. A credible technician knows when the job is beyond his or her level of expertise and knows when to ask for help. In most organizations, if you find that you cannot address a customer's problem, there are policies and procedures for passing the problem to more

18

experienced personnel or to personnel with more resources. This process of passing the problem up organizational levels is often called **escalating**. Don't be afraid to escalate when you have exhausted your efforts or knowledge. Customers appreciate a technician who cares enough about the customer's problem to take it to his or her boss.

Also, credibility implies integrity and honesty. If you've made a mistake, don't attempt to hide the fact—not with your customer or with your boss. Everyone makes mistakes, but you don't need to compound the problem by lack of integrity or by not assuming responsibility for what has happened. Accept responsibility and do what you can to make it right. When you take this approach to your mistakes, your credibility with your customer (and your boss) rises.

Also, know the law with respect to your work. For instance, know the laws concerning the use of software, and follow them. Don't use or install pirated software (copies of software made in violation of the licensing agreement with the original purchaser). In an organization, there may be many people who do not know what is legal and what is illegal concerning software installations. You, however, are expected to know. Set an example by personally committing yourself to using only legally obtained software on your own PC and on your company's or customers' PCs. When asked if certain actions are legal, have the answer or know how to get it. Not only will you be viewed by others as someone who can be trusted, but this kind of integrity and honesty is rewarded in other ways as well.

Professionalism

Customers want a technician to look professional and to behave in a professional manner. Dress appropriately for the environment. For example, don't arrive at a customer site in a T-shirt and shorts or use the phone without permission. Consider yourself a guest at the customer site. See Chapter 7 concerning how to handle yourself on a site visit: what to do and not to do.

Perform your work in a professional manner. If a customer is angry, allow the customer to vent, keeping your own professional distance. Remain calm and nondefensive. (You do, however, have the right to expect a customer not to talk to you in an abusive way.)

PROVIDING GOOD SERVICE ON SUPPORT CALLS

Customers want good service. Even though each customer is different and may expect slightly different results, there are certain things that consistently constitute good service in the eyes of most customers. Universally, customers define good service from a PC technician as follows:

- The technician responds within a reasonable time and completes the work within a reasonable time.

- For on-site visits, the technician is prepared for the service call.

- The work is done right the first time.

- The price for the work is reasonable and competitive.

- The technician exhibits good interpersonal skills.

- If the work extends beyond a brief on-site visit or phone call, the technician keeps the customer informed about the progress of the work.

PLANNING FOR GOOD SERVICE

Whether you support PCs on the phone, on-site, or in a shop, you need a plan to follow when you approach a service call. Chapter 7 gave many guidelines and specific suggestions about PC troubleshooting from a technical point of view. This section steps back from those details to survey the entire service situation—from the first contact with the customer to closing the call. Follow these general guidelines when supporting computers and their users. You will find more specific instructions on how to implement this guide later in the chapter.

Taking the Initial Call

Almost every support project starts with a phone call, and your company likely has a policy with very specific instructions on the information you should take when recording that initial call. Follow the guidelines of your company.

Don't assume that an on-site visit is necessary until you have asked questions and asked the caller to check and try some simple things while on the phone with you. For example, the customer can check cable connections, power, and monitor settings, and can look for POST error messages. Only after you have determined that the problem cannot be easily resolved on the phone should you make an appointment to go to the customer's location or ask the customer to bring the PC to you. If an on-site visit is needed, make an appointment and fill out the proper documentation (discussed below) while the caller is on the phone.

Customer Service Policies

It is extremely important to know what your company's policies are about customer service. You might need to refer questions about warranties, licenses, documentation, or procedures to other support personnel or customer relations personnel. Also, there may be questions that your organization does not want you to answer, such as questions about upcoming releases of software or new products, or what your personal or company experience has been supporting particular hardware or software.

Be clear on how your organization wants you to handle these situations, and stay current on new information. You might find it helpful to make friends with employees in other departments to which you might refer customers, so that you know whom to call and how to route a difficult or critical situation to someone with special experience or knowledge.

18

Troubleshooting

With the preliminaries out of the way, if you now are ready to enter the actual troubleshooting part of the conversation or on-site visit, follow these general guidelines to effective troubleshooting:

- First, let the customer explain the problem in his or her own way. Take notes, and then interview the customer about the problem. Do your best to understand what the problem is. (See Chapter 7 for specific questions you can ask.)

- Search for answers. If the answers to specific questions or problems are not evident, become a researcher. Learn to use the online documentation, expert systems, and other resources that your company provides.

- Develop your troubleshooting skills. Remember the skills learned throughout this book. One paramount skill of troubleshooting is to isolate the problem. Check for user error. What works and what doesn't work? What has changed since the system last worked? Reduce the system to essentials. Check the simple things first. Use the troubleshooting guidelines in Appendix E to help you think of approaches to test and try.

- If you have given the problem your best, but still haven't solved it, ask for help. Ask a coworker to listen and offer suggestions as you describe the problem. Sometimes just talking with someone else about the problem will help you think more clearly.

Asking for Help

The ability to recognize that you cannot solve a particular problem and that it is time to ask for help is learned from experience. Once you have made a reasonable effort to help, and it seems clear that you are unlikely to be successful, don't waste a customer's valuable time. Ask a coworker for help or escalate the problem by following your company policy to direct the problem to someone more experienced.

Documentation and Other Aids

Keeping written records of support calls is an extremely effective way of building your own knowledge base. Record how a customer initially presented a problem, what you discovered the problem to actually be, how you made that discovery, and how the problem was finally solved. Remember, it's a real waste of time when a problem has to be researched more than once. Write down what you know. Writing can help you think. But more importantly, once you have solved a problem, recording the process helps you retain the knowledge you have gained. Some forms to help you do this are presented later in the chapter.

MAKING A SERVICE CALL

When a technician makes a service call, customers expect him or her to have not only technical skills but interpersonal skills as well. Prepare for a service call by reviewing information given you by whoever took the call. For example:

- You should know the problem you are going to address.

- You should know what computer, software, and hardware need servicing.

- You should know the urgency of the situation.

- You should arrive with a complete set of equipment that is in order, including tool kit, flashlight, multimeter, grounding strap and mat, and bootable disks that have been scanned for viruses.

- You should dress in an appropriate manner, which is partly determined by the customer site. Your dress for servicing PCs on shop floors might not be appropriate for servicing PCs in executive offices.

Set a realistic time for the appointment (one that you can expect to keep) and arrive on time. If you are unavoidably delayed, call the customer and let him or her know what to expect. When you arrive at the customer's site, greet the customer in a friendly manner. Use Mr. or Ms. and last names rather than first names when addressing the customer, unless you are certain that the customer expects you to use first names. Don't let the first thing you do be the paperwork, but rather let it be listening:

- Listen carefully to the customer explain the problem.

- Allow the customer to say everything he or she wants to say before you make suggestions or offer solutions.

- When talking with the customer, judge the technical knowledge that the customer has, and speak with the customer at that level.

- Never speak to the customer in a condescending or patronizing way.

As you work, be as unobtrusive as possible. Don't make a big mess. Keep your tools and papers out of the customer's way. Don't use the phone or sit in the customer's desk chair without permission. If the customer needs to attend to his or her own work while you are present, do whatever is necessary to accommodate that. Remember that you are a guest at the customer's site, and act accordingly.

Express genuine concern for the customer's problem and predicament. Even though you want a customer to have confidence in your skills to resolve the problem, you do not want to project the attitude that the problem is not serious.

Keep the customer informed:

- Once you have collected enough information, explain to the customer what the problem is and what you must do to fix it, giving the details to the degree that the customer wants.

18

- When choices are to be made, state the customer's options in such a way that you are not unfairly favoring the solution that makes the most money for you as the technician or for your company.

Allow the customer time to be fully satisfied that all is working before you close the call. Does the printer work? Print a test page. Does the network connection work? Can the customer log on to the network and access data on it? If you changed anything on the PC after you booted it, reboot one more time to make sure that you have not caused a problem with the boot. When you have fixed the problem, it's tempting to stop right there. However, double-check that you have not caused another problem with your "fix." Take the time to convince yourself and the customer that he or she can simply go back to work after you leave.

After the problem is fixed and the fix tested, one of the final steps in your call should be to review the service call with the customer. Summarize the instructions and explanations you have given during the call. This is an appropriate time to fill out your paperwork and explain to the customer what you have written. However, if the customer is not interested or does not have the time to listen, then don't pressure him or her to do so.

Before you leave, if you see things that the customer can do to prevent this same problem or some other problem from occurring, share that knowledge with the customer. Explain preventive maintenance to the customer (such as deleting temporary files from the hard drive or cleaning the mouse). Most customers don't have preventive maintenance contracts for their PCs and appreciate your taking the time to show them how they themselves can take better care of their computers.

PHONE SUPPORT

Providing good phone support requires much more interaction with customers than any other type of PC support. To give clear instructions to the customer, you must be able to visualize what the customer is seeing at his or her PC. Customers may or may not have technical knowledge, and may be only slightly computer-literate. Patience is required if the customer must be told each key to type or command button to click. Help-desk support requires excellent communication skills, good phone manners, and lots of patience and empathy.

One important skill in help-desk support is learning to make few, if any, assumptions. It's important to have the caller check the very simplest things, such as making sure that the PC or monitor is plugged into a power source and making sure that cables are securely and correctly connected. As your help-desk skills improve, you will learn to think through the process just as though you were sitting in front of the PC yourself. Drawing diagrams and taking notes as you talk can be very helpful.

Depending on the scope of the computer hardware and software a help-desk supports, the kinds of calls you receive can fall within a limited range or can include a wide range of problems. If the range of problems is not too vast, documenting help-desk calls can be very helpful, especially if you organize your documentation in such a way that you can readily refer back to it the next time you need to address a similar problem. In your documentation, if you carefully record the problem's symptoms and what you did toward a solution, you can make a call can go very smoothly by simply following your own instructions created from past calls.

As with on-site service calls, give the user the opportunity to make sure that all is working before you close the call. If you terminate the call too soon and the problem is not completely resolved, it can be very frustrating to the customers, because it might be difficult to get you back on the line.

If you spend long hours on the phone at a help-desk, use a headset instead of a regular phone. Your ears and neck will greatly benefit. Learn how to use your telephone system well, so that you don't accidentally disconnect someone. If you are accidentally disconnected, call back immediately. Don't eat or drink while on the phone. If you must put callers on hold, tell them how long it will be before you get back to them. When the call is over, wait for the caller to hang up first. Don't complain about your job, about your company, or about other companies or products to your customers. A little small talk is okay and is sometimes beneficial in easing a tense situation, but keep it upbeat and positive.

LEARNING TO BE A BETTER COMMUNICATOR

Most people assume they are good communicators—that others understand what they are saying and that they in turn understand others. However, learning to be a good communicator begins with understanding that everyone has room for improvement. Almost anyone can improve his or her communications skills by following some specific guidelines; this section presents those guidelines as they apply to PC support technicians. For the PC technician, on-the-job training often involves only technical training, and communication skills are not included. Yet, without good communication skills, even a good technician won't be able to effectively deliver his or her support. Customers often form their opinion of your organization on the basis of the way you communicate with them.

Communicating on the Phone

When someone calls asking for help-desk support, you must control the call, especially at the beginning. Follow these steps at the beginning of a service call.

- Identify yourself and your organization. (Follow the guidelines of your employer as to what to say.)

- Ask for and write down the name and phone number of the caller. Ask for spelling if necessary. If your help-desk supports businesses, get the name of the business that the caller represents.

- Your company might require that you obtain a licensing or warrantee number to determine if the customer is entitled to receive your support free of charge, or that you obtain a credit card number, if the customer is paying by the call. Get whatever information you need at this point to determine that you should provide service before you continue by addressing the problem. It might be necessary to

18

refer the call to someone else in the organization, such as a customer service representative.

- Open the conversation up for the caller to describe his or her problem.

Be certain to get a caller's name down correctly, and use that name correctly as you speak. You must have a phone number in case you are disconnected during the call or need to call back later. As a caller describes his or her problem, listen carefully, focus on the call, and don't allow yourself to be distracted.

Show Concern for the Customer's Situation

Empathy goes a long way toward successful communication. Put yourself in the customer's situation and express your concern for his or her problem, so that the customer no longer feels alone in the situation. Another way of saying this is that you should take ownership of the problem. It was just the customer's problem, but now it's the customer's problem and it's also your problem. Ways to communicate that attitude are saying things like, "I understand." "You've really had it rough!" "That's terrible." "I know you must be frustrated." "I'm sorry you're having such a hard time."

Express Confidence

Someone asking for your help, either on-site, on a phone call, or in a repair shop, wants and needs you to express confidence as you communicate. Confidence does not mean that you always have the answers, but you should convey the attitude that if you don't have the answer, you can and will direct them to those who do. Ways to communicate this to your customer are:

- Speak calmly.

- Ask questions in a systematic way. A good way to do this is to have a list of questions written down to refer to.

- Take your time and pause when necessary. Don't allow the urgency of a situation to fluster you.

- Plan ahead how you will handle a situation in which you don't know what to do. For example, you can say, "Excuse me while I check with my coworkers," or you can say, "I've got to research this; I'll get back to you shortly." Be sure to say exactly when you will call back or return to the customer's desk.

- Don't be defensive about the software or hardware you are supporting, or about your own degree of knowledge or experience.

- Adjust to the level of technical ability your customer has. Don't talk down to the customer, but also don't use terms and expressions that the customer will not understand.

Handling Difficult Situations

Be prepared to handle difficult situations when communicating with a customer on the phone or face to face. Here are a few guidelines.

When the Customer Is Not Knowledgeable.   A help-desk call is the most difficult situation to handle when a customer is not knowledgeable about how to use a computer. When on-site, you can put a PC in good repair without depending on a customer to help you, but when trying to solve a problem over the phone with a customer as your only eyes, ears, and hands, a computer-illiterate user can present a very challenging situation. Here are some tips as to how to handle this situation.

- Don't use computer jargon while talking. Describe things in a way that the customer can understand. For example, instead of saying, "Open File Manager," say, "Do you see the yellow filing cabinet that has File Manager written underneath? Using your left mouse button, double-click on it."

- Don't ask the customer to do something that might destroy settings or files, without first having him or her back them up carefully. If you think the customer can't handle what you need done, then ask for some on-site help.

- Frequently ask the customer what he or she sees on the screen, to help you track the keystrokes and action.

- Follow along at your own PC. It's easier to direct the customer, keystroke by keystroke, if you are doing the same things.

- Give the customer plenty of opportunity to ask questions.

- Compliment the customer whenever you can, to help the customer gain confidence.

- If you determine that the customer is not able to help you solve the problem without a great amount of coaching, you may need to request that the caller have someone with more experience call you. Do this in a tactful manner, using expressions such as, "I think I need to discuss your problem with your on-site technical support. Could you have him or her call me?" This might become necessary if your or the customer's time is valuable, and you simply cannot take the extra time that is required to guide him or her through each step that needs to be done.

When the Customer Is Overly Confident.   Sometimes a customer is proud of what he or she knows about computers and wants to give advice, take charge of a call, withhold information that he or she judges that you don't need to know, or execute commands at the computer without sharing them with you, so that you don't have enough information to follow along. A situation like this must be handled with tact and respect for the customer. Here are a few tips.

- When you can do so, compliment the customer concerning his or her knowledge, experience, or insight. Let the customer know that you respect what he or

18

she knows. If the customer does not feel that he or she must prove or establish his or her knowledge, then it is much easier for the customer to relax and be more helpful.

- Ask the customer's advice. Say something like, "What do you think the problem is?" Do this for two reasons. First, to let customers know that you respect their knowledge, and second, because they might have the answer.

- Slow the conversation down. You can say, "Please slow down. You're moving too fast for me to follow. Help me understand."

- Don't back off from using the problem-solving skills you know how to practice. You must still have the customer check the simple things, but direct the conversation with tact. For example, you can say, "I know you've probably already gone over these simple things, but could we just do them again together?"

- Be very careful not to accuse the customer of making a mistake.

- Use technical language in a way that conveys that you expect the customer to understand you.

When the Customer Complains.   Many times when you are on-site or on the phone, a customer will complain to you about your organization, your computer, your service, or the service and product of another company. Studies have shown that a dissatisfied customer who complains is more likely to continue to use your product or service than a dissatisfied customer who does not let you know. Consider the complaint to be helpful feedback that can lead to a better product or service and better customer relationships. A PC support person is expected to handle these complaints in a professional manner. Here are a few suggestions on to how to do that.

- Listen to the complaint. Consider it valuable feedback.

- Remember that a genuine, empathic apology for whatever the customer has experienced can be very helpful. See if that allows you to move on to solving the problem. If it does, don't spend a lot of time finding out exactly whom the customer dealt with and what exactly happened to upset him or her.

- Don't be defensive. Everyone and every company makes mistakes. It's better to leave the customer with the impression that you and your company are listening and willing to admit mistakes and learn from them than to defend yourself, your product, or your company.

- Empathize with the customer. Show that you are concerned about the problem.

- If the customer is complaining about a product or service that is not from your company, don't start off by saying, "That's not our problem." Instead, listen to the customer complain. Don't appear as though you don't care.

- If the complaint is against you or your product, identify the underlying problem if you can. Ask questions and take notes. Then pass these notes on to whoever in your organization needs to know. The complaint might be used to improve the product or service.

When the Customer Is Angry.   I once worked as the fourth and final level of support at a help-desk. When calls arrived at my desk, three tiers of support under me had already given up. The customer was at the highest level of frustration and impatience. In a situation like this, if the customer is also angry, special consideration must be given. Allow the customer to be angry. You might be angry, too, in a similar situation. Listen carefully to what the customer is saying. Ask questions. Be an active listener, and let the customer know that he or she is not being ignored. Look for the underlying problem and take notes if the customer is also complaining. Stay calm. Don't take the anger personally. Give the customer a little time to vent, and apologize when you can. Then start the conversation from the beginning, asking questions, taking notes, and problem solving. When the customer realizes that you are helping, doing your best, respecting his or her needs, and solving the problem, the anger will subside.

When the Customer Does Not Want to End a Phone Call.   Some customers like to talk and don't want to end a phone call. In this situation, when you have finished the work and are ready to hang up, you can ease the caller into the end of the call by doing these things:

- Ask if there is anything that needs more explanation.

- Briefly summarize the main points of the call, and then say something like, "That about does it. Call if you need more help."

- Be silent about new issues. Answer only with "yes" or "no." Don't take the bait by engaging in a new topic.

- Don't get frustrated. As a last resort, you can say, "I'm sorry, but I must go now."

When a Customer Is Beginning to Get Upset.   When you sense that a customer is beginning to get angry or upset, try these things to control the situation and get things back on track.

- If you have made a mistake, admit it and apologize.

- Apologize for the situation even if you don't think you're at fault.

- Summarize what you have both agreed on or observed so far in the conversation. In so doing, you are establishing and reinforcing points of agreement.

- Point out ways that you think communication could be improved. For example, you might say, "I'm sorry, but I'm having trouble understanding what you want. Could you please slow down, and let's take this one step at a time."

- Reassure the customer that you will work on the problem until it is solved.

18

WHEN YOU CAN'T SOLVE THE PROBLEM

You are not going to be able to solve every computer problem you encounter. It's important to have a plan as to what you'll do when you have run out of ideas and things to try. Knowing how to escalate a problem to those higher in the support chain is one of the first things you should learn on a new job. Each organization will have procedures in place as to how to do this, and it is essential that you familiarize yourself with your company's specific escalation policies and procedures. When escalation involves the customer, generally follow these guidelines:

- Before you escalate, first ask knowledgeable coworkers for suggestions toward solving the problem, which might save you and your customer the time and effort it takes to escalate.

- Know your company's policy as to how to escalate. What documents do you fill out? Who gets them? Do you remain the responsible "support" party, or does the person now addressing the problem become the new contact? Are you expected to still keep in touch with the customer and the problem, or are you totally out of the picture?

- Document the escalation. In the documentation, describe the problem as clearly as you can while keeping the description brief and concise. Engineers and other support personnel are normally very busy people and don't have the time to read long pages of information, but they also don't have the time to investigate for information that you already knew but failed to pass on.

- Pass the problem on according to the proper channels of your organization. This might mean a phone call, an online entry in a database, or an e-mail message.

- Tell the customer that you are passing the problem on to someone who is more experienced and has access to more extensive resources. Let the customer know when he or she should expect this new support person to call. In most cases, the person who receives the escalation will immediately contact the customer and assume responsibility for the problem. However, you should follow through, at least to the point where you know that the new person and the customer have made contact.

- If you check back with the customer only to find out that the other support person has not called or followed through to the customer's satisfaction, don't lay blame or point fingers. Just do whatever you can within your company guidelines to help. Your call to the customer will go a long way toward helping in the situation.

RECORDKEEPING AND INFORMATION TOOLS

Most service organizations have many of the tools you will need to do your job, including forms, online recordkeeping, procedures, and manuals. In some cases, help-desk support personnel may have software to help them do their jobs, such as programs that support the remote control of customers' PCs (one example is pcANYWHERE), an online help utility, or a problem-solving tool developed specifically for their help-desk.

There are several types of resources, records, and information tools that can help you with your work. These include:

- *Copies of software or hardware you are expected to support*: Specific software or hardware that you support must be available to you to test, observe, and study, and to use to recreate a customer's problem whenever possible.

- *User documentation*: You should have a copy of the same documentation that the user sees and be familiar with it.

- *Technical documentation*: Products, including both hardware and software, will likely have more technical documentation than just a user manual. This technical documentation should be made available to you by a company when you support its product.

- *Online help*: Online help targeted specifically to field technicians and help-desk technicians is often available. This online help will probably include a search engine that works by topics, words, error messages, and the like. An additional feature of some online help software is the ability for support personnel to write annotations directly into the online text, so that they and other technicians can benefit from new information gained. Some organizations have one or more persons whose sole responsibility is to keep this online help current.

- *Expert systems*: Expert systems software is designed and written to help solve problems. It uses databases of known facts and rules to simulate human experts' reasoning and decision-making processes. Expert systems for PC technicians work by posing questions about a problem, to be answered either by the technician or by the customer. The response to each question will trigger another question from the software, until the expert system arrives at a possible solution or solutions. Many expert systems are "intelligent," meaning that the system will record your input and use it in subsequent sessions to select more questions to ask and things to try. Expert systems are fun to use and develop, and they can be wonderful assets in a support organization.

- *Call tracking*: Call tracking can be done online or on paper. Most organizations will have a call-tracking system that tracks (1) the date, time, and length of help-desk or on-site calls, (2) causes and solutions to problems already addressed, (3) who did what, and when, and (4) how each call was officially resolved. Call-tracking software or documents can also be vehicles used to escalate calls when necessary and to track the escalation. In addition, if an organization knows who its customers are (for example, who the registered users of its software are), this information will probably be made available to the call-tracking system. For small organizations, you might have to develop your own call-tracking system.

18

TRACKING SERVICE CALLS AND HELP-DESK CALLS

Sometimes an organization will already have documents for tracking service calls, help-desk calls, and work done by bench technicians. The main goal of these records may be to determine how much to charge a customer or how personnel spends its time. However, keeping your own records of what you have done as a PC technician can help you in several ways. By developing your own personal records or by using what is already in place at your company, you can become more responsible for the outcome of your work and its future direction. Good support records can help you do the following:

- Determine how you spend your time, what you work on the most, and what common problems you consistently see

- Solve future problems, because you have a record of what happened the last time you encountered a similar problem

- Project where you need training or information

- Discover patterns that can help you identify what preventive maintenance or user training could be done to help prevent recurring problems

Keep records of service calls, help-desk calls, or work that is brought into your shop. Occasionally take the time to sit down and review these records; look for patterns, trends, and other insights that can help you redirect your focus or do your job better. Below are some suggestions for this reporting, but if your employer already has a tool, use it—and, by all means, if these suggestions don't fit your situation, revise them so that they do. Note that these forms are not designed to be used to track charges and payments, customer information needed for billing, or time reporting. Their sole purpose is to help you, the technician, track your work so that you can do a better job.

You might want to track this information in a database or spreadsheet on a computer, rather than on single sheets of paper. However, the disadvantage of using a computer is that you may not have access to the computer when you are working at a customer site or even at a workbench. When you are working at a help-desk, a computerized recordkeeping system might be appropriate, if you are not already using your PC for a variety of other tasks while handling the call, as is often the case at a help-desk.

Some professional technicians find it helpful to attach a label to the inside of a PC cover that they have serviced. The technician puts a brief statement about the service, the date, and his or her name on the label. If the PC ever comes back into the shop, the label gives the technician enough information to cross-reference past service to more detailed documentation kept on file in the shop. The label can also be helpful to other technicians who later service the PC.

But whatever method you choose to use, it's important to keep a well-organized log of all service work you do. This is especially important when warranties are involved. When a customer calls you back after service, even if it's a year or more later, you should be able to easily locate your records of what happened when he or she came to you for service.

Form to Track a Service Call

A form to track a service call is shown in Figure 18-1. The form is designed to track the initial information taken over the phone, so that you can take it with you to the call, and be prepared when you get on-site. The first two blocks on the form—Initial Request and Initial Action—should be filled out when the call is first received. The last part of the form can be filled out at the end of the service call, preferably before you leave the site, while all is still fresh in your mind. You might want to include a second page on the form for taking notes as you work, or you can use the back of the form. On the form, you will want to be certain that you get an accurate description of the initial symptoms that precipitated the call, a clear description of the underlying problem, and what was done to solve it. This information is the heart of the reason you're keeping the record—to help you identify and solve similar problems in the future.

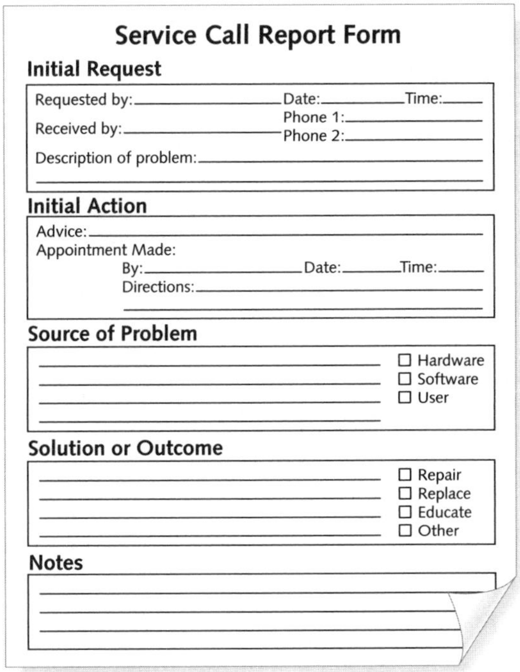

Service Call Report Form

Initial Request

Requested by: ______ Date: ______ Time: ______
Received by: ______ Phone 1: ______ Phone 2: ______
Description of problem: ______

Initial Action

Advice: ______
Appointment Made:
By: ______ Date: ______ Time: ______
Directions: ______

Source of Problem

☐ Hardware
☐ Software
☐ User

Solution or Outcome

☐ Repair
☐ Replace
☐ Educate
☐ Other

Notes

Figure 18-1 Service Call Report Form

Form to Track a Help-Desk Call

Help-desk calls can be less stressful than on-site calls, and can free you to keep better records while the work is in progress. Keep a pad of reporting forms on your desk and fill out the form as you are talking with the customer. Since help-desks are usually focused on a particular system or customer group, the form can probably be customized, too. The form in Figure 18-2 is generic, and you will probably want to revise it to suit your individual work. Since many help-desk calls result in one or more follow-up calls, room for the follow-up calls is included. Remember that when someone calls your help desk, you must stay in control, especially at the beginning of the call, long enough to get the vital information you need to handle the call, including the customer's full name, location (if appropriate), phone number, and brief description of the problem. Then, as you proceed with the call, take notes.

Again, the challenge is to not allow the call to go so hurriedly that you don't have time to write down what is happening—or later you won't be able to make sense of your notes! However, don't frustrate the caller by requiring too much time for taking notes, although some time is necessary.

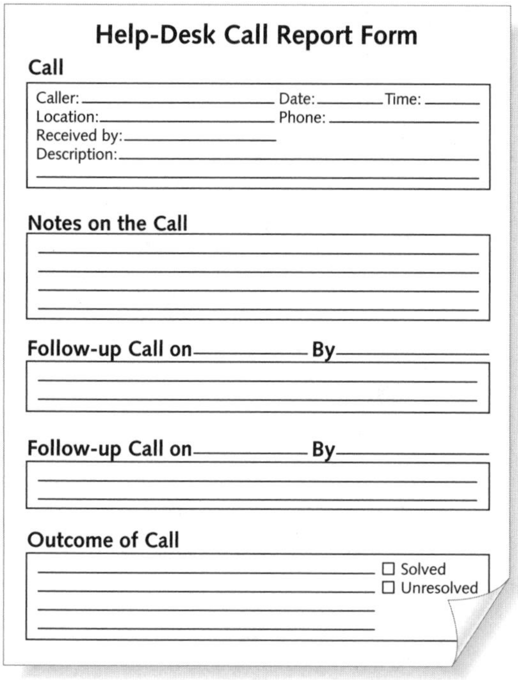

Figure 18-2 Help-Desk Call Report Form

When the call is completed, fill out the last part of the form, Outcome of the Call. Put in your notes what you did or said that resolved the problem, or why the problem is not resolved. By comparing these notes to the description of the problem at the top of the form, over a period of time, you will see patterns emerge that can help you come to some conclusions and solve future problems that are similar.

Form to Track Work Coming into Your Shop

If you are a shop owner, or the manager of a PC repair shop, you will, most likely, be responsible for designing intake and processing forms to handle services, charges, billing, and payments on work that comes to your shop. This business-oriented recordkeeping is beyond the scope of this chapter. However, as a repair technician, you will want a method or form to track the actual work done in such a way as to help you perform your work better. The purpose of the form shown in Figure 18-3 is to track one thing—the work done—so as to have a record of problems, their causes, and solutions, which can help you establish trends to make future work easier. The form can also be used to track when a customer is notified to pick up equipment, and when equipment is actually picked up. Including the customer's work and home phone numbers makes it convenient to call the customer to ask a question or get permission to perform the work, if necessary.

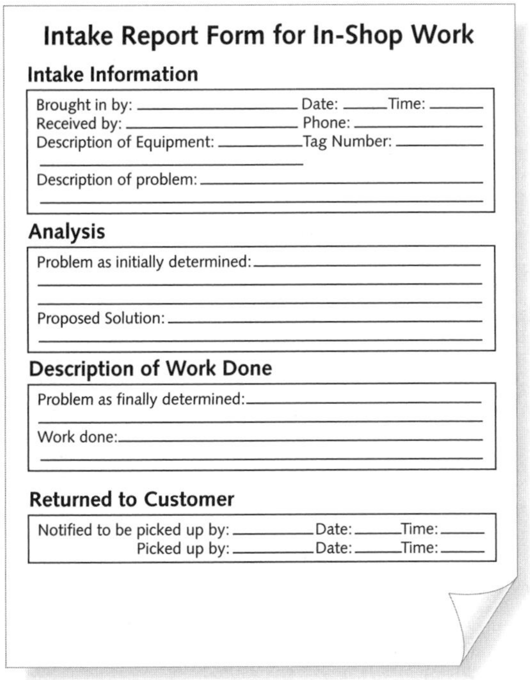

Intake Report Form for In-Shop Work

Intake Information

Brought in by: ______ Date: ______ Time: ______
Received by: ______ Phone: ______
Description of Equipment: ______ Tag Number: ______
Description of problem: ______

Analysis

Problem as initially determined: ______
Proposed Solution: ______

Description of Work Done

Problem as finally determined: ______
Work done: ______

Returned to Customer

Notified to be picked up by: ______ Date: ______ Time: ______
Picked up by: ______ Date: ______ Time: ______

Figure 18-3 Intake Report Form for In-Shop Work

Professional Organizations and Certifications

The work done by PC technicians has been viewed as a profession only within the past few years, and, as with other budding professions, professional organizations and certifications take a while to develop and to become recognized by the industry. The one most significant certifying organization for PC technicians is the **Computing Technology Industry Association** (**CompTIA**, pronounced "comp-tee-a"). CompTIA sponsors the A+ Certification Program, including managing the A+ Service Technician Certification Examination, which measures the knowledge of job tasks and behaviors expected of entry-level technicians. To become certified, you must pass two test modules: the core test and one of two other specialty tests, either for Microsoft Windows or for the Macintosh operating system. This book is designed to fully prepare you for the A+ Certification core test and Microsoft Windows specialty test. A+ Certification is gaining increasing industry recognition, so it should be your first choice for certification as a PC technician. As evidence of this industry recognition, these companies now include A+ Certification in their requirements for employment:

- Compaq Computer Corporation requires that all work done under its warranty agreements be done by A+ Certified personnel.

- Digital Equipment Corporation requires A+ Certification for all international and domestic warranty work.

- Entex Information Services requires that all service employees have A+ Certification.

- GE Capital Services requires that all service employees have A+ Certification one year after hire.

- InaCom requires A+ Certification as a core competency for all service providers.

- Okidata requires that all field service technicians have A+ Certification.

- Packard Bell requires all employees to be certified within 90 days of hire.

Some other companies where A+ Certification is mandatory are:

- Aetna U.S. Healthcare

- BancTec, Inc.

- Computer Data, Inc.

- Computer Sciences Corp.

- Delta Airlines

- Dow Jones & Company

- FBI, U.S. Department of Justice

- Gateway 2000

- New Horizons

- Tandy Corporation

- TSS IBM

- USAir

- Vanstar

- Wang

CompTIA has over 6,000 members that include every major company that manufacturers, distributes, or publishes computer-related products and services. For more information about CompTIA and A+ Certification, see the CompTIA Web site at www.comptia.org.

WHY CERTIFICATION?

Many people work as PC technicians without any formal classroom training or certification. However, by having certification or an advanced technical degree, you prove to yourself, your customers, and your employers that you are prepared to do the work and are committed to being educated in your chosen profession. Here are some reasons for seeking certification and advanced degrees:

- They are recognized proof of competence and achievement.

- They improve your job opportunities.

- They create a higher level of customer confidence.

- They often qualify you for other training and/or degrees.

STAYING ABREAST OF NEW TECHNOLOGY

In addition to becoming certified and seeking advanced degrees, the professional PC technician should also stay abreast of new technology. With the ever-changing technology of today, this can be quite a challenge. Resources that help include: on-the-job training, books, magazines, the Internet, trade shows, interaction with colleagues, seminars, and workshops. Some magazines that routinely include excellent articles explaining new technology in detail are *PC Magazine, PC Today, Computer Shopper, PC Computing,* and *PC World.* Probably the best-known trade show is COMDEX and Windows World, where you can view the latest technology, hear industry leaders speak, and network with vast numbers of organizations and people. For more information about COMDEX and Windows World, see the Web site www.comdex.com.

Throughout this book you'll find references to Web sites for more information about a particular technology. In addition, try the Web sites listed in Table 18-1 for excellent up-to-date technical information about PCs:

Table 18-1   Technical support Web sites

Web Site	Responsible Organization
www.aserve.net	Advanced Services Network
www.byte.com	BYTE Magazine
www.cnet.com	CNET.Inc.
www.cybercollege.com	CyberCollege
www.datafellows.com	Data Fellows Inc.
www.disktrend.com	DISK/TREND, Inc.
www.modems.com	Zoom Telephonics, Inc.
www.pc-today.com	PC Today Online
www.pcwebopedia.com	Sandy Bay Software, Inc.

18

Table 18-1 Technical support Web sites (continued)

Web Site	Responsible Organization
www.pcworld.com	PC World
www.sangoma.com	Sangoma Technologies, Inc.
www.sysdoc.com	Tom's Hardware Guide
www.tcp.ca	The Computer Paper
www.windows95.com	Steve Jenkins and Jenesys, LLC.
www.zdnet.com	ZDNet

Staying up-to-date concerning new technology begins with an attitude and commitment to self-improvement. Your education is primarily your own responsibility, and only secondarily the responsibility of your employer. Take advantage of opportunities presented by your employer for training, but remember that a personal commitment to continue to learn is more important than any training program offered by your employer.

PROTECTING SOFTWARE COPYRIGHTS

As a computer support technician, you will be faced with the legal issues and practices surrounding the distribution of software. When someone purchases software from a software vendor, that person has only purchased the right to *use* the software, but does not legally *own* the software, and therefore does not have the right to distribute the software. A professional PC technician should understand and follow the laws that apply to the sale and distribution of software.

As a PC technician you will be called upon to install, upgrade, and customize software. You need to know where your responsibility lies in upholding the law especially as it applies to software copyright. **Copyright** is intended to legally protect the intellectual property rights of organizations or individuals to creative works, whether they be books, images, or, in the case of this discussion, software. While the original owner of a copyright is the originator of a creative work, copyright can be transferred from one entity to another.

The Federal Copyright Act of 1976 was designed in part to protect **software copyrights** by requiring that only legally obtained copies of software be used; the law also allows for one backup copy of software to be made. Making unauthorized copies of original software violates the Federal Copyright Act of 1976, and is called **software piracy**, or, more officially, software copyright infringement. Making a copy of software and then selling it or giving it away are both violations of the law. Because it is so easy to do this, and because so many people do it, many people don't realize that they're breaking the law. Normally only the person who violated the copyright law is liable for infringement; however, in some cases, an employer or supervisor is also held responsible, even when the copies were made without the employer's knowledge. The Business Software Alliance (a membership organization of software manufacturers and vendors) has estimated that 26% of the business software in the United States is obtained illegally and that, in 1995, the worldwide illegal use of software cost the software industry more than $13 billion.

Vendors may sometimes sell counterfeit software by installing unauthorized software on computers for sale. This practice is called **hard-disk loading**. Vendors have even been known to counterfeit disk labels and Certificates of Authenticity. Warning signs that software purchased from vendors is pirated include:

- No end-user license is included.

- There is no mail-in product registration card.

- Software is installed on a new PC, but documentation and original disks are not included in the package.

- Documentation is photocopied, or disks have handwritten labels.

Several technological methods have been attempted to prevent people from making copies of software. These methods include making distribution disks copy-resistant and putting holographic images on software packages. Nontechnical methods include stiffer fines and sentences for infringement and more aggressive lawsuits.

In the past few years, site licensing, whereby a company can purchase the rights to use multiple copies of software, has grown in popularity. There are many ways that software is licensed today in order to accommodate the growing demands of companies that distribute software to PCs from network servers or execute software directly off the server. Read the licensing agreement of any software to determine the terms of distribution.

One of two associations committed to the prevention of software piracy is the Software Publishers Association, a nonprofit organization that educates the public and enforces copyright laws. Their Web address is www.spa.org, and their antipiracy hotline is 1-800-388-7478. Another organization is the Business Software Alliance, which manages the BSA Anti-Piracy Hotline at 1-888-NOPIRACY. The BSA can also be reached at their e-mail address: software@bsa.org. Their Web site is www.bsa.org. These associations are made up of hundreds of software manufacturers and publishers in North and Latin America, Europe, and Asia. They are promoting software raids on large and small companies, and, in the U.S., are receiving the cooperation of the United States government to prosecute offenders.

WHAT DOES THE LAW SAY?

The Federal Copyright Act of 1976 protects the exclusive rights of copyright holders. It gives legal users the right to make one backup copy. Other rights are based on what the copyright holder allows. Employers can be held liable when employees make illegal copies of software, with or without the employer's knowledge. In 1990, the United States Congress passed the Software Rental Amendment Act, which prevents the renting, leasing, lending, or sharing of software without the expressed written permission of the copyright holder. In 1992, Congress instituted criminal penalties for software copyright infringement, which include imprisonment for up to five years and/or fines of up to $250,000, for the unlawful reproduction or distribution of 10 or more copies of software. In short, it is illegal for a person to give an unauthorized copy of software to another individual, even if they both work for the same organization.

18

WHAT ARE YOUR RESPONSIBILITIES TO THE LAW?

Your first responsibility as an individual user is to use only software that has been purchased or licensed for your use. As an employee of a company that has a site license to use multiple copies of the software, your responsibility is to comply with the license agreement, whatever that is. It is also your responsibility to purchase only legitimate software. Purchasers of counterfeit or copied software face the risk of corrupted files, virus-infected disks, inadequate documentation, lack of technical support and upgrades, as well as the legal penalties for using pirated software.

CHAPTER SUMMARY

- Customers want and expect more than just technical proficiency from a PC technician.

- Customers expect a technician to keep a positive and helpful attitude, to remain professional at all times, and to put the needs of the customer above all else.

- A PC technician is expected to respond to a call for service within a reasonable time, to be prepared for the service call, and to do the work right the first time.

- Good communication skills are important attributes of a PC technician.

- A PC technician is a guest at the customer site and should act like a guest.

- Keeping records of service calls, help-desk calls, and bench work is important to identifying trends and the need for training or information, and to helping with future problem solving.

- When tracking a service call, phone call, or bench work, always record the symptoms, the originating problem, and the solution. This information will help in future problem solving.

- CompTIA (Computing Technology Industry Association) sponsors A+ Certification, the industry-accepted certification for the PC technician.

- Staying abreast of new technology can be done by attending trade shows, reading trade magazines, researching on the Internet, and attending seminars and workshops.

- Software piracy—the use of software obtained in violation of the copyright owner's specific terms—is against the law. A professional PC technician is committed to not using or installing pirated software.

- The Business Software Alliance and the Software Publishers Association are two associations committed to controlling software piracy.

KEY TERMS

- **A+ Certification** — A certification awarded by CompTIA (The Computing Technology Industry Association) that measures a PC technician's knowledge of the skills and behaviors expected of entry-level PC technicians. Many companies require that their service technicians have A+ Certification.

- **Call tracking** — A system that tracks the dates, times, and transactions of help-desk or on-site PC support calls, including the problem presented, the issues addressed, who did what, and when and how each call was resolved.

- **Computing Technology Industry Association (CompTIA)** — A membership trade association that sponsors A+ Certification, a valuable certification for PC technicians.

- **Escalating** — The process of a technician passing a customer's problem to higher organizational levels, if he or she cannot address the problem.

- **Expert systems** — Computerized software that uses a database of known facts and rules to simulate a human expert's reasoning and decision-making processes.

- **Hard-disk loading** — The illegal practice of installing unauthorized software on computers for sale. Hard-disk loading can typically be identified by the absence of original disks in the original system's shipment.

- **Holographic images** — A three-dimensional image (created by holography) that is made up of a light interference pattern preserved in a medium such as photographic film and which changes when the angle of view changes. Because making unofficial copies of holographic images is extremely difficult, they are often used to tag products, such as software packages, as original, making it difficult to distribute illegal copies.

- **Software copyrights** — Copyright is a legal concept (covered by the Federal Copyright Act of 1976) that encompasses the protection of the rights of an originator of a creative work, which can include software. With the exception of archival backups, copyrighted programs are illegal to copy without specific authorization from the copyright holder.

- **Software piracy** — Making unauthorized copies of original copyrighted software.

- **Technical documentation** — The technical reference manuals, included with software packages and peripherals, that provide directions for installation, usage, and troubleshooting.

- **User documentation** — Manuals, online documentation, instructions, and tutorials designed specifically for the user.

18

REVIEW QUESTIONS

1. Assume that you are a customer who wants to have a personal computer repaired. List five main characteristics that you would want to see in your PC repairperson.

2. List and briefly discuss five practices that should be followed to make a technician a better customer-oriented service person.

3. What is one thing you should do when you receive a phone call requesting on-site support, before you make an appointment?

4. What can you do if you cannot make an on-site call in a manner that is considered timely to the client?

5. You make an appointment to do an on-site repair, but you are detained and find out that you will be late. What is the best thing to do?

6. When you arrive for an on-site service call, how important is your greeting? What would be a good greeting to start off a good business relationship?

7. When making an on-site service call, what should you do before making any changes to software, or before taking the case off a computer?

8. What should you do after finishing your PC repair?

9. What would be a good strategy to follow if a conflict arises between you and your customer?

10. Why is it wise to make a follow-up telephone call to a customer after the repair is done?

11. When someone calls your help-desk, what is the first thing you should do?

12. What is one thing you can do to help a caller who needs phone support and is not a competent computer user?

13. Describe what you should do when a customer complains to you about a product or service that your company provides.

14. What are some things you can do to make your work at a help-desk easier?

15. What is one printed source that you can use to stay abreast of new technology?

16. Why is it important to be a certified technician?

17. Examine the software license of some software currently installed on your PC. Is it legal to have this software installed on your PC at work and also installed on your PC at home?

18. List three things to check when you are considering the purchase of software to know that the software is not pirated.

19. What two associations educate and protect against software piracy?

20. What organization offers PC technician certification?

PROJECTS

A+ CERTIFICATION

Go to CompTIA's Web site, www.comptia.org, and print out sample test questions for the A+ Certification exam. Include questions from the core test and one of the two operating system sample tests. Answer the questions for these sample tests. On the basis of the sample test, how prepared do you think you are to take the A+ exam?

PRACTICING HELP-DESK SKILLS

Work with a partner. One of you play the role of the customer, and the other the role of the help-desk technician. The customer calls, saying, "My computer won't work." The technician should lead the conversation by asking questions. Ask the appropriate questions to determine exactly what the problem is, and then check all cable connections for PC, monitor, mouse, keyboard, and power. Write down the questions you ask, using the form in this chapter for tracking a help-desk call. (Don't forget to ask the customer's name, phone number, and so on.)

CUSTOMER RELATIONSHIPS

Work in a small discussion group of three to four people. Come prepared by writing a paragraph describing the worst situation in which you might realistically be found when servicing a PC. Read the paragraph to the group. Have the group discuss what is the appropriate thing to do in this situation. Under the paragraph, write two column headings, Do and Don't. Write down the suggestions of the group for each column. For example, here is one sample paragraph for your discussion:

You respond to a customer call by traveling across town in heavy traffic to the customer's place of business. He insists that you arrive promptly that same day, even though the call didn't come until 4:00 pm. The customer told you on the phone that the PC would not boot. You had him check all connections and switches, over the phone, but all seemed well. When you get to the site, the customer is angry because you took so long arriving and threatens to report you. When you check the PC, you discover that the monitor cable is not plugged into the computer case. What do you say and do?

18

A SELF-STUDY OF NEW TECHNOLOGY

Select a new hardware or software feature or product and do a self-directed study of the subject. Use magazines, books, and the Internet. Collect the information in a file folder and let it be the first folder of many that you keep on new technology. Some suggestions for your study are:

- Digital cameras
- DVD technology
- Windows 98
- Windows NT 5.0

ILLEGAL SOFTWARE

1. Search in Windows 95 Help for ways to identify illegal Microsoft software. Print out the warning signs that might indicate that software installed on your newly purchased PC, or available on a retail store shelf, might be illegal.

2. If you believe you have unknowingly purchased illegal software, see the Software Publishers Association Web site at www.spa.org to find out what you can do about your situation.

INTERNET SEARCH

1. Log on to the Internet and do a Web search. Enter the key words PC+troubleshooting, and list and describe five of the sites found. Also enter the key words PC+certification, and list three sites found.

2. In the chapter under the heading, "Staying Abreast of New Technology," select three of the Web sites listed and access the sites. Write one paragraph for each site describing what type of technical information is available on the site to help a PC technician.

APPENDIX A: ERROR MESSAGES AND THEIR MEANINGS

The following table of error messages and their meanings can help when you are diagnosing computer problems.

Error Message	Meaning of the Error Message and What to Do
Bad sector writing or reading to drive	Sector markings on the disk may be fading. Try ScanDisk or reformat the disk.
Bad command or file not found	The DOS command just executed cannot be interpreted, or DOS cannot find the program file specified in the command line. Check the spelling of the filename and check that the path to the program file has been given to DOS.
Beeps during POST	Before the video is checked, during POST, the ROM BIOS communicates error messages with a series of beeps. Each BIOS manufacturer has its own beep codes, but the following are typical of many BIOS codes.
One single beep followed by 3, 4, or 5 beeps	Systemboard problems, possibly with DMA, CMOS setup chip, timer, or system bus
Two beeps	The POST numeric code is displayed on the monitor.
Two beeps followed by 3, 4, or 5 beeps	First 64K of RAM has errors.
Three beeps followed by 3, 4, or 5 beeps	Keyboard controller failed or video controller failed.
Four beeps followed by 2, 3, or 4 beeps	Serial or parallel ports, system timer, or time of day
Continuous beeps	Power supply
Configuration/CMOS error	Setup information does not agree with the actual hardware the computer found during boot. Check setup for errors.
Insufficient memory	This error happens under Windows when too many applications are open. Close some applications. A reboot may help.
Fixed disk error	The OS cannot locate the hard drive, or the controller card is not responding.
Hard drive not found	Computer cannot find the hard drive that setup told it to expect. Check cables, connections, and power supply.
Incorrect DOS version	You are attempting to use a DOS command such as FORMAT. When DOS looks at the FORMAT.COM program file, it finds that the file belongs to a different version of DOS than the one that is now running. Use the DOS software from the same version that you are running.

Appendix A   (Continued)

Error Message	Meaning of the Error Message and What to Do
Invalid drive specification	The computer is unable to find a hard drive or a floppy drive that setup tells it to expect. The hard drive may have a corrupted partition table.
Invalid or missing COMMAND.COM	This may be caused by a nonbooting disk in drive A. Remove the disk and boot from drive C. COMMAND.COM on drive C may have been erased.
No boot device available	The hard drive is not formatted, or the format is corrupted, and there is no disk in drive A. Boot from a floppy and examine your hard drive for corruption.
Non-system disk or disk error	COMMAND.COM or one of two DOS hidden files is missing from the disk in drive A or the hard drive. Remove the disk in drive A and boot from the hard drive.
Not ready reading drive A: Abort, Retry, Fail?	The disk in drive A is missing, is not formatted, or is corrupted. Try another disk.
Numeric codes during POST	Sometimes numeric codes are used to communicate errors at POST. Some examples include:
Code in the 100 range	Systemboard errors
Code in the 200 range	RAM errors
Code in the 300 range	Keyboard errors
Code in the 500 range	Video controller errors
Code in the 600 range	Floppy drive errors
Code in the 700 range	Coprocessor errors
Code in the 900 range	Parallel port errors
Code in the 1100-1200 range	Systemboard errors
Code in the 1300 range	Game controller or joystick errors
Code in the 1700 range	Hard drive errors
Code in the 6000 range	SCSI device or network card errors
Code in the 7300 range	Floppy drive errors
Track 0 bad, disk not usable	This usually occurs when you attempt to format a floppy disk using the wrong format type. Check the disk type and compare to the format command type specified.
Write-protect error writing drive A:	Let the computer write to the disk by setting the switch on a 3.5-inch disk or removing the tape on a 5.25-inch disk.

APPENDIX B: HARD DRIVE TYPES

As you remember, when you set up your system, you must tell it what hard drive type you are using. BIOS provides you a list of drive types to select from as well as the option of specifying a user-defined drive type. Unfortunately, this list is largely outdated because today's hard drives are much larger than any on the BIOS drive list, so the user-defined drive type is the optioned used most often today. Nonetheless, the BIOS of almost every PC continues to offer the same list of "old" drive types, and it is still helpful to understand where the list comes from and what it means. The first hard drive types were established by IBM and a list of them was first included in its BIOS for the IBM XT 286 computers in 1985. When a hard drive is installed on a microcomputer, setup is told the drive type, and this information is written to CMOS. The system BIOS then knows the logical layout of the hard drive. As the kinds of hard drives increased, so did the list of drive types. IBM later added more types to its list, and Compaq and other manufacturers introduced their own lists. Other companies writing BIOS also introduced their own lists.

At the bottom of the list of drive types, System BIOS offers a user the option to specify a user-defined hard drive type which can be used for larger drives. In most lists, this type is number 47 or 48. When you specify this type, you must tell setup the specifications of your drive, although some BIOS will autodetect the drive for you, so that you donít need to enter any information about the drive.

Following are two tables, the first listing drive types from the IBM BIOS list, and the second with drive types from the Phoenix BIOS list.

Table B-1   IBM Hard Drive Types

Drive Type	Tracks	Heads	Sectors Per Track	Write Precomp	Capacity (MB)
1	306	4	17	128	10
2	615	4	17	300	20
3	615	6	17	300	32
4	940	8	17	512	64
5	940	6	17	512	48
6	615	4	17	NONE	20
7	462	8	17	256	30
8	733	5	17	NONE	30
9	900	15	17	110	112
10	820	3	17	NONE	20
11	855	5	17	NONE	35
12	855	7	17	NONE	50
13	306	8	17	128	20
14	733	7	17	NONE	40
15	NOT USED				
16	612	4	17	0	20
17	977	5	17	300	40

Table B-1   IBM Hard Drive Types (Continued)

Drive Type	Tracks	Heads	Sectors Per Track	Write Precomp	Capacity (MB)
18	977	7	17	none	56
19	1024	5	17	512	60
20	733	5	17	300	30
21	733	7	17	300	42
22	733	5	17	300	30
23	306	4	17	0	10
24	612	4	17	305	21

Table B-2   Phoenix BIOS Drive Types

Drive Type	Tracks	Heads	Sectors Per Track	Write Precomp	Capacity (MB)
25	615	4	17	0	20
26	1024	4	17	none	35
27	1024	5	17	none	44
28	1024	8	17	none	70
29	512	8	17	256	35
30	615	2	17	615	10
31	989	5	17	0	42
32	1020	15	17	none	130
33	615	4	26	none	32
34	820	6	26	none	65
35	1024	9	17	1024	80
36	1024	5	17	512	44
37	1024	5	26	512	68
38	823	10	17	256	70
39	615	4	17	128	21
40	615	8	17	128	42
41	917	15	17	none	120
42	1023	15	17	none	132
43	823	10	17	512	71
44	820	6	17	none	42
45	1024	5	17	none	44
46	925	9	17	none	71
47	699	7	17	256	42
48	user-defined				

APPENDIX C: ASCII COLLATING SEQUENCE

ASCII (American Standard Code for Information Interchange) is a coding system that is used by personal computers to store character data, such as letters of the alphabet, numerals, some symbols, and certain control characters. There are 128 characters defined by the standard ASCII character set. Each ASCII character is assigned an 8-bit code that converts to a decimal number from 0 to 127. The first 31 values are used for control characters and can be used to send commands to a printer or other peripheral devices. Files that store data as ASCII characters are sometimes called ASCII files, ASCII text files, or simply text files. These files can be read by most editors and word processors and are considered the universal file format for personal computers. Autoexec.bat is one example of an ASCII file.

In addition to the standard ASCII character set, some manufacturers use an extended ASCII character set that is specific to their equipment and is not necessarily compatible with other computers. The extended ASCII character sets use the codes 128 through 255. The table below lists the standard ASCII character set. Note that items 2 through 32 are not included; these represent ASCII control characters that are used to communicate with peripheral devices.

Table C-1   Standard ASCII Character Set

Item Number	Symbol	Meaning	ASCII in Decimal Representation	ASCII in Binary Representation	ASCII in Hex Representation
1	.	Null	0	0000 0000	0
33.	b/	Space	32	0010 0000	20
34.	!	Exclamation point	33	0010 0001	21
35.	"	Quotation mark	34	0010 0010	22
36.	#	Number sign	35	0010 0011	23
37.	$	Dollar sign	36	0010 0100	24
38.	%	Percent sign	37	0010 0101	25
39.	&	Ampersand	38	0010 0110	26
40.	'	Apostrophe, prime sign	39	0010 0111	27
41.	(	Opening parenthesis	40	0010 1000	28
42.	)	Closing parenthesis	41	0010 1001	29
43.	*	Asterisk	42	0010 1010	2A
44.	+	Plus sign	43	0010 1011	2B
45.	,	Comma	44	0010 1100	2C
46.	-	Hyphen, Minus sign	45	0010 1101	2D
47.	.	Period, Decimal point	46	0010 1110	2E
48.	/	Slant	47	0010 1111	2F
49.	0		48	0011 0000	30
50.	1		49	0011 0001	31

Table C-1   Standard ASCII Character Set   (Continued)

Item Number	Symbol	Meaning	ASCII in Decimal Representation	ASCII in Binary Representation	ASCII in Hex Representation
51.	2		50	0011 0010	32
52.	3		51	0011 0011	33
53.	4		52	0011 0100	34
54.	5		53	0011 0101	35
55.	6		54	0011 0110	36
56.	7		55	0011 0111	37
57.	8		56	0011 1000	38
58.	9		57	0011 1001	39
59.	:	Colon	58	0011 1010	3A
60.	;	Semicolon	59	0011 1011	3B
61.	<	Less than sign	60	0011 1100	3C
62.	=	Equal sign	61	0011 1101	3D
63.	>	Greater than sign	62	0011 1110	3E
64.	?	Question mark	63	0011 1111	3F
65.	@	Commercial at sign	64	0100 0000	40
66.	A		65	0100 0001	41
67.	B		66	0100 0010	42
68.	C		67	0100 0011	43
69.	D		68	0100 0100	44
70.	E		69	0100 0101	45
71.	F		70	0100 0110	46
72.	G		71	0100 0111	47
73.	H		72	0100 1000	48
74.	I		73	0100 1001	49
75.	J		74	0100 1010	4A
76.	K		75	0100 1011	4B
77.	L		76	0100 1100	4C
78.	M		77	0100 1101	4D
79.	N		78	0100 1110	4E
80.	O		79	0100 1111	4F
81.	P		80	0101 0000	50
82.	Q		81	0101 0001	51
83.	R		82	0101 0010	52
84.	S		83	0101 0011	53

Table C-1   Standard ASCII Character Set   (Continued)

Item Number	Symbol	Meaning	ASCII in Decimal Representation	ASCII in Binary Representation	ASCII in Hex Representation
85.	T		84	0101 0100	54
86.	U		85	0101 0101	55
87.	V		86	0101 0110	56
88.	W		87	0101 0111	57
89.	X		88	0101 1000	58
90.	Y		89	0101 1001	59
91.	Z		90	0101 1010	5A
92.	[	Opening bracket	91	0101 1011	5B
93.	\	Reverse slant	92	0101 1100	5C
94.	]	Closing bracket	93	0101 1101	5D
95.	^	Caret	94	0101 1110	5E
96.	_	Underscore	95	0101 1111	5F
97.	'	Grave accent	96	0110 0000	60
98.	a		97	0110 0001	61
99.	b		98	0110 0010	62
100.	c		99	0110 0011	63
101.	d		100	0110 0100	64
102.	e		101	0110 0101	65
103.	f		102	0110 0110	66
104.	g		103	0110 0111	67
105.	h		104	0110 1000	68
106.	i		105	0110 1001	69
107.	j		106	0110 1010	6A
108.	k		107	0110 1011	6B
109.	l		108	0110 1100	6C
110.	m		109	0110 1101	6D
111.	n		110	0110 1110	6E
112.	o		111	0110 1111	6F
113.	p		112	0111 0000	70
114.	q		113	0111 0001	71
115.	r		114	0111 0010	72
116.	s		115	0111 0011	73
117.	t		116	0111 0100	74

C

Table C-1   Standard ASCII Character Set   (Continued)

Item Number	Symbol	Meaning	ASCII in Decimal Representation	ASCII in Binary Representation	ASCII in Hex Representation
118.	u		117	0111 0101	75
119.	v		118	0111 0110	76
120.	w		119	0111 0111	77
121.	x		120	0111 1000	78
122.	y		121	0111 1001	79
123.	z		122	0111 1010	7A
124.	{	Opening brace	123	0111 1011	7B
125.	|	Split vertical bar	124	0111 1100	7C
126.	}	Closing brace	125	0111 1101	7D
127.	~	Tilde	126	0111 1110	7E

APPENDIX D: THE HEXIDECIMAL NUMBER SYSTEM AND MEMORY ADDRESSING

Fundamental to understanding how computers work is understanding the number system and the coding system that computers use to store data and communicate with each other. Early attempts to invent an electronic computing device met with disappointing results as long as inventors tried to use our own decimal number system with the digits 0–9. No electronic device could be invented that would dependably hold 10 different numeric values. Attempts during the 1940s involved using vacuum tubes that held varying quantities of electrical charge. A very small charge would be a 1, a little more would be a 2, and so on up to 9, the strongest charge. Measuring the charge later to determine what number it represented just wasn't reliable, because the electrical charges fluctuated too much. Then John Atanasoff came up with the brilliant idea of not measuring the charge at all. He proposed using only two digits in the number system, one represented by the presence of a charge and one represented by the absence of a charge. The existing technology could handle that.

What number system only uses 2 digits? Invented by Ada Lovelace many years before, the binary number system uses only the two digits 0 and 1. Under Atanasoff's design, all numbers and other characters would be converted to this binary number system, and all storage, comparisons, and arithmetic would be done using it. Even today, this is one of the basic principles of computers. Every character or digit entered into a computer is first converted into a series of 0s and 1s. Many coding schemes and techniques have been invented to manipulate these 0s and 1s, affectionately called **bits** for binary digits.

The most widespread binary coding scheme for microcomputers, which is recognized as the microcomputer standard, is called the ASCII (American Standard Code for Information Interchange) coding system. (Appendix C lists the binary code for most of the characters used.) In ASCII, each character is assigned an 8-bit code called a **byte**. Table D-1 lists the terms used in the discussion of how numbers are stored in computers.

Table D-1   Computer Terminology

Term	Definition
bit	A numeral in the binary number system: a 0 or a 1
byte	8 bits
kilobyte	1,024 bytes, which is 2^{10}, which is often rounded to 1,000 bytes
megabyte	Either 1,024 kilobytes or 1,000 kilobytes, depending on what has come to be standard practice in different situations. For example, when calculating floppy disk capacities, 1 megabyte = 1,000 kilobytes. But when calculating hard drive capacity, traditionally, 1 megabyte = 1,024 kilobytes.
gigabyte	1,000 megabytes or 1024 megabytes, depending on what has come to be standard practice in different situations.
ASCII	Coding scheme used for microcomputers that assigns an 8-bit code to all characters and symbols
hex	Short for hexadecimal. A number system based on 16 values (called base 16), which is explained in detail below. Uses the sixteen numerals 0, 1, 2, 3, 4, 5, 6, 7, 8, 9, A, B, C, D, E, F.

Working with the binary number system is quite tedious for human beings, but working in the binary system is easy for computers. Therefore, a compromise arose. Human beings use the decimal system;

computers use the binary system. We meet somewhere in the middle with the hexadecimal number system (shortened to hex system). It is much easier for computers to convert binary numbers into hex numbers than into decimal, and it is much easier for human beings to read hex numbers than to read binary numbers.

LEARNING TO "THINK HEX"

One skill a knowledgeable computer support person must have is the ability to read hex numbers and convert hex to decimal and decimal to hex. One reason you might find this a complicated task is that you might not thoroughly understand the concept of place value as applied to any number system including our own decimal system. And so you begin there.

Your friend Joe, in Figure D-1, is a widget packer in the shipping department of the ACE Widget Co. Joe can ship single widgets, or he can pack them in boxes, cartons, crates, and truck loads. He packs widgets three to a box, and three boxes of widgets are packed into one carton. Three cartons of widgets are packed into one crate, and three crates of widgets will all fit into one truck load. He is not allowed to pack more widgets into boxes, cartons, crates, or truck loads than those specified. Neither is he allowed to send out a box, carton, crate, or truck load that is not completely filled.

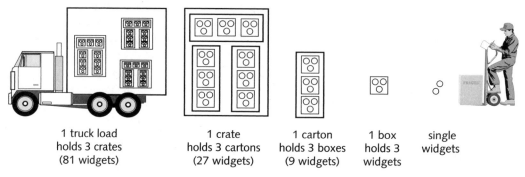

| 1 truck load holds 3 crates (81 widgets) | 1 crate holds 3 cartons (27 widgets) | 1 carton holds 3 boxes (9 widgets) | 1 box holds 3 widgets | single widgets |

Figure D-1   Joe in the shipping department

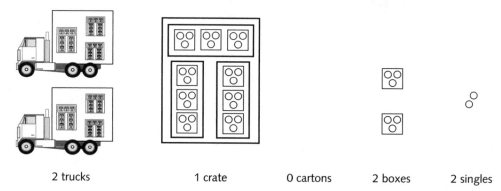

| 2 trucks | 1 crate | 0 cartons | 2 boxes | 2 singles |

Figure D-2   Joe's shipment of 197 widgets: 2 trucks, 1 crate, 0 cartons, 2 boxes, and a group of 2 singles

Joe receives an order to ship out 197 widgets. How does he ship them? The answer is shown in Figure D-2. Joe sends out 2 truck loads, 1 crate, no cartons, 2 boxes, and 2 single widgets for a total of 197 widgets. You have just converted the decimal number (base 10) 197 into the ternary number (base 3) 21022. Ternary numbers are grouped by 3s. The numerals in this number system are 0, 1, and 2. When

D

you get to the next value after 2, instead of counting on up to 3, you move one place value to the left and begin again with 1 in that position, which represents 3. In fact, whatever base you are working in, a one in each place value is equal to the base you are working in raised to a power. In the right-most place, the based is raised to the power of 0, in the next place over, the base is raised to the power of 1, in the next place over the base is raised to the power of 2, and so on. So, in base 3, a one in the right-most place is equal to 1×3^0 or 1, a one in the next position to the left is equal to 1×3^1 or 3, a one in the next position to the left is equal to 1×3^2 or 9, and so on. So, counting in base 3 goes like this: 0, 1, 2, 10, 11, 12, 20, 21, 22, 100, 101 and so on. Similarly in base 10, a one in the right-most place is equal to 1×10^0 or 1, a one in the next position to the left is equal to 1×10^1 or 10, a one in the next position to the left is equal to 1×10^2 or 100, and so on. And in base 16, or hexadecimal, a one in the right-most place is equal to 1×16^0 or 1, a one in the next position to the left is equal to 1×16^1 or 16, a one in the next position to the left is equal to 1×16^2 or 256, and so on. Because our system has only nine single-digit numerals, hexadecimal must use letters as well, as you will see below.

Now, back to Joe, who is really deciding how to pack widgets by counting in different number systems. Counting in different number systems is a matter of how you group values. How many units (or widgets) go in each group? In our decimal number system, we group by 10, probably because we all have 10 fingers. In the hex number system, we group by 16. If Joe were shipping in groups of 16, as in Figure D-3, single widgets could be shipped out up to 15, but 16 widgets would make one box. Sixteen boxes would make one carton, which would contain 16 * 16, or 256, widgets. Sixteen cartons would make one crate, which would contain 256 * 16, or 4,096, widgets.

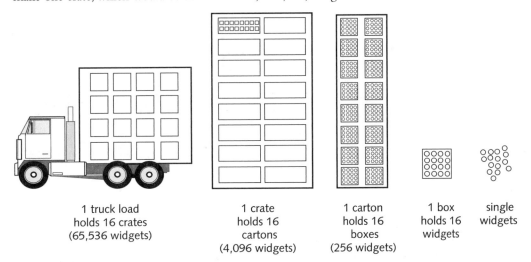

1 truck load	1 crate	1 carton	1 box	single
holds 16 crates	holds 16	holds 16	holds 16	widgets
(65,536 widgets)	cartons	boxes	widgets	
	(4,096 widgets)	(256 widgets)		

Figure D-3   Widgets displayed in truck loads, crates, cartons, boxes, and singles grouped in 16s

Suppose Joe receives an order for 197 widgets to be packed in groups of 16. He will not be able to fill a carton (256 widgets), so he ships out 12 boxes and 5 single widgets:

12 * 16=192, and 192 + 5=197

You approach an obstacle if you attempt to write the number in hex. How are you going to express 12 boxes and 5 singles? You need a single numeral in hex that represents 12 in decimal. To improvise, you use the letters of the alphabet for the numbers 10–15. Table D-2 shows numerals expressed in decimal, hex, and binary numbering systems. In the second column in Table D-2, you are counting in the hex number system. For example, 12 is represented with a C. So you say that Joe packs C boxes and 5 singles. The hex number for decimal 197 is C5 (see Figure D-4).

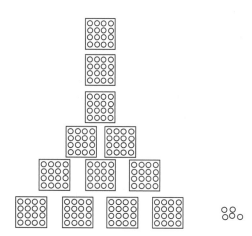

Figure D-4   Hex C5 represented as C boxes and 5 singles = 197 decimal

Table D-2   Decimal, hex, and binary values

Decimal	Hex	Binary	Decimal	Hex	Binary
0	0	0	22	16	10110
1	1	1	23	17	10111
2	2	10	24	18	11000
3	3	11	25	19	11001
4	4	100	26	1A	11010
5	5	101	27	1B	11011
6	6	110	28	1C	11100
7	7	111	29	1D	11101
8	8	1000	30	1E	11110
9	9	1001	31	1F	11111
10	A	1010	32	20	100000
11	B	1011	33	21	100001
12	C	1100	34	22	100010
13	D	1101	35	23	100011
14	E	1110	36	24	100100
15	F	1111	37	25	100101
16	10	10000	38	26	100110
17	11	10001	39	27	100111
18	12	10010	40	28	101000
19	13	10011	41	29	101001
20	14	10100	42	2A	101010
21	15	10101	43	2B	101011

Table D-2   Decimal, hex, and binary values (Continued)

Decimal	Hex	Binary	Decimal	Hex	Binary
44	2C	101100	54	36	110110
45	2D	101101	55	37	110111
46	2E	101110	56	38	111000
47	2F	101111	57	39	111001
48	30	110000	58	3A	111010
49	31	110001	59	3B	111011
50	32	110010	60	3C	111100
51	33	110011	61	3D	111101
52	34	110100	62	3E	111110
53	35	110101			

Practice a little. Fill in the following table:

Table D-3

Decimal Value	Hex Value
14	
259	
75	
	FF
1,024	
	A11

BINARY NUMBER SYSTEM

It was stated earlier that it is easier for the computer to convert from binary to hex or from hex to binary than between binary and decimal. You will see just how easy. Recall that the binary number system only has two digits, or bits: 0 and 1. If your friend Joe in shipping operated a "binary" shipping system, he would pack like this: two widgets in a box, two boxes in one carton, two cartons in one crate, and two crates in one truckload. In Figure D-5, Joe is asked to pack 13 widgets. He packs 1 crate (8 widgets), 1 carton (4 widgets), no boxes, and 1 single. The number 13 in binary is 1101.

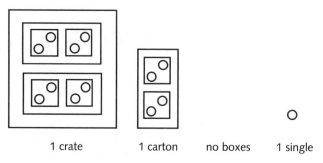

| 1 crate | 1 carton | no boxes | 1 single |

Figure D-5   Binary 1101 = 13 displayed as crates, cartons, boxes, and singles

The largest 4–bit number in binary is 1111. This number in decimal and hex is:

$$
\begin{aligned}
\text{binary } 1111 = \;&1 \text{ group of } 8 = 8 \\
&1 \text{ group of } 4 = 4 \\
&1 \text{ group of } 2 = 2 \\
&1 \text{ single } = 1
\end{aligned}
$$

TOTAL = 15

1111 (binary) = 15 (decimal) = F (hex)

This last fact is very important for working with computers: F (hex) = 1111 (binary). It takes 4 bits to make the largest single–numeral hex numeral, so every hex numeral can be converted into a 4–digit binary number. When converting from hex to binary, take each hex numeral and convert it to a 4-bit binary number. Fortunately, when working with computers, you will almost never be working with more than 2 hex numerals at a time. Here are some examples:

1. Convert hex F8 to binary: F = 1111, and 8 = 1000. Therefore,
   F8 = 11111000 (usually written 1111 1000)

2. Convert hex 9A to binary: 9 = 1001, and A = 1010. Therefore, 9A = 1001 1010

3. Convert binary 101110 to hex. First, group in groups of 4, adding leading zeros as necessary: 0010 1110
   Then convert each group of 4 to a single hex numeral: 0010 = 2, and 1110 = E
   The hex number is 2E.

Writing Conventions

Sometimes when you are dealing with hex, binary, and decimal numbers, it is not always clear which number system is being used. If you see a letter in the number, you know the number is a hex number. Binary numbers are usually written in groups of four bits. To make it clear that a number is a hex number, often a lower case h is placed after the number like this: 2Eh. This convention is used in this book.

MEMORY ADDRESSING

Computers often display memory addresses in the hex number system. You must either "think in hex" or convert to decimal. It's really easier, with a little practice, to think in hex. Here's the way it works:

Memory addresses are displayed as two hex numbers. An example is C800:5

The part C800 is called the **segment address**, and the 5 is called the **offset**. The offset value can have as many as four hex digits. The actual memory address is calculated by adding a zero to the right of the segment address and adding the offset value like this: C800:5=C8000+5=C8005

The first 640K of memory is called conventional memory. Look at how that memory is addressed. If 1 kilobyte = 1,024 bytes: 640K=640*1,024=655,360

There are 655,360 memory addresses in conventional memory. Each memory address can hold 1 byte, or 8 bits, of either data or program instructions. The decimal value 655,360 converted to hex is A0000. Conventional memory addresses begin with 00000 and end with A0000 minus 1 or 9FFFF. Written in segment-and-offset form, conventional memory addresses range from 0000:0 to 9FFF:F.

The next address after 9FFF:F, the last address in conventional memory, is the first address of upper memory. Upper memory is defined as the memory addresses from 640K through 1,024K - 1. The first address in upper memory is A0000, and the last address is FFFFF. Written in segment-and-offset terms, upper memory addresses range from A000:0 to FFFF:F.

Here is one way to organize the conversion of a large hex value such as FFFFF to decimal (remember F in hex equals 15 in decimal):

F F F F F
$15 \times 16^0 = 15 \times 1 =$ 15
$15 \times 16^1 = 15 \times 16 =$ 240
$15 \times 16^2 = 15 \times 256 =$ 3,840
$15 \times 16^3 = 15 \times 496 =$ 61,440
$15 \times 16^4 = 15 \times 65,536 =$ 983,040

Remember that FFFFF is the last memory address in upper memory. The very next memory address is the first address of extended memory, which is defined as memory above 1 MB. If you add 1 to the number above, you get 1,048,576, which is equal to 1024×1024, which is the definition of 1 megabyte.

DISPLAYING MEMORY WITH DOS DEBUG

In Figure D-6 you see the results of the beginning of upper memory displayed. The DOS DEBUG command displays the contents of memory. Memory addresses are displayed in hex segment-and-offset values. To enter DEBUG, type the following command at the C prompt:

```
c:\> DEBUG
```

Type the following dump command to display the beginning of upper memory (the hyphen in the commmand is the DEBUG command prompt):

```
-d A000:0
```

Memory is displayed showing 16 bytes on each line. The A area of memory (the beginning of upper memory) is not used unless the computer is using a monochrome monitor. In Figure D-6, the area contains nothing but continuous 1s in binary or Fs in hex. The ASCII interpretation is on the right side. To view the next group of memory addresses, you can type **d** at the hyphen and press **Enter**. DEBUG displays the next 128 addresses.

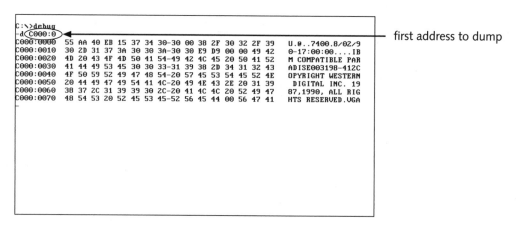

Figure D-6   Memory dump: `-d A000:0`

The A and B ranges of upper memory addresses (upper memory addresses that begin with A or B when written in hex) are used for monochrome monitors. The C range contains the video BIOS for a color monitor. Figure D-7 shows the dump of the beginning of the C range.

```
C:\>debug
-d C000:0                                              ←—— first address to dump
C000:0000  55 AA 40 EB 15 37 34 30-30 00 38 2F 30 32 2F 39   U.@..7400.8/02/9
C000:0010  30 2D 31 37 3A 30 30 3A-30 30 E9 D9 00 00 49 42   0-17:00:00....IB
C000:0020  4D 20 43 4F 4D 50 41 54-49 42 4C 45 20 50 41 52   M COMPATIBLE PAR
C000:0030  41 44 49 53 45 30 30 33-31 39 38 2D 34 31 32 43   ADISE003198-412C
C000:0040  4F 50 59 52 49 47 48 54-20 57 45 53 54 45 52 4E   OPYRIGHT WESTERN
C000:0050  20 44 49 47 49 54 41 4C-20 49 4E 43 2E 20 31 39    DIGITAL INC. 19
C000:0060  38 37 2C 31 39 39 30 2C-20 41 4C 4C 20 52 49 47   87,1990, ALL RIG
C000:0070  48 54 53 20 52 45 53 45-52 56 45 44 00 56 47 41   HTS RESERVED.UGA
```

Figure D-7   Memory dump: `-d C000:0`

There is more than one way, in fact there are many ways, that the same segment-and-offset value can be identified. Try these commands to display the same upper memory addresses:

```
-d C000:0
-d BFF1:00F0
-d BFFF:0010
-d BEEE:1120
```

In summary, reading and understanding binary and hex numbers are essential skills to managing computers. All data is stored in binary in a computer and is often displayed in hex. Memory addresses are often displayed in hex segment-and-offset terms. An address in memory can be written in a variety of segment and offset values. The actual memory address is calculated by placing one zero to the right side of the segment address and adding the resulting value to the offset value.

APPENDIX E: TROUBLESHOOTING GUIDELINES

This appendix brings together all the troubleshooting guidelines covered in the text and is designed to serve as a central point of reference when you are solving computer problems. The appendix is divided into sections by topic to help you locate information, but when you are not certain of the source of the problem, try browsing through the entire appendix, which may help you identify the source of the problem you are addressing. The suggestions made here are only meant to be summary guidelines. See the related chapters for complete explanations and procedures.

Below is a table that indexes the troubleshooting problems addressed in this appendix, indicating the type of problem you may find yourself addressing, where in the appendix you can find troubleshooting guides, and which chapter in the book contains more details about the problem.

These troubleshooting guidelines are regularly updated. See the Course Technology Web site for the latest version. If you would like to submit an item to be included in future versions of the guidelines, go to the Web site www.course.com and search for *A Guide to Managing and Maintaining Your PC* by Jean Andrews.

Description of Problem	Appendix E Page	Chapter Reference
Floppy Drive Problems	E-2	4, 6
Problems with the Mouse	E-4	4, 11 (mouse problems with OS installation)
Hard Drive Problems	E-4	5, 6
Keyboard Problems	E-5	4
Monitor Problems	E-6	4
Printer Problems	E-8	7
Network Printer Problems	E-11	16
Modem Problems	E-11	15
CD-ROM Drive Problems	E-13	8, 11 (installing Windows 95 for CD-ROM), 13
Backup Tape Drive Problems	E-15	17
The Computer Does Not Boot	E-16	1, 2 (complete discussion of the boot process); 12 (Windows NT startup problems; 6 (boot problems related to the hard drive)
Problems after the Computer Boots	E-18	11 (software problems under Windows 3.x and Windows 95); 12 (software problems under Windows NT)
Memory Problems with DOS and Windows 3.x	E-18	9
Power Supply Problems	E-19	10
Windows 3.x Installation Problems	E-20	11
Software Installation Problems	E-21	11
Hardware Device Installation Problems under Windows 95	E-21	See Index for individual devices
Windows NT Boot Problems	E-22	12
Network Problems	E-22	16

Don't open your computer's case until you read this warning. Removing, replacing, and modifying pieces of hardware inside your computer without following the necessary precautions can cause you and your computer serious damage. The most common risk to a computer is posed by the discharge of static electricity, which can destroy circuit boards and chips. However, accessing the insides of the power supply or monitor can pose serious safety risks to you as well. These dangers can be avoided. To ensure safety in your work setting, follow every precaution listed in the *Read This Before You Begin* section of this book's Preface.

FLOPPY DRIVE PROBLEMS

General failure reading drive A, Abort, Retry, Fail?

The problem may come from several sources including:

- An error in the application you are currently running
- The operating system you are currently running
- The system BIOS or CMOS setup (they may not be correctly configured)
- The floppy disk in the drive
- The floppy drive
- The floppy drive controller card
- The cable from the controller card to the drive
- The power supply
- The power supply cable to the drive (it may be loose or disconnected)
- The command just issued (it may contain a mistake or may be the wrong command)
- The drive latch (it may not be closed or the disk may be incorrectly inserted)
- The drive read/write head (it might be dirty)

Try the following:

- Remove the floppy disk. Does the shuttle window move freely?
- Do you see any dirt, hair, or trash on the disk's Mylar surface?
- Does the disk spin freely inside the housing cover?
- Some new disks simply need a little loosening up. Put the disk back in the drive and try again.
- Does the light on the correct drive go on when you try to access it? Maybe you are trying to access the B drive, but the disk is in the A drive.
- Will another disk work in the drive? If so, the problem is probably caused by the disk, not the drive. There is an exception to this statement. The drive may be out of alignment. If it is, the drive will be unable to read a floppy disk formatted in another drive that has a different (correct) alignment, although it may read a disk that is formatted with its own alignment. To test this possibility, try several disks, and note if the drive only reads those disks that it has recently formatted. If so, then you've probably located the problem. You probably will want to replace the drive.
- Does the drive light come on at all? If not, then the problem may be with the software or the hardware. Try to access the disk with a different software program.
- What does work? Can DOS access the drive with a simple DIR A:? Can File Manager or Explorer access the disk? How about CHKDSK A:?
- Reboot the machine and try again. Many problems with computers disappear with a simple reboot. If a soft boot doesn't do it, try a hard boot.

■ If the light doesn't come on even then, suspect that the source of your problem is the power to the drive or the hardware connections inside the case.

■ Does a second floppy drive work? If both lights refuse to come on, suspect the power supply or the floppy drive controller card.

■ Has this drive been used recently? Perhaps the system setup has lost CMOS data. The system may think it has a 720K drive when it really has a 1.44 MB drive. Access Setup and check the drive specifications.

■ Try cleaning the drive's read/write heads. Use a head cleaning kit that includes a paper disk and a cleaning solution.

If none of the above solves the problem, it is time to go inside the case. Turn off the computer and open the computer case.

E

■ Check every connection from the systemboard to the drive.

■ Check the power cable connection.

■ Remove the controller card of the problem drive. Using a clean white eraser, erase and clean the edge connector and reseat the board.

■ Take the power cable from a second, working floppy drive and put it on the nonworking one to eliminate the power cable as the problem.

■ Replace the data cable and try the drive again. Exchange the controller card. If that does not work, exchange the drive itself and try again.

■ If the drive still does not work, suspect the systemboard or the ROM BIOS on the systemboard.

Non-system disk or disk error. Replace and strike any key when ready.

This error message appears when you are booting from a disk that does not have the operating system on it. Replace the disk and try to boot again.

Invalid or missing COMMAND.COM

This error message appears when DOS is loading, and the two hidden files are present but COMMAND.COM is not present, is corrupt, or is the wrong version. Boot from a bootable disk that has COMMAND.COM, and then copy the file to the disk that you want to be bootable.

Invalid Drive Specification

This error message appears when you are trying to access a drive that the operating system does not know is available.

Not ready reading drive A:, Abort, Retry, Fail?

This error occurs when the disk in drive A is not readable. Maybe the disk is missing or is inserted incorrectly. The disk may have a bad boot record, errors in the FAT, or bad sectors. Try using Nuts & Bolts to examine the disk for corruption.

Track 0 bad, disk not usable

This message typically appears when you are trying to format a disk using the wrong disk type.

Write-protect error writing drive A:

This error occurs when the disk is write-protected and the application is trying to write to it.

PROBLEMS WITH THE MOUSE

The cursor on the screen is difficult to move with the mouse

The rollers inside the mouse housing collect dirt and dust and occasionally need cleaning. Remove the cover to the mouse ball from the bottom of the mouse. These usually come off with a simple press and shift motion. Clean the rollers with a cotton swab dipped in a very small amount of liquid soap.

HARD DRIVE PROBLEMS

When troubleshooting hard drive problems, always begin by interviewing the user, asking questions such as the following:

- Was the computer recently moved?
- Was any new hardware recently installed?
- Was any new software recently installed?
- Was any software recently reconfigured or upgraded?
- Has the computer had a history of similar problems?

Hard drive does not boot

This error may occur for any number of reasons. Try the following:

- Confirm that both the monitor and computer switches are turned on.
- Try using a bootable floppy disk, then log on to drive C:. If you have a Windows 95 rescue disk, you can use SCANDISK, CHKDSK, or FDISK to examine the system.
- If the PC will not boot from the boot disk, verify that the boot disk is good. Try using it in a different computer. To protect against viruses, write-protect it first.
- Check to be sure that the power cable and disk controller cable connections are good and are correctly oriented.
- If the drive still does not boot, try performing the following procedures in order:
  - Reconnect or swap the drive data cable.
  - Reseat or exchange the drive adapter card.
  - Exchange the hard drive with one you know is in working condition and try to boot from that.
- A bad power supply or a bad systemboard also may cause a disk boot failure. If the problem is solved by exchanging one of the above modules, try reinstalling the old module to verify that the problem was not caused by a bad connection.
- System files (COMMAND.COM, IO.SYS, MSDOS.SYS) may be damaged, missing, or mis-matched, which can keep a hard disk from booting. You can see if they are of the same version by typing DIR/AH. This will show the hidden system files and their dates. If COMMAND.COM and the hidden files have different dates, then they are usually mixed and incompatible versions. Boot a Rescue or system DOS disk from drive A (make sure you are using the same DOS version).
- Restore hidden system files on drive C: A:\>SYS C:.
- Run SCANDISK.
- Boot from the Nuts & Bolts rescue disk.
- Run a current version of an antivirus program.

Drive retrieves and saves data slowly

This may be caused by fragmented files that have been updated, modified, and spread over different portions of the disk. Run DEFRAG to rewrite fragmented files to contiguous sectors.

Also, verify that the hard disk drivers are properly installed.

Computer will not recognize a newly installed hard disk

Consider the following if the disk is brand new or has no information you want to keep on it.

■ Does the manual state that you must first do a "low-level" format or run Disk Manager? IDE drives are already low-level formatted. Older drives require the user to perform this routine.
■ Has the FDISK utility been successfully run? Choose Display Partition Information from the FDISK menu to verify the status.
■ FORMAT C:/S is the last required "format" step. Has this been done?
■ Has the CMOS setup been correctly configured?
■ Are there any drivers to install?
■ Are there any DIP switches or jumpers that must be set?
■ Has the data cable been properly connected? Verify that the cable stripes are connected to pin 1 on the edge connectors of both the card and cable.
■ Call the drive manufacturer if the above steps are not productive.

KEYBOARD PROBLEMS

Because of the low cost of keyboards, most often if a keyboard does not work, the solution is to replace it. However, there are a few simple things you can do to repair one that is not working.

A few keys don't work

■ Remove the cap on the bad key with a chip extractor. Spray contact cleaner into the key well. Repeatedly depress the contact in order to clear it out. Don't use rubbing alcohol to clean the key well, as it can add a residue to the contact.
■ If this method of cleaning solves the problem, then clean the adjacent keys as well.

The keyboard does not work at all

■ Is the cable plugged in securely?
■ If the cable connection is good and the keyboard still does not work, connect a working keyboard of the same type to the computer. If the second keyboard works, you have verified that the problem is in the keyboard and not in the computer.
■ If the second keyboard does not work, connect the first keyboard to a computer that works properly. If this works, then the problem must be with the original computer.
■ If the problem is in the keyboard, check the cable.
■ If possible, swap the existing cable with a cable known to be good, perhaps from an old, discarded keyboard. Sometimes a wire in a PC keyboard cable becomes pinched or broken. Most cables can be easily separated and detached from the keyboard by removing the few screws that hold the keyboard case together, then simply unplugging the cable. Be careful as you work; don't allow the key caps to fall out!
■ If the problem is not the cable, replace the keyboard.
■ If the problem is with the computer, consider the following: On the systemboard, the two chips that affect the keyboard functions are the keyboard chip and the ROM BIOS chip. You might choose to swap each of these chips on the systemboard. Otherwise the entire systemboard may have to be replaced.

Key continues to repeat after being released

■ The problem may be a dirty contact. Some debris has conductive properties and can therefore short the gap between the contacts, causing the key to repeat. Try cleaning the key switch with contact cleaner.

- Very high humidity and excess moisture may short key switch contacts and cause keys to repeat. The problem will usually resolve itself once the humidity level returns to normal. You can hasten the drying process by using a fan (not a hot hair dryer) to blow air at the keyboard.

Keys produce the wrong characters

This problem is usually caused by a bad chip on the keyboard. Try swapping the keyboard for one you know is good. If the problem goes away, replace the original keyboard with a new one.

MONITOR PROBLEMS

Poor cable connections or bad contrast/brightness adjustments cause many monitor problems.

Power light (LED) does not go on, no picture

- Is the monitor plugged in?
- Verify that the wall outlet works by plugging in a lamp, radio, etc.
- If the monitor power cord is plugged into a power strip or surge protector, verify that the power strip is turned on, and the monitor is also turned on.
- If the monitor power cord is plugged into the back of the computer, verify that the connection is tight, and that the computer is turned on.

Power LED light is on, no picture on power up

- Check the contrast adjustment. If there's no change, then leave it at a middle setting.
- Check the brightness adjustment. If there's no change, then leave it at a middle setting.
- Is the cable connected securely to the computer?
- If the monitor-to-computer cable detaches from the monitor, exchange it for a cable you know is good or check the cable for continuity (Chapter 10).
- If this solves the problem, reattach the old cable to verify that the problem was not simply a bad connection.
- Confirm that the proper system configuration has been set up. Some older systemboards have a jumper or DIP switch that can be used to select the monitor type.
- Trade with a different monitor of the same type. For example, trade a color SVGA for another color SVGA.
- Test the monitor that isn't working on a computer that works with another monitor.
- Test a monitor you know is good on the computer you suspect to be bad. If you think the monitor is bad, make sure that it also fails to work on a good computer.
- Check the CMOS settings or software configuration on the computer.
- Trade a good video card for the video card you suspect is bad.
- Test the video card you think is bad on a computer that works. Test a video card you know is good on the computer that you suspect may be bad. Whenever possible, try to do both. If the card you think is bad works on a computer you know is good, then the card is good. If the card doesn't work on either machine, you have probably found the source of your problem.
- If the video card has some socketed chips that appear dirty or corroded, consider removing them and trying to clean the pins. You can use a clean pencil eraser to do this. But normally, if the problem is a bad video card, the most cost-effective measure is to replace the card.
- Use Nuts & Bolts Discover Pro to test the RAM on the systemboard.
- Trade the systemboard for one you know is good. Sometimes, though rarely, a peripheral chip on the systemboard of the computer causes the problem.

Power on, but monitor displays the wrong characters

■ Wrong characters are usually not the result of a bad monitor, but a problem with the video card. Trade the video card for one you know is good.
■ If the new video card doesn't work, exchange the systemboard. Sometimes a bad chip, ROM or RAM, on the systemboard will display the wrong characters on the monitor.

Monitor flickers and/or has wavy lines

■ Check the cable. Monitor flicker can be caused by poor cable connections.
■ Check if something in the office is providing a high amount of electrical noise. For example, you may be able to stop a flicker by moving the office fan to a different outlet. Bad fluorescent lights or large speakers have also been known to cause interference. Two monitors placed very close together may also cause problems.
■ If the vertical scan frequency (the refresh rate at which the screen is drawn) is below 60 Hz, a screen flicker may appear in the normal course of operation.
■ Try a different monitor set in the same location. Does the same thing happen to the new monitor? If so, suspect interference.
■ Check Control Panel, Display, Settings to see if a high resolution (greater than 800×600 with more than 256 colors) is selected. Consider these issues:
    ■ The video card may not support this resolution/color setting
    ■ There may not be enough video RAM; 2 MB may be required.
    ■ The added (socketed) video RAM may be of a different speed than the soldered memory.
■ Does the monitor have a degauss button that is provided to eliminate accumulated or stray magnetic fields? If so, press it.

No graphics display or the screen goes blank when loading certain programs

■ A special graphics or video accelerator card is defective or not present.
■ Software is not configured to do graphics, or the software does not recognize the installed graphics card.
■ The video card may not support this resolution and/or color setting.
■ There may not be enough video RAM; 2MB may be required.
■ The added (socketed) video RAM may be of a different speed than the soldered memory.
■ The wrong adapter/display type is selected. Start Windows 95 from Safe Mode to reset display ("How to" is covered in Chapter 11).

Screen goes blank 30 seconds or one minute after not touching the keyboard

■ A "green" systemboard (which follows energy-saving standards) used with an Energy Star monitor can be configured to go into a Standby or Doze mode after a period of inactivity.
■ Try to change the doze features in CMOS, using a menu option such as Power Management, or in Windows 95, using Control Panel, Display, Screen Saver.
■ Some monitors have a Power Save switch on the back of the monitor. This may not be switched to your desired setting.

Poor quality color display

■ Read the documentation for the monitor for explanations of the color-adjusting buttons on the outside of the monitor, which are used to fine-tune the color.

- Exchange video cards.
- Add more video RAM; 2 MB or 4 MB may be required for higher resolutions.
- Check if there is a fan or large speaker (which has large magnets) or another monitor nearby that may be causing interference.

Picture out of focus, or out of adjustment

- Check the adjustment knobs on the control panel on the outside of the monitor.
- There are adjustments that can be made inside the monitor that may solve the problem. If you have not been trained to work inside the monitor, take the monitor to a service center for adjustments.

Crackling sound

An accumulation of dirt or dust inside the unit may be the cause. Someone trained to work on the inside of the monitor can vacuum the inside.

PRINTER PROBLEMS

When troubleshooting printer problems, first determine that the problem is truly with the printer. The problem may be the computer hardware communicating with the printer, the applications software using the printer, the printer driver, the printer cable, or the printer. Ask these questions and try these things:

- Is the printer turned on, and is the printer online?
- Is the correct printer selected as the default printer?
- Will the printer work with an applications program other than the one currently running?
- Is the printer using the correct driver? Does the driver need updating? Is the driver correctly installed?
- Is there enough available hard drive space for the software to create temporary print files?
- Can you move the printer to another computer and print from it? Will another printer work on this computer?

After you are convinced that the problem is not with the computer hardware or software, but is indeed a problem with the printer itself, you are ready for the following troubleshooting guide. Also see the printer documentation for troubleshooting steps to solve printer problems.

Laser printer problems

The printer documentation can be very helpful and most often contains a phone number for technical support for the printer manufacturer. A good test for a printer is to print the manufacturer's test page from the PC, not just directly from the printer. From Windows 95, access **Control Panel** and double-click on **Printers**. Right-click on the printer you want to test. Select the **Properties** options. Click on **Print Test Page** to send a test page to the printer.

Printer never leaves warm-up mode

The warming up message should disappear as soon as the printer establishes communication with the PC. If it doesn't, try the following:

- Turn the printer off and disconnect the cable to the computer.
- Turn on the printer. If it now displays a Ready message, the problem is communication between the printer and the computer.
- Verify that the cable is connected to the correct printer port, not to a serial port.
- Verify that data to the installed printer is being sent to the parallel port. For example, access the **Properties** box of the installed printer as described above. Verify that the print is being sent to LPT1.
- Replace the cable.

A Paper Out message displays

■ Remove the paper tray. Be sure there is paper in the tray. Carefully replace the tray, being certain that the tray is fully inserted in the slot.
■ Check the lever mechanism that falls into a slot on the tray when no paper is present. Is it jammed or bent?

A Toner Low message displays, or print is irregular or light

■ Remove the toner cartridge from the printer, tap the cartridge to redistribute the toner supply, and replace it in the printer. To avoid flying toner, don't shake the cartridge too hard. This is really just a temporary fix for a cartridge low on toner. Plan to replace the toner cartridge in the printer soon.
■ Extreme humidity may cause the toner to clump in the cartridge and give the same error message.

A Paper Jam message displays

■ If paper is jammed inside the printer, follow the directions in the printer documentation to remove the paper. Don't jerk the paper from the printer mechanism, but carefully pull evenly on the paper.
■ If there is no jammed paper, then remove the tray and check the metal plate at the bottom of the tray. Can it move up and down freely? If not, replace the tray with a new tray.
■ When you insert the tray in the printer, does the printer lift the plate as the tray is inserted? If not, the lift mechanism may need repairing.

One or more white streaks appear in the print

■ Remove the toner cartridge, tap it to redistribute the toner supply, and replace the cartridge.
■ Check the printer manual for specific directions as to what part may need replacing when this problem occurs.

Print appears speckled

Try replacing the cartridge. If the problem continues, the power supply assembly may be damaged.

Printed images are distorted

■ Check for debris that might be interfering with the printer operation.
■ Replace the toner cartridge.

Dot matrix printer problems

A number of problems can arise with dot matrix printers.

Print quality is poor

■ Begin with the ribbon. Does it advance normally while the carriage moves back and forth? Is it placed correctly in the ribbon guide? Replace the ribbon.
■ If the ribbon still does not advance properly, check the printer's advance mechanism.
■ Adjust the print head spacing. There is usually a lever adjustment that can alter the distance between the print head and the plate.
■ Check the print head for dirt. Make sure it's not hot before you touch it. If there is a build-up, wipe off each wire with a cotton swab dipped in alcohol or contact cleaner.

Printer self-test works, but printing from a computer application program does not work

■ To perform a printer self-test, see the printer documentation. If this test indicates that the printer itself is functioning correctly, communication from the PC may be the problem.
■ Check cable connections. Is the printer online?

Print head moves back and forth, but nothing prints

- Check the ribbon. Is it installed correctly between the plate and the print head?
- Does the ribbon advance properly?

Ink jet printer problems

A number of problems can arise with ink jet printers.

Print quality is poor

- Is the paper being used specifically designed for ink jet printers?
- Is the ink supply low, or is there a partially clogged nozzle? (This may happen if the printer has been idle for several days.) If so, follow the printer's documentation to clean each nozzle.
- Is the print head too close to, or too far from, the paper?

Printing is intermittent or absent

- Is the correct printer driver installed?
- Is the ink supply low?
- Are nozzles clogged?
- Replace the ink cartridges or replenish the ink supply. Follow the directions in the printer documentation.

NETWORK PRINTER PROBLEMS

First determine that the problem is not a physical problem with the printer. Problems with network printing may be caused by the printer, the network to the printer, or the computer trying to use the printer. You can isolate the problem by finding the answers to the following questions:

- Is the printer online?
- Is the network printer on the remote PC configured correctly?
- Is the correct network printer selected on the remote PC?
- Is there enough hard disk space available on the remote PC?
- Can you print successfully from another application on the remote PC?
- Can you print successfully from the host PC using the identical application?
- If you print to a file and then send the file to the host PC, does it print successfully? If this works, then the problem is with data transmission. If this does not work, then the problem is with the application or print driver on the remote PC.
- For DOS applications, you may need to exit the application before printing occurs.

MODEM PROBLEMS

The modem does not respond

To address this problem, answer the following questions and try the following approaches:

- Is the modem plugged into the phone jack?
- Is the external modem plugged into the computer? Is the connection solid?
- There are two jacks on a modem. Are the lines reversed?
- Is the phone line working? Plug in a phone. Is there a dial tone?
- Do you need to dial an extra character to get an outside line (such as 9 or 8)?

- Has the modem ever worked, or is this a new installation? If it is a new installation, check these things:
    - Is the computer short on RAM or hard drive space? Try closing all other applications currently running.
    - Is the modem set to the same COM port and IRQ that the software is set to?
    - Is another device also configured to the same COM port or IRQ that the modem is using?
    - For an internal modem, check the DIP switches and jumpers. Do they agree with the modem properties in the OS?
    - Try moving an internal modem to a different expansion slot. For an external modem using a serial port card, move the serial port card to a different slot.
    - For an external modem, use a different serial cable.
    - Did the software correctly initialize the modem? If you did not give the correct modem type to the software, it may be trying to send the wrong initialization command. Try AT&F. (Under Windows 95, click **Start**, **Settings**, **Control Panel**. Double-click **Modem**. Select the modem and click **Modem Properties**, **Connections**, **Advanced Connection Settings**. Enter the **AT** command under Extra Settings.) Retry the modem.

The modem says that there is no dial tone, even though you can hear it

- The modem may not be able to detect the dial tone, even if you can hear it. Try unplugging any other equipment plugged into this same phone line, such as a Fax machine.
- Try giving the ATX0 command before you dial. Enter the command under Advanced Settings as described above.
- Straighten your phone lines! Don't let them get all twisted and crossed up with other heavy electrical lines.

The modem dials and then says that the other end is busy, even when you know that it is not

- This can happen with international calls; the modem does not recognize the signal as a ring. Using communications software that allows you to enter AT commands (such as ProCom Plus), try entering the ATX0 command before entering the command to dial.
- Straighten the phone lines and remove extra equipment, as described above.

The modem and the receiving modem take a very long time to negotiate the connection

- This is probably due to a noisy phone line. Try calling again or using a different number.
- Remove other equipment from your line. A likely suspect is a credit card machine.
- Turn off data compression and try again.
- Turn off error correction and try again.
- Try forcing your modem to use a slower speed.

During a connection, it sounds as if the handshaking starts all over again

Modems normally do this if the phone line is noisy and causes much data to get corrupted; it's called **retraining**, and sometimes it can solve the problem as the modems renegotiate, compensating for the noisy line. Do the things listed above to clear your line of equipment and twisted phone lines.

File transfers are too slow

Does your modem support data compression? Check that the modem is configured for it.

The modem loses connection at odd times or is slow

■ Check the communications software for the speed assigned to the modem. Many times people set the communications software speed for the modem speed instead of for the port speed, which is what the software is asking for. (It should be about four times the modem speed.)

■ You may have a noisy phone line. Try the connection using two modems of the same brand and model. If performance is better, the problem is most likely the phone line because two modems of the same brand and model are best able to compensate for a noisy phone line.

■ Is the phone line from the modem to the jack too long? About 4 feet is the upper limit; otherwise, electromagnetic interference may be the problem.

■ Straighten the phone lines and clear the line of any extra equipment.

■ Reinstall the modem. Allow Windows 95 to detect the modem for you and install its own drivers.

The modem drops the connection and gives the NO CARRIER message

■ Most likely the connection was first dropped by the remote modem. Is someone trying to use a phone extension on this line?

■ Disable call waiting. To do this, put ★70, before the dialing number. Some communications software has a setting to disable call waiting. If not, you can put these four characters in the Extra Settings box of Advanced Connections Settings.

■ Remove extra equipment from the line and straighten the phone lines.

When the weather is bad, the connection often disconnects

This is caused by a dirty phone line. Does your line make extra noises at these times? Remove any extra equipment and straighten the lines.

Whenever large files are downloaded, some of the data is lost

Make sure that hardware flow control is on and that software flow control is off, for the software, the COM port, and the modem.

The connection fails whenever large files are uploaded or downloaded

There may be a buffer overflow. Try these things to gain better control of data flow:

■ Make sure that hardware flow control is on and that software flow control is off, for the software, the COM port, and the modem.

■ Is the serial port speed set too high for the UART chip you have? Lower the port speed.

■ For an external modem, try a different serial port cable.

You get nothing but garbage across the connection

■ Check the port settings. Try 8 databits, no parity, and one stop bit (8, No, and 1).

■ Slow down the port speed.

■ Slow down the modem speed.

CD-ROM DRIVE PROBLEMS

Problems when installing the CD-ROM drive

CD-ROM drivers can be loaded from the AUTOEXEC.BAT and CONFIG.SYS files. See the CD-ROM installation guide for specific commands for your drive. Here are two examples:

In the CONFIG.SYS file: `DEVICE =C:\CDSYS\SLCD.SYS /D:MSCD001`

In AUTOEXEC.BAT: `C:\DOS\MSCDEX.EXE /D:MSCD001 /L:D /M:8`

Try creating a bootable disk with these commands and the referenced files. (Modify the paths to point to drive A.)

The error message (Invalid Drive Specification) appears while trying to access the drive

- Check that there are no errors in the command lines in the CONFIG.SYS or AUTOEXEC.BAT file according to the documentation that came with the CD-ROM. Did you get an error message during booting, such as Bad Command or File Not Found?
- Reseat the adapter card and check cable connections.
- The MSCDEX.EXE program may not be loaded. Is the entry placed too late in AUTOEXEC.BAT after the command to load Windows?
- Try a different version of MSCDEX. Look for this file in the \DOS directory and change the path in front of the filename in AUTOEXEC.BAT to point to that version.

The install process is terminated with the message "MSCDEX.EXE not found"

MSCDEX.EXE must be copied onto the hard drive. Put it in the \DOS directory, then restart the install process. Sometimes MSCDEX is placed in the Windows directory, and sometimes a copy is put in the newly created CD-ROM directory.

The error message "Not Enough Drive Letters" appears during booting

Increase the number of allowed drive letters with the LASTDRIVE line in CONFIG.SYS: LASTDRIVE=Z.

Conflict errors exist

These will appear during booting as error messages, or they will cause some other device to fail to operate. The IRQ and the I/O address of your CD-ROM should be in the documentation. If not, call the manufacturer's technical support for this information.

Computer does not recognize CD-ROM (no prompt for the designated CD-ROM drive)

Check the following configurations:

- When using DOS, does the CONFIG.SYS file contain a CD device command line?
- Does the AUTOEXEC.BAT file call MSCDEX.EXE? Is MSCDEX.EXE placed in the correct directory? (A correct Windows 95 installation will not need to have MSCDEX.EXE in the AUTOEXEC.BAT file.)
- Is MSCDEX.EXE on the hard drive?
- For Windows 95, has the CD-ROM driver been installed?
- Check to see if another device is using the same port settings or IRQ number. See Control Panel, System Icon, Device Manager.

Check the following connections:

- Is the power cable attached to the CD-ROM?
- Is the data cable attached to the CD-ROM and to the controller?

- Is the stripe on the data cable correctly aligned to pin 1? (Look for an arrow or small 1 printed on the drive. For a best guess, pin 1 is usually next to the power connector.)
- Is the correct master/slave jumper set? For example, if both the hard drive and the CD-ROM drive are hooked up to the same ribbon cable, one must be designated master (the one attached to the end connector), and the other slave (the one attached to the middle connector).

No sound

- Is the sound cable attached between the CD-ROM and the analog audio connector on the sound card?
- Are the speakers turned on?
- Is the speaker volume turned down? (Check both the speaker itself and the OS volume control.)
- Are the speakers plugged into the line "Out" or "Spkr" port of the sound card?
- Is the transformer for the speaker plugged into an electrical outlet on one end and into the speakers on the other end?
- Is the volume control for Windows turned down? (To check, click Start, Programs, Accessories, Multimedia, Volume Control.)
- Does the sound card have a "diagnose" file on the Install floppy disk?
- Reinstall the sound card drivers.
- Is another device using the same I/O address or IRQ number?
- To check for a bad connection, remove and reinstall the sound card.
- Replace the sound card with one you know is good.

BACKUP TAPE DRIVE PROBLEMS

There are a number of different tape drives that may cause different types of problems.

A minicartridge does not work

- Verify that the minicartridge is write-enabled if you are trying to write data.
- Are you inserting the minicartridge correctly? Check the user guide.
- Check that you are using the correct type of minicartridge. See the user guide.
- Is the minicartridge formatted? The format is done by the software and can take an hour or more.
- Retension the tape. Use the backup software to do this. Some tape drives require this, and others do not. Retension fast forwards and rewinds the tape to eliminate loose spots on the tape.
- Take the minicartridge out and reboot. Try the minicartridge again.
- Try using a new minicartridge. The old one may have worn out.
- Just as with floppy disks, if the tape was removed from the drive while the drive light was still on, the data being written at that time may not be readable.

Data transfer is slow

- Does the tape software have an option for optimizing speed or data compression? Try turning one and then the other off and on.
- Some tape drives can use an optional accelerator card to speed up data transfer. See the tape drive user guide.
- Try a new minicartridge
- If the tape drive can do so, completely erase the tape and reformat it. Be sure that the tape drive has the ability to perform this procedure before you tell the software to do so.
- If you have installed an accelerator card, verify that the card is connected to the tape drive.
- Check that there is enough memory for the software to run.

The drive does not work after the installation

- Check that pin 1 is oriented correctly to the data cable at both ends.
- Check for a resource conflict. The tape drive normally requires an IRQ, DMA channel, and I/O address.
- For DOS, check the entries in CONFIG.SYS and AUTOEXEC.BAT.

The drive fails intermittently or generates errors

- The tape might be worn out. Try a new tape.
- Clean the read/write head of the tape drive. See the tape drive user guide for directions.
- For an external tape drive, move the drive as far as you can from the monitor and computer case.
- Reformat the tape.
- Retension the tape.
- Verify that you are using the correct tape type and tape format

THE COMPUTER DOES NOT BOOT

Blank screen, the PC appears "dead"

- Are there any burnt parts or odors? Any loose cable connections?
- Is the computer plugged in?
- Are *all* the switches turned on? Computer? Monitor? Surge protector? Uninterruptible power supply? Separate circuit breaker?
- Is the wall outlet (or surge protector) good?
- If the fan is not running, turn off the computer, open the case, and check the connections to the power supply. Are they secure? Are all cards securely seated?
- Check the voltage output from the power supply. ("How to" is covered in Chapter 10.)
- Remove all nonessential expansion cards (modem, sound card, mouse) one at a time. Verify that they are not drawing too much power and pulling the system down.
- It is possible that the expansion cards are all good, but the power supply is not capable of supplying enough current for all the add-on boards.
- It may be that there are too many cards and the computer is overheating. The temperature inside the case should not exceed 113° F.
- Excessive dust insulates components and causes them to overheat. Vacuum the entire unit, especially the power supply's fan vent.
- Trade the power supply for one you know is good. Be certain to follow the black-to-black rule when attaching the power cords to the systemboard.
- Is there strong magnetic or electrical interference? Sometimes an old monitor will emit too much static and EMF (electromagnetic force) and bring a whole system down.
- If the fan is running, reseat or trade the CPU, BIOS, or RAM. A POST code diagnostic card is a great help at this point.
- Sometimes a dead computer can be fixed by simply disassembling it and reseating cables, adapter cards, socketed chips, and SIMMs. Bad connections and corrosion are common problems.
- Check jumpers, DIP switches, and CMOS settings.
- Is the system in a Doze or Sleep mode? Many "green" systems can be programmed through CMOS to suspend the monitor or even the drive if the keyboard and/or CPU has been inactive for a few minutes. Pressing any key will usually resume exactly where the user left off.
- If the battery is dead, or dying, it may cause problems. Sometimes, after a long holiday, a weak battery will cause the CMOS to forget its configuration.

- Use a POST code diagnostic card to check systemboard components.
- Exchange the systemboard.

The computer does not recognize all installed RAM or SIMMs

- Are CMOS settings correct?
- Run a diagnostic software such as PC Technician to test memory.
- Are RAM or SIMM modules properly seated?
- Look for bent pins, or chips installed the wrong way, on cache memory. Look for loose SIMM modules.
- Place your fingers on the individual chips. Sometimes a bad chip will be noticeably hotter than the other chips.
- Make sure the RAM or SIMMs have the correct or consistent part number. For example, if there are four installed SIMMs, they usually must be the same size (in megabytes) and same speed (in nanoseconds).
- Reseat the SIMM memory modules.
- Trade SIMMs one at a time. For example, if the system only recognizes 6 out of 8 megabytes of RAM, swap the last two SIMM modules. Did the amount of recognized RAM change?
- Use SIMM modules with the same part number. (See Chapter 9 for details.)
- A trace on the systemboard may be bad. If this is the case, you may have to replace the entire systemboard.

Error messages appear during booting

- When a PC boots, one beep after POST indicates that all is well. If you hear more than one beep, look up the beep code in Appendix A.
- If error messages appear on the screen, then video is working. Look up the error message in Appendix A if the message on the screen is not clear.
- If a problem arises during a soft boot, try a hard boot. A soft boot may not work because TSRs are not always "kicked out" of RAM with a soft boot, or an ISA bus may not be initialized correctly.
- Boot from a floppy disk. You should boot to an A prompt. If you are successful, the problem is in the hard drive subsystem and/or the software on the drive.
- Can you access the hard drive from the A prompt?
- If you can get a C prompt, then the problem is in the software that is used on the hard drive to boot, such as the partition table, master boot record, operating system hidden files, or command interface files. See the suggestions for hard drive problems.
- Run diagnostic software (Nuts & Bolts or PC Technician) to test for hard drive hardware problems.
- Check all connections, and reseat all boards.
- Reduce the system to essentials. Remove any unnecessary hardware such as expansion cards, and then try to boot again.

Windows 95 does not load correctly

- Boot into Safe mode and then try booting normally. While in Safe Mode, if any changes were made in Control Panel just before the problem occurred, undo the changes.
- Try booting from the Nuts & Bolts rescue disk.

PROBLEMS AFTER THE COMPUTER BOOTS

- If you suspect that software may be the source of the problem, try diagnostic software such as Nuts & Bolts Disk Tune or ScanDisk before reloading the software package.

- Suspect the applications software using the device. Try another application or reinstall the software.
- If you suspect that hardware is the source of the problem, first isolate the problem by removing devices and trading good components for suspected bad ones, one at a time. Be aware that the problem may be a resource conflict.
- Check the voltage output from the power supply with a multimeter.
- Check jumpers, DIP switches, and CMOS settings for the devices.
- Suspect a corrupted device driver. Reinstall the driver.

MEMORY PROBLEMS WITH DOS AND WINDOWS 3.x

A TSR will not load high

- Are all command lines present in CONFIG.SYS and AUTOEXEC.BAT?
- Make sure that the DEVICEHIGH= commands in CONFIG.SYS are ordered so that the larger TSRs are placed first in the larger UMBs. There may not be enough upper memory addresses available to load the last ones.
- MEMMAKER does a very good job of choosing the best order of loading TSRs. Try it.
- Some TSRs do not work from upper memory, so test them before assuming that all is well.

A device does not work or the system hangs

These memory conflicts may cause a device to stop working or the system to hang:

- Two expansion boards are using the same upper memory addresses.
- DOS has created and is using a UMB in the same memory addresses used by an expansion board.

Two expansion boards using the same upper memory addresses

- Read the documentation for each board for upper memory addresses in use. If the documentation is missing, try to get the information using the MEM command or Nuts & Bolts Discover Pro.
- Some expansion boards have DIP switches or jumpers that allow you to substitute one set of memory addresses for another. Change the settings to avoid the conflict.
- You may change the memory addresses by adding a parameter to the command line that loads the device driver for the expansion board.

When UMBs and expansion boards conflict

- Read the documentation for each board for upper memory addresses in use.
- Use the Exclude option to the EMM386.EXE command line. For example, to exclude CC000–CFFFF from the addresses used by UMBs, use this command line:
DEVICE=C:\DOS\EMM386.EXE. NOEMS X=CC00 - CFFF
- Reboot your computer to activate the change.

POWER SUPPLY PROBLEMS

Symptoms of problems with the power supply or the house current to the PC are:

- The computer stops or hangs for no reason. Sometimes it may even reboot itself.
- Memory errors appear occasionally.
- Data is written incorrectly to the hard drive.
- The keyboard stops working at odd times.
- The systemboard fails or is damaged.
- The power supply overheats and becomes hot to the touch.

Try these things:

- What other devices are using the same house circuit? Remove a copy machine, laser printer, or other heavy equipment from the same circuit.
- Measure the voltage output of the power supply, or exchange it for one you know is good.
- Install an electrical conditioner to monitor and condition the voltage to the PC.

The fan on the power supply stops working

The problem may be a faulty power supply, or it may be caused by a short somewhere else in the system drawing too much power. This section is about troubleshooting a short somewhere else in the system.

- Don't operate the PC with the fan not working. Computers without cooling fans can quickly overheat and damage chips.
- Turn the power off and remove all power cord connections to all components, including P8 and P9, and all power cords to drives. Turn the power back on. If the fan comes on, the problem is probably with one of the systems you disconnected, not with the power supply.
- Turn the power off and reconnect the power cords to the drives. If the fan comes on, you can eliminate the drives as the problem. If the fan does not come on, try one drive after another until you identify the drive with the short.
- If the drives are not the problem, suspect the systemboard subsystem. With the power off, reconnect all power cords to the drives.
- Turn the power off and remove the power to the systemboard by disconnecting P8 and P9. Turn the power back on.
- If the fan comes back on, the problem is probably not the power supply but a short in one of the components powered by P8 and P9. The power to the systemboard also powers interface cards.
- Remove all interface cards and reconnect P8 and P9.
- If the fan still works, the problem is with one of the interface cards. If the fan does not work, the problem is with the systemboard or something still connected to it.
- Check for missing standoffs that may be allowing the systemboard to ground to the computer case.
- Look for damage on the bottom side of the systemboard that may be causing shorted circuits on the board.
- Frayed wires on cable connections can also cause shorts. Disconnect hard drive cables connected directly to the systemboard. Power up with P8 and P9 connected, but all cables disconnected from the systemboard. If the fan comes on, the problem is with one of the systems you disconnected.
- Never replace a damaged systemboard with a good one without first testing the power supply. You don't want to subject another good board to possible damage.

WINDOWS 3.x INSTALLATION PROBLEMS

Setup continues to ask for the same installation disk

Remove the disk from the floppy drive and verify that you have the correct disk. Open and close the shuttle window several times and try the disk again. The disk may be defective.

Setup does not list the hardware you have on your system

- Check the documentation for your hardware to see if you can substitute an alternate brand and model. This is only a short-term fix, because applications software might have trouble with the alternate printer driver.
- Look for a driver to download from the Microsoft support Web site or from the manufacturer's Web site.

You don't have enough hard drive space for the installation

- Use CHKDSK/F, erase lost clusters, and defragment the drive before the installation.
- Look for temporary files or applications software that you no longer use, which can be deleted.
- Run the Custom Setup and choose to not install the accessories, including wallpaper, when given the opportunity to make this decision.

Setup hangs during the installation

- Setup is probably having trouble detecting the hardware present. Reboot to DOS. Add the /I option to the Setup command line to bypass the search for hardware: `C:>A:SETUP /1`
- You must now select the hardware manually. See the documentation for the hardware for answers to the questions that Setup asks about the hardware.
- Another possibility is a virus. Run a virus scan program on the hard drive from the DOS prompt.

Windows will not boot after the installation is complete

- Boot to the DOS C prompt. Change directories to the Windows directory and enter SETUP at the DOS prompt like this: `C:>WINDOWS> SETUP`
- Check the hardware installed and make changes as necessary.
- Check the CONFIG.SYS and AUTOEXEC.BAT files for TSRs, and comment these lines out to make the cleanest boot possible.

After the installation, the mouse does not work in Windows

- Verify that the mouse works in DOS before you load Windows. Load the mouse driver in either the CONFIG.SYS or AUTOEXEC.BAT file.
- Boot to the DOS prompt and test the mouse. Try to edit a file using EDIT.COM. If the mouse driver loaded correctly, you should have the use of the mouse in this editor.
- Try a different mouse driver. Did the mouse manufacturer provide one with the mouse?
- After you have the mouse working in DOS, try loading Windows again.

SOFTWARE INSTALLATION PROBLEMS

Windows does not allow software to be installed

There may have been some restrictions placed on Windows to prevent software from being installed or uninstalled by the user. Look in the Progman.ini file for a section labeled [RESTRICTIONS]. These restrictions can prevent program groups from being added to and deleted from Program Manager. Among other restrictions, look for the line EditLevel=. Any EditLevel above 0 can hamper a program installation. Comment out the restriction and reboot.

Message "Insufficient Disk Space"

- Erase lost clusters and defragment the drive before the installation.
- Look for temporary files or applications software that you no longer use, which can be deleted.
- Run a Custom Setup that allows you to install only some of the application.

The software is installed, but when you first execute it, it tells you that an environmental variable is not defined

■ Is a SET command in AUTOEXEC.BAT placed after the WIN command, causing it not to be executed before Windows is loaded?

■ A SET PATH command put into AUTOEXEC.BAT by the software installation program may have an error.

The problem is unknown; the software just does not work after the installation

■ Wrong configuration information may have been given to the installation program. If you suspect that this is the problem, begin again, giving the correct information.

■ Try reinstalling the software and carefully watch for error messages. Before you begin again, use the uninstall program that comes with the software to completely uninstall the software.

■ If there is no uninstall program, use a third-party uninstaller, or erase all files that the installation program copied to the hard drive, and remove the directories it created.

■ Look in AUTOEXEC.BAT and CONFIG.SYS files for errors. Restore the original AUTOEXEC.BAT, CONFIG.SYS, Win.ini, Progman.ini, and System.ini files, and begin again, at the beginning of the installation process.

■ Try to execute some portion of the software such as the Help utility. Look for information about installation requirements. Consult your documentation and technical support for the software.

■ After the installation is complete and the software is working, update your backup copies of AUTOEXEC.BAT, CONFIG.SYS, System.ini, Win.ini, and Progman.ini so that they, too, reflect the changes the applications software made to these configuration files.

HARDWARE DEVICE INSTALLATION PROBLEMS UNDER WINDOWS 95

The device is not in the supported list of devices

When Windows 95 cannot identify a new hardware device, you can select the device from the list of devices supported by the OS. If your device is not in the list, provide a device driver from the manufacturer (click **Have Disk**), or use a substitute (see the device documentation for a recommendation).

Windows 95 cannot use a 16-bit driver

■ Contact the manufacturer of the device for an updated driver, or ask them to recommend a substitute driver.

■ If the 16-bit device driver has an install program, run the install program under either DOS or Windows 3.x, depending on what the install program requires. It makes the correct entries in the AUTOEXEC.BAT and CONFIG.SYS files and copies the driver files to the hard drive. You should then be able to install the device in Windows 95 with no problems.

Problems installing a legacy card (not PnP)

■ Problems installing a legacy card under Windows 95 are generally caused by resource conflicts with other legacy cards.

■ See Device Manager for the resources being used by other legacy cards already installed.

■ Change the jumpers or DIP switches on one of the devices to force it to use a different resource.

WINDOWS NT BOOT PROBLEMS

Errors display during the boot process

Don't attempt to log on. Reboot and select the Last Known Good configuration at bootup.

■ Use anti-virus software to scan for viruses.

Windows NT will not boot

Boot using the three Windows NT boot disks. Have the Windows NT emergency repair disk available. When the Start menu displays, select all options and execute the menu. Follow the directions on screen. You may be asked to provide the original Windows NT CD-ROM or a previously prepared Windows NT emergency repair disk.

NETWORK PROBLEMS

Windows 95 Dial-up Problems

If you experience problems when using Windows 95 Dial-Up Networking to dial into a host computer, they may be caused by the modem. See the troubleshooting guidelines for modems above, to eliminate the modem as the source of the problem.

Cannot make a connection

Because Dial-Up Networking involves so many different components, first find out what works and what doesn't work. Find out the answers to these questions:

■ Does the modem work? Compare the printout of a Modemlog.txt file that was made during a successful connection from another PC to the Modemlog.txt file generated when trying to connect from this PC, to identify at what point in the connection an error occurs. (For Windows 95 to log modem events to the Modemlog.txt file, double-click on **Modems** in Control Panel, and then select the modem, click **Properties**, **Connection**, **Advanced**, and turn on **Recording to a log file**.)
■ Are all components installed? Check for the Dial-Up Adapter and TCP/IP, and check the configuration of each.
■ Check the Dial-Up Networking connection icon for errors. Is the phone number correct? Does the number need to include a 9 for you to get an outside line? Has a 1 been added in front of the number by mistake?
■ Reboot your PC and try again.
■ Try removing and reinstalling each network component. Begin with TCP/IP.
■ Try dialing the number manually from a phone. Do you hear beeps on the other end?
■ Try another phone number.
■ Sometimes older copies of the Windows socket DLL may be interfering with the current Windows 95 version. (Windows 95 may be finding and executing the older DLL before it finds the newer one.) Search for and rename any files named WINSOCK.DLL except the one in the Windows\System directory.

You can connect, but you get the message, "Unable to resolve hostname..."

This means that TCP/IP is not able to determine how to route a request to a host. Right-click on the **Dial-Up Networking** connection icon, select **Properties**, and check for these things:

■ Under Server Type, is TCP/IP the only network protocol allowed?
■ Under TCP/IP settings, check the IP addresses of the DNS servers.

- Is **Using the default gateway** selected?
- Try *not* selecting IP header compression.

After connection, you get the error: "Unable to establish a compatible set of network protocols"

The error is most likely to be caused by a problem with the installation and configuration of Dial-Up Networking and/or TCP/IP. Try these things:

- Verify that Dial-Up Adapter and TCP/IP are installed and configured correctly.
- Remove and reinstall TCP/IP. Be sure to reboot after the installation.
- Try putting the PCs in different workgroups. Sometimes problems arise when two PCs using Windows 95 are in the same workgroup.
- Windows 95 can write the events of PPP processing a call to a log file. Create the PPPLog.txt file on a PC that makes a successful connection, and compare it to the log file of your bad connection. You might be able to see exactly when the problem began. To turn on **Logging events to the file**, double-click the **Network** icon in **Control Panel**. Click **Dial-Up Adapter**, click **Properties**, select the **Advanced** tab, and select **Record a log file**. On the Value list, click **Yes**, and then click **OK**. Reboot the PC. The file PPPLog.txt is created in the Windows folder as the connection is made and used.

When you double-click on the network browser, the modem does not dial automatically

Right-click on the network browser icon and select **Properties** from the drop-down menu. Under the Connection tab, check **Connect to the Internet as needed**.

Problems with TCP/IP Under Windows 95 or Windows NT

- For Windows NT, at the command prompt, enter IPCONFIG, or, for Windows 95, go to Explorer and double-click on **WinIPcfg** in the Windows 95 folder. If the TCP/IP configuration is correct, then for static IP addressing, the IP address, subnet mask, and default gateway will display, along with the adapter address. If DHCP is used for dynamic IP addressing and no IP address has yet been assigned, the IP address should read 0.0.0.0.
- Next try the loopback address test. Enter the command PING 127.0.0.1. If this works, most likely TCP/IP is configured correctly.
- If you have been assigned an IP address, PING it. If you get any errors up to this point, then assume that the problem is on your PC. Check the installation and configuration of each component. Remove and reinstall each component and watch for error messages. Compare the configuration to that of a PC that is working, on the same network.
- Next PING the IP address of your default gateway. If it does not respond, then the problem may be with the gateway or with the network to the gateway.
- Now try to PING the host computer you are trying to reach. If it does not respond, then the problem may be with the host computer or with the network to the computer.
- If you substitute a URL for the IP address in the PING command, and the PING works, then you can conclude that DNS works. If an IP address works, but the URL does not work, the problem lies with DNS. Try this: PING Microsoft.com.

GLOSSARY

3D RAM Special video RAM designed to improve 3D graphics simulation.

32-bit flat memory mode A protected processing mode for the CPU that can process programs written in 32-bit code. NT is a full 32-bit OS.

A

A+ Certification A certification awarded by CompTIA (the Computing Technology Industry Association) that measures a PC technician's knowledge of the skills and behaviors expected of entry-level PC technicians. Many companies require that their service technicians have A+ Certification.

Adapter address A 6-byte hex hardware address unique to each NIC card and assigned by manufacturers. The address is often printed on the adapter. An example is 00 00 0C 08 2F 35.

Adapter card Also called an Interface Card. A small circuit board inserted in an expansion slot and used to communicate between the system bus and a peripheral device.

Address Resolution Protocol (ARP) A method used by TCP/IP that dynamically or automatically translates IP addresses into physical network addresses such as Ethernet IDs or Token Ring MAC addresses.

Administrator account In Windows NT, an account that grants to the administrator(s) rights and permissions to all hardware and software resources such as the right to add, delete, and change accounts and to change hardware configurations.

Advanced SCSI programming interface (ASPI) A popular device driver that enables operating systems to communicate with the SCSI host adapter. (The "A" originally stood for Adaptec.)

Alternate gateway An alternate router that is used if the default gateway is down. *See* Gateway.

Alternating current (AC) Current that cycles back and forth rather than traveling in only one direction. Normally between 110 and 115 AC volts are supplied from a standard wall outlet.

Ammeter A meter that measures electrical current in amps.

Ampere (A) or amp A unit of measurement for electrical current. One volt across a resistance of one ohm will produce a flow of one amp.

Amplifier repeater A repeater that amplifies whatever it receives regardless of its source.

Analog signals Signals that have an infinite number of values within a range of possible values. An example is the transmission of sound, in wave format, over traditional telephone lines. Compare to Digital signal.

Analog-to-digital converter (A/D or ADC) A component on a sound card that samples and converts analog sound into digital values that can be stored on hard drives.

Anti-Virus (AV) software Utility programs that prevent infection, or scan a system to detect and remove viruses. Norton AntiVirus and McAfee Associates Virus Scan are two popular AV packages.

Application layer The layer of the OSI model responsible for interfacing with the user or application using the network.

Applications software Programs that perform a specific task, such as word processing, database management, or mathematical calculations (for example, Word, WordPerfect, and Excel).

Asynchronous SRAM A slow version of SRAM that does not work in step with the CPU clock speed.

AT command set A set of commands used by a PC to control a modem. AT is the ATtention command, which alerts a modem to prepare to receive additional commands. For example, ATDT means attention and listen for a dial tone.

ATTRIB command A DOS command that can display file attributes and even lock files so that they are "read-only" and cannot be modified (for example, ATTRIB +R FILENAME makes FILENAME a read-only file).

Authoring software Software that allows the user to incorporate text, sound, graphics, photos, animations, and video into one continuous show.

Auto-detecting BIOS A feature on newer system BIOS and hard drives that provides for auto-detection when identifying and configuring a new hard drive in the CMOS setup.

AUTOEXEC.BAT One startup file on an MS-DOS computer. It tells the computer what commands or programs to execute automatically after bootup.

Autorange meter A multimeter that senses the quantity of input and sets the range accordingly.

B

Back end In a client/server environment, the application on the server that processes requests for data from the client.

Backbone A network used to link several networks together. For example, several Token Rings and Ethernets may be connected using a single FDDI backbone.

Back up (v), Backup (n) To make a second copy of important files or data. Backups can be made by saving a file with a different name or by copying files to a different disk or to a tape drive.

Backup catalog A backup set that displays a list of the files and folders previously backed up. *See* backup set.

Backup set The name for the set of files you backed up. For example, perhaps only the C:\data and C:\mail directories were backed up. DATA and MAIL might be used as the backup set names. *See* backup set.

Backup Windows NT domain controller (BDC) A computer on a network that holds a read-only copy of the SAM (Security Accounts Manager) database.

Bandwidth The range of frequencies that a communications cable or channel can carry. In general use, the term refers to the volume of data that can travel on a bus or over a cable.

Bank An area on the systemboard that contains slots for memory modules (typically labeled bank 0, 1, 2, and 3).

Batch file A text file containing a series of DOS instructions to the computer, telling it to perform a specific task (for example, AUTOEXEC.BAT is a batch file that contains a series of startup commands).

Baud rate A line speed of communication between two devices such as a computer and a printer or a modem. This speed is measured in the number of times a signal changes in one second.

Beam detect mirror Detects the initial presence of a laser printer's laser beam by reflecting the beam to an optical fiber.

Binding Associating an OSI layer to a layer above it or below it.

BIOS (basic input/output system) Firmware that controls much of a computer's input/output functions, such as communication with disk drives, the printer, RAM chips, and the monitor.

Bit-map file A type of graphics file in which the image is written as a series of 0s and 1s. These files have the extension .BMP and can be loaded into paint programs to be edited and printed.

Boot loader menu In Windows NT, a startup menu that gives the user the choice between Windows NT and another OS such as Windows 95.

Boot partition The hard drive partition where the Windows NT operating system is stored. The system partition and the boot partition may be different partitions.

Boot sector virus An infectious program that can replace the boot program with a modified, infected version of the boot command utilities, often causing boot and data retrieval problems.

Bootable disk For DOS, a floppy disk that can upload the operating system files necessary for computer startup. It must have the two hidden system files IO.SYS and MSDOS.SYS, and also COMMAND.COM.

Break code A code produced when a key is released. *See* Make code.

Bridge A hardware device or box, coupled with software at the Data Link Layer, used to connect similar networks and network segments. *See* Router.

Buck-boost regulator A line-interactive UPS that offers good line conditioning and has an automatic voltage regulator that boosts the voltage during electrical sags.

Buffer A temporary memory area where data is kept before being written to a hard drive or sent to a printer, thus reducing the number of writes when devices communicate at different speeds.

Burst SRAM Memory that is more expensive and slightly faster than pipelined burst SRAM. Data is sent as a two-step process; the data address is sent, and then the data itself is sent without interruption.

Burst transfer A means of sending data across the bus, with one packet immediately following the next, without waiting for clock beats and/or addressing of the information being sent.

Bus Strips of parallel wires or printed circuits used to transmit electronic signals on the systemboard to other devices. Most Pentium systems use a 32-bit bus.

Bus enumerator A component of Windows 95 Plug-and-Play that locates all devices on a particular bus and inventories the resource requirements for these devices.

Bus mouse A mouse that plugs into a bus adapter card and has a round, 9-pin mini-DIN connector.

Bus network architecture A network design in which nodes are connected in line with one another, with no centralized point of contact.

Bus speed The speed at which the data on the systemboard is moving.

C

Cache controller The microchip on the systemboard that controls the memory cache to static RAM.

Call tracking A system that tracks the dates, times, and transactions of help-desk or on-site PC support calls, including the problem presented, the issues addressed, who did what, and when and how each call was resolved.

Cards Adapter boards or interface cards placed into expansion slots to expand the functions of a computer, allowing it to communicate with external devices such as monitors or printers.

Carrier A reference signal used to activate a phone line to confirm a continuous frequency; used to indicate that two computers are ready to receive or transmit data via modems.

Carrier Sense Multiple Access with Collision Detection (CSMA/CD) A feature used in ethernet networks whereby packets are sent after listening for a silence, and are resent if a collision is detected.

CD or CHDIR command A DOS command to change directories (for example, CD\WINDOWS would change the directory to the Windows directory, and CD\ would return to the Root directory).

Chain A group of clusters used to hold a single file.

Checksum A method of error checking of transmitted data, whereby the digits are added up and their sum compared to an expected sum.

Child, parent, grandparent backup method A plan for backing up and reusing tapes or removable disks by rotating them each week (child), month (parent), and year (grandparent).

Chip set A set of chips on the systemboard that collectively controls the memory cache, external buses, and some peripherals.

CHKDSK command A DOS command that checks for some hard drive errors and displays possible problems (for example, CHKDSK C: is used to check drive C).

CHS (cylinders, heads, sectors) The traditional method by which BIOS reads and writes to hard drives by addressing the correct cylinder, head, and sector.

Circuit boards Computer components, such as the main systemboard or an adapter board, that have electronic circuits and chips.

Clamping voltage The maximum voltage allowed through a surge suppressor, such as 175 or 330 volts.

Classless addresses Class C network addresses a service provider owns and then subleases to small companies.

Clock speed The speed at which the CPU operates, usually expressed in MHz. A Pentium may have a speed of 150 MHz, while a Pentium II may operate at 233 MHz.

Clone Originally, a computer that was compatible with IBM computer hardware and MS-DOS software. Today, the word clone often refers to no-name Intel and Microsoft compatibles.

Cluster One or more sectors that constitute the smallest unit of space on a disk for storing data (also referred to as a file allocation unit). Files are written to the disk as groups of whole clusters.

Cluster chain A series of clusters used to hold a single file.

.CMD files Windows NT batch files that contain a list of commands to be executed as a group.

CMOS (complementary metal oxide conductor) A type of microchip that requires relatively less electricity and produces less heat than other types of chips. The configuration chip on the systemboard is an example of a CMOS chip.

COAST (cache on a stick) Chips on a module available for pipelined burst synchronous SRAM.

CODEC (COder/DECoder) A method of compressing and later decompressing sound, animation, and video files. MPEG is a common example.

Collision In an ethernet network, when transmitted packets of data are sent at the same time and collide. Ethernet will first listen for silence before it transmits, and it will stop and resend if a collision occurs.

Color depth The number of possible colors used by the monitor. Determines the number of bits used to compose one pixel. One of two characteristics (the other is screen resolution) that determine the amount of data sent to the video card to build one screen.

Color space conversion Converting images to RGB values before they are displayed. Processing is faster if the video card does the conversion instead of the CPU.

Comment lines Documentation lines that are ignored by the OS or software executing a list of instructions. A REM in front of a line will turn an AUTOEXEC command into a comment. A semicolon will turn an .ini file line into a comment.

Common access method (CAM) A standard adapter driver used by SCSI.

Compressed drive A drive whose format has been reorganized, in order to store more data. A compressed drive is really not a drive at all; it's actually a type of file, typically with a host drive called H.

Computing Technology Industry Association (CompTIA) A membership trade association that sponsors A+ Certification, a valuable certification for PC technicians.

Configuration data Also called setup information. Information about the computer's hardware, such as what type of hard drive, floppy drive, or monitor is present, along with other detailed settings.

Configuration manager A component of Windows 95 Plug-and-Play that controls the configuration process of all devices and communicates these configurations to the devices.

Configuration parameter Another name for the value names and values of the registry, which is information in the Windows registry.

Connection protocol In networking, confirming that a good connection is made before transmitting data to the other end. To accomplish this, most network applications use TCP rather than UDP.

Connectionless protocol When UDP is used and a connection is not required before sending a packet. Consequently, there is no guarantee that the packet will arrive at its destination. An example of a UDP transmission is a broadcast to all nodes on a network.

Constant linear velocity (CLV) A CD-ROM format in which the spacing of data is consistent on the CD, but the speed of the disc varies depending on whether the drive is reading near the center or the edge of the disc.

Contention-based system A system in which each computer contends for the opportunity to transmit on the network. If there is a collision, a computer waits a random amount of time and resends.

Continuity A continuous, unbroken path for the flow of electricity. A "continuity test" can determine whether or not internal wiring is still intact.

Control blade A laser printer component that prevents too much toner from sticking to the cylinder surface.

Controlled-access unit (CAU) A centralized hub on a Token Ring network. *See* Multistation access unit.

Controller board An adapter board used to interface between the computer and a device such as a scanner.

Coprocessor A chip or portion of the CPU that helps the microprocessor perform calculations and speeds up computations and data manipulations dramatically.

Copy backup A full backup that does not change the archive attributes of files and folders, so that incremental and differential backups don't "sense" this backup.

COPY command A DOS command that copies files from one location to another (for example, COPY FILE.EXT A: is used to copy the file named FILE.EXT to the disk in drive A).

Corrupted files Data and program files that are damaged for any of a variety of reasons, ranging from power spikes to user error.

CPU (central processing unit) Also called a microprocessor. The heart and brain of the computer, which receives data input, processes the information, and executes instructions.

Cross-linked clusters Errors caused when files appear to share the same disk space, according to the file allocation table.

Crosstalk The interference that one wire, in a twisted pair, may produce in the other.

D

DAC (Digital-to-Analog Converter) A component that converts digital data back into analog signals just before output from the computer. For example, DAC technology is used to convert digital sound to analog sound just before playback to the speakers.

Daily copy backup Backs up all files that have changed during a day, but does not change the archive attributes of files; in this way, incremental and differential backups don't "sense" the backup.

Data bits The number of bits used to make up a transmitted character or value. PC communication will typically use 8 data bits and 1 stop bit for communicating data over phone lines.

Data cartridge A type of tape medium typically used for backups. Full-sized data cartridges are $4 \times 6 \times \frac{5}{8}$ inches in size. A minicartridge is only $3\frac{1}{4} \times 2\frac{1}{2} \times \frac{3}{8}$ inches.

Data communications equipment (DCE) The hardware, usually a dial-up modem, that provides the connection between a data terminal and a communication line.

Data compression Reducing the size of files by various techniques such as using a shortcut code to represent repeated data.

Data line protectors Surge protectors designed to protect the telephone line to a modem.

Data Link layer The OSI layer that disassembles packets and reassembles data into packets.

Data path The size of a bus, such as a 32-bit-wide data path in a PCI bus.

Data terminal equipment (DTE) This term refers to both the computer and a remote terminal or other computer to which it is attached.

Datagrams Packets of data that travel between networks from a sender to a receiver. A datagram typically includes an IP header, address information, a checksum, and data.

De facto standard A standard that does not have an official backing, but is considered a standard because of widespread use and acceptance by the industry.

DEBUG utility A DOS utility that shows exactly what is written in memory, using the hexadecimal numbering system to display memory addresses and data.

Default gateway The main gateway or unit that will send or receive packets addressed to other networks.

Default Windows printer The printer that Windows software will use unless the user specifies another printer.

Defragment To "optimize" or rewrite a file to a disk in one continuous chain, thus speeding up data retrieval.

DEL command A DOS command that deletes files (for example, DEL A:FILE.EXT deletes the file named FILE.EXT from drive A).

DELTREE command A DOS command used to delete a directory, all its subdirectories, and all files within it (for example, DELTREE DIRNAME deletes the directory named DIRNAME and everything in it).

Demodulation When digital data that has been converted to analog data is converted back to digital data. *See* Modulation.

Desktop publishing Using a microcomputer for tasks once done by graphic designers, typesetters, and print shops, to produce professional-quality, camera-ready output.

Device driver A small program that tells the computer how to communicate with an input/output device such as a printer or modem.

Device Manager A Windows 95 program that allows the user to view and set hardware configurations.

Diagnostic cards Adapter cards designed to discover and report computer errors and conflicts at POST time (before the computer boots up), often by displaying a number on the card.

Diagnostic software Utility programs that help troubleshoot computer systems. Some DOS diagnostic utilities are CHKDSK and SCANDISK. PC Technician is an example of a third-party diagnostic program.

Dial-Up Networking A Windows application that allows a PC to remotely connect to a network through a phone line. A Dial-Up Network icon can be found under My Computer.

Differential backup Backs up only files that have changed or have been created since the last *full* backup. When recovering data, only two backups are needed: the full backup and the last differential backup.

Differential SCSI device A device (with a cable up to 75 feet long) that sends signals through a pair of wires and is less vulnerable to noise than single-ended SCSI devices. *See* Single-ended SCSI devices.

Digital signal A signal that has only a finite number of values in the range of possible values. An example is the transmission of data over a serial cable as bits, where there are only two values: 0 and 1.

Digital video disc (DVD) A faster, larger CD-ROM format that can read older CDs, store over 4 gigabytes of data, and hold full-length motion picture videos.

DIMM (dual in-line memory module) A miniature circuit board that has a 64-bit path, unlike SIMMs, which have a 32-bit path. Because Pentium processors require a 64-bit path, you must install two SIMMs at a time, but you can install DIMMs one at a time.

DIP switch (dual in-line packet switch) A switch that has only two settings, and can be used to set configurations such as modem COM ports or printer setup.

Direct current (DC) Current that travels in only one direction (the type of electricity provided by batteries). Computer power supplies transform AC current to low DC current.

Directory A DOS table that contains file information such as name, size, time, and date of last modification, and the cluster number of the file's beginning location.

Disk cache A method whereby recently retrieved data and adjacent data from a hard drive are read into memory in advance, anticipating the next CPU request. Also a process by which data written to the hard drive is accumulated in memory to reduce the number of writes to the drive.

Disk compression Compressing data on a hard drive to allow more data to be written to the drive.

Disk duplexing An improvement of disk mirroring, whereby redundant data is written to two or more drives, and each hard drive has its own adapter card. This provides greater protection than disk mirroring.

Disk editor A powerful tool for editing any part of a disk, including the partition table, directory entries, DOS boot record, and FAT.

Disk mirroring A strategy whereby the same data is written to two hard drives in a computer, to safeguard against hard drive failure. Disk mirroring uses only a single adapter for two drives.

Disk striping Treating multiple hard drives as a single volume. Data is written across the multiple drives in small segments, in order to increase performance and logical disk volume, and, when parity is also used, to provide fault tolerance. RAID 5 is disk striping with an additional drive for parity.

Disk thrashing A condition that results when the hard drive is excessively used for virtual memory because RAM is full. It dramatically slows down processing and can cause premature hard drive failure.

DISKCOPY command A DOS command that copies the entire contents of one disk to another disk of the same type, while formatting the destination disk so that the two will be identical (for example, DISKCOPY A: A: makes a duplicate floppy disk using drive A).

Display adapter Another name for a video controller card.

Display power management signaling (DPMS) Energy Star standard specifications that allow for the video card and monitor to go into sleep mode simultaneously.

DMA (direct memory access) controller A chip or chip logic on the systemboard that provides channels that a device may use to send data directly to memory, bypassing the CPU.

Docking station A system that is designed to connect to a portable or notebook computer for downloading and uploading data and for sharing local peripheral devices.

Documentation Manuals, tutorials, and help files that provide information that a user needs in order to use a computer system or software application.

Domain A logical group of networked computers, such as those on a college campus, that share a centralized directory database of user account information and security for the entire domain.

Domain name A unique, text-based name that identifies an IP (Internet address). Typically, domain names in the United States end in .edu, .gov, .com, .org, or .net. Domain names also include a country code, such as .uk for the United Kingdom.

Domain name system or **domain name service (DNS)** A database on a top-level domain name server that keeps track of assigned domain names and their corresponding IP addresses.

Double conversion The process by which the in-line UPS converts the AC power to battery power in DC form and then back to AC power.

Doze time The time before an Energy Star or "green" system will reduce 80% of its activity.

DriveSpace A utility that compresses data on a disk drive, creating a single large file on the disk to hold all the compressed files.

Drop height The height that the manufacturer states that a drive can be dropped without making the drive unusable.

Dual boot The ability to boot using two different operating systems, such as Windows NT and Windows 95. However, programs cannot be shared between Windows NT and the other OS.

Dual ported When the video chip set (input) and the RAM DAC (output) can access video memory at the same time. A special kind of video RAM is required.

Dual voltage CPU A CPU that requires two different voltages, one for internal processing and the other for I/O processing.

Dynamic Host Configuration Protocol (DHCP) The protocol of a server that manages dynamically assigned IP addresses. DHCP is supported by both Windows 95 and Windows NT.

Dynamic IP address An assigned IP address that is used for the current session only. When the session is terminated, the IP address is returned to the list of available addresses.

Dynamic RAM (DRAM) The most commonly used type of system memory with access speeds ranging from 70 to 50 nanoseconds, requiring refreshing every few milliseconds.

Dynamic routing Routing tables that are automatically updated as new information about routes becomes known and is shared by one router with another. Compare to static routing.

E

EDO (extended data output) memory A type of RAM that may be 10-20% faster than conventional RAM because it eliminates the delay before it issues the next memory address.

EEPROM (electrically erasable programmable ROM) chip A type of chip in which higher voltage may be applied to one of the pins to erase its previous memory before a new instruction set is electronically written.

EISA (Extended Standard Industry Architecture) bus A 32-bit bus that can transfer 4 bytes at a time at a speed of about 20 MHz.

Electrostatic discharge (ESD) Another name for static electricity, which can damage chips and destroy systemboards, even though it may not be felt or seen with the naked eye.

ELF (Extremely Low Frequency) Very low-frequency monitor emission of magnetic fields. ELF guidelines are established to ensure that computers are safe and energy efficient.

Embedded SCSI devices Devices that contain their own host adapter, whereby the SCSI interface is built into the device.

EMM386.EXE A DOS utility that creates upper memory blocks (commonly used in pre-Windows 95 systems).

Encrypting virus A type of virus that transforms itself into a nonreplicating program in order to avoid detection. It transforms itself back into a replicating program in order to spread.

Energy Star systems "Green" systems that satisfy the EPA requirements to decrease the overall consumption of electricity.

Enhanced BIOS A newer BIOS that has been written to accommodate the larger-capacity gigabyte drives.

Enhanced IDE technology A newer drive standard that allows systems to recognize drives larger than 528 MB and to handle up to four devices on the same adapter.

Environment subsystems A Windows NT user mode process in which a subsystem runs an application in its own private memory address space as a virtual machine. (Compare to integral subsystems.)

EPROM (erasable programmable ROM) chip A type of chip with a special window that allows the current memory contents to be erased with special ultraviolet light so that the chip can be reprogrammed. Many BIOS chips are EPROMs.

ERASE command A DOS command that deletes or erases files (for example, ERASE FILE.EXT deletes the file named FILE.EXT from the current disk).

Error correction The ability of some modems to identify transmission errors and then automatically request another transmission.

Escalating The process of a technician passing a customer's problem to higher organizational levels, if he or she cannot address the problem.

ESD *See* Electrostatic discharge.

Ethernet The most popular network topology used today. It uses Carrier Sense Multiple Access with Collision Detection (CSMA/CD) and can be physically configured as a bus or star network.

Event Viewer A Windows NT utility that tracks and logs events as they are performed by the applications, processes, or user actions. Accessed by: clicking Start, Programs, Administrative Tools, and then selecting Event Viewer.

Executive Services _ In Windows NT, a subsystem running in kernel mode that interfaces between the user mode and HAL.

Expanded memory (EMS) Memory outside of the conventional linearly addressed memory that is accessed in 16K segments, or pages, by way of a window to upper memory.

Expert systems Computerized software that uses a database of known facts and rules to simulate a human expert's reasoning and decision-making processes.

Extended memory Memory above the initial 1024 KB, or 1 MB, area.

External cache Static cache memory, stored on the systemboard, that is not part of the CPU (also called Level 2 or L2 cache).

F

Fake parity chip A parity generator chip designed to simulate parity checking so that the user can use less expensive nonparity memory modules on a systemboard that expects parity memory.

Fatal system error An error that prevents the OS from loading. An example is a damaged registry.

Fault tolerance The degree to which a system can tolerate failures. Adding redundant components, such as disk mirroring or disk duplexing, is a way to build in fault tolerance.

FDDI (Fiber Distributed Data Interface) Pronounced "fiddy." A ring-based network, similar to Token Ring, that does not require a centralized hub. FDDI often uses only fiber-optic cabling.

Ferroresonant regulator A UPS device that contains a magnetic coil that can retain a power charge that can be used during a brownout to raise the voltage at switching time.

FIFO (first-in first-out) A method of storing and retrieving data from a table or stack, whereby the first element stored is the first one retrieved.

FIFO buffer A buffer on a 16550 UART chip that solves the problem of lost data, which sometimes occurred with the older 16450 UART chips.

File A collection of related records or lines that can be written to disk and assigned a name (for example, a simple letter or a payroll file containing data about employees).

File allocation table (FAT) A DOS table at the beginning of a disk that tracks where files are stored on the disk according to the file allocation units used by the files.

File allocation units *See* Cluster.

File virus A virus that inserts virus code into an executable program and can spread whenever that program is accessed.

Firmware Software that is permanently etched onto a chip.

Fixed frequency Monitors that only support a single refresh rate. Compare to multiscan monitors, which support different video cards and different refresh rates.

Flash memory A type of RAM that can electronically hold memory even when the power is off.

Flash ROM ROM that can be reprogrammed or changed without replacing chips.

Flow control When using modems, a method of controlling the flow of data from a sending PC by having the receiving PC send a message to the sending device to stop or start data flow. Xon/Xoff is an example of a flow control protocol.

FM (Frequency Modulation) method A method of synthesizing sound by making a mathematical approximation of the musical sound wave. MIDI may use FM synthesis or wavetable synthesis.

Folder A Windows directory for a collection of related files (for instance, a person may find it convenient to create a MYDATA directory, or folder, in which to store personal files).

Format To prepare a disk for use by creating a FAT and root directory on the disk. During formatting, any data on the disk is lost.

FPM (fast page mode) memory An earlier memory mode used before the introduction of EDO memory.

Fragmentation The condition that occurs when files are not written in single chains on a disk.

Fragmented files Files that are spread out over different portions of the disk so that they are not in contiguous clusters.

Frame A small, standardized packet of data that also includes header and trailer information as well as error-checking codes.

Frame buffer An area of memory on a video controller that is used to store the data to be displayed on the screen.

Front end In a client/server environment, the application on the client that makes use of data stored on the server.

FTP (File Transfer Protocol) An Internet standard that provides for the transfer of files from one computer to another. FTP can be used at a command prompt, or with a GUI interface, which is available with FTP software or with a Web browser. When using a Web browser, enter the command "ftp" in the browser URL line instead of the usual "http://" used to locate a Web site.

FTP server or **FTP site** A computer that stores files that can be downloaded by FTP.

Full backup A complete backup, whereby all of the files on the hard drive are backed up each time the backup procedure is performed. It is the safest backup method, but it takes the most time.

G

Gateway A device or process that connects networks with different protocols. *See* Bridge and Router.

General Protection Fault (GPF) error A Windows error that occurs when a program attempts to access a memory address that is not available or is no longer assigned to it.

Genlock A standard for video-capturing cards that refers to the ability of the card to capture a single unique frame of video, rather than "sampling" pieces of adjoining frames.

Gigabyte Approximately 1 billion bytes of data (actually 2 to the 30th power, or 1,073,741,824 bytes).

Graphics accelerator A type of video card that has an on-board processor that can substantially increase speed and boost graphical and video performance.

Green monitor A monitor that is designed to conserve energy by using such techniques as sleep or doze mode.

Green Standards Standards that mean that a computer or device can go into sleep or doze mode when not in use, thus saving energy and helping the environment.

Ground mat An antistatic mat designed for electronic workbenches to dissipate static electricity. It often uses a wire attached to the ground connection, in a standard electrical outlet.

Ground strap An antistatic wrist strap used to dissipate static electricity. Typically grounded by attaching an alligator clip to the computer chassis or to a nearby grounded antistatic mat.

Group files Windows 3.x files with the .grp file extension that contain information about a program group and related programs; program groups are displayed in Program Manager.

GUI (graphical user interface) A user interface, such as the Windows interface, that uses graphics or icons on the screen for running programs and entering information.

H

Half-life The time it takes for a medium storing data to weaken to half of its strength. Magnetic media, including traditional hard drives and floppy disks, have a half-life of 5 to 7 years.

Handshaking When two modems begin to communicate, the initial agreement made as to how to send and receive data. It often occurs when you hear the modem making noises as the dial-up is completed.

Hard disk removable drives High-capacity drives, such as Zip or Jaz drives, that have disks that can be removed like floppy disks.

Hard drive standby time The amount of time before a hard drive will shut down to conserve energy.

Hard-disk loading The illegal practice of installing unauthorized software on computers for sale. Hard-disk loading can typically be identified by the absence of original disks in the original system's shipment.

Hardware The physical machinery that constitutes the computer system, such as the monitor, the keyboard, the system unit, and the printer.

Hardware abstraction layer (HAL) The low-level part of Windows NT, written specifically for each CPU technology, so that only the HAL must change when platform components change.

Hardware cache A disk cache that is contained in RAM chips built right on the disk controller.

Hardware Compatibility List (HCL) The list of all computers and peripheral devices that have been tested and are officially supported by Windows NT. (*See* www. microsoft.com/hwtest)

Hardware profiles Configuration information about memory, CPU, and OS, for a PC. A PC may have more than one profile. For example, a docking station PC may have two profiles, one with and one without the notebook PC docked.

Hardware tree A database built each time Windows 95 starts up that contains a list of installed components and the resources they use.

Header Information sent ahead of data being transferred over a network to identify it to receiving protocols. An IP header consists of things such as header and datagram length, flags, checksum, addresses, and so on.

Heap A memory block set aside for a program's data. If the heap fills up, an "Out of memory" error may occur, even if there is plenty of regular RAM left, especially in 16-bit applications.

Heat sink A piece of metal, with cooling fins, that can be attached to or mounted on an integrated circuit (such as the CPU) to dissipate heat.

Hertz (Hz) Unit of measurement for frequency, calculated in terms of vibrations, or cycles, per second. For example, a Pentium CPU may have a speed of 233 MHz (megahertz). For 16-bit stereo sound, 44,100 Hz is used.

High memory area (HMA) The first 64K of extended memory. The method of storing part of DOS in the high memory area is called loading DOS high.

High-capacity floppy drives Large storage devices such as the Iomega 3.5-inch Zip drive, which stores 100 MB of data.

High-level format Formatting performed by means of the DOS FORMAT program (for example, FORMAT C:/S formats drive C and writes systems files to the drive).

HIMEM.SYS A utility that makes memory above 640K available.

Hive A physical segment of the NT registry that is stored in a disk file.

Holographic images A three-dimensional image (created by holography) that is made up of a light interference pattern preserved in a medium such as photographic film and which changes when the angle of view changes. Because making unofficial copies of holographic images is extremely difficult, they are often used to tag products, such as software packages, as original, making it difficult to distribute illegal copies.

Hop count The number of routers a packet must pass through in a network in order to reach its destination.

Host adapter The circuit board that controls a SCSI bus that supports as many as eight separate devices, one of which is a host adapter that controls communication with the PC.

Host drive Typically drive H on a compressed drive. *See* Compressed drive.

Hot swapping A system feature, desirable in file servers, whereby a hard drive can be removed and exchanged without powering down a computer.

HTTP (Hypertext Transfer Protocol) The common transfer protocol used by Internet browsers on the World Wide Web.

Hub A network device or box that provides a central location to connect cables.

I

I/O (input/output) address table A table that stores the memory addresses assigned to I/O devices controlled by the system BIOS or device drivers. Also called interrupt vector table or vector table.

I/O (input/output) card A card that often contains serial, parallel, and game ports on the same adapter board.

Inband signaling In modem communication, the name of the signalling used by software flow control, which sends a message to pause transmission by sending a special control character in the same channel (or band) that data is sent in.

Incremental backup A time-saving backup method that only backs up files changed or newly created since the last full or incremental backup. Multiple incremental backups might be required when recovering lost data.

Infestation Any unwanted program that is unknowingly transmitted to a computer and is designed to do varying degrees of damage to data and software. There are a number of different types of infestations, including viruses, Trojan Horses, Worms, and time bombs, among others.

Initialization files Configuration information for Windows. WIN.INI and SYSTEM.INI are the two most important Windows initialization files.

In-line UPS A UPS that continually provides power through a battery-powered circuit, and, because it requires no switching, ensures continuous power to the user.

Instruction set The set of instructions, on the CPU chip, that the computer can perform directly (such as ADD and MOVE).

Integral subsystems Windows NT user mode processes used to provide services to the rest of the system and the applications the system supports. (Compare to environment subsystems.)

Integrated Device Electronics (IDE) drive A hard drive whose disk controller is integrated into the drive, eliminating the need for a signal cable and thus increasing speed, as well as reducing price.

Intelligent hubs Network hubs that can be remotely controlled at a console, using network software. These hubs can monitor a network and report errors or problems.

Intelligent UPS A UPS connected to a computer by a serial cable that can be monitored and controlled by software on the computer.

Interleave To write data in nonconsecutive sectors around a track, so that time is not wasted waiting for the disk to make a full revolution before the next sector is read.

Internal cache Memory cache that is faster than external cache, and is contained inside the 80486 and Pentium chips (also referred to as primary, Level 1, or L1 cache).

Internet The worldwide collection of over a million hosts that can communicate with each other using TCP/IP. The lowercase *internet* simply means multiple networks connected together.

Internet Control Message Protocol (ICMP) Part of the IP layer that is used to transmit error messages and other control messages to hosts and routers.

Internet Network Information Center (InterNIC) The central group that assigns and keeps track of all Internet IP addresses on the organizational level.

Internet Service Provider (ISP) A commercial group that provides a user with software for Internet access for a monthly fee. AOL, Prodigy, GTE, and CompuServe are four large ISPs.

Internetwork Two or more networks connected together, such as a LAN and a WAN joined together.

Interpolative scaling A method used to fill in the gaps in an image to produce a more realistic-looking display when a small video window is enlarged to full-screen size.

Interrupt descriptor table Another name for the I/O address table.

Interrupt handler A program that services a device when the CPU handles an IRQ request for service.

Interrupt vector table *See* I/O address table.

Intranet A private internet used by a large company over a fairly wide geographical area.

IP (Internet Protocol) address A 32-bit "dotted-decimal" address consisting of four numbers separated by periods used to uniquely identify a device on a network that uses TCP/IP protocols. The first numbers identify the network; the last number identifies a host. An example of an IP address is 206.96.103.114.

IPX/SPX A protocol developed and used by Novell NetWare for LANs. The IPX portion of the protocol works at the Network layer, which is responsible for routing, and the SPX portion of the protocol manages error checking at the Transport layer.

IRQ (interrupt request) number A number that is assigned to a device and is used to signal the CPU for servicing (for example, the normal IRQ number for COM1 is IRQ 4).

ISA bus An 8-bit Industry Standard Architecture bus used on the original 8088 PC. Sixteen-bit ISA buses were designed for the 286 AT. ISA buses are often used on Pentium systemboards.

ISDN (Integrated services digital network) A communications standard that can carry digital data simultaneously over two channels on a single pair of wires, at about five times the speed of regular phone lines.

J

Joule A measure of energy equal to the work done when a current of one ampere is passed through a resistance of one ohm for one second.

JPEG (Joint Photographic Experts Group) A "lossy" graphical compression scheme that allows the user to control the amount of data that is averaged and sacrificed as file size is reduced. It is a common Internet file format. *See* Lossy compression.

Jumpers Small, plastic-coated conductive shorting blocks that are installed on pins on circuit boards to close or complete a circuit to configure the board. They are often labeled JP 1, JP 2, and so on.

K

Kernel mode A Windows NT "privileged" processing mode that has access to hardware components.

Keyboard A common input device through which data and instructions may be typed into computer memory.

Keys Setting names of the Windows 95 Registry.

L

Lands Microscopic flat areas on the surface of a compact disc that separate pits. Lands and pits are used to represent data as either a 0 or a 1.

Large Mode A format that supports hard drives that range from 504 MB to 1 GB, mapping the data to conform to the 504 MB barrier before the address information is passed to the operating system.

Legacy device An older device or adapter card that does not support Plug-and-Play, and may have to be manually configured through jumpers or DIP switches.

Let-through The maximum voltage allowed through a surge suppressor to the device being protected.

Level 1 cache *See* Internal cache.

Level 2 cache *See* External cache.

Limited token Applies to a FDDI network. A token sent that allows a receiving station to communicate only with the sending station, thus providing continuous communication between the two stations.

Line conditioners Devices that regulate, or condition, the power, providing continuous voltage during brownouts or spikes.

Line protocol A protocol used over phone lines to allow a connection to a network. Also called bridging protocol. The most popular line protocol is PPP (Point-to-Point Protocol).

Line-interactive UPS A variation of a standby UPS that shortens switching time by always keeping the inverter from AC to DC working, so that there is no charge-up time for the inverter.

Load size The largest amount of memory that a driver needs to initialize itself and to hold its data. It is almost always a little larger than the size of the program file.

Loading high The process of loading a driver or TSR into upper memory.

Local bus A bus connecting adapters directly to the local processor bus. On 80486 computers, it is usually a 32-bit bus running at the same clock speed as the CPU.

Logic parity A fake parity chip designed to simulate parity checking so that the user can use less expensive nonparity memory modules on a systemboard that expects parity memory.

Logical block addressing (LBA) A method in which the operating system views the drive as one long linear list of LBAs, permitting larger drive sizes to be accessed by the OS.

Logical unit number (LUN) Also called SCSI ID. A number from 0 to 7 assigned to each SCSI device attached to a SCSI chain.

Lossless compression A method that substitutes special characters for repeating patterns without image degradation. A substitution table is used to restore the compressed image to its original form.

Lossy compression A method that drops unnecessary data, but with image and sound loss. JPEG allows the user to control the amount of loss, which is inversely related to the image size.

Lost allocation units See Lost clusters.

Lost clusters Also called lost allocation units. Lost file fragments that, according to the file allocation table, contain data that does not belong to any file. In DOS, the command CHKDSK/F can free these fragments.

Low-level format A process, usually performed at the factory, that electronically creates the hard drive cylinders and tests for bad spots on the disk surface.

M

MAC (Media Access Control) An element of Data Link layer protocol that provides compatibility with the NIC used by the Physical layer. An adapter address is often called a MAC address.

Macro A small sequence of commands, contained within a document, that can be automatically executed when the document is loaded, or executed later by pressing a predetermined keystroke.

Macro virus A virus that can hide in the macros of a document file. Typically, viruses do not reside in data or document files.

Magneto-optical (MO) drives Removable, rewritable, high-capacity drives that combine magnetic and optical disc technology.

Make code A code produced by pressing a key. See Break code.

Master boot record (MBR) The record written at the beginning of a disk, containing information about the disk as well as startup programs.

MCA (Micro Channel Architecture) bus A proprietary IBM PS/2 bus, seldom seen today, with a width of 16 or 32 bits and multiple master control, which allowed for multitasking.

MD or MKDIR command A DOS command used to create a directory on a drive (for example, MD C:\MYDATA will create a directory in drive C called MYDATA).

Megahertz (Mhz) One million hertz. CPU speed is measured in MHz (for example, a Pentium II may have a speed of 233 MHz).

MEM command A DOS utility used to display program and driver usage, as well as conventional, extended, and HMA memory (for example, MEM/C/P displays a complete listing of memory one screen at a time).

MemMaker A DOS utility that can increase the amount of conventional memory available to DOS-based software applications, by loading drivers and TSRs into upper memory.

Memory cache A small amount of faster RAM that stores recently retrieved data, in anticipation of what the CPU will next request, thus speeding up access.

Memory caching Using a small amount of faster RAM to store recently retrieved data, in anticipation of what the CPU will next request, thus speeding up access.

Memory conflict A problem that occurs when two programs attempt to use the same memory address at the same time. This may cause the computer to "hang."

Memory leak A problem caused when an application does not release the memory addresses assigned to it when it unloads, causing the memory heaps to have less and less memory for new applications.

Memory management The process of increasing available conventional memory, required by DOS-based programs, accomplished by loading device drivers and TSRs into upper memory.

Memory mapping Assigning addresses to both RAM and ROM during the boot process.

Memory paging Swapping blocks of RAM memory to an area of the hard drive to serve as virtual memory when RAM memory is low.

Memory-resident virus A virus that can stay lurking in memory, even after its host program is terminated.

Middleware Software necessary for an application on a client to pass requests to a server, and for a server to respond with data. Microsoft's **Open Database Connectivity (ODBC)** is an example of middleware.

Minicartridge A tape drive cartridge that is only 3¼ × 2½ × ⅜ inches. It is small enough to allow two drives to fit into a standard 5½-inch drive bay of a PC case.

Minifile system In Windows NT boot process, a simplified file system that is started so that Ntldr (NT Loader) can read files from either a FAT or an NTFS file system.

MIRROR command A DOS command that can be used to save the partition table of a hard drive to a floppy disk.

MMX (Multimedia Extensions) technology A variation of the Pentium processor designed to manage and speed up high-volume input/output needed for graphics, motion video, animation, and sound.

Modem From MOdulate/DEModulate. A device that modulates digital data from a computer to an analog format that can be sent over telephone lines, then demodulates it back into digital form.

Modem speed The speed a modem can transmit data along a phone line measured in bits per second (bps). Two communicating modems must talk at the same speed for data transmission to be successful.

Modem-eliminator A "null modem" that allows two data terminal equipment (DTE) devices to communicate by means of a special cable in which the transmit and receive wires are cross-connected.

Modulation Converting binary or digital data into an analog signal that can be sent over standard telephone lines.

Monitor The most commonly used output device for displaying text and graphics on a computer (for example, a 15-inch SVGA monitor).

Mouse A pointing and input device that allows the user to move the cursor around the screen and select programs with the click of a button.

MPC (Multimedia Personal Computer) specifications The minimum standards created by Microsoft and a consortium of hardware manufacturers for multimedia PCs.

MPEG (Moving Pictures Experts Group) A processing-intensive standard for data compression for motion pictures that tracks movement from one frame to the next, and only stores the new data that has changed.

MSDOS.SYS A read-only, hidden MS-DOS system file that must be on the boot disk for a system to boot successfully.

Multibank DRAM (MDRAM) A special kind of RAM that is able to use a full 128-bit bus path without requiring the full 4 MB of RAM.

Multiframe dialog When a token is sent that allows a receiving station to communicate only with the sending station, thus providing continuous communication between the two stations.

Multimedia A type of computer presentation that combines text, graphics, animations, photos, sound, and/or full-motion video.

Multimeter Either a voltmeter or an ammeter that can also measure resistance in ohms or as continuity, depending on a switch setting.

Multipartite virus A combination of a boot sector virus and a file virus. It can hide in either type of program.

Multiplier The factor by which the bus speed is multiplied to get the CPU clock speed.

Multiscan monitor A monitor that can work within a range of frequencies, and thus can work with different standards and video adapters. It offers a variety of refresh rates.

Multisession A CD feature that allows data to be read (or written) on a disc recorded in more than one session. This is important if the disc was only partially filled during the first write.

Multistation access unit (MSAU or MAU) A centralized hub device used to connect IBM Token Ring network stations.

Multithreading The ability of an application under Windows NT to pass more than one function (thread) to the kernel at the same time, such as when one thread is performing a print job while another reads a file.

Musical Instrument Digital Interface (MIDI) Pronounced "middy," a standard for transmitting sound from musical devices, such as electronic keyboards, to computers where it can be digitally stored.

N

Nearest active downstream neighbor (NADN) The next station to receive a token in a token ring.

Nearest active upstream neighbor (NAUN) The station that has just sent a token to the nearest active downstream neighbor in a token ring.

NetBEUI (NetBIOS Extended User Interface) A proprietary Microsoft networking protocol used only by Windows-based systems, and limited to LANs because it does not support routing.

NetBT (NetBIOS over TCP/IP) An alternative Microsoft NetBEUI component designed to interface with TCP/IP networks.

Network interface card (NIC) A network adapter board that plugs into a computer's systemboard and provides a port on the back of the card to connect a PC to a network.

Network layer The OSI layer responsible for routing packets.

Network mask That portion of an IP address that identifies the network.

Node Each computer, workstation, or device on a network.

Noise An extraneous, unwanted signal, often over an analog phone line, that can cause communication interference or transmission errors. Possible sources are fluorescent lighting, radios, TVs, or bad wiring.

Non-memory-resident virus A virus that is terminated when the host program is closed. Compare to memory-resident virus.

Nonparity memory Slightly less expensive, 8-bit memory without error checking, used on Macs and recently in DOS PCs.

Normal backup A full backup that sets the archive attributes of all files and folders it backs up so that later backups can sense that a current backup exists.

Normal mode The traditional method of accessing a hard drive by which the BIOS reads and writes to hard drives by addressing the correct cylinder, head, and sector. *See* CHS.

Norton Disk Doctor (NDD) A third-party utility designed to automatically repair many hard disk and floppy disk problems, including those in the drive's boot sector, FAT, and data areas.

NT Hardware Qualifier This utility, found on the Windows NT installation CD-ROM, examines your system to determine if all hardware present qualifies for Windows NT.

NT virtual DOS machine (NTVDM) An emulated environment in which a 16-bit DOS application or a Windows 3.x application resides within Windows NT with its own memory space or WOW (Win 16 application on a Win 32 platform). (*See* WOW.)

Ntldr (NT Loader) The component of Windows NT that loads the operating system on Intel-based systems.

NTSC (National Television Standards Committee) An organization that sets standards for such devices as video-capturing cards.

Null modem cable *See* Modem-eliminator.

O

Octet A traditional term for each of the four 8-bit numbers that make up an IP address. For example, the IP address 206.96.103.114 has four octets.

Ohms The standard unit of measurement for electrical resistance. Resistors are rated in ohms.

On-board BIOS Basic input/output system services found on a supporting circuit board such as a controller card.

On-board ports Ports that are directly on the systemboard, such as a built-in keyboard port or on-board serial port.

Open Systems Interconnect (OSI) A seven-layer (Application, Presentation, Session, Transport, Network, Data Link, Physical) model of communications supported by a network. Refers to software and firmware only.

Operating system Programs that control the computer's input and output operations, such as saving files and managing memory. Windows, OS/2, Mac OS, and UNIX are operating systems.

Operating system format A high-level format. *See* High-level format.

Out-of-band signaling The type of signalling used by hardware flow control, which sends a message to pause transmission by using channels (or bands) not used for data.

P

Packet Network segments of data that also include header, destination addresses, and trailer information.

Page Memory allocated in 4K or 16K segments within a page frame.

Page fault A program interrupt that occurs when an application requests data or instructions stored in virtual memory.

Page frame A 64K upper memory area divided into four equal-sized pages through which the memory manager swaps data.

Page-in The process in which the memory manager goes to the hard drive to return the data from a swap file to RAM.

Page-out The process in which, when RAM is full, the memory manager takes a page and moves it to the swap file.

Parallel port A female port on the computer that can transmit data in parallel, 8 bits at a time, and is usually used with a printer. The DOS names for parallel ports are LPT1 and LPT2.

Parity An error-checking scheme in which the bits in a byte are added to determine the value of a ninth, or "parity," bit. The value of the parity bit is set to either 0 or 1 to provide an even number of ones for even parity or an odd number of ones for odd parity.

Parity error An error that occurs when the number of 1s in the byte is not in agreement with the expected number.

Parity generator chip A fake parity chip designed to simulate parity checking so that the user can use less expensive nonparity memory modules on a systemboard that expects parity memory. *See* Fake parity chip.

Parity memory Nine-bit memory in which the 9th bit is used for error checking. Older DOS PCs almost always use parity chips.

Partition table A table written at the very beginning of a hard drive that describes the number and location of all partitions, and identifies the boot partition.

Passive network A network, such as Ethernet, in which the computers, not dedicated network devices, drive the signals over the network.

PATH command A DOS command that tells the OS where to look for executable files (for example, the PATH command in an AUTOEXEC.BAT file might be PATH C:\DOS;C:\WINDOWS which tells the OS to look for executable files first in the DOS directory and then in the Windows directory).

PC Card Also called PCMCIA card. A credit-card-sized adapter card that can be slid into a slot in the side of many notebook computers and used for connection to modems, networks, and CD-ROM drives.

PC Card slot Also called a PCMCIA card slot. An expansion slot on a notebook computer, into which a PC Card is inserted.

PC-compatible A computer that uses an Intel (or compatible) processor and can run DOS and Windows.

PCI (peripheral component interconnect) bus A bus common on Pentium computers that runs at speeds of up to 33 MHz, with a 32-bit-wide data path.

PCI (peripheral component interconnect) expansion slot Slots found on most Pentium systemboards. They can accept 32- or 64-bit adapter cards, and allow the card to interface with the PCI bus.

PCMCIA (Personal Computer Memory Card International Association) card *See* PC Card.

PCMCIA card slot *See* PC Card slot.

Peripheral devices Devices that are attached to the computer to enhance its capabilities, such as the monitor, printer, and mouse.

Phase-dual or PD optical drives A type of optical hard drive that is rewritable and may store several gigabytes of data, yet can also read traditional CD-ROMs.

Physical layer The OSI layer responsible for interfacing with the network media (cabling).

Pipeline burst cache The most common cache on systemboards today, which is slightly slower than other types of cache, but is less expensive.

Pipelined burst SRAM A less-expensive SRAM that uses more clock cycles per transfer than non-pipelined burst SRAM, but does not significantly slow down the process.

Pipelining A process that allows a CPU to begin processing a new instruction as soon as the preceding instruction moves to the next stage, thus providing faster throughput.

Pits Recessed areas on the surface of a compact disc, separating Lands. Lands and pits represent data as either a 0 or a 1.

Pixels Small dots on a fine horizontal scan line that are illuminated to create an image on the monitor.

Plug-and-Play (PnP) A technology in which the operating system and BIOS are designed to automatically configure new hardware devices to eliminate system resource conflicts (such as IRQ and port conflicts).

Plug-and-Play BIOS Basic input/output system for Plug-and-Play devices that are designed to be automatically recognized by the computer upon installation.

Polling A process by which the CPU checks the status of connected devices to determine if they are ready to send or receive data.

Polymorphic virus A type of virus that changes its distinguishing characteristics as it replicates itself. Mutating in this way makes it more difficult for AV software to recognize the presence of the virus.

Port A physical connector at the back of a computer that allows a cable from a peripheral device, such as a printer, mouse, or modem, to be attached.

Port settings The configuration parameters of communications devices such as COM1, COM2, or COM3, including IRQ settings.

Port speed The communication speed between a DTE (computer) and a DCE (modem). As a general rule, the port speed should be about four times as fast as the modem speed.

Portable Operating System Interface (POSIX) A set of standards adopted to allow operating systems (such as UNIX and NT) and their applications to port from one platform to another.

POST (power-on self-test) A self-diagnostic program used to perform a simple test of the CPU, RAM, and various I/O devices. The POST is performed when the computer is first turned on.

Power conditioners Line conditioners that regulate, or condition, the power, providing continuous voltage during brownouts.

Power supply A box inside the computer case that supplies power to the systemboard and other installed devices. Power supplies normally provide between 5 and 12 volts DC.

Power-on self-test *See* POST.

PPP (Point-to-Point Protocol) A common way PCs with modems can connect to an internet. The Windows Dial-Up Networking utility, found under My Computer, uses PPP.

Presentation layer The OSI layer that compresses and decompresses data and interfaces with the Application layer and the Session layer.

Primary cache *See* Internal cache.

Primary domain controller (PDC) The computer that controls the directory database of user accounts, group accounts, and computer accounts on a Windows NT domain.

Printer A peripheral output device that produces printed output to paper. Different types of printers include dot matrix, ink-jet, and laser.

Process An executing instance of a program and its resources. There can be more than one process running for a program at the same time. One process for a program happens each time the program is loaded into memory or executed.

Program A set of step-by-step instructions to a computer. Some are burned directly into chips, while others are written in languages such as BASIC or C++.

Program information file (PIF) A file used by a DOS application that describes the environment the DOS program uses. Used in Windows 3.x.

Program jump In a program, an instruction that causes control to be sent to a memory address other than the next sequential address.

Proprietary When a company has exclusive rights to manufacture and/or market a product. Proprietary computer components are typically more difficult to find and more expensive to buy.

Protected mode A mode used by 80286 and newer systems that can address more than 1 MB of memory. It controls memory addresses that a program can access. (Windows 95 runs in protected mode.)

Protocol A set of preestablished rules for communication. Examples of protocols are modem parity settings and the way in which header and trailer information in a data packet is formatted.

Pulse code modulation (PCM) A method of sampling sound in a reduced, digitized format, by recording differences between successive digital samples instead of their full values.

Q

Quarter-Inch Committee or **quarter-inch cartridge (QIC)** A name of a standardized method used to write data to tape. Backups made with the Windows 95 System Tools Backup utility have a .QIC extension.

R

RAID (Redundant Array of Inexpensive Disks or **Redundant Array of Independent Disks)** Several methods of configuring multiple hard drives to store data to increase logical volume size and improve performance, and so that if one hard drive fails, the data is still available from another hard drive.

RAM (random access memory) Temporary memory stored on chips or modules such as SIMMs inside the computer. Information in RAM disappears when the computer's power is turned off.

RAM drive A memory area configured as a virtual hard drive, such as drive D, so that frequently used programs can be accessed faster. It is the opposite of virtual memory.

RD or RMDIR command A DOS command to remove an unwanted directory (for example, RD C:\OLDDIR). You must delete all files in the directory to be removed, prior to using this command.

Real mode A mode used by older 8088 systems whereby the CPU can only address 1 MB of memory, and DOS programs can access memory addresses that may be used by other programs.

RECOVER command A DOS command that recovers files that were lost because of a corrupted file allocation table.

Reduced write current A method whereby less current is used to write data to tracks near the center of the disk, where the bits are closer together.

Refresh The process of periodically rewriting the data on dynamic RAM.

Registration database A Windows 3.x database used to store configuration information. REGEDIT loads REG.DAT and displays a list of applications that Windows has registered.

Re-marked chips Chips that have been used and returned to the factory, marked again, and sent out. The surface of the chips may be dull or scratched.

Remote control Controlling a computer or other device from a remote location (for example, when a person controls a computer from another computer connected by a phone line).

Removable drives High-capacity drives, such as Zip or Jaz drives, that have disks that can be removed like floppy disks.

Repeater A device that amplifies weakened signals on a network.

Rescue disk A disk that can be used to start up a computer when the hard drive fails to boot.

Resistance The degree to which a device opposes or resists the flow of electricity. As the electrical resistance increases, the current decreases. (*See* Ohms and Resistor.)

Resistor An electronic device that resists or opposes the flow of electricity. A resistor can be used to reduce the amount of electricity being supplied to an electronic component.

Resource arbitrator A Plug-and-Play component that decides which resources are assigned to which devices.

Resource management The Plug-and-Play process of allocating resources to devices at startup.

Retension A tape maintenance procedure that fast forwards and then rewinds the tape to eliminate loose spots on the tape.

Reverse Address Resolution Protocol (RARP) Translates the unique hardware NIC addresses into IP addresses (the reverse of ARP).

RISC (reduced instruction set computer) chips Chips that incorporate only the most frequently used instructions, so that the computer operates faster (for example, the PowerPC uses RISC chips).

Roaming users Users who can move from PC to PC within a Windows NT network, with their profiles following them.

ROM (read-only memory) chips Chips that contain programming code and cannot be erased.

Root directory The main directory on the computer (often represented as C:\ on a hard drive), which typically contains other directories, such as Windows and MSOffice.

Route discovery When a router rebuilds its router tables on the basis of new information.

Router A device or box that connects networks. A router transfers a packet to other networks only when the packet is addressed to a station outside its network. The router can make intelligent decisions as to which network is the best route to use to send data to a distant network. *See* Bridge.

Router table Tables of network addresses that also include the best possible routes (regarding tick count and hop count) to these networks. *See* Tick count and Hop count.

Runtime configuration A Plug-and-Play ongoing process that monitors changes in system devices, such as the removal of a PC Card on a notebook computer or the docking of a notebook computer to a docking station.

S

Safe mode The mode in which Windows 95 is loaded with minimum configuration and drivers in order to allow the correction of system errors. To enter Safe mode, press F5 or F8 when "Starting Windows 95" is displayed.

SAM (security accounts manager) A portion of the Windows NT registry that manages the account database that contains accounts, policies, and other pertinent information about the domain.

Sample size Refers to samples taken when converting a signal from analog to digital. Sample size is a measure of the amount of storage allocated to storing a single measurement of a single sample. The larger the sample size, the more accurate the value and the larger the file sizes needed to store the data.

Sampling Part of the process of converting sound or video from analog to digital format, whereby a sound wave or image is measured at uniform time intervals and saved as a series of smaller representative blocks. *See* Sampling rate.

Sampling rate The rate of samples taken of an analog signal over a period of time, usually expressed as samples per second or Hertz. For example, 44,100 Hz is the sampling rate used for 16-bit stereo.

SCAM (SCSI configuration automatically) A method in which SCSI devices and the host adapter are Plug-and-Play-compliant, and the user does not need to manually set the ID on the device.

Scanning mirror A component of a laser printer. An octagonal mirror that can be directed in a sweeping motion to cover the entire length of a laser printer drum.

SCSI (small computer system interface) A faster system-level interface with a host adapter and a bus that can daisy-chain as many as seven other devices.

SCSI bus A faster bus standard used for peripheral devices tied together in a daisy chain.

SCSI bus adapter chip The chip mounted on the logic board of a hard drive that allows the drive to be a part of a SCSI bus system.

SCSI ID *See* Logical unit number.

SCSI-1 The oldest SCSI bus standard, established in 1986, which requires an 8-bit parallel bus with optional parity checking.

SCSI-2 An improved version of SCSI-1 with several new features and options added. Although compatible, the additional features found in SCSI-2 will be ignored by SCSI-1 devices.

Segmentation To split a large Ethernet into smaller segments that are connected to each other by bridges or routers. This is done to prevent congestion as the number of nodes increases.

Sequential access A method of data access used by tape drives whereby data is written or read sequentially from the beginning to the end of the tape or until the desired data is found.

Serial mouse A mouse that uses a serial port and has a female DB-9 plug.

Serial ports Male ports on the computer used for transmitting data serially, one bit at a time. They are commonly used for modems and mice, and in DOS are called COM1 or COM2.

Session layer The OSI layer that makes and manages a connection between two nodes of the network.

SGRAM (Synchronous Graphics RAM) Memory designed specifically for the video card processing that can synchronize itself with the CPU bus clock.

Shadow RAM, Shadowing ROM ROM programming code copied into RAM to speed up the system operation, because of the faster access speed of RAM.

Signal-regenerating repeater A repeater that "reads" the signal on the network and then creates an exact duplicate of the signal, thus amplifying the signal without also amplifying unwanted noise that is mixed with the signal.

SIMM (single in-line memory modules) Miniature circuit boards that are used in newer computers in place of traditional RAM chips. These mini-boards hold 8, 16, or 32 MB on a single module.

Single instruction multiple data (SIMD) An MMX process that allows the CPU to execute a single instruction simultaneously on multiple pieces of data rather than by repetitive looping.

Single voltage CPU A CPU that requires one voltage for both internal and I/O operations.

Single-ended SCSI device A SCSI device that uses half the number of wires in the cable that a differential device uses, and is limited in the cable length.

Sleep mode A mode used in many "green" computers that allows them to be programmed through CMOS to suspend the monitor or even the drive if the keyboard and/or CPU have been inactive for a set number of minutes.

SLIP (Serial Line Internet Protocol) An early version of line protocol designed for home users connecting to the Internet. SLIP lacks reliable error checking and has mostly been replaced by PPP.

Slot A socket on the systemboard into which adapter boards or interface cards can be installed.

SMARTDrive A hard drive cache program that comes with Windows 3.x and DOS that can be executed as a TSR from the AUTOEXEC.BAT file.

SMTP (Simple Mail Transfer Protocol) A common protocol used to send e-mail across a network.

Socket A virtual connection from one computer to another such as that between a client and a server. Higher-level protocols such as HTTP use a socket to pass data between two computers. A socket is assigned a number for the current session, which is used by the high-level protocol.

Software Computer programs or instructions to perform a specific task. Software may be operating systems or applications software such as a word-processing or spreadsheet program.

Software cache A disk cache that is stored on the hard drive as software and uses RAM to hold the cache. It is usually loaded into memory as a TSR.

Software copyrights Copyright is a legal concept (covered by the Federal Copyright Act of 1976) that encompasses the protection of the rights of an originator of a creative work, which can include software. With the exception of archival backups, copyrighted programs are illegal to copy without specific authorization from the copyright holder.

Software piracy Making unauthorized copies of original copyrighted software.

SRAM *See* Static RAM.

Stack A place in memory where information, such as addresses of pending tasks for the CPU, is kept.

Standby time The time before a "green" system will reduce 92% of its activity.

Standby UPS A UPS that quickly switches from an AC power source to a battery-powered source during a brownout or outage.

Standoffs Small plastic spacers placed on the bottom of the main systemboard, to raise it off the chassis, so that its components will not short out on the metal case.

Star network architecture A network design in which nodes are connected at a centralized location.

Start bit A bit that is used to signal the approach of data.

Static electricity *See* Electrostatic discharge.

Static IP addresses IP addresses permanently assigned to a workstation. In Windows 95, this can be done under Dial-Up Networking, Server Type, TCP/IP settings. Specify an IP address.

Static RAM (SRAM) RAM chips that retain information without the need for refreshing as long as the power is on. They are more expensive than traditional DRAM.

Static routing When routing tables do not automatically change and must be manually edited. Windows NT and Windows 95 support only static routing.

Stealth virus A virus that actively conceals itself by temporarily removing itself from an infected file that is about to be examined, and then hiding a copy of itself elsewhere on the drive.

Stop bit A bit that is used to signal the end of a block of data.

Subnet mask Defines which portion of an IP address identifies the network, and which portion identifies the host. A 1 in the mask indicates that the bit is part of the network address, and a 0 indicates that the bit is part of the host address. For example, the subnet mask 255.255.192.0, in binary, is 11111111.11111111.11000000.00000000. Therefore, the network address is the first two octets and the first two bits of the third octet. The rest of the IP address refers to the host.

Subnetworks or **subnets** Divisions of a large network, consisting of smaller separate networks (to prevent congestion). Each subnetwork is assigned a logical network IP name.

Subtree One of five main keys that make up the Windows NT registry. Examples are HKEY_CURRENT_USER and HKEY_LOCAL_MACHINE.

Surge suppressor A device or power strip designed to protect electronic equipment from power surges and spikes.

Suspend time The time before a "green" system will reduce 99% of its activity. After this time, the system needs a warm-up time so that the CPU, monitor, and hard drive can reach full activity.

Swapping A method of freeing some memory by moving a "page" of data temporarily to a swap file on the hard drive; it can later be copied from disk back into memory.

Synchronous DRAM Modules that are more expensive than SIMM modules and can operate at various speeds, depending on the bus speed, whereas SIMMs only operate at a single speed.

Synchronous SRAM SRAM that is faster and more expensive than asynchronous SRAM. It requires a clock signal to validate its control signals, enabling the cache to run in step with the CPU.

System BIOS Basic input/output system chip(s) residing on the systemboard that control(s) normal I/O to such areas as system memory and video display.

System partition The active partition of the hard drive containing the boot record and the specific files required to load Windows NT.

System variable A variable that has been given a name and a value; it becomes available to the operating system, Windows, and applications software programs.

Systemboard The main board in the computer, also called the motherboard. The CPU, ROM chips, SIMMs, and interface cards are plugged into the systemboard.

Systemboard mouse A mouse that plugs into a round mouse port on the systemboard.

T

TCP/IP (Transmission Control Protocol/ Internet Protocol) The suite of protocols developed to support the Internet. TCP is responsible for error checking, and IP is responsible for routing.

Technical documentation The technical reference manuals, included with software packages and peripherals, that provide directions for installation, usage, and troubleshooting.

Telephony A term describing the technology of converting sound to signals that can travel over telephone lines.

Telephony Application Programming Interface (TAPI) A standard developed by Intel and Microsoft that can be used by 32-bit Windows 95 communications programs for communicating over phone lines.

Temp directory A location to which inactive applications and data can be moved as a swap file, while Windows continues to process current active applications.

Temporary file A file that is created by Windows applications, to save temporary data, and that may or may not be deleted when the application is unloaded.

Terminating resistor The resistor added at the end of a SCSI chain to dampen the voltage at the end of the chain. *See* Termination.

Termination A process necessary to prevent interference of data transmission caused by an echo effect of power at the end of a chain. *See* Terminating resistor.

Thermal grease A special compound placed on processors to facilitate the transfer of heat from the top of the CPU to a heat sink.

Tick count The time required for a packet to reach its destination. One tick equals 1/18 of a second.

Token A small frame on a Token Ring network that constantly travels around the ring in only one direction. When a station seizes the token, it controls the channel until its message is sent.

Token ring A network that is logically a ring, but stations are connected to a centralized multistation access unit (MAU) in a star formation. Network communication is controlled by a token.

Toner cavity A container in a laser printer that is filled with toner. The black resin toner is used to form the printed image on paper.

Trailer The part of a packet that follows the data and contains information used by some protocols for error checking.

Transceiver The bidirectional (transmitter and receiver) component on a NIC that is responsible for signal conversion and monitors for data collision.

Transformer A device that converts AC to DC or DC to AC current. A computer power supply is basically a transformer.

Transport layer The OSI layer that verifies data and requests a resend when the data is corrupted.

TREE command A DOS command that shows the disk directories in a graphical layout similar to a family tree (for example, TREE/F shows every filename in all branches of the tree).

Trojan horse A type of infestation that hides or disguises itself as a useful program, yet is designed to cause damage at a later time.

TSR (terminate and stay resident) program A program that is loaded into memory but is not immediately executed, such as a screen saver or a memory-resident antivirus program.

Turbo mode A means of doubling the clock speed by pressing a button on the case of some older computers. (Actually the turbo switch cuts the speed in half to run slower applications.)

U

UART (Universal Asynchronous Receiver-Transmitter chip) A chip that controls serial ports. It sets protocol and converts parallel data bits coming from the system bus into serial bits.

Ultra-SCSI Also called Fast-20 or Fast SCSI. A technology that offers 20 MB/sec burst transfers across 8-bit paths and 40 MB/sec burst transfers across wide 16-bit paths.

UNDELETE command A DOS command that retrieves previously deleted files, provided that their locations have not been written over.

UNFORMAT command A DOS command that performs recovery from an accidental FORMAT, and may also repair a damaged partition table if the partition table was previously saved with MIRROR/PARTN.

Universal serial bus (USB) A bus developed by Intel Corporation, intended to be used by low-volume I/O devices such as modems, joysticks, touch pads, trackballs, and mice.

Upper memory The memory addresses from 640K up to 1024K, originally reserved for system BIOS but now used for device drivers and TSRs.

Upper memory block (UMB) A group of consecutive memory addresses in RAM from 640K to 1 MB that can be used by device drivers and TSRs.

UPS (Uninterruptible Power Supply) A device designed to provide a backup power supply during a power failure. Basically, a UPS is a battery backup system with an ultrafast sensing device.

URL (Universal Resource Locator) A unique address that identifies the domain name, path, or filename of a World Wide Web site. Microsoft's URL address is: http://www.microsoft.com/

User account In Windows NT, the information, stored in the SAM database, that defines an NT user, including user name, password, memberships, and rights.

User Datagram Protocol (UDP) A connection-less protocol that does not require a connection to send a packet and does not guarantee that the packet arrives at its destination.

User documentation Manuals, online documentation, instructions, and tutorials designed specifically for the user.

User mode The portion of Windows NT that provides an interface between the OS and applications or users. User mode has access to hardware resources through the kernel mode.

User profile In Windows NT, a personal profile about the user kept in the NT registry, which enables the user's desktop settings and other operating parameters to be retained from one session to another.

Utility software Software packages, such as Nuts & Bolts, Norton Utilities, and PC Tools, that provide the means for data recovery and repair, virus detection, and the creation of backups.

V

V.34 standard A communications standard that transmits at 28,800 bps and/or 33,600 bps.

Value data In Windows 95 and NT, the name and the value of a setting for a key in the registry.

VCACHE A built-in Windows 95 32-bit software cache that doesn't take up conventional memory space or upper memory space, as SmartDrive does.

Vector table *See* I/O address table.

VESA (Video Electronics Standards Association) VL bus A bus used on 80486 computers for connecting 32-bit adapters directly to the local processor bus.

Video card An interface card installed in the computer to control the monitor.

Video controller card A card installed in the computer that controls the monitor. Another name for display adapter.

Video driver A program that tells the computer how to effectively communicate with the video adapter card and monitor. It is often found on a disk that is shipped with the card.

Video memory Microchips on the video card that hold the data that is being passed from the computer to the monitor. Higher resolution often requires more video memory.

Video RAM or **VRAM** RAM on video cards that allows simultaneous access from both the input and output processes.

Video-capturing card A multimedia card that can capture input video and convert the frames into motion files or still clips that can be stored on disk.

Virtual device drivers (VDD) or VxD drivers Programs that emulate the DOS device drivers for hardware devices in Windows 95 and Windows NT.

Virtual file allocation table (VFAT) A variation of the original DOS 16-bit FAT that allows for long filenames used in Windows 95.

Virtual machines (VM) Multiple logical machines created within one physical machine by Windows, allowing applications to make serious errors without disturbing other programs.

Virtual memory Hard disk space used as though it is RAM in order to increase total RAM in a system. Because hard drives are much slower than RAM access, virtual memory is relatively slow.

Virtual Memory Manager A Windows 95 or NT program that controls the page table, swapping 4K pages in and out of physical RAM to and from the hard drive.

Virus A program that often has an incubation period, is infectious, and is intended to cause damage. A virus program might destroy data and programs or damage a disk drive's boot sector.

Virus signature The distinguishing characteristics or patterns of a particular virus. Typically, AV signature updates for new viruses can be downloaded monthly from the Internet.

Volt A measure of the potential difference in electrical "pressure." One volt is the potential generated by 1 ampere of current flowing through 1 ohm of resistance. A computer power supply usually provides four separate voltages: +12V, -12V, +5V, and -5V.

Voltage A potential difference in electrical "pressure" that causes current to flow, measured in volts. (*See* Volts.)

Voltage regulator module (VRM) socket Converts the system power supply voltage to the voltage required by the CPU.

Voltmeter A device for measuring electrical voltage.

W

Wait state A clock tick in which nothing happens, used to ensure that the microprocessor isn't getting ahead of slower components. A 0-wait state is preferable to a 1-wait state.

Watt The unit used to measure power. A typical computer may use a power supply that provides 200 watts.

Wavetable A table of stored sample sounds used to synthesize sound by reconstructing the sound from digital data using actual samples of sounds from real instruments.

Wide SCSI A type of SCSI that allows for 16- to 32-bit parallel data transfer. It has not become a standard in the PC environment.

Windows Custom Setup A setup feature that allows user customization of such things as directory locations, wallpaper settings, font selections, and many other features.

Windows Express Setup A setup feature that automatically installs Windows in the most commonly used fashion.

Windows Internet Naming Service (WINS) A Microsoft resolution service with a distributed database that tracks relationships between domain names and IP addresses. Compare to DNS.

Windows NT file system (NTFS) A file system first introduced with Windows NT that provides improved security, disk storage, file compression, and long filenames.

Windows NT registry A database containing all configuration information, including the user profile and hardware settings. The NT registry is not compatible with the Windows 95 registry.

Workgroup In Windows NT, a logical group of computers and users in which administration, resources, and security are distributed throughout the network, without centralized management or security.

Worm An infestation designed to copy itself repeatedly to memory, on drive space, or on a network until little memory or disk space remains.

WOW (Win 16 on Win 32) A group of programs provided by Windows NT to create a virtual DOS environment that emulates a 16-bit Windows environment, protecting the rest of the NT OS from 16-bit applications.

WRAM (window RAM) Dual-ported video RAM that is faster and less expensive than VRAM. It has its own internal bus on the chip, with a data path that is 256 bits wide.

Write precompensation A method whereby data is written faster to the tracks that are near the center of a disk.

X

XCOPY command A faster external DOS COPY program that can copy subdirectories (for example, XCOPY *.* A:/S will copy all files from the current directory, including subdirectories and their files, to drive A).

Y

YUV A scheme of determining color by specifying brightness or luminance (Y), the color or hue (U), and the intensity or saturation (V).

Z

ZIF (zero insertion force) socket A chip socket that has a small locking lever attached to its side. If the lever is raised, the CPU can be easily lifted out of its socket.

INDEX

A

A+ Certification, 959–60, 966
ACIA chip, 776
active partition, Windows NT, 596–97
Adaptec AVA-1502 ISA-to-SCSI host
  adapter, 409–11
adapter addresses, 821, 855–57, 886
adapter cards, *See also* cards
  defined, 234, 250
  hard drive/CPU interface, 11
  hard drive installation, 265
  IDE drives, 234, 236
Add New Hardware Wizard, 564–68
add-on devices. *See* peripheral devices
Add Printer Wizard, Windows NT,
  622–24
Add/Remove Programs, Windows NT,
  643–44
Address Resolution Protocol (ARP),
  854, 886
administrator accounts, 612, 652
Advanced Port Settings dialog, 777
Advanced SCSI Programming Interface
  (ASPI), 242, 250
alignment, floppy drives, 161, 162, 163
Alpha chip, 93
alternate gateways, 857, 886
alternating current (AC), 490
  backup power, 505
AMD chip sets, 98–99
  K5, 92, 93
  K6, 93
  X86 chip names, 89
American Megatrends Inc. (AMI), 99
ammeters, 488
amperes (amps), 488, 490
  measuring, 493
amplifier repeaters, 814, 886
amplifiers, 385
analog signals
  converting to digital signals, 659–60,
    763–64
  defined, 804
analog-to-digital converters (A/D or
  ADC), 674, 697
AND operator, bitwise, 861
antivirus (AV) software, 901, 909–11, 934
AOL4FREE program, 906
Apple Computer Corporation, 6
Application layer, 824, 825, 827,
  870–72, 887

applications software, 25–35, 422
  associating file extensions with, 522
  categories, 25
  configuration errors, 533
  conflicts, 533–40
  for devices, 391–92
  executing, 49–50
    DOS, 27–29
    Windows, 30–35
  .INI files, 521–24
  installing, 25, 272
    Windows 3.x, 530–33
    Windows NT, 643–44
  legacy, 27, 634–37
  minimizing, memory usage and, 542
  operation of, 25–30
  registration of, 526
  scanners, 392
  serial numbers, 531
  suites, 25
  testing, 532
  Windows NT registry and, 638
applications swap files, 456
arithmetic logic units, Pentium chip, 90
ARP (Address Resolution Protocol), 854
ASCII
  defined, C-1, D-1
  files, C-1
  standard character set, C-1–4
ASPI standard, 242, 250
  host adapter support, 408
associations, creating in File Manager, 522
asynchronous communication, modems,
  774
asynchronous SRAM, 435–36, 475
ATA-2 standard, 237
Atanasoff, John, D-1
ATAPI standard, 237
ATA standard, 237
AT bus, 110
AT commands, 787–89, 803, 804, 924,
  925–27
ATTRIB command, 161, 165, 213,
  250, 338
  hiding files with, 322
  unhiding MSDOS.SYS with, 556
  unhiding root directory files with, 322
authoring software, 385, 422
auto-answer, modems, 774
auto-detecting BIOS, 268, 327

AUTOEXEC.BAT, 27, 214
  backing up, 68–69
  commenting lines in, 527
  copying to rescue disk, 71–72
  debugging, 69
  defined, 66, 75, 445
  editing, 68–69
  error messages, 322
  functions, 66–67
  hiding, 322
  loading high from, 452, 454
  loading TSRs high, 450–51
  network files and parameters, 844–45
  SET command placement, 532–33
  TSRs executed from, 445
  updating to include CD-ROM drive
    access, 417, 418
  in Windows 95, 71, 461
autorange meters, 492
Award Software, 99
azimuth skew, floppy drives, 161

B

backbones, 816, 887
back end applications, 830–31, 887
backup catalogs, 934
BACKUP command, 165, 233
backup domain controller (BDC), 610,
  652
backups, 72, 75, 312, 314, 324, 911–32,
  933
  child, parent, and grandparent method,
    917, 918
  differential, 918, 934
  full, 918, 935
  hard drive, 272, 368
  importance of, 290
  incremental, 918
  .INI files, 521
  managing tapes, 928–29
  normal, 935
  removable drives, 912
  scheduling, 918
  scheduling with Windows NT, 924
  software, 368
  tape drives, 912–17
  verifying tapes or disks, 931–32
backup sets, 934
backup software, 918–29
  Windows 95 Backup utility, 919–22
  Windows NT Backup utility, 922–29

backward compatibility
  defined, 588
  Windows NT, 588–89, 599
  Windows programs, 545
bad sectors, 310
bandwidth, 669, 698
banks, systemboards, 468–72, 476
base file record, 595
base memory. *See* conventional memory
basic input/output system (BIOS), 12
batch (.BAT) files, 13, 27, 214, 217, 219, 365
  defined, 250
batteries, configuration data problems and, 53
baud rate, 765, 804
beam detect mirrors, in laser printers, 693, 698
Bell 212A standard, 767
bench technicians, 334
binary number system, 7, D-5–6
binding, to OSI layers, 856, 887
BIOS, *See also* Plug-and-Play (PnP)
  BIOS; ROM BIOS; ROM BIOS
  Startup Program; System BIOS
  auto-detecting, 268, 327
  CHS (normal mode), 199
  compatibility, 102–3, 200–201
  defined, 12, 37
  enhanced (LBA mode), 199, 200, 251, 267
  ESCD, 102, 563
  identifying, 563
  for large-capacity drives, 200, 267
  on-board, 47, 57, 75
  sources of, 100–101
  upgrading, 102, 200–201, 267
  video, 57, 436
BIOS Features Setup, 750
bit map files, 386, 422
bits, D-1
bitwise AND operator, 861
blackouts, 511
blocks, 205
bootable disks, *See also* rescue disks
  creating, 68–69, 164
    in DOS, 147–48, 151, 338, 366
    in Windows 3.x, 157
  defined, 369
BootDelay, 557
boot disks, Windows NT, 629–31
BootFailSafe, 557
booting, 13, *See also* rebooting
  with DOS, 66–67
  error messages, 363, E-15–17
  hard, 64–65, 164
  problems following, 364
  problems following Windows installation, 529
  process, 64–71
  soft, 65, 164

troubleshooting, 324–25, 361–64, E-4, E-15–17, E-21–22
  Windows, 67–68
  Windows 95, 69–71
  Windows NT, 624–33
BOOT.INI, 627
BootKeys, 557
boot loader menu, 627, 636, 652
BootMenu, 557
BootMenuDefault, 557
BootMenuDelay, 557
BootMulti, 557
boot partition, Windows NT, 597, 652
boot record
  contents, 292
  damaged, 291–99, 318–20
  defined, 271
  errors, 320
  examining, 292–98
  recovery, 292, 293, 298
boot sector viruses, 902, 934
BootWarm, 558
BootWin, 557
brand-name PCs, 704, 706, 754
break code, 175, 182
bridges, 814, 821–22, 887, *See also* routers
  ISDN and, 801
  protocols, 833
brownouts, 498, 507, 510, 511
browsers, 829, 872
  installing, 870
buck-boost, 510
BUFFERS= command, 66, 232, 446, 545
buffers
  defined, 232, 250, 446, 477
  FIFO, 397, 422
  number of, 545
burst SRAM, 435, 477
burst transfer, 240, 251
bus enumerator, Plug-and-Play, 562–63, 580
buses, 8, 108–18, 126
  comparisons, 116
  defined, 108
  EISA, 108, 111, 112, 116
  functions of, 108–9
  ISA 8-bit, 108, 109–10, 111, 116, 117
  ISA 16-bit, 108, 110, 111, 116
  local, 108, 111, 112–13
  MCA, 108, 111, 112
  PCI, 108, 111, 114–16, 117
  universal serial (USB), 118
  VESA VL, 111, 112–13, 116
  video controller cards, 178
bus masters, 115–16
bus mouse, 180, 182, 392
bus network architecture, 811, 887
bus speed, 88, 126
  changing, 117
  comparisons, 116
  in Pentium computers, 90
  performance and, 117–18

bus width, video cards, 670
buttons, mouse, 3
bytes, D-1

C

C> prompt, 67
cables, 3, 4
  data, 12
  floppy drives, 734
  hard drive data, 737
  IDE data, 740
  for networks, 812–13
  null modem, 838–40
  power, floppy drives, 169–70
  SCSI, 753
cache, 8, *See also* disk cache
  external, 432
  internal, 88, 432
  jumper settings, 717–18
  levels of, 107
  MMX technology and, 667
  static, 107
cache controller, 107, 126, 432
caddies, CD-ROM drives, 412
Caller ID, 774
call tracking, for PC technicians, 955–59, 966
cameras, digital, 687–88, 697
CAM standard, 242, 251
  host adapter support, 408
cards, *See also* adapter cards
  defined, 4, 37
  video, 2
carpal tunnel syndrome (CTS), 172
Carrier Detect (CD) light, modems, 774
carriers, modems, 773, 804
carrier sense multiple access with collision detection (CMSA/CD), 812, 887
case cover, installing, 751–52
cathode ray tube monitors, 175–76
CAU (controlled access unit), 815
CCITT standards, 766, 802
  CCITT V.32, 767
  CCITT V.32bis, 767
  CCITT V.34, 767, 806
  CCITT V.42, 767, 772
  CCITT V.42bis, 767, 772
CD command, 28–29, 211, 251
CD-ROM drives, 385, 411–20
  cables, 415–16
  caddies, 412
  care of, 414
  constant linear velocity (CLV), 412
  device driver installation, 416
  installing, 272, 413–14, 415–20, 739–41
  interface card installation, 415
  MPC3 specifications, 663
  multi-session feature, 412
  not recognized, 419
  power-saving features, 412
  power to, 416
  systemboard interface, 413

testing, 416
transfer rate, 412
troubleshooting, 417–20, 686–87, E-12–14
updating rescue disk, 417
CD-ROMs
care of, 414, 531
lands and pits, 411, 422, 423
loading Windows 95 from, 72
read-writable, 912
Central Point Anti-Virus (CPAV), 342
central processing units (CPUs), 6–8, 37, 87–99
bus clock selection jumper settings, 715
components, 125
cooling fans, 94, 498–99, 720–21, E-18
CPU core to bus clock ratio selection jumper settings, 715–16
dual voltage, 96, 126
history, 88–89
installing, 719–22
Intel, 80–81, 88–89
I/O address table used by, 59, 60–61
IRQ processing, 62
memory address assignments by, 437–38
MMX Pentium, 658, 697
MPC3 specifications, 662–63
Pentium Pro, 658
rating, 87–88
RISC technology, 93–94
single voltage, 96, 128
slots, 94–95
sockets, 94–95
speed, 87, 118–19
voltage regulator, 96
voltage selection jumper settings, 717
certification, for PC technicians, 959–61
chains, 221, 251
change directory (CD) command, 28–29, 211, 251
charge-coupled device (CCD) technology, 687–88
chat rooms, 829
CHDIR command, 211, 251
Check It Diagnostic Kit, 341
checksum, 773, 804
Cheyenne AntiVirus software, 909, 910–11
child directories, 209, *See also* subdirectories
child, parent, and grandparent backup method, 917, 918, 934
chip sets, 8, 96–99, 125
AMD, 89, 92, 93, 98–99
Cyrix, 89, 92, 93, 98–99
defined, 96
Intel, 6, 87, 96–99
manufacturers, 98
SiS, 98

systemboard, 87–94
Triton II, 96
Triton III, 96
VIA, 98
CHKDSK command, 152–53, 161, 163, 182, 201, 233, 338, 527
for lost clusters, 310
options, 152
CHS mode, for large-capacity drives, 199, 251
circuit boards, 8, 37, *See also* cards
RAM chips on, 430
CISC chips, 93
clamping voltage, 506, 513
classless addresses, 861–62, 887
clean phone lines, 766
Clear to Send (CTS) signal, modems, 774
Client for Microsoft Networks, 837–38, 868
cloaking techniques, 903–4
clocks, modem, 774
clock speed, 87, 88, 126
overdrive mode, 89
in Pentium computers, 90
clones, 704, 706, 754, 755
cluster chains, 148, 182
clusters
cross-linked, 23, 251
file allocation table, 201, 302–4
floppy disks, 145–46, 182
hard drive organization, 194–95
lost, 223, 252, 310, 327
.CMD files, 934
CMOS chips, 7–8, 48
backing up and restoring configuration data, 53–56
changing configuration data, 52
storage of configuration data, 51–52, 119–21
CMOS RAM clearance, jumper settings, 719
CMOS settings, 748–51
Advanced Chip Set setup, 121
Advanced CMOS setup, 120–21
maintaining records, 73
SCSI setup, 275
setup, 7, 37, 430
Standard CMOS setup, 120
CMSA/CD, 812, 887
COAST (cache on a stick), 436, 477, 717
coaxial cable, 812, 813
CODEC compression, 666, 698
collisions, between packets, 812, 887
color, monitor display, 178
color depth, video cards, 670, 698
color space conversion, 664–65, 698
COM1, 393, 394
COM1 Properties box, 777
COM2, 393
combo cards, 820
.COM files, 13, 27

Comité Consultatif Internationale de Télégraphie et Téléphonie (CCITT), 766, 802
COMMAND.COM, 67, 161
on bootable disks, 148, 151
internal and external DOS commands, 151
missing, 322
in Windows 95 environment, 71
command-driven interfaces, 15
command line, viewing in Windows 3.x, 31–32
comment lines
in AUTOEXE.BAT and CONFIG.SIS, 527, 580
in .INI files, 523, 580
Common Access Method (CAM), 242, 251
communications
computer-hardware-to-modem, 775–83
layers, 760–63
MPC3 specifications, 666
networking levels, 823–27
over phone lines, 762
physical, 760–62, 802
virtual, 760–63, 802
communication skills, PC technicians, 949–54
communication software, 786–96
pcANYWHERE, 786, 789–90, 793–96
ProComm Plus, 786, 790–91
software-to-modem communication, 787–92
software-to-software communication, 792–96
Communications Port Properties box, 778
compatibility, backward. *See* backward compatibility
COM ports
COM1, 779
COM2, 779
for modems, 779
compressed drives
cautions, 225–26, 367
creating, 225–30
defined, 226, 251
installing Windows on, 527
uncompressing, 230
compressed files, 225
compressed volume files (CVF), 226, 228
compression, *See also* data compression; disk compression
CODEC, 666
data, 772
lossless, 666, 698
lossy, 699
ratios, 772
computer case, installing systemboard in, 728

computer-hardware-to-modem communications, 775–83
Computing Technology Industry Association (CompTIA), 959–60, 966
CONFIG.SYS
  commenting lines in, 527
  copying to rescue disk, 71–72
  debugging, 69
  defined, 66
  editing, 68–69
  error messages, 322
  hiding, 322
  HIMEM.SYS loaded from, 445–47
  loading drivers from CD-ROM, 72
  network files and parameters, 844–45
  SCSI device drivers, 242
  updating to include CD-ROM drive access, 417, 418
  in Windows 95, 70, 461
configuration data
  backing up and restoring, 53–56
  conflicts, 100
  defined, 50, 75
  hard drive installation and, 267–68
  loss of, 53
  maintaining records, 73, 366–67
  read by ROM BIOS Startup program, 47
  storage of
    CMOS chips, 51–56, 119–21
    DIP switches, 50–51
    jumpers, 52
configuration files. See initialization (.INI) files
configuration manager, Plug-and-Play, 562–63, 580
conflicts
  applications software, 533–40
  configuration data, 100
  defined, 63, 75
  DIP switches, 63
  .DLL files, 533–35
  DMA channels, 124
  expansion boards, 466–67, E-17
  I/O addresses, 63, 387
  IRQ, 63, 386–87
  jumper settings, 63
  legacy devices, 568–69
  locking up, 466
  peripheral devices, 100, 386, 387, 403–5, 419
  resolving, 63, 64, 403–5
  software, 533–40
  troubleshooting, 466
  upper memory blocks (UMBs), 457, 467
  Windows 3.x, 533–40
connectionless protocols, 854, 887
connection protocols, 854, 887
connections, troubleshooting, E-21
Console icon, 592
constant linear velocity (CLV), 412, 422

continuity, 493, 513
Control 3 for Windows 95, 574
control blade, in laser printers, 694, 698
CONTROL.INI, 68, 521, 522
controlled access unit (CAU), 815, 887
controllers/controller boards
  defined, 251
  DMA, 63, 75, 124
  DRAM, 178
  floppy drives, 12, 142
  hard drive, 11, 234, 238
  SCSI, 238
  video, 178
Control Panel
  device driver settings, 389–91
  Windows NT, 624–25
conventional memory, 440–41
  defined, 439
  device drivers, 60
  inadequacy of, 440
cooling fans, 94, 498–99, 720–21, E-18
coprocessors, 6, 37, 89
Copy backup, 923, 934
COPY command, 155, 182
  for bad sectors, 310
  Windows 3.x, 157, 158
Copy Disk command, Windows 3.x, 157
copyrights, 962–64, 966
corrupted files
  data, 323, 327
  .DLL, 539–40
  hidden, 321–22
  program, 323, 327
  registry, 520, 526–27, 571–72
  system, 321–22
corrupted sector/track markings, 322–23
cover, removing, 166–68
C prompt, 26
CPUs. See central processing units (CPUs)
Create Directory command, Windows 3.x, 215–16
cross-linked clusters, 223, 251
crosstalk, 813, 887
CRT monitors, 175–76
Ctrl-Alt-Del booting, 65
Ctrl-Alt-Del logon, Windows NT, 612
current
  alternating, 490
  direct, 490
  measuring, 493
  resistance and, 489
  voltage and, 488, 489
current directory, 26
current drive, 26
customers
  external, 942
  internal, 942
customer service
  communication skills and, 949–54
  complaints, 952–54

customer satisfaction with, 942–43, 950–54
  policies, 945
  support calls, 944–54
Custom Setup, Windows 3.x, 527, 529
CVF files, 226, 228
CyberMedia
  First Aid 97, 340
  Oil Change, 340
cylinders, hard drives, 192
Cyrix chip sets, 98–99
  6x86, 92, 98
  6x86L, 92
  M2, 92, 93
  X86 chip names, 89

D

DAC (digital to analog converter), 666, 698
Daily copy backup, 924, 934
damaged boot record, 318–20
damaged FAT, 321
damaged files, 309–12
  bad sectors, 310
  erased files, 310–11
  lost clusters, 310
  preventing, 312
  recovering with utility software, 311–12
  recovering with Windows 95 and DOS, 309, 310
damaged partition tables, 318–20
damaged root directory, 321
data
  bits, 782, 804
  compression, modems, 772
  sent over networks, 810
data cables, 12
  floppy drives, 142
  reconnecting, 170–71
  twist in, 168
  unplugging, 168
data cartridges, for tape drives, 914, 916, 934, 935
data communications equipment. See DCE
data compression, 251, See also compression; disk compression
data files
  corrupted, 323, 327
  storage of, 367
data frames, 827
datagrams, 853, 887
data line protectors, 507, 513
Data Link layer, 824, 826, 827, 887
data path, 87, 109, 126
data recovery, 291–313
  boot record damage, 291–99
  file allocation table damage, 299–309
  file damage, 309–12
  technology, 293–98
Data SRAM chips, 717
data terminal equipment. See DTE

data throughput, 116

data transfer mode, in software-to-software communication, 792

date, of creation or last update, 150

.DAT files, 365

DC bias charge, laser printers, 695

DCE (Data Communications Equipment), 395, 775, 802, 804
DCE speed, 778

DEBUG utility
boot record examination with, 293–98
defined, 327
directory repair, 307–9
displaying memory with, D-7–8
file allocation table restoration, 301, 304–5
recovering damaged files, 312
subdirectory dump with, 210
viewing FAT with, 202–5

decimal number system, 7

dedicated servers, 830–31

de facto standards, 787, 805

default directory, 26

default drive, 26

default gateways, 857, 887

default Windows printer, 37

DEFRAG command, 221, 312, 338, 527

defragmentation, 221–22, 251, 290, 527, 529, 545

Defragmenter utility, 221–22

DEL command, 153, 182

Delete command, Windows 3.x, 157, 158

Delete Folder command, Windows 95, 218

DELTREE command, 156, 182, 212, 251

demodulation, 763, 805

desktop
defined, 16
Windows 95, 552–56
Windows NT, 591, 592

desktop-publishing devices, 383–84, 422

destructive low-level formatting, 323

DETCRASH.LOG, 552

Detection Log (DETLOG.TXT), 552

DEVICE= command, 66, 72, 242, 389, 392
CD-ROM installation, 417
HIMEM.SYS executed by, 445, 447
RAM drive creation, 444

device drivers, 389–91
CD-ROM drives, 416
defined, 3, 37, 57, 251, 387
installation problems, E-20
installing, 389–91, 644–45
loading high, 449–50
memory address storage, 60
SCSI, 242
16-bit, 564, 568
System BIOS vs., 58
TSRs, 389
UART, 397

video cards, 391
Windows NT, 638, 644–45

DEVICEHIGH= command, 449, 466

Device Manager, 37, 410–11, 677

devices. See peripheral devices

DHCP, 851–52, 888

diagnostic cards, 339, 369

diagnostic software, 339–40, 369

Dial-Up Adapter, 836–37
setting up, 867–68

Dial-Up Networking (DUN), 832–38, 885, 888
Client for Microsoft Networks, 837–38
creating connection, 833–36
Dial-Up Adapter, 836–37
operation of, 832–33
setting up, 868–69
troubleshooting, 882–83

differential backups, 918, 934

differential SCSI devices, 408–9, 422

digital to analog converter (DAC), 666, 698

digital cameras, 687–88, 697

digital diagnostic disks, 162

Digital Equipment Company (DEC)
Alpha chip, 93
MIPS chip, 93

digital phone lines, 799

digital signals
converting to analog signals, by modems, 763–64
converting analog signals to, 659–60, 675
defined, 805

digital video disc (DVD) technology, 688–90, 697, 698

DIMMs
defined, 106, 126, 430, 432–33, 477
installing, 473–74, 722
module size, 435
selecting, 472–73
speeds, 433
used modules, 435

DIN connectors, 174–75

DIP switches
configuration data storage, 47, 50–51
defined, 50, 75
hard drive installation and, 263
maintaining records of, 367
memory conflicts and, 63
modem settings, 742–45
peripheral devices, 388

DIR command, 163, 201, 210

Direct Cable Connect, 838–40, 885

direct current (DC), 490, 513

direct memory access (DMA) controller chip, 63, 75, 124

directories
changing, 28–29
changing default, 211
child, 209

creating with Windows 3.x, 215
current, 26
damaged, 306–7
default, 26
defined, 26, 182
deleting, 212
deleting with Windows 3.x, 216
hard drive organization, 194
parent, 209
removing, 211–12
repairing, 307–9
root, 26, 149–51

directory database, 610

directory structure, displaying, 212

directory trees, deleting, 156

dirty phone lines, 766, 769, 772
retraining, 798

disaster recovery planning, 931–32, 933

Disctec PD RoadRunner Express, 248

disk cache
defined, 230, 251
in DOS, 231–32
hardware, 231, 232
memory cache vs., 232
software, 231, 232
in Windows 3.x, 231
in Windows 95, 232

disk caching, 446

disk compression, 225–30, See also compression; data compression
cautions, 225–26, 367
defined, 225, 251
in DOS, 225–26
uncompression, 230
in Windows 3.x, 225–26
in Windows 95, 226–30

DISKCOPY command, 154, 182, 292

Disk Copy command, Windows 95, 160

disk duplexing, 930, 934

disk manager software, 200

disk mirroring, 930, 935

disks. See floppy disks; hard drives

disk striping, 929, 935

disk thrashing, 551, 580

display adapters, 62, 75

Display Power Management Signaling (DPMS), 504, 513

display readout, external modems, 774

.DLL files, 349–50
corrupted, 539–40
identifying, 539–40
software conflicts and, 533–35

DLL Unloader, 539–40

DMA channels
conflicts, 124
defined, 63
purpose, 64

DMA (direct memory access) controller chip, 63, 75, 124

DMA (dynamic memory access) chip, 106

DNS (Domain Name Service), 853–54, 886

docking stations, 406, 422

documentation
defined, 370
maintaining, 72–73
preventive maintenance, 900
record books, 366
Windows 3.x files, 530

documents, launching in Windows 3.x, 33

domain names
defined, 852, 886, 888
resolution of, 852–53

Domain Name Service (DNS), 853–54, 886, 888

domains, Windows NT, 587, 609–11, 652

DOS
advantages/disadvantages, 21
backward compatibility, 439
booting with, 66–67
buffers, 232
defined, 13, 20
disk compression in, 225–26
dual boot with Windows 95, 559–60
executing programs in, 27–29
files renamed by Windows 95, 560
hard drive management under Windows 95, 233
interface, 15
limitations, 14–15
MemMaker with, 454–55
memory divisions, 7
memory limitations, 439
memory management with, 445–55
memory problems, troubleshooting, E-18–19
multiple operating system installation, 276–77
recovering damaged files with, 309
16-bit programming in, 546–47
in virtual machines, 548–49
with Windows 3.x, 20–21
with Windows 95, 21

DOS applications
in Windows 95, 460–63
in Windows NT, 593, 634–35, 637

DOS boot record (DBR), 271, See also master boot record (MBR)

DOS commands
external, 151
floppy disks, 151–56
FTP, 873
hard drive management, 208–14
internal, 151

DOS=HIGH,UMB command, 448–49

DOS-like commands, Windows NT, 591–93

dot matrix printers, 360, E-10

dot pitch, monitors, 177

DoubleBuffer, 557

double conversion, 510, 513

DoubleSpace, 226–27

Doze mode, monitors, 353–54

doze time, 502, 513

DRAM. See dynamic RAM (DRAM)

drive mapping, network, 875–79

drives, See also floppy drives; hard drive; removable drives; tape drives
A, data cable twist and, 168, 171–72
C, 195
current, 26
default, 26
removable, 244–49

DriveSpace, 226–30, 251

drive testing software, 161–64

drop height, removable drives, 247, 251

Drvspace, 557

DTE (Data Terminal Equipment), 395, 775, 802, 805
DTE speed, 776, 778

dual boot
defined, 652
Windows 95, 559–63, 580
Windows NT, 594, 597

dual in-line memory modules. See DIMMs

dual porting, 669, 698

dual voltage CPUs, 96, 126

DUMP command, 295–97

DUN. See dial-up networking (DUN)

duplexing, 930, 934

DVD (digital video disc) technology, 688–90, 697, 698

DVMs (digital voltage meters). See multimeters

dynamic data exchange, 524

Dynamic Host Configuration Protocol (DHCP), 851–52, 888

dynamic IP addresses, 851–52, 888

dynamic link libraries, .DLL file conflicts, 533–35

dynamic memory access (DMA) chip, 106

dynamic RAM (DRAM), 105–6, 107
defined, 127, 431, 477
refreshing, 431–32
synchronous, 434, 479
video controller cards, 178

dynamic routing, 862, 888

E

EDIT.COM, 161, 338, 446, 461

EDO memory, 106, 127, 434, 477

EEPROM, 103, 430, 477

EIDE drives, 236, 244, 252
vs. SCSI drives, 243, 244

EISA bus, 108, 111, 112, 116, 127

electrical system, 486–87

electricity, 486–90
amps, 488
current, 488
damage from, 73

measures of, 490
ohms, 489
voltage, 487, 488
wattage, 489–90

electrostatic discharge (ESD)
damage from, 73, 335, 370
defined, 73, 75, 370
protecting against, 166, 264, 335–36

ELF (extremely low frequency) emissions, 673, 698

e-mail, 829
software, installing, 870
viruses in, 907

embedded components, 86

embedded SCSI devices, 238, 251

emergencies, 343–44
disaster recovery planning, 931–32, 933

emergency repair disk (ERD), Windows NT, 631–33

EMM386.EXE, 447–55, 530
defined, 445, 447, 477
using HIMEM.SYS with, 451–52
in Windows 95, 461

EMS memory. See expanded memory (EMS)

encrypting viruses, 903–4, 935

Energy Star systems, 501–5, 513
computers, 501–3
monitors, 503–5

enhanced BIOS (LBA mode), for large-capacity drives, 199, 200, 251, 267

enhanced IDE (EIDE) drives. See EIDE drives

enhanced keyboards, 2

environment
defined, 17
multitasking, 17
operating, 18–20

environmental subsystems, Windows NT, 604, 652

environmental variables, not defined, 532–33

EPROM, 430, 477

equalization stage, modems, 773–74

ERASE command, 153, 182

erased files, recovering, 310–11

eraser heads, read/write head, 144

ergonomic keyboards, 2, 173

error correction protocols, modems, 772–73, 802, 805

error messages
Bad command or file not found, A-1
Bad Sector or Sector Not Found, 322
Bad sector writing or reading to drive, A-1
beeps during POST, A-1
Command file not found, 322
Configuration/CMOS error, 273, A-1
corrupted system files, 321–22
during booting, 363
Fixed disk error, A-1

General failure reading drive A: Abort, Retry, Fail?, 162–63, 165, E–2–3
hard drive, 314
Hard drive not found, 273, 274, A-1
Incorrect DOS version, 165, A-1
Insufficient Disk Space, E-19
Insufficient memory, A-1
Invalid drive specification, 165, 418, A-2, E-3
Invalid or missing COMMAND.COM, 164–65, A-2, E-3
Invalid system disk, 321
MSCDEX.EXE not found, 418
No boot device available, 273, A-2
Non-system disk or disk error, 66, 148, 164, 321, A-2, E-3
Not Enough Drive Letters, 418
Not reading drive A:, Abort, Retry, Fail?, 165, 291, A-2, E-3
numeric codes during POST, A-2
Object not found, 525
Out of Memory, 540
Track 0 bad, disk not usable, 165, A-2, E-3
Window NT startup, 633
Write-protect error writing drive A:, 165, A-2, E-3
errors
  applications software, configuration, 533
  boot record, 320
  device installation conflict, 419
  fatal system, 624, 652
  General Protection Fault (GFP), 533, 540–41
  hard drive does not boot, E-4
  hard drive not recognized, E-5
  hard drive retrieves and saves data slowly, E-4
  loading high, 465–66
  memory, 540–41
  parity, 106, 128
  registration, 525
escalating, 944, 954, 966
ESCD BIOS, 102, 563
ESD. See electrostatic discharge (ESD)
establishing carriers, modems, 773
Ethernet, 811–14, 885, 888
  bus design, 811
  cards, 819–21
  networks, 819
  star design, 811
Eudora Light, 870
even parity, 106, 433
Event Viewer, 648–49, 652
exception interrupts, 123
executive services, Windows NT, 603
.EXE files, 13, 27
expanded memory (EMS), 442–43
  defined, 439, 442, 477
  page frames, 442–43
  simulating, 451–52

expansion, maintaining records of, 367
expansion boards, See also cards
  memory, 436
  memory conflicts, 466–67, E-17
  ROM chips on, 100, 430
  for scanners, 392
  UMB conflicts, 467
expansion slots, 8, 264
  8-bit, 109
  16-bit, 110
  32-bit, 112
  ISA, 116
  PCI, 114, 755
  VESA local bus, 112–13
expert systems software, 955, 966
Express Setup, Windows 3.x, 527, 581
extended data output memory. See EDO memory
extended memory, 442
  availability, 454
  defined, 439, 477
external cache, 107, 127, 432
external devices, 387
external DOS commands, 151
external modems, 387, 763
  operation of, 774
  UART chips on, 778–79
external tape drives, 913–14

F

fake parity, 433–34, 477
fans, 94, 498–99, 720–21, E-18
Fast-ATA, 237
fast page mode memory. See FPM memory
FAT. See file allocation table (FAT)
fatal system errors, 624, 652
fault tolerance, RAID and, 929, 935
FC.EXE, 161
FDISK command, 161, 195, 233, 268–70, 338
  for damaged partition table, 318, 319
  /MBR, 319
female ports, 393
ferroresonant regulators, 508, 509, 513
Fiber Distributed Data Interface (FDDI) networks, 816–18, 819, 888
  FDDI cards, 820–21
  FDDI networks, 816–18, 819
fiber-optic cables, 813
FIFO buffers, 397, 422, 776, 777
file allocation table (FAT)
  damaged, 299–309, 321
  file system, 594–96
  floppy disks, 148–49, 150, 182
  fragmentation shown by, 221
  hard drives, 194–95, 201–5
  recovering damaged files, 311–12
  restoring with DEBUG, 304–5
  for root directory files, 207–8
  second copy of, 305
  technology, 202–4, 301–5

viewing with DEBUG utility, 202–5, 305–6
  virtual (VFAT), 205
  writing, 301–3
file allocation units. See clusters
file attributes
  displaying, 213
  root directory, 150–51, 206
file extensions
  associating with applications, 522
  defined, 13
file headers, 323
File Manager
  creating file associations in, 522
  disk commands, 156–58
  hard drive management with, 214–17
  root directory organization with, 365
FILENAME.INI, contents, 521
filenames
  defined, 13
  long, 13, 150, 205
file properties
  in Windows 3.x, 216–17
  in Windows 95, 218–19
FILES= command, 66, 446
files, See also program files
  ASCII, C-1
  compressing, 225
  damaged, 309–12
  data, corrupted, 323
  data storage in, 194
  defined, 13, 37
  erasing, 153
  fragmented, 148, 182
  hidden, 66
  organizing into subdirectories, 209
  program, corrupted, 323
  recovering, 153, 154
  system, corrupted, 321–22
file systems, Windows NT, 594–96
file transfer, 872–75
  using FTP utilities, 872–73
  using Internet service providers, 873–75
File Transfer Protocol. See FTP
file viruses, 903, 935
firmware, 430, See also ROM
  defined, 2, 37, 430
  modems, 772
  peripheral devices, 388
First Aid 97, 340
fixed frequency monitors, 673, 698
flash memory
  defined, 477
  uses of, 434
Flash ROM, 6, 37, 771
  defined, 99, 103, 477
  downloading, 1–3–4
  modems, 774
  upgrading BIOS with, 58, 102, 103–5
flat memory mode, 626, 627

floppy disks, *See also* formatting floppy disks
  3½, 142, 145, 146
  5¼, 142
  bootable, 68–69, 147–48, 151
  boot sector viruses, 902
  checking, 152–53
  clusters, 145–46
  copying, 154–55
  DOS commands, 151–56
  double-density, 142, 145
  erasing files, 153
  error messages, 164–65
  formatting, 143–51, 156, 159
  high-density, 142, 145
  incorrectly formatted, 145
  logical data storage, 145–46
  physical data storage, 143–45
  recovering files, 153, 154
  sectors, 143–45, 146
  storage capacity, 146
  tracks, 143–45, 146
  types, 142, 149
  volume labels, 152
  Windows 3.x commands, 156–58
  Windows 95 commands, 158–60
floppy drives, 11–12, 142–72
  adding, 171–72
  cable, 734
  changing disk type, 171
  connections, 142–43
  controllers, 12, 142
  data cable, 142, 168
  data recovery, 291–313
  drive light, 163
  error messages, 162–63, 164–65
  half-life, 247
  installing, 733–36
  measuring power output to, 497
  MPC3 specifications, 663
  non-working, 160–65
  port connection, 734
  power cable, 169–70
  read/write head, 144
  replacing, 160, 165–71
  solving drive problems, 163–64
  testing, 161–64
  troubleshooting, E-2–3
flow control
  defined, 803, 805
  hardware, 779–80
  modems, 779–80
  software, 779–80
FM synthesis, 666, 675, 697, 698
folders
  creating, 217–18
  defined, 217, 252
  deleting, 218
  hard drive organization, 194
fonts, memory and, 544
FORMAT command, 146, 151, 165, 338
  drive C:, 233

high-level formatting, 271
  options, 151–52
  Windows 95, 159
FORMAT.EXE, 161
formatting floppy disks, 143–51, 182
  bootable, 147–48, 151
  creating tracks and sectors, 146
  DOS commands, 151–52
  file allocation table, 148–49
  incorrectly, 145
  master boot record, 147–48
  root directory, 149–51
  Windows 3.x, 156
  Windows 95, 159
formatting hard drives, 220–33, *See also* hard drives
  high-level, 220–21, 271, 327
  low-level, 220, 235, 262, 327
  OS, 220
  partitioning, 220
  reversing, 213–14
  root directory creation, 206
FPM memory, 434, 477
F-Protect (F-PROT), 342
fragmentation
  causes, 221
  defined, 148, 182, 252
  of hard drives, 221–22
frame buffers, 664, 696, 697, 698
frames, 773, 805
  OSI layer network model and, 827
  sent over networks, 810
front end applications, 830–31, 888
front panel connectors, 729–31
FTP, 829, 871, 888
  from DOS command prompt, 873
  transferring files with, 872–75
  utility software, 872–75
Fujitsu DynaMO 230 Parallel Port drive, 248
full backups, 918, 935

G

game port connectors, 401
game ports, 393–94
Gang of Nine, 112
gateways, 823, 888
  alternate, 857, 886
  default, 857, 887
GDI memory heap, 540, 542, 544
GDI program, Windows 95, 546, 547
General Protection Fault (GPF) errors, 433, 477
  software conflicts, 533
  in Windows 3.x, 540–41
general-purpose I/O cards, 400–403
genlock, 385, 422
gigabytes, 199, 252, D-1
gold leads, matching, 434
GPF errors. *See* General Protection Fault (GPF) errors
grandparent backups, 917

graphical user interface (GUI), 16, 37
graphics accelerators, 669, 697, 698
green monitors, 178, 182, E-7
Green Standards, 501, 513
Green Star computers, 501–5
Green systemboards, 353–54
grounding out, preventing, 723–25
ground leads, 495
ground mats, 335, 336, 755
ground straps, 335, 336, 755
group (.GRP) files, 527, 580
guard tones, 773
guest computers, in Direct Cable Connection, 839–40
GUI. *See* graphical user interface (GUI)

H

half-life, removable drives, 247, 252
handshaking, 764–65, 768, 773–74, 802
  defined, 805
  error correction protocol, 772–73
  retraining, 798
hard booting, 64–65, 164
hard-coded, 101
hard copy, 3
hard disks. *See* hard drives
hard drive failure
  crashes, 11, 315–17
  data access, 317
  preparing for, 317–18
  recovery utilities, 283–89
hard drive installation, 262–67
  adapter cards, 265
  DIP switches, 263
  expansion slots, 264
  high-level formatting, 271
  IDE drives, 262
  jumper settings, 263–64
  large-capacity drives, 263
  partitioning, 268–71
  precautions, 262–67
  problem resolution, 272–74
  SCSI drives, 262, 275–76
  setup, 267–68
  software installation, 271–72
  technical support, 274
  tower cases, 265
  universal bay kits, 264–65
hard drives, 10–11, *See also* formatting hard drives
  backing up, 272, 290
  backups, 368
  bootable, 271
  boot sector viruses, 902
  capacity, 196–201
  changing BIOS, 200–201
  CMOS settings, 749
  components, 233–34
  controller, 11, 234, 238
  crashes, 315–17
  cylinders, 192
  data cable, 737

data fading, 11
data recovery, 291, 313–24
defined, 11
defragmenting, 290, 527, 529
deleting temporary files, 900
EIDE, 236, 244
emergency procedures, 343–44
error messages, 314
formatting, 206, 213–14, 220–33, 235, 262, 271, 327
fragmentation, 221–22
half-life, 247, 252
hard-disk loading, 963, 966
hardware problems, 313
heads, 192, 197
IDE, 233, 234–36, 262
inadequate space, 529, 532
installing, 262–77, 736–38
large-capacity, 199–201, 263
logical, 193–208
managing
  with DOS commands, 208–14
  with DOS under Windows 95, 233
  with Windows 3.x, 214–17
  with Windows 95, 217–19
MFM, 233, 234, 262
moving, 200–201
MPC3 specifications, 663
not booting, 324–25, E-4
not recognized, 325–26, E-5
operating systems and, 193–95
optimizing, 529
partitioning, 195, 220
physical, 192–93, 195–96
platters, 192, 193, 197
power output to, measuring, 497
precautions, 289–90
problem prevention, 290–91
problem resolution, 314–17
reduced write current, 193
removable, 247–49, 252
RLL, 233, 234, 262
root directory organization, 365
scanning, 290
SCSI, 233, 234, 236–44, 262
sectors, 192
sectors per track, 196–97
slow, 325, E-4
software problems, 313
standby time, 502, 513
System BIOS support, 196
technology, 233–44
tracks, 192
translation methods, 197–99
troubleshooting, 313–26, E-4–5
types, B-1–2
whining, 315
write precompression, 193
hardware, *See also* hard drives; peripheral devices
  defined, 2, 37

inside the case, 4–12
installation, Windows NT, 644–46
interface cards, 8–9
networking, 819–23
not listed in Windows setup, 529
on-board BIOS, 47, 57, 75
outside the case, 2–4
peripheral devices, 387–88
power supply, 10
ROM BIOS Startup program survey of, 47
secondary storage, 10–12
selecting, 707
software management of, 46–64
systemboard, 4–8
Windows NT support, 590–91, 616–17
hardware abstraction layer (HAL), 590, 606–7, 652
hardware cache, 231, 232, 252
hardware compatibility list (HCL), 591, 616, 653
hardware configuration. *See* configuration data
hardware conflicts. *See* conflicts
hardware devices. *See* peripheral devices
hardware flow control, 779–80, 781
hardware interrupts, 123
hardware profiles, Windows NT, 589, 638, 653
hardware tree, Plug-and-Play, 562–63, 580
Hayes Microcomputer Products, 787
HDD LED connector, 730, 731
header information, 323
headers, for data packets, 810, 888
heads, hard drives, 192, 197
heaps, 540, 542, 544, 580
heat sensors, 94
heat sinks, 94, 127, 721
Helix Software, 341, *See also* Nuts & Bolts
help-desk support, 334, 948–49
  tracking calls, 955–58
hertz (Hz), 675, 698
hexadecimal number system, 7, 441, 467, D-2–5
  memory addressing, D-6–7
  values, D-1–5
  writing conventions, D-6
hidden files, 66, *See also* ATTRIB command
  exposing, 322
  missing or corrupted, 321–22
high-level formatting, 220, 271, 327
high memory area, 439, 442, 478
HIMEM.SYS, 338, 445–47, 530
  defined, 445, 478
  using with EMM386.EXE, 451–52
  in Windows 95, 461
hives, 640–41, 653
HKEY_CLASSES_ROOT, 571, 640, 642

HKEY_CURRENT_CONFIG, 571, 640, 642
HKEY_CURRENT_USER, 571, 640, 641, 642
HKEY_DYN_DATA, 571
HKEY_LOCAL_MACHINE, 571, 640, 641, 642, 643
HKEY_USER, 640, 642
HKEY_USERS, 571
hoax viruses, 907
holographic images, 966
hop counts, 822, 888
host adapters
  matching to SCSI devices, 407–9
  SCSI bus, 237, 243, 252, 392
  SCSI ID settings, 275
  for a single device, 409–11
host computers
  defined, 810
  in Direct Cable Connection, 839–40
  mapping remote drive to, 878–79
host drives, 226, 252
hot swapping, 407, 422, 931, 935
HST standard, 767
HTTP, 829, 871, 889
hub centering, floppy drives, 161
hubs
  defined, 819, 889
  intelligent, 811, 889
  in star networks, 811
humidity, hard drive failure and, 290
Hypertext Transfer Protocol. *See* HTTP
hysteresis, floppy drives, 161

I

IANA, 851, 852
IBM Corporation
  8088 PCs, ISA 8-bit bus, 109
  AT, ISA 16-bit bus, 110
  RS 6000 chip, 93
ICMP (Internet Control Message Protocol), 854, 889
icon-driven interfaces, 16–17, 37
IDE controller ports
  for CD-ROM drives, 739, 741
  CD-ROM installation, 739
IDE drives, 233, 234–36, 262
  adapter cards, 86, 234, 236
  defined, 252
  installation, 262
  low-level formatting, 235–36, 319, 323
  operating system and, 235
  sectors per track, 235
IDE HDD Auto Detection, 749
IEEE, 823
image sensing, digital cameras, 687–88
inband signaling, 780, 805
In Control 2 for Windows 3.x, 535–39
In Control 3 for Windows 95, 535
incremental backups, 918, 935
incubation periods, viruses, 902

infestations, 932, 933, *See also* viruses
  basics, 901–2
  cloaking techniques, 903–4
  damage caused by, 904
  defined, 901, 935
  hiding places, 902–3
  hoaxes, 907
  protecting against, 907–8, 909–11
  spread of, 905–6
  symptoms, 908–9
  types of, 901
  viruses, 901–11
infrared sensors, 688
initialization, by ROM BIOS, 56–57
initialization (.INI) files, 68, 365, 521–24
  backing up, 521, 524, 531
  defined, 521, 580
  editing, 521–24
  file sections, 521
  Keynames, 521
  maximum file size, 523
  monitoring during installation, 535–39
  restarting Windows after changing, 521
  Windows 3.x, 520–24
ink jet printers, 695, 696
  troubleshooting, 360–61, E-10
in-line UPS, 508, 509–10, 513
input devices, 2, *See also* peripheral
  devices
  MPC3 specifications, 665
Institute of Electrical and Electronics
  Engineers (IEEE), 823
instruction execution unit, virtual
  machine, 608
instruction set, 93, 127
insufficient memory problems, 541–43
integral subsystems, Windows NT, 604,
  653
Integrated Device Electronics (IDE)
  drives. *See* IDE drives
integrated services digital network. *See*
  ISDN
Intel Corporation, *See also* Pentium
  computers
  486DX, 88, 89
  486SL, 89
  486SX, 88, 89
  80386DX, 88, 89
  80386SX, 88, 89
  chips, 6, 87, 96–99
  Classic Pentium, 80–81, 88
  in notebook computers, 89
intelligent hubs, 811, 889
intelligent UPS, 510–11, 513
Intel MMX Pentium CPUs, 658, 697
interface cards, 8–9, *See also* cards
interlaced monitors, 177
interleave, 262, 327
internal cache, 88, 107, 127, 432
internal data path size. *See* word size
internal devices, 387
internal DOS commands, 151

internal modems, 387, 763, *See also*
  modems
  installing, 742–45
  network cards, 8–9
  UART chips on, 778–79
internal tape drives, 913–14
International Organization for
  Standardization (ISO), 823
Internet, 847–81
  connecting to, 849, 867–70
  defined, 886, 889
  domain name resolution, 852–53
  IP addresses, 849–52
  Microsoft Technical Support Web site,
    577–78
  operations, 848
  routing using TCP/IP, 853–58
Internet Assigned Numbers Authority
  (IANA), 851, 852
Internet Control Message Protocol
  (ICMP), 854, 889
Internet Explorer, 590, 870
Internet Network Information Center
  (InterNiC), 849, 852, 889
Internet Protocol addresses. *See* IP
  addresses
Internet service providers (ISPs)
  defined, 889
  file transfer through, 873–75
  Internet access via, 849
internetwork packet
  exchange/sequenced packet exchange.
  See IPX/SPX
internetworks, 889
InterNIC, 849, 852, 889
interpolative scaling, 664, 696, 698
interrupt descriptor table. *See* I/O address
  table
interrupt handlers, 122, 127
interrupt request number. *See* IRQ
interrupts
  conflicts, 124
  IRQs, 121–24
  types of, 122
interrupt vector table. *See* I/O address
  table
intranets, 829, 889
I/O addresses
  default ranges, 123
  defined, 60
  maintaining lists of, 123
  memory conflicts, 63
  purpose, 64
I/O address table
  CPU use of, 59, 60–61
  defined, 59, 75
  IRQ numbers, 121–24
  peripheral devices, 387, 393
I/O cards, 9, 400–403, 422
Iomega drives
  Jaz, 247
  Zip, 247

IO.SYS, 66, 70, 148, 161
IP addresses, 849–52, 886
  classes of, 850–52
  classless, 861–62
  defined, 889
  dynamic, 851–52, 888
  IP version 6 (IPv6) standard, 852
  physical addresses and, 855–57
  shortage of, 851
  static, 851, 881, 886, 891
  subnets, 858–61
IPX/SPX, 826, 889
IRQ, 58–59, 62, 121–24
  conflicts, 63, 386–87
  defined, 58, 75
  peripheral device assignments, 386–87,
    393
  purpose, 64
  request handlers, 59
IRQ numbers
  default, 123
  I/O address table, 121–24
  maintaining lists of, 123
ISA buses
  8-bit, 108, 109–10, 111, 116, 117, 127
  16-bit, 108, 110, 111, 116, 127
ISDN, 799–802, 803
  connection options, 801
  defined, 805
  requirements for, 800
ISO, 823

J

Jaz drives, 912
joules, 506, 513
JPEG format, 688, 698
jump, program, 14, 38
jumpers
  configuration data stored by, 52
  defined, 52
  hard drive installation and, 263–64
  peripheral devices, 388
  voltage regulation, 96
jumper settings, 712–19, 755
  cache memory selection, 717–18
  CD-ROM drives, 739
  changing, 52
  closed position, 714
  CMOS RAM clearance, 719
  CPU bus clock selection, 715
  CPU core to bus clock ratio selection,
    715–16
  CPU voltage selection, 717
  documentation, 714
  hard drive, 736
  maintaining records of, 367
  memory conflicts and, 63
  for modems, 743–45
  open position, 714
  parking the jumper, 715
  SCSI host adapters, 746

K

K56flex standard, 767
kernel mode, Windows NT, 605–6
kernel program, Windows 95, 546, 547
keyboards, 172–75
    connectors, 174–75
    defined, 2, 37
    mouse ports in, 173
    troubleshooting, 350, 351–52, E-5–6
    types, 173
key lock connector, 730
Keynames, in .INI files, 521
keys
    Windows 95 registry, 570, 571, 580
    Windows NT registry, 638
kilobytes, D-1
kilovolt-amperes (kVA), 507
KRNL386.EXE, 609

L

L1 cache. See internal cache
L2 cache. See external cache
LABEL command, 152
Label Disk command, Windows 3.x, 157
lands, 411, 422
LANs (local area networks), define, 810
large-capacity drives
    BIOS issues, 267
    CHS mode, 199
    defined, 199
    enhanced BIOS or LBA mode, 200
    installing, 263
    lack of BIOS support for, 200–201
    large mode, 199
    translation for, 199
large mode, for large-capacity drives, 199, 252
laser printers, 384, 690–95, 697
    cleaning, 691, 692
    conditioning, 691, 692
    developing, 691, 694–95
    fusing, 691, 695
    transferring, 691, 695
    troubleshooting, 357–60, E-8–9
    writing, 691, 693–94
Last Known Good configuration, 628–29
launching, documents, in Windows 3.x, 33
LBA. See logical block addressing (LBA)
LCD monitors, 175
LCD panel, external modems, 774
legacy devices
    defined, 564, 580
    installation, 564–69
    troubleshooting, 568–69
legacy software, 27, 634–37
let-through, 506, 513
level 1 cache. See internal cache
level 2 cache. See external cache
limited tokens, 817, 889
LIM memory, 443
linear addressing, 442

line conditioners, 507–8, 513
line-interactive UPS, 510, 513
line protocols, 833, 889
liquid crystal display monitors. See LCD monitors
LOADHIGH= command, 449, 450
loading high
    defined, 449, 478
    device drivers, 449–50
    DOS, 442
    errors, 465–66
    TSRs, 449, 450–51
loading speed, RAM drives and, 444
load size, 449–50, 478
LoadTop, 558
local area networks. See LANs (local area networks)
local buses, 108, 111, 112–13, 127
locking up, memory conflicts and, 466
logfiles, monitoring memory leaks with, 542–43
logical block addressing (LBA), 200, 267
    defined, 252
    EIDE drives, 237
logical cluster number (LCN), 594
logical (virtual) communication, 760–63
logical drives, 195–96, 228–29
logical unit number (LUN), 238, 252
logic boards, 142
logic parity, 433, 478
Logo, 557
long filenames
    VFAT and, 205
    Windows 95, 13, 150
loop-back plugs, 339
loop-back tests, 339
lossless compression, 666, 698
lossy compression, 699
lost clusters, 213, 252, 310, 327
Lotus Corporation, expanded memory, 443
Lovelace, Ada, D-1
low-level formatting, 220, 327
    cautions, 319, 323
    destructive, 323
    hard drives, 262
    IDE drives, 235
    nondestructive, 323
LUN (logical unit number), 238, 252

M

MAC (media access control), 821, 885, 889
McAfee ViruScan (SCAN), 342
Mace Cache, 231
Macintosh
    computers, 6
    operating system, 24
macros, 903, 935
macro viruses, 903, 935
magneto-optical drives, 248, 252
maintenance, preventive, 898–901

make code, 175, 182
Make System Disk command, Windows 3.x, 157
male ports, 393
master boot program, 66
master boot record (MBR), 269
    contents, 147
    defined, 147, 182
    restoring, 319
    viruses in, 902
    Windows NT, 626, 627
master boot sector, 269
master file table (MFT), 594, 595
Max-Blast Disk Manager, 200
MCA bus, 108, 111, 112, 127
MD command, 209–10, 252
MDRAM, 671, 699
media access control (MAC) addresses, 821, 885, 889
Media Player, 680
megabytes, D-1
megahertz (MHz), 87, 127
MEM command, 447, 450
    defined, 478
    memory reports using, 452–54
    options, 447
MEM.EXE, 161
MemMaker, 454–55, 478
memory
    conventional, 439, 440–41
    defined, 437
    DOS divisions, 7
    DOS limitations, 439, 440
    EMS, 439, 442–43, 451–52, 477
    errors, in Windows 3.x, 540–41
    expanded, 439, 442–43, 477
    General Protection Fault (GPF) errors, 433, 477, 533, 540–41
    high memory area, 439, 442
    installing, 473–74
    insufficient, 541–43
    LIM, 443
    logical organization of, 437
    module selection, 472–73
    nonvolatile, 7
    optimizing, 527
    pages, 465, 478
    parity, 433
    primary storage, 7, 10, 430
    problems in DOS, E-17
    problems in Window 3.x, E-17
    secondary storage, 10–12
    speed, 433
    systemboard, 432–33
    upgrading, 468–74
    upper, 439, 440, 441
    virtual, 44
    volatile, 7
memory addresses, 7, See also I/O addresses
    assignment of, 437–38
    defined, 437

devices sharing, 466–67
hexadecimal number system, D-6–7
linear addressing, 442
maximum, 87
physical memory and, 437–39
Plug-and-Play cards and, 437
protected mode, 541
real mode, 541
video, 441
memory cache
defined, 127, 432, 478
disk cache vs., 232
in Pentium computers, 90
memory chips
buying, 433–35
re-marked, 435, 479
used modules, 435
memory conflicts. *See* conflicts
memory heaps, 542
defined, 540
memory leaks and, 542
types of, 540
memory leaks, 540, 543–44, 580
memory management
defined, 441, 445, 478
with DOS, 445–55
error prevention, 465–67
software, 442
troubleshooting, 464–67
Window 95, 460–64
Windows 3.x, 445–60, 540–44
Windows NT, 464–65, 606–7
memory mapping
defined, 438, 478
memory map areas, 439
page frames, 442–43, 478
memory modules
buying, 433–35
types of, 432–33
memory paging, 549–51, 580
memory reports, using MEM command, 452–54
memory-resident viruses, 906, 935
memory tests
POST, 726–27
systemboard testing with, 723–27
MEM reports, troubleshooting, 465–66
menu-driven interfaces, 15–16
menu heap, contents, 540
MFM drives, 233, 234, 262
Microchannel Architecture bus.
See MCA bus
microprocessors. *See* central processing
units (CPUs)
Microsoft Technical Support Web site, 577–78
middleware, 831, 889
MIDI format, 675, 696, 699
MIDI interface, MPC3 specifications, 665
minicartridges
for tape drives, 914, 916, 934, 935
troubleshooting, E-14

minifile system drivers, Windows NT, 626, 627, 653
minimizing applications, memory usage and, 542
MIPS chip, 93
MIRROR command, 213, 253, 318
mirrors
beam detect, 693, 698
scanning, 693
MKDIR command, 209–10, 252
MMX technology, 88, 91, 658, 697, 699
advantages of, 667–68
MNP standards, 767, 772
modem eliminator, 395–96, 423
Modem Properties box, 670, 765, 769, 776–77
modems, 387, 759–99, 802, 805
analog/digital conversion, 763–64
applications software, 391
baud rate, 765
communication software, 786–96
COM ports, 779
configuring, 783–86
data compression, 772
error correction protocols, 772–73
external, 387, 763, 774, 778–79, 783
features, 774–75
56 Kbps, 771–72
firmware, 772
flow control, 779–80
handshaking, 764–65, 768
installing, 742–45, 783–86
internal, 8–9, 387, 763, 778–79, 783
modem speed, 765–66, 776, 802, 805
modem-to-modem communication, 761
noise, 764
port speed, 779
rating, 764
reducing speed of, 769
RS-232c serial port communication, 781–82
software-to-modem communication, 787–92
speed limitations, 766
standards, 766–71, 802
33.6, 768–69
transmission speed, 776
transmission standards, 767
troubleshooting, 796–99, E-10–12
modulation, 763, 805
monitors, 175–78
blank screen, 353–54, 361–62, E-7, E-15–16
color display, 178
defined, 2, 37
dot pitch, 177
Energy Star, 503–5
features, 672–73
flickering, 353
green, 178, 182, E-7
interlaced, 177
multiscan, 177, 182

non-interlaced, 177
no picture, 352–53, E-6–7
poor picture, 355, E-7–8
power light (LED), 352–53, E-6
refresh rate, 177
resolution, 177, 178
screen size, 176
Standby/Doze mode, 353–54
touch screen, 62
troubleshooting, 350, 352–56, E-6–8
VGA settings, 356
video BIOS, 57
video drivers, 355–56
wrong characters, 353
MORE.COM, 161
motherboard. *See* systemboard
motherboard BIOS. *See* System BIOS
Motorola Corporation, 6
mouse, 179–81
bus, 180, 182, 392
buttons, 3, 179
cleaning, 181
defined, 3, 37
IRQs, 59
problems following Windows installation, 529–30
PS-2 compatible, 180
serial port, 180, 183, 392
systemboard, 180, 183
troubleshooting, E-4, E-19
MOUSE.INI, 68
mouse ports, on keyboards, 2, 173
Move command, Windows 3.x, 157, 158
MPC (Multimedia Personal Computer)
standards, 384–85
MPC specifications, 661–67, 699
defined, 661
MPC1, 666–67
MPC2, 666–67
MPC3, 662–66
MPEG format, 663, 696, 699
MPEG-2 controller cards, 689
MSAU (multistation access unit), 815–16, 890
MSBACKUP command, 233
MSCDEX.EXE, 161, 338, 418
MSD command
identifying BIOS with, 563
resolving resource conflicts with, 404–5
MSD.EXE, 397–98
MS-DOS. *See* DOS
MSDOS.SYS, 66, 148, 161, 580
contents, 557–58
customizing Windows 95 installation
with, 556–58
in Windows 95 environment, 70–71
Multibank DRAM (MDRAM), 671, 699
Multiframe dialogs, 817, 890
multimedia devices, 384–85
Multimedia Marketing Council, 384
multimedia PCs
defined, 658

MPC specifications, 661–67
requirements, 661–68
multimedia presentations, 384, 423
Multimedia Properties, 680–81
multimedia technology, 657–96
  digital cameras, 687–88
  digital video disc (DVD), 688–90
  goals of, 657, 658–59
  printers, 690–96
  sound cards, 674–87
  video cards, 668–72
multimeters, 491–97, 514
  autorange, 492
  display, 491
  measuring power output to drives, 497
  measuring power output to system-
    board, 495–97
  measuring voltage with, 492–93
  test probes, 492
multipartite viruses, 903, 935
multiplier
  changing, 117
  defined, 127
  in Pentium computers, 90
  performance and, 117
multiprocessing, 88
multiscan monitors, 177, 182
multisession feature, CD-ROM drives,
  412, 423
multistation access unit (MSAU), 815–16,
  890
multitasking
  defined, 17
  environment, 17
  SCSI bus support, 244
  swap files and, 456
  Windows NT, 589
multithreading, 605, 608, 653

N

nanoseconds, 433
nearest active downstream neighbor
  (NADN), 816, 890
nearest active upstream neighbor
  (NAUN), 816, 890
NetBIOS, 871
NetBIOS Extended User Interface
  (NETBEUI), 829, 871, 890
NetBIOS over TCP/IP (NetBT), 854, 890
NET.CFG, 845, 846
NetSync, WebPatch, 340
NetWare (Novell), 827, 844
Network, 557
network adapters
  installing using Windows 95, 842
  installing using Windows NT, 840–41
network administration, Windows NT,
  612–16
Network Basic Input/Output System
  (NetBIOS), 871
network cards, 8–9

network drive mapping, 875–79
  from remote to host computer, 878–79
  preparing a Windows NT host com-
    puter for, 875–77
network drives, 843–44
networked PCs
  disconnecting network cable, 846
  logging off the network, 844
  reconnecting to network, 846
  restoring network configurations, 846
  saving network files and parameters,
    844–45
  servicing, 843–46
  troubleshooting, 843
  verifying availability of network
    resources, 846
  verifying network-readiness, 843–46
network file service (NFS) software, 875
networking
  dial-up, 832–38
  Direct Cable Connection, 838–40
  domain model, 609–11
  Internet and, 847–81
  print services, 830, 884
  troubleshooting, 882–84, E-21–22
  with Windows 95, 831–40, 842
  Windows NT, 609–16
  with Windows NT Workstation, 831–41
  workgroup model, 609–11
networking hardware, 819–23
networking software, 827–31
  component relationships, 828
  network applications, 829–30
network interface cards (NICs), 819–21,
  885, 890
Network layer, 824, 826, 827, 890
network mask, 857–58, 890
network printers, troubleshooting, E-10
networks
  dedicated servers, 830–31
  defined, 810
  Ethernet, 811–14, 819
  FDDI, 816–18, 819
  logging off, 844
  OSI layer model, 823–27
  passive, 812, 890
  peer-to-peer, 830–31
  protocol, 829
  saving files and parameters to disk,
    844–45
  servicing PCs on, 843–46
  token ring, 815–16, 819
  types of, 810–19
Network Solutions, Inc. (NSI), 849
network stations, 810
NETWORKS.WRI, 530
New Folder command, Windows 95,
  217–18
New Hardware Wizard, 677
NICs. See network interface cards (NICs)
NO CARRIER message, 798
nodes, 810, 826, 890

NOEMS switch, 448
noise, modem, 764, 805
noisy phone lines, 766, 769, 772
  retraining, 798
nondestructive low-level formatting, 323
non-interlaced monitors, 177
non-memory-resident viruses, 906, 935
nonparity DRAM, 105
nonparity memory, 433–34, 478
non-system disks, 148, 164
nonvolatile memory, 7
Normal, removable drives, 248
normal mode, 199, 253
Norton Anti-Virus (NAV), 342
Norton Cache, 231
Norton Utilities, 73, 277, 278–83, 341
  boot record restoration, 291
  configuration data backup and restora-
    tion, 53–56
  defragmentation, 221
  Disk Doctor, 278, 280, 299, 300, 311,
    319, 320–21
  Disk Editor, 280, 299, 300, 305–7,
    311–12, 327
  file allocation table restoration, 299–301
  File Compare, 280
  file recovery, 280, 311–12
  Help features, 281–82
  Image, 279, 317–18
  monitoring .INI file changes in, 534
  partition table restoration, 319
  Protection, 279
  Registry Editor, 280
  Registry Tracker, 280, 574–77
  Rescue Disk, 279, 281–83, 320
  Speed Disk, 280
  System Doctor, 278
  System Genie, 280
  UnErase Wizard, 280
notebook computers
  CPU model numbers, 89
  flash memory for, 434
  PC card slots, 406–7
NTBACKUP command, 924, 927–28
NTDETECT.COM, 626, 627
NTDOS.SYS, 608
NT Hardware Qualifier, 616–17, 653
NTHQ.TXT, 617
NTIO.SYS, 608
NT Loader (NTLDR), 626, 627, 653
NTOSKRNL.EXE, 626, 627
NTSC video capturing cards, 385, 422
NTVDM.EXE, 608
NT virtual DOS machine (NTVDM), 607
  customizing for DOS applications,
    634–35
  defined, 604–5, 653
null modem cable, 395–96
null modem cables, 838–40
number systems, 7
Nuts & Bolts, 73, 161, 277, 283–89, 341
  boot record restoration, 291, 298

Discover Pro, 283, 542, 547
Disk Minder, 283, 284–85, 286, 298, 319
  file allocation table restoration, 301
  hard drive failure, 283–89
  Image, 283, 285–88
  partition table restoration, 319
  Registry Wizard, 572
  Rescue Disk, 283, 288–89
  WinGauge, 283
  WinGauge Pro, 542

O

object linking, 524
.OCA files, 350
octets, 850, 890
.OCX files, 349–50
odd parity, 106, 433
offset, D-7
ohms, 489, 490, 514
Oil Change, 340
Olympus PowerMO 230 drive, 248
on-board BIOS, 47, 57, 75
on-board ports, 119, 127
online help, for PC technicians, 955
Open Database Connectivity (ODBC), 831, 889
Open Systems Interconnect (OSI). See OSI layer network model
operating environment, 18–20
operating system (OS), 12, 13–24
  applications software and, 25, 49–50
  command-driven interfaces, 15
  defined, 38
  execution of, 13–14
  functions, 14
  hard drive organization and, 193–95
  hardware management by, 46
  icon-driven interfaces, 16–17
  IDE drives and, 235
  loading, 66
  Macintosh, 24
  menu-driven interfaces, 15–16
  multiple, 276–77
  system configuration by, 49
  terms, 17–24
  UNIX, 24
operation system (OS) formatting. See high-level formatting
optical fiber cable, 813
optimization, of Windows 3.x, 544–45
OS. See operating system (OS)
OS/2, 22, 23
OS boot record, Windows NT, 626, 627
OSI layer network model, 823–27, 885, 890
  Application layer, 824, 825, 827, 870–72, 887
  binding to, 856, 887
  data frames, 827
  Data Link layer, 824, 826, 827, 887

Network layer, 824, 826, 827, 890
Physical layer, 824, 826, 827, 890
Presentation layer, 824, 825, 827, 890
Session layer, 824, 825–26, 827, 870, 891
Transport layer, 870, 892
out-of-band signaling, 805
output devices, 2, See also peripheral devices
  MPC3 specifications, 665
overdrive mode, 89
overhead projectors, with LCD panels, 385

P

packet Internet groper (PING), 883–84
packets
  collisions between, 812
  defined, 890
  routing of, 853–54
  sent over networks, 810
page composition software, 383–84
page faults, 551, 580
page frames, 442–43, 478
page-in, 551, 581
page-out, 551, 581
pages, 465, 478
parallel port connectors, 732–33
parallel ports
  25-pin, 400, 401
  default assignments, 393–94
  defined, 423
  identifying, 393
  for peripheral devices, 393, 400
parallel transmission, 9
parameter RAM (PRAM), 7
parent backups, 917
parent directories, 209
parity, 782
  defined, 105, 106, 128
  even, 106, 433
  fake, 433–34, 477
  logic, 433, 478
  odd, 106, 433
parity DRAM, 105–6
parity errors, 106, 128
parity generator chips, 433, 478
parity memory, 433, 478
partitions
  active, 268
  creating, 220, 268–71
  extended, 268
  hard drives, 195
  master boot record, 269
  master boot sector, 269
  number of, 268
  value of, 271
  Windows NT, 596–97
partition tables, 195, 268–70, 327
  damaged, 318–20
  displaying, 213
  restoring, 318–20
  saving to disk, 272

passive networks, 812, 890
passwords, startup (power-on), 52
path, 27
PATH command, 27–28, 67, 214, 217, 219, 253
path size, 88
pcANYWHERE, 786, 789–90, 793–96
PC Cache, 231
PC cards, 406–7, 423, 434
PC card slots, 406–7, 423
PC-compatible computers, 704, 755
PC-Diagnosys, 340
PC Handyman, 341
PCI bridge, 114, 115
PCI bus, 108, 111, 114–16, 117
  defined, 128
  standard, 98
PCI expansion slots, 755
PCM, (pulse code modulation), 666, 699
PCMCIA slots, 406–7, 423
PCs. See personal computers
PC-Technician, 339
PC technicians, 334, 941–64
  characteristics of, 943–44
  communication by, 949–54
  customer satisfaction and, 942–43
  escalating, 944
  help-desk support, 948–49
  job functions, 334
  professional organizations and certificates, 959–61
  recordkeeping, 954–59
  support calls, 944–54
  technical support Web sites, 961–62
PC-to-modem communication, 761
PC Tools, 221, 277, 290, 319, 341
  boot record restoration, 299
  DISKFIX, 301, 319
  file allocation table restoration, 301
  PCSHELL, 301
peer-to-peer networks, 830–31
Pentium computers, 88, 90–93
  Classic, 88, 90–91
  competitors, 92–93
  II, 91
  local bus, SIMMs configuration, 470–71
  MMX, 88, 91
  Pro, 91
Pentium Pro CPUs, 658
performance
  bus speed and, 117–18
  Windows NT, 599
peripheral devices, 381–420
  applications software for, 391–92
  CD-ROM drives, 411–20
  conflicts, 100, 386, 387, 403–5
  connecting, 747
  defined, 2, 38
  desktop-publishing devices, 383–84
  device drivers, 389–91
  DIP switches, 388

external, 387
firmware, 388
general-purpose I/O cards, 400–403
hard-coded memory addresses, 101
hardware, 387–88
internal, 387
I/O addresses, 121–24
IRQ assignments, 393
jumpers, 388
legacy devices, 564–69
multimedia, 384–85
for notebook computers, 406–7
parallel port connections, 400
Plug-and-Play, 388, 564–65
principles for adding, 386
researching, 382, 387–88
SCSI devices, 407–11
serial port connections, 392, 393–400
sharing memory addresses, 466–67
system resources for, 58–63
troubleshooting, 350, 351–61
types of, 2–4
Windows 95 installation, 564–69, E-20
Permanent RAM. *See* PRAM
permanent swap files, 457–60
personal computers
assembly process, 709–54
case cover installation, 751–52
CD-ROM drive installation, 739–41
CMOS settings, 748–51
CPU installation, 719–22
floppy disk installation, 733–35
hard drive installation, 736–38
modem installation, 742–45
operating system installation, 748–51
peripheral connections, 748
scanner connections, 753
SCSI host adapter installation, 745–47
serial and parallel port connections, 732–33
sound card installation, 741–42
speaker installation, 747
systemboard installation, 728–32
systemboard jumper settings, 712–19
systemboard RAM installation, 722
systemboard testing, 723–27
video card installation, 748
brand-name PCs, 704
buying, 382
clones, 704
complete packages, 707–8
functional requirements, 705
intended purposes, 704–5
PC-compatible, 704, 755
preparing to build, 708–9
selecting, 704
selecting components for, 709–10
shipping, 900–901
personal computers (PCs), 6
phase-dual (PD) optical drives, 246, 247, 248, 253

Phoenix BIOS, 99, B-1, B-2
phone lines
clean, 766
communication over, 762
digital, 799
dirty (noisy), 766, 769, 772, 798
modem speeds and, 766
physical communication, 760–62
Physical layer, 824, 826, 827, 890
physical memory, 430–36
memory addresses and, 437–39
PIFs (program information files), 461–62, 479
PING, 883–84, E-22
pipeline burst cache, 107, 128
pipelined burst SRAM, 435, 478
pitch, modems, 773
pits, 411, 423
pixels, 2, 37, 177, 183
Pizazz Plus, 450
platters, 192, 193, 197
Plug-and-Play (PnP)
cards, memory addresses and, 437
defined, 75, 128, 253, 562, 581
ESCD, 102, 563
hardware device installation, 564–65
IRQ numbers and, 124
modems, 774
modem settings, 744–45
operating systems, 63
operation of, 562–63
peripheral devices, 388
removable drives, 247
UART chips, 397
Plug-and-Play (PnP) BIOS, 101–2, 563
advantages of, 69–70
defined, 63, 581
processing, 70
pointing devices, 179–81
Point-to-Point Protocol (PPP), 829, 832, 890
polling, 123, 128
polymorphic viruses, 903, 936
portable operating system interface (POSIX), 599, 653
ports, 3, 4
defined, 2, 37
disabling, 119
IDE controller, 739, 741
on-board, 119
parallel connectors, 732–33
serial connectors, 732–33
port settings, 805
for UART protocols, 782
port speed, modems, 776, 779, 806
POSIX (portable operating system interface), 599, 653
POST (power-on self test), 45, 56–57, 62, 726–27
booting and, 65
defined, 75, 370
diagnostic cards, 339

floppy drive error messages, 162–63
hardware problems, 314
non-system disks, 148
steps in, 65
three beeps during, 273
Windows NT, 626
power cables, floppy drives, 169–70
power conditioners, 505, 507–8, 514
power light (LED), monitors, 352–53, E-6
Power Management Setup, 502
power-on passwords, 52
power output
to drives, 497
to systemboard, 495–97
power-saving features
CD-ROM drives, 412
Green Standards, 501–5, 513
power spikes, 507, 511
power supply, 4, 10, 37
connections, 124, 491
exchanging, 498–501
fan, 94, 498–99, E-18
installing, 500–501
measuring voltage of, 493–97
troubleshooting, 498–99, E-17–18
upgrading, 499–500
voltage measurement, 490–97
power switch, turning off and on, 65
PPP (Point-to-Point Protocol), 829, 832, 890
PRAM, 7, 102
Presentation layer, 824, 825, 827, 890
preventive maintenance, 898–901, 932
plan, 898–90
when moving equipment, 900–901
primary cache. *See* internal cache
primary domain controller (PDC), 610, 653
primary storage, 7, 10, 430
printers
defined, 3, 38
dot matrix, 360, E-9–10
improving performance, 695–96
ink jet, 360–61, 695, 696, E-10
laser, 357–60, 384, 690–95, 697, E-8–9
multimedia technology, 690–96
network, E-10
parallel ports for, 400
shared, 880–81
troubleshooting, 350, 357–61, E-8–10
Windows NT Workstation installation, 622–24
PRINTERS.WRI, 530
Print Manager, 544
print services, 880–81
network, 830, 880–81
shared printers, 880–81
private circuits, 799
processes, Windows NT, 607–8, 653
ProComm, 391
ProComm Plus, 786, 790–91
professional organizations, 959–60

profiles, Windows NT, 612
PROGMAN.INI, 68, 521, 522
program files
  copying into RAM, 29–30
  corrupted, 323, 327
  defined, 13
  executing in DOS, 27–29
  executing in Windows, 29–30
  locating, 27–29
program information files (PIFs), 461–62, 479
program jump, 14, 38
programs, 2, 38
PROMPT command, 67
properties, of shortcuts (Windows 95), 34
Properties command
  Windows 3.x, 158, 216–17
  Windows 95, 218–19
Properties sheets, for DOS application, 461–62
proprietary devices, video controller cards, 178
proprietary systems, 706, 754, 755
protected mode
  defined, 460, 479, 541, 581
  Windows 95 installation in, 551
protocols, 394–95
  bridging (line), 833
  connection, 854
  connectionless, 854
  defined, 890
  for modems, 764–65
PS/2-compatible mouse, 180
PS/2 connectors, 174–75
pulse code modulation (PCM), 666, 699

Q

QBASIC.EXE, 338
Quarterdeck Corp., WINProbe, 340
Quarter-Inch Committee (QIC) standards, 915, 936

R

radial alignment, floppy drives, 162
RAID, 912, 929–31, 933, 936
RAM, 105–6, See also dynamic RAM (DRAM); static RAM (SRAM)
  chips, 6–7
  copying program files into, 29–30
  defined, 38, 430
  on expansion boards, 436
  installing on systemboard, 722–23
  MPC3 specifications, 663
  not recognized, 362–63, E-16
  refreshing, 106
  shadow, 60, 100
  video, 436
  volatility of, 430
  Windows 95 requirements, 468
RAM DAC technology, 669
RAM drives, 444, 479

random access memory. See RAM
RARP (Reverse Address Resolution Protocol), 854, 891
RCP/IP, routing using, 853–58
RD command, 211–12, 253
README.WRI, 530
read-only files, creating, 322
read-only memory. See ROM
read-writable CDs, 912
read/write heads, 11, 147
  cleaning, 164
  defined, 144
real mode
  defined, 460, 479, 541, 581
  Windows 95, 551
  Windows NT, 627
rebooting, See also booting
  hard booting, 64–65, 164
  soft booting, 65, 164
record books, maintaining setup data in, 366–67
recordkeeping
  by PC technicians, 954–59
  preventive maintenance, 900
Record Sound dialog box, 682
RECOVER command, 148, 154, 183, 310
rectifiers, 490
reduced write current, hard drives, 193, 253
refresh, 106, 128
refresh rate, monitors, 177
REGEDIT.EXE, 524–27, 573–74
.REG files, registering applications with, 526
registration
  during installation, 526
  errors related to, 525
registration database (REG.DAT), 524–27
  corrupted, 520, 526
  defined, 520, 524, 581
  rebuilding, 526–27
Registration Info Editor (REGEDIT.EXE), 524–27, 573–74
registry, Windows 3.x, 524–27
  corrupted, rebuilding, 526–27
  dynamic data exchange, 524
  object linking, 524
  SETUP.REG, 524–26
registry, Windows 95, 367, 551, 570–77
  corrupted, recovering, 571–72
  modifying, 572–74
  organization of, 570–71
  searching, 573–74
  tracking changes during installation, 574–77
registry, Windows NT, 594, 631, 637–46
  backing up, 646
  components, 638
  hardware installation, 644–46
  logical organization, 638–39, 641–43
  physical organization, 640–41

Registry Editor, 639–43
  software installation, 643–44
  subkeys, 638, 641–43
  values, 638, 641–43
REGSVR.EXE utility, 526
re-marked chips, 435, 479
REM command, 527
Remote Access Service (RA), 875–77
remote computers, mapping to host computers, 878–79
remote control
  with pcANYWHERE, 794–96
  in software-to-software communication, 792, 806
removable drives, 244–49
  advantages, 245
  defined, 253
  drop height, 247, 251
  half-life, 247
  hard disk, 247–48, 252
  high-capacity, 247
  installing, 249
  magneto-optical, 245, 248
  phase-dual (PD) optical, 246, 247, 248
  selecting, 246–47
  technologies, 246
Rename command, Windows 3.x, 158
repeaters, 814, 885, 891
  amplifier, 814, 886
repetitive looping, 661, 667
repetitive stress injury (RSI), 172
request handlers, 59
rescue disks, 338, See also bootable disks
  booting from, 164, 289
  creating, 53–56, 159, 160, 272, 366
    with Norton Utilities Rescue Disk, 279, 281–83
    with Nuts & Bolts Rescue Disk, 288–89
  defined, 183
  files, 161
  keeping, 71–72
  updating to include CD-ROM drive access, 417
  using, 56
reset switch connector, 730
resistance, 489, 514
  current and, 489
  voltage and, 489
resistors, 489, 514
resolution, monitors, 177, 178
resource arbitrator, Plug-and-Play, 562–63, 581
resource conflicts. See conflicts
resources
  checking, 531
  hardware survey, 47–48
  management, Plug-and-Play, 562, 581
  used by serial ports, 399–400
retensioning, minicartridge tapes, 916, 936
retraining, 798

Reverse Address Resolution Protocol
(RARP), 854, 891
Rhapsody, 24
RISC chips, 93–94, 128
RLL drives, 233, 234, 262
RMDIR command, 211–12, 253
roaming users, 612, 653
ROM, *See also* shadow RAM
  defined, 2, 6, 7, 38, 430
  EEPROM, 103, 430, 477
  EPROM, 430, 477
  on expansion boards, 430, 436
  firmwear, 388, 430
  memory address assignments, 437
  on systemboard, 430
ROM BIOS, 45, 56–64, 99–105, *See also*
  BIOS; ROM BIOS Startup Program
  compatibility needs, 99
  configuring and initializing computer
    by, 56–57
  defined, 12, 37, 56, 430
  functions of, 56
  hardware control by, 57–58
  memory address storage, 60
  upgrading with Flash ROM, 58
ROM BIOS Startup Program, 45, 57, *See
  also* BIOS; ROM BIOS
  booting with DOS, 66
  defined, 12–13
  hardware resources survey, 47–48
  operating system loaded by, 48
  operation of, 61–62
root directories, 26
  creating, 149–51, 206
  damaged, 306–7, 321
  defined, 183, 253
  file information, 150–51
  hard drives, 205–8
  minimizing number of files in, 365
  organizing, 365
  repairing, 307–9
  technology, 207–8
  unhiding files in, 322
rotational speed, floppy drives, 162
route discovery, 822, 891
routers, 814, 822, 856–57
  defined, 891
  multiple, 857, 858
  routing of, 853
router tables, 822, 891
routing
  dynamic, 862, 888
  static, 862
  TCP/IP, 856–57
RS-232c serial port communication,
  781–82, 787
RS-232 port, 393
RS 6000 chip, 93
RTS/CTS protocol, 779
Rubenking, Neil, 535

Run command
  in Windows 3.x, 33
  in Windows 95, 34, 35
runtime configuration, Plug-and-Play,
  562, 581

S

safe mode, 561–62, 581
sampling
  sound cards and, 674, 675, 699
  sound waves, 659–61, 699
SCAM (SCSI configuration
  automatically), 240, 253, 423
SCAM-compliant SCSI devices, 409
scan code, 175
SCANDISK command, 153, 223–24
  for lost clusters, 310
  options, 153
SCANDISK.EXE, 161, 338
SCANDISK.INI, 161
Scangal for Windows, 392
scanners, 383–84
  applications software, 392
  black-and-white, 386
  connecting, 753
  host adapters, 410
  installation, 392
scanning mirrors, in laser printers, 693
screen savers, memory and, 544
SCSI bus, 237–44
  configuration, 240, 241
  defined, 237, 253, 327
  interface software, 242
  multitasking support, 244
  SCSI-1, 238, 239, 253
  SCSI-2, 238, 240, 253
  system components, 240–42
  termination, 240–42
  ultra SCSI, 238, 240, 254
  wide SCSI, 238, 240, 254
SCSI bus adapter chip (SBAC), 238, 253
SCSI cables, for scanners, 753
SCSI devices, 407–11
  compatibility, 238
  defined, 238
  device drivers, 242, 275–76
  differential, 408–9, 422
  embedded, 238, 251
  host adapters, 237, 243, 252, 275, 392,
    407–11
  installing, 249
  SCAM-compliant, 409
  single-ended, 408–9, 423
SCSI drives, 233, 234, 236–44, 262
  CD-ROM, installing, 413–14
  CMOS setup, 275
  controllers, 238
  device drivers, 275–76
  vs. EIDE drives, 243, 244
  installing, 249, 262, 275–76
  low-level formatting, 319
  terminating resistors, 275

SCSI host adapters, installing, 745–47
SCSI ID, 238, 249, 253, 275
secondary storage, 10–12
sector markings, corrupted, 322–23
sectors
  bad, 310
  creating, 146
  floppy disks, 143–45
  hard drives, 192
sectors per track
  hard drives, 196–97
  IDE drives, 235
security, Windows NT, 590, 599
security accounts manager (SAM) database, 610, 653
segment address, D-7
segmentation, 814, 885, 891
Select Drive command, Windows 3.x,
  157
semicolons, creating comment lines with,
  523
sensitivity, floppy drives, 162
sequential access, tape drives, 912, 936
Serial Line Internet Protocol (SLIP), 833,
  891
serial mouse, 180, 183, 392
serial numbers, for applications software,
  531
serial port communications, 781–82
serial port connectors, 732–33
serial ports
  9-pin, 393–95
  25-pin, 393–95, 396
  default assignments, 393–94
  defined, 392, 423
  identifying, 393
  for peripheral devices, 392, 393–400
  resources used by, 399–400
  UART chip, 397–99
serial transmission, 9
servers, 609
  dedicated, 830–31
service calls, tracking, 955–59
servicing, networked PCs, 843–46
Session layer, 824, 825–26, 827, 891
  network services, 870–72
SET command, 456, 532–33
setup data. *See* configuration data
SETUPLOG.TXT, 552
Setup program
  installation problems, 527–29
  Windows 3.x options, 527
  Windows 95, 551–52
  Windows NT registry and, 638
SETUP.REG, 524, 525
SETVER.EXE, 161
SGRAM, 672, 697, 699
shadowing ROM. *See* shadow RAM
shadow RAM, 100, 438
  defined, 60, 75, 479
  disabling, 443

shared printers, 880–81
SHARE.EXE, 460
shielded twisted pair (STP) cable, 813
short circuits, 495, 499
shortcuts
  creating, 552–55
  defined, 552
  icons, 34
signal-regenerating repeaters, 814, 891
SIMD process, 667, 699
SIMMs, 6, 38
  adding, 468
  defined, 106, 430, 432–33, 468
  installation, 468–72
  installing, 473–74, 722–23
  module size, 435
  not recognized, 362–63, E-16
  parity, 433
  Pentium local bus, 470–71
  selecting, 472–73
  speeds, 433
  used modules, 435
Simple Mail Transfer Protocol (SMTP),
  829, 871, 891
single-ended SCSI devices, 408–9, 423
single in-line memory modules. See
  SIMMs
single instruction multiple data (SIMD)
  process, 667, 699
single threading, 605, 608
single voltage CPUs, 96, 128
SiS, chip sets, 98
16-bit applications
  in DOS, 546–47
  in Windows 95, 460–63, 546–47, 549
  in Windows NT, 636–37
16-bit drivers, 564, 568
  real mode, 460–62
sleep mode, 501, 514
SLIP (Serial Line Internet Protocol), 833,
  891
slots, 75, 94–95
Small Computer Systems Interface. See
  SCSI
SMARTDrive, 231, 253
SMARTDRV.EXE, 460, 530
smoking, hard drive life span and, 290
SMTP, 829, 871, 891
sockets, 94–95, 826, 891
  Internet connections, 871
soft booting, 65, 164
software, 12–35, See also applications software; operating system (OS)
  backing up, 368
  communications, 786–96
  copyrights, 962–64, 966
  defined, 2, 12, 38
  hardware management by, 46–64
  installation problems, E-19–20
  networking, 827–31
  piracy, 962–63, 966
  precautions, 367–68

selecting, 706–7
software-to-modem communication,
  787–92
software-to-software communication,
  792–96
troubleshooting, 349–50, E-21
software cache, 231, 232, 254
software flow control, 779–80
software interrupts, 123
sound
  files, 675
  playback, 676
  recording, 682–83
  troubleshooting, 419–20, E-14
  in Windows 95, 678–84
sound application software, 684–86
sound cards, 385, 386, 674–87, 696
  digital-to-analog conversion, 675
  drivers, 677–78
  installing, 676–77, 697, 741–42
  MPC3 specifications, 665–66
  sample size and rate, 674–75
  Sound Blaster compatibility, 674
  sound playback, 676
  storing sound files, 675
  troubleshooting, 686–87
sound waves
  digitizing, 659–61
  sampling, 659–61
SPARC chip, 93
speaker connector, 730, 731
speakers, 385
  installing, 747
  MPC3 specifications, 666
spikes, 507, 511
SRAM chips, 717
SRAM. See static RAM (SRAM)
stack, 122, 128
Stacker, 226
Standby Mode, monitors, 353–54
standby time, 502, 513, 514
standby UPS, 509, 514
standoffs, 723–25, 755
star network architecture, 811, 891
start bits, 774, 806
Start menu, adding shortcuts to, 554–56
StartUp folders, adding shortcuts to,
  554–56
Startup Menu
  dual boot, 560–63
  safe mode, 561–62
startup passwords, 52
static cache memory, 107
static electricity. See electrostatic discharge
  (ESD)
static IP addressing, 851, 881, 886, 891
static RAM (SRAM), 107
  advantages of, 432
  asynchronous, 435–36, 476
  burst, 435, 477
  COAST, 436, 477
  defined, 105, 128, 431, 479

pipelined burst, 435, 478
  single chips, 436
  synchronous, 435
static routing, 862, 891
static shielding bags, 335
static straps, 335
stealth viruses, 904, 936
stop bits, 774, 783, 806
storage. See memory
subdirectories, 26, 208
  creating, 209–10
  file information, 150
  hard drive organization, 194
subkeys, Windows NT registry, 638,
  641–43
subnetworks (subnets), 822, 858–61
  addressing, 859, 860
  defined, 859, 892
  masks, 859, 862, 891–92
subsystems, Windows NT, 603–5
subtrees, Windows NT registry, 638, 639,
  653
suites, 25
Sun Microsystems, SPARC chip, 93
Super PC-Kwick Cache, 231
SuperVGA monitors, 175
support calls, 944–54
  troubleshooting, 946
surge suppressors (surge protectors),
  505–7, 514
suspend time, 502, 514
swap files, 444, 527, 545
  applications, 456
  creating virtual memory with, 457–60
  defined, 456
  optimizing Windows with, 457
  permanent, 457–60
  temporary, 456–59
swapping, 456, 479
switching time, 509
Symantec
  Norton Utilities, 341
  PC Handyman, 341
  PC Tools, 341
synchronous DRAM, 434, 479
synchronous graphics RAM (SGRAM),
  672, 697, 699
synchronous SRAM, 435, 479
SyQuest Technology
  EZFlyer 230, 247–48
  Syjet drive, 247–48
SYS C: command, 233
SYS.COM, 161, 338
SYS command, 164, 322
Sysedit, 522
SYSINI.WRI, 530
System 7.5x, 24
System BIOS
  compatibility needs, 99
  defined, 12, 57–58, 75, 99, 430
  device drivers vs., 58
  functions of, 57–58

hard drive support, 196
hard drive type and, B-1–2
on-board, 57
total, 100–101
systemboard
  front panel connectors, 729–31
  grounding out, 723–25
  installing in computer case, 728
  jumper settings, 712–19
  layout, 713
  memory test, 723–27
  RAM installation, 722–23
systemboard mouse, 180, 183
systemboards, 4–8, 38, 83–124
  banks, 468–72, 476
  buses, 108–18
  CD-ROM drive interface, 413
  chip sets, 87–94
  components, 5, 6–8, 84–86
  DMA controllers, 124
  embedded components, 86
  expansion slots, 109, 110, 112–14, 116
  IRQ, 121–24
  manufacturers, 86
  memory, 432–33, 468–72
  power supply connections, 124
  proprietary components, 86
  RAM, 105–7
  ROM BIOS, 99–105, 430
  selecting, 84–86
  testing power output to, 495–97
  types of, 84–86
  voltages, 124
  wait states, 108
system clock, 7, 87
System Configuration Editor (Sysedit),
  522
SYSTEM.DA0, 571–72
SYSTEM.DAT, 571, 572
system disks. See bootable disks
system files, corrupted, 321–22
system heap, 540
SYSTEM.INI, 68
  contents, 521
  editing, 522
system partitions, Windows NT, 596–97,
  653
System Properties box, Windows NT,
  624–25
system variables, 456, 479
System Virtual Machine, 548–49

T
T1 lines, 799
TAG SRAM chips, 717
tape backup systems, 72, 928–29
tape drives, 912–17, 933
  computer interface, 913–15
  disadvantages, 912
  external/internal, 913–14
  tapes used by, 914–15
  troubleshooting, 916–17, E-14–15

TAPI, 666
Taskbar Properties sheet, 552–53
Task Manager, 646–48
TCP/IP, 826, 886, 892
  IP addresses for, 849
  other networks and, 847–48
  protocols, 853–54
  routing, 856–57
  troubleshooting, 883–84, E-21–22
  with Windows 95, 862–65
  with Windows NT, 862–66
technical documentation, 955, 966
technical support Web sites, 961–62
technicians. See PC technicians
telephony, 666, 699
Telephony Application Programming
  Interface (TAPI), 666, 699
Telnet, 830
temp directory, 456, 479
\TEMP directory, deleting files from, 900
Tempo, 24
temporary files, 456, 457–59, 479
TEMP variable, 456
terminate and stay resident programs. See
  TSRs
terminating resistors, 239, 254, 275, 753
termination, 240–42, 254
TestDrive, 161
text string heap, 540
thermal grease, 720–21, 756
thicknet, 813
thinnet, 813
32-bit flat memory mode, 626, 627, 652
32-bit programming, 545, 546–47
32-bit protected mode drivers, 460–61
threading
  multi-, 605, 608
  single, 605, 608
  Windows NT, 605, 607–8
3-pin connector, 730, 731
3D RAM, 672, 697
386SPART.PAR, 457
throughput performance, 116
tick counts, 822, 892
time, of creation or last update, 150
tin leads, matching, 434
token ring cards, 820–21
token ring networks, 815–16, 819
tokens, 816, 892
  limited, 817, 889
toner, 694–95, E-9
toner cavity, 694, 699
tool kit, 336
Toray PC Phasewriter Dual drive, 248
touchpads, 179, 180–81
touch screen monitors, 62
Touchstone Software, Check It
  Diagnostic Kit, 341
tower cases, hard drive installation, 265
traces, 8
trackball, 179, 180–81

track markings, corrupted, 322–23
tracks
  creating, 146
  floppy disks, 143–45
  hard drives, 192
  sectors per, 196–97, 198, 235
trailers, for data packets, 810, 892
training (modems), 764, 802
transceivers, 820
transformers, 490, 514
transistor-transistor logic (TTL) chips, 7
translation
  BIOS and, 200
  defined, 197
  hard drives, 197–99
  large-capacity drives, 199, 200
  large mode, 199
  for zone bit recording, 198
Transmission Control Protocol/Internet
  Protocol. See TCP/IP
transmission speed, modems, 776
Transport layer, network services,
  870–72, 892
TREE command, 212, 254
Triton II chip set, 96
Triton III chip set, 96
Trojan horses, 901–2, 904, 906
troubleshooting, 333–68, E-1–22
  booting, 324–25, 361–64, E-4, E-15–17
  CD-ROM drives, 417–20, 686–87,
    E-12–14
  comment lines for, 523
  devising a course of action, 347–50
  Dial-Up Networking, 882–83
  DOS memory problems, E-17
  emergencies, 343–44
  floppy drives, E-2–3
  hard drives, 313–26, E-4–5
  intermittent problems, 350
  isolating computer problems, 343–50
  keyboards, 350, 351–52, E-5–6
  memory management, 464–67
  modems, 796–99, E-10–12
  monitors, 350, 352–56, E-6–8
  mouse, E-4, E-19
  networking, 843, 882–84
  network printing, 884
  peripheral devices, 351–64
  perspectives, 334
  power supply, E-17–18
  preparation, 364–68
  printers, 350, 357–61, E-8–10
  protection, 334–36
  rules, 345–47
  software problems, 349–50, E-19–20
  sound, E-14
  sound cards, 686–87
  support calls, 946
  tape drives, 916–17, E-14–15
  TCP/IP, 883–84
  tools, 337–41

user interaction, 347–48
viruses, 342–43
Windows 3.x memory problems, E-17
TSRs
creating RAM drive with, 444
defined, 67, 75, 445, 479
device drivers, 389
execution of, 445
loading high, 449, 450–51, 465–66,
E-17
memory management, 445
minimizing, 545
T-switch, 696
TTL chips, 7–8
Tuff TEST-Pro, 339
turbo mode, 89, 128
TWAIN technology, 687
twisted pair cable, 812–13
TYPE command, 27

U

UART chips, 397–99, 776–79, 803
defined, 423, 806
determining type of, 397
on external and internal modems,
778–79
maximum port speeds, 776
Plug-and-Play compliant, 397
port settings, 782
protocols, 782–83
RS-232c serial port communication
and, 781–82
UDP (User Datagram Protocol), 854,
892
ultra SCSI, 238, 240, 254
UNDELETE command, 153, 154, 183,
310–11, 338
UNERASE command, 310
UNFORMAT command, 213–14, 254,
272, 318
uninterruptible power supplies (UPSs),
505, 508–11, 514
buying, 511
in-line, 508, 509–10, 513
intelligent, 510–11, 513
line-interactive, 510
standby, 509
universal bay kits, 264–65
universal resource locators (URLs), 871,
892
universal serial bus (USB), 86, 118, 128
UNIX operating system, 24, 827
unshielded twisted pair (UTP) cable, 812,
813
upper memory, 440, 441
addresses, 64
BIOS programs, 62
defined, 439, 479
devices drivers, 60
upper memory blocks (UMBs)
creating, 448–49

defined, 449, 479
expansion board conflicts, 467, E-17
memory reports, 452–54
UPS. See uninterruptible power supplies
(UPSs)
URLs, 871, 892
USB. See universal serial bus (USB)
U.S. Department of Defense (DOD), 847
user accounts
creating, 613–16
defined, 612
profiles, 612
roaming users, 612
Windows NT, 612–16
USER.DA0, 571–72
USER.DAT, 571, 572
User Datagram Protocol (UDP), 854,
892
user documentation, 955, 966
user heap, 540
user input, MPC3 specifications, 665
user mode, Windows NT, 603–5
user profiles, Windows NT, 638
user program, Windows 95, 546, 547
users, interacting with, 347–48
utility software, 277–91, 327, 370, See also
Norton Utilities; Nuts & Bolts; PC
Tools
general purpose, 341
recovering damaged files with, 311–12
for updates and fixes, 340–41
UTP cable, 812, 813

V

value data, Windows 95 registry, 570, 581
values
Windows 95 registry, 570
Windows NT registry, 638, 641–43
.VBX files, 350
VCACHE, 232, 254
vector tables. See I/O address table
VESA VL bus, 111, 112–13, 116, 128
VFAT, 205, 254
VGA monitors, 175
VGA settings, returning to, 356
VIA, chip sets, 98
video
drivers, 355–56, 370
memory, 38, 441
output, 175–78
systemboard support, 86
video BIOS, 57, 436
video-capturing cards, 385, 386, 422, 423
video cards, 62, 178, 183, 668–72, 696,
697
buses, 178
defined, 2, 38
device drivers, 391
installing, 747
memory on card, 178
proprietary devices, 178

temporary installation, 725–26
video memory, 669–72, 700
video controllers, 668
video hardware, MPC3 specifications, 664
video RAM (VRAM), 178, 430, 436,
671, 700
virtual cluster number (VCN), 595
virtual communication, 760–63, 802
virtual device drivers, 460, 480, 609
virtual file allocation table (VFAT), 205,
254
virtual machines, 545, 548–49, 581
Windows NT, 604, 608–9
virtual memory
creating with swap files, 457–60
defined, 44, 480
management in Windows 95, 463–64
Virtual Memory Manager, 549–51
viruses, 323, 901–11, 932, 933, See also
infestations
boot sector, 902, 934
eliminating, 909
in e-mail messages, 907
encrypting, 903–4
file, 903, 935
handling, 342
hiding places, 902–3
incubation periods, 902
macro, 903, 935
master boot, 903
memory-resident, 906, 935
multipartite, 903, 935
non-memory-resident, 906, 935
polymorphic, 903, 936
reducing threat of, 342–43
replication of, 905–6
stealth, 903–4, 936
symptoms, 908–9
warning signs, 342–43
virus scan programs, 342–43
virus signatures, 903, 936
VMM32.EXE, 460
voice/data capability, modems, 774
volatile memory, 7
voltage
clamping, 506, 513
current and, 488, 489
defined, 487, 514
measuring, 490–97
of power supply, measuring, 493–97
resistance and, 489
systemboards, 124
voltage regulator module (VRM) socket,
721, 756
Voltage regulators, 96
volt-amperes (VA), 507
voltmeters, 487, 514
volts, 487, 490, 514
volume boot record, 271
Volume Control dialog box, 680
volume labels, floppy disks, 152
volumes, hard drives, 195

VRAM, 671, 700
  video controller cards, 178
VRM (voltage regulator module), 721
  VRM Header, 721
VSAFE, 342
VSHARE.386, 460
VxD drivers, 460

W

wait states, 108, 128
wallpaper, memory and, 544
WANs (wide area networks)
  connections, 861–62
  defined, 810–11
wattage, 489–90, 514
  estimating needs, 499–500
wavetable synthesis, 666, 696, 700
Web browsers. *See* browsers
WebPatch, 340
Web servers, Windows NT, 590
whining, hard drives, 315
wide area networks. *See* WANs (wide
  area networks)
wide SCSI, 238, 240, 254
Win 16 on Win 32 (WOW), 604, 609
WIN386, 454
WIN386.SWP, 457
WIN command, 32, 67
window RAM (WRAM), 672, 697, 700
Windows 3.x, 13
  advantages and disadvantages, 21
  Custom Setup, 527, 529, 581
  disk compression in, 225–26
  documentation files, 530
  dual boot with Windows 95, 559–60
  386 enhanced mode, 457
  Express Setup, 527, 581
  hard drive management, 214–17
  improvements over DOS, 30
  initialization files, 520–24
  installing, 271–72, 527–30, E-17
  interface, 15–16
  managing floppy drives with, 156–58
  memory errors, 540–41
  memory management, 445–60, 540–44
  memory problems, 541–44, E-18–19
  multiple operating system installation,
    276–77
  multitasking, 18
  operating environment, 18–19, 20–21
  optimizing, 544–45
  organizing root directory with, 365
  registration database, 524–27
  reinstalling, 527
  software conflicts, 533–40
  software execution, 30–33
  software installation, 530–33
  standard mode, 457
  system directory files, backing up,
    534–35
Windows 3.x applications, in Windows
  NT environment, 593
Windows 95, 13, 545–77
  advantages and disadvantages, 22
  applications software execution in,
    34–35
  Backup utility, 919–22
  booting with, 69–71
  compared to DOS and Windows 3.x,
    545–51
  compared to Windows NT, 588–94, 608
  connecting to the Internet with, 867–70
  customizing the desktop, 552–55
  customizing with MSDOS.SYS,
    556–58
  device driver installation, 389, E-20
  Dial-Up Networking, troubleshooting,
    E-21–22
  disk cache, 232
  disk compression in, 226–30
  DOS files renamed by, 277, 560
  dual boot with DOS and Windows 3.x,
    559–60
  Energy Star monitor recognition, 504
  floppy drive management with, 158–60
  hard drive management, 217–19, 233
  improvements over DOS, 30
  installing, 271–72, 551–52, 750–51
    custom, 556–60, 581
    multiple operating system, 276–77
    over DOS and Windows 3.x, 559
    tracking changes during, 574–77
  interface, 16
  loading problems, 364, E-17
  long filenames, 13
  memory management, 437, 460–64
  memory paging, 549–51
  multitasking, 18
  network adapters, 842
  networking with, 831–40, 842
  operating environment, 18, 21
  RAM required for, 468
  recovering damaged files with, 309
  registry, 367, 551, 570–77
  Setup, 551–52
  16-bit support, 460–63, 546–47, 549
  sound with, 678–84
  Startup menu, 560–62
  swap files, 463–64
  TCP/IP with, 862–65
  32-bit programming, 545, 546–47
  upgrading to Windows NT, 594–97
  virtual machines, 548–49
  virtual memory management in,
    463–64
Windows Explorer, hard drive management with, 217–19
Windows Internet Naming Service
  (WINS), 853–54, 886, 892
Windows NT, 827
  Backup utility, 922–29
  host computer, network drive mapping,
    875–77
  network adapters, 840–41
  Scheduler service, 924–25
  TCP/IP with, 862–66
Windows NT Diagnostics, 650
Windows NT file system (NTFS),
  594–96
Windows NT Registry Editor, 639–43
Windows NT Server, 609
Windows NT Workstation, 545, 587–650
  advantages, 23, 588
  backward compatibility, 588
  boot disks, 629–31
  boot process, 624–33, E-21
  Command Prompt, 591–93
  compatibility, 599
  Control Panel, 624–25
  defined, 22, 609
  desktop, 591, 592
  diagnostic tools, 646–50
  domains, 609–11
  DOS-like commands, 591–93
  emergency repair disk (ERD), 631–33
  Event Viewer, 648–49, 652
  expandability, 598
  features, 589–93
  files needed for booting, 628
  file systems, 594–96
  as first operating system, 622
  goals, 598–99
  hard drive partitions, 596–97
  hardware compatibility, 590–91, 616–17
  installation, 616–24
  kernel mode, 605–6
  Last Known Good configuration,
    628–29
  legacy software, 634–37
  local printer installation, 622–24
  memory management, 437, 440, 464–65
  memory module, 606–7
  modular concept, 599–607
  network files and parameters, 845
  networking with, 609–16, 831–40, 842
  performance, 599
  portability, 598
  processes, 607–8
  registry, 594, 631, 637–46
  reliability, 599
  as second operating system, 618–22
  security, 599
  Task Manager, 646–48
  threading, 605, 607–8
  upgrading to, 594–97
  user mode, 603–5
  virtual machine, 604, 608–9
  Windows 95 compared to, 588–94, 608
  workgroups, 609–11

INDEX

Windows Sockets (WinSock) protocol,
  853–54
Windows for Workgroups, 13
WindSock, 542
Windsor Technologies, Inc.
  PC-Diagnosys, 340
  PC-Technician, 339
WINFILE.INI, 521, 522
WIN.INI, 68, 521, 522
WININI.WRI, 530
WINProbe, 340
WINS (Windows Internet Naming
  Service), 853–54, 886, 892
word size, 87, 88

workgroups, 609–11
workstations, 609
World Wide Web (WWW), 847
worms, 901–2, 904, 936
WOW32.DLL, 609
WOWEXE.EXE, 609
WRAM, 672, 697, 700
write precompression, 193, 254
write-protection, error messages, 165

X

x2 standard, 767
XCOPY command, 155, 183
XCOPY.EXE, 161

Xoff control, 780
Xon control, 780
Xon/Xoff protocol, 779

Y

YUV color space, 664–65, 700

Z

ZIF (zero insertion force), 95–96
ZIF sockets, 719–20, 756
zone bit recording, 198